35.99 x

Managerial Accounting

coleraine
nrc
northern regional college
Learning Resource Centre

Managerial Accounting

Twelfth Edition

Ray H. Garrison, D.B.A., CPA
Professor Emeritus
Brigham Young University

Eric W. Noreen, Ph.D., CMA
Professor Emeritus
University of Washington

Peter C. Brewer, Ph.D., CPA
Miami University—Oxford, Ohio

McGraw-Hill Irwin

Boston   Burr Ridge, IL   Dubuque, IA   Madison, WI   New York   San Francisco   St. Louis
Bangkok   Bogotá   Caracas   Kuala Lumpur   Lisbon   London   Madrid   Mexico City
Milan   Montreal   New Delhi   Santiago   Seoul   Singapore   Sydney   Taipei   Toronto

Dedication

*To our families and
to our many
colleagues who use this book.*

McGraw-Hill
Irwin

MANAGERIAL ACCOUNTING, ALTERNATE ISE

Published by McGraw-Hill/Irwin, a business unit of The McGraw-Hill Companies, Inc., 1221 Avenue of the
Americas, New York, NY, 10020. Copyright © 2008 by The McGraw-Hill Companies, Inc. All rights reserved.
No part of this publication may be reproduced or distributed in any form or by any means, or stored in a
database or retrieval system, without the prior written consent of The McGraw-Hill Companies, Inc., including,
but not limited to, in any network or other electronic storage or transmission, or broadcast for distance learning.

Some ancillaries, including electronic and print components, may not be available to customers outside the
United States.

This book is printed on acid-free paper.

1 2 3 4 5 6 7 8 9 0 SDB/SDB 0 9 8 7
Printed in China

ISBN   978-0-07-110113-4
MHID   0-07-110113-6

About the Authors

Ray H. Garrison is emeritus professor of accounting at Brigham Young University, Provo, Utah. He received his BS and MS degrees from Brigham Young University and his DBA degree from Indiana University.

As a certified public accountant, Professor Garrison has been involved in management consulting work with both national and regional accounting firms. He has published articles in *The Accounting Review, Management Accounting*, and other professional journals. Innovation in the classroom has earned Professor Garrison the Karl G. Maeser Distinguished Teaching Award from Brigham Young University.

Eric W. Noreen is a globe-trotting academic who has held appointments at institutions in the United States, Europe, and Asia. He is emeritus professor of accounting at the University of Washington.

He received his BA degree from the University of Washington and MBA and PhD degrees from Stanford University. A Certified Management Accountant, he was awarded a Certificate of Distinguished Performance by the Institute of Certified Management Accountants.

Professor Noreen has served as associate editor of *The Accounting Review* and the *Journal of Accounting and Economics*. He has numerous articles in academic journals including: the *Journal of Accounting Research*; the *Accounting Review*; the *Journal of Accounting and Economics*; *Accounting Horizons*; *Accounting, Organizations and Society*; *Contemporary Accounting Research*; the *Journal of Management Accounting Research*; and the *Review of Accounting Studies*.

Professor Noreen has won a number of awards from students for his teaching.

Peter C. Brewer

is a professor in the Department of Accountancy at Miami University, Oxford, Ohio. He holds a BS degree in accounting from Penn State University, an MS degree in accounting from the University of Virginia, and a PhD from the University of Tennessee. He has published 30 articles in a variety of journals including: *Management Accounting Research*, the *Journal of Information Systems*, *Cost Management*, *Strategic Finance*, the *Journal of Accountancy*, *Issues in Accounting Education*, and the *Journal of Business Logistics*.

Professor Brewer is a member of the editorial boards of *Issues in Accounting Education* and the *Journal of Accounting Education*. His article *"Putting Strategy into the Balanced Scorecard"* won the 2003 International Federation of Accountants' Articles of Merit competition and his articles *"Using Six Sigma to Improve the Finance Function"* and *"Lean Accounting: What's It All About?"* were awarded the Institute of Management Accountants' Lybrand Gold and Silver Medals in 2005 and 2006. He has received Miami University's Richard T. Farmer School of Business Teaching Excellence Award and has been recognized on two occasions by the Miami University Associated Student Government for "making a remarkable commitment to students and their educational development." He is a leading thinker in undergraduate management accounting curriculum innovation and is a frequent presenter at various professional and academic conferences.

Prior to joining the faculty at Miami University, Professor Brewer was employed as an auditor for Touche Ross in the firm's Philadelphia office. He also worked as an internal audit manager for the Board of Pensions of the Presbyterian Church (U.S.A.). He frequently collaborates with companies such as Harris Corporation, Ghent Manufacturing, Cintas, Ethicon Endo-Surgery, Schneider Electric, Lenscrafters, and Fidelity Investments in a consulting or case writing capacity.

Garrison—Leading Textbook, Leading Technology

The wide array of technology assets that come with *Managerial Accounting* aren't add-ons thrown in at the last minute: They're extensions of the textbook itself, that work in unison to make managerial accounting as easy as possible to learn.

You may be tempted to put aside your CD and registration cards, planning to "get to them later"; you may even want to discard them outright. **Don't do it!** These supplements can offer you tremendous help as you go through the course; the sooner you become familiar with them, the sooner you can enjoy the immense benefits they have to offer.

Here's what you need to know to get the most out of *Managerial Accounting*'s technology package.

iPod Content

Harness the power of one of the most popular technology tools you use today—the Apple iPod. Our innovative approach allows you to download audio and video presentations right into your iPod and take learning materials with you wherever you go.

You just need to visit the Online Learning Center at **www.mhhe.com/garrison12e** to download our iPod content. For each chapter of the book you will be able to download audio narrated lecture presentations, managerial accounting videos, and even self-quizzes designed for use on various versions of iPods. The iPod content can be downloaded quickly and easily from the enclosed DVD without the need to spend the additional download time.

It makes review and study time as easy as putting on headphones.

Topic Tackler Plus

Topic Tackler provides focused help on the two most challenging topics in every chapter. How do you use Topic Tackler? Take your pick:

- Watch a short, high-quality video presentation.
- Review the topic highlights with a graphical slide show.
- Practice on numerous interactive exercises.
- Follow the links to more information on the World Wide Web.

However you want to use it, Topic Tackler is the perfect tool for review sessions, or just for some quick reinforcement as you read. Look for the Topic Tackler icon while you read—that means you'll find Topic Tackler ready to help you on that particular subject.

Turn to the inside front cover to learn how to get started using Topic Tackler!

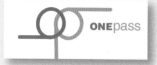

One Pass eliminates the frustration of remembering multiple access codes for different online resources. Now you can use the access code found on your OnePass card to register and create one password for access to your book's online resources. By having just one access code for everything, you can go back and forth between tutorials as you study.

Student Supplements

McGraw-Hill's Homework Manager®

Practice makes perfect, and when it comes to managerial accounting, there's often no better practice than working with the numbers yourself. *Managerial Accounting* provides a great many problems for your instructor to assign or for you to do on your own, but there are only so many problems you can fit into a textbook. That's where McGraw-Hill's Homework Manager comes in.

McGraw-Hill's Homework Manager duplicates problems from the textbook in a convenient, online format. You can work problems and receive instant feedback on your answers, taking as many tries as you want. Because McGraw-Hill's Homework Manager uses specialized algorithms to generate values for each problem, it can produce infinite variations of certain text problems just by changing the values—you can practice on the same problem as many times as you need to, with fresh figures to work with every time.

Your instructor will have already decided whether to make McGraw-Hill's Homework Manager a part of your course, and he or she will create a course account and generate the assignments for you to do. Your McGraw-Hill's Homework Manager user guide will include an access code enabling you to enroll; refer to the guide for help in creating your account. Talk to your instructor to be sure McGraw-Hill's Homework Manager is available for you as you begin the course.

Online Learning Center (OLC)

When it comes to getting the most out of your textbook, the Online Learning Center is the place to start. The OLC follows *Managerial Accounting* chapter by chapter, offering all kinds of supplementary help for you as you read. OLC features include:

- Learning objectives
- Chapter overviews
- Internet-based activities
- Self-grading quizzes
- Links to text references
- Links to professional resources on the Web
- Job opportunity information
- Internet factory tours

Before you even start reading Chapter 1, go to this address and bookmark it:

www.mhhe.com/garrison12e

Remember, your Online Learning Center was created specifically to accompany *Managerial Accounting*—so don't let this great resource pass you by!

Topic Tackler Plus

Available on the text Web site, Topic Tackler Plus helps you master difficult concepts in managerial accounting through a creative, interactive learning process. Designed for study outside the classroom, this material delves into chapter concepts with graphical slides and diagrams, Web links, video clips, and animations, all centered around engaging exercises designed to put you in control of your learning of managerial accounting topics.

Workbook/Study Guide

MHID: 0073203025
ISBN-13: 9780073203027

This study aid provides suggestions for studying chapter material, summarizes essential points in each chapter, and tests your knowledge using self-test questions and exercises.

Ready Notes

MHID: 0073203092
ISBN-13: 9780073203096

This booklet provides Ready Slide exhibits in a workbook format for efficient note taking.

Student Lecture Aid

MHID: 0073203033
ISBN-13: 9780073203034

Much like the Ready Notes, this booklet offers a hard-copy version of all the Teaching Transparencies. You can annotate the material during the lecture and take notes in the space provided.

Working Papers

MHID: 0073203017
ISBN-13: 9780073203010

This study aid contains forms that help you organize your solutions to homework problems.

Excel® Templates

Prepared by Jack Terry of ComSource Associates, Inc., this spreadsheet-based software uses Excel to solve selected problems and cases in the text. These selected problems and cases are identified in the margin of the text with an appropriate icon. The Student Excel Templates are only available on the text's Web site.

Telecourse Guide

MHID: 0073203009
ISBN-13: 9780073203003

This study guide ties the Dallas County Community College Telecourse directly to this text.

Practice Set

MHID: 0073396192
ISBN-13: 9780073396194

Authored by Janice L. Cobb of Texas Christian University, *Doing the Job of the Managerial Accountant* is a real-world application for the Introductory Managerial Accounting student. The case is based on an actual growing, entrepreneurial manufacturing company that is complex enough to demonstrate the decisions management must make, yet simple enough that a sophomore student can easily understand the entire operations of the company. The case requires the student to do tasks they would perform working as the managerial accountant for the company. The required tasks are directly related to the concepts learned in all managerial accounting classes. The practice set can be used by the professor as a teaching tool for class lectures, as additional homework assignments, or as a semester project.

Acknowledgments

Suggestions have been received from many of our colleagues throughout the world. Each of those who have offered comments and suggestions has our thanks.

The efforts of many people are needed to develop and improve a text. Among these people are the reviewers and consultants who point out areas of concern, cite areas of strength, and make recommendations for change. In this regard, the following professors provided feedback that was enormously helpful in preparing the twelfth edition of **Managerial Accounting**:

Helen Adams, University of Washington
Gilda Agacer, Monmouth University
Natalie Allen, Texas A&M University–College Station
Thomas Arcuri, FCCJ–South Campus
John Armstrong, Nichols College
Kashi R. Balachandran, New York University
Ben Bean, Utah Valley State College–Orem
Deborah F. Beard, Southeast Missouri State University
Linda Benz, KCTCS Jefferson Community and Technical College
Sak Bhamornsiri, UNCC
Brenda Bindschatel, Green River Community College
Karen Bird, University of Michigan
Steven Black, College of Eastern Utah, San Juan Campus
Philip Blanchard, University of Arizona
Marv Bouillon, Iowa State University
Alisa Brink, Florida State University
Robert Bromley, Central Michigan University
William Burch, Houston Community College
Janet Butler, Texas State University–San Marcos
Ronald Bytnar, South Suburban College
Richard Calvasina, University of West Florida
Linda Campbell, Siena Heights University
Valrie Chambers, Texas A&M University–Corpus Christi
Dave Champagne, Antelope Valley College
Chiaho Chang, Montclair State University
Dr. Jo Ann Christensen, Louisiana Tech University
Earl Clay, Cape Cod Community College
Deb Cosgrove, University of Nebraska–Lincoln
Nancy Coster, University of California, Irvine
Barbara Croteau, Santa Rosa Junior College
Kathy Crusto-Way, Tarrant County College, Southeast Campus
Alan Czyzewski, Indiana State University
David L. Davis, Tallahassee Community College
Patricia Doherty, Boston University
Michael Dole, Marquette University
B. Duckworth, University of Wisconsin, Baraboo
Cathy Duffy, Carthage College
Rita Dufour, Northeast Wisconsin Technical College
Robert Dunn, Georgia Institute Tech
Rafik Z. Elias, California State University–LA
Terry G. Elliott, Morehead State University
Richard Emery, Linfield College
Dr. Andrew Felo, Pennsylvania State University School of Graduate Professional Studies—Great Valley
Tom Finnicum, Oklahoma State University

Ronald Flinn, Creighton University–Omaha
Drew Fountaine, Somona State University
M. Lou Fowler, Missouri Western State College
Bob Geiges, Ottawa University
Louis Giuliano, Thomas Jefferson University, Department of General Studies
Dr. Marina R. Grau, Houston Community College
Sharon Green, Duquesne University
Dr. Dennis P. Greer, Utah Valley State College
Cindy Gruber, Marquette University
Joseph Hagan, East Carolina University
Julie Hansen, Mesa College
Susan Hass, Simmons College
Betsy Haywood-Sullivan, Rider University
Candice Heino, Anoka Ramsey Community College
Norma Holter, Towson University
Susan B. Hughes, Butler University
Laura Ilcisin, University of Nebraska–Omaha
Wayne C. Ingalls, University of Maine
Sharon Jackson, Samford University
Bob Jensen, Trinity College
Mary Jepperson, College of Saint Benedict/Saint John's University
Gene Johnson, Clark College
Shondra Johnson, Bradley University
Leland Jordan, Christopher Newport University
Robert Kachur, Richard Stockton College of NJ
Janice Kerber, Durham Tech Community College
M. Khaitan, Massachusetts Bay Community College
Floyd Kirby, Jacksonville State University
Shirly A. Kleiner, Johnson County Community College
Christine Kloezeman, Glendale Community College
Carol Knapp, University of Oklahoma
Ridgway Knight, Loyola Marymount University
John Koeplin, University of San Francisco
Steven J. LaFave, Augsberg College
C. Andrew Lafond, Philadelphia University
Joseph Larkin, Saint Joseph's University
Dan Law, Gonzaga University
Richard Lee, University of California Berkeley Extension
William R. Link, University of Missouri–St. Louis
Harold Little, Western Kentucky University
Lawrence B. Logan, University of Massachusetts–Dartmouth
Cynthia Lovick, Austin Community College
Jordan Lowe, Arizona State University West
Suzanne Lowensohn, Colorado State University

James Lukawitz, University of Memphis
Tom Madden, University of California–Irvine
Sitikantha Mahapatra, California State University–Long Beach
S. A. Marino, SUNY/Westchester Community College
Ariel Markelevich, Baruch College–CUNY
Danny G. Matthews, Midwestern State University
R. K. McCabe, Colorado State University
Barbara McElroy, Susquehanna University
Paul McGee, Salem State College
Philip Meader, New Hampshire Community
    Technical College–Stratham
Scott I. Meisel, Morehead State University
Chris Metcalfe, Miami University
Jon Mikkelsen, Monterey Peninsula College
Paula Miller, Collin County Community College
Valerie Milliron, California State University–Chico
Susan Minke, Indiana Purdue at Fort Wayne
Andrew Morgret, University of Memphis
Matthew Mouritsen, Weber State University
Ann B. Murphy, Metropolitan State College of Denver
Ramesh Narasimhan, Montclair State University
Patricia Newbanks, Iowa State University
Peter F. Oehlers, West Chester University
Aileen Ormiston, Mesa Community College
Paul R. Pahoresky, Keller Graduate School of Management
    and Weatherhead School of Management
Viola Persia, Stony Brook University
Jo Ann Pinto, Montclair State University
Margaret Pollard, American River College
Peter Poznanski, Cleveland State
Cheryl Prachyl, University of Texas–Arlington
Nova Randolph, Shawnee Community College
Ahmed Riahi-Belkaoui, University of Illinois–Chicago
Kelly Richmond, University of North Carolina–Greensboro
Laura K. Rickett, Kent State University
Juan Rivera, University of Notre Dame
Walter A. Robbins, University of Alabama
Michael Robinson, Baylor University
Margo Rock, Hillsborough Community College–Tampa
Luther L. Ross, Sr., Central Piedmont Community College
Pamela J. Rouse, Butler University
Karen Russom, North Harris College
Dr. P.N. Saksena, Indiana University South Bend

James Schaefer, University Of Evansville
Nancy Schrumpf, Parkland College
Mike Schumacher, Gardner-Webb University
Mike Schuster, Portland State University
Dr. Robert J. Sellani, Nova Southeastern University
Karen Shastri, University of Pittsburgh
Lewis Shaw, Suffolk University–Dakar
John W. Shishoff, University of Dayton
Lily Sieux, CSU East Bay
Tom Sill, Northwest University
Jack Simon, University of Nevada–Reno
Jack Simon, Golden Gate University
William E. Smith, Xavier University
Talitha Smith, Auburn University
Jill Smith, Idaho State University
Henry C. Smith, III, Otterbein College
Roxanne Spindle, Virginia Commwealth University
Jim Stanley, Lower Columbia College
Victor Stanton, Stanford University
I. Stapleton, Modesto Junior College
Carolyn Strand Norman, Viriginia Commonwealth University
Gracelyn Stuart, Palm Beach Community College–Boca Raton
Holly Sudano, Florida State University
Stephen Sullivan, St. Joseph's University
John J. Surdick, Xavier University
Diane Tanner, University of North Florida
Linda Tarrago, Hillsborough Community College
Wendy Tietz, Kent State University
Vicki Trammel Spencer, Northeastern State University
Greg Treadwell, Cameron University
Carmelita Troy, Naval Postgraduate School
Mark A. Turner, Stephen F. Austin State University
Thomas Vickman, University of Minnesota
Lisa M. Victoravich, Florida State University
Larry Walther, University of Texas–Arlington
Gerald P. Weinstein, John Carroll University
Stephen Welborn, University of Redlands
Steve Welter, Parkland College
Judith Zander, Grossmont College
Bert J. Zarb, Embry-Riddle Aeronautical University
Jim Zeigler, Bowling Green State University–Bowling Green
Lin Zheng, Georgia College and State University
Nan Zhou, Binghamton University

We are grateful for the outstanding support from McGraw-Hill. In particular, we would like to thank Stewart Mattson, Editorial Director; Tim Vertovec, Executive Editor; Sarah Wood, Developmental Editor; Krista Bettino, Executive Marketing Manager; Pat Frederickson, Lead Project Manager; Debra Sylvester, Production Supervisor; Kami Carter, Senior Designer; Ira Roberts, Manager of Publishing Services; Brian Nacik, Media Project Manager; Elizabeth Mavetz, Senior Media Tech Producer; and Lori Kramer, Photo Research Coordinator.

Finally, we would like to thank Beth Woods and Barbara Schnathorst for working so hard to ensure an error-free twelfth edition. The authors also wish to thank Linda and Michael Bamber for inspiring the creation of the 10-K Research and Application exercises that are included in the end-of-chapter materials throughout the book.

We are grateful to the Institute of Certified Management Accountants for permission to use questions and/or unofficial answers from past Certificate in Management Accounting (CMA) examinations. Likewise, we thank the American Institute of Certified Public Accountants, the Society of Management Accountants of Canada, and the Chartered Institute of Management Accountants (United Kingdom) for permission to use (or to adapt) selected problems from their examinations. These problems bear the notations CPA, SMA, and CIMA respectively.

Ray H. Garrison • Eric Noreen • Peter Brewer

Brief Contents

Contents

Chapter **3**

Systems Design: Job-Order Costing 91

Chapter **4**

Systems Design: Process Costing 149

Chapter 5

**Cost Behavior: Analysis
and Use   187**

Chapter 6

**Cost-Volume-Profit
Relationships   232**

Chapter 11

Flexible Budgets and Overhead Analysis   474

Chapter 12

Segment Reporting and Decentralization   515

Chapter 13

Relevant Costs for Decision Making 577

Chapter 14

Capital Budgeting Decisions 625

Chapter 15

"How Well Am I Doing?" Statement of Cash Flows   682

Managerial Accounting and the Business Environment

The Role of Management Accounting

BUSINESS FOCUS

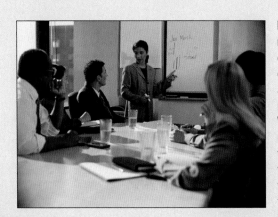

It is estimated that 95% of all finance professionals work inside corporations, governments, and other organizations, integrating accounting with operations and reporting to the outside world. While some of the effort expended by these people relates to financial accounting, the profession needs to further stress the role management accountants play within organizations supporting decision making, planning, and control. In short, the emphasis in business and the role of accounting should be more about *doing* business rather than tabulating and reporting historical financial results.

Management accounting is undergoing a renaissance in response to technological changes, globalization, and growing risk management concerns. In these challenging times, management accountants help "steady the ship" by acting as their organizations' interpreters, sage advisors, and ethical "keepers of the numbers." Managers understand that good business results come from dynamic processes, procedures, and practices that are well designed and properly implemented and managed. Certified Management Accountants are qualified to help their fellow managers achieve good business results because they have earned an advanced certification that addresses all important aspects of accounting inside organizations. ∎

Source: Conversation with Paul Sharman, CEO of the Institute of Management Accountants.

Learning Objectives

After studying Chapter 1, you should be able to:

LO1 Identify the major differences and similarities between financial and managerial accounting.

LO2 Understand the role of management accountants in an organization.

LO3 Understand the basic concepts underlying Lean Production, the Theory of Constraints (TOC), and Six Sigma.

LO4 Understand the importance of upholding ethical standards.

Managerial accounting is concerned with providing information to managers—that is, people inside an organization who direct and control its operations. In contrast, **financial accounting** is concerned with providing information to stockholders, creditors, and others who are outside an organization. Managerial accounting provides the essential data that are needed to run organizations. Financial accounting provides the essential data that are used by outsiders to judge a company's past financial performance.

Managerial accountants prepare a variety of reports. Some reports focus on how well managers or business units have performed—comparing actual results to plans and to benchmarks. Some reports provide timely, frequent updates on key indicators such as orders received, order backlog, capacity utilization, and sales. Other analytical reports are prepared as needed to investigate specific problems such as a decline in the profitability of a product line. And yet other reports analyze a developing business situation or opportunity. In contrast, financial accounting is oriented toward producing a limited set of specific prescribed annual and quarterly financial statements in accordance with generally accepted accounting principles (GAAP).

The chapter begins with discussions of globalization and the meaning of strategy. Next, it describes the information needs of management and how the role of managerial accounting differs from financial accounting. Finally, the chapter provides an overview of the organizational context within which management accounting operates—including discussions of organizational structure, process management, technology in business, the importance of ethics, corporate governance, and enterprise risk management.

Globalization

The world has become much more intertwined over the last 20 years. Reductions in tariffs, quotas, and other barriers to free trade; improvements in global transportation systems; explosive expansion in Internet usage; and increasing sophistication in international markets have created a truly global marketplace. Exhibit 1–1 illustrates this tremendous growth in international trade from the standpoint of the United States and some of its key trading partners. Panel A of the exhibit shows the dollar value of imports (stated in billions of dollars) into the United States from six countries; Panel B shows the dollar value of exports from the United States to those same six countries. As you can see, the increase in import and export activity from 1990 to 2004 was huge. In particular, trade with China expanded enormously as did trade with Mexico and Canada, which participate in the North American Free Trade Agreement (NAFTA).

In a global marketplace, a company that has been very successful in its local market may suddenly find itself facing competition from halfway around the globe. For example, in the 1980s American automobile manufacturers began losing market share to Japanese competitors who offered American consumers higher quality cars at lower prices. For consumers, this type of heightened international competition promises a greater variety of goods and services, at higher quality and lower prices. However, heightened international competition threatens companies that may have been quite profitable in their own local markets.

Although globalization leads to greater competition, it also means greater access to new markets, customers, and workers. For example, the emerging markets of China, India, Russia, and Brazil contain more than 2.5 billion potential customers and workers.[1] Many companies such as FedEx, McDonald's, and Nike are actively seeking to grow

---

[1] *The Economist: Pocket World in Figures 2004,* Profile Books Ltd., London, U.K.

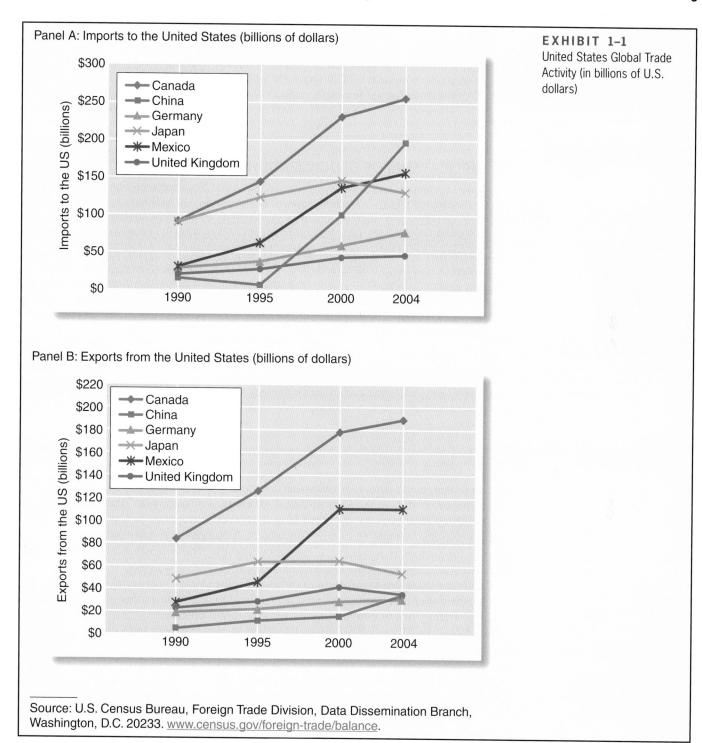

Panel A: Imports to the United States (billions of dollars)

EXHIBIT 1–1
United States Global Trade Activity (in billions of U.S. dollars)

Panel B: Exports from the United States (billions of dollars)

Source: U.S. Census Bureau, Foreign Trade Division, Data Dissemination Branch, Washington, D.C. 20233. www.census.gov/foreign-trade/balance.

their sales by investing in emerging markets. In addition, the movement of jobs from the United States and Western Europe to other parts of the world has been notable in recent years. For example, one study estimates that by the end of the decade more than 825,000 financial services and high-tech jobs will transfer from Western Europe to less expensive labor markets such as India, China, Africa, Eastern Europe, and Latin America.[2]

---

[2] "Job Exports: Europe's Turn," *BusinessWeek,* April 19, 2004, p. 50.

The Internet fuels the globalization phenomenon by providing companies with greater access to geographically dispersed customers, employees, and suppliers. While the number of Internet users worldwide more than doubled during the first four years of the new millennium, as of 2004, more than 87% of the world's population was still not connected to the Internet. This suggests that the Internet's impact on global business has yet to fully develop.

THE IMPLICATIONS OF GLOBALIZATION

International competition goes hand-in-hand with globalization. China's entrance into the global marketplace has highlighted this stark reality for many U.S. companies. For example, from 2000 to 2003, China's wooden bedroom furniture exports to the United States increased by more than 233% to a total of $1.2 billion. During this same time, the number of workers employed by U.S. furniture manufacturers dropped by about a third, or a total of 35,000 workers.

However, globalization means more than international competition. It brings opportunities for companies to enter new markets. FedEx has pushed hard to be an important player in the emerging Asian cargo market. FedEx makes 622 weekly flights to and from Asian markets, including service to 224 Chinese cities. FedEx currently has 39% of the U.S.–China express market and it plans to pursue continuous growth in that region of the world.

Sources: Ted Fishman, "How China Will Change Your Business," *Inc.* magazine, March 2005, pp. 70–84; Matthew Boyle, "Why FedEx is Flying High," *Fortune*, November 1, 2004, pp. 145–150.

Strategy

Even more than in the past, companies that now face global competition must have a viable *strategy* for succeeding in the marketplace. A **strategy** is a "game plan" that enables a company to attract customers by distinguishing itself from competitors. The focal point of a company's strategy should be its target customers. A company can only succeed if it creates a reason for customers to choose it over a competitor. These reasons, or what are more formally called *customer value propositions,* are the essence of strategy.

Customer value propositions tend to fall into three broad categories—*customer intimacy, operational excellence,* and *product leadership*. Companies that adopt a *customer intimacy* strategy are in essence saying to their target customers, "The reason that you should choose us is because we understand and respond to your individual needs better than our competitors." Ritz-Carlton, Nordstrom, and Starbucks rely primarily on a customer intimacy value proposition for their success. Companies that pursue the second customer value proposition, called *operational excellence,* are saying to their target customers, "The reason that you should choose us is because we can deliver products and services faster, more conveniently, and at a lower price than our competitors." Southwest Airlines, Wal-Mart, and The Vanguard Group are examples of companies that succeed first and foremost because of their operational excellence. Companies pursuing the third customer value proposition, called *product leadership,* are saying to their target customers, "The reason that you should choose us is because we offer higher quality products than our competitors." BMW, Cisco Systems, and W.L. Gore (the creator of GORE-TEX® fabrics) are examples of companies that succeed because of their product leadership. Although one company may offer its customers a combination of these three customer value propositions, one usually outweighs the others in terms of importance.[3]

---

[3]   These three customer value propositions were defined by Michael Treacy and Fred Wiersema in "Customer Intimacy and Other Value Disciplines," *Harvard Business Review,* January/February 1993, pp. 84–93.

OPERATIONAL EXCELLENCE COMES TO THE DIAMOND BUSINESS

An average engagement ring purchased from Blue Nile, an Internet diamond retailer, costs $5,200 compared to $9,500 if purchased from Tiffany & Co., a bricks-and-mortar retailer. Why is there such a difference? There are three reasons. First, Blue Nile allows wholesalers to sell directly to customers using its website. In the brick-and-mortar scenario, diamonds change hands as many as seven times before being sold to a customer—passing through various cutters, wholesalers, brokers, and retailers, each of whom demands a profit. Second, Blue Nile carries very little inventory and incurs negligible overhead. Diamonds are shipped directly from wholesalers after they have been purchased by a customer—no retail outlets are necessary. Bricks-and-mortar retailers tie up large amounts of money paying for the inventory and employees on their showroom floors. Third, Blue Nile generates a high volume of transactions by selling to customers anywhere in the world; therefore, it can accept a lower profit margin per transaction than local retailers, who complete fewer transactions with customers within a limited geographic radius.

Perhaps you are wondering why customers are willing to trust an Internet retailer when buying an expensive item such as a diamond. The answer is that all of the diamonds sold through Blue Nile's website are independently certified by the Gemological Institute of America in four categories—carat count, type of cut, color, and clarity. In essence, Blue Nile has turned diamonds into a commodity and is using an operational excellence customer value proposition to generate annual sales of $154 million.

Source: Victoria Murphy, "Romance Killer," *Forbes*, November 29, 2004, pp. 97–101.

The Work of Management and the Need for Managerial Accounting Information

Every organization—large and small—has managers. Someone must be responsible for formulating strategy, making plans, organizing resources, directing personnel, and controlling operations. This is true of the Bank of America, the Peace Corps, the University of Illinois, the Red Cross, and the Coca-Cola Corporation, as well as the local 7-Eleven convenience store. In this chapter, we will use a particular organization—Good Vibrations, Inc.—to illustrate the work of management. What we have to say about the management of Good Vibrations, however, is very general and can be applied to virtually any organization.

Good Vibrations runs a chain of retail outlets that sells a full range of music CDs. The chain's stores are concentrated in Pacific Rim cities such as Sydney, Singapore, Hong Kong, Beijing, Tokyo, and Vancouver. The company has found that the best way to generate sales, and profits, is to create an exciting shopping environment following a customer intimacy strategy. Consequently, the company puts a great deal of effort into planning the layout and decor of its stores—which are often quite large and extend over several floors in key downtown locations. Management knows that different types of clientele are attracted to different kinds of music. The international rock section is generally decorated with bold, brightly colored graphics, and the aisles are purposely narrow to create a crowded feeling much like one would experience at a popular nightclub on Friday night. In contrast, the classical music section is wood-paneled and fully sound insulated, with the rich, spacious feeling of a country club meeting room.

Managers at Good Vibrations like managers everywhere, carry out three major activities—*planning, directing and motivating,* and *controlling.* **Planning** involves establishing a basic strategy, selecting a course of action, and specifying how the action will be implemented. **Directing and motivating** involves mobilizing people to carry out plans and run routine operations. **Controlling** involves ensuring that the plan is actually carried out and is appropriately modified as circumstances change. Management accounting information plays a vital role in these basic management activities—but most particularly in the planning and control functions.

Planning

An important part of planning is to identify alternatives and then to select from among the alternatives the one that best fits the organization's strategy and objectives. The basic objective of Good Vibrations is to earn profits for the owners of the company by providing superior service at competitive prices in as many markets as possible. To further this strategy, every year top management carefully considers a range of options, or alternatives, for expanding into new geographic markets. This year management is considering opening new stores in Shanghai, Los Angeles, and Auckland.

When making this choice, management must balance the potential benefits of opening a new store against the costs and demands on the company's resources. Management knows from bitter experience that opening a store in a major new market is a big step that cannot be taken lightly. It requires enormous amounts of time and energy from the company's most experienced, talented, and busy professionals. When the company attempted to open stores in both Beijing and Vancouver in the same year, resources were stretched too thinly. The result was that neither store opened on schedule, and operations in the rest of the company suffered. Therefore, Good Vibrations plans very carefully before entering a new market.

Among other data, top management looks at the sales volumes, profit margins, and costs of the company's established stores in similar markets. These data, supplied by the management accountant, are combined with projected sales volume data at the proposed new locations to estimate the profits that would be generated by the new stores. In general, virtually all important alternatives considered by management in the planning process impact revenues or costs, and management accounting data are essential in estimating those impacts.

After considering all of the alternatives, Good Vibrations' top management decided to open a store in the booming Shanghai market in the third quarter of the year, but to defer opening any other new stores to another year. As soon as this decision was made, detailed plans were drawn up for all parts of the company that would be involved in the Shanghai opening. For example, the Personnel Department's travel budget was increased, since it would be providing extensive on-site training to the new personnel hired in Shanghai.

As in the case of the Personnel Department, the plans of management are often expressed formally in **budgets,** and the term *budgeting* is generally used to describe this part of the planning process. Budgets are usually prepared under the direction of the **controller,** who is the manager in charge of the Accounting Department. Typically, budgets are prepared annually and represent management's plans in specific, quantitative terms. In addition to a travel budget, the Personnel Department will be given goals in terms of new hires, courses taught, and detailed breakdowns of expected expenses. Similarly, the store managers will be given targets for sales volume, profit, expenses, pilferage losses, and employee training. Good Vibrations' management accountants will collect, analyze, and summarize these data in the form of budgets.

Directing and Motivating

In addition to planning for the future, managers oversee day-to-day activities and try to keep the organization functioning smoothly. This requires motivating and directing people. Managers assign tasks to employees, arbitrate disputes, answer questions, solve on-the-spot problems, and make many small decisions that affect customers and employees. In effect, directing is that part of a manager's job that deals with the routine and the here and now. Managerial accounting data, such as daily sales reports, are often used in this type of day-to-day activity.

Controlling

In carrying out the **control** function, managers seek to ensure that the plan is being followed. **Feedback,** which signals whether operations are on track, is the key to effective control. In sophisticated organizations, this feedback is provided by various detailed reports. One of these reports, which compares budgeted to actual results, is called a **performance report.** Performance reports suggest where operations are not proceeding as planned and where some parts of the organization may require additional attention. For example, the manager of the new Shanghai store will be given sales volume, profit, and expense targets. As the year progresses, performance reports will be constructed that compare actual sales volume, profit, and expenses to the targets. If the actual results fall below the targets, top management will be alerted that the Shanghai store requires more attention. Experienced personnel can be flown in to help the new manager, or top management may conclude that its plans need to be revised. As we shall see in later chapters, one of the central purposes of managerial accounting is to provide this kind of feedback to managers.

The End Results of Managers' Activities

When a customer enters a Good Vibrations store, the results of management's planning, directing and motivating, and controlling activities will be evident in the many details that make the difference between a pleasant and an irritating shopping experience. The store will be clean, fashionably decorated, and logically laid out. Featured artists' videos will be displayed on TV monitors throughout the store, and the background rock music will be loud enough to send older patrons scurrying for the classical music section. Popular CDs will be in stock, and the latest hits will be available for private listening on earphones. Specific titles will be easy to find. Regional music, such as CantoPop in Hong Kong, will be prominently featured. Checkout clerks will be alert, friendly, and efficient. In short, what the customer experiences doesn't simply happen; it is the result of the efforts of managers who must visualize and then fit together the processes that are needed to get the job done.

The Planning and Control Cycle

Exhibit 1–2 (page 8) depicts the work of management in the form of the *planning and control cycle*. The **planning and control cycle** involves the smooth flow of management activities from planning through directing and motivating, controlling, and then back to planning again. All of these activities involve decision making, which is the hub around which the other activities revolve.

Comparison of Financial and Managerial Accounting

Financial accounting reports are prepared for external parties such as shareholders and creditors, whereas managerial accounting reports are prepared for managers inside the organization. This contrast in orientation results in a number of major differences between financial and managerial accounting, even though they often rely on the same underlying financial data. Exhibit 1–3 (page 8) summarizes these differences.

As shown in Exhibit 1–3, financial and managerial accounting differ not only in their user orientation but also in their emphasis on the past and the future, in the type of data provided to users, and in several other ways. These differences are discussed in the following paragraphs.

> **LEARNING OBJECTIVE 1**
> Identify the major differences and similarities between financial and managerial accounting.

Emphasis on the Future

Since *planning* is such an important part of the manager's job, managerial accounting has a strong future orientation. In contrast, financial accounting primarily summarizes past financial transactions. These summaries may be useful in planning, but only to a point. The future is not simply a reflection of what has happened in the past. Changes are constantly taking place in economic conditions, customer needs and desires, competitive conditions, and so on. All of these changes demand that the manager's planning be based in large part on estimates of what will happen rather than on summaries of what has already happened.

Topic Tackler

PLUS

1–1

EXHIBIT 1–2
The Planning and Control Cycle

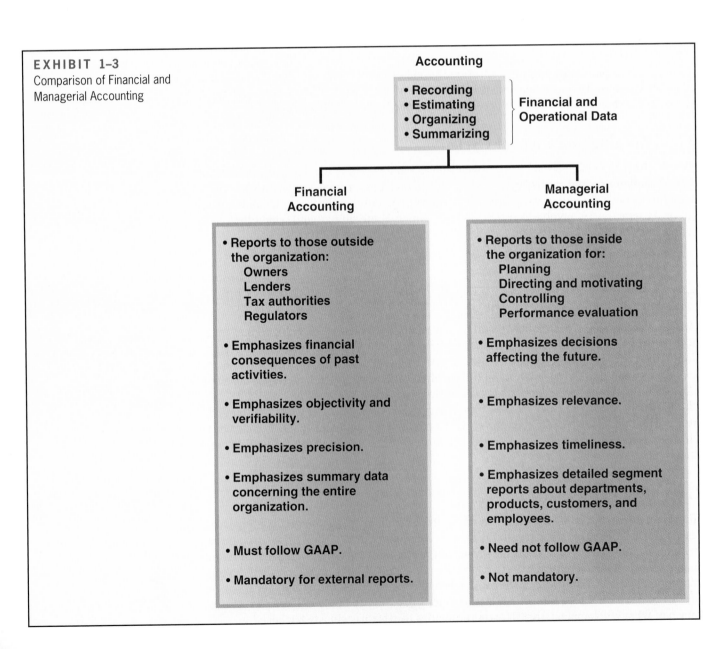

EXHIBIT 1–3
Comparison of Financial and
Managerial Accounting

Relevance of Data

Financial accounting data should be objective and verifiable. However, for internal uses managers want information that is relevant even if it is not completely objective or verifiable. By relevant, we mean *appropriate for the problem at hand.* For example, it is difficult to verify estimated sales volumes for a proposed new store at Good Vibrations, but this is exactly the type of information that is most useful to managers. Managerial accounting should be flexible enough to provide whatever data are relevant for a particular decision.

Less Emphasis on Precision

Making sure that dollar amounts are accurate down to the last dollar or penny takes time and effort. While that kind of accuracy is required for external reports, most managers would rather have a good estimate immediately than wait for a more precise answer later. For this reason, managerial accountants often place less emphasis on precision than financial accountants do. For example, in a decision involving hundreds of millions of dollars, estimates that are rounded off to the nearest million dollars are probably good enough. In addition to placing less emphasis on precision than financial accounting, managerial accounting places much more weight on nonmonetary data. For example, data about customer satisfaction may be routinely used in managerial accounting reports.

Segments of an Organization

Financial accounting is primarily concerned with reporting for the company as a whole. By contrast, managerial accounting focuses much more on the parts, or **segments,** of a company. These segments may be product lines, sales territories, divisions, departments, or any other categorization that management finds useful. Financial accounting does require some breakdowns of revenues and costs by major segments in external reports, but this is a secondary emphasis. In managerial accounting, segment reporting is the primary emphasis.

Generally Accepted Accounting Principles (GAAP)

Financial accounting statements prepared for external users must comply with generally accepted accounting principles (GAAP). External users must have some assurance that the reports have been prepared in accordance with a common set of ground rules. These common ground rules enhance comparability and help reduce fraud and misrepresentation, but they do not necessarily lead to the type of reports that would be most useful in internal decision making. For example, if management at Good Vibrations is considering selling land to finance a new store, they need to know the current market value of the land. However, GAAP requires that the land be stated at its original, historical cost on financial reports. The more relevant data for the decision—the current market value—is ignored under GAAP.

Managerial accounting is not bound by GAAP. Managers set their own rules concerning the content and form of internal reports. The only constraint is that the expected benefits from using the information should outweigh the costs of collecting, analyzing, and summarizing the data. Nevertheless, as we shall see in subsequent chapters, it is undeniably true that financial reporting requirements have heavily influenced management accounting practice.

Managerial Accounting—Not Mandatory

Financial accounting is mandatory; that is, it must be done. Various outside parties such as the Securities and Exchange Commission (SEC) and the tax authorities require periodic financial statements. Managerial accounting, on the other hand, is not mandatory. A company is completely free to do as much or as little as it wishes. No regulatory bodies or other outside agencies specify what is to be done, or, for that matter, whether anything is to be done at all. Since managerial accounting is completely optional, the important question is always, "Is the information useful?" rather than, "Is the information required?"

Organizational Structure

LEARNING OBJECTIVE 2
Understand the role of management accountants in an organization.

Management must accomplish its objectives by working through people. Presidents of companies like Good Vibrations could not possibly execute all of their company's strategies alone; they must rely on other people. This is done by creating an organizational structure that permits effective *decentralization.*

Decentralization

Decentralization is the delegation of decision-making authority throughout an organization by giving managers the authority to make decisions relating to their area of responsibility. Some organizations are more decentralized than others. Because of Good Vibrations' geographic dispersion and the peculiarities of local markets, the company is highly decentralized.

Good Vibrations' president (often synonymous with the term chief executive officer, or CEO) sets the broad strategy for the company and makes major strategic decisions such as opening stores in new markets; however, much of the remaining decision-making authority is delegated to managers at various levels throughout the organization. Each of the company's numerous retail stores has a store manager as well as a separate manager for each music category such as international rock and classical/jazz. In addition, the company has support departments such as a central Purchasing Department and a Personnel Department.

The Functional View of Organizations

Exhibit 1–4 shows Good Vibrations' organizational structure in the form of an **organization chart.** The purpose of an organization chart is to show how responsibility is divided among

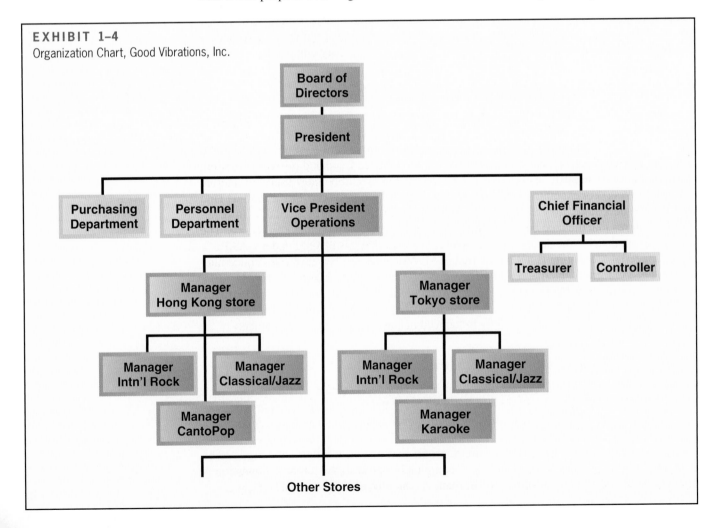

EXHIBIT 1–4
Organization Chart, Good Vibrations, Inc.

managers and to show formal lines of reporting and communication, or *chain of command.* Each box depicts an area of management responsibility, and the lines between the boxes show the lines of formal authority between managers. The chart tells us, for example, that the store managers are responsible to the operations vice president. In turn, the operations vice president is responsible to the company president, who in turn is responsible to the board of directors. Following the lines of authority and communication on the organization chart, we can see that the manager of the Hong Kong store would ordinarily report to the operations vice president rather than directly to the president of the company.

Informal relationships and channels of communication often develop outside the formal reporting relationships on the organization chart as a result of personal contacts between managers. The informal structure does not appear on the organization chart, but it is often vital to effective operations.

Line and Staff Relationships

An organization chart also depicts *line* and *staff* positions in an organization. A person in a **line** position is *directly* involved in achieving the basic objectives of the organization. A person in a **staff** position, by contrast, is only *indirectly* involved in achieving those basic objectives. Staff positions provide assistance to line positions or other parts of the organization, but they do not have direct authority over line positions. Refer again to the organization chart in Exhibit 1–4. Because the basic objective of Good Vibrations is to sell recorded music at a profit, those managers whose areas of responsibility are directly related to selling music occupy line positions. These positions, which are shown in a darker color in the exhibit, include the managers of the various music departments in each store, the store managers, the operations vice president, the president, and the board of directors.

By contrast, the manager of the central Purchasing Department occupies a staff position, since the only purpose of the Purchasing Department is to serve the line departments by doing their purchasing for them. However, both line and staff managers have authority over the employees in their own departments.

The Chief Financial Officer

As previously mentioned, in the United States the manager of the accounting department is often known as the *controller.* The controller in turn reports to the *Chief Financial Officer (CFO).* The **Chief Financial Officer** is the member of the top management team who is responsible for providing timely and relevant data to support planning and control activities and for preparing financial statements for external users. An effective CFO is considered a key member of the top management team whose advice is sought in all major decisions. The CFO is a highly paid professional who has command over the technical details of accounting and finance, who can provide leadership to other professionals in his or her department, who can analyze new and evolving situations, who can communicate technical data to others in a simple and clear manner, and who is able to work well with top managers from other disciplines. More than ever, the accountants who work under the CFO focus their efforts on supporting the needs of their co-workers in line positions:

> Growing numbers of management accountants spend the bulk of their time as internal consultants or business analysts within their companies. Technological advances have liberated them from the mechanical aspects of accounting. They spend less time preparing standardized reports and more time analyzing and interpreting information. Many have moved from the isolation of accounting departments to be physically positioned in the operating departments with which they work. Management accountants work on cross-functional teams, have extensive face-to-face communications with people throughout their organizations, and are actively involved in decision making. . . . They are trusted advisors.[4]

---

[4] Gary Siegel Organization, *Counting More, Counting Less: Transformations in the Management Accounting Profession, The 1999 Practice Analysis of Management Accounting,* Institute of Management Accountants, Montvale, NJ, August 1999, p. 3.

WHAT DOES IT TAKE?

A controller at McDonald's describes the characteristics needed by its most successful management accountants as follows:

> [I]t's a given that you know your accounting cold. You're expected to know the tax implications of proposed courses of action. You need to understand cost flows and information flows. You have to be very comfortable with technology and be an expert in the company's business and accounting software. You have to be a generalist. You need a working knowledge of what people do in marketing, engineering, human resources, and other departments. You need to understand how the processes, departments, and functions work together to run the business. You'll be expected to contribute ideas at planning meetings, so you have to see the big picture, keep a focus on the bottom line, and think strategically.

Source: Gary Siegel, James E. Sorensen, and Sandra B. Richtermeyer, "Becoming a Business Partner: Part 2," *Strategic Finance*, October 2003, pp. 37–41. Used with permission from the Institute of Management Accountants (IMA), Montvale, N.J., USA, www.imanet.org.

Process Management

LEARNING OBJECTIVE 3
Understand the basic concepts underlying Lean Production, the Theory of Constraints (TOC), and Six Sigma.

As discussed at the beginning of this chapter, the last two decades have been a period of tremendous turmoil and change in the business environment. Competition in many industries has become worldwide in scope, and the pace of innovation in products and services has accelerated. This has been good news for consumers, since intensified competition has generally led to lower prices, higher quality, and more choices. However, for businesses intensified global competition has presented serious challenges. More than ever companies are realizing that they must complement the functional view of their operations with a cross-functional orientation that seeks to improve the *business processes* that deliver customer value.

A **business process** is a series of steps that are followed in order to carry out some task in a business. It is quite common for the linked set of steps comprising a business process to span departmental boundaries. The term *value chain* is often used when we look at how the functional departments of an organization interact with one another to form business processes. A **value chain,** as shown in Exhibit 1–5, consists of the major business functions that add value to a company's products and services. The customer's needs are most effectively met by coordinating the business processes that span these functions.

This section discusses three different approaches to managing and improving business processes—Lean Production, the Theory of Constraints (TOC), and Six Sigma. Although each is unique in certain respects, they all share the common theme of focusing on managing and improving business processes.

Topic Tackler

PLUS

1–2

EXHIBIT 1–5
Business Functions Making Up the Value Chain

Research and Development	Product Design	Manufacturing	Marketing	Distribution	Customer Service

Lean Production

Traditionally, managers in manufacturing companies have sought to maximize production so as to spread the costs of investments in equipment and other assets over as many units as possible. In addition, managers have traditionally felt that an important part of their jobs was to keep everyone busy on the theory that idleness wastes money. These traditional views, often aided and abetted by traditional management accounting practices, resulted in a number of practices that have come under criticism in recent years.

In a traditional manufacturing company, work is *pushed* through the system in order to produce as much as possible and to keep everyone busy—even if products cannot be immediately sold. This almost inevitably results in large inventories of *raw materials, work in process,* and *finished* goods. **Raw materials** are the materials that are used to make a product. **Work in process** inventories consist of units of product that are only partially complete and will require further work before they are ready for sale to a customer. **Finished goods** inventories consist of units of product that have been completed but have not yet been sold to customers.

The *push* process in traditional manufacturing starts by accumulating large amounts of raw material inventories from suppliers so that operations can proceed smoothly even if unanticipated disruptions occur. Next, enough materials are released to workstations to keep everyone busy. When a workstation completes its tasks, the partially completed goods (i.e., work in process) are "pushed" forward to the next workstation regardless of whether that workstation is ready to receive them. The result is that partially completed goods stack up, waiting for the next workstation to become available. They may not be completed for days, weeks, or even months. Additionally, when the units are finally completed, customers may or may not want them. If finished goods are produced faster than the market will absorb, the result is bloated finished goods inventories.

Although some may argue that maintaining large amounts of inventory has its benefits, it clearly has its costs. According to experts, in addition to tying up money, maintaining inventories encourages inefficient and sloppy work, results in too many defects, and dramatically increases the amount of time required to complete a product. For example, when partially completed goods are stored for long periods of time before being processed by the next workstation, defects introduced by the preceding workstation go unnoticed. If a machine is out of calibration or incorrect procedures are being followed, many defective units will be produced before the problem is discovered. And when the defects are finally discovered, it may be very difficult to track down the source of the problem. In addition, units may be obsolete or out of fashion by the time they are finally completed.

Large inventories of partially completed goods create many other problems that are best discussed in more advanced courses. These problems are not obvious—if they were, companies would have long ago reduced their inventories. Managers at Toyota are credited with the insight that large inventories often create many more problems than they solve. Toyota pioneered what is known today as *Lean Production*.

The Lean Thinking Model   The **lean thinking model** is a five-step management approach that organizes resources such as people and machines around the flow of business processes and that pulls units through these processes in response to customer orders. The result is lower inventories, fewer defects, less wasted effort, and quicker customer response times. Exhibit 1–6 (page 14) depicts the five stages of the lean thinking model.

The first step is to identify the value to customers in specific products and services. The second step is to identify the *business process* that delivers this value to customers.[5] As discussed earlier, the linked set of steps comprising a business process typically span the departmental boundaries that are specified in an organization chart. The third step is to organize work arrangements around the flow of the business process. This is often accomplished by creating what is known as a *manufacturing cell*. The cellular approach takes employees

---

[5]   The Lean Production literature uses the term *value stream* rather than *business process.*

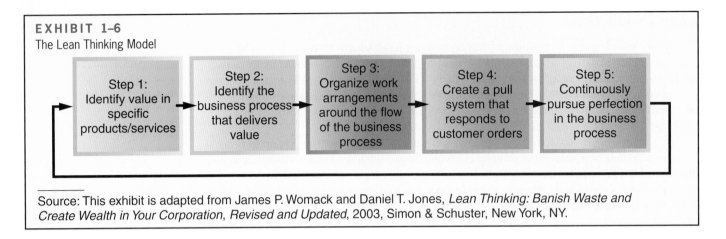

EXHIBIT 1–6
The Lean Thinking Model

Step 1: Identify value in specific products/services → Step 2: Identify the business process that delivers value → Step 3: Organize work arrangements around the flow of the business process → Step 4: Create a pull system that responds to customer orders → Step 5: Continuously pursue perfection in the business process

Source: This exhibit is adapted from James P. Womack and Daniel T. Jones, *Lean Thinking: Banish Waste and Create Wealth in Your Corporation, Revised and Updated*, 2003, Simon & Schuster, New York, NY.

and equipment from departments that were previously separated from one another and places them side-by-side in a work space called a *cell*. The equipment within the cell is aligned in a sequential manner that follows the steps of the business process. Each employee is trained to perform all the steps within his or her own manufacturing cell.

The fourth step in the lean thinking model is to create a pull system where production is not initiated until a customer has ordered a product. Inventories are reduced to a minimum by purchasing raw materials and producing units only as needed to meet customer demand. Under ideal conditions, a company operating a pull system would purchase only enough materials each day to meet that day's needs. Moreover, the company would have no goods still in process at the end of the day, and all goods completed during the day would be shipped immediately to customers. As this sequence suggests, work takes place "just-in-time" in the sense that raw materials are received by each manufacturing cell just in time to go into production, manufactured parts are completed just in time to be assembled into products, and products are completed just in time to be shipped to customers. Not surprisingly, this facet of the lean thinking model is often called **just-in-time** production, or **JIT** for short.

The change from *push* to *pull* production is more profound than it may appear. Among other things, producing only in response to a customer order means that workers will be idle whenever demand falls below the company's production capacity. This can be an extremely difficult cultural change for an organization. It challenges the core beliefs of many managers and raises anxieties in workers who have become accustomed to being kept busy all of the time.

The fifth step of the lean thinking model is to continuously pursue perfection in the business process. In a traditional company, parts and materials are inspected for defects when they are received from suppliers, and assembled units are inspected as they progress along the production line. In a Lean Production system, the company's suppliers are responsible for the quality of incoming parts and materials. And instead of using quality inspectors, the company's production workers are directly responsible for spotting defective units. A worker who discovers a defect immediately stops the flow of production. Supervisors and other workers go to the cell to determine the cause of the problem and correct it before any further defective units are produced. This procedure ensures that problems are quickly identified and corrected.

The lean thinking model can also be used to improve the business processes that link companies together. The term **supply chain management** is commonly used to refer to the coordination of business processes across companies to better serve end consumers. For example Procter & Gamble and Costco coordinate their business processes to ensure that Procter & Gamble's products, such as Bounty, Tide, and Crest, are on Costco's shelves when customers want them. Both Procter & Gamble and Costco realize that their mutual success depends on working together to ensure Procter & Gamble's products are available to Costco's customers.

THE POWER OF LEAN

Lean thinking can benefit all types of businesses. For example, Dell Inc.'s lean production system can produce a customized personal computer within 36 hours. Even more impressive, Dell doesn't start ordering components and assembling computers until orders are booked. By ordering right before assembly, Dell's parts are on average 60 days newer than those of its competitors, which translates into a 6% profit advantage in components alone.

In the service arena, Jefferson Pilot Financial (JPF) realized that "[l]ike an automobile on the assembly line, an insurance policy goes through a series of processes, from initial application to underwriting, or risk assessment, to policy issuance. With each step, value is added to the work in progress—just as a car gets doors or a coat of paint." Given this realization, JPF organized its work arrangements into a cellular layout and synchronized the rate of output to the pace of customer demand. JPF's lean thinking enabled it to reduce attending physician statement turnaround times by 70%, decrease labor costs 26%, and reduce reissue errors by 40%.

Sources: Gary McWilliams, "Whirlwind on the Web," *BusinessWeek*, April 7, 1997, p. 134; Stephen Pritchard, "Inside Dell's Lean Machine," *Works Management*, December 2002, pp. 14–16; and Cynthia Karen Swank, "The Lean Service Machine," *Harvard Business Review*, October 2003, pp. 123–129.

The Theory of Constraints (TOC)

A **constraint** is anything that prevents you from getting more of what you want. Every individual and every organization faces at least one constraint, so it is not difficult to find examples of constraints. You may not have enough time to study thoroughly for every subject *and* to go out with your friends on the weekend, so time is your constraint. United Airlines has only a limited number of loading gates available at its busy Chicago O'Hare hub, so its constraint is loading gates. Vail Resorts has only a limited amount of land to develop as homesites and commercial lots at its ski areas, so its constraint is land.

The **Theory of Constraints (TOC)** is based on the insight that effectively managing the constraint is a key to success. As an example, long waiting periods for surgery are a chronic problem in the National Health Service (NHS), the government-funded provider of health care in the United Kingdom. The diagram in Exhibit 1–7 illustrates a simplified version of the steps followed by a surgery patient. The number of patients who can be processed through each step in a day is indicated in the exhibit. For example, appointments for outpatient visits can be made for as many as 100 referrals from general practitioners in a day.

The constraint, or *bottleneck,* in the system is determined by the step that has the smallest capacity—in this case surgery. The total number of patients processed through the entire system cannot exceed 15 per day—the maximum number of patients who can be treated in surgery. No matter how hard managers, doctors, and nurses try to improve the processing rate elsewhere in the system, they will never succeed in driving down wait lists until the capacity

EXHIBIT 1–7
Processing Surgery Patients at an NHS Facility (simplified)*

General practitioner referral	Appointment made	Outpatient visit	Add to surgery waiting list	Surgery	Follow-up visit	Discharge
100 patients per day	100 patients per day	50 patients per day	150 patients per day	15 patients per day	60 patients per day	140 patients per day

*This diagram originally appeared in the February 1999 issue of the U.K. magazine *Health Management*.

of surgery is increased. In fact, improvements elsewhere in the system—particularly before the constraint—are likely to result in even longer waiting times and more frustrated patients and health care providers. Thus, to be effective, improvement efforts must be focused on the constraint. A business process, such as the process for serving surgery patients, is like a chain. If you want to increase the strength of a chain, what is the most effective way to do this? Should you concentrate your efforts on strengthening the strongest link, all the links, or the weakest link? Clearly, focusing your effort on the weakest link will bring the biggest benefit.

The procedure to follow to strengthen the chain is clear. First, identify the weakest link, which is the constraint. In the case of the NHS, the constraint is surgery. Second, do not place a greater strain on the system than the weakest link can handle—if you do, the chain will break. In the case of the NHS, more referrals than surgery can accommodate lead to unacceptably long waiting lists. Third, concentrate improvement efforts on strengthening the weakest link. In the case of the NHS, this means finding ways to increase the number of surgeries that can be performed in a day. Fourth, if the improvement efforts are successful, eventually the weakest link will improve to the point where it is no longer the weakest link. At that point, the new weakest link (i.e., the new constraint) must be identified, and improvement efforts must be shifted over to that link. This simple sequential process provides a powerful strategy for optimizing business processes.

IN BUSINESS

WATCH WHERE YOU CUT COSTS

At one hospital, the emergency room became so backlogged that its doors were closed to the public and patients were turned away for over 36 hours in the course of a single month. It turned out, after investigation, that the constraint was not the emergency room itself; it was the housekeeping staff. To cut costs, managers at the hospital had laid off housekeeping workers. This created a bottleneck in the emergency room because rooms were not being cleaned as quickly as the emergency room staff could process new patients. Thus, laying off some of the lowest paid workers at the hospital had the effect of forcing the hospital to idle some of its most highly paid staff and most expensive equipment!

Source: Tracey Burton-Houle, "AGI Continues to Steadily Make Advances with the Adaptation of TOC into Healthcare," www.goldratt.com/toctquarterly/august2002.htm.

Six Sigma

Six Sigma is a process improvement method that relies on customer feedback and fact-based data gathering and analysis techniques to drive process improvement. Motorola and General Electric are closely identified with the emergence of the Six Sigma movement. Technically, the term Six Sigma refers to a process that generates no more than 3.4 defects per million opportunities. Because this rate of defects is so low, Six Sigma is sometimes associated with the term *zero defects*.

The most common framework used to guide Six Sigma process improvement efforts is known as DMAIC (pronounced: du-may-ik), which stands for Define, Measure, Analyze, Improve, and Control. As summarized in Exhibit 1–8, the Define stage of the process focuses on defining the scope and purpose of the project, the flow of the current process, and the customer's requirements. The Measure stage is used to gather baseline performance data concerning the existing process and to narrow the scope of the project to the most important problems. The Analyze stage focuses on identifying the root causes of the problems that were identified during the Measure stage. The Analyze stage often reveals that the process includes many *activities that do not add value to the product or service*. Activities that customers are not willing to pay for because they add no value are known as **non-value-added**

Stage	Goals
Define	Establish the scope and purpose of the project. Diagram the flow of the current process. Establish the customer's requirements for the process.
Measure	Gather baseline performance data related to the existing process. Narrow the scope of the project to the most important problems.
Analyze	Identify the root cause(s) of the problems identified in the Measure stage.
Improve	Develop, evaluate, and implement solutions to the problems.
Control	Ensure that problems remain fixed. Seek to improve the new methods over time.

Source: Peter C. Brewer and Nancy A. Bagranoff, "Near Zero-Defect Accounting with Six Sigma," *Journal of Corporate Accounting and Finance,* January-February 2004, pp. 67–72.

EXHIBIT 1–8
The Six Sigma DMAIC
Framework

activities and such activities should be eliminated wherever possible. During the Improve stage potential solutions are developed, evaluated, and implemented to eliminate non-value-added activities and any other problems uncovered in the Analyze stage. Finally, the objective in the Control stage is to ensure that the problems remain fixed and that the new methods are improved over time.[6]

Managers must be very careful when attempting to translate Six Sigma improvements into financial benefits. There are only two ways to increase profits—decrease costs or increase sales. Cutting costs may seem easy—lay off workers who are no longer needed because of improvements such as eliminating non-value-added activities. However, if this approach is taken, employees quickly get the message that process improvements lead to job losses and they will understandably resist further improvement efforts. If improvement is to continue, employees must be convinced that the end result of improvement will be more secure rather than less secure jobs. This can only happen if management uses tools such as Six Sigma to generate more business rather than to cut the workforce.

Technology in Business

Technology is being harnessed in many ways by businesses. In this section we will discuss two of these ways—e-commerce and enterprise systems.

E-Commerce

E-commerce refers to business that is conducted using the Internet. At the start of the new millennium, e-commerce was riding high. The stock prices of dot.com companies (companies that focus on generating revenue exclusively through the Internet) were climbing by leaps and bounds. On January 30, 2000, more than 20 dot.com companies, such as Pets.com and Epidemic.com, paid as much as $3 million for 30-second commercials during the Super Bowl. However, by November of that same year, prospects for dot.com companies began to worsen as companies such as Pets.com, Garden.com and Furniture.com all failed. By the spring of 2001, EToys had folded and monthly statistics for dot.com layoffs and closures had peaked at 17,554 and 64, respectively. In short, the dot.com collapse was under way.[7]

---

[6] Peter C. Brewer, "Six Sigma Helps a Company Create a Culture of Accountability," *Journal of Organizational Excellence,* Summer 2004, pp. 45–59.

[7] Time line published by BBC News at http://news.bbc.co.uk.

Since the collapse of the dot.com bubble in 2001, e-commerce has slowly been rebuilding momentum. Internet advertising is projected to exceed $12 billion per year before the end of the decade.[8] And while e-commerce has already had a major impact on the sale of books, music, and airline tickets, it appears that companies such as Blue Nile, eBay, Amazon.com, Lending Tree, and Expedia will continue to disrupt and redefine other markets such as the jewelry, real estate, and hotel industries.[9] In addition to dot.com companies, established brick-and-mortar companies such as General Electric, Wells Fargo, and Target will undoubtedly continue to expand into cyberspace—both for business-to-business transactions and for retailing.

The growth in e-commerce is occurring because the Internet has important advantages over more conventional marketplaces for many kinds of transactions. For example, the Internet is an ideal technology for streamlining the mortgage lending process. Customers can complete loan applications over the Internet rather than tying up the time of a staffperson in an office. And data and funds can be sent back and forth electronically.

Nevertheless, while building a successful dot.com business remains a tenuous and high-risk proposition, e-commerce is here to stay. The stock prices of dot.com companies will rise and fall, but the benefits that the Internet provides to businesses and their customers will ensure that e-commerce grows.

IN BUSINESS

INTERNET INNOVATIONS

Companies continue to develop new ways of using the Internet to improve their performance. Below is a summary of intriguing Internet applications categorized into four descriptive groups.

1. Collaboration
   - Eli Lilly has a website where scientific problems are posed to its global workforce. The best solutions earn cash rewards.
   - Lockheed Martin used the Internet to help 80 of its suppliers from around the world to collaborate in designing and building a new stealth fighter plane.

2. Customer Service
   - General Motors uses the Internet to auction off vehicles with expired leases.
   - IndyMac Bancorp uses the Internet to link its nationwide network of loan brokers to its central computers. Using these links, the brokers can electronically submit and then monitor their clients' loan applications.

3. Management
   - CareGroup's approximately 2,500 doctors are rated on 20 criteria related to the care they provide for insured patients. The results are summarized on digital report cards that have helped spot inefficiencies, saving the company $4 million annually.
   - Bristol-Myers Squibb uses the Internet to speed up drug research and development. The Web-based system has reduced by one-third the time needed to develop new medications.

4. Cutting Edge
   - Fresh Direct is an on-line grocer in New York City. Using the Internet to streamline order processing, the company is able to charge prices as much as 35% below its competitors.
   - eArmyU is a virtual Internet-based university that provides educational opportunities to 40,000 geographically dispersed U.S. soldiers.

Source: Heather Green, "The Web Smart 50," *BusinessWeek*, November 24, 2003, pp. 82–106.

---

[8] Stephen Baker, "Where the Real Internet Money Is Made," *BusinessWeek*, December 27, 2004, p. 99.

[9] Timothy J. Mullaney, "E-Biz Strikes Again!" *BusinessWeek*, May 10, 2004, pp. 80–90.

Enterprise Systems[10]

Historically, most companies implemented specific software programs to support specific business functions. The accounting department would select its own software applications to meet its needs, while manufacturing would select different software programs to support its needs. The separate systems were not integrated and could not easily pass data back and forth. The end result was data duplication and data inconsistencies coupled with lengthy customer response times and high costs.

An **enterprise system** is designed to overcome these problems by integrating data across an organization into a single software system that enables all employees to have simultaneous access to a common set of data. There are two keys to the data integration inherent in an enterprise system. First, all data are recorded only once in the company's centralized digital data repository known as a database. When data are added to the database or are changed, the new information is simultaneously and immediately available to everyone across the organization. Second, the unique data elements contained within the database can be linked together. For example, one data element, such as a customer identification number, can be related to other data elements, such as that customer's address, billing history, shipping history, merchandise returns history, and so on. The ability to forge such relationships among data elements explains why this type of database is called a *relational database*.

Data integration helps employees communicate with one another and it also helps them communicate with their suppliers and customers. For example, consider how the *customer relationship management* process is improved when enterprise-wide information resides in one location. Whether meeting the customer's needs requires accessing information related to billing (an accounting function), delivery status (a distribution function), price quotes (a marketing function), or merchandise returns (a customer service function) the required information is readily available to the employee interacting with the customer. Though expensive and risky to install, the benefits of data integration have led many companies to invest in enterprise systems.

IN BUSINESS

THE BENEFITS OF DATA INTEGRATION

Nike's old supply-chain system was tenuously connected by 27 different computer systems, most of which could not talk to one another. The results for Nike were predictable—retailers ran out of hot-selling sneakers and were saddled with duds that didn't sell. Nike spent $500 million to fix the problem and the results have been impressive—the lead time for getting new sneaker styles to retail shelves has been cut from nine to six months. The percentage of shoes that Nike makes without a firm order from a retailer has dropped from 30% to 3%.

Agri Beef Company's enterprise system enables its accounts payable process to accomplish in two check runs what used to require 22 check runs. As Treasurer Kim Stuart commented: "Now we can post transactions straight through to another division's general ledger account . . . That change alone saves us 200 [labor] hours a month."

Sources: Stanley Holmes, "The New Nike," *BusinessWeek*, September 20, 2004, pp. 78–86; Doug Bartholomew, "The ABC's of ERP," *CFO-IT*, Fall 2004, pp. 19–21.

The Importance of Ethics in Business

A series of major financial scandals involving Enron, Tyco International, HealthSouth, Adelphia Communications, WorldCom, Global Crossing, Rite Aid, and other companies have raised deep concerns about ethics in business. The managers and companies involved in these scandals have suffered mightily—from huge fines to jail terms and financial

LEARNING OBJECTIVE 4
Understand the importance of upholding ethical standards.

---

[10] *Enterprise systems* is a broad term that encompasses many enterprise-wide computer applications such as customer relationship management and supply chain management systems. Perhaps the most frequently mentioned type of enterprise system is an Enterprise Resource Planning (ERP) system.

collapse. And the recognition that ethical behavior is absolutely essential for the functioning of our economy has led to numerous regulatory changes—some of which we will discuss in a later section on corporate governance. But why is ethical behavior so important? This is not a matter of just being "nice." Ethical behavior is the lubricant that keeps the economy running. Without that lubricant, the economy would operate much less efficiently—less would be available to consumers, quality would be lower, and prices would be higher.

Take a very simple example. Suppose that dishonest farmers, distributors, and grocers knowingly tried to sell wormy apples as good apples and that grocers refused to take back wormy apples. What would you do as a consumer of apples? Go to another grocer? But what if all grocers acted this way? What would you do then? You would probably either stop buying apples or you would spend a lot of time inspecting apples before buying them. So would everyone else. Now notice what has happened. Because farmers, distributors, and grocers could not be trusted, sales of apples would plummet and those who did buy apples would waste a lot of time inspecting them minutely. Everyone loses. Farmers, distributors; and grocers make less money; consumers enjoy fewer apples; and consumers waste time looking for worms. In other words, without fundamental trust in the integrity of businesses, the economy would operate much less efficiently. James Surowiecki summed up this point as follows:

> [F]lourishing economies require a healthy level of trust in the reliability and fairness of everyday transactions. If you assumed every potential deal was a rip-off or that the

NO TRUST—NO ENRON

Jonathan Karpoff reports on a particularly important, but often overlooked, aspect of the Enron debacle:

> As we know, some of Enron's reported profits in the late 1990s were pure accounting fiction. But the firm also had legitimate businesses and actual assets. Enron's most important businesses involved buying and selling electricity and other forms of energy. [Using Enron as an intermediary, utilities that needed power bought energy from producers with surplus generating capacity.] Now when an electric utility contracts to buy electricity, the managers of the utility want to make darned sure that the seller will deliver the electrons exactly as agreed, at the contracted price. There is no room for fudging on this because the consequences of not having the electricity when consumers switch on their lights are dire. . . .
>
> This means that the firms with whom Enron was trading electricity . . . had to trust Enron. And trust Enron they did, to the tune of billions of dollars of trades every year. But in October 2001, when Enron announced that its previous financial statements overstated the firm's profits, it undermined such trust. As everyone recognizes, the announcement caused investors to lower their valuations of the firm. Less understood, however, was the more important impact of the announcement; by revealing some of its reported earnings to be a house of cards, Enron sabotaged its reputation. The effect was to undermine even its legitimate and (previously) profitable operations that relied on its trustworthiness.
>
> This is why Enron melted down so fast. Its core businesses relied on the firm's reputation. When that reputation was wounded, energy traders took their business elsewhere. . . .

Energy traders lost their faith in Enron, but what if no other company could be trusted to deliver on its commitments to provide electricity as contracted? In that case, energy traders would have nowhere to turn. As a direct result, energy producers with surplus generating capacity would be unable to sell their surplus power. As a consequence, their existing customers would have to pay higher prices. And utilities that did not have sufficient capacity to meet demand on their own would have to build more capacity, which would also mean higher prices for their consumers. So a general lack of trust in companies such as Enron would ultimately result in overinvestment in energy-generating capacity and higher energy prices for consumers.

Source: Jonathan M. Karpoff, "Regulation vs. Reputation in Preventing Corporate Fraud," *UW Business,* Spring 2002, pp. 28–30 products you were buying were probably going to be lemons, then very little business would get done. More important, the costs of the transactions that did take place would be exorbitant, since you'd have to do enormous work to investigate each deal and you'd have to rely on the threat of legal action to enforce every contract. For an economy to prosper, what's needed is not a Pollyannaish faith that everyone else has your best interests at heart—"caveat emptor" [buyer beware] remains an important truth—but a basic confidence in the promises and commitments that people make about their products and services.[11]

Thus, for the good of everyone—including profit-making companies—it is vitally important that business be conducted within an ethical framework that builds and sustains trust.

The Institute of Management Accountants (IMA) of the United States has adopted an ethical code called the *Statement of Ethical Professional Practice* that describes in some detail the ethical responsibilities of management accountants. Even though the code was specifically developed for management accountants, it has much broader application.

Code of Conduct for Management Accountants

The IMA's Statement of Ethical Professional Practice consists of two parts that are presented in full in Exhibit 1–9 (page 22). The first part provides general guidelines for ethical behavior. In a nutshell, a management accountant has ethical responsibilities in four broad areas: first, to maintain a high level of professional competence; second, to treat sensitive matters with confidentiality; third, to maintain personal integrity; and fourth, to disclose information in a credible fashion. The second part of the code specifies what should be done if an individual finds evidence of ethical misconduct. We recommend that you stop at this point and read all of Exhibit 1–9.

The IMA's code of conduct provides sound, practical advice for management accountants and managers. Most of the rules in the code are motivated by a very practical consideration—if these rules were not generally followed in business, then the economy and all of us would suffer. Consider the following specific examples of the consequences of not abiding by the code:

- Suppose employees could not be trusted with confidential information. Then top managers would be reluctant to distribute such information within the company and, as a result, decisions would be based on incomplete information and operations would deteriorate.

- Suppose employees accepted bribes from suppliers. Then contracts would tend to go to suppliers who pay the highest bribes rather than to the most competent suppliers. Would you like to fly in aircraft whose wings were made by the subcontractor who paid the highest bribe? Would you fly as often? What would happen to the airline industry if its safety record deteriorated due to shoddy workmanship on contracted parts and assemblies?

- Suppose the presidents of companies routinely lied in their annual reports and financial statements. If investors could not rely on the basic integrity of a company's financial statements, they would have little basis for making informed decisions. Suspecting the worst, rational investors would pay less for securities issued by companies and may not be willing to invest at all. As a consequence, companies would have less money for productive investments—leading to slower economic growth, fewer goods and services, and higher prices.

---

[11] James Surowiecki, "A Virtuous Cycle," *Forbes*, December 23, 2002, pp. 248–256. Reprinted by Permission of Forbes Magazine©2006 Forbes Inc.

EXHIBIT 1–9
IMA Statement of Ethical
Professional Practice

Members of IMA shall behave ethically. A commitment to ethical professional practice includes: overarching principles that express our values, and standards that guide our conduct.

PRINCIPLES

IMA's overarching ethical principles include: Honesty, Fairness, Objectivity, and Responsibility. Members shall act in accordance with these principles and shall encourage others within their organizations to adhere to them.

STANDARDS

A member's failure to comply with the following standards may result in disciplinary action.

I. COMPETENCE

Each member has a responsibility to:
1. Maintain an appropriate level of professional expertise by continually developing knowledge and skills.
2. Perform professional duties in accordance with relevant laws, regulations, and technical standards.
3. Provide decision support information and recommendations that are accurate, clear, concise, and timely.
4. Recognize and communicate professional limitations or other constraints that would preclude responsible judgment or successful performance of an activity.

II. CONFIDENTIALITY

Each member has a responsibility to:
1. Keep information confidential except when disclosure is authorized or legally required.
2. Inform all relevant parties regarding appropriate use of confidential information. Monitor subordinates' activities to ensure compliance.
3. Refrain from using confidential information for unethical or illegal advantage.

III. INTEGRITY

Each member has a responsibility to:
1. Mitigate actual conflicts of interest. Regularly communicate with business associates to avoid apparent conflicts of interest. Advise all parties of any potential conflicts.
2. Refrain from engaging in any conduct that would prejudice carrying out duties ethically.
3. Abstain from engaging in or supporting any activity that might discredit the profession.

IV. CREDIBILITY

Each member has a responsibility to:
1. Communicate information fairly and objectively.
2. Disclose all relevant information that could reasonably be expected to influence an intended user's understanding of the reports, analyses, or recommendations.
3. Disclose delays or deficiencies in information, timeliness, processing, or internal controls in conformance with organization policy and/or applicable law.

RESOLUTION OF ETHICAL CONFLICT

In applying the Standards of Ethical Professional Practice, you may encounter problems identifying unethical behavior or resolving an ethical conflict. When faced with ethical issues, you should follow your organization's established policies on the resolution of such conflict. If these policies do not resolve the ethical conflict, you should consider the following courses of action:
1. Discuss the issue with your immediate supervisor except when it appears that the supervisor is involved. In that case, present the issue to the next level. If you cannot achieve a satisfactory resolution, submit the issue to the next management level. If your immediate superior is the chief executive officer or equivalent, the acceptable reviewing authority may be a group such as the audit committee, executive committee, board of directors, board of trustees, or owners. Contact with levels above the immediate superior should be initiated only with your superior's knowledge, assuming he or she is not involved. Communication of such problems to authorities or individuals not employed or engaged by the organization is not considered appropriate, unless you believe there is a clear violation of the law.
2. Clarify relevant ethical issues by initiating a confidential discussion with an IMA Ethics Counselor or other impartial advisor to obtain a better understanding of possible courses of action.
3. Consult your own attorney as to legal obligations and rights concerning the ethical conflict.

As these examples suggest, if ethical standards were not generally adhered to, everyone would suffer—businesses as well as consumers. Essentially, abandoning ethical standards would lead to a lower standard of living with lower-quality goods and services, less to choose from, and higher prices. In short, following ethical rules such as those in the Statement of Ethical Professional Practice is absolutely essential for the smooth functioning of an advanced market economy.

WHO IS TO BLAME?

Don Keough, a retired Coca-Cola executive, recalls that, "In my time, CFOs [Chief Financial Officers] were basically tough, smart, and mean. Bringing good news wasn't their function. They were the truth-tellers." But that had changed by the late 1990s in some companies. Instead of being truth-tellers, CFOs became corporate spokesmen, guiding stock analysts in their quarterly earnings estimates—and then making sure those earnings estimates were beaten using whatever means necessary, including accounting tricks and in some cases outright fraud. But does the buck stop there?

A survey of 179 CFOs published in May 2004 showed that only 38% of those surveyed believed that pressure to use aggressive accounting techniques to improve results had lessened relative to three years earlier. And 20% of those surveyed said the pressure had increased over the past three years. Where did the respondents say the pressure was coming from? Personal greed, weak boards of directors, and overbearing Chief Executive Officers (CEOs) topped the list. Who is to blame? Perhaps that question is less important than focusing on what is needed—greater personal integrity and less emphasis on meeting quarterly earnings estimates.

Sources: Jeremy Kahn, "The Chief Freaked Out Officer," *Fortune*, December 9, 2002, pp. 197–202, and Don Durfee, "After the Scandals: It's Better (and Worse) Than You Think," *CFO*, May 2004, p. 29.

Company Codes of Conduct

Many companies have adopted formal ethical codes of conduct. These codes are generally broad-based statements of a company's responsibilities to its employees, its customers, its suppliers, and the communities in which the company operates. Codes rarely spell out specific do's and don'ts or suggest proper behavior in a specific situation. Instead, they give broad guidelines. For example, Exhibit 1–10 (page 24) shows Johnson & Johnson's code of ethical conduct, which it refers to as a Credo. Johnson & Johnson created its Credo in 1943 and today it is translated into 36 languages. Johnson & Johnson surveys its employees every two to three years to obtain their impressions of how well the company adheres to its ethical principles. If the survey reveals shortcomings, corrective actions are taken.[12]

It bears emphasizing that establishing a code of ethical conduct, such as Johnson & Johnson's Credo, is meaningless if employees, and in particular top managers, do not adhere to it when making decisions. If top managers continue to say, in effect, that they will only be satisfied with bottom-line results and will accept no excuses, they are building a culture that implicitly coerces employees to engage in unethical behavior to get ahead. This type of unethical culture is contagious. In fact, one survey showed that "[t]hose who engage in unethical behavior often justify their actions with one or more of the following reasons: (1) the organization expects unethical behavior, (2) everyone else is unethical, and/or (3) behaving unethically is the only way to get ahead."[13]

---

[12]   www.jnj.com/our_company/our_credo

[13]   Michael K. McCuddy, Karl E. Reichardt, and David Schroeder, "Ethical Pressures: Fact or Fiction?" *Management Accounting* 74, no. 10, pp. 57–61.

EXHIBIT 1–10
The Johnson & Johnson Credo

Johnson & Johnson Credo

We believe our first responsibility is to the doctors, nurses and patients, to mothers and fathers and all others who use our products and services. In meeting their needs everything we do must be of high quality. We must constantly strive to reduce our costs in order to maintain reasonable prices. Customers' orders must be serviced promptly and accurately. Our suppliers and distributors must have an opportunity to make a fair profit.

We are responsible to our employees, the men and women who work with us throughout the world. Everyone must be considered as an individual. We must respect their dignity and recognize their merit. They must have a sense of security in their jobs. Compensation must be fair and adequate, and working conditions clean, orderly and safe. We must be mindful of ways to help our employees fulfill their family responsibilities. Employees must feel free to make suggestions and complaints. There must be equal opportunity for employment, development and advancement for those qualified. We must provide competent management, and their actions must be just and ethical.

We are responsible to the communities in which we live and work and to the world community as well. We must be good citizens—support good works and charities and bear our fair share of taxes. We must encourage civic improvements and better health and education. We must maintain in good order the property we are privileged to use, protecting the environment and natural resources.

Our final responsibility is to our stockholders. Business must make a sound profit. We must experiment with new ideas. Research must be carried on, innovative programs developed and mistakes paid for. New equipment must be purchased, new facilities provided and new products launched. Reserves must be created to provide for adverse times. When we operate according to these principles, the stockholders should realize a fair return.

IN BUSINESS

WHERE WOULD YOU LIKE TO WORK?

Nearly all executives claim that their companies maintain high ethical standards; however, not all executives walk the talk. Employees usually know when top executives are saying one thing and doing another and they also know that these attitudes spill over into other areas. Working in companies where top managers pay little attention to their own ethical rules can be extremely unpleasant. Several thousand employees in many different organizations were asked if they would recommend their company to prospective employees. Overall, 66% said that they would. Among those employees who believed that their top management strives to live by the company's stated ethical standards, the number of recommenders jumped to 81%. But among those who believed top management did not follow the company's stated ethical standards, the number was just 21%.

Source: Jeffrey L. Seglin, "Good for Goodness' Sake," *CFO*, October 2002, pp. 75–78.

Codes of Conduct on the International Level

The Code of Ethics for Professional Accountants, issued by the International Federation of Accountants (IFAC), governs the activities of all professional accountants throughout the world, regardless of whether they are practicing as independent CPAs, employed in government service, or employed as internal accountants.[14]

In addition to outlining ethical requirements in matters dealing with integrity and objectivity, resolution of ethical conflicts, competence, and confidentiality, the IFAC's code also outlines the accountant's ethical responsibilities in other matters such as those relating to

---

[14]   A copy of this code can be obtained on the International Federation of Accountants' website www.ifac.org.

taxes, independence, fees and commissions, advertising and solicitation, the handling of monies, and cross-border activities. Where cross-border activities are involved, the IFAC ethical requirements must be followed if they are stricter than the ethical requirements of the country in which the work is being performed.

Corporate Governance

Effective *corporate governance* enhances stockholders' confidence that a company is being run in their best interests rather than in the interests of top managers. **Corporate governance** is the system by which a company is directed and controlled. If properly implemented, the corporate governance system should provide incentives for the board of directors and top management to pursue objectives that are in the interests of the company's owners and it should provide for effective monitoring of performance.[15] Many would argue that, in addition to protecting the interests of stockholders, an effective corporate governance system also should protect the interests of the company's many other *stakeholders*—its customers, creditors, employees, suppliers, and the communities within which it operates. These parties are referred to as stakeholders because their welfare is tied to the company's performance.

Unfortunately, history has repeatedly shown that unscrupulous top managers, if unchecked, can exploit their power to defraud stakeholders. This unpleasant reality became all too clear in 2001 when the fall of Enron kicked off a wave of corporate scandals. These scandals were characterized by financial reporting fraud and misuse of corporate funds at the very highest levels—including CEOs and CFOs. While this was disturbing in itself, it also indicated that the institutions intended to prevent such abuses weren't working, thus raising fundamental questions about the adequacy of the existing corporate governance system. In an attempt to respond to these concerns, the U.S. Congress passed the most important reform of corporate governance in many decades—*The Sarbanes-Oxley Act of 2002.*

IN BUSINESS

SPILLED MILK AT PARMALAT

Corporate scandals have not been limited to the United States. In 2003, Parmalat, a publicly traded dairy company in Italy, went bankrupt. The CEO, Calisto Tanzi, admitted to manipulating the books for more than a decade so that he could skim off $640 million to cover losses at various of his family businesses. But the story doesn't stop there. Parmalat's balance sheet contained $13 billion in nonexistent assets, including a $5 billion Bank of America account that didn't exist. All in all, Parmalat was the biggest financial fraud in European history.

Source: Gail Edmondson, David Fairlamb, and Nanette Byrnes, "The Milk Just Keeps on Spilling," *BusinessWeek*, January 26, 2004, pp. 54–58.

The Sarbanes-Oxley Act of 2002

The **Sarbanes-Oxley Act of 2002** was intended to protect the interests of those who invest in publicly traded companies by improving the reliability and accuracy of corporate financial reports and disclosures. We would like to highlight six key aspects of the legislation.[16]

---

[15]   This definition of corporate governance was adapted from the 2004 report titled OECD Principles of Corporate Governance published by the Organization for Economic Co-Operation and Development.

[16]   A summary of the Sarbanes-Oxley Act of 2002 can be obtained from the American Institute of Certified Public Accountants (AICPA) website www.aicpa.org/info/sarbanes_oxley_summary.

First, the Act requires that both the CEO and CFO certify in writing that their company's financial statements and accompanying disclosures fairly represent the results of operations—with possible jail time if a CEO or CFO certifies results that they know are false. This creates very powerful incentives for the CEO and CFO to ensure that the financial statements contain no misrepresentations.

Second, the Act established the Public Company Accounting Oversight Board to provide additional oversight over the audit profession. The Act authorizes the Board to conduct investigations, to take disciplinary actions against audit firms, and to enact various standards and rules concerning the preparation of audit reports.

Third, the Act places the power to hire, compensate, and terminate the public accounting firm that audits a company's financial reports in the hands of the audit committee of the board of directors. Previously, management often had the power to hire and fire its auditors. Furthermore, the Act specifies that all members of the audit committee must be independent, meaning that they do not have an affiliation with the company they are overseeing, nor do they receive any consulting or advisory compensation from the company.

Fourth, the Act places important restrictions on audit firms. Historically, public accounting firms earned a large part of their profits by providing consulting services to the companies that they audited. This provided the appearance of a lack of independence since a client that was dissatisfied with an auditor's stance on an accounting issue might threaten to stop using the auditor as a consultant. To avoid this possible conflict of interests, the Act prohibits a public accounting firm from providing a wide variety of nonauditing services to an audit client.

Fifth, the Act requires that a company's annual report contain an *internal control report*. Internal controls are put in place by management to provide assurance to investors that financial disclosures are reliable. The report must state that it is management's responsibility to establish and maintain adequate internal controls and it must contain an assessment by management of the effectiveness of its internal control structure. The internal control report is accompanied by an opinion from the company's audit firm as to whether management's assessment of its internal control over financial reporting is fairly stated.[17]

Finally, the Act establishes severe penalties of as many as 20 years in prison for altering or destroying any documents that may eventually be used in an official proceeding and as many as 10 years in prison for managers who retaliate against a so-called whistle-blower who goes outside the chain of command to report misconduct. Collectively, these six aspects of the Sarbanes-Oxley Act of 2002 should help reduce the incidence of fraudulent financial reporting.

IN BUSINESS

SARBANES-OXLEY: AN EXPENSIVE PIECE OF LEGISLATION

You wouldn't think 169 words could be so expensive! But that is the case with what is known as Section 404 of The Sarbanes-Oxley Act of 2002 that requires a publicly traded company's annual report to contain an internal control report certified by its auditors. Estimates indicate that compliance with this provision will cost the Fortune 1000 companies alone about $6 billion annually—much of which will go to public accounting firms in fees. With the increased demand for audit services, public accounting firms such as KPMG, PriceWaterhouseCoopers, Ernst & Young, and Deloitte are returning to campuses to hire new auditors in large numbers and students are flocking to accounting classes.

Source: Holman W. Jenkins Jr., "Thinking Outside the Sarbox," *The Wall Street Journal*, November 24, 2004, p. A13.

---

[17]   The Public Company Accounting Oversight Board's Auditing Standard No. 2 requires the audit firm to issue a second opinion on whether its client maintained effective internal control over the financial reporting process. This opinion is in addition to the opinion regarding the fairness of management's assessment of the effectiveness of its own internal controls.

Enterprise Risk Management

Businesses face risks every day. Some risks are foreseeable. For example, a company could reasonably be expected to foresee the possibility of a natural disaster or a fire destroying its centralized data storage facility. Companies respond to this type of risk by maintaining off-site backup data storage facilities. Other risks are unforeseeable. For example, in 1982 Johnson & Johnson never could have imagined that a deranged killer would insert poison into bottles of Tylenol and then place these tainted bottles on retail shelves, ultimately killing seven people.[18] Johnson & Johnson—guided by the first line of its Credo (see page 24)—responded to this crisis by acting to reduce the risks faced by its customers and itself. First, it immediately recalled and destroyed 31 million bottles of Tylenol with a retail value of $100 million to reduce the risk of additional fatalities. Second, it developed the tamper-resistant packaging that we take for granted today to reduce the risk that the same type of crime could be repeated in the future.

Every business strategy or decision involves risks. **Enterprise risk management** is a process used by a company to proactively identify and manage those risks.

Identifying and Controlling Business Risks

Companies should identify foreseeable risks before they occur rather than react to unfortunate events that have already happened. The left-hand column of Exhibit 1–11 (page 28) provides 12 examples of business risks. This list is not exhaustive, rather its purpose is to illustrate the diverse nature of business risks that companies face. Whether the risks relate to the weather, computer hackers, complying with the law, employee theft, financial reporting, or strategic decision making, they all have one thing in common. If the risks are not managed effectively, they can infringe on a company's ability to meet its goals.

Once a company identifies its risks, it can respond to them in various ways such as accepting, avoiding, sharing, or reducing the risk. Perhaps the most common risk management tactic is to reduce risks by implementing specific controls. The right-hand column of Exhibit 1–11 provides an example of a control that could be implemented to help reduce each of the risks mentioned in the left-hand column of the exhibit.

In conclusion, a sophisticated enterprise risk management system cannot guarantee that all risks are eliminated. Nonetheless, many companies understand that managing risks is a superior alternative to reacting, perhaps too late, to unfortunate events.

MANAGING WEATHER RISK

The National Oceanic and Atmospheric Administration claims that the weather influences one-third of the U.S. gross domestic product. In 2004, the word *unseasonable* was used by more than 120 publicly traded companies to explain unfavorable financial performance. Indeed, it would be easy to conclude that the weather poses an uncontrollable risk to businesses, right? Wrong! Weather risk management is a growing industry with roughly 80 companies offering weather risk management services to clients.

For example, Planalytics is a weather consulting firm that helps Wise Metal Group, a manufacturer of aluminum can sheeting, to manage its natural gas purchases. Wise's $3 million monthly gas bill fluctuates sharply depending on the weather. Planalytics' software helps Wise plan its gas purchases in advance of changing temperatures. Beyond influencing natural gas purchases, the weather can also delay the boats that deliver Wise's raw materials and it can affect Wise's sales to the extent that cooler weather conditions lead to a decline in canned beverage sales.

Source: Abraham Lustgarten, "Getting Ahead of the Weather," *Fortune,* February 7, 2005, pp. 87–94.

---

[18] Tamara Kaplan, "The Tylenol Crisis: How Effective Public Relations Saved Johnson & Johnson," in Glen Broom, Allen Center, and Scott Cutlip, *Effective Public Relations,* Prentice Hall, Upper Saddle River, NJ.

EXHIBIT 1–11
Identifying and Controlling
Business Risks

Examples of Business Risks	Examples of Controls to Reduce Business Risks
• Intellectual assets being stolen from computer files	• Create firewalls that prohibit computer hackers from corrupting or stealing intellectual property
• Products harming customers	• Develop a formal and rigorous new product testing program
• Losing market share due to the unforeseen actions of competitors	• Develop an approach for legally gathering information about competitors' plans and practices
• Poor weather conditions shutting down operations	• Develop contingency plans for overcoming weather-related disruptions
• A website malfunctioning	• Thoroughly test the website before going "live" on the Internet
• A supplier strike halting the flow of raw materials	• Establish a relationship with two companies capable of providing needed raw materials
• A poorly designed incentive compensation system causing employees to make bad decisions	• Create a balanced set of performance measures that motivates the desired behavior
• Financial statements unfairly reporting the value of inventory	• Count the physical inventory on hand to make sure that it agrees with the accounting records
• An employee stealing assets	• Segregate duties so that the same employee does not have physical custody of an asset and the responsibility of accounting for it
• An employee accessing unauthorized information	• Create password-protected barriers that prohibit employees from obtaining information not needed to do their jobs
• Inaccurate budget estimates causing excessive or insufficient production	• Implement a rigorous budget review process
• Failing to comply with equal employment opportunity laws	• Create a report that tracks key metrics related to compliance with the laws

The Certified Management Accountant (CMA)

An individual who possesses the necessary qualifications and who passes a rigorous professional exam earns the right to be known as a *Certified Management Accountant (CMA)*. In addition to the prestige that accompanies a professional designation, CMAs are often given greater responsibilities and higher compensation than those who do not have such a designation. Information about becoming a CMA and the CMA program can be accessed on the Institute of Management Accountants' (IMA) website www.imanet.org or by calling 1-800-638-4427.

To become a Certified Management Accountant, the following four steps must be completed:

1. File an Application for Admission and register for the CMA examination.
2. Pass all four parts of the CMA examination within a three-year period.
3. Satisfy the experience requirement of two continuous years of professional experience in management and/or financial accounting prior to or within seven years of passing the CMA examination.
4. Comply with the Statement of Ethical Professional Practice.

HOW'S THE PAY?

The Institute of Management Accountants has created the following table that allows an individual to estimate what his salary would be as a management accountant. (The table below applies specifically to men. A similar table exists for women.)

			Your Calculation
Start with this base amount		$74,779	$74,779
If you are top-level management	ADD	$15,893	
OR, if you are senior-level management	ADD	$6,369	
OR, if you are entry-level management	SUBTRACT	$21,861	
Number of years in the field _____	TIMES	$355	
If you have an advanced degree	ADD	$13,861	
OR, if you have no degree	SUBTRACT	$19,289	
If you hold the CMA	ADD	$13,619	
If you hold the CPA	ADD	$6,832	
If you have had one or more career interruptions	SUBTRACT	$13,367	
Your estimated salary level			_____

For example, if you make it to top-level management in ten years, have an advanced degree and a CMA, and no career interruptions, your estimated salary would be $121,702 [$74,779 + $15,893 + (10 × $355) + $13,861 + $13,619].

Source: David L. Schroeder and Karl E. Reichardt, "2004 Salary Survey," *Strategic Finance*, June 2005, pp. 28–43.

Summary

Successful companies follow strategies that differentiate themselves from competitors. Strategies often focus on three customer value propositions—customer intimacy, operational excellence, and product leadership.

Most organizations rely on decentralization to some degree. Decentralization is formally depicted in an organization chart that shows who works for whom and which units perform line and staff functions.

Lean Production, the Theory of Constraints, and Six Sigma are three management approaches that focus on business processes. Lean Production organizes resources around business processes and pulls units through those processes in response to customer orders. The result is lower inventories, fewer defects, less wasted effort, and quicker customer response times. The Theory of Constraints emphasizes the importance of managing an organization's constraints. Since the constraint is whatever is holding back the organization, improvement efforts usually must be focused on the constraint to be effective. Six Sigma uses the DMAIC (Define, Measure, Analyze, Improve, and Control) framework to eliminate non-value-added activities and to improve processes.

E-commerce and enterprise systems are being used to reshape business practices. An enterprise system integrates data across the organization in a single software system that makes the same data available to all managers.

Ethical behavior is the foundation of a successful market economy. If we cannot trust others to act ethically in their business dealings with us, we will be inclined to invest less, scrutinize purchases more, and generally waste time and money trying to protect ourselves from the unscrupulous—resulting in fewer goods available to consumers at higher prices and lower quality.

Unfortunately, trust in our corporate governance system has been undermined in recent years by numerous high-profile financial reporting scandals. The Sarbanes-Oxley Act of 2002 was passed with the objective of improving the reliability of the financial disclosures provided by publicly traded companies.

Glossary

At the end of each chapter, a list of key terms for review is given, along with the definition of each term. (These terms are printed in boldface where they are defined in the chapter.) Carefully study each term to be sure you understand its meaning. The list for Chapter 1 follows.

Budget A detailed plan for the future, usually expressed in formal quantitative terms. (p. 6)

Business process A series of steps that are followed to carry out some task in a business. (p. 12)

Chief Financial Officer (CFO) The member of the top management team who is responsible for providing timely and relevant data to support planning and control activities and for preparing financial statements for external users. (p. 11)

Constraint Anything that prevents an organization or individual from getting more of what it wants. (p. 15)

Control The process of instituting procedures and then obtaining feedback to ensure that all parts of the organization are functioning effectively and moving toward overall company goals. (p. 6)

Controller The member of the top management team who is responsible for providing relevant and timely data to managers and for preparing financial statements for external users. The controller reports to the CFO. (p. 6)

Controlling Ensuring that the plan is actually carried out and is appropriately modified as circumstances change. (p. 5)

Corporate governance The system by which a company is directed and controlled. If properly implemented it should provide incentives for top management to pursue objectives that are in the interests of the company and it should effectively monitor performance. (p. 25)

Decentralization The delegation of decision-making authority throughout an organization by providing managers with the authority to make decisions relating to their area of responsibility. (p.10)

Directing and motivating Mobilizing people to carry out plans and run routine operations. (p. 5)

Enterprise system A software system that integrates data from across an organization into a single centralized database that enables all employees to access a common set of data. (p. 19)

Enterprise risk management A process used by a company to help identify the risks that it faces and to develop responses to those risks that enable the company to be reasonably assured of meeting its goals. (p. 27)

Feedback Accounting and other reports that help managers monitor performance and focus on problems and/or opportunities that might otherwise go unnoticed. (p. 6)

Financial accounting The phase of accounting concerned with providing information to stockholders, creditors, and others outside the organization. (p. 2)

Finished goods Units of product that have been completed but have not yet been sold to customers. (p. 13)

Just-in-time (JIT) A production and inventory control system in which materials are purchased and units are produced only as needed to meet actual customer demand. (p. 14)

Lean thinking model A five-step management approach that organizes resources around the flow of business processes and that pulls units through these processes in response to customer orders. (p. 13)

Line A position in an organization that is directly related to the achievement of the organization's basic objectives. (p. 11)

Managerial accounting The phase of accounting concerned with providing information to managers for use inside the organization. (p. 2)

Non-value-added activities Activities that consume resources but do not add value for which customers are willing to pay. (p. 16)

Organization chart A diagram of a company's organizational structure that depicts formal lines of reporting, communication, and responsibility between managers. (p. 10)

Performance report A detailed report comparing budgeted data to actual data. (p. 7)

Planning Selecting a course of action and specifying how the action will be implemented. (p. 5)

Planning and control cycle The flow of management activities through planning, directing and motivating, and controlling, and then back to planning again. (p. 7)

Raw materials Materials that are used to make a product. (p. 13)

Sarbanes-Oxley Act of 2002 Legislation enacted to protect the interests of stockholders who invest in publicly traded companies by improving the reliability and accuracy of the disclosures provided to them. (p. 25)

Segment Any part of an organization that can be evaluated independently of other parts and about which the manager seeks financial data. Examples include a product line, a sales territory, a division, or a department. (p. 9)

Six Sigma A method that relies on customer feedback and objective data gathering and analysis techniques to drive process improvement. (p. 16)

Staff A position in an organization that is only indirectly related to the achievement of the organization's basic objectives. Such positions provide service or assistance to line positions or to other staff positions. (p. 11)

Strategy A "game plan" that enables a company to attract customers by distinguishing itself from competitors. (p. 4)

Supply chain management A management approach that coordinates business processes across companies to better serve end consumers. (p. 14)

Theory of Constraints (TOC) A management approach that emphasizes the importance of managing constraints. (p. 15)

Value chain The major business functions that add value to a company's products and services such as research and development, product design, manufacturing, marketing, distribution, and customer service. (p. 12)

Work in process Units of product that are only partially complete and will require further work before they are ready for sale to a customer. (p. 13)

Questions

1-1	What is the basic difference in orientation between financial and managerial accounting?
1-2	What is meant by a business strategy?
1-3	Describe the three broad categories of customer value propositions.
1-4	Describe the three major activities of a manager.
1-5	What are the four steps in the planning and control cycle?
1-6	What are the major differences between financial and managerial accounting?
1-7	Distinguish between line and staff positions in an organization.
1-8	Describe the basic responsibilities of the Chief Financial Officer.
1-9	What are the three main categories of inventories in a manufacturing company?
1-10	What are the five steps in the lean thinking model?
1-11	What are the major benefits from successful implementation of the lean thinking model?
1-12	Describe what is meant by a "pull" production system.
1-13	Where does the Theory of Constraints recommend that improvement efforts be focused?
1-14	Briefly describe Six Sigma.
1-15	Describe the five stages in the Six Sigma DMAIC Framework.
1-16	What is an enterprise system supposed to accomplish?
1-17	Why is adherence to ethical standards important for the smooth functioning of an advanced market economy?
1-18	Describe what is meant by corporate governance.
1-19	Briefly describe what is meant by enterprise risk management.

 Exercises

EXERCISE 1-1 The Roles of Managers and Management Accountants [LO1, LO2]
A number of terms that relate to organizations, the work of management, and the role of managerial accounting are listed below:

Budgets	Controller
Decentralization	Directing and motivating
Feedback	Financial accounting
Line	Managerial accounting
Nonmonetary data	Performance report
Planning	Precision
Staff	Chief Financial Officer

Choose the term or terms above that most appropriately complete the following statements:

1. A position on the organization chart that is directly related to achieving the basic objectives of an organization is called a _____ position.

2. When _____, managers oversee day-to-day activities and keep the organization functioning smoothly.

3. The plans of management are expressed formally in _____.

4. _____ consists of identifying alternatives, selecting from among the alternatives the one that is best for the organization, and specifying what actions will be taken to implement the chosen alternative.

5. A _____ position provides service or assistance to other parts of the organization and does not directly achieve the basic objectives of the organization.

6. The delegation of decision-making authority throughout an organization by allowing managers at various operating levels to make key decisions relating to their area of responsibility is called _____.

7. Managerial accounting places less emphasis on _____ and more emphasis on _____ than financial accounting.

8. _____ is concerned with providing information for the use of those who are inside the organization, whereas _____ is concerned with providing information for the use of those who are outside the organization.

9. The accounting and other reports coming to management that are used in controlling the organization are called _____.

10. The manager in charge of the accounting department is generally known as the _____.

11. A detailed report to management comparing budgeted data with actual data for a specific time period is called a _____.

12. The _____ is the member of the top management team who is responsible for providing timely and relevant data to support planning and control activities and for preparing financial statements for external users.

EXERCISE 1–2 The Business Environment [LO3]
A number of terms are listed below:

corporate governance	Theory of Constraints	budget
enterprise risk management	value chain	Six Sigma
nonconstraint	enterprise system	pulls
customer value proposition	lean thinking model	constraint
Internet	business process	strategy
Just-In-Time	non-value-added activity	supply chain management

Required:
Choose the term or terms from the above list that most appropriately completes each of the following statements:

1. A company can only succeed if it creates a reason for customers to choose it over a competitor; in short, a _____.

2. Increasing the rate of output of a(n) _____ as the result of an improvement effort is unlikely to have much effect on profits.

3. A(n) _____ is a game plan that enables a company to attract customers by distinguishing itself from competitors.

4. A(n) _____ consists of business functions that add value to a company's products and services such as research and development, product design, manufacturing, marketing, distribution, and customer service.

5. A(n) _____ integrates data from across an organization into a single centralized database that enables all employees to access a common set of data.

6. A production and inventory control system in which materials are purchased and units are produced only as needed to meet actual customer demand is known as _____.

7. A management approach that coordinates business processes across companies to better serve end consumers is known as _____.

8. The process used by a company to help identify the risks that it faces and to develop responses to those risks so that the company is reasonably assured of meeting its goals is known as _____.

9. The system by which a company is directed and controlled is called _____.

10. The _____ fuels the globalization phenomenon by providing companies with greater access to geographically dispersed customers, employees, and suppliers.

11. A(n) _____ is anything that prevents an organization or individual from getting more of what it wants.

12. The management approach that emphasizes the importance of managing constraints is known as the _____.

13. The _____ is a five-step management approach that organizes resources around the flow of business processes and that _____ units through those processes in response to customer orders.

14. A(n) _____ is a detailed plan for the future, usually expressed in formal quantitative terms.

15. A(n) _____ is a series of steps that are followed to carry out some task in a business.

16. _____ is a method that relies on customer feedback and objective data gathering and analysis techniques to drive process improvement.

17. A(n) _____ consumes resources but does not add value for which customers are willing to pay.

EXERCISE 1–3 Ethics in Business [LO4]

Mary Karston was hired by a popular fast-food restaurant as an order-taker and cashier. Shortly after taking the job, she was shocked to overhear an employee bragging to a friend about shortchanging customers. She confronted the employee who then snapped back: "Mind your own business. Besides, everyone does it and the customers never miss the money." Mary didn't know how to respond to this aggressive stance.

Required:

What would be the practical consequences on the fast-food industry and on consumers if cashiers generally shortchanged customers at every opportunity?

Problems

PROBLEM 1–4 Ethics and the Manager [LO4]

Richmond, Inc., operates a chain of department stores located in the northwest that has steadily grown to its present size of 44 stores. Two years ago, the board of directors of Richmond approved a large-scale remodeling of its stores to attract a more upscale clientele.

Before finalizing these plans, two stores were remodeled as a test. Linda Perlman, assistant controller, was asked to oversee the financial reporting for these test stores, and she and other management personnel were offered bonuses based on the sales growth and profitability of these stores. While completing the financial reports, Perlman discovered a sizable inventory of outdated goods that should have been discounted for sale or returned to the manufacturer. She discussed the situation with her management colleagues; the consensus was to ignore reporting this inventory as obsolete, since reporting it would diminish the financial results and their bonuses.

Required:

1. According to the IMA's Statement of Ethical Professional Practice, would it be ethical for Perlman *not* to report the inventory as obsolete?
2. Would it be easy for Perlman to take the ethical action in this situation?

(CMA, adapted)

PROBLEM 1–5 Preparing an Organization Chart [LO2]

Bristow University is a large private school located in the Midwest. The university is headed by a president who has five vice presidents reporting to him. These vice presidents are responsible for, respectively, auxiliary services, admissions and records, academics, financial services (controller), and the physical plant.

In addition, the university has managers over several areas who report to these vice presidents. These include managers over central purchasing, the university press, and the university bookstore, all of whom report to the vice president for auxiliary services; managers over computer services and over accounting and finance, who report to the vice president for financial services;

and managers over grounds and custodial services and over plant and maintenance, who report to the vice president for physical plant.

The university has four colleges—business, humanities, fine arts, and engineering and quantitative methods—and a law school. Each of these units has a dean who is responsible to the academic vice president. Each college has several departments.

Required:
1. Prepare an organization chart for Bristow University.
2. Which of the positions on your chart would be line positions? Why would they be line positions? Which would be staff positions? Why?
3. Which of the positions on your chart would have need for accounting information? Explain.

PROBLEM 1–6 Ethics; Just-In-Time (JIT) Purchasing [LO3, LO4]
(The situation described below was adapted from a case published by the Institute of Management Accountants' Committee on Ethics.*)

WIW is a publicly owned corporation that makes various control devices used in manufacturing mechanical equipment. J.B. is the president of WIW, Tony is the purchasing agent, and Diane is J.B.'s executive assistant. All three have been with WIW for about five years. Charlie is WIW's controller and has been with the company for two years.

J.B.: Hi, Charlie, come on in. Diane said you had a confidential matter to discuss. What's on your mind?
Charlie: J.B., I was reviewing our increased purchases from A-1 Warehouse Sales last week and wondered why our volume has tripled in the past year. When I discussed this with Tony he seemed a bit evasive and tried to dismiss the issue by stating that A-1 can give us one-day delivery on our orders.
J.B.: Well, Tony is right. You know we have been trying to implement just-in-time and have been trying to get our inventory down.
Charlie: We still have to look at the overall cost. A-1 is more of a jobber than a warehouse. After investigating orders placed with them, I found that only 10% are delivered from their warehouse and the other 90% are drop-shipped from the manufacturers. The average markup by A-1 is 30%, which amounted to about $600,000 on our orders for the past year. If we had ordered directly from the manufacturers when A-1 didn't have an item in stock, we could have saved about $540,000 ($600,000 × 90%). In addition, some of the orders were late and not complete.
J.B.: Now look, Charlie, we get quick delivery on most items, and who knows how much we are saving by not having to stock this stuff in advance or worry about it becoming obsolete. Is there anything else on your mind?
Charlie: Well, J.B., as a matter of fact, there is. I ordered a Dun & Bradstreet credit report on A-1 and discovered that Mike Bell is the principal owner. Isn't he your brother-in-law?
J.B.: Sure he is. But don't worry about Mike. He understands this JIT approach. Besides, he's looking out for our interests.
Charlie (to himself): This conversation has been enlightening, but it doesn't really respond to my concerns. Can I legally or ethically ignore this apparent conflict of interests?

Required:
1. Would Charlie be justified in ignoring this situation, particularly since he is not the purchasing agent? In preparing your answer, consider the IMA's Standards of Ethical Conduct.
2. State the specific steps Charlie should follow to resolve this matter.

PROBLEM 1–7 Ethics in Business [LO4]
Consumers and attorney generals in more than 40 states accused a prominent nationwide chain of auto repair shops of misleading customers and selling them unnecessary parts and services, from brake jobs to front-end alignments. Lynn Sharpe Paine reported the situation as follows in "Managing for Organizational Integrity," *Harvard Business Review,* March-April, 1994:

> In the face of declining revenues, shrinking market share, and an increasingly competitive market . . . management attempted to spur performance of its auto centers. . . . The automotive service advisers were given product-specific sales quotas—sell so many springs, shock absorbers, alignments, or brake jobs per shift—and paid a commission based on sales. . . . [F]ailure to meet quotas could lead to a transfer or a reduction in work hours. Some employees spoke of the "pressure, pressure, pressure" to bring in sales.

*Neil Holmes, ed., "Ethics," *Management Accounting* 73, no. 8 (February 1992), p. 16. Used with permission from the Institute of Management Accountants (IMA), Montvale, N.J., USA, www.imanet.org.

This pressure-cooker atmosphere created conditions under which employees felt that the only way to satisfy top management was by selling products and services to customers that they didn't really need.

Suppose all automotive repair businesses routinely followed the practice of attempting to sell customers unnecessary parts and services.

Required:

1. How would this behavior affect customers? How might customers attempt to protect themselves against this behavior?
2. How would this behavior probably affect profits and employment in the automotive service industry?

PROBLEM 1–8 Line and Staff Positions [LO2]

Special Alloys Corporation manufactures a variety of specialized metal products for industrial use. Most of the revenues are generated by large contracts with companies that have government defense contracts. The company also develops and markets parts to the major automobile companies. It employs many metallurgists and skilled technicians because most of its products are made from highly sophisticated alloys.

The company recently signed two large contracts; as a result, the workload of Wayne Washburn, the general manager, has become overwhelming. To relieve some of this overload, Mark Johnson was transferred from the Research Planning Department to the general manager's office. Johnson, who has been a senior metallurgist and supervisor in the Research Planning Department, was given the title "assistant to the general manager."

Washburn assigned several responsibilities to Johnson in their first meeting. Johnson will oversee the testing of new alloys in the Product Planning Department and be given the authority to make decisions as to the use of these alloys in product development; he will also be responsible for maintaining the production schedules for one of the new contracts. In addition to these duties, he will be required to meet with the supervisors of the production departments regularly to consult with them about production problems they may be experiencing. Washburn expects to be able to manage the company much more efficiently with Johnson's help.

Required:

1. Positions within organizations are often described as having (a) line authority or (b) staff authority. Describe what is meant by these two terms.
2. Of the responsibilities assigned to Mark Johnson as assistant to the general manager, which tasks have line authority and which have staff authority?
3. Identify and discuss the conflicts Mark Johnson may experience in the production departments as a result of his new responsibilities.

(CMA, adapted)

RESEARCH AND APPLICATION 1–9   [LO1, LO2, and LO4]

The questions in this exercise are based on one of the fastest growing food retailers in the United States—Whole Foods Market, Inc. To answer the questions, you will need to download Whole Foods Market's 2004 Annual Report and 10-K/A at www.wholefoodsmarket.com/investor/annualreports.html. In addition, you'll need to download the company's mission statement (which it refers to as a Declaration of Interdependence) at www.wholefoodsmarket.com/company/declaration.html and its code of conduct and ethics at www.wholefoodsmarket.com/investor/codeofconduct.pdf. You do not need to print these documents in order to answer the questions.

Required:

1. What is Whole Foods Market's strategy for success in the marketplace? Does the company rely primarily on a customer intimacy, operational excellence, or product leadership customer value proposition? What evidence supports your conclusion?
2. What business risks does Whole Foods Market face that may threaten its ability to satisfy stockholder expectations? What are some examples of control activities that the company could use to reduce these risks? (Hint: Focus on pages 11–15 of the 10-K/A.)
3. Create an excerpt of an organization chart for Whole Foods Market. Do not try to create an organization chart for the entire company—it would be overwhelming! Pick a portion of the

company and depict how the company organizes itself. (Hint: Study the 2004 Global All-Stars mentioned in the annual report and refer to page 16 of the 10-K/A.) Mention by name three employees that occupy line positions and three employees that occupy staff positions.

4. Compare and contrast Whole Foods Market's mission statement with the Johnson & Johnson Credo shown on page 24.

5. Compare and contrast Whole Foods Market's mission statement and its code of conduct and ethics.

6. Is Whole Foods Market's Annual Report and 10-K/A primarily a financial accounting document or a managerial accounting document? What evidence supports your conclusion? (Hint: Refer to Exhibit 1–3 in the text.)

Chapter 2

Learning Objectives

After studying Chapter 2, you should be able to:

LO1 Identify and give examples of each of the three basic manufacturing cost categories.

LO2 Distinguish between product costs and period costs and give examples of each.

LO3 Prepare an income statement including calculation of the cost of goods sold.

LO4 Prepare a schedule of cost of goods manufactured.

LO5 Understand the differences between variable costs and fixed costs.

LO6 Understand the differences between direct and indirect costs.

LO7 Define and give examples of cost classifications used in making decisions: differential costs, opportunity costs, and sunk costs.

LO8 (Appendix 2A) Properly account for labor costs associated with idle time, overtime, and fringe benefits.

LO9 (Appendix 2B) Identify the four types of quality costs and explain how they interact.

LO10 (Appendix 2B) Prepare and interpret a quality cost report.

Cost Terms, Concepts, and Classifications

Costs Add Up

Understanding costs and how they behave is critical in business. Labor Ready is a company based in Tacoma, Washington, that fills temporary manual labor jobs throughout the United States, Canada, and the UK—issuing over 6 million paychecks each year to more than half a million laborers. For example, food vendors at the Seattle Mariners' Safeco Field hire Labor Ready workers to serve soft drinks and food at baseball games. Employers are charged about $11 per hour for this service. Since Labor Ready pays its workers only about $6.50 per hour and offers no fringe benefits and has no national competitors, this business would appear to be a gold mine generating about $4.50 per hour in profit. However, the company must maintain 687 hiring offices, each employing a permanent staff of four to five persons. Those costs, together with payroll taxes, workmen's compensation insurance, and other administrative costs, result in a margin of only about 5%, or a little over 50¢ per hour. ■

Source: Catie Golding, "Short-Term Work, Long-Term Profits," *Washington CEO*, January 2000, pp. 10–12.

As explained in Chapter 1, the work of management focuses on (1) planning, which includes setting objectives and outlining how to attain these objectives; and (2) control, which includes the steps taken to ensure that objectives are realized. To carry out these planning and control responsibilities, managers need *information* about the organization. This information often relates to the *costs* of the organization.

In managerial accounting, the term *cost* is used in many different ways. The reason is that there are many types of costs, and these costs are classified differently according to the immediate needs of management. For example, managers may want cost data to prepare external financial reports, to prepare planning budgets, or to make decisions. Each different use of cost data demands a different classification and definition of costs. For example, the preparation of external financial reports requires the use of historical cost data, whereas decision making may require predictions about future costs.

In this chapter, we discuss many of the possible uses of cost data and how costs are defined and classified for each use. Our first task is to explain how costs are classified for the purpose of preparing external financial reports—particularly in manufacturing companies. To set the stage for this discussion, we begin the chapter by defining some terms commonly used in manufacturing.

General Cost Classifications

All types of organizations incur costs—governmental, not-for-profit, manufacturing, retail, and service. Generally, the kinds of costs that are incurred and the way in which these costs are classified depend on the type of organization. For this reason, we will consider in our discussion the cost characteristics of a variety of organizations—manufacturing, merchandising, and service.

Our initial focus in this chapter is on manufacturing companies, since their basic activities include most of the activities found in other types of organizations. Manufacturing companies such as Texas Instruments, Ford, and DuPont are involved in acquiring raw materials, producing finished goods, marketing, distributing, billing, and almost every other business activity. Therefore, an understanding of costs in a manufacturing company can be very helpful in understanding costs in other types of organizations.

In this chapter, we introduce cost concepts that apply to diverse organizations including fast-food outlets such as Kentucky Fried Chicken, Pizza Hut, and Taco Bell; movie studios such as Disney, Paramount, and United Artists; consulting firms such as Accenture and McKinsey; and your local hospital. The exact terms used in these industries may not be the same as those used in manufacturing, but the same basic concepts apply. With some slight modifications, these basic concepts also apply to merchandising companies such as Wal-Mart, The Gap, 7-Eleven, Nordstrom, and Tower Records. With that in mind, let's begin our discussion of manufacturing costs.

Topic Tackler

PLUS

2–1

Manufacturing Costs

Most manufacturing companies separate manufacturing costs into three broad categories: direct materials, direct labor, and manufacturing overhead. A discussion of each of these categories follows.

Direct Materials   The materials that go into the final product are called **raw materials.** This term is somewhat misleading, since it seems to imply unprocessed natural resources like wood pulp or iron ore. Actually, raw materials refer to any materials that are used in the final product; and the finished product of one company can become the raw materials of

LEARNING OBJECTIVE 1
Identify and give examples of each of the three basic manufacturing cost categories.

another company. For example, the plastics produced by Du Pont are a raw material used by Compaq Computer in its personal computers. One study of 37 manufacturing industries found that materials costs averaged about 55% of sales revenues.[1]

Raw materials may include both *direct* and *indirect materials*. **Direct materials** are those materials that become an integral part of the finished product and whose costs can be conveniently traced to the finished product. This would include, for example, the seats that Airbus purchases from subcontractors to install in its commercial aircraft and the tiny electric motor Panasonic uses in its DVD players.

Sometimes it isn't worth the effort to trace the costs of relatively insignificant materials to end products. Such minor items would include the solder used to make electrical connections in a Sony TV or the glue used to assemble an Ethan Allen chair. Materials such as solder and glue are called **indirect materials** and are included as part of manufacturing overhead, which is discussed later in this section.

Direct Labor   **Direct labor** consists of labor costs that can be easily (i.e., physically and conveniently) traced to individual units of product. Direct labor is sometimes called *touch labor,* since direct labor workers typically touch the product while it is being made. Examples of direct labor include assembly-line workers at Toyota, carpenters at the home builder Kaufman and Broad, and electricians who install equipment on aircraft at Bombardier Learjet.

Labor costs that cannot be physically traced to the creation of products, or that can be traced only at great cost and inconvenience, are termed **indirect labor.** Just like indirect materials, indirect labor is treated as part of manufacturing overhead. Indirect labor includes the labor costs of janitors, supervisors, materials handlers, and night security guards. Although the efforts of these workers are essential to production, it would be either impractical or impossible to accurately trace their costs to specific units of product. Hence, such labor costs are treated as indirect labor.

IN BUSINESS

IS SENDING JOBS OVERSEAS ALWAYS A GOOD IDEA?

In recent years, many companies have sent jobs from high labor-cost countries such as the United States to lower labor-cost countries such as India and China. But is chasing labor cost savings always the right thing to do? In manufacturing, the answer is no. Typically, total direct labor costs are around 7% to 15% of cost of goods sold. Since direct labor is such a small part of overall costs, the labor savings realized by "offshoring" jobs can easily be overshadowed by a decline in supply chain efficiency that occurs simply because production facilities are located farther from the ultimate customers. The increase in inventory carrying costs and obsolescence costs coupled with slower response to customer orders, not to mention foreign currency exchange risks, can more than offset the benefits of employing geographically dispersed low-cost labor.

One manufacturer of casual wear in Los Angeles, California, understands the value of keeping jobs close to home in order to maintain a tightly knit supply chain. The company can fill orders for as many as 160,000 units in 24 hours. In fact, the company carries less than 30 days' inventory and is considering fabricating clothing only after orders are received from customers rather than attempting to forecast what items will sell and making them in advance. How would they do this? The company's entire supply chain—including weaving, dyeing, and sewing—is located in downtown Los Angeles, eliminating shipping delays.

Source: Robert Sternfels and Ronald Ritter, "When Offshoring Doesn't Make Sense," *The Wall Street Journal,* October 19, 2004, p. B8.

---

[1] Germain Boer and Debra Jeter, "What's New About Modern Manufacturing? Empirical Evidence on Manufacturing Cost Changes," *Journal of Management Accounting Research,* volume 5, pp. 61–83.

Major shifts have taken place and continue to take place in the structure of labor costs in some industries. Sophisticated automated equipment, run and maintained by skilled indirect workers, is increasingly replacing direct labor. Indeed, direct labor averages only about 10% of sales revenues in manufacturing. In some companies, direct labor has become such a minor element of cost that it has disappeared altogether as a separate cost category. Nevertheless, the vast majority of manufacturing and service companies throughout the world continue to recognize direct labor as a separate cost category.

Manufacturing Overhead **Manufacturing overhead,** the third element of manufacturing cost, includes all costs of manufacturing except direct materials and direct labor. Manufacturing overhead includes items such as indirect materials; indirect labor; maintenance and repairs on production equipment; and heat and light, property taxes, depreciation, and insurance on manufacturing facilities. A company also incurs costs for heat and light, property taxes, insurance, depreciation, and so forth, associated with its selling and administrative functions, but these costs are not included as part of manufacturing overhead. Only those costs associated with *operating the factory* are included in manufacturing overhead. Across large numbers of manufacturing companies, manufacturing overhead averages about 16% of sales revenues.[2]

Various names are used for manufacturing overhead, such as *indirect manufacturing cost, factory overhead,* and *factory burden.* All of these terms are synonyms for *manufacturing overhead.*

Nonmanufacturing Costs

Nonmanufacturing costs are often divided into two categories: (1) *selling costs* and (2) *administrative costs.* **Selling costs** include all costs that are incurred to secure customer orders and get the finished product to the customer. These costs are sometimes called *order-getting* and *order-filling* costs. Examples of selling costs include advertising, shipping, sales travel, sales commissions, sales salaries, and costs of finished goods warehouses.

Administrative costs include all executive, organizational, and clerical costs associated with the *general management* of an organization rather than with manufacturing or selling. Examples of administrative costs include executive compensation, general accounting, secretarial, public relations, and similar costs involved in the overall, general administration of the organization *as a whole.*

Nonmanufacturing costs are also often called selling, general, and administrative (SG&A) costs.

Product Costs versus Period Costs

In addition to classifying costs as manufacturing or nonmanufacturing costs, there are other ways to look at costs. For instance, they can also be classified as either *product costs* or *period costs.* To understand the difference between product costs and period costs, we must first discuss the matching principle from financial accounting.

Generally, costs are recognized as expenses on the income statement in the period that benefits from the cost. For example, if a company pays for liability insurance in advance for

LEARNING OBJECTIVE 2
Distinguish between product costs and period costs and give examples of each.

---

[2] J. Miller, A. DeMeyer, and J. Nakane, *Benchmarking Global Manufacturing* (Homewood, IL: Richard D. Irwin), Chapter 2. The Boer and Jeter article cited on the previous page contains a similar finding concerning the magnitude of manufacturing overhead.

two years, the entire amount is not considered an expense of the year in which the payment is made. Instead, one-half of the cost would be recognized as an expense each year. The reason is that both years—not just the first year—benefit from the insurance payment. The unexpensed portion of the insurance payment is carried on the balance sheet as an asset called prepaid insurance.

The *matching principle* is based on the *accrual* concept that *costs incurred to generate a particular revenue should be recognized as expenses in the same period that the revenue is recognized.* This means that if a cost is incurred to acquire or make something that will eventually be sold, then the cost should be recognized as an expense only when the sale takes place—that is, when the benefit occurs. Such costs are called *product costs.*

Product Costs

For financial accounting purposes, **product costs** include all costs involved in acquiring or making a product. In the case of manufactured goods, these costs consist of direct materials, direct labor, and manufacturing overhead. Product costs "attach" to units of product as the goods are purchased or manufactured, and they remain attached as the goods go into inventory awaiting sale. Product costs are initially assigned to an inventory account on the balance sheet. When the goods are sold, the costs are released from inventory as expenses (typically called cost of goods sold) and matched against sales revenue. Since product costs are initially assigned to inventories, they are also known as **inventoriable costs.**

We want to emphasize that product costs are not necessarily treated as expenses in the period in which they are incurred. Rather, as explained above, they are treated as expenses in the period in which the related products *are sold.* This means that a product cost such as direct materials or direct labor might be incurred during one period but not recorded as an expense until a following period when the completed product is sold.

Period Costs

Period costs are all the costs that are not product costs. For example, sales commissions and the rental costs of administrative offices are period costs. Period costs are not included as part of the cost of either purchased or manufactured goods; instead, period costs are expensed on the income statement in the period in which they are incurred using the usual rules of accrual accounting. Keep in mind that the period in which a cost is incurred is not necessarily the period in which cash changes hands. For example, as discussed earlier, the costs of liability insurance are spread across the periods that benefit from the insurance—regardless of the period in which the insurance premium is paid.

As suggested above, *all selling and administrative expenses are considered to be period costs.* Advertising, executive salaries, sales commissions, public relations, and other nonmanufacturing costs discussed earlier are all examples of period costs. They will appear on the income statement as expenses in the period in which they are incurred.

Prime Cost and Conversion Cost

Two more cost categories are often used in discussions of manufacturing costs—*prime cost* and *conversion cost.* These terms are quite easy to define. **Prime cost** is the sum of direct materials cost and direct labor cost. **Conversion cost** is the sum of direct labor cost and manufacturing overhead cost. The term *conversion cost* is used to describe direct labor and manufacturing overhead because these costs are incurred to convert materials into the finished product.

Exhibit 2–1 (page 44) contains a summary of the cost terms that we have introduced so far.

DISSECTING THE VALUE CHAIN

United Colors of Benetton, an Italian apparel company headquartered in Ponzano, is unusual in that it is involved in all activities in the "value chain" from clothing design through manufacturing, distribution, and ultimate sale to customers in Benetton retail outlets. Most companies are involved in only one or two of these activities. Looking at this company allows us to see how costs are distributed across the entire value chain. A recent income statement from the company contained the following data:

	Millions of Euros	Percent of Revenues
Revenue......................................	1,686	100.0%
Cost of sales	929	55.1
Selling and administrative expenses:		
Payroll and related cost	125	7.4
Distribution and transport.....................	30	1.8
Sales commissions	74	4.4
Advertising and promotion	54	3.2
Depreciation and amortization	78	4.6
Other expenses	179	10.6
Total selling and administrative expenses	540	32.0%

Even though this company spends large sums on advertising and runs its own shops, the cost of sales is still quite high in relation to the revenue—55.1% of revenue. And despite the company's lavish advertising campaigns, advertising and promotion costs amounted to only 3.2% of revenue. (Note: One U.S. dollar was worth about 0.7331 euros at the time of this financial report.)

PRODUCT COSTS AND PERIOD COSTS: A LOOK ACROSS INDUSTRIES

Cost of goods sold and selling and administrative expenses expressed as a percentage of sales differ across companies and industries. For example, the data below summarize the median cost of goods sold as a percentage of sales and the median selling and administrative expense as a percentage of sales for eight different industries. Why do you think the percentages in each column differ so dramatically?

Industry	Cost of Goods Sold ÷ Sales	Selling and Administrative Expense ÷ Sales
Aerospace and Defense	79%	9%
Beverages	52%	34%
Computer Software and Services	34%	38%
Electrical Equipment and Components....	64%	21%
Healthcare Services	82%	6%
Oil and Gas	90%	3%
Pharmaceuticals	31%	41%
Restaurants	78%	8%

Source: Lori Calabro, "Controlling the Flow," *CFO*, February 2005, p. 46–50.

EXHIBIT 2–1
Summary of Cost Terms

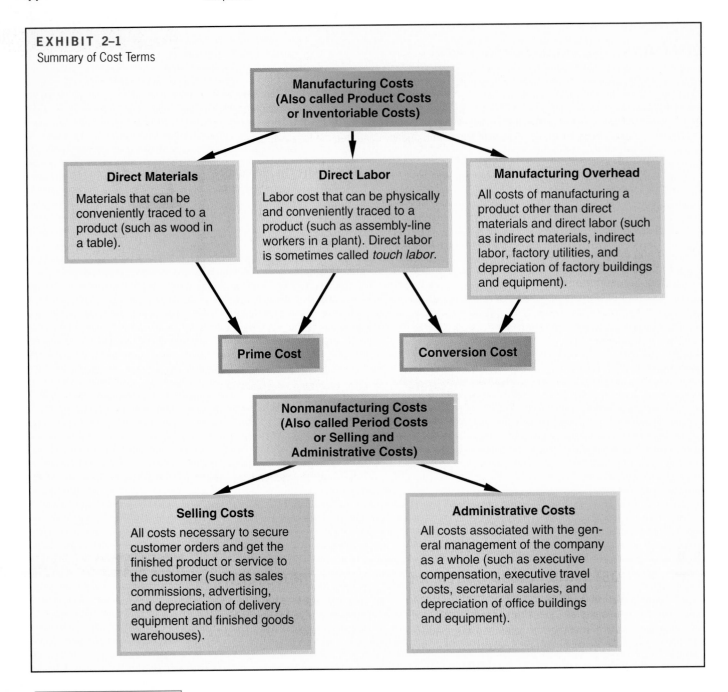

Manufacturing Costs
(Also called Product Costs
or Inventoriable Costs)

Direct Materials

Materials that can be conveniently traced to a product (such as wood in a table).

Direct Labor

Labor cost that can be physically and conveniently traced to a product (such as assembly-line workers in a plant). Direct labor is sometimes called *touch labor*.

Manufacturing Overhead

All costs of manufacturing a product other than direct materials and direct labor (such as indirect materials, indirect labor, factory utilities, and depreciation of factory buildings and equipment).

Prime Cost

Conversion Cost

Nonmanufacturing Costs
(Also called Period Costs
or Selling and
Administrative Costs)

Selling Costs

All costs necessary to secure customer orders and get the finished product or service to the customer (such as sales commissions, advertising, and depreciation of delivery equipment and finished goods warehouses).

Administrative Costs

All costs associated with the general management of the company as a whole (such as executive compensation, executive travel costs, secretarial salaries, and depreciation of office buildings and equipment).

IN BUSINESS

BLOATED SELLING AND ADMINISTRATIVE EXPENSES

Selling and administrative expenses tend to creep up during economic booms—creating problems when the economy falls into recession. Ron Nicol, a partner at the Boston Consulting Group, found that selling and administrative expenses at America's 1000 largest companies grew at an average rate of 1.7% per year between 1985 and 1996 and then exploded to an average of 10% growth per year between 1997 and 2000. If companies had maintained their historical balance between sales revenues on the one hand and selling and administrative expenses on the other hand, Nicol calculates that selling and administrative expenses would have been about $500 million lower in the year 2000 for the average company on his list.

Source: Jon E. Hilsenrath, "The Outlook: Corporate Dieting Is Far from Over," *The Wall Street Journal*, July 9, 2001, p. A1.

Cost Classifications on Financial Statements

In this section of the chapter, we compare the cost classifications used on the financial statements of manufacturing and merchandising companies. The financial statements prepared by a *manufacturing* company are more complex than the statements prepared by a merchandising company because a manufacturing company must produce its goods as well as market them. The production process involves many costs that do not exist in a merchandising company, and these costs must be properly accounted for on the manufacturing company's financial statements. We begin by explaining how these costs are shown on the balance sheet followed by the income statement.

Topic Tackler

PLUS

2–2

The Balance Sheet

The balance sheet, or statement of financial position, of a manufacturing company is similar to that of a merchandising company. However, their inventory accounts differ. A merchandising company has only one class of inventory—goods purchased from suppliers for resale to customers. In contrast, manufacturing companies have three classes of inventories—*raw materials*, *work in process*, and *finished goods*. **Raw materials** are the materials that are used to make a product. **Work in process** consists of units of product that are only partially complete and will require further work before they are ready for sale to a customer. **Finished goods** consist of completed units of product that have not yet been sold to customers. Ordinarily, the sum total of these three categories of inventories is the only amount shown on the balance sheet in external reports. However, the footnotes to the financial statements often provide more detail.

We will use two companies—Graham Manufacturing and Reston Bookstore—to illustrate the concepts discussed in this section. Graham Manufacturing is located in Portsmouth, New Hampshire, and makes precision brass fittings for yachts. Reston Bookstore is a small bookstore in Reston, Virginia, specializing in books about the Civil War.

The footnotes to Graham Manufacturing's Annual Report reveal the following information concerning its inventories:

Graham Manufacturing Corporation Inventory Accounts		
	Beginning Balance	Ending Balance
Raw materials	$ 60,000	$ 50,000
Work in process	90,000	60,000
Finished goods	125,000	175,000
Total inventory accounts	$275,000	$285,000

Graham Manufacturing's raw materials inventory consists largely of brass rods and brass blocks. The work in process inventory consists of partially completed brass fittings. The finished goods inventory consists of brass fittings that are ready to be sold to customers.

In contrast, the inventory account at Reston Bookstore consists entirely of the costs of books the company has purchased from publishers for resale to the public. In merchandising companies like Reston, these inventories may be called *merchandise inventory*. The beginning and ending balances in this account appear as follows:

Reston Bookstore Inventory Account		
	Beginning Balance	Ending Balance
Merchandise Inventory	$100,000	$150,000

LEARNING OBJECTIVE 3
Prepare an income statement including calculation of the cost of goods sold.

The Income Statement

Exhibit 2–2 compares the income statements of Reston Bookstore and Graham Manufacturing. For purposes of illustration, these statements contain more detail about cost of goods sold than you will generally find in published financial statements.

At first glance, the income statements of merchandising and manufacturing companies like Reston Bookstore and Graham Manufacturing are very similar. The only apparent difference is in the labels of some of the entries in the computation of the cost of goods sold. In the exhibit, the computation of cost of goods sold relies on the following basic equation for inventory accounts:

Basic Equation for Inventory Accounts

$$\text{Beginning balance} + \text{Additions to inventory} = \text{Ending balance} + \text{Withdrawals from inventory}$$

The logic underlying this equation, which applies to any inventory account, is illustrated in Exhibit 2–3. The beginning inventory consists of any units that are in the inventory at the beginning of the period. Additions are made to the inventory during the period. The sum of the beginning balance and the additions to the account is the total amount of inventory available. During the period, withdrawals are made from inventory. The ending balance is whatever is left at the end of the period after the withdrawals.

EXHIBIT 2–2
Comparative Income Statements: Merchandising and Manufacturing Companies

Merchandising Company
Reston Bookstore

The cost of merchandise inventory purchased from outside suppliers during the period.

Sales		$1,000,000
Cost of goods sold:		
Beginning merchandise inventory	$100,000	
Add: Purchases	650,000	
Goods available for sale	750,000	
Deduct: Ending merchandise inventory	150,000	600,000
Gross margin		400,000
Selling and administrative expenses:		
Selling expense	100,000	
Administrative expense	200,000	300,000
Net operating income		$ 100,000

Manufacturing Company
Graham Manufacturing

The manufacturing costs associated with the goods that were finished during the period. (See Exhibit 2–4 for details.)

Sales		$1,500,000
Costs of goods sold:		
Beginning finished goods inventory	$125,000	
Add: Cost of goods manufactured	850,000	
Goods available for sale	975,000	
Deduct: Ending finished goods inventory	175,000	800,000
Gross margin		700,000
Selling and administrative expenses:		
Selling expense	250,000	
Administrative expense	300,000	550,000
Net operating income		$ 150,000

EXHIBIT 2–3
Inventory Flows

Beginning balance + Additions   = Total available   − Withdrawals   = Ending balance

These concepts are used to determine the cost of goods sold for a merchandising company like Reston Bookstore as follows:

Cost of Goods Sold in a Merchandising Company

Beginning merchandise inventory + Purchases = Ending merchandise inventory + Cost of goods sold

or

Cost of goods sold = Beginning merchandise inventory + Purchases − Ending merchandise inventory

To determine the cost of goods sold in a merchandising company, we only need to know the beginning and ending balances in the Merchandise Inventory account and the purchases. Total purchases can be easily determined in a merchandising company by simply adding together all purchases from suppliers.

The cost of goods sold for a manufacturing company like Graham Manufacturing is determined as follows:

Cost of Goods Sold in a Manufacturing Company

Beginning finished goods inventory + Cost of goods manufactured = Ending finished goods inventory + Cost of goods sold

or

Cost of goods sold = Beginning finished goods inventory + Cost of goods manufactured − Ending finished goods inventory

To determine the cost of goods sold in a manufacturing company, we need to know the *cost of goods manufactured* and the beginning and ending balances in the Finished Goods inventory account. The **cost of goods manufactured** consists of the manufacturing costs associated with goods that were *finished* during the period. The cost of goods manufactured for Graham Manufacturing is derived in the *schedule of cost of goods manufactured* shown in Exhibit 2–4 (page 48).

Schedule of Cost of Goods Manufactured

At first glance, the **schedule of cost of goods manufactured** in Exhibit 2–4 appears complex and perhaps even intimidating. However, it is all quite logical. The schedule of cost of goods manufactured contains the three elements of product costs that we discussed earlier—direct materials, direct labor, and manufacturing overhead.

LEARNING OBJECTIVE 4
Prepare a schedule of cost of goods manufactured.

EXHIBIT 2–4
Schedule of Cost of Goods Manufactured

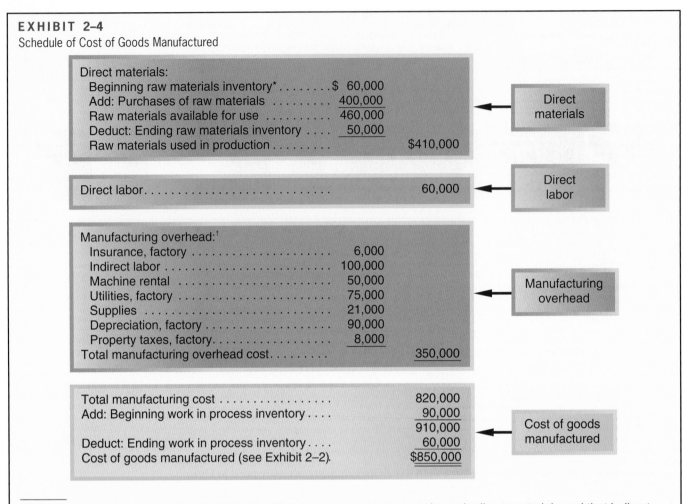

Direct materials:
　Beginning raw materials inventory* . . . . $ 60,000
　Add: Purchases of raw materials 400,000
　Raw materials available for use 460,000
　Deduct: Ending raw materials inventory 50,000
　Raw materials used in production . . . . 　　　　　$410,000　　　　← Direct materials

Direct labor. . . . . 　　　　　60,000　　　　← Direct labor

Manufacturing overhead:†
　Insurance, factory 6,000
　Indirect labor 100,000
　Machine rental 50,000
　Utilities, factory 75,000
　Supplies 21,000
　Depreciation, factory 90,000
　Property taxes, factory. 8,000
　Total manufacturing overhead cost. . . . . 　　　　　350,000　　　　← Manufacturing overhead

Total manufacturing cost 820,000
Add: Beginning work in process inventory 90,000
　　　　　　　　　　　　　　　　　　　　　 910,000　　　　← Cost of goods manufactured
Deduct: Ending work in process inventory 60,000
Cost of goods manufactured (see Exhibit 2–2). $850,000

---

*We assume in this example that the Raw Materials inventory account contains only direct materials and that indirect materials are carried in a separate Supplies account. Using a Supplies account for indirect materials is a common practice. In Chapter 3, we discuss the procedure to be followed if *both* direct and indirect materials are carried in a single account.
†In Chapter 3 we will see that the manufacturing overhead section of the Schedule of Cost of Goods Manufactured can be considerably simplified by using a *predetermined manufacturing overhead rate.*

The direct materials cost of $410,000 is not the cost of raw materials purchased during the period—it is the cost of raw materials *used* during the period. The purchases of raw materials are added to the beginning balance to determine the cost of the materials available for use. The ending raw materials inventory is deducted from this amount to arrive at the cost of raw materials used in production. The sum of the three manufacturing cost elements—materials, direct labor, and manufacturing overhead—is the total manufacturing cost of $820,000. However, you'll notice that this is *not* the same thing as the cost of goods manufactured for the period of $850,000. The subtle distinction between the total manufacturing cost and the cost of goods manufactured is very easy to miss. Some of the materials, direct labor, and manufacturing overhead costs incurred during the period relate to goods that are not yet completed. As stated above, the cost of goods manufactured consists of the manufacturing costs associated with the goods that were finished during the period. Consequently, adjustments need to be made to the total manufacturing cost of the period for the partially completed goods that were in process at the beginning and at the end of the period. The costs that relate to goods that are not yet completed are shown in the work in process inventory figures at the bottom of the schedule. Note that the beginning work in process inventory must be added to the manufacturing costs of the period, and the ending work in process inventory must be deducted, to arrive at the cost of goods manufactured. Since the Work in Process account declined by $30,000 during the year ($90,000 − $60,000), this explains the $30,000 difference between the total manufacturing cost and the cost of goods manufactured.

Product Cost Flows

Earlier in the chapter, we defined product costs as costs incurred to either purchase or manufacture goods. For manufactured goods, these costs consist of direct materials, direct labor, and manufacturing overhead. It will be helpful at this point to look briefly at the flow of costs in a manufacturing company. This will help us understand how product costs move through the various accounts and how they affect the balance sheet and the income statement.

Exhibit 2–5 illustrates the flow of costs in a manufacturing company. Raw materials purchases are recorded in the Raw Materials inventory account. When raw materials are used in production, their costs are transferred to the Work in Process inventory account as direct materials. Notice that direct labor cost and manufacturing overhead cost are added directly to Work in Process. Work in Process can be viewed most simply as products on an assembly line. The direct materials, direct labor, and manufacturing overhead costs added to Work in Process in Exhibit 2–5 are the costs needed to complete these products as they move along this assembly line.

Notice from the exhibit that as goods are completed, their costs are transferred from Work in Process to Finished Goods. Here the goods await sale to customers. As goods are sold, their costs are transferred from Finished Goods to Cost of Goods Sold. At this point the various costs required to make the product are finally recorded as an expense. Until that point, these costs are in inventory accounts on the balance sheet.

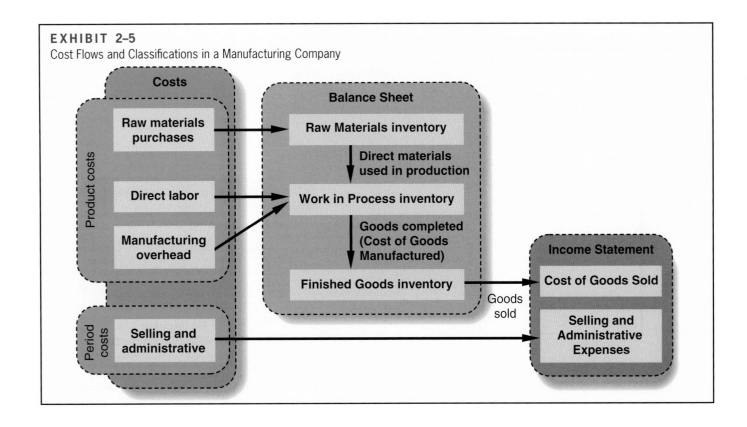

EXHIBIT 2–5
Cost Flows and Classifications in a Manufacturing Company

Inventoriable Costs

As stated earlier, product costs are often called inventoriable costs. The reason is that these costs go directly into inventory accounts as they are incurred (first into Work in Process and then into Finished Goods), rather than going into expense accounts. Thus, they are termed *inventoriable costs. This is a key concept because such costs can end up on the balance sheet as assets if goods are only partially completed or are unsold at the end of a period.* To illustrate this point, refer again to Exhibit 2–5. At the end of the period, the materials, labor, and overhead costs that are associated with the units in the Work in Process and Finished Goods inventory accounts will appear on the balance sheet as assets. As explained earlier, these costs will not become expenses until the goods are completed and sold.

Selling and administrative expenses are not involved in making a product. For this reason, they are not treated as product costs but rather as period costs that are expensed as they are incurred, as shown in Exhibit 2–5.

An Example of Cost Flows

To provide an example of cost flows in a manufacturing company, assume that a company's annual insurance cost is $2,000. Three-fourths of this amount ($1,500) applies to factory operations, and one-fourth ($500) applies to selling and administrative activities. Therefore, $1,500 of the $2,000 insurance cost would be a product (inventoriable) cost and would be added to the cost of the goods produced during the year. This concept is illustrated in Exhibit 2–6, where $1,500 of insurance cost is added to Work in Process.

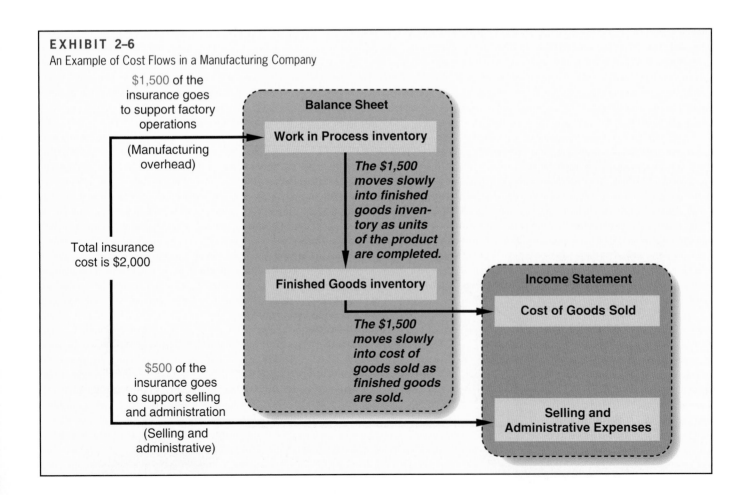

EXHIBIT 2–6
An Example of Cost Flows in a Manufacturing Company

Purpose of Cost Classification	Cost Classifications	EXHIBIT 2–7 Summary of Cost Classifications

Preparing external financial statements	• Product costs (inventoriable)
	  • Direct materials
	  • Direct labor
	  • Manufacturing overhead
	• Period costs (expensed)
	  • Nonmanufacturing costs
	    • Selling costs
	    • Administrative costs	

Predicting cost behavior in response to changes in activity	• Variable cost (proportional to activity) • Fixed cost (constant in total)	
Assigning costs to cost objects such as departments or products	• Direct cost (can be easily traced) • Indirect cost (cannot be easily traced)	
Making decisions	• Differential cost (differs between alternatives) • Sunk cost (past cost not affected by a decision) • Opportunity cost (forgone benefit)	
Cost of quality (Appendix)	• Prevention costs • Appraisal costs • Internal failure costs • External failure costs	

As shown in the exhibit, this portion of the year's insurance cost will not become an expense until the goods that are produced during the year are sold—which may not happen until the following year or even later. Until the goods are sold, the $1,500 will be part of inventories—either Work in Process or Finished Goods—along with the other costs of producing the goods.

By contrast, the $500 of insurance cost that applies to the company's selling and administrative activities will be expensed immediately.

Thus far, we have been mainly concerned with classifications of manufacturing costs for the purpose of determining inventory valuations on the balance sheet and cost of goods sold on the income statement in external financial reports. However, costs are used for many other purposes, and each purpose requires a different classification of costs. We will consider several different purposes for cost classifications in the remaining sections of this chapter. These purposes and the corresponding cost classifications are summarized in Exhibit 2–7. To help keep the big picture in mind, we suggest that you refer back to this exhibit frequently as you progress through the rest of this chapter.

Cost Classifications for Predicting Cost Behavior

Quite frequently, it is necessary to predict how a certain cost will behave in response to a change in activity. For example, a manager at Qwest may want to estimate the impact a 5% increase in long-distance calls would have on the company's total electric bill. **Cost behavior** refers to how a cost reacts to changes in the level of activity. As the activity level rises and falls, a particular cost may rise and fall as well—or it may remain constant. For planning purposes, a manager must be able to anticipate which of these will happen; and if a cost can be expected to change, the manager must be able to estimate how much it will change. To help make such distinctions, costs are often categorized as variable or fixed.

LEARNING OBJECTIVE 5
Understand the differences between variable costs and fixed costs.

Variable Cost

A **variable cost** is a cost that varies, in total, in direct proportion to changes in the level of activity. The activity can be expressed in many ways, such as units produced, units sold, miles driven, beds occupied, lines of print, hours worked, and so forth. A good example of a variable cost is direct materials. The cost of direct materials used during a period will vary, in total, in direct proportion to the number of units that are produced. To illustrate this idea, consider the Saturn Division of GM. Each auto requires one battery. As the output of autos increases and decreases, the number of batteries used will increase and decrease proportionately. If auto production goes up 10%, then the number of batteries used will also go up 10%. The concept of a variable cost is shown graphically in Exhibit 2–8.

The graph on the left-hand side of Exhibit 2–8 illustrates that the *total* variable cost rises and falls as the activity level rises and falls. This idea is presented below, assuming that a Saturn's battery costs $24:

Number of Autos Produced	Cost per Battery	Total Variable Cost— Batteries
1	$24	$24
500	$24	$12,000
1,000	$24	$24,000

While total variable costs change as the activity level changes, it is important to note that a variable cost is constant if expressed on a *per unit* basis. For example, the per unit cost of batteries remains constant at $24 even though the total cost of the batteries increases and decreases with activity.

There are many examples of costs that are variable with respect to the products and services provided by a company. In a manufacturing company, variable costs include items such as direct materials, shipping costs, and sales commissions and some elements of manufacturing overhead such as lubricants. We will also usually assume that direct labor is a variable cost, although direct labor may act more like a fixed cost in some situations as we shall see in a later chapter. In a merchandising company, the variable costs

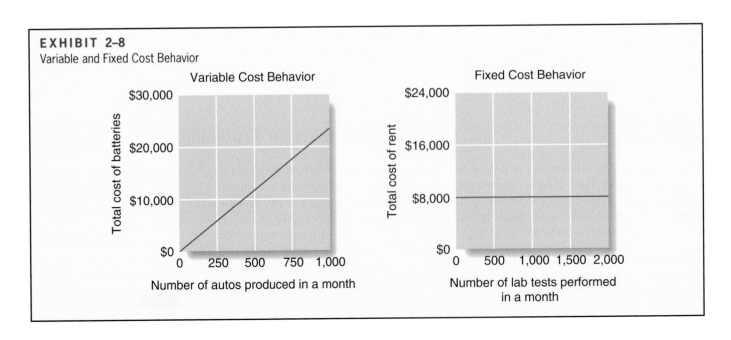

EXHIBIT 2–8
Variable and Fixed Cost Behavior

of carrying and selling products include items such as cost of goods sold, sales commissions, and billing costs. In a hospital, the variable costs of providing health care services to patients would include the costs of the supplies, drugs, meals, and perhaps nursing services.

When we say that a cost is variable, we ordinarily mean that it is variable with respect to the amount of goods or services the organization produces. However, costs can be variable with respect to other things. For example, the wages paid to employees at a Blockbuster Video outlet will depend on the number of hours the store is open and not strictly on the number of videos rented. In this case, we would say that wage costs are variable with respect to the hours of operation. Nevertheless, when we say that a cost is variable, we ordinarily mean it is variable with respect to the amount of goods and services produced. This could be how many Jeep Cherokees are produced, how many videos are rented, how many patients are treated, and so on.

IN BUSINESS

BROWN IS THINKING GREEN

United Parcel Service (UPS) truck drivers travel more than 1.3 billion miles annually to deliver more than 4.5 billion packages. Therefore, it should come as no surprise that fuel is a huge variable cost for the company. Even if UPS can shave just a penny of cost from each mile driven, the savings can be enormous. This explains why UPS is so excited about swapping its old diesel powered trucks for diesel-electric hybrid vehicles, which have the potential to cut fuel costs by 50%. Beyond the savings for UPS, the environment would also benefit from the switch since hybrid vehicles cut emissions by 90%. As UPS television commercials ask, "What can Brown do for you?" Thanks to diesel-electric technology, the answer is that Brown can help make the air you breathe a little bit cleaner.

Source: Charles Haddad and Christine Tierney, "FedEx and Brown Are Going Green," *BusinessWeek*, August 4, 2003, pp. 60–62.

Fixed Cost

A **fixed cost** is a cost that remains constant, in total, regardless of changes in the level of activity. Unlike variable costs, fixed costs are not affected by changes in activity. Consequently, as the activity level rises and falls, total fixed costs remain constant unless influenced by some outside force, such as a price change. Rent is a good example of a fixed cost. Suppose the Mayo Clinic rents a machine for $8,000 per month that tests blood samples for the presence of leukemia cells. The $8,000 monthly rental cost will be incurred regardless of the number of tests that may be performed during the month. The concept of a fixed cost is shown graphically on the right-hand side of Exhibit 2–8.

Very few costs are completely fixed. Most will change if activity changes enough. For example, suppose that the capacity of the leukemia diagnostic machine at the Mayo Clinic is 2,000 tests per month. If the clinic wishes to perform more than 2,000 tests in a month, it would be necessary to rent an additional machine, which would cause a jump in the fixed costs. When we say a cost is fixed, we mean it is fixed within some *relevant range*. The **relevant range** is the range of activity within which the assumptions about variable and fixed costs are valid. For example, the assumption that the rent for diagnostic machines is $8,000 per month is valid within the relevant range of 0 to 2,000 tests per month.

Fixed costs can create confusion if they are expressed on a per unit basis. This is because the average fixed cost per unit increases and decreases *inversely* with changes in activity. In the Mayo Clinic, for example, the average cost per test will fall as the number

FOOD COSTS AT A LUXURY HOTEL

The Sporthotel Theresa (http://www.theresa.at/), owned and operated by the Egger family, is a four star hotel located in Zell im Zillertal, Austria. The hotel features access to hiking, skiing, biking, and other activities in the Ziller alps as well as its own fitness facility and spa.

Three full meals a day are included in the hotel room charge. Breakfast and lunch are served buffet-style while dinner is a more formal affair with as many as six courses. A sample dinner menu appears below:

> Tyrolean cottage cheese with homemade bread
> ***
> Salad bar
> ***
> Broccoli-terrine with saddle of venison and smoked goose-breast
> Or
> Chicken-liver parfait with gorgonzola-cheese ravioli and port-wine sauce
> ***
> Clear vegetable soup with fine vegetable strips
> Or
> Whey-yoghurt juice
> ***
> Roulade of pork with zucchini, ham and cheese on pesto ribbon noodles and saffron sauce
> Or
> Roasted filet of Irish salmon and prawn with spring vegetables and sesame mash
> Or
> Fresh white asparagus with scrambled egg, fresh herbs, and parmesan
> Or
> Steak of Tyrolean organic beef
> ***
> Strawberry terrine with homemade chocolate ice cream
> Or
> Iced Viennese coffee

The chef, Stefan Egger, believes that food costs are roughly proportional to the number of guests staying at the hotel; that is, they are a variable cost. He must order food from suppliers two or three days in advance, but he adjusts his purchases to the number of guests who are currently staying at the hotel and their consumption patterns. In addition, guests make their selections from the dinner menu early in the day, which helps Stefan plan which foodstuffs will be required for dinner. Consequently, he is able to prepare just enough food so that all guests are satisfied and yet waste is held to a minimum.

Source: Conversation with Stefan Egger, chef at the Sporthotel Theresa.

of tests performed increases because the $8,000 rental cost will be spread over more tests. Conversely, as the number of tests performed in the clinic declines, the average cost per test will rise as the $8,000 rental cost is spread over fewer tests. This concept is illustrated in the table below:

Monthly Rental Cost	Number of Tests Performed	Average Cost per Test
$8,000	10	$800
$8,000	500	$16
$8,000	2,000	$4

EXHIBIT 2–9
Summary of Variable and Fixed
Cost Behavior

Cost	Behavior of the Cost (within the relevant range)	
	In Total	Per Unit
Variable cost	Total variable cost increases and decreases in proportion to changes in the activity level.	Variable cost per unit remains constant.
Fixed cost	Total fixed cost is not affected by changes in the activity level within the relevant range.	Fixed cost per unit decreases as the activity level rises and increases as the activity level falls.

EXHIBIT 2–9
Summary of Variable and Fixed
Cost Behavior

Note that if the Mayo Clinic performs only 10 tests each month, the rental cost of the equipment will average $800 per test. But if 2,000 tests are performed each month, the average cost will drop to only $4 per test. More will be said later about the misunderstandings created by this variation in average unit costs.

Examples of fixed costs include straight-line depreciation, insurance, property taxes, rent, supervisory salaries, administrative salaries, and advertising.

A summary of both variable and fixed cost behavior is presented in Exhibit 2–9.

THE POWER OF SHRINKING AVERAGE FIXED COST PER UNIT

Intel has recently built five new computer chip manufacturing facilities that have put its competitors on the defensive. Each plant can produce chips using a 12-inch wafer that is imprinted with 90-nanometer circuit lines that are 0.1% of the width of a human hair. These plants can produce 1.25 million chips a day, or about 375 million chips a year. Better yet, these new plants slash Intel's production costs in half since each plant's volume of output is 2.5 times greater than any of Intel's seven older plants. Building a computer chip manufacturing facility is a very expensive undertaking due to the required investment in fixed equipment costs. So why are Intel's competitors on the defensive? Because they are struggling to match Intel's exceptionally low average fixed cost per unit of output. Or, in an economist's terms, they are struggling to match Intel's economies of scale.

Source: Cliff Edwards, "Intel," *BusinessWeek*, March 8, 2004, pp. 56–64.

Cost Classifications for Assigning Costs to Cost Objects

Costs are assigned to cost objects for a variety of purposes including pricing, preparing profitability studies, and controlling spending. A **cost object** is anything for which cost data are desired—including products, customers, jobs, and organizational subunits. For purposes of assigning costs to cost objects, costs are classified as either *direct* or *indirect*.

LEARNING OBJECTIVE 6
Understand the differences between direct and indirect costs.

Direct Cost

A **direct cost** is a cost that can be easily and conveniently traced to a specified cost object. The concept of direct cost extends beyond just direct materials and direct labor. For example, if Reebok is assigning costs to its various regional and national sales offices, then the salary of the sales manager in its Tokyo office would be a direct cost of that office.

Indirect Cost

An **indirect cost** is a cost that cannot be easily and conveniently traced to a specified cost object. For example, a Campbell Soup factory may produce dozens of varieties of canned soups. The factory manager's salary would be an indirect cost of a particular variety such as chicken noodle soup. The reason is that the factory manager's salary is incurred as a consequence of running the entire factory—it is not incurred to produce any one soup variety. *To be traced to a cost object such as a particular product, the cost must be caused by the cost object.* The factory manager's salary is called a *common cost* of producing the various products of the factory. A **common cost** is a cost that is incurred to support a number of cost objects but cannot be traced to them individually. A common cost is a type of indirect cost.

A particular cost may be direct or indirect, depending on the cost object. While the Campbell Soup factory manager's salary is an *indirect* cost of manufacturing chicken noodle soup, it is a *direct* cost of the manufacturing division. In the first case, the cost object is chicken noodle soup. In the second case, the cost object is the entire manufacturing division.

Cost Classifications for Decision Making

LEARNING OBJECTIVE 7
Define and give examples of cost classifications used in making decisions: differential costs, opportunity costs, and sunk costs.

Costs are an important feature of many business decisions. In making decisions, it is essential to have a firm grasp of the concepts *differential cost, opportunity cost,* and *sunk cost.*

Differential Cost and Revenue

Decisions involve choosing between alternatives. In business decisions, each alternative will have costs and benefits that must be compared to the costs and benefits of the other available alternatives. A difference in costs between any two alternatives is known as a **differential cost.** A difference in revenues between any two alternatives is known as **differential revenue.**

A differential cost is also known as an **incremental cost,** although technically an incremental cost should refer only to an increase in cost from one alternative to another; decreases in cost should be referred to as *decremental costs.* Differential cost is a broader term, encompassing both cost increases (incremental costs) and cost decreases (decremental costs) between alternatives.

The accountant's differential cost concept can be compared to the economist's marginal cost concept. In speaking of changes in cost and revenue, the economist uses the terms *marginal cost* and *marginal revenue.* The revenue that can be obtained from selling one more unit of product is called marginal revenue, and the cost involved in producing one more unit of product is called marginal cost. The economist's marginal concept is basically the same as the accountant's differential concept applied to a single unit of output.

IN BUSINESS

THE COST OF A HEALTHIER ALTERNATIVE

McDonald's is under pressure from critics to address the health implications of its menu. In response, McDonald's switched from partially hydrogenated vegetable oil to fry foods to a new soybean oil that cuts trans-fat levels by 48% even though the soybean oil is much more expensive than the partially hydrogenated vegetable oil and it lasts only half as long. What were the cost implications of this change? A typical McDonald's restaurant uses 500 pounds of the relatively unhealthy oil per week at a cost of about $186. In contrast, the same restaurant would need to use 1,000 pounds of the new soybean oil per week at a cost of about $571. This is a differential cost of $385 per restaurant per week. This may seem like a small amount of money until the calculation is expanded to include 13,000 McDonald's restaurants operating 52 weeks a year. Now, the total tab for a more healthy frying oil rises to about $260 million per year.

Source: Matthew Boyle, "Can You Really Make Fast Food Healthy?" *Fortune,* August 9, 2004, pp. 134–139.

Differential costs can be either fixed or variable. To illustrate, assume that Nature Way Cosmetics, Inc., is thinking about changing its marketing method from distribution through retailers to distribution by a network of neighborhood sales representatives. Present costs and revenues are compared to projected costs and revenues in the following table:

	Retailer Distribution (present)	Sales Representatives (proposed)	Differential Costs and Revenues
Revenues (Variable)	$700,000	$800,000	$100,000
Cost of goods sold (Variable)	350,000	400,000	50,000
Advertising (Fixed)	80,000	45,000	(35,000)
Commissions (Variable)	0	40,000	40,000
Warehouse depreciation (Fixed)	50,000	80,000	30,000
Other expenses (Fixed)	60,000	60,000	0
Total expenses	540,000	625,000	85,000
Net operating income	$160,000	$175,000	$ 15,000

According to the above analysis, the differential revenue is $100,000 and the differential costs total $85,000, leaving a positive differential net operating income of $15,000 under the proposed marketing plan.

The decision of whether Nature Way Cosmetics should stay with the present retail distribution or switch to sales representatives could be made on the basis of the net operating incomes of the two alternatives. As we see in the above analysis, the net operating income under the present distribution method is $160,000, whereas the net operating income with sales representatives is estimated to be $175,000. Therefore, using sales representatives is preferred, since it would result in $15,000 higher net operating income. Note that we would have arrived at exactly the same conclusion by simply focusing on the differential revenues, differential costs, and differential net operating income, which also show a $15,000 advantage for sales representatives.

In general, only the differences between alternatives are relevant in decisions. Those items that are the same under all alternatives and that are not affected by the decision can be ignored. For example, in the Nature Way Cosmetics example above, the "Other expenses" category, which is $60,000 under both alternatives, can be ignored, since it has no effect on the decision. If it were removed from the calculations, the sales representatives would still be preferred by $15,000. This is an extremely important principle in management accounting that we will revisit in later chapters.

USING THOSE EMPTY SEATS

Cancer patients who seek specialized or experimental treatments must often travel far from home. Flying on a commercial airline can be an expensive and grueling experience for these patients. Priscilla Blum noted that many corporate jets fly with empty seats and she wondered why these seats couldn't be used for cancer patients. Taking the initiative, she founded Corporate Angel Network (www. corpangelnetwork.org), an organization that arranges free flights on some 1,500 jets from over 500 companies. There are no tax breaks for putting cancer patients in empty corporate jet seats, but filling an empty seat with a cancer patient doesn't involve any significant incremental cost. Since its founding, Corporate Angel Network has provided over 16,000 free flights.

Sources: Scott McCormack, "Waste Not, Want Not," *Forbes*, July 26, 1999, p. 118. Roger McCaffrey, "A True Tale of Angels in the Sky," *The Wall Street Journal*, February, 2002, p. A14. Helen Gibbs, Communication Director, Corporate Angel Network, private communication.

Opportunity Cost

Opportunity cost is the potential benefit that is given up when one alternative is selected over another. To illustrate this important concept, consider the following examples:

Example 1 Vicki has a part-time job that pays $200 per week while attending college. She would like to spend a week at the beach during spring break, and her employer has agreed to give her the time off, but without pay. The $200 in lost wages would be an opportunity cost of taking the week off to be at the beach.

Example 2 Suppose that Neiman Marcus is considering investing a large sum of money in land that may be a site for a future store. Rather than invest the funds in land, the company could invest the funds in high-grade securities. If the land is acquired, the opportunity cost is the investment income that could have been realized by purchasing the securities instead.

Example 3 Steve is employed by a company that pays him a salary of $38,000 per year. He is thinking about leaving the company and returning to school. Since returning to school would require that he give up his $38,000 salary, the forgone salary would be an opportunity cost of seeking further education.

Opportunity costs are not usually found in the accounting records of an organization, but they are costs that must be explicitly considered in every decision a manager makes. Virtually every alternative involves an opportunity cost. In Example 3 above, for instance, the higher income that could be realized in future years as a result of returning to school is an opportunity cost of staying in his present job.

Sunk Cost

A **sunk cost** is a cost *that has already been incurred* and that cannot be changed by any decision made now or in the future. Because sunk costs cannot be changed by any decision, they are not differential costs. And because only differential costs are relevant in a decision, sunk costs can and should be ignored.

To illustrate a sunk cost, assume that a company paid $50,000 several years ago for a special-purpose machine. The machine was used to make a product that is now obsolete and is no longer being sold. Even though in hindsight purchasing the machine may have been unwise, the $50,000 cost has already been incurred and cannot be undone. And it would be folly to continue making the obsolete product in a misguided attempt to "recover" the original cost of the machine. In short, the $50,000 originally paid for the machine is a sunk cost that should be ignored in current decisions.

IN BUSINESS

THE SUNK COST TRAP

Hal Arkes, a psychologist at Ohio University, asked 61 college students to assume they had mistakenly purchased tickets for both a $50 and a $100 ski trip for the same weekend. They could go on only one of the ski trips and would have to throw away the unused ticket. He further asked them to assume that they would actually have more fun on the $50 trip. Most of the students reported that they would go on the less enjoyable $100 trip. The larger cost mattered more to the students than having more fun. However, the sunk costs of the tickets should have been totally irrelevant in this decision. No matter which trip was selected, the actual total cost was $150—the cost of both tickets. And since this cost does not differ between the alternatives, it should be ignored. Like these students, most people have a great deal of difficulty ignoring sunk costs when making decisions.

Source: John Gourville and Dilip Soman, "Pricing and the Psychology of Consumption," *Harvard Business Review,* September 2002, pp. 92–93.

Summary

In this chapter, we have looked at some of the ways in which managers classify costs. How the costs will be used—for preparing external reports, predicting cost behavior, assigning costs to cost objects, or decision making—will dictate how the costs are classified.

For purposes of valuing inventories and determining expenses for the balance sheet and income statement, costs are classified as either product costs or period costs. Product costs are assigned to inventories and are considered assets until the products are sold. At the point of sale, product costs become cost of goods sold on the income statement. In contrast, period costs are taken directly to the income statement as expenses in the period in which they are incurred.

In a merchandising company, product cost is whatever the company paid for its merchandise. For external financial reports in a manufacturing company, product costs consist of all manufacturing costs. In both kinds of companies, selling and administrative costs are considered to be period costs and are expensed as incurred.

For purposes of predicting how costs will react to changes in activity, costs are classified into two categories—variable and fixed. Variable costs, in total, are strictly proportional to activity. The variable cost per unit is constant. Fixed costs, in total, remain at the same level for changes in activity that occur within the relevant range. The average fixed cost per unit decreases as the number of units increases.

For purposes of assigning costs to cost objects such as products or departments, costs are classified as direct or indirect. Direct costs can be conveniently traced to cost objects. Indirect costs cannot be conveniently traced to cost objects.

For purposes of making decisions, the concepts of differential cost and revenue, opportunity cost, and sunk cost are vitally important. Differential costs and revenues are the costs and revenues that differ between alternatives. Opportunity cost is the benefit that is forgone when one alternative is selected over another. Sunk cost is a cost that occurred in the past and cannot be altered. Differential costs and opportunity costs should be carefully considered in decisions. Sunk costs are always irrelevant in decisions and should be ignored.

These various cost classifications are *different* ways of looking at costs. A particular cost, such as the cost of cheese in a taco served at Taco Bell, could be a manufacturing cost, a product cost, a variable cost, a direct cost, and a differential cost—all at the same time. Taco Bell is a manufacturer of fast food. The cost of the cheese in a taco is a manufacturing cost and, as such, it would be a product cost as well. In addition, the cost of cheese is variable with respect to the number of tacos served and it is a direct cost of serving tacos. Finally, the cost of the cheese in a taco is a differential cost of making and serving the taco.

Review Problem 1: Cost Terms

Many new cost terms have been introduced in this chapter. It will take you some time to learn what each term means and how to properly classify costs in an organization. Consider the following example: Chippen Corporation manufactures furniture, including tables. Selected costs are given below:

1. The tables are made of wood that costs $100 per table.
2. The tables are assembled by workers, at a wage cost of $40 per table.
3. Workers making the tables are supervised by a factory supervisor who is paid $38,000 per year.
4. Electrical costs are $2 per machine-hour. Four machine-hours are required to produce a table.
5. The depreciation on the machines used to make the tables totals $10,000 per year. The machines have no resale value and do not wear out through use.
6. The salary of the president of the company is $100,000 per year.
7. The company spends $250,000 per year to advertise its products.
8. Salespersons are paid a commission of $30 for each table sold.
9. Instead of producing the tables, the company could rent its factory space for $50,000 per year.

Required:

Classify these costs according to the various cost terms used in the chapter. *Carefully study the classification of each cost.* If you don't understand why a particular cost is classified the way it is, reread the section of the chapter discussing the particular cost term. The terms *variable cost* and *fixed cost* refer to how costs behave with respect to the number of tables produced in a year.

Solution to Review Problem 1

	Variable Cost	Fixed Cost	Period (Selling and Administrative) Cost	Product Cost			Sunk Cost	Opportunity Cost
				Direct Materials	Direct Labor	Manufacturing Overhead		
1. Wood used in a table ($100 per table)	X			X				
2. Labor cost to assemble a table ($40 per table)	X				X			
3. Salary of the factory supervisor ($38,000 per year)		X				X		
4. Cost of electricity to produce tables ($2 per machine-hour)	X					X		
5. Depreciation of machines used to produce tables ($10,000 per year)		X				X	X*	
6. Salary of the company president ($100,000 per year)		X	X					
7. Advertising expense ($250,000 per year)		X	X					
8. Commissions paid to salespersons ($30 per table sold)	X		X					
9. Rental income forgone on factory space								X†

*This is a sunk cost because the outlay for the equipment was made in a previous period.
†This is an opportunity cost because it represents the potential benefit that is lost or sacrificed as a result of using the factory space to produce tables. Opportunity cost is a special category of cost that is not ordinarily recorded in an organization's accounting books. To avoid possible confusion with other costs, we will not attempt to classify this cost in any other way except as an opportunity cost.

Review Problem 2: Schedule of Cost of Goods Manufactured and Income Statement

The following information has been taken from the accounting records of Klear-Seal Corporation for last year:

Selling expenses	$140,000
Raw materials inventory, January 1	$90,000
Raw materials inventory, December 31	$60,000
Utilities, factory	$36,000
Direct labor cost	$150,000
Depreciation, factory	$162,000
Purchases of raw materials	$750,000
Sales	$2,500,000
Insurance, factory	$40,000
Supplies, factory	$15,000
Administrative expenses	$270,000
Indirect labor	$300,000
Maintenance, factory	$87,000
Work in process inventory, January 1	$180,000
Work in process inventory, December 31	$100,000
Finished goods inventory, January 1	$260,000
Finished goods inventory, December 31	$210,000

Management wants these data organized in a better format so that financial statements can be prepared for the year.

Required:
1. Prepare a schedule of cost of goods manufactured as in Exhibit 2–4.
2. Compute the cost of goods sold as in Exhibit 2–2.
3. Prepare an income statement.

Solution to Review Problem 2

1.

Klear-Seal Corporation Schedule of Cost of Goods Manufactured For the Year Ended December 31		
Direct materials:		
Raw materials inventory, January 1	$ 90,000	
Add: Purchases of raw materials	750,000	
Raw materials available for use	840,000	
Deduct: Raw materials inventory, December 31	60,000	
Raw materials used in production		$ 780,000
Direct labor		150,000
Manufacturing overhead:		
Utilities, factory	36,000	
Depreciation, factory	162,000	
Insurance, factory	40,000	
Supplies, factory	15,000	
Indirect labor	300,000	
Maintenance, factory	87,000	
Total manufacturing overhead cost		640,000
Total manufacturing cost		1,570,000
Add: Work in process inventory, January 1		180,000
		1,750,000
Deduct: Work in process inventory, December 31		100,000
Cost of goods manufactured		$1,650,000

2. The cost of goods sold would be computed as follows:

Finished goods inventory, January 1	$ 260,000
Add: Cost of goods manufactured	1,650,000
Goods available for sale	1,910,000
Deduct: Finished goods inventory, December 31	210,000
Cost of goods sold	$1,700,000

3.

Klear-Seal Corporation Income Statement For the Year Ended December 31		
Sales		$2,500,000
Cost of goods sold (above)		1,700,000
Gross margin		800,000
Selling and administrative expenses:		
Selling expenses	$140,000	
Administrative expenses	270,000	410,000
Net operating income		$ 390,000

Glossary

Administrative costs All executive, organizational, and clerical costs associated with the general management of an organization rather than with manufacturing or selling. (p. 41)

Common cost A cost that is incurred to support a number of cost objects but that cannot be traced to them individually. For example, the wage cost of the pilot of a 747 airliner is a common cost of all of the passengers on the aircraft. Without the pilot, there would be no flight and no passengers. But no part of the pilot's wage is caused by any one passenger taking the flight. (p. 56)

Conversion cost Direct labor cost plus manufacturing overhead cost. (p. 42)

Cost behavior The way in which a cost reacts to changes in the level of activity. (p. 51)

Cost object Anything for which cost data are desired. Examples of cost objects are products, customers, jobs, and parts of the organization such as departments or divisions. (p. 55)

Cost of goods manufactured The manufacturing costs associated with the goods that were finished during the period. (p. 47)

Differential cost A difference in cost between two alternatives. Also see *Incremental cost.* (p. 56)

Differential revenue The difference in revenue between two alternatives. (p. 56)

Direct cost A cost that can be easily and conveniently traced to a specified cost object. (p. 55)

Direct labor Factory labor costs that can be easily traced to individual units of product. Also called *touch labor.* (p. 40)

Direct materials Materials that become an integral part of a finished product and whose costs can be conveniently traced to it. (p. 40)

Finished goods Units of product that have been completed but not yet sold to customers. (p. 45)

Fixed cost A cost that remains constant, in total, regardless of changes in the level of activity within the relevant range. If a fixed cost is expressed on a per unit basis, it varies inversely with the level of activity. (p. 53)

Incremental cost An increase in cost between two alternatives. Also see *Differential cost.* (p. 56)

Indirect cost A cost that cannot be easily and conveniently traced to a specified cost object. (p. 56)

Indirect labor The labor costs of janitors, supervisors, materials handlers, and other factory workers that cannot be conveniently traced to particular products. (p. 40)

Indirect materials Small items of material such as glue and nails that may be an integral part of a finished product, but whose costs cannot be easily or conveniently traced to it. (p. 40)

Inventoriable costs Synonym for *product costs.* (p. 42)

Manufacturing overhead All manufacturing costs except direct materials and direct labor. (p. 41)

Opportunity cost The potential benefit that is given up when one alternative is selected over another. (p. 58)

Period costs Costs that are taken directly to the income statement as expenses in the period in which they are incurred or accrued. (p. 42)

Prime cost Direct materials cost plus direct labor cost. (p. 42)

Product costs All costs that are involved in acquiring or making a product. In the case of manufactured goods, these costs consist of direct materials, direct labor, and manufacturing overhead. Also see *Inventoriable costs.* (p. 42)

Raw materials Any materials that go into the final product. (pp. 39, 45)

Relevant range The range of activity within which assumptions about variable and fixed cost behavior are valid. (p. 53)

Schedule of cost of goods manufactured A schedule showing the direct materials, direct labor, and manufacturing overhead costs incurred during a period and the portion of those costs that are assigned to Work in Process and Finished Goods. (p. 47)

Selling costs All costs that are incurred to secure customer orders and get the finished product or service into the hands of the customer. (p. 41)

Sunk cost A cost that has already been incurred and that cannot be changed by any decision made now or in the future. (p. 58)

Variable cost A cost that varies, in total, in direct proportion to changes in the level of activity. A variable cost is constant per unit. (p. 52)

Work in process Units of product that are only partially complete. (p. 45)

Appendix 2A: Further Classification of Labor Costs

Idle time, overtime, and fringe benefits associated with direct labor workers pose particular problems in accounting for labor costs. Are these costs a part of the costs of direct labor or are they something else?

LEARNING OBJECTIVE 8
Properly account for labor costs associated with idle time, overtime, and fringe benefits.

IN BUSINESS

THE BIG THREE WRESTLE WITH FRINGE BENEFITS

When companies hire employees they have to pay more than just salaries and wages. Providing fringe benefits to employees, such as retirement and medical benefits, can be very costly. The Big Three U. S. automobile manufacturers (Ford, General Motors, and DaimlerChrysler) understand the costs associated with providing fringe benefits all too well. DaimlerChrysler's retirement and medical costs run $450 per vehicle higher than the likes of Toyota and Honda. Worse yet, the same costs for General Motors are $1,200 higher per vehicle than its Japanese rivals. The Big Three combined have approximately $15 billion in annual health and retirement expenses.

Source: David Welch, "A Contract the Big Three Can Take to the Bank," *BusinessWeek*, September 29, 2003, p. 46.

Idle Time

Machine breakdowns, materials shortages, power failures, and the like result in idle time. The labor costs incurred during idle time may be treated as a manufacturing overhead cost rather than as a direct labor cost. This approach spreads such costs over all the production of a period rather than just the jobs that happen to be in process when breakdowns or other disruptions occur.

To give an example of how the cost of idle time may be handled, assume that a press operator earns $12 per hour. If the press operator is paid for a normal 40-hour workweek but is idle for 3 hours during a given week due to breakdowns, labor cost would be allocated as follows:

Direct labor ($12 per hour × 37 hours)	$444
Manufacturing overhead (idle time: $12 per hour × 3 hours)	36
Total cost for the week	$480

Overtime Premium

The overtime premium paid to factory workers (direct labor as well as indirect labor) is usually considered to be part of manufacturing overhead and is not assigned to any particular order. At first glance this may seem strange, since overtime is always spent working on some particular order. Why not charge that order for the overtime cost? The reason is that it would be considered unfair and arbitrary to charge an overtime premium against a particular order simply because the order *happened* to fall on the tail end of the daily production schedule.

To illustrate, assume that two batches of goods, order A and order B, each take three hours to complete. The production run on order A is scheduled early in the day, but the production run on order B is scheduled late in the afternoon. By the time the run on order B is completed, two hours of overtime have been logged. The necessity to work overtime was a result of the fact that total production exceeded the regular time available. Order B was no more responsible for the overtime than was order A. Therefore, managers feel that all production should share in the premium charge that resulted. This is considered a more equitable way of handling overtime premium because it doesn't penalize one run simply because it happens to occur late in the day.

Let us again assume that a press operator in a plant earns $12 per hour. She is paid time and a half for overtime (time in excess of 40 hours a week). During a given week, she works 45 hours and has no idle time. Her labor cost for the week would be allocated as follows:

Direct labor ($12 per hour × 45 hours)	$540
Manufacturing overhead (overtime premium: $6 per hour × 5 hours)	30
Total cost for the week.	$570

Observe from this computation that only the overtime premium of $6 per hour is charged to the overhead account—*not* the entire $18 earned for each hour of overtime work ($12 regular rate per hour × 1.5 hours = $18).

Labor Fringe Benefits

Labor fringe benefits are made up of employment-related costs paid by the employer and include the costs of insurance programs, retirement plans, various supplemental unemployment benefits, and hospitalization plans. The employer also pays the employer's share of Social Security, Medicare, workers' compensation, federal employment tax, and state unemployment insurance. These costs often add up to as much as 30% to 40% of base pay.

Many companies treat all such costs as indirect labor by adding them to manufacturing overhead. Other companies treat the portion of fringe benefits that relates to direct labor as additional direct labor cost. This approach is conceptually superior, since the fringe benefits provided to direct labor workers clearly represent an added cost of their services.

Appendix 2B: Cost of Quality

A company may have a product with a high-quality design that uses high-quality components, but if the product is poorly assembled or has other defects, the company will have high warranty repair costs and dissatisfied customers. People who are dissatisfied with a product are unlikely to buy the product again. They are also likely to tell others about their bad experiences. This is the worst possible sort of advertising. To prevent such problems, companies expend a great deal of effort to reduce defects. The objective is to have high *quality of conformance.*

Quality of Conformance

A product that meets or exceeds its design specifications and is free of defects that mar its appearance or degrade its performance is said to have high **quality of conformance.** Note that if an economy car is free of defects, it can have a quality of conformance that is just as high as a defect-free luxury car. The purchasers of economy cars cannot expect their cars to be as opulently equipped as luxury cars, but they can and do expect them to be free of defects.

LEARNING OBJECTIVE 9
Identify the four types of quality costs and explain how they interact.

Preventing, detecting, and dealing with defects causes costs that are called *quality costs* or the *cost of quality.* The use of the term *quality cost* is confusing to some people. It does not refer to costs such as using a higher-grade leather to make a wallet or using 14K gold instead of gold-plating in jewelry. Instead, the term **quality cost** refers to all of the costs that are incurred to prevent defects or that result from defects in products.

WHO IS LAUGHING NOW?

There was time when Hyundai's product quality was the laughing stock of the automobile industry. However, in 2004 Hyundai's vehicles tied Toyota and Honda for the top spot in J.D. Power and Associates' study of initial vehicle quality. In that same year, *Consumer Reports* rated Hyundai's Sonata the most reliable car on the road. Why the dramatic turnabout? The company expanded its quality department to 1,000 employees—a tenfold increase—and required the department to report directly to the company's chairman, Mong-Koo Chung. Now, employees are paid bonuses for sharing and implementing ideas for improvement. "At Hyundai's Asian factory outside Seoul, workers have dropped 25,000 ideas into the suggestion box, of which 30% have been adopted." When test drives revealed a flaw in the Sonata's front door, it took engineers two months to create a solution that cost 40 cents per car. Had the same problem occurred a few years ago, one manager at Hyundai commented "we'd probably leave it."

Source: Joann Muller and Robyn Meredith, "Last Laugh," *Forbes*, April, 18, 2005, pp. 98–104.

Quality costs can be broken down into four broad groups. Two of these groups—known as *prevention costs* and *appraisal costs*—are incurred in an effort to keep defective products from falling into the hands of customers. The other two groups of costs—known as *internal failure costs* and *external failure costs*—are incurred because defects are produced despite efforts to prevent them. Examples of specific costs involved in each of these four groups are given in Exhibit 2B–1.

Several things should be noted about the quality costs shown in the exhibit. First, quality costs don't relate to just manufacturing; rather, they relate to all the activities in a company from initial research and development (R&D) through customer service. Second, the number

Prevention Costs	Internal Failure Costs
Systems development	Net cost of scrap
Quality engineering	Net cost of spoilage
Quality training	Rework labor and overhead
Quality circles	Reinspection of reworked products
Statistical process control activities	Retesting of reworked products
Supervision of prevention activities	Downtime caused by quality problems
Quality data gathering, analysis, and reporting	Disposal of defective products
Quality improvement projects	Analysis of the cause of defects in production
Technical support provided to suppliers	Re-entering data because of keying errors
Audits of the effectiveness of the quality system	Debugging software errors

Appraisal Costs	External Failure Costs
Test and inspection of incoming materials	Cost of field servicing and handling complaints
Test and inspection of in-process goods	Warranty repairs and replacements
Final product testing and inspection	Repairs and replacements beyond the warranty period
Supplies used in testing and inspection	Product recalls
Supervision of testing and inspection activities	Liability arising from defective products
Depreciation of test equipment	Returns and allowances arising from quality problems
Maintenance of test equipment	Lost sales arising from a reputation for poor quality
Plant utilities in the inspection area	
Field testing and appraisal at customer site	

EXHIBIT 2B–1
Typical Quality Costs

of costs associated with quality is very large; total quality cost can be quite high unless management gives this area special attention. Finally, the costs in the four groupings are quite different. We will now look at each of these groupings more closely.

Prevention Costs

Generally, the most effective way to manage quality costs is to avoid having defects in the first place. It is much less costly to prevent a problem from ever happening than it is to find and correct the problem after it has occurred. **Prevention costs** support activities whose purpose is to reduce the number of defects. Companies employ many techniques to prevent defects including statistical process control, quality engineering, training, and a variety of other Six Sigma tools.

Note from Exhibit 2B–1 that prevention costs include activities relating to quality circles and statistical process control. **Quality circles** consist of small groups of employees that meet on a regular basis to discuss ways to improve quality. Both management and workers are included in these circles. Quality circles are widely used and can be found in manufacturing companies, utilities, health care organizations, banks, and many other organizations.

Statistical process control is a technique that is used to detect whether a process is in or out of control. An out-of-control process results in defective units and may be caused by a miscalibrated machine or some other factor. In statistical process control, workers use charts to monitor the quality of units that pass through their workstations. With these charts, workers can quickly spot processes that are out of control and that are creating defects. Problems can be immediately corrected and further defects prevented rather than waiting for an inspector to catch the defects later.

Note also from the list of prevention costs in Exhibit 2B–1 that some companies provide technical support to their suppliers as a way of preventing defects. Particularly in just-in-time (JIT) systems, such support to suppliers is vital. In a JIT system, parts are delivered from suppliers just in time and in just the correct quantity to fill customer orders. There are no parts stockpiles. If a defective part is received from a supplier, the part cannot be used and the order for the ultimate customer cannot be filled on time. Hence, every part received from a supplier must be free of defects. Consequently, companies that use JIT often require that their suppliers use sophisticated quality control programs such as statistical process control and that their suppliers certify that they will deliver parts and materials that are free of defects.

Appraisal Costs

Any defective parts and products should be caught as early as possible in the production process. **Appraisal costs,** which are sometimes called *inspection costs,* are incurred to identify defective products *before* the products are shipped to customers. Unfortunately, performing appraisal activities doesn't keep defects from happening again, and most managers now realize that maintaining an army of inspectors is a costly (and ineffective) approach to quality control.

The late professor John K. Shank of Dartmouth College once stated, "The old-style approach was to say, 'We've got great quality. We have 40 quality control inspectors in the factory.' Then somebody realized that if you need 40 inspectors, it must be a lousy factory. So now the trick is to run a factory without any quality control inspectors; each employee is his or her own quality control person."[1]

Employees are increasingly being asked to be responsible for their own quality control. This approach, along with designing products to be easy to manufacture properly, allows quality to be built into products rather than relying on inspection to get the defects out.

Internal Failure Costs

Failure costs are incurred when a product fails to conform to its design specifications. Failure costs can be either internal or external. **Internal failure costs** result from identifying

---

[1]   Robert W. Casey, "The Changing World of the CEO," *PPM World* 24, no. 2, p. 31.

defects before they are shipped to customers. These costs include scrap, rejected products, reworking of defective units, and downtime caused by quality problems. In some companies, as little as 10% of the company's products make it through the production process without rework of some kind. Of course, the more effective a company's appraisal activities, the greater the chance of catching defects internally and the greater the level of internal failure costs. This is the price that is paid to avoid incurring external failure costs, which can be devastating.

External Failure Costs

External failure costs result when a defective product is delivered to a customer. As shown in Exhibit 2B–1, external failure costs include warranty repairs and replacements, product recalls, liability arising from legal action against a company, and lost sales arising from a reputation for poor quality. Such costs can decimate profits.

In the past, some managers have taken the attitude, "Let's go ahead and ship everything to customers, and we'll take care of any problems under the warranty." This attitude generally results in high external failure costs, customer ill will, and declining market share and profits.

THE HIGH COST OF EXTERNAL FAILURES IN HEALTH CARE

Poor quality management has plagued the American health-care industry for years. At least 100,000 patients are killed every year due to external failures and $500 billion a year is spent on avoidable medical costs. These alarming statistics fueled $27 billion in malpractice costs in 2003. Fortunately, change appears on the horizon. Some hospitals are beginning to measure performance and issue report cards rather than assuming that their doctors' decisions and practices are always correct. For example, when newly created reports informed managers at Utah's Intermountain LDS Hospital that their doctors were frequently inducing expectant mothers prematurely for convenience sake, they clamped down by requiring more prudent medical practices. The LDS Hospital is also finding that small investments in prevention are reaping huge savings in money and lives. The hospital's annual deaths from congestive heart failure have dropped 22% simply by creating and enforcing the use of a checklist to ensure that all patients receive the proper medications before being discharged from the hospital.

Source: Robert Langreth, "Fixing Hospitals," *Forbes*, June 20, 2005, pp. 68–76.

Distribution of Quality Costs

Quality costs for U.S. companies have been found to range between 10% and 20% of total sales, whereas experts say that these costs should be more in the 2% to 4% range. How does a company reduce its total quality cost? The answer lies in how the quality costs are distributed. Refer to the graph in Exhibit 2B–2 (page 68), which shows total quality costs as a function of the quality of conformance.

The graph shows that when the quality of conformance is low, total quality cost is high and that most of this cost consists of costs of internal and external failure. A low quality of conformance means that a high percentage of units are defective and hence the company has high failure costs. However, as a company spends more and more on prevention and appraisal, the percentage of defective units drops (the percentage of defect-free units increases). This results in lower internal and external failure costs. Ordinarily, total quality cost drops rapidly as the quality of conformance increases. Thus, a company can reduce its total quality cost by focusing its efforts on prevention and appraisal. The cost savings from reduced defects usually swamp the costs of the additional prevention and appraisal efforts.

The graph in Exhibit 2B–2 has been drawn so that the total quality cost is minimized when the quality of conformance is less than 100%. However, some experts contend that the total quality cost is not minimized until the quality of conformance is 100% and there are no

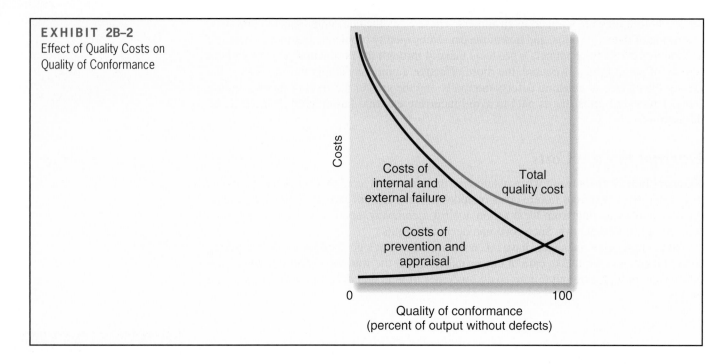

EXHIBIT 2B–2
Effect of Quality Costs on
Quality of Conformance

Costs

Costs of
internal and
external failure

Total
quality cost

Costs of
prevention and
appraisal

0

100

Quality of conformance
(percent of output without defects)

defects. Indeed, many companies have found that the total quality costs seem to keep dropping even when the quality of conformance approaches 100% and defect rates get as low as 1 in a million units. Others argue that total quality cost eventually increases as the quality of conformance increases. However, in most companies this does not seem to happen until the quality of conformance is very close to 100% and defect rates are very close to zero.

As a company's quality program becomes more refined and as its failure costs begin to fall, prevention activities usually become more effective than appraisal activities. Appraisal can only find defects, whereas prevention can eliminate them. The best way to prevent defects from happening is to design processes that reduce the likelihood of defects and to continually monitor processes using statistical process control methods.

Quality Cost Reports

As an initial step in quality improvement programs, companies often construct a *quality cost report* that provides an estimate of the financial consequences of the company's current level of defects. A **quality cost report** details the prevention costs, appraisal costs, and costs of internal and external failures that arise from the company's current quality control efforts. Managers are often shocked by the magnitude of these costs. A typical quality cost report is shown in Exhibit 2B–3.

Several things should be noted from the data in the exhibit. First, Ventura Company's quality costs are poorly distributed in both years, with most of the costs due to either internal failure or external failure. The external failure costs are particularly high in Year 1 in comparison to other costs.

Second, note that the company increased its spending on prevention and appraisal activities in Year 2. As a result, internal failure costs went up in that year (from $2 million in Year 1 to $3 million in Year 2), but external failure costs dropped sharply (from $5.15 million in Year 1 to only $2 million in Year 2). Because of the increase in appraisal activity in Year 2, more defects were caught inside the company before they were shipped to customers. This resulted in more cost for scrap, rework, and so forth, but saved huge amounts in warranty repairs, warranty replacements, and other external failure costs.

Third, note that as a result of greater emphasis on prevention and appraisal, *total* quality cost decreased in Year 2. As continued emphasis is placed on prevention and appraisal in

EXHIBIT 2B–3
Quality Cost Report

	Year 1		Year 2	
Ventura Company Quality Cost Report For Years 1 and 2	Amount	Percent*	Amount	Percent*
Prevention costs:				
Systems development	$ 270,000	0.54%	$ 400,000	0.80%
Quality training	130,000	0.26%	210,000	0.42%
Supervision of prevention activities	40,000	0.08%	70,000	0.14%
Quality improvement projects	210,000	0.42%	320,000	0.64%
Total prevention cost	650,000	1.30%	1,000,000	2.00%
Appraisal costs:				
Inspection	560,000	1.12%	600,000	1.20%
Reliability testing	420,000	0.84%	580,000	1.16%
Supervision of testing and inspection	80,000	0.16%	120,000	0.24%
Depreciation of test equipment	140,000	0.28%	200,000	0.40%
Total appraisal cost	1,200,000	2.40%	1,500,000	3.00%
Internal failure costs:				
Net cost of scrap	750,000	1.50%	900,000	1.80%
Rework labor and overhead	810,000	1.62%	1,430,000	2.86%
Downtime due to defects in quality	100,000	0.20%	170,000	0.34%
Disposal of defective products	340,000	0.68%	500,000	1.00%
Total internal failure cost	2,000,000	4.00%	3,000,000	6.00%
External failure costs:				
Warranty repairs	900,000	1.80%	400,000	0.80%
Warranty replacements	2,300,000	4.60%	870,000	1.74%
Allowances	630,000	1.26%	130,000	0.26%
Cost of field servicing	1,320,000	2.64%	600,000	1.20%
Total external failure cost	5,150,000	10.30%	2,000,000	4.00%
Total quality cost	$9,000,000	18.00%	$7,500,000	15.00%

*As a percentage of total sales. In each year sales totaled $50,000,000.

future years, total quality cost should continue to decrease. That is, future increases in prevention and appraisal costs should be more than offset by decreases in failure costs. Moreover, appraisal costs should also decrease as more effort is placed in prevention.

EXTERNAL FAILURE; IT'S WORSE THAN YOU THINK

Venky Nagar and Madhav Rajan investigated quality costs at 11 manufacturing plants of a large U.S. company. They found that total quality costs were about 7% of sales. Moreover, they found that external failure costs as usually measured grossly understate the true impact of external failures on the company's profits. In addition to the obvious costs of repairing defective products that are under warranty, defective products sold to customers negatively impact the company's reputation and hence future sales. Statistical analysis of the data from the manufacturing plants indicated that a $1 increase in external failure costs such as warranty repairs was associated with a $26 decrease in cumulative future sales and a $10.40 cumulative decrease in future profits.

Source: Venky Nagar and Madhav V. Rajan, "The Revenue Implications of Financial and Operational Measures of Product Quality," *The Accounting Review* 76, no. 4, October 2001, pp. 495–513.

Quality Cost Reports in Graphic Form

As a supplement to the quality cost report shown in Exhibit 2B–3, companies frequently prepare quality cost information in graphic form. Graphic presentations include pie charts, bar graphs, trend lines, and so forth. The data for Ventura Company from Exhibit 2B–3 are presented in bar graph form in Exhibit 2B–4.

The first bar graph in Exhibit 2B–4 is scaled in terms of dollars of quality cost, and the second is scaled in terms of quality cost as a percentage of sales. In both graphs, the data are "stacked" upward. That is, appraisal costs are stacked on top of prevention costs, internal failure costs are stacked on top of the sum of prevention costs plus appraisal costs, and so forth. The percentage figures in the second graph show that total quality cost equals 18% of sales in Year 1 and 15% of sales in Year 2, the same as reported earlier in Exhibit 2B–3.

Data in graphic form help managers to see trends more clearly and to see the magnitude of the various costs in relation to each other. Such graphs are easily prepared using computer graphics and spreadsheet applications.

Uses of Quality Cost Information

A quality cost report has several uses. First, quality cost information helps managers see the financial significance of defects. Managers usually are not aware of the magnitude of their quality costs because these costs cut across departmental lines and are not normally tracked and accumulated by the cost system. Thus, when first presented with a quality cost report, managers often are surprised by the amount of cost attributable to poor quality.

Second, quality cost information helps managers identify the relative importance of the quality problems faced by their companies. For example, the quality cost report may show that scrap is a major quality problem or that the company is incurring huge warranty costs. With this information, managers have a better idea of where to focus their efforts.

Third, quality cost information helps managers see whether their quality costs are poorly distributed. In general, quality costs should be distributed more toward prevention and appraisal activities and less toward failures.

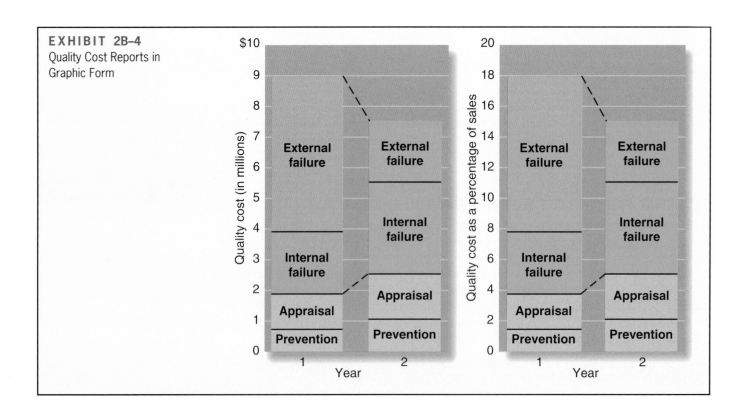

EXHIBIT 2B–4
Quality Cost Reports in Graphic Form

Counterbalancing these uses, three limitations of quality cost information should be recognized. First, simply measuring and reporting quality costs does not solve quality problems. Problems can be solved only by taking action. Second, results usually lag behind quality improvement programs. Initially, total quality cost may even increase as quality control systems are designed and installed. Decreases in quality costs may not begin to occur until the quality program has been in effect for some time. And third, the most important quality cost, lost sales arising from customer ill will, is usually omitted from the quality cost report because it is difficult to estimate.

Typically, during the initial years of a quality improvement program, the benefits of compiling a quality cost report outweigh the costs and limitations of the reports. As managers gain experience in balancing prevention and appraisal activities, the need for quality cost reports often diminishes.

International Aspects of Quality

Many of the tools used in quality management today were developed in Japan after World War II. In statistical process control, Japanese companies borrowed heavily from the work of W. Edwards Deming. However, Japanese companies are largely responsible for quality circles, JIT, the idea that quality is everyone's responsibility, and the emphasis on prevention rather than on inspection.

In the 1980s, quality reemerged as a pivotal factor in the market. Many companies now find that it is impossible to effectively compete without a very strong quality program in place. This is particularly true of companies that wish to compete in the European market.

The ISO 9000 Standards

The International Organization for Standardization (ISO), based in Geneva, Switzerland, has established quality control guidelines known as the **ISO 9000 standards.** Many companies and organizations in Europe will buy only from ISO 9000-certified suppliers. This means that the suppliers must demonstrate to a certifying agency that:

1. A quality control system is in use, and the system clearly defines an expected level of quality.
2. The system is fully operational and is backed up with detailed documentation of quality control procedures.
3. The intended level of quality is being achieved on a sustained, consistent basis.

The key to receiving certification under the ISO 9000 standards is documentation. It's one thing for a company to say that it has a quality control system in operation, but it's quite a different thing to be able to document the steps in that system. Under ISO 9000, this documentation must be so detailed and precise that if all the employees in a company were suddenly replaced, the new employees could use the documentation to make the product exactly as it was made by the old employees. Even companies with good quality control systems find that it takes up to two years of painstaking work to develop this detailed documentation. But companies often find that compiling this documentation results in improvements in their quality systems.

The ISO 9000 standards have become an international measure of quality. Although the standards were developed to control the quality of goods sold in European countries, they have become widely accepted elsewhere as well. Companies in the United States that export to Europe often expect their own suppliers to comply with ISO 9000 standards, since these exporters must document the quality of the materials going into their products as part of their own ISO 9000 certification.

The ISO program for certification of quality management programs is not limited to manufacturing companies. The American Institute of Certified Public Accountants was the first professional membership organization in the United States to win recognition under an ISO certification program.

IN BUSINESS

ISO 9000 STANDARDS: WHERE IS THE PAYOFF?

The International Organization for Standardization (ISO) has established over 15,000 standards during its existence. As of 2003, more than 600,000 companies worldwide had received some form of ISO certification. Organizations such as Northrop Grumman, Ford, and some units of the United States government require their suppliers to be ISO certified. Nonetheless, many companies are beginning to question whether the effort expended to become certified is worth it. According to Bill Robinson, who supervised more than 50 ISO certifications at Lucent Technologies, ISO certification "can help drive a company to a plateau level of performance, but it will keep it at that level and, in fact, stifle improvement." Arunas Chesonis, CEO of Paetec Communications in Rochester, New York, is de-emphasizing ISO in favor of Six Sigma because he believes ISO "is not one of the better systems for process improvement." Furthermore, research has shown that although ISO 9000 certification may be necessary to maintain current levels of financial performance (in cases where a company's customers require their suppliers to be certified), it has a very limited effect on improving financial performance.

Source: Stephanie Clifford, "So Many Standards to Follow, So Little Payoff," *Inc.* magazine, May 2005, pp. 25–27.

Summary (Appendix 2B)

Defects cause costs, which can be classified into prevention costs, appraisal costs, internal failure costs, and external failure costs. Prevention costs are incurred to keep defects from happening. Appraisal costs are incurred to ensure that defective products, once made, are not shipped to customers. Internal failure costs are incurred as a consequence of detecting defective products before they are shipped to customers. External failure costs are the consequences (in terms of repairs, servicing, and lost future business) of delivering defective products to customers. Most experts agree that management effort should be focused on preventing defects. Small investments in prevention can lead to dramatic reductions in appraisal costs and costs of internal and external failure.

Quality costs are summarized on a quality cost report. This report shows the types of quality costs being incurred and their significance and trends. The report helps managers understand the importance of quality costs, spot problem areas, and assess the way in which the quality costs are distributed.

Glossary (Appendix 2B)

Appraisal costs Costs that are incurred to identify defective products before the products are shipped to customers. (p. 66)

External failure costs Costs that are incurred when a product or service that is defective is delivered to a customer. (p. 67)

Internal failure costs Costs that are incurred as a result of identifying defective products before they are shipped to customers. (p. 66)

ISO 9000 standards Quality control requirements issued by the International Organization for Standardization that relate to products sold in European countries. (p. 71)

Prevention costs Costs that are incurred to keep defects from occurring. (p. 66)

Quality circles Small groups of employees that meet on a regular basis to discuss ways of improving quality. (p. 66)

Quality cost Costs that are incurred to prevent defective products from falling into the hands of customers or that are incurred as a result of defective units. (p. 64)

Quality cost report A report that details prevention costs, appraisal costs, and the costs of internal and external failures. (p. 68)

Quality of conformance The degree to which a product or service meets or exceeds its design specifications and is free of defects or other problems that mar its appearance or degrade its performance. (p. 64)

Statistical process control A charting technique used to monitor the quality of work being done in a workstation for the purpose of immediately correcting any problems. (p. 66)

Questions

2-1   What are the three major elements of product costs in a manufacturing company?

2-2   Distinguish between the following: (a) direct materials, (b) indirect materials, (c) direct labor, (d) indirect labor, and (e) manufacturing overhead.

2-3   Explain the difference between a product cost and a period cost.

2-4   Describe how the income statement of a manufacturing company differs from the income statement of a merchandising company.

2-5   Describe the schedule of cost of goods manufactured. How does it tie into the income statement?

2-6   Describe how the inventory accounts of a manufacturing company differ from the inventory account of a merchandising company.

2-7   Why are product costs sometimes called inventoriable costs? Describe the flow of such costs in a manufacturing company from the point of incurrence until they finally become expenses on the income statement.

2-8   Is it possible for costs such as salaries or depreciation to end up as assets on the balance sheet? Explain.

2-9   What is meant by the term *cost behavior?*

2-10   "A variable cost is a cost that varies per unit of product, whereas a fixed cost is constant per unit of product." Do you agree? Explain.

2-11   How do fixed costs create difficulties in costing units of product?

2-12   Why is manufacturing overhead considered an indirect cost of a unit of product?

2-13   Define the following terms: differential cost, opportunity cost, and sunk cost.

2-14   Only variable costs can be differential costs. Do you agree? Explain.

2-15   (Appendix 2A) Mary Adams is employed by Acme Company. Last week she worked 34 hours assembling one of the company's products and was idle 6 hours due to material shortages. Acme's employees are engaged at their workstations for a normal 40-hour week. Ms. Adams is paid $15 per hour. Allocate her earnings between direct labor cost and manufacturing overhead cost.

2-16   (Appendix 2A) John Olsen operates a stamping machine on the assembly line of Drake Manufacturing Company. Last week Mr. Olsen worked 45 hours. His basic wage rate is $14 per hour, with time and a half for overtime (time worked in excess of 40 hours per week). Allocate Mr. Olsen's wages for the week between direct labor cost and manufacturing overhead cost.

2-17   (Appendix 2B) Costs associated with the quality of conformance can be broken down into four broad groups. What are these four groups and how do they differ?

2-18   (Appendix 2B) In their efforts to reduce the total cost of quality, should companies generally focus on decreasing prevention costs and appraisal costs?

2-19   (Appendix 2B) What is probably the most effective way to reduce a company's total quality costs?

2-20   (Appendix 2B) What are the main uses of quality cost reports?

2-21   (Appendix 2B) Why are managers often unaware of the magnitude of quality costs?

 ## Exercises

EXERCISE 2-1 Classifying Manufacturing Costs [LO1]

The PC Works assembles custom computers from components supplied by various manufacturers. The company is very small and its assembly shop and retail sales store are housed in a single facility in a Redmond, Washington, industrial park. Listed below are some of the costs that are incurred at the company.

Required:

For each cost, indicate whether it would most likely be classified as direct labor, direct materials, manufacturing overhead, marketing and selling, or an administrative cost.

1.   The cost of a hard drive installed in a computer.
2.   The cost of advertising in the *Puget Sound Computer User* newspaper.
3.   The wages of employees who assemble computers from components.
4.   Sales commissions paid to the company's salespeople.
5.   The wages of the assembly shop's supervisor.
6.   The wages of the company's accountant.
7.   Depreciation on equipment used to test assembled computers before release to customers.
8.   Rent on the facility in the industrial park.

EXERCISE 2-2 Classification of Costs as Period or Product Cost [LO2]

A product cost is also known as an inventoriable cost. Classify the following costs as either product (inventoriable) costs or period (noninventoriable) costs in a manufacturing company:

1. Depreciation on salespersons' cars.
2. Rent on equipment used in the factory.
3. Lubricants used for maintenance of machines.
4. Salaries of finished goods warehouse personnel.
5. Soap and paper towels used by factory workers at the end of a shift.
6. Factory supervisors' salaries.
7. Heat, water, and power consumed in the factory.
8. Materials used for boxing products for shipment overseas. (Units are not normally boxed.)
9. Advertising costs.
10. Workers' compensation insurance on factory employees.
11. Depreciation on chairs and tables in the factory lunchroom.
12. The wages of the receptionist in the administrative offices.
13. Lease cost of the corporate jet used by the company's executives.
14. Rent on rooms at a Florida resort for holding of the annual sales conference.
15. Attractively designed box for packaging the company's product—breakfast cereal.

EXERCISE 2-3 Constructing an Income Statement [LO3]

Last month CyberGames, a computer game retailer, had total sales of $1,450,000, selling expenses of $210,000, and administrative expenses of $180,000. The company had beginning merchandise inventory of $240,000, purchased additional merchandise inventory for $950,000, and had ending merchandise inventory of $170,000.

Required:
Prepare an income statement for the company for the month.

EXERCISE 2-4 Prepare a Schedule of Cost of Goods Manufactured [LO4]

Lompac Products manufactures a variety of products in its factory. Data for the most recent month's operations appear below:

Beginning raw materials inventory	$ 60,000
Purchases of raw materials	$690,000
Ending raw materials inventory	$ 45,000
Direct labor.	$135,000
Manufacturing overhead.	$370,000
Beginning work in process inventory	$120,000
Ending work in process inventory.	$130,000

Required:
Prepare a schedule of cost of goods manufactured for the company for the month.

EXERCISE 2-5 Classification of Costs as Fixed or Variable [LO5]

Below are a number of costs that are incurred in a variety of organizations.

Required:
Classify each cost as being variable or fixed with respect to the number of units of product or services sold by the organization by placing an *X* in the appropriate column.

	Cost Behavior	
Cost Item	Variable	Fixed
1. X-ray film used in the radiology lab at Virginia Mason Hospital in Seattle		
2. The costs of advertising a Madonna rock concert in New York City		
3. Rental cost of a McDonald's restaurant building in Hong Kong		
4. The electrical costs of running a roller coaster at Magic Mountain		
5. Property taxes on your local cinema		
6. Commissions paid to salespersons at Nordstrom		
7. Property insurance on a Coca-Cola bottling plant		
8. The costs of synthetic materials used to make Nike running shoes		
9. The costs of shipping Panasonic televisions to retail stores		
10. The cost of leasing an ultra-scan diagnostic machine at the American Hospital in Paris		

EXERCISE 2-6 Identifying Direct and Indirect Costs [LO6]

Northwest Hospital is a full-service hospital that provides everything from major surgery and emergency room care to outpatient clinics.

Required:

For each cost incurred at Northwest Hospital, indicate whether it would most likely be a direct cost or an indirect cost of the specified cost object by placing an *X* in the appropriate column.

	Cost	Cost Object	Direct Cost	Indirect Cost
Ex.	Catered food served to patients	A particular patient	X	
1.	The wages of pediatric nurses	The pediatric department		
2.	Prescription drugs	A particular patient		
3.	Heating the hospital	The pediatric department		
4.	The salary of the head of pediatrics	The pediatric department		
5.	The salary of the head of pediatrics	A particular pediatric patient		
6.	Hospital chaplain's salary	A particular patient		
7.	Lab tests by outside contractor	A particular patient		
8.	Lab tests by outside contractor	A particular department		

EXERCISE 2-7 Differential, Opportunity, and Sunk Costs [LO7]

Northwest Hospital is a full-service hospital that provides everything from major surgery and emergency room care to outpatient clinics. The hospital's Radiology Department is considering replacing an old inefficient X-ray machine with a state-of-the-art digital X-ray machine. The new machine would provide higher quality X-rays in less time and at a lower cost per X-ray. It would also require less power and would use a color laser printer to produce easily readable X-ray images. Instead of investing the funds in the new X-ray machine, the Laboratory Department is lobbying the hospital's management to buy a new DNA analyzer.

Required:

For each of the items below, indicate by placing an *X* in the appropriate column whether it should be considered a differential cost, an opportunity cost, or a sunk cost in the decision to replace the old X-ray machine with a new machine. If none of the categories apply for a particular item, leave all columns blank.

	Item	Differential Item	Opportunity Cost	Sunk Cost
Ex.	Cost of X-ray film used in the old machine............	X		
1.	Cost of the old X-ray machine			
2.	The salary of the head of the Radiology Department ...			
3.	The salary of the head of the Pediatrics Department ...			
4.	Cost of the new color laser printer...................			
5.	Rent on the space occupied by Radiology			
6.	The cost of maintaining the old machine			
7.	Benefits from a new DNA analyzer			
8.	Cost of electricity to run the X-ray machines			

EXERCISE 2-8 (Appendix 2A) Classification of Overtime Cost [LO8]

Several days ago you took your TV set into a shop to have some repair work done. When you later picked up the set, the bill showed a $75 charge for labor. This charge represented two hours of service time—$30 for the first hour and $45 for the second.

When questioned about the difference in hourly rates, the shop manager explained that work on your set was started at 4 o'clock in the afternoon. By the time work was completed two hours later at 6 o'clock, an hour of overtime had been put in by the repair technician. The second hour therefore contained a charge for an "overtime premium," since the company had to pay the repair technician time and a half for any work in excess of eight hours per day. The shop manager further explained that the shop was working overtime to "catch up a little" on its backlog of repairs, but it still needed to maintain a "decent" profit margin on the technicians' time.

Required:
1. Do you agree with the shop's computation of the service charge on your job?
2. Assume that the shop pays its technicians $14 per hour for the first eight hours worked in a day and $21 per hour for any additional time worked in a day. Prepare computations to show how the cost of the repair technician's time for the day (nine hours) should be allocated between direct labor cost and general overhead cost on the shop's books.
3. Under what circumstances might the shop be justified in charging an overtime premium for repair work on your set?

EXERCISE 2-9 (Appendix 2B) Classification of Quality Costs [LO9]

Listed below are a number of costs that are incurred in connection with a company's quality control system.

a.	Product testing.	k.	Net cost of scrap.
b.	Product recalls.	l.	Depreciation of test equipment.
c.	Rework labor and overhead.	m.	Returns and allowances arising from poor
d.	Quality circles.		quality.
e.	Downtime caused by defects.	n.	Disposal of defective products.
f.	Cost of field servicing.	o.	Technical support to suppliers.
g.	Inspection of goods.	p.	Systems development.
h.	Quality engineering.	q.	Warranty replacements.
i.	Warranty repairs.	r.	Field testing at customer site.
j.	Statistical process control.	s.	Product design.

Required:
1. Classify each of the costs above into one of the following categories: prevention cost, appraisal cost, internal failure cost, or external failure cost.
2. Which of the costs in (1) above are incurred in an effort to keep poor quality of conformance from occurring? Which of the costs in (1) above are incurred because poor quality of conformance has occurred?

EXERCISE 2-10 Product Cost Flows; Product versus Period Costs [LO2, LO3]

The Devon Motor Company produces motorcycles. During April, the company purchased 8,000 batteries at a cost of $10 per battery. Devon withdrew 7,600 batteries from the storeroom during the month. Of these, 100 were used to replace batteries in motorcycles used by the company's traveling sales staff. The remaining 7,500 batteries withdrawn from the storeroom were placed in motorcycles being produced by the company. Of the motorcycles in production during April, 90% were completed and transferred from work in process to finished goods. Of the motorcycles completed during the month, 30% were unsold at April 30.

There were no inventories of any type on April 1.

Required:
1. Determine the cost of batteries that would appear in each of the following accounts at April 30:
    a. Raw Materials.
    b. Work in Process.
    c. Finished Goods.
    d. Cost of Goods Sold.
    e. Selling Expense.
2. Specify whether each of the above accounts would appear on the balance sheet or on the income statement at April 30.

EXERCISE 2-11 Preparation of Schedule of Costs of Goods Manufactured and Cost of Goods Sold [LO1, LO3, LO4]

The following cost and inventory data are taken from the accounting records of Mason Company for the year just completed:

Costs incurred:	
Direct labor cost	$70,000
Purchases of raw materials.	$118,000
Indirect labor.	$30,000
Maintenance, factory equipment.	$6,000
Advertising expense	$90,000

Insurance, factory equipment	$800
Sales salaries	$50,000
Rent, factory facilities	$20,000
Supplies	$4,200
Depreciation, office equipment	$3,000
Depreciation, factory equipment	$19,000

	Beginning of the Year	End of the Year
Inventories:		
Raw materials	$7,000	$15,000
Work in process	$10,000	$5,000
Finished goods	$20,000	$35,000

Required:
1. Prepare a schedule of cost of goods manufactured in good form.
2. Prepare the cost of goods sold section of Mason Company's income statement for the year.

EXERCISE 2-12 Classification of Costs as Variable or Fixed and as Selling and Administrative or Product [LO2, LO5]

Below are listed various costs that are found in organizations.
1. Hamburger buns in a Wendy's outlet.
2. Advertising by a dental office.
3. Apples processed and canned by Del Monte.
4. Shipping canned apples from a Del Monte plant to customers.
5. Insurance on a Bausch & Lomb factory producing contact lenses.
6. Insurance on IBM's corporate headquarters.
7. Salary of a supervisor overseeing production of printers at Hewlett-Packard.
8. Commissions paid to Encyclopedia Britannica salespersons.
9. Depreciation of factory lunchroom facilities at a General Electric plant.
10. Steering wheels installed in BMWs.

Required:

Classify each cost as being either variable or fixed with respect to the number of units produced and sold. Also classify each cost as either a selling and administrative cost or a product cost. Prepare your answer sheet as shown below. Place an *X* in the appropriate columns to show the proper classification of each cost.

	Cost Behavior		Selling and Administrative	Product
Cost Item	Variable	Fixed	Cost	Cost

EXERCISE 2-13 (Appendix 2A) Classification of Labor Costs [LO8]

Paul Clark is employed by Aerotech Products and assembles a component part for one of the company's product lines. He is paid $14 per hour for regular time and time and a half (i.e., $21 per hour) for all work in excess of 40 hours per week.

Required:
1. Assume that during a given week Paul is idle for five hours due to machine breakdowns and that he is idle for four more hours due to material shortages. No overtime is recorded for the week. Allocate Paul's wages for the week between direct labor cost and manufacturing overhead cost.
2. Assume that during the following week Paul works a total of 48 hours. He has no idle time for the week. Allocate Paul's wages for the week between direct labor cost and manufacturing overhead cost.
3. Paul's company provides an attractive package of fringe benefits for its employees. This package includes a retirement program and a health insurance program. Explain two ways that the company could handle the costs of its direct laborers' fringe benefits in its cost records.

Problems

PROBLEM 2-14 Cost Classification [LO2, LO5, LO6]
Listed below are a number of costs typically found in organizations.
1. Property taxes, factory.
2. Boxes used for packaging detergent produced by the company.
3. Salespersons' commissions.
4. Supervisor's salary, factory.
5. Depreciation, executive autos.
6. Wages of workers assembling computers.
7. Insurance, finished goods warehouses.
8. Lubricants for machines.
9. Advertising costs.
10. Microchips used in producing calculators.
11. Shipping costs on merchandise sold.
12. Magazine subscriptions, factory lunchroom.
13. Thread in a garment factory.
14. Billing costs.
15. Executive life insurance.
16. Ink used in textbook production.
17. Fringe benefits, assembly-line workers.
18. Yarn used in sweater production.
19. Wages of receptionist, executive offices.

Required:
Prepare an answer sheet with column headings as shown below. For each cost item, indicate whether it would be variable or fixed with respect to the number of units produced and sold; and then whether it would be a selling cost, an administrative cost, or a manufacturing cost. If it is a manufacturing cost, indicate whether it would typically be treated as a direct cost or an indirect cost with respect to units of product. Three sample answers are provided for illustration.

Cost Item	Variable or Fixed	Selling Cost	Administrative Cost	Manufacturing (Product) Cost Direct	Manufacturing (Product) Cost Indirect
Direct labor	V			X	
Executive salaries	F		X		
Factory rent	F				X

PROBLEM 2-15 (Appendix 2A) Allocating Labor Costs [LO8]
Mark Hansen is employed by Eastern Products, Inc., and works on the company's assembly line. Mark's basic wage rate is $20 per hour. The company's union contract states that employees are to be paid time and a half (i.e., $30 per hour) for any work in excess of 40 hours per week.

Required:
1. Suppose that in a given week Mark works 46 hours. Compute Mark's total wages for the week. How much of this amount would be allocated to direct labor cost? To manufacturing overhead cost?
2. Suppose in another week that Mark works 48 hours but is idle for 3 hours during the week due to machine breakdowns. Compute Mark's total wages for the week. How much of this amount would be allocated to direct labor cost? To manufacturing overhead cost?
3. Eastern Products, Inc., has an attractive package of fringe benefits that costs the company $6 for each hour of employee time (either regular time or overtime). During a particular week, Mark works 50 hours but is idle for 2 hours due to material shortages. Compute Mark's total wages and fringe benefits for the week. If the company treats all fringe benefits as part of manufacturing overhead cost, how much of Mark's wages and fringe benefits for the week would be allocated to direct labor cost? To manufacturing overhead cost?
4. Refer to the data in (3) above. If the company treats that part of fringe benefits relating to direct labor as added direct labor cost, how much of Mark's wages and fringe benefits for the week will be allocated to direct labor cost? To manufacturing overhead cost?

PROBLEM 2-16 Classification of Costs [LO1, LO2, LO5, LO7]

Wollogong Group Ltd. of New South Wales, Australia, acquired its factory building about 10 years ago. For several years the company has rented out a small annex attached to the rear of the building. The company has received a rental income of $30,000 per year on this space. The renter's lease will expire soon, and rather than renewing the lease, the company has decided to use the space itself to manufacture a new product.

Direct materials cost for the new product will total $80 per unit. To have a place to store finished units of product, the company will rent a small warehouse nearby. The rental cost will be $500 per month. In addition, the company must rent equipment for use in producing the new product; the rental cost will be $4,000 per month. Workers will be hired to manufacture the new product, with direct labor cost amounting to $60 per unit. The space in the annex will continue to be depreciated on a straight-line basis, as in prior years. This depreciation is $8,000 per year.

Advertising costs for the new product will total $50,000 per year. A supervisor will be hired to oversee production; her salary will be $1,500 per month. Electricity for operating machines will be $1.20 per unit. Costs of shipping the new product to customers will be $9 per unit.

To provide funds to purchase materials, meet payrolls, and so forth, the company will have to liquidate some temporary investments. These investments are presently yielding a return of about $3,000 per year.

Required:

Prepare an answer sheet with the following column headings:

Name of the Cost	Variable Cost	Fixed Cost	Product Cost			Period (Selling and Administrative) Cost	Opportunity Cost	Sunk Cost
			Direct Materials	Direct Labor	Manufacturing Overhead			

List the different costs associated with the new product decision down the extreme left column (under Name of the Cost). Then place an *X* under each heading that helps to describe the type of cost involved. There may be *X*'s under several column headings for a single cost. (For example, a cost may be a fixed cost, a period cost, and a sunk cost; you would place an *X* under each of these column headings opposite the cost.)

PROBLEM 2-17 Cost Classification [LO5, LO6]

Various costs associated with the operation of factories are given below:

1. Electricity used in operating machines.
2. Rent on a factory building.
3. Cloth used in drapery production.
4. Production superintendent's salary.
5. Wages of laborers assembling a product.
6. Depreciation of air purification equipment used in furniture production.
7. Janitorial salaries.
8. Peaches used in canning fruit.
9. Lubricants needed for machines.
10. Sugar used in soft-drink production.
11. Property taxes on the factory.
12. Wages of workers painting a product.
13. Depreciation on cafeteria equipment.
14. Insurance on a building used in producing helicopters.
15. Cost of rotor blades used in producing helicopters.

Required:

Classify each cost as either variable or fixed with respect to the number of units produced and sold. Also indicate whether each cost would typically be treated as a direct cost or an indirect cost with respect to units of product. Prepare your answer sheet as shown below:

Cost Item	Cost Behavior		To Units of Product	
	Variable	Fixed	Direct	Indirect
Example: Factory insurance		X		X

PROBLEM 2-18 (Appendix 2B) Quality Cost Report [LO9, LO10]

In response to intensive foreign competition, the management of Florex Company has attempted over the past year to improve the quality of its products. A statistical process control system has been installed and other steps have been taken to decrease the amount of warranty and other field costs, which have been trending upward over the past several years. Costs relating to quality and quality control over the last two years are given below:

	Costs (in thousands)	
	This Year	Last Year
Inspection	$900	$750
Quality engineering	$570	$420
Depreciation of test equipment.	$240	$210
Rework labor	$1,500	$1,050
Statistical process control.	$180	$0
Cost of field servicing	$900	$1,200
Supplies used in testing	$60	$30
Systems development	$750	$480
Warranty repairs.	$1,050	$3,600
Net cost of scrap.	$1,125	$630
Product testing	$1,200	$810
Product recalls	$750	$2,100
Disposal of defective products	$975	$720

Sales have been flat over the past few years, at $75,000,000 per year. A great deal of money has been spent in the effort to upgrade quality, and management is anxious to see whether or not the effort has been effective.

Required:

1. Prepare a quality cost report that contains data for both this year and last year. Carry percentage computations to two decimal places.
2. Prepare a bar graph showing the distribution of the various quality costs by category.
3. Prepare a written evaluation to accompany the reports you have prepared in (1) and (2) above. This evaluation should discuss the distribution of quality costs in the company, changes in this distribution that you see taking place, the reasons for changes in costs in the various categories, and any other information that would be of value to management.

PROBLEM 2-19 Schedule of Cost of Goods Manufactured; Income Statement; Cost Behavior [LO1, LO2, LO3, LO4, LO5]

Various cost and sales data for Meriwell Company for the just completed year appear in the worksheet below:

	A	B
1	Finished goods inventory, beginning	$20,000
2	Finished goods inventory, ending	$40,000
3	Depreciation, factory	$27,000
4	Administrative expenses	$110,000
5	Utilities, factory	$8,000
6	Maintenance, factory	$40,000
7	Supplies, factory	$11,000
8	Insurance, factory	$4,000
9	Purchases of raw materials	$125,000
10	Raw materials inventory, beginning	$9,000
11	Raw materials inventory, ending	$6,000
12	Direct labor	$70,000
13	Indirect labor	$15,000
14	Work in process inventory, beginning	$17,000
15	Work in process inventory, ending	$30,000
16	Sales	$500,000
17	Selling expenses	$80,000

Required:
1. Prepare a schedule of cost of goods manufactured.
2. Prepare an income statement.
3. Assume that the company produced the equivalent of 10,000 units of product during the year just completed. What was the average cost per unit for direct materials? What was the average cost per unit for factory depreciation?
4. Assume that the company expects to produce 15,000 units of product during the coming year. What average cost per unit and what total cost would you expect the company to incur for direct materials at this level of activity? For factory depreciation? (In preparing your answer, assume that direct materials is a variable cost and that depreciation is a fixed cost; also assume that depreciation is computed on a straight-line basis.)
5. As the manager responsible for production costs, explain to the president any difference in the average costs per unit between (3) and (4) above.

PROBLEM 2-20 Classification of Salary Cost as a Period or Product Cost [LO2]

You have just been hired by Ogden Company to fill a new position that was created in response to rapid growth in sales. It is your responsibility to coordinate shipments of finished goods from the factory to distribution warehouses located in various parts of the United States so that goods will be available as orders are received from customers.

The company is unsure how to classify your annual salary in its cost records. The company's cost analyst says that your salary should be classified as a manufacturing (product) cost; the controller says that it should be classified as a selling expense; and the president says that it doesn't matter which way your salary cost is classified.

Required:
1. Which viewpoint is correct? Why?
2. From the point of view of the reported net operating income for the year, is the president correct in his statement that it doesn't matter which way your salary cost is classified? Explain.

PROBLEM 2-21 Classification of Various Costs [LO1, LO2, LO5, LO7]

Staci Valek began dabbling in pottery several years ago as a hobby. Her work is quite creative, and it has been so popular with friends and others that she has decided to quit her job with an aerospace firm and manufacture pottery full time. The salary from Staci's aerospace job is $3,800 per month.

Staci will rent a small building near her home to use as a place for manufacturing the pottery. The rent will be $500 per month. She estimates that the cost of clay and glaze will be $2 for each finished piece of pottery. She will hire workers to produce the pottery at a labor rate of $8 per pot. To sell her pots, Staci feels that she must advertise heavily in the local area. An advertising agency states that it will handle all advertising for a fee of $600 per month. Staci's brother will sell the pots; he will be paid a commission of $4 for each pot sold. Equipment needed to manufacture the pots will be rented at a cost of $300 per month.

Staci has already paid the legal and filing fees associated with incorporating her business in the state. These fees amounted to $500. A small room has been located in a tourist area that Staci will use as a sales office. The rent will be $250 per month. A phone installed in the room for taking orders will cost $40 per month. In addition, a recording device will be attached to the phone for taking after-hours messages.

Staci has some money in savings that is earning interest of $1,200 per year. These savings will be withdrawn and used to get the business going. For the time being, Staci does not intend to draw any salary from the new company.

Required:
1. Prepare an answer sheet with the following column headings:

Name of the Cost	Variable Cost	Fixed Cost	Product Cost			Period (Selling and Administrative) Cost	Opportunity Cost	Sunk Cost
			Direct Materials	Direct Labor	Manufacturing Overhead			

List the different costs associated with the new company down the extreme left column (under Name of Cost). Then place an *X* under each heading that helps to describe the type of cost involved. There may be *X*'s under several column headings for a single cost. (That is, a cost may be a fixed cost, a period cost, and a sunk cost; you would place an *X* under each of these column headings opposite the cost.)

Under the Variable Cost column, list only those costs that would be variable with respect to the number of units of pottery that are produced and sold.

2.   All of the costs you have listed above, except one, would be differential costs between the alternatives of Staci producing pottery or staying with the aerospace firm. Which cost is *not* differential? Explain.

PROBLEM 2-22 (Appendix 2B) Analyzing a Quality Cost Report [LO10]

Mercury, Inc., produces pagers at its plant in Texas. In recent years, the company's market share has been eroded by stiff competition from overseas. Price and product quality are the two key areas in which companies compete in this market.

A year ago, the company's pagers had been ranked low in product quality in a consumer survey. Shocked by this result, Jorge Gomez, Mercury's president, initiated a crash effort to improve product quality. Gomez set up a task force to implement a formal quality improvement program. Included on this task force were representatives from the Engineering, Marketing, Customer Service, Production, and Accounting departments. The broad representation was needed because Gomez believed that this was a companywide program and that all employees should share the responsibility for its success.

After the first meeting of the task force, Holly Elsoe, manager of the Marketing Department, asked John Tran, production manager, what he thought of the proposed program. Tran replied, "I have reservations. Quality is too abstract to be attaching costs to it and then to be holding you and me responsible for cost improvements. I like to work with goals that I can see and count! I'm nervous about having my annual bonus based on a decrease in quality costs; there are too many variables that we have no control over."

Mercury's quality improvement program has now been in operation for one year. The company's most recent quality cost report is shown below.

Mercury, Inc. Quality Cost Report (in thousands)		
	This Year	Last Year
Prevention costs:		
Machine maintenance	$ 120	$ 70
Training suppliers	10	0
Quality circles	20	0
Total prevention costs	150	70
Appraisal costs:		
Incoming inspection	40	20
Final testing.	90	80
Total appraisal costs.	130	100
Internal failure costs:		
Rework.	130	50
Scrap	70	40
Total internal failure costs	200	90
External failure costs:		
Warranty repairs	30	90
Customer returns	80	320
Total external failure costs.	110	410
Total quality cost.	$ 590	$ 670
Total production cost	$4,800	$4,200

As they were reviewing the report, Elsoe asked Tran what he now thought of the quality improvement program. Tran replied. "I'm relieved that the new quality improvement program hasn't hurt our bonuses, but the program has increased the workload in the Production Department. It is true that customer returns are way down, but the pagers that were returned by customers to retail outlets were rarely sent back to us for rework."

Required:

1.   Expand the company's quality cost report by showing the costs in both years as percentages of both total production cost and total quality cost. Carry all computations to one decimal place. By analyzing the report, determine if Mercury, Inc.'s quality improvement program has been successful. *List specific evidence to support your answer.*

2. Do you expect the improvement program as it progresses to continue to increase the workload in the Production Department?
3. Jorge Gomez believed that the quality improvement program was essential and that Mercury, Inc., could no longer afford to ignore the importance of product quality. Discuss how Mercury, Inc., could measure the cost of *not* implementing the quality improvement program.

(CMA, adapted)

PROBLEM 2-23 Cost Classification and Cost Behavior [LO2, LO5, LO6]

The Dorilane Company specializes in producing a set of wood patio furniture consisting of a table and four chairs. The set enjoys great popularity, and the company has ample orders to keep production going at its full capacity of 2,000 sets per year. Annual cost data at full capacity follow:

Factory labor, direct	$118,000
Advertising	$50,000
Factory supervision	$40,000
Property taxes, factory building	$3,500
Sales commissions.	$80,000
Insurance, factory.	$2,500
Depreciation, office equipment.	$4,000
Lease cost, factory equipment	$12,000
Indirect materials, factory	$6,000
Depreciation, factory building	$10,000
General office supplies (billing)	$3,000
General office salaries	$60,000
Direct materials used (wood, bolts, etc.)	$94,000
Utilities, factory.	$20,000

Required:
1. Prepare an answer sheet with the column headings shown below. Enter each cost item on your answer sheet, placing the dollar amount under the appropriate headings. As examples, this has been done already for the first two items in the list above. Note that each cost item is classified in two ways: first, as variable or fixed with respect to the number of units produced and sold; and second, as a selling and administrative cost or a product cost. (If the item is a product cost, it should also be classified as either direct or indirect as shown.)

	Cost Behavior		Selling or Administrative	Product Cost	
Cost Item	Variable	Fixed	Cost	Direct	Indirect*
Factory labor, direct	$118,000			$118,000	
Advertising		$50,000	$50,000		

*To units of product.

2. Total the dollar amounts in each of the columns in (1) above. Compute the average product cost of one patio set.
3. Assume that production drops to only 1,000 sets annually. Would you expect the average product cost of one set to increase, decrease, or remain unchanged? Explain. No computations are necessary.
4. Refer to the original data. The president's brother-in-law has considered making himself a patio set and has priced the necessary materials at a building supply store. The brother-in-law has asked the president if he could purchase a patio set from the Dorilane Company "at cost," and the president agreed to let him do so.
   a. Would you expect any disagreement between the two men over the price the brother-in-law should pay? Explain. What price does the president probably have in mind? The brother-in-law?
   b. Since the company is operating at full capacity, what cost term used in the chapter might be justification for the president to charge the full, regular price to the brother-in-law and still be selling "at cost"?

PROBLEM 2-24 Variable and Fixed Costs; Subtleties of Direct and Indirect Costs [LO5, LO6]

Madison Seniors Care Center is a nonprofit organization that provides a variety of health services to the elderly. The center is organized into a number of departments, one of which is the meals-on-wheels program that delivers hot meals to seniors in their homes on a daily basis. Below are listed a number of costs of the center and the meals-on-wheels program.

example   The cost of groceries used in meal preparation.
 a. The cost of leasing the meals-on-wheels van.
 b. The cost of incidental supplies such as salt, pepper, napkins, and so on.
 c. The cost of gasoline consumed by the meals-on-wheels van.
 d. The rent on the facility that houses Madison Seniors Care Center, including the meals-on-wheels program.
 e. The salary of the part-time manager of the meals-on-wheels program.
 f. Depreciation on the kitchen equipment used in the meals-on-wheels program.
 g. The hourly wages of the caregiver who drives the van and delivers the meals.
 h. The costs of complying with health safety regulations in the kitchen.
 i. The costs of mailing letters soliciting donations to the meals-on-wheels program.

Required:

For each cost listed above, indicate whether it is a direct or indirect cost of the meals-on-wheels program, whether it is a direct or indirect cost of particular seniors served by the program, and whether it is variable or fixed with respect to the number of seniors served. Use the below form for your answer.

		Direct or Indirect Cost of the Meals-on-Wheels Program		Direct or Indirect Cost of Particular Seniors Served by the Meals-on-Wheels Program		Variable or Fixed with Respect to the Number of Seniors Served by the Meals-on-Wheels Program	
Item	Description	Direct	Indirect	Direct	Indirect	Variable	Fixed
example	The cost of groceries used in meal preparation	X		X		X	

PROBLEM 2-25 Schedule of Cost of Goods Manufactured; Income Statement [LO1, LO2, LO3, LO4]

Swift Company was organized on March 1 of the current year. After five months of start-up losses, management had expected to earn a profit during August. Management was disappointed, however, when the income statement for August also showed a loss. August's income statement follows:

Swift Company Income Statement For the Month Ended August 31		
Sales.		$450,000
Less operating expenses:		
Indirect labor cost	$ 12,000	
Utilities	15,000	
Direct labor cost	70,000	
Depreciation, factory equipment.	21,000	
Raw materials purchased	165,000	
Depreciation, sales equipment	18,000	
Insurance	4,000	
Rent on facilities	50,000	
Selling and administrative salaries	32,000	
Advertising	75,000	462,000
Net operating loss.		$(12,000)

After seeing the $12,000 loss for August, Swift's president stated, "I was sure we'd be profitable within six months, but our six months are up and this loss for August is even worse than July's. I think it's time to start looking for someone to buy out the company's assets—if we don't, within a few months there won't be any assets to sell. By the way, I don't see any reason to look for a new controller. We'll just limp along with Sam for the time being."

The company's controller resigned a month ago. Sam, a new assistant in the controller's office, prepared the income statement above. Sam has had little experience in manufacturing operations. Additional information about the company follows:

a. Some 60% of the utilities cost and 75% of the insurance apply to factory operations. The remaining amounts apply to selling and administrative activities.

b. Inventory balances at the beginning and end of August were:

	August 1	August 30
Raw materials	$ 8,000	$13,000
Work in process	$16,000	$21,000
Finished goods	$40,000	$60,000

c. Only 80% of the rent on facilities applies to factory operations; the remainder applies to selling and administrative activities.

The president has asked you to check over the income statement and make a recommendation as to whether the company should look for a buyer for its assets.

Required:

1. As one step in gathering data for a recommendation to the president, prepare a schedule of cost of goods manufactured for August.
2. As a second step, prepare a new income statement for August.
3. Based on your statements prepared in (1) and (2) above, would you recommend that the company look for a buyer?

PROBLEM 2-26 Ethics and the Manager [LO2]

M. K. Gallant is president of Kranbrack Corporation, a company whose stock is traded on a national exchange. In a meeting with investment analysts at the beginning of the year, Gallant had predicted that the company's earnings would grow by 20% this year. Unfortunately, sales have been less than expected for the year, and Gallant concluded within two weeks of the end of the fiscal year that it would be impossible to ultimately report an increase in earnings as large as predicted unless some drastic action was taken. Accordingly, Gallant has ordered that wherever possible, expenditures should be postponed to the new year—including canceling or postponing orders with suppliers, delaying planned maintenance and training, and cutting back on end-of-year advertising and travel. Additionally, Gallant ordered the company's controller to carefully scrutinize all costs that are currently classified as period costs and reclassify as many as possible as product costs. The company is expected to have substantial inventories of work in process and finished goods at the end of the year.

Required:

1. Why would reclassifying period costs as product costs increase this period's reported earnings?
2. Do you believe Gallant's actions are ethical? Why or why not?

PROBLEM 2-27 Schedule of Cost of Goods Manufactured; Income Statement; Cost Behavior [LO1, LO2, LO3, LO4, LO5]

Selected account balances for the year ended December 31 are provided below for Superior Company:

Selling and administrative salaries.........	$110,000
Insurance, factory.....................	$8,000
Utilities, factory.......................	$45,000
Purchases of raw materials	$290,000
Indirect labor	$60,000
Direct labor..........................	?
Advertising expense...................	$80,000
Cleaning supplies, factory	$7,000
Sales commissions	$50,000
Rent, factory building.................	$120,000
Maintenance, factory	$30,000

Inventory balances at the beginning and end of the year were as follows:

	Beginning of the Year	End of the Year
Raw materials.	$40,000	$10,000
Work in process	?	$35,000
Finished goods	$50,000	?

The total manufacturing costs for the year were $683,000; the goods available for sale totaled $740,000; and the cost of goods sold totaled $660,000.

Required:
1. Prepare a schedule of cost of goods manufactured and the cost of goods sold section of the company's income statement for the year.
2. Assume that the dollar amounts given above are for the equivalent of 40,000 units produced during the year. Compute the average cost per unit for direct materials used and the average cost per unit for rent on the factory building.
3. Assume that in the following year the company expects to produce 50,000 units. What average cost per unit and total cost would you expect to be incurred for direct materials? For rent on the factory building? (Assume that direct materials is a variable cost and that rent is a fixed cost.)
4. As the manager in charge of production costs, explain to the president the reason for any difference in average cost per unit between (2) and (3) above.

PROBLEM 2-28 Working with Incomplete Data from the Income Statement and Schedule of Cost of Goods Manufactured [LO3, LO4]
Supply the missing data in the following cases. Each case is independent of the others.

	Case 1	Case 2	Case 3	Case 4
Direct materials	$4,500	$6,000	$5,000	$3,000
Direct labor.	?	$3,000	$7,000	$4,000
Manufacturing overhead	$5,000	$4,000	?	$9,000
Total manufacturing costs	$18,500	?	$20,000	?
Beginning work in process inventory	$2,500	?	$3,000	?
Ending work in process inventory	?	$1,000	$4,000	$3,000
Sales	$30,000	$21,000	$36,000	$40,000
Beginning finished goods inventory	$1,000	$2,500	?	$2,000
Cost of goods manufactured	$18,000	$14,000	?	$17,500
Goods available for sale.	?	?	?	?
Ending finished goods inventory	?	$1,500	$4,000	$3,500
Cost of goods sold	$17,000	?	$18,500	?
Gross margin	$13,000	?	$17,500	?
Operating expenses.	?	$3,500	?	?
Net operating income.	$4,000	?	$5,000	$9,000

PROBLEM 2-29 Income Statement; Schedule of Cost of Goods Manufactured [LO1, LO2, LO3, LO4]
Visic Corporation, a manufacturing company, produces a single product. The following information has been taken from the company's production, sales, and cost records for the just completed year.

Production in units	29,000
Sales in units	?
Ending finished goods inventory in units	?
Sales in dollars.	$1,300,000
Costs:	
Advertising	$105,000
Entertainment and travel	$40,000
Direct labor.	$90,000
Indirect labor.	$85,000
Raw materials purchased.	$480,000

Building rent (production uses 80% of the space; administrative and sales offices use the rest)		$40,000
Utilities, factory.		$108,000
Royalty paid for use of production patent, $1.50 per unit produced		?
Maintenance, factory		$9,000
Rent for special production equipment, $7,000 per year plus $0.30 per unit produced.		?
Selling and administrative salaries.		$210,000
Other factory overhead costs		$6,800
Other selling and administrative expenses.		$17,000

	Beginning of the Year	End of the Year
Inventories:		
Raw materials	$20,000	$30,000
Work in process	$50,000	$40,000
Finished goods	$0	?

The finished goods inventory is being carried at the average unit production cost for the year. The selling price of the product is $50 per unit.

Required:
1. Prepare a schedule of cost of goods manufactured for the year.
2. Compute the following:
   - *a.* The number of units in the finished goods inventory at the end of the year.
   - *b.* The cost of the units in the finished goods inventory at the end of the year.
3. Prepare an income statement for the year.

Cases

CASE 2-30 Missing Data; Income Statement; Schedule of Cost of Goods Manufactured
[LO1, LO2, LO3, LO4]

"I was sure that when our battery hit the market it would be an instant success," said Roger Strong, founder and president of Solar Technology, Inc. "But just look at the gusher of red ink for the first quarter. It's obvious that we're better scientists than we are businesspeople." The data to which Roger was referring follow:

Solar Technology, Inc. Income Statement For the Quarter Ended March 31		
Sales (32,000 batteries)		$ 960,000
Less operating expenses:		
Selling and administrative salaries	$110,000	
Advertising	90,000	
Maintenance, factory.	43,000	
Indirect labor cost	120,000	
Cleaning supplies, factory.	7,000	
Purchases of raw materials.	360,000	
Rental cost, facilities	75,000	
Insurance, factory	8,000	
Depreciation, office equipment	27,000	
Utilities	80,000	
Depreciation, factory equipment	100,000	
Direct labor cost	70,000	
Travel, salespersons	40,000	1,130,000
Net operating loss		$ (170,000)

"At this rate we'll be out of business within a year," said Cindy Zhang, the company's accountant. "But I've double-checked these figures, so I know they're right."

Solar Technology was organized at the beginning of the current year to produce and market a revolutionary new solar battery. The company's accounting system was set up by Margie Wallace, an experienced accountant who recently left the company to do independent consulting work. The statement above was prepared by Zhang, her assistant.

"We may not last a year if the insurance company doesn't pay the $226,000 it owes us for the 8,000 batteries lost in the warehouse fire last week," said Roger. "The insurance adjuster says our claim is inflated, but he's just trying to pressure us into a lower figure. We have the data to back up our claim, and it will stand up in any court."

On April 3, just after the end of the first quarter, the company's finished goods storage area was swept by fire and all 8,000 unsold batteries were destroyed. (These batteries were part of the 40,000 units completed during the first quarter.) The company's insurance policy states that the company will be reimbursed for the "cost" of any finished batteries destroyed or stolen. Zhang has determined this cost as follows:

$$\frac{\text{Total costs for the quarter}}{\text{Batteries produced during the quarter}} = \frac{\$1,130,000}{40,000 \text{ units}}$$

$$= \$28.25 \text{ per unit}$$

$$8,000 \text{ batteries} \times \$28.25 \text{ per unit} = \$226,000$$

The following additional information is available on the company's activities during the quarter ended March 31:

a.   Inventories at the beginning and end of the quarter were as follows:

	Beginning of the Quarter	End of the Quarter
Raw materials	$0	$10,000
Work in process.	$0	$50,000
Finished goods	$0	?

b.   Eighty percent of the rental cost for facilities and 90% of the utilities cost relate to manufacturing operations. The remaining amounts relate to selling and administrative activities.

Required:

1.   What conceptual errors, if any, were made in preparing the income statement above?
2.   Prepare a schedule of cost of goods manufactured for the first quarter.
3.   Prepare a corrected income statement for the first quarter. Your statement should show in detail how the cost of goods sold is computed.
4.   Do you agree that the insurance company owes Solar Technology, Inc., $226,000? Explain your answer.

CASE 2-31 Inventory Computations from Incomplete Data [LO3, LO4]

Hector P. Wastrel, a careless employee, left some combustible materials near an open flame in Salter Company's plant. The resulting explosion and fire destroyed the entire plant and administrative offices. Justin Quick, the company's controller, and Constance Trueheart, the operations manager, were able to save only a few bits of information as they escaped from the roaring blaze.

"What a disaster," cried Justin. "And the worst part is that we have no records to use in filing an insurance claim."

"I know," replied Constance. "I was in the plant when the explosion occurred, and I managed to grab only this brief summary sheet that contains information on one or two of our costs. It says that our direct labor cost this year has totaled $180,000 and that we have purchased $290,000 in raw materials. But I'm afraid that doesn't help much; the rest of our records are just ashes."

"Well, not completely," said Justin. "I was working on the year-to-date income statement when the explosion knocked me out of my chair. I instinctively held onto the page I was working on, and from what I can make out, our sales to date this year have totaled $1,200,000 and our gross margin rate has been 40% of sales. Also, I can see that our goods available for sale to customers has totaled $810,000 at cost."

"Maybe we're not so bad off after all," exclaimed Constance. "My sheet says that prime cost has totaled $410,000 so far this year and that manufacturing overhead is 70% of conversion cost. Now if we just had some information on our beginning inventories."

"Hey, look at this," cried Justin. "It's a copy of last year's annual report, and it shows what our inventories were when this year started. Let's see, raw materials was $18,000, work in process was $65,000, and finished goods was $45,000.

"Super," yelled Constance. "Let's go to work."

To file an insurance claim, the company must determine the amount of cost in its inventories as of the date of the fire. You may assume that all materials used in production during the year were direct materials.

Required:

Determine the amount of cost in the Raw Materials, Work in Process, and Finished Goods inventory accounts as of the date of the fire. (Hint: One way to proceed would be to reconstruct the various schedules and statements that would have been affected by the company's inventory accounts during the period.)

RESEARCH AND APPLICATION 2-32 [LO1, LO2, LO5, LO6]

To answer the questions in this exercise, you will need to download Dell, Inc.'s 2005 Form 10-K at www.dell.com/downloads/global/corporate/sec/10k-fy05.pdf. You can view this document on your computer screen; you do not need to print this document to answer the questions.

Required:

1. What is Dell's strategy for success in the marketplace? Does the company rely primarily on a customer intimacy, operational excellence, or product leadership customer value proposition? What evidence supports your conclusion?

2. What business risks does Dell face that may threaten its ability to satisfy stockholder expectations? What are some examples of control activities that the company could use to reduce these risks? (Hint: Focus on pages 7–10 of the 10-K.)

3. How has the Sarbanes-Oxley Act of 2002 explicitly affected the disclosures contained in Dell's 10-K report? (Hint: Focus on pages 34–35, 59, and 76–78.)

4. Is Dell a merchandiser or a manufacturer? What information contained in the 10-K supports your answer?

5. What are some examples of direct and indirect inventoriable costs for Dell? Why has Dell's gross margin (in dollars) steadily increased from 2003 to 2005, yet the gross margin as a percent of net revenue has only increased slightly?

6. What is the inventory balance on Dell's January 28, 2005 balance sheet? Why is the inventory balance so small compared to the other current asset balances? What competitive advantage does Dell derive from its low inventory levels? Page 27 of Dell's 10-K reports a figure called the cash conversion cycle. The cash conversion cycle for Dell has consistently been negative. Is this a good sign for Dell or a bad sign? Why?

7. Describe some of the various types of operating expenses incurred by Dell. Why are these expenses treated as period costs?

8. List four different cost objects for Dell. For each cost object, mention one example of a direct cost and an indirect cost.

Systems Design: Job-Order Costing

Two College Students Succeeding as Entrepreneurs

When the University of Dayton athletic department needed 2,000 customized T-shirts to give away at its first home basketball game of the year, it chose University Tees to provide the shirts. A larger competitor could have been chosen, but University Tees won the order because of its fast customer response time, low price, and high quality.

University Tees is a small business that was started in February 2003 by two Miami University seniors—Joe Haddad and Nick Dadas (see the company's website at www.universitytees.com). The company creates the artwork for customized T-shirts and then relies on carefully chosen suppliers to manufacture the product.

Accurately calculating the cost of each potential customer order is critically important to University Tees because the company needs to be sure that the price exceeds the cost associated with satisfying the order. The costs include the cost of the T-shirts themselves, printing costs (which vary depending on the quantity of shirts produced and the number of colors printed per shirt), silk screen costs (which also vary depending on the number of colors included in a design), shipping costs, and the artwork needed to create a design. The company also takes into account its competitors' pricing strategies when developing its own price quotes. ■

Source: Conversation with Joe Haddad, cofounder of University Tees.

Learning Objectives

After studying Chapter 3, you should be able to:

LO1 Distinguish between process costing and job-order costing and identify companies that would use each costing method.

LO2 Identify the documents used in a job-order costing system.

LO3 Compute predetermined overhead rates and explain why estimated overhead costs (rather than actual overhead costs) are used in the costing process.

LO4 Understand the flow of costs in a job-order costing system and prepare appropriate journal entries to record costs.

LO5 Apply overhead cost to Work in Process using a predetermined overhead rate.

LO6 Prepare schedules of cost of goods manufactured and cost of goods sold.

LO7 Use T-accounts to show the flow of costs in a job-order costing system.

LO8 Compute underapplied or overapplied overhead cost and prepare the journal entry to close the balance in Manufacturing Overhead to the appropriate accounts.

LO9 (Appendix 3A) Understand the implications of basing the predetermined overhead rate on activity at capacity rather than on estimated activity for the period.

As discussed in Chapter 2, product costing is the process of assigning costs to the products and services provided by a company. An understanding of this costing process is vital to managers, because the way in which a product or service is costed can have a substantial impact on reported profits, as well as on key management decisions.

The essential purpose of any managerial costing system should be to provide cost data to help managers plan, control, direct, and make decisions. Nevertheless, external financial reporting and tax reporting requirements often heavily influence how costs are accumulated and summarized on managerial reports. This is true of product costing.

In this chapter and in Chapter 4, we use *absorption costing* to determine product costs. This method was also used in Chapter 2. In **absorption costing,** all manufacturing costs, both fixed and variable, are assigned to units of product—units are said to *fully absorb manufacturing costs*. Later, in Chapter 7, we look at an alternative to absorption costing known as *variable costing.* Chapter 7 also discusses the strengths and weaknesses of the two approaches.

Most countries—including the United States—require some form of absorption costing for both external financial reporting and for tax reporting. In addition, the vast majority of companies throughout the world also use absorption costing for managerial accounting purposes. Since absorption costing is the most common approach to product costing, we discuss it first and then deal with alternatives in subsequent chapters.

Process and Job-Order Costing

In computing the cost of a product or a service, managers are faced with a difficult problem. Many costs (such as rent) do not change much from month to month, whereas production may change frequently, with production going up in one month and then down in another. In addition to variations in the level of production, several different products or services may be produced in a given period in the same facility. Under these conditions, how is it possible to accurately determine the cost of a product or service? In practice, assigning costs to products and services involves averaging across time and across products. The way in which this averaging is carried out depends heavily on the type of production process. Two costing systems are commonly used in manufacturing and in many service companies; these two systems are known as *process costing* and *job-order costing.*

Process Costing

A **process costing system** is used in situations where the company produces many units of a single product for long periods. Examples include producing paper at Weyerhaeuser, refining aluminum ingots at Reynolds Aluminum, mixing and bottling beverages at Coca-Cola, and making wieners at Oscar Meyer. All of these industries are characterized by an essentially homogeneous product that flows through the production process on a continuous basis.

Process costing systems accumulate costs in a particular operation or department for an entire period (month, quarter, year) and then divide this total cost by the number of units produced during the period. The basic formula for process costing is:

$$\text{Unit product cost} = \frac{\text{Total manufacturing cost}}{\text{Total units produced}}$$

Since one unit of product is indistinguishable from any other unit of product, each unit produced during the period is assigned the same average cost. This costing technique results in a broad, average unit cost figure that applies to homogeneous units flowing in a continuous stream out of the production process.

Job-Order Costing

A **job-order costing system** is used in situations where many *different* products are produced each period. For example, a Levi Strauss clothing factory would typically make many different types of jeans for both men and women during a month. A particular order might consist of 1,000 stonewashed men's blue denim jeans, style number A312. This order of 1,000 jeans is called a *batch* or a *job*. In a job-order costing system, costs are traced and allocated to jobs and then the costs of the job are divided by the number of units in the job to arrive at an average cost per unit.

Other examples of situations where job-order costing would be used include large-scale construction projects managed by Bechtel International, commercial aircraft produced by Boeing, greeting cards designed and printed by Hallmark, and airline meals prepared by LSG SkyChefs. All of these examples are characterized by diverse outputs. Each Bechtel project is unique and different from every other—the company may be simultaneously constructing a dam in Zaire and a bridge in Indonesia. Likewise, each airline orders a different type of meal from LSG SkyChefs' catering service.

Job-order costing is also used extensively in service industries. Hospitals, law firms, movie studios, accounting firms, advertising agencies, and repair shops, for example, all use a variation of job-order costing to accumulate costs for accounting and billing purposes. Although the detailed example of job-order costing provided in the following section deals with a manufacturing company, the same basic concepts and procedures are used by many service organizations.

The record-keeping and cost assignment problems are more complex when a company sells many different products and services than when it has only a single product. Since the products are different, the costs are typically different. Consequently, cost records must be maintained for each distinct product or job. For example, an attorney in a large criminal law practice would ordinarily keep separate records of the costs of advising and defending each client. And the Levi Strauss factory mentioned above would keep separate track of the costs of filling orders for particular styles of jeans. Thus, a job-order costing system requires more effort than a process costing system. Nevertheless, job-order costing is used by more than half the manufacturers in the United States.

In this chapter, we focus on the design of a job-order costing system. In the following chapter, we focus on process costing and also look more closely at the similarities and differences between the two costing methods.

Job-Order Costing—An Overview

To introduce job-order costing, we will follow a specific job as it progresses through the manufacturing process. This job consists of two experimental couplings that Yost Precision Machining has agreed to produce for Loops Unlimited, a manufacturer of roller coasters. Couplings connect the cars on the roller coaster and are a critical component in the performance and safety of the ride. Before we begin our discussion, recall from the previous chapter that companies generally classify manufacturing costs into three broad categories: (1) direct materials, (2) direct labor, and (3) manufacturing overhead. As we study the operation of a job-order costing system, we will see how each of these three types of costs is recorded and accumulated.

LEARNING OBJECTIVE 2
Identify the documents used in a job-order costing system.

Yost Precision Machining is a small company in Michigan that specializes in fabricating precision metal parts that are used in a variety of applications ranging from deep-sea exploration vehicles to the inertial triggers in automobile air bags. The company's top managers gather every morning at 8:00 A.M. in the company's conference room for the daily planning meeting. Attending the meeting this morning are: Jean Yost, the company's president; David Cheung, the marketing manager; Debbie Turner, the production manager; and Marcus White, the company controller. The president opened the meeting:

Jean: The production schedule indicates we'll be starting Job 2B47 today. Isn't that the special order for experimental couplings, David?

David: That's right. That's the order from Loops Unlimited for two couplings for their new roller coaster ride for Magic Mountain.

Debbie: Why only two couplings? Don't they need a coupling for every car?

David: Yes. But this is a completely new roller coaster. The cars will go faster and will be subjected to more twists, turns, drops, and loops than on any other existing roller coaster. To hold up under these stresses, Loops Unlimited's engineers had to completely redesign the cars and couplings. They want to thoroughly test the design before proceeding to large-scale production. So they want us to make just two of these new couplings for testing purposes. If the design works, then we'll have the inside track on the order to supply couplings for the whole ride.

Jean: We agreed to take on this initial order at our cost just to get our foot in the door. Marcus, will there be any problem documenting our cost so we can get paid?

Marcus: No problem. The contract with Loops stipulates that they will pay us an amount equal to our cost of goods sold. With our job-order costing system, I can tell you that number on the day the job is completed.

Jean: Good. Is there anything else we should discuss about this job at this time? No? Well then let's move on to the next item of business.

Measuring Direct Materials Cost

Topic Tackler

PLUS

3–1

Yost Precision Machining will require four G7 Connectors and two M46 Housings to make the two experimental couplings for Loops Unlimited. If this were a standard product, it already would have a *bill of materials*. A **bill of materials** is a document that lists the type and quantity of each type of direct material needed to complete a unit of product. In this case, there is no established bill of materials, so Yost's production staff determined the materials requirements from the blueprints submitted by the customer. Each coupling requires two connectors and one housing, so to make two couplings, four connectors and two housings are required.

A *production order* is issued when an agreement has been reached with the customer concerning the quantities, prices, and shipment date for the order. The Production Department then prepares a *materials requisition form* similar to the form in Exhibit 3–1. The **materials requisition form** is a detailed source document that specifies the type and quantity of materials to be drawn from the storeroom and identifies the job that will be charged for the cost of the materials. The form is used to control the flow of materials into production and also for making entries in the accounting records.

The Yost Precision Machining materials requisition form in Exhibit 3–1 shows that the company's Milling Department has requisitioned two M46 Housings and four G7 Connectors for the Loops Unlimited job, which has been designated as Job 2B47. A production worker presents the completed form to the storeroom clerk who then issues the specified materials to the worker. The storeroom clerk is not allowed to release materials without a completed and properly authorized materials requisition form.

Job Cost Sheet

After being notified that the production order has been issued, the Accounting Department prepares a *job cost sheet* like the one presented in Exhibit 3–2. A **job cost sheet** is a form prepared for a job that records the materials, labor, and manufacturing overhead costs charged to that job.

EXHIBIT 3–1
Materials Requisition Form

Materials Requistion Number __14873__   Date __March 2__
Job Number to Be Charged __2B47__
Department __Milling__

Description	Quantity	Unit Cost	Total Cost
M46 Housing	2	$124	$248
G7 Connector	4	$103	412
			$660

Authorized
Signature __Bill White__

After direct materials are issued, the Accounting Department records their costs directly on the job cost sheet. Note from Exhibit 3–2, for example, that the $660 cost for direct materials shown earlier on the materials requisition form has been charged to Job 2B47 on its job cost sheet. The requisition number 14873 from the materials requisition form is also recorded on the job cost sheet to make it easier to identify the source document for the direct

EXHIBIT 3–2
Job Cost Sheet

JOB COST SHEET

Job Number __2B47__   Date Initiated __March 2__
                                   Date Completed _____
Department __Milling__   Units Completed _____
Item __Special order coupling__
For Stock _____

Direct Materials		Direct Labor			Manufacturing Overhead		
Req. No.	Amount	Ticket	Hours	Amount	Hours	Rate	Amount
14873	$660	843	5	$45			

Cost Summary		Units Shipped		
Direct Materials	$	Date	Number	Balance
Direct Labor	$			
Manufacturing Overhead	$			
Total Cost	$			
Unit Product Cost	$			

materials charge. Job cost sheets serve as a subsidiary ledger to the Work in Process account because the detailed records that they provide for the jobs in process add up to the balance in Work in Process.

Measuring Direct Labor Cost

Direct labor cost is handled similarly to direct materials cost. Direct labor consists of labor charges that are easily traced to a particular job. Labor charges that cannot be easily traced directly to any job are treated as part of manufacturing overhead. As discussed in the previous chapter, this latter category of labor costs is called *indirect labor* and includes tasks such as maintenance, supervision, and cleanup.

Workers use *time tickets* to record the time they spend on each job and task. A completed **time ticket** is an hour-by-hour summary of the employee's activities throughout the day. An example of an employee time ticket is shown in Exhibit 3–3. When working on a specific job, the employee enters the job number on the time ticket and notes the amount of time spent on that job. When not assigned to a particular job, the employee records the nature of the indirect labor task (such as cleanup and maintenance) and the amount of time spent on the task.

At the end of the day, the time tickets are gathered and the Accounting Department enters the direct labor-hours and costs on individual job cost sheets. (See Exhibit 3–2 for an example of how direct labor costs are entered on the job cost sheet.) The daily time tickets are source documents that are used as the basis for labor cost entries into the accounting records.

The system we have just described is a manual method for recording and posting labor costs. Today many companies rely on computerized systems and no longer record labor time by hand on sheets of paper. One computerized approach uses bar codes to capture data. Each employee and each job has a unique bar code. When beginning work on a job, the employee scans three bar codes using a handheld device much like the bar code readers at grocery store check-out stands. The first bar code indicates that a job is being started; the second is the unique bar code on the employee's identity badge; and the third is the unique bar code of the job itself. This information is fed automatically via an electronic network to a computer that notes the time and records all of the data. When the task is completed, the employee scans a bar code indicating the task is complete, the bar code on his or her identity badge, and the bar code attached to the job. This information is relayed to the computer that again notes the time, and a time ticket is automatically prepared. Since all of the source data is already in computer files, the labor costs can be automatically posted to job cost sheets (or their electronic equivalents). Computers, coupled with technology such as bar codes, can eliminate much of the drudgery involved in routine bookkeeping activities while at the same time increasing timeliness and accuracy.

EXHIBIT 3–3
Employee Time Ticket

Time Ticket No. 843 Date March 3

Employee Mary Holden Station 4

Started	Ended	Time Completed	Rate	Amount	Job Number
7:00	12:00	5.0	$9	$45	2B47
12:30	2:30	2.0	9	18	2B50
2:30	3:30	1.0	9	9	Maintenance
Totals		8.0		$72	

Supervisor R. W. Pace

BUCKING THE TREND: USING PEOPLE INSTEAD OF MACHINES

For decades overhead costs have been going up and labor costs have been going down as companies have replaced people with machines. However, at the French automaker Renault, the exact opposite has been happening with its new, no-frills vehicle called the Logan. The Logan was intentionally stripped of costly design elements and unnecessary technology so that the car could be sold for $6,000 in emerging Eastern European markets. The car's simplified design enables Renault's manufacturing plant in Romania to assemble the car almost entirely with people instead of robots. The monthly pay for a line worker at Renault's Romanian plant is $324 versus an average of more than $4,700 per worker in Western European countries. Thanks in part to low-cost labor, Logan's production costs are estimated to be just $1,089 per unit.

The Logan is finding buyers not only in emerging markets but also in more advanced Western European nations where customers have been clamoring for the car. Renault expects sales for the Logan to climb to one million vehicles by 2010—adding $341 million to its profits.

Source: Gail Edmondson and Constance Faivre d'Arcier, "Got 5,000 Euros? Need a New Car?" *BusinessWeek*, July 4, 2005, p. 49.

Application of Manufacturing Overhead

Topic Tackler

PLUS

3–2

Recall that product costs include manufacturing overhead as well as direct materials and direct labor. Therefore, manufacturing overhead also needs to be recorded on the job cost sheet. However, assigning manufacturing overhead to a specific job involves some difficulties. There are three reasons for this:

1. Manufacturing overhead is an *indirect cost.* This means that it is either impossible or difficult to trace these costs to a particular product or job.
2. Manufacturing overhead consists of many different items ranging from the grease used in machines to the annual salary of the production manager.
3. Even though output may fluctuate due to seasonal or other factors, total manufacturing overhead costs tend to remain relatively constant due to the presence of fixed costs.

> **LEARNING OBJECTIVE 3**
> Compute predetermined overhead rates and explain why estimated overhead costs (rather than actual overhead costs) are used in the costing process.

Given these problems, overhead costs are usually assigned to products using an allocation process. This allocation of overhead costs is accomplished by selecting an *allocation base* that is common to all of the company's products and services. An **allocation base** is a measure such as direct labor-hours (DLH) or machine-hours (MH) that is used to assign overhead costs to products and services.

The most widely used allocation bases are direct labor-hours and direct labor cost, with machine-hours and even units of product (where a company has only a single product) also used to some extent.

Manufacturing overhead is commonly applied to products using *a predetermined overhead rate.* The **predetermined overhead rate** is computed by dividing the total estimated manufacturing overhead cost for the period by the estimated total amount of the allocation base as follows:

$$\text{Predetermined overhead rate} = \frac{\text{Estimated total manufacturing overhead cost}}{\text{Estimated total amount of the allocation base}}$$

Note that the predetermined overhead rate is based on estimates rather than actual results. This is because the *predetermined* overhead rate is computed *before* the period begins and is used to *apply* overhead cost to jobs throughout the period. The process of assigning overhead cost to jobs is called **overhead application.** The formula for determining the amount of overhead cost to apply to a particular job is:

$$\begin{array}{c} \text{Overhead applied to} \\ \text{a particular job} \end{array} = \begin{array}{c} \text{Predetermined} \\ \text{overhead rate} \end{array} \times \begin{array}{c} \text{Amount of the allocation} \\ \text{base incurred by the job} \end{array}$$

For example, if the predetermined overhead rate is $8 per direct labor-hour, then $8 of overhead cost is *applied* to a job for each direct labor-hour incurred by the job. When the allocation base is direct labor-hours, the formula becomes:

$$\frac{\text{Overhead applied to}}{\text{a particular job}} = \frac{\text{Predetermined}}{\text{overhead rate}} \times \frac{\text{Actual direct labor-hours}}{\text{charged to the job}}$$

Using the Predetermined Overhead Rate   To illustrate the steps involved in computing and using a predetermined overhead rate, let's return to Yost Precision Machining. The company has estimated its total manufacturing overhead costs will be $320,000 for the year and its total direct labor-hours will be 40,000. Its predetermined overhead rate for the year would be $8 per direct labor-hour, as shown below:

$$\text{Predetermined overhead rate} = \frac{\text{Estimated total manufacturing overhead cost}}{\text{Estimated total amount of the allocation base}}$$

$$= \frac{\$320,000}{40,000 \text{ direct labor-hours}}$$

$$= \$8 \text{ per direct labor-hour}$$

The job cost sheet in Exhibit 3–4 indicates that 27 direct labor-hours (i.e., DLHs) were charged to Job 2B47. Therefore, a total of $216 of manufacturing overhead cost would be applied to the job:

$$\frac{\text{Overhead applied to}}{\text{Job 2B47}} = \frac{\text{Predetermined}}{\text{overhead rate}} \times \frac{\text{Actual direct labor-hours}}{\text{charged to Job 2B47}}$$

$$= \$8 \text{ per DLH} \times 27 \text{ DLHs}$$

$$= \$216 \text{ of overhead applied to Job 2B47}$$

This amount of overhead has been entered on the job cost sheet in Exhibit 3–4. Note that this is *not* the actual amount of overhead caused by the job. Actual overhead costs are *not* assigned to jobs—if that could be done, the costs would be direct costs, not overhead. The overhead assigned to the job is simply a share of the total overhead that was estimated at the beginning of the year. A **normal cost system,** which we have been describing, applies overhead to jobs by multiplying a predetermined overhead rate by the actual amount of the allocation base incurred by the jobs.

Overhead may be applied as direct labor-hours are charged to jobs, or all of the overhead can be applied at once when the job is completed. The choice is up to the company. However, if a job is not completed at the end of the accounting period, overhead should be applied to that job so as to value work in process inventory.

The Need for a Predetermined Rate

Instead of using a predetermined rate, a company could wait until the end of the accounting period to compute an actual overhead rate based on the *actual* total manufacturing costs and the *actual* total units in the allocation base for the period. However, managers cite several reasons for using predetermined overhead rates instead of actual overhead rates:

1. They would like to know the accounting system's valuation of completed jobs *before* the end of the accounting period. Suppose, for example, that Yost Precision Machining waits until the end of the year to compute its overhead rate. Then the cost of goods sold for Job 2B47 would not be known until the close of the year, even though the job was completed and shipped to the customer in March. This problem can be reduced by computing the actual overhead rate more frequently, but that immediately leads to another problem as discussed below.
2. If actual overhead rates are computed frequently, seasonal factors in overhead costs or in the allocation base can produce fluctuations in the overhead rates. For example, the costs

EXHIBIT 3–4
A Completed Job Cost Sheet

JOB COST SHEET

Job Number _2B47_   Date Initiated _March 2_

                                     Date Completed _March 8_

Department _Milling_

Item _Special order coupling_   Units Completed   2

For Stock _____

Direct Materials		Direct Labor			Manufacturing Overhead		
Req. No.	Amount	Ticket	Hours	Amount	Hours	Rate	Amount
14873	$ 660	843	5	$ 45	27	$8/DLH	$216
14875	506	846	8	60			
14912	238	850	4	21			
	$1,404	851	10	54			
			27	$180			

Cost Summary		Units Shipped		
Direct Materials	$1,404	Date	Number	Balance
Direct Labor	$ 180	March 8	—	2
Manufacturing Overhead	$ 216			
Total Product Cost	$1,800			
Unit Product Cost	$ 900*			

*$1,800 ÷ 2 units = $900 per unit.

of heating and cooling a production facility in Illinois will be highest in the winter and summer months and lowest in the spring and fall. If an overhead rate were computed each month or each quarter, the predetermined overhead rate would go up in the winter and summer and down in the spring and fall. Two identical jobs, one completed in the winter and one completed in the spring, would be assigned different costs if the overhead rate were computed on a monthly or quarterly basis. Managers generally feel that such fluctuations in overhead rates and costs serve no useful purpose and are misleading.

3. The use of a predetermined overhead rate simplifies record keeping. To determine the overhead cost to apply to a job, the accounting staff at Yost Precision Machining simply multiplies the direct labor-hours recorded for the job by the predetermined overhead rate of $8 per direct labor-hour.

For these reasons, most companies use predetermined overhead rates rather than actual overhead rates in their cost accounting systems.

Choice of an Allocation Base for Overhead Cost

Ideally, the allocation base used in the predetermined overhead rate should *drive* the overhead cost. A **cost driver** is a factor, such as machine-hours, beds occupied, computer time, or flight-hours, that causes overhead costs. If a base is used to compute overhead rates that does not "drive" overhead costs, then the result will be inaccurate overhead rates and distorted product costs. For example, if direct labor-hours is used to allocate overhead, but in reality overhead has little to do with direct labor-hours, then products with high direct labor-hour requirements will be overcosted.

Most companies use direct labor-hours or direct labor cost as the allocation base for manufacturing overhead. However, as discussed in earlier chapters, major shifts are taking place in the structure of costs. In the past, direct labor accounted for up to 60% of the cost of many products, with overhead cost making up only a portion of the remainder. This situation has been changing for two reasons. First, sophisticated automated equipment has taken over functions that used to be performed by direct labor workers. Since the costs of acquiring and maintaining such equipment are classified as overhead, this increases overhead while decreasing direct labor. Second, products are becoming more sophisticated and complex and are changed more frequently. This increases the need for highly skilled indirect workers such as engineers. As a result of these two trends, direct labor is decreasing relative to overhead as a component of product costs.

In companies where direct labor and overhead costs have been moving in opposite directions, it would be difficult to argue that direct labor "drives" overhead costs. Accordingly, managers in some companies use *activity-based costing* principles to redesign their cost accounting systems. Activity-based costing is designed to more accurately reflect the demands that products, customers, and other cost objects make on overhead resources. The activity-based approach is discussed in more detail in Chapter 8.

We hasten to add that although direct labor may not be an appropriate allocation base in some industries, in others it continues to be a significant driver of manufacturing overhead. Indeed, most manufacturing companies in the United States continue to use direct labor as the primary or secondary allocation base for manufacturing overhead. The key point is that the allocation base used by the company should really drive, or cause, overhead costs, and direct labor is not always an appropriate allocation base.

IN BUSINESS

WAIST MANAGEMENT

Research from the University of Michigan suggests that a company's health-care costs are driven to a significant extent by the weight of its employees. Workers who are overweight can cost as much as $1,500 more per year to insure than other workers. So what is a company to do? Park Place Entertainment, a casino operator with more than 7,000 employees, decided to attack the problem by holding a weight-loss contest. Over two years, the company's workforce dropped 20 tons of weight. After the contest, 12 diabetics were able to stop using medications that cost $13,300 per year per employee. Additionally, the company believes that its contest caused a decline in absenteeism and an increase in productivity.

Source: Jill Hecht Maxwell, "Worker Waist Management," *Inc.* magazine, August 2004, p. 32; Jessi Hempel, "Dieting for Dollars," *BusinessWeek*, November 3, 2003, p. 10.

IN BUSINESS

UNDERSTANDING COST DRIVERS CAN BE TRICKY BUSINESS

Conventional wisdom in the health-care industry was that costs could be reduced by reducing a patient's length of stay in a hospital. It seemed logical that reducing the number of days that a patient spends in the hospital should reduce the cost of treating that patient. However, researchers John Evans, Yuhchang Hwang, and Nandu Nagarajan provide evidence within one hospital that when doctors were motivated to reduce length of stay, it did not reduce costs. Doctors compensated for a reduction in length of stay by increasing the number of procedures performed per patient per day. Thus, any potential savings from reducing one cost driver—length of stay—were offset by cost increases caused by increasing another cost driver—number of procedures performed per patient per day.

Source: John H. Evans, Yuhchang Hwang, and Nandu J. Nagarajan, "Management Control and Hospital Cost Reduction: Additional Evidence," *Journal of Accounting and Public Policy*, Spring 2001, pp. 73–88.

Computation of Unit Costs

With the application of Yost Precision Machining's $216 of manufacturing overhead to the job cost sheet in Exhibit 3–4, the job cost sheet is complete except for two final steps. First, the totals for direct materials, direct labor, and manufacturing overhead are transferred to the Cost Summary section of the job cost sheet and added together to obtain the total cost for the job. Then the total product cost ($1,800) is divided by the number of units (2) to obtain the unit product cost ($900). As indicated earlier, *this unit product cost is an average cost and should not be interpreted as the cost that would actually be incurred if another unit were produced.* Much of the actual overhead costs would not change if another unit were produced, so the incremental cost of an additional unit is something less than the average unit cost of $900.

The completed job cost sheet will serve as the basis for valuing unsold units in ending inventory and for determining cost of goods sold.

Summary of Document Flows

The sequence of events discussed above is summarized in Exhibit 3–5 (page 102). A careful study of the flow of documents in this exhibit provides a good overview of the overall operation of a job-order costing system.

In the 8:00 A.M. daily planning meeting on March 9, Jean Yost, the president of Yost Precision Machining, once again drew attention to Job 2B47, the experimental couplings:

Jean: I see Job 2B47 is completed. Let's get those couplings shipped immediately to Loops Unlimited so they can get their testing program under way. Marcus, how much are we going to bill Loops for those two units?

Marcus: Because we agreed to sell the experimental couplings at cost, we will be charging Loops Unlimited just $900 a unit.

Jean: Fine. Let's hope the couplings work out and we make some money on the big order later.

Job-Order Costing—The Flow of Costs

We are now ready to take a more detailed look at the flow of costs through the company's general ledger. To illustrate, we shall consider a single month's activity for Rand Company, a producer of gold and silver commemorative medallions. Rand Company has two jobs in process during April, the first month of its fiscal year. Job A, a special minting of 1,000 gold medallions commemorating the invention of motion pictures, was started during March. By the end of March, $30,000 in manufacturing costs had been recorded for the job. Job B, an order for 10,000 silver medallions commemorating the fall of the Berlin Wall, was started in April.

LEARNING OBJECTIVE 4
Understand the flow of costs in a job-order costing system and prepare appropriate journal entries to record costs.

The Purchase and Issue of Materials

On April 1, Rand Company had $7,000 in raw materials on hand. During the month, the company purchased on account an additional $60,000 in raw materials. The purchase is recorded in journal entry (1) below:

(1)

Raw Materials	60,000	
Accounts Payable		60,000

As explained in the previous chapter, Raw Materials is an asset account. Thus, when raw materials are purchased, they are initially recorded as an asset—not as an expense.

EXHIBIT 3-5
The Flow of Documents in a Job-Order Costing System

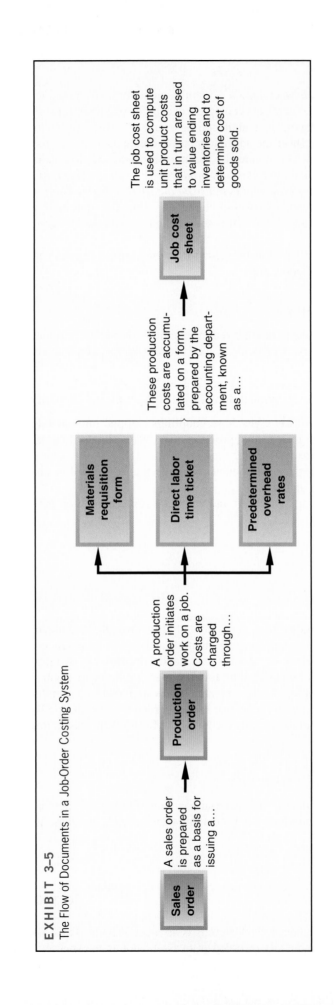

Issue of Direct and Indirect Materials   During April, $52,000 in raw materials were requisitioned from the storeroom for use in production. These raw materials included $50,000 of direct and $2,000 of indirect materials. Entry (2) records issuing the materials to the production departments.

(2)

Work in Process	50,000	
Manufacturing Overhead	2,000	
Raw Materials		52,000

The materials charged to Work in Process represent direct materials for specific jobs. These costs are also recorded on the appropriate job cost sheets. This point is illustrated in Exhibit 3–6, where $28,000 of the $50,000 in direct materials is charged to Job A's cost sheet and the remaining $22,000 is charged to Job B's cost sheet. (In this example, all data are presented in summary form and the job cost sheet is abbreviated.)

The $2,000 charged to Manufacturing Overhead in entry (2) represents indirect materials used in production during April. Observe that the Manufacturing Overhead account is separate from the Work in Process account. The purpose of the Manufacturing Overhead account is to accumulate all manufacturing overhead costs as they are incurred during a period.

Before leaving Exhibit 3–6 we need to point out one additional thing. Notice from the exhibit that the job cost sheet for Job A contains a beginning balance of $30,000. We stated earlier that this balance represents the cost of work done during March that has been carried forward to April. Also note that the Work in Process account contains the same $30,000 balance. *The reason the $30,000 appears in both places is that the Work in Process account is a control account and the job cost sheets form a subsidiary ledger. Thus, the Work in Process account contains a summarized total of all costs appearing on the individual job cost sheets for all jobs in process at any given point in time.* (Since Rand Company had only Job A in process at the beginning of April, Job A's $30,000 balance on that date is equal to the balance in the Work in Process account.)

Labor Cost

As work is performed each day employee time tickets are filled out by workers, collected, and forwarded to the Accounting Department. In the Accounting Department, wages are

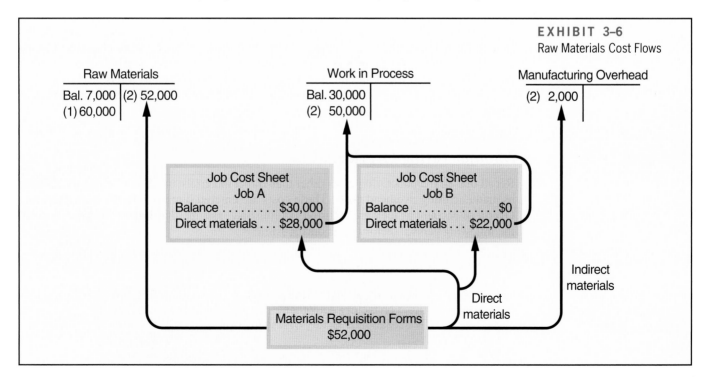

EXHIBIT 3–6
Raw Materials Cost Flows

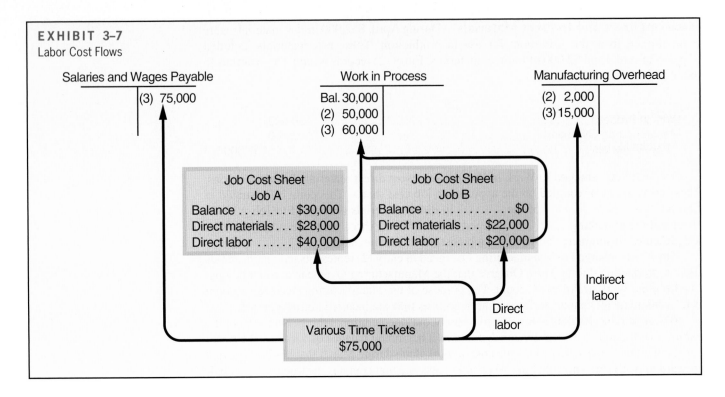

EXHIBIT 3-7
Labor Cost Flows

computed and the resulting costs are classified as either direct or indirect labor. In April, $60,000 was recorded for direct labor and $15,000 for indirect labor. The following entry summarizes those accruals:

(3)

Work in Process	60,000	
Manufacturing Overhead	15,000	
Salaries and Wages Payable		75,000

Only the direct labor cost of $60,000 is added to the Work in Process account. At the same time that direct labor costs are added to Work in Process, they are also added to the individual job cost sheets, as shown in Exhibit 3–7. During April, $40,000 of direct labor cost was charged to Job A and the remaining $20,000 was charged to Job B.

The labor costs charged to Manufacturing Overhead represent the indirect labor costs of the period, such as supervision, janitorial work, and maintenance.

Manufacturing Overhead Costs

Recall that all manufacturing costs other than direct materials and direct labor are classified as manufacturing overhead costs. These costs are entered directly into the Manufacturing Overhead account as they are incurred. To illustrate, assume that Rand Company incurred the following general factory costs during April:

Utilities (heat, water, and power)	$21,000
Rent on factory equipment	16,000
Miscellaneous factory overhead costs	3,000
Total	$40,000

The following entry records the incurrence of these costs:

(4)

Manufacturing Overhead	40,000	
Accounts Payable*		40,000

*Accounts such as Cash may also be credited

In addition, assume that during April, Rand Company recognized $13,000 in accrued property taxes and that $7,000 in prepaid insurance expired on factory buildings and equipment. The following entry records these items:

(5)

Manufacturing Overhead	20,000	
Property Taxes Payable		13,000
Prepaid Insurance		7,000

Finally, assume that the company recognized $18,000 in depreciation on factory equipment during April. The following entry records the accrual of this depreciation:

(6)

Manufacturing Overhead	18,000	
Accumulated Depreciation		18,000

In short, *all* manufacturing overhead costs are recorded directly into the Manufacturing Overhead account as they are incurred. It is important to understand that Manufacturing Overhead is a control account for many—perhaps thousands—of subsidiary accounts such as Indirect Materials, Indirect Labor, Factory Utilities, and so forth. As the Manufacturing Overhead account is debited for costs during a period, the various subsidiary accounts are also debited. In the example above and also in the assignment material for this chapter, for the sake of brevity we omit the entries to the subsidiary accounts.

> **LEARNING OBJECTIVE 5**
> Apply overhead cost to
> Work in Process using a
> predetermined overhead
> rate.

Applying Manufacturing Overhead

Since actual manufacturing costs are charged to the Manufacturing Overhead control account rather than to Work in Process, how are manufacturing overhead costs assigned to Work in Process? The answer is, by means of the predetermined overhead rate. Recall from our discussion earlier in the chapter that a predetermined overhead rate is established at the beginning of each year. The rate is calculated by dividing the estimated total manufacturing overhead cost for the year by the estimated total amount of the allocation base (measured in machine-hours, direct labor-hours, or some other base). The predetermined overhead rate is then used to apply overhead costs to jobs. For example, if direct labor-hours is the allocation base, overhead cost is applied to each job by multiplying the predetermined overhead rate by the number of direct labor-hours charged to the job.

To illustrate, assume that Rand Company's predetermined overhead rate is $6 per machine-hour. Also assume that during April, 10,000 machine-hours were worked on Job A and 5,000 machine-hours were worked on Job B (a total of 15,000 machine-hours). Thus, $90,000 in overhead cost ($6 per machine-hour × 15,000 machine-hours = $90,000) would be applied to Work in Process. The following entry records the application of Manufacturing Overhead to Work in Process:

(7)

Work in Process	90,000	
Manufacturing Overhead		90,000

The flow of costs through the Manufacturing Overhead account is shown in Exhibit 3–8 (page 106).

EXHIBIT 3–8
The Flow of Costs in
Overhead Application

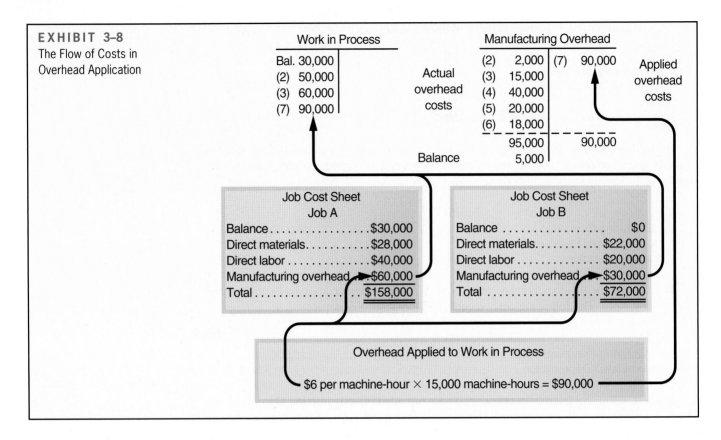

The actual overhead costs in the Manufacturing Overhead account in Exhibit 3–8 are the costs that were added to the account in entries (2)–(6). Observe that the incurrence of these actual overhead costs [entries (2)–(6)] and the application of overhead to Work in Process [entry (7)] represent two separate and entirely distinct processes.

The Concept of a Clearing Account   The Manufacturing Overhead account operates as a clearing account. As we have noted, actual factory overhead costs are debited to the account as they are incurred throughout the year. At certain intervals during the year (usually when a job is completed), overhead cost is applied to the job using the predetermined overhead rate, and Work in Process is debited and Manufacturing Overhead is credited. This sequence of events is illustrated below:

**Manufacturing Overhead
(a clearing account)**

Actual overhead costs are charged to this account as they are incurred throughout the period.	Overhead is applied to Work in Process using the predetermined overhead rate.

As we emphasized earlier, the predetermined overhead rate is based entirely on estimates of what overhead costs are *expected* to be, and it is established before the year begins. As a result, the overhead cost applied during a year will almost certainly turn out to be more or less than the actual overhead cost incurred. For example, notice from Exhibit 3–8 that Rand Company's actual overhead costs for the period are $5,000 greater than the overhead cost that has been applied to Work in Process, resulting in a $5,000 debit balance in the Manufacturing Overhead account. We will reserve discussion of what to do with this $5,000 balance until the next section, Problems of Overhead Application.

For the moment, we can conclude by noting from Exhibit 3–8 that the cost of a completed job consists of the actual direct materials cost of the job, the actual direct labor cost of the job, and the manufacturing overhead cost *applied* to the job. Pay particular attention to the following subtle but important point: *Actual overhead costs are not charged to jobs; actual overhead costs do not appear on the job cost sheet nor do they appear in the Work in Process account. Only the applied overhead cost, based on the predetermined overhead rate, appears on the job cost sheet and in the Work in Process account.*

Nonmanufacturing Costs

In addition to manufacturing costs, companies also incur selling and administrative costs. As explained in the previous chapter, these costs should be treated as period expenses and charged directly to the income statement. *Nonmanufacturing costs should not go into the Manufacturing Overhead account.* To illustrate the correct treatment of nonmanufacturing costs, assume that Rand Company incurred $30,000 in selling and administrative salary costs during April. The following entry summarizes the accrual of those salaries:

(8)

Salaries Expense	30,000	
Salaries and Wages Payable		30,000

Assume that depreciation on office equipment during April was $7,000. The entry is as follows:

(9)

Depreciation Expense	7,000	
Accumulated Depreciation		7,000

Pay particular attention to the difference between this entry and entry (6) where we recorded depreciation on factory equipment. In journal entry (6), depreciation on factory equipment was debited to Manufacturing Overhead and is therefore a product cost. In journal entry (9) above, depreciation on office equipment is debited to Depreciation Expense. Depreciation on office equipment is considered to be a period expense rather than a product cost.

Finally, assume that advertising was $42,000 and that other selling and administrative expenses in April totaled $8,000. The following entry records these items:

(10)

Advertising Expense....................................	42,000	
Other Selling and Administrative Expense...................	8,000	
Accounts Payable*		50,000

*Other accounts, such as Cash may be credited.

The amounts in entries (8) through (10) all go directly into expense accounts—they have no effect on product costs. The same will be true of any other selling and administrative expenses incurred during April, including sales commissions, depreciation on sales equipment, rent on office facilities, insurance on office facilities, and related costs.

Cost of Goods Manufactured

When a job has been completed, the finished output is transferred from the production departments to the finished goods warehouse. By this time, the accounting department will have charged the job with direct materials and direct labor cost, and manufacturing overhead will have been applied using the predetermined overhead rate. A transfer of costs is made within the costing system that *parallels* the physical transfer of goods to the finished goods warehouse. The costs of the completed job are transferred out of the Work in Process account and into the Finished Goods account. The sum of all amounts transferred between these two accounts represents the cost of goods manufactured for the period.

LEARNING OBJECTIVE 6
Prepare schedules of cost of goods manufactured and cost of goods sold.

In the case of Rand Company, assume that Job A was completed during April. The following entry transfers the cost of Job A from Work in Process to Finished Goods:

(11)

| Finished Goods . . . . | 158,000 | |
| Work in Process . . . . | | 158,000 |

The $158,000 represents the completed cost of Job A, as shown on the job cost sheet in Exhibit 3–8. Since Job A was the only job completed during April, the $158,000 also represents the cost of goods manufactured for the month.

Job B was not completed by the end of the month, so its cost will remain in the Work in Process account and carry over to the next month. If a balance sheet is prepared at the end of April, the cost accumulated thus far on Job B will appear as an asset— "Work in process inventory".

Cost of Goods Sold

As finished goods are shipped to customers, their accumulated costs are transferred from the Finished Goods account to the Cost of Goods Sold account. If an entire job is shipped at one time, then the entire cost appearing on the job cost sheet is transferred into the Cost of Goods Sold account. In most cases, however, only a portion of the units involved in a particular job will be immediately sold. In these situations, the unit product cost must be used to determine how much product cost should be removed from Finished Goods and charged to Cost of Goods Sold.

For Rand Company, we will assume 750 of the 1,000 gold medallions in Job A were shipped to customers on account by the end of the month for total sales revenue of $225,000. Since 1,000 units were produced and the total cost of the job from the job cost sheet was $158,000, the unit product cost was $158. The following journal entries would record the sale (all sales were on account):

(12)

| Accounts Receivable . . . . | 225,000 | |
| Sales . . . . | | 225,000 |

(13)

Cost of Goods Sold	118,500	
Finished Goods		118,500
(750 units × $158 per unit = $118,500)		

LEARNING OBJECTIVE 7
Use T-accounts to show the flow of costs in a job-order costing system.

Entry (13) completes the flow of costs through the job-order costing system.

Summary of Cost Flows

To pull the entire Rand Company example together, journal entries (1) through (13) are summarized in Exhibit 3–9. The flow of costs through the accounts is presented in T-account form in Exhibit 3–10 (page 110).

Exhibit 3–11 (page 111) presents a schedule of cost of goods manufactured and a schedule of cost of goods sold for Rand Company. Note particularly from Exhibit 3–11 that the manufacturing overhead cost on the schedule of cost of goods manufactured is the overhead applied to jobs during the month—not the actual manufacturing overhead costs incurred. The reason for this can be traced back to journal entry (7) and the T-account for Work in Process that appears in Exhibit 3–10. Under a normal costing system as illustrated in this chapter, applied—not actual—overhead costs are applied to jobs and thus to Work in Process inventory. In contrast, in Chapter 2 actual overhead costs were assigned to Work in Process and included in the schedule of cost of goods manufactured. This is because we had not introduced the concept of normal costing in that chapter.

EXHIBIT 3–9
Summary of Rand Company
Journal Entries

(1)

| Raw Materials.. | 60,000 | |
| Accounts Payable..................................... | | 60,000 |

(2)

Work in Process.......................................	50,000	
Manufacturing Overhead	2,000	
Raw Materials.....................................		52,000

(3)

Work in Process.......................................	60,000	
Manufacturing Overhead	15,000	
Salaries and Wages Payable		75,000

(4)

| Manufacturing Overhead .... | 40,000 | |
| Accounts Payable..................................... | | 40,000 |

(5)

Manufacturing Overhead	20,000	
Property Taxes Payable		13,000
Prepaid Insurance..................................		7,000

(6)

| Manufacturing Overhead .... | 18,000 | |
| Accumulated Depreciation .... | | 18,000 |

(7)

| Work in Process....................................... | 90,000 | |
| Manufacturing Overhead .... | | 90,000 |

(8)

| Salaries Expense .... | 30,000 | |
| Salaries and Wages Payable .... | | 30,000 |

(9)

| Depreciation Expense .... | 7,000 | |
| Accumulated Depreciation .... | | 7,000 |

(10)

Advertising Expense....................................	42,000	
Other Selling and Administrative Expense....................	8,000	
Accounts Payable.....................................		50,000

(11)

| Finished Goods....................................... | 158,000 | |
| Work in Process.................................... | | 158,000 |

(12)

| Accounts Receivable .... | 225,000 | |
| Sales.. | | 225,000 |

(13)

| Cost of Goods Sold .... | 118,500 | |
| Finished Goods .... | | 118,500 |

EXHIBIT 3–10
Summary of Cost Flows—Rand Company

Accounts Receivable

Bal.	XX		
(12)	225,000		

Prepaid Insurance

Bal.	XX		
		(5)	7,000

Raw Materials

Bal.	7,000	(2)	52,000
(1)	60,000		
Bal.	15,000		

Work in Process

Bal.	30,000	(11)	158,000
(2)	50,000		
(3)	60,000		
(7)	90,000		
Bal.	72,000		

Finished Goods

Bal.	10,000	(13)	118,500
(11)	158,000		
Bal.	49,500		

Accumulated Depreciation

		Bal.	XX
		(6)	18,000
		(9)	7,000

Manufacturing Overhead

(2)	2,000	(7)	90,000
(3)	15,000		
(4)	40,000		
(5)	20,000		
(6)	18,000		
Bal.	5,000		

Accounts Payable

		Bal.	XX
		(1)	60,000
		(4)	40,000
		(10)	50,000

Salaries and Wages Payable

		Bal.	XX
		(3)	75,000
		(8)	30,000

Property Taxes Payable

		Bal.	XX
		(5)	13,000

Capital Stock

		Bal.	XX

Retained Earnings

		Bal.	XX

Sales

		(12)	225,000

Cost of Goods Sold

(13)	118,500		

Salaries Expense

(8)	30,000		

Depreciation Expense

(9)	7,000		

Advertising Expense

(10)	42,000		

Other Selling and Administrative Expense

(10)	8,000		

Explanation of entries:
(1) Raw materials purchased.
(2) Direct and indirect materials issued into production.
(3) Direct and indirect factory labor cost incurred.
(4) Utilities and other factory costs incurred.
(5) Property taxes and insurance incurred on the factory.
(6) Depreciation recorded on factory assets.
(7) Overhead cost applied to Work in Process.
(8) Administrative salaries expense incurred.
(9) Depreciation recorded on office equipment.
(10) Advertising and other selling and administrative expense incurred.
(11) Cost of goods manufactured transferred into finished goods.
(12) Sale of Job A recorded.
(13) Cost of goods sold recorded for Job A.

Cost of Goods Manufactured

Direct materials:

Raw materials inventory, beginning	$ 7,000	
Add: Purchases of raw materials	60,000	
Total raw materials available	67,000	
Deduct: Raw materials inventory, ending	15,000	
Raw materials used in production	52,000	
Less indirect materials included in manufacturing overhead.................................	2,000	$ 50,000
Direct labor......................................		60,000
Manufacturing overhead applied to work in process		90,000
Total manufacturing costs		200,000
Add: Beginning work in process inventory		30,000
		230,000
Deduct: Ending work in process inventory		72,000
Cost of goods manufactured		$158,000

Cost of Goods Sold

Finished goods inventory, beginning	$ 10,000
Add: Cost of goods manufactured	158,000
Goods available for sale	168,000
Deduct: Finished goods inventory, ending	49,500
Unadjusted cost of goods sold	118,500
Add: Underapplied overhead	5,000
Adjusted cost of goods sold	$123,500

*Note that the underapplied overhead is added to cost of goods sold. If overhead were overapplied, it would be deducted from cost of goods sold.

Note also, as shown in Exhibit 3–11, that the cost of goods manufactured for the month ($158,000) agrees with the amount transferred from Work in Process to Finished Goods for the month as recorded earlier in entry (11). Also note that this $158,000 is used in computing the cost of goods sold for the month.

An income statement for April is presented in Exhibit 3–12. Observe that the cost of goods sold on this statement ($123,500) is carried down from Exhibit 3–11.

EXHIBIT 3–12
Income Statement

Rand Company Income Statement For the Month Ending April 30		
Sales		$225,000
Cost of goods sold ($118,500 + $5,000)...........		123,500
Gross margin		101,500
Selling and administrative expenses:		
Salaries expense	$30,000	
Depreciation expense........................	7,000	
Advertising expense.........................	42,000	
Other expense	8,000	87,000
Net operating income..........................		$ 14,500

Problems of Overhead Application

LEARNING OBJECTIVE 8
Compute underapplied or overapplied overhead cost and prepare the journal entry to close the balance in Manufacturing Overhead to the appropriate accounts.

We need to consider two complications relating to overhead application: (1) the computation of underapplied and overapplied overhead; and (2) the disposition of any balance remaining in the Manufacturing Overhead account at the end of a period.

Underapplied and Overapplied Overhead

Since the predetermined overhead rate is established before the period begins and is based entirely on estimated data, the overhead cost applied to Work in Process will generally differ from the amount of overhead cost actually incurred. In the case of Rand Company, for example, the predetermined overhead rate of $6 per hour was used to apply $90,000 of overhead cost to Work in Process, whereas actual overhead costs for April proved to be $95,000 (see Exhibit 3–8). The difference between the overhead cost applied to Work in Process and the actual overhead costs of a period is called either **underapplied** or **overapplied overhead.** For Rand Company, overhead was underapplied because the applied cost ($90,000) was $5,000 less than the actual cost ($95,000). If the situation had been reversed and the company had applied $95,000 in overhead cost to Work in Process while incurring actual overhead costs of only $90,000, then the overhead would have been overapplied.

What is the cause of underapplied or overapplied overhead? The causes can be complex, and a full explanation will have to wait for later chapters. Nevertheless, the basic problem is that the method of applying overhead to jobs using a predetermined overhead rate assumes that actual overhead costs will be proportional to the actual amount of the allocation base incurred during the period. If, for example, the predetermined overhead rate is $6 per machine-hour, then it is assumed that actual overhead costs incurred will be $6 for every machine-hour that is actually worked. There are at least two reasons why this may not be true. First, much of the overhead often consists of fixed costs that do not change as the number of machine-hours incurred goes up or down. Second, spending on overhead items may or may not be under control. If individuals who are responsible for overhead costs do a good job, those costs should be less than were expected at the beginning of the period. If they do a poor job, those costs will be more than expected. As we indicated above, however, a fuller explanation of the causes of underapplied and overapplied overhead will have to wait for later chapters.

To illustrate what can happen, suppose that two companies—Turbo Crafters and Black & Howell—have prepared the following estimated data for the coming year:

	Turbo Crafters	Black & Howell
Allocation base	Machine-hours	Direct materials cost
Estimated manufacturing overhead cost (a)	$300,000	$120,000
Estimated total amount of the allocation base (b)	75,000 machine-hours	$80,000 direct materials cost
Predetermined overhead rate (a) ÷ (b)	$4 per machine-hour	150% of direct materials cost

Note that when the allocation base is dollars (such as direct materials cost in the case of Black & Howell) the predetermined overhead rate is expressed as a percentage of the allocation base. When dollars are divided by dollars, the result is a percentage.

Now assume that because of unexpected changes in overhead spending and changes in demand for the companies' products, the *actual* overhead cost and the actual activity recorded during the year in each company are as follows:

	Turbo Crafters	Black & Howell
Actual manufacturing overhead cost	$290,000	$130,000
Actual total amount of the allocation base	68,000 machine-hours	$90,000 direct materials cost

For each company, note that the actual data for both cost and the allocation base differ from the estimates used in computing the predetermined overhead rate. This results in underapplied and overapplied overhead as follows:

	Turbo Crafters	Black & Howell
Actual manufacturing overhead cost	$290,000	$130,000
Manufacturing overhead cost applied to Work in Process during the year:		
Predetermined overhead rate (a)	$4 per machine-hour	150% of direct materials cost
Actual total amount of the allocation base (b)	68,000 machine-hours	$ 90,000 direct materials cost
Manufacturing overhead applied (a) × (b)	$272,000	$135,000
Underapplied (overapplied) manufacturing overhead	$ 18,000	$ (5,000)

For Turbo Crafters, notice that the amount of overhead cost applied to Work in Process ($272,000) is less than the actual overhead cost for the year ($290,000). Therefore, overhead is underapplied. Also, notice that the original estimate of overhead for Turbo Crafters ($300,000) is not directly involved in this computation. Its impact is felt only through the $4 predetermined overhead rate.

For Black & Howell, the amount of overhead cost applied to Work in Process ($135,000) is greater than the actual overhead cost for the year ($130,000), so overhead is overapplied.

A summary of the concepts discussed above is presented in Exhibit 3–13.

Disposition of Underapplied or Overapplied Overhead Balances

The underapplied or overapplied balance remaining in the Manufacturing Overhead account at the end of a period is treated in one of two ways:

1. Closed out to Cost of Goods Sold.
2. Allocated between Work in Process, Finished Goods, and Cost of Goods Sold in proportion to the overhead applied during the current period that is in the ending balances of these accounts.

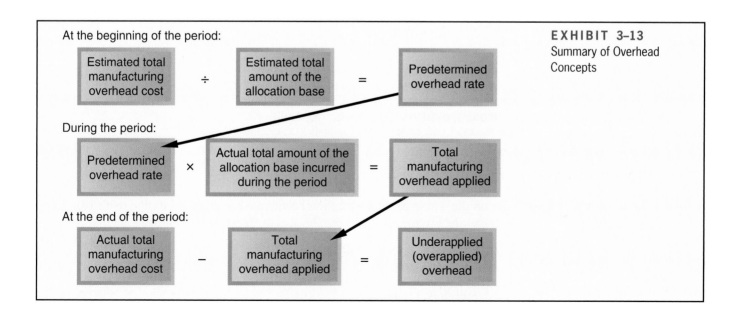

EXHIBIT 3–13
Summary of Overhead Concepts

The second method, which allocates the underapplied or overapplied overhead among ending inventories and Cost of Goods Sold, is equivalent to using an "actual" overhead rate and is for that reason considered by many to be more accurate than the first method. Consequently, if the amount of underapplied or overapplied overhead is material, many accountants would insist that the second method be used. In problem assignments, we will always indicate which method you are to use for disposing of underapplied or overapplied overhead.

Closed Out to Cost of Goods Sold   As mentioned above, closing out the balance in Manufacturing Overhead to Cost of Goods Sold is simpler than the allocation method. Returning to the example of Rand Company, the entry to close the $5,000 of underapplied overhead to Cost of Goods Sold is as follows:

(14)

| Cost of Goods Sold | 5,000 | |
| Manufacturing Overhead | | 5,000 |

Note that because the Manufacturing Overhead account has a debit balance, Manufacturing Overhead must be credited to close out the account. This has the effect of increasing Cost of Goods Sold for April to $123,500:

Unadjusted cost of goods sold [from entry (13)]	$118,500
Add underapplied overhead [entry (14) above]	5,000
Adjusted cost of goods sold	$123,500

After this adjustment has been made, Rand Company's income statement for April will appear as shown earlier in Exhibit 3–12.

Allocated between Accounts   Allocation of underapplied or overapplied overhead between Work in Process, Finished Goods, and Cost of Goods Sold is more accurate than closing the entire balance into Cost of Goods Sold. This allocation assigns overhead costs to where they would have gone in the first place had it not been for the errors in estimating the predetermined overhead rate.

Had Rand Company chosen to allocate the underapplied overhead among the inventory accounts and Cost of Goods Sold, it would first be necessary to determine the amount of overhead that had been applied during April to each of the accounts. The computations would have been as follows:

Overhead applied in work in process inventory, April 30	$30,000	33.33%
Overhead applied in finished goods inventory, April 30		
($60,000/1,000 units = $60 per unit) × 250 units	15,000	16.67%
Overhead applied in cost of goods sold, April		
($60,000/1,000 units = $60 per unit) × 750 units	45,000	50.00%
Total overhead applied	$90,000	100.00%

Based on the above percentages, the underapplied overhead (i.e., the debit balance in Manufacturing Overhead) would be allocated as shown in the following journal entry:

Work in Process (33.33% × $5,000)	1,666.50	
Finished Goods (16.67% × $5,000)	833.50	
Cost of Goods Sold (50.00% × $5,000)	2,500.00	
Manufacturing Overhead		5,000.00

Note that the first step in the allocation was to determine the amount of overhead applied in each of the accounts. For Finished Goods, for example, the total amount of overhead applied to Job A, $60,000, was divided by the total number of units in Job A, 1,000 units, to arrive at the average overhead applied of $60 per unit. Since 250 units from Job A were still in ending finished goods inventory, the amount of overhead applied in the Finished Goods Inventory account was $60 per unit multiplied by 250 units or $15,000 in total.

If overhead had been overapplied, the entry above would have been just the reverse, since a credit balance would have existed in the Manufacturing Overhead account.

A General Model of Product Cost Flows

Exhibit 3–14 presents a T-account model of the flow of costs in a product costing system. This model applies as much to a process costing system as it does to a job-order costing system. This model can be very helpful in understanding how costs enter a system, flow through it, and finally end up as Cost of Goods Sold on the income statement.

Multiple Predetermined Overhead Rates

Our discussion in this chapter has assumed that there is a single predetermined overhead rate for an entire factory called a **plantwide overhead rate.** This is a fairly common practice—particularly in smaller companies. But in larger companies, *multiple predetermined overhead*

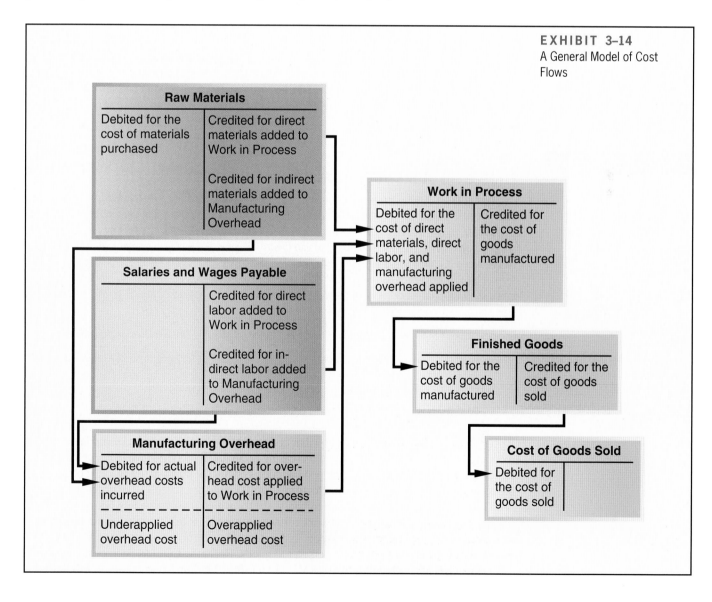

EXHIBIT 3–14
A General Model of Cost Flows

rates are often used. In a **multiple predetermined overhead rate** system each production department may have its own predetermined overhead rate. Such a system, while more complex, is more accurate, since it can reflect differences across departments in how overhead costs are incurred. For example, overhead might be allocated based on direct labor-hours in departments that are relatively labor intensive and based on machine-hours in departments that are relatively machine intensive. When multiple predetermined overhead rates are used, overhead is applied in each department according to its own overhead rate as a job proceeds through the department.

Job-Order Costing in Service Companies

Job-order costing is also used in service organizations such as law firms, movie studios, hospitals, and repair shops, as well as in manufacturing companies. In a law firm, for example, each client is considered to be a "job," and the costs of that job are accumulated day by day on a job cost sheet as the client's case is handled by the firm. Legal forms and similar inputs represent the direct materials for the job; the time expended by attorneys represents the direct labor; and the costs of secretaries, clerks, rent, depreciation, and so forth, represent the overhead.

In a movie studio such as Columbia Pictures, each film produced by the studio is a "job," and costs for direct materials (costumes, props, film, etc.) and direct labor (actors, directors, and extras) are charged to each film's job cost sheet. A share of the studio's overhead costs, such as utilities, depreciation of equipment, wages of maintenance workers, and so forth, is also charged to each film.

In sum, job-order costing is a versatile and widely used costing method that may be encountered in virtually any organization that provides diverse products or services.

MANAGING JOB COSTS IN A SERVICE BUSINESS

IBM has created a software program called Professional Marketplace to match IBM employees with client needs. "Using Marketplace, IBM consultants working for customers can search through 100 job classifications and 10,000 skills, figuring out who inside IBM is available, where they are located and roughly how much it costs the company to use them." Thus far, the results have been encouraging. IBM has reduced its reliance on outside contractors by 5% to 7% and its consultants spend more of their time in billable work. Furthermore, IBM's senior consultants can search across the globe for available employees with particular niche skills with the click of a mouse instead of having to rely on numerous time-consuming phone calls and emails.

Source: Charles Forelle, "IBM Tool Deploys Employees Efficiently," *The Wall Street Journal*, July 14, 2005, p. B3.

Use of Information Technology

Earlier in the chapter we discussed how bar code technology can be used to record labor time—reducing the drudgery in that task and increasing accuracy. Bar codes have many other uses.

In a company with a well-developed bar code system, the manufacturing cycle begins with the receipt of a customer's order in electronic form. Until very recently, the order would have been received via electronic data interchange (EDI), which involves a network of computers linking organizations. An EDI network allows companies to electronically exchange business documents and other information that extend into all areas of business activity from ordering raw materials to shipping completed goods. Recently, EDI has been challenged by a far cheaper web-based alternative—XML (Extensible Markup Language), an extension of

HTML (Hypertext Markup Language). HTML uses codes to tell your web browser how to display information on your screen, but the computer doesn't know what the information is—it just displays it. XML provides additional tags that identify the kind of information that is being exchanged. For example, price data might be coded as <price> 14.95 <price>. When your computer reads this data and sees the tags <price> surrounding 14.95, your computer will immediately know that this is a price. XML tags can designate many different kinds of information—customer orders, medical records, bank statements, and so on—and the tags will indicate to your computer how to display, store, and retrieve the information. Office Depot is an early adopter of XML, which it is using to facilitate e-commerce with its big customers.

Once an order has been received via EDI or in the form of an XML file, the computer draws up a list of required raw materials and sends out electronic purchase orders to suppliers. When materials arrive at the company's plant from the suppliers, bar codes that have been applied by the suppliers are scanned to update inventory records and to trigger payment for the materials. The bar codes are scanned again when the materials are requisitioned for use in production. At that point, the computer credits the Raw Materials inventory account for the amount and type of goods requisitioned and charges the Work in Process inventory account.

A unique bar code is assigned to each job. This bar code is scanned to update Work in Process records for labor and other costs incurred in the manufacturing process. When goods are completed, another scan is performed to transfer the cost and quantity of goods from the Work in Process inventory account to the Finished Goods inventory account, or to charge Cost of Goods Sold for goods ready to be shipped.

Goods ready to be shipped are packed into containers that are bar coded with information that includes the customer number, the type and quantity of goods being shipped, and the order number. This bar code is then used for preparing billing information and for tracking the packed goods until placed on a carrier for shipment to the customer. Some customers require that the packed goods be bar coded with point-of-sale labels that can be scanned at retail check-out counters. These scans allow the retailer to update inventory records, verify price, and generate a customer receipt.

RFID: THE NEXT GENERATION BEYOND BAR CODES

Bar code technology has revolutionized how organizations gather data. However, bar code readers cannot read a bar code more than a few feet away nor can they read a bar code that is not visible. This creates inefficiencies when companies attempt to track large amounts of raw materials, finished goods or merchandise inventory. Radio Frequency Identification Systems (RFID) overcome these inherent limitations of bar codes. For example, a tractor trailer full of merchandise with RFID tags can be "read" without even opening the trailer doors.

According to Kurt Salmon Associates, RFID technology can lower warehousing and distribution costs by 3% to 5% largely because employees no longer need to scan the bar code on each item. Companies such as Home Depot, Marks & Spencer, Metro AG, Procter & Gamble, and Wal-Mart are moving quickly to adopt RFID technology. In fact, Wal-Mart is requiring its top 100 suppliers to "put RFID tags on all of their pallets, cases, cartons and high margin items."

A survey conducted by *PC* Magazine indicates that more than half of the companies in the automotive, consumer goods, and transportation and logistics industries plan to adopt RFID. Some experts believe that, once technological advances drop the cost of an RFID tag from 25–30 cents down to 5 cents, this technology will be very widely adopted.

Sources: Meredith Levinson, "The RFID Imperative," *CIO* Magazine, December 2003 (www.cio.com/archive/120103/retail.html) and "Here Comes RFID Chips," *PC* Magazine, October 18, 2005, pp. 31–33.

In short, bar code technology is being integrated into many areas of business activity. When combined with EDI or XML, it eliminates a lot of clerical drudgery and allows companies to capture and exchange more data and to analyze and report information much more quickly and completely and with less error than with manual systems.

MANAGING DIVERSITY WITH TECHNOLOGY

Andersen Windows, Inc. of Bayport, Minnesota, has a software program that enables it to produce just about any window configuration that a customer might order. The program—which works on most standard Microsoft® Windows platforms—allows customers to select from any of the company's large selection of standard window and door sizes and styles. Customers can add the features and options they want with an easy "point-and-click" until they've configured the desired units. Placing the order after final selections are made is just as easy—the window order can be sent electronically into Andersen's back office system where it is automatically fulfilled. The entire process is highly automated and very efficient, yet it enables the customer a high degree of flexibility.

Source: Andersen® Intelligent Quote, used by permission of Andersen Windows, Inc.

Summary

Job-order costing and process costing are widely used to track costs. Job-order costing is used in situations where the organization offers many different products or services, such as in furniture manufacturing, hospitals, and legal firms. Process costing is used where units of product are homogeneous, such as in flour milling or cement production.

Materials requisition forms and labor time tickets are used to assign direct materials and direct labor costs to jobs in a job-order costing system. Manufacturing overhead costs are assigned to jobs using a predetermined overhead rate. The predetermined overhead rate is determined before the period begins by dividing the estimated total manufacturing cost for the period by the estimated total amount of the allocation base for the period. The most frequently used allocation bases are direct labor-hours and machine-hours. Overhead is applied to jobs by multiplying the predetermined overhead rate by the actual amount of the allocation base used by the job.

Since the predetermined overhead rate is based on estimates, the actual overhead cost incurred during a period may be more or less than the amount of overhead cost applied to production. Such a difference is referred to as underapplied or overapplied overhead. The underapplied or overapplied overhead for a period can be either closed out to Cost of Goods Sold or allocated between Work in Process, Finished Goods, and Cost of Goods Sold. When overhead is underapplied, manufacturing overhead costs have been understated and therefore inventories and/or expenses must be adjusted upwards. When overhead is overapplied, manufacturing overhead costs have been overstated and therefore inventories and/or expenses must be adjusted downwards.

Review Problem: Job-Order Costing

Hogle Corporation is a manufacturer that uses job-order costing. On January 1, the beginning of its fiscal year, the company's inventory balances were as follows:

Raw materials	$20,000
Work in process	$15,000
Finished goods	$30,000

The company applies overhead cost to jobs on the basis of machine-hours worked. For the current year, the company estimated that it would work 75,000 machine-hours and incur $450,000 in manufacturing overhead cost. The following transactions were recorded for the year:
a.   Raw materials were purchased on account, $410,000.
b.   Raw materials were requisitioned for use in production, $380,000 ($360,000 direct materials and $20,000 indirect materials).

c. The following costs were accrued for employee services: direct labor, $75,000; indirect labor, $110,000; sales commissions, $90,000; and administrative salaries, $200,000.
d. Sales travel costs were $17,000.
e. Utility costs in the factory were $43,000.
f. Advertising costs were $180,000.
g. Depreciation was recorded for the year, $350,000 (80% relates to factory operations, and 20% relates to selling and administrative activities).
h. Insurance expired during the year, $10,000 (70% relates to factory operations, and the remaining 30% relates to selling and administrative activities).
i. Manufacturing overhead was applied to production. Due to greater than expected demand for its products, the company worked 80,000 machine-hours during the year.
j. Goods costing $900,000 to manufacture according to their job cost sheets were completed during the year.
k. Goods were sold on account to customers during the year for a total of $1,500,000. The goods cost $870,000 to manufacture according to their job cost sheets.

Required:
1. Prepare journal entries to record the preceding transactions.
2. Post the entries in (1) above to T-accounts (don't forget to enter the beginning balances in the inventory accounts).
3. Is Manufacturing Overhead underapplied or overapplied for the year? Prepare a journal entry to close any balance in the Manufacturing Overhead account to Cost of Goods Sold. Do not allocate the balance between ending inventories and Cost of Goods Sold.
4. Prepare an income statement for the year.

Solution to Review Problem

1.
a.	Raw Materials	410,000	
	Accounts Payable		410,000
b.	Work in Process	360,000	
	Manufacturing Overhead	20,000	
	Raw Materials		380,000
c.	Work in Process	75,000	
	Manufacturing Overhead	110,000	
	Sales Commissions Expense	90,000	
	Administrative Salaries Expense	200,000	
	Salaries and Wages Payable		475,000
d.	Sales Travel Expense	17,000	
	Accounts Payable		17,000
e.	Manufacturing Overhead	43,000	
	Accounts Payable		43,000
f.	Advertising Expense	180,000	
	Accounts Payable		180,000
g.	Manufacturing Overhead	280,000	
	Depreciation Expense	70,000	
	Accumulated Depreciation		350,000
h.	Manufacturing Overhead	7,000	
	Insurance Expense	3,000	
	Prepaid Insurance		10,000

i. The predetermined overhead rate for the year would be computed as follows:

$$\frac{\text{Predetermined}}{\text{overhead rate}} = \frac{\text{Estimated total manufacturing overhead cost}}{\text{Estimated total amount of the allocation base}}$$

$$= \frac{\$450,000}{75,000 \text{ machine-hours}}$$

$$= \$6 \text{ per machine-hour}$$

Based on the 80,000 machine-hours actually worked during the year, the company would have applied $480,000 in overhead cost to production: $6 per machine-hour × 80,000 machine-hours = $480,000. The following entry records this application of overhead cost:

	Work in Process	480,000	
	Manufacturing Overhead		480,000
j.	Finished Goods	900,000	
	Work in Process		900,000
k.	Accounts Receivable	1,500,000	
	Sales		1,500,000
	Cost of Goods Sold	870,000	
	Finished Goods		870,000

2.

Accounts Receivable

(k)	1,500,000	

Prepaid Insurance

		(h)	10,000

Raw Materials

Bal.	20,000	(b)	380,000
(a)	410,000		
Bal.	50,000		

Work in Process

Bal.	15,000	(j)	900,000
(b)	360,000		
(c)	75,000		
(i)	480,000		
Bal.	30,000		

Finished Goods

Bal.	30,000	(k)	870,000
(j)	900,000		
Bal.	60,000		

Manufacturing Overhead

(b)	20,000	(i)	480,000
(c)	110,000		
(e)	43,000		
(g)	280,000		
(h)	7,000		
	460,000		480,000
		Bal.	20,000

Accumulated Depreciation

		(g)	350,000

Accounts Payable

		(a)	410,000
		(d)	17,000
		(e)	43,000
		(f)	180,000

Salaries and Wages Payable

		(c)	475,000

Sales

		(k)	1,500,000

Cost of Goods Sold

(k)	870,000	

Sales Commissions Expense

(c)	90,000	

Administrative Salaries Expense

(c)	200,000	

Sales Travel Expense

(d)	17,000	

Advertising Expense

(f)	180,000	

Depreciation Expense

(g)	70,000	

Insurance Expense

(h)	3,000	

3. Manufacturing overhead is overapplied for the year. The entry to close it out to Cost of Goods Sold is as follows:

Manufacturing Overhead	20,000	
Cost of Goods Sold.		20,000

4.

Hogle Corporation Income Statement For the Year Ended December 31		
Sales.		$1,500,000
Cost of goods sold ($870,000 − $20,000)		850,000
Gross margin		650,000
Selling and administrative expenses:		
Sales commissions expense	$ 90,000	
Administrative salaries expense	200,000	
Sales travel expense	17,000	
Advertising expense	180,000	
Depreciation expense	70,000	
Insurance expense	3,000	560,000
Net operating income		$ 90,000

Glossary

Absorption costing A costing method that includes all manufacturing costs—direct materials, direct labor, and both variable and fixed manufacturing overhead—in the cost of a product. (p. 92)

Allocation base A measure of activity such as direct labor-hours or machine-hours that is used to assign costs to cost objects. (p. 97)

Bill of materials A document that shows the quantity of each type of direct material required to make a product. (p. 94)

Cost driver A factor, such as machine-hours, beds occupied, computer time, or flight-hours, that causes overhead costs. (p. 99)

Job cost sheet A form prepared for a job that records the materials, labor, and manufacturing overhead costs charged to that job. (p. 94)

Job-order costing system A costing system used in situations where many different products, jobs, or services are produced each period. (p. 93)

Materials requisition form A detailed source document that specifies the type and quantity of materials to be drawn from the storeroom and that identifies the job that will be charged for the cost of those materials. (p. 94)

Multiple predetermined overhead rates A costing system with multiple overhead cost pools with a different predetermined overhead rate for each cost pool, rather than a single predetermined overhead rate for the entire company. Each production department is often treated as a separate overhead cost pool. (p. 116)

Normal cost system A costing system in which overhead costs are applied to a job by multiplying a predetermined overhead rate by the actual amount of the allocation base incurred by the job. (p. 98)

Overapplied overhead A credit balance in the Manufacturing Overhead account that occurs when the amount of overhead cost applied to Work in Process exceeds the amount of overhead cost actually incurred during a period. (p. 112)

Overhead application The process of charging manufacturing overhead cost to job cost sheets and to the Work in Process account. (p. 97)

Plantwide overhead rate A single predetermined overhead rate that is used throughout a plant. (p. 115)

Predetermined overhead rate A rate used to charge manufacturing overhead cost to jobs that is established in advance for each period. It is computed by dividing the estimated total manufacturing overhead cost for the period by the estimated total amount of the allocation base for the period. (p. 97)

Process costing system A costing system used in situations where a single, homogeneous product (such as cement or flour) is produced for long periods of time. (p. 92)

Time ticket A detailed source document that is used to record the amount of time an employee spends on various activities. (p. 96)

Underapplied overhead A debit balance in the Manufacturing Overhead account that occurs when the amount of overhead cost actually incurred exceeds the amount of overhead cost applied to Work in Process during a period. (p. 112)

Appendix 3A: The Predetermined Overhead Rate and Capacity

Companies typically base their predetermined overhead rates on the estimated, or budgeted, amount of the allocation base for the upcoming period. This is the method that is used in the chapter, but it is a practice that has come under severe criticism.[1] An example will be very helpful in understanding why. Prahad Corporation manufactures music CDs for local recording studios. The company's CD duplicating machine is capable of producing a new CD every 10 seconds from a master CD. The company leases the CD duplicating machine for $180,000 per year, and this is the company's only manufacturing overhead cost. With allowances for setups and maintenance, the machine is theoretically capable of producing up to 900,000 CDs per year. However, due to weak retail sales of CDs, the company's commercial customers are unlikely to order more than 600,000 CDs next year. The company uses machine time as the allocation base for applying manufacturing overhead to CDs. These data are summarized below:

Prahad Corporation Data	
Total manufacturing overhead cost.	$180,000 per year
Allocation base—machine time per CD	10 seconds per CD
Capacity	900,000 CDs per year
Budgeted output for next year	600,000 CDs

If Prahad follows common practice and computes its predetermined overhead rate using estimated or budgeted figures, then its predetermined overhead rate for next year would be $0.03 per second of machine time computed as follows:

$$\text{Predetermined overhead rate} = \frac{\text{Estimated total manufacturing overhead cost}}{\text{Estimated total amount of the allocation base}}$$

$$= \frac{\$180,000}{600,000 \text{ CDs} \times 10 \text{ seconds per CD}}$$

$$= \$0.03 \text{ per second}$$

Since each CD requires 10 seconds of machine time, each CD will be charged for $0.30 of overhead cost.

Critics charge that there are two problems with this procedure. First, if predetermined overhead rates are based on budgeted activity, then the unit product costs will fluctuate depending on the budgeted level of activity for the period. For example, if the budgeted output for the year was only 300,000 CDs, the predetermined overhead rate would be $0.06 per second of machine time or $0.60 per CD rather than $0.30 per CD. In general, if budgeted output falls, the overhead cost per unit will increase; it will appear that the CDs cost more to make. Managers may then be tempted to increase prices at the worst possible time—just as demand is falling.

Second, critics charge that under the traditional approach, products are charged for resources that they don't use. When the fixed costs of capacity are spread over estimated

---

[1] Institute of Management Accountants, *Measuring the Cost of Capacity: Statements on Management Accounting, Number 4Y*, Montvale, NJ; Thomas Klammer, ed., *Capacity Measurement and Improvement: A Manager's Guide to Evaluating and Optimizing Capacity Productivity* (Chicago: CAM-I, Irwin Professional Publishing); and C. J. McNair, "The Hidden Costs of Capacity," *The Journal of Cost Management* (Spring 1994), pp. 12–24.

activity, the units that are produced must shoulder the costs of unused capacity. That is why the applied overhead cost per unit increases as the level of activity falls. The critics argue that products should be charged only for the capacity that they use; they should not be charged for the capacity they don't use. This can be accomplished by basing the predetermined overhead rate on capacity as follows:

$$\text{Predetermined overhead rate based on capacity} = \frac{\text{Estimated total manufacturing overhead cost at capacity}}{\text{Estimated total amount of the allocation base at capacity}}$$

$$= \frac{\$180,000}{900,000 \text{ CDs} \times 10 \text{ seconds per CD}}$$

$$= \$0.02 \text{ per second}$$

Since the predetermined overhead rate is $0.02 per second, the overhead cost applied to each CD would be $0.20. This charge is constant and would not be affected by the level of activity during a period. If output falls, the charge would still be $0.20 per CD.

This method will almost certainly result in underapplied overhead. If actual output at Prahad Corporation is 600,000 CDs, then only $120,000 of overhead cost would be applied to products ($0.20 per CD × 600,000 CDs). Since the actual overhead cost is $180,000, there would be underapplied overhead of $60,000. In another departure from tradition, the critics suggest that the underapplied overhead that results from idle capacity should be separately disclosed on the income statement as the Cost of Unused Capacity—a period expense. Disclosing this cost as a lump sum on the income statement, rather than burying it in Cost of Goods Sold or ending inventories, makes it much more visible to managers.

Official pronouncements do not prohibit basing predetermined overhead rates on capacity for external reports.[2] Nevertheless, basing the predetermined overhead rate on estimated or budgeted activity is a long-established practice in industry, and some managers and accountants may object to the large amounts of underapplied overhead that would often result from using capacity to determine predetermined overhead rates. And some may insist that the underapplied overhead be allocated among Cost of Goods Sold and ending inventories—which would defeat the purpose of basing the predetermined overhead rate on capacity.

RESOURCE CONSUMPTION ACCOUNTING

Clopay Plastic Products Company, headquartered in Cincinnati, Ohio, recently implemented a pilot application of a German cost accounting system known in the United States as Resource Consumption Accounting (RCA). One of the benefits of RCA is that it uses the estimated total amount of the allocation base at capacity to calculate overhead rates and to assign costs to cost objects. This makes idle capacity visible to managers who can react to this information by either growing sales or taking steps to reduce the amount and cost of available capacity. It also ensures that products are only charged for the resources used to produce them.

Clopay's old cost system spread all of the company's manufacturing overhead costs over the units produced. So, if Clopay's senior managers decided to discontinue what appeared to be an unprofitable product, the unit costs of the remaining products would increase as the fixed overhead costs of the newly idled capacity were spread over the remaining products.

Source: B. Douglas Clinton and Sally A. Webber, "Here's Innovation in Management Accounting with Resource Consumption Accounting," *Strategic Finance,* October 2004, pp. 21–26.

---

[2] Institute of Management Accountants, *Measuring the Cost of Capacity,* pp. 46–47.

Questions

3-1   Why aren't actual overhead costs traced to jobs just as direct materials and direct labor costs are traced to jobs?

3-2   When would job-order costing be used instead of process costing?

3-3   What is the purpose of the job cost sheet in a job-order costing system?

3-4   What is a predetermined overhead rate, and how is it computed?

3-5   Explain how a sales order, a production order, a materials requisition form, and a labor time ticket are involved in producing and costing products.

3-6   Explain why some production costs must be assigned to products through an allocation process.

3-7   Why do companies use predetermined overhead rates rather than actual manufacturing overhead costs to apply overhead to jobs?

3-8   What factors should be considered in selecting a base to be used in computing the predetermined overhead rate?

3-9   If a company fully allocates all of its overhead costs to jobs, does this guarantee that a profit will be earned for the period?

3-10   What account is credited when overhead cost is applied to Work in Process? Would you expect the amount applied for a period to equal the actual overhead costs of the period? Why or why not?

3-11   What is underapplied overhead? Overapplied overhead? What disposition is made of these amounts at the end of the period?

3-12   Provide two reasons why overhead might be underapplied in a given year.

3-13   What adjustment is made for underapplied overhead on the schedule of cost of goods sold? What adjustment is made for overapplied overhead?

3-14   Sigma Company applies overhead cost to jobs on the basis of direct labor cost. Job A, which was started and completed during the current period, shows charges of $5,000 for direct materials, $8,000 for direct labor, and $6,000 for overhead on its job cost sheet. Job B, which is still in process at year-end, shows charges of $2,500 for direct materials and $4,000 for direct labor. Should any overhead cost be added to Job B at year-end? Explain.

3-15   A company assigns overhead cost to completed jobs on the basis of 125% of direct labor cost. The job cost sheet for Job 313 shows that $10,000 in direct materials has been used on the job and that $12,000 in direct labor cost has been incurred. If 1,000 units were produced in Job 313, what is the unit product cost?

3-16   What is a plantwide overhead rate? Why are multiple overhead rates, rather than a plantwide overhead rate, used in some companies?

3-17   What happens to overhead rates based on direct labor when automated equipment replaces direct labor?

3-18   (Appendix 3A) If the plant is operated at less than capacity and the predetermined overhead rate is based on the estimated total units in the allocation base at capacity, will overhead ordinarily be overapplied or underapplied?

3-19   (Appendix 3A) Rather than netting underapplied overhead against Cost of Goods Sold or Cost of Goods Sold and ending inventories, some critics suggest an alternative way to disclose underapplied overhead. What is this alternative method?

Exercises

EXERCISE 3-1 Process Costing and Job-Order Costing [LO1]
Which method of determining product costs, job-order costing or process costing, would be more appropriate in each of the following situations?
a.   An Elmer's glue factory.
b.   A textbook publisher such as McGraw-Hill.
c.   An Exxon oil refinery.
d.   A facility that makes Minute Maid frozen orange juice.
e.   A Scott paper mill.

f.   A custom home builder.
g.   A shop that customizes vans.
h.   A manufacturer of specialty chemicals.
i.   An auto repair shop.
j.   A Firestone tire manufacturing plant.
k.   An advertising agency.
l.   A law office.

EXERCISE 3-2 Job-Order Costing Documents [LO2]

Cycle Gear Corporation has incurred the following costs on job number W456, an order for 20 special sprockets to be delivered at the end of next month.

Direct materials:
   On April 10, requisition number 15673 was issued for 20 titanium blanks to be used in the special order. The blanks cost $15.00 each.
   On April 11, requisition number 15678 was issued for 480 hardened nibs also to be used in the special order. The nibs cost $1.25 each.

Direct labor:
   On April 12, Jamie Unser worked from 11:00 AM until 2:45 PM on Job W456. He is paid $9.60 per hour.
   On April 18, Melissa Chan worked from 8:15 AM until 11:30 AM on Job W456. She is paid $12.20 per hour.

Required:
1.   On what documents would these costs be recorded?
2.   How much cost should have been recorded on each of the documents for Job W456?

EXERCISE 3-3 Compute the Predetermined Overhead Rate [LO3]

Harris Fabrics computes its predetermined overhead rate annually on the basis of direct labor hours. At the beginning of the year it estimated that its total manufacturing overhead would be $134,000 and the total direct labor would be 20,000 hours. Its actual total manufacturing overhead for the year was $123,900 and its actual total direct labor was 21,000 hours.

Required:
Compute the company's predetermined overhead rate for the year.

EXERCISE 3-4 Prepare Journal Entries [LO4]

Larned Corporation recorded the following transactions for the just completed month.
a. $80,000 in raw materials were purchased on account.
b. $71,000 in raw materials were requisitioned for use in production. Of this amount, $62,000 was for direct materials and the remainder was for indirect materials.
c.   Total labor wages of $112,000 were incurred. Of this amount, $101,000 was for direct labor and the remainder was for indirect labor.
d.   Additional manufacturing overhead costs of $175,000 were incurred.

Required:
Record the above transactions in journal entries.

EXERCISE 3-5 Apply Overhead [LO5]

Luthan Company uses a predetermined overhead rate of $23.40 per direct labor-hour. This predetermined rate was based on 11,000 estimated direct labor-hours and $257,400 of estimated total manufacturing overhead.

   The company incurred actual total manufacturing overhead costs of $249,000 and 10,800 total direct labor-hours during the period.

Required:
Determine the amount of manufacturing overhead that would have been applied to units of product during the period.

EXERCISE 3-6 Applying Overhead; Cost of Goods Manufactured [LO5, LO6, LO8]

The following cost data relate to the manufacturing activities of Chang Company during the just completed year:

Manufacturing overhead costs incurred:	
Indirect materials...	$15,000
Indirect labor..	130,000
Property taxes, factory	8,000
Utilities, factory	70,000
Depreciation, factory...	240,000
Insurance, factory	10,000
Total actual manufacturing overhead costs incurred.........	$473,000
Other costs incurred:	
Purchases of raw materials (both direct and indirect)........	$400,000
Direct labor cost	$60,000
Inventories:	
Raw materials, beginning	$20,000
Raw materials, ending	$30,000
Work in process, beginning..................................	$40,000
Work in process, ending	$70,000

The company uses a predetermined overhead rate to apply overhead cost to production. The rate for the year was $25 per machine-hour. A total of 19,400 machine-hours was recorded for the year.

Required:
1. Compute the amount of under- or overapplied overhead cost for the year.
2. Prepare a schedule of cost of goods manufactured for the year.

EXERCISE 3-7 Prepare T-Accounts [LO7, LO8]

Jurvin Enterprises recorded the following transactions for the just completed month. The company had no beginning inventories.
a. $94,000 in raw materials were purchased for cash.
b. $89,000 in raw materials were requisitioned for use in production. Of this amount, $78,000 was for direct materials and the remainder was for indirect materials.
c. Total labor wages of $132,000 were incurred and paid. Of this amount, $112,000 was for direct labor and the remainder was for indirect labor.
d. Additional manufacturing overhead costs of $143,000 were incurred and paid.
e. Manufacturing overhead costs of $152,000 were applied to jobs using the company's predetermined overhead rate.
f. All of the jobs in progress at the end of the month were completed and shipped to customers.
g. The underapplied or overapplied overhead for the period was closed out to Cost of Goods Sold.

Required:
1. Post the above transactions to T-accounts.
2. Determine the cost of goods sold for the period.

EXERCISE 3-8 Under- and Overapplied Overhead [LO8]

Osborn Manufacturing uses a predetermined overhead rate of $18.20 per direct labor-hour. This predetermined rate was based on 12,000 estimated direct labor-hours and $218,400 of estimated total manufacturing overhead.

The company incurred actual total manufacturing overhead costs of $215,000 and 11,500 total direct labor-hours during the period.

Required:
1. Determine the amount of underapplied or overapplied manufacturing overhead for the period.
2. Assuming that the entire amount of the underapplied or overapplied overhead is closed out to Cost of Goods Sold, what would be the effect of the underapplied or overapplied overhead on the company's gross margin for the period?

EXERCISE 3-9 Applying Overhead in a Service Company [LO2, LO3, LO5]

Leeds Architectural Consultants began operations on January 2. The following activity was recorded in the company's Work in Process account for the first month of operations:

Work in Process

Costs of subcontracted work	230,000	To completed projects	390,000
Direct staff costs	75,000		
Studio overhead	120,000		

Leeds Architectural Consultants is a service firm, so the names of the accounts it uses are different from the names used in manufacturing firms. Costs of Subcontracted Work is comparable to Direct Materials; Direct Staff Costs is the same as Direct Labor; Studio Overhead is the same as Manufacturing Overhead; and Completed Projects is the same as Finished Goods. Apart from the difference in terms, the accounting methods used by the company are identical to the methods used by manufacturing companies.

Leeds Architectural Consultants uses a job-order costing system and applies studio overhead to Work in Process on the basis of direct staff costs. At the end of January, only one job was still in process. This job (Lexington Gardens Project) had been charged with $6,500 in direct staff costs.

Required:
1. Compute the predetermined overhead rate that was in use during January.
2. Complete the following job cost sheet for the partially completed Lexington Gardens Project.

Job Cost Sheet—Lexington Gardens Project As of January 31	
Costs of subcontracted work	$?
Direct staff costs	?
Studio overhead	?
Total cost to January 31	$?

EXERCISE 3-10 Journal Entries and T-accounts [LO4, LO5, LO7]

The Polaris Company uses a job-order costing system. The following data relate to October, the first month of the company's fiscal year.
a. Raw materials purchased on account, $210,000.
b. Raw materials issued to production, $190,000 ($178,000 direct materials and $12,000 indirect materials).
c. Direct labor cost incurred, $90,000; indirect labor cost incurred, $110,000.
d. Depreciation recorded on factory equipment, $40,000.
e. Other manufacturing overhead costs incurred during October, $70,000 (credit Accounts Payable).
f. The company applies manufacturing overhead cost to production on the basis of $8 per machine-hour. There were 30,000 machine-hours recorded for October.
g. Production orders costing $520,000 according to their job cost sheets were completed during October and transferred to Finished Goods.
h. Production orders that had cost $480,000 to complete according to their job cost sheets were shipped to customers during the month. These goods were sold on account at 25% above cost.

Required:
1. Prepare journal entries to record the information given above.
2. Prepare T-accounts for Manufacturing Overhead and Work in Process. Post the relevant information above to each account. Compute the ending balance in each account, assuming that Work in Process has a beginning balance of $42,000.

EXERCISE 3-11 Applying Overhead in a Service Company; Journal Entries [LO4, LO5, LO8]

Vista Landscaping uses a job-order costing system to track the costs of its landscaping projects. The company provides garden design and installation services for its clients. The table below provides data concerning the three landscaping projects that were in progress during April. There was no work in process at the beginning of April.

	Project		
	Harris	Chan	James
Designer-hours............	120	100	90
Direct materials cost........	$4,500	$3,700	$1,400
Direct labor cost	$9,600	$8,000	$7,200

Actual overhead costs were $30,000 for April. Overhead costs are applied to projects on the basis of designer-hours since most of the overhead is related to the costs of the garden design studio. The predetermined overhead rate is $90 per designer-hour. The Harris and Chan projects were completed in April; the James project was not completed by the end of the month.

Required:
1. Compute the amount of overhead cost that would have been charged to each project during April.
2. Prepare a journal entry showing the completion of the Harris and Chan projects and the transfer of costs to the Completed Projects (i.e., Finished Goods) account.
3. What is the balance in the Work in Process account at the end of the month?
4. What is the balance in the Overhead account at the end of the month? What is this balance called?

EXERCISE 3-12 Varying Predetermined Overhead Rates [LO3, LO5]
Kingsport Containers, Ltd, of the Bahamas experiences wide variation in demand for the 200-liter steel drums it fabricates. The leakproof, rustproof steel drums have a variety of uses from storing liquids and bulk materials to serving as makeshift musical instruments. The drums are made to order and are painted according to the customer's specifications—often in bright patterns and designs. The company is well known for the artwork that appears on its drums. Unit product costs are computed on a quarterly basis by dividing each quarter's manufacturing costs (materials, labor, and overhead) by the quarter's production in units. The company's estimated costs, by quarter, for the coming year follow:

	Quarter			
	First	Second	Third	Fourth
Direct materials	$240,000	$120,000	$ 60,000	$180,000
Direct labor	128,000	64,000	32,000	96,000
Manufacturing overhead	300,000	220,000	180,000	260,000
Total manufacturing costs	$668,000	$404,000	$272,000	$536,000
Number of units to be produced........	80,000	40,000	20,000	60,000
Estimated unit product cost	$8.35	$10.10	$13.60	$8.93

Management finds the variation in unit costs to be confusing and difficult to work with. It has been suggested that the problem lies with manufacturing overhead, since it is the largest element of cost. Accordingly, you have been asked to find a more appropriate way of assigning manufacturing overhead cost to units of product. After some analysis, you have determined that the company's overhead costs are mostly fixed and therefore show little sensitivity to changes in the level of production.

Required:
1. The company uses a job-order costing system. How would you recommend that manufacturing overhead cost be assigned to production? Be specific, and show computations.
2. Recompute the company's unit product costs in accordance with your recommendations in (1) above.

EXERCISE 3-13 Applying Overhead; Journal Entries; Disposition of Underapplied or Overapplied Overhead [LO4, LO7, LO8]

The following information is taken from the accounts of Latta Company. The entries in the T-accounts are summaries of the transactions that affected those accounts during the year.

	Manufacturing Overhead		
(a)	460,000	(b)	390,000
Bal.	70,000		

	Work in Process		
Bal.	15,000	(c)	710,000
	260,000		
	85,000		
(b)	390,000		
Bal.	40,000		

	Finished Goods		
Bal.	50,000	(d)	640,000
(c)	710,000		
Bal.	120,000		

	Cost of Goods Sold		
(d)	640,000		

The overhead that had been applied to production during the year is distributed among the ending balances in the accounts as follows:

Work in Process, ending	$ 19,500
Finished Goods, ending	58,500
Cost of Goods Sold	312,200
Overhead applied	$390,000

For example, of the $40,000 ending balance in Work in Process, $19,500 was overhead that had been applied during the year.

Required:
1. Identify reasons for entries (a) through (d).
2. Assume that the company closes any balance in the Manufacturing Overhead account directly to Cost of Goods Sold. Prepare the necessary journal entry.
3. Assume instead that the company allocates any balance in the Manufacturing Overhead account to the other accounts in proportion to the overhead applied in their ending balances. Prepare the necessary journal entry, with supporting computations.

EXERCISE 3-14 (Appendix 3A) Overhead Rates and Capacity Issues [LO3, LO5, LO8, LO9]

Security Pension Services helps clients to set up and administer pension plans that are in compliance with tax laws and regulatory requirements. The firm uses a job-order costing system in which overhead is applied to clients' accounts on the basis of professional staff hours charged to the accounts. Data concerning two recent years appear below:

	2008	2007
Estimated professional staff hours to be charged to clients' accounts	4,600	4,500
Estimated overhead cost	$310,500	$310,500
Professional staff hours available	6,000	6,000

"Professional staff hours available" is a measure of the capacity of the firm. Any hours available that are not charged to clients' accounts represent unused capacity.

Required:
1. Marta Brinksi is an established client whose pension plan was set up many years ago. In both 2007 and 2008, only 2.5 hours of professional staff time were charged to Ms. Brinksi's account. If the company bases its predetermined overhead rate on the estimated overhead cost and the estimated professional staff hours to be charged to clients, how much overhead cost would have been applied to Ms. Brinksi's account in 2007? In 2008?

2. Suppose that the company bases its predetermined overhead rate on the estimated overhead cost and the estimated professional staff hours to be charged to clients as in (1) above. Also suppose that the actual professional staff hours charged to clients' accounts and the actual overhead costs turn out to be exactly as estimated in both years. By how much would the overhead be under- or overapplied in 2007? In 2008?

3. Refer back to the data concerning Ms. Brinksi in (1) above. If the company bases its predetermined overhead rate on the estimated overhead cost and the *professional staff hours available,* how much overhead cost would have been applied to Ms. Brinksi's account in 2007? In 2008?

4. Suppose that the company bases its predetermined overhead rate on the estimated overhead cost and the professional staff hours available as in (3) above. Also suppose that the actual professional staff hours charged to clients' accounts and the actual overhead costs turn out to be exactly as estimated in both years. By how much would the overhead be under- or overapplied in 2007? In 2008?

EXERCISE 3-15 Departmental Overhead Rates [LO2, LO3, LO5]
White Company has two departments, Cutting and Finishing. The company uses a job-order cost system and computes a predetermined overhead rate in each department. The Cutting Department bases its rate on machine-hours, and the Finishing Department bases its rate on direct labor cost. At the beginning of the year, the company made the following estimates:

	Department	
	Cutting	Finishing
Direct labor-hours	6,000	30,000
Machine-hours	48,000	5,000
Manufacturing overhead cost	$360,000	$486,000
Direct labor cost	$50,000	$270,000

Required:
1. Compute the predetermined overhead rate to be used in each department.
2. Assume that the overhead rates that you computed in (1) above are in effect. The job cost sheet for Job 203, which was started and completed during the year, showed the following:

	Department	
	Cutting	Finishing
Direct labor-hours	6	20
Machine-hours	80	4
Materials requisitioned	$500	$310
Direct labor cost	$70	$150

    Compute the total overhead cost applied to Job 203.
3. Would you expect substantially different amounts of overhead cost to be assigned to some jobs if the company used a plantwide overhead rate based on direct labor cost, rather than using departmental rates? Explain. No computations are necessary.

EXERCISE 3-16 Applying Overhead; T-accounts; Journal Entries [LO3, LO4, LO5, LO7, LO8]
Harwood Company is a manufacturer that operates a job-order costing system. Overhead costs are applied to jobs on the basis of machine-hours. At the beginning of the year, management estimated that the company would incur $192,000 in manufacturing overhead costs and work 80,000 machine-hours.

Required:
1. Compute the company's predetermined overhead rate.
2. Assume that during the year the company works only 75,000 machine-hours and incurs the following costs in the Manufacturing Overhead and Work in Process accounts:

Manufacturing Overhead				Work in Process		
(Maintenance)	21,000		?	(Direct materials)	710,000	
(Indirect materials)	8,000			(Direct labor)	90,000	
(Indirect labor)	60,000			(Overhead)	?	
(Utilities)	32,000					
(Insurance)	7,000					
(Depreciation)	56,000					

Copy the data in the T-accounts above onto your answer sheet. Compute the amount of overhead cost that would be applied to Work in Process for the year and make the entry in your T-accounts.

3. Compute the amount of under- or overapplied overhead for the year and show the balance in your Manufacturing Overhead T-account. Prepare a journal entry to close out the balance in this account to Cost of Goods Sold.

4. Explain why the manufacturing overhead was under- or overapplied for the year.

EXERCISE 3-17 Applying Overhead; Journal Entries; T-accounts [LO3, LO4, LO5, LO7]

Dillon Products manufactures various machined parts to customer specifications. The company uses a job-order costing system and applies overhead cost to jobs on the basis of machine-hours. At the beginning of the year, it was estimated that the company would work 240,000 machine-hours and incur $4,800,000 in manufacturing overhead costs.

The company spent the entire month of January working on a large order for 16,000 custom-made machined parts. The company had no work in process at the beginning of January. Cost data relating to January follow:

a. Raw materials purchased on account, $325,000.
b. Raw materials requisitioned for production, $290,000 (80% direct materials and 20% indirect materials).
c. Labor cost incurred in the factory, $180,000 (one-third direct labor and two-thirds indirect labor).
d. Depreciation recorded on factory equipment, $75,000.
e. Other manufacturing overhead costs incurred, $62,000 (credit Accounts Payable).
f. Manufacturing overhead cost was applied to production on the basis of 15,000 machine-hours actually worked during the month.
g. The completed job was moved into the finished goods warehouse on January 31 to await delivery to the customer. (In computing the dollar amount for this entry, remember that the cost of a completed job consists of direct materials, direct labor, and *applied* overhead.)

Required:
1. Prepare journal entries to record items (a) through (f) above [ignore item (g) for the moment].
2. Prepare T-accounts for Manufacturing Overhead and Work in Process. Post the relevant items from your journal entries to these T-accounts.
3. Prepare a journal entry for item (g) above.
4. Compute the unit product cost that will appear on the job cost sheet.

Problems

PROBLEM 3-18 Comprehensive Problem [LO3, LO4, LO5, LO7, LO8]

Gold Nest Company of Guandong, China, is a family-owned enterprise that makes birdcages for the South China market. A popular pastime among older Chinese men is to take their pet birds on daily excursions to teahouses and public parks where they meet with other bird owners to talk and play mahjong. A great deal of attention is lavished on these birds, and the birdcages are often elaborately constructed from exotic woods and contain porcelain feeding bowls and silver roosts. Gold Nest Company makes a broad range of birdcages that it sells through an extensive network of street vendors who receive commissions on their sales. The Chinese currency is the renminbi, which is denoted by Rmb. All of the company's transactions with customers, employees, and suppliers are conducted in cash; there is no credit.

The company uses a job-order costing system in which overhead is applied to jobs on the basis of direct labor cost. At the beginning of the year, it was estimated that the total direct labor cost for the year would be Rmb200,000 and the total manufacturing overhead cost would be Rmb330,000. At the beginning of the year, the inventory balances were as follows:

Raw Materials	Rmb25,000
Work in Process........	Rmb10,000
Finished Goods	Rmb40,000

During the year, the following transactions were completed:
a. Raw materials purchased for cash, Rmb275,000.
b. Raw materials requisitioned for use in production, Rmb280,000 (materials costing Rmb220,000 were charged directly to jobs; the remaining materials were indirect).
c. Costs for employee services were incurred as follows:

Direct labor	Rmb180,000
Indirect labor	Rmb72,000
Sales commissions	Rmb63,000
Administrative salaries........	Rmb90,000

d. Rent for the year was Rmb18,000 (Rmb13,000 of this amount related to factory operations, and the remainder related to selling and administrative activities).
e. Utility costs incurred in the factory, Rmb57,000.
f. Advertising costs incurred, Rmb140,000.
g. Depreciation recorded on equipment, Rmb100,000. (Rmb88,000 of this amount was on equipment used in factory operations; the remaining Rmb12,000 was on equipment used in selling and administrative activities.)
h. Manufacturing overhead cost was applied to jobs, Rmb ___?___.
i. Goods that had cost Rmb675,000 to manufacture according to their job cost sheets were completed during the year.
j. Sales for the year totaled Rmb1,250,000. The total cost to manufacture these goods according to their job cost sheets was Rmb700,000.

Required:
1. Prepare journal entries to record the transactions for the year.
2. Prepare T-accounts for inventories, Manufacturing Overhead, and Cost of Goods Sold. Post relevant data from your journal entries to these T-accounts (don't forget to enter the beginning balances in your inventory accounts). Compute an ending balance in each account.
3. Is Manufacturing Overhead underapplied or overapplied for the year? Prepare a journal entry to close any balance in the Manufacturing Overhead account to Cost of Goods Sold.
4. Prepare an income statement for the year. (Do not prepare a schedule of cost of goods manufactured; all of the information needed for the income statement is available in the journal entries and T-accounts you have prepared.)

PROBLEM 3-19 Journal Entries; T-Accounts; Cost Flows [LO4, LO5, LO7]
Almeda Products, Inc., uses a job-order costing system. The company's inventory balances on April 1, the start of its fiscal year, were as follows:

Raw materials	$32,000
Work in process	$20,000
Finished goods	$48,000

During the year, the following transactions were completed:
a. Raw materials were purchased on account, $170,000.
b. Raw materials were issued from the storeroom for use in production, $180,000 (80% direct and 20% indirect).
c. Employee salaries and wages were accrued as follows: direct labor, $200,000; indirect labor, $82,000; and selling and administrative salaries, $90,000.
d. Utility costs were incurred in the factory, $65,000.
e. Advertising costs were incurred, $100,000.

f.   Prepaid insurance expired during the year, $20,000 (90% related to factory operations, and 10% related to selling and administrative activities).

g.   Depreciation was recorded, $180,000 (85% related to factory assets, and 15% related to selling and administrative assets).

h.   Manufacturing overhead was applied to jobs at the rate of 175% of direct labor cost.

i.   Goods that cost $700,000 to manufacture according to their job cost sheets were transferred to the finished goods warehouse.

j.   Sales for the year totaled $1,000,000 and were all on account. The total cost to manufacture these goods according to their job cost sheets was $720,000.

Required:

1.   Prepare journal entries to record the transactions for the year.

2.   Prepare T-accounts for Raw Materials, Work in Process, Finished Goods, Manufacturing Overhead, and Cost of Goods Sold. Post the appropriate parts of your journal entries to these T-accounts. Compute the ending balance in each account. (Don't forget to enter the beginning balances in the inventory accounts.)

3.   Is Manufacturing Overhead underapplied or overapplied for the year? Prepare a journal entry to close this balance to Cost of Goods Sold.

4.   Prepare an income statement for the year. (Do not prepare a schedule of cost of goods manufactured; all of the information needed for the income statement is available in the journal entries and T-accounts you have prepared.)

PROBLEM 3-20 T-accounts; Applying Overhead [LO5, LO7, LO8]
Hudson Company's trial balance as of January 1, the beginning of its fiscal year, is given below:

Cash..........................	$ 7,000	
Accounts Receivable	18,000	
Raw Materials	9,000	
Work in Process...............	20,000	
Finished Goods	32,000	
Prepaid Insurance	4,000	
Plant and Equipment	210,000	
Accumulated Depreciation		$ 53,000
Accounts Payable		38,000
Capital Stock		160,000
Retained Earnings.............		49,000
Total	$300,000	$300,000

Hudson Company is a manufacturer that uses a job-order costing system. During the year, the following transactions took place:

a.   Raw materials purchased on account, $40,000.

b.   Raw materials were requisitioned for use in production, $38,000 (85% direct and 15% indirect).

c.   Factory utility costs incurred, $19,100.

d.   Depreciation was recorded on plant and equipment, $36,000. Three-fourths of the depreciation related to factory equipment, and the remainder related to selling and administrative equipment.

e.   Advertising expense incurred, $48,000.

f.   Costs for salaries and wages were incurred as follows:

Direct labor	$45,000
Indirect labor	$10,000
Administrative salaries	$30,000

g.   Prepaid insurance expired during the year, $3,000 (80% related to factory operations, and 20% related to selling and administrative activities).

h.   Miscellaneous selling and administrative expenses incurred, $9,500.

i.   Manufacturing overhead was applied to production. The company applies overhead on the basis of $8 per machine-hour; 7,500 machine-hours were recorded for the year.

j.   Goods that cost $140,000 to manufacture according to their job cost sheets were transferred to the finished goods warehouse.

k.   Sales for the year totaled $250,000 and were all on account. The total cost to manufacture these goods according to their job cost sheets was $130,000.

l.   Collections from customers during the year totaled $245,000.

m.   Payments to suppliers on account during the year, $150,000; payments to employees for salaries and wages, $84,000.

Required:

1.   Prepare a T-account for each account in the company's trial balance and enter the opening balances shown above.

2.   Record the transactions above directly into the T-accounts. Prepare new T-accounts as needed. Key your entries to the letters (a) through (m) above. Find the ending balance in each account.

3.   Is manufacturing overhead underapplied or overapplied for the year? Make an entry in the T-accounts to close any balance in the Manufacturing Overhead account to Cost of Goods Sold.

4.   Prepare an income statement for the year. (Do not prepare a schedule of cost of goods manufactured; all of the information needed for the income statement is available in the T-accounts.)

PROBLEM 3-21 Cost Flows; T-Accounts; Income Statement [LO3, LO5, LO6, LO7, LO8]
Supreme Videos, Inc., produces short musical videos for sale to retail outlets. The company's balance sheet accounts as of January 1, the beginning of its fiscal year, are given below.

Supreme Videos, Inc. Balance Sheet January 1		
Assets		
Current assets:		
Cash		$ 63,000
Accounts receivable.		102,000
Inventories:		
Raw materials (film, costumes)	$ 30,000	
Work in process	45,000	
Finished videos awaiting sale	81,000	156,000
Prepaid insurance		9,000
Total current assets		330,000
Studio and equipment	730,000	
Less accumulated depreciation	210,000	520,000
Total assets		$850,000
Liabilities and Stockholders' Equity		
Accounts payable		$160,000
Capital stock	$420,000	
Retained earnings.	270,000	690,000
Total liabilities and stockholders' equity		$850,000

Since the videos differ in length and in complexity of production, the company uses a job-order costing system to determine the cost of each video produced. Studio (manufacturing) overhead is charged to videos on the basis of camera-hours of activity. At the beginning of the year, the company estimated that it would work 7,000 camera-hours and incur $280,000 in studio overhead cost. The following transactions were recorded for the year:

a.   Film, costumes, and similar raw materials purchased on account, $185,000.

b.   Film, costumes, and other raw materials issued to production, $200,000 (85% of this material was considered direct to the videos in production, and the other 15% was considered indirect).

c.   Utility costs incurred in the production studio, $72,000.

d.   Depreciation recorded on the studio, cameras, and other equipment, $84,000. Three-fourths of this depreciation related to actual production of the videos, and the remainder related to equipment used in marketing and administration.

e. Advertising expense incurred, $130,000.

f. Costs for salaries and wages were incurred as follows:

Direct labor (actors and directors)	$ 82,000
Indirect labor (carpenters to build sets, costume designers, and so forth)	$110,000
Administrative salaries	$ 95,000

g. Prepaid insurance expired during the year, $7,000 (80% related to production of videos, and 20% related to marketing and administrative activities).

h. Miscellaneous marketing and administrative expenses incurred, $8,600.

i. Studio (manufacturing) overhead was applied to videos in production. The company recorded 7,250 camera-hours of activity during the year.

j. Videos that cost $550,000 to produce according to their job cost sheets were transferred to the finished videos warehouse to await sale and shipment.

k. Sales for the year totaled $925,000 and were all on account. The total cost to produce these videos according to their job cost sheets was $600,000.

l. Collections from customers during the year totaled $850,000.

m. Payments to suppliers on account during the year, $500,000; payments to employees for salaries and wages, $285,000.

Required:

1. Prepare a T-account for each account on the company's balance sheet and enter the beginning balances.

2. Record the transactions directly into the T-accounts. Prepare new T-accounts as needed. Key your entries to the letters (a) through (m) above. Find the ending balance in each account.

3. Is the Studio (manufacturing) Overhead account underapplied or overapplied for the year? Make an entry in the T-accounts to close any balance in the Studio Overhead account to Cost of Goods Sold.

4. Prepare an income statement for the year. (Do not prepare a schedule of cost of goods manufactured; all of the information needed for the income statement is available in the T-accounts.)

PROBLEM 3-22 T-accounts; Overhead Rates; Journal Entries [LO2, LO3, LO4, LO5, LO7]

AOZT Volzhskije Motory of St. Petersburg, Russia, makes marine motors for vessels ranging in size from harbor tugs to open-water icebreakers. (The Russian currency is the ruble, which is denoted by RUR. All currency amounts below are in thousands of RUR.)

The company uses a job-order costing system. Only three jobs—Job 208, Job 209, and Job 210—were worked on during May and June. Job 208 was completed on June 20; the other two jobs were uncompleted on June 30. Job cost sheets on the three jobs are given below:

	Job Cost Sheet		
	Job 208	Job 209	Job 210
May costs incurred:*			
Direct materials.	RUR9,500	RUR5,100	RUR —
Direct labor	RUR8,000	RUR3,000	RUR —
Manufacturing overhead.	RUR11,200	RUR4,200	RUR —
June costs incurred:			
Direct materials.	RUR —	RUR6,000	RUR7,200
Direct labor	RUR4,000	RUR7,500	RUR8,500
Manufacturing overhead.	RUR ?	RUR ?	RUR ?

*Jobs 208 and 209 were started during May.

The following additional information is available:

a. Manufacturing overhead is applied to jobs on the basis of direct labor cost.

b. Balances in the inventory accounts at May 31 were:

Raw Materials.	RUR30,000
Work in Process	RUR?
Finished Goods	RUR50,000

Required:

1. Prepare T-accounts for Raw Materials, Work in Process, Finished Goods, and Manufacturing Overhead. Enter the May 31 balances given above; in the case of Work in Process, compute the May 31 balance and enter it into the Work in Process T-account.

2. Prepare journal entries for *June* as follows:

    a. Prepare an entry to record the issue of materials into production and post the entry to appropriate T-accounts. (In the case of direct materials, it is not necessary to make a separate entry for each job.) Indirect materials used during June totaled RUR3,600.

    b. Prepare an entry to record the incurrence of labor cost and post the entry to appropriate T-accounts. (In the case of direct labor cost, it is not necessary to make a separate entry for each job.) Indirect labor cost totaled RUR7,000 for June.

    c. Prepare an entry to record the incurrence of RUR19,400 in various actual manufacturing overhead costs for June. (Credit Accounts Payable.) Post this entry to the appropriate T-accounts.

3. What apparent predetermined overhead rate does the company use to assign overhead cost to jobs? Using this rate, prepare a journal entry to record the application of overhead cost to jobs for June (it is not necessary to make a separate entry for each job). Post this entry to appropriate T-accounts.

4. As stated earlier, Job 208 was completed during June. Prepare a journal entry to show the transfer of this job off of the production line and into the finished goods warehouse. Post the entry to appropriate T-accounts.

5. Determine the balance at June 30 in the Work in Process inventory account. How much of this balance consists of costs charged to Job 209? To Job 210?

PROBLEM 3-23 Multiple Departments; Overhead Rates; Under- or Overapplied Overhead [LO3, LO5, LO8]

Hobart, Evans, and Nix is a small law firm that contains 10 partners and 12 support persons. The firm employs a job-order costing system to accumulate costs chargeable to each client, and it is organized into two departments—the Research and Documents Department and the Litigation Department. The firm uses predetermined overhead rates to charge the costs of these departments to its clients. At the beginning of the year, the firm's management made the following estimates for the year:

	Department	
	Research and Documents	Litigation
Research-hours	24,000	—
Direct attorney-hours	9,000	18,000
Legal forms and supplies	$16,000	$5,000
Direct attorney cost	$450,000	$900,000
Departmental overhead cost.	$840,000	$360,000

The predetermined overhead rate in the Research and Documents Department is based on research-hours, and the rate in the Litigation Department is based on direct attorney cost.

The costs charged to each client are made up of three elements: legal forms and supplies used, direct attorney costs incurred, and an applied amount of overhead from each department in which work is performed on the case.

Case 418-3 was initiated on February 23 and completed on May 16. During this period, the following costs and time were recorded on the case:

	Department	
	Research and Documents	Litigation
Research-hours	26	—
Direct attorney-hours	7	114
Legal forms and supplies	$80	$40
Direct attorney cost.	$350	$5,700

Required:

1. Compute the predetermined overhead rate used during the year in the Research and Documents Department. Compute the rate used in the Litigation Department.
2. Using the rates you computed in (1) above, compute the total overhead cost applied to Case 418-3.
3. What would be the total cost charged to Case 418-3? Show computations by department and in total for the case.
4. At the end of the year, the firm's records revealed the following actual cost and operating data for all cases handled during the year:

	Department	
	Research and Documents	Litigation
Research-hours	26,000	—
Direct attorney-hours	8,000	15,000
Legal forms and supplies.	$19,000	$6,000
Direct attorney cost	$400,000	$750,000
Departmental overhead cost	$870,000	$315,000

Determine the amount of under- or overapplied overhead cost in each department for the year.

PROBLEM 3-24 Journal Entries; T-Accounts; Disposition of Underapplied or Overapplied Overhead
[LO3, LO4, LO5, LO7, LO8]
Film Specialties, Inc., operates a small production studio in which advertising films are made for TV and other uses. The company uses a job-order costing system to accumulate costs for each film produced. The company's trial balance as of May 1, the start of its fiscal year, is given as follows:

Cash	$ 60,000	
Accounts Receivable.	210,000	
Materials and Supplies	130,000	
Films in Process	75,000	
Finished Films.	860,000	
Prepaid Insurance.	90,000	
Studio and Equipment.	5,200,000	
Accumulated Depreciation		$1,990,000
Accounts Payable		700,000
Salaries and Wages Payable.		35,000
Capital Stock.		2,500,000
Retained Earnings		1,400,000
Total	$6,625,000	$6,625,000

Film Specialties, Inc., uses a Production Overhead account to record all transactions relating to overhead costs and applies overhead costs to jobs on the basis of camera-hours. For the current year, the company estimated that it would incur $1,350,000 in production overhead costs, and film 15,000 camera-hours. During the year, the following transactions were completed:
a. Materials and supplies purchased on account, $690,000.
b. Materials and supplies issued from the storeroom for use in production of various films, $700,000 (80% direct to the films and 20% indirect).
c. Utility costs incurred in the production studio, $90,000.
d. Costs for employee salaries and wages were incurred as follows:

Actors, directors, and camera crew	$1,300,000
Indirect labor costs of support workers	$230,000
Marketing and administrative salaries	$650,000

e. Advertising costs incurred, $800,000.

f. Prepaid insurance expired during the year, $70,000. Of this amount, $60,000 related to the operation of the production studio, and the remaining $10,000 related to the company's marketing and administrative activities.

g. Depreciation recorded for the year, $650,000 (80% represented depreciation of the production studio, cameras, and other production equipment; the remaining 20% represented depreciation of facilities and equipment used in marketing and administrative activities).

h. Rental costs incurred on various facilities and equipment used in production of films, $360,000; and rental costs incurred on equipment used in marketing and administrative activities, $40,000.

i. Production overhead was applied to jobs filmed during the year. The company recorded 16,500 camera-hours.

j. Films that cost $3,400,000 to produce according to their job cost sheets were completed during the year. The films were transferred to the finished films storeroom to await delivery to customers.

k. Sales of films for the year (all on account) totaled $6,000,000. The total cost to produce these films was $4,000,000 according to their job cost sheets.

l. Collections on account from customers during the year, $5,400,000.

m. Cash payments made during the year; to creditors on account, $2,500,000; and to employees for salaries and wages, $2,200,000.

Required:

1. Prepare journal entries to record the year's transactions.

2. Prepare a T-account for each account in the company's trial balance and enter the opening balances given above. Post your journal entries to the T-accounts. Prepare new T-accounts as needed. Compute the ending balance in each account.

3. Is production overhead underapplied or overapplied for the year? Prepare the necessary journal entry to close the balance in Production Overhead to Cost of Films Sold.

4. Prepare an income statement for the year. (Do not prepare a schedule of cost of goods manufactured; all of the information needed for the income statement is available in the T-accounts.)

PROBLEM 3-25 Multiple Departments; Applying Overhead [LO3, LO5, LO8]

High Desert Potteryworks makes a variety of pottery products that it sells to retailers such as Home Depot. The company uses a job-order costing system in which predetermined overhead rates are used to apply manufacturing overhead cost to jobs. The predetermined overhead rate in the Molding Department is based on machine-hours, and the rate in the Painting Department is based on direct labor cost. At the beginning of the year, the company's management made the following estimates:

	Department	
	Molding	Painting
Direct labor-hours.	12,000	60,000
Machine-hours	70,000	8,000
Direct materials cost.	$510,000	$650,000
Direct labor cost	$130,000	$420,000
Manufacturing overhead cost	$602,000	$735,000

Job 205 was started on August 1 and completed on August 10. The company's cost records show the following information concerning the job:

	Department	
	Molding	Painting
Direct labor-hours.	30	85
Machine-hours	110	20
Materials placed into production.	$470	$332
Direct labor cost	$290	$680

Required:

1. Compute the predetermined overhead rate used during the year in the Molding Department. Compute the rate used in the Painting Department.
2. Compute the total overhead cost applied to Job 205.
3. What would be the total cost recorded for Job 205? If the job contained 50 units, what would be the unit product cost?
4. At the end of the year, the records of High Desert Potteryworks revealed the following *actual* cost and operating data for all jobs worked on during the year:

	Department	
	Molding	Painting
Direct labor-hours.	10,000	62,000
Machine-hours	65,000	9,000
Direct materials cost.	$430,000	$680,000
Direct labor cost	$108,000	$436,000
Manufacturing overhead cost	$570,000	$750,000

What was the amount of under- or overapplied overhead in each department at the end of the year?

PROBLEM 3-26 (Appendix 3A) Predetermined Overhead Rate and Capacity [LO3, LO5, LO8, LO9]

Platinum Tracks, Inc., is a small audio recording studio located in Los Angeles. The company handles work for advertising agencies—primarily for radio ads—and has a few singers and bands as clients. Platinum Tracks handles all aspects of recording from editing to making a digital master from which CDs can be copied. The competition in the audio recording industry in Los Angeles has always been tough, but it has been getting even tougher over the last several years. The studio has been losing customers to newer studios that are equipped with more up-to-date equipment and that are able to offer very attractive prices and excellent service. Summary data concerning the last two years of operations follow:

	2008	2007
Estimated hours of studio service	800	1,000
Estimated studio overhead cost.	$160,000	$160,000
Actual hours of studio service provided.	500	750
Actual studio overhead cost incurred.	$160,000	$160,000
Hours of studio service at capacity	1,600	1,600

The company applies studio overhead to recording jobs on the basis of the hours of studio service provided. For example, 40 hours of studio time were required to record, edit, and master the *Verde Baja* music CD for a local Latino band. All of the studio overhead is fixed, and the actual overhead cost incurred was exactly as estimated at the beginning of the year in both 2007 and 2008.

Required:

1. Platinum Tracks computes its predetermined overhead rate at the beginning of each year based on the estimated studio overhead and the estimated hours of studio service for the year. How much overhead would have been applied to the *Verde Baja* job if it had been done in 2007? In 2008? By how much would overhead have been under- or overapplied in 2007? In 2008?
2. The president of Platinum Tracks has heard that some companies in the industry have changed to a system of computing the predetermined overhead rate at the beginning of each year based on the estimated studio overhead for the year and the hours of studio service that could be provided at capacity. He would like to know what effect this method would have on job costs. How much overhead would have been applied using this method to the *Verde Baja* job if it had been done in 2007? In 2008? By how much would overhead have been under- or overapplied in 2007 using this method? In 2008?
3. How would you interpret the under- or overapplied overhead that results from using studio hours at capacity to compute the predetermined overhead rate?
4. What fundamental business problem is Platinum Tracks facing? Which method of computing the predetermined overhead rate is likely to be more helpful in facing this problem? Explain.

PROBLEM 3-27 T-Account Analysis of Cost Flows [LO3, LO6, LO8]

Selected ledger accounts of Moore Company are given below for the just completed year:

Raw Materials			
Bal. 1/1	15,000	Credits	?
Debits	120,000		
Bal. 12/31	25,000		

Manufacturing Overhead			
Debits	230,000	Credits	?

Work in Process			
Bal. 1/1	20,000	Credits	470,000
Direct materials	90,000		
Direct labor	150,000		
Overhead	240,000		
Bal. 12/31	?		

Factory Wages Payable			
Debits	185,000	Bal. 1/1	9,000
		Credits	180,000
		Bal. 12/31	4,000

Finished Goods			
Bal. 1/1	40,000	Credits	?
Debits	?		
Bal. 12/31	60,000		

Cost of Goods Sold		
Debits	?	

Required:

1. What was the cost of raw materials put into production during the year?
2. How much of the materials in (1) above consisted of indirect materials?
3. How much of the factory labor cost for the year consisted of indirect labor?
4. What was the cost of goods manufactured for the year?
5. What was the cost of goods sold for the year (before considering under- or overapplied overhead)?
6. If overhead is applied to production on the basis of direct labor cost, what rate was in effect during the year?
7. Was manufacturing overhead under- or overapplied? By how much?
8. Compute the ending balance in the Work in Process inventory account. Assume that this balance consists entirely of goods started during the year. If $8,000 of this balance is direct labor cost, how much of it is direct materials cost? Manufacturing overhead cost?

PROBLEM 3-28 Schedule of Cost of Goods Manufactured; Overhead Analysis [LO3, LO5, LO6, LO7]

Gitano Products operates a job-order costing system and applies overhead cost to jobs on the basis of direct materials *used in production* (*not* on the basis of raw materials purchased). In computing a predetermined overhead rate at the beginning of the year, the company's estimates were: manufacturing overhead cost, $800,000; and direct materials to be used in production, $500,000. The company has provided the following data in the form of an Excel worksheet:

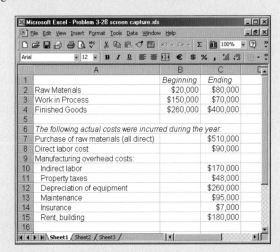

Required:

1. *a.*   Compute the predetermined overhead rate for the year.
    b.   Compute the amount of under- or overapplied overhead for the year.
2. Prepare a schedule of cost of goods manufactured for the year.
3. Compute the Cost of Goods Sold for the year. (Do not include any under- or overapplied overhead in your Cost of Goods Sold figure.) What options are available for disposing of under- or overapplied overhead?
4. Job 215 was started and completed during the year. What price would have been charged to the customer if the job required $8,500 in direct materials and $2,700 in direct labor cost and the company priced its jobs at 25% above the job's cost according to the accounting system?
5. Direct materials made up $24,000 of the $70,000 ending Work in Process inventory balance. Supply the information missing below:

Direct materials	$24,000
Direct labor.	?
Manufacturing overhead	?
Work in process inventory	$70,000

PROBLEM 3-29 Predetermined Overhead Rate; Disposition of Under- or Overapplied Overhead
[LO3, LO8]

Bieler & Cie of Altdorf, Switzerland, makes furniture using the latest automated technology. The company uses a job-order costing system and applies manufacturing overhead cost to products on the basis of machine-hours. The following estimates were used in preparing the predetermined overhead rate at the beginning of the year:

Machine-hours	75,000
Manufacturing overhead cost.	Sfr900,000

The currency in Switzerland is the Swiss franc, which is denoted by Sfr.

During the year, a glut of furniture on the market resulted in cutting back production and a buildup of furniture in the company's warehouse. The company's cost records revealed the following actual cost and operating data for the year:

Machine-hours	60,000
Manufacturing overhead cost	Sfr850,000
Inventories at year-end:	
Raw materials	Sfr30,000
Work in process (includes overhead applied of 36,000)	Sfr100,000
Finished goods (includes overhead applied of 180,000).	Sfr500,000
Cost of goods sold (includes overhead applied of 504,000).	Sfr1,400,000

Required:

1. Compute the company's predetermined overhead rate.
2. Compute the under- or overapplied overhead.
3. Assume that the company closes any under- or overapplied overhead directly to Cost of Goods Sold. Prepare the appropriate journal entry.
4. Assume that the company allocates any under- or overapplied overhead to Work in Process, Finished Goods, and Cost of Goods Sold on the basis of the amount of overhead applied that remains in each account at the end of the year. Prepare the journal entry to show the allocation for the year.
5. How much higher or lower will net operating income be if the under- or overapplied overhead is allocated rather than closed directly to Cost of Goods Sold?

PROBLEM 3-30 Journal Entries; T-Accounts; Comprehensive Problem; Financial Statements; [LO3, LO4, LO5, LO6, LO7, LO8]

Froya Fabrikker A/S of Bergen, Norway, is a small company that manufactures specialty heavy equipment for use in North Sea oil fields. (The Norwegian currency is the krone, which is denoted by Nkr.) The company uses a job-order costing system and applies manufacturing overhead cost to jobs on the basis of direct labor-hours. At the beginning of the year, the following estimates were made for the purpose of computing the predetermined overhead rate: manufacturing overhead cost, Nkr360,000; and direct labor-hours, 900.

The following transactions took place during the year (all purchases and services were acquired on account):

a. Raw materials were purchased for use in production, Nkr200,000.
b. Raw materials were requisitioned for use in production (all direct materials), Nkr185,000.
c. Utility bills were incurred, Nkr70,000 (90% related to factory operations, and the remainder related to selling and administrative activities).
d. Salary and wage costs were incurred:

Direct labor (975 hours)	Nkr230,000
Indirect labor.	Nkr90,000
Selling and administrative salaries	Nkr110,000

e. Maintenance costs were incurred in the factory, Nkr54,000.
f. Advertising costs were incurred, Nkr136,000.
g. Depreciation was recorded for the year, Nkr95,000 (80% related to factory equipment, and the remainder related to selling and administrative equipment).

h. Rental cost incurred on buildings, Nkr120,000 (85% related to factory operations, and the remainder related to selling and administrative facilities).
i. Manufacturing overhead cost was applied to jobs, Nkr ___?___ .
j. Cost of goods manufactured for the year, Nkr770,000.
k. Sales for the year (all on account) totaled Nkr1,200,000. These goods cost Nkr800,000 to manufacture according to their job cost sheets.

The balances in the inventory accounts at the beginning of the year were:

Raw Materials	Nkr30,000
Work in Process	Nkr21,000
Finished Goods	Nkr60,000

Required:

1. Prepare journal entries to record the preceding data.
2. Post your entries to T-accounts. (Don't forget to enter the beginning inventory balances above.) Determine the ending balances in the inventory accounts and in the Manufacturing Overhead account.
3. Prepare a schedule of cost of goods manufactured.
4. Prepare a journal entry to close any balance in the Manufacturing Overhead account to Cost of Goods Sold. Prepare a schedule of cost of goods sold.
5. Prepare an income statement for the year.
6. Job 412 was one of the many jobs started and completed during the year. The job required Nkr8,000 in direct materials and 39 hours of direct labor time at a total direct labor cost of Nkr9,200. The job contained only four units. If the company bills at a price 60% above the unit product cost on the job cost sheet, what price per unit would have been charged to the customer?

PROBLEM 3-31 Plantwide versus Departmental Overhead Rates; Under- or Overapplied Overhead
[LO3, LO5, LO8]

"Blast it!" said David Wilson, president of Teledex Company. "We've just lost the bid on the Koopers job by $2,000. It seems we're either too high to get the job or too low to make any money on half the jobs we bid."

Teledex Company manufactures products to customers' specifications and operates a job-order costing system. Manufacturing overhead cost is applied to jobs on the basis of direct labor cost. The following estimates were made at the beginning of the year:

	Department			
	Fabricating	Machining	Assembly	Total Plant
Direct labor..................	$200,000	$100,000	$300,000	$600,000
Manufacturing overhead........	$350,000	$400,000	$ 90,000	$840,000

Jobs require varying amounts of work in the three departments. The Koopers job, for example, would have required manufacturing costs in the three departments as follows:

	Department			
	Fabricating	Machining	Assembly	Total Plant
Direct materials...............	$3,000	$200	$1,400	$4,600
Direct labor..................	$2,800	$500	$6,200	$9,500
Manufacturing overhead........	?	?	?	?

The company uses a plantwide overhead rate to apply manufacturing overhead cost to jobs.

Required:
1. Assuming use of a plantwide overhead rate:
   a. Compute the rate for the current year.
   b. Determine the amount of manufacturing overhead cost that would have been applied to the Koopers job.
2. Suppose that instead of using a plantwide overhead rate, the company had used a separate predetermined overhead rate in each department. Under these conditions:
   a. Compute the rate for each department for the current year.
   b. Determine the amount of manufacturing overhead cost that would have been applied to the Koopers job.
3. Explain the difference between the manufacturing overhead that would have been applied to the Koopers job using the plantwide rate in question 1 (b) above and using the departmental rates in question 2 (b).
4. Assume that it is customary in the industry to bid jobs at 150% of total manufacturing cost (direct materials, direct labor, and applied overhead). What was the company's bid price on the Koopers job? What would the bid price have been if departmental overhead rates had been used to apply overhead cost?
5. At the end of the year, the company assembled the following *actual* cost data relating to all jobs worked on during the year.

	Department			
	Fabricating	Machining	Assembly	Total Plant
Direct materials...............	$190,000	$16,000	$114,000	$320,000
Direct labor..................	$210,000	$108,000	$262,000	$580,000
Manufacturing overhead........	$360,000	$420,000	$84,000	$864,000

Compute the under- or overapplied overhead for the year (a) assuming that a plantwide overhead rate is used, and (b) assuming that departmental overhead rates are used.

Cases

CASE 3-32 (Appendix 3A) Ethics; Predetermined Overhead Rate and Capacity [LO5, LO8, LO9]

Pat Miranda, the new controller of Vault Hard Drives, Inc., has just returned from a seminar on the choice of the activity level in the predetermined overhead rate. Even though the subject did not sound exciting at first, she found that there were some important ideas presented that should get a hearing at her company. After returning from the seminar, she arranged a meeting with the production manager, J. Stevens, and the assistant production manager, Marvin Washington.

Pat: I ran across an idea that I wanted to check out with both of you. It's about the way we compute predetermined overhead rates.

J.: We're all ears.

Pat: We compute the predetermined overhead rate by dividing the estimated total factory overhead for the coming year by the estimated total units produced for the coming year.

Marvin: We've been doing that as long as I've been with the company.

J.: And it has been done that way at every other company I've worked at, except at most places they divide by direct labor-hours.

Pat: We use units because it is simpler and we basically make one product with minor variations. But, there's another way to do it. Instead of dividing the estimated total factory overhead by the estimated total units produced for the coming year, we could divide by the total units produced at capacity.

Marvin: Oh, the Sales Department will love that. It will drop the costs on all of our products. They'll go wild over there cutting prices.

Pat: That is a worry, but I wanted to talk to both of you first before going over to Sales.

J.: Aren't you always going to have a lot of underapplied overhead?

Pat: That's correct, but let me show you how we would handle it. Here's an example based on our budget for next year.

Budgeted (estimated) production	160,000 units
Budgeted sales	160,000 units
Capacity	200,000 units
Selling price	$60 per unit
Variable manufacturing cost	$15 per unit
Total manufacturing overhead cost (all fixed)	$4,000,000
Administrative and selling expenses (all fixed)	$2,700,000
Beginning inventories	$0

Traditional Approach to Computation of the Predetermined Overhead

$$\frac{\text{Estimated total manufacturing overhead cost, } \$4,000,000}{\text{Estimated total units produced, } 160,000} = \$25 \text{ per unit}$$

Budgeted Income Statement		
Revenue (160,000 units × $60 per unit)		$9,600,000
Cost of goods sold:		
Variable manufacturing (160,000 units × $15 per unit)	$2,400,000	
Manufacturing overhead applied		
(160,000 units × $25 per unit)	4,000,000	6,400,000
Gross margin		3,200,000
Administrative and selling expenses		2,700,000
Net operating income		$ 500,000

**New Approach to Computation of the Predetermined Overhead Rate
Using Capacity in the Denominator**

$$\frac{\text{Estimated total manufacturing overhead cost, \$4,000,000}}{\text{Total units at capacity, 200,000}} = \$20 \text{ per unit}$$

Budgeted Income Statement		
Revenue (160,000 units × $60 per unit)		$9,600,000
Cost of goods sold:		
Variable manufacturing (160,000 units × $15 per unit).........	$2,400,000	
Manufacturing overhead applied		
(160,000 units × $20 per unit)	3,200,000	5,600,000
Gross margin		4,000,000
Cost of unused capacity [(200,000 units − 160,000 units)		
× $20 per unit]		800,000
Selling and administrative expenses		2,700,000
Net operating income		$ 500,000

J.: Whoa!! I don't think I like the looks of that "Cost of unused capacity." If that thing shows up on the income statement, someone from headquarters is likely to come down here looking for some people to lay off.

Marvin: I'm worried about something else too. What happens when sales are not up to expectations? Can we pull the "hat trick"?

Pat: I'm sorry, I don't understand.

J.: Marvin's talking about something that happens fairly regularly. When sales are down and profits look like they are going to be lower than the president told the owners they were going to be, the president comes down here and asks us to deliver some more profits.

Marvin: And we pull them out of our hat.

J.: Yeah, we just increase production until we get the profits we want.

Pat: I still don't understand. You mean you increase sales?

J.: Nope, we increase production. We're the production managers, not the sales managers.

Pat: I get it. Since you have produced more, the sales force has more units it can sell.

J.: Nope, the marketing people don't do a thing. We just build inventories and that does the trick.

Required:

In all of the questions below, assume that the predetermined overhead rate under the traditional method is $25 per unit, and under the new method it is $20 per unit. Also assume that under the traditional method any under- or overapplied overhead is taken directly to the income statement as an adjustment to Cost of Goods Sold.

1.   Suppose actual production is 160,000 units. Compute the net operating incomes that would be realized under the traditional and new methods if actual sales are 150,000 units and everything else turns out as expected.

2.   How many units would have to be produced under each of the methods in order to realize the budgeted net operating income of $500,000 if actual sales are 150,000 units and everything else turns out as expected?

3.   What effect does the new method based on capacity have on the volatility of net operating income?

4.   Will the "hat trick" be easier or harder to perform if the new method based on capacity is used?

5.   Do you think the "hat trick" is ethical?

CASE 3-33 Critical Thinking; Interpretation of Manufacturing Overhead Rates [LO3, LO5]

Kelvin Aerospace, Inc., manufactures parts such as rudder hinges for the aerospace industry. The company uses a job-order costing system with a plantwide predetermined overhead rate based on direct labor-hours. On December 16, 2007, the company's controller made a preliminary estimate of the predetermined overhead rate for the year 2008. The new rate was based on the estimated total manufacturing overhead cost of $3,402,000 and the estimated 63,000 total direct labor-hours for 2008:

$$\text{Predetermined overhead rate} = \frac{\$3,402,000}{63,000 \text{ hours}}$$

$$= \$54 \text{ per direct labor-hour}$$

This new predetermined overhead rate was communicated to top managers in a meeting on December 19. The rate did not cause any comment because it was within a few pennies of the overhead rate that had been used during 2007. One of the subjects discussed at the meeting was a proposal by the production manager to purchase an automated milling machine built by Sunghi Industries. The president of Kelvin Aerospace, Harry Arcany, agreed to meet with the sales representative from Sunghi Industries to discuss the proposal.

On the day following the meeting, Mr. Arcany met with Jasmine Chang, Sunghi Industries' sales representative. The following discussion took place:

Arcany: Wally, our production manager, asked me to meet with you since he is interested in installing an automated milling machine. Frankly, I'm skeptical. You're going to have to show me this isn't just another expensive toy for Wally's people to play with.

Chang: This is a great machine with direct bottom-line benefits. The automated milling machine has three major advantages. First, it is much faster than the manual methods you are using. It can process about twice as many parts per hour as your present milling machines. Second, it is much more flexible. There are some up-front programming costs, but once those have been incurred, almost no setup is required to run a standard operation. You just punch in the code for the standard operation, load the machine's hopper with raw material, and the machine does the rest.

Arcany: What about cost? Having twice the capacity in the milling machine area won't do us much good. That center is idle much of the time anyway.

Chang: I was getting there. The third advantage of the automated milling machine is lower cost. Wally and I looked over your present operations, and we estimated that the automated equipment would eliminate the need for about 6,000 direct labor-hours a year. What is your direct labor cost per hour?

Arcany: The wage rate in the milling area averages about $32 per hour. Fringe benefits raise that figure to about $41 per hour.

Chang: Don't forget your overhead.

Arcany: Next year the overhead rate will be $54 per hour.

Chang: So including fringe benefits and overhead, the cost per direct labor-hour is about $95.

Arcany: That's right.

Chang: Since you can save 6,000 direct labor-hours per year, the cost savings would amount to about $570,000 a year. And our 60-month lease plan would require payments of only $348,000 per year.

Arcany: That sounds like a no-brainer. When can you install the equipment?

Shortly after this meeting, Mr. Arcany informed the company's controller of the decision to lease the new equipment, which would be installed over the Christmas vacation period. The controller realized that this decision would require a recomputation of the predetermined overhead rate for the year 2008 since the decision would affect both the manufacturing overhead and the direct labor-hours for the year. After talking with both the production manager and the sales representative from Sunghi Industries, the controller discovered that in addition to the annual lease cost of $348,000, the new machine would also require a skilled technician/programmer who would have to be hired at a cost of $50,000 per year to maintain and program the equipment. Both of these costs would be included in factory overhead. There would be no other changes in total manufacturing overhead cost, which is almost entirely fixed. The controller assumed that the new machine would result in a reduction of 6,000 direct labor-hours for the year from the levels that had initially been planned.

When the revised predetermined overhead rate for the year 2008 was circulated among the company's top managers, there was considerable dismay.

Required:

1. Recompute the predetermined rate assuming that the new machine will be installed. Explain why the new predetermined overhead rate is higher (or lower) than the rate that was originally estimated for the year 2008.
2. What effect (if any) would this new rate have on the cost of jobs that do not use the new automated milling machine?

3. Why would managers be concerned about the new overhead rate?

4. After seeing the new predetermined overhead rate, the production manager admitted that he probably wouldn't be able to eliminate all of the 6,000 direct labor-hours. He had been hoping to accomplish the reduction by not replacing workers who retire or quit, but that had not been possible. As a result, the real labor savings would be only about 2,000 hours—one worker. Given this additional information, evaluate the original decision to acquire the automated milling machine from Sunghi Industries.

CASE 3-34 Ethics and the Manager [LO3, LO5, LO8]

Terri Ronsin had recently been transferred to the Home Security Systems Division of National Home Products. Shortly after taking over her new position as divisional controller, she was asked to develop the division's predetermined overhead rate for the upcoming year. The accuracy of the rate is of some importance, since it is used throughout the year and any overapplied or underapplied overhead is closed out to Cost of Goods Sold at the end of the year. National Home Products uses direct labor-hours in all of its divisions as the allocation base for manufacturing overhead.

To compute the predetermined overhead rate, Terri divided her estimate of the total manufacturing overhead for the coming year by the production manager's estimate of the total direct labor-hours for the coming year. She took her computations to the division's general manager for approval but was quite surprised when he suggested a modification in the base. Her conversation with the general manager of the Home Security Systems Division, Harry Irving, went like this:

Ronsin: Here are my calculations for next year's predetermined overhead rate. If you approve, we can enter the rate into the computer on January 1 and be up and running in the job-order costing system right away this year.

Irving: Thanks for coming up with the calculations so quickly, and they look just fine. There is, however, one slight modification I would like to see. Your estimate of the total direct labor-hours for the year is 440,000 hours. How about cutting that to about 420,000 hours?

Ronsin: I don't know if I can do that. The production manager says she will need about 440,000 direct labor-hours to meet the sales projections for the year. Besides, there are going to be over 430,000 direct labor-hours during the current year and sales are projected to be higher next year.

Irving: Teri, I know all of that. I would still like to reduce the direct labor-hours in the base to something like 420,000 hours. You probably don't know that I had an agreement with your predecessor as divisional controller to shave 5% or so off the estimated direct labor-hours every year. That way, we kept a reserve that usually resulted in a big boost to net operating income at the end of the fiscal year in December. We called it our Christmas bonus. Corporate headquarters always seemed as pleased as punch that we could pull off such a miracle at the end of the year. This system has worked well for many years, and I don't want to change it now.

Required:

1. Explain how shaving 5% off the estimated direct labor-hours in the base for the predetermined overhead rate usually results in a big boost in net operating income at the end of the fiscal year.

2. Should Terri Ronsin go along with the general manager's request to reduce the direct labor-hours in the predetermined overhead rate computation to 420,000 direct labor-hours?

RESEARCH AND APPLICATION 3-35   [LO1, LO2, LO5, LO6]

The questions in this exercise are based on Toll Brothers, Inc., one of the largest home builders in the United States. To answer the questions, you will need to download Toll Brothers' 2004 annual report (www.tollbrothers.com/homesearch/servlet/HomeSearch?app=IRannual) and Form 10-K (www.tollbrothers.com/homesearch/servlet/HomeSearch?app=IR10K). You do not need to print these documents to answer the questions.

America's Luxury Home Builder™

Required:

1. What is Toll Brothers' strategy for success in the marketplace? Does the company rely primarily on a customer intimacy, operational excellence, or product leadership customer value proposition? What evidence supports your conclusion?

2. What business risks does Toll Brothers face that may threaten the company's ability to satisfy stockholder expectations? What are some examples of control activities that the company could use to reduce these risks? (Hint: Focus on pages 10–11 of the 10-K.)

3.   Would Toll Brothers be more likely to use process costing or job-order costing? Why?

4.   What are some examples of Toll Brothers' direct material costs? Would you expect the bill of materials for each of Toll Brothers' homes to be the same or different? Why?

5.   Describe the types of direct labor costs incurred by Toll Brothers. Would Toll Brothers use employee time tickets at their home sites under construction? Why or why not?

6.   What are some examples of overhead costs that are incurred by Toll Brothers?

7.   Some companies establish prices for their products by marking up their full manufacturing cost (i.e., the sum of direct materials, direct labor, and manufacturing overhead costs). For example, a company may set prices at 150% of each product's full manufacturing cost. Does Toll Brothers price its houses using this approach?

8.   How does Toll Brothers assign manufacturing overhead costs to cost objects? From a financial reporting standpoint, why does the company need to assign manufacturing overhead costs to cost objects?

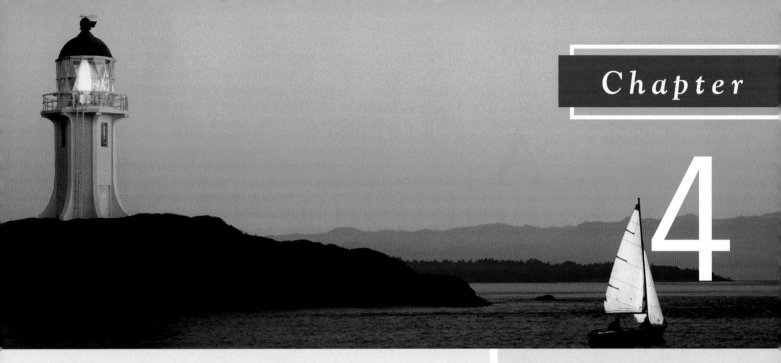

Systems Design: Process Costing

Costing the "Quicker-Picker-Upper"

If you have ever spilled milk, there is a good chance that you used Bounty paper towels to clean up the mess. Procter & Gamble (P&G) manufactures Bounty in two main processing departments—Paper Making and Paper Converting. In the Paper Making Department, wood pulp is converted into paper and then spooled into 2,000 pound rolls. In the Paper Converting Department, two of the 2,000 pound rolls of paper are simultaneously unwound into a machine that creates a two-ply paper towel that is decorated, perforated, and embossed to create texture. The large sheets of paper towels that emerge from this process are wrapped around a cylindrical cardboard core measuring eight feet in length. Once enough sheets wrap around the core, the eight foot roll is cut into individual rolls of Bounty that are sent down a conveyor to be wrapped, packed and shipped.

In this type of manufacturing environment, costs cannot be readily traced to individual rolls of Bounty; however, given the homogeneous nature of the product, the total costs incurred in the Paper Making Department can be spread uniformly across its output of 2,000 pound rolls of paper. Similarly, the total costs incurred in the Paper Converting Department (including the cost of the 2,000 pound rolls that are transferred in from the Paper Making Department) can be spread uniformly across the number of cases of Bounty produced.

P&G uses a similar costing approach for many of its products such as Tide, Crest toothpaste, and Pringles. ■

Source: Conversation with Brad Bays, formerly a Procter & Gamble financial executive.

Learning Objectives

After studying Chapter 4, you should be able to:

LO1 Record the flow of materials, labor, and overhead through a process costing system.

LO2 Compute the equivalent units of production using the weighted-average method.

LO3 Compute the cost per equivalent unit using the weighted-average method.

LO4 Assign costs to units using the weighted-average method.

LO5 (Appendix 4A) Compute the equivalent units of production using the FIFO method.

LO6 (Appendix 4A) Compute the cost per equivalent unit using the FIFO method.

LO7 (Appendix 4A) Assign costs to units using the FIFO method.

LO8 (Appendix 4B) Allocate service department costs to operating departments using the direct method.

LO9 (Appendix 4B) Allocate service department costs to operating departments using the step-down method.

A s explained in Chapter 3, job-order costing and process costing are two common methods for determining unit product costs. A job-order costing system is used when many different jobs or products are worked on each period. Examples of industries that use job-order costing include furniture manufacturing, special-order printing, shipbuilding, and many types of service organizations.

By contrast, **process costing** is most commonly used in industries that convert raw materials into homogeneous (i.e., uniform) products, such as bricks, soda, or paper, on a continuous basis. Examples of companies that would use process costing include Reynolds Aluminum (aluminum ingots), Scott Paper (toilet paper), General Mills (flour), Exxon (gasoline and lubricating oils), Coppertone (sunscreens), and Kellogg (breakfast cereals). In addition, process costing is sometimes used in companies with assembly operations. A form of process costing may also be used in utilities that produce gas, water, and electricity.

Our purpose in this chapter is to explain how product costing works in a process costing system.

Comparison of Job-Order and Process Costing

In some ways process costing is very similar to job-order costing, and in some ways it is very different. In this section, we focus on these similarities and differences to provide a foundation for the detailed discussion of process costing that follows.

Similarities between Job-Order and Process Costing

Much of what you learned in Chapter 3 about costing and cost flows applies equally well to process costing in this chapter. We are not throwing out all that we have learned about costing and starting from "scratch" with a whole new system. The similarities between job-order and process costing can be summarized as follows:

1. Both systems have the same basic purposes—to assign material, labor, and manufacturing overhead costs to products and to provide a mechanism for computing unit product costs.
2. Both systems use the same basic manufacturing accounts, including Manufacturing Overhead, Raw Materials, Work in Process, and Finished Goods.
3. The flow of costs through the manufacturing accounts is basically the same in both systems.

As can be seen from this comparison, much of the knowledge that you have already acquired about costing is applicable to a process costing system. Our task now is to refine and extend your knowledge to process costing.

Differences between Job-Order and Process Costing

There are three differences between job-order and process costing. First, process costing is used when a company produces a continuous flow of units that are indistinguishable from one another. Job-order costing is used when a company produces many different jobs that have unique production requirements. Second, under process costing, it makes no sense to try to identify materials, labor, and overhead costs with a particular customer order (as we did with job-order costing), since each order is just one of many that are filled from a continuous flow of virtually identical units from the production line. Accordingly, process costing accumulates costs by department (rather than by order) and assigns these costs uniformly to all units that pass through the department during a period. Job cost sheets (which we used for

Job-Order Costing	Process Costing
1. Many different jobs are worked on during each period, with each job having different production requirements.	1. A single product is produced either on a continuous basis or for long periods of time. All units of product are identical.
2. Costs are accumulated by individual job.	2. Costs are accumulated by department.
3. Unit costs are computed *by job* on the job cost sheet.	3. Unit costs are computed *by department.*

EXHIBIT 4–1
Differences between Job-Order and Process Costing

job-order costing) are not used to accumulate costs. Third, process costing systems compute unit costs by department. This differs from job-order costing where unit costs are computed by job on the job cost sheet. Exhibit 4–1 summarizes the differences just described.

Cost Flows in Process Costing

Before going through a detailed example of process costing, it will be helpful to see how manufacturing costs flow through a process costing system.

Processing Departments

A **processing department** is an organizational unit where work is performed on a product and where materials, labor, or overhead costs are added to the product. For example, a Nalley's potato chip factory might have three processing departments—one for preparing potatoes, one for cooking, and one for inspecting and packaging. A brick factory might have two processing departments—one for mixing and molding clay into brick form and one for firing the molded brick. Some products and services may go through a number of processing departments, while others may go through only one or two. Regardless of the number of processing departments, they all have two essential features. First, the activity in the processing department must be performed uniformly on all of the units passing through it. Second, the output of the processing department must be homogeneous; in other words, all of the units produced must be identical.

Products in a process costing environment, such as bricks or potato chips, typically flow in sequence from one department to another as in Exhibit 4–2.

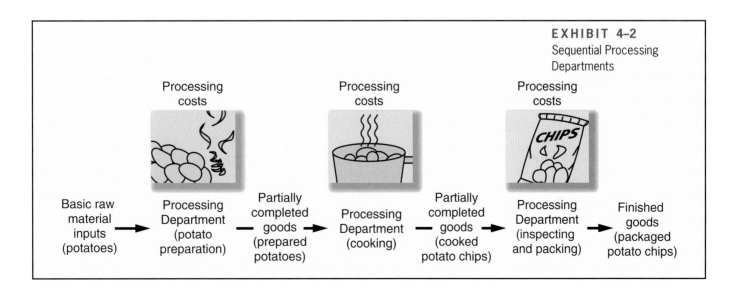

EXHIBIT 4–2
Sequential Processing Departments

Processing costs

Processing costs

Processing costs

Basic raw material inputs (potatoes) → Processing Department (potato preparation) — Partially completed goods (prepared potatoes) → Processing Department (cooking) — Partially completed goods (cooked potato chips) → Processing Department (inspecting and packing) → Finished goods (packaged potato chips)

COCA-COLA'S PROCESSING DEPARTMENTS

In 2004, the Coca-Cola Company sold more than $21 billion of products in over 200 countries. The company offers a virtual tour of its bottling process at www2.coca-cola.com/ourcompany/aboutbottling.html. Some of the key processing steps described at this website include washing and rinsing bottles, mixing and blending ingredients, filling and capping bottles, and labeling and packaging bottles. Raw material costs are added at various stages during this process. For example, sugar, filtered water, carbon dioxide, and syrup are added during the mixing and blending stage of the process. Bottle caps are added during the filling and capping step and paper labels are added during the labeling and packaging stage.

Coca-Cola's manufacturing process is well suited for process costing because it produces a continuous stream of identical bottles of soda. The material costs and conversion costs that are incurred at the various stages of the production process can be assigned to products by spreading them evenly over the total volume of production.

Sources: The Coca-Cola Company 2004 annual report and www2.coca-cola.com/ourcompany/aboutbottling.html.

The Flow of Materials, Labor, and Overhead Costs

Cost accumulation is simpler in a process costing system than in a job-order costing system. In a process costing system, instead of having to trace costs to hundreds of different jobs, costs are traced to only a few processing departments.

A T-account model of materials, labor, and overhead cost flows in a process costing system is shown in Exhibit 4–3. Several key points should be noted from this exhibit. First,

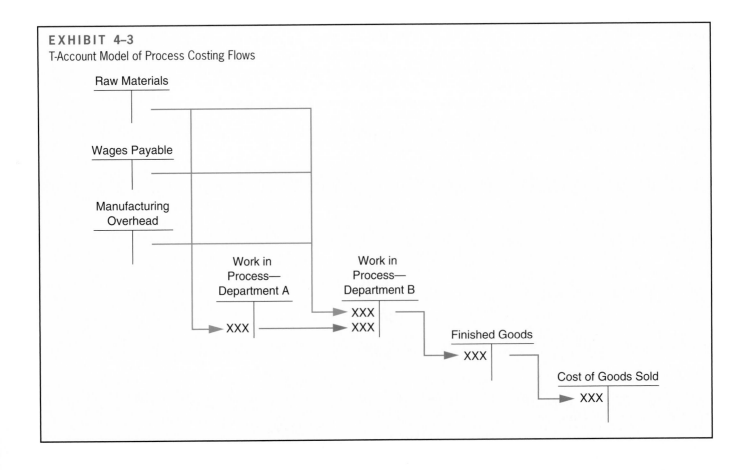

EXHIBIT 4–3
T-Account Model of Process Costing Flows

note that a separate Work in Process account is maintained for *each processing department.* In contrast, in a job-order costing system the entire company may have only one Work in Process account. Second, note that the completed production of the first processing department (Department A in the exhibit) is transferred to the Work in Process account of the second processing department (Department B). After further work in Department B, the completed units are then transferred to Finished Goods. (In Exhibit 4–3, we show only two processing departments, but a company can have many processing departments.)

Finally, note that materials, labor, and overhead costs can be added in *any* processing department—not just the first. Costs in Department B's Work in Process account would consist of the materials, labor, and overhead costs incurred in Department B plus the costs attached to partially completed units transferred in from Department A (called transferred-in costs).

Materials, Labor, and Overhead Cost Entries

To complete our discussion of cost flows in a process costing system, in this section we show journal entries relating to materials, labor, and overhead costs at Megan's Classic Cream Soda, a company that has two processing departments—Formulating and Bottling. In the Formulating Department, ingredients are checked for quality and then mixed and injected with carbon dioxide to create bulk cream soda. In the Bottling Department, bottles are checked for defects, filled with cream soda, capped, visually inspected again for defects, and then packed for shipping.

LEARNING OBJECTIVE 1
Record the flow of materials, labor, and overhead through a process costing system.

Materials Costs   As in job-order costing, materials are drawn from the storeroom using a materials requisition form. Materials can be added in any processing department, although it is not unusual for materials to be added only in the first processing department, with subsequent departments adding only labor and overhead costs as the partially completed units move along toward completion.

At Megan's Classic Cream Soda, some materials (i.e., water, flavors, sugar, and carbon dioxide) are added in the Formulating Department and some materials (i.e., bottles, caps, and packing materials) are added in the Bottling Department. The journal entry to record the materials used in the first processing department, the Formulating Department, is as follows:

| Work in Process—Formulating | XXX | |
| Raw Materials | | XXX |

The journal entry to record the materials used in the second processing department, the Bottling Department, is as follows:

| Work in Process—Bottling | XXX | |
| Raw Materials | | XXX |

Labor Costs   In process costing, labor costs are traced to departments—not to individual jobs. The following journal entry records the labor costs in the Formulating Department at Megan's Classic Cream Soda:

| Work in Process—Formulating | XXX | |
| Salaries and Wages Payable | | XXX |

A similar entry would be made to record labor costs in the Bottling Department.

Overhead Costs   In process costing, as in job-order costing, predetermined overhead rates are usually used. Manufacturing overhead cost is applied to units of product as they move through the department. The following journal entry records the overhead cost for the Formulating Department:

| Work in Process—Formulating | XXX | |
| Manufacturing Overhead | | XXX |

A similar entry would be made to record manufacturing overhead costs in the Bottling Department.

Completing the Cost Flows   Once processing has been completed in a department, the units are transferred to the next department for further processing, as illustrated in the T-accounts in Exhibit 4–3. The following journal entry transfers the cost of partially completed units from the Formulating Department to the Bottling Department:

Work in Process—Bottling	XXX	
Work in Process—Formulating		XXX

After processing has been completed in the Bottling Department, the costs of the completed units are transferred to the Finished Goods inventory account:

Finished Goods	XXX	
Work in Process—Bottling.		XXX

Finally, when a customer's order is filled and units are sold, the cost of the units is transferred to Cost of Goods Sold:

Cost of Goods Sold	XXX	
Finished Goods		XXX

To summarize, the cost flows between accounts are basically the same in a process costing system as they are in a job-order costing system. The only difference at this point is that in a process costing system each department has a separate Work in Process account.

We now turn our attention to Double Diamond Skis, a company that manufactures a high-performance deep-powder ski, and that uses process costing to determine its unit product costs. The company's production process is illustrated in Exhibit 4–4. Skis go through a sequence of five processing departments, starting with the Shaping and Milling Department and ending with the Finishing and Pairing Department. The basic idea in process costing is to add together all of the costs incurred in a department during a period and then spread those costs uniformly across the units processed in that department during that period. As we shall see, applying this simple idea involves a few complications.

Equivalent Units of Production

Topic Tackler
PLUS
4–1

After materials, labor, and overhead costs have been accumulated in a department, the department's output must be determined so that unit product costs can be computed. The difficulty is that a department usually has some partially completed units in its ending inventory. It does not seem reasonable to count these partially completed units as equivalent to fully completed units when counting the department's output. Therefore, these partially completed units are translated into an *equivalent* number of fully completed units. In process costing, this translation is done using the following formula:

Equivalent units = Number of partially completed units × Percentage completion

As the formula states, **equivalent units** is defined as the product of the number of partially completed units and the percentage completion of those units. Roughly speaking, the equivalent units is the number of complete units that could have been obtained from the materials and effort that went into the partially complete units.

For example, suppose the Molding Department at Double Diamond has 500 units in its ending work in process inventory that are 60% complete. These 500 partially complete units are equivalent to 300 fully complete units (500 × 60% = 300). Therefore, the ending work in process inventory contains 300 equivalent units. These equivalent units would be added to any units completed during the period to determine the period's output for the department—called the *equivalent units of production.*

EXHIBIT 4–4
The Production Process at Double Diamond Skis*

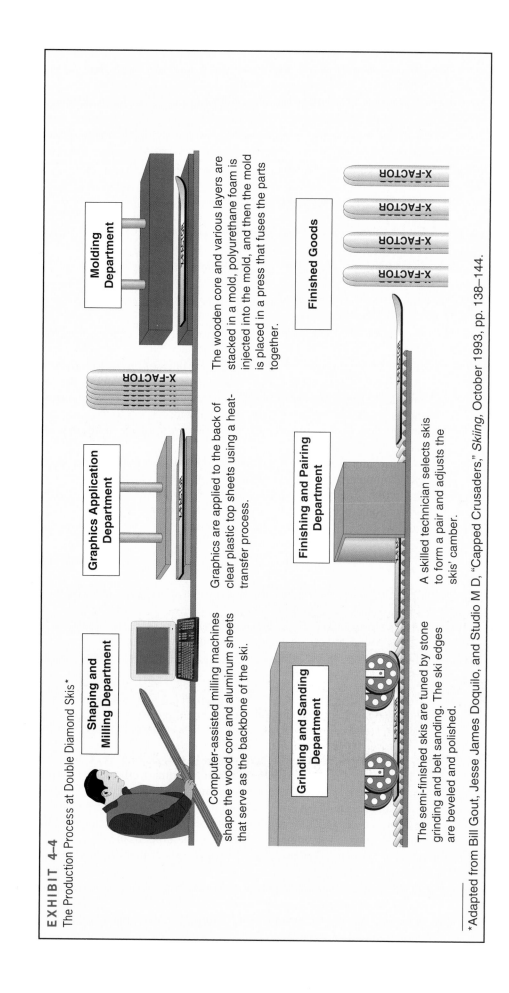

Shaping and Milling Department

Computer-assisted milling machines shape the wood core and aluminum sheets that serve as the backbone of the ski.

Graphics Application Department

Graphics are applied to the back of clear plastic top sheets using a heat-transfer process.

Molding Department

The wooden core and various layers are stacked in a mold, polyurethane foam is injected into the mold, and then the mold is placed in a press that fuses the parts together.

Grinding and Sanding Department

The semi-finished skis are tuned by stone grinding and belt sanding. The ski edges are beveled and polished.

Finishing and Pairing Department

A skilled technician selects skis to form a pair and adjusts the skis' camber.

Finished Goods

X-FACTOR

* Adapted from Bill Gout, Jesse James Doquilo, and Studio M D, "Capped Crusaders," *Skiing*, October 1993, pp. 138–144.

Equivalent units of production for a period can be computed in different ways. In this chapter, we discuss the *weighted-average method.* In Appendix 4A, we discuss the *FIFO method.* The **FIFO method** of process costing is a method in which equivalent units and unit costs relate only to work done during the current period. In contrast, the **weighted-average method** blends together units and costs from the current period with units and costs from the prior period. In the weighted-average method, the **equivalent units of production** for a department are the number of units transferred to the next department (or to finished goods) plus the equivalent units in the department's ending work in process inventory.

Weighted-Average Method

LEARNING OBJECTIVE 2
Compute the equivalent units of production using the weighted-average method.

Under the weighted-average method, a department's equivalent units are computed as follows:

**Weighted-Average Method
(a separate calculation is made for each cost category in
each processing department)**

$$\text{Equivalent units of production} = \text{Units transferred to the next department or to finished goods} + \text{Equivalent units in ending work in process inventory}$$

Note that the computation of the equivalent units of production involves adding the number of units transferred out of the department to the equivalent units in the department's ending inventory. There is no need to compute the equivalent units for the units transferred out of the department—they are 100% complete with respect to the work done in that department or they would not be transferred out. In other words, each unit transferred out of the department is counted as one equivalent unit.

Consider the Shaping and Milling Department at Double Diamond. This department uses computerized milling machines to precisely shape the wooden core and metal sheets that will be used to form the backbone of the ski. (See Exhibit 4–4 for an overview of the production process at Double Diamond.) The following activity took place in the department in May.

		Percent Complete	
Shaping and Milling Department	Units	Materials	Conversion
Beginning work in process	200	55%	30%
Units started into production during May	5,000		
Units completed during May and transferred to the next department	4,800	100%*	100%*
Ending work in process	400	40%	25%

*It is always assumed that units transferred out of a department are 100% complete with respect to the processing done in that department.

Note the use of the term *conversion* in the table above. **Conversion cost,** as defined in Chapter 2, is direct labor cost plus manufacturing overhead cost. In process costing, conversion cost may be treated as a single element of product cost.

Note that the beginning work in process inventory was 55% complete with respect to materials costs and 30% complete with respect to conversion costs. This means that 55% of the materials costs required to complete the units in the department had already been incurred. Likewise, 30% of the conversion costs required to complete the units had already been incurred.

Two equivalent unit figures must be computed—one for materials and one for conversion. These computations are shown in Exhibit 4–5.

Note that the computations in Exhibit 4–5 ignore the fact that the units in the beginning work in process inventory were partially complete. For example, the 200 units in beginning

Shaping and Milling Department	Materials	Conversion
Units transferred to the next department	4,800	4,800
Ending work in process:		
Materials: 400 units × 40% complete	160	
Conversion: 400 units × 25% complete		100
Equivalent units of production	4,960	4,900

EXHIBIT 4–5
Equivalent Units of Production:
Weighted-Average Method

inventory were already 30% complete with respect to conversion costs. Nevertheless, the weighted-average method is concerned only with the 4,900 equivalent units that are in ending inventories and in units transferred to the next department; it is not concerned with the fact that the beginning inventory was already partially complete. In other words, the 4,900 equivalent units computed using the weighted-average method include work that was accomplished in prior periods. This is a key point in the weighted-average method and it is easy to overlook.

Exhibit 4–6 provides an alternative way of looking at the computation of equivalent units of production. Study this exhibit carefully before going on.

CUTTING CONVERSION COSTS

Cemex SA, the world's third largest cement maker, owns 54 plants. Each of these plants consumes 800 tons of fuel a day heating kilns to 2,700 degrees Fahrenheit. Not surprisingly, energy costs account for 40% of the company's overall conversion costs. Historically, Cemex relied exclusively on coal to heat its kilns; however, faced with soaring coal prices and shrinking profits, the company desperately needed a cheaper fuel. Cemex turned its attention to an oil industry waste product called *petroleum coke* that burns hotter than coal and costs half as much. The company spent about $150 million to convert its kilns to burn petroleum coke. Overall, Cemex has cut its energy bills by 17%, helping it earn higher profit margins than its biggest rivals.

Source: John Lyons, "Expensive Energy? Burn Other Stuff, One Firm Decides," *The Wall Street Journal*, September 1, 2004, pp. A1 and A8.

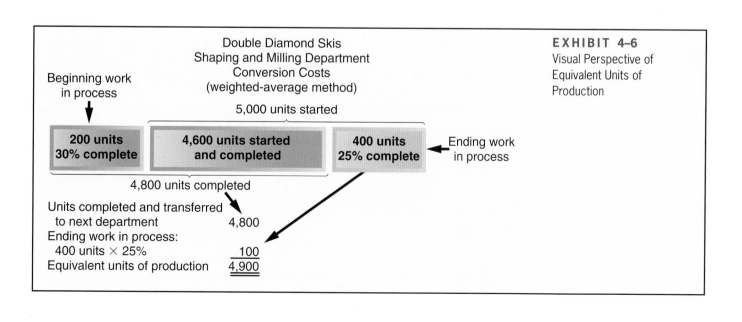

EXHIBIT 4–6
Visual Perspective of Equivalent Units of Production

Compute and Apply Costs

LEARNING OBJECTIVE 3
Compute the cost per equivalent unit using the weighted-average method.

In the last section we computed the equivalent units of production for materials and for conversion at Double Diamond Skis. In this section we will compute the cost per equivalent unit for materials and for conversion. We will then use these costs to value ending work in process and finished goods inventories. Exhibit 4–7 displays all of the data concerning May's operations in the Shaping and Milling Department that we will need to complete these tasks.

EXHIBIT 4–7
Shaping and Milling Department Data for May Operations

Work in process, beginning:	
Units in process	200
Stage of completion with respect to materials	55%
Stage of completion with respect to conversion	30%
Costs in the beginning inventory:	
Materials cost	$ 9,600
Conversion cost	5,575
Total cost in the beginning inventory	$ 15,175
Units started into production during the period	5,000
Units completed and transferred out	4,800
Costs added to production during the period:	
Materials cost	$368,600
Conversion cost	350,900
Total cost added in the department	$719,500
Work in process, ending:	
Units in process	400
Stage of completion with respect to materials	40%
Stage of completion with respect to conversion	25%

Cost per Equivalent Unit—Weighted-Average Method

In the weighted-average method, the cost per equivalent unit is computed as follows:

Weighted-Average Method
(a separate calculation is made for each cost category in each processing department)

$$\text{Cost per equivalent unit} = \frac{\substack{\text{Cost of beginning} \\ \text{work in process inventory}} + \substack{\text{Cost added} \\ \text{during the period}}}{\text{Equivalent units of production}}$$

Note that the numerator is the sum of the cost of beginning work in process inventory and of the cost added during the period. Thus, the weighted-average method blends together costs from the prior and current periods. That is why it is called the weighted-average method; it averages together units and costs from both the prior and current periods.

The costs per equivalent unit for materials and for conversion are computed below for the Shaping and Milling Department for May:

Shaping and Milling Department Costs per Equivalent Unit		
	Materials	Conversion
Cost of beginning work in process inventory	$ 9,600	$ 5,575
Costs added during the period	368,600	350,900
Total cost (a)	$378,200	$356,475
Equivalent units of production (see the computations in the previous section) (b)	4,960	4,900
Cost per equivalent unit (a) ÷ (b)	$76.25	$72.75

Applying Costs—Weighted-Average Method

The costs per equivalent unit are used to value units in ending inventory and units that are transferred to the next department. For example, each unit transferred out of Double Diamond's Shaping and Milling Department to the Graphics Application Department, as depicted in Exhibit 4–4, will carry with it a cost of $149 ($76.25 for materials cost and $72.75 for conversion cost). Since 4,800 units were transferred out in May to the next department, the total cost assigned to those units would be $715,200 (4,800 units × $149 per unit).

A complete accounting of the costs of both ending work in process inventory and the units transferred out appears below:

Shaping and Milling Department
Costs of Ending Work in Process Inventory and the Units Transferred Out

	Materials	Conversion	Total
Ending work in process inventory:			
Equivalent units of production (materials: 400 units × 40% complete; conversion: 400 units × 25% complete) (a)	160	100	
Cost per equivalent unit (see above) (b)	$76.25	$72.75	
Cost of ending work in process inventory (a) × (b)	$12,200	$7,275	$19,475
Units completed and transferred out:			
Units transferred to the next department (a)	4,800	4,800	
Cost per equivalent unit (see above) (b)	$76.25	$72.75	
Cost of units transferred out (a) × (b)	$366,000	$349,200	$715,200

Topic Tackler
PLUS
4–2

In each case, the equivalent units are multiplied by the cost per equivalent unit to determine the cost assigned to the units. This is done for each cost category—in this case, materials and conversion. The equivalent units for the units completed and transferred out are simply the number of units transferred to the next department because they would not have been transferred unless they were complete.

The costs assigned to ending work in process inventory and to the units transferred out reconcile with the costs we started with in Exhibit 4–7 as shown below:

Shaping and Milling Department
Cost Reconciliation

Costs to be accounted for:	
Cost of beginning work in process inventory (Exhibit 4–7)	$ 15,175
Costs added to production during the period (Exhibit 4–7)	719,500
Total cost to be accounted for	$734,675
Costs accounted for as follows:	
Cost of ending work in process inventory (see above)	$ 19,475
Cost of units transferred out (see above)	715,200
Total cost accounted for	$734,675

The $715,200 cost of the units transferred to the next department, Graphics Application, will be accounted for in that department as "costs transferred in." It will be treated in the process costing system as just another category of costs like materials or conversion costs. The only difference is that the costs transferred in will always be 100% complete with respect to the work done in the Graphics Applications Department. Costs are passed on from one department to the next in this fashion, until they reach the last processing department, Finishing and Pairing. When the products are completed in this last department, their costs are transferred to finished goods.

Operation Costing

The costing systems discussed in Chapters 3 and 4 represent the two ends of a continuum. On one end is job-order costing, which is used by companies that produce many different items—generally to customers' specifications. On the other end is process costing, which is used by companies that produce homogeneous products in large quantities. Between these two extremes there are many hybrid systems that include characteristics of both job-order and process costing. One of these hybrids is called *operation costing*.

Operation costing is used in situations where products have some common characteristics and some individual characteristics. Shoes, for example, have common characteristics in that all styles involve cutting and sewing that can be done on a repetitive basis, using the same equipment and following the same basic procedures. Shoes also have individual characteristics—some are made of expensive leathers and others may be made using inexpensive synthetic materials. In a situation such as this, where products have some common characteristics but also must be processed individually, operation costing may be used to determine product costs.

As mentioned above, operation costing is a hybrid system that employs aspects of both job-order and process costing. Products are typically processed in batches when operation costing is used, with each batch charged for its own specific materials. In this sense, operation costing is similar to job-order costing. However, labor and overhead costs are accumulated by operation or by department, and these costs are assigned to units as in process costing. If shoes are being produced, for example, each shoe is charged the same per unit conversion cost, regardless of the style involved, but it is charged with its specific materials cost. Thus, the company is able to distinguish between styles in terms of materials, but it is able to employ the simplicity of a process costing system for labor and overhead costs.

Examples of other products for which operation costing may be used include electronic equipment (such as semiconductors), textiles, clothing, and jewelry (such as rings, bracelets, and medallions). Products of this type are typically produced in batches, but they can vary considerably from model to model or from style to style in terms of the cost of raw material inputs. Therefore, an operation costing system is well suited for providing cost data.

Summary

Process costing is used in situations where homogeneous products or services are produced on a continuous basis. Costs flow through the manufacturing accounts in basically the same way in a process costing system as in a job-order costing system. However, costs are accumulated by department rather than by job in process costing.

In process costing, the equivalent units of production must be determined for each cost category in each department. Under the weighted-average method, the equivalent units of production equals the number of units transferred out to the next department or to finished goods plus the equivalent units in ending work in process inventory. The equivalent units in ending inventory equals the product of the number of partially completed units in ending work in process inventory and their percentage of completion with respect to the specific cost category.

Under the weighted-average method, the cost per equivalent unit for a specific cost category is computed by adding the cost of beginning work in process inventory and the cost added during the period and then dividing the result by the equivalent units of production. The cost per equivalent unit is then used to value the ending work in process inventory and the units transferred out to the next department or to finished goods.

Costs are transferred from one department to the next until the last processing department. At that point, the cost of completed units is transferred to finished goods.

Review Problem: Process Cost Flows and Costing Units

Luxguard Home Paint Company produces exterior latex paint, which it sells in one-gallon containers. The company has two processing departments—Base Fab and Finishing. White paint, which is used as a base for all the company's paints, is mixed from raw ingredients in the Base Fab Department. Pigments are then added to the basic white paint, the pigmented paint is squirted under pressure into one-gallon containers, and the containers are labeled and packed for shipping in the Finishing Department. Information relating to the company's operations for April follows:

a. Issued raw materials for use in production: Base Fab Department, $851,000; and Finishing Department, $629,000.

b. Incurred direct labor costs: Base Fab Department, $330,000; and Finishing Department, $270,000.

c. Applied manufacturing overhead cost: Base Fab Department, $665,000; and Finishing Department, $405,000.

d. Transferred basic white paint from the Base Fab Department to the Finishing Department, $1,850,000.

e. Transferred paint that had been prepared for shipping from the Finishing Department to Finished Goods, $3,200,000.

Required:

1. Prepare journal entries to record items (a) through (e) above.

2. Post the journal entries from (1) above to T-accounts. The balance in the Base Fab Department's Work in Process account on April 1 was $150,000; the balance in the Finishing Department's Work in Process account was $70,000. After posting entries to the T-accounts, find the ending balance in each department's Work in Process account.

3. Determine the cost of ending work in process inventories and of units transferred out of the Base Fab Department in April. The following additional information is available regarding production in the Base Fab Department during April:

Production data:	
Units (gallons) in process, April 1: materials 100% complete, labor and overhead 60% complete	30,000
Units (gallons) started into production during April	420,000
Units (gallons) completed and transferred to the Finishing Department	370,000
Units (gallons) in process, April 30: materials 50% complete, labor and overhead 25% complete	80,000
Cost data:	
Work in process inventory, April 1:	
Materials	$ 92,000
Labor	21,000
Overhead	37,000
Total cost of work in process	$ 150,000
Cost added during April:	
Materials	$ 851,000
Labor	330,000
Overhead	665,000
Total cost added during April	$1,846,000

Solution to Review Problem

1.	*a.*	Work in Process—Base Fab Department	851,000	
		Work in Process—Finishing Department	629,000	
		Raw Materials		1,480,000
	b.	Work in Process—Base Fab Department	330,000	
		Work in Process—Finishing Department	270,000	
		Salaries and Wages Payable		600,000

c. Work in Process—Base Fab Department   665,000
   Work in Process—Finishing Department   405,000
     Manufacturing Overhead   1,070,000
d. Work in Process—Finishing Department   1,850,000
   Work in Process—Base Fab Department.   1,850,000
e. Finished Goods   3,200,000
   Work in Process—Finishing Department   3,200,000

2.

Raw Materials

| Bal. | XXX | (a) | 1,480,000 |

Salaries and Wages Payable

| | | (b) | 600,000 |

Work in Process—Base Fab Department

Bal.	150,000	(d)	1,850,000
(a)	851,000		
(b)	330,000		
(c)	665,000		
Bal.	146,000		

Manufacturing Overhead

| (Various actual costs) | | (c) | 1,070,000 |

Work in Process—Finishing Department

Bal.	70,000	(e)	3,200,000
(a)	629,000		
(b)	270,000		
(c)	405,000		
(d)	1,850,000		
Bal.	24,000		

Finished Goods

| Bal. | XXX | | |
| (e) | 3,200,000 | | |

3. First, we must compute the equivalent units of production for each cost category:

Base Fab Department Equivalent Units of Production	Materials	Labor	Overhead
Units transferred to the next department	370,000	370,000	370,000
Ending work in process inventory (materials: 80,000 units × 50% complete; labor: 80,000 units × 25% complete; overhead: 80,000 units × 25% complete)	40,000	20,000	20,000
Equivalent units of production	410,000	390,000	390,000

Then we must compute the cost per equivalent unit for each cost category:

Base Fab Department Costs per Equivalent Unit	Materials	Labor	Overhead
Costs:			
Cost of beginning work in process inventory	$ 92,000	$ 21,000	$ 37,000
Costs added during the period	851,000	330,000	665,000
Total cost (a)	$943,000	$351,000	$702,000
Equivalent units of production (b)	410,000	390,000	390,000
Cost per equivalent unit (a) ÷ (b)	$2.30	$0.90	$1.80

The costs per equivalent unit can then be applied to the units in ending work in process inventory and the units transferred out as follows:

Base Fab Department Costs of Ending Work in Process Inventory and the Units Transferred Out	Materials	Labor	Overhead	Total
Ending work in process inventory:				
Equivalent units of production	40,000	20,000	20,000	
Cost per equivalent unit	$2.30	$0.90	$1.80	
Cost of ending work in process inventory . . .	$92,000	$18,000	$36,000	$146,000
Units completed and transferred out:				
Units transferred to the next department . . .	370,000	370,000	370,000	
Cost per equivalent unit	$2.30	$0.90	$1.80	
Cost of units completed and transferred out . .	$851,000	$333,000	$666,000	$1,850,000

Glossary

Conversion cost Direct labor cost plus manufacturing overhead cost. (p. 156)

Equivalent units The product of the number of partially completed units and their percentage of completion with respect to a particular cost. Equivalent units are the number of complete whole units one could obtain from the materials and effort contained in partially completed units. (p. 154)

Equivalent units of production (weighted-average method) The units transferred to the next department (or to finished goods) during the period plus the equivalent units in the department's ending work in process inventory. (p. 156)

FIFO method A method of accounting for cost flows in a process costing system in which equivalent units and unit costs relate only to work done during the current period. (p. 156)

Operation costing A hybrid costing system used when products have some common characteristics and some individual characteristics. (p. 160)

Process costing A costing method used when essentially homogeneous products are produced on a continuous basis. (p. 150)

Processing department An organizational unit where work is performed on a product and where materials, labor, or overhead costs are added to the product. (p. 151)

Weighted-average method A method of process costing that blends together units and costs from both the current and prior periods. (p. 156)

Appendix 4A: FIFO Method

The FIFO method of process costing differs from the weighted-average method in two ways: (1) the computation of equivalent units, and (2) the way in which costs of beginning inventory are treated. The FIFO method is generally considered more accurate than the weighted-average method, but it is more complex. The complexity is not a problem for computers, but the FIFO method is a little more difficult to understand and to learn than the weighted-average method.

Equivalent Units—FIFO Method

The computation of equivalent units under the FIFO method differs from the computation under the weighted-average method in two ways.

> **LEARNING OBJECTIVE 5**
> Compute the equivalent units of production using the FIFO method.

First, the "units transferred out" is divided into two parts. One part consists of the units from the beginning inventory that were completed and transferred out, and the other part consists of the units that were both *started* and *completed* during the current period.

Second, full consideration is given to the amount of work expended during the current period on units in the *beginning* work in process inventory as well as on units in the ending inventory. Thus, under the FIFO method, both beginning and ending inventories are converted to an equivalent units basis. For the beginning inventory, the equivalent units represent the work done to *complete* the units; for the ending inventory, the equivalent units represent the work done to bring the units to a stage of partial completion at the end of the period (the same as with the weighted-average method):

The formula for computing the equivalent units of production under the FIFO method is more complex than under the weighted-average method:

FIFO Method
(a separate calculation is made for each cost category
in each processing department)

Equivalent units of production = Equivalent units to complete beginning work in process inventory*

+ Units started and completed during the period

+ Equivalent units in ending work in process inventory

$$
\begin{array}{c}
\text{*Equivalent units to} \\
\text{complete beginning work} \\
\text{in process inventory}
\end{array} =
\begin{array}{c}
\text{Units in beginning} \\
\text{work in process} \\
\text{inventory}
\end{array} \times
\left(
100\% -
\begin{array}{c}
\text{Percentage completion} \\
\text{of beginning work in} \\
\text{process inventory}
\end{array}
\right)
$$

Or, the equivalent units of production can also be determined as follows:

Equivalent units of production = Units transferred out

+ Equivalent units in ending work in process inventory

− Equivalent units in beginning work in process inventory

To illustrate the FIFO method, refer again to the data for the Shaping and Milling Department at Double Diamond Skis. The department completed and transferred 4,800 units to the Graphics Application Department during May. Since 200 of these units came from the beginning inventory, the Shaping and Milling Department must have started and completed 4,600 units during May. The 200 units in the beginning inventory were 55% complete with respect to materials and only 30% complete with respect to conversion costs when the month started. Thus, to complete these units the department must have added another 45% of materials costs (100% − 55% = 45%) and another 70% of conversion costs (100% − 30% = 70%). Following this line of reasoning, the equivalent units for the department for May would be computed as shown in Exhibit 4A–1.

Comparison of Equivalent Units of Production under the Weighted-Average and FIFO Methods

Stop at this point and compare the data in Exhibit 4A–1 with the data in Exhibit 4–5 in the chapter, which shows the computation of equivalent units under the weighted-average method. Also refer to Exhibit 4A–2, which compares the two methods.

The essential difference between the two methods is that the weighted-average method blends work and costs from the prior period with work and costs in the current period,

	Materials	Conversion
To complete beginning work in process:		
Materials: 200 units × (100% − 55%)*	90	
Conversion: 200 units × (100% − 30%)*.............		140
Units started and completed during the period	4,600†	4,600†
Ending work in process:		
Materials: 400 units × 40% complete	160	
Conversion: 400 units × 25% complete..............		100
Equivalent units of production	4,850	4,840

*This is the work needed to complete the units in beginning inventory.
†5,000 units started − 400 units in ending work in process = 4,600 units started and completed. This can also be computed as 4,800 units completed and transferred to the next department − 200 units in beginning work in process inventory. The FIFO method assumes that the units in beginning inventory are finished first.

EXHIBIT 4A–1
Equivalent Units of Production: FIFO Method

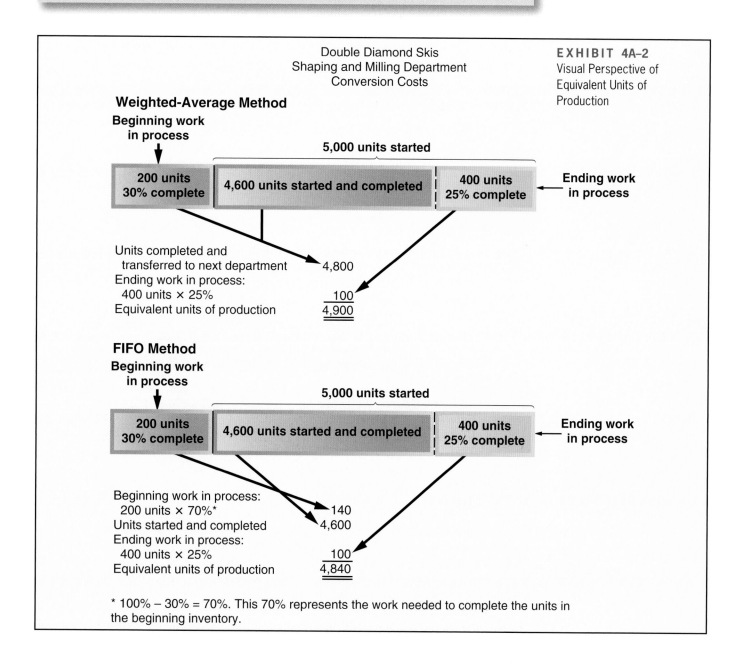

EXHIBIT 4A–2
Visual Perspective of Equivalent Units of Production

whereas the FIFO method separates the two periods. To see this more clearly, consider the following reconciliation of the two calculations of equivalent units:

Shaping and Milling Department	Materials	Conversion
Equivalent units—weighted-average method	4,960	4,900
Less equivalent units in beginning inventory:		
200 units × 55%.	110	
200 units × 30%.		60
Equivalent units of production—FIFO method.	4,850	4,840

From the above, it is evident that the FIFO method removes the equivalent units that were already in beginning inventory from the equivalent units as defined using the weighted-average method. Thus, the FIFO method isolates the equivalent units due to work performed during the current period. The weighted-average method blends together the equivalent units already in beginning inventory with the equivalent units due to work performed in the current period.

Cost per Equivalent Unit—FIFO Method

LEARNING OBJECTIVE 6
Compute the cost per equivalent unit using the FIFO method.

In the FIFO method, the cost per equivalent unit is computed as follows:

FIFO Method
(a separate calculation is made for each cost category in each processing department)

$$\text{Cost per equivalent unit} = \frac{\text{Cost added during the period}}{\text{Equivalent units of production}}$$

Unlike the weighted-average method, in the FIFO method the cost per equivalent unit is based only on the costs incurred in the department in the current period.

The costs per equivalent unit for materials and for conversion are computed below for the Shaping and Milling Department for May:

Shaping and Milling Department Costs per Equivalent Unit—FIFO method	Materials	Conversion
Cost added during the period (a)	$368,600	$350,900
Equivalent units of production (b)	4,850	4,840
Cost per equivalent unit (a) ÷ (b)	$76.00	$72.50

LEARNING OBJECTIVE 7
Assign costs to units using the FIFO method.

Applying Costs—FIFO Method

The costs per equivalent unit are used to value units in ending inventory and units that are transferred to the next department. For example, each unit transferred out of the Shaping and Milling Department to the Graphics Application Department will carry with it a cost of $148.50—$76.00 for materials cost and $72.50 for conversion cost. Since 4,800 units were transferred out in May to the next department, the total cost assigned to those units would be $712,800 (4,800 units × $148.50 per unit).

A complete accounting of the costs of both ending work in process inventory and the units transferred out appears below. It is more complicated than the weighted average method. This is because the cost of the units transferred out consists of three separate components: (1) the cost of beginning work in process inventory; (2) the cost to complete the units in beginning work in process inventory; and (3) the cost of units started and completed during the period.

| Shaping and Milling Department | | | |
| Costs of Ending Work in Process Inventory and Units Transferred Out—FIFO Method | | | |
	Materials	Conversion	Total
Ending work in process inventory:			
Equivalent units of production			
(see Exhibit 4A–1) (a)......................	160	100	
Cost per equivalent unit (see above) (b)	$76.00	$72.50	
Cost of ending work in process inventory			
(a) × (b)	$12,160	$7,250	$19,410
Units transferred out:			
Cost in beginning work in process inventory ...	$9,600	$5,575	$15,175
Cost to complete the units in beginning work in process inventory:			
Equivalent units of production required to			
complete the units in beginning inventory			
(see Exhibit 4A–1) (a)...................	90	140	
Cost per equivalent unit (see above) (b).......	$76.00	$72.50	
Cost to complete the units in beginning			
inventory (a) × (b)	$6,840	$10,150	$16,990
Cost of units started and completed this period:			
Units started and completed this period			
(see Exhibit 4A–1) (a).....................	4,600	4,600	
Cost per equivalent unit (see above) (b)	$76.00	$72.50	
Cost of units started and completed this period			
(a) × (b)	$349,600	$333,500	$683,100
Total cost of units transferred out			$715,265

Again, note that the cost of the units transferred out consists of three distinct components—the cost of beginning work in process inventory, the cost to complete the units in beginning inventory, and the cost of units started and completed during the period. This is a major difference between the weighted-average and FIFO methods.

The costs assigned to ending work in process inventory and to the units transferred out reconcile with the costs we started with in Exhibit 4–7 as shown below:

| Shaping and Milling Department | |
Cost Reconciliation	
Costs to be accounted for:	
Cost of beginning work in process inventory (Exhibit 4–7)	$ 15,175
Costs added to production during the period (Exhibit 4–7).........	719,500
Total cost to be accounted for..................................	$734,675
Costs accounted for as follows:	
Cost of ending work in process inventory (see above)	$ 19,410
Cost of units transferred out (see above)	715,265
Total cost accounted for	$734,675

The $715,265 cost of the units transferred to the next department, Graphics Application, will be accounted for in that department as "costs transferred in." As in the weighted-average method, this cost will be treated in the process costing system as just another category of costs like materials or conversion costs. The only difference is that the costs transferred in will always be 100% complete with respect to the work done in the Graphics Applications Department. Costs are passed on from one department to the next in this fashion, until they reach the last processing department, Finishing and Pairing. When the products are completed in this last department, their costs are transferred to finished goods.

A Comparison of Costing Methods

In most situations, the weighted-average and FIFO methods will produce very similar unit costs. If there never are any ending inventories, as in an ideal Lean Production environment, the two methods will produce identical results. The reason for this is that without any ending inventories, no costs can be carried forward into the next period and the weighted-average method will base the unit costs on just the current period's costs—just as in the FIFO method. If there *are* ending inventories, either erratic input prices or erratic production levels would also be required to generate much of a difference in unit costs under the two methods. This is because the weighted-average method will blend the unit costs from the prior period with the unit costs of the current period. Unless these unit costs differ greatly, the blending will not make much difference.

Nevertheless, from the standpoint of cost control, the FIFO method is superior to the weighted-average method. Current performance should be measured in relation to costs of the current period only, and the weighted-average method mixes costs of the current period with costs of the prior period. Thus, under the weighted-average method, the manager's apparent performance in the current period is influenced by what happened in the prior period. This problem does not arise under the FIFO method because the FIFO method makes a clear distinction between costs of prior periods and costs incurred during the current period. For the same reason, the FIFO method also provides more up-to-date cost data for decision-making purposes.

On the other hand, the weighted-average method is simpler to apply than the FIFO method, but computers can handle the additional calculations with ease once they have been appropriately programmed.

Appendix 4B: Service Department Allocations

Most large organizations have both *operating departments* and *service departments*. The central purposes of the organization are carried out in the operating departments. In contrast, service departments do not directly engage in operating activities. Instead, they provide services or assistance to the operating departments. Examples of operating departments include the Surgery Department at Mt. Sinai Hospital, the Geography Department at the University of Washington, the Marketing Department at Allstate Insurance Company, and production departments at manufacturers such as Mitsubishi, Hewlett-Packard, and Michelin. In process costing, the processing departments are all operating departments. Examples of service departments include Cafeteria, Internal Auditing, Human Resources, Cost Accounting, and Purchasing.

The overhead costs of operating departments commonly include allocations of costs from the service departments. To the extent that service department costs are classified as production costs, they should be included in unit product costs and thus must be allocated to operating departments in a process costing system.

Three approaches are used to allocate the costs of service departments to other departments: the direct method, the step-down method, and the reciprocal method. These three methods are discussed in the following sections. However, before getting into the details of these methods, a few words are in order concerning *interdepartmental services*.

Interdepartmental Services   Many service departments provide services to each other, as well as to operating departments. For example, the Cafeteria Department provides meals for all employees, including those assigned to other service departments, as well as to employees of the operating departments. In turn, the Cafeteria Department may receive services from other service departments, such as from Custodial Services or from Personnel. Services provided between service departments are known as *interdepartmental* or *reciprocal* *services.*

Direct Method

The *direct method* is the simplest of the three cost allocation methods. It ignores the services provided by a service department to other service departments (e.g., reciprocal services) and allocates all service department costs directly to operating departments. Even if a service department (such as Personnel) provides a large amount of service to another service department (such as the cafeteria), no allocations are made between the two departments. Rather, all costs are allocated *directly* to the operating departments, bypassing the other service departments. Hence the term *direct method.*

IN BUSINESS

GENERAL MOTORS TRIMS SUPPORT STAFF

In difficult economic times, companies frequently look to cut costs within their service departments. Because workers in service departments are not directly involved in making the products that their companies sell, they are often viewed as more expendable than their counterparts employed in operating departments. For example, General Motors (GM) responded to a slowdown in vehicle sales by telling many of its service departments to reduce their headcount by 10%. GM's operating departments were also asked to cut back, but only 3% to 7%.

Source: Dave Guilford, "GM Trims 10% in Some Areas," *Automotive News*, April 7, 2003, p.1.

For an example of the direct method, consider Mountain View Hospital, which has two service departments and two operating departments as shown below. The hospital allocates its Hospital Administration costs on the basis of employee-hours and its Custodial Services costs on the basis of square feet occupied.

	Service Departments		Operating Departments		
	Hospital Administration	Custodial Services	Laboratory	Patient Care	Total
Departmental costs before allocation	$360,000	$90,000	$261,000	$689,000	$1,400,000
Employee hours	12,000	6,000	18,000	30,000	66,000
Space occupied— square feet	10,000	200	5,000	45,000	60,200

The direct method of allocating the hospital's service department costs to the operating departments is shown in Exhibit 4B–1 (page 170). Several things should be noted in this exhibit. First, the employee-hours of the Hospital Administration Department and the Custodial Services Department are ignored when allocating the costs of Hospital Administration using the direct method. *Under the direct method, any of the allocation base attributable to the*

EXHIBIT 4B–1
Direct Method of Allocation

	Service Departments		Operating Departments		
	Hospital Administration	Custodial Services	Laboratory	Patient Care	Total
Departmental costs before allocation	$360,000	$90,000	$261,000	$689,000	$1,400,000
Allocation:					
Hospital Administration costs ($^{18}\!/_{48}$, $^{30}\!/_{48}$)*.	(360,000)		135,000	225,000	
Custodial Services costs ($^{5}\!/_{50}$, $^{45}\!/_{50}$)†.		(90,000)	9,000	81,000	
Total cost after allocation	$ 0	$ 0	$405,000	$995,000	$1,400,000

*Based on the employee-hours in the two operating departments, which are 18,000 hours + 30,000 hours = 48,000 hours.
†Based on the square feet occupied by the two operating departments, which is 5,000 square feet + 45,000 square feet = 50,000 square feet.

service departments themselves is ignored; only the amount of the allocation base attributable to the operating departments is used in the allocation. Note that the same rule is used when allocating the costs of the Custodial Services Department. Even though the Hospital Administration and Custodial Services departments occupy some space, this is ignored when the Custodial Services costs are allocated. Finally, note that after all allocations have been completed, all of the service department costs are contained in the two operating departments.

Although the direct method is simple, it is less accurate than the other methods because it ignores interdepartmental services.

Step-Down Method

Unlike the direct method, the *step-down method* provides for allocation of a service department's costs to other service departments, as well as to operating departments. The step-down method is sequential. The sequence typically begins with the department that provides the greatest amount of service to other service departments. After its costs have been allocated, the process continues, step by step, ending with the department that provides the least amount of services to other service departments. This step procedure is illustrated in graphic form in Exhibit 4B–2.

Exhibit 4B–3 shows the details of the step-down method. Note the following three key points about these allocations. First, under Allocation in Exhibit 4B–3, you see two allocations, or steps. In the first step, the costs of Hospital Administration are allocated to another service department (Custodial Services) as well as to the operating departments. In contrast to the direct method, the allocation base for Hospital Administration costs now includes the employee-hours for Custodial Services as well as for the operating departments. However, the allocation base still excludes the employee-hours for Hospital Administration itself. *In both the direct and step-down methods, any amount of the allocation base attributable to the service department whose cost is being allocated is always ignored.* Second, looking again at Exhibit 4B–3, note that in the second step under the Allocation heading, the cost of Custodial Services is allocated to the two operating departments, and none of the cost is allocated to Hospital Administration even though Hospital Administration occupies space in the building. *In the step-down method, any amount of the allocation base that is attributable to a service department whose cost has already been allocated is ignored.* After a service department's costs have been allocated, costs of other service departments are not reallocated back to it. Third, note that the cost of

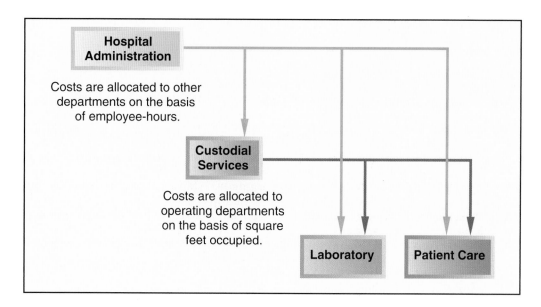

Custodial Services allocated to other departments in the second step ($130,000) in Exhibit 4B–3 includes the costs of Hospital Administration that were allocated to Custodial Services in the first step in Exhibit 4B–3.

Reciprocal Method

The *reciprocal method* gives full recognition to interdepartmental services. Under the step-down method discussed above only partial recognition of interdepartmental services is possible. The step-down method always allocates costs forward—never backward. The reciprocal method, by contrast, allocates service department costs in *both* directions. Thus, since Custodial Services in the prior example provides services for Hospital Administration, part of Custodial Services' costs will be allocated *back* to Hospital Administration if the reciprocal method is used. At the same time, part of Hospital Administration's costs will be allocated *forward* to Custodial Services. Reciprocal allocation requires the use of simultaneous linear equations and is beyond the scope of this book. Examples of the reciprocal method can be found in more advanced cost accounting texts.

EXHIBIT 4B–3
Step-Down Method of Allocation

	Service Departments		Operating Departments		
	Hospital Administration	Custodial Services	Laboratory	Patient Care	Total
Departmental costs before allocation	$360,000	$ 90,000	$261,000	$ 689,000	$1,400,000
Allocation:					
Hospital Administration costs ($6/54$, $18/54$, $30/54$)*	(360,000)	40,000	120,000	200,000	
Custodial Services costs ($5/50$, $45/50$)†		(130,000)	13,000	117,000	
Total cost after allocation	$ 0	$ 0	$394,000	$1,006,000	$1,400,000

*Based on the employee-hours in Custodial Services and the two operating departments, which are 6,000 hours + 18,000 hours + 30,000 hours = 54,000 hours.
†As in Exhibit 4B–1, this allocation is based on the square feet occupied by the two operating departments.

Questions

4-1 Under what conditions would it be appropriate to use a process costing system?

4-2 In what ways are job-order and process costing similar?

4-3 Why is cost accumulation easier in a process costing system than it is in a job-order costing system?

4-4 How many Work in Process accounts are maintained in a company that uses process costing?

4-5 Assume that a company has two processing departments—Mixing and Firing. Prepare a journal entry to show a transfer of partially completed units from the Mixing Department to the Firing Department.

4-6 Assume that a company has two processing departments—Mixing followed by Firing. Explain what costs might be added to the Firing Department's Work in Process account during a period.

4-7 What is meant by the term *equivalent units of production* when the weighted-average method is used?

4-8 Watkins Trophies, Inc., produces thousands of medallions made of bronze, silver, and gold. The medallions are identical except for the materials used in their manufacture. What costing system would you advise the company to use?

4-9 (Appendix 4A) How does the computation of equivalent units under the FIFO method differ from the computation of equivalent units under the weighted-average method?

4-10 (Appendix 4A) From the standpoint of cost control, why is the FIFO method superior to the weighted-average method?

4-11 (Appendix 4B) What is the difference between a service department and an operating department?

4-12 (Appendix 4B) How are service department costs assigned to products?

4-13 (Appendix 4B) What are interdepartmental services?

4-14 (Appendix 4B) How are interdepartmental service costs handled under the direct method?

4-15 (Appendix 4B) How are service department costs allocated to other departments under the step-down method?

Exercises

EXERCISE 4-1 Process Costing Journal Entries [LO1]

Quality Brick Company produces bricks in two processing departments—Molding and Firing. Information relating to the company's operations in March follows:

a. Raw materials were issued for use in production: Molding Department, $23,000; and Firing Department, $8,000.

b. Direct labor costs were incurred: Molding Department, $12,000; and Firing Department, $7,000.

c. Manufacturing overhead was applied: Molding Department, $25,000; and Firing Department, $37,000.

d. Unfired, molded bricks were transferred from the Molding Department to the Firing Department. According to the company's process costing system, the cost of the unfired, molded bricks was $57,000.

e. Finished bricks were transferred from the Firing Department to the finished goods warehouse. According to the company's process costing system, the cost of the finished bricks was $103,000.

f. Finished bricks were sold to customers. According to the company's process costing system, the cost of the finished bricks sold was $101,000.

Required:
Prepare journal entries to record items (a) through (f) above.

EXERCISE 4-2 Computation of Equivalent Units—Weighted-Average Method [LO2]

Clonex Labs, Inc., uses a process costing system. The following data are available for one department for October:

		Percent Completed	
	Units	Materials	Conversion
Work in process, October 1	30,000	65%	30%
Work in process, October 31	15,000	80%	40%

The department started 175,000 units into production during the month and transferred 190,000 completed units to the next department.

Required:

Compute the equivalent units of production for October assuming that the company uses the weighted-average method of accounting for units and costs.

EXERCISE 4-3 Cost per Equivalent Unit—Weighted-Average Method [LO3]

Superior Micro Products uses the weighted-average method in its process costing system. Data for the Assembly Department for May appear below:

	Materials	Labor	Overhead
Work in process, May 1.	$ 18,000	$ 5,500	$ 27,500
Cost added during May.	$238,900	$80,300	$401,500
Equivalent units of production.	35,000	33,000	33,000

Required:

Compute the cost per equivalent unit for materials, for labor, and for overhead.

EXERCISE 4-4 Applying Costs to Units—Weighted-Average Method [LO4]

Data concerning a recent period's activity in the Prep Department, the first processing department in a company that uses process costing, appear below:

	Materials	Conversion
Equivalent units of production in ending work in process.	300	100
Cost per equivalent unit	$31.56	$9.32

A total of 1,300 units were completed and transferred to the next processing department during the period.

Required:

Compute the cost of the units transferred to the next department during the period and the cost of ending work in process inventory.

EXERCISE 4-5 (Appendix 4A) Computation of Equivalent Units—FIFO Method [LO5]

QualCon, Inc., produces wine bottles for vintners in a process that starts in the Melt and Mold Department. Data concerning that department's operations in the most recent period appear below:

Beginning work in process:	
Units in process	400
Stage of completion with respect to materials	75%
Stage of completion with respect to conversion	25%
Units started into production during the month	42,600
Units completed and transferred out	42,500
Ending work in process:	
Units in process	500
Stage of completion with respect to materials	80%
Stage of completion with respect to conversion	30%

Required:

QualCon uses the FIFO method in its process costing system. Compute the equivalent units of production for the period for the Melt and Mold Department.

EXERCISE 4-6 (Appendix 4A) Cost per Equivalent Unit—FIFO Method [LO6]

Superior Micro Products uses the FIFO method in its process costing system. Data for the Assembly Department for May appear below:

	Materials	Labor	Overhead
Cost added during May	$193,320	$62,000	$310,000
Equivalent units of production	27,000	25,000	25,000

Required:

Compute the cost per equivalent unit for materials, for labor, for overhead, and in total.

EXERCISE 4-7 (Appendix 4A) Applying Costs to Units—FIFO Method [LO7]

Data concerning a recent period's activity in the Mixing Department, the first processing department in a company that uses process costing, appear below:

	Materials	Conversion
Cost of work in process inventory at the beginning of the period	$2,700	$380
Equivalent units of production in the ending work in process inventory	800	200
Equivalent units of production required to complete the beginning work in process inventory	400	700
Cost per equivalent unit for the period	$4.40	$1.30

A total of 8,000 units were completed and transferred to the next processing department during the period. Beginning work in process inventory consisted of 1,000 units and ending work in process inventory consisted of 2,000 units.

Required:

Compute the cost of the units transferred to the next department during the period and the cost of ending work in process inventory.

EXERCISE 4-8 (Appendix 4B) Direct Method [LO8]

Seattle Western University has provided the following data to be used in its service department cost allocations:

	Service Departments		Operating Departments	
	Administration	Facility Services	Undergraduate Programs	Graduate Programs
Departmental costs before allocations	$2,400,000	$1,600,000	$26,800,000	$5,700,000
Student credit-hours			20,000	5,000
Space occupied—square feet	25,000	10,000	70,000	30,000

Required:

Using the direct method, allocate the costs of the service departments to the two operating departments. Allocate administrative costs on the basis of student credit-hours and facility services costs on the basis of space occupied.

EXERCISE 4-9 (Appendix 4B) Step-Down Method [LO9]

Madison Park Co-op, a whole foods grocery and gift shop, has provided the following data to be used in its service department cost allocations:

	Service Departments		Operating Departments	
	Administration	Janitorial	Groceries	Gifts
Departmental costs before allocations	$150,000	$40,000	$2,320,000	$950,000
Employee-hours	320	160	3,100	740
Space occupied—square feet	250	100	4,000	1,000

Required:

Using the step method, allocate the costs of the service departments to the two operating departments. Allocate administrative costs first on the basis of employee-hours and then janitorial costs on the basis of space occupied.

EXERCISE 4-10 Process Costing Journal Entries [LO1]

Chocolaterie de Geneve, SA, is located in a French-speaking canton in Switzerland. The company makes chocolate truffles that are sold in popular embossed tins. The company has two processing departments—Cooking and Molding. In the Cooking Department, the raw ingredients for the truffles are mixed and then cooked in special candy-making vats. In the Molding Department, the melted chocolate and other ingredients from the Cooking Department are carefully poured into molds and decorative flourishes are applied by hand. After cooling, the truffles are packed for sale. The company uses a process costing system. The T-accounts below show the flow of costs through the two departments in April (all amounts are in Swiss francs):

Work in Process—Cooking

Balance 4/1	8,000	Transferred out	160,000
Direct materials	42,000		
Direct labor	50,000		
Overhead	75,000		

Work in Process—Molding

Balance 4/1	4,000	Transferred out	240,000
Transferred in	160,000		
Direct labor	36,000		
Overhead	45,000		

Required:

Prepare journal entries showing the flow of costs through the two processing departments during April.

EXERCISE 4-11 Equivalent Units and Cost per Equivalent Unit—Weighted-Average Method [LO2, LO3]

Pureform, Inc., manufactures a product that passes through two departments. Data for a recent month for the first department follow:

	Units	Materials	Labor	Overhead
Work in process, beginning	5,000	$4,320	$1,040	$1,790
Units started in process	45,000			
Units transferred out	42,000			
Work in process, ending	8,000			
Cost added during the month		$52,800	$21,500	$32,250

The beginning work in process inventory was 80% complete with respect to materials and 60% complete with respect to labor and overhead. The ending work in process inventory was 75% complete with respect to materials and 50% complete with respect to labor and overhead.

Required:

Assume that the company uses the weighted-average method of accounting for units and costs.

1. Compute the equivalent units for the month's activity for the first department.
2. Determine the costs per equivalent unit for the month.

EXERCISE 4-12 (Appendix 4A) Equivalent Units and Cost per Equivalent Unit—FIFO Method [LO5, LO6]

Refer to the data for Pureform, Inc., in Exercise 4-11.

Required:

Assume that the company uses the FIFO method of accounting for units and costs.

1. Compute the equivalent units for the month's activity for the first department.
2. Determine the costs per equivalent unit for the month.

EXERCISE 4-13 (Appendix 4A) Cost Reconciliation—FIFO Method [LO9]

Jarvene Corporation uses the FIFO method in its process costing system. The following data are for the most recent month of operations in one of the company's processing departments:

Units in beginning inventory.	400	
Units started into production	3,000	
Units in ending inventory	300	
Units transferred to the next department	3,100	

	Materials	Conversion
Percentage completion of beginning inventory	80%	40%
Percentage completion of ending inventory	70%	60%

The cost of beginning inventory according to the company's costing system was $11,040 of which $5,231 was for materials and the remainder was for conversion cost. The costs added during the month amounted to $132,730. The costs per equivalent unit for the month were:

	Materials	Conversion
Cost per equivalent unit	$25.40	$18.20

Required:

1. Compute the total cost per equivalent unit for the month.
2. Compute the equivalent units of material and of conversion costs in the ending inventory.
3. Compute the equivalent units of material and of conversion costs that were required to complete the beginning inventory.
4. Determine the number of units started and completed during the month.
5. Determine the costs of ending inventory and units transferred out.

EXERCISE 4-14 Equivalent Units—Weighted-Average Method [LO2]

Alaskan Fisheries, Inc., processes salmon for various distributors. Two departments are involved—Cleaning and Packing. Data relating to pounds of salmon processed in the Cleaning Department during July are presented below:

	Pounds of Salmon	Percent Completed*
Work in process, July 1.	20,000	30%
Started into production during July.	380,000	—
Work in process, July 31.	25,000	60%

*Labor and overhead only.

All materials are added at the beginning of processing in the Cleaning Department.

Required:

Compute the equivalent units for July for the Cleaning Department, assuming that the company uses the weighted-average method of accounting for units.

EXERCISE 4-15 (Appendix 4A) Equivalent Units—FIFO Method [LO5]

Refer to the data for Alaskan Fisheries, Inc., in Exercise 4–11.

Required:

Prepare a quantity schedule and a computation of equivalent units for July for the Cleaning Department assuming that the company uses the FIFO method of accounting for units.

EXERCISE 4-16 (Appendix 4B) Step-Down Method [LO9]

The Ferre Publishing Company has three service departments and two operating departments. Selected data from a recent period on the five departments follow:

| | Service Departments | | | Operating Departments | | |
	Administration	Janitorial	Maintenance	Binding	Printing	Total
Overhead costs.....................	$140,000	$105,000	$48,000	$275,000	$430,000	$998,000
Number of employees...............	60	35	140	315	210	760
Square feet of space occupied	15,000	10,000	20,000	40,000	100,000	185,000
Hours of press time.................				30,000	60,000	90,000

The company allocates service department costs by the step method in the following order: Administration (number of employees), Janitorial (space occupied), and Maintenance (hours of press time).

Required:

Using the step-down method, allocate the service department costs to the operating departments.

EXERCISE 4-17 (Appendix 4B) Direct Method [LO8]

Refer to the data for the Ferre Publishing Company in Exercise 4-16.

Required:

Assuming that the company uses the direct method rather than the step-down method to allocate service department costs, how much overhead cost would be assigned to each operating department?

EXERCISE 4-18 Equivalent Units and Cost per Equivalent Unit—Weighted-Average Method
[LO2, LO3, LO4]

Helox, Inc., manufactures a product that passes through two production processes. Data for May for the first process follow:

	Units	Completion with Respect to Materials	Completion with Respect to Conversion
Work in process inventory, May 1	5,000	100%	40%
Work in process inventory, May 31	10,000	100%	30%
Materials cost in work in process			
inventory, May 1		$1,500	
Conversion cost in work in process			
inventory, May 1		$4,000	
Units started into production		180,000	
Units transferred to the next process........		175,000	
Materials cost added during May		$54,000	
Conversion cost added during May		$352,000	

Required:

1. Assume that the company uses the weighted-average method of accounting for units and costs. Determine the equivalent units for May for the first process.
2. Compute the costs per equivalent unit for May for the first process.
3. Determine the total cost of ending work in process inventory and the total cost of units transferred to the next process in May.

Problems

PROBLEM 4-19 Equivalent Units, Cost per Equivalent Unit, Applying Costs—Weighted-Average Method
[LO2, LO3, LO4]
Sunspot Beverages, Ltd., of Fiji makes blended tropical fruit drinks in two stages. Fruit juices are extracted from fresh fruits and then blended in the Blending Department. The blended juices are then bottled and packed for shipping in the Bottling Department. The following information pertains to the operations of the Blending Department for June. (The currency in Fiji is the Fijian dollar.)

		A	B	C	D	E
				Percent	Completed	
2			Units	Materials	Conversion	
3	Work in process, beginning		20,000	100%	75%	
4	Started into production		180,000			
5	Completed and transferred out		160,000			
6	Work in process, ending		40,000	100%	25%	
7						
8				Materials	Conversion	
9	Work in process, beginning			$25,200	$24,800	
10	Cost added during June			$334,800	$238,700	
11						
12						

Required:
Assume that the company uses the weighted-average method.
1. Determine the equivalent units for June for the first process.
2. Compute the costs per equivalent unit for June for the first process.
3. Determine the total cost of ending work in process inventory and the total cost of units transferred to the next process in June.
4. Prepare a report that reconciles the total costs assigned to the ending work in process inventory and the units transferred out with the costs in beginning inventory and costs added during the period.

PROBLEM 4-20 (Appendix 4A) Equivalent Units, Cost per Equivalent Unit, Applying Costs—FIFO Method
[LO5, LO6, LO7]
Refer to the data for the Blending Department of Sunspot Beverages, Ltd., in Problem 4-19. Assume that the company uses the FIFO method rather than the weighted-average method in its process costing system.

Required:
1. Determine the equivalent units for June for the first process.
2. Compute the costs per equivalent unit for June for the first process.
3. Determine the total cost of ending work in process inventory and the total cost of units transferred to the next process in June.
4. Prepare a report that reconciles the total costs assigned to the ending work in process inventory and the units transferred out with the costs in beginning inventory and costs added during the period.

PROBLEM 4-21 Equivalent Units; Applying Costs—Weighted-Average Method [LO2, LO3, LO4]

Builder Products, Inc., manufactures a caulking compound that goes through three processing stages prior to completion. Information on work in the first department, Cooking, is given below for May:

Production data:

Units in process, May 1; materials 100% complete;	
labor and overhead 80% complete	10,000
Units started into production during May.	100,000
Units completed and transferred out.	95,000
Units in process, May 31; materials 60% complete;	
labor and overhead 20% complete	?
Cost data:	
Work in process inventory, May 1:	
Materials cost.	$1,500
Labor cost	$1,800
Overhead cost	$5,400
Cost added during May:	
Materials cost.	$154,500
Labor cost	$22,700
Overhead cost	$68,100

Materials are added at several stages during the cooking process, whereas labor and overhead costs are incurred uniformly. The company uses the weighted-average method.

Required:

1. Compute the equivalent units of production.
2. Compute the costs per equivalent unit for May.
3. Determine the cost of ending work in process inventory and of the units transferred to the Molding Department.
4. Prepare a cost reconciliation between the costs determined in part (3) above and the cost of beginning inventory and costs added during the period.

PROBLEM 4-22 (Appendix 4A) Equivalent Units; Applying Costs—FIFO Method [LO5, LO6, LO7]

Selzik Company makes super-premium cake mixes that go through two processing departments, Blending and Packaging. The following activity was recorded in the Blending Department during July:

Production data:

Units in process, July 1 (materials 100%		
complete; conversion 30% complete).	10,000	
Units started into production	170,000	
Units completed and transferred to Packaging.	?	
Units in process, July 31 (materials 100%		
complete; conversion 40% complete	20,000	
Cost data:		
Work in process inventory, July 1:		
Materials cost.	$ 8,500	
Conversion cost	4,900	$ 13,400
Cost added during the month:		
Materials cost.	139,400	
Conversion cost	244,200	383,600
Total cost.		$397,000

All materials are added at the beginning of work in the Blending Department. The company uses the FIFO method.

Required:

1. Compute the equivalent units of production.
2. Compute the costs per equivalent unit for July.

3. Determine the cost of ending work in process inventory and of the units transferred to the Wiring Department.
4. Prepare a cost reconciliation between the costs determined in part (3) above and the cost of beginning inventory and costs added during the period.

PROBLEM 4-23 (Appendix 4B) Step-Down Method [LO9]

Woodbury Hospital has three service departments and three operating departments. Estimated cost and operating data for all departments in the hospital for the forthcoming quarter are presented in the table below:

| | Service Departments | | | Operating Departments | | | |
	Housekeeping Services	Food Services	Admin. Services	Laboratory	Radiology	General Hospital	Total
Variable costs	$ 0	$193,860	$158,840	$243,600	$304,800	$ 74,500	$ 975,600
Fixed costs	87,000	107,200	90,180	162,300	215,700	401,300	1,063,680
Total cost	$87,000	$301,060	$249,020	$405,900	$520,500	$475,800	$2,039,280
Meals served			800	2,000	1,000	68,000	71,800
Percentage of peak-period needs—Food Services			0.8%	2.4%	1.6%	95.2%	100%
Square feet of space	5,000	13,000	6,500	10,000	7,500	108,000	150,000
Files processed				14,000	7,000	25,000	46,000
Percentage of peak-period needs—Admin. Services.				30%	20%	50%	100%

The costs of the service departments are allocated by the step-down method using the allocation bases and in the order shown in the following table:

Service Department	Costs Incurred	Base for Allocation
Housekeeping Services	Fixed	Square feet of space
Food Services.	Variable	Meals served
	Fixed	Peak-period needs—Food Services
Administrative Services.	Variable	Files processed
	Fixed	Peak-period needs—Admin. Services

All billing in the hospital is done through Laboratory, Radiology, or General Hospital. The hospital's administrator wants the costs of the three service departments allocated to these three billing centers.

Required:

Prepare the cost allocation desired by the hospital administrator. (Use the step-down method.) Include under each billing center the direct costs of the center, as well as the costs allocated from the service departments.

PROBLEM 4-24 Interpreting a Production Report—Weighted-Average Method [LO2, LO3, LO4]

Cooperative San José of southern Sonora state in Mexico makes a unique syrup using cane sugar and local herbs. The syrup is sold in small bottles and is prized as a flavoring for drinks and for use in desserts. The bottles are sold for $12 each. (The Mexican currency is the peso and is denoted by $.) The first stage in the production process is carried out in the Mixing Department, which removes foreign matter from the raw materials and mixes them in the proper proportions in large vats. The company uses the weighted-average method in its process costing system.

A hastily prepared report for the Mixing Department for April appears below:

Quantity Schedule	
Units to be accounted for:	
Work in process, April 1 (materials 90% complete; conversion 80% complete)	30,000
Started into production	200,000
Total units to be accounted for	230,000
Units accounted for as follows:	
Transferred to next department	190,000
Work in process, April 30 (materials 75% complete; conversion 60% complete)	40,000
Total units accounted for	230,000
Cost to be accounted for:	
Work in process, April 1	$ 98,000
Cost added during the month	827,000
Total cost to be accounted for	$925,000
Cost accounted for as follows:	
Transferred to next department	$805,600
Work in process, April 30	119,400
Total cost accounted for	$925,000

Cooperative San José has just been acquired by another company, and the management of the acquiring company wants some additional information about Cooperative San José's operations.

Required:
1. What were the equivalent units for the month?
2. What were the costs per equivalent unit for the month? The beginning inventory consisted of the following costs: materials, $67,800; and conversion cost, $30,200. The costs added during the month consisted of: materials, $579,000; and conversion cost, $248,000.
3. How many of the units transferred to the next department were started and completed during the month?
4. The manager of the Mixing Department, anxious to make a good impression on the new owners, stated, "Materials prices jumped from about $2.50 per unit in March to $3 per unit in April, but due to good cost control I was able to hold our materials cost to less than $3 per unit for the month." Should this manager be rewarded for good cost control? Explain.

PROBLEM 4-25 Analysis of Work in Process T-Account—Weighted-Average Method
[LO1, LO2, LO3, LO4]

Weston Products manufactures an industrial cleaning compound that goes through three processing departments—Grinding, Mixing, and Cooking. All raw materials are introduced at the start of work in the Grinding Department. The Work in Process T-account for the Grinding Department for a recent month is given below:

Work in Process—Grinding Department

Inventory, May 1 (18,000 pounds, labor and overhead 1/3 complete)	21,800	Completed and transferred to mixing (__?__ pounds)	__?__
May costs added:			
Raw materials (167,000 pounds)	133,400		
Labor and overhead	226,800		
Inventory, May 31 (15,000 pounds, labor and overhead 2/3 complete)	__?__		

The May 1 work in process inventory consists of $14,600 in materials cost and $7,200 in labor and overhead cost. The company uses the weighted-average method to account for units and costs.

Required:

1. Determine the equivalent units of production for May.
2. Determine the costs per equivalent unit for May.
3. Determine the cost of the units completed and transferred to Grinding during May and the cost of ending work in process inventory.
4. What criticism can be made of the unit costs that you have computed if they are used to evaluate how well costs have been controlled?

PROBLEM 4-26 Equivalent Units; Costing of Inventories; Journal Entries—Weighted-Average Method
[LO1, LO2, LO3, LO4]
You are employed by Spirit Company, a manufacturer of digital watches. The company's chief financial officer is trying to verify the accuracy of the ending work in process and finished goods inventories prior to closing the books for the year. You have been asked to assist in this verification. The year-end balances shown on Spirit Company's books are as follows:

	Units	Costs
Work in process, December 31 (labor and overhead 50% complete)	300,000	$660,960
Finished goods, December 31	200,000	$1,009,800

Materials are added to production at the beginning of the manufacturing process, and overhead is applied to each product at the rate of 60% of direct labor cost. There was no finished goods inventory at the beginning of the year. A review of Spirit Company's inventory and cost records has disclosed the following data:

		Costs	
	Units	Materials	Labor
Work in process, January 1 (labor and overhead 80% complete)	200,000	$200,000	$315,000
Started into production	1,000,000		
Cost added during the year:			
Materials cost		$1,300,000	
Labor cost			$1,995,000
Units completed during the year	900,000		

The company uses the weighted-average method.

Required:

1. Determine the equivalent units and costs per equivalent unit for materials, labor, and overhead for the year.
2. Determine the amount of cost that should be assigned to the ending work in process and finished goods inventories.
3. Prepare the necessary correcting journal entry to adjust the work in process and finished goods inventories to the correct balances as of December 31.
4. Determine the cost of goods sold for the year assuming there is no under- or overapplied overhead.

(CPA, adapted)

PROBLEM 4-27 Cost Flows [LO1]
Lubricants, Inc., produces a special kind of grease that is widely used by race car drivers. The grease is produced in two processing departments: Refining and Blending. Raw materials are introduced at various points in the Refining Department.

The following incomplete Work in Process account is available for the Refining Department for March:

Work in Process—Refining Department

March 1 inventory (20,000 gallons; materials 100% complete; labor and overhead 90% complete) 38,000	Completed and transferred to blending (___?___ gallons) ?
March costs added:	
Raw oil materials	
(390,000 gallons) 495,000	
Direct labor 72,000	
Overhead 181,000	
March 31 inventory (40,000 gallons; materials 75% complete; labor and overhead 25% complete) ?	

The March 1 work in process inventory in the Refining Department consists of the following cost elements: raw materials, $25,000; direct labor, $4,000; and overhead, $9,000.

Costs incurred during March in the Blending Department were: materials used, $115,000; direct labor, $18,000; and overhead cost applied to production, $42,000. The company uses the weighted-average method in its process costing.

Required:

1. Prepare journal entries to record the costs incurred in both the Refining Department and Blending Department during March. Key your entries to the items (a) through (g) below.
   a. Raw materials were issued for use in production.
   b. Direct labor costs were incurred.
   c. Manufacturing overhead costs for the entire factory were incurred, $225,000. (Credit Accounts Payable.)
   d. Manufacturing overhead cost was applied to production using a predetermined overhead rate.
   e. Units that were complete with respect to processing in the Refining Department were transferred to the Blending Department, $740,000.
   f. Units that were complete with respect to processing in the Blending Department were transferred to Finished Goods, $950,000.
   g. Completed units were sold on account, $1,500,000. The Cost of Goods Sold was $900,000.
2. Post the journal entries from (1) above to T-accounts. The following account balances existed at the beginning of March. (The beginning balance in the Refining Department's Work in Process account is given above.)

Raw Materials.	$618,000
Work in Process—Blending Department.	$65,000
Finished Goods.	$20,000

After posting the entries to the T-accounts, find the ending balance in the inventory accounts and the manufacturing overhead account.

Cases

CASE 4-28 Ethics and the Manager, Understanding the Impact of Percentage Completion on Profit [LO2, LO3, LO4]

Gary Stevens and Mary James are production managers in the Consumer Electronics Division of General Electronics Company, which has several dozen plants scattered in locations throughout the world. Mary manages the plant located in Des Moines, Iowa, while Gary manages the plant in El Segundo, California. Production managers are paid a salary and get an additional bonus equal to 5% of their base salary if the entire division meets or exceeds its target profits for the year. The bonus is determined in March after the company's annual report has been prepared and issued to stockholders.

Shortly after the beginning of the new year, Mary received a phone call from Gary that went like this:

Gary: How's it going, Mary?

Mary: Fine, Gary. How's it going with you?

Gary: Great! I just got the preliminary profit figures for the division for last year and we are within $200,000 of making the year's target profits. All we have to do is pull a few strings, and we'll be over the top!

Mary: What do you mean?

Gary: Well, one thing that would be easy to change is your estimate of the percentage completion of your ending work in process inventories.

Mary: I don't know if I can do that, Gary. Those percentage completion figures are supplied by Tom Winthrop, my lead supervisor, who I have always trusted to provide us with good estimates. Besides, I have already sent the percentage completion figures to corporate headquarters.

Gary: You can always tell them there was a mistake. Think about it, Mary. All of us managers are doing as much as we can to pull this bonus out of the hat. You may not want the bonus check, but the rest of us sure could use it.

The final processing department in Mary's production facility began the year with no work in process inventories. During the year, 210,000 units were transferred in from the prior processing department and 200,000 units were completed and sold. Costs transferred in from the prior department totaled $39,375,000. No materials are added in the final processing department. A total of $20,807,500 of conversion cost was incurred in the final processing department during the year.

Required:

1. Tom Winthrop estimated that the units in ending inventory in the final processing department were 30% complete with respect to the conversion costs of the final processing department. If this estimate of the percentage completion is used, what would be the Cost of Goods Sold for the year?

2. Does Gary Stevens want the estimated percentage completion to be increased or decreased? Explain why.

3. What percentage completion would result in increasing reported net operating income by $200,000 over the net operating income that would be reported if the 30% figure were used?

4. Do you think Mary James should go along with the request to alter estimates of the percentage completion?

CASE 4-29 Second Department—Weighted-Average Method [LO2, LO3, LO4]

"I think we goofed when we hired that new assistant controller," said Ruth Scarpino, president of Provost Industries. "Just look at this production report that he prepared for last month for the Finishing Department. I can't make heads or tails out of it."

Finishing Department costs:	
Work in process inventory, April 1, 450 units; materials 100% complete; conversion 60% complete	$ 8,208*
Costs transferred in during the month from the preceding department, 1,950 units	17,940
Materials cost added during the month (materials are added when processing is 50% complete in the Finishing Department)	6,210
Conversion costs incurred during the month	13,920
Total departmental costs	$46,278

Finishing Department costs assigned to:	
Units completed and transferred to finished goods, 1,800 units at $25.71 per unit	$46,278
Work in process inventory, April 30, 600 units; materials 0% complete; conversion 35% complete	0
Total departmental costs assigned	$46,278

*Consists of cost transferred in, $4,068; materials cost, $1,980; and conversion cost, $2,160.

"He's struggling to learn our system," replied Frank Harrop, the operations manager. "The problem is that he's been away from process costing for a long time, and it's coming back slowly."

"It's not just the format of his report that I'm concerned about. Look at that $25.71 unit cost that he's come up with for April. Doesn't that seem high to you?" said Ms. Scarpino.

"Yes, it does seem high; but on the other hand, I know we had an increase in materials prices during April, and that may be the explanation," replied Mr. Harrop. "I'll get someone else to redo this report and then we may be able to see what's going on."

Provost Industries manufactures a ceramic product that goes through two processing departments—Molding and Finishing. The company uses the weighted-average method in its process costing.

Required:

1. Prepare a report for the Finishing Department for April showing how much cost should have been assigned to the units completed and transferred to finished goods and to the ending work in process inventory.
2. Explain to the president why the unit cost on the new assistant controller's report is so high.

CASE 4-30 (Appendix 4A) Second Department—FIFO Method [LO5, LO6, LO7]

Refer to the data for Provost Industries in the preceding case. Assume that the company uses the FIFO method to account for units and costs.

Required:

1. Prepare a report for the Finishing Department for April showing how much cost should have been assigned to the units completed and transferred to finished goods and to the ending work in process.
2. As stated in the case, the company experienced an increase in materials prices during April. Would the effects of this price increase tend to show up more under the weighted-average method or under the FIFO method? Why?

CASE 4-31 Step-Down Method versus Direct Method [LO8, LO9]

"This is really an odd situation," said Jim Carter, general manager of Highland Publishing Company. "We get most of the jobs we bid on that require a lot of press time in the Printing Department, yet profits on those jobs are never as high as they ought to be. On the other hand, we lose most of the jobs we bid on that require a lot of time in the Binding Department. I would be inclined to think that the problem is with our overhead rates, but we're already computing separate overhead rates for each department. So what else could be wrong?"

Highland Publishing Company is a large organization that offers a variety of printing and binding work. The Printing and Binding departments are supported by three service departments. The costs of these service departments are allocated to other departments in the order listed below. (For each service department, use the allocation base that provides the best measure of service provided, as discussed in the chapter.)

Department	Total Labor-Hours	Square Feet of Space Occupied	Number of Employees	Machine-Hours	Direct Labor-Hours
Personnel.............	20,000	4,000	10		
Custodial Services........	30,000	6,000	15		
Maintenance	50,000	20,000	25		
Printing................	90,000	80,000	40	150,000	60,000
Binding................	260,000	40,000	120	30,000	175,000
	450,000	150,000	210	180,000	235,000

Budgeted overhead costs in each department for the current year are shown below (no distinction is made between variable and fixed costs):

Personnel	$ 360,000
Custodial Services	141,000
Maintenance	201,000
Printing	525,000
Binding	373,500
Total budgeted cost........	$1,600,500

Because of its simplicity, the company has always used the direct method to allocate service department costs to the two operating departments.

Required:

1. Using the step-down method, allocate the service department costs to the operating departments. Then compute predetermined overhead rates for the current year using machine-hours as the allocation base in the Printing Department and direct labor-hours as the allocation base in the Binding Department.
2. Repeat (1) above, this time using the direct method. Again compute predetermined overhead rates in the Printing and Binding departments.
3. Assume that during the current year the company bids on a job that requires machine and labor time as follows:

	Machine-Hours	Direct Labor-Hours
Printing Department	15,400	900
Binding Department	800	2,000
Total hours	16,200	2,900

   a. Determine the amount of overhead cost that would be assigned to the job if the company used the overhead rates developed in (1) above. Then determine the amount of overhead cost that would be assigned to the job if the company used the overhead rates developed in (2) above.
   b. Explain to Mr. Carter, the general manager, why the step-down method provides a better basis for computing predetermined overhead rates than the direct method.

RESEARCH AND APPLICATION 4–32   [LO1]

The questions in this exercise are based on Anheuser-Busch Companies, Inc. The company had almost $15 billion in net sales in 2004. Although the company derives revenue from various sources, we are going to focus on the company's core business—beer manufacturing. To answer the questions, you will need to download and view an on-line tour of the company's beer brewing process at www.budweisertours.com/docs/onlinetour/Tour2.htm.

Required:

1. List each of the processing departments in Anheuser-Busch's brewing process. For each department, identify any raw materials that are added to production within that department,.
2. Would you expect Anheuser-Busch's brewing process to require fairly large amounts of manufacturing overhead costs? Why or why not?
3. Prepare a T-account model of the process costing flows for Anheuser-Busch that is similar to the one shown in Exhibit 4–3 on page 152. You need not take the diagram beyond the first two processes: Mashing and Straining.
4. Why might Anheuser-Busch use a form of operation costing as described on page 160?

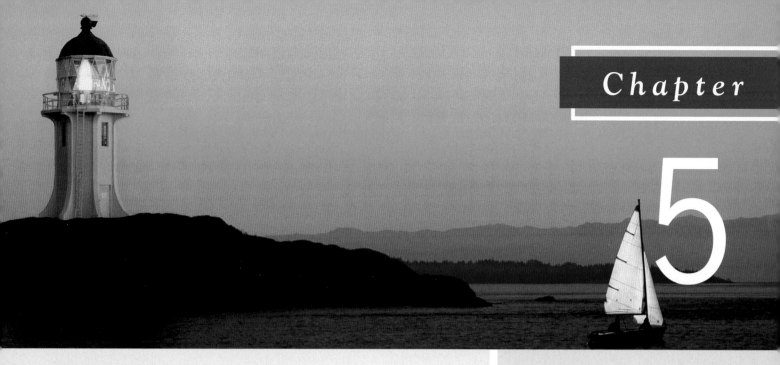

Cost Behavior Analysis and Use

The Business of Art Sculpture

Shidoni Foundry, located in Tesuque, New Mexico, is a fine art casting and fabrication facility. The process of creating a bronze or other metal sculpture is complex. The artist creates the sculpture using modeling clay and then hires a foundry such as Shidoni to produce the actual metal sculpture. Shidoni craftspeople make a rubber mold from the clay model then use that mold to make a wax version of the original. The wax is in turn used to make a ceramic casting mold, and finally the bronze version is cast. Both the wax and the ceramic casting mold are destroyed in the process of making the metal casting, but the rubber mold is not and can be reused to make additional castings.

The surface of the metal sculpture can be treated with various patinas. One of the accompanying photos shows Harry Gold, the shop's patina artist, applying a patina to a metal sculpture with brush and blowtorch. The other photo shows a finished sculpture with patinas applied.

The artist is faced with a difficult business decision. The rubber mold for a small figure such as the seated Indian in the accompanying photo costs roughly $500; the mold for a life-size figure such as the cowboy costs $3,800 to $5,000. This is just for the mold! Fortunately, as discussed above, a number of metal castings can be made from each mold. However, each life-size casting costs $8,500 to $11,000. In contrast, a casting of the much smaller Indian sculpture would cost about $750. Given the fixed costs of the mold and variable costs of the casting, finish treatments, and bases, the artist must decide how many castings to produce and how to price them. The fewer the castings, the greater the rarity factor, and hence the higher the price that can be charged to art lovers. However, in that case, the fixed costs of making the mold must be spread across fewer items. The artist must make sure not to price the sculptures so high that the investment in molds and in the castings cannot be recovered. ■

Learning Objectives

After studying Chapter 5, you should be able to:

LO1 Understand how fixed and variable costs behave and how to use them to predict costs.

LO2 Use a scattergraph plot to diagnose cost behavior.

LO3 Analyze a mixed cost using the high-low method.

LO4 Prepare an income statement using the contribution format.

LO5 (Appendix 5A) Analyze a mixed cost using the least-squares regression method.

Source: Conversations with Shidoni personnel, including Bill Rogers and Harry Gold, and Shidoni literature. See www.shidoni.com for more information concerning the company.

In Chapter 2, we stated that costs can be classified by behavior. Cost behavior refers to how a cost will change as the level of activity changes. Managers who understand how costs behave can predict how costs will change under various alternatives. Conversely, attempting to make decisions without a thorough understanding of cost behavior patterns can lead to disaster. For example, cutting back production of a product line might result in far less cost savings than managers assume if they confuse fixed costs with variable costs—leading to a drop in profits. To avoid such problems, managers must be able to accurately predict what costs will be at various activity levels.

This chapter briefly reviews the definitions of variable and fixed costs and then discusses the behavior of these costs in greater depth than in Chapter 2. The chapter also introduces the concept of a mixed cost, which is a cost that has both variable and fixed cost elements. The chapter concludes by introducing a new income statement format—called the *contribution format*—in which costs are organized by behavior rather than by the traditional functions of production, sales, and administration.

Types of Cost Behavior Patterns

Topic Tackler

PLUS

5–1

In Chapter 2 we mentioned only variable and fixed costs. In this chapter we will examine a third cost behavior pattern, known as a *mixed* or *semivariable* cost. All three cost behavior patterns—variable, fixed, and mixed—are found in most organizations. The relative proportion of each type of cost in an organization is known as its **cost structure.** For example, an organization might have many fixed costs but few variable or mixed costs. Alternatively, it might have many variable costs but few fixed or mixed costs. In this chapter, we will concentrate on gaining a fuller understanding of the behavior of each type of cost. In the next chapter, we explore how cost structure impacts decisions.

COST STRUCTURE: A MANAGEMENT CHOICE

Some managers are thriftier than others. Kenneth Iverson built Nucor Steel into the most successful U.S. steel company of recent years by developing a whole new approach to steel-making using cost-efficient minimills. Iverson ran his company with few layers of management and a commitment to employees that everyone would be treated alike. Workers were "dissuaded from joining a union by high wages and a series of No's—no management dining rooms, no company yachts, no company planes, no first-class travel for executives, and no support staff to pamper the upper echelons." Iverson ran the largest steel company in the U.S. with only 20 people in his headquarters. "By responding to market signals, focusing on a single major product line, and treating his employees with respect and compassion, Mr. Iverson contributed immensely to the industrial rebirth in this country."

Source: Donald F. Barnett and Robert W. Crandall, "Remembering a Man of Steel," *The Wall Street Journal,* April 23, 2002, p. B4.

LEARNING OBJECTIVE 1
Understand how fixed and variable costs behave and how to use them to predict costs.

Variable Costs

We explained in Chapter 2 that a variable cost is a cost whose total dollar amount varies in direct proportion to changes in the activity level. If the activity level doubles, the total variable cost also doubles. If the activity level increases by only 10%, then the total variable cost increases by 10% as well.

ADVERTISING ON THE WEB

Many companies spend a growing portion of their advertising budgets on web-based contextual advertising. Here is an example of how it works. A tour company specializing in trips to Belize would like to steer consumers interested in Belize vacations to its website. The tour company partners with National Geographic and Quigo Technologies, a software company, to ensure that every time a visitor reads a National Geographic article mentioning the word Belize, a pop-up advertisement contains a link to the tour company's website. The tour company pays 50 cents each time a visitor clicks on that link. The 50 cents is split between iExplore.com, National Geographic's on-line business, and Quigo Technologies. For the tour company, this form of advertising is a clear example of a variable cost. The cost per click is constant at 50 cents per unit, but the total advertising cost rises as the number of clicks increases.

The challenge for software developers at companies such as Quigo Technologies, Google, and Yahoo is to write programs that intelligently select ads that are relevant to the context of a given web page. Providing superior contextual relevance increases the likelihood that web surfers will click on an advertisement, which in turn increases the revenue generated. Quigo Technologies' Michael Yavonditte claims that his company's ads are clicked on 0.7% of the time versus 0.2% for competitors.

Source: Chana R. Schoenberger, "Out of Context" *Forbes*, November 29, 2004, pp. 64–68.

We also found in Chapter 2 that a variable cost remains constant if expressed on a *per unit* basis. To provide an example, consider Nooksack Expeditions, a small company that provides daylong whitewater rafting excursions on rivers in the North Cascade Mountains. The company provides all of the necessary equipment and experienced guides, and it serves gourmet meals to its guests. The meals are purchased from an exclusive caterer for $30 a person for a daylong excursion. If we look at the cost of the meals on a *per person* basis, it remains constant at $30. This $30 cost per person will not change, regardless of how many people participate in a daylong excursion. The behavior of this variable cost, on both a per unit and a total basis, is tabulated as follows:

Number of Guests	Cost of Meals per Guest	Total Cost of Meals
250	$30	$7,500
500	$30	$15,000
750	$30	$22,500
1,000	$30	$30,000

The idea that a variable cost is constant per unit but varies in total with the activity level is crucial to understanding cost behavior patterns. We shall rely on this concept repeatedly in this chapter and in chapters ahead.

Exhibit 5–1 (page 190) illustrates variable cost behavior. Note that the graph of the total cost of the meals slants upward to the right. This is because the total cost of the meals is directly proportional to the number of guests. In contrast, the graph of the per unit cost of meals is flat because the cost of the meals per guest is constant at $30.

The Activity Base   For a cost to be variable, it must be variable *with respect to something*. That "something" is its *activity base*. An **activity base** is a measure of whatever causes the incurrence of variable cost. An activity base is sometimes referred to as a *cost driver*. Some of the most common activity bases are direct labor-hours, machine-hours, units produced, and units sold. Other examples of activity bases (cost drivers) include the number of miles driven by salespersons, the number of pounds of laundry cleaned by a hotel, the

EXHIBIT 5–1
Variable Cost Behavior

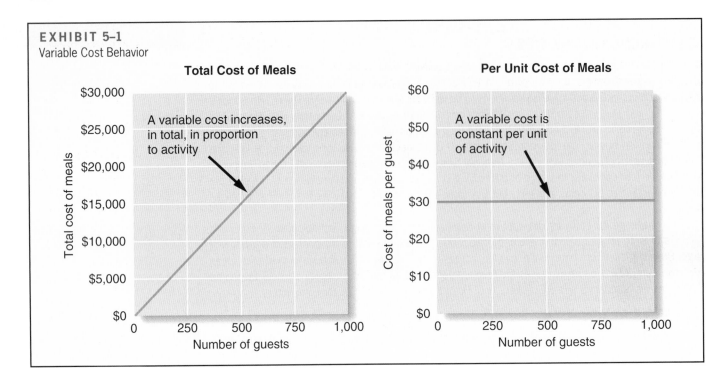

number of calls handled by technical support staff at a software company, and the number of beds occupied in a hospital.

People sometimes get the notion that if a cost doesn't vary with production or with sales, then it is not a variable cost. This is not correct. As suggested by the range of bases listed above, costs are caused by many different activities within an organization. Whether a cost is variable or fixed depends on whether it is caused by the activity under consideration. For example, when analyzing the cost of service calls under a product warranty, the relevant activity measure is the number of service calls made. Those costs that vary in total with the number of service calls made are the variable costs of making service calls.

Nevertheless, unless stated otherwise, you can assume that the activity base under consideration is the total volume of goods and services provided by the organization. So, for example, if we ask whether direct materials at Ford is a variable cost, the answer is yes, since the cost of direct materials is variable with respect to Ford's total volume of output. We will specify the activity base only when it is something other than total output.

IN BUSINESS

COPING WITH THE FALLOUT FROM SEPTEMBER 11

Costs can change for reasons that have nothing to do with changes in volume. Filterfresh is a company that services coffee machines located in commercial offices—providing milk, sugar, cups, and coffee. The company's operations were profoundly affected by the security measures many companies initiated after the terrorist attacks on the World Trade Center and the Pentagon on September 11, 2001. Heightened security at customer locations means that Filterfresh's 250 deliverymen can no longer casually walk through a customer's lobby with a load of supplies. Now a guard typically checks the deliveryman's identification and paperwork at the loading dock and may search the van before permitting the deliveryman access to the customer's building. These delays have added an average of about an hour per day to each route, which means that Filterfresh needs 24 more delivery people to do the same work it did prior to September 11. That's a 10% increase in cost without any increase in the amount of coffee sold.

Source: Anna Bernasek, "The Friction Economy," *Fortune,* February 18, 2002, pp. 104–112.

EXHIBIT 5–2
Examples of Variable Costs

Type of Organization	Costs that Are Normally Variable with Respect to Volume of Output
Merchandising company	Cost of goods (merchandise) sold

Manufacturing company	Direct materials
	Direct labor*
	Variable elements of manufacturing overhead:
	    Indirect materials
	    Lubricants
	    Supplies
	    Power

Both merchandising and manufacturing companies	Variable elements of selling and administrative costs:
	    Commissions
	    Shipping costs

Service organizations	Supplies, travel

*Direct labor may or may not be variable in practice. See the discussion later in this chapter.

Extent of Variable Costs   The number and type of variable costs in an organization will depend in large part on the organization's structure and purpose. A public utility like Florida Power and Light, with large investments in equipment, will tend to have few variable costs. Most of the costs are associated with its plant, and these costs tend to be insensitive to changes in levels of service provided. A manufacturing company like Black and Decker, by contrast, will often have many variable costs; these costs will be associated with both manufacturing and distributing its products to customers.

A merchandising company like Wal-Mart or J. K. Gill will usually have a high proportion of variable costs in its cost structure. In most merchandising companies, the cost of merchandise purchased for resale, a variable cost, constitutes a very large component of total cost. Service companies, by contrast, have diverse cost structures. Some service companies, such as the Skippers restaurant chain, have fairly large variable costs because of the costs of their raw materials. On the other hand, service companies involved in consulting, auditing, engineering, dental, medical, and architectural activities have very large fixed costs in the form of expensive facilities and highly trained salaried employees.

Some of the more frequently encountered variable costs are listed in Exhibit 5–2 above. This exhibit is not a complete listing of all costs that can be considered variable. Moreover, some of the costs listed in the exhibit may behave more like fixed than variable costs in some organizations and in some circumstances. We will see examples of this later in the chapter. Nevertheless, Exhibit 5–2 provides a useful listing of many of the costs that normally would be considered variable with respect to the volume of output.

True Variable versus Step-Variable Costs

Not all variable costs have exactly the same behavior pattern. Some variable costs behave in a *true variable* or *proportionately variable* pattern. Other variable costs behave in a *step-variable* pattern.

True Variable Costs   Direct materials is a true or proportionately variable cost because the amount used during a period will vary in direct proportion to the level of production activity. Moreover, any amounts purchased but not used can be stored and carried forward to the next period as inventory.

Step-Variable Costs   The cost of a resource that is obtainable only in large chunks and that increases or decreases only in response to fairly wide changes in activity is known as a **step-variable cost.** For example, the wages of skilled repair technicians are often considered

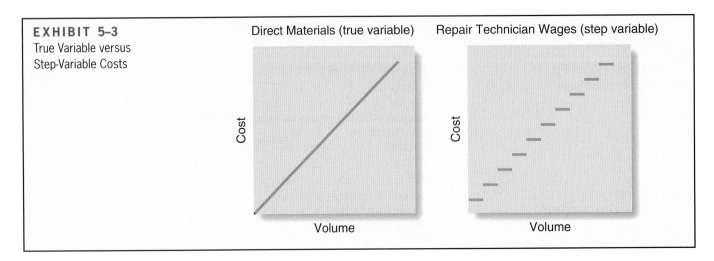

EXHIBIT 5–3
True Variable versus
Step-Variable Costs

Direct Materials (true variable)   Repair Technician Wages (step variable)

to be a step-variable cost. Such a technician's time can only be obtained in large chunks—it is difficult to hire a skilled technician on anything other than a full-time basis. Moreover, any technician's time not currently used cannot be stored as inventory and carried forward to the next period. If the time is not used effectively, it is gone forever. Furthermore, a repair technician can work at a leisurely pace if pressures are light but intensify his or her efforts if pressures build up. For this reason, small changes in the level of production may have no effect on the number of technicians employed by the company.

Exhibit 5–3 contrasts the behavior of a step-variable cost with the behavior of a true variable cost. Notice that the cost of repair technicians changes only with fairly wide changes in volume and that additional technicians come in large, indivisible chunks. Great care must be taken in working with these kinds of costs to prevent "fat" from building up in an organization. There may be a tendency to employ additional help more quickly than needed, and there is a natural reluctance to lay people off when volume declines.

IN BUSINESS

WHAT GOES UP DOESN'T NECESSARILY COME DOWN

The traditional view of variable costs is that they behave similarly in response to either increases or decreases in activity. However, the results of a research study using data from 7,629 companies spanning a 20-year period suggests otherwise. In this study, a 1% increase in sales corresponded with a 0.55% increase in selling and administrative costs, while a 1% decrease in sales corresponded with a 0.35% decrease in selling and administrative costs. These results suggest that many costs do not mechanistically increase or decrease in response to changes in the activity base; rather they change in response to managers' decisions about how to react to changes in the level of the activity base.

"When volume falls, managers must decide whether to maintain committed resources and bear the costs of operating with unutilized capacity or reduce committed resources and incur the adjustment costs of retrenching and, if volume is restored, replacing committed resources at a later date." Managers faced with these choices are less likely to reduce expenses when they perceive that a decrease in activity level is temporary or when the cost of adjusting committed resources is high.

Source: Mark C. Anderson, Rajiv D. Banker, and Surya N. Janakiraman, "Are Selling, General, and Administrative Costs 'Sticky'?" *Journal of Accounting Research*, March 2003, pp. 47–63.

The Linearity Assumption and the Relevant Range   Except in the case of step-variable costs, we ordinarily assume a strictly linear relationship between cost and volume. Economists correctly point out that many costs that the accountant classifies as variable actually behave in a *curvilinear* fashion; that is, the relation between cost and activity is a curve. A curvilinear cost is illustrated in Exhibit 5–4.

Although many costs are not strictly linear, a curvilinear cost can be satisfactorily approximated with a straight line within a narrow band of activity known as the *relevant range*. The **relevant range** is that range of activity within which the assumptions made about cost behavior

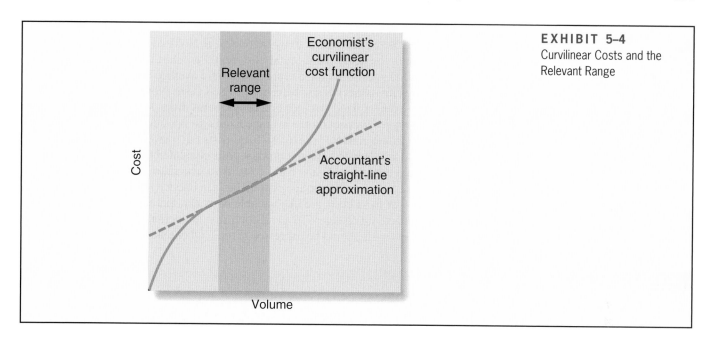

EXHIBIT 5–4
Curvilinear Costs and the
Relevant Range

are reasonably valid. For example, note that the dashed line in Exhibit 5–4 approximates the curvilinear cost with very little loss of accuracy within the shaded relevant range. However, outside of the relevant range this particular straight line is a poor approximation to the curvilinear cost relationship. Managers should always keep in mind that assumptions made about cost behavior may be invalid if activity falls outside of the relevant range.

Fixed Costs

In our discussion of cost behavior patterns in Chapter 2, we stated that total fixed costs remain constant within the relevant range of activity. To continue the Nooksack Expeditions example, assume the company rents a building for $500 per month to store its equipment. Within the relevant range, the total amount of rent paid is the same regardless of the number of guests the company takes on its expeditions during any given month. Exhibit 5–5 depicts this cost behavior pattern.

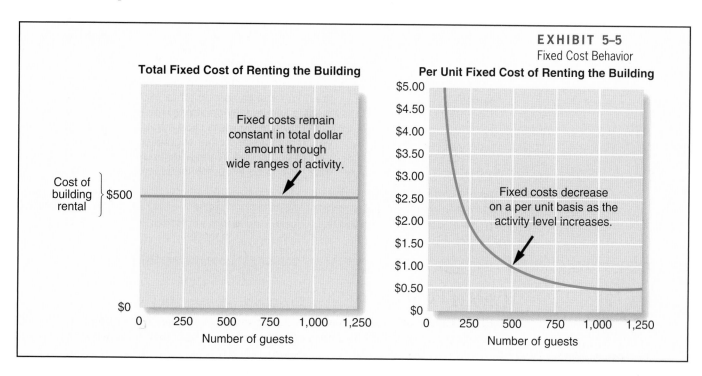

EXHIBIT 5–5
Fixed Cost Behavior

Since fixed costs remain constant in total, the average fixed cost *per unit* becomes progressively smaller as the level of activity increases. If Nooksack Expeditions has only 250 guests in a month, the $500 fixed rental cost would amount to an average of $2 per guest. If there are 1,000 guests, the fixed rental cost would average only 50 cents per guest. Exhibit 5–5 illustrates this aspect of the behavior of fixed costs. Note that as the number of guests increases, the average fixed cost per unit drops, but it drops at a decreasing rate. The first guests have the biggest impact on the average fixed cost per unit.

It is necessary in some contexts to express fixed costs on an average per unit basis. For example, in Chapter 2 we showed how unit product costs computed for use in external financial statements contain both variable and fixed costs. As a general rule, however, we caution against expressing fixed costs on an average per unit basis in internal reports because it creates the false impression that fixed costs are like variable costs and that total fixed costs actually change as the level of activity changes. To avoid confusion in internal reporting and decision-making situations, fixed costs should be expressed in total rather than on a per unit basis.

IN BUSINESS

COSTING THE TREK

Jackson Hole Llamas is owned and operated by Jill Aanonsen/Hodges and David Hodges. The company provides guided tours to remote areas of Yellowstone National Park and the Jedediah Smith Wilderness, with the llamas carrying the baggage for the multiday treks.

Jill and David operate out of their ranch in Jackson Hole, Wyoming, leading about 10 trips each summer season. All food is provided as well as tents and sleeping pads. Based on the number of guests on a trip, Jill and David will decide how many llamas will go on the trip and how many will remain on the ranch. Llamas are transported to the trailhead in a special trailer.

The company has a number of costs, some of which are listed below:

Cost	Cost Behavior
Food and beverage costs	Variable with respect to the number of guests and the length of the trip in days.
Truck and trailer operating costs	Variable with respect to the number of miles to the trailhead.
Guide wages	Step variable; Jill and David serve as the guides on most trips and hire guides only for larger groups.
Costs of providing tents	Variable with respect to the number of guests and length of the trip in days. Jackson Hole Llamas owns its tents, but they wear out through use and must be repaired or eventually replaced.
Cost of feeding llamas	Variable with respect to the number of guests, and hence the number of llamas, on a trip. [Actually, the cost of feeding llamas may *decrease* with the number of guests on a trip. When a llama is on a trek, it lives off the land—eating grasses and other vegetation found in meadows and along the trail. When a llama is left on the ranch, it may have to be fed purchased feed.]
Property taxes	Fixed.

Source: Jill Aanonsen/Hodges and David Hodges, owners and operators of Jackson Hole Llamas, www.jhllamas.com.

Types of Fixed Costs

Fixed costs are sometimes referred to as capacity costs, since they result from outlays made for buildings, equipment, skilled professional employees, and other items needed to provide the basic capacity for sustained operations. For planning purposes, fixed costs can be viewed as either *committed* or *discretionary.*

Committed Fixed Costs   Investments in facilities, equipment, and the basic organization that can't be significantly reduced even for short periods of time without making fundamental changes are referred to as **committed fixed costs.** Examples of such costs include depreciation of buildings and equipment, real estate taxes, insurance expenses, and salaries of top management and operating personnel. Even if operations are interrupted or cut back, committed fixed costs remain largely unchanged in the short term. During a recession, for example, a company won't usually eliminate key executive positions or sell off key facilities—the basic organizational structure and facilities ordinarily are kept intact. The costs of restoring them later are likely to be far greater than any short-run savings that might be realized.

Once a decision is made to acquire committed fixed resources, the company may be locked into that decision for many years to come. Consequently, such commitments should be made only after careful analysis of the available alternatives. Investment decisions involving committed fixed costs will be examined in Chapter 14.

Discretionary Fixed Costs   **Discretionary fixed costs** (often referred to as *managed fixed costs*) usually arise from *annual* decisions by management to spend on certain fixed cost items. Examples of discretionary fixed costs include advertising, research, public relations, management development programs, and internships for students.

Two key differences exist between discretionary fixed costs and committed fixed costs. First, the planning horizon for a discretionary fixed cost is short term—usually a single year. By contrast, committed fixed costs have a planning horizon that encompasses many years. Second, discretionary fixed costs can be cut for short periods of time with minimal damage to the long-run goals of the organization. For example, spending on management development programs can be reduced because of poor economic conditions. Although some unfavorable consequences may result from the cutback, it is doubtful that these consequences would be as great as those that would result if the company decided to economize by laying off key personnel.

Whether a particular cost is regarded as committed or discretionary may depend on management's strategy. For example, during recessions when the level of home building is down, many construction companies lay off most of their workers and virtually disband operations. Other construction companies retain large numbers of employees on the payroll, even though the workers have little or no work to do. While these latter companies may be faced with short-term cash flow problems, it will be easier for them to respond quickly when economic conditions improve. And the higher morale and loyalty of their employees may give these companies a significant competitive advantage.

The most important characteristic of discretionary fixed costs is that management is not locked into its decisions regarding such costs. Discretionary costs can be adjusted from year to year or even perhaps during the course of a year if necessary.

IN BUSINESS

A TWIST ON FIXED AND VARIABLE COSTS

Mission Controls designs and installs automation systems for food and beverage manufacturers. At most companies, when sales drop and cost cutting is necessary, top managers lay off workers. The founders of Mission Controls decided to do something different when sales drop—they slash their own salaries before they even consider letting any of their employees go. This makes their own salaries somewhat variable, while the wages and salaries of workers act more like fixed costs. The payoff is a loyal and committed workforce.

Source: Christopher Caggiano, "Employment, Guaranteed for Life," *Inc.* magazine, October 15, 2002, p. 74.

The Trend toward Fixed Costs The trend in many industries is toward greater fixed costs relative to variable costs. Chores that used to be performed by hand have been taken over by machines. For example, grocery clerks at stores like Safeway and Kroger used to key in prices by hand on cash registers. Now, most stores are equipped with barcode readers that enter price and other product information automatically. In general, competition has created pressure to give customers more value for their money—a demand that often can only be satisfied by automating business processes. For example, an H & R Block employee used to fill out tax returns for customers by hand and the advice given to a customer largely depended on the knowledge of that particular employee. Now, sophisticated computer software based on the accumulated knowledge of many experts is used to complete tax returns, and the software provides tax planning and other advice tailored to the customer's needs.

As automation intensifies, the demand for "knowledge" workers—those who work primarily with their minds rather than their muscles—has grown tremendously. Since knowledge workers tend to be salaried, highly trained, and difficult to replace, the costs of compensating these workers are often relatively fixed and are committed rather than discretionary.

IN BUSINESS

A NEW TWIST ON SENDING JOBS OFFSHORE

SeaCode (www.sea-code.com) is a San Diego based company that offers a new twist on the popular practice of outsourcing jobs from the United States to foreign countries with lower labor costs. The company houses 600 computer programmers from around the world on a cruise ship three miles off the coast of Los Angeles. This "floating tech factory" is subject to the labor laws of whatever flag the boat chooses to fly rather than to U.S. labor laws. SeaCode pays its "knowledge workers" $1,500 to $1,800 per month, which is below prevailing salaries on the U.S. mainland but exceeds the salaries in many countries. The company claims that it has been inundated with resumes of college graduates from across the globe.

SeaCode's clients get access to highly skilled labor at a lower cost than would have to be paid for similar jobs housed on U.S. soil. In addition, rather than having to fly half way around the world to places such as India or China to oversee projects, U.S. managers can fly to Los Angeles and in a brief time be three miles off the California coast checking on the status of "offshore" operations.

Source: Reed Tucker, "Will a Floating Tech Factory Fly?" *Fortune*, September 5, 2005, p. 28.

Is Labor a Variable or a Fixed Cost? As the preceding discussion suggests, wages and salaries may be fixed or variable. The behavior of wage and salary costs will differ from one country to another, depending on labor regulations, labor contracts, and custom. In some countries, such as France, Germany, and Japan, management has little flexibility in adjusting the labor force to changes in business activity. In countries such as the United States and the United Kingdom, management typically has much greater latitude. However, even in these less restrictive environments, managers may choose to treat employee compensation as a fixed cost for several reasons.

First, many managers are reluctant to decrease their workforce in response to short-term declines in sales. These managers realize that the success of their businesses hinges on retaining highly skilled and trained employees. If these valuable workers are laid off, it is unlikely that they would ever return or be easily replaced. Furthermore, laying off workers undermines the morale of those employees who remain.

Second, managers do not want to be caught with a bloated payroll in an economic downturn. Therefore, managers are reluctant to add employees in response to short-term increases in sales. Instead, more and more companies rely on temporary and part-time workers to take up the slack when their permanent, full-time employees are unable to handle all of the demand for their products and services. In such companies, labor costs are a complex mixture of fixed and variable costs.

LABOR AT SOUTHWEST AIRLINES

Starting with a $10,000 investment in 1966, Herb Kelleher built Southwest Airlines into the most profitable airline in the United States. Prior to stepping down as president and CEO of the airline in 2001, Kelleher wrote: "The thing that would disturb me most to see after I'm no longer CEO is layoffs at Southwest. Nothing kills your company's culture like layoffs. Nobody has ever been furloughed here, and that is unprecedented in the airline industry. It's been a huge strength of ours . . . We could have furloughed at various times and been more profitable, but I always thought that was shortsighted. You want to show your people that you value them and you're not going to hurt them just to get a little money in the short run."

Because of this commitment by management to the company's employees, all wages and salaries are basically committed fixed costs at Southwest Airlines.

Source: Herb Kelleher, "The Chairman of the Board Looks Back," *Fortune*, May 28, 2001, pp. 63–76.

Many major companies have undergone waves of downsizing in recent years in which large numbers of employees—particularly managers—have lost their jobs. This downsizing may seem to suggest that even management salaries should be regarded as variable costs, but this would not be a valid conclusion. Downsizing has largely been the result of attempts to reengineer business processes and cut costs rather than a response to a decline in sales activity. This underscores an important, but subtle, point. Fixed costs can change—they just don't change in response to small changes in activity.

In sum, there is no clear-cut answer to the question "Is labor a variable or fixed cost?" It depends on how much flexibility management has to adjust the workforce and management's strategy. Nevertheless, unless otherwise stated, we will assume in this text that direct labor is a variable cost. This assumption is more likely to be valid for companies in the United States than in countries where employment laws permit much less flexibility.

THE REGULATORY BURDEN

The late Peter F. Drucker, a renowned observer of business and society, claimed that "the driving force behind the steady growth of temps [and outsourcing of work] . . . is the growing burden of rules and regulations for employers." U.S. laws and regulations concerning employees require companies to file multiple reports—and any breach, even if unintentional, can result in punishment. According to the Small Business Administration, the owner of a small or midsize business spends up to a quarter of his or her time on employment-related paperwork and the cost of complying with government regulations (including tax report preparation) is over $5,000 per employee per year. "No wonder that employers . . . complain bitterly that they have no time to work on products and services. . . . They no longer chant the old mantra 'People are our greatest asset.' Instead, they claim 'People are our greatest liability.'" To the extent that the regulatory burden leads to a decline in permanent full-time employees and an increase in the use of temporary employees and outsourcing, labor costs are converted from fixed to variable costs. While this is not the intent of the regulations, it is a consequence.

Source: Peter F. Drucker, "They're Not Employees, They're People," *Harvard Business Review*, February 2002.

Fixed Costs and the Relevant Range

The concept of the relevant range, which was introduced in the discussion of variable costs, is also important in understanding fixed costs—particularly discretionary fixed costs. The levels of discretionary fixed costs are typically decided at the beginning of the year and depend on the needs of planned programs such as advertising and training. The scope of these programs will depend, in turn, on the overall anticipated level of activity for the year. At very high levels of activity, programs are often broadened or expanded. For example, if the company hopes to increase sales by 25%, it would probably plan for much larger advertising costs than if no sales increase were planned. So the *planned* level of activity might affect total discretionary fixed costs. However, once the total discretionary fixed costs have been budgeted, they are unaffected by the *actual* level of activity. For example, once the advertising budget has been established and spent, it will not be affected by how many units are actually sold. Therefore, the cost is fixed with respect to the *actual* number of units sold.

Discretionary fixed costs are easier to adjust than committed fixed costs. They also tend to be less "lumpy." Committed fixed costs consist of costs such as buildings, equipment, and the salaries of key personnel. It is difficult to buy half a piece of equipment or to hire a quarter of a product-line manager, so the step pattern depicted in Exhibit 5–6 is typical for such costs. The relevant range of activity for a fixed cost is the range of activity over which the graph of the cost is flat as in Exhibit 5–6. As a company expands its level of activity, it may outgrow its present facilities, or the key management team may need to be expanded. The result, of course, will be increased committed fixed costs as larger facilities are built and as new management positions are created.

One reaction to the step pattern depicted in Exhibit 5–6 is to conclude that discretionary and committed fixed costs are really just step-variable costs. To some extent this is true, since *almost* all costs can be adjusted in the long run. There are two major differences, however, between the step-variable costs depicted earlier in Exhibit 5–3 and the fixed costs depicted in Exhibit 5–6.

The first difference is that the step-variable costs can often be adjusted quickly as conditions change, whereas once fixed costs have been set, they usually can't be changed easily. A step-variable cost such as the wages of repair technicians, for example, can be adjusted upward or downward by hiring and laying off technicians. By contrast, once a company has signed a lease for a building, it is locked into that level of lease cost for the life of the contract.

The second difference is that the *width of the steps* depicted for step-variable costs is much narrower than the width of the steps depicted for the fixed costs in Exhibit 5–6. The width of the steps relates to volume or level of activity. For step-variable costs, the width of a step might be 40 hours of activity per week in the case of repair technicians. For fixed costs, however, the width of a step might be *thousands* or even *tens of thousands* of hours of activity. In essence, the width of the steps for step-variable costs is generally so narrow that these costs can be treated essentially as variable costs for most purposes. The width of the steps for fixed costs, on the other hand, is so wide that these costs should be treated as entirely fixed within the relevant range.

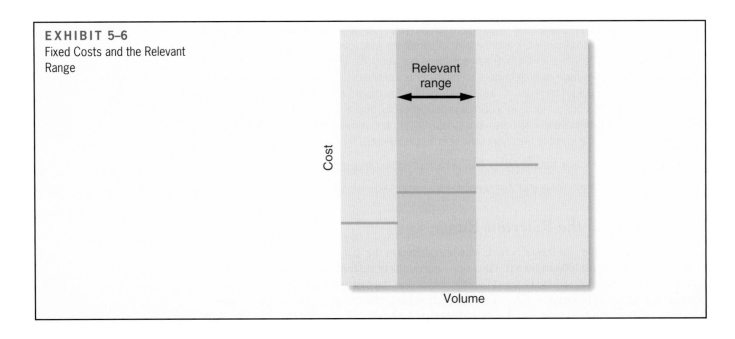

EXHIBIT 5–6
Fixed Costs and the Relevant Range

Mixed Costs

A **mixed cost** contains both variable and fixed cost elements. Mixed costs are also known as semivariable costs. To continue the Nooksack Expeditions example, the company must pay a license fee of $25,000 per year plus $3 per rafting party to the state's Department of Natural Resources. If the company runs 1,000 rafting parties this year, then the total fees paid to the state would be $28,000, made up of $25,000 in fixed cost plus $3,000 in variable cost. Exhibit 5–7 depicts the behavior of this mixed cost.

Even if Nooksack fails to attract any customers, the company will still have to pay the license fee of $25,000. This is why the cost line in Exhibit 5–7 intersects the vertical cost axis at the $25,000 point. For each rafting party the company organizes, the total cost of the state fees will increase by $3. Therefore, the total cost line slopes upward as the variable cost of $3 per party is added to the fixed cost of $25,000 per year.

Since the mixed cost in Exhibit 5–7 is represented by a straight line, the following equation for a straight line can be used to express the relationship between a mixed cost and the level of activity:

$$Y = a + bX$$

In this equation,

Y = The total mixed cost

a = The total fixed cost (the vertical intercept of the line)

b = The variable cost per unit of activity (the slope of the line)

X = The level of activity

Since the variable cost per unit equals the slope of the straight line, the steeper the slope, the higher the variable cost per unit.

In the case of the state fees paid by Nooksack Expeditions, the equation is written as follows:

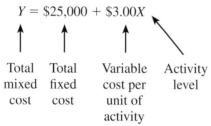

$$Y = \$25,000 + \$3.00X$$

| Total mixed cost | Total fixed cost | Variable cost per unit of activity | Activity level |

This equation makes it easy to calculate the total mixed cost for any level of activity within the relevant range. For example, suppose that the company expects to

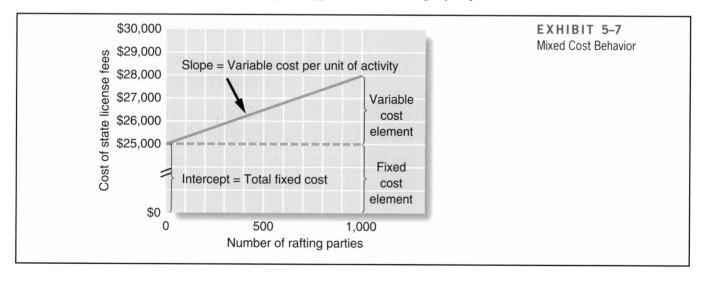

EXHIBIT 5–7
Mixed Cost Behavior

organize 800 rafting parties in the next year. The total state fees would be calculated as follows:

$$Y = \$25{,}000 + (\$3.00 \text{ per rafting party} \times 800 \text{ rafting parties})$$

$$= \$27{,}400$$

COST BEHAVIOR IN THE U.S. AND JAPAN

A total of 257 American and 40 Japanese manufacturing companies responded to a questionnaire concerning their management accounting practices. Among other things, the companies were asked whether they classified certain costs as variable, semivariable, or fixed. Some of the results are summarized in Exhibit 5–8. Note that companies do not all classify costs in the same way. For example, roughly 45% of the U.S. companies classify material-handling labor costs as variable, 35% as semivariable, and 20% as fixed. Also note that the Japanese companies are much more likely than U.S. companies to classify labor costs as fixed.

Source: NAA Tokyo Affiliate, "Management Accounting in the Advanced Management Surrounding—Comparative Study on Survey in Japan and U.S.A."

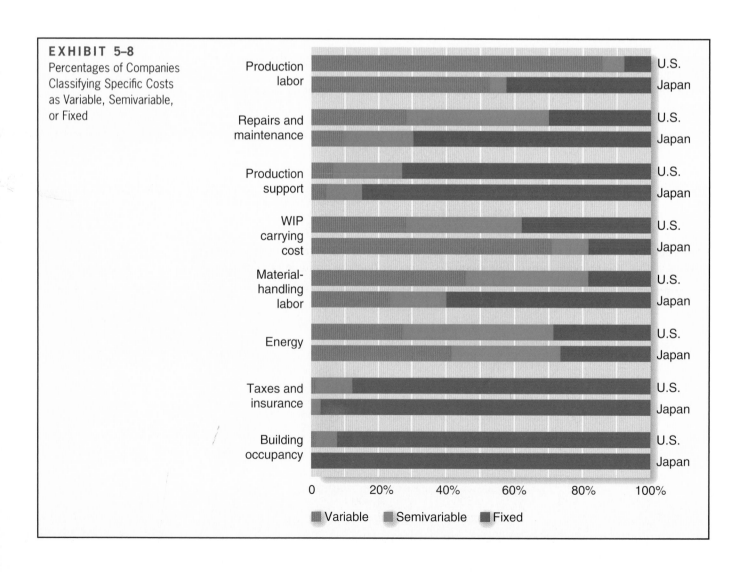

EXHIBIT 5–8
Percentages of Companies Classifying Specific Costs as Variable, Semivariable, or Fixed

The Analysis of Mixed Costs

Mixed costs are very common. For example, the cost of providing X-ray services to patients at the Harvard Medical School Hospital is a mixed cost. The costs of equipment depreciation and radiologists' and technicians' salaries are fixed, but the costs of X-ray film, power, and supplies are variable. At Southwest Airlines, maintenance costs are a mixed cost. The company incurs fixed costs for renting maintenance facilities and for keeping skilled mechanics on the payroll, but the costs of replacement parts, lubricating oils, tires, and so forth, are variable with respect to how often and how far the company's aircraft are flown.

The fixed portion of a mixed cost represents the minimum cost of having a service *ready and available* for use. The variable portion represents the cost incurred for *actual consumption* of the service, thus it varies in proportion to the amount of service actually consumed.

How does management go about actually estimating the fixed and variable components of a mixed cost? The most common methods used in practice are *account analysis* and the *engineering approach.*

In **account analysis,** an account is classified as either variable or fixed based on the analyst's prior knowledge of how the cost in the account behaves. For example, direct materials would be classified as variable and a building lease cost would be classified as fixed because of the nature of those costs. The total fixed cost of an organization is the sum of the costs for the accounts that have been classified as fixed. The variable cost per unit is estimated by dividing the sum of the costs for the accounts that have been classified as variable by the total activity.

The **engineering approach** to cost analysis involves a detailed analysis of what cost behavior should be, based on an industrial engineer's evaluation of the production methods

OPERATIONS DRIVE COSTS

White Grizzly Adventures is a snowcat skiing and snowboarding company in Meadow Creek, British Columbia, that is owned and operated by Brad and Carole Karafil. The company shuttles 12 guests to the top of the company's steep and tree-covered terrain in a single snowcat. Guests stay as a group at the company's lodge for a fixed number of days and are provided healthy gourmet meals.

Brad and Carole must decide each year when snowcat operations will begin in December and when they will end in early spring, and how many nonoperating days to schedule between groups of guests for maintenance and rest. This decision affects a variety of costs. Examples of costs that are fixed and variable with respect to the number of days of operation at White Grizzly include:

Cost	Cost Behavior—Fixed or Variable with Respect to Days of Operation
Property taxes	Fixed
Summer road maintenance and tree clearing	Fixed
Lodge depreciation	Fixed
Snowcat operator and guides	Variable
Cooks and lodge help	Variable
Snowcat depreciation	Variable
Snowcat fuel	Variable
Food*	Variable

*The costs of food served to guests theoretically depend on the number of guests in residence. However, the lodge is almost always filled to its capacity of 12 persons when the snowcat operation is running, so food costs can be considered to be driven by the days of operation.

Source: Brad & Carole Karafil, owners and operators of White Grizzly Adventures, www.whitegrizzly.com.

to be used, the materials specifications, labor requirements, equipment usage, production efficiency, power consumption, and so on. For example, Pizza Hut might use the engineering approach to estimate the cost of preparing and serving a particular take-out pizza. The cost of the pizza would be estimated by carefully costing the specific ingredients used to make the pizza, the power consumed to cook the pizza, and the cost of the container the pizza is delivered in. The engineering approach must be used in those situations where no past experience is available concerning activity and costs. In addition, it is sometimes used together with other methods to improve the accuracy of cost analysis.

Account analysis works best when analyzing costs at a fairly aggregated level, such as the cost of serving patients in the emergency room (ER) of Cook County General Hospital. The costs of drugs, supplies, forms, wages, equipment, and so on, can be roughly classified as variable or fixed and a mixed cost formula for the overall cost of the emergency room can be estimated fairly quickly. However, this method does not recognize that some of the accounts may have both fixed and variable cost elements. For example, the cost of electricity for the ER is a mixed cost. Most of the electricity is a fixed cost because it is used for heating and lighting. However, the consumption of electricity increases with activity in the ER since diagnostic equipment, operating theater lights, defibrillators, and so on, all consume electricity. The most effective way to estimate the fixed and variable elements of such a mixed cost may be to analyze past records of cost and activity data. These records should reveal whether electrical costs vary significantly with the number of patients and if so, by how much. The remainder of this section explains how to conduct such an analysis of past cost and activity data.

Dr. Derek Chalmers, the chief executive officer of Brentline Hospital, motioned Kinh Nguyen, the chief financial officer of the hospital, into his office.

MANAGERIAL ACCOUNTING IN ACTION
The Issue

BRENTLINE
HOSPITAL

Derek: I wanted to talk to you about our maintenance expenses. They seem to be bouncing around a lot. Over the last half year or so they have been as low as $7,400 and as high as $9,800 per month.

Kinh: That type of variation is normal for maintenance expenses.

Derek: But we budgeted a constant $8,400 a month. Can't we do a better job of predicting what these costs are going to be? And how do we know when we've spent too much in a month? Shouldn't there be some explanation for these variations?

Kinh: Now that you mention it, we are in the process of tightening up our budgeting process. Our first step is to break all of our costs down into fixed and variable components.

Derek: How will that help?

Kinh: Well, it will permit us to predict what the level of costs will be. Some costs are fixed and shouldn't change much. Other costs go up and down as our activity goes up and down. The trick is to figure out what is driving the variable component of the costs.

Derek: What about the maintenance costs?

Kinh: My guess is that the variations in maintenance costs are being driven by our overall level of activity. When we treat more patients, our equipment is used more intensively, which leads to more maintenance expense.

Derek: How would you measure the level of overall activity? Would you use patient-days?

Kinh: I think so. Each day a patient is in the hospital counts as one patient-day. The greater the number of patient-days in a month, the busier we are. Besides, our budgeting is all based on projected patient-days.

Derek: Okay, so suppose you are able to break the maintenance costs down into fixed and variable components. What will that do for us?

Kinh: Basically, I will be able to predict what maintenance costs should be as a function of the number of patient-days.

Derek: I can see where that would be useful. We could use it to predict costs for budgeting purposes.

Kinh: We could also use it as a benchmark. Based on the actual number of patient-days for a period, I can predict what the maintenance costs should have been. We can compare this to the actual spending on maintenance.

Derek: Sounds good to me. Let me know when you get the results.

Diagnosing Cost Behavior with a Scattergraph Plot

Kinh Nguyen began his analysis of maintenance costs by collecting cost and activity data for a number of recent months. Those data are displayed below:

LEARNING OBJECTIVE 2
Use a scattergraph plot to diagnose cost behavior.

Month	Activity Level: Patient-Days	Maintenance Cost Incurred
January	5,600	$7,900
February	7,100	$8,500
March	5,000	$7,400
April	6,500	$8,200
May	7,300	$9,100
June...........	8,000	$9,800
July	6,200	$7,800

The first step in analyzing the cost and activity data is to plot the data on a scattergraph. This plot immediately reveals any nonlinearities or other problems with the data. The scattergraph of maintenance costs versus patient-days at Brentline Hospital is shown in the top half of Exhibit 5–9 (page 204). Two things should be noted about this scattergraph:

1. The total maintenance cost, Y, is plotted on the vertical axis. Cost is known as the **dependent variable,** since the amount of cost incurred during a period depends on the level of activity for the period. (That is, as the level of activity increases, total cost will also ordinarily increase.)
2. The activity, X (patient-days in this case), is plotted on the horizontal axis. Activity is known as the **independent variable,** since it causes variations in the cost.

From the scattergraph, it is evident that maintenance costs do increase with the number of patient-days. In addition, the scattergraph reveals that the relation between maintenance costs and patient-days is approximately *linear.* In other words, the points lie more or less along a straight line. Such a straight line has been drawn using a ruler in the bottom half of Exhibit 5–9. Cost behavior is considered **linear** whenever a straight line is a reasonable approximation for the relation between cost and activity. Note that the data points do not fall exactly on the straight line. This will almost always happen in practice; the relation is seldom perfectly linear.

Note that the straight line in Exhibit 5–9 has been drawn through the point representing 7,300 patient-days and a total maintenance cost of $9,100. Drawing the straight line through one of the data points helps make a quick-and-dirty estimate of variable and fixed costs. The vertical intercept where the straight line crosses the Y axis—in this case, about $3,300—is the rough estimate of the fixed cost. The variable cost can be quickly estimated by subtracting the estimated fixed cost from the total cost at the point lying on the straight line.

Total maintenance cost for 7,300 patient-days (a point falling on the straight line)	$9,100
Less estimated fixed cost (the vertical intercept)	3,300
Estimated total variable cost for 7,300 patient-days.......	$5,800

The average variable cost per unit at 7,300 patient-days is computed as follows:

$$\text{Variable cost per unit} = \$5,800 \div 7,300 \text{ patient-days}$$

$$= \$0.79 \text{ per patient-day (rounded)}$$

EXHIBIT 5–9
Scattergraph Method of Cost
Analysis

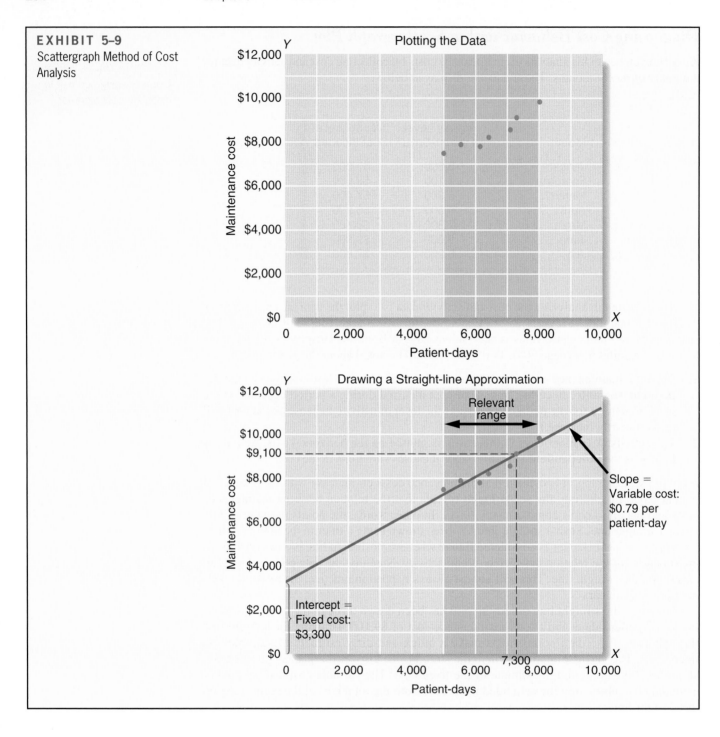

Combining the estimate of the fixed cost and the estimate of the variable cost per patient-day, we can express the relation between cost and activity as follows:

$$Y = \$3,300 + \$0.79X$$

where X is the number of patient-days.

We hasten to add that this *is* a quick-and-dirty method of estimating the fixed and variable cost elements of a mixed cost; it is seldom used in practice when the financial implications of a decision based on the data are significant. However, setting aside the estimates of the fixed and variable cost elements, plotting the data on a scattergraph is an essential diagnostic step that is too often overlooked. Suppose, for example, we had

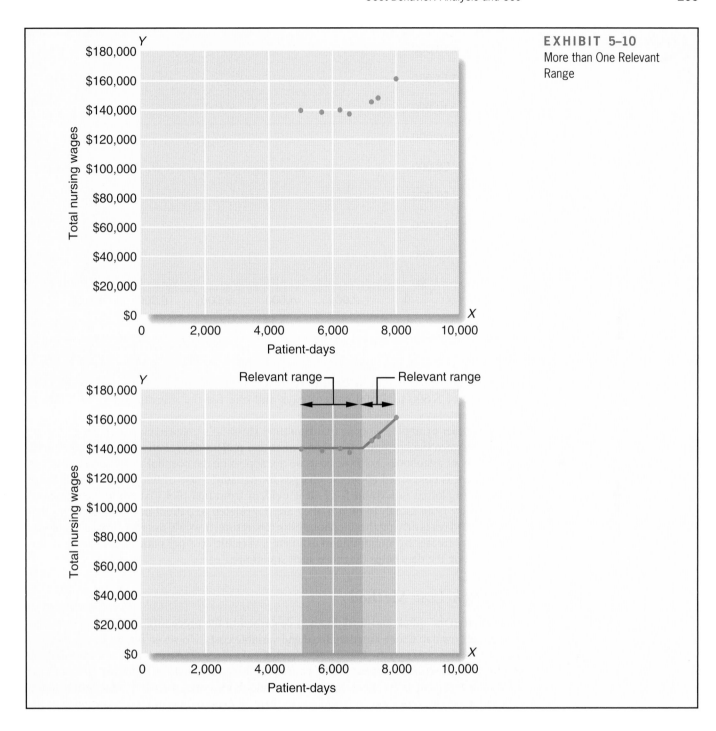

EXHIBIT 5–10
More than One Relevant
Range

been interested in the relation between total nursing wages and the number of patient-days at the hospital. The permanent, full-time nursing staff can handle up to 7,000 patient-days in a month. Beyond that level of activity, part-time nurses must be called in to help out. The cost and activity data for nurses are plotted on the scattergraph in Exhibit 5–10. Looking at that scattergraph, it is evident that two straight lines would do a much better job of fitting the data than a single straight line. Up to 7,000 patient-days, total nursing wages are essentially a fixed cost. Above 7,000 patient-days, total nursing wages are a mixed cost. This happens because, as stated above, the permanent, full-time nursing staff can handle up to 7,000 patient-days in a month. Above that level, part-time nurses are called in to help, which adds to the cost. Consequently, two straight lines

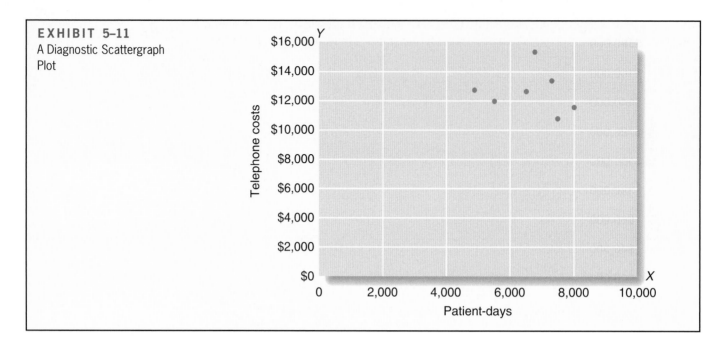

EXHIBIT 5–11
A Diagnostic Scattergraph Plot

(and two equations) would be used to represent total nursing wages—one for the relevant range of 5,600 to 7,000 patient-days and one for the relevant range of 7,000 to 8,000 patient-days.

As another example, suppose that Brentline Hospital's management is interested in the relation between the hospital's telephone costs and patient-days. Patients are billed directly for their use of telephones, so those costs do not appear on the hospital's cost records. Rather, management is concerned about the charges for the staff's use of telephones. The data for this cost are plotted in Exhibit 5–11. It is evident from that plot that while the telephone costs do vary from month to month, they are not related to patient-days. Something other than patient-days is driving the telephone bills. Therefore, it would not make sense to analyze this cost any further by attempting to estimate a variable cost per patient-day for telephone costs. Plotting the data helps diagnose such situations.

The High-Low Method

LEARNING OBJECTIVE 3
Analyze a mixed cost using the high-low method.

In addition to the quick-and-dirty method described in the preceding section, more precise methods are available for estimating fixed and variable costs. However, it must be emphasized that fixed and variable costs should be computed only if a scattergraph plot confirms that the relation is approximately linear. In the case of maintenance costs at Brentline Hospital, the relation does appear to be linear. In the case of telephone costs, there isn't any clear relation between telephone costs and patient-days, so there is no point in estimating how much of the cost varies with patient-days.

Assuming that the scattergraph plot indicates a linear relation between cost and activity, the fixed and variable cost elements of a mixed cost can be estimated using the *high-low method* or the *least-squares regression method*. The high-low method is based on the rise-over-run formula for the slope of a straight line. As discussed above, if the relation between cost and activity can be represented by a straight line, then the slope of the straight line is equal to the variable cost per unit of activity. Consequently, the following formula can be used to estimate the variable cost.

$$\text{Variable cost} = \text{Slope of the line} = \frac{\text{Rise}}{\text{Run}} = \frac{Y_2 - Y_1}{X_2 - X_1}$$

To analyze mixed costs with the **high-low method,** begin by identifying the period with the lowest level of activity and the period with the highest level of activity. The period with the lowest activity is selected as the first point in the above formula and the period with the highest activity is selected as the second point. Consequently, the formula becomes:

$$\text{Variable cost} = \frac{Y_2 - Y_1}{X_2 - X_1} = \frac{\text{Cost at the high activity level} - \text{Cost at the low activity level}}{\text{High activity level} - \text{Low activity level}}$$

or

$$\text{Variable cost} = \frac{\text{Change in cost}}{\text{Change in activity}}$$

Therefore, when the high-low method is used, the variable cost is estimated by dividing the difference in cost between the high and low levels of activity by the change in activity between those two points.

To return to the Brentline Hospital example, using the high-low method, we first identify the periods with the highest and lowest *activity*—in this case, June and March. We then use the activity and cost data from these two periods to estimate the variable cost component as follows:

	Patient-Days	Maintenance Cost Incurred
High activity level (June).	8,000	$9,800
Low activity level (March).	5,000	7,400
Change.	3,000	$2,400

$$\text{Variable cost} = \frac{\text{Change in cost}}{\text{Change in activity}} = \frac{\$2,400}{3,000 \text{ patient-days}} = \$0.80 \text{ per patient-day}$$

Having determined that the variable maintenance cost is 80 cents per patient-day, we can now determine the amount of fixed cost. This is done by taking the total cost at *either* the high or the low activity level and deducting the variable cost element. In the computation below, total cost at the high activity level is used in computing the fixed cost element:

Fixed cost element = Total cost − Variable cost element

= $9,800 − ($0.80 per patient-day × 8,000 patient-days)

= $3,400

Both the variable and fixed cost elements have now been isolated. The cost of maintenance can be expressed as $3,400 per month plus 80 cents per patient-day or as:

$$Y = \$3,400 + \$0.80X$$

↑ ↑

Total maintenance cost   Total patient-days

The data used in this illustration are shown graphically in Exhibit 5–12 (page 208). Notice that a straight line has been drawn through the points corresponding to the low and high levels of activity. In essence, that is what the high-low method does—it draws a straight line through those two points.

Sometimes the high and low levels of activity don't coincide with the high and low amounts of cost. For example, the period that has the highest level of activity may not have the highest amount of cost. Nevertheless, the costs at the highest and lowest levels of *activity* are always used to analyze a mixed cost under the high-low method. The reason is that the analyst would like to use data that reflect the greatest possible variation in activity.

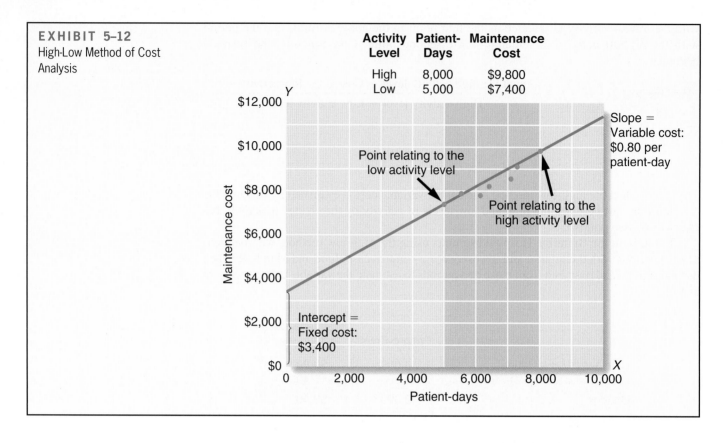

EXHIBIT 5–12
High-Low Method of Cost Analysis

Activity Level	Patient-Days	Maintenance Cost
High	8,000	$9,800
Low	5,000	$7,400

The high-low method is very simple to apply, but it suffers from a major (and sometimes critical) defect—it utilizes only two data points. Generally, two data points are not enough to produce accurate results. Additionally, the periods with the highest and lowest activity tend to be unusual. A cost formula that is estimated solely using data from these unusual periods may misrepresent the true cost behavior during normal periods. Such a distortion is evident in Exhibit 5–12. The straight line should probably be shifted down somewhat so that it is closer to more of the data points. For these reasons, other methods of cost analysis that use all of the data will generally be more accurate than the high-low method. A manager who chooses to use the high-low method should do so with a full awareness of its limitations.

Fortunately, computer software makes it very easy to use sophisticated statistical methods, such as *least-squares regression,* that use all of the data and that are capable of providing much more information than just the estimates of variable and fixed costs. The details of these statistical methods are beyond the scope of this text, but the basic approach is discussed below. Nevertheless, even if the least-squares regression approach is used, it is always a good idea to plot the data in a scattergraph. By simply looking at the scattergraph, you can quickly verify whether it makes sense to fit a straight line to the data using least-squares regression or some other method.

The Least-Squares Regression Method

The **least-squares regression method,** unlike the high-low method, uses all of the data to separate a mixed cost into its fixed and variable components. A *regression line* of the form $Y = a + bX$ is fitted to the data, where a represents the total fixed cost and b represents the variable cost per unit of activity. The basic idea underlying the least-squares regression method is illustrated in Exhibit 5–13 using hypothetical data points. Notice from the exhibit that the deviations from the plotted points to the regression line are measured vertically on the graph. These vertical deviations are called the regression errors. There is nothing mysterious about the least-squares regression method. It simply computes the regression line that minimizes the sum of these squared errors. The formulas

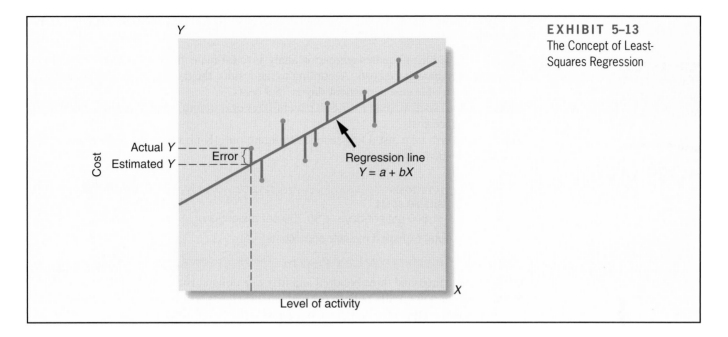

EXHIBIT 5-13
The Concept of Least-Squares Regression

that accomplish this are fairly complex and involve numerous calculations, but the principle is simple.

Fortunately, computers are adept at carrying out the computations required by the least-squares regression formulas. The data—the observed values of X and Y—are entered into the computer, and software does the rest. In the case of the Brentline Hospital maintenance cost data, a statistical software package on a personal computer can calculate the following least-squares regression estimates of the total fixed cost (a) and the variable cost per unit of activity (b):

$$a = \$3,431$$

$$b = \$0.759$$

Therefore, using the least-squares regression method, the fixed element of the maintenance cost is \$3,431 per month and the variable portion is 75.9 cents per patient-day.

In terms of the linear equation $Y = a + bX$, the cost formula can be written as

$$Y = \$3,431 + \$0.759X$$

where activity (X) is expressed in patient-days.

While a statistical software application was used in this example to calculate the values of a and b, the estimates can also be computed using a spreadsheet application such as Microsoft® Excel. In Appendix 5A to this chapter, we show how this can be done.

In addition to estimates of the intercept (fixed cost) and slope (variable cost per unit), least-squares regression software ordinarily provides a number of other very useful statistics. One of these statistics is the R^2, which is a measure of "goodness of fit." The R^2 tells us the percentage of the variation in the dependent variable (cost) that is explained by variation in the independent variable (activity). The R^2 varies from 0% to 100%, and the higher the percentage, the better. In the case of the Brentline Hospital maintenance cost data, the R^2 is 0.90, which indicates that 90% of the variation in maintenance costs is explained by the variation in patient-days. This is reasonably high and is an indication of a good fit. On the other hand, a low R^2 would be an indication of a poor fit. You should always plot the data in a scattergraph, but it is particularly important to check the data visually when the R^2 is low. A quick look at the scattergraph can reveal that there is little relation between the cost and the activity or that the relation is something other than a simple straight line. In such cases, additional analysis would be required.

After completing the analysis of maintenance costs, Kinh Nguyen met with Dr. Derek Chalmers to discuss the results.

Kinh: We used least-squares regression analysis to estimate the fixed and variable components of maintenance costs. According to the results, the fixed cost per month is $3,431 and the variable cost per patient-day is 75.9 cents.

Derek: Okay, so if we plan for 7,800 patient-days next month, what is your estimate of the maintenance costs?

Kinh: That will take just a few seconds to figure out. [Kinh wrote the following calculations on a pad of paper.]

Fixed costs	$3,431
Variable costs:	
7,800 patient-days × $0.759 per patient-day	5,920
Total expected maintenance costs	$9,351

Derek: Nine thousand three hundred and fifty *one* dollars; isn't that a bit *too* precise?

Kinh: Sure. I don't really believe the maintenance costs will be exactly this figure. However, based on the information we have, this is the best estimate we can come up with.

Derek: This type of estimate will be a lot better than just guessing like we have done in the past. Thanks. I hope to see more of this kind of analysis.

Multiple Regression Analysis

In the discussion thus far, we have assumed that a single factor such as patient-days drives the variable cost component of a mixed cost. This assumption is acceptable for many mixed costs, but in some situations the variable cost element may be driven by a number of factors. For example, shipping costs may depend on both the number of units shipped *and* the weight of the units. In a situation such as this, *multiple regression* is necessary. **Multiple regression** is an analytical method that is used when the dependent variable (i.e., cost) is caused by more than one factor. Although adding more factors, or variables, makes the computations more complex, the principles involved are the same as in the simple least-squares regressions discussed above.

The Contribution Format Income Statement

LEARNING OBJECTIVE 4
Prepare an income statement using the contribution format.

Separating costs into fixed and variable elements helps to predict costs and provide benchmarks. As we will see in later chapters, separating costs into fixed and variable elements is also often crucial in making decisions. This crucial distinction between fixed and variable costs is at the heart of the **contribution approach** to constructing income statements. The unique thing about the contribution approach is that it provides managers with an income statement that clearly distinguishes between fixed and variable costs and therefore facilitates planning, control, and decision making.

Why a New Income Statement Format?

An income statement prepared using the *traditional approach,* as illustrated in Chapter 2, is organized in a "functional" format—emphasizing the functions of production, administration, and sales. No attempt is made to distinguish between fixed and variable costs. Under the heading "Administrative expense," for example, both variable and fixed costs are lumped together.

Although an income statement prepared in the functional format may be useful for external reporting purposes, it has serious limitations when used for internal purposes. Internally, managers need cost data organized in a format that will facilitate planning, control, and decision making. As we shall see in chapters ahead, these tasks are much easier when cost data are available in a fixed and variable format. The contribution format income statement has been developed in response to these needs.

The Contribution Approach

Topic Tackler

PLUS

5–2

Exhibit 5–14 uses a simple example to compare a contribution approach income statement to the traditional approach discussed in Chapter 2.

Notice that the contribution approach separates costs into fixed and variable categories, first deducting variable expenses from sales to obtain the *contribution margin*. The **contribution margin** is the amount remaining from sales revenues after variable expenses have been deducted. This amount *contributes* toward covering fixed expenses and then toward profits for the period.

The contribution format income statement is used as an internal planning and decision-making tool. Its emphasis on cost behavior facilitates cost-volume-profit analysis (such as we shall be doing in the next chapter), management performance appraisals, and budgeting. Moreover, the contribution approach helps managers organize data pertinent to numerous decisions such as product-line analysis, pricing, use of scarce resources, and make or buy analysis. All of these topics are covered in later chapters.

EXHIBIT 5–14
Comparison of the Contribution Income Statement with the Traditional Income Statement (the data are given)

Traditional Approach (costs organized by function)				Contribution Approach (costs organized by behavior)			
Sales			$12,000	Sales			$12,000
Cost of goods sold			6,000*	Variable expenses:			
Gross margin			6,000	Variable production		$2,000	
Selling and administrative expenses:				Variable selling		600	
Selling	$3,100*			Variable administrative		400	3,000
Administrative	1,900*	5,000		Contribution margin			9,000
Net operating income			$ 1,000	Fixed expenses:			
				Fixed production		4,000	
				Fixed selling		2,500	
				Fixed administrative		1,500	8,000
				Net operating income			$ 1,000

*Contains both variable and fixed expenses. This is the income statement for a manufacturing company; thus, when the income statement is placed in the contribution format, the "cost of goods sold" is divided between variable production costs and fixed production costs. If this were the income statement for a *merchandising* company (which simply purchases completed goods from a supplier), then the cost of goods sold would be *all* variable.

Summary

As we shall see in later chapters, the ability to predict how costs respond to changes in activity is critical for making decisions, controlling operations, and evaluating performance. Three major classifications of costs were discussed in this chapter—variable, fixed, and mixed. Mixed costs consist of variable and fixed elements and can be expressed in equation form as $Y = a + bX$, where X is the activity, Y is the cost, a is the fixed cost element, and b is the variable cost per unit of activity.

Several methods can be used to estimate the fixed and variable cost components of a mixed cost using past records of cost and activity. If the relation between cost and activity appears to be linear based on a scattergraph plot, then the variable and fixed components of the mixed cost can be estimated using the quick-and-dirty method, the high-low method, or the least-squares regression method. The quick-and-dirty method is based on drawing a straight line and then using the slope and the intercept of the straight line to estimate the variable and fixed cost components of the mixed cost. The high-low method implicitly draws a straight line through the points of lowest activity and highest activity. In most situations, the least-squares regression method is preferred to both the quick-and-dirty and high-low methods. Computer software is widely available for using the least-squares regression method. These software applications provide a variety of useful statistics along with estimates of the intercept (fixed cost) and slope (variable cost per unit). Nevertheless, even when least-squares regression is used, the data should be plotted to confirm that the relationship is really a straight line.

Managers use costs organized by behavior to help make many decisions. The contribution format income statement can aid decision making because it classifies costs by cost behavior (i.e., variable versus fixed) rather than by the functions of production, administration, and sales.

Review Problem 1: Cost Behavior

Neptune Rentals operates a boat rental service. Consider the following costs of the company over the relevant range of 5,000 to 8,000 hours of operating time for its boats:

	Hours of Operating Time			
	5,000	6,000	7,000	8,000
Total costs:				
Variable costs	$ 20,000	$?	$?	$?
Fixed costs	168,000	?	?	?
Total costs	$188,000	$?	$?	$?
Cost per hour:				
Variable cost	$?	$?	$?	$?
Fixed cost	?	?	?	?
Total cost per hour	$?	$?	$?	$?

Required:

Compute the missing amounts, assuming that cost behavior patterns remain unchanged within the relevant range of 5,000 to 8,000 hours.

Solution to Review Problem 1

The variable cost per hour can be computed as follows:

$$\$20,000 \div 5,000 \text{ hours} = \$4 \text{ per hour}$$

Therefore, the missing amounts are as follows:

	Hours of Operating Time			
	5,000	6,000	7,000	8,000
Total costs:				
Variable costs				
(@ $4 per hour)	$ 20,000	$ 24,000	$ 28,000	$ 32,000
Fixed costs	168,000	168,000	168,000	168,000
Total costs	$188,000	$192,000	$196,000	$200,000
Cost per hour:				
Variable cost	$ 4.00	$ 4.00	$ 4.00	$ 4.00
Fixed cost	33.60	28.00	24.00	21.00
Total cost per hour	$ 37.60	$ 32.00	$ 28.00	$ 25.00

Observe that the total variable costs increase in proportion to the number of hours of operating time, but that these costs remain constant at $4 if expressed on a per hour basis.

In contrast, the total fixed costs do not change with changes in the level of activity. They remain constant at $168,000 within the relevant range. With increases in activity, however, the fixed cost per hour decreases, dropping from $33.60 per hour when the boats are operated 5,000 hours a period to only $21.00 per hour when the boats are operated 8,000 hours a period. *Because of this troublesome aspect of fixed costs, they are most easily (and most safely) dealt with on a total basis, rather than on a unit basis, in cost analysis work.*

Review Problem 2: High-Low Method

The administrator of Azalea Hills Hospital would like a cost formula linking the administrative costs involved in admitting patients to the number of patients admitted during a month. The admitting department's costs and the number of patients admitted during the immediately preceding eight months are given in the following table:

Month	Number of Patients Admitted	Admitting Department Costs
May	1,800	$14,700
June	1,900	$15,200
July	1,700	$13,700
August	1,600	$14,000
September	1,500	$14,300
October	1,300	$13,100
November	1,100	$12,800
December	1,500	$14,600

Required:
1. Use the high-low method to establish the fixed and variable components of admitting costs.
2. Express the fixed and variable components of admitting costs as a cost formula in the form $Y = a + bX$.

Solution to Review Problem 2
1. The first step in the high-low method is to identify the periods of the lowest and highest activity. Those periods are November (1,100 patients admitted) and June (1,900 patients admitted).

   The second step is to compute the variable cost per unit using those two data points:

Month	Number of Patients Admitted	Admitting Department Costs
High activity level (June)	1,900	$15,200
Low activity level (November)	1,100	12,800
Change	800	$ 2,400

$$\text{Variable cost} = \frac{\text{Change in cost}}{\text{Change in activity}} = \frac{\$2,400}{800 \text{ patients admitted}} = \$3 \text{ per patient admitted}$$

   The third step is to compute the fixed cost element by deducting the variable cost element from the total cost at either the high or low activity. In the computation below, the high point of activity is used:

   Fixed cost element = Total cost − Variable cost element

   = $15,200 − ($3 per patient admitted × 1,900 patients admitted)

   = $9,500

2. The cost formula is $Y = \$9,500 + \$3X$.

Glossary

Account analysis A method for analyzing cost behavior in which an account is classified as either variable or fixed based on the analyst's prior knowledge of how the cost in the account behaves. (p. 201)

Activity base A measure of whatever causes the incurrence of a variable cost. For example, the total cost of X-ray film in a hospital will increase as the number of X-rays taken increases. Therefore, the number of X-rays is the activity base that explains the total cost of X-ray film. (p. 189)

Committed fixed costs Investments in facilities, equipment, and basic organizational structure that can't be significantly reduced even for short periods of time without making fundamental changes. (p. 195)

Contribution approach An income statement format that organizes costs by their behavior. Costs are separated into variable and fixed categories rather than being separated according to organizational functions. (p. 210)

Contribution margin The amount remaining from sales revenues after all variable expenses have been deducted. (p. 211)

Cost structure The relative proportion of fixed, variable, and mixed costs in an organization. (p. 188)

Dependent variable A variable that responds to some causal factor; total cost is the dependent variable, as represented by the letter Y, in the equation $Y = a + bX$. (p. 203)

Discretionary fixed costs Those fixed costs that arise from annual decisions by management to spend on certain fixed cost items, such as advertising and research. (p. 195)

Engineering approach A detailed analysis of cost behavior based on an industrial engineer's evaluation of the inputs that are required to carry out a particular activity and of the prices of those inputs. (p. 201)

High-low method A method of separating a mixed cost into its fixed and variable elements by analyzing the change in cost between the high and low activity levels. (p. 206)

Independent variable A variable that acts as a causal factor; activity is the independent variable, as represented by the letter X, in the equation $Y = a + bX$. (p. 203)

Least-squares regression method A method of separating a mixed cost into its fixed and variable elements by fitting a regression line that minimizes the sum of the squared errors. (p. 208)

Linear cost behavior Cost behavior is said to be linear whenever a straight line is a reasonable approximation for the relation between cost and activity. (p. 203)

Mixed cost A cost that contains both variable and fixed cost elements. (p. 199)

Multiple regression An analytical method required when variations in a dependent variable are caused by more than one factor. (p. 210)

R^2 A measure of goodness of fit in least-squares regression analysis. It is the percentage of the variation in the dependent variable that is explained by variation in the independent variable. (p. 209)

Relevant range The range of activity within which assumptions about variable and fixed cost behavior are reasonably valid. (p. 192)

Step-variable cost The cost of a resource that is obtainable only in large chunks and that increases and decreases only in response to fairly wide changes in activity. (p. 191)

Appendix 5A: Least-Squares Regression Using Microsoft® Excel

LEARNING OBJECTIVE 5
Analyze a mixed cost using the least-squares regression method.

The least-squares regression method for estimating a linear relationship is based on the equation for a straight line:

$$Y = a + bX$$

As explained in the chapter, least-squares regression selects the values for the intercept a and the slope b that minimize the sum of the squared errors. The following formulas, which are derived in statistics and calculus texts, accomplish that objective:

$$b = \frac{n(\Sigma XY) - (\Sigma X)(\Sigma Y)}{n(\Sigma X^2) - (\Sigma X)^2}$$

$$a = \frac{(\Sigma Y) - b(\Sigma X)}{n}$$

where:

X = The level of activity (independent variable)

Y = The total mixed cost (dependent variable)

a = The total fixed cost (the vertical intercept of the line)

b = The variable cost per unit of activity (the slope of the line)

n = Number of observations

Σ = Sum across all n observations

Manually performing the calculations required by the formulas is tedious at best. Fortunately, statistical software packages are widely available that perform the calculations automatically. Spreadsheet software, such as Microsoft® Excel, can also be used to do least-squares regression—although it requires a little more work than using a specialized statistical application.

To illustrate how Excel can be used to calculate the intercept a, the slope b, and the R^2, we will use the Brentline Hospital data for maintenance costs on page 203. The worksheet in Exhibit 5A–1 contains the data and the calculations.

As you can see, the X values (the independent variable) have been entered in cells B4 through B10. The Y values (the dependent variable) have been entered in cells C4 through C10. The slope, intercept, and R^2 are computed using the Excel functions INTERCEPT, SLOPE, and RSQ. You must specify the range of cells for the Y values and for the X values.

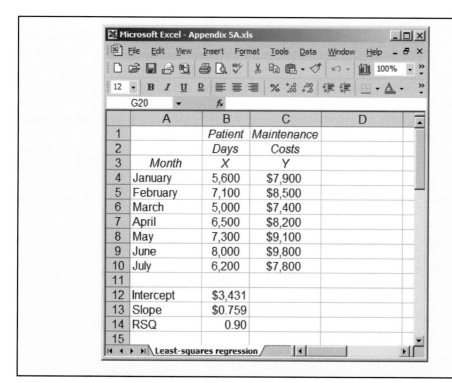

EXHIBIT 5A–1
The Least-Squares Regression Worksheet for Brentline Hospital

EXHIBIT 5A–2
A Scattergraph Plot of the
Brentline Hospital Data

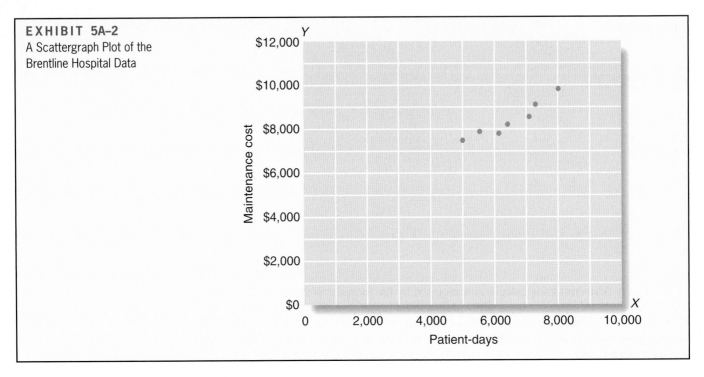

In Exhibit 5A–1, cell B12 contains the formula =INTERCEPT(C4:C10,B4:B10); cell B13 contains the formula =SLOPE(C4:C10,B4:B10); and cell B14 contains the formula =RSQ(C4:C10,B4:B10).

According to the calculations carried out by Excel, the fixed maintenance cost (the intercept) is $3,431 per month and the variable cost (the slope) is $0.759 per patient-day. Therefore, the cost formula for maintenance cost is:

$$Y = a + bX$$

$$Y = \$3,431 + \$0.759X$$

Note that the R^2 (i.e., RSQ) is 0.90, which—as previously discussed—is quite good and indicates that 90% of the variation in maintenance costs is explained by the variation in patient-days.

Plotting the data is easy in Excel. Select the range of values that you would like to plot—in this case, cells B4:C10. Then select the Chart Wizard tool on the toolbar and make the appropriate choices in the various dialogue boxes that appear. When you are finished, you should have a scattergraph that looks like the plot in Exhibit 5A–2. Note that the relation between cost and activity is approximately linear, so it is reasonable to fit a straight line to the data as we have implicitly done with the least-squares regression.

Questions

5-1 Distinguish between (*a*) a variable cost, (*b*) a fixed cost, and (*c*) a mixed cost.

5-2 What effect does an increase in volume have on—
   a. Unit fixed costs?
   b. Unit variable costs?
   c. Total fixed costs?
   d. Total variable costs?

5-3 Define the following terms: (*a*) cost behavior and (*b*) relevant range.

5-4 What is meant by an *activity base* when dealing with variable costs? Give several examples of activity bases.

5-5 Distinguish between (*a*) a variable cost, (*b*) a mixed cost, and (*c*) a step-variable cost. Plot the three costs on a graph, with activity plotted horizontally and cost plotted vertically.

5-6 Managers often assume a strictly linear relationship between cost and volume. How can this practice be defended in light of the fact that many costs are curvilinear?

5-7   Distinguish between discretionary fixed costs and committed fixed costs.
5-8   Classify the following fixed costs as normally being either committed or discretionary:
    a.   Depreciation on buildings.
    b.   Advertising.
    c.   Research.
    d.   Long-term equipment leases.
    e.   Pension payments to the company's retirees.
    f.   Management development and training.
5-9   Does the concept of the relevant range apply to fixed costs? Explain.
5-10   What is the major disadvantage of the high-low method?
5-11   Give the general formula for a mixed cost. Which term represents the variable cost? The fixed cost?
5-12   What is meant by the term *least-squares regression?*
5-13   What is the difference between ordinary least-squares regression analysis and multiple regression analysis?
5-14   What is the difference between a contribution approach income statement and a traditional approach income statement?
5-15   What is the contribution margin?

Exercises

EXERCISE 5-1 Fixed and Variable Cost Behavior [LO1]

Espresso Express operates a number of espresso coffee stands in busy suburban malls. The fixed weekly expense of a coffee stand is $1,200 and the variable cost per cup of coffee served is $0.22.

Required:
1.   Fill in the following table with your estimates of total costs and cost per cup of coffee at the indicated levels of activity for a coffee stand. Round off the cost of a cup of coffee to the nearest tenth of a cent.

	Cups of Coffee Served in a Week		
	2,000	2,100	2,200
Fixed cost	?	?	?
Variable cost	?	?	?
Total cost	?	?	?
Cost per cup of coffee served.........	?	?	?

2.   Does the cost per cup of coffee served increase, decrease, or remain the same as the number of cups of coffee served in a week increases? Explain.

EXERCISE 5-2 Scattergraph Analysis [LO2]

Oki Products, Ltd., has observed the following processing costs at various levels of activity over the last 15 months:

Month	Units Processed	Processing Cost
1	4,500	$38,000
2	11,000	$52,000
3	12,000	$56,000
4	5,500	$40,000
5	9,000	$47,000
6	10,500	$52,000
7	7,500	$44,000
8	5,000	$41,000
9	11,500	$52,000
10	6,000	$43,000
11	8,500	$48,000
12	10,000	$50,000
13	6,500	$44,000
14	9,500	$48,000
15	8,000	$46,000

Required:
1. Prepare a scattergraph using the above data. Plot cost on the vertical axis and activity on the horizontal axis. Fit a line to your plotted points using a ruler.
2. Using the quick-and-dirty method, what is the approximate monthly fixed cost? The approximate variable cost per unit processed? Show your computations.

EXERCISE 5-3 High-Low Method [LO3]
The Cheyenne Hotel in Big Sky, Montana, has accumulated records of the total electrical costs of the hotel and the number of occupancy-days over the last year. An occupancy-day represents a room rented out for one day. The hotel's business is highly seasonal, with peaks occurring during the ski season and in the summer.

Month	Occupancy-Days	Electrical Costs
January	1,736	$4,127
February.	1,904	$4,207
March.	2,356	$5,083
April	960	$2,857
May	360	$1,871
June.	744	$2,696
July.	2,108	$4,670
August	2,406	$5,148
September	840	$2,691
October	124	$1,588
November.	720	$2,454
December	1,364	$3,529

Required:
1. Using the high-low method, estimate the fixed cost of electricity per month and the variable cost of electricity per occupancy-day. Round off the fixed cost to the nearest whole dollar and the variable cost to the nearest whole cent.
2. What other factors other than occupancy-days are likely to affect the variation in electrical costs from month to month?

EXERCISE 5-4 Contribution Format Income Statement [LO4]
The Alpine House, Inc., is a large retailer of winter sports equipment. An income statement for the company's Ski Department for a recent quarter is presented below:

The Alpine House, Inc. Income Statement—Ski Department For the Quarter Ended March 31		
Sales		$150,000
Less cost of goods sold		90,000
Gross margin		60,000
Less operating expenses:		
Selling expenses	$30,000	
Administrative expenses.	10,000	40,000
Net operating income.		$ 20,000

Skis sell, on the average, for $750 per pair. Variable selling expenses are $50 per pair of skis sold. The remaining selling expenses are fixed. The administrative expenses are 20% variable and 80% fixed. The company does not manufacture its own skis; it purchases them from a supplier for $450 per pair.

Required:
1. Prepare an income statement for the quarter using the contribution approach.
2. For every pair of skis sold during the quarter, what was the contribution toward covering fixed expenses and toward earning profits?

EXERCISE 5-5 (Appendix 5A) Least-Squares Regression [LO5]

EZ Rental Car offers rental cars in an off-airport location near a major tourist destination in Florida. Management would like to better understand the behavior of the company's costs. One of those costs is the cost of washing cars. The company operates its own car wash facility in which each rental car that is returned is thoroughly cleaned before being released for rental to another customer. Management believes that the costs of operating the car wash should be related to the number of rental returns. Accordingly, the following data have been compiled:

Month	Rental Returns	Car Wash Costs
January	2,310	$10,113
February	2,453	$12,691
March	2,641	$10,905
April	2,874	$12,949
May	3,540	$15,334
June	4,861	$21,455
July	5,432	$21,270
August	5,268	$19,930
September	4,628	$21,860
October	3,720	$18,383
November	2,106	$9,830
December	2,495	$11,081

Required:
Using least-squares regression, estimate the fixed cost and variable cost elements of monthly car wash costs. The fixed cost element should be estimated to the nearest dollar and the variable cost element to the nearest cent.

EXERCISE 5-6 Cost Behavior; Contribution Format Income Statement [LO1, LO4]

Harris Company manufactures and sells a single product. A partially completed schedule of the company's total and per unit costs over the relevant range of 30,000 to 50,000 units produced and sold annually is given below:

	Units Produced and Sold		
	30,000	40,000	50,000
Total costs:			
Variable costs	$180,000	?	?
Fixed costs	300,000	?	?
Total costs	$480,000	?	?
Cost per unit:			
Variable cost	?	?	?
Fixed cost	?	?	?
Total cost per unit	?	?	?

Required:
1. Complete the schedule of the company's total and unit costs above.
2. Assume that the company produces and sells 45,000 units during the year at a selling price of $16 per unit. Prepare a contribution format income statement for the year.

EXERCISE 5-7 High-Low Method; Scattergraph Analysis [LO2, LO3]

The following data relating to units shipped and total shipping expense have been assembled by Archer Company, a wholesaler of large, custom-built air-conditioning units for commercial buildings:

Month	Units Shipped	Total Shipping Expense
January	3	$1,800
February	6	$2,300
March	4	$1,700
April	5	$2,000
May	7	$2,300
June	8	$2,700
July	2	$1,200

Required:
1. Using the high-low method, estimate a cost formula for shipping expense.
2. The president of the company has no confidence in the high-low method and would like you to check out your results using a scattergraph.
    a. Prepare a scattergraph, using the data given above. Plot cost on the vertical axis and activity on the horizontal axis. Use a ruler to fit a straight line to your plotted points.
    b. Using your scattergraph, estimate the approximate variable cost per unit shipped and the approximate fixed cost per month with the quick-and-dirty method.
3. What factors, other than the number of units shipped, are likely to affect the company's total shipping expense? Explain.

EXERCISE 5-8 (Appendix 5A) Least-Squares Regression [LO5]
Refer to the data for Archer Company in Exercise 5-7.

Required:
1. Using the least-squares regression method, estimate the cost formula for shipping expense.
2. If you also completed Exercise 5-7, prepare a simple table comparing the variable and fixed cost elements of shipping expense as computed under the quick-and-dirty scattergraph method, the high-low method, and the least-squares regression method.

EXERCISE 5-9 Cost Behavior; High-Low Method [LO1, LO3]
Hoi Chong Transport, Ltd., operates a fleet of delivery trucks in Singapore. The company has determined that if a truck is driven 105,000 kilometers during a year, the average operating cost is 11.4 cents per kilometer. If a truck is driven only 70,000 kilometers during a year, the average operating cost increases to 13.4 cents per kilometer. (The Singapore dollar is the currency used in Singapore.)

Required:
1. Using the high-low method, estimate the variable and fixed cost elements of the annual cost of truck operation.
2. Express the variable and fixed costs in the form $Y = a + bX$.
3. If a truck were driven 80,000 kilometers during a year, what total cost would you expect to be incurred?

EXERCISE 5-10 High-Low Method; Predicting Cost [LO1, LO3]
The Lakeshore Hotel's guest-days of occupancy and custodial supplies expense over the last seven months were:

Month	Guest-Days of Occupancy	Custodial Supplies Expense
March	4,000	$7,500
April	6,500	$8,250
May	8,000	$10,500
June	10,500	$12,000
July	12,000	$13,500
August	9,000	$10,750
September	7,500	$9,750

Guest-days is a measure of the overall activity at the hotel. For example, a guest who stays at the hotel for three days is counted as three guest-days.

Required:
1. Using the high-low method, estimate a cost formula for custodial supplies expense.
2. Using the cost formula you derived above, what amount of custodial supplies expense would you expect to be incurred at an occupancy level of 11,000 guest-days?

EXERCISE 5-11 Scattergraph Analysis; High-Low Method [LO2, LO3]
Refer to the data for Lakeshore Hotel in Exercise 5-10.

Required:
1. Prepare a scattergraph using the data from Exercise 5-10. Plot cost on the vertical axis and activity on the horizontal axis. Using a ruler, fit a line to your plotted points.
2. Using the quick-and-dirty method, what is the approximate monthly fixed cost? The approximate variable cost per guest-day?
3. Scrutinize the points on your graph and explain why the high-low method would or would not yield an accurate cost formula in this situation.

EXERCISE 5-12 High-Low Method; Predicting Cost [LO1, LO3]
St. Mark's Hospital contains 450 beds. The average occupancy rate is 80% per month. In other words, on average, 80% of the hospital's beds are occupied by patients. At this level of occupancy, the hospital's operating costs are $32 per occupied bed per day, assuming a 30-day month. This $32 figure contains both variable and fixed cost elements.

During June, the hospital's occupancy rate was only 60%. A total of $326,700 in operating cost was incurred during the month.

Required:
1. Using the high-low method, estimate:
   a. The variable cost per occupied bed on a daily basis.
   b. The total fixed operating costs per month.
2. Assume an occupancy rate of 70% per month. What amount of total operating cost would you expect the hospital to incur?

EXERCISE 5-13 (Appendix 5A) Least-Squares Regression [LO1, LO5]
George Caloz & Frères, located in Grenchen, Switzerland, makes prestige high-end custom watches in small lots. The company has been in operation since 1856. One of the company's products, a platinum diving watch, goes through an etching process. The company has observed etching costs as follows over the last six weeks:

Week	Units	Total Etching Cost
1	4	SFr18
2	3	17
3	8	25
4	6	20
5	7	24
6	2	16
	30	SFr120

The Swiss currency is the Swiss Franc, which is denoted by SFr.

For planning purposes, management would like to know the amount of variable etching cost per unit and the total fixed etching cost per week.

Required:
1. Using the least-squares regression method, estimate the variable and fixed elements of etching cost.
2. Express the cost data in (1) above in the form $Y = a + bX$.
3. If the company processes five units next week, what would be the expected total etching cost?

Problems

PROBLEM 5-14 (Appendix 5A) Scattergraph; Cost Behavior; Least-Squares Regression Method [LO1, LO2, LO5]
Professor John Morton has just been appointed chairperson of the Finance Department at Westland University. In reviewing the department's cost records, Professor Morton has found the following total cost associated with Finance 101 over the last several terms:

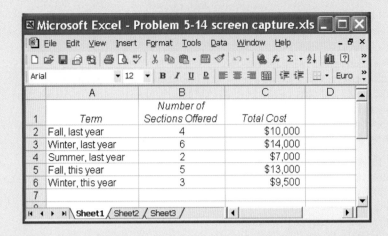

Professor Morton knows that there are some variable costs, such as amounts paid to graduate assistants, associated with the course. He would like to have the variable and fixed costs separated for planning purposes.

Required:

1. Using the least-squares regression method, estimate the variable cost per section and the total fixed cost per term for Finance 101.
2. Express the cost data derived in (1) above in the linear equation form $Y = a + bX$.
3. Assume that because of the small number of sections offered during the Winter Term this year, Professor Morton will have to offer eight sections of Finance 101 during the Fall Term. Compute the expected total cost for Finance 101. Can you see any problem with using the cost formula from (2) above to derive this total cost figure? Explain.
4. Prepare a scattergraph and fit a line to the plotted points using the cost formula expressed in (2) above.

PROBLEM 5-15 Contribution Format versus Traditional Income Statement [LO4]

Marwick's Pianos, Inc., purchases pianos from a large manufacturer and sells them at the retail level. The pianos cost, on the average, $2,450 each from the manufacturer. Marwick's Pianos, Inc., sells the pianos to its customers at an average price of $3,125 each. The selling and administrative costs that the company incurs in a typical month are presented below:

Costs	Cost Formula
Selling:	
Advertising	$700 per month
Sales salaries and commissions	$950 per month, plus 8% of sales
Delivery of pianos to customers.	$30 per piano sold
Utilities	$350 per month
Depreciation of sales facilities	$800 per month
Administrative:	
Executive salaries	$2,500 per month
Insurance	$400 per month
Clerical.	$1,000 per month, plus $20 per piano sold
Depreciation of office equipment	$300 per month

During August, Marwick's Pianos, Inc., sold and delivered 40 pianos.

Required:

1. Prepare an income statement for Marwick's Pianos, Inc., for August. Use the traditional format, with costs organized by function.
2. Redo (1) above, this time using the contribution format, with costs organized by behavior. Show costs and revenues on both a total and a per unit basis down through contribution margin.
3. Refer to the income statement you prepared in (2) above. Why might it be misleading to show the fixed costs on a per unit basis?

PROBLEM 5-16 Cost Behavior; High-Low Method; Contribution Format Income Statement [LO1, LO3, LO4]

Morrisey & Brown, Ltd., of Sydney is a merchandising company that is the sole distributor of a product that is increasing in popularity among Australian consumers. The company's income statements for the three most recent months follow:

Morrisey & Brown, Ltd. Income Statements For the Three Months Ending September 30			
	July	August	September
Sales in units.	4,000	4,500	5,000
Sales revenue	A$400,000	A$450,000	A$500,000
Less cost of goods sold	240,000	270,000	300,000
Gross margin.	160,000	180,000	200,000
Less operating expenses:			
Advertising expense	21,000	21,000	21,000
Shipping expense	34,000	36,000	38,000
Salaries and commissions	78,000	84,000	90,000
Insurance expense	6,000	6,000	6,000
Depreciation expense.	15,000	15,000	15,000
Total operating expenses	154,000	162,000	170,000
Net operating income	A$ 6,000	A$ 18,000	A$ 30,000

(Note: Morrisey & Brown, Ltd.'s Australian-formatted income statement has been recast in the format common in the United States. The Australian dollar is denoted here by A$.)

Required:
1. Identify each of the company's expenses (including cost of goods sold) as either variable, fixed, or mixed.
2. Using the high-low method, separate each mixed expense into variable and fixed elements. State the cost formula for each mixed expense.
3. Redo the company's income statement at the 5,000-unit level of activity using the contribution format.

PROBLEM 5-17 Identifying Cost Behavior Patterns [LO1]

A number of graphs displaying cost behavior patterns are shown below. The vertical axis on each graph represents total cost, and the horizontal axis represents level of activity (volume).

Required:
1. For each of the following situations, identify the graph below that illustrates the cost behavior pattern involved. Any graph may be used more than once.
   a. Cost of raw materials used.
   b. Electricity bill—a flat fixed charge, plus a variable cost after a certain number of kilowatt-hours are used.
   c. City water bill, which is computed as follows:

First 1,000,000 gallons or less.	$1,000 flat fee
Next 10,000 gallons	$0.003 per gallon used
Next 10,000 gallons	$0.006 per gallon used
Next 10,000 gallons	$0.009 per gallon used
Etc.	Etc.

   d. Depreciation of equipment, where the amount is computed by the straight-line method. When the depreciation rate was established, it was anticipated that the obsolescence factor would be greater than the wear and tear factor.
   e. Rent on a factory building donated by the city, where the agreement calls for a fixed fee payment unless 200,000 labor-hours or more are worked, in which case no rent need be paid.
   f. Salaries of maintenance workers, where one maintenance worker is needed for every 1,000 hours of machine-hours or less (that is, 0 to 1,000 hours requires one maintenance worker, 1,001 to 2,000 hours requires two maintenance workers, etc.)
   g. Cost of raw materials, where the cost starts at $7.50 per unit and then decreases by 5 cents per unit for each of the first 100 units purchased, after which it remains constant at $2.50 per unit.

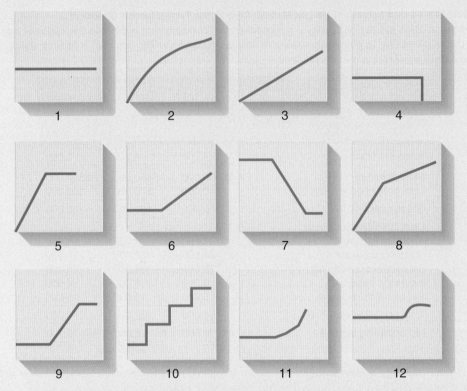

h.   Rent on a factory building donated by the county, where the agreement calls for rent of
     $100,000 less $1 for each direct labor-hour worked in excess of 200,000 hours, but a mini-
     mum rental payment of $20,000 must be paid.

i.   Use of a machine under a lease, where a minimum charge of $1,000 is paid for up to 400
     hours of machine time. After 400 hours of machine time, an additional charge of $2 per hour
     is paid up to a maximum charge of $2,000 per period.

2.   How would a knowledge of cost behavior patterns such as those above be of help to a manager in
     analyzing the cost structure of his or her company?

(CPA, adapted)

PROBLEM 5-18 High-Low and Scattergraph Analysis [LO2, LO3]

Pleasant View Hospital of British Columbia has just hired a new chief administrator who is anxious to
employ sound management and planning techniques in the business affairs of the hospital. Accordingly, she has directed her assistant to summarize the cost structure of the various departments so that
data will be available for planning purposes.

The assistant is unsure how to classify the utilities costs in the Radiology Department since these
costs do not exhibit either strictly variable or fixed cost behavior. Utilities costs are very high in the
department due to a CAT scanner that draws a large amount of power and is kept running at all times.
The scanner can't be turned off due to the long warm-up period required for its use. When the scanner
is used to scan a patient, it consumes an additional burst of power. The assistant has accumulated the
following data on utilities costs and use of the scanner since the first of the year.

Month	Number of Scans	Utilities Cost
January	60	$2,200
February.	70	$2,600
March.	90	$2,900
April	120	$3,300
May	100	$3,000
June.	130	$3,600
July.	150	$4,000
August	140	$3,600
September	110	$3,100
October	80	$2,500

The chief administrator has informed her assistant that the utilities cost is probably a mixed cost that will have to be broken down into its variable and fixed cost elements by use of a scattergraph. The assistant feels, however, that if an analysis of this type is necessary, then the high-low method should be used, since it is easier and quicker. The controller has suggested that there may be a better approach.

Required:
1. Using the high-low method, estimate a cost formula for utilities. Express the formula in the form $Y = a + bX$. (The variable rate should be stated in terms of cost per scan.)
2. Prepare a scattergraph using the data given. (The number of scans should be placed on the horizontal axis, and utilities cost should be placed on the vertical axis.) Fit a straight line to the plotted points using a ruler and estimate a cost formula for utilities using the quick-and-dirty method.

PROBLEM 5-19 (Appendix 5A) Least-Squares Regression Method [LO5]
Refer to the data for Pleasant View Hospital in Problem 5-18.

Required:
1. Using the least-squares regression method, estimate a cost formula for utilities. (Round the variable cost to two decimal places.)
2. Refer to the graph prepared in part (2) of Problem 5-18. Explain why in this case the high-low method would be the least accurate of the three methods in deriving a cost formula.

PROBLEM 5-20 (Appendix 5A) Least-Squares Regression Analysis; Contribution Format Income Statement [LO4, LO5]
Milden Company has an exclusive franchise to purchase a product from the manufacturer and distribute it on the retail level. As an aid in planning, the company has decided to start using the contribution format income statement internally. To have data to prepare such a statement, the company has analyzed its expenses and developed the following cost formulas:

Cost	Cost Formula
Cost of goods sold	$35 per unit sold
Advertising expense.	$210,000 per quarter
Sales commissions	6% of sales
Shipping expense	?
Administrative salaries	$145,000 per quarter
Insurance expense.	$9,000 per quarter
Depreciation expense	$76,000 per quarter

Management has concluded that shipping expense is a mixed cost, containing both variable and fixed cost elements. Units sold and the related shipping expense over the last eight quarters follow:

Quarter	Units Sold (000)	Shipping Expense
Year 1:		
First	10	$119,000
Second	16	$175,000
Third	18	$190,000
Fourth	15	$164,000
Year 2:		
First	11	$130,000
Second	17	$185,000
Third	20	$210,000
Fourth	13	$147,000

Milden Company's president would like a cost formula derived for shipping expense so that a budgeted income statement using the contribution approach can be prepared for the next quarter.

Required:
1. Using the least-squares regression method, estimate a cost formula for shipping expense. (Since the Units Sold above are in thousands of units, the variable cost you compute will also be in thousands of units. It can be left in this form, or you can convert your variable cost to a per unit basis by dividing it by 1,000.)

2. In the first quarter of Year 3, the company plans to sell 12,000 units at a selling price of $100 per unit. Prepare a contribution format income statement for the quarter.

PROBLEM 5-21 High-Low Method; Predicting Cost [LO1, LO3]

Nova Company's total overhead costs at various levels of activity are presented below:

Month	Machine-Hours	Total Overhead Cost
April	70,000	$198,000
May	60,000	$174,000
June.	80,000	$222,000
July.	90,000	$246,000

Assume that the total overhead costs above consist of utilities, supervisory salaries, and maintenance. The breakdown of these costs at the 60,000 machine-hour level of activity is:

Utilities (variable)	$ 48,000
Supervisory salaries (fixed).	21,000
Maintenance (mixed)	105,000
Total overhead cost.	$174,000

Nova Company's management wants to break down the maintenance cost into its variable and fixed cost elements.

Required:
1. Estimate how much of the $246,000 of overhead cost in July was maintenance cost. (Hint: to do this, it may be helpful to first determine how much of the $246,000 consisted of utilities and supervisory salaries. Think about the behavior of variable and fixed costs!)
2. Using the high-low method, estimate a cost formula for maintenance.
3. Express the company's *total* overhead costs in the linear equation form $Y = a + bX$.
4. What total overhead costs would you expect to be incurred at an operating activity level of 75,000 machine-hours?

PROBLEM 5-22 High-Low Method; Cost of Goods Manufactured [LO1, LO3]

Amfac Company manufactures a single product. The company keeps careful records of manufacturing activities from which the following information has been extracted:

	Level of Activity	
	March–Low	June–High
Number of units produced.	6,000	9,000
Cost of goods manufactured.	$168,000	$257,000
Work in process inventory, beginning.	$9,000	$32,000
Work in process inventory, ending	$15,000	$21,000
Direct materials cost per unit	$6	$6
Direct labor cost per unit.	$10	$10
Manufacturing overhead cost, total.	?	?

The company's manufacturing overhead cost consists of both variable and fixed cost elements. To have data available for planning, management wants to determine how much of the overhead cost is variable with units produced and how much of it is fixed per month.

Required:
1. For both March and June, estimate the amount of manufacturing overhead cost added to production. The company had no under- or overapplied overhead in either month. (Hint: A useful way to proceed might be to construct a schedule of cost of goods manufactured.)
2. Using the high-low method, estimate a cost formula for manufacturing overhead. Express the variable portion of the formula in terms of a variable rate per unit of product.
3. If 7,000 units are produced during a month, what would be the cost of goods manufactured? (Assume that work in process inventories do not change and that there is no under- or overapplied overhead cost for the month.)

PROBLEM 5-23 High-Low Method; Predicting Cost [LO1, LO3]

Sawaya Co., Ltd., of Japan is a manufacturing company whose total factory overhead costs fluctuate considerably from year to year according to increases and decreases in the number of direct labor-hours worked in the factory. Total factory overhead costs (in Japanese yen, denoted ¥) at high and low levels of activity for recent years are given below:

	Level of Activity	
	Low	High
Direct labor-hours	50,000	75,000
Total factory overhead costs	¥14,250,000	¥17,625,000

The factory overhead costs above consist of indirect materials, rent, and maintenance. The company has analyzed these costs at the 50,000-hour level of activity as follows:

Indirect materials (variable)	¥5,000,000
Rent (fixed)	6,000,000
Maintenance (mixed)	3,250,000
Total factory overhead costs	¥14,250,000

To have data available for planning, the company wants to break down the maintenance cost into its variable and fixed cost elements.

Required:

1. Estimate how much of the ¥17,625,000 factory overhead cost at the high level of activity consists of maintenance cost. (Hint: To do this, it may be helpful to first determine how much of the ¥17,625,000 consists of indirect materials and rent. Think about the behavior of variable and fixed costs!)
2. Using the high-low method, estimate a cost formula for maintenance.
3. What *total* factory overhead costs would you expect the company to incur at an operating level of 70,000 direct labor-hours?

Cases

CASE 5-24 Scattergraph Analysis; Selection of an Activity Base [LO2]

Angora Wraps of Pendleton, Oregon, makes fine sweaters out of pure angora wool. The business is seasonal, with the largest demand during the fall, the winter, and Christmas holidays. The company must ramp up production each summer to meet estimated demand.

The company has been analyzing its costs to determine which costs are fixed and variable for planning purposes. Below are data for the company's activity and direct labor costs over the last year.

Month	Thousands of Units Produced	Number of Paid Days	Direct Labor Cost
January	98	20	$14,162
February	76	20	$12,994
March	75	21	$15,184
April	80	22	$15,038
May	85	22	$15,768
June	102	21	$15,330
July	52	19	$13,724
August	136	21	$14,162
September	138	22	$15,476
October	132	23	$15,476
November	86	18	$12,972
December	56	21	$14,074

The number of workdays varies from month to month due to the number of weekdays, holidays, and days of vacation in the month. The paid days include paid vacations (in July) and paid holidays (in November and December). The number of units produced in a month varies depending on demand and the number of workdays in the month.

The company has eight workers who are classified as direct labor.

Required:
1. Plot the direct labor cost and units produced on a scattergraph. (Place cost on the vertical axis and units produced on the horizontal axis.)
2. Plot the direct labor cost and number of paid days on a scattergraph. (Place cost on the vertical axis and the number of paid days on the horizontal axis.)
3. Which measure of activity—number of units produced or paid days—should be used as the activity base for explaining direct labor cost? Explain

CASE 5-25 (Appendix 5A) Least-Squares Regression; Scattergraph; Comparison of Activity Bases [LO2, LO5]

The Hard Rock Mining Company is developing cost formulas for management planning and decision-making purposes. The company's cost analyst has concluded that utilities cost is a mixed cost, and he is attempting to find a base with which the cost might be closely correlated. The controller has suggested that tons mined might be a good base to use in developing a cost formula. The production superintendent disagrees; she thinks that direct labor-hours would be a better base. The cost analyst has decided to try both bases and has assembled the following information:

Quarter	Tons Mined (000)	Direct Labor-Hours (000)	Utilities Cost
Year 1:			
First	15	5	$50,000
Second	11	3	$45,000
Third	21	4	$60,000
Fourth	12	6	$75,000
Year 2:			
First	18	10	$100,000
Second	25	9	$105,000
Third	30	8	$85,000
Fourth	28	11	$120,000

Required:
1. Using tons mined as the independent (X) variable:
   a. Determine a cost formula for utilities cost using the least-squares regression method. (The variable cost you compute will be in thousands of tons. It can be left in this form, or you can convert your variable cost to a per ton basis by dividing it by 1,000.)
   b. Prepare a scattergraph and plot the tons mined and utilities cost. (Place cost on the vertical axis and tons mined on the horizontal axis.) Fit a straight line to the plotted points using the cost formula determined in (*a*) above.
2. Using direct labor-hours as the independent (X) variable, repeat the computations in (*a*) and (*b*) above.
3. Would you recommend that the company use tons mined or direct labor-hours as a base for planning utilities cost?

CASE 5-26 (Appendix 5A) Analysis of Mixed Costs, Job-Order Costing, and Activity-Based Costing [LO1, LO2, LO5]

Hokuriku-Seika Co., Ltd., of Yokohama, Japan, is a subcontractor to local manufacturing companies. The company specializes in precision metal cutting using focused high-pressure water jets and high-energy lasers. The company has a traditional job-order costing system in which direct labor and direct materials costs are assigned directly to jobs, but factory overhead is applied to jobs using a predetermined overhead rate with direct labor-hours as the activity base. Management uses this job cost data for valuing cost of goods sold and inventories for external reports. For internal decision making, management has largely ignored this cost data since direct labor costs are basically fixed and management believes overhead costs actually have little to do with direct labor-hours. Recently, management has become interested in activity-based costing (ABC) as a way of estimating job costs and other costs for decision-making purposes.

Management assembled a cross-functional team to design a prototype ABC system. Electrical costs were among the first factory overhead costs investigated by the team. Electricity is used to provide light, to power equipment, and to heat the building in the winter and cool it in the summer. The ABC team proposed allocating electrical costs to jobs based on machine-hours since running the machines consumes significant amounts of electricity. Data assembled by the team concerning actual direct labor-hours, machine-hours, and electrical costs over a recent eight-week period appear below. (The Japanese currency is the yen, which is denoted by ¥.)

	Direct Labor-Hours	Machine-Hours	Electrical Costs
Week 1........	8,920	7,200	¥ 77,100
Week 2........	8,810	8,200	84,400
Week 3........	8,950	8,700	80,400
Week 4........	8,990	7,200	75,500
Week 5........	8,840	7,400	81,100
Week 6........	8,890	8,800	83,300
Week 7........	8,950	6,400	79,200
Week 8........	8,990	7,700	85,500
Total..........	71,340	61,600	¥646,500

To help assess the effect of the proposed change to machine-hours as the allocation base, the eight-week totals were converted to annual figures by multiplying them by six.

	Direct Labor-Hours	Machine-Hours	Electrical Costs
Estimated annual total (eight-week total above × 6).............	428,040	369,600	¥3,879,000

Required:
1. Assume that the estimated annual totals from the above table are used to compute the company's predetermined overhead rate. What would be the predetermined overhead rate for electrical costs if the allocation base is direct labor-hours? Machine-hours?
2. Hokuriku-Seika Co. intends to bid on a job for a shipyard that would require 350 direct labor-hours and 270 machine-hours. How much electrical cost would be charged to this job using the predetermined overhead rate computed in (1) above if the allocation base is direct labor-hours? Machine-hours?
3. Prepare a scattergraph in which you plot direct labor-hours on the horizontal axis and electrical costs on the vertical axis. Prepare another scattergraph in which you plot machine-hours on the horizontal axis and electrical costs on the vertical axis. Do you agree with the ABC team that machine-hours is a better allocation base for electrical costs than direct labor-hours? Why?
4. Using machine-hours as the measure of activity, estimate the fixed and variable components of electrical costs using least-squares regression.
5. How much electrical cost do you think would actually be caused by the shipyard job in (2) above? Explain.
6. What factors, apart from direct labor-hours and machine-hours, are likely to affect consumption of electrical power in the company?

CASE 5-27 Analysis of Mixed Costs in a Pricing Decision [LO1 and LO2, LO3, or LO5]
Maria Chavez owns a catering company that serves food and beverages at parties and business functions. Chavez's business is seasonal, with a heavy schedule during the summer months and holidays and a lighter schedule at other times.

One of the major events Chavez's customers request is a cocktail party. She offers a standard cocktail party and has estimated the cost per guest as follows:

Food and beverages	$15.00
Labor (0.5 hrs. @ $10.00/hr.)	5.00
Overhead (0.5 hrs. @ $13.98/hr.)	6.99
Total cost per guest	$26.99

The standard cocktail party lasts three hours and Chavez hires one worker for every six guests, so that works out to one-half hour of labor per guest. These workers are hired only as needed and are paid only for the hours they actually work.

When bidding on cocktail parties, Chavez adds a 15% markup to yield a price of about $31 per guest. She is confident about her estimates of the costs of food and beverages and labor but is not as comfortable with the estimate of overhead cost. The $13.98 overhead cost per labor hour was determined by dividing total overhead expenses for the last 12 months by total labor hours for the same period. Monthly data concerning overhead costs and labor-hours follow:

Month	Labor-Hours	Overhead Expenses
January	2,500	$ 55,000
February	2,800	59,000
March	3,000	60,000
April	4,200	64,000
May	4,500	67,000
June	5,500	71,000
July	6,500	74,000
August	7,500	77,000
September	7,000	75,000
October	4,500	68,000
November	3,100	62,000
December	6,500	73,000
Total	57,600	$805,000

Chavez has received a request to bid on a 180-guest fund-raising cocktail party to be given next month by an important local charity. (The party would last the usual three hours.) She would like to win this contract because the guest list for this charity event includes many prominent individuals that she would like to land as future clients. Maria is confident that these potential customers would be favorably impressed by her company's services at the charity event.

Required:
1. Estimate the contribution to profit of a standard 180-guest cocktail party if Chavez charges her usual price of $31 per guest. (In other words, by how much would her overall profit increase?)
2. How low could Chavez bid for the charity event in terms of a price per guest and still not lose money on the event itself?
3. The individual who is organizing the charity's fund-raising event has indicated that he has already received a bid under $30 from another catering company. Do you think Chavez should bid below her normal $31 per guest price for the charity event? Why or why not?

(CMA, adapted)

RESEARCH AND APPLICATION 5-28 [LO1, LO2, LO3, LO4, LO5]
(APPENDIX 5A)

The questions in this exercise are based on Blue Nile, Inc. To answer the questions, you will need to download Blue Nile's 2004 Form 10-K at http://investor.bluenile.com/phoenix.zhtml?c=177247&p=irol-reportsAnnual. You do not need to print this document to answer the questions. You will need the information at the top of the next page to answer the questions.

	2004				2005	
	Quarter 1	Quarter 2	Quarter 3	Quarter 4	Quarter 1	Quarter 2
Net sales	?	?	?	?	$44,116	$43,826
Cost of sales	?	?	?	?	$34,429	$33,836
Gross profit	?	?	?	?	$9,687	$9,990
Selling, general, and administrative expense	$5,308	$5,111	$5,033	$7,343	$6,123	$6,184
Operating income...	?	?	?	?	$3,564	$3,806

Required:

1. What is Blue Nile's strategy for success in the marketplace? Does the company rely primarily on a customer intimacy, operational excellence, or product leadership customer value proposition? What evidence from the 10-K supports your conclusion?

2. What business risks does Blue Nile face that may threaten its ability to satisfy stockholder expectations? What are some examples of control activities that the company could use to reduce these risks? (Hint: Focus on pages 8–19 of the 10-K.) Are some of the risks faced by Blue Nile difficult to reduce through control activities? Explain.

3. Is Blue Nile a merchandiser or a manufacturer? What information contained in the 10-K supports your answer?

4. Using account analysis, would you label cost of sales and selling, general, and administrative expense as variable, fixed, or mixed costs? Why? (Hint: focus on pages 24–26 and 38 of the 10-K.) Cite one example of a variable cost, step-variable cost, discretionary fixed cost, and committed fixed cost for Blue Nile.

5. Fill in the blanks in the table above based on information contained in the 10-K. Using the high-low method, estimate the variable and fixed cost elements of the quarterly selling, general, and administrative expense. Express Blue Nile's variable and fixed selling, general, and administrative expenses in the form $Y = a + bX$.

6. Using the least-squares regression method, estimate a cost formula for selling, general, and administrative expense. Are these estimates the same or different from those obtained using the high-low method? Why?

7. Prepare a contribution format income statement for the third quarter of 2005 assuming that Blue Nile's net sales were $45,500 and its cost of sales as a percentage of net sales remained unchanged from the prior quarter.

8. How would you describe Blue Nile's cost structure? Is Blue Nile's cost of sales as a percentage of sales higher or lower than competitors with bricks and mortar jewelry stores?

Chapter

6

Cost-Volume-Profit Relationships

What Happened to the Profit?

BUSINESS FOCUS

Chip Conley is CEO of Joie de Vivre Hospitality, a company that owns and operates 28 hospitality businesses in northern California. Conley summed up the company's experience after the dot.com crash and 9/11 as follows: "In the history of American hotel markets, no hotel market has ever seen a drop in revenues as precipitous as the one in San Francisco and Silicon Valley in the last two years. On average, hotel revenues . . . dropped 40% to 45%. . . . We've been fortunate that our breakeven point is lower than our competition's. . . . But the problem is that the hotel business is a fixed-cost business. So in an environment where you have those precipitous drops and our costs are moderately fixed, our net incomes—well, they're not incomes anymore, they're losses." ■

Source: Karen Dillon, "Shop Talk," *Inc* magazine, December 2002, pp. 111–114.

Cost-volume-profit (CVP) analysis is a powerful tool that helps managers understand the relationships among cost, volume, and profit. CVP analysis focuses on how profits are affected by the following five factors:

1. Selling prices.
2. Sales volume.
3. Unit variable costs.
4. Total fixed costs.
5. Mix of products sold.

Because CVP analysis helps managers understand how profits are affected by these key factors, it is a vital tool in many business decisions. These decisions include what products and services to offer, what prices to charge, what marketing strategy to use, and what cost structure to implement. To help understand the role of CVP analysis in business decisions, consider the case of Acoustic Concepts, Inc., a company founded by Prem Narayan.

Prem, who was a graduate student in engineering at the time, started Acoustic Concepts to market a radical new speaker he had designed for automobile sound systems. The speaker, called the Sonic Blaster, uses an advanced microprocessor and proprietary software to boost amplification to awesome levels. Prem contracted with a Taiwanese electronics manufacturer to produce the speaker. With seed money provided by his family, Prem placed an order with the manufacturer and ran advertisements in auto magazines.

The Sonic Blaster was an almost immediate success, and sales grew to the point that Prem moved the company's headquarters out of his apartment and into rented quarters in a nearby industrial park. He also hired a receptionist, an accountant, a sales manager, and a small sales staff to sell the speakers to retail stores. The accountant, Bob Luchinni, had worked for several small companies where he had acted as a business advisor as well as accountant and bookkeeper. The following discussion occurred soon after Bob was hired:

MANAGERIAL ACCOUNTING IN ACTION
The Issue

Accoustic Concepts, Inc.

Prem: Bob, I've got a lot of questions about the company's finances that I hope you can help answer.

Bob: We're in great shape. The loan from your family will be paid off within a few months.

Prem: I know, but I am worried about the risks I've taken on by expanding operations. What would happen if a competitor entered the market and our sales slipped? How far could sales drop without putting us into the red? Another question I've been trying to resolve is how much our sales would have to increase to justify the big marketing campaign the sales staff is pushing for.

Bob: Marketing always wants more money for advertising.

Prem: And they are always pushing me to drop the selling price on the speaker. I agree with them that a lower price will boost our volume, but I'm not sure the increased volume will offset the loss in revenue from the lower price.

Bob: It sounds like these questions are all related in some way to the relationships among our selling prices, our costs, and our volume. I shouldn't have a problem coming up with some answers.

Prem: Can we meet again in a couple of days to see what you have come up with?

Bob: Sounds good. By then I'll have some preliminary answers for you as well as a model you can use for answering similar questions in the future.

The Basics of Cost-Volume-Profit (CVP) Analysis

Bob Luchinni's preparation for his forthcoming meeting with Prem begins where our study of cost behavior in the preceding chapter left off—with the contribution income statement. The contribution income statement emphasizes the behavior of costs and therefore is extremely helpful to managers in judging the impact on profits of changes in selling price, cost, or volume. Bob will base his analysis on the following contribution income statement he prepared last month:

Acoustic Concepts, Inc. Contribution Income Statement For the Month of June		
	Total	Per Unit
Sales (400 speakers)	$100,000	$250
Variable expenses	60,000	150
Contribution margin	40,000	$100
Fixed expenses	35,000	
Net operating income	$ 5,000	

Notice that sales, variable expenses, and contribution margin are expressed on a per unit basis as well as in total on this contribution income statement. The per unit figures will be very helpful to Bob in some of his calculations. Note that this contribution income statement has been prepared for management's use inside the company and would not ordinarily be made available to those outside the company.

Contribution Margin

LEARNING OBJECTIVE 1
Explain how changes in activity affect contribution margin and net operating income.

As explained in the previous chapter, contribution margin is the amount remaining from sales revenue after variable expenses have been deducted. Thus, it is the amount available to cover fixed expenses and then to provide profits for the period. Notice the sequence here—contribution margin is used *first* to cover the fixed expenses, and then whatever remains goes toward profits. If the contribution margin is not sufficient to cover the fixed expenses, then a loss occurs for the period. To illustrate with an extreme example, assume that Acoustic Concepts sells only one speaker during a particular month. The company's income statement would appear as follows:

Contribution Income Statement Sales of 1 Speaker		
	Total	Per Unit
Sales (1 speaker)	$ 250	$250
Variable expenses	150	150
Contribution margin	100	$100
Fixed expenses	35,000	
Net operating loss	$(34,900)	

For each additional speaker the company sells during the month, $100 more in contribution margin becomes available to help cover the fixed expenses. If a second speaker is sold, for example, then the total contribution margin will increase by $100 (to a total of $200) and the company's loss will decrease by $100, to $34,800:

Contribution Income Statement Sales of 2 Speakers		
	Total	Per Unit
Sales (2 speakers)	$ 500	$250
Variable expenses	300	150
Contribution margin	200	$100
Fixed expenses	35,000	
Net operating loss	$(34,800)	

If enough speakers can be sold to generate $35,000 in contribution margin, then all of the fixed expenses will be covered and the company will *break even* for the month—that is, it will show neither profit nor loss but just cover all of its costs. To reach the break-even point, the company will have to sell 350 speakers in a month, since each speaker sold yields $100 in contribution margin:

Contribution Income Statement Sales of 350 Speakers		
	Total	Per Unit
Sales (350 speakers)	$87,500	$250
Variable expenses	52,500	150
Contribution margin	35,000	$100
Fixed expenses	35,000	
Net operating income	$ 0	

Computation of the break-even point is discussed in detail later in the chapter; for the moment, note that the **break-even point** is the level of sales at which profit is zero.

Once the break-even point has been reached, net operating income will increase by the amount of the unit contribution margin for each additional unit sold. For example, if 351 speakers are sold in a month, then the net operating income for the month will be $100, since the company will have sold 1 speaker more than the number needed to break even:

Contribution Income Statement Sales of 351 Speakers		
	Total	Per Unit
Sales (351 speakers)	$87,750	$250
Variable expenses	52,650	150
Contribution margin	35,100	$100
Fixed expenses	35,000	
Net operating income	$ 100	

If 352 speakers are sold (2 speakers above the break-even point), the net operating income for the month will be $200. If 353 speakers are sold (3 speakers above the break-even point), the net operating income for the month will be $300, and so forth. To estimate the profit at any sales volume above the break-even point, simply multiply the number of units sold in excess of the break-even point by the unit contribution margin. The result represents the anticipated profits for the period. Or, to estimate the effect of a planned increase in sales on profits, simply multiply the increase in units sold by the unit contribution margin. The result will be the expected increase in profits. To illustrate, if Acoustic Concepts is currently selling 400 speakers per month and plans to increase sales to 425 speakers per month, the anticipated impact on profits can be computed as follows:

Increased number of speakers to be sold	25
Contribution margin per speaker	× $100
Increase in net operating income.	$2,500

These calculations can be verified as follows:

| | Sales Volume | | | |
	400 Speakers	425 Speakers	Difference (25 Speakers)	Per Unit
Sales (@ $250 per speaker).......	$100,000	$106,250	$6,250	$250
Variable expenses (@ $150 per speaker)..........	60,000	63,750	3,750	150
Contribution margin	40,000	42,500	2,500	$100
Fixed expenses	35,000	35,000	0	
Net operating income	$ 5,000	$ 7,500	$2,500	

To summarize, if sales are zero, the company's loss would equal its fixed expenses. Each unit that is sold reduces the loss by the amount of the unit contribution margin. Once the break-even point has been reached, each additional unit sold increases the company's profit by the amount of the unit contribution margin.

CVP Relationships in Graphic Form

LEARNING OBJECTIVE 2
Prepare and interpret a cost-volume-profit (CVP) graph.

The relationships among revenue, cost, profit, and volume are illustrated on a **cost-volume-profit (CVP) graph.** A CVP graph highlights CVP relationships over wide ranges of activity. To help explain his analysis to Prem Narayan, Bob Luchinni decided to prepare a CVP graph for Acoustic Concepts.

Preparing the CVP Graph   In a CVP graph (sometimes called a *break-even chart*), unit volume is represented on the horizontal (X) axis and dollars on the vertical (Y) axis. Preparing a CVP graph involves three steps as depicted in Exhibit 6–1:

1. Draw a line parallel to the volume axis to represent total fixed expense. For Acoustic Concepts, total fixed expenses are $35,000.

EXHIBIT 6–1
Preparing the CVP Graph

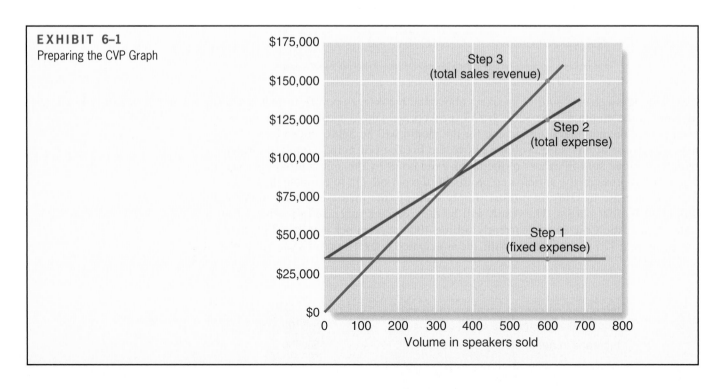

2. Choose some volume of unit sales and plot the point representing total expense (fixed and variable) at the activity level you have selected. In Exhibit 6–1, Bob Luchinni chose a volume of 600 speakers. Total expense at that activity level is:

Fixed expense	$35,000
Variable expense (600 speakers × $150 per speaker)	90,000
Total expense	$125,000

After the point has been plotted, draw a line through it back to the point where the fixed expense line intersects the dollars axis.

3. Again choose some volume of unit sales and plot the point representing total sales dollars at the activity level you have selected. In Exhibit 6–1, Bob Luchinni again chose a volume of 600 speakers. Sales at that activity level total $150,000 (600 speakers × $250 per speaker). Draw a line through this point back to the origin.

The interpretation of the completed CVP graph is given in Exhibit 6–2. The anticipated profit or loss at any given level of sales is measured by the vertical distance between the total revenue line (sales) and the total expense line (variable expense plus fixed expense).

The break-even point is where the total revenue and total expense lines cross. The break-even point of 350 speakers in Exhibit 6–2 agrees with the break-even point computed earlier.

As discussed earlier, when sales are below the break-even point—in this case, 350 units—the company suffers a loss. Note that the loss (represented by the vertical distance between the total expense and total revenue lines) gets bigger as sales decline. When sales are above the break-even point, the company earns a profit and the size of the profit (represented by the vertical distance between the total revenue and total expense lines) increases as sales increase.

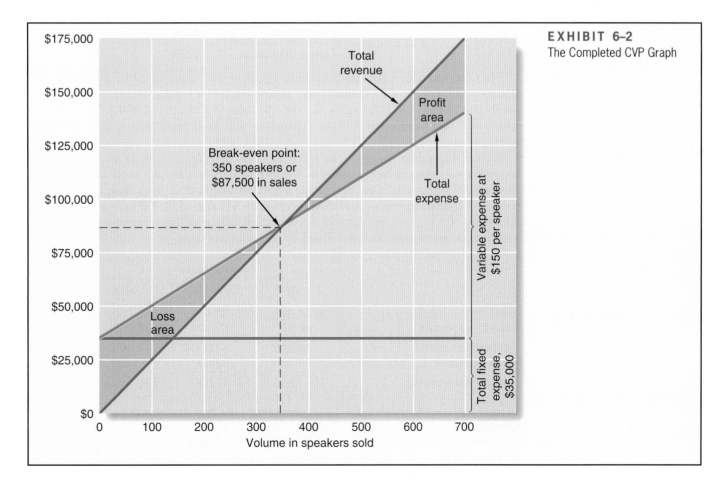

EXHIBIT 6–2
The Completed CVP Graph

LEARNING OBJECTIVE 3
Use the contribution margin ratio (CM ratio) to compute changes in contribution margin and net operating income resulting from changes in sales volume.

Contribution Margin Ratio (CM Ratio)

In the previous section, we explored how cost-volume-profit relationships can be visualized. In this section, we show how the *contribution margin ratio* can be used in cost-volume-profit calculations. As the first step, we have added a column to Acoustic Concepts' contribution format income statement in which sales revenues, variable expenses, and contribution margin are expressed as a percentage of sales:

	Total	Per Unit	Percent of Sales
Sales (400 speakers)	$100,000	$250	100%
Variable expenses	60,000	150	60%
Contribution margin	40,000	$100	40%
Fixed expenses	35,000		
Net operating income	$ 5,000		

The contribution margin as a percentage of sales is referred to as the **contribution margin ratio (CM ratio).** This ratio is computed as follows:

$$\text{CM ratio} = \frac{\text{Contribution margin}}{\text{Sales}}$$

For Acoustic Concepts, the computations are:

$$\text{CM ratio} = \frac{\text{Total contribution margin}}{\text{Total sales}} = \frac{\$40,000}{\$100,000} = 40\%$$

In a company such as Acoustic Concepts that has only one product, the CM ratio can also be computed on a per unit basis as follows:

$$\text{CM ratio} = \frac{\text{Unit contribution margin}}{\text{Unit selling price}} = \frac{\$100}{\$250} = 40\%$$

The CM ratio shows how the contribution margin will be affected by a change in total sales. Acoustic Concepts' CM ratio of 40% means that for each dollar increase in sales, total contribution margin will increase by 40 cents ($1 sales × CM ratio of 40%). Net operating income will also increase by 40 cents, assuming that fixed costs are not affected by the increase in sales.

As this illustration suggests, *the impact on net operating income of any given dollar change in total sales can be computed by simply applying the CM ratio to the dollar change.* For example, if Acoustic Concepts plans a $30,000 increase in sales during the coming month, the contribution margin should increase by $12,000 ($30,000 increase in sales × CM ratio of 40%). As we noted above, net operating income will also increase by $12,000 if fixed costs do not change. This is verified by the following table:

	Sales Volume			Percent of Sales
	Present	Expected	Increase	
Sales	$100,000	$130,000	$30,000	100%
Variable expenses	60,000	78,000*	18,000	60%
Contribution margin	40,000	52,000	12,000	40%
Fixed expenses	35,000	35,000	0	
Net operating income	$ 5,000	$ 17,000	$12,000	

*$130,000 expected sales ÷ $250 per unit = 520 units. 520 units × $150 per unit = $78,000.

The CM ratio is particularly valuable in situations where the dollar sales of one product must be traded off against the dollar sales of another product. In this situation, products that yield the greatest amount of contribution margin per dollar of sales should be emphasized.

Some Applications of CVP Concepts

Bob Luchinni, the accountant at Acoustic Concepts, wanted to demonstrate to the company's president Prem Narayan how the concepts developed on the preceding pages can be used in planning and decision making. Bob gathered the following basic data:

LEARNING OBJECTIVE 4
Show the effects on contribution margin of changes in variable costs, fixed costs, selling price, and volume.

	Per Unit	Percent of Sales
Selling price	$250	100%
Variable expenses	150	60%
Contribution margin	$100	40%

Recall that fixed expenses are $35,000 per month. Bob Luchinni will use these data to show the effects of changes in variable costs, fixed costs, sales price, and sales volume on the company's profitability in a variety of situations.

Change in Fixed Cost and Sales Volume   Acoustic Concepts is currently selling 400 speakers per month at $250 per speaker for total monthly sales of $100,000. The sales manager feels that a $10,000 increase in the monthly advertising budget would increase monthly sales by $30,000 to a total of 520 units. Should the advertising budget be increased? The following table shows the financial impact of the proposed change in the monthly advertising budget:

	Current Sales	Sales with Additional Advertising Budget	Difference	Percent of Sales
Sales	$100,000	$130,000	$30,000	100%
Variable expenses	60,000	78,000*	18,000	60%
Contribution margin	40,000	52,000	12,000	40%
Fixed expenses	35,000	45,000†	10,000	
Net operating income	$ 5,000	$ 7,000	$ 2,000	

*520 units × $150 per unit = $78,000.
†$35,000 + additional $10,000 monthly advertising budget = $45,000.

Assuming no other factors need to be considered, the increase in the advertising budget should be approved because it would increase net operating income by $2,000. There are two shorter ways to arrive at this solution. The first alternative solution follows:

Alternative Solution 1

Expected total contribution margin:	
$130,000 × 40% CM ratio	$52,000
Present total contribution margin:	
$100,000 × 40% CM ratio	40,000
Incremental contribution margin	12,000
Change in fixed expenses:	
Less incremental advertising expense	10,000
Increased net operating income	$ 2,000

Topic Tackler

PLUS

6–1

Because in this case only the fixed costs and the sales volume change, the solution can be presented in an even shorter format, as follows:

Alternative Solution 2

Incremental contribution margin:	
$30,000 × 40% CM ratio	$12,000
Less incremental advertising expense	10,000
Increased net operating income	$ 2,000

Notice that this approach does not depend on knowledge of previous sales. Also note that it is unnecessary under either shorter approach to prepare an income statement. Both of the alternative solutions involve an **incremental analysis**—they consider only those items of revenue, cost, and volume that will change if the new program is implemented. Although in each case a new income statement could have been prepared, the incremental approach is simpler and more direct and focuses attention on the specific changes that would occur as a result of the decision.

Change in Variable Costs and Sales Volume   Refer to the original data. Recall that Acoustic Concepts is currently selling 400 speakers per month. Prem is considering the use of higher-quality components, which would increase variable costs (and thereby reduce the contribution margin) by $10 per speaker. However, the sales manager predicts that using higher-quality components would increase sales to 480 speakers per month. Should the higher-quality components be used?

The $10 increase in variable costs would decrease the unit contribution margin by $10—from $100 down to $90.

Solution

Expected total contribution margin with higher-quality components:	
480 speakers × $90 per speaker	$43,200
Present total contribution margin:	
400 speakers × $100 per speaker	40,000
Increase in total contribution margin	$ 3,200

According to this analysis, the higher-quality components should be used. Since fixed costs would not change, the $3,200 increase in contribution margin shown above should result in a $3,200 increase in net operating income.

Change in Fixed Cost, Sales Price, and Sales Volume   Refer to the original data and recall again that Acoustic Concepts is currently selling 400 speakers per month. To increase sales, the sales manager would like to cut the selling price by $20 per speaker and increase the advertising budget by $15,000 per month. The sales manager believes that if these two steps are taken, unit sales will increase by 50% to 600 speakers per month. Should the changes be made?

A decrease in the selling price of $20 per speaker would decrease the unit contribution margin by $20 down to $80.

Solution

Expected total contribution margin with lower selling price:	
600 speakers × $80 per speaker	$48,000
Present total contribution margin:	
400 speakers × $100 per speaker	40,000
Incremental contribution margin	8,000
Change in fixed expenses:	
Less incremental advertising expense.	15,000
Reduction in net operating income	$ (7,000)

According to this analysis, the changes should not be made. The $7,000 reduction in net operating income that is shown above can be verified by preparing comparative income statements as follows:

	Present 400 Speakers per Month		Expected 600 Speakers per Month		
	Total	Per Unit	Total	Per Unit	Difference
Sales	$100,000	$250	$138,000	$230	$38,000
Variable expenses	60,000	150	90,000	150	30,000
Contribution margin	40,000	$100	48,000	$ 80	8,000
Fixed expenses	35,000		50,000*		15,000
Net operating income (loss)	$ 5,000		$ (2,000)		$ (7,000)

*35,000 + Additional monthly advertising budget of $15,000 = $50,000.

DELTA ATTEMPTS TO BOOST TICKET SALES

The United States Transportation Department ranked the Cincinnati/Northern Kentucky International Airport (CNK) as the second most expensive airport in the country. Because of its high ticket prices, CNK airport officials estimated that they were losing 28% of Cincinnati-area travelers—about 2,500 people per day—to five surrounding airports that offered lower fares. Delta Airlines, which has 90% of the traffic at CNK, attempted to improve the situation by introducing SimpliFares. The program, which Delta touted with a $2 million media campaign, not only lowered fares but also reduced the ticket change fee from $100 to $50. From a cost-volume-profit standpoint, Delta was hoping that the increase in discretionary fixed advertising costs and the decrease in sales revenue realized from lower ticket prices would be more than offset by an increase in sales volume.

Source: James Pilcher, "New Delta Fares Boost Ticket Sales," *The Cincinnati Enquirer,* September 3, 2004, pp. A1 and A12.

Change in Variable Cost, Fixed Cost, and Sales Volume   Refer to Acoustic Concepts' original data. As before, the company is currently selling 400 speakers per month. The sales manager would like to pay salespersons a sales commission of $15 per speaker sold, rather than the flat salaries that now total $6,000 per month. The sales manager is confident that the change would increase monthly sales by 15% to 460 speakers per month. Should the change be made?

Solution   Changing the sales staff's compensation from salaries to commissions would affect both fixed and variable expenses. Fixed expenses would decrease by $6,000, from $35,000 to $29,000. Variable expenses per unit would increase by $15, from $150 to $165, and the unit contribution margin would decrease from $100 to $85.

Expected total contribution margin with sales staff on commissions:	
460 speakers × $85 per speaker	$39,100
Present total contribution margin:	
400 speakers × $100 per speaker	40,000
Decrease in total contribution margin	(900)
Change in fixed expenses:	
Add salaries avoided if a commission is paid	6,000
Increase in net operating income	$ 5,100

According to this analysis, the changes should be made. Again, the same answer can be obtained by preparing comparative income statements:

	Present 400 Speakers per Month		Expected 460 Speakers per Month		
	Total	Per Unit	Total	Per Unit	Difference
Sales.	$100,000	$250	$115,000	$250	$15,000
Variable expenses.	60,000	150	75,900	165	15,900
Contribution margin.	40,000	$100	39,100	$ 85	900
Fixed expenses.	35,000		29,000		(6,000)*
Net operating income	$ 5,000		$ 10,100		$ 5,100

*Note: A *reduction* in fixed expenses has the effect of *increasing* net operating income.

Change in Selling Price   Refer to the original data where Acoustic Concepts is currently selling 400 speakers per month. The company has an opportunity to make a bulk sale of 150 speakers to a wholesaler if an acceptable price can be negotiated. This sale would not disturb the company's regular sales and would not affect the company's total fixed expenses. What price per speaker should be quoted to the wholesaler if Acoustic Concepts wants to increase its total monthly profits by $3,000?

Solution

Variable cost per speaker	$150
Desired profit per speaker:	
$3,000 ÷ 150 speakers	20
Quoted price per speaker.	$170

Notice that fixed expenses are not included in the computation. This is because fixed expenses are not affected by the bulk sale, so all of the additional contribution margin increases the company's profits.

Break-Even Analysis

Break-even analysis is an aspect of CVP analysis that is designed to answer questions such as how far could sales drop before the company begins to lose money?

Topic Tackler

PLUS

6–2

Break-Even Computations

Earlier in the chapter we defined the break-even point as the level of sales at which the company's profit is zero. The break-even point can be computed using either the *equation method* or the *contribution margin method*—the two methods are equivalent.

The Equation Method   The **equation method** translates the contribution format income statement illustrated earlier in the chapter into equation form as follows:

$$\text{Profits} = (\text{Sales} - \text{Variable expenses}) - \text{Fixed expenses}$$

Rearranging this equation slightly yields the following equation, which is widely used in CVP analysis:

$$\text{Sales} = \text{Variable expenses} + \text{Fixed expenses} + \text{Profits}$$

At the break-even point, profits are zero. Therefore, the break-even point can be computed by finding the point where sales equal the total of the variable expenses plus the fixed expenses. For Acoustic Concepts, the break-even point in unit sales, Q, can be computed as follows:

$$\text{Sales} = \text{Variable expenses} + \text{Fixed expenses} + \text{Profits}$$

$$\$250Q = \$150Q + \$35{,}000 + \$0$$

$$\$100Q = \$35{,}000$$

$$Q = \$35{,}000 \div \$100 \text{ per speaker}$$

$$Q = 350 \text{ speakers}$$

where:

$$Q = \text{Quantity of speakers sold}$$

$$\$250 = \text{Unit selling price}$$

$$\$150 = \text{Unit variable expenses}$$

$$\$35{,}000 = \text{Total fixed expenses}$$

The break-even point in total sales dollars can be computed by multiplying the break-even level of unit sales by the selling price per unit:

$$350 \text{ speakers} \times \$250 \text{ per speaker} = \$87{,}500$$

The break-even point in total sales dollars, X, can also be computed as follows:

$$\text{Sales} = \text{Variable expenses} + \text{Fixed expenses} + \text{Profits}$$

$$X = 0.60X + \$35{,}000 + \$0$$

$$0.40X = \$35{,}000$$

$$X = \$35{,}000 \div 0.40$$

$$X = \$87{,}500$$

where:

$$X = \text{Total sales dollars}$$
$$0.60 = \text{Variable expense ratio (Variable expenses} \div \text{Sales)}$$
$$\$35,000 = \text{Total fixed expenses}$$

Note that in the above analysis the *variable expense ratio* is used. The **variable expense ratio** is the ratio of variable expense to sales. It can be computed by dividing the total variable expense by the total sales, or in a single product analysis, it can be computed by dividing the variable cost per unit by the unit selling price.

Also note that the use of the ratios in the above analysis yields a break-even point expressed in sales dollars rather than in units sold. If desired, the break-even point in units sold can be computed as follows:

$$\$87,500 \div \$250 \text{ per speaker} = 350 \text{ speakers}$$

The Contribution Margin Method   The **contribution margin method** is a shortcut version of the equation method already described. The approach centers on the idea discussed earlier that each unit sold provides a certain amount of contribution margin that goes toward covering fixed costs. To find how many units must be sold to break even, divide the total fixed expenses by the unit contribution margin:

$$\text{Break-even point in units sold} = \frac{\text{Fixed expenses}}{\text{Unit contribution margin}}$$

Each speaker generates a contribution margin of $100 ($250 selling price, less $150 variable expenses). Since the total fixed expenses are $35,000, the break-even point in unit sales is computed as follows:

$$\frac{\text{Fixed expenses}}{\text{Unit contribution margin}} = \frac{\$35,000}{\$100 \text{ per speaker}} = 350 \text{ speakers}$$

A variation of this method uses the CM ratio instead of the unit contribution margin. The result is the break-even point in total sales dollars rather than in total units sold.

$$\text{Break-even point in total sales dollars} = \frac{\text{Fixed expenses}}{\text{CM ratio}}$$

In the Acoustic Concepts example, the calculation is as follows:

$$\frac{\text{Fixed expenses}}{\text{CM ratio}} = \frac{\$35,000}{0.40} = \$87,500$$

LEARNING OBJECTIVE 6
Determine the level of sales needed to achieve a desired target profit.

This approach, based on the CM ratio, is particularly useful when a company has multiple products and wishes to compute a single break-even point for the company as a whole. More is said on this point later in the chapter.

Target Profit Analysis

CVP formulas can be used to determine the sales volume needed to achieve a target profit. Suppose that Prem Narayan of Acoustic Concepts wishes to earn a target profit of $40,000 per month. How many speakers would have to be sold?

The CVP Equation   One approach is to use the equation method. Instead of solving for the unit sales where profits are zero, solve for the unit sales where profits are $40,000.

$$\text{Sales} = \text{Variable expenses} + \text{Fixed expenses} + \text{Profits}$$
$$\$250Q = \$150Q = \$35,000 = \$40,000$$
$$\$100Q = \$75,000$$
$$Q = \$75,000 \div \$100 \text{ per speaker}$$
$$Q = 750 \text{ speakers}$$

where:

$$Q = \text{Quantity of speakers sold}$$

$$\$250 = \text{Unit selling price}$$

$$\$150 = \text{Unit variable expenses}$$

$$\$35,000 = \text{Total fixed expenses}$$

$$\$40,000 = \text{Target profit}$$

Thus, the target profit can be achieved by selling 750 speakers per month, which represents $187,500 in total sales ($250 per speaker × 750 speakers).

COSTS ON THE INTERNET

The company eToys, which sells toys over the Internet, lost $190 million in 1999 on sales of $151 million. One big cost was advertising. eToys spent about $37 on advertising for each $100 of sales. (Other e-tailers were spending even more—in some cases, up to $460 on advertising for each $100 in sales!)

eToys did have some advantages relative to bricks-and-mortar stores such as Toys "R" Us. eToys had much lower inventory costs since it only needed to keep on hand one or two of a slow-moving item, whereas a traditional store has to fully stock its shelves. And bricks-and-mortar retail spaces in malls and elsewhere do cost money—on average, about 7% of sales. However, e-tailers such as eToys have their own set of disadvantages. Customers "pick and pack" their own items at a bricks-and-mortar outlet, but e-tailers have to pay employees to carry out this task. This costs eToys about $33 for every $100 in sales. And the technology to sell over the Internet is not free. eToys spent about $29 on its website and related technology for every $100 in sales. However, many of these costs of selling over the Internet are fixed. Toby Lenk, the CEO of eToys, estimated that the company would pass its break-even point somewhere between $750 and $900 million in sales—representing less than 1% of the market for toys. eToys did not make this goal and laid off 70% of its employees in January 2001. Subsequently, eToys was acquired by KBToys.com.

Sources: Erin Kelly, "The Last e-Store on the Block," *Fortune*, September 18, 2000, pp. 214–220; Jennifer Couzin, *The Industry Standard*, January 4, 2001.

The Contribution Margin Approach   A second approach involves expanding the contribution margin formula to include the target profit:

$$\text{Unit sales to attain the target profit} = \frac{\text{Fixed expenses} + \text{Target profit}}{\text{Unit contribution margin}}$$

$$= \frac{\$35,000 + \$40,000}{\$100 \text{ per speaker}}$$

$$= 750 \text{ speakers}$$

This approach gives the same answer as the equation method because it is simply a shortcut version of the equation method. Similarly, the dollar sales needed to attain the target profit can be computed as follows:

$$\text{Dollar sales to attain target profit} = \frac{\text{Fixed expenses} + \text{Target profit}}{\text{CM ratio}}$$

$$= \frac{\$35,000 + \$40,000}{0.40}$$

$$= \$187,500$$

The Margin of Safety

LEARNING OBJECTIVE 7
Compute the margin of
safety and explain its
significance.

The **margin of safety** is the excess of budgeted (or actual) sales dollars over the break-even volume of sales dollars. It is the amount by which sales can drop before losses are incurred. The higher the margin of safety, the lower the risk of not breaking even and incurring a loss. The formula for its calculation is:

$$\text{Margin of safety} = \text{Total budgeted (or actual) sales} - \text{Break-even sales}$$

The margin of safety can also be expressed in percentage form by dividing the margin of safety in dollars by total dollar sales:

$$\text{Margin of safety percentage} = \frac{\text{Margin of safety in dollars}}{\text{Total budgeted (or actual) sales in dollars}}$$

The calculation of the margin of safety for Acoustic Concepts is:

Sales (at the current volume of 400 speakers) (a)	$100,000
Break-even sales (at 350 speakers).	87,500
Margin of safety (in dollars) (b).	$ 12,500
Margin of safety as a percentage of sales, (b) ÷ (a)	12.5%

This margin of safety means that at the current level of sales and with the company's current prices and cost structure, a reduction in sales of $12,500, or 12.5%, would result in just breaking even.

In a single-product company like Acoustic Concepts, the margin of safety can also be expressed in terms of the number of units sold by dividing the margin of safety in dollars by the selling price per unit. In this case, the margin of safety is 50 speakers ($12,500 ÷ $250 per speaker = 50 speakers).

IN BUSINESS

COMPUTING MARGIN OF SAFETY FOR A SMALL BUSINESS

Sam Calagione owns Dogfish Head Craft Brewery, a microbrewery in Rehobeth Beach, Delaware. He charges distributors as much as $100 per case for his premium beers such as World Wide Stout. The high-priced microbrews bring in $800,000 in operating income on revenue of $7 million. Calagione reports that his raw ingredients and labor costs for one case of World Wide Stout are $30 and $16, respectively. Bottling and packaging costs are $6 per case. Gas and electric costs are about $10 per case.

If we assume that World Wide Stout is representative of all Dogfish microbrews, then we can compute the company's margin of safety in five steps. First, variable cost as a percentage of sales is 62% [($30 + $16 + $6 + $10)/$100]. Second, the contribution margin ratio is 38% (1 − 0.62). Third, Dogfish's total fixed cost is $1,860,000 [($7,000,000 × 0.38) − $800,000]. Fourth, the break-even point in sales dollars is $4,894,737 ($1,860,000/0.38). Fifth, the margin of safety is $2,105,263 ($7,000,000 − $4,894,737).

Source: Patricia Huang, "Château Dogfish," *Forbes*, February 28, 2005, pp. 57–59.

MANAGERIAL ACCOUNTING IN ACTION

The Wrap-up

Accoustic Concepts, Inc.

Prem Narayan and Bob Luchinni met to discuss the results of Bob's analysis.

Prem: Bob, everything you have shown me is pretty clear. I can see what impact some of the sales manager's suggestions would have on our profits. Some of those suggestions are quite good and others are not so good. I am concerned that our margin of safety is only 50 speakers. What can we do to increase this number?

Bob: Well, we have to increase total sales or decrease the break-even point or both.

Prem: And to decrease the break-even point, we have to either decrease our fixed expenses or increase our unit contribution margin?

Bob: Exactly.

Prem: And to increase our unit contribution margin, we must either increase our selling price or decrease the variable cost per unit?

Bob: Correct.

Prem: So what do you suggest?

Bob: Well, the analysis doesn't tell us which of these to do, but it does indicate we have a potential problem here.

Prem: If you don't have any immediate suggestions, I would like to call a general meeting next week to discuss ways we can work on increasing the margin of safety. I think everyone will be concerned about how vulnerable we are to even small downturns in sales.

CVP Considerations in Choosing a Cost Structure

Cost structure refers to the relative proportion of fixed and variable costs in an organization. Managers often have some latitude in trading off between these two types of costs. For example, fixed investments in automated equipment can reduce variable labor costs. In this section, we discuss the choice of a cost structure. We introduce the concept of *operating leverage,* which plays a key role in determining the impact of cost structure on profit stability.

Cost Structure and Profit Stability

Which cost structure is better—high variable costs and low fixed costs, or the opposite? No single answer to this question is possible; each approach has its advantages. To show what we mean, refer to the income statements given below for two blueberry farms. Bogside Farm depends on migrant workers to pick its berries by hand, whereas Sterling Farm has invested in expensive berry-picking machines. Consequently, Bogside Farm has higher variable costs, but Sterling Farm has higher fixed costs:

	Bogside Farm		Sterling Farm	
	Amount	Percent	Amount	Percent
Sales	$100,000	100%	$100,000	100%
Variable expenses	60,000	60%	30,000	30%
Contribution margin	40,000	40%	70,000	70%
Fixed expenses	30,000		60,000	
Net operating income	$ 10,000		$ 10,000	

Which farm has the better cost structure? The answer depends on many factors, including the long-run trend in sales, year-to-year fluctuations in the level of sales, and the attitude of the owners toward risk. If sales are expected to exceed $100,000 in the future, then Sterling Farm probably has the better cost structure. The reason is that its CM ratio is higher, and its profits will therefore increase more rapidly as sales increase. To illustrate, assume that each farm experiences a 10% increase in sales without any increase in fixed costs. The new income statements would be as follows:

	Bogside Farm		Sterling Farm	
	Amount	Percent	Amount	Percent
Sales	$110,000	100%	$110,000	100%
Variable expenses	66,000	60%	33,000	30%
Contribution margin	44,000	40%	77,000	70%
Fixed expenses	30,000		60,000	
Net operating income	$ 14,000		$ 17,000	

Sterling Farm has experienced a greater increase in net operating income due to its higher CM ratio even though the increase in sales was the same for both farms.

What if sales drop below $100,000? What are the farms' break-even points? What are their margins of safety? The computations needed to answer these questions are shown below using the contribution margin method:

	Bogside Farm	Sterling Farm
Fixed expenses	$ 30,000	$ 60,000
Contribution margin ratio	÷ 0.40	÷ 0.70
Break-even in total sales dollars	$ 75,000	$ 85,714
Total current sales (a).	$100,000	$100,000
Break-even sales	75,000	85,714
Margin of safety in sales dollars (b)	$ 25,000	$ 14,286
Margin of safety as a percentage of sales, (b) ÷ (a)	25.0%	14.3%

Bogside Farm's margin of safety is greater and its contribution margin ratio is lower than Sterling Farm. Therefore Bogside Farm is less vulnerable to downturns than Sterling Farm. Due to its lower contribution margin ratio, Bogside Farm will not lose contribution margin as rapidly as Sterling Farm when sales decline. Thus, Bogside Farm's profit will be less volatile. We saw earlier that this is a drawback when sales increase, but it provides more protection when sales drop. And because its break-even point is lower, Bogside Farm can suffer a larger sales decline before losses emerge.

To summarize, without knowing the future, it is not obvious which cost structure is better. Both have advantages and disadvantages. Sterling Farm, with its higher fixed costs and lower variable costs, will experience wider swings in net operating income as sales fluctuate, with greater profits in good years and greater losses in bad years. Bogside Farm, with its lower fixed costs and higher variable costs, will enjoy greater profit stability and will be more protected from losses during bad years, but at the cost of lower net operating income in good years.

IN BUSINESS

A LOSING COST STRUCTURE

Both JetBlue and United Airlines use an Airbus 235 to fly from Dulles International Airport near Washington, DC, to Oakland, California. Both planes have a pilot, copilot, and four flight attendants. That is where the similarity ends. Based on 2002 data, the pilot on the United flight earned $16,350 to $18,000 a month compared to $6,800 per month for the JetBlue pilot. United's senior flight attendants on the plane earned more than $41,000 per year; whereas the JetBlue attendants were paid $16,800 to $27,000 per year. Largely because of the higher labor costs at United, its costs of operating the flight were more than 60% higher than JetBlue's costs. Due to intense fare competition from JetBlue and other low-cost carriers, United was unable to cover its higher operating costs on this and many other flights. Consequently, United went into bankruptcy at the end of 2002.

Source: Susan Carey, "Costly Race in the Sky," *The Wall Street Journal*, September 9, 2002, pp. B1 and B3.

Operating Leverage

LEARNING OBJECTIVE 8
Compute the degree of operating leverage at a particular level of sales and explain how it can be used to predict changes in net operating income.

A lever is a tool for multiplying force. Using a lever, a massive object can be moved with only a modest amount of force. In business, *operating leverage* serves a similar purpose. **Operating leverage** is a measure of how sensitive net operating income is to a given percentage change in dollar sales. Operating leverage acts as a multiplier. If operating leverage is high, a small percentage increase in sales can produce a much larger percentage increase in net operating income.

Operating leverage can be illustrated by returning to the data for the two blueberry farms. We previously showed that a 10% increase in sales (from $100,000 to $110,000 in each farm) results in a 70% increase in the net operating income of Sterling Farm (from $10,000 to $17,000) and only a 40% increase in the net operating income of Bogside Farm (from $10,000 to $14,000). Thus, for a 10% increase in sales, Sterling Farm experiences a much greater percentage increase in profits than does Bogside Farm. Therefore, Sterling Farm has greater operating leverage than Bogside Farm.

The **degree of operating leverage** at a given level of sales is computed by the following formula:

$$\text{Degree of operating leverage} = \frac{\text{Contribution margin}}{\text{Net operating income}}$$

The degree of operating leverage is a measure, at a given level of sales, of how a percentage change in sales volume will affect profits. To illustrate, the degree of operating leverage for the two farms at $100,000 sales would be computed as follows:

$$\text{Bogside Farm:} \frac{\$40,000}{\$10,000} = 4$$

$$\text{Sterling Farm:} \frac{\$70,000}{\$10,000} = 7$$

Since the degree of operating leverage for Bogside Farm is 4, the farm's net operating income grows four times as fast as its sales. Similarly, Sterling Farm's net operating income grows seven times as fast as its sales. Thus, if sales increase by 10%, then we can expect the net operating income of Bogside Farm to increase by four times this amount, or by 40%, and the net operating income of Sterling Farm to increase by seven times this amount, or by 70%.

	(1) Percent Increase in Sales	(2) Degree of Operating Leverage	Percent Increase in Net Operating Income (1) × (2)
Bogside Farm.......	10%	4	40%
Sterling Farm	10%	7	70%

What is responsible for the higher operating leverage at Sterling Farm? The only difference between the two farms is their cost structure. If two companies have the same total revenue and same total expense but different cost structures, then the company with the higher proportion of fixed costs in its cost structure will have higher operating leverage. Referring back to the original example on page 247, when both farms have sales of $100,000 and total expenses of $90,000, one-third of Bogside Farm's costs are fixed but two-thirds of Sterling Farm's costs are fixed. As a consequence, Sterling's degree of operating leverage is higher than Bogside's.

The degree of operating leverage is not a constant; it is greatest at sales levels near the break-even point and decreases as sales and profits rise. The following table shows the degree of operating leverage for Bogside Farm at various sales levels. (Data used earlier for Bogside Farm are shown in color.)

Sales	$75,000	$80,000	$100,000	$150,000	$225,000
Variable expenses	45,000	48,000	60,000	90,000	135,000
Contribution margin (a)......	30,000	32,000	40,000	60,000	90,000
Fixed expenses	30,000	30,000	30,000	30,000	30,000
Net operating income (b)	$ 0	$ 2,000	$ 10,000	$ 30,000	$ 60,000
Degree of operating leverage, (a) ÷ (b)	∞	16	4	2	1.5

Thus, a 10% increase in sales would increase profits by only 15% (10% × 1.5) if sales were previously $225,000, as compared to the 40% increase we computed earlier at the $100,000 sales level. The degree of operating leverage will continue to decrease the farther the company moves from its break-even point. At the break-even point, the degree of operating leverage is infinitely large ($30,000 contribution margin ÷ $0 net operating income = ∞).

OPERATING LEVERAGE: A KEY TO PROFITABLE E-COMMERCE

Did you ever wonder why Expedia and eBay were among the first Internet companies to become profitable? One big reason is because they sell information products rather than physical products. For example, when somebody buys a physical product, such as a book from Amazon.com, the company needs to purchase a copy of the book from the publisher, process it, and ship it; hence, Amazon.com's gross margins are around 26%. However, once Expedia covers its fixed overhead costs, the extra expense incurred to provide service to one more customer is practically zero; therefore, the incremental revenue provided by that customer "falls to the bottom line."

In the first quarter of 2002, Expedia doubled its sales to $116 million and reported net income of $5.7 million compared to a loss of $17.6 million in the first quarter of 2001. This is the beauty of having a high degree of operating leverage. Sales growth can quickly translate to profit growth when variable costs are negligible. Of course, operating leverage has a dark side—if Expedia's sales plummet, its profits will nosedive as well.

Source: Timothy J. Mullaney and Robert D. Hof, "Finally, the Pot of Gold," *BusinessWeek*, June 24, 2002, pp. 104–106.

The degree of operating leverage can be used to quickly estimate what impact various percentage changes in sales will have on profits, without the necessity of preparing detailed income statements. As shown by our examples, the effects of operating leverage can be dramatic. If a company is near its break-even point, then even small percentage increases in sales can yield large percentage increases in profits. *This explains why management will often work very hard for only a small increase in sales volume.* If the degree of operating leverage is 5, then a 6% increase in sales would translate into a 30% increase in profits.

Structuring Sales Commissions

Companies usually compensate salespeople by paying them a commission based on sales, a salary, or a combination of the two. Commissions based on sales dollars can lead to lower profits. To illustrate, consider Pipeline Unlimited, a producer of surfing equipment. Salespeople for the company sell the company's products to retail sporting goods stores throughout

North America and the Pacific Basin. Data for two of the company's surfboards, the XR7 and Turbo models, appear below:

	Model	
	XR7	Turbo
Selling price	$695	$749
Variable expenses	344	410
Contribution margin	$351	$339

Which model will salespeople push hardest if they are paid a commission of 10% of sales revenue? The answer is the Turbo, since it has the higher selling price and hence the larger commission. On the other hand, from the standpoint of the company, profits will be greater if salespeople steer customers toward the XR7 model since it has the higher contribution margin.

To eliminate such conflicts, commissions can be based on contribution margin rather than on selling price. If this is done, the salespersons will want to sell the mix of products that maximizes contribution margin. Providing that fixed costs are not affected by the sales mix, maximizing the contribution margin will also maximize the company's profit.[1] In effect, by maximizing their own compensation, salespersons will also maximize the company's profit.

IN BUSINESS

AN ALTERNATIVE APPROACH TO SALES COMMISSIONS

Thrive Networks, located in Concord, Massachusetts, used to pay its three salesmen based on individually earned commissions. This system seemed to be working fine as indicated by the company's sales growth from $2.7 million in 2002 to $3.6 million in 2003. However, the company felt there was a better way to motivate and compensate its salesmen. It pooled commissions across the three salesmen and compensated them collectively. The new approach was designed to build teamwork and leverage each salesman's individual strengths. Jim Lippie, the director of business development, was highly skilled at networking and generating sales leads. John Barrows, the sales director, excelled at meeting with prospective clients and producing compelling proposals. Nate Wolfson, the CEO and final member of the sales team, was the master at closing the deal. The new approach has worked so well that Wolfson plans to use three-person sales teams in his offices nationwide.

Source: Cara Cannella, "Kill the Commissions," *Inc.* magazine, August 2004, p. 38.

Sales Mix

Before concluding our discussion of CVP concepts, we need to consider the impact of changes in *sales mix* on a company's profit.

The Definition of Sales Mix

The term **sales mix** refers to the relative proportions in which a company's products are sold. The idea is to achieve the combination, or mix, that will yield the greatest amount of profits. Most companies have many products, and often these products are not equally profitable.

LEARNING OBJECTIVE 9
Compute the break-even point for a multiproduct company and explain the effects of shifts in the sales mix on contribution margin and the break-even point.

---

[1] This also assumes the company has no production constraint. If it does, the sales commissions should be modified. See the Profitability Appendix at the end of the book.

Hence, profits will depend to some extent on the company's sales mix. Profits will be greater if high-margin rather than low-margin items make up a relatively large proportion of total sales.

Changes in the sales mix can cause perplexing variations in a company's profits. A shift in the sales mix from high-margin items to low-margin items can cause total profits to decrease even though total sales may increase. Conversely, a shift in the sales mix from low-margin items to high-margin items can cause the reverse effect—total profits may increase even though total sales decrease. It is one thing to achieve a particular sales volume; it is quite another to sell the most profitable mix of products.

KODAK: GOING DIGITAL

Kodak dominates the film industry in the U.S., selling two out of every three rolls of film. It also processes 40% of all film dropped off for developing. Unfortunately for Kodak, this revenue stream is rapidly declining due to competition from digital cameras, which do not use film at all. To counter this threat, Kodak has moved into the digital market with its own line of digital cameras and various services, but sales of digital products undeniably cut into the company's film business. "Chief Financial Officer Robert Brust has 'stress-tested' profit models based on how quickly digital cameras may spread. If half of homes go digital, . . . Kodak's sales would rise 10% a year—but profits would go up only 8% a year. Cost cuts couldn't come fast enough to offset a slide in film sales and the margin pressure from selling cheap digital cameras." The sales mix is moving in the wrong direction, given the company's current cost structure and competitive prices.

Source: Bruce Upbin, "Kodak's Digital Moment," *Forbes*, August 21, 2000, pp. 106–112.

Sales Mix and Break-Even Analysis

If a company sells more than one product, break-even analysis is more complex than discussed to this point. The reason is that different products will have different selling prices, different costs, and different contribution margins. Consequently, the break-even point depends on the mix in which the various products are sold. To illustrate, consider Sound Unlimited, a small company that imports DVDs from France. At present, the company sells two DVDs: the Le Louvre DVD, a multimedia free-form tour of the famous art museum in Paris; and the Le Vin DVD, which features the wines and wine-growing regions of France. The company's September sales, expenses, and break-even point are shown in Exhibit 6–3.

As shown in the exhibit, the break-even point is $60,000 in sales, which was computed by dividing the company's fixed expenses of $27,000 by its overall CM ratio of 45%. However, this is the break-even only if the company's sales mix does not change. Currently, the Le Louvre DVD is responsible for 20% and the Le Vin DVD for 80% of the company's dollar sales. Assuming this sales mix does not change, if total sales are $60,000, the sales of the Le Louvre DVD would be $12,000 (20% of $60,000) and the sales of the Le Vin DVD would be $48,000 (80% of $60,000). As shown in Exhibit 6–3, at these levels of sales, the company would indeed break even. But $60,000 in sales represents the break-even point for the company only if the sales mix does not change. *If the sales mix changes, then the break-even point will also usually change.* This is illustrated by the results for October in which the sales mix shifted away from the more profitable Le Vin DVD (which has a 50% CM ratio) toward the less profitable Le Louvre CD (which has a 25% CM ratio). These results appear in Exhibit 6–4.

Although sales have remained unchanged at $100,000, the sales mix is exactly the reverse of what it was in Exhibit 6–3, with the bulk of the sales now coming from the less profitable Le Louvre DVD. Notice that this shift in the sales mix has caused both the overall CM ratio and total profits to drop sharply from the prior month even though total sales are the same. The overall CM ratio has dropped from 45% in September to only 30% in October, and net operating income has dropped from $18,000 to only $3,000. In addition, with the

EXHIBIT 6–3
Multiproduct Break-Even Analysis

Sound Unlimited
Contribution Income Statement
For the Month of September

	Le Louvre DVD		Le Vin DVD		Total	
	Amount	Percent	Amount	Percent	Amount	Percent
Sales	$20,000	100%	$80,000	100%	$100,000	100%
Variable expenses	15,000	75%	40,000	50%	55,000	55%
Contribution margin	$ 5,000	25%	$40,000	50%	45,000	45%
Fixed expenses					27,000	
Net operating income					$ 18,000	

Computation of the break-even point:

$$\frac{\text{Fixed expenses}}{\text{Overall CM ratio}} = \frac{\$27,000}{0.45} = \$60,000$$

Verification of the break-even point:

	Le Louvre DVD	Le Vin DVD	Total
Current dollar sales	$20,000	$80,000	$100,000
Percentage of total dollar sales	20%	80%	100%
Sales at the break-even point	$12,000	$48,000	$60,000

	Le Louvre DVD		Le Vin DVD		Total	
	Amount	Percent	Amount	Percent	Amount	Percent
Sales	$12,000	100%	$48,000	100%	$ 60,000	100%
Variable expenses	9,000	75%	24,000	50%	33,000	55%
Contribution margin	$ 3,000	25%	$24,000	50%	27,000	45%
Fixed expenses					27,000	
Net operating income					$ 0	

EXHIBIT 6–4
Multiproduct Break-Even Analysis: A Shift in Sales Mix (see Exhibit 6–3)

Sound Unlimited
Contribution Income Statement
For the Month of October

	Le Louvre DVD		Le Vin DVD		Total	
	Amount	Percent	Amount	Percent	Amount	Percent
Sales	$80,000	100%	$20,000	100%	$100,000	100%
Variable expenses	60,000	75%	10,000	50%	70,000	70%
Contribution margin	$20,000	25%	$10,000	50%	30,000	30%
Fixed expenses					27,000	
Net operating income					$ 3,000	

Computation of the break-even point:

$$\frac{\text{Fixed expenses}}{\text{Overall CM ratio}} = \frac{\$27,000}{0.30} = \$90,000$$

drop in the overall CM ratio, the company's break-even point is no longer $60,000 in sales. Since the company is now realizing less average contribution margin per dollar of sales, it takes more sales to cover the same amount of fixed costs. Thus, the break-even point has increased from $60,000 to $90,000 in sales per year.

In preparing a break-even analysis, some assumption must be made concerning the sales mix. Usually the assumption is that it will not change. However, if the sales mix is expected to change, then this must be explicitly considered in any CVP computations.

PLAYING THE CVP GAME

In 2002, General Motors (GM) gave away almost $2,600 per vehicle in customer incentives such as price cuts and 0% financing. "The pricing sacrifices have been more than offset by volume gains, most of which have come from trucks and SUVs, like the Chevy Suburban and the GMC Envoy, which generate far more profit for the company than cars. Lehman Brothers analysts estimate that GM will sell an additional 395,000 trucks and SUVs and an extra 75,000 cars in 2002. The trucks, however, are the company's golden goose, hauling in an average [contribution margin] . . . of about $7,000, compared with just $4,000 for the cars. All told, the volume gains could bring in an additional $3 billion [in profits]."

Source: Janice Revell, "GM's Slow Leak," *Fortune*, October 28, 2002, pp. 105–110.

Assumptions of CVP Analysis

A number of assumptions commonly underlie CVP analysis:

1. Selling price is constant. The price of a product or service will not change as volume changes.
2. Costs are linear and can be accurately divided into variable and fixed elements. The variable element is constant per unit, and the fixed element is constant in total over the entire relevant range.
3. In multiproduct companies, the sales mix is constant.
4. In manufacturing companies, inventories do not change. The number of units produced equals the number of units sold.

While these assumptions may be violated in practice, the results of CVP analysis are often "good enough" to be quite useful. Perhaps the greatest danger lies in relying on simple CVP analysis when a manager is contemplating a large change in volume that lies outside of the relevant range. For example, a manager might contemplate increasing the level of sales far beyond what the company has ever experienced before. However, even in these situations the model can be adjusted as we have done in this chapter to take into account anticipated changes in selling prices, fixed costs, and the sales mix that would otherwise violate the assumptions mentioned above. For example, in a decision that would affect fixed costs, the change in fixed costs can be explicitly taken into account as illustrated earlier in the chapter in the Acoustic Concepts example on pages 239–242.

Summary

CVP analysis is based on a simple model of how profits respond to prices, costs, and volume. This model can be used to answer a variety of critical questions such as what is the company's break-even volume, what is its margin of safety, and what is likely to happen if specific changes are made in prices, costs, and volume.

A CVP graph depicts the relationships between sales volume in units on the one hand and fixed expenses, variable expenses, total expenses, total sales, and profits on the other hand. The CVP graph is useful for developing intuition about how costs and profits respond to changes in sales volume.

The contribution margin ratio is the ratio of the total contribution margin to total sales. This ratio can be used to quickly estimate what impact a change in total sales would have on net operating income. The ratio is also useful in break-even analysis.

The break-even point is the level of sales (in units or in dollars) at which the company just breaks even. The break-even point can be computed using several different techniques that are all based on the simple CVP model. With slight modifications, the same techniques can be used to compute the level of sales required to attain a target profit.

The margin of safety is the amount by which the company's current sales exceeds break-even sales.

The degree of operating leverage allows quick estimation of what impact a given percentage change in sales would have on the company's net operating income. The higher the degree of operating leverage, the greater is the impact on the company's profits. The degree of operating leverage is not constant—it depends on the company's current level of sales.

The profits of a multiproduct company are affected by its sales mix. Changes in the sales mix can affect the break-even point, margin of safety, and other critical factors.

Review Problem: CVP Relationships

Voltar Company manufactures and sells a specialized cordless telephone for high electromagnetic radiation environments. The company's contribution format income statement for the most recent year is given below:

	Total	Per Unit	Percent of Sales
Sales (20,000 units)	$1,200,000	$60	100%
Variable expenses	900,000	45	? %
Contribution margin	300,000	$15	? %
Fixed expenses	240,000		
Net operating income	$ 60,000		

Management is anxious to increase the company's profit and has asked for an analysis of a number of items.

Required:
1. Compute the company's CM ratio and variable expense ratio.
2. Compute the company's break-even point in both units and sales dollars. Use the equation method.
3. Assume that sales increase by $400,000 next year. If cost behavior patterns remain unchanged, by how much will the company's net operating income increase? Use the CM ratio to compute your answer.
4. Refer to the original data. Assume that next year management wants the company to earn a profit of at least $90,000. How many units will have to be sold to meet this target profit?
5. Refer to the original data. Compute the company's margin of safety in both dollar and percentage form.
6. *a.* Compute the company's degree of operating leverage at the present level of sales.
   b. Assume that through a more intense effort by the sales staff, the company's sales increase by 8% next year. By what percentage would you expect net operating income to increase? Use the degree of operating leverage to obtain your answer.
   c. Verify your answer to (*b*) by preparing a new contribution format income statement showing an 8% increase in sales.
7. In an effort to increase sales and profits, management is considering the use of a higher-quality speaker. The higher-quality speaker would increase variable costs by $3 per unit, but management could eliminate one quality inspector who is paid a salary of $30,000 per year. The sales manager estimates that the higher-quality speaker would increase annual sales by at least 20%.
   a. Assuming that changes are made as described above, prepare a projected contribution format income statement for next year. Show data on a total, per unit, and percentage basis.
   b. Compute the company's new break-even point in both units and dollars of sales. Use the contribution margin method.
   c. Would you recommend that the changes be made?

Solution to Review Problem

1.

$$\text{CM ratio} = \frac{\text{Unit contribution margin}}{\text{Selling price}} = \frac{\$15}{\$60} = 25\%$$

$$\text{Variable expense ratio} = \frac{\text{Variable expense}}{\text{Selling price}} = \frac{\$45}{\$60} = 75\%$$

2.

$$\text{Sales} = \text{Variable expenses} + \text{Fixed expenses} + \text{Profits}$$

$$\$60Q = \$45Q + \$240,000 + \$0$$

$$\$15Q = \$240,000$$

$$Q = \$240,000 \div \$15 \text{ per unit}$$

$$Q = 16,000 \text{ units; or at } \$60 \text{ per unit, } \$960,000$$

Alternative solution:

$$X = 0.75X + \$240,000 + \$0$$

$$0.25X = \$240,000$$

$$X = \$240,000 \div 0.25$$

$$X = \$960,000; \text{ or at } \$60 \text{ per unit, } 16,000 \text{ units}$$

3.

Increase in sales	$400,000
Multiply by the CM ratio	× 25%
Expected increase in contribution margin	$100,000

Since the fixed expenses are not expected to change, net operating income will increase by the entire $100,000 increase in contribution margin computed above.

4. Equation method:

$$\text{Sales} = \text{Variable expenses} + \text{Fixed expenses} + \text{Profits}$$

$$\$60Q = \$45Q + \$240,000 + \$90,000$$

$$\$15Q = \$330,000$$

$$Q = \$330,000 \div \$15 \text{ per unit}$$

$$Q = 22,000 \text{ units}$$

Contribution margin method:

$$\frac{\text{Fixed expenses} + \text{Target profit}}{\text{Contribution margin per unit}} = \frac{\$240,000 + \$90,000}{\$15 \text{ per unit}} = 22,000 \text{ units}$$

5.

$$\text{Margin of safety in dollars} = \text{Total sales} - \text{Break-even sales}$$

$$= \$1,200,000 - \$960,000 = \$240,000$$

$$\text{Margin of safety percentage} = \frac{\text{Margin of safety in dollars}}{\text{Total sales}} = \frac{\$240,000}{\$1,200,000} = 20\%$$

6. *a.*

$$\text{Degree of operating leverage} = \frac{\text{Contribution margin}}{\text{Net operating income}} = \frac{\$300,000}{\$60,000} = 5$$

b.

Expected increase in sales	8%
Degree of operating leverage	× 5
Expected increase in net operating income	40%

c.   If sales increase by 8%, then 21,600 units (20,000 × 1.08 = 21,600) will be sold next year. The new contribution format income statement would be as follows:

	Total	Per Unit	Percent of Sales
Sales (21,600 units)	$1,296,000	$60	100%
Variable expenses	972,000	45	75%
Contribution margin	324,000	$15	25%
Fixed expenses	240,000		
Net operating income	$ 84,000		

Thus, the $84,000 expected net operating income for next year represents a 40% increase over the $60,000 net operating income earned during the current year:

$$\frac{\$84,000 - \$60,000}{\$60,000} = \frac{\$24,000}{\$60,000} = 40\% \text{ increase}$$

Note from the income statement above that the increase in sales from 20,000 to 21,600 units has increased *both* total sales and total variable expenses. It is a common error to overlook the increase in variable expenses when preparing a projected contribution format income statement.

7.   a.   A 20% increase in sales would result in 24,000 units being sold next year: 20,000 units × 1.20 = 24,000 units.

	Total	Per Unit	Percent of Sales
Sales (24,000 units)	$1,440,000	$60	100%
Variable expenses	1,152,000	48*	80%
Contribution margin	288,000	$12	20%
Fixed expenses	210,000†		
Net operating income	$ 78,000		

*$45 + $3 = $48; $48 ÷ $60 = 80%.
†$240,000 − $30,000 = $210,000.

Note that the change in per unit variable expenses results in a change in both the per unit contribution margin and the CM ratio.

b. $$\text{Break-even point in unit sales} = \frac{\text{Fixed expenses}}{\text{Unit contribution margin}}$$

$$= \frac{\$210,000}{\$12 \text{ per unit}} = 17,500 \text{ units}$$

$$\text{Break-even point in dollar sales} = \frac{\text{Fixed expenses}}{\text{CM ratio}}$$

$$= \frac{\$210,000}{0.20} = \$1,050,000$$

c.   Yes, based on these data the changes should be made. The changes increase the company's net operating income from the present $60,000 to $78,000 per year. Although the changes also result in a higher break-even point (17,500 units as compared to the present 16,000 units), the company's margin of safety actually becomes greater than before:

Margin of safety in dollars = Total sales − Break-even sales

= $1,440,000 − $1,050,000 = $390,000

As shown in (5) above, the company's present margin of safety is only $240,000. Thus, several benefits will result from the proposed changes.

Glossary

Break-even point The level of sales at which profit is zero. The break-even point can also be defined as the point where total sales equals total expenses or as the point where total contribution margin equals total fixed expenses. (p. 235)

Contribution margin method A method of computing the break-even point in which the fixed expenses are divided by the contribution margin per unit. (p. 244)

Contribution margin ratio (CM ratio) A ratio computed by dividing contribution margin by dollar sales. (p. 238)

Cost-volume-profit (CVP) graph A graphical representation of the relationships between an organization's revenues, costs, and profits on the one hand and its sales volume on the other hand. (p. 236)

Degree of operating leverage A measure, at a given level of sales, of how a percentage change in sales will affect profits. The degree of operating leverage is computed by dividing contribution margin by net operating income. (p. 249)

Equation method A method of computing the break-even point that relies on the equation Sales = Variable expenses + Fixed expenses + Profits. (p. 243)

Incremental analysis An analytical approach that focuses only on those costs and revenues that change as a result of a decision. (p. 240)

Margin of safety The excess of budgeted (or actual) dollar sales over the break-even dollar sales. (p. 246)

Operating leverage A measure of how sensitive net operating income is to a given percentage change in dollar sales. (p. 249)

Sales mix The relative proportions in which a company's products are sold. Sales mix is computed by expressing the sales of each product as a percentage of total sales. (p. 251)

Variable expense ratio A ratio computed by dividing variable expenses by dollar sales (p. 244)

Questions

6-1   What is meant by a product's contribution margin ratio? How is this ratio useful in planning business operations?

6-2   Often the most direct route to a business decision is an incremental analysis. What is meant by an *incremental analysis?*

6-3   Company A's costs are mostly variable, whereas Company B's costs are mostly fixed. When sales increase, which company will tend to realize the greatest increase in profits? Explain.

6-4   What is meant by the term *operating leverage?*

6-5   What is meant by the term *break-even point?*

6-6   Name three approaches to break-even analysis. Briefly explain how each approach works.

6-7   In response to a request from your immediate supervisor, you have prepared a CVP graph portraying the cost and revenue characteristics of your company's product and operations. Explain how the lines on the graph and the break-even point would change if (*a*) the selling price per unit decreased, (*b*) fixed cost increased throughout the entire range of activity portrayed on the graph, and (*c*) variable cost per unit increased.

6-8   What is meant by the margin of safety?

6-9   What is meant by the term *sales mix?* What assumption is usually made concerning sales mix in CVP analysis?

6-10   Explain how a shift in the sales mix could result in both a higher break-even point and a lower net income.

Exercises

EXERCISE 6-1 Preparing a Contribution Format Income Statement [LO1]

Whirly Corporation's most recent income statement is shown below:

	Total	Per Unit
Sales (10,000 units)............	$350,000	$35.00
Less variable expenses.........	200,000	20.00
Contribution margin............	150,000	$15.00
Less fixed expenses	135,000	
Net operating income	$ 15,000	

Required:
Prepare a new contribution format income statement under each of the following conditions (consider each case independently):
1. The sales volume increases by 100 units.
2. The sales volume decreases by 100 units.
3. The sales volume is 9,000 units.

EXERCISE 6-2 Prepare a Cost-Volume-Profit (CVP) Graph [LO2]
Karlik Enterprises has a single product whose selling price is $24 and whose variable cost is $18 per unit. The company's monthly fixed expense is $24,000.

Required:
1. Prepare a cost-volume-profit graph for the company up to a sales level of 8,000 units.
2. Estimate the company's break-even point in unit sales using your cost-volume-profit graph.

EXERCISE 6-3 Computing and Using the CM Ratio [LO3]
Last month when Holiday Creations, Inc., sold 50,000 units, total sales were $200,000, total variable expenses were $120,000, and total fixed expenses were $65,000.

Required:
1. What is the company's contribution margin (CM) ratio?
2. Estimate the change in the company's net income if it were to increase its total sales by $1,000.

EXERCISE 6-4 Changes in Variable Costs, Fixed Costs, Selling Price, and Volume [LO4]
Data for Hermann Corporation are shown below:

	Per Unit	Percent of Sales
Selling price.................	$90	100%
Less variable expenses........	63	70
Contribution margin...........	$27	30%

Fixed expenses are $30,000 per month and the company is selling 2,000 units per month.
Required:
1. The marketing manager argues that a $5,000 increase in the monthly advertising budget would increase monthly sales by $9,000. Should the advertising budget be increased?
2. Refer to the original data. Management is considering using higher-quality components that would increase the variable cost by $2 per unit. The marketing manager believes the higher-quality product would increase sales by 10% per month. Should the higher-quality components be used?

EXERCISE 6-5 Compute the Break-Even Point [LO5]
Mauro Products has a single product, a woven basket whose selling price is $15 and whose variable cost is $12 per unit. The company's monthly fixed expenses are $4,200.
Required:
1. Solve for the company's break-even point in unit sales using the equation method.
2. Solve for the company's break-even point in sales dollars using the equation method and the CM ratio.
3. Solve for the company's break-even point in unit sales using the contribution margin method.
4. Solve for the company's break-even point in sales dollars using the contribution margin method and the CM ratio.

EXERCISE 6-6 Compute the Level of Sales Required to Attain a Target Profit [LO6]

Lin Corporation has a single product whose selling price is $120 and whose variable cost is $80 per unit. The company's monthly fixed expense is $50,000.

Required:
1. Using the equation method, solve for the unit sales that are required to earn a target profit of $10,000.
2. Using the contribution margin approach, solve for the dollar sales that are required to earn a target profit of $15,000.

EXERCISE 6-7 Compute the Margin of Safety [LO7]

Molander Corporation is a distributor of a sun umbrella used at resort hotels. Data concerning the next month's budget appear below:

Selling price	$30 per unit
Variable expense.	$20 per unit
Fixed expense.	$7,500 per month
Unit sales	1,000 units per month

Required:
1. Compute the company's margin of safety.
2. Compute the company's margin of safety as a percentage of its sales.

EXERCISE 6-8 Compute and Use the Degree of Operating Leverage [LO8]

Engberg Company installs lawn sod in home yards. The company's most recent monthly contribution format income statement follows:

	Amount	Percent of Sales
Sales	$80,000	100%
Variable expenses	32,000	40%
Contribution margin	48,000	60%
Fixed expenses	38,000	
Net operating income.	$10,000	

Required:
1. Compute the company's degree of operating leverage.
2. Using the degree of operating leverage, estimate the impact on net income of a 5% increase in sales.
3. Verify your estimate from part (2) above by constructing a new contribution format income statement for the company assuming a 5% increase in sales.

EXERCISE 6-9 Compute the Break-Even Point for a Multiproduct Company [LO9]

Lucido Products markets two computer games: Claimjumper and Makeover. A contribution format income statement for a recent month for the two games appears below:

	Claimjumper	Makeover	Total
Sales	$30,000	$70,000	$100,000
Less variable expenses	20,000	50,000	70,000
Contribution margin	$10,000	$20,000	30,000
Less fixed expenses			24,000
Net operating income			$ 6,000

Required:
1. Compute the overall contribution margin (CM) ratio for the company.
2. Compute the overall break-even point for the company in sales dollars.
3. Verify the overall break-even point for the company by constructing a contribution format income statement showing the appropriate levels of sales for the two products.

EXERCISE 6-10 Break-Even Analysis; Target Profit; Margin of Safety; CM Ratio [LO1, LO3, LO5, LO6, LO7]

Menlo Company manufactures and sells a single product. The company's sales and expenses for last quarter follow:

	Total	Per Unit
Sales	$450,000	$30
Less variable expenses	180,000	12
Contribution margin	270,000	$18
Less fixed expenses	216,000	
Net operating income	$ 54,000	

Required:

1. What is the quarterly break-even point in units sold and in sales dollars?
2. Without resorting to computations, what is the total contribution margin at the break-even point?
3. How many units would have to be sold each quarter to earn a target profit of $90,000? Use the contribution margin method. Verify your answer by preparing a contribution format income statement at the target sales level.
4. Refer to the original data. Compute the company's margin of safety in both dollar and percentage terms.
5. What is the company's CM ratio? If sales increase by $50,000 per quarter and there is no change in fixed expenses, by how much would you expect quarterly net operating income to increase?

EXERCISE 6-11 Break-Even Analysis and CVP Graphing [LO2, LO4, LO5]

The Hartford Symphony Guild is planning its annual dinner-dance. The dinner-dance committee has assembled the following expected costs for the event:

Dinner (per person)	$18
Favors and program (per person)	$2
Band	$2,800
Rental of ballroom	$900
Professional entertainment during intermission........	$1,000
Tickets and advertising	$1,300

The committee members would like to charge $35 per person for the evening's activities.

Required:

1. Compute the break-even point for the dinner-dance (in terms of the number of persons who must attend).
2. Assume that last year only 300 persons attended the dinner-dance. If the same number attend this year, what price per ticket must be charged in order to break even?
3. Refer to the original data ($35 ticket price per person). Prepare a CVP graph for the dinner-dance from a zero level of activity up to 600 tickets sold. Number of persons should be placed on the horizontal *(X)* axis, and dollars should be placed on the vertical *(Y)* axis.

EXERCISE 6-12 Using a Contribution Format Income Statement [LO1, LO4]

Miller Company's most recent contribution format income statement is shown below:

	Total	Per Unit
Sales (20,000 units).........	$300,000	$15.00
Variable expenses	180,000	9.00
Contribution margin	120,000	$6.00
Fixed expenses	70,000	
Net operating income........	$ 50,000	

Required:

Prepare a new contribution format income statement under each of the following conditions (consider each case independently):

1. The sales volume increases by 15%.
2. The selling price decreases by $1.50 per unit, and the sales volume increases by 25%.

3. The selling price increases by $1.50 per unit, fixed expenses increase by $20,000, and the sales volume decreases by 5%.
4. The selling price increases by 12%, variable expenses increase by 60 cents per unit, and the sales volume decreases by 10%.

EXERCISE 6-13 Missing Data; Basic CVP Concepts [LO1, LO9]

Fill in the missing amounts in each of the eight case situations below. Each case is independent of the others. (Hint: One way to find the missing amounts would be to prepare a contribution income statement for each case, enter the known data, and then compute the missing items.)

a. Assume that only one product is being sold in each of the four following case situations:

Case	Units Sold	Sales	Variable Expenses	Contribution Margin per Unit	Fixed Expenses	Net Operating Income (Loss)
1	15,000	$180,000	$120,000	?	$50,000	?
2	?	$100,000	?	$10	$32,000	$8,000
3	10,000	?	$70,000	$13	?	$12,000
4	6,000	$300,000	?	?	$100,000	$(10,000)

b. Assume that more than one product is being sold in each of the four following case situations:

Case	Sales	Variable Expenses	Average Contribution Margin (Percent)	Fixed Expenses	Net Operating Income (Loss)
1	$500,000	?	20%	?	$7,000
2	$400,000	$260,000	?	$100,000	?
3	?	?	60%	$130,000	$20,000
4	$600,000	$420,000	?	?	$(5,000)

EXERCISE 6-14 Break-Even and Target Profit Analysis [LO3, LO4, LO5, LO6]

Lindon Company is the exclusive distributor for an automotive product that sells for $40 per unit and has a CM ratio of 30%. The company's fixed expenses are $180,000 per year.

Required:
1. What are the variable expenses per unit?
2. Using the equation method:
    a. What is the break-even point in units and sales dollars?
    b. What sales level in units and in sales dollars is required to earn an annual profit of $60,000?
    c. Assume that by using a more efficient shipper, the company is able to reduce its variable expenses by $4 per unit. What is the company's new break-even point in units and sales dollars?
3. Repeat (2) above using the contribution margin method.

EXERCISE 6-15 Operating Leverage [LO4, LO8]

Magic Realm, Inc., has developed a new fantasy board game. The company sold 15,000 games last year at a selling price of $20 per game. Fixed costs associated with the game total $182,000 per year, and variable costs are $6 per game. Production of the game is entrusted to a printing contractor. Variable costs consist mostly of payments to this contractor.

Required:
1. Prepare a contribution format income statement for the game last year and compute the degree of operating leverage.
2. Management is confident that the company can sell 18,000 games next year (an increase of 3,000 games, or 20%, over last year). Compute:
    a. The expected percentage increase in net operating income for next year.
    b. The expected total dollar net operating income for next year. (Do not prepare an income statement; use the degree of operating leverage to compute your answer.)

EXERCISE 6-16 Break-Even and Target Profit Analysis [LO4, LO5, LO6]
Outback Outfitters sells recreational equipment. One of the company's products, a small camp stove, sells for $50 per unit. Variable expenses are $32 per stove, and fixed expenses associated with the stove total $108,000 per month.

Required:
1. Compute the break-even point in number of stoves and in total sales dollars.
2. If the variable expenses per stove increase as a percentage of the selling price, will it result in a higher or a lower break-even point? Why? (Assume that the fixed expenses remain unchanged.)
3. At present, the company is selling 8,000 stoves per month. The sales manager is convinced that a 10% reduction in the selling price would result in a 25% increase in monthly sales of stoves. Prepare two contribution income statements, one under present operating conditions, and one as operations would appear after the proposed changes. Show both total and per unit data on your statements.
4. Refer to the data in (3) above. How many stoves would have to be sold at the new selling price to yield a minimum net operating income of $35,000 per month?

EXERCISE 6-17 Multiproduct Break-Even Analysis [LO9]
Olongapo Sports Corporation is the distributor in the Philippines of two premium golf balls—the Flight Dynamic and the Sure Shot. Monthly sales and the contribution margin ratios for the two products follow:

	Product		
	Flight Dynamic	Sure Shot	Total
Sales	P150,000	P250,000	P400,000
CM ratio.	80%	36%	?

Fixed expenses total P183,750 per month. (The currency in the Philippines is the peso, which is denoted by P.)

Required:
1. Prepare a contribution format income statement for the company as a whole. Carry computations to one decimal place.
2. Compute the break-even point for the company based on the current sales mix.
3. If sales increase by P100,000 a month, by how much would you expect net operating income to increase? What are your assumptions?

Problems

PROBLEM 6-18 Basic CVP Analysis [LO1, LO3, LO4, LO5, LO8]
Feather Friends, Inc., distributes a high-quality wooden birdhouse that sells for $20 per unit. Variable costs are $8 per unit, and fixed costs total $180,000 per year.

Required:
Answer the following independent questions:
1. What is the product's CM ratio?
2. Use the CM ratio to determine the break-even point in sales dollars.
3. Due to an increase in demand, the company estimates that sales will increase by $75,000 during the next year. By how much should net operating income increase (or net loss decrease) assuming that fixed costs do not change?
4. Assume that the operating results for last year were:

Sales	$400,000
Variable expenses	160,000
Contribution margin	240,000
Fixed expenses	180,000
Net operating income.	$60,000

a. Compute the degree of operating leverage at the current level of sales.
b. The president expects sales to increase by 20% next year. By what percentage should net operating income increase?

5. Refer to the original data. Assume that the company sold 18,000 units last year. The sales manager is convinced that a 10% reduction in the selling price, combined with a $30,000 increase in advertising, would cause annual sales in units to increase by one-third. Prepare two contribution income statements, one showing the results of last year's operations and one showing the results of operations if these changes are made. Would you recommend that the company do as the sales manager suggests?

6. Refer to the original data. Assume again that the company sold 18,000 units last year. The president does not want to change the selling price. Instead, he wants to increase the sales commission by $1 per unit. He thinks that this move, combined with some increase in advertising, would increase annual sales by 25%. By how much could advertising be increased with profits remaining unchanged? Do not prepare an income statement; use the incremental analysis approach.

PROBLEM 6-19 Basics of CVP Analysis; Cost Structure [LO1, LO3, LO4, LO5, LO6]

Due to erratic sales of its sole product—a high-capacity battery for laptop computers—PEM, Inc., has been experiencing difficulty for some time. The company's contribution format income statement for the most recent month is given below:

Sales (19,500 units × $30 per unit)	$585,000
Variable expenses	409,500
Contribution margin	175,500
Fixed expenses	180,000
Net operating loss	$ (4,500)

Required:

1. Compute the company's CM ratio and its break-even point in both units and dollars.
2. The president believes that a $16,000 increase in the monthly advertising budget, combined with an intensified effort by the sales staff, will result in an $80,000 increase in monthly sales. If the president is right, what will be the effect on the company's monthly net operating income or loss? (Use the incremental approach in preparing your answer.)
3. Refer to the original data. The sales manager is convinced that a 10% reduction in the selling price, combined with an increase of $60,000 in the monthly advertising budget, will cause unit sales to double. What will the new contribution format income statement look like if these changes are adopted?
4. Refer to the original data. The Marketing Department thinks that a fancy new package for the laptop computer battery would help sales. The new package would increase packaging costs by 75 cents per unit. Assuming no other changes, how many units would have to be sold each month to earn a profit of $9,750?
5. Refer to the original data. By automating certain operations, the company could reduce variable costs by $3 per unit. However, fixed costs would increase by $72,000 each month.
   a. Compute the new CM ratio and the new break-even point in both units and dollars.
   b. Assume that the company expects to sell 26,000 units next month. Prepare two contribution format income statements, one assuming that operations are not automated and one assuming that they are. (Show data on a per unit and percentage basis, as well as in total, for each alternative.)
   c. Would you recommend that the company automate its operations? Explain.

PROBLEM 6-20 Sales Mix; Multiproduct Break-Even Analysis [LO9]

Gold Star Rice, Ltd., of Thailand exports Thai rice throughout Asia. The company grows three varieties of rice—Fragrant, White, and Loonzain. (The currency in Thailand is the baht, which is denoted by B.) Budgeted sales by product and in total for the coming month are shown below:

	Product							
	White		Fragrant		Loonzain		Total	
Percentage of total sales	20%		52%		28%		100%	
Sales	B150,000	100%	B390,000	100%	B210,000	100%	B750,000	100%
Less variable expenses	108,000	72%	78,000	20%	84,000	40%	270,000	36%
Contribution margin	B 42,000	28%	B312,000	80%	B126,000	60%	480,000	64%
Less fixed expenses							449,280	
Net operating income.							B30,720	

$$\text{Break-even point in sales dollars} = \frac{\text{Fixed expenses}}{\text{CM ratio}} = \frac{B449,280}{0.64} = B702,000$$

As shown by these data, net operating income is budgeted at B30,720 for the month and break-even sales at B702,000.

Assume that actual sales for the month total B750,000 as planned. Actual sales by product are: White, B300,000; Fragrant, B180,000; and Loonzain, B270,000.

Required:

1. Prepare a contribution format income statement for the month based on actual sales data. Present the income statement in the format shown above.
2. Compute the break-even point in sales dollars for the month based on your actual data.
3. Considering the fact that the company met its B750,000 sales budget for the month, the president is shocked at the results shown on your income statement in (1) above. Prepare a brief memo for the president explaining why both the operating results and the break-even point in sales dollars are different from what was budgeted.

PROBLEM 6-21 Basic CVP Analysis; Graphing [LO1, LO2, LO4, LO5]

The Fashion Shoe Company operates a chain of women's shoe shops around the country. The shops carry many styles of shoes that are all sold at the same price. Sales personnel in the shops are paid a substantial commission on each pair of shoes sold (in addition to a small basic salary) in order to encourage them to be aggressive in their sales efforts.

The following worksheet contains cost and revenue data for Shop 48 and is typical of the company's many outlets:

	Per Pair of Shoes
Selling price	$ 30.00
Variable expenses:	
Invoice cost	$ 13.50
Sales commission	4.50
Total variable expenses	$ 18.00
	Annual
Fixed expenses:	
Advertising	$ 30,000
Rent	20,000
Salaries	100,000
Total fixed expenses	$150,000

Required:

1. Calculate the annual break-even point in dollar sales and in unit sales for Shop 48.
2. Prepare a CVP graph showing cost and revenue data for Shop 48 from a zero level of activity up to 17,000 pairs of shoes sold each year. Clearly indicate the break-even point on the graph.
3. If 12,000 pairs of shoes are sold in a year, what would be Shop 48's net operating income or loss?
4. The company is considering paying the store manager of Shop 48 an incentive commission of 75 cents per pair of shoes (in addition to the salesperson's commission). If this change is made, what will be the new break-even point in dollar sales and in unit sales?
5. Refer to the original data. As an alternative to (4) above, the company is considering paying the store manager 50 cents commission on each pair of shoes sold in excess of the break-even point. If this change is made, what will be the shop's net operating income or loss if 15,000 pairs of shoes are sold?

6. Refer to the original data. The company is considering eliminating sales commissions entirely in its shops and increasing fixed salaries by $31,500 annually. If this change is made, what will be the new break-even point in dollar sales and in unit sales for Shop 48? Would you recommend that the change be made? Explain.

PROBLEM 6-22 Break-Even Analysis; Pricing [LO1, LO4, LO5]
Minden Company introduced a new product last year for which it is trying to find an optimal selling price. Marketing studies suggest that the company can increase sales by 5,000 units for each $2 reduction in the selling price. The company's present selling price is $70 per unit, and variable expenses are $40 per unit. Fixed expenses are $540,000 per year. The present annual sales volume (at the $70 selling price) is 15,000 units.

Required:
1. What is the present yearly net operating income or loss?
2. What is the present break-even point in units and in dollar sales?
3. Assuming that the marketing studies are correct, what is the *maximum* profit that the company can earn yearly? At how many units and at what selling price per unit would the company generate this profit?
4. What would be the break-even point in units and in sales dollars using the selling price you determined in (3) above (e.g., the selling price at the level of maximum profits)? Why is this break-even point different from the break-even point you computed in (2) above?

PROBLEM 6-23 Graphing; Incremental Analysis; Operating Leverage [LO2, LO4, LO5, LO6, LO8]
Angie Silva has recently opened The Sandal Shop in Brisbane, Australia, a store that specializes in fashionable sandals. Angie has just received a degree in business and she is anxious to apply the principles she has learned to her business. In time, she hopes to open a chain of sandal shops. As a first step, she has prepared the following analysis for her new store:

Sales price per pair of sandals	$40
Variable expense per pair of sandals.	16
Contribution margin per pair of sandals.	$24
Fixed expense per year:	
Building rental.	$15,000
Equipment depreciation	7,000
Selling	20,000
Administrative.	18,000
Total fixed expense	$60,000

Required:
1. How many pairs of sandals must be sold each year to break even? What does this represent in total sales dollars?
2. Prepare a CVP graph for the store from a zero level of activity up to 4,000 pairs of sandals sold each year. Indicate the break-even point on your graph.
3. Angie has decided that she must earn at least $18,000 the first year to justify her time and effort. How many pairs of sandals must be sold to reach this target profit?
4. Angie now has two salespersons working in the store—one full time and one part time. It will cost her an additional $8,000 per year to convert the part-time position to a full-time position. Angie believes that the change would bring in an additional $25,000 in sales each year. Should she convert the position? Use the incremental approach. (Do not prepare an income statement.)
5. Refer to the original data. During the first year, the store sold only 3,000 pairs of sandals and reported the following operating results:

Sales (3,000 pairs)	$120,000
Less variable expenses	48,000
Contribution margin	72,000
Less fixed expenses	60,000
Net operating income	$ 12,000

   a.   What is the store's degree of operating leverage?

   b.   Angie is confident that with a more intense sales effort and with a more creative advertising program she can increase sales by 50% next year. What would be the expected percentage increase in net operating income? Use the degree of operating leverage to compute your answer.

PROBLEM 6-24 Break-Even and Target Profit Analysis [LO5, LO6]

The Shirt Works sells a large variety of tee shirts and sweatshirts. Steve Hooper, the owner, is thinking of expanding his sales by hiring local high school students, on a commission basis, to sell sweatshirts bearing the name and mascot of the local high school.

These sweatshirts would have to be ordered from the manufacturer six weeks in advance, and they could not be returned because of the unique printing required. The sweatshirts would cost Mr. Hooper $8 each with a minimum order of 75 sweatshirts. Any additional sweatshirts would have to be ordered in increments of 75.

Since Mr. Hooper's plan would not require any additional facilities, the only costs associated with the project would be the costs of the sweatshirts and the costs of the sales commissions. The selling price of the sweatshirts would be $13.50 each. Mr. Hooper would pay the students a commission of $1.50 for each shirt sold.

Required:

1.   To make the project worthwhile, Mr. Hooper would require a $1,200 profit for the first three months of the venture. What level of sales in units and in dollars would be required to reach this target net operating income? Show all computations.

2.   Assume that the venture is undertaken and an order is placed for 75 sweatshirts. What would be Mr. Hooper's break-even point in units and in sales dollars? Show computations and explain the reasoning behind your answer.

PROBLEM 6-25 Sales Mix; Break-Even Analysis; Margin of Safety [LO7, LO9]

Island Novelties, Inc., of Palau makes two products, Hawaiian Fantasy and Tahitian Joy. Present revenue, cost, and sales data for the two products follow:

	Hawaiian Fantasy	Tahitian Joy
Selling price per unit.	$15	$100
Variable expenses per unit.	$9	$20
Number of units sold monthly.	20,000	5,000

Fixed expenses total $475,800 per year. The Republic of Palau uses the U.S. dollar as its currency.

Required:

1.   Assuming the sales mix given above, do the following:

   a.   Prepare a contribution format income statement showing both dollar and percent columns for each product and for the company as a whole.

   b.   Compute the break-even point in dollars for the company as a whole and the margin of safety in both dollars and percent.

2.   The company has developed a new product to be called Samoan Delight. Assume that the company could sell 10,000 units at $45 each. The variable expenses would be $36 each. The company's fixed expenses would not change.

   a.   Prepare another contribution format income statement, including sales of the Samoan Delight (sales of the other two products would not change).

   b.   Compute the company's new break-even point in dollars and the new margin of safety in both dollars and percent.

3.   The president of the company examines your figures and says, "There's something strange here. Our fixed costs haven't changed and you show greater total contribution margin if we add the new product, but you also show our break-even point going up. With greater contribution margin, the break-even point should go down, not up. You've made a mistake somewhere." Explain to the president what has happened.

PROBLEM 6-26 Sales Mix; Commission Structure; Multiproduct Break-Even Analysis [LO9]
Carbex, Inc., produces cutlery sets out of high-quality wood and steel. The company makes a standard cutlery set and a deluxe set and sells them to retail department stores throughout the country. The standard set sells for $60, and the deluxe set sells for $75. The variable expenses associated with each set are given below (in cost per set):

	Standard	Deluxe
Production costs........................	$15.00	$30.00
Sales commissions (15% of sales price)........	$9.00	$11.25

The company's fixed expenses each month are:

Advertising..........	$105,000
Depreciation.........	$21,700
Administrative........	$63,000

Salespersons are paid on a commission basis to encourage them to be aggressive in their sales efforts. Mary Parsons, the financial vice president, watches sales commissions carefully and has noted that they have risen steadily over the last year. For this reason, she was shocked to find that even though sales have increased, profits for the current month—May—are down substantially from April. Sales, in sets, for the last two months are given below:

	Standard	Deluxe	Total
April	4,000	2,000	6,000
May.........	1,000	5,000	6,000

Required:
1. Prepare contribution format income statements for April and May. Use the following headings:

	Standard		Deluxe		Total	
	Amount	Percent	Amount	Percent	Amount	Percent
Sales						
Etc.						

Place the fixed expenses only in the Total column. Do not show percentages for the fixed expenses.
2. Explain why there is a difference in net operating income between the two months, even though the same *total* number of sets was sold in each month.
3. What can be done to the sales commissions to optimize the sales mix?
4. *a.*   Using April's figures, what was the break-even point for the month in sales dollars?
    b.   Has May's break-even point gone up or down from that of April? Explain your answer without calculating the break-even point for May.

PROBLEM 6-27 Various CVP Questions: Break-Even Point; Cost Structure; Target Sales [LO1, LO3, LO4, LO5, LO6, LO8]

Northwood Company manufactures basketballs. The company has a ball that sells for $25. At present, the ball is manufactured in a small plant that relies heavily on direct labor workers. Thus, variable costs are high, totaling $15 per ball.

Last year, the company sold 30,000 of these balls, with the following results:

Sales (30,000 balls).........	$750,000
Variable expenses	450,000
Contribution margin	300,000
Fixed expenses	210,000
Net operating income........	$ 90,000

Required:

1. Compute (a) the CM ratio and the break-even point in balls, and (b) the degree of operating leverage at last year's sales level.
2. Due to an increase in labor rates, the company estimates that variable costs will increase by $3 per ball next year. If this change takes place and the selling price per ball remains constant at $25, what will be the new CM ratio and break-even point in balls?
3. Refer to the data in (2) above. If the expected change in variable costs takes place, how many balls will have to be sold next year to earn the same net operating income ($90,000) as last year?
4. Refer again to the data in (2) above. The president feels that the company must raise the selling price of its basketballs. If Northwood Company wants to maintain *the same CM ratio as last year,* what selling price per ball must it charge next year to cover the increased labor costs?
5. Refer to the original data. The company is discussing the construction of a new, automated manufacturing plant. The new plant would slash variable costs per ball by 40%, but it would cause fixed costs per year to double. If the new plant is built, what would be the company's new CM ratio and new break-even point in balls?
6. Refer to the data in (5) above.
   a. If the new plant is built, how many balls will have to be sold next year to earn the same net operating income ($90,000) as last year?
   b. Assume the new plant is built and that next year the company manufactures and sells 30,000 balls (the same number as sold last year). Prepare a contribution income statement and compute the degree of operating leverage.
   c. If you were a member of top management, would you have been in favor of constructing the new plant? Explain.

PROBLEM 6-28 Interpretive Questions on the CVP Graph [LO2, LO5]

A CVP graph such as the one shown on the next page is a useful technique for showing relationships between an organization's costs, volume, and profits.

Required:

1. Identify the numbered components in the CVP graph.
2. State the effect of each of the following actions on line 3, line 9, and the break-even point. For line 3 and line 9, state whether the action will cause the line to:

   Remain unchanged.
   Shift upward.
   Shift downward.
   Have a steeper slope (i.e., rotate upward).
   Have a flatter slope (i.e., rotate downward).
   Shift upward *and* have a steeper slope.
   Shift upward *and* have a flatter slope.
   Shift downward *and* have a steeper slope.
   Shift downward *and* have a flatter slope.

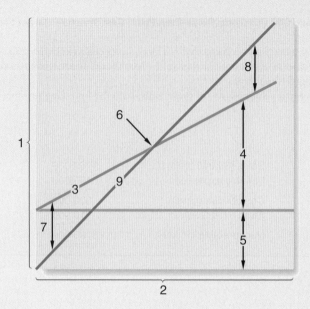

In the case of the break-even point, state whether the action will cause the break-even point to:

    Remain unchanged.
    Increase.
    Decrease.
    Probably change, but the direction is uncertain.

Treat each case independently.

x.   *Example.*   Fixed costs are reduced by $5,000 per period.
        Answer (see choices above):   Line 3:   Shift downward.
                                  Line 9:   Remain unchanged.
                                  Break-even point: Decrease.

a.   The unit selling price is increased from $18 to $20.
b.   Unit variable costs are decreased from $12 to $10.
c.   Fixed costs are increased by $3,000 per period.
d.   Two thousand more units are sold during the period than were budgeted.
e.   Due to paying salespersons a commission rather than a flat salary, fixed costs are reduced by $8,000 per period and unit variable costs are increased by $3.
f.   Due to an increase in the cost of materials, both unit variable costs and the selling price are increased by $2.
g.   Advertising costs are increased by $10,000 per period, resulting in a 10% increase in the number of units sold.
h.   Due to automating an operation previously done by workers, fixed costs are increased by $12,000 per period and unit variable costs are reduced by $4.

PROBLEM 6-29 Changes in Fixed and Variable Costs; Break-Even and Target Profit Analysis [LO4, LO5, LO6]

Neptune Company produces toys and other items for use in beach and resort areas. A small, inflatable toy has come onto the market that the company is anxious to produce and sell. The new toy will sell for $3 per unit. Enough capacity exists in the company's plant to produce 16,000 units of the toy each month. Variable costs to manufacture and sell one unit would be $1.25, and fixed costs associated with the toy would total $35,000 per month.

The company's Marketing Department predicts that demand for the new toy will exceed the 16,000 units that the company is able to produce. Additional manufacturing space can be rented from another company at a fixed cost of $1,000 per month. Variable costs in the rented facility would total $1.40 per unit, due to somewhat less efficient operations than in the main plant.

Required:
1.   Compute the monthly break-even point for the new toy in units and in total sales dollars. Show all computations in good form.

2. How many units must be sold each month to make a monthly profit of $12,000?
3. If the sales manager receives a bonus of 10 cents for each unit sold in excess of the break-even point, how many units must be sold each month to earn a return of 25% on the monthly investment in fixed costs?

PROBLEM 6-30 Changes in Cost Structure; Break-Even Analysis; Operating Leverage; Margin of Safety [LO4, LO5, LO7, LO8]

Morton Company's contribution format income statement for last month is given below:

Sales (15,000 units × $30 per unit)........	$450,000
Less variable expenses.................	315,000
Contribution margin....................	135,000
Less fixed expenses....................	90,000
Net operating income...................	$ 45,000

The industry in which Morton Company operates is quite sensitive to cyclical movements in the economy. Thus, profits vary considerably from year to year according to general economic conditions. The company has a large amount of unused capacity and is studying ways of improving profits.

Required:

1. New equipment has come onto the market that would allow Morton Company to automate a portion of its operations. Variable costs would be reduced by $9 per unit. However, fixed costs would increase to a total of $225,000 each month. Prepare two contribution format income statements, one showing present operations and one showing how operations would appear if the new equipment is purchased. Show an Amount column, a Per Unit column, and a Percent column on each statement. Do not show percentages for the fixed costs.
2. Refer to the income statements in (1) above. For both present operations and the proposed new operations, compute (a) the degree of operating leverage, (b) the break-even point in dollars, and (c) the margin of safety in both dollar and percentage terms.
3. Refer again to the data in (1) above. As a manager, what factor would be paramount in your mind in deciding whether to purchase the new equipment? (Assume that ample funds are available to make the purchase.)
4. Refer to the original data. Rather than purchase new equipment, the marketing manager is thinking about changing the company's marketing strategy. Rather than pay sales commissions, which are currently included in variable expenses, the company would pay salespersons fixed salaries and would invest heavily in advertising. The marketing manager claims this new approach would increase unit sales by 30% without any change in selling price; the company's new monthly fixed expenses would be $180,000; and its net operating income would increase by 20%. Compute the break-even point in sales dollars for the company under the new marketing strategy. Do you agree with the marketing manager's proposal?

Cases

CASE 6-31 Break-Evens for Individual Products in a Multiproduct Company [LO5, LO9]

Cheryl Montoya picked up the phone and called her boss, Wes Chan, the vice president of marketing at Piedmont Fasteners Corporation: "Wes, I'm not sure how to go about answering the questions that came up at the meeting with the president yesterday."

"What's the problem?"

"The president wanted to know the break-even point for each of the company's products, but I am having trouble figuring them out."

"I'm sure you can handle it, Cheryl. And, by the way, I need your analysis on my desk tomorrow morning at 8:00 sharp in time for the follow-up meeting at 9:00."

Piedmont Fasteners Corporation makes three different clothing fasteners in its manufacturing facility in North Carolina. Data concerning these products appear below:

	Velcro	Metal	Nylon
Normal annual sales volume	100,000	200,000	400,000
Unit selling price	$1.65	$1.50	$0.85
Variable cost per unit	$1.25	$0.70	$0.25

Total fixed expenses are $400,000 per year.

All three products are sold in highly competitive markets, so the company is unable to raise its prices without losing unacceptable numbers of customers.

The company has an extremely effective just-in-time manufacturing system, so there are no beginning or ending work in process or finished goods inventories.

Required:
1. What is the company's over-all break-even in total sales dollars?
2. Of the total fixed costs of $400,000, $20,000 could be avoided if the Velcro product were dropped, $80,000 if the Metal product were dropped, and $60,000 if the Nylon product were dropped. The remaining fixed costs of $240,000 consist of common fixed costs such as administrative salaries and rent on the factory building that could be avoided only by going out of business entirely.
   a. What is the break-even point in units for each product?
   b. If the company sells exactly the break-even quantity of each product, what will be the overall profit of the company? Explain this result.

CASE 6-32 Cost Structure; Break-Even; Target Profits [LO4, LO5, LO6]
Pittman Company is a small but growing manufacturer of telecommunications equipment. The company has no sales force of its own; rather, it relies completely on independent sales agents to market its products. These agents are paid a commission of 15% of selling price for all items sold.

Barbara Cheney, Pittman's controller, has just prepared the company's budgeted income statement for next year. The statement follows:

Pittman Company Budgeted Income Statement For the Year Ended December 31		
Sales		$16,000,000
Manufacturing costs:		
Variable	$7,200,000	
Fixed overhead	2,340,000	9,540,000
Gross margin		6,460,000
Selling and administrative costs:		
Commissions to agents	2,400,000	
Fixed marketing costs	120,000*	
Fixed administrative costs	1,800,000	4,320,000
Net operating income		2,140,000
Less fixed interest cost		540,000
Income before income taxes		1,600,000
Less income taxes (30%)		480,000
Net income		$ 1,120,000

*Primarily depreciation on storage facilities.

As Barbara handed the statement to Karl Vecci, Pittman's president, she commented, "I went ahead and used the agents' 15% commission rate in completing these statements, but we've just learned that they refuse to handle our products next year unless we increase the commission rate to 20%."

"That's the last straw," Karl replied angrily. "Those agents have been demanding more and more, and this time they've gone too far. How can they possibly defend a 20% commission rate?"

"They claim that after paying for advertising, travel, and the other costs of promotion, there's nothing left over for profit," replied Barbara.

"I say it's just plain robbery," retorted Karl. "And I also say it's time we dumped those guys and got our own sales force. Can you get your people to work up some cost figures for us to look at?"

"We've already worked them up," said Barbara. "Several companies we know about pay a 7.5% commission to their own salespeople, along with a small salary. Of course, we would have to handle all promotion costs, too. We figure our fixed costs would increase by $2,400,000 per year, but that would be more than offset by the $3,200,000 (20% × $16,000,000) that we would avoid on agents' commissions."

The breakdown of the $2,400,000 cost follows:

Salaries:	
Sales manager..............	$ 100,000
Salespersons...............	600,000
Travel and entertainment........	400,000
Advertising...................	1,300,000
Total.......................	$2,400,000

"Super," replied Karl. "And I noticed that the $2,400,000 is just what we're paying the agents under the old 15% commission rate."

"It's even better than that," explained Barbara. "We can actually save $75,000 a year because that's what we're having to pay the auditing firm now to check out the agents' reports. So our overall administrative costs would be less."

"Pull all of these numbers together and we'll show them to the executive committee tomorrow," said Karl. "With the approval of the committee, we can move on the matter immediately."

Required:
1. Compute Pittman Company's break-even point in sales dollars for next year assuming:
   a. That the agents' commission rate remains unchanged at 15%.
   b. That the agents' commission rate is increased to 20%.
   c. That the company employs its own sales force.
2. Assume that Pittman Company decides to continue selling through agents and pays the 20% commission rate. Determine the volume of sales that would be required to generate the same net income as contained in the budgeted income statement for next year.
3. Determine the volume of sales at which net income would be equal regardless of whether Pittman Company sells through agents (at a 20% commission rate) or employs its own sales force.
4. Compute the degree of operating leverage that the company would expect to have on December 31 at the end of next year assuming:
   a. That the agents' commission rate remains unchanged at 15%.
   b. That the agents' commission rate is increased to 20%.
   c. That the company employs its own sales force.
   Use income *before* income taxes in your operating leverage computation.
5. Based on the data in (1) through (4) above, make a recommendation as to whether the company should continue to use sales agents (at a 20% commission rate) or employ its own sales force. Give reasons for your answer.

(CMA, adapted)

CASE 6-33 Break-Even Analysis with Step Fixed Costs [LO5, LO6]

The Pediatric Department at Wymont General Hospital has a capacity of 90 beds and operates 24 hours a day every day. The measure of activity in the department is patient-days, where one patient-day represents one patient occupying a bed for one day. The average revenue per patient-day is $130 and the average variable cost per patient-day is $50. The fixed cost of the department (not including personnel costs) is $454,000.

The only personnel directly employed by the Pediatric Department are aides, nurses, and supervising nurses. The hospital has minimum staffing requirements for the department based on total annual patient-days in Pediatrics. Hospital requirements, beginning at the minimum expected level of activity, follow:

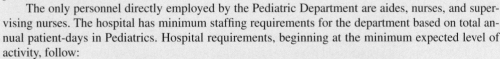

Annual Patient-Days	Aides	Nurses	Supervising Nurses
10,000–14,000	21	11	4
14,001–17,000	22	12	4
17,001–23,725	22	13	4
23,726–25,550	25	14	5
25,551–27,375	26	14	5
27,376–29,200	29	16	6

These staffing levels represent full-time equivalents, and it should be assumed that the Pediatric Department always employs only the minimum number of required full-time equivalent personnel.

Average annual salaries for each class of employee are: aides, $18,000; nurses, $26,000; and supervising nurses, $36,000.

Required:

1. Compute the total fixed costs (including the salaries of aides, nurses, and supervising nurses) in the Pediatric Department for each level of activity shown above (i.e., total fixed costs at the 10,000–14,000 patient-day level of activity, total fixed costs at the 14,001–17,000 patient-day level of activity, etc.).
2. Compute the minimum number of patient-days required for the Pediatric Department to break even.
3. Determine the minimum number of patient-days required for the Pediatric Department to earn an annual "profit" of $200,000.

(CPA, adapted)

RESEARCH AND APPLICATION 6-34　[LO3, LO4, LO5, LO6, LO7, LO8, LO9]

The questions in this exercise are based on the Benetton Group, a company headquartered in Italy and known in the United States primarily for one of its brands of fashion apparel—United Colors of Benetton. To answer the questions, you will need to download the Benetton Group's 2004 Annual Report at www.benetton.com/investors. You do not need to print this document to answer the questions.

Required:

1. How do the formats of the income statements shown on pages 33 and 50 of Benetton's annual report differ from one another (disregard everything beneath the line titled "income from operations")? Which expenses shown on page 50 appear to have been reclassified as variable selling costs on page 33?
2. Why do you think cost of sales is included in the computation of contribution margin on page 33?
3. Perform two separate computations of Benetton's break-even point in euros. For the first computation, use data from 2003. For the second computation, use data from 2004. Why do the numbers that you computed differ from one another?
4. What sales volume would have been necessary in 2004 for Benetton to attain a target income from operations of €300 million?
5. Compute Benetton's margin of safety using data from 2003 and 2004. Why do your answers for the two years differ from one another?
6. What is Benetton's degree of operating leverage in 2004? If Benetton's sales in 2004 had been 6% higher than what is shown in the annual report, what income from operations would the company have earned? What percentage increase in income from operations does this represent?
7. What income from operations would Benetton have earned in 2004 if it had invested an additional €10 million in advertising and promotions and realized a 3% increase in sales? As an alternative, what income from operations would Benetton have earned if it not only invested an additional €10 million in advertising and promotions but also raised its sales commission rate to 6% of sales, thereby generating a 5% increase in sales? Which of these two scenarios would have been preferable for Benetton?
8. Assume that total sales in 2004 remained unchanged at €1,686 million (as shown on pages 33 and 50); however, the Casual sector sales were €1,554 million, the Sportswear and Equipment sector sales were €45million, and the Manufacturing and Other sector sales were €87 million. What income from operations would Benetton have earned with this sales mix? (Hint: look at pages 36 and 37 of the annual report.) Why is the income from operations under this scenario different from what is shown in the annual report?

Variable Costing: A Tool for Management

IBM's $2.5 Billion Investment in Technology

When it comes to state-of-the-art in automation, IBM's $2.5 billion semiconductor manufacturing facility in East Fishkill, New York, is tough to beat. The plant uses wireless networks, 600 miles of cable, and more than 420 servers to equip itself with what IBM claims is more computing power than NASA uses to launch a space shuttle.

Each batch of 25 wafers (one wafer can be processed into 1,000 computer chips) travels through the East Fishkill plant's manufacturing process without ever being touched by human hands. A computer system "looks at orders and schedules production runs . . . adjusts schedules to allow for planned maintenance and . . . feeds vast reams of production data into enterprise-wide management and financial-reporting systems." The plant can literally run itself as was the case a few years ago when a snowstorm hit and everyone went home while the automated system continued to manufacture computer chips until it ran out of work.

In a manufacturing environment such as this, labor costs are insignificant and fixed overhead costs are huge. There is a strong temptation to build inventories and increase profits without increasing sales. How can this be done you ask? It would seem logical that producing more units would have no impact on profits unless the units were sold, right? Wrong! As we will discover in this chapter, absorption costing—the most widely used method of determining product costs—can artificially increase profits by increasing the quantity of units produced. ■

Source: Ghostwriter, "Big Blue's $2.5 Billion Sales Tool," *Fortune*, September 19, 2005, pp. 316F–316J.

Learning Objectives

After studying Chapter 7, you should be able to:

LO1 Explain how variable costing differs from absorption costing and compute unit product costs under each method.

LO2 Prepare income statements using both variable and absorption costing.

LO3 Reconcile variable costing and absorption costing net operating incomes and explain why the two amounts differ.

LO4 Understand the advantages and disadvantages of both variable and absorption costing.

Two general approaches are used in manufacturing companies for costing products for the purposes of valuing inventories and cost of goods sold. One approach, called *absorption costing,* was discussed in Chapter 3. Absorption costing is generally used for external financial reports. The other approach, called *variable costing,* is preferred by some managers for internal decision making and must be used when an income statement is prepared in the contribution format. Ordinarily, absorption costing and variable costing produce different figures for net operating income, and the difference can be quite large. In addition to showing how these two methods differ, we will consider the arguments for and against each costing method and we will show how management decisions can be affected by the costing method chosen.

Overview of Absorption and Variable Costing

LEARNING OBJECTIVE 1
Explain how variable costing differs from absorption costing and compute unit product costs under each method.

As discussed in the last two chapters, the contribution format income statement and cost-volume-profit (CVP) analysis are valuable management tools. Both of these tools emphasize cost behavior and require that managers carefully distinguish between variable and fixed costs. Absorption costing, which was discussed in Chapters 2 and 3, assigns both variable and fixed manufacturing costs to products—mingling them in a way that makes it difficult for managers to distinguish between them. In contrast, variable costing focuses on *cost behavior*—clearly separating fixed from variable costs. One of the strengths of variable costing is that it harmonizes with both the contribution approach and the CVP concepts discussed in the preceding chapter.

Absorption Costing

As discussed in Chapter 3, **absorption costing** treats *all* manufacturing costs as product costs, regardless of whether they are variable or fixed. The cost of a unit of product under the absorption costing method consists of direct materials, direct labor, and *both* variable and fixed manufacturing overhead. Thus, absorption costing allocates a portion of fixed manufacturing overhead cost to each unit of product, along with the variable manufacturing costs. Because absorption costing includes all manufacturing costs in product costs, it is frequently referred to as the *full cost* method.

Variable Costing

Under **variable costing,** only those manufacturing costs that vary with output are treated as product costs. This would usually include direct materials, direct labor, and the variable portion of manufacturing overhead. Fixed manufacturing overhead is not treated as a product cost under this method. Rather, fixed manufacturing overhead is treated as a period cost and, like selling and administrative expenses, it is expensed in its entirety each period. Consequently, the cost of a unit of product in inventory or in cost of goods sold under the variable costing method does not contain any fixed manufacturing overhead cost. Variable costing is sometimes referred to as *direct costing* or *marginal costing.*

Selling and Administrative Expense

To complete this summary comparison of absorption and variable costing, we need to briefly consider the handling of selling and administrative expenses. These expenses are never treated as product costs, regardless of the costing method. Thus, under absorption and variable costing, variable and fixed selling and administrative expenses are always treated as period costs and are expensed as incurred.

Exhibit 7–1 summarizes the classification of costs under both absorption and variable costing.

Absorption Costing		Variable Costing
Product costs	Direct materials	**Product costs**
	Direct labor	
	Variable manufacturing overhead	
	Fixed manufacturing overhead	
Period costs	Variable selling and administrative expenses	**Period costs**
	Fixed selling and administrative expenses	

EXHIBIT 7–1
Cost Classifications—
Absorption versus Variable
Costing

Unit Cost Computations

To illustrate the computation of unit product costs under both absorption and variable costing, consider Boley Company, a small company that produces a single product and that has the following cost structure:

Number of units produced each year	6,000
Variable costs per unit:	
Direct materials	$2
Direct labor.	$4
Variable manufacturing overhead	$1
Variable selling and administrative expenses	$3
Fixed costs per year:	
Fixed manufacturing overhead	$30,000
Fixed selling and administrative expenses	$10,000

Topic Tackler

PLUS

7–1

Required:
1. Compute the unit product cost under absorption costing.
2. Compute the unit product cost under variable costing.

Solution

Absorption Costing	
Direct materials	$ 2
Direct labor	4
Variable manufacturing overhead	1
Total variable manufacturing cost.	7
Fixed manufacturing overhead ($30,000 ÷ 6,000 units of product)	5
Unit product cost	$12
Variable Costing	
Direct materials	$ 2
Direct labor	4
Variable manufacturing overhead	1
Unit product cost	$ 7

(Under variable costing, the $30,000 fixed manufacturing overhead is a period expense along with selling and administrative expenses.)

Under the absorption costing method, *all* manfacturing costs, variable and fixed, are included when determining the unit product cost. Thus, if the company sells a unit of product and absorption costing is being used, then $12 (consisting of $7 variable cost and $5 fixed cost) will be deducted on the income statement as cost of goods sold. Similarly, any unsold units will be carried as inventory on the balance sheet at $12 each.

Under the variable costing method, only the variable manfacturing costs are included in product costs. Thus, if the company sells a unit of product, only $7 will be deducted as cost of goods sold, and unsold units will be carried as inventory on the balance sheet at only $7 each.

IN BUSINESS

THE BEHAVIORAL SIDE OF CALCULATING UNIT PRODUCT COSTS

In 2004, Andreas STIHL, a manufacturer of chain saws and other landscaping products, asked its U.S. subsidiary, STIHL Inc., to replace its absorption costing income statements with the variable costing approach. From a computer systems standpoint, the change was not disruptive because STIHL used an enterprise system called SAP that accommodates both absorption and variable costing. However, from a behavioral standpoint, STIHL felt the change could be very disruptive. For example, STIHL's senior managers were keenly aware that the variable costing approach reported lower unit product costs than the absorption costing approach. Given this reality, the sales force might be inclined to erroneously conclude that each product had magically become more profitable, thereby justifying ill-advised price reductions. Because of behavioral concerns such as this, STIHL worked hard to educate its employees how to interpret a variable costing income statement.

Source: Carl S. Smith, "Going for GPK: STIHL Moves Toward This Costing System in the United States," *Strategic Finance*, April 2005, pp. 36–39.

IN BUSINESS

SCRUTINIZING VARIABLE MANUFACTURING COSTS AT FORD

Jim Padilla, the chief operating officer at the Ford Motor Company, believes in ranking vehicles by the amount of contribution margin earned. In other words, for internal decision-making purposes he views direct materials, direct labor, and variable manufacturing overhead as product costs and fixed manufacturing overhead as a period cost. Historically, Ford has been willing to sell small cars that get good gas mileage at a loss to boost the company's average fuel economy and air-pollution emission ratings. Padilla is committed to scaling back this practice. He believes the company should give serious consideration to discontinuing any car that cannot generate enough sales to cover its variable production costs.

Source: Alex Taylor III, "Bill's Brand-New Ford," *Fortune*, June 28, 2004, pp. 68–76.

Income Comparison of Absorption and Variable Costing

LEARNING OBJECTIVE 2
Prepare income statements using both variable and absorption costing.

Exhibit 7–2 displays income statements prepared under the absorption and variable costing approaches. In preparing these statements, we use the data for Boley Company presented earlier, along with other information about the company as given below:

Units in beginning inventory	0
Units produced.	6,000
Units sold	5,000
Units in ending inventory	1,000
Selling price per unit	$20
Selling and administrative expenses:	
Variable per unit	$3
Fixed per year	$10,000

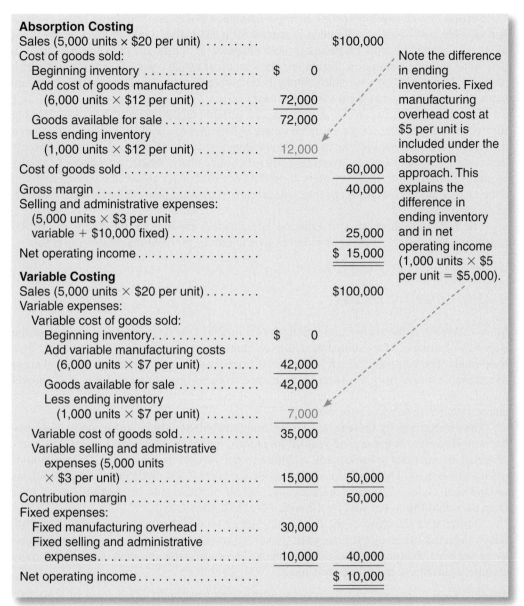

EXHIBIT 7–2
Comparison of Absorption and Variable Costing—Boley Company

Absorption Costing

Sales (5,000 units × $20 per unit)		$100,000
Cost of goods sold:		
Beginning inventory	$ 0	
Add cost of goods manufactured		
(6,000 units × $12 per unit)	72,000	
Goods available for sale	72,000	
Less ending inventory		
(1,000 units × $12 per unit)	12,000	
Cost of goods sold		60,000
Gross margin		40,000
Selling and administrative expenses:		
(5,000 units × $3 per unit		
variable + $10,000 fixed)		25,000
Net operating income		$ 15,000

Variable Costing

Sales (5,000 units × $20 per unit)		$100,000
Variable expenses:		
Variable cost of goods sold:		
Beginning inventory.	$ 0	
Add variable manufacturing costs		
(6,000 units × $7 per unit)	42,000	
Goods available for sale	42,000	
Less ending inventory		
(1,000 units × $7 per unit)	7,000	
Variable cost of goods sold.	35,000	
Variable selling and administrative		
expenses (5,000 units		
× $3 per unit)	15,000	50,000
Contribution margin		50,000
Fixed expenses:		
Fixed manufacturing overhead	30,000	
Fixed selling and administrative		
expenses.	10,000	40,000
Net operating income		$ 10,000

Note the difference in ending inventories. Fixed manufacturing overhead cost at $5 per unit is included under the absorption approach. This explains the difference in ending inventory and in net operating income (1,000 units × $5 per unit = $5,000).

    Several observations should be made concerning the income statements in Exhibit 7–2. First, the net operating incomes under the two costing methods are not the same. The net operating income under absorption costing is higher than under variable costing by $5,000. Why is this? Under absorption costing, each of the units produced during the period is assigned $5 of fixed manufacturing overhead cost (see the unit cost computations on page 277). This is true of the 1,000 units in ending inventory as well as the 5,000 units that were sold. Consequently, the ending inventory under absorption costing contains $5,000 of fixed manufacturing overhead and the cost of goods sold contains $25,000 of fixed manufacturing overhead. In contrast, the entire $30,000 of fixed manufacturing overhead is expensed under variable costing. As a direct result, the net operating income under variable costing is $5,000 higher than under absorption costing. In effect, the $5,000 of fixed manufacturing overhead in ending inventory under absorption costing is deferred to the future period in which these units are sold. This $5,000 of fixed manufacturing overhead cost in the ending inventory is referred to as **fixed manufacturing overhead cost deferred in inventory.** In general, under absorption costing, when inventories increase, some of the fixed manufacturing costs of the current period are reported on the balance sheet as part of the ending inventories rather than on the income statement as part of cost of goods sold.

Topic Tackler

PLUS

7–2

Second, the absorption costing income statement makes no distinction between fixed and variable costs—a distinction that is crucial for CVP analysis and for much of the planning and control concepts discussed in later chapters. It is difficult or even impossible to determine from an absorption costing income statement which costs are variable and which are fixed. In contrast, on a variable costing income statement the fixed and variable costs are explicitly identified—making CVP analysis far easier.

The difference between the absorption and variable costing approaches to accounting for fixed manufacturing costs centers on timing. Advocates of variable costing say that fixed manufacturing costs should be expensed immediately in total, whereas advocates of absorption costing say that fixed manufacturing costs should be charged against revenues gradually as units of product are sold. Any units of product not sold under absorption costing result in fixed manfacturing costs being inventoried and carried forward on the balance sheet *as assets* to the next period.

The following discussion of Emerald Isle Knitters expands on the discussion of the absorption and variable costing approaches to accounting for fixed manufacturing costs.

Extended Comparison of Income Data

**MANAGERIAL
ACCOUNTING
IN ACTION**

The Issue

Mary O'Meara is the owner and manager of Emerald Isle Knitters, Ltd., located in the Republic of Ireland. Mary started the company three years ago with cash loaned to her by a local bank. The company, which has only 10 employees, manufactures a traditional wool fisherman's sweater from a pattern Mary learned from her grandmother. Like most apparel manufacturers, Emerald Isle Knitters sells its product to department stores and clothing store chains rather than to retail customers.

The sweater was an immediate success, and the company sold all of its first year's production. However, in the second year of operations, one of the company's major customers canceled its order due to bankruptcy, and the company ended the year with a large inventory of unsold sweaters. The third year of operations was a great year in contrast to the disastrous second year. Sales rebounded dramatically, and all of the unsold production carried over from the second year was sold by the end of the third year.

Shortly after the close of the third year, Mary met with her accountant Sean MacLafferty to discuss the results for the year. (Note: All of the company's business is transacted using the euro, denoted by €, as the currency. The euro is the common currency of many member countries of the European Union.)

Mary: Sean, I am confused! Last year, we reported a net operating income of €30,000, which was higher than I expected given the big order that was cancelled by a major customer. This year we reported a net operating income of €90,000, which is lower than I expected given our dramatic rebound in sales. My intuition in terms of predicting our financial performance has been dead wrong for two years in a row. What's going on?

Sean: I think the source of confusion is the rules of financial accounting that we must follow when preparing financial statements for the bank. I have always felt that complying with these rules may be necessary for external reporting purposes, but that relying on them for internal decision-making purposes is misleading.

Mary: What other options do we have? Frankly, I have always assumed that there is only one way to prepare an income statement.

Sean: Most people make the same assumption. However, when it comes to internal reporting, we can use another income statement approach that I think you'll find more intuitive. How about if I prepare income statements for the last three years using what is called the variable costing approach and we'll compare them to the income statements that we have been using for the bank—which, by the way, are called absorption costing income statements. You can compare the two sets of numbers and decide which approach you prefer.

Mary: Sounds good. Let me know when you are ready to meet again.

EXHIBIT 7–3
Basic Data for Absorption and Variable Costing Income Statements—Emerald Isle Knitters, Ltd.

Basic Data

Selling price per unit sold	€20
Variable manufacturing cost per unit produced	€7
Fixed manufacturing overhead costs per year	€150,000
Variable selling and administrative expenses per unit sold	€1
Fixed selling and administrative expenses per year	€90,000

	Year 1	Year 2	Year 3	Three Years Together
Units in beginning inventory	0	0	5,000	0
Units produced	25,000	25,000	25,000	75,000
Units sold	25,000	20,000	30,000	75,000
Units in ending inventory	0	5,000	0	0

Unit Product Costs	Year 1	Year 2	Year 3	
Under variable costing (variable manufacturing costs only)	€7	€7	€7	
Under absorption costing:				
Variable manufacturing costs	€7	€7	€7	
Fixed manufacturing overhead costs (€150,000 spread				
over the number of units produced in each year)	6	6	6	
Total absorption cost per unit	€13	€13	€13	

Immediately after the meeting with Mary, Sean put together the data and financial reports that appear in Exhibit 7–3. (All financial statements have been reformatted to be closer to U.S. standards.)

The basic data needed to prepare both income statements appear in Exhibit 7–3. The absorption costing income statements as reported to the bank for the last three years appear in the top half of Exhibit 7–4 (page 282). The variable costing income statements that Sean prepared for the last three years appear in the bottom half of Exhibit 7–4.

Note that Emerald Isle Knitters maintained a steady rate of production of 25,000 sweaters per year. However, sales varied from year to year. In Year 1, production and sales were equal. In Year 2, production exceeded sales due to the canceled order. In Year 3, sales recovered and exceeded production. As a consequence, inventories did not change during Year 1, inventories increased during Year 2, and inventories decreased during Year 3. The change in inventories during the year is the key to understanding how absorption costing differs from variable costing. Note that when inventories increase in Year 2, absorption costing net operating income exceeds variable costing net operating income. When inventories decrease in Year 3, the opposite occurs—variable costing net operating income exceeds absorption costing net operating income. And when inventories do not change as in Year 1, there is no difference in net operating income between the two methods. Why is this? The reasons are discussed below and are briefly summarized in Exhibit 7–5 (page 283).[1]

1. When production and sales are equal, as in Year 1 for Emerald Isle Knitters, net operating income will generally be the same regardless of whether absorption or variable costing is used. The reason is as follows: The *only* difference that can exist between absorption and variable costing net operating income is the amount of fixed manufacturing

LEARNING OBJECTIVE 3
Reconcile variable costing and absorption costing net operating incomes and explain why the two amounts differ.

---

[1] The discussions in this chapter concerning differences between absorption and variable costing net operating incomes assume that the LIFO inventory flow assumption is used.

EXHIBIT 7–4
Absorption and Variable Costing Income Statements—Emerald Isle Knitters, Ltd.

Absorption Costing

	Year 1		Year 2		Year 3		Three Years Together	
Sales		€500,000		€400,000		€600,000		€1,500,000
Cost of goods sold:								
Beginning inventory	€ 0		€ 0		€ 65,000		€ 0	
Add cost of goods manufactured (25,000 units × €13 per unit)	325,000		325,000		325,000		975,000	
Goods available for sale	325,000		325,000		390,000		975,000	
Less ending inventory (5,000 units × €13 per unit)	0		65,000		0		0	
Cost of goods sold		325,000		260,000		390,000		975,000
Gross margin		175,000		140,000		210,000		525,000
Selling and administrative expenses		115,000*		110,000*		120,000*		345,000
Net operating income		€ 60,000		€ 30,000		€ 90,000		€ 180,000

*The selling and administrative expenses are computed as follows:
Year 1: 25,000 units × €1 per unit variable + €90,000 fixed = €115,000.
Year 2: 20,000 units × €1 per unit variable + €90,000 fixed = €110,000.
Year 3: 30,000 units × €1 per unit variable + €90,000 fixed = €120,000.

Variable Costing

	Year 1		Year 2		Year 3		Three Years Together	
Sales		€500,000		€400,000		€600,000		€1,500,000
Variable expenses:								
Variable cost of goods sold:								
Beginning inventory	€ 0		€ 0		€ 35,000		€ 0	
Add variable manufacturing costs (25,000 units × €7 per unit)	175,000		175,000		175,000		525,000	
Goods available for sale	175,000		175,000		210,000		525,000	
Less ending inventory (5,000 units × €7 per unit)	0		35,000		0		0	
Variable cost of goods sold	175,000*		140,000*		210,000*		525,000*	
Variable selling and administrative expenses (€1 per unit sold)	25,000		20,000		30,000		75,000	
		200,000		160,000		240,000		600,000
Contribution margin		300,000		240,000		360,000		900,000
Fixed expenses:								
Fixed manufacturing overhead	150,000		150,000		150,000		450,000	
Fixed selling and administrative expenses	90,000		90,000		90,000		270,000	
		240,000		240,000		240,000		720,000
Net operating income		€ 60,000		€ 0		€120,000		€ 180,000

*The variable cost of goods sold could have been computed more simply as follows:
Year 1: 25,000 units sold × €7 per unit = €175,000.
Year 2: 20,000 units sold × €7 per unit = €140,000.
Year 3: 30,000 units sold × €7 per unit = €210,000.

Relation between Production and Sales for the Period	Effect on Inventories	Relation between Absorption and Variable Costing Net Operating Incomes
Production = Sales	No change in inventories	Absorption costing net operating income = Variable costing net operating income
Production > Sales	Inventories increase	Absorption costing net operating income > Variable costing net operating income*
Production < Sales	Inventories decrease	Absorption costing net operating income < Variable costing net operating income†

*Net operating income is higher under absorption costing, since fixed manufacturing overhead cost is *deferred* in inventory under absorption costing as inventories increase.
†Net operating income is lower under absorption costing, since fixed manufacturing overhead cost is *released* from inventory under absorption costing as inventories decrease.

EXHIBIT 7–5
Comparative Income Effects—Absorption and Variable Costing

overhead recognized as expense on the income statement. When everything that is produced in the year is sold, all of the fixed manufacturing overhead assigned to units of product under absorption costing becomes part of the current year's cost of goods sold. Under variable costing, the total fixed manufacturing overhead flows directly to the income statement as an expense. So under either method, when production equals sales (and hence inventories do not change), all the fixed manufacturing overhead incurred during the year flows through to the income statement as an expense. And therefore, the net operating income under the two methods is the same.

2. When production exceeds sales, the net operating income reported under absorption costing will generally be higher than the net operating income reported under variable costing (see Year 2 in Exhibit 7–4). This occurs because under absorption costing, part of the fixed manufacturing overhead cost of the current period is deferred in inventory. In Year 2, for example, €30,000 of fixed manufacturing overhead cost (5,000 units × €6 per unit) has been applied to units in ending inventory. These costs are excluded from cost of goods sold.

    Under variable costing, however, *all* of the fixed manufacturing overhead cost of Year 2 has been immediately expensed. As a result, the net operating income for Year 2 under variable costing is €30,000 *lower* than it is under absorption costing. Exhibit 7–6

	Year 1	Year 2	Year 3
Variable costing net operating income	€60,000	€ 0	€120,000
Add fixed manufacturing overhead costs deferred in inventory under absorption costing (5,000 units × €6 per unit)		30,000	
Deduct fixed manufacturing overhead costs released from inventory under absorption costing (5,000 units × €6 per unit)			(30,000)
Absorption costing net operating income	€60,000	€30,000	€ 90,000

EXHIBIT 7–6
Reconciliation of Variable Costing and Absorption Costing—Net Operating Income Data from Exhibit 7–4

contains a reconciliation of the variable costing and absorption costing net operating incomes.

3. When production is less than sales, the net operating income reported under the absorption costing approach will generally be less than the net operating income reported under the variable costing approach (see Year 3 in Exhibit 7–4). This happens with absorption costing because fixed manufacturing overhead costs that were previously deferred in the prior period's inventory are released as part of the current period's cost of goods sold. This is known as **fixed manufacturing overhead cost released from inventory.** In Year 3, for example, the €30,000 in fixed manufacturing overhead cost deferred in inventory under the absorption approach from Year 2 to Year 3 is released from inventory because these units were sold. As a result, the cost of goods sold for Year 3 contains not only all of the fixed manufacturing overhead cost for Year 3 (since all that was produced in Year 3 was sold in Year 3) but €30,000 of fixed manufacturing overhead cost from Year 2 as well.

By contrast, under variable costing only the fixed manufacturing overhead cost of Year 3 have been charged against Year 3. The result is that net operating income under variable costing is €30,000 *higher* than it is under absorption costing. Exhibit 7–6 contains a reconciliation of the variable costing and absorption costing net operating incomes for Year 3.

4. Over an *extended* period of time, the cumulative net operating incomes reported under absorption costing and variable costing will tend to be the same. The reason is that over the long run sales can't exceed production, nor can production much exceed sales. The shorter the time period, the more the net operating incomes will tend to differ.

THE HOUSE OF CARDS AT GILLETTE

Alfred M. Zeien was the successful CEO of Gillette Co. for eight years, leading the company to earnings growth rates of 15% to 20% per year. However, as his successor discovered, some of this profit growth was an illusion based on building inventories. William H. Steele, an analyst with Bank of America Securities, alleges: "There is no question Gillette was making its numbers (in part) by aggressively selling to the trade, and building inventories." Within a three-year period, Gillette's inventories of finished goods had increased by over 40% (to $1.3 billion) even though Gillette's sales had barely increased.

How can building inventories increase profits without any increase in sales? It's fairly simple. When a company produces more units than it sells fixed manufacturing overhead is deferred in ending inventory, thereby increasing profits.

Source: William C. Symonds, "The Big Trim at Gillette," *BusinessWeek*, November 8, 1999, p. 42.

Effect of Changes in Production on Net Operating Income

In the Emerald Isle Knitters example in the preceding section, production was constant and sales fluctuated over the three-year period. Since sales fluctuated, the income statements Sean MacLafferty presented in Exhibit 7–4 allowed us to see the effect of changes in sales on net operating income under both variable and absorption costing.

To further investigate the differences between variable and absorption costing, Sean next put together the hypothetical example in Exhibit 7–7. In this hypothetical example, sales are constant and production fluctuates (the opposite of Exhibits 7–3 and 7–4). The purpose of Exhibit 7–7 and the income statements shown in Exhibit 7–8 is to illustrate for Mary O'Meara the effect of changes in *production* on net operating income under both variable and absorption costing.

EXHIBIT 7–7

Basic Data to Demonstrate the Sensitivity of Costing Methods to Changes in Production

Basic Data

Selling price per unit sold		€20
Variable manufacturing cost per unit produced		€7
Fixed manufacturing overhead costs per year		€150,000
Variable selling and administrative expenses per unit sold		€1
Fixed selling and administrative expenses per year		€90,000

	Year 1	Year 2	Year 3
Units in beginning inventory	0	0	5,000
Units produced	25,000	30,000	20,000
Units sold	25,000	25,000	25,000
Units in ending inventory	0	5,000	0

Unit Product Costs	Year 1	Year 2	Year 3
Under variable costing (variable manufacturing costs only)	€ 7.00	€ 7.00	€ 7.00
Under absorption costing			
Variable manufacturing costs	€ 7.00	€ 7.00	€ 7.00
Fixed manufacturing overhead costs (€150,000 spread			
over the number of units produced in each year)	6.00	5.00	7.50
Total absorption cost per unit	€13.00	€12.00	€14.50

Variable Costing

Net operating income is *not* affected by changes in production under variable costing. Notice from Exhibit 7–8 (page 286) that net operating income is the same for all three years under variable costing, although production exceeds sales in one year and is less than sales in another year. In short, a change in production has no impact on net operating income when variable costing is used.

Absorption Costing

Net operating income *is* affected by changes in production under absorption costing. As shown in Exhibit 7–8, net operating income under absorption costing goes up in Year 2 and then goes down in Year 3. Note particularly that net operating income goes up and down between these two years *even though the same number of units is sold in each year.* The reason for this effect can be traced to fixed manufacturing overhead costs that shift between periods under absorption costing as a result of changes in inventory.

As shown in Exhibit 7–7, production exceeds sales in Year 2, resulting in an increase of 5,000 units in inventory. Each unit produced during Year 2 is assigned €5 in fixed manufacturing overhead costs (see the unit cost computations in Exhibit 7–7). Therefore, €25,000 (5,000 units × €5 per unit) of the fixed manufacturing overhead costs of Year 2 are not expensed in that year but rather are added to the inventory account (along with the variable manufacturing costs). The net operating income of Year 2 rises sharply, because these costs are deferred in inventories, even though the same number of units is sold in Year 2 as in the other years.

The reverse effect occurs in Year 3. Since sales exceed production in Year 3, that year is forced to cover all of its own fixed manufacturing overhead costs as well as the fixed manufacturing overhead costs carried forward in inventory from Year 2. A substantial drop in net operating income during Year 3 results from the release of fixed manufacturing overhead costs from inventories despite the fact that the same number of units is sold in that year as in the other years.

EXHIBIT 7-8
Absorption and Variable Costing Income Statements—Changes in Production Scenario.

Absorption Costing

	Year 1		Year 2		Year 3	
Sales (25,000 units)		€500,000		€500,000		€500,000
Cost of goods sold:						
Beginning inventory	€ 0		€ 0		€ 60,000	
Add cost of goods manufactured	325,000*		360,000*		290,000*	
Goods available for sale	325,000		360,000		350,000	
Less ending inventory	0		60,000†		0	
Cost of goods sold		325,000		300,000		350,000
Gross margin		175,000		200,000		150,000
Selling and administrative expenses (25,000 units × €1 per unit variable + €90,000 fixed)		115,000		115,000		115,000
Net operating income		€ 60,000		€ 85,000		€ 35,000

*Cost of goods manufactured:
Year 1: 25,000 units × €13.00 per unit = €325,000.
Year 2: 30,000 units × €12.00 per unit = €360,000.
Year 3: 20,000 units × €14.50 per unit = €290,000.
†Ending inventory, Year 2: 5,000 units × €12 per unit = €60,000.

Variable Costing

	Year 1		Year 2		Year 3	
Sales (25,000 units)		€500,000		€500,000		€500,000
Variable expenses:						
Variable cost of goods sold:						
Beginning inventory	€ 0		€ 0		€ 35,000	
Add variable manufacturing costs at €7 per unit produced	175,000		210,000		140,000	
Goods available for sale	175,000		210,000		175,000	
Less ending inventory	0		35,000*		0	
Variable cost of goods sold	175,000		175,000		175,000	
Variable selling and administrative expenses	25,000		25,000		25,000	
		200,000		200,000		200,000
Contribution margin		300,000		300,000		300,000
Fixed expenses:						
Fixed manufacturing overhead	150,000		150,000		150,000	
Fixed selling and administrative expenses	90,000		90,000		90,000	
		240,000		240,000		240,000
Net operating income		€ 60,000		€ 60,000		€ 60,000

*Ending inventory, Year 2: 5,000 units × €7 per unit = €35,000.

	Year 1	Year 2	Year 3
Variable costing net operating income............	€60,000	€60,000	€60,000
Add fixed manufacturing overhead costs deferred in inventory under absorption costing (5,000 units × €5 per unit)		25,000	
Deduct fixed manufacturing overhead costs released from inventory under absorption costing (5,000 units × €5 per unit)................................			(25,000)
Absorption costing net operating income..........	€60,000	€85,000	€35,000

EXHIBIT 7–9
Reconciliation of Variable Costing and Absorption Costing—Net Operating Income Data from Exhibit 7–8

The variable costing and absorption costing net operating incomes are reconciled in Exhibit 7–9. This exhibit shows that the differences in net operating income can be traced to the effects of changes in inventories on absorption costing net operating income. Under absorption costing, fixed manufacturing overhead costs are deferred in inventory when inventories increase and are released from inventory when inventories decrease.

IN BUSINESS

eBAY EASES THE PAIN OF EXCESS INVENTORY

Companies can accumulate excess inventory for numerous reasons. For example, overly optimistic sales forecasts can result in too much inventory. Or, as we have learned in this chapter, managers can inflate absorption costing net income by producing excess inventory. Regardless of the cause, eBay is coming to the rescue of companies whose warehouses are bursting at the seams. More than 71 companies, including Motorola, Dell, and IBM, are selling outdated inventory using eBay's auction services. Using eBay enables these companies to recoup 45% of the product's usual selling price compared to 15–20% using other disposal methods. eBay estimates that big company sales on its website now total $500 million a year. In fact, eBay reports that Motorola alone unloads $1 million of outdated cell phones per month.

Source: Brian Grow and Sheridan Prasso, "Excess Inventory? eBay to the Rescue," *BusinessWeek*, September 9, 2002, p. 8.

After checking all of his work, Sean discussed his results with Mary.

Sean: I have some calculations I would like to show you. These exhibits should help explain why our net operating income didn't increase this year as much as you thought it should have.

Mary: This first exhibit (i.e., Exhibit 7–4) looks like it just summarizes our income statements for the last three years.

Sean: Not exactly. There are actually two sets of income statements on this exhibit. The absorption costing income statements are the ones I originally prepared and we submitted to the bank. Below the absorption costing income statements is another set of income statements.

Mary: Those are the ones labeled variable costing.

Sean: That's right. You can see that the net operating incomes are the same for the two sets of income statements in our first year of operations, but they differ for the other two years.

Mary: I'll say! The variable costing statements indicate that we just broke even in the second year instead of earning a €30,000 profit. And the increase in net operating

MANAGERIAL ACCOUNTING IN ACTION

The Wrap-up

income between the second and third years is €120,000 instead of just €60,000. I don't know how you came up with two different net operating income figures, but the variable costing net operating income seems to be much closer to the truth. The second year was almost a disaster. We barely sold enough sweaters to cover all of our fixed costs.

Sean: You and I both know that, but the accounting rules view the situation a little differently. If we produce more than we sell, the accounting rules require that we take some of the fixed manufacturing cost and assign it to the units that end up on the balance sheet in ending inventories.

Mary: That surprises me given that I thought accountants were always supposed to err on the side of being conservative. Since when is it conservative to call an expense an asset?

Sean: While I tend to agree with you, some accountants would argue otherwise because . . .

Mary: Honestly, I am not interested in the various arguments. All I know is that we don't make any money just producing sweaters. If absorption costing lets a company boost its net operating income by making more sweaters—and not selling any of them—that makes no sense to me.

Sean: Me neither.

Mary: Well, if our bank wants us to use absorption costing, then that is what we'll continue to do for it. However, is there any reason why we can't use the variable costing method inside the company? The statements are easier for me to understand, and the net operating income figures make more sense to me.

Sean: I don't see why we can't do both. Making the adjustment from one method to the other is very simple.

Mary: Good. Let's make the switch.

Choosing a Costing Method

LEARNING OBJECTIVE 4
Understand the advantages and disadvantages of both variable and absorption costing.

The Impact on the Manager

Like Mary O'Meara, opponents of absorption costing argue that shifting fixed manufacturing overhead cost between periods can be confusing and can lead to misinterpretations and even to faulty decisions. Look again at the data in Exhibit 7–8; a manager might wonder why net operating income went up substantially in Year 2 under absorption costing when sales remained the same as in the prior year. Was it a result of lower selling costs, more efficient operations, or was some other factor involved? One cannot say by simply looking at the absorption costing income statement. Then in Year 3, net operating income drops sharply, even though the same number of units is sold as in the other two years. Why would income rise in one year and then drop in the next? The figures seem erratic and contradictory and can lead to confusion and a loss of confidence in the integrity of the financial data.

By contrast, the variable costing income statements in Exhibit 7–8 are clear and easy to understand. Sales remain constant over the three-year period covered in the exhibit, so both contribution margin and net operating income also remain constant. The statements are consistent with what managers would expect to see under the circumstances, so they tend to generate confidence rather than confusion.

To avoid mistakes when absorption costing is used, readers of financial statements should be alert to changes in inventory levels. Under absorption costing, if inventories increase, fixed manufacturing overhead costs are deferred in inventories, which in turn increases net operating income. If inventories decrease, fixed manufacturing overhead costs are released from inventories, which in turn decreases net operating income. Thus, when absorption costing is used, fluctuations in net operating income can be due to changes in inventories rather than to changes in sales.

THE PERVERSE EFFECTS OF ABSORPTION COSTING AT NISSAN

Jed Connelly, the top American executive at Nissan North America, admits: "We had a lot of excess production that we had to force on the market." Nissan liked to run its factories at capacity, regardless of how well the cars were selling, because under its bookkeeping rules (presumably absorption costing), the factories would then generate a profit. As a consequence, Nissan dealers had to slash prices and offer big rebates to sell their cars. According to *Fortune* magazine, "Years of discounting and distress sales seriously undercut the value of the Nissan brand. While Toyota stood for quality, customers came to Nissan to get a better deal."

Source: Alex Taylor III, "The Man Who Wants to Change Japan Inc.," *Fortune*, December 20, 1999, pp. 189–198.

CVP Analysis and Absorption Costing

Absorption costing is widely used for both internal and external reports. Many companies use the absorption approach exclusively because of its focus on *full* costing of units of product. A weakness of the method, however, is its inability to work well with CVP analysis.

To illustrate, refer again to Exhibit 7–3. Let us compute the break-even point for Emerald Isle Knitters. To obtain the break-even point, we divide total fixed costs by the contribution margin per unit:

Selling price per unit	€	20
Variable costs per unit (manufacturing and selling)		8
Contribution margin per unit	€	12
Fixed manufacturing overhead costs	€150,000	
Fixed selling and administrative costs	90,000	
Total fixed costs	€240,000	

$$\frac{\text{Break-even point}}{\text{in unit sales}} = \frac{\text{Total fixed expenses}}{\text{Contribution margin per unit}} = \frac{€240{,}000}{€12 \text{ per unit}} = 20{,}000 \text{ units}$$

The break-even point is 20,000 units. Notice from Exhibit 7–3 that in Year 2 the company sold exactly 20,000 units, the break-even volume. Under the contribution approach, using variable costing, the company does break even in Year 2, showing zero net operating income. *Under absorption costing, however, the company shows a positive net operating income of €30,000 for Year 2* (see Exhibit 7–4). How can this be? How can absorption costing produce a positive net operating income when the company sold exactly the break-even volume of units?

The answer lies in the fact that €30,000 in fixed manufacturing overhead costs were deferred in inventory during Year 2 under absorption costing and therefore did not appear as expenses. By deferring these fixed manufacturing overhead costs in inventory, the income statement shows a profit even though the company sold exactly the break-even volume of units. Absorption costing runs into similar kinds of difficulty in other areas of CVP analysis, which assumes that variable costing is being used.

Decision Making

Under absorption costing, fixed manufacturing overhead costs appear to be variable with respect to the number of units sold, but they are not. For example, in Exhibit 7–3, the absorption unit product cost is €13, but the variable portion of this cost is only €7. Since the product costs are stated on a per unit basis, managers may mistakenly believe that if another unit is produced, it will cost the company €13.

The misperception that absorption unit product costs are variable can lead to many problems, including inappropriate pricing decisions and decisions to drop products that are in fact profitable. These problems with absorption costing product costs will be discussed more fully in later chapters.

External Reporting and Income Taxes

Practically speaking, absorption costing is required for external reports in the United States. A company that attempts to use variable costing on its external financial reports runs the risk that its auditors may not accept the financial statements as conforming to generally accepted accounting principles (GAAP).[2] Tax law on this issue is clear-cut. Under the Tax Reform Act of 1986, a form of absorption costing must be used when filling out income tax forms.

Even if a company must use absorption costing for its external reports, a manager can, as Mary O'Meara suggests, use variable costing income statements for internal reports. No particular accounting problems are created by using *both* costing methods—the variable costing method for internal reports and the absorption costing method for external reports. As we demonstrated earlier in Exhibits 7–6 and 7–9, the adjustment from variable costing net operating income to absorption costing net operating income is a simple one that can be easily made at the end of the accounting period.

Top executives are typically evaluated based on the earnings reported to shareholders on the company's external financial reports. This creates a problem for top executives who might otherwise favor using variable costing for internal reports. They may feel that since they are evaluated based on absorption costing reports, decisions should also be based on absorption costing data.

IN BUSINESS

ABSORPTION COSTING AROUND THE WORLD

Absorption costing is the norm for external financial reports around the world. After the fall of communism, accounting methods were changed in Russia to bring them into closer agreement with accounting methods used in the West. One result was the adoption of absorption costing.

Source: Adolf J. H. Enthoven, "Russia's Accounting Moves West," *Strategic Finance*, July 1999, pp. 32–37.

---

[2] The situation is actually slightly ambiguous concerning whether absorption costing is strictly required. Official pronouncements do not actually prohibit variable costing. And some companies expense significant elements of their fixed manufacturing costs on their external reports. Nevertheless, the reality is that most accountants believe that absorption costing is required for external reporting and a manager who argues otherwise is likely to be unsuccessful.

Advantages of Variable Costing and the Contribution Approach

As stated earlier, even if the absorption approach is used for external reporting purposes, variable costing, together with the contribution format income statement, is an appealing alternative for internal reports. The advantages of variable costing can be summarized as follows:

1. Data required for CVP analysis can be taken directly from a contribution format income statement. These data are not available on a conventional absorption costing income statement.
2. Under variable costing, the profit for a period is not affected by changes in inventories. Other things remaining the same (i.e., selling prices, costs, sales mix, etc.), profits move in the same direction as sales when variable costing is used.
3. Managers often assume that unit product costs are variable costs. This is a problem under absorption costing, since unit product costs are a combination of both fixed and variable costs. Under variable costing, unit product costs do not contain fixed costs.
4. The impact of fixed costs on profits is emphasized under the variable costing and contribution approach. The total amount of fixed costs appears explicitly on the income statement, highlighting that the whole amount of fixed costs must be covered for the company to be truly profitable. In contrast, under absorption costing, the fixed costs are mingled together with the variable costs and are buried in cost of goods sold and ending inventories.
5. Variable costing data make it easier to estimate the profitability of products, customers, and other business segments. With absorption costing, profitability is obscured by arbitrary fixed cost allocations. These issues will be discussed in later chapters.
6. Variable costing ties in with cost control methods such as standard costs and flexible budgets, which will be covered in later chapters.
7. Variable costing net operating income is closer to net cash flow than absorption costing net operating income. This is particularly important for companies with potential cash flow problems.

With all of these advantages, one might wonder why absorption costing continues to be used almost exclusively for external reporting and why it is the predominant choice for internal reports as well. This is partly due to tradition, but absorption costing is also attractive to many accountants and managers because they believe it better matches costs with revenues. Advocates of absorption costing argue that *all* manufacturing costs must be assigned to products in order to properly match the costs of producing units of product with their revenues when they are sold. The fixed costs of depreciation, taxes, insurance, supervisory salaries, and so on, are just as essential to manufacturing products as are the variable costs.

Advocates of variable costing argue that fixed manufacturing costs are not really the costs of any particular unit of product. These costs are incurred to have the *capacity* to make products during a particular period and will be incurred even if nothing is made during the period. Moreover, whether a unit is made or not, the fixed manufacturing costs will be exactly the same. Therefore, variable costing advocates argue that fixed manufacturing costs are not part of the costs of producing a particular unit of product and thus the matching principle dictates that fixed manufacturing costs should be charged to the current period.

At any rate, absorption costing is the generally accepted method for preparing mandatory external financial reports and income tax returns. Probably because of the cost and possible confusion of maintaining two separate costing systems—one for external reporting and one for internal reporting—most companies use absorption costing for both external and internal reports.

Variable Costing and the Theory of Constraints

The Theory of Constraints (TOC), which was introduced in Chapter 1, suggests that the key to improving a company's profits is managing its constraints. For reasons that will be discussed in Chapter 13, this requires careful identification of each product's variable costs.

Consequently, companies involved in TOC use a form of variable costing. One difference is that the TOC approach generally considers direct labor to be a fixed cost. As discussed in earlier chapters, in many companies direct labor is not really a variable cost. Even though direct labor workers may be paid on an hourly basis, many companies have a commitment—sometimes enforced in labor contracts or by law—to guarantee workers a minimum number of paid hours. In TOC companies, there are two additional reasons to consider direct labor a fixed cost.

First, direct labor is not usually the constraint. In the simplest cases, the constraint is a machine. In more complex cases, the constraint is a policy (such as a poorly designed compensation scheme for salespersons) that prevents the company from using its resources more effectively. If direct labor is not the constraint, there is no reason to increase it. Hiring more direct labor would increase costs without increasing the output of salable products and services.

Second, TOC emphasizes continuous improvement to maintain competitiveness. Without committed and enthusiastic employees, sustained continuous improvement is virtually impossible. Since layoffs often have devastating effects on employee morale, managers involved in TOC are extremely reluctant to lay off employees.

For these reasons, most managers in TOC companies regard direct labor as a committed fixed cost rather than a variable cost. Hence, in the modified form of variable costing used in TOC companies, direct labor is not usually classified as a product cost.

Impact of Lean Production

As discussed in this chapter, variable and absorption costing will produce different net operating incomes whenever the number of units produced is different from the number of units sold—in other words, whenever there is a change in the number of units in inventory. We have also learned that absorption costing net operating income can be erratic, sometimes moving in a direction that is opposite from the movement in sales.

When companies use Lean Production methods, these problems are reduced. The erratic movement of net operating income under absorption costing and the difference in net operating income between absorption and variable costing occur because of changes in the number of units in inventory. Under Lean Production, goods are produced to customers' orders and the goal is to eliminate finished goods inventories entirely and reduce work in process inventory to almost nothing. If there is very little inventory, then changes in inventories will be very small and both variable and absorption costing will show basically the same net operating income. With very little inventory, absorption costing net operating income usually moves in the same direction as movements in sales.

Of course, the cost of a unit of product will still be different between variable and absorption costing, as explained earlier in the chapter. But when Lean Production is used, the differences in net operating income will largely disappear.

Summary

Variable and absorption costing are alternative methods of determining unit product costs. Under variable costing, only those manufacturing costs that vary with output are treated as product costs. This includes direct materials, variable overhead, and ordinarily direct labor. Fixed manufacturing overhead is treated as a period cost and it is expensed on the income statement as incurred. By contrast, absorption costing treats fixed manufacturing overhead as a product cost, along with direct materials, direct labor, and variable overhead. Under both costing methods, selling and administrative expenses are treated as period costs and they are expensed on the income statement as incurred.

Since absorption costing treats fixed manufacturing overhead as a product cost, a portion of fixed manufacturing overhead is assigned to each unit as it is produced. If units of product are unsold at the end of a period, then the fixed manufacturing overhead cost attached to those units is carried with them into the inventory account and deferred to a future period. When these units are later sold, the fixed manufacturing overhead cost attached to them is released from the inventory account and charged against income as part of cost of goods sold. Thus, under absorption costing, it is possible to defer a portion of the fixed manufacturing overhead cost from one period to a future period through the inventory account.

Unfortunately, this shifting of fixed manufacturing overhead cost between periods can cause erratic fluctuations in net operating income and can result in confusion and unwise decisions. To guard against mistakes when they interpret income statement data, managers should be alert to changes in inventory levels or unit product costs during the period.

Practically speaking, variable costing can't be used externally for either financial or tax reporting. However, it may be used internally by managers for planning and control purposes. The variable costing approach works well with CVP analysis.

Review Problem: Contrasting Variable and Absorption Costing

Dexter Corporation produces and sells a single product, a wooden hand loom for weaving small items such as scarves. Selected cost and operating data relating to the product for two years are given below:

Selling price per unit	$50
Manufacturing costs:	
Variable per unit produced:	
Direct materials.	$11
Direct labor	$6
Variable overhead	$3
Fixed per year.	$120,000
Selling and administrative costs:	
Variable per unit sold	$4
Fixed per year.	$70,000

	Year 1	Year 2
Units in beginning inventory	0	2,000
Units produced during the year.	10,000	6,000
Units sold during the year	8,000	8,000
Units in ending inventory.	2,000	0

Required:
1. Assume the company uses absorption costing.
   a. Compute the unit product cost in each year.
   b. Prepare an income statement for each year.
2. Assume the company uses variable costing.
   a. Compute the unit product cost in each year.
   b. Prepare an income statement for each year.
3. Reconcile the variable costing and absorption costing net operating incomes.

Solution to Review Problem
1. *a.* Under absorption costing, all manufacturing costs, variable and fixed, are included in unit product costs:

	Year 1	Year 2
Direct materials.	$11	$11
Direct labor	6	6
Variable manufacturing overhead	3	3
Fixed manufacturing overhead		
($120,000 ÷ 10,000 units)	12	
($120,000 ÷ 6,000 units)		20
Unit product cost.	$32	$40

b. The absorption costing income statements follow:

	Year 1		Year 2	
Sales (8,000 units × $50 per unit)............		$400,000		$400,000
Cost of goods sold:				
Beginning inventory.....................	$0		$ 64,000	
Add cost of goods manufactured				
(10,000 units × $32 per unit;				
6,000 units × $40 per unit).............	320,000		240,000	
Goods available for sale	320,000		304,000	
Less ending inventory				
(2,000 units × $32 per				
unit; 0 units × $40 per unit)	64,000	256,000	0	304,000
Gross margin		144,000		96,000
Selling and administrative				
expenses (8,000 units × $4 per				
unit + $70,000)		102,000		102,000
Net operating income		$ 42,000		$ (6,000)

2. a. Under variable costing, only the variable manufacturing costs are included in unit product costs:

	Year 1	Year 2
Direct materials.........................	$11	$11
Direct labor	6	6
Variable manufacturing overhead	3	3
Unit product cost	$20	$20

b. The variable costing income statements follow. Notice that the variable cost of goods sold is computed in a simpler, more direct manner than in the examples provided earlier. On a variable costing income statement, this simple approach or the more complex approach illustrated earlier is acceptable for computing the cost of goods sold.

	Year 1		Year 2	
Sales (8,000 units × $50 per unit)............		$400,000		$400,000
Variable expenses:				
Variable cost of goods sold				
(8,000 units × $20 per unit)	$160,000		$160,000	
Variable selling and administrative				
expenses (8,000 units ×				
$4 per unit)	32,000	192,000	32,000	192,000
Contribution margin		208,000		208,000
Fixed expenses:				
Fixed manufacturing overhead	120,000		120,000	
Fixed selling and administrative				
expenses.........................	70,000	190,000	70,000	190,000
Net operating income		$ 18,000		$ 18,000

3. The reconciliation of the variable and absorption costing net operating incomes follows:

	Year 1	Year 2
Variable costing net operating income	$18,000	$18,000
Add fixed manufacturing overhead costs deferred in inventory under absorption costing (2,000 units × $12 per unit)	24,000	
Deduct fixed manufacturing overhead costs released from inventory under absorption costing (2,000 units × $12 per unit)		(24,000)
Absorption costing net operating income	$42,000	$(6,000)

Glossary

Absorption costing A costing method that includes all manufacturing costs—direct materials, direct labor, and both variable and fixed manufacturing overhead—in unit product costs. (p. 276)

Fixed manufacturing overhead cost deferred in inventory The portion of the fixed manufacturing overhead cost of a period that goes into ending inventory under the absorption costing method. (p. 279)

Fixed manufacturing overhead cost released from inventory The fixed manufacturing overhead cost of a *prior* period that becomes an expense of the current period under the absorption costing method. (p. 284)

Variable costing A costing method that includes only variable manufacturing costs—direct materials, direct labor, and variable manufacturing overhead—in unit product costs. (p. 276)

Questions

7-1 What is the basic difference between absorption costing and variable costing?

7-2 Are selling and administrative expenses treated as product costs or as period costs under variable costing?

7-3 Explain how fixed manufacturing overhead costs are shifted from one period to another under absorption costing.

7-4 What arguments can be advanced in favor of treating fixed manufacturing overhead costs as product costs?

7-5 What arguments can be advanced in favor of treating fixed manufacturing overhead costs as period costs?

7-6 If production and sales are equal, which method would you expect to show the higher net operating income, variable costing or absorption costing? Why?

7-7 If production exceeds sales, which method would you expect to show the higher net operating income, variable costing or absorption costing? Why?

7-8 If fixed manufacturing overhead costs are released from inventory under absorption costing, what does this tell you about the level of production in relation to the level of sales?

7-9 Parker Company had $5,000,000 in sales and reported a $300,000 loss in its annual report to stockholders. According to a CVP analysis prepared for management's use, $5,000,000 in sales is the break-even point for the company. Did the company's inventory level increase, decrease, or remain unchanged? Explain.

7-10 Under absorption costing, how is it possible to increase net operating income without increasing sales?

7-11 How is the use of variable costing limited?

7-12 How does Lean Production reduce or eliminate the difference in reported net operating income between absorption and variable costing?

Exercises

EXERCISE 7-1 Variable and Absorption Costing Unit Product Costs [LO1]

Ida Sidha Karya Company is a family-owned company located in the village of Gianyar on the island of Bali in Indonesia. The company produces a handcrafted Balinese musical instrument called a gamelan that is similar to a xylophone. The sounding bars are cast from brass and hand-filed to attain just the right sound. The bars are then mounted on an intricately hand-carved wooden base. The gamelans are sold for 850 (thousand) rupiahs. (The currency in Indonesia is the rupiah, which is denoted by Rp.) Selected data for the company's operations last year follow (all currency values are in thousands of rupiahs):

Units in beginning inventory.	0
Units produced.	250
Units sold.	225
Units in ending inventory	25
Variable costs per unit:	
Direct materials	Rp100
Direct labor.	Rp320
Variable manufacturing overhead.	Rp40
Variable selling and administrative.	Rp20
Fixed costs:	
Fixed manufacturing overhead.	Rp60,000
Fixed selling and administrative.	Rp20,000

Required:
1. Assume that the company uses absorption costing. Compute the unit product cost for one gamelan.
2. Assume that the company uses variable costing. Compute the unit product cost for one gamelan.

EXERCISE 7-2 Variable Costing Income Statement; Explanation of Difference in Net Operating Income [LO2]

Refer to the data in Exercise 7-1 for Ida Sidha Karya Company. An absorption costing income statement prepared by the company's accountant appears below (all currency values are in thousands of rupiahs):

Sales (225 units × Rp8500 per unit)		Rp191,250
Less cost of goods sold:		
Beginning inventory.	Rp 0	
Add cost of goods manufactured		
(250 units × Rp __?__ per unit).	175,000	
Goods available for sale	175,000	
Less ending inventory		
(25 units × R __?__ per unit).	17,500	157,500
Gross margin.		33,750
Less selling and administrative expenses:		
Variable selling and administrative	4,500	
Fixed selling and administrative.	20,000	24,500
Net operating income		Rp 9,250

Required:
1. Determine how much of the ending inventory of Rp17,500 consists of fixed manufacturing overhead cost deferred in inventory to the next period.
2. Prepare an income statement for the year using the variable costing method. Explain the difference in net operating income between the two costing methods.

EXERCISE 7-3 Reconciliation of Absorption and Variable Costing Net Operating Incomes [LO3]

Jorgansen Lighting, Inc., manufactures heavy-duty street lighting systems for municipalities. The company uses variable costing for internal management reports and absorption costing for external reports to shareholders, creditors, and the government. The company has provided the following data:

	Year 1	Year 2	Year 3
Inventories:			
Beginning (units)	200	170	180
Ending (units).........................	170	180	220
Variable costing net operating income........	$1,080,400	$1,032,400	$996,400

The company's fixed manufacturing overhead per unit was constant at $560 for all three years.

Required:

1. Determine each year's absorption costing net operating income. Present your answer in the form of a reconciliation report such as the one shown in Exhibit 7–6.
2. In Year 4, the company's variable costing net operating income was $984,400 and its absorption costing net operating income was $1,012,400. Did inventories increase or decrease during Year 4? How much fixed manufacturing overhead cost was deferred or released from inventory during Year 4?

EXERCISE 7-4 Evaluating Absorption and Variable Costing as Alternative Costing Methods [LO4]

The questions below pertain to two different scenarios involving a manufacturing company. In each scenario, the cost structure of the company is constant from year to year. Selling prices, unit variable costs, and total fixed costs are the same every year. However, unit sales and/or unit production levels may vary from year to year.

Required:

1. Consider the following data for scenario A:

	Year 1	Year 2	Year 3	Year 4
Variable costing net operating income	$510,600	$510,600	$510,600	$510,600
Absorption costing net operating income	$577,290	$636,518	$471,082	$361,500

   a. Were unit sales constant from year to year? Explain.
   b. What was the relation between unit sales and unit production levels in each year? For each year, indicate whether inventories grew or shrank.

2. Consider the following data for scenario B:

	Year 1	Year 2	Year 3	Year 4
Variable costing net operating income..........	$770,600	$640,600	$380,600	$510,600
Absorption costing net operating income........	$603,745	$603,745	$603,745	$603,745

   a. Were unit sales constant from year to year? Explain.
   b. What was the relation between unit sales and unit production levels in each year? For each year, indicate whether inventories grew or shrank.

3. Given the patterns of net operating income in scenarios A and B above, which costing method, variable costing or absorption costing, do you believe provides a better reflection of economic reality? Explain.

EXERCISE 7-5 Variable Costing Unit Product Cost and Income Statement; Break-Even [LO1, LO2]

Chuck Wagon Grills, Inc., makes a single product—a handmade specialty barbecue grill that it sells for $210. Data for last year's operations follow:

Units in beginning inventory.	0
Units produced.	20,000
Units sold	19,000
Units in ending inventory	1,000

Variable costs per unit:		
Direct materials	$	50
Direct labor.		80
Variable manufacturing overhead.		20
Variable selling and administrative		10
Total variable cost per unit	$	160

Fixed costs:	
Fixed manufacturing overhead.	$700,000
Fixed selling and administrative	285,000
Total fixed costs	$985,000

Required:

1. Assume that the company uses variable costing. Compute the unit product cost for one barbecue grill.
2. Assume that the company uses variable costing. Prepare an income statement for the year using the contribution format.
3. What is the company's break-even point in terms of the number of barbecue grills sold?

EXERCISE 7-6 Absorption Costing Unit Product Cost and Income Statement [LO1, LO2]

Refer to the data in Exercise 7-5 for Chuck Wagon Grills. Assume in this exercise that the company uses absorption costing.

Required:

1. Compute the unit product cost for one computer desk.
2. Prepare an income statement for the year.

EXERCISE 7-7 Variable and Absorption Costing Unit Product Costs and Income Statements [LO1, LO2]

Lynch Company manufactures and sells a single product. The following costs were incurred during the company's first year of operations:

Variable costs per unit:	
Manufacturing:	
Direct materials.	$6
Direct labor	$9
Variable manufacturing overhead	$3
Variable selling and administrative	$4

Fixed costs per year:	
Fixed manufacturing overhead.	$300,000
Fixed selling and administrative expenses	$190,000

During the year, the company produced 25,000 units and sold 20,000 units. The selling price of the company's product is $50 per unit.

Required:

1. Assume that the company uses the absorption costing method:
   a. Compute the unit product cost.
   b. Prepare an income statement for the year.
2. Assume that the company uses the variable costing method:
   a. Compute the unit product cost.
   b. Prepare an income statement for the year.

EXERCISE 7-8 Inferring Costing Method; Unit Product Cost [LO1, LO4]

Sierra Company incurs the following costs to produce and sell a single product.

Variable costs per unit:	
Direct materials	$9
Direct labor.....................................	$10
Manufacturing overhead.......................	$5
Selling and administrative expenses	$3
Fixed costs per year:	
Fixed manufacturing overhead..................	$150,000
Fixed selling and administrative expenses........	$400,000

During the last year, 25,000 units were produced and 22,000 units were sold. The Finished Goods inventory account at the end of the year shows a balance of $72,000 for the 3,000 unsold units.

Required:

1. Is the company using absorption costing or variable costing to cost units in the Finished Goods inventory account? Show computations to support your answer.
2. Assume that the company wishes to prepare financial statements for the year to issue to its stockholders.
   a. Is the $72,000 figure for Finished Goods inventory the correct amount to use on these statements for external reporting purposes? Explain.
   b. At what dollar amount *should* the 3,000 units be carried in the inventory for external reporting purposes?

EXERCISE 7-9 Variable Costing Income Statement; Reconciliation [LO2, LO3]

Whitman Company has just completed its first year of operations. The company's accountant has prepared an absorption costing income statement for the year:

Whitman Company Income Statement		
Sales (35,000 units at $25 per unit).....................		$875,000
Cost of goods sold:		
Beginning inventory...........................	$ 0	
Add cost of goods manufactured (40,000 units at $16 per unit)	640,000	
Goods available for sale.........................	640,000	
Less ending inventory (5,000 units at $16 per unit)	80,000	560,000
Gross margin		315,000
Selling and administrative expenses		280,000
Net operating income		$ 35,000

The company's selling and administrative expenses consist of $210,000 per year in fixed expenses and $2 per unit sold in variable expenses. The $16 per unit product cost given above is computed as follows:

Direct materials..	$ 5
Direct labor	6
Variable manufacturing overhead	1
Fixed manufacturing overhead ($160,000 ÷ 40,000 units)........	4
Unit product cost.....................................	$16

Required:

1. Redo the company's income statement in the contribution format using variable costing.
2. Reconcile any difference between the net operating income on your variable costing income statement and the net operating income on the absorption costing income statement above.

Problems

PROBLEM 7-10 Variable Costing Income Statement; Reconciliation [LO2, LO3]
During Heaton Company's first two years of operations, the company reported absorption costing net operating income as follows:

	Year 1	Year 2
Sales (@ $25 per unit)	$1,000,000	$1,250,000
Less cost of goods sold:		
Beginning inventory.	0	90,000
Add cost of goods manufactured (@ $18 per unit).	810,000	810,000
Goods available for sale	810,000	900,000
Less ending inventory (@ $18 per unit).	90,000	0
Cost of goods sold	720,000	900,000
Gross margin	280,000	350,000
Less selling and administrative expenses*	210,000	230,000
Net operating income	$ 70,000	$ 120,000

*$2 per unit variable; $130,000 fixed each year.

The company's $18 unit product cost is computed as follows:

Direct materials	$ 4
Direct labor.	7
Variable manufacturing overhead	1
Fixed manufacturing overhead ($270,000 ÷ 45,000 units).	6
Unit product cost	$18

Production and cost data for the two years are:

	Year 1	Year 2
Units produced.	45,000	45,000
Units sold	40,000	50,000

Required:
1. Prepare a variable costing income statement for each year.
2. Reconcile the absorption costing and the variable costing net operating income figures for each year.

PROBLEM 7-11 Variable and Absorption Costing Unit Product Costs and Income Statements; Explanation of Difference in Net Operating Income [LO1, LO2, LO3]
High Country, Inc., produces and sells many recreational products. The company has just opened a new plant to produce a folding camp cot that will be marketed throughout the United States. The following cost and revenue data relate to May, the first month of the plant's operation:

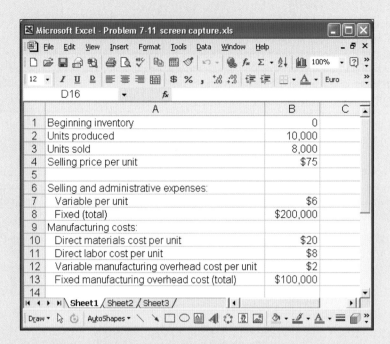

Management is anxious to see how profitable the new camp cot will be and has asked that an income statement be prepared for May.

Required:
1. Assume that the company uses absorption costing.
   a. Determine the unit product cost.
   b. Prepare an income statement for May.
2. Assume that the company uses the contribution approach with variable costing.
   a. Determine the unit product cost.
   b. Prepare an income statement for May.
3. Explain the reason for any difference in the ending inventory balance under the two costing methods and the impact of this difference on reported net operating income.

PROBLEM 7-12 Comprehensive Problem with Labor Fixed [LO1, LO2, LO3, LO4]
Far North Telecom, Ltd., of Ontario, has organized a new division to manufacture and sell specialty cellular telephones. The division's monthly costs are shown below:

 e**X**cel

Manufacturing costs:	
Variable costs per unit:	
Direct materials	$48
Variable manufacturing overhead	$2
Fixed manufacturing overhead costs (total)	$360,000
Selling and administrative costs:	
Variable	12% of sales
Fixed (total)	$470,000

Far North Telecom regards all of its workers as full-time employees and the company has a long-standing no layoff policy. Furthermore, production is highly automated. Accordingly, the company includes its labor costs in its fixed manufacturing overhead. The cellular phones sell for $150 each. During September, the first month of operations, the following activity was recorded:

Units produced.......	12,000
Units sold	10,000

Required:
1. Compute the unit product cost under:
   a. Absorption costing.
   b. Variable costing.

2. Prepare an income statement for September using absorption costing.
3. Prepare an income statement for September using variable costing.
4. Assume that the company must obtain additional financing in order to continue operations. As a member of top management, would you prefer to rely on the statement in (2) above or in (3) above when meeting with a group of prospective investors?
5. Reconcile the absorption costing and variable costing net operating income figures in (2) and (3) above.

PROBLEM 7-13 Absorption and Variable Costing; Production Constant, Sales Fluctuate [LO1, LO2, LO3, LO4]

Tami Tyler opened Tami's Creations, Inc., a small manufacturing company, at the beginning of the year. Getting the company through its first quarter of operations placed a considerable strain on Ms. Tyler's personal finances. The following income statement for the first quarter was prepared by a friend who has just completed a course in managerial accounting at State University.

Tami's Creations, Inc. Income Statement For the Quarter Ended March 31		
Sales (28,000 units)		$1,120,000
Less variable expenses:		
Variable cost of goods sold*	$462,000	
Variable selling and administrative	168,000	630,000
Contribution margin		490,000
Less fixed expenses:		
Fixed manufacturing overhead	300,000	
Fixed selling and administrative	200,000	500,000
Net operating loss.		$ (10,000)

*Consists of direct materials, direct labor, and variable manufacturing overhead.

Ms. Tyler is discouraged over the loss shown for the quarter, particularly since she had planned to use the statement as support for a bank loan. Another friend, a CPA, insists that the company should be using absorption costing rather than variable costing, and argues that if absorption costing had been used the company would probably have reported at least some profit for the quarter.

At this point, Ms. Tyler is manufacturing only one product, a swimsuit. Production and cost data relating to the swimsuit for the first quarter follow:

Units produced.	30,000
Units sold	28,000
Variable costs per unit:	
Direct materials.	$3.50
Direct labor	$12.00
Variable manufacturing overhead	$1.00
Variable selling and administrative expenses	$6.00

Required:

1. Complete the following:
   a. Compute the unit product cost under absorption costing.
   b. Redo the company's income statement for the quarter using absorption costing.
   c. Reconcile the variable and absorption costing net operating income (loss) figures.
2. Was the CPA correct in suggesting that the company really earned a "profit" for the quarter? Explain.
3. During the second quarter of operations, the company again produced 30,000 units but sold 32,000 units. (Assume no change in total fixed costs.)
   a. Prepare an income statement for the quarter using variable costing.
   b. Prepare an income statement for the quarter using absorption costing.
   c. Reconcile the variable costing and absorption costing net operating income figures.

PROBLEM 7-14 Prepare and Reconcile Variable Costing Statements [LO1, LO2, LO3, LO4]

Denton Company manufactures and sells a single product. Cost data for the product are given below:

Variable costs per unit:		
Direct materials....................	$	7
Direct labor		10
Variable manufacturing overhead		5
Variable selling and administrative		3
Total variable costs per unit.............	$	25
Fixed costs per month:		
Fixed manufacturing overhead	$315,000	
Fixed selling and administrative	245,000	
Total fixed cost per month	$560,000	

The product sells for $60 per unit. Production and sales data for July and August, the first two months of operations, follow:

	Units Produced	Units Sold
July	17,500	15,000
August	17,500	20,000

The company's Accounting Department has prepared absorption costing income statements for July and August as presented below:

	July	August
Sales	$900,000	$1,200,000
Less cost of goods sold:		
Beginning inventory	0	100,000
Add cost of goods manufactured	700,000	700,000
Goods available for sale	700,000	800,000
Less ending inventory.....................	100,000	0
Cost of goods sold	600,000	800,000
Gross margin	300,000	400,000
Less selling and administrative expenses........	290,000	305,000
Net operating income.....................	$ 10,000	$ 95,000

Required:

1. Determine the unit product cost under:
   a. Absorption costing.
   b. Variable costing.
2. Prepare variable costing income statements for July and August using the contribution approach.
3. Reconcile the variable costing and absorption costing net operating income figures.
4. The company's Accounting Department has determined the company's break-even point to be 16,000 units per month, computed as follows:

$$\frac{\text{Fixed cost per month, \$560,000}}{\text{Unit contribution margin, \$35 per unit}} = 16,000 \text{ units}$$

"I'm confused," said the president. "The accounting people say that our break-even point is 16,000 units per month, but we sold only 15,000 units in July, and the income statement they prepared shows a $10,000 profit for that month. Either the income statement is wrong or the break-even point is wrong." Prepare a brief memo for the president, explaining what happened on the July income statement.

PROBLEM 7-15 Incentives Created by Absorption Costing; Ethics and the Manager [LO2, LO4]
Carlos Cavalas, the manager of Echo Products' Brazilian Division, is trying to decide what production schedule to set for the last quarter of the year. The Brazilian Division had planned to sell 3,600 units during the year, but by September 30 only the following activity had been reported:

	Units
Inventory, January 1	0
Production	2,400
Sales	2,000
Inventory, September 30	400

The division can rent warehouse space to store up to 1,000 units. The minimum inventory level that the division should carry is 50 units. Mr. Cavalas is aware that production must be at least 200 units per quarter in order to retain a nucleus of key employees. Maximum production capacity is 1,500 units per quarter.

Demand has been soft, and the sales forecast for the last quarter is only 600 units. Due to the nature of the division's operations, fixed manufacturing overhead is a major element of product cost.

Required:
1. Assume that the division is using variable costing. How many units should be scheduled for production during the last quarter of the year? (The basic formula for computing the required production for a period in a company is: Expected sales + Desired ending inventory − Beginning inventory = Required production.) Show computations and explain your answer. Will the number of units scheduled for production affect the division's reported income or loss for the year? Explain.
2. Assume that the division is using absorption costing and that the divisional manager is given an annual bonus based on divisional operating income. If Mr. Cavalas wants to maximize his division's operating income for the year, how many units should be scheduled for production during the last quarter? [See the formula in (1) above.] Explain.
3. Identify the ethical issues involved in the decision Mr. Cavalas must make about the level of production for the last quarter of the year.

PROBLEM 7-16 Variable Costing Income Statements; Sales Constant, Production Varies; JIT Impact
[LO1, LO2, LO3, LO4]
"This makes no sense at all," said Bill Sharp, president of Essex Company. "We sold the same number of units this year as we did last year, yet our profits have more than doubled. Who made the goof—the computer or the people who operate it?" The statements to which Mr. Sharp was referring are shown below (absorption costing basis):

	Year 1	Year 2
Sales (20,000 units each year)	$700,000	$700,000
Less cost of goods sold	460,000	400,000
Gross margin	240,000	300,000
Less selling and administrative expenses	200,000	200,000
Net operating income	$ 40,000	$100,000

The statements above show the results of the first two years of operation. In the first year, the company produced and sold 20,000 units; in the second year, the company again sold 20,000 units, but it increased production as shown below:

	Year 1	Year 2
Production in units	20,000	25,000
Sales in units	20,000	20,000
Variable manufacturing cost per unit produced	$8	$8
Variable selling and administrative expense per unit sold	$1	$1
Fixed manufacturing overhead costs (total)	$300,000	$300,000

Essex Company applies fixed manufacturing overhead costs to its only product on the basis of *each year's production.* (Thus, a new fixed manufacturing overhead rate is computed each year, as in Exhibit 7–7.)

Required:

1. Compute the unit product cost for each year under:
   a. Absorption costing.
   b. Variable costing.
2. Prepare a variable costing income statement for each year, using the contribution approach.
3. Reconcile the variable costing and absorption costing net operating income figures for each year.
4. Explain to the president why, under absorption costing, the net operating income for Year 2 was higher than the net operating income for Year 1, although the same number of units was sold in each year.
5. a. Explain how operations would have differed in Year 2 if the company had been using JIT inventory methods.
   b. If JIT had been in use during Year 2, what would the company's net operating income have been under absorption costing? Explain the reason for any difference between this income figure and the figure reported by the company in the statements above.

PROBLEM 7-17 Prepare and Interpret Income Statements; Changes in Both Sales and Production; JIT [LO1, LO2, LO3, LO4]

Starfax, Inc., manufactures a small part that is widely used in various electronic products such as home computers. Operating results for the first three years of activity were as follows (absorption costing basis):

	Year 1	Year 2	Year 3
Sales	$800,000	$640,000	$800,000
Cost of goods sold:			
Beginning inventory	0	0	200,000
Add cost of goods manufactured	580,000	600,000	560,000
Goods available for sale	580,000	600,000	760,000
Less ending inventory	0	200,000	140,000
Cost of goods sold	580,000	400,000	620,000
Gross margin	220,000	240,000	180,000
Selling and administrative expenses	190,000	180,000	190,000
Net operating income (loss)	$ 30,000	$ 60,000	$ (10,000)

In the latter part of Year 2, a competitor went out of business and in the process dumped a large number of units on the market. As a result, Starfax's sales dropped by 20% during Year 2 even though production increased during the year. Management had expected sales to remain constant at 50,000 units; the increased production was designed to provide the company with a buffer of protection against unexpected spurts in demand. By the start of Year 3, management could see that inventory was excessive and that spurts in demand were unlikely. To reduce the excessive inventories, Starfax cut back production during Year 3, as shown below:

	Year 1	Year 2	Year 3
Production in units	50,000	60,000	40,000
Sales in units	50,000	40,000	50,000

Additional information about the company follows:

a. The company's plant is highly automated. Variable manufacturing costs (direct materials, direct labor, and variable manufacturing overhead) total only $2 per unit, and fixed manufacturing overhead costs total $480,000 per year.
b. Fixed manufacturing overhead costs are applied to units of product on the basis of each year's production. (That is, a new fixed manufacturing overhead rate is computed each year, as in Exhibit 7–7.)

c.   Variable selling and administrative expenses were $1 per unit sold in each year. Fixed selling and administrative expenses totaled $140,000 per year.

d.   The company uses a FIFO inventory flow assumption.

Starfax's management can't understand why profits doubled during Year 2 when sales dropped by 20% and why a loss was incurred during Year 3 when sales recovered to previous levels.

Required:

1.   Prepare variable costing income statements for each year using the contribution approach.

2.   Refer to the absorption costing income statements above.

   a.   Compute the unit product cost in each year under absorption costing. (Show how much of this cost is variable and how much is fixed.)

   b.   Reconcile the variable costing and absorption costing net operating income figures for each year.

3.   Refer again to the absorption costing income statements. Explain why net operating income was higher in Year 2 than it was in Year 1 under the absorption approach, in light of the fact that fewer units were sold in Year 2 than in Year 1.

4.   Refer again to the absorption costing income statements. Explain why the company suffered a loss in Year 3 but reported a profit in Year 1 although the same number of units was sold in each year.

5.   *a.*   Explain how operations would have differed in Year 2 and Year 3 if the company had been using JIT inventory methods.

   b.   If JIT had been used during Year 2 and Year 3, what would the company's net operating income (or loss) have been in each year under absorption costing? Explain the reason for any differences between these income figures and the figures reported by the company in the statements above.

Cases

CASE 7-18 Ethics and the Manager; Absorption Costing Income Statements [LO2, LO4]

Guochang Li was hired as chief executive officer (CEO) in late November by the board of directors of ContactGlobal, a company that produces an advanced global positioning system (GPS) device. The previous CEO had been fired by the board of directors due to a series of shady business practices including shipping defective GPS devices to dealers.

Guochang felt that his first priority was to restore employee morale—which had suffered during the previous CEO's reign. He was particularly anxious to build a sense of trust between himself and the company's employees. His second priority was to prepare the budget for the coming year, which the board of directors wanted to review in their December 15 meeting.

After hammering out the details in meetings with key managers, Guochang was able to put together a budget that he felt the company could realistically meet during the coming year. That budget appears below:

Basic budget data	
Units in beginning inventory	0
Units produced	400,000
Units sold	400,000
Units in ending inventory	0
Variable costs per unit:	
Direct materials.	$ 57.20
Direct labor	15.00
Variable manufacturing overhead	5.00
Variable selling and administrative	10.00
Total variable cost per unit.	$ 87.20
Fixed costs:	
Fixed manufacturing overhead	$ 6,888,000
Fixed selling and administrative	4,560,000
Total fixed costs.	$11,448,000

ContactGlobal Budgeted Income Statement (absorption method)		
Sales (400,000 units × $120 per unit)		$48,000,000
Cost of goods sold:		
Beginning inventory.	$ 0	
Add cost of goods manufactured		
(400,000 units × $94.42 per unit)	37,768,000	
Goods available for sale	37,768,000	
Less ending inventory	0	37,768,000
Gross margin		10,232,000
Selling and administrative expenses:		
Variable selling and administrative		
(400,000 units × $10 per unit)	4,000,000	
Fixed selling and administrative.	4,560,000	8,560,000
Net operating income		$ 1,672,000

The board of directors made it clear that this budget was not as ambitious as they had hoped. The most influential member of the board stated that "managers should have to stretch to meet profit goals." After some discussion, the board decided to set a profit goal of $2,000,000 for the coming year. To provide strong incentives, the board agreed to pay out very substantial bonuses to top managers of $10,000 to $25,000 each if this profit goal was eventually met. The bonus would be all-or-nothing. If actual net operating income turned out to be $2,000,000 or more, the bonus would be paid. Otherwise, no bonus would be paid.

Required:
1. Assuming that the company does not build up its inventory (i.e., production equals sales) and its selling price and cost structure remain the same, how many units of the GPS device would have to be sold to meet the net operating income goal of $2,000,000?
2. Verify your answer to (1) above by constructing a revised budget and budgeted absorption costing income statement that yields a net operating income of $2,000,000.
3. Unfortunately, by October of the next year it had become clear that the company would not be able to make the $2,000,000 target profit. In fact, it looked like the company would wind up the year as originally planned, with sales of 400,000 units, no ending inventories, and a profit of $1,672,000.

   Several managers who were reluctant to lose their year-end bonuses approached Guochang and suggested that the company could still show a profit of $2,000,000. The managers pointed out that at the present rate of sales, there was enough capacity to produce tens of thousands of additional GPS devices for the warehouse and thereby shift fixed manufacturing overhead costs to another year. If sales are 400,000 units for the year and the selling price and cost structure remain the same, how many units would have to be produced in order to show a profit of at least $2,000,000 under absorption costing?
4. Verify your answer to (3) above by constructing an absorption costing income statement.
5. Do you think Guochang Li should approve the plan to build ending inventories in order to attain the target profit?
6. What advice would you give to the board of directors concerning how they determine bonuses in the future?

CASE 7-19 The Case of the Plummeting Profits; JIT Impact [LO2, LO3, LO4]
"These statements can't be right," said Ben Yoder, president of Rayco, Inc. "Our sales in the second quarter were up by 25% over the first quarter, yet these income statements show a precipitous drop in net operating income for the second quarter. Those accounting people have fouled something up." Mr. Yoder was referring to the following statements (absorption costing basis):

Rayco, Inc. Income Statements For the First Two Quarters	First Quarter		Second Quarter	
Sales		$480,000		$600,000
Cost of goods sold:				
Beginning inventory	$ 80,000		$140,000	
Add cost of goods manufactured.........	300,000		180,000	
Goods available for sale	380,000		320,000	
Less ending inventory.................	140,000		20,000	
Cost of goods sold	240,000		300,000	
Add underapplied overhead	—	240,000	72,000	372,000
Gross margin		240,000		228,000
Selling and administrative expenses........		200,000		215,000
Net operating income..................		$ 40,000		$ 13,000

After studying the statements briefly, Mr. Yoder called in the controller to see if the mistake in the second quarter could be located before the figures were released to the press. The controller stated, "I'm sorry to say that those figures are correct, Ben. I agree that sales went up during the second quarter, but the problem is in production. You see, we budgeted to produce 15,000 units each quarter, but a strike on the west coast among some of our suppliers forced us to cut production in the second quarter back to only 9,000 units. That's what caused the drop in net operating income."

Mr. Yoder was confused by the controller's explanation. He replied, "This doesn't make sense. I ask you to explain why net operating income dropped when sales went up and you talk about production! So what if we had to cut back production? We still were able to increase sales by 25%. If sales go up, then net operating income should go up. If your statements can't show a simple thing like that, then it's time for some changes in your department!"

Budgeted production and sales for the year, along with actual production and sales for the first two quarters, are given below:

	Quarter			
	First	Second	Third	Fourth
Budgeted sales (units).............	12,000	15,000	15,000	18,000
Actual sales (units)...............	12,000	15,000	—	—
Budgeted production (units)........	15,000	15,000	15,000	15,000
Actual production (units)	15,000	9,000	—	—

The company's plant is heavily automated, and fixed manufacturing overhead amounts to $180,000 each quarter. Variable manufacturing costs are $8 per unit. The fixed manufacturing overhead is applied to units of product at a rate of $12 per unit (based on the budgeted production shown above). Any under- or overapplied overhead is closed directly to cost of goods sold for the quarter. The company had 4,000 units in inventory to start the first quarter and uses the FIFO inventory flow assumption. Variable selling and administrative expenses are $5 per unit.

Required:
1. What characteristic of absorption costing caused the drop in net operating income for the second quarter and what could the controller have said to explain the problem?
2. Prepare a variable costing income statement for each quarter using the contribution approach.
3. Reconcile the absorption costing and the variable costing net operating income figures for each quarter.
4. Identify and discuss the advantages and disadvantages of using the variable costing method for internal reporting purposes.
5. Assume that the company had introduced JIT (just-in-time) at the beginning of the second quarter. (Sales and production during the first quarter remain the same.)
   a. How many units would have been produced during the second quarter under JIT?
   b. Starting with the third quarter, would you expect any difference between the net operating income reported under absorption costing and under variable costing? Explain why there would or would not be any difference.

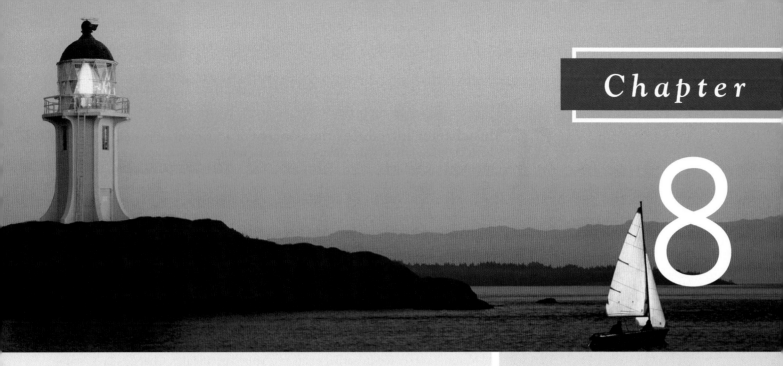

Activity-Based Costing: A Tool to Aid Decision Making

Learning Objectives

After studying Chapter 8, you should be able to:

LO1 Understand activity-based costing and how it differs from a traditional costing system.

LO2 Assign costs to cost pools using a first-stage allocation.

LO3 Compute activity rates for cost pools.

LO4 Assign costs to a cost object using a second-stage allocation.

LO5 Use activity-based costing to compute product and customer margins.

LO6 (Appendix 8A) Prepare an action analysis report using activity-based costing data and interpret the report.

LO7 (Appendix 8B) Use activity-based costing techniques to compute unit product costs for external reports.

The Payoff from Activity-Based Costing

BUSINESS FOCUS

Implementing an activity-based costing system can be expensive. To be worth the cost, the system must actually be used to make decisions and increase profits. Insteel Industries manufactures a range of products, such as concrete reinforcing steel, industrial wire, and bulk nails, for the construction, home furnishings, appliance, and tire manufacturing industries. The company implemented an activity-based costing system at its manufacturing plant in Andrews, South Carolina, and immediately began using activity-based data to make strategic and operating decisions.

In terms of strategic decisions, Insteel dropped some unprofitable products, raised prices on others, and in some cases even discontinued relationships with unprofitable customers. Insteel realized that simply discontinuing products and customers does not improve profits. The company needed to either redeploy its freed-up capacity to increase sales or eliminate its freed-up capacity to reduce costs. Insteel chose to redeploy its freed-up capacity and used its activity-based costing system to identify which new business opportunities to pursue.

In terms of operational improvements, Insteel's activity-based costing system revealed that its 20 most expensive activities consumed 87% of the plant's $21.4 million in costs. Almost $4.9 million was being consumed by non-value-added activities. Teams were formed to reduce scrap costs, material handling and freight costs, and maintenance costs. Within one year, scrap and maintenance costs had been cut by $1,800,000 and freight costs by $550,000. Overall, non-value-added activity costs dropped from 23% to 17% of total costs. ■

Source: V.G. Narayanan and R. Sarkar, "The Impact of Activity-Based Costing on Managerial Decisions at Insteel Industries—A Field Study," *Journal of Economics & Management Strategy*, Summer 2002, pp. 257–288.

This chapter introduces the concept of *activity-based costing* which has been embraced by a wide variety of manufacturing, service, and nonprofit organizations including American Express, The Association of Neurological Surgeons, Cambridge Hospital Community Health Network, Carrier Corporation, Dana Corporation, Dialysis Clinic, GE Medical Systems, Hallmark, ITT Automotive North America, Maxwell Appliance Controls, Pillsbury, Tampa Electric Company, and the U.S. Postal Service. **Activity-based costing (ABC)** is a costing method that is designed to provide managers with cost information for strategic and other decisions that potentially affect capacity and therefore "fixed" as well as variable costs. Activity-based costing is ordinarily used as a supplement to, rather than as a replacement for, a company's usual costing system. Most organizations that use activity-based costing have two costing systems—the official costing system that is used for preparing external financial reports and the activity-based costing system that is used for internal decision making and for managing activities.

This chapter focuses primarily on ABC applications in manufacturing to provide a contrast with the material presented in earlier chapters. More specifically, Chapters 2, 3, and 4 focused on traditional absorption costing systems used by manufacturing companies to calculate unit product costs for the purpose of valuing inventories and determining cost of goods sold for external financial reports. In contrast, this chapter explains how manufacturing companies can use activity-based costing rather than traditional methods to calculate unit product costs for the purposes of managing overhead and making decisions. Chapter 7 had a similar purpose. That chapter focused on how to use variable costing to aid decisions that do not affect fixed costs. This chapter extends that idea to show how activity-based costing can be used to aid decisions that potentially affect fixed costs as well as variable costs.

Activity-Based Costing: An Overview

LEARNING OBJECTIVE 1
Understand activity-based costing and how it differs from a traditional costing system.

As stated above, traditional absorption costing is designed to provide data for external financial reports. In contrast, activity-based costing is designed to be used for internal decision making. As a consequence, activity-based costing differs from traditional cost accounting in three ways. In activity-based costing:

1. Nonmanufacturing as well as manufacturing costs may be assigned to products, but only on a cause-and-effect basis.
2. Some manufacturing costs may be excluded from product costs.
3. Numerous overhead cost pools are used, each of which is allocated to products and other cost objects using its own unique measure of activity.

Each of these departures from traditional cost accounting practice will be discussed in turn.

IN BUSINESS

SHEDDING LIGHT ON PRODUCT PROFITABILITY

Reichhold, Inc., one of the world's leading suppliers of synthetic materials, adopted activity-based costing to help shed light on the profitability of its various products. Reichhold's prior cost system used one allocation base, reactor hours, to assign overhead costs to products. The ABC system uses four additional activity measures—preprocess preparation hours, thin-tank hours, filtration hours, and waste disposal costs per batch—to assign costs to products. Reichhold has rolled out ABC to all 19 of its North American plants because the management team believes that ABC helps improve the company's "capacity management, cycle times, value-added pricing decisions, and analysis of product profitability."

Source: Edward Blocher, Betty Wong, and Christopher McKittrick, "Making Bottom-Up ABC Work at Reichhold, Inc.," *Strategic Finance*, April 2002, pp. 51–55.

How Costs Are Treated under Activity-Based Costing

Nonmanufacturing Costs and Activity-Based Costing

In traditional cost accounting, only manufacturing costs are assigned to products. Selling and administrative expenses are treated as period expenses and are not assigned to products. However, many of these nonmanufacturing costs are also part of the costs of producing, selling, distributing, and servicing specific products. For example, commissions paid to salespersons, shipping costs, and warranty repair costs can be easily traced to individual products. In this chapter, we will use the term *overhead* to refer to nonmanufacturing costs as well as to indirect manufacturing costs. In activity-based costing, products are assigned all of the overhead costs—nonmanufacturing as well as manufacturing—that they can reasonably be supposed to have caused. In essence, we will be determining the entire cost of a product rather than just its manufacturing cost. The focus in Chapters 2, 3, and 4 was on determining just the manufacturing cost of a product.

Manufacturing Costs and Activity-Based Costing

In traditional cost accounting systems, *all* manufacturing costs are assigned to products—even manufacturing costs that are not caused by the products. For example, in Chapter 3 we learned that a predetermined plantwide overhead rate is computed by dividing *all* budgeted manufacturing overhead costs by a measure of budgeted activity such as direct labor-hours. This approach spreads *all* manufacturing overhead costs across products based on each product's direct labor-hour usage. In contrast, activity-based costing systems purposely do not assign two types of manufacturing overhead costs to products.

Manufacturing overhead includes costs such as the factory security guard's wages, the plant controller's salary, and the cost of supplies used by the plant manager's secretary. These types of costs are assigned to products in a traditional absorption costing system even though they are totally unaffected by which products are made during a period. In contrast, activity-based costing systems do not arbitrarily assign these types of costs, which are called *organization-sustaining* costs, to products. Activity-based costing treats these types of costs as period expenses rather than product costs.

Additionally, in a traditional absorption costing system, the costs of unused, or idle, capacity are assigned to products. If the budgeted level of activity declines, the overhead rate and unit product costs increase as the increasing costs of idle capacity are spread over a smaller base. In contrast, in activity-based costing, products are only charged for the costs of the capacity they use—not for the costs of capacity they don't use. This provides more stable unit product costs and is consistent with the goal of assigning to products only the costs of the resources that they use.[1]

Cost Pools, Allocation Bases, and Activity-Based Costing

Throughout the 19th century and most of the 20th century, cost system designs were simple and satisfactory. Typically, either one plantwide overhead cost pool or a number of departmental overhead cost pools was used to assign overhead costs to products. The plantwide and departmental approaches always had one thing in common—they relied on allocation bases such as direct labor-hours and machine-hours for allocating overhead costs to products. In the labor-intensive production processes of many years ago, direct labor was the most common choice for an overhead allocation base because it represented a large component of product costs, direct labor-hours were closely tracked, and many managers believed that direct labor-hours, the total volume of units produced, and overhead costs were highly

---

[1]   Appendix 3A discusses how the costs of idle capacity can be accounted for as a period cost in an income statement. This treatment highlights the cost of idle capacity rather than burying it in inventory and cost of goods sold. The procedures laid out in this chapter for activity-based costing have the same end effect.

correlated. (Three variables, such as direct labor-hours, the total volume of units produced, and overhead costs, are highly correlated if they tend to move together.) Given that most companies at the time were producing a very limited variety of products that required similar resources to produce, allocation bases such as direct labor-hours, or even machine-hours, worked fine because in fact there was probably little difference in the overhead costs attributable to different products.

Then conditions began to change. As a percentage of total cost, direct labor began declining and overhead began increasing. Many tasks previously done by direct laborers were being performed by automated equipment—a component of overhead. Companies began creating new products and services at an ever-accelerating rate that differed in volume, batch size, and complexity. Managing and sustaining this product diversity required investing in many more overhead resources, such as production schedulers and product design engineers, that had no obvious connection to direct labor-hours or machine-hours. In this new environment, continuing to rely exclusively on a limited number of overhead cost pools and traditional allocation bases posed the risk that reported unit product costs would be distorted and, therefore, misleading when used for decision-making purposes.

Activity-based costing, thanks to advances in technology that make more complex cost systems feasible, provides an alternative to the traditional plantwide and departmental approaches to defining cost pools and selecting allocation bases. The activity-based approach has appeal in today's business environment because it uses more cost pools and unique measures of activity to better understand the costs of managing and sustaining product diversity.

In activity-based costing, an **activity** is any event that causes the consumption of overhead resources. An **activity cost pool** is a "bucket" in which costs are accumulated that relate to a single activity measure in the ABC system. An **activity measure** is an allocation base in an activity-based costing system. The term *cost driver* is also used to refer to an activity measure because the activity measure should "drive" the cost being allocated. The two most common types of activity measures are *transaction drivers* and *duration drivers*. **Transaction drivers** are simple counts of the number of times an activity occurs such as the number of bills sent out to customers. **Duration drivers** measure the amount of time required to perform an activity such as the time spent preparing individual bills for customers. In general, duration drivers are more accurate measures of resource consumption than transaction drivers, but they take more effort to record. For that reason, transaction drivers are often used in practice.

Traditional cost systems rely exclusively on allocation bases that are driven by the volume of production. On the other hand, activity-based costing defines five levels of activity—unit-level, batch-level, product-level, customer-level, and organization-sustaining—that largely do *not* relate to the volume of units produced. The costs and corresponding activity measures for unit-level activities do relate to the volume of units produced; however, the remaining categories do not. These levels are described as follows:[2]

1. **Unit-level activities** are performed each time a unit is produced. The costs of unit-level activities should be proportional to the number of units produced. For example, providing power to run processing equipment would be a unit-level activity since power tends to be consumed in proportion to the number of units produced.
2. **Batch-level activities** are performed each time a batch is handled or processed, regardless of how many units are in the batch. For example, tasks such as placing purchase orders, setting up equipment, and arranging for shipments to customers are batch-level activities. They are incurred once for each batch (or customer order). Costs at the batch level depend on the number of batches processed rather than on the number of units produced, the number of units sold, or other measures of volume. For example, the cost of setting up a machine for batch processing is the same regardless of whether the batch contains one or thousands of items.
3. **Product-level activities** relate to specific products and typically must be carried out regardless of how many batches are run or units of product are produced or sold. For

2   Robin Cooper, "Cost Classification in Unit-Based and Activity-Based Manufacturing Cost Systems," *Journal of Cost Management,* Fall 1990, pp. 4–14.

example, activities such as designing a product, advertising a product, and maintaining a product manager and staff are all product-level activities.

4. **Customer-level activities** relate to specific customers and include activities such as sales calls, catalog mailings, and general technical support that are not tied to any specific product.

5. **Organization-sustaining activities** are carried out regardless of which customers are served, which products are produced, how many batches are run, or how many units are made. This category includes activities such as heating the factory, cleaning executive offices, providing a computer network, arranging for loans, preparing annual reports to shareholders, and so on.

Many companies throughout the world continue to base overhead allocations on direct labor-hours or machine-hours. In situations where overhead costs and direct labor-hours are highly correlated or in situations where the goal of the overhead allocation process is to prepare external financial reports, this practice makes sense. However, if plantwide overhead costs do not move in tandem with plantwide direct labor-hours or machine-hours, product costs will be distorted—with the potential of distorting decisions made within the company.

DINING IN THE CANYON

Western River Expeditions (www.westernriver.com) runs river rafting trips on the Colorado, Green, and Salmon rivers. One of its most popular trips is a six-day trip down the Grand Canyon, which features famous rapids such as Crystal and Lava Falls as well as the awesome scenery accessible only from the bottom of the Grand Canyon. The company runs trips of one or two rafts, each of which carries two guides and up to 18 guests. The company provides all meals on the trip, which are prepared by the guides.

In terms of the hierarchy of activities, a guest can be considered as a unit and a raft as a batch. In that context, the wages paid to the guides are a batch-level cost since each raft requires two guides regardless of the number of guests in the raft. Each guest is given a mug to use during the trip and to take home at the end of the trip as a souvenir. The cost of the mug is a unit-level cost since the number of mugs given away is strictly proportional to the number of guests on a trip.

What about the costs of food served to guests and guides—is this a unit-level cost, a batch-level cost, a product-level cost, or an organization-sustaining cost? At first glance, it might be thought that food costs are a unit-level cost—the greater the number of guests, the higher the food costs. However, that is not quite correct. Standard menus have been created for each day of the trip. For example, the first night's menu might consist of shrimp cocktail, steak, cornbread, salad, and cheesecake. The day before a trip begins, all of the food needed for the trip is taken from the central warehouse and packed in modular containers. It isn't practical to finely adjust the amount of food for the actual number of guests planned to be on a trip—most of the food comes prepackaged in large lots. For example, the shrimp cocktail menu may call for two large bags of frozen shrimp per raft and that many bags will be packed regardless of how many guests are expected on the raft. Consequently, the costs of food are not a unit-level cost that varies with the number of guests actually on a trip. Instead, the costs of food are a batch-level cost.

Source: Conversations with Western River Expeditions personnel.

Designing an Activity-Based Costing (ABC) System

Experts agree on several essential characteristics of any successful implementation of activity-based costing. First, the initiative to implement activity-based costing must be strongly supported by top management. Second, the design and implementation of an ABC system should be the responsibility of a cross-functional team rather than of the accounting department. The team should include representatives from each area that will use the data

Topic Tackler

PLUS

8–1

provided by the ABC system. Ordinarily, this would include representatives from marketing, production, engineering, and top management as well as technically trained accounting staff. An outside consultant who specializes in activity-based costing may serve as an advisor to the team. And third, the ABC data should be linked to how people are evaluated and rewarded. This ensures that the system will not be ignored.

The reason for insisting on strong top-management support and a multifunction team approach is rooted in the fact that it is difficult to implement changes in organizations unless those changes have the full support of those who are affected. This is particularly true if, as recommended above, the ABC system is used in evaluating and rewarding managers. Unless the managers who are directly affected by these changes have a say, resistance will be inevitable. In addition, designing a good ABC system requires intimate knowledge of many parts of the organization's overall operations. This knowledge can only come from the people who are familiar with those operations.

Top managers must support the initiative for two reasons. First, without leadership from top management, some managers may not see any reason to change. Second, if top managers do not support the ABC system and continue to evaluate and reward employees based on traditional (non-ABC) cost data, their subordinates will quickly get the message that ABC is not important and they will abandon the ABC initiative. Time after time, when accountants have attempted to implement an ABC system on their own without top-management support and active cooperation from other managers, the results have been ignored.

MANAGERIAL ACCOUNTING IN ACTION
The Issue

Classic Brass, Inc. makes two main product lines for luxury yachts—standard stanchions and custom compass housings. The president of the company, John Towers, recently attended a management conference at which activity-based costing was discussed. Following the conference, he called a meeting of the company's top managers to discuss what he had learned. Attending the meeting were production manager Susan Richter, the marketing manager Tom Olafson, and the accounting manager Mary Goodman. He began the conference by distributing the company's income statement that Mary Goodman had prepared a few hours earlier (see Exhibit 8–1):

John: Well, it's official. Our company has sunk into the red for the first time in its history—a loss of $1,250.

Tom: I don't know what else we can do! Given our successful efforts to grow sales of the custom compass housings, I was expecting to see a boost to our bottom line, not a net loss. Granted, we have been losing even more bids than usual for standard stanchions because of our recent price increase, but . . .

EXHIBIT 8–1
Classic Brass Income Statement

Classic Brass Income Statement Year Ended December 31, 2005		
Sales		$3,200,000
Cost of goods sold:		
Direct materials	$ 975,000	
Direct labor	351,250	
Manufacturing overhead*	1,000,000	2,326,250
Gross margin		873,750
Selling and administrative expenses:		
Shipping expenses	65,000	
Marketing expenses	300,000	
General administrative expenses	510,000	875,000
Net operating income		($ 1,250)

*The company's traditional cost system allocates manufacturing overhead to products using a plantwide overhead rate and machine-hours as the allocation base. Inventory levels did not change during the year.

John: Do you think our prices for standard stanchions are too high?

Tom: No, I don't think our prices are too high. I think our competitors' prices are too low. In fact, I'll bet they are pricing below their cost.

Susan: Why would our competitors price below their cost?

Tom: They are out to grab market share.

Susan: What good is more market share if they are losing money on every unit sold?

John: I think Susan has a point. Mary, what is your take on this?

Mary: If our competitors are pricing standard stanchions below cost, shouldn't they be losing money rather than us? If our company is the one using accurate information to make informed decisions while our competitors are supposedly clueless, then why is our "bottom line" taking a beating? Unfortunately, I think we may be the ones shooting in the dark, not our competitors.

John: Based on what I heard at the conference that I just attended, I am inclined to agree. One of the presentations at the conference dealt with activity-based costing. As the speaker began describing the usual insights revealed by activity-based costing systems, I was sitting in the audience getting an ill feeling in my stomach.

Mary: Honestly John, I have been claiming for years that our existing cost system is okay for external reporting, but it is dangerous to use it for internal decision making. It sounds like you are on board now, right?

John: Yes.

Mary: Well then, how about if all of you commit the time and energy to help me build a fairly simple activity-based costing system that may shed some light on the problems we are facing?

John: Let's do it. I want each of you to appoint one of your top people to a special "ABC team" to investigate how we cost products.

Like most other ABC implementations, the ABC team decided that its new ABC system would supplement, rather than replace, the existing cost accounting system, which would continue to be used for external financial reports. The new ABC system would be used to prepare special reports for management decisions such as bidding on new business.

The accounting manager drew the chart appearing in Exhibit 8–2 to explain the general structure of the ABC model to her team members. Cost objects such as products generate activities. For example, a customer order for a custom compass housing requires the activity of preparing a production order. Such an activity consumes resources. A production order uses a sheet of paper and takes time to fill out. And consumption of resources causes costs. The greater the number of sheets used to fill out production orders and the greater the amount of time devoted to filling out such orders, the greater the cost. Activity-based costing attempts to trace through these relationships to identify how products and customers affect costs.

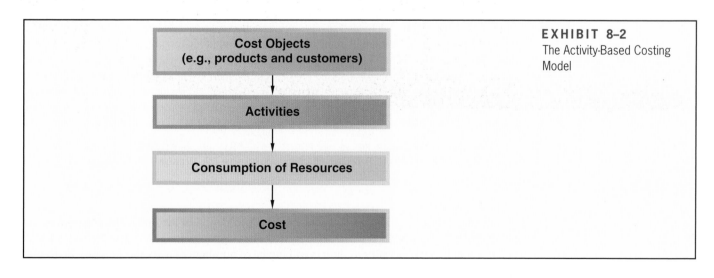

EXHIBIT 8–2
The Activity-Based Costing Model

As in most other companies, the ABC team at Classic Brass felt that the company's traditional cost accounting system adequately measured the direct materials and direct labor costs of products since these costs are directly traced to products. Therefore, the ABC study would be concerned solely with the other costs of the company—manufacturing overhead and selling and administrative costs.

The team felt it was important to carefully plan how it would go about implementing the new ABC system at Classic Brass. Accordingly, it broke down the implementation process into five steps:

Steps for Implementing Activity-Based Costing:

1. Define activities, activity cost pools, and activity measures.
2. Assign overhead costs to activity cost pools.
3. Calculate activity rates.
4. Assign overhead costs to cost objects using the activity rates and activity measures.
5. Prepare management reports.

Step 1: Define Activities, Activity Cost Pools, and Activity Measures

The first major step in implementing an ABC system is to identify the activities that will form the foundation for the system. This can be difficult, time-consuming, and involves a great deal of judgment. A common procedure is for the individuals on the ABC implementation team to interview people who work in overhead departments and ask them to describe their major activities. Ordinarily, this results in a very long list of activities.

IN BUSINESS

IS E-TAILING REALLY EASIER?

The company art.com™ sells prints and framed prints over the web. An activity-based costing study identified the following 12 activities carried out in the company:

1. Service customers
2. Website optimization
3. Merchandise inventory selection and management
4. Purchasing and receiving
5. Customer acquisition and retention—paid-for marketing
6. Customer acquisition and retention—revenue share marketing (affiliate group)
7. Sustain information system
8. Sustain business—administration
9. Sustain business—production
10. Maintain facility—administrative
11. Maintain facility—production
12. Sustain business—executive

For example, the activity "merchandise inventory selection and management" involves scanning, describing, classifying, and linking each inventory item to search options on the company's website. "Staff must carefully manage each change to the database, which is similar to adding and removing inventory items from the shelf of a store. They annotate added inventory items and upload them into the system, as well as remove obsolete and discontinued items. . . . The number of inventory items for an e-tailer is typically much greater than for a brick-and-mortar [store], which is a competitive advantage, but experience shows managing a large inventory consumes substantial resources."

Source: Thomas L. Zeller, David R. Kublank, and Philip G. Makris, "How art.com™ Uses ABC to Succeed," *Strategic Finance*, March 2001, pp. 25–31. Reprinted with permission from the IMA, Montvale, NJ, USA, www.imanet.org.

The length of such lists of activities poses a problem. On the one hand, the greater the number of activities tracked in the ABC system, the more accurate the costs are likely to be. On the other hand, a complex system involving large numbers of activities is costly to design, implement, maintain, and use. Consequently, the original lengthy list of activities is usually reduced to a handful by combining similar activities. For example, several actions may be involved in handling and moving raw materials—from receiving raw materials on the loading dock to sorting them into the appropriate bins in the storeroom. All of these activities might be combined into a single activity called material handling.

When combining activities in an ABC system, activities should be grouped together at the appropriate level. Batch-level activities should not be combined with unit-level activities or product-level activities with batch-level activities and so on. In general, it is best to combine only those activities that are highly correlated with each other within a level. For example, the number of customer orders received is likely to be highly correlated with the number of completed customer orders shipped, so these two batch-level activities (receiving and shipping orders) can usually be combined with little loss of accuracy.

At Classic Brass, the ABC team, in consultation with top managers, selected the following *activity cost pools* and *activity measures:*

Activity Cost Pools at Classic Brass	
Activity Cost Pool	**Activity Measure**
Customer orders	Number of customer orders
Product design	Number of product designs
Order size	Machine-hours
Customer relations	Number of active customers
Other	Not applicable

The *Customer Orders* cost pool will be assigned all costs of resources that are consumed by taking and processing customer orders, including costs of processing paperwork and any costs involved in setting up machines for specific orders. The activity measure for this cost pool is simply the number of customer orders received. This is a batch-level activity, since each order generates work that occurs regardless of whether the order is for one unit or 1,000 units.

The *Product Design* cost pool will be assigned all costs of resources consumed by designing products. The activity measure for this cost pool is the number of products designed. This is a product-level activity because the amount of design work on a new product does not depend on the number of units ultimately ordered or batches ultimately run.

The *Order Size* cost pool will be assigned all costs of resources consumed as a consequence of the number of units produced, including the costs of miscellaneous factory supplies, power to run machines, and some equipment depreciation. This is a unit-level activity since each unit requires some of these resources. The activity measure for this cost pool is machine-hours.

The *Customer Relations* cost pool will be assigned all costs associated with maintaining relations with customers, including the costs of sales calls and the costs of entertaining customers. The activity measure for this cost pool is the number of customers the company has on its active customer list. The Customer Relations cost pool represents a customer-level activity.

The *Other* cost pool will be assigned all overhead costs that are not associated with customer orders, product design, the size of the orders, or customer relations. These costs mainly consist of organization-sustaining costs and the costs of unused, idle capacity. These costs *will not* be assigned to products because they represent resources that are *not* consumed by products.

It is unlikely that any other company would use exactly the same activity cost pools and activity measures that were selected by Classic Brass. Because of the amount of judgment involved, the number and definitions of the activity cost pools and activity measures used by companies vary considerably.

The Mechanics of Activity-Based Costing

Step 2: Assign Overhead Costs to Activity Cost Pools

Exhibit 8–3 shows the annual overhead costs (both manufacturing and nonmanufacturing) that Classic Brass intends to assign to its activity cost pools. Notice the data in the exhibit are organized by department (e.g., Production, Marketing, and General Administrative). This is because the data have been extracted from the company's general ledger. General ledgers usually classify costs within the departments where the costs are incurred. For example, salaries, supplies, rent, and so forth incurred in the marketing department are charged to that department. The functional orientation of the general ledger mirrors the presentation of costs in the absorption income statement in Exhibit 8–1. In fact, you'll notice the total costs for the Production Department in Exhibit 8–3 ($1,000,000) equal the total manufacturing overhead costs from the income statement in Exhibit 8–1. Similarly, the total costs for the General Administrative and Marketing Departments in Exhibit 8–3 ($510,000 and $300,000) equal the marketing and general and administrative expenses shown in Exhibit 8–1.

Three costs included in the income statement in Exhibit 8–1—direct materials, direct labor, and shipping—are excluded from the costs shown in Exhibit 8–3. The ABC team purposely excluded these costs from Exhibit 8–3 because the existing cost system can accurately trace direct materials, direct labor, and shipping costs to products. There is no need to incorporate these direct costs in the activity-based allocations of indirect costs.

Classic Brass's activity-based costing system will divide the nine types of overhead costs in Exhibit 8–3 among its activity cost pools via an allocation process called *first-stage allocation*. The **first-stage allocation** in an ABC system is the process of assigning functionally organized overhead costs derived from a company's general ledger to the activity cost pools.

First-stage allocations are usually based on the results of interviews with employees who have first-hand knowledge of the activities. For example, Classic Brass needs to allocate $500,000 of indirect factory wages to its five activity cost pools. These allocations will be more accurate if the employees who are classified as indirect factory workers (e.g., supervisors, engineers, and quality inspectors) are asked to estimate what percentage of their time is spent dealing with customer orders, with product design, with processing units of product (i.e., order size), and with customer relations. These interviews are conducted with considerable care. Those who are interviewed must thoroughly understand what the activities encompass and what is expected of them in the interview. In addition, departmental managers are typically interviewed to determine how the nonpersonnel costs should be distributed across the activity cost pools. For example, the Classic Brass production manager would be interviewed to determine how the $300,000 of factory equipment depreciation (shown in

EXHIBIT 8–3
Annual Overhead Costs (both Manufacturing and Nonmanufacturing) at Classic Brass

Production Department:		
Indirect factory wages.................	$500,000	
Factory equipment depreciation.........	300,000	
Factory utilities......................	120,000	
Factory building lease.................	80,000	$1,000,000
General Administrative Department:		
Administrative wages and salaries.......	400,000	
Office equipment depreciation..........	50,000	
Administrative building lease...........	60,000	510,000
Marketing Department:..................		
Marketing wages and salaries..........	250,000	
Selling expenses.....................	50,000	300,000
Total overhead cost....................		$1,810,000

ABC HELPS A DAIRY UNDERSTAND ITS COSTS

Kemps LLC, headquartered in Minneapolis, Minnesota, produces dairy products such as milk, yogurt, and ice cream. The company implemented an ABC system that helped managers understand the impact of product and customer diversity on profit margins. The ABC model "captured differences in how the company entered orders from customers (customer phone call, salesperson call, fax, truck-driver entry, EDI, or Internet), how it packaged orders (full stacks of six cases, individual cases, or partial break-pack cases for small orders), how it delivered orders (commercial carriers or its own fleet, including route miles), and time spent by the driver at each customer location."

Kemps' ABC system helped the company acquire a large national customer because it identified "the specific manufacturing, distribution, and order handling costs associated with serving this customer." The ability to provide the customer with accurate cost information built a trusting relationship that distinguished Kemps from other competitors. Kemps also used its ABC data to transform unprofitable customers into profitable ones. For example, one customer agreed to accept a 13% price increase, to eliminate two low-volume products, and to begin placing full truckload orders rather than requiring partial truckload shipments, thereby lowering Kemps' costs by $150,000 per year.

Source: Robert S. Kaplan and Steven R. Anderson, "Time-Driven Activity-Based Costing," *Harvard Business Review*, November 2004, pp. 131–139.

Exhibit 8–3) should be allocated to the activity cost pools. The key question that the production manager would need to answer is "What percentage of the available machine capacity is consumed by each activity such as the number of customer orders or the number of units processed (i.e., size of orders)?"

The results of the interviews at Classic Brass are displayed in Exhibit 8–4 (page 320). For example, factory equipment depreciation is distributed 20% to Customer Orders, 60% to Order Size, and 20% to the Other cost pool. The resource in this instance is machine time. According to the estimates made by the production manager, 60% of the total available machine time was used to actually process units to fill orders. This percentage is entered in the Order Size column. Each customer order requires setting up, which also requires machine time. This activity consumes 20% of the total available machine time and is entered under the Customer Orders column. The remaining 20% of available machine time represents idle time and is entered under the Other column.

Exhibit 8–4 and many of the other exhibits in this chapter are presented in the form of Excel spreadsheets. All of the calculations required in activity-based costing can be done by hand. Nevertheless, setting up an activity-based costing system on a spreadsheet or using special ABC software can save a lot of work—particularly in situations involving many activity cost pools and in organizations that periodically update their ABC systems.

We will not go into the details of how all of the percentages in Exhibit 8–4 were determined. However, note that 100% of the factory building lease has been assigned to the Other cost pool. Classic Brass has a single production facility. It has no plans to expand or to sublease any excess space. The cost of this production facility is treated as an organization-sustaining cost because there is no way to avoid even a portion of this cost if a particular product or customer were to be dropped. (Remember that organization-sustaining costs are assigned to the Other cost pool and are not allocated to products.) In contrast, some companies have separate facilities for manufacturing specific products. The costs of these separate facilities could be directly traced to the specific products.

Once the percentage distributions in Exhibit 8–4 have been established, it is easy to allocate costs to the activity cost pools. The results of this first-stage allocation are displayed in Exhibit 8–5 (page 320). Each cost is allocated across the activity cost pools by multiplying it by the percentages in Exhibit 8–4. For example, the indirect factory wages of $500,000 are

EXHIBIT 8–4

Results of Interviews: Distribution of Resource Consumption across Activity Cost Pools

| | Activity Cost Pools | | | | | |
A	Customer Orders	Product Design	Order Size	Customer Relations	Other	Totals
Production Department:						
Indirect factory wages	25%	40%	20%	10%	5%	100%
Factory equipment depreciation	20%	0%	60%	0%	20%	100%
Factory utilities	0%	10%	50%	0%	40%	100%
Factory building lease	0%	0%	0%	0%	100%	100%
General Administrative Department:						
Administrative wages and salaries	15%	5%	10%	30%	40%	100%
Office equipment depreciation	30%	0%	0%	25%	45%	100%
Administrative building lease	0%	0%	0%	0%	100%	100%
Marketing Department:						
Marketing wages and salaries	22%	8%	0%	60%	10%	100%
Selling expenses	10%	0%	0%	70%	20%	100%

EXHIBIT 8–5

First-Stage Allocations to Activity Cost Pools

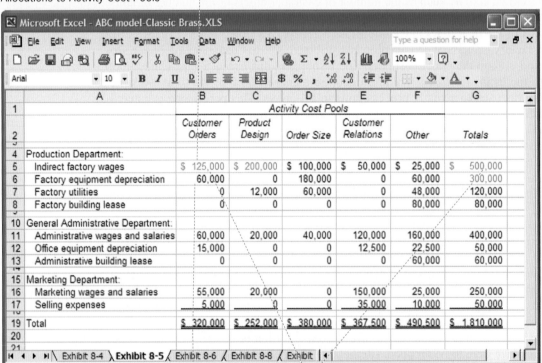

| | Activity Cost Pools | | | | | |
A	Customer Orders	Product Design	Order Size	Customer Relations	Other	Totals
Production Department:						
Indirect factory wages	$ 125,000	$ 200,000	$ 100,000	$ 50,000	$ 25,000	$ 500,000
Factory equipment depreciation	60,000	0	180,000	0	60,000	300,000
Factory utilities	0	12,000	60,000	0	48,000	120,000
Factory building lease	0	0	0	0	80,000	80,000
General Administrative Department:						
Administrative wages and salaries	60,000	20,000	40,000	120,000	160,000	400,000
Office equipment depreciation	15,000	0	0	12,500	22,500	50,000
Administrative building lease	0	0	0	0	60,000	60,000
Marketing Department:						
Marketing wages and salaries	55,000	20,000	0	150,000	25,000	250,000
Selling expenses	5,000	0	0	35,000	10,000	50,000
Total	$ 320,000	$ 252,000	$ 380,000	$ 367,500	$ 490,500	$ 1,810,000

Exhibit 8–4 shows that Customer Orders consume 25% of the resources represented by the $500,000 of indirect factory wages.

$$25\% \times \$500,000 = \$125,000$$

Other entries in the table are computed in a similar fashion.

multiplied by the 25% entry under Customer Orders in Exhibit 8–4 to arrive at the $125,000 entry under Customer Orders in Exhibit 8–5. Similarly, the indirect factory wages of $500,000 are multiplied by the 40% entry under Product Design in Exhibit 8–4 to arrive at the $200,000 entry under Product Design in Exhibit 8–5. All of the entries in Exhibit 8–5 are computed in this way.

Now that the first-stage allocations to the activity cost pools have been completed, the next step is to compute the activity rates.

Step 3: Calculate Activity Rates

The activity rates that will be used for assigning overhead costs to products and customers are computed in Exhibit 8–6. The ABC team determined the total activity for each cost pool that would be required to produce the company's present product mix and to serve its present customers. These numbers are listed in Exhibit 8–6. For example, the ABC team found that 400 new product designs are required each year to serve the company's present customers. The activity rates are computed by dividing the *total* cost for each activity by its *total* activity. For example, the $320,000 total annual cost for the Customer Orders cost pool (which was computed in Exhibit 8–5) is divided by the total of 1,000 customer orders per year to arrive at the activity rate of $320 per customer order. Similarly, the $252,000 *total* cost for the Product Design cost pool is divided by the *total* number of designs (i.e., 400 product designs) to determine the activity rate of $630 per design. Note that an activity rate is not computed for the *Other* category of costs. This is because the Other cost pool consists of organization-sustaining costs and costs of idle capacity that are not allocated to products and customers. Overall profits must be large enough to cover these unallocated costs. Also note that the activity rates represent *average* costs. For example, the average cost of a customer order is $320.

The rates in Exhibit 8–6 indicate that *on average* a customer order consumes resources that cost $320; a product design consumes resources that cost $630; a unit of product consumes resources that cost $19 per machine-hour; and maintaining relations with a customer consumes resources that cost $1,470. Note that these are *average* figures. Some members of the ABC design team at Classic Brass argued that it would be unfair to charge all new products the same $630 product design cost regardless of how much

Topic Tackler

PLUS

8–2

EXHIBIT 8–6
Computation of Activity Rates

Microsoft Excel - ABC model-Classic Brass.XLS

File   Edit   View   Insert   Format   Tools   Data   Window   Help   Type a question for help

Arial   10   B I U $ %

	A	B	C	D	E	F
1	Activity Cost Pools	(a) Total Cost*	(b) Total Activity		(a) ÷ (b) Activity Rate	
2	Customer orders	$320,000	1,000	orders	$320	per order
3	Product design	$252,000	400	designs	$630	per design
4	Order size	$380,000	20,000	MHs	$19	per MH
5	Customer relations	$367,500	250	customers	$1,470	per customer
6	Other	$490,500	Not applicable		Not applicable	
8	*From Exhibit 8-5.					
9						

Exhibit 8-4 / Exhibit 8-5 \ **Exhibit 8-6** / Exhibit 8 design time they actually require. After discussing the pros and cons, the team concluded that it would not be worth the effort at the present time to keep track of actual design time spent on each new product. They felt that the benefits of increased accuracy would not be great enough to justify the higher cost of implementing and maintaining the more detailed costing system. Similarly, some team members were uncomfortable assigning the same $1,470 cost to each customer. Some customers are undemanding—ordering standard products well in advance of their needs. Others are very demanding and consume large amounts of marketing and administrative staff time. These are generally customers who order customized products, who tend to order at the last minute, and who change their minds. While everyone agreed with this observation, the data that would be required to measure individual customers' demands on resources was not currently available. Rather than delay implementation of the ABC system, the team decided to defer such refinements to a later date.

Before proceeding further, it would be helpful to get a better idea of the overall process of assigning costs to products and other cost objects in an ABC system. Exhibit 8–7 provides a visual perspective of the ABC system at Classic Brass. We recommend that you carefully go over this exhibit. In particular, note that the Other category, which contains organization-sustaining costs and costs of idle capacity, is not allocated to products or customers.

Step 4: Assign Overhead Costs to Cost Objects

LEARNING OBJECTIVE 4
Assign costs to a cost object using a second-stage allocation.

The fourth step in the implementation of activity-based costing is called *second-stage allocation*. In the **second-stage allocation**, activity rates are used to apply overhead costs to products and customers. First, we will illustrate how to assign costs to products followed by an example of how to assign costs to customers.

The data needed by the ABC team to assign overhead costs to Classic Brass's two products—standard stanchions and custom compass housings—are as follows:

Standard Stanchions

1. This product line does not require any new design resources.
2. 30,000 units were ordered during the year, comprising 600 separate orders.
3. Each stanchion requires 35 minutes of machine time for a total of 17,500 machine-hours.

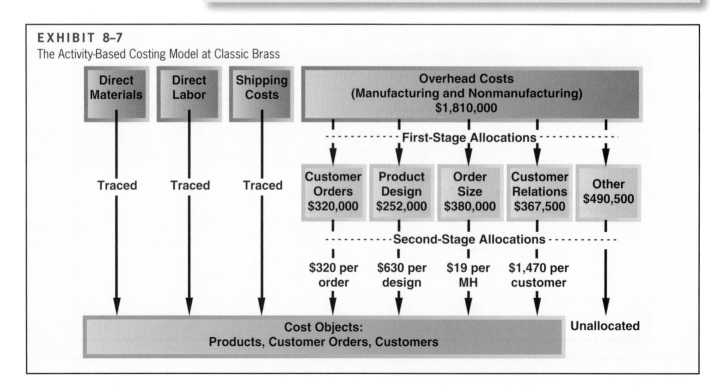

EXHIBIT 8–7
The Activity-Based Costing Model at Classic Brass

Custom Compass Housings

1. This is a custom product that requires new design resources.
2. There were 400 orders for custom compass housings. Orders for this product are placed separately from orders for standard stanchions.
3. There were 400 custom designs prepared. One custom design was prepared for each order.
4. Since some orders were for more than one unit, a total of 1,250 custom compass housings were produced during the year. A custom compass housing requires an average of 2 machine-hours for a total of 2,500 machine-hours.

Notice, 600 customer orders were placed for standard stanchions and 400 customer orders were placed for custom compass housings, for a total of 1,000 customer orders. All 400 product designs related to custom compass housings; none related to standard stanchions. Producing 30,000 standard stanchions required 17,500 machine-hours and producing 1,250 custom compass housings required 2,500 machine-hours, for a total of 20,000 machine-hours.

Exhibit 8–8 illustrates how overhead costs are assigned to the standard stanchions and custom compass housings. For example, the exhibit shows that $192,000 of overhead costs are assigned from the Customer Orders activity cost pool to the standard stanchions ($320 per order × 600 orders). Similarly, $128,000 of overhead costs are assigned from the Customer Orders activity cost pool to the custom compass housings ($320 per order × 400 orders). The Customer Orders cost pool contained a total of $320,000 (see Exhibit 8–5 or 8–6) and this total amount has been assigned to the two products ($192,000 + $128,000 = $320,000).

EXHIBIT 8–8
Assigning Overhead Costs to Products

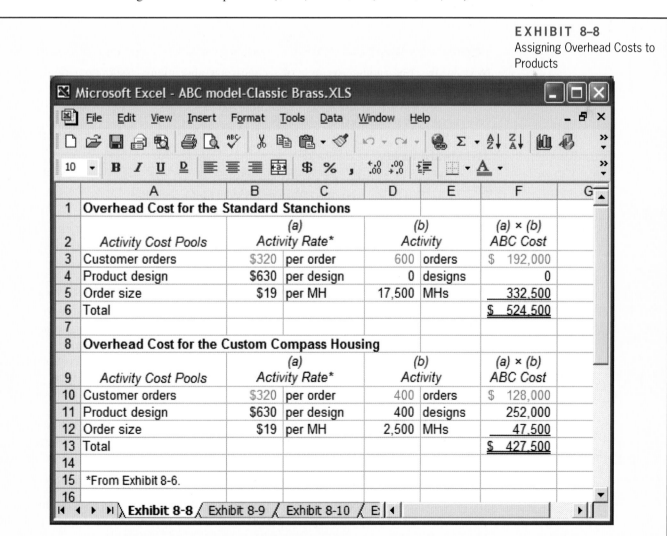

Overhead Cost for the Standard Stanchions

Activity Cost Pools	(a) Activity Rate*		(b) Activity		(a) × (b) ABC Cost
Customer orders	$320	per order	600	orders	$ 192,000
Product design	$630	per design	0	designs	0
Order size	$19	per MH	17,500	MHs	332,500
Total					$ 524,500

Overhead Cost for the Custom Compass Housing

Activity Cost Pools	(a) Activity Rate*		(b) Activity		(a) × (b) ABC Cost
Customer orders	$320	per order	400	orders	$ 128,000
Product design	$630	per design	400	designs	252,000
Order size	$19	per MH	2,500	MHs	47,500
Total					$ 427,500

*From Exhibit 8-6.

Exhibit 8–8 shows that a total of $952,000 of overhead costs is assigned to Classic Brass's two product lines—$524,500 to standard stanchions and $427,500 to custom compass housings. This amount is less than the $1,810,000 of overhead costs included in the ABC system. Why? The total amount of overhead assigned to products does not match the total amount of overhead cost in the ABC system because the ABC team purposely did not assign the $367,500 of Customer Relations and $490,500 of Other costs to products. The Customer Relations activity is a customer-level activity and the Other activity is an organization-sustaining activity—neither activity is caused by products. As shown below, when the Customer Relations and Other activity costs are added to the $952,000 of overhead costs assigned to products, the total is $1,810,000.

	Standard Stanchions	Custom Compass Housings	Total
Overhead Costs Assigned to Products			
Customer orders.......................	$192,000	$128,000	$ 320,000
Product design	0	252,000	252,000
Order size............................	332,500	47,500	380,000
Subtotal..............................	$524,500	$427,500	952,000
Overhead Costs not Assigned to Products			
Customer relations			367,500
Other.................................			490,500
Subtotal..............................			858,000
Total overhead cost			$1,810,000

Next, we describe another example of second-stage allocation—assigning activity costs to customers.

The data needed by the design team to assign overhead costs to one of its company's customers—Windward Yachts—are as follows:

Windward Yachts

1. The company placed a total of three orders.
   a. Two orders were for 150 standard stanchions per order.
   b. One order was for a single custom compass housing unit.
2. A total of 177 machine-hours were used to fulfill the three customer orders.
   a. The 300 standard stanchions required 175 machine-hours.
   b. The custom compass housing required 2 machine-hours.
3. Windward Yachts is one of 250 customers served by Classic Brass.

Exhibit 8–9 illustrates how the ABC system assigns overhead costs to this customer. As shown in Exhibit 8–9, the ABC team calculated that $6,423 of overhead costs should be assigned to Windward Yachts. The exhibit shows that Windward Yachts is assigned $960 ($320 per order × 3 orders) of overhead costs from the Customer Orders activity cost pool; $630 ($630 per design × 1 design) from the Product Design cost pool; $3,363 ($19 per machine-hour × 177 machine-hours) from the Order Size cost pool; and $1,470 ($1,470 per customer × 1 customer) from the Customer Relations cost pool.

With second-stage allocations complete, the ABC design team was ready to turn its attention to creating reports that would help explain the company's first ever net operating loss.

Step 5: Prepare Management Reports

The most common management reports prepared with ABC data are product and customer profitability reports. These reports help companies channel their resources to their most profitable

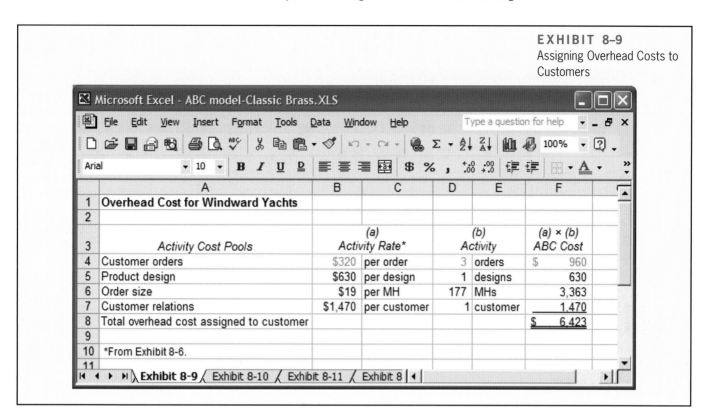

EXHIBIT 8–9
Assigning Overhead Costs to Customers

growth opportunities while at the same time highlighting products and customers that drain profits. We begin by illustrating a product profitability report followed by a customer profitability report.

The Classic Brass ABC team realized that the profit from a product, also called the *product margin,* is a function of the product's sales and the direct and indirect costs that the product causes. The ABC cost allocations shown in Exhibit 8–8 only summarize each product's indirect (i.e., overhead) costs. Therefore, to compute a product's profit (i.e., product margin), the design team needed to gather each product's sales and direct costs in addition to the overhead costs previously computed. The pertinent sales and direct cost data for each product are shown below. Notice the numbers in the total column agree with the income statement in Exhibit 8–1.

> **LEARNING OBJECTIVE 5**
> Use activity-based costing to compute product and customer margins.

	Standard Stanchions	Custom Compass Housings	Total
Sales	$2,660,000	$540,000	$3,200,000
Direct costs:			
Direct materials.	$905,500	$69,500	$975,000
Direct labor	$263,750	$87,500	$351,250
Shipping	$60,000	$5,000	$65,000

Having gathered the above data, the design team created the product profitability report shown in Exhibit 8–10 (page 326). The report revealed that standard stanchions are profitable, with a positive product margin of $906,250, whereas the custom compass housings are unprofitable, with a negative product margin of $49,500. Keep in mind that the product profitability report purposely does not include the costs in the Customer Relations and Other activity cost pools. These costs, which total $858,000, were excluded from the report because they are not caused by the products. Customer Relations costs are caused by customers, not products. The Other costs are organization-sustaining costs that are not caused by any particular product.

EXHIBIT 8–10
Product Margins—Activity-Based Costing

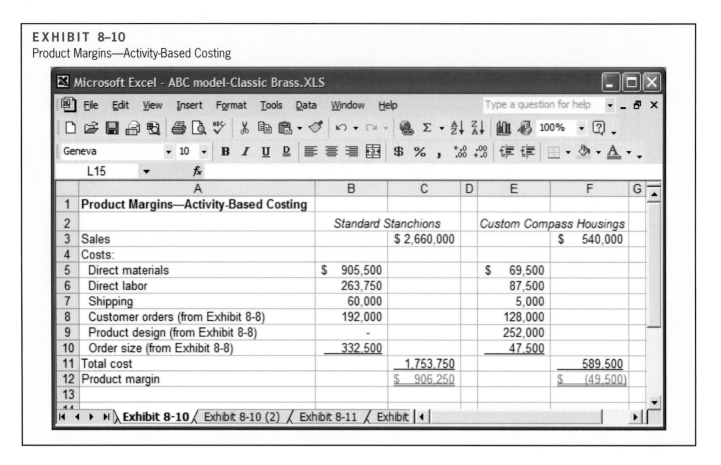

The product margins can be reconciled with the company's net operating income as follows:

	Standard Stanchions	Custom Compass Housings	Total
Sales (See Exhibit 8–10)	$2,660,000	$540,000	$3,200,000
Total costs (See Exhibit 8–10)	1,753,750	589,500	2,343,250
Product margins (See Exhibit 8–10)	$ 906,250	$ (49,500)	856,750
Overhead costs not assigned to products:			
Customer relations			367,500
Other.			490,500
Total			858,000
Net operating income			$ (1,250)

Next, the design team created a customer profitability report for Windward Yachts. Similar to the product profitability report, the design team needed to gather data concerning sales to Windward Yachts and the direct material, direct labor, and shipping costs associated with those sales. Those data are presented below:

	Windward Yachts
Sales	$11,350
Direct costs:	
Direct material costs	$2,123
Direct labor costs	$1,900
Shipping costs	$205

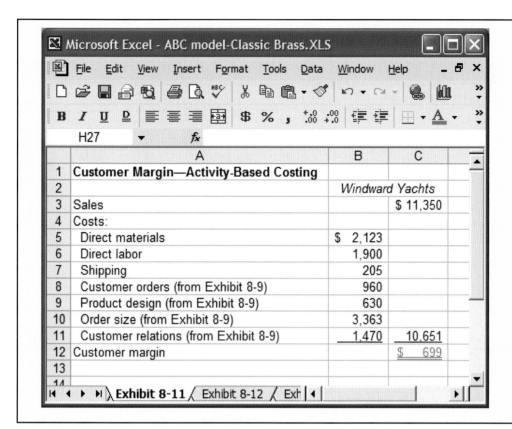

EXHIBIT 8–11
Customer Margin—
Activity-Based Costing

EXHIBIT 8–11
Customer Margin—
Activity-Based Costing

The spreadsheet shows:

		Windward Yachts
1	Customer Margin—Activity-Based Costing	
2		Windward Yachts
3	Sales	$ 11,350
4	Costs:	
5	Direct materials	$ 2,123
6	Direct labor	1,900
7	Shipping	205
8	Customer orders (from Exhibit 8-9)	960
9	Product design (from Exhibit 8-9)	630
10	Order size (from Exhibit 8-9)	3,363
11	Customer relations (from Exhibit 8-9)	1,470 10,651
12	Customer margin	$ 699

Using these data and the data from Exhibit 8–9, the design team created the customer profitability report shown in Exhibit 8–11. The report revealed that the customer margin for Windward Yachts is $699. A similar report could be prepared for each of Classic Brass's 250 customers, thereby enabling the company to cultivate relationships with its most profitable customers, while taking steps to reduce the negative impact of unprofitable customers.

IN BUSINESS

FINDING THAT GOLDEN TOP 20%

According to Meridien Research of Newton, Massachusetts, 20% of a bank's customers generate about 150% of its profits. At the other end of the spectrum, 30% of a bank's customers drain 50% of its profits. The question becomes how do banks identify which customers are in that golden top 20%? For many banks, the answer is revealed through customer relationship management software that provides activity-based costing capability.

"We had some customers that we thought, on the surface, would be very profitable, with an average of $300,000 in business accounts," said Jerry Williams, chairman and chief executive officer of First Bancorp. "What we didn't pull out was the fact that some write more than 275 checks a month. Once you apply the labor costs, it's not a profitable customer."

Meridien Research estimates that large commercial banks are increasing their spending on customer profitability systems by 14% a year with total annual expenditures exceeding $6 billion dollars.

Source: Joseph McKendrick, "Your Best Customers May Be Different Tomorrow," *Bank Technology News,* July 2001, pp. 1–4.

Comparison of Traditional and ABC Product Costs

The ABC team used a two-step process to compare its traditional and ABC product costs. First, the team reviewed the product margins reported by the traditional cost system. Then, they contrasted the differences between the traditional and ABC product margins.

EXHIBIT 8–12
Product Margins—Traditional Costing System

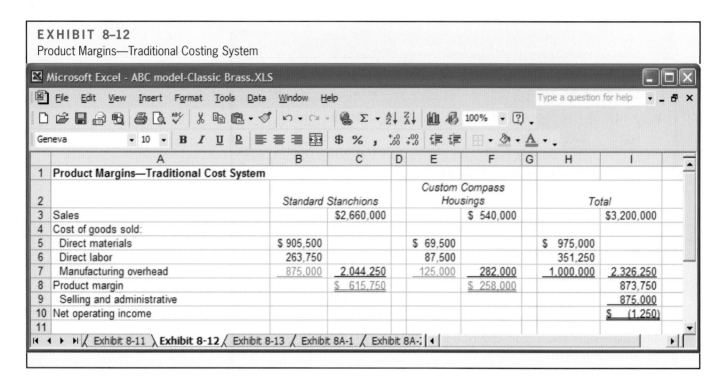

	A	B	C	D	E	F	G	H	I
1	**Product Margins—Traditional Cost System**								
2			*Standard Stanchions*			*Custom Compass Housings*			*Total*
3	Sales		$2,660,000			$ 540,000			$3,200,000
4	Cost of goods sold:								
5	Direct materials	$ 905,500			$ 69,500			$ 975,000	
6	Direct labor	263,750			87,500			351,250	
7	Manufacturing overhead	875,000	2,044,250		125,000	282,000		1,000,000	2,326,250
8	Product margin		$ 615,750			$ 258,000			873,750
9	Selling and administrative								875,000
10	Net operating income								$ (1,250)
11									

⏮ ◀ ▶ ⏭ ╲ Exhibit 8-11 ╲ **Exhibit 8-12** ╱ Exhibit 8-13 ╱ Exhibit 8A-1 ╱ Exhibit 8A-╵ ◀ |

Product Margins Computed Using the Traditional Cost System

Classic Brass's traditional cost system assigns only manufacturing costs to products—this includes direct materials, direct labor, and manufacturing overhead. Selling and administrative costs are not assigned to products. Exhibit 8–12 shows the product margins reported by Classic Brass's traditional cost system. We will explain how these margins were calculated in three steps. First, the sales and direct materials and direct labor cost data are the same numbers used by the ABC team to prepare Exhibit 8–10. In other words, the traditional cost system and the ABC system treat these three pieces of revenue and cost data identically.

Second, the traditional cost system uses a plantwide overhead rate to assign manufacturing overhead costs to products. The numerator for the plantwide overhead rate is $1,000,000, which is the total amount of manufacturing overhead shown on the income statement in Exhibit 8–1. The footnote in Exhibit 8–1 mentions that the traditional cost system uses machine-hours to assign manufacturing overhead costs to products. The Order Size activity in Exhibit 8–6 used 20,000 machine-hours as its level of activity. These same 20,000 machine-hours would be used in the denominator of the plantwide overhead rate, which is computed as follows:

$$\text{Plantwide overhead rate} = \frac{\text{Total estimated manufacturing overhead}}{\text{Total estimated machine-hours}}$$

$$= \frac{\$1,000,000}{20,000 \text{ machine-hours}}$$

$$= \$50 \text{ per machine-hour}$$

Since 17,500 machine-hours were worked on standard stanchions, this product line is assigned $875,000 (17,500 machine-hours × $50 per machine-hour) of manufacturing overhead cost. Similarly, the custom compass housings required 2,500 machine-hours, so this product line is assigned $125,000 (2,500 machine-hours × $50 per machine-hour) of manufacturing overhead cost. The sales of each product minus its cost of goods sold equals the product margin of $615,750 for standard stanchions and $258,000 for custom compass housings.

Notice, the net operating loss of $1,250 shown in Exhibit 8–12 agrees with the loss reported in the income statement in Exhibit 8–1 and with the loss shown in the table immediately benneath Exhibit 8–10. The company's *total* sales, *total* costs, and its resulting net operating loss are the same regardless of whether you are looking at the absorption income statement in Exhibit 8–1, the ABC product profitability analysis depicted on page 326, or the traditional product profitability analysis in Exhibit 8–12. Although the "total pie" remains constant across the traditional and ABC systems, what differs is how the pie is divided between the two product lines. The traditional product margin calculations suggest that standard stanchions are generating a product margin of $615,750 and the custom compass housings a product margin of $258,000. However, these product margins differ from the ABC product margins reported in Exhibit 8–10. Indeed, the traditional cost system is sending misleading signals to Classic Brass's managers about each product's profitability. Let's explain why.

The Differences between ABC and Traditional Product Costs

The changes in product margins caused by switching from the traditional cost system to the activity-based costing system are shown below:

	Standard Stanchions	Custom Compass Housings
Product margins—traditional	$615,750	$258,000
Product margins—ABC	906,250	(49,500)
Change in reported product margins	$290,500	($307,500)

The traditional cost system overcosts the standard stanchions and consequently reports an artificially low product margin for this product. The switch to an activity-based view of product profitability increases the product margin on standard stanchions by $290,500. In contrast, the traditional cost system undercosts the custom compass housings and reports an artificially high product margin for this product. The switch to activity-based costing decreases the product margin on custom compass housings by $307,500.

The reasons for the change in reported product margins between the two costing methods are revealed in Exhibit 8–13 (page 330). The top portion of the exhibit shows each product's direct and indirect cost assignments as reported by the traditional cost system in Exhibit 8–12. For example, Exhibit 8–13 includes the following costs for standard stanchions: direct materials, $905,500; direct labor, $263,750; and manufacturing overhead, $875,000. Each of these costs corresponds with those reported in Exhibit 8–12. Notice, the selling and administrative costs of $875,000 are purposely not allocated to products because these costs are considered to be period costs. Similarly, the bottom portion of Exhibit 8–13 summarizes the direct and indirect cost assignments as reported by the activity-based costing system in Exhibit 8–10. The only new information in Exhibit 8–13 is shown in the two columns of percentages. The first column of percentages shows the percentage of each cost assigned to standard stanchions. For example, the $905,500 of direct materials cost traced to standard stanchions is 92.9% of the company's total direct materials cost of $975,000. The second column of percentages does the same thing for custom compass housings.

There are three reasons why the traditional and activity-based costing systems report different product margins. First, Classic Brass's traditional cost system allocates *all* manufacturing overhead costs to products. This forces both products to absorb all manufacturing overhead costs regardless of whether they actually consumed the costs that were allocated to them. The ABC system does not assign the manufacturing overhead costs consumed by the Customer Relations activity to products because these costs are caused by customers, not specific products. It also does not assign the manufacturing overhead costs included in the Other activity to products because these organization-sustaining and unused capacity costs

EXHIBIT 8–13
A Comparison of Traditional and Activity-Based Cost Assignments

	Standard Stanchions		Custom Compass Housings		Total
	(a)	(a) ÷ (c)	(b)	(b) ÷ (c)	(c)
Traditional Cost System	Amount	%	Amount	%	Amount
Direct materials	$ 905,500	92.9%	$ 69,500	7.1%	$ 975,000
Direct labor.	263,750	75.1%	87,500	24.9%	351,250
Manufacturing overhead.	875,000	87.5%	125,000	12.5%	1,000,000
Total cost assigned to products	$2,044,250		$282,000		2,326,250
Selling and administrative					875,000
Total cost					$3,201,250
Activity-Based Costing System					
Direct costs:					
Direct materials.	$ 905,500	92.9%	$ 69,500	7.1%	$ 975,000
Direct labor	263,750	75.1%	87,500	24.9%	351,250
Shipping	60,000	92.3%	5,000	7.7%	65,000
Indirect costs:					
Customer orders.	192,000	60.0%	128,000	40.0%	320,000
Product design	0	0.0%	252,000	100.0%	252,000
Order size	332,500	87.5%	47,500	12.5%	380,000
Total cost assigned to products	$1,753,750		$589,500		2,343,250
Costs not assigned to products:					
Customer relations					367,500
Other.					490,500
Total cost					$3,201,250

are not caused by any particular product. From an ABC point of view, assigning these costs to products is inherently arbitrary and counterproductive.

Second, Classic Brass's traditional cost system allocates all of the manufacturing overhead costs using a volume-related allocation base—machine-hours—that may or may not reflect what actually causes the costs. In other words, in the traditional system, 87.5% of each manufacturing overhead cost is implicitly assigned to standard stanchions and 12.5% is assigned to custom compass housings. For example, the traditional cost system inappropriately assigns 87.5% of costs of the Customer Orders activity (a batch-level activity) to standard stanchions even though the ABC system revealed that standard stanchions caused only 60% of these costs. Conversely, the traditional cost system assigns only 12.5% of these costs to custom compass housings even though this product caused 40% of these costs. Similarly, the traditional cost system assigns 87.5% of the costs of the Product Design activity (a product-level activity) to standard stanchions even though the standard stanchions caused none of these costs. All of the costs of the Product Design activity, rather than just 12.5%, should be assigned to custom compass housings. The result is that traditional cost systems overcost high-volume products (such as the standard stanchions) and undercost low-volume products (such as the custom compass housings) because they assign batch-level and product-level costs using volume-related allocation bases.

The third reason the product margins differ between the two cost systems is that the ABC system assigns the nonmanufacturing overhead costs caused by products to those products on a cause-and-effect basis. The traditional cost system disregards these costs because they are classified as period costs. The ABC system directly traces shipping costs to products and includes the nonmanufacturing overhead costs caused by products in the activity cost pools that are assigned to products.

COMPARING ACTIVITY-BASED AND TRADITIONAL PRODUCT COSTS

Airco Heating and Air Conditioning (Airco), located in Van Buren, Arkansas, implemented an ABC system to better understand the profitability of its products. The ABC system assigned $4,458,605 of overhead costs to eight activities as follows:

Activity Cost Pool	Total Cost	Total Activity		Activity Rate
Machines	$ 435,425	73,872	machine-hours	$5.89
Data record maintenance	132,597	14	products administered	$9,471.21
Material handling	1,560,027	16,872	products	$92.46
Product changeover	723,338	72	setup hours	$10,046.36
Scheduling	24,877	2,788	production runs	$8.92
Raw material receiving	877,107	2,859	receipts	$306.79
Product shipment	561,014	13,784,015	miles	$0.04
Customer service	144,220	2,533	customer contacts	$56.94
Total	$4,458,605			

Airco's managers were surprised by the fact that 55% [($1,560,027 + $877,107) ÷ $4,458,605] of its overhead resources were consumed by material handling and receiving activities. They responded by reducing the raw material and part transport distances within the facility. In addition, they compared the traditional and ABC product margin percentages (computed by dividing each product's margin by the sales of the product) for the company's seven product lines of air conditioners as summarized below:

	Product						
	5-Ton	6-Ton	7.5 Ton	10-Ton	12.5 Ton	15-Ton	20-Ton
Traditional product margin %	−20%	4%	40%	−4%	20%	42%	70%
ABC product margin %	−15%	−8%	50%	1%	−6%	40%	69%

In response to the ABC data, Airco decided to explore the possibility of raising prices on 5-ton, 6-ton, and 12.5-ton air conditioners while at the same time seeking to reduce overhead consumption by these products.

Source: Heather Nachtmann and Mohammad Hani Al-Rifai, "An Application of Activity-Based Costing in the Air Conditioner Manufacturing Industry," *The Engineering Economist* 49, Issue 3, 2004, pp. 221–236.

The ABC design team presented the results of its work in a meeting attended by all of the top managers of Classic Brass, including the president John Towers, the production manager Susan Richter, the marketing manager Tom Olafson, and the accounting manager Mary Goodman. The ABC team brought with them copies of the chart showing the ABC design (Exhibit 8–7), and the table comparing the traditional and ABC cost assignments (Exhibit 8–13). After the formal presentation by the ABC team, the following discussion took place:

John: I would like to personally thank the ABC team for all of the work they have done and for an extremely interesting presentation. I am now beginning to wonder about a lot of the decisions we have made in the past using our old cost accounting system. According to the ABC analysis, we had it all backwards. We are losing money on the custom products and making a fistful on the standard products.

Mary: I have to admit that I had no idea that the Product Design work for custom compass housings was so expensive! I knew burying these costs in our plantwide overhead rate was penalizing standard stanchions, but I didn't understand the magnitude of the problem.

Susan: I never did believe we were making a lot of money on the custom jobs. You ought to see all of the problems they create for us in production.

Tom: I hate to admit it, but the custom jobs always seem to give us headaches in marketing, too.

John: If we are losing money on custom compass housings, why not suggest to our customers that they go elsewhere for that kind of work?

Tom: Wait a minute, we would lose a lot of sales.

Susan: So what, we would save a lot more costs.

Mary: Maybe yes, maybe no. Some of the costs would not disappear if we were to drop the custom business.

Tom: Like what?

Mary: Well Tom, I believe you said that about 10% of your time is spent dealing with new products. As a consequence, 10% of your salary was allocated to the Product Design cost pool. If we were to drop all of the products requiring design work, would you be willing to take a 10% pay cut?

Tom: I trust you're joking.

Mary: Do you see the problem? Just because 10% of your time is spent on custom products doesn't mean that the company would save 10% of your salary if the custom products were dropped. Before we take a drastic action like dropping the custom products, we should identify which costs are really relevant.

John: I think I see what you are driving at. We wouldn't want to drop a lot of products only to find that our costs really haven't changed much. It is true that dropping the products would free up resources like Tom's time, but we had better be sure we have some good use for those resources *before* we take such an action.

As this discussion among the managers of Classic Brass illustrates, caution should be exercised before taking an action based on an ABC analysis such as the one shown in Exhibits 8–10 and 8–11. The product and customer margins computed in these exhibits are a useful starting point for further analysis, but managers need to know what costs are really affected before taking any action such as dropping a product or customer or changing the prices of products or services. Appendix 8A shows how an *action analysis report* can be constructed to help managers make such decisions. An **action analysis report** provides more detail about costs and how they might adjust to changes in activity than the ABC analysis presented in Exhibits 8–10 and 8–11.

Targeting Process Improvements

Activity-based costing can also be used to identify activities that would benefit from process improvements. Indeed, this is the most widely cited benefit of activity-based costing by managers.[3] When used in this way, activity-based costing is often called *activity-based management.* Basically, **activity-based management** involves focusing on activities to eliminate waste, decrease processing time, and reduce defects. Activity-based management is used in organizations as diverse as manufacturing companies, hospitals, and the U.S. Marine Corps. When "40 percent of the cost of running a hospital involves storing, collecting and moving information," there is obviously a great deal of room for eliminating waste.[4]

The first step in any improvement program is to decide what to improve. The Theory of Constraints approach discussed in Chapter 1 is a powerful tool for targeting the area in an organization whose improvement will yield the greatest benefit. Activity-based management provides another approach. The activity rates computed in activity-based costing can provide valuable clues concerning where there is waste and opportunity for improvement. For example, looking at the activity rates in Exhibit 8–6, managers at Classic Brass may conclude that $320 to process a customer order is far too expensive for an activity that adds

---

[3] Dan Swenson, "The Benefits of Activity-Based Cost Management to the Manufacturing Industry," *Journal of Management Accounting Research* 7, pp. 167–180.

[4] Kambiz Foroohar, "Rx: Software," *Forbes,* April 7, 1997, p. 114.

no value to the product. As a consequence, they may target customer order processing for process improvement using Six Sigma as discussed in Chapter 1.

Benchmarking is another way to leverage the information in activity rates. **Benchmarking** is a systematic approach to identifying the activities with the greatest room for improvement. It is based on comparing the performance in an organization with the performance of other, similar organizations known for their outstanding performance. If a particular part of the organization performs far below the world-class standard, managers will be likely to target that area for improvement.

COSTS IN HEALTH CARE

Owens & Minor, a $3 billion medical supplies distributor, offers an activity-based billing option to its customers. Instead of charging a fixed amount for items that are ordered by customers, the charges are based on activities required to fill the order as well as on the cost of the item ordered. For example, Owens & Minor charges extra for weekend deliveries. These charges encourage customers to reduce their weekend delivery requests. This results in decreased costs for Owens & Minor, which can then be passed on to customers in the form of lower charges for the specific items that are ordered. As many as 25% of Owens & Minor's 4,000 health care customers have used this billing option to identify and realize cost reduction opportunities. For example, Bill Wright of Sutter Health in Sacramento, California, said that Owens & Minor's activity-based billing has motivated his company to eliminate weekend deliveries, place more items per order, align purchase quantities with prepackaged specifications, and transmit orders electronically. The end result is that one Sutter affiliate decreased its purchasing costs from 4.25% of product costs to 3.75%. In all, Owens & Minor has identified about 250 activity-driven procurement costs that hospitals can manage more efficiently to reduce costs.

Source: Todd Shields, "Hospitals Turning to Activity-Based Costing to Save and Measure Distribution Costs," *Healthcare Purchasing News*, November 2001, pp. 14–15.

PROCESS IMPROVEMENTS HELP NURSES

Providence Portland Medical Center (PPMC) used ABC to improve one of the most expensive and error-prone processes within its nursing units—ordering, distributing, and administering medications to patients. To the surprise of everyone involved, the ABC data showed that "medication-related activities made up 43% of the nursing unit's total operating costs." The ABC team members knew that one of the root causes of this time-consuming process was the illegibility of physician orders that are faxed to the pharmacy. Replacing the standard fax machine with a much better $5,000 machine virtually eliminated unreadable orders and decreased follow-up telephone calls by more than 90%—saving the hospital $500,000 per year. In total, the ABC team generated improvement ideas that offered $1 million of net savings in redeployable resources. "This amount translates to additional time that nurses and pharmacists can spend on direct patient care."

Source: "How ABC Analysis Will Save PPMC Over $1 Million a Year," *Financial Analysis, Planning & Reporting*, November 2003, pp. 6–10.

Activity-Based Costing and External Reports

Since activity-based costing generally provides more accurate product costs than traditional costing methods, why isn't it used for external reports? Some companies *do* use activity-based costing in their external reports, but most do not.[5] There are a number of reasons for

---

[5] Appendix 8B illustrates how a variation of activity-based costing can be used to develop product costs for external reports.

this. First, external reports are less detailed than internal reports prepared for decision making. On the external reports, individual product costs are not reported. Cost of goods sold and inventory valuations are disclosed, but these accounts are not broken down by product. If some products are undercosted and some are overcosted, the errors tend to cancel each other when the product costs are added together.

Second, it is often very difficult to make changes in a company's accounting system. The official cost accounting systems in most large companies are usually embedded in complex computer programs that have been modified in-house over the course of many years. It is extremely difficult to make changes in such computer programs without causing numerous bugs.

Third, an ABC system such as the one described in this chapter does not conform to generally accepted accounting principles (GAAP). As discussed in Chapter 2, product costs computed for external reports must include all of the manufacturing costs and only manufacturing costs; but in an ABC system as described in this chapter, product costs exclude some manufacturing costs and include some nonmanufacturing costs. It is possible to adjust the ABC data at the end of the period to conform to GAAP, but that requires more work.

Fourth, auditors are likely to be uncomfortable with allocations that are based on interviews with the company's personnel. Such subjective data can be easily manipulated by management to make earnings and other key variables look more favorable.

For all of these reasons, most companies confine their ABC efforts to special studies for management, and they do not attempt to integrate activity-based costing into their formal cost accounting systems.

The Limitations of Activity-Based Costing

Implementing an activity-based costing system is a major project that requires substantial resources. And once implemented, an activity-based costing system is more costly to maintain than a traditional costing system—data concerning numerous activity measures must be periodically collected, checked, and entered into the system. The benefits of increased accuracy may not outweigh these costs.

Activity-based costing produces numbers, such as product margins, that are at odds with the numbers produced by traditional costing systems. But managers are accustomed to using traditional costing systems to run their operations and traditional costing systems are often used in performance evaluations. Essentially, activity-based costing changes the rules of the game. It is a fact of human nature that changes in organizations, particularly those that alter the rules of the game, inevitably face resistance. This underscores the importance of top management support and the full participation of line managers, as well as the accounting staff, in any activity-based costing initiative. If activity-based costing is viewed as an accounting initiative that does not have the full support of top management, it is doomed to failure.

In practice, most managers insist on fully allocating all costs to products, customers, and other costing objects in an activity-based costing system—including the costs of idle capacity and organization-sustaining costs. This results in overstated costs and understated margins and mistakes in pricing and other critical decisions.

Activity-based costing data can easily be misinterpreted and must be used with care when used in making decisions. Costs assigned to products, customers, and other cost objects are only *potentially* relevant. Before making any significant decisions using activity-based costing data, managers must identify which costs are really relevant for the decision at hand. See Appendix 8A for more details.

As discussed in the previous section, reports generated by the best activity-based costing systems do not conform to generally accepted accounting principles. Consequently, an organization involved in activity-based costing should have two cost systems—one for internal use and one for preparing external reports. This is costlier than maintaining just one system and may cause confusion about which system is to be believed and relied on.

A CRITICAL PERSPECTIVE OF ABC

Marconi is a Portuguese telecommunications company that encountered problems with its ABC system. The company's production managers felt that 23% of the costs included in the system were common costs that should not be allocated to products and that allocating these costs to products was not only inaccurate, but also irrelevant to their operational cost reduction efforts. Furthermore, Marconi's front-line workers resisted the ABC system because they felt it might be used to weaken their autonomy and to justify downsizing, outsourcing, and work intensification. They believed that ABC created a "turkeys queuing for Christmas syndrome" because they were expected to volunteer information to help create a cost system that could eventually lead to their demise. These two complications created a third problem—the data necessary to build the ABC cost model was provided by disgruntled and distrustful employees. Consequently, the accuracy of the data was questionable at best. In short, Marconi's experiences illustrate some of the challenges that complicate real-world ABC implementations.

Source: Maria Major and Trevor Hopper, "Managers Divided: Implementing ABC in a Portuguese Telecommunications Company," *Management Accounting Research*, June 2005, pp. 205–229.

THE SURVEY SAYS . . .

Professors John Innes, Falconer Mitchell, and Donald Sinclair have conducted two surveys designed to study ABC adoption trends within the United Kingdom across a five-year time span. The professors' initial survey results are based on responses from 352 of the U.K.'s largest companies, while the follow-up survey results obtained five years later are based on responses from 177 of the U.K.'s largest companies.

The initial survey results indicated that 21% of respondents were currently using ABC, 29.6% were considering ABC adoption, 13.3% had rejected ABC after considering its implementation, and 36.1% were not considering ABC. Five years later the follow-up survey showed that 17.5% of respondents were currently using ABC, 20.3% were considering ABC adoption, 15.3% had rejected ABC after considering implementation, and 46.9% were not considering ABC. The professors summarized their findings by saying "These results are indicative of no growth in the popularity of ABC, and are consistent with both a leveling off in interest in it and the adoption of it over this five-year period."

Source: John Innes, Falconer Mitchell, and Donald Sinclair, "Activity-Based Costing in the U.K.'s Largest Companies: A Comparison of 1994 and 1999 Survey Results," *Management Accounting Research*, September 2000, pp. 349–362.

Summary

Traditional cost accounting methods suffer from several defects that can result in distorted costs for decision-making purposes. All manufacturing costs—even those that are not caused by any specific product—are allocated to products. And nonmanufacturing costs that are caused by products are not assigned to products. Traditional methods also allocate the costs of idle capacity to products. In effect, products are charged for resources that they don't use. And finally, traditional methods tend to place too much reliance on unit-level allocation bases such as direct labor and machine-hours. This results in overcosting high-volume products and undercosting low-volume products and can lead to mistakes when making decisions.

Activity-based costing estimates the costs of the resources consumed by cost objects such as products and customers. The activity-based costing approach assumes that cost objects generate activities that in turn consume costly resources. Activities form the link between costs and cost objects.

Activity-based costing is concerned with overhead—both manufacturing overhead and selling and administrative overhead. The accounting for direct labor and direct materials is usually the same under traditional and ABC costing methods.

To build an ABC system, companies typically choose a small set of activities that summarize much of the work performed in overhead departments. Associated with each activity is an activity cost pool. To the extent possible, overhead costs are directly traced to these activity cost pools. The remaining overhead costs are allocated to the activity cost pools in the first-stage allocation. Interviews with managers often form the basis for these allocations.

An activity rate is computed for each cost pool by dividing the costs assigned to the cost pool by the measure of activity for the cost pool. Activity rates provide useful information to managers concerning the costs of performing overhead activities. A particularly high cost for an activity may trigger efforts to improve the way the activity is carried out in the organization.

In the second-stage allocation, the activity rates are used to apply costs to cost objects such as products and customers. The costs computed under activity-based costing are often quite different from the costs generated by a company's traditional cost accounting system. While the ABC system is almost certainly more accurate, managers should nevertheless exercise caution before making decisions based on the ABC data. Some of the costs may not be avoidable and hence would not be relevant.

Review Problem: Activity-Based Costing

Ferris Corporation makes a single product—a fire-resistant commercial filing cabinet—that it sells to office furniture distributors. The company has a simple ABC system that it uses for internal decision making. The company has two overhead departments whose costs are listed below:

Manufacturing overhead	$500,000
Selling and administrative overhead	300,000
Total overhead costs	$800,000

The company's ABC system has the following activity cost pools and activity measures:

Activity Cost Pool	Activity Measure
Assembling units	Number of units
Processing orders	Number of orders
Supporting customers	Number of customers
Other	Not applicable

Costs assigned to the "Other" activity cost pool have no activity measure; they consist of the costs of unused capacity and organization-sustaining costs—neither of which are assigned to orders, customers, or the product.

Ferris Corporation distributes the costs of manufacturing overhead and of selling and administrative overhead to the activity cost pools based on employee interviews, the results of which are reported below:

Distribution of Resource Consumption Across Activity Cost Pools					
	Assembling Units	Processing Orders	Supporting Customers	Other	Total
Manufacturing overhead	50%	35%	5%	10%	100%
Selling and administrative overhead	10%	45%	25%	20%	100%
Total activity	1,000 units	250 orders	100 customers		

Required:
1. Perform the first-stage allocation of overhead costs to the activity cost pools as in Exhibit 8–5.
2. Compute activity rates for the activity cost pools as in Exhibit 8–6.
3. OfficeMart is one of Ferris Corporation's customers. Last year, OfficeMart ordered filing cabinets four different times. OfficeMart ordered a total of 80 filing cabinets during the year. Construct a table as in Exhibit 8–9 showing the overhead costs attributable to OfficeMart.
4. The selling price of a filing cabinet is $595. The cost of direct materials is $180 per filing cabinet, and direct labor is $50 per filing cabinet. What is the customer margin of OfficeMart? See Exhibit 8–11 for an example of how to complete this report.

Solution to Review Problem

1. The first-stage allocation of costs to the activity cost pools appears below:

	Activity Cost Pools				
	Assembling Units	Processing Orders	Supporting Customers	Other	Total
Manufacturing overhead	$250,000	$175,000	$25,000	$50,000	$500,000
Selling and administrative overhead	30,000	135,000	75,000	60,000	300,000
Total cost..................	$280,000	$310,000	$100,000	$110,000	$800,000

2. The activity rates for the activity cost pools are:

Activity Cost Pools	(a) Total Cost	(b) Total Activity	(a) ÷ (b) Activity Rate
Assembling units............	$280,000	1,000 units	$280 per unit
Processing orders...........	$310,000	250 orders	$1,240 per order
Supporting customers........	$100,000	100 customers	$1,000 per customer

3. The overhead cost attributable to OfficeMart would be computed as follows:

Activity Cost Pools	(a) Activity Rate	(b) Activity	(a) × (b) ABC Cost
Assembling units	$280 per unit	80 units	$22,400
Processing orders	$1,240 per order	4 orders	$4,960
Supporting customers	$1,000 per customer	1 customer	$1,000

4. The customer margin can be computed as follows:

Sales ($595 per unit × 80 units)		$47,600
Costs:		
Direct materials ($180 per unit × 80 units)	$14,400	
Direct labor ($50 per unit × 80 units)...........	4,000	
Unit-related overhead (above)	22,400	
Order-related overhead (above)...............	4,960	
Customer-related overhead (above)	1,000	46,760
Customer margin		$ 840

Glossary

Action analysis report A report showing what costs have been assigned to a cost object, such as a product or customer, and how difficult it would be to adjust the cost if there is a change in activity. (p. 332)

Activity An event that causes the consumption of overhead resources in an organization. (p. 312)

Activity-based costing (ABC) A costing method based on activities that is designed to provide managers with cost information for strategic and other decisions that potentially affect capacity and therefore fixed as well as variable costs. (p. 310)

Activity-based management (ABM) A management approach that focuses on managing activities as a way of eliminating waste and reducing delays and defects. (p. 332)

Activity cost pool A "bucket" in which costs are accumulated that relate to a single activity measure in an activity-based costing system. (p. 312)

Activity measure An allocation base in an activity-based costing system; ideally, a measure of the amount of activity that drives the costs in an activity cost pool. (p. 312)

Batch-level activities Activities that are performed each time a batch of goods is handled or processed, regardless of how many units are in the batch. The amount of resource consumed depends on the number of batches run rather than on the number of units in the batch. (p. 312)

Benchmarking A systematic approach to identifying the activities with the greatest potential for improvement. (p. 333)

Customer-level activities Activities that are carried out to support customers but that are not related to any specific product. (p. 313)

Duration driver A measure of the amount of time required to perform an activity. (p. 312)

First-stage allocation The process by which overhead costs are assigned to activity cost pools in an activity-based costing system. (p. 318)

Organization-sustaining activities Activities that are carried out regardless of which customers are served, which products are produced, how many batches are run, or how many units are made. (p. 313)

Product-level activities Activities that relate to specific products that must be carried out regardless of how many units are produced and sold or batches run. (p. 312)

Second-stage allocation The process by which activity rates are used to apply costs to products and customers in activity-based costing. (p. 322)

Transaction driver A simple count of the number of times an activity occurs. (p. 312)

Unit-level activities Activities that are performed each time a unit is produced. (p. 312)

Appendix 8A: ABC Action Analysis

LEARNING OBJECTIVE 6
Prepare an action analysis report using activity-based costing data and interpret the report.

A conventional ABC analysis, such as the one presented in Exhibits 8–10 and 8–11 in the chapter, has several important limitations. Referring back to Exhibit 8–10, recall that the custom compass housings show a negative product margin of $49,500. Because of this apparent loss, managers were considering dropping this product. However, as the discussion among the managers revealed, it is unlikely that all of the $589,500 cost of the product would be avoided if it were dropped. Some of these costs would continue even if the product were totally eliminated. *Before* taking action, it is vital to identify which costs would be avoided and which costs would continue. Only those costs that can be avoided are relevant in the decision. Moreover, many of the costs are managed costs that would require explicit management action to eliminate. If the custom compass housings product line were eliminated, the direct materials cost would be avoided without any explicit management action—the materials simply wouldn't be ordered. On the other hand, if the custom compass housings were dropped, explicit management action would be required to eliminate the salaries of overhead workers that are assigned to this product.

Simply shifting these managed costs to other products would not solve anything. These costs would have to be eliminated or the resources *shifted to the constraint* to have any benefit to the company. While eliminating the cost is obviously beneficial, redeploying the resources is only beneficial if the resources are shifted to the constraint in the process. If the resources are redeployed to a work center that is not a constraint, it would increase the excess capacity in that work center—which has no direct benefit to the company.

In addition, if some overhead costs need to be eliminated as a result of dropping a product, specific managers must be held responsible for eliminating those costs or the reductions are unlikely to occur. If no one is specifically held responsible for eliminating the costs, they will almost certainly continue to be incurred. Without external pressure, managers usually avoid cutting costs in their areas of responsibility. The action analysis report developed in this appendix is intended to help top managers identify what costs are relevant in a decision and to place responsibility for the elimination of those costs on the appropriate managers.

Activity Rates—Action Analysis Report

Constructing an action analysis report begins with the results of the first-stage allocation, which is reproduced as Exhibit 8A–1 (page 340). In contrast to the conventional ABC analysis covered in the chapter, the calculation of the activity rates for an action analysis report is a bit more involved. In addition to computing an overall activity rate for each activity cost pool, an activity rate is computed for each cell in Exhibit 8A–1. The computations of activity rates for the action analysis are carried out in Exhibit 8A–2 (page 340). For example, the $125,000 cost of indirect factory wages for the Customer Orders cost pool is divided by the total activity for that cost pool—1,000 orders—to arrive at the activity rate of $125 per customer order for indirect factory wages. Similarly, the $200,000 cost of indirect factory wages for the Product Design cost pool is divided by the total activity for that cost pool—400 designs—to arrive at the activity rate of $500 per design for indirect factory wages. Note that the totals at the bottom of Exhibit 8A–2 agree with the overall activity rates in Exhibit 8–6 in the chapter. Exhibit 8A–2, which shows the activity rates for the action analysis report, contains more detail than Exhibit 8–6, which contains the activity rates for the conventional ABC analysis.

Assignment of Overhead Costs to Products—Action Analysis Report

Similarly, computing the overhead costs to be assigned to products for an action analysis report involves more detail than for a conventional ABC analysis. The computations for Classic Brass are carried out in Exhibit 8A–3 (page 341). For example, the activity rate of $125 per customer order for indirect factory wages is multiplied by 600 orders for the standard stanchions to arrive at the cost of $75,000 for indirect factory wages in Exhibit 8A–3. Instead of just a single cost number for each cost pool as in the conventional ABC analysis, we now have an entire cost matrix showing much more detail. Note that the column totals for the cost matrix in Exhibit 8A–3 agree with the ABC costs for stanchions in Exhibit 8–8. Indeed, the conventional ABC analysis of Exhibit 8–10 can be easily constructed using the column totals at the bottom of the cost matrices in Exhibit 8A–3. In contrast, the action analysis report will be based on the row totals at the right of the cost matrices in Exhibit 8A–3. In addition, the action analysis report will include a simple color-coding scheme that will help managers identify how easily the various costs can be adjusted.

EXHIBIT 8A–1
First-Stage Allocations to Activity Cost Pools

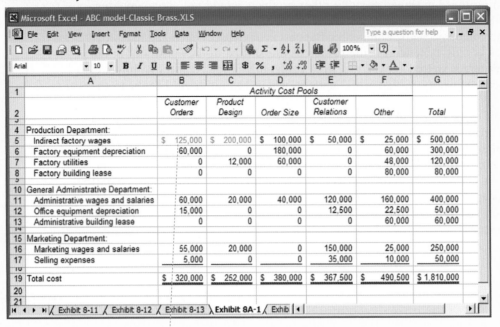

	Customer Orders	Product Design	Order Size	Customer Relations	Other	Total
Activity Cost Pools						
Production Department:						
Indirect factory wages	$ 125,000	$ 200,000	$ 100,000	$ 50,000	$ 25,000	$ 500,000
Factory equipment depreciation	60,000	0	180,000	0	60,000	300,000
Factory utilities	0	12,000	60,000	0	48,000	120,000
Factory building lease	0	0	0	0	80,000	80,000
General Administrative Department:						
Administrative wages and salaries	60,000	20,000	40,000	120,000	160,000	400,000
Office equipment depreciation	15,000	0	0	12,500	22,500	50,000
Administrative building lease	0	0	0	0	60,000	60,000
Marketing Department:						
Marketing wages and salaries	55,000	20,000	0	150,000	25,000	250,000
Selling expenses	5,000	0	0	35,000	10,000	50,000
Total cost	$ 320,000	$ 252,000	$ 380,000	$ 367,500	$ 490,500	$ 1,810,000

EXHIBIT 8A–2
Computation of the Activity Rates for the Action Analysis Report

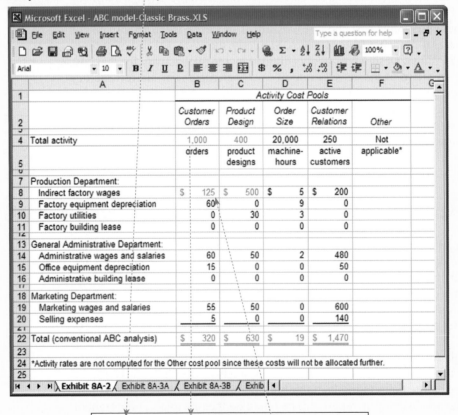

	Customer Orders	Product Design	Order Size	Customer Relations	Other
Activity Cost Pools					
Total activity	1,000 orders	400 product designs	20,000 machine-hours	250 active customers	Not applicable*
Production Department:					
Indirect factory wages	$ 125	$ 500	$ 5	$ 200	
Factory equipment depreciation	60	0	9	0	
Factory utilities	0	30	3	0	
Factory building lease	0	0	0	0	
General Administrative Department:					
Administrative wages and salaries	60	50	2	480	
Office equipment depreciation	15	0	0	50	
Administrative building lease	0	0	0	0	
Marketing Department:					
Marketing wages and salaries	55	50	0	600	
Selling expenses	5	0	0	140	
Total (conventional ABC analysis)	$ 320	$ 630	$ 19	$ 1,470	

*Activity rates are not computed for the Other cost pool since these costs will not be allocated further.

$125,000 ÷ 1,000 orders = $125 per order.

Other entries in the table are computed similarly.

Microsoft Excel - ABC model-Classic Brass.XLS

File   Edit   View   Insert   Format   Tools   Data   Window   Help

Arial   10   B I U

	A	B	C	D	E	F
1	**Action Analysis Cost Matrix for Standard Stanchions**					
3			*Activity Cost Pools*			
4		*Customer Orders*	*Product Design*	*Order Size*	*Customer Relations*	*Total*
6	Total activity for stanchions	600		17,500	Not	
7		orders	product designs	machine-hours	applicable	
9	Production Department:					
10	Indirect factory wages	$ 75,000	$ 0	$ 87,500		$ 162,500
11	Factory equipment depreciation	36,000	0	157,500		193,500
12	Factory utilities	0	0	52,500		52,500
13	Factory building lease	0	0	0		0
15	General Administrative Department:					
16	Administrative wages and salaries	36,000	0	35,000		71,000
17	Office equipment depreciation	9,000	0	0		9,000
18	Administrative building lease	0	0	0		0
20	Marketing Department:					
21	Marketing wages and salaries	33,000	0	0		33,000
22	Selling expenses	3,000	0	0		3,000
24	Total (conventional ABC analysis)	$ 192,000	$ 0	$ 332,500		$ 524,500
25						

Exhibit 8A-2 **Exhibit 8A-3A** Exhibit 8A-3B Exhibit

From Exhibit 8A–2, the activity rate for indirect factory wages for the Customer Orders cost pool is $125 per order.

$125 per order × 600 orders = $75,000

Other entries in the table are computed in a similar way.

Microsoft Excel - ABC model-Classic Brass.XLS

File   Edit   View   Insert   Format   Tools   Data   Window   Help

Arial   10   B I U

J35

	A	B	C	D	E	F
1	**Action Analysis Cost Matrix for the Custom Compass Housings**					
3			*Activity Cost Pools*			
4		*Customer Orders*	*Product Design*	*Order Size*	*Customer Relations*	*Total*
6	Total activity for custom compass housings	400	400	2,500	Not	
7		order	product design	machine-hours	applicable	
9	Production Department:					
10	Indirect factory wages	$ 50,000	$ 200,000	$ 12,500		$ 262,500
11	Factory equipment depreciation	24,000	0	22,500		46,500
12	Factory utilities	0	12,000	7,500		19,500
13	Factory building lease	0	0	0		0
15	General Administrative Department:					
16	Administrative wages and salaries	24,000	20,000	5,000		49,000
17	Office equipment depreciation	6,000	0	0		6,000
18	Administrative building lease	0	0	0		0
20	Marketing Department:					
21	Marketing wages and salaries	22,000	20,000	0		42,000
22	Selling expenses	2,000	0	0		2,000
24	Total (conventional ABC analysis)	$ 128,000	$ 252,000	$ 47,500		$ 427,500
25						
26						

Exhibit 8A-3B Exhibit 8A-5 Activity rates Stanchions

From Exhibit 8A–2, the activity rate for indirect factory wages for the Customer Orders cost pool is $125 per order.

$125 per order × 400 order = $50,000

Other entries in the table are computed in a similar way.

Green: *Costs that adjust automatically to changes in activity without management action.*

Direct materials
Shipping costs

Yellow: *Costs that could, in principle, be adjusted to changes in activity, but management action would be required.*

Direct labor
Indirect factory wages
Factory utilities
Administrative wages and salaries
Office equipment depreciation
Marketing wages and salaries
Selling expenses

Red: *Costs that would be very difficult to adjust to changes in activity and management action would be required.*

Factory equipment depreciation
Factory building lease
Administrative building lease

Ease of Adjustment Codes

The ABC team constructed Exhibit 8A–4 to aid managers in the use of the ABC data. In this exhibit, each cost has been assigned an *ease of adjustment code*—Green, Yellow, or Red. The **ease of adjustment code** reflects how easily the cost could be adjusted to changes in activity.[6] "Green" costs are those costs that would adjust more or less automatically to changes in activity without any action by managers. For example, direct materials costs would adjust to changes in orders without any action being taken by managers. If a customer does not order stanchions, the direct materials for the stanchions would not be required and would not be ordered. "Yellow" costs are those costs that could be adjusted in response to changes in activity, but such adjustments require management action; the adjustment is not automatic. The ABC team believes, for example, that direct labor costs should be included in the Yellow category. Managers must make difficult decisions and take explicit action to increase or decrease, in aggregate, direct labor costs—particularly since the company has a no lay-off policy. "Red" costs are costs that could be adjusted to changes in activity only with a great deal of difficulty, and the adjustment would require management action. The building leases fall into this category, since it would be very difficult and expensive to break the leases.

The Action Analysis View of the ABC Data

Looking at Exhibit 8A–3, the totals on the right-hand side of the table indicate that the $427,500 of overhead cost for the custom compass housings consists of $262,500 of indirect factory wages, $46,500 of factory equipment depreciation, and so on. These data are displayed in Exhibit 8A–5, which shows an action analysis of the custom compass housings product. An action analysis report shows what costs have been assigned to the cost object, such as a product or customer, and how difficult it would be to adjust the cost if there is a change in activity. Note that the Red margin at the bottom of Exhibit 8A–5, ($49,500), is exactly the same as the product margin for the custom compass housings in Exhibit 8–10 in the chapter.

The cost data in the action analysis in Exhibit 8A–5 are arranged by the color coded ease of adjustment. All of the Green costs—those that adjust more or less automatically

---

[6]   The idea of using colors to code how easily costs can be adjusted was suggested to us at a seminar put on by Boeing and by an article by Alfred King, "Green Dollars and Blue Dollars: The Paradox of Cost Reduction," *Journal of Cost Management,* Fall 1993, pp. 44–52.

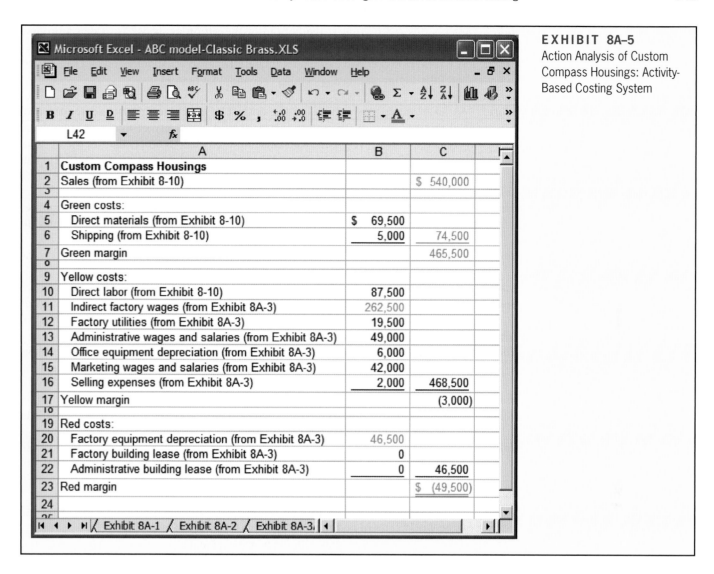

EXHIBIT 8A–5
Action Analysis of Custom
Compass Housings: Activity-
Based Costing System

to changes in activity—appear together at the top of the list of costs. These costs total $74,500 and are subtracted from the sales of $540,000 to yield a Green margin of $465,500. The same procedure is followed for the Yellow and Red costs. This action analysis indicates what costs would have to be cut and how difficult it would be to cut them if the custom compass housings product were dropped. Prior to making any decision about dropping products, the managers responsible for the costs must agree to either eliminate the resources represented by those costs or to transfer the resources to an area in the organization that really needs the resources—namely, a constraint. If managers do not make such a commitment, it is likely that the costs would continue to be incurred. As a result, the company would lose the sales from the products without really saving the costs.

After the action analysis was prepared by the ABC team, top management at Classic Brass met once again to review the results of the ABC analysis.

John: When we last met, we had discussed the advisability of discontinuing the custom compass housings product line. I understand that the ABC team has done some additional analysis to help us in making this decision.

Mary: That's right. The action analysis report we put together indicates how easy it would be to adjust each cost and where specific cost savings would have to come from if we were to drop the custom compass housings.

John: What's this red margin at the bottom of the action analysis? Isn't that a product margin?

Mary: Yes, it is. However, we call it a red margin because we should stop and think very, very carefully before taking any actions based on that margin.

John: Why is that?

Mary: As an example, we subtracted the costs of factory equipment depreciation to arrive at that red margin. We doubt that we could avoid any of that cost if we were to drop custom orders. We use the same machines on custom orders that we use on standard products. The factory equipment has no resale value, and it does not wear out through use.

John: What about this yellow margin?

Mary: Yellow means proceed with a great deal of caution. To get to the yellow margin we deducted from sales numerous costs that could be adjusted only if the managers involved are willing to eliminate resources or shift them to the constraint.

John: If I understand the yellow margin correctly, the apparent loss of $3,000 on the custom compass housings is the result of the indirect factory wages of $262,500.

Susan: Right, that's basically the wages of our design engineers.

John: I am uncomfortable with the idea of laying off any of our designers for numerous reasons. So where does that leave us?

Mary: What about raising prices on our custom products?

Tom: We should be able to do that. We have been undercutting the competition to make sure that we won bids on custom work because we thought it was a very profitable thing to do.

John: Why don't we just charge directly for design work?

Tom: Some of our competitors already do that. However, I don't think we would be able to charge enough to cover our design costs.

John: Can we do anything to make our design work more efficient so it costs us less? I'm not going to lay anyone off, but if we make the design process more efficient, we could lower the charge for design work and spread those costs across more customers.

Susan: That may be possible. I'll form a Six Sigma team to look at it.

John: Let's get some benchmark data on design costs. If we set our minds to it, I'm sure we can be world class in no time.

Susan: Okay. Mary, will you help with the benchmark data?

Mary: Sure.

John: Let's meet again in about a week to discuss our progress. Is there anything else on the agenda for today?

The points raised in the preceding discussion are extremely important. By measuring the resources consumed by products (and other cost objects), an ABC system provides a much better basis for decision making than a traditional cost accounting system that spreads overhead costs around without much regard for what might be causing the overhead. A well-designed ABC system provides managers with estimates of potentially relevant costs that can be a very useful starting point for management analysis.

Summary (Appendix 8A)

The action analysis report illustrated in this appendix is a valuable addition to the ABC toolkit. An action analysis report provides more information for decision making than a conventional ABC analysis. The action analysis report makes it clear where costs would have to be adjusted in the organization as a result of an action. In a conventional ABC analysis, a cost such as $320 for processing an order represents costs from many parts of the organization. If an order is dropped, there will be little pressure to actually eliminate the $320 cost unless it is clear where the costs are incurred and which managers would be responsible for reducing the cost. In contrast, an action analysis report traces the costs

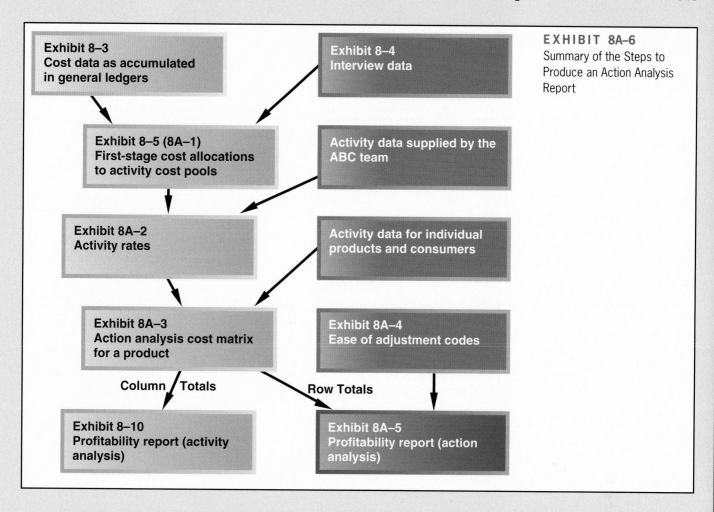

EXHIBIT 8A-6
Summary of the Steps to Produce an Action Analysis Report

to where they are incurred in the organization and makes it much easier to assign responsibility to managers for reducing costs. In addition, an action analysis report provides information concerning how easily a cost can be adjusted. Costs that cannot be adjusted are not relevant in a decision.

Exhibit 8A–6 summarizes all of the steps required to create both an action analysis report as illustrated in this appendix and an activity analysis as shown in the chapter.

Review Problem: Activity Analysis Report

Refer to the data for Ferris Corporation in the Review Problem at the end of the chapter on pages 336–337.

Required:

1. Compute activity rates for Ferris Corporation as in Exhibit 8A–2.
2. Using Exhibit 8A–3 as a guide, construct a table showing the overhead costs for the OfficeMart orders described in requirement (3) of the Review Problem at the end of the chapter.
3. The management of Ferris Corporation has assigned ease of adjustment codes to costs as follows:

Cost	Ease of Adjustment Code
Direct materials	Green
Direct labor.	Yellow
Manufacturing overhead	Yellow
Selling and administrative overhead	Red

Using Exhibit 8A–5 as a guide, prepare an action analysis of the OfficeMart orders.

Solution to Review Problem

1. The activity rates for the activity cost pools are:

	Assembling Units	Processing Orders	Supporting Customers
Total activity	1,000 units	250 orders	100 customers
Manufacturing overhead	$250	$ 700	$ 250
Selling and administrative overhead	30	540	750
Total	$280	$1,240	$1,000

2. The overhead cost for the four orders of a total of 80 filing cabinets would be computed as follows:

	Assembling Units	Processing Orders	Supporting Customers	Total
Activity	80 units	4 orders	1 customer	
Manufacturing overhead	$20,000	$2,800	$ 250	$23,050
Selling and administrative overhead	2,400	2,160	750	5,310
Total	$22,400	$4,960	$1,000	$28,360

3. The action analysis report is:

Sales		$47,600
Green costs:		
Direct materials	$14,400	14,400
Green margin		33,200
Yellow costs:		
Direct labor	4,000	
Manufacturing overhead	23,050	27,050
Yellow margin		6,150
Red costs:		
Selling and administrative overhead	5,310	5,310
Red margin		$ 840

Glossary (Appendix 8A)

Ease of adjustment codes Costs are coded as Green, Yellow, or Red—depending on how easily the cost could be adjusted to changes in activity. "Green" costs adjust automatically to changes in activity. "Yellow" costs could be adjusted in response to changes in activity, but such adjustments require management action; the adjustment is not automatic. "Red" costs could be adjusted to changes in activity only with a great deal of difficulty and would require management action. (p. 342)

Appendix 8B: Using a Modified Form of Activity-Based Costing to Determine Product Costs for External Reports

This chapter has emphasized using activity-based costing information in internal decisions. However, a modified form of activity-based costing can also be used to develop product costs for external financial reports. For this purpose, product costs include *all* manufacturing overhead costs—including organization-sustaining costs and the costs of idle capacity—and exclude all nonmanufacturing costs, even costs that are clearly caused by the products.

LEARNING OBJECTIVE 7
Use activity-based costing techniques to compute unit product costs for external reports.

The simplest absorption costing systems as described in Chapter 3 assign manufacturing overhead costs to products using a single factory-wide predetermined overhead rate based on direct labor-hours or machine-hours. When activity-based costing is used to assign manufacturing overhead costs to products, a predetermined overhead rate is computed for each activity cost pool. An example will make this difference clear.

Maxtar Industries manufactures high-quality smoker/barbecue units. The company has two product lines—Premium and Standard. The company has traditionally applied manufacturing overhead costs to these products using a plantwide predetermined overhead rate based on direct labor-hours. Exhibit 8B–1 details how the unit product costs of the two product lines are computed using the company's traditional costing system. The unit product cost of the Premium product line is $71.60 and the unit product cost of the Standard product line is $53.70 according to this traditional costing system.

Maxtar Industries has recently experimented with an activity-based costing approach to determining its unit product costs for external reporting purposes. The company's activity-based costing system has three activity cost pools: (1) supporting direct labor; (2) setting up machines; and (3) parts administration. The top of Exhibit 8B–2 (page 348)

EXHIBIT 8B–1
Maxtar Industries' Traditional Costing System

Basic Data

| Total estimated manufacturing overhead cost | $1,520,000 |
| Total estimated direct labor-hours | 400,000 DLHs |

	Premium	Standard
Direct materials per unit	$40.00	$30.00
Direct labor per unit	$24.00	$18.00
Direct labor-hours per unit	2.0 DLHs	1.5 DLHs
Units produced	50,000 units	200,000 units

Computation of the Predetermined Overhead Rate

$$\text{Predetermined overhead rate} = \frac{\text{Total estimated manufacturing overhead}}{\text{Total estimated amount of the allocation base}}$$

$$= \frac{\$1,520,000}{400,000 \text{ DLHs}} = \$3.80 \text{ per DLH}$$

Traditional Unit Product Costs

	Premium	Standard
Direct materials	$40.00	$30.00
Direct labor	24.00	18.00
Manufacturing overhead (2.0 DLHs × $3.80 per DLH; 1.5 DLHs × $3.80 per DLH)	7.60	5.70
Unit product cost	$71.60	$53.70

displays basic data concerning these activity cost pools. Note that the total estimated overhead cost in these three costs pools, $1,520,000, agrees with the total estimated overhead cost in the company's traditional costing system. The company's activity-based costing system simply provides an alternative way to allocate the company's manufacturing overhead across the two products.

The activity rates for the three activity cost pools are computed in the second table in Exhibit 8B–2. For example, the total cost in the "setting up machines" activity cost pool, $480,000, is divided by the total activity associated with that cost pool, 800 setups, to determine the activity rate of $600 per setup.

EXHIBIT 8B–2
Maxtar Industries' Activity-Based Costing System

Basic Data

Activities and Activity Measures	Estimated Overhead Cost	Premium	Standard	Total
Supporting direct labor (DLHs)	$ 800,000	100,000	300,000	400,000
Setting up machines (setups)	480,000	600	200	800
Parts administration (part types)	240,000	140	60	200
Total manufacturing overhead cost	$1,520,000			

Computation of Activity Rates

Activities	(a) Estimated Overhead Cost	(b) Total Expected Activity	(a) ÷ (b) Activity Rate
Supporting direct labor.......	$800,000	400,000 DLHs	$2 per DLH
Setting up machines	$480,000	800 setups	$600 per setup
Parts administration	$240,000	200 part types	$1,200 per part type

Assigning Overhead Costs to Products:

Overhead Cost for the Premium Product

Activity Cost Pools	(a) Activity Rate	(b) Activity	(a) × (b) ABC Cost
Supporting direct labor	$2 per DLH	100,000 DLHs	$200,000
Setting up machines	$600 per setup	600 setups	360,000
Parts administration	$1,200 per part type	140 part types	168,000
Total			$728,000

Overhead Cost for the Standard Product

Activity Cost Pools	(a) Activity Rate	(b) Activity	(a) × (b) ABC Cost
Supporting direct labor.......	$2 per DLH	300,000 DLHs	$600,000
Setting up machines	$600 per setup	200 setups	120,000
Parts administration	$1,200 per part type	60 part types	72,000
Total			$792,000

Activity-Based Costing Product Costs

	Premium	Standard
Direct materials	$40.00	$30.00
Direct labor	24.00	18.00
Manufacturing overhead ($728,000 ÷ 50,000 units; $792,000 ÷ 200,000 units)	14.56	3.96
Unit product cost	$78.56	$51.96

The activity rates are used to allocate overhead costs to the two products in the third table in Exhibit 8B–2. For example, the activity rate for the "setting up machines" activity cost pool, $600 per setup, is multiplied by the Premium product line's 600 setups to determine the $360,000 machine setup cost allocated to the Premium product line. The overhead cost per unit is determined at the bottom of this table by dividing the total overhead cost by the number of units produced. For example, the Premium product line's total overhead cost of $728,000 is divided by 50,000 units to determine the $14.56 overhead cost per unit.

The table at the bottom of Exhibit 8B–2 displays the activity-based costing unit product costs. Note that these unit product costs differ from those computed using the company's traditional costing system in Exhibit 8B–1. Because the activity-based costing system contains both a batch-level (setting up machines) and a product-level (parts administration) activity cost pool, the unit product costs under activity-based costing follow the usual pattern in which overhead costs are shifted from the high-volume to the low-volume product. The unit product cost of the Standard product line, the high-volume product, has gone down from $53.70 under the traditional costing system to $51.96 under activity-based costing. In contrast, the unit product cost of the Premium product line, the low-volume product, has increased from $71.60 under the traditional costing system to $78.56 under activity-based costing. Instead of arbitrarily assigning most of the costs of setting up machines and of parts administration to the high-volume product, the activity-based costing system more accurately assigns these costs to the two products.

Questions

8-1   In what fundamental ways does activity-based costing differ from traditional costing methods such as those described in Chapters 2 and 3?

8-2   Why is direct labor a poor base for allocating overhead in many companies?

8-3   Why is top management support crucial when attempting to implement an activity-based costing system?

8-4   What are unit-level, batch-level, product-level, customer-level, and organization-sustaining activities?

8-5   What types of costs should not be assigned to products in an activity-based costing system?

8-6   Why are there two stages of allocation in activity-based costing?

8-7   Why is the first stage of the allocation process in activity-based costing often based on interviews?

8-8   When activity-based costing is used, why do manufacturing overhead costs often shift from high-volume products to low-volume products?

8-9   How can the activity rates (i.e., cost per activity) for the various activities be used to target process improvements?

8-10   Why is the activity-based costing described in this chapter unacceptable for external financial reports?

8-11   (Appendix 8A) Why should reports such as those in Exhibits 8–10 and 8–11 be supplemented with an action analysis report such as in Exhibit 8A–5 when making decisions about products or customers?

Exercises

EXERCISE 8-1 ABC Cost Hierarchy [LO1]

The following activities occur at Greenwich Corporation, a company that manufactures a variety of products.

a.   Receive raw materials from suppliers.

b.   Manage parts inventories.

c.   Do rough milling work on products.
d.   Interview and process new employees in the personnel department.
e.   Design new products.
f.   Perform periodic preventive maintenance on general-use equipment.
g.   Use the general factory building.
h.   Issue purchase orders for a job.

Required:
Classify each of the activities above as either a unit-level, batch-level, product-level, or organization-sustaining activity.

EXERCISE 8-2 First-Stage Allocation [LO2]
SecuriCorp operates a fleet of armored cars that make scheduled pickups and deliveries in the Los Angeles area. The company is implementing an activity-based costing system that has four activity cost pools: Travel, Pickup and Delivery, Customer Service, and Other. The activity measures are miles for the Travel cost pool, number of pickups and deliveries for the Pickup and Delivery cost pool, and number of customers for the Customer Service cost pool. The Other cost pool has no activity measure. The following costs will be assigned using the activity-based costing system:

Driver and guard wages	$ 720,000
Vehicle operating expense	280,000
Vehicle depreciation	120,000
Customer representative salaries and expenses.	160,000
Office expenses	30,000
Administrative expenses	320,000
Total cost	$1,630,000

The distribution of resource consumption across the activity cost pools is as follows:

	Travel	Pickup and Delivery	Customer Service	Other	Totals
Driver and guard wages.	50%	35%	10%	5%	100%
Vehicle operating expense.	70%	5%	0%	25%	100%
Vehicle depreciation.	60%	15%	0%	25%	100%
Customer representative salaries and expenses.	0%	0%	90%	10%	100%
Office expenses.	0%	20%	30%	50%	100%
Administrative expenses	0%	5%	60%	35%	100%

Required:
Carry out the first stage allocations of costs to activity cost pools as illustrated in Exhibit 8–5.

EXERCISE 8-3 Compute Activity Rates [LO3]
Green Thumb Gardening is a small gardening service that uses activity-based costing to estimate costs for pricing and other purposes. The proprietor of the company believes that costs are driven primarily by the size of customer lawns, the size of customer garden beds, the distance to travel to customers, and the number of customers. In addition, the cost of maintaining garden beds depends on whether the beds are low maintenance beds (mainly ordinary trees and shrubs) or high maintenance beds (mainly flowers and exotic plants). Accordingly, the company uses the five activity cost pools listed below:

Activity Cost Pool	Activity Measure
Caring for lawn.	Square feet of lawn
Caring for garden beds—low maintenance	Square feet of low-maintenance beds
Caring for garden beds—high maintenance.	Square feet of high-maintenance beds
Travel to jobs	Miles
Customer billing and service	Number of customers

The company has already carried out its first stage allocations of costs and has summarized its annual costs and activity as follows:

Activity Cost Pool	Estimated Overhead Cost	Expected Activity
Caring for lawn	$72,000	150,000 square feet of lawn
Caring for garden beds— low maintenance	$26,400	20,000 square feet of low-maintenance beds
Caring for garden beds— high maintenance	$41,400	15,000 square feet of high-maintenance beds
Travel to jobs	$3,250	12,500 miles
Customer billing and service........	$8,750	25 customers

Required:
Compute the activity rate for each of the activity cost pools.

EXERCISE 8-4 Second-Stage Allocation [LO4]
Klumper Corporation is a diversified manufacturer of industrial goods. The company's activity-based costing system contains the following six activity cost pools and activity rates:

Activity Cost Pool	Activity Rates
Labor related............	$6.00 per direct labor-hour
Machine related	$4.00 per machine-hour
Machine setups..........	$50.00 per setup
Production orders	$90.00 per order
Shipments..............	$14.00 per shipment
Product sustaining........	$840.00 per product

Activity data have been supplied for the following two products:

	Total Expected Activity	
	K425	M67
Number of units produced per year	200	2,000
Direct labor-hours	80	500
Machine-hours.......................	100	1,500
Machine setups	1	4
Production orders......................	1	4
Shipments	1	10
Product sustaining	1	1

Required:
Determine the total overhead cost that would be assigned to each of the products listed above in the activity-based costing system.

EXERCISE 8-5 Product and Customer Profitability Analysis [LO4, LO5]
Thermal Rising, Inc., makes paragliders for sale through specialty sporting goods stores. The company has a standard paraglider model, but also makes custom-designed paragliders. Management has designed an activity-based costing system with the following activity cost pools and activity rates:

Activity Cost Pool	Activity Rate
Manufacturing volume	$26 per direct labor-hour
Order processing	$284 per order
Custom design processing........	$186 per custom design
Customer service..............	$379 per customer

Management would like an analysis of the profitability of a particular customer, Big Sky Outfitters, which has ordered the following products over the last 12 months:

	Standard Model	Custom Design
Number of gliders	20	3
Number of orders	1	3
Number of custom designs...........	0	3
Direct labor-hours per glider..........	26.35	28.0
Selling price per glider	$1,850	$2,400
Direct materials cost per glider........	$564	$634

The company's direct labor rate is $19.50 per hour.

Required:

Using the company's activity-based costing system, compute the profitability of each of the two products ordered by Big Sky Outfitters and the overall profitability of this customer.

EXERCISE 8-6 (Appendix 8A) Preparing an Action Analysis Report [LO6]

Hard Driver Corporation produces private label golf clubs for pro shops throughout North America. The company uses activity-based costing to evaluate the profitability of serving its customers. This analysis is based on categorizing the company's costs as follows, using the ease of adjustment color coding scheme described in Appendix 8A:

	Ease of Adjustment Code
Direct materials	Green
Direct labor	Yellow
Indirect labor	Yellow
Factory equipment depreciation	Red
Factory administration	Red
Selling and administrative wages and salaries	Red
Selling and administrative depreciation	Red
Marketing expenses	Yellow

Management would like to evaluate the profitability of a particular customer—the Grouse Mountain Golf Club of Avon, Colorado. Over the last 12 months, this customer submitted one order for 120 golf clubs that had to be produced in two batches due to differences in product labeling requested by the customer. Summary data concerning the order appear below:

Number of clubs	120
Number of orders	1
Number of batches	2
Direct labor-hour per club	0.4
Selling price per club..............	$49.00
Direct materials cost per club	$27.65
Direct labor rate per hour...........	$22.00

A cost analyst working in the controller's office at the company has already produced the action analysis cost matrix for the Grouse Mountain Golf Club that appears below:

Action Analysis Cost Matrix for Grouse Mountain Golf Club

| | Activity Cost Pools | | | | |
	Volume	Batch Processing	Order Processing	Customer Service	Total
Activity	48 direct labor-hours	2 batches	1 order	1 customer	
Manufacturing overhead:					
Indirect labor	$ 57.60	$52.40	$ 3.40	$ 0.00	$ 113.40
Factory equipment depreciation.	216.00	0.60	0.00	0.00	216.60
Factory administration	31.20	0.50	15.00	245.00	291.70
Selling and administrative overhead:					
Wages and salaries	21.60	0.00	42.00	324.00	387.60
Depreciation.	0.00	0.00	7.00	21.00	28.00
Marketing expenses.	268.80	0.00	65.00	376.00	709.80
Total	$595.20	$53.50	$132.40	$966.00	$1,747.10

Required:

Prepare an action analysis report showing the profitability of the Grouse Mountain Golf Club. Include direct materials and direct labor costs in the report. Use Exhibit 8A–5 as a guide for organizing the report.

EXERCISE 8-7 (Appendix 8B) Activity-Based Costing Product Costs for External Reports [LO7]

Pryad Corporation makes ultra-lightweight backpacking tents. Data concerning the company's two product lines appear below:

	Deluxe	Standard
Direct materials per unit	$60.00	$45.00
Direct labor per unit	$9.60	$7.20
Direct labor-hours per unit.	0.8 DLHs	0.6 LHs
Estimated annual production.	10,000 units	70,000 units

The company has a traditional costing system in which manufacturing overhead is applied to units based on direct labor-hours. Data concerning manufacturing overhead and direct labor-hours for the upcoming year appear below:

Estimated total manufacturing overhead.	$290,000
Estimated total direct labor-hours.	50,000 DLHs

Required:

1. Determine the unit product costs of the Deluxe and Standard products under the company's traditional costing system.
2. The company is considering replacing its traditional costing system for determining unit product costs for external reports with an activity-based costing system. The activity-based costing system would have the following three activity cost pools:

| | Estimated | Expected Activity | | |
Activities and Activity Measures	Overhead Cost	Deluxe	Standard	Total
Supporting direct labor (direct labor-hours)	$150,000	8,000	42,000	50,000
Batch setups (setups)	60,000	200	50	250
Safety testing (tests)	80,000	80	20	100
Total manufacturing overhead cost	$290,000			

Determine the unit product costs of the Deluxe and Standard products under the activity-based costing system.

EXERCISE 8-8 Activity Measures [LO1]
Listed below are activities that you have observed at Ming Corporation, a manufacturing company. Each activity has been classified as a unit-level, batch-level, product-level, or customer-level activity.

Activity	Activity Classification	Examples of Activity Measures
a. Direct labor workers assemble a product	Unit-level	
b. Products are designed by engineers.	Product-level	
c. Equipment is set up.	Batch-level	
d. Machines are used to shape and cut materials.	Unit-level	
e. Monthly bills are sent out to regular customers.	Customer-level	
f. Materials are moved from the receiving dock to production lines	Batch-level	
g. All completed units are inspected for defects	Unit-level	

Required:
Complete the table by providing examples of activity measures for each activity.

EXERCISE 8-9 Computing ABC Product Costs [LO3, LO4]
Fogerty Company makes two products, titanium Hubs and Sprockets. Data regarding the two products follow:

	Direct Labor-Hours per Unit	Annual Production
Hubs	0.80	10,000 units
Sprockets.	0.40	40,000 units

Additional information about the company follows:
a.   Hubs require $32 in direct materials per unit, and Sprockets require $18.
b.   The direct labor wage rate is $15 per hour.
c.   Hubs are more complex to manufacture than Sprockets and they require special equipment.
d.   The ABC system has the following activity cost pools:

Activity Cost Pool	Activity Measure	Estimated Overhead Cost	Activity Total	Activity Hubs	Activity Sprockets
Machine setups	Number of setups	$72,000	400	100	300
Special processing.	Machine-hours	$200,000	5,000	5,000	—
General factory	Direct labor-hours	$816,000	24,000	8,000	16,000

Required:
1.   Compute the activity rate for each activity cost pool.
2.   Determine the unit cost of each product according to the ABC system, including direct materials and direct labor.

EXERCISE 8-10 First-Stage Allocations [LO2]
The operations vice president of Security Home Bank has been interested in investigating the efficiency of the bank's operations. She has been particularly concerned about the costs of handling routine transactions at the bank and would like to compare these costs at the bank's various branches. If the branches with the most efficient operations can be identified, their methods can be studied and then replicated

elsewhere. While the bank maintains meticulous records of wages and other costs, there has been no attempt thus far to show how those costs are related to the various services provided by the bank. The operations vice president has asked your help in conducting an activity-based costing study of bank operations. In particular, she would like to know the cost of opening an account, the cost of processing deposits and withdrawals, and the cost of processing other customer transactions.

The Westfield branch of Security Home Bank has submitted the following cost data for last year:

Teller wages	$160,000
Assistant branch manager salary	75,000
Branch manager salary	80,000
Total	$315,000

Virtually all of the other costs of the branch—rent, depreciation, utilities, and so on—are organization-sustaining costs that cannot be meaningfully assigned to individual customer transactions such as depositing checks.

In addition to the cost data above, the employees of the Westfield branch have been interviewed concerning how their time was distributed last year across the activities included in the activity-based costing study. The results of those interviews appear below:

Distribution of Resource Consumption Across Activities

	Opening Accounts	Processing Deposits and Withdrawals	Processing Other Customer Transactions	Other Activities	Totals
Teller wages	5%	65%	20%	10%	100%
Assistant branch manager salary.........	15%	5%	30%	50%	100%
Branch manager salary	5%	0%	10%	85%	100%

Required:
Prepare the first-stage allocation for the activity-based costing study. (See Exhibit 8–5 for an example of a first-stage allocation.)

EXERCISE 8-11 Computing and Interpreting Activity Rates [LO3]
(This exercise is a continuation of Exercise 8-10; it should be assigned *only* if Exercise 8-10 is also assigned.) The manager of the Westfield branch of Security Home Bank has provided the following data concerning the transactions of the branch during the past year:

Activity	Total Activity at the Westfield Branch
Opening accounts	500 new accounts opened
Processing deposits and withdrawals..........	100,000 deposits and withdrawals processed
Processing other customer transactions........	5,000 other customer transactions processed

The lowest costs reported by other branches for these activities are displayed below:

Activity	Lowest Cost Among All Security Home Bank Branches
Opening accounts	$26.75 per new account
Processing deposits and withdrawals	$1.24 per deposit or withdrawal
Processing other customer transactions	$11.86 per other customer transaction

Required:
1. Using the first-stage allocation from Exercise 8-10 and the above data, compute the activity rates for the activity-based costing system. (Use Exhibit 8-6 as a guide.) Round all computations to the nearest whole cent.
2. What do these results suggest to you concerning operations at the Westfield branch?

EXERCISE 8-12 Second-Stage Allocation to an Order [LO4]

Durban Metal Products, Ltd., of the Republic of South Africa makes specialty metal parts used in applications ranging from the cutting edges of bulldozer blades to replacement parts for Land Rovers. The company uses an activity-based costing system for internal decision-making purposes. The company has four activity cost pools as listed below:

Activity Cost Pool	Activity Measure	Activity Rate
Order size.............	Number of direct labor-hours	R16.85 per direct labor-hour
Customer orders........	Number of customer orders	R320.00 per customer order
Product testing.........	Number of testing hours	R89.00 per testing hour
Selling	Number of sales calls	R1,090.00 per sales call

Note: The currency in South Africa is the Rand, denoted here by R.

The managing director of the company would like information concerning the cost of a recently completed order for heavy-duty trailer axles. The order required 200 direct labor-hours, 4 hours of product testing, and 2 sales calls.

Required:

Prepare a report showing the overhead cost of the order for heavy-duty trailer axles according to the activity-based costing system. What is the total overhead cost assigned to the order?

EXERCISE 8-13 (Appendix 8A) Second-Stage Allocation to an Order Using the Action Analysis Approach [LO4, LO6]

This exercise should be assigned in conjunction with Exercise 8–12.

The results of the first-stage allocation of the activity-based costing system at Durban Metal Products, Ltd., in which the activity rates were computed, appear below:

	Order Size	Customer Orders	Product Testing	Selling
Manufacturing:				
Indirect labor	R 8.25	R180.00	R30.00	R 0.00
Factory depreciation	8.00	0.00	40.00	0.00
Factory utilities	0.10	0.00	1.00	0.00
Factory administration	0.00	48.00	18.00	30.00
Selling and administrative:				
Wages and salaries...........	0.50	80.00	0.00	800.00
Depreciation	0.00	12.00	0.00	40.00
Taxes and insurance	0.00	0.00	0.00	20.00
Selling expenses	0.00	0.00	0.00	200.00
Total overhead cost.............	R16.85	R320.00	R89.00	R1,090.00

Required:

1. Prepare a report showing the overhead cost of the order for heavy-duty trailer axles discussed in Exercise 8–12. (Use Exhibit 8A–3 as a guide.) What is the total overhead cost of the order?
2. Explain the two different perspectives this report gives to managers concerning the nature of the overhead costs involved in the order. (Hint: Look at the row and column totals of the report you have prepared.)

EXERCISE 8-14 Cost Hierarchy [LO1]

CD Express, Inc., provides CD duplicating services to software companies. The customer provides a master CD from which CD Express makes copies. An order from a customer can be for a single copy or for thousands of copies. Most jobs are broken down into batches to allow smaller jobs, with higher priorities, to have access to the machines.

Following are listed a number of activities carried out at CD Express.

a. Sales representatives' periodic visits to customers to keep them informed about the services provided by CD Express.
b. Ordering labels from the printer for a particular CD.

c.   Setting up the CD duplicating machine to make copies from a particular master CD.
d.   Loading the automatic labeling machine with labels for a particular CD.
e.   Visually inspecting CDs and placing them by hand into protective plastic cases prior to shipping.
f.   Preparation of the shipping documents for the order.
g.   Periodic maintenance of equipment.
h.   Lighting and heating the company's production facility.
i.   Preparation of quarterly financial reports.

Required:
Classify each of the activities above as either a unit-level, batch-level, product-level, customer-level, or organization-sustaining activity. (An order to duplicate a particular CD is a product-level activity.) Assume the order is large enough that it must be broken down into batches.

EXERCISE 8-15 Second-Stage Allocation and Margin Calculations [LO4, LO5]
Foam Products, Inc., makes foam seat cushions for the automotive and aerospace industries. The company's activity-based costing system has four activity cost pools, which are listed below along with their activity measures and activity rates:

Activity Cost Pool	Activity Measure	Activity Rate
Volume.	Number of direct labor-hours	$5.55 per direct labor-hour
Batch processing	Number of batches	$107.00 per batch
Order processing	Number of orders	$275.00 per order
Customer service	Number of customers	$2,463.00 per customer

The company just completed a single order from Interstate Trucking for 1,000 custom seat cushions. The order was produced in two batches. Each seat cushion required 0.25 direct labor-hours. The selling price was $20 per unit, the direct materials cost was $8.50 per unit, and the direct labor cost was $6.00 per unit. This was Interstate Trucking's only order during the year.

Required:
Using Exhibit 8–11 as a guide, prepare a report showing the customer margin on sales to Interstate Trucking for the year.

EXERCISE 8-16 (Appendix 8A) Second-Stage Allocations and Margin Calculations Using the Action Analysis Approach [LO4, LO6]
Refer to the data for Foam Products, Inc., in Exercise 8–15 and the following additional details concerning the activity rates in the activity-based costing system:

		Activity Rates		
	Volume	Batch Processing	Order Processing	Customer Service
Manufacturing overhead:				
Indirect labor	$0.60	$60.00	$ 20.00	$ 0.00
Factory equipment depreciation	4.00	17.00	0.00	0.00
Factory administration	0.10	7.00	25.00	150.00
Selling and administrative overhead:				
Wages and salaries	0.40	20.00	160.00	1,600.00
Depreciation	0.00	3.00	10.00	38.00
Marketing expenses	0.45	0.00	60.00	675.00
Total	$5.55	$107.00	$275.00	$2,463.00

Management has provided their ease of adjustment codes for the purpose of preparing action analyses.

	Ease of Adjustment Code
Direct materials	Green
Direct labor	Yellow
Manufacturing overhead:	
Indirect labor	Yellow
Factory equipment depreciation	Red
Factory administration	Red
Selling and administrative overhead:	
Wages and salaries	Red
Depreciation.	Red
Marketing expenses.	Yellow

Required:

Using Exhibit 8A–5 as a guide, prepare an action analysis report on the order from Interstate Trucking. Ignore customer service costs.

EXERCISE 8-17 Cost Hierarchy and Activity Measures [LO1]

Vapo Ingman Oy, a Finnish manufacturing company, makes a variety of products at its plant outside Helsinki. Listed below are activities that you have observed at the plant.
a. Machine settings are changed between batches of different products.
b. Parts inventories are maintained in the storeroom. (Each product requires its own unique parts.)
c. Products are milled on a milling machine.
d. New employees are hired by the personnel office.
e. New products are designed.
f. Periodic maintenance is performed on general-purpose production equipment.
g. A bill is sent to a customer who is late in making payments.
h. Yearly taxes are paid on the company's facilities.
i. Purchase orders are issued for materials to be used in production.

Required:
1. Classify each of the activities above as either a unit-level, batch-level, product-level, customer-level, or organization-sustaining activity.
2. Where possible, for each activity name one or more activity measures that might be used to assign costs generated by the activity to products or customers.

EXERCISE 8-18 Comprehensive Activity-Based Costing Exercise [LO2, LO3, LO4, LO5]

Advanced Products Corporation has supplied the following data from its activity-based costing system:

Overhead Costs	
Wages and salaries	$300,000
Other overhead costs.	100,000
Total overhead costs	$400,000

Activity Cost Pool	Activity Measure	Total Activity for the Year
Volume related	Number of direct labor-hours	20,000 DLHs
Order related	Number of orders	400 orders
Customer support.	Number of customers	200 customers
Other	These costs are not allocated to products or customers	Not applicable

	Distribution of Resource Consumption Across Activity Cost Pools				
	Volume Related	Order Related	Customer Support	Other	Total
Wages and salaries	40%	30%	20%	10%	100%
Other overhead costs.	30%	10%	20%	40%	100%

During the year, Advanced Products completed one order for a new customer, Shenzhen Enterprises. This customer did not order any other products during the year. Data concerning that order follow:

Data concerning the Shenzhen Enterprises Order	
Units ordered	10 units
Direct labor-hours.	2 DLHs per unit
Selling price	$300 per unit
Direct materials	$180 per unit
Direct labor.	$50 per unit

Required:
1. Prepare a report showing the first-stage allocations of overhead costs to the activity cost pools. (Use Exhibit 8–5 as a guide.)
2. Compute the activity rates for the activity cost pools. (Use Exhibit 8–6 as a guide.)
3. Prepare a report showing the overhead costs for the order from Shenzhen Enterprises, including customer support costs.
4. Prepare a report showing the customer margin for Shenzhen Enterprises. (Use Exhibit 8–11 as a guide.)

EXERCISE 8-19 (Appendix 8A) Comprehensive Activity-Based Costing Exercise [LO2, LO3, LO4, LO6]

Refer to the data for Advanced Products Corporation in Exercise 8–18.

Required:
1. Using Exhibit 8A–1 as a guide, prepare a report showing the first-stage allocations of overhead costs to the activity cost pools.
2. Using Exhibit 8A–2 as a guide, compute the activity rates for the activity cost pools.
3. Using Exhibit 8A–3 as a guide, prepare a report showing the overhead costs for the order from Shenzhen Enterprises including customer support costs.
4. Using Exhibit 8–11 as a guide, prepare an activity analysis report showing the customer margin for Shenzhen Enterprises.
5. Using Exhibit 8A–5 as a guide, prepare an action analysis report showing the customer margin for Shenzhen Enterprises. Direct materials should be coded as a Green cost, direct labor and wages and salaries as Yellow costs, and other overhead costs as a Red cost.
6. What action, if any, do you recommend as a result of the above analyses?

EXERCISE 8-20 Activity-Based Costing Product Costs for External Reports [LO7]

Harrison Company makes two products and uses a traditional costing system in which a single plant-wide predetermined overhead rate is computed based on direct labor-hours. Data for the two products for the upcoming year follow:

	Rascon	Parcel
Direct materials cost per unit	$13.00	$22.00
Direct labor cost per unit.	$6.00	$3.00
Direct labor-hours per unit	0.40	0.20
Number of units produced.	20,000	80,000

These products are customized to some degree for specific customers.

Required:
1. The company's manufacturing overhead costs for the year are expected to be $576,000. Using the company's traditional costing system, compute the unit product costs for the two products.
2. Management is considering an activity-based costing system in which half of the overhead would continue to be allocated on the basis of direct labor-hours and half would be allocated on the basis of engineering design time. The Rascon product is expected to need 3,000 engineering design hours and the Parcel product is also expected to need 3,000 engineering design hours. Compute the unit product costs for the two products using the proposed ABC system.
3. Explain why the product costs differ between the two systems.

EXERCISE 8-21 Calculating and Interpreting Activity-Based Costing Data [LO3, LO4]

Hiram's Lakeside is a popular restaurant located on Lake Washington in Seattle. The owner of the restaurant has been trying to better understand costs at the restaurant and has hired a student intern to conduct an activity-based costing study. The intern, in consultation with the owner, identified three major activities and then completed the first-stage allocations of costs to the activity cost pools. The results appear below.

Activity Cost Pool	Activity Measure	Total Cost	Total Activity
Serving a party of diners........	Number of parties served	$33,000	6,000 parties
Serving a diner	Number of diners served	$138,000	15,000 diners
Serving drinks	Number of drinks ordered	$24,000	10,000 drinks

The above costs include all of the costs of the restaurant except for organization-sustaining costs such as rent, property taxes, and top-management salaries. A group of diners who ask to sit at the same table are counted as a party. Some costs, such as the costs of cleaning linen, are the same whether one person is at a table or the table is full. Other costs, such as washing dishes, depend on the number of diners served.

Prior to the activity-based costing study, the owner knew very little about the costs of the-restaurant. She knew that the total cost for the month (including organization-sustaining costs) was $240,000 and that 15,000 diners had been served. Therefore, the average cost per diner was $16.

Required:
1. According to the activity-based costing system, what is the total cost of serving each of the following parties of diners? (You can use the simplified approach described at the end of the chapter.)
   a. A party of four diners who order three drinks in total.
   b. A party of two diners who do not order any drinks.
   c. A lone diner who orders two drinks.
2. Convert the total costs you computed in (1) above to costs per diner. In other words, what is the average cost per diner for serving each of the following parties of diners?
   a. A party of four diners who order three drinks in total.
   b. A party of two diners who do not order any drinks.
   c. A lone diner who orders two drinks.
3. Why do the costs per diner for the three different parties differ from each other and from the overall average cost of $16 per diner?

Problems

PROBLEM 8-22 Evaluating the Profitability of Services [LO2, LO3, LO4, LO5]
Gallatin Carpet Cleaning is a small, family-owned business operating out of Bozeman, Montana. For its services, the company has always charged a flat fee per hundred square feet of carpet cleaned. The current fee is $28 per hundred square feet. However, there is some question about whether the company is actually making any money on jobs for some customers—particularly those located on remote ranches that require considerable travel time. The owner's daughter, home for the summer from college, has suggested investigating this question using activity-based costing. After some discussion, a simple system consisting of four activity cost pools seemed to be adequate. The activity cost pools and their activity measures appear below:

Activity Cost Pool	Activity Measure	Activity for the Year
Cleaning carpets	Square feet cleaned (00s)	20,000 hundred square feet
Travel to jobs	Miles driven	60,000 miles
Job support	Number of jobs	2,000 jobs
Other (costs of idle capacity and organization-sustaining costs)	None	Not applicable

The total cost of operating the company for the year is $430,000, which includes the following costs:

Wages	$150,000
Cleaning supplies...................	40,000
Cleaning equipment depreciation........	20,000
Vehicle expenses	80,000
Office expenses	60,000
President's compensation	80,000
Total cost	$430,000

Resource consumption is distributed across the activities as follows:

	Distribution of Resource Consumption Across Activities				
	Cleaning Carpets	Travel to Jobs	Job Support	Other	Total
Wages	70%	20%	0%	10%	100%
Cleaning supplies.	100%	0%	0%	0%	100%
Cleaning equipment depreciation.	80%	0%	0%	20%	100%
Vehicle expenses	0%	60%	0%	40%	100%
Office expenses	0%	0%	45%	55%	100%
President's compensation	0%	0%	40%	60%	100%

Job support consists of receiving calls from potential customers at the home office, scheduling jobs, billing, resolving issues, and so on.

Required:
1. Using Exhibit 8–5 as a guide, prepare the first-stage allocation of costs to the activity cost pools.
2. Using Exhibit 8–6 as a guide, compute the activity rates for the activity cost pools.
3. The company recently completed a 5 hundred square-foot carpet-cleaning job at the Flying N Ranch—a 75-mile round-trip journey from the company's offices in Bozeman. Compute the cost of this job using the activity-based costing system.
4. The revenue from the Flying N Ranch was $140 (5 hundred square-feet at $28 per hundred square feet). Using Exhibit 8–9 as a guide, prepare a report showing the margin from this job.
5. What do you conclude concerning the profitability of the Flying N Ranch job? Explain.
6. What advice would you give the president concerning pricing jobs in the future?

PROBLEM 8-23 (Appendix 8A) Evaluating the Profitability of Services Using an Action Analysis [LO2, LO3, LO4, LO6]

Refer to the data for Gallatin Carpet Cleaning in Problem 8-22.

Required:
1. Using Exhibit 8A–1 as a guide, prepare the first-stage allocation of costs to the activity cost pools.
2. Using Exhibit 8A–2 as a guide, compute the activity rates for the activity cost pools.
3. The company recently completed a 5 hundred square-foot carpet-cleaning job at the Flying N Ranch—a 75-mile round-trip journey from the company's offices in Bozeman. Compute the cost of this job using the activity-based costing system.
4. The revenue from the Flying N Ranch was $140 (5 hundred square-feet at $28 per hundred square feet). Using Exhibit 8A–5 as a guide, prepare an action analysis report of the Flying N Ranch job. The president of Gallatin Carpet Cleaning considers all of the company's costs to be Green costs except for office expenses, which are coded Yellow, and his own compensation, which is coded Red. The people who do the actual carpet cleaning are all trained part-time workers who are paid only for work actually done.
5. What do you conclude concerning the profitability of the Flying N Ranch job? Explain.
6. What advice would you give the president concerning pricing jobs in the future?

PROBLEM 8-24 Activity-Based Costing as an Alternative to Traditional Product Costing [LO7]

Siegel Company manufactures a product that is available in both a deluxe model and a regular model. The company has manufactured the regular model for years. The deluxe model was introduced several years ago to tap a new segment of the market. Since introduction of the deluxe model, the company's profits have steadily declined and management has become increasingly concerned about the accuracy of its costing system. Sales of the deluxe model have been increasing rapidly.

Manufacturing overhead is assigned to products on the basis of direct labor-hours. For the current year, the company has estimated that it will incur $900,000 in manufacturing overhead cost and produce 5,000 units of the deluxe model and 40,000 units of the regular model. The deluxe model requires two hours of direct labor time per unit, and the regular model requires one hour. Material and labor costs per unit are as follows:

	Model	
	Deluxe	Regular
Direct materials........	$40	$25
Direct labor	$14	$7

Required:

1. Using direct labor-hours as the base for assigning overhead cost to products, compute the predetermined overhead rate. Using this rate and other data from the problem, determine the unit product cost of each model.

2. Management is considering using activity-based costing to apply manufacturing overhead cost to products for external financial reports. The activity-based costing system would have the following four activity cost pools:

Activity Cost Pool	Activity Measure	Estimated Overhead Costs
Purchasing..........	Purchase orders issued	$204,000
Processing..........	Machine-hours	182,000
Scrap/rework........	Scrap/rework orders issued	379,000
Shipping............	Number of shipments	135,000
		$900,000

Activity Measure	Expected Activity		
	Deluxe	Regular	Total
Purchase orders issued	200	400	600
Machine-hours	20,000	15,000	35,000
Scrap/rework orders issued	1,000	1,000	2,000
Number of shipments	250	650	900

Using Exhibit 8–6 as a guide, determine the predetermined overhead rate (i.e., activity rates) for each of the four activity cost pools.

3. Using the predetermined overhead rates you computed in part (2) above, do the following:

   a. Compute the total amount of manufacturing overhead cost that would be applied to each model using the activity-based costing system. After these totals have been computed, determine the amount of manufacturing overhead cost per unit of each model.

   b. Compute the unit product cost of each model (materials, labor, and manufacturing overhead).

4. From the data you have developed in parts (1) through (3) above, identify factors that may account for the company's declining profits.

PROBLEM 8-25 Activity-Based Costing and Bidding on Jobs [LO2, LO3, LO4]
Mercer Asbestos Removal Company removes potentially toxic asbestos insulation and related products from buildings. There has been a long-simmering dispute between the company's estimator and the work supervisors. The on-site supervisors claim that the estimators do not adequately distinguish between routine work such as removal of asbestos insulation around heating pipes in older homes and nonroutine work such as removing asbestos-contaminated ceiling plaster in industrial buildings. The on-site supervisors believe that nonroutine work is far more expensive than routine work and should bear higher customer charges. The estimator sums up his position in this way: "My job is to measure the area to be cleared of asbestos. As directed by top management, I simply multiply the square footage by $2.50 to determine the bid price. Since our average cost is only $2.175 per square foot, that leaves enough cushion to take care of the additional costs of nonroutine work that shows up. Besides, it is difficult to know what is routine or not routine until you actually start tearing things apart."

To shed light on this controversy, the company initiated an activity-based costing study of all of its costs. Data from the activity-based costing system follow:

Activity Cost Pool	Activity Measure	Total Activity
Job size	Thousands of square feet	800 thousand square feet
Estimating and job setup	Number of jobs	500 jobs*
Working on nonroutine jobs	Number of nonroutine jobs	100 nonroutine jobs
Other (costs of idle capacity and organization-sustaining costs)	Not applicable; these costs are not allocated to jobs	

*The 100 nonroutine jobs are included in the total of 500 jobs. Both nonroutine jobs and routine jobs require estimating and setup.

Wages and salaries	$ 300,000
Disposal fees	700,000
Equipment depreciation	90,000
On-site supplies	50,000
Office expenses	200,000
Licensing and insurance	400,000
Total cost	$1,740,000

	Distribution of Resource Consumption Across Activities				
	Job Size	Estimating and Job Setup	Working on Nonroutine Jobs	Other	Total
Wages and salaries	50%	10%	30%	10%	100%
Disposal fees	60%	0%	40%	0%	100%
Equipment depreciation	40%	5%	20%	35%	100%
On-site supplies	60%	30%	10%	0%	100%
Office expenses	10%	35%	25%	30%	100%
Licensing and insurance	30%	0%	50%	20%	100%

Required:
1. Using Exhibit 8–5 as a guide, perform the first-stage allocation of costs to the activity cost pools.
2. Using Exhibit 8–6 as a guide, compute the activity rates for the activity cost pools.
3. Using the activity rates you have computed, determine the total cost and the average cost per thousand square feet of each of the following jobs according to the activity-based costing system.
   a. A routine 1,000-square-foot asbestos removal job.
   b. A routine 2,000-square-foot asbestos removal job.
   c. A nonroutine 2,000-square-foot asbestos removal job.
4. Given the results you obtained in (3) above, do you agree with the estimator that the company's present policy for bidding on jobs is adequate?

PROBLEM 8-26 Second Stage Allocations and Product Margins [LO4, LO5]

Pixel Studio, Inc., is a small company that creates computer-generated animations for films and television. Much of the company's work consists of short commercials for television, but the company also does realistic computer animations for special effects in movies.

The young founders of the company have become increasingly concerned with the economics of the business—particularly since many competitors have sprung up recently in the local area. To help understand the company's cost structure, an activity-based costing system has been designed. Three major activities are carried out in the company: animation concept, animation production, and contract administration. The animation concept activity is carried out at the contract proposal stage when the company bids on projects. This is an intensive activity that involves individuals from all parts of the company in creating story boards and prototype stills to be shown to the prospective client. Once a project is accepted by the client, the animation goes into production and contract administration begins. Almost all of the work involved in animation production is done by the technical staff, whereas the administrative staff is largely responsible for contract administration. The activity cost pools and their activity measures are listed below:

Activity Cost Pool	Activity Measure	Activity Rate
Animation concept	Number of proposals	$6,040 per proposal
Animation production	Minutes of completed animation	$7,725 per minute
Contract administration.	Number of contracts	$6,800 per contract

These activity rates include all of the company' costs, except for the costs of idle capacity and organization-sustaining costs. There are no direct labor or direct materials costs.

Preliminary analysis using these activity rates has indicated that the local commercial segment of the market may be unprofitable. This segment is highly competitive. Producers of local commercials may ask three or four companies like Pixel Studio to bid, which results in an unusually low ratio of accepted contracts to bids. Furthermore, the animation sequences tend to be much shorter for local commercials than for other work. Since animation work is billed at fairly standard rates according to the running time of the completed animation, this means that the revenues from these short projects tend to be below average. Data concerning activity in the local commercial market appear below:

Activity Measure	Local Commercials
Number of proposals.	25
Minutes of animation	5
Number of contracts	10

The total sales from the 10 contracts for local commercials was $180,000.

Required:
1. Determine the cost of the local commercials market. (Think of the local commercials market as a product.)
2. Prepare a report showing the product margin of the local commercials market. (Remember, this company has no direct materials or direct labor costs.)
3. What would you recommend to management concerning the local commercials market?

PROBLEM 8-27 (Appendix 8A) Second Stage Allocations and Product Margins [LO4, LO6]
Refer to the data for Pixel Studio, Inc., in Problem 8–26. In addition, the company has provided the following details concerning its activity rates:

	Activity Rates		
	Animation Concept	Animation Production	Contract Administration
Technical staff salaries.	$4,000	$6,000	$1,600
Animation equipment depreciation.	360	1,125	0
Administrative wages and salaries.	1,440	150	4,800
Supplies costs	120	300	160
Facility costs	120	150	240
Total	$6,040	$7,725	$6,800

Management has provided the following ease of adjustment codes for the various costs:

	Ease of Adjustment Code
Technical staff salaries.	Red
Animation equipment depreciation	Red
Administrative wages and salaries	Yellow
Supplies costs	Green
Facility costs	Red

These codes created some controversy. In particular, some administrators objected to coding their own salaries Yellow, while the technical staff salaries were coded Red. However, the founders of the firm overruled these objections by pointing out that "our technical staff is our most valuable asset. Good animators are extremely difficult to find, and they would be the last to go if we had to cut back."

Required:
1. Using Exhibit 8A–3 as a guide, determine the cost of the local commercials market. (Think of the local commercial market as a product.)
2. Using Exhibit 8A–5 as a guide, prepare an action analysis report concerning the local commercial market. (This company has no direct materials or direct labor costs.)
3. What would you recommend to management concerning the local commercial market?

PROBLEM 8-28 Activity-Based Costing as an Alternative to Traditional Product Costing [LO7]

For many years, Zapro Company manufactured a single product called a mono-relay. Then three years ago, the company automated a portion of its plant and at the same time introduced a second product called a bi-relay which has become increasingly popular. The bi-relay is a more complex product, requiring one hour of direct labor time per unit to manufacture and extensive machining in the automated portion of the plant. The mono-relay requires only 0.75 hour of direct labor time per unit and only a small amount of machining. Manufacturing overhead costs are currently assigned to products on the basis of direct labor-hours.

Despite the growing popularity of the company's new bi-relay, profits have been declining steadily. Management is beginning to believe that there may be a problem with the company's costing system. Material and labor costs per unit are as follows:

	Mono-Relay	Bi-Relay
Direct materials	$35	$48
Direct labor (0.75 hour and 1.0 hour @ $12 per hour)	$9	$12

Management estimates that the company will incur $1,000,000 in manufacturing overhead costs during the current year and 40,000 units of the mono-relay and 10,000 units of the bi-relay will be produced and sold.

Required:
1. Compute the predetermined manufacturing overhead rate assuming that the company continues to apply manufacturing overhead cost on the basis of direct labor-hours. Using this rate and other data from the problem, determine the unit product cost of each product.
2. Management is considering using activity-based costing to apply manufacturing overhead cost to products for external financial reports. Some preliminary work has been done and the data that have been collected are displayed below in the form of an Excel spreadsheet.

	A	B	C	D	E	F
2	Activity Cost Pool (and Activity Measure)	Estimated Overhead Costs	Total	Mono-Relay	Bi-Relay	
3	Maintaining parts inventory (number of part types)	$ 180,000	225	75	150	
4	Processing purchase orders (number of orders)	90,000	1,000	800	200	
5	Quality control (number of tests)	230,000	5,750	2,500	3,250	
6	Machine-related (machine-hours)	500,000	10,000	4,000	6,000	
7	Total overhead cost	$ 1,000,000				

Determine the predetermined overhead rate (i.e., activity rate) for each of the four activity cost pools.

3. Using the predetermined manufacturing overhead rates you computed in part (2) above, do the following:
   a. Determine the total amount of manufacturing overhead cost that would be applied to each product using the activity-based costing system. After these totals have been computed, determine the amount of manufacturing overhead cost per unit of each product.
   b. Compute the unit product cost of each product.
4. Look at the data you have computed in parts (1) through (3) above. In terms of manufacturing overhead costs, what factors make the bi-relay more costly to produce than the mono-relay? Is the bi-relay as profitable as management believes? Explain.

PROBLEM 8-29 Activity-Based Costing as an Alternative to Traditional Product Costing [LO7]

Ellix Company manufactures two models of ultra-high fidelity speakers, the X200 model and the X99 model. Data regarding the two products follow:

Product	Direct Labor-Hours	Annual Production	Total Direct Labor-Hours
X200........	1.8 DLHs per unit	5,000 units	9,000 DLHs
X99.........	0.9 DLHs per unit	30,000 units	27,000 DLHs
			36,000 DLHs

Additional information about the company follows:
a. Model X200 requires $72 in direct materials per unit, and model X99 requires $50.
b. The direct labor rate is $10 per hour.
c. The company has always used direct labor-hours as the base for applying manufacturing overhead cost to products.
d. Model X200 is more complex to manufacture than model X99 and requires the use of special equipment.
e. Because of the special work required in (d) above, the company is considering the use of activity-based costing to apply manufacturing overhead cost to products. Three activity cost pools have been identified as follows:

Activity Cost Pool	Activity Measure	Total Cost	Expected Activity		
			Model X200	Model X99	Total
Machine setups	Number of setups	$ 360,000	50	100	150
Special processing	Machine-hours	180,000	12,000	0	1,200
General factory........	Direct labor-hours	1,260,000	9,000	27,000	36,000
		$1,800,000			

Required:
1. Assume that the company continues to use direct labor-hours as the base for applying overhead cost to products.
   a. Compute the predetermined overhead rate.
   b. Compute the unit product cost of each model.
2. Assume that the company decides to use activity-based costing to apply overhead cost to products.
   a. Compute the activity rate for each activity cost pool. Also compute the amount of overhead cost that would be applied to each model.
   b. Determine the unit product cost of each model.
3. Explain why overhead cost shifted from the high-volume model to the low-volume model under activity-based costing.

CASE 8-30 (Appendix 8A) Comprehensive Activity-Based Costing Case [LO2, LO3, LO4, LO6]

Classic Windows is a small company that builds specialty wooden windows for local builders. For years the company has assigned overhead costs to products based on direct labor-hours (DLHs). However, the company's president became interested in activity-based costing after reading an article about activity-based costing in a trade journal. An activity-based costing design team was put together, and within a few months a simple system consisting of four activity cost pools had been created. The activity cost pools and their activity measures appear below:

Activity Cost Pool	Activity Measure	Total Activity for the Year
Making windows	Direct labor-hours	100,000 DLHs
Processing orders	Number of orders	2,000 orders
Customer relations	Number of customers	100 customers
Other (costs of idle capacity and organization-sustaining costs)	None	Not applicable

The Processing Orders activity cost pool includes order taking, job setup, job scheduling, and so on. Direct materials and direct labor are directly assigned to jobs in both the traditional and activity-based costing systems. The total overhead cost (both nonmanufacturing and manufacturing) for the year is $1,370,000 and includes the following costs:

Manufacturing overhead costs:		
Indirect factory wages..................	$400,000	
Production equipment depreciation	300,000	
Other factory costs	80,000	$ 780,000
Selling and administrative expenses:		
Administrative wages and salaries	300,000	
Office expenses	40,000	
Marketing expenses	250,000	590,000
Total overhead cost		$1,370,000

Based largely on interviews with employees, the distribution of resource consumption across the activities has been estimated as follows:

Distribution of Resource Consumption Across Activities					
	Making Windows	Processing Orders	Customer Relations	Other	Total
Indirect factory wages	30%	40%	10%	20%	100%
Production equipment depreciation	90%	0%	0%	10%	100%
Other factory costs...................	30%	0%	0%	70%	100%
Administrative wages and salaries......	0%	20%	30%	50%	100%
Office expenses.....................	0%	30%	10%	60%	100%
Marketing expenses..................	0%	0%	60%	40%	100%

Management of the company is particularly interested in measuring the profitability of two customers. One of the customers, Kuszik Builders, is a low-volume purchaser. The other, Western Homes, is a relatively high-volume purchaser. Details of these two customers' orders for the year appear below:

	Kuszik Builders	Western Homes
Number of orders during the year........	2 orders	3 orders
Total direct labor-hours.................	300 DLHs	2,000 DLHs
Total sales	$12,500	$68,000
Total direct materials..................	$4,200	$18,500
Total direct labor cost.................	$5,400	$36,000

Required:

1. The company's traditional costing system applies manufacturing overhead to jobs strictly on the direct labor-hours. Using this traditional approach, carry out the following steps:
   a. Compute the predetermined manufacturing overhead rate.
   b. Compute the total margin for all of the windows ordered by Kuszik Builders according to the traditional costing system. Do the same for Western Homes.
2. Using activity-based costing, do the following:
   a. Using Exhibit 8–5 as a guide, perform the first-stage allocation of costs to the activity cost pools.
   b. Using Exhibit 8A–2 as a guide, compute the activity rates for the activity cost pools.
   c. Compute the overhead costs of serving each of the two customers. (You will need to construct a table like Exhibit 8A–3 for each of the customers. However, unlike Exhibit 8A–3, you should fill in the column for Customer Relations as well as the other columns. Exhibit 8A–3 was constructed for a product; in this case we are interested in a customer.)
   d. Management has provided the following ease of adjustment codes to use in action analysis reports:

	Ease of Adjustment Code
Direct materials	Green
Direct labor	Yellow
Indirect factory wages	Yellow
Production equipment depreciation........	Yellow
Other factory costs....................	Yellow
Administrative wages and salaries	Red
Office expenses.......................	Yellow
Marketing expenses....................	Yellow

   Using Exhibit 8A–5 as a guide, prepare an action analysis report showing the margin on business with Kuszik Builders. Repeat for Western Homes.
3. Does Classic Windows appear to be losing money on either customer? Do the traditional and activity-based costing systems agree concerning the profitability of the customers? If they do not agree, which costing system do you believe? Why?

CASE 8-31 Activity-Based Costing and Pricing [LO7]

Java Source, Inc. (JSI), is a processor and distributor of a variety of blends of coffee. The company buys coffee beans from around the world and roasts, blends, and packages them for resale. JSI offers a large variety of different coffees that it sells to gourmet shops in one-pound bags. The major cost of the coffee is raw materials. However, the company's predominantly automated roasting, blending, and packing processes require a substantial amount of manufacturing overhead. The company uses relatively little direct labor.

Some of JSI's coffees are very popular and sell in large volumes, while a few of the newer blends sell in very low volumes. JSI prices its coffees at manufacturing cost plus a markup of 25%, with some adjustments made to keep the company's prices competitive.

For the coming year, JSI's budget includes estimated manufacturing overhead cost of $2,200,000. JSI assigns manufacturing overhead to products on the basis of direct labor-hours. The expected direct labor cost totals $600,000, which represents 50,000 hours of direct labor time. Based on the sales budget and expected raw materials costs, the company will purchase and use $5,000,000 of raw materials (mostly coffee beans) during the year.

The expected costs for direct materials and direct labor for one-pound bags of two of the company's coffee products appear below.

	Kenya Dark	Viet Select
Direct materials	$4.50	$2.90
Direct labor (0.02 hours per bag)	$0.24	$0.24

JSI's controller believes that the company's traditional costing system may be providing misleading cost information. To determine whether or not this is correct, the controller has prepared an analysis of the year's expected manufacturing overhead costs, as shown in the following table:

Activity Cost Pool	Activity Measure	Expected Activity for the Year	Expected Cost for the Year
Purchasing	Purchase orders	2,000 orders	$ 560,000
Material handling	Number of setups	1,000 setups	193,000
Quality control.	Number of batches	500 batches	90,000
Roasting	Roasting hours	95,000 roasting hours	1,045,000
Blending	Blending hours	32,000 blending hours	192,000
Packaging.	Packaging hours	24,000 packaging hours	120,000
Total manufacturing overhead cost			$2,200,000

Data regarding the expected production of Kenya Dark and Viet Select coffees are presented below.

	Kenya Dark	Viet Select
Expected sales	80,000 pounds	4,000 pounds
Batch size	5,000 pounds	500 pounds
Setups	2 per batch	2 per batch
Purchase order size	20,000 pounds	500 pounds
Roasting time per 100 pounds	1.5 roasting hours	1.5 roasting hours
Blending time per 100 pounds	0.5 blending hours	0.5 blending hours
Packaging time per 100 pounds	0.3 packaging hours	0.3 packaging hours

Required:
1. Using direct labor-hours as the base for assigning manufacturing overhead cost to products, do the following:
   a. Determine the predetermined overhead rate that will be used during the year.
   b. Determine the unit product cost of one pound of the Kenya Dark coffee and one pound of the Viet Select coffee.
2. Using activity-based costing as the basis for assigning manufacturing overhead cost to products, do the following:
   a. Determine the total amount of manufacturing overhead cost assigned to the Kenya Dark coffee and to the Viet Select coffee for the year.
   b. Using the data developed in (2a) above, compute the amount of manufacturing overhead cost per pound of the Kenya Dark coffee and the Viet Select coffee. Round all computations to the nearest whole cent.
   c. Determine the unit product cost of one pound of the Kenya Dark coffee and one pound of the Viet Select coffee.
3. Write a brief memo to the president of JSI explaining what you have found in (1) and (2) above and discussing the implications to the company of using direct labor as the base for assigning manufacturing overhead cost to products.

(CMA, adapted)

RESEARCH AND APPLICATION 8-32   [LO1, LO2, LO3]

The questions in this exercise are based on JetBlue Airways Corporation. To answer the questions, you will need to download JetBlue's 2004 10-K/A at www.hoovers.com. Once at this website, do a search for JetBlue Airways. Click on the matching company name and then click on the link called SEC filings. Download the 2004 10-K/A. You do not need to print the 10-K/A to answer the questions.

Required:

1. What is JetBlue's strategy for success in the marketplace? Does the company rely primarily on a customer intimacy, operational excellence, or product leadership customer value proposition? What evidence supports your conclusion?
2. What business risks does JetBlue face that may threaten the company's ability to satisfy stockholder expectations? What are some examples of control activities that the company could use to reduce these risks? (Hint: Focus on pages 17–23 of the 10-K/A).
3. How can the concept of unit-level activities be applied to an airline? More specifically, what are two examples of unit-level activities for JetBlue? What steps has JetBlue taken to manage these unit-level activities more efficiently?
4. How can the concept of batch-level activities be applied to an airline? What are two examples of batch-level activities for JetBlue? What steps has JetBlue taken to manage these batch-level activities more efficiently?
5. What is one example of a customer-level activity and an organization-sustaining activity for JetBlue?
6. Give an example of a transaction driver and a duration driver that could be used to assign fuel costs to a particular flight departure. Which of the two activity measures would be more accurate and why?

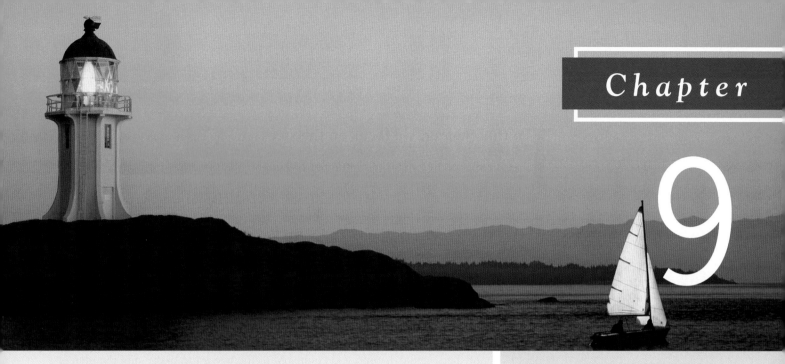

Profit Planning

Lilo & Stitch on Budget

The full-length feature cartoon *Tarzan* grossed about $450 million worldwide for the Walt Disney Company. However, production costs got out of control. The company traditionally manages film production by focusing on meeting the planned release date—paying little attention to costs. In the case of *Tarzan*, production fell behind schedule due to the tendency of animation teams to add more eye-dazzling complexity to each production. At one point, it was estimated that 190,000 individual drawings would be needed to complete the film in contrast to the 130,000 drawings needed to complete *The Lion King*. To meet *Tarzan*'s release date, workers were pulled off other productions and were often paid at overtime rates. The size of the film crew eventually reached 573, which was nearly twice the size of the crew that had made *The Lion King*. With animators earning salaries in the hundreds of thousands of dollars, the cost implications were staggering.

Thomas S. Schumacher, Disney's feature-animation chief, was charged with dramatically reducing the cost of future films while making sure that the audience wouldn't notice any decline in quality. *Lilo & Stitch* was the first film to be produced with this goal in mind. The process began by prioritizing where the money was to be spent. The budget for music was kept generous; animation costs were cut by controlling the small details that add big costs with little effect on the quality of the film. For example, animators wanted to draw cute designs on the shirts worn by Nani, Lilo's big sister. However, adding this level of detail on every frame in which Nani appears in the film would have added about $250,000 in cost. By controlling such details, *Lilo & Stitch* was finished on time and at a cost of about $80 million. This contrasted with a cost of more than $150 million for *Tarzan*. ■

Source: Bruce Orwall, "Comics Stripped: At Disney, String of Weak Cartoons Leads to Cost Cuts," *The Wall Street Journal*, June 18, 2002, pp. A1 and A8.

Learning Objectives

After studying Chapter 9, you should be able to:

LO1 Understand why organizations budget and the processes they use to create budgets.

LO2 Prepare a sales budget, including a schedule of expected cash collections.

LO3 Prepare a production budget.

LO4 Prepare a direct materials budget, including a schedule of expected cash disbursements for purchases of materials.

LO5 Prepare a direct labor budget.

LO6 Prepare a manufacturing overhead budget.

LO7 Prepare a selling and administrative expense budget.

LO8 Prepare a cash budget.

LO9 Prepare a budgeted income statement.

LO10 Prepare a budgeted balance sheet.

I n this chapter, we focus on the steps taken by businesses to achieve their planned levels of profits—a process called *profit planning*. Profit planning is accomplished by preparing a number of budgets that together form an integrated business plan known as the *master budget*. The master budget is an essential management tool that communicates management's plans throughout the organization, allocates resources, and coordinates activities.

The Basic Framework of Budgeting

A **budget** is a quantitative plan for acquiring and using resources over a specified time period. Individuals often create household budgets that balance their income and expenditures for food, clothing, housing, and so on while providing for some savings. Once the budget is established, actual spending is compared to the budget to make sure the plan is being followed. Companies use budgets in a similar way, although the amount of work and underlying details involved far exceed a personal budget.

In an organization, the term **master budget** refers to a summary of a company's plans including specific targets for sales, production, and financing activities. The master budget—which culminates in a cash budget, a budgeted income statement, and a budgeted balance sheet—formally lays out the financial aspects of management's plans for the future and assists in monitoring actual expenditures relative to those plans.

Budgets are used for two distinct purposes—*planning* and *control*. **Planning** involves developing goals and preparing various budgets to achieve those goals. **Control** involves the steps taken by management to increase the likelihood that all parts of the organization are working together to achieve the goals set down at the planning stage. To be effective, a good budgeting system must provide for both planning and control. Good planning without effective control is a waste of time and effort.

Advantages of Budgeting

Organizations realize many benefits from budgeting including:

1. Budgets *communicate* management's plans throughout the organization.
2. Budgets force managers to *think about* and plan for the future. In the absence of the necessity to prepare a budget, many managers would spend all of their time dealing with daily emergencies.
3. The budgeting process provides a means of *allocating resources* to those parts of the organization where they can be used most effectively.
4. The budgeting process can uncover potential *bottlenecks* before they occur.
5. Budgets *coordinate* the activities of the entire organization by *integrating* the plans of its various parts. Budgeting helps to ensure that everyone in the organization is pulling in the same direction.
6. Budgets define goals and objectives that can serve as *benchmarks* for evaluating subsequent performance.

Responsibility Accounting

Most of what we say in this chapter and in the next three chapters is concerned with *responsibility accounting*. The basic idea underlying **responsibility accounting** is that a manager should be held responsible for those items—and *only* those items—that the manager can actually control to a significant extent. Each line item (i.e., revenue or cost) in the budget is made the responsibility of a manager who is held responsible for subsequent deviations between

BRINGING ORDER OUT OF CHAOS

Consider the following situation encountered by one of the authors at a mortgage banking company: For years, the company operated with virtually no system of budgets whatsoever. Management contended that budgeting wasn't well suited to the company's type of operation. Moreover, management pointed out that the company was already profitable. Indeed, outwardly the company gave every appearance of being a well-managed, smoothly operating organization. A careful look within, however, disclosed that day-to-day operations were far from smooth, and often approached chaos. The average day involved putting out one brush fire after another. The Cash account was always at crisis levels. At the end of a day, no one ever knew whether enough cash would be available the next day to cover required loan closings. Departments were uncoordinated, and it was not uncommon to find that one department was pursuing a course of action that conflicted with the goals of another department. Employee morale was low, and turnover was high. Employees complained bitterly that when a job was well done, nobody ever knew about it.

The company was bought out by a new group of stockholders who required that an integrated budgeting system be established to control operations. Within one year's time, significant changes were evident. Brush fires were rare. Careful planning virtually eliminated the problems that had been experienced with cash, and departmental efforts were coordinated and directed toward predetermined overall company goals. Although the employees were initially wary of the new budgeting program, they became "converted" when they experienced its positive effects. The more efficient operations caused profits to jump dramatically. Communication increased throughout the organization. When a job was well done, everybody knew about it. As one employee stated, "For the first time, we know what the company expects of us."

budgeted goals and actual results. In effect, responsibility accounting *personalizes* accounting information by holding individuals responsible for revenues and costs. This concept is central to any effective profit planning and control system. Someone must be held responsible for each cost or else no one will be responsible and the cost will inevitably grow out of control.

Being held responsible for financial performance does not mean that the manager is penalized if actual results do not measure up to the budgeted goals. However, the manager should take the initiative to correct any unfavorable discrepancies, should understand the source of significant favorable or unfavorable discrepancies, and should be prepared to explain the reasons for discrepancies to higher management. The point of an effective responsibility accounting system is to make sure that nothing "falls through the cracks," that the organization reacts quickly and appropriately to deviations from its plans, and that the organization learns from the feedback it gets by comparing budgeted goals to actual results. The point is *not* to penalize individuals for missing targets.

Choosing a Budget Period

Operating budgets ordinarily cover a one-year period corresponding to the company's fiscal year. Many companies divide their budget year into four quarters. The first quarter is then subdivided into months, and monthly budgets are developed. The last three quarters may be carried in the budget as quarterly totals only. As the year progresses, the figures for the second quarter are broken down into monthly amounts, then the third-quarter figures are broken down, and so forth. This approach has the advantage of requiring periodic review and reappraisal of budget data throughout the year.

Continuous or *perpetual budgets* are used by a significant number of organizations. A **continuous** or **perpetual budget** is a 12-month budget that rolls forward one month (or quarter) as the current month (or quarter) is completed. In other words, one month (or quarter) is added to the end of the budget as each month (or quarter) comes to a close. This approach keeps managers focused at least one year ahead so that they do not become too narrowly focused on short-term results.

In this chapter, we will look at one-year operating budgets. However, using basically the same techniques, operating budgets can be prepared for periods that extend over many years. It may be difficult to accurately forecast sales and required data much beyond a year, but even rough estimates can be invaluable in uncovering potential problems and opportunities that would otherwise be overlooked.

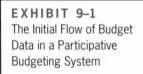

KEEPING CURRENT

Jim Bell, Hunstman Corp.'s director of corporate finance, says that his company must frequently update its budgets and its forecasts to meet the demands of investors, creditors, and others. The company updates its annual budget each month, using the most recent data, to provide greater accuracy as the year unfolds. The budget is also used together with sophisticated modeling software to evaluate what effects decisions and various changes in input prices and other parameters might have on future results.

Source: Tim Reason, "Partial Clearing," *CFO*, December 2002, pp. 73–76.

The Self-Imposed Budget

The success of a budget program is largely determined by the way a budget is developed. In the most successful budget programs, managers actively participate in preparing their own budgets rather than having them imposed from above. The participative approach is particularly effective when budgets are used to evaluate a manager's performance because imposing expectations from above and then penalizing employees who do not meet those expectations will generate resentment rather than cooperation and commitment. In fact, many managers believe that being empowered to create their own *self-imposed budgets* is the most effective method of budget preparation. A **self-imposed budget** or **participative budget,** as illustrated in Exhibit 9–1, is a budget that is prepared with the full cooperation and participation of managers at all levels.

EXHIBIT 9–1
The Initial Flow of Budget Data in a Participative Budgeting System

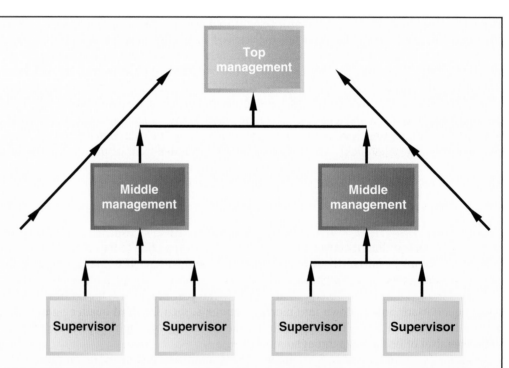

The initial flow of budget data in a participative system is from lower levels of responsibility to higher levels of responsibility. Each person with responsibility for cost control will prepare his or her own budget estimates and submit them to the next higher level of management. These estimates are reviewed and consolidated as they move upward in the organization.

Self-imposed budgets have a number of advantages:

1. Individuals at all levels of the organization are recognized as members of the team whose views and judgments are valued by top management.
2. Budget estimates prepared by front-line managers are often more accurate and reliable than estimates prepared by top managers who have less intimate knowledge of markets and day-to-day operations.
3. Motivation is generally higher when individuals participate in setting their own goals than when the goals are imposed from above. Self-imposed budgets create commitment.
4. A manager who is not able to meet a budget that has been imposed from above can always say that the budget was unrealistic and impossible to meet. With a self-imposed budget, this excuse is not available.

One important limitation of self-imposed budgeting is that lower-level managers may allow too much *budgetary slack*. Since the manager who creates the budget will be held accountable for actual results that deviate from the budget, the manager will have a natural tendency to submit a budget that is easy to attain (i.e., the manager will build slack into the budget). For this reason, budgets prepared by lower-level managers should be scrutinized by higher levels of management. Questionable items should be discussed and modified as appropriate. Without such a review, self-imposed budgets may be too slack, resulting in suboptimal performance.

As these comments suggest, all levels in the organization should work together to produce the budget. Lower-level managers are more familiar with day-to-day operations than top managers. Top managers should have a more strategic perspective than lower-level managers. Each level of responsibility in an organization should contribute its unique knowledge and perspective in a cooperative effort to develop an integrated budget. Nevertheless, a self-imposed approach to setting budgets works best when all managers understand the organization's strategy. Otherwise, the budgets proposed by the lower-level managers will lack coherent direction. Chapter 10 discusses in greater detail how a company can go about formulating its strategy and communicating it throughout the organization.

Unfortunately, most companies do not follow the budgeting process we have described. Typically, top managers initiate the budgeting process by issuing profit targets. Lower-level managers are directed to prepare budgets that meet those targets. The difficulty is that the targets set by top managers may be unrealistically high or may allow too much slack. If the targets are too high and employees know they are unrealistic, motivation will suffer. If the targets allow too much slack, waste will occur. Unfortunately, top managers are often not in a position to know whether the targets are appropriate. Admittedly, a self-imposed budgeting system may lack sufficient strategic direction and lower-level managers may be tempted to build slack into their budgets. Nevertheless, because of the motivational advantages of self-imposed budgets, top managers should be cautious about imposing inflexible targets from above.

Human Factors in Budgeting

The success of a budget program also depends on the degree to which top management accepts the budget program as a vital part of the company's activities and the way in which top management uses budgeted data.

If a budget program is to be successful, it must have the complete acceptance and support of the persons who occupy key management positions. If lower or middle management personnel sense that top management is lukewarm about budgeting, or if they sense that top management simply tolerates budgeting as a necessary evil, then their own attitudes will reflect a similar lack of enthusiasm. Budgeting is hard work, and if top management is not enthusiastic about and committed to the budget program, then it is unlikely that anyone else in the organization will be either.

In administering the budget program, it is particularly important that top management not use the budget to pressure or blame employees. Using budgets in such negative ways will breed hostility, tension, and mistrust rather than cooperation and productivity. Unfortunately, the budget is too often used as a pressure device and excessive emphasis is placed on "meeting the budget" under all circumstances. Rather than being used as a weapon, the budget should be used as a positive instrument to assist in establishing goals, measuring operating results, and isolating areas that need attention.

The human aspects of budgeting are extremely important. The remainder of the chapter deals with technical aspects of budgeting, but do not lose sight of the human aspects. The purpose of the budget is to motivate people and to coordinate their efforts. This purpose is undermined if managers become preoccupied with the technical aspects or if the budget is used in a rigid and inflexible manner to control people.

IN BUSINESS

WHO CARES ABOUT BUDGETS?

Towers Perrin, a consulting firm, reports that the bonuses of more than two out of three corporate managers are based on meeting targets set in annual budgets. "Under this arrangement, managers at the beginning of a year all too often argue that their targets should be lowered because of tough business conditions, when in fact conditions are better than projected. If their arguments are successful, they can easily surpass the targets."

Source: Ronald Fink and Towers Perrin, "Riding the Bull: The 2000 Compensation Survey," *CFO*, June 2000, pp. 45–60.

How challenging should budget targets be? Some experts argue that budget targets should be very challenging and should require managers to stretch to meet goals. Even the most capable managers may have to scramble to meet such a "stretch budget" and they may not always succeed. In practice, most companies set their budget targets at a "highly achievable" level. A highly achievable budget may be challenging, but it can almost always be met by competent managers exerting reasonable effort.

Bonuses based on meeting and exceeding budgets are often a key element of management compensation. Typically, no bonus is paid unless the budget is met. The bonus often increases when the budget target is exceeded, but the bonus is usually capped out at some level. For obvious reasons, managers who have such a bonus plan or whose performance is evaluated based on meeting budget targets usually prefer to be evaluated based on highly achievable budgets rather than on stretch budgets. Moreover, highly achievable budgets may help build a manager's confidence and generate greater commitment to the budget. And finally, highly achievable budgets may result in less undesirable behavior at the end of budgetary periods by managers who are intent on earning their bonuses. Examples of such undesirable behaviors are presented in several of the In Business boxes in this chapter.

IN BUSINESS

BIASING FORECASTS

A manager's compensation is often tied to the budget. Typically, no bonus is paid unless a minimum performance hurdle such as 80% of the budget target is attained. Once that hurdle is passed, the manager's bonus increases until a cap is reached. That cap is often set at 120% of the budget target.

This common method of tying a manager's compensation to the budget has some serious negative side effects. For example, a marketing manager for a big beverage company intentionally grossly understated demand for the company's products for an upcoming major holiday so that the budget target for revenues would be low and easy to beat. Unfortunately, the company tied its production to this biased forecast and ran out of products to sell during the height of the holiday selling season.

As another example, near the end of the year another group of managers announced a price increase of 10% effective January 2 of the following year. Why would they do this? By announcing this price increase, managers hoped that customers would order before the end of the year, helping managers meet their sales targets for the current year. Sales in the following year would, of course, drop. What trick would managers pull to meet their sales targets next year in the face of this drop in demand?

Sources: Michael C. Jensen, "Corporate Budgeting Is Broken—Let's Fix It," *Harvard Business Review*, November 2001; and Michael C. Jensen, "Why Pay People to Lie?" *The Wall Street Journal*, January 8, 2001, p. A32.

The Budget Committee

A standing **budget committee** is usually responsible for overall policy relating to the budget program and for coordinating the preparation of the budget itself. This committee may consist of the president; vice presidents in charge of various functions such as sales, production, and purchasing; and the controller. Difficulties and disputes relating to the budget are resolved by the budget committee. In addition, the budget committee approves the final budget.

Disputes can (and do) erupt over budget matters. Because budgets allocate resources, the budgeting process determines to a large extent which departments get more resources and which get less. Also, the budget sets the benchmarks used to evaluate managers and their departments. Therefore, it should not be surprising that managers take the budgeting process very seriously and invest considerable energy and emotion in ensuring that their interests, and those of their departments, are protected. Because of this, the budgeting process can easily degenerate into an interoffice brawl in which the ultimate goal of working together toward common goals is forgotten.

Running a successful budgeting program that avoids interoffice battles requires considerable interpersonal skills in addition to purely technical skills. But even the best interpersonal skills will fail if, as discussed earlier, top management uses the budget process to inappropriately pressure employees or to assign blame.

IN BUSINESS

BETTER THAN BUDGETS?

Borealis is a company headquartered in Copenhagen, Denmark, that produces polymers for the plastics industry. Thomas Boesen, the company's financial controller, felt that the traditional budgeting process had outlived its usefulness—markets were changing so fast that the budget was out of date within weeks of its publication. Moreover, since budgets were used to control and evaluate the performance of managers, they were subject to considerable gaming behavior that reduced their accuracy and usefulness. So over a five-year period the company phased out its traditional budgets and replaced them with rolling forecasts and several other management tools. Instead of holding managers to a budget, targets based on competitors' performance were set for variable costs, fixed costs, and operating margins. Managers were given the freedom to spend money as needed to meet these competitive benchmarks. Since the rolling forecasts of financial results were not used to control spending or to evaluate managers' performance, managers had little incentive to "game the system," and hence the forecasts were more accurate than those obtained through the traditional budgeting process.

Source: Professor Bjorn Jorgensen, *Borealis*, Harvard Business School Case 9-102-048, Rev: May 9, 2002.

The Master Budget: An Overview

Topic Tackler
PLUS

9–1

The master budget consists of a number of separate but interdependent budgets. Exhibit 9–2 (page 378) provides an overview of the various parts of the master budget and how they are related.

The first step in the budgeting process is the preparation of the **sales budget,** which is a detailed schedule showing the expected sales for the budget period. An accurate sales budget is the key to the entire budgeting process. As illustrated in Exhibit 9–2, all other parts of the master budget depend on the sales budget. If the sales budget is inaccurate, the rest of the budget will be inaccurate. The sales budget is based on the company's sales forecast, which may require the use of sophisticated mathematical models and statistical tools. We will not go into the details of how sales forecasts are made. This is a subject that is most appropriately covered in marketing courses.

The sales budget helps determine how many units need to be produced. Thus, the production budget is prepared after the sales budget. The production budget in turn is used to determine the budgets for manufacturing costs including the direct materials budget, the

EXHIBIT 9–2
The Master Budget
Interrelationships

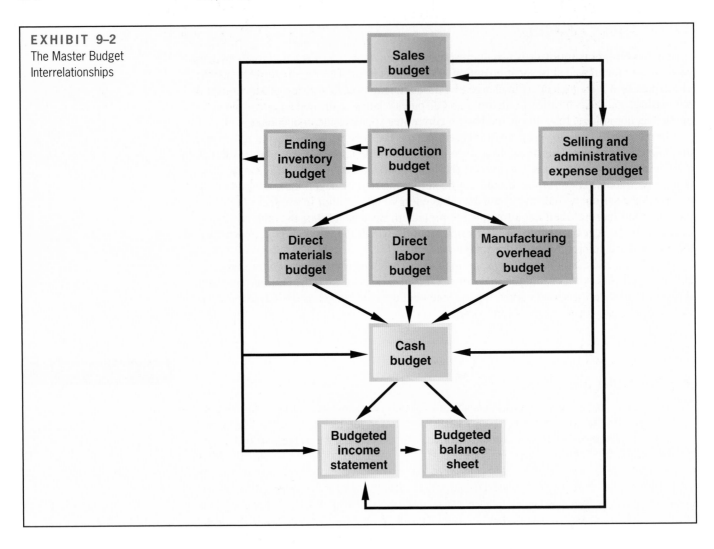

direct labor budget, and the manufacturing overhead budget. These budgets are then combined with data from the sales budget and the selling and administrative expense budget to determine the *cash budget*. A **cash budget** is a detailed plan showing how cash resources will be acquired and used. Observe from Exhibit 9–2 that all of the operating budgets have an impact on the cash budget. After the cash budget is prepared, the budgeted income statement and then the budgeted balance sheet can be prepared.

IN BUSINESS

BE REALISTIC

Gillette, the company that makes razors and other consumer products, got into trouble trying to meet increasingly unrealistic sales targets. The buyer at one of the company's big retail customers told Gillette's new CEO, Jim Kilts, that "he always waited until the last week of the quarter to order anything from Gillette 'because I know that you will always cut a deal.' To hit their numbers each quarter, [the Gillette salepersons] were willing to do anything—offer cut-rate deals, rearrange product packaging— whatever it took to make the sale." This resulted in artificially large sales at the end of the quarter— disrupting production schedules and loading the retail stores with excess inventory at discounted prices that would have to be sold off before more inventory would be ordered from Gillette.

Source: Katrina Brooker, "Jim Kilts Is an Old-School Curmudgeon," *Fortune,* December 30, 2002, pp. 95–102.

Preparing the Master Budget

Tom Wills is the majority stockholder and chief executive officer of Hampton Freeze, Inc., a company he started in 2006. The company makes premium popsicles using only natural ingredients and featuring exotic flavors such as tangy tangerine and minty mango. The company's business is highly seasonal, with most of the sales occurring in spring and summer.

MANAGERIAL ACCOUNTING IN ACTION

The Issue

In 2007, the company's second year of operations, a major cash crunch in the first and second quarters almost forced the company into bankruptcy. In spite of this cash crunch, 2007 turned out to be a very successful year in terms of both cash flow and net income. Partly as a result of that harrowing experience, Tom decided toward the end of 2007 to hire a professional financial manager. Tom interviewed several promising candidates for the job and settled on Larry Giano, who had considerable experience in the packaged foods industry. In the job interview, Tom questioned Larry about the steps he would take to prevent a recurrence of the 2007 cash crunch:

Tom: As I mentioned earlier, we are going to end 2007 with a very nice profit. What you may not know is that we had some very big financial problems this year.

Larry: Let me guess. You ran out of cash sometime in the first or second quarter.

Tom: How did you know?

Larry: Most of your sales are in the second and third quarter, right?

Tom: Sure, everyone wants to buy popsicles in the spring and summer, but nobody wants them when the weather turns cold.

Larry: So you don't have many sales in the first quarter?

Tom: Right.

Larry: And in the second quarter, which is the spring, you are producing like crazy to fill orders?

Tom: Sure.

Larry: Do your customers, the grocery stores, pay you the day you make your deliveries?

Tom: Are you kidding? Of course not.

Larry: So in the first quarter, you don't have many sales. In the second quarter, you are producing like crazy, which eats up cash, but you aren't paid by your customers until long after you have paid your employees and suppliers. No wonder you had a cash problem. I see this pattern all the time in food processing because of the seasonality of the business.

Tom: So what can we do about it?

Larry: The first step is to predict the magnitude of the problem before it occurs. If we can predict early in the year what the cash shortfall is going to be, we can go to the bank and arrange for credit before we really need it. Bankers tend to be leery of panicky people who show up begging for emergency loans. They are much more likely to make the loan if you look like you are in control of the situation.

Tom: How can we predict the cash shortfall?

Larry: You can put together a cash budget. While you're at it, you might as well do a master budget. You'll find it is well worth the effort.

Tom: I don't like budgets. They are too confining. My wife budgets everything at home, and I can't spend what I want.

Larry: Can I ask a personal question?

Tom: What?

Larry: Where did you get the money to start this business?

Tom: Mainly from our family's savings. I get your point. We wouldn't have had the money to start the business if my wife hadn't been forcing us to save every month.

Larry: Exactly. I suggest you use the same discipline in your business. It is even more important here because you can't expect your employees to spend your money as carefully as you would.

With the full backing of Tom Wills, Larry Giano set out to create a master budget for the company for the year 2008. In his planning for the budgeting process, Larry drew up the following list of documents that would be a part of the master budget:

1. A sales budget, including a schedule of expected cash collections.
2. A production budget (a merchandise purchases budget would be used in a merchandising company).
3. A direct materials budget, including a schedule of expected cash disbursements for purchases of materials.
4. A direct labor budget.
5. A manufacturing overhead budget.
6. An ending finished goods inventory budget.
7. A selling and administrative expense budget.
8. A cash budget.
9. A budgeted income statement.
10. A budgeted balance sheet.

Larry felt it was important to have everyone's cooperation in the budgeting process, so he asked Tom to call a companywide meeting to explain the budgeting process. At the meeting there was initially some grumbling, but Tom was able to convince nearly everyone of the necessity for planning and getting better control over spending. It helped that the cash crisis earlier in the year was still fresh in everyone's minds. As much as some people disliked the idea of budgets, they liked their jobs more.

In the months that followed, Larry worked closely with all of the managers involved in the master budget, gathering data from them and making sure that they understood and fully supported the parts of the master budget that would affect them. In subsequent years, Larry hoped to turn the whole budgeting process over to the managers and to take a more advisory role.

The interdependent documents that Larry Giano prepared for Hampton Freeze are Schedules 1 through 10 of his company's master budget. In this section, we will study these schedules.

LEARNING OBJECTIVE 2
Prepare a sales budget, including a schedule of expected cash collections.

The Sales Budget

The sales budget is the starting point in preparing the master budget. As shown earlier in Exhibit 9–2, all other items in the master budget, including production, purchases, inventories, and expenses, depend on it.

The sales budget is constructed by multiplying budgeted unit sales by the selling price. Schedule 1 contains the quarterly sales budget for Hampton Freeze for the year 2008. Notice from the schedule that the company plans to sell 100,000 cases of popsicles during the year, with sales peaking in the third quarter.

A schedule of expected cash collections, such as the one that appears in Schedule 1 for Hampton Freeze, is prepared after the sales budget. This schedule will be needed later to prepare the cash budget. Cash collections consist of collections on credit sales made to customers in prior periods plus collections on sales made in the current budget period. At Hampton Freeze all sales are on credit; furthermore, experience has shown that 70% of sales are collected in the quarter in which the sale is made and the remaining 30% are collected in the following quarter. For example, 70% of the first quarter sales of $200,000 (or $140,000) is collected during the first quarter and 30% (or $60,000) is collected during the second quarter.

PREDICTING DEMAND

O'Reilly Auto Parts uses sophisticated demand software from Nonstop Solutions to forecast seasonal variations in sales. For example, monthly sales of windshield wiper blades vary from 25,000 in the summer to 50,000 in the winter. Demand software uses weather data, economic trends, and other information to make forecasts and can even learn from its past mistakes.

Source: Chana R. Schoenberger, "The Weakest Link," *Forbes*, October 1, 2001, pp. 114–115.

SCHEDULE 1

Microsoft Excel - Hampton Freeze.xls

File Edit View Insert Format Tools Data Window Help   Type a question for help

Arial   10   **B** *I* <u>U</u>

C39

	A	B	C	D	E	F
1		Hampton Freeze, Inc.				
2		Sales Budget				
3		For the Year Ended December 31, 2008				
4						
5		*Quarter*				
6		*1*	*2*	*3*	*4*	*Year*
7	Budgeted sales in cases	10,000	30,000	40,000	20,000	100,000
8	Selling price per case	$ 20.00	$ 20.00	$ 20.00	$ 20.00	$ 20.00
9	Total sales	$200,000	$600,000	$800,000	$400,000	$2,000,000
10						
11	Percentage of sales collected in the period of the sale			70%		
12	Percentage of sales collected in the period after the sale			30%		
13		70%	30%			
14		Schedule of Expected Cash Collections				
15	Accounts receivable, beginning balance[1]	$ 90,000				$ 90,000
16	First-quarter sales[2]	140,000	$ 60,000			200,000
17	Second-quarter sales[3]		420,000	$180,000		600,000
18	Third-quarter sales[4]			560,000	$240,000	800,000
19	Fourth-quarter sales[5]	-	-	-	280,000	280,000
20	Total cash collections[6]	$230,000	$480,000	$740,000	$520,000	$1,970,000
21						
22						

Schedule 1 / Schedule 2 / Schedule 3 / Schedule 4 / Schedule 5 /

Ready   NUM

---

[1]Cash collections from last year's fourth-quarter sales. See the beginning-of-year balance sheet on page 394.
[2]$200,000 × 70%; $200,000 × 30%.
[3]$600,000 × 70%; $600,000 × 30%.
[4]$800,000 × 70%; $800,000 × 30%.
[5]$400,000 × 70%.
[6]Uncollected fourth-quarter sales appear as accounts receivable on the company's end-of-year balance sheet (see Schedule 10 on page 395).

The Production Budget

The production budget is prepared after the sales budget. The **production budget** lists the number of units that must be produced to satisfy sales needs and to provide for the desired ending inventory. Production needs can be determined as follows:

LEARNING OBJECTIVE 3
Prepare a production budget.

Budgeted unit sales	XXXX
Add desired ending inventory.......	XXXX
Total needs	XXXX
Less beginning inventory	XXXX
Required production..............	XXXX

Note that production requirements are influenced by the desired level of the ending inventory. Inventories should be carefully planned. Excessive inventories tie up funds and create storage problems. Insufficient inventories can lead to lost sales or last-minute, high-cost production efforts. At Hampton Freeze, management believes that an ending inventory equal to 20% of the next quarter's sales strikes the appropriate balance.

Schedule 2 contains the production budget for Hampton Freeze. The first row in the production budget contains the budgeted sales, which have been taken directly from the sales budget (Schedule 1). The total needs for the first quarter are determined by adding together the budgeted sales of 10,000 cases for the quarter and the desired ending inventory of 6,000 cases. As discussed above, the ending inventory is intended to provide some cushion in case problems develop in production or sales increase unexpectedly. Since the budgeted sales for the second quarter are 30,000 cases and management would like the ending inventory in each quarter to equal 20% of the following quarter's sales, the desired ending inventory for the first quarter is 6,000 cases (20% of 30,000 cases). Consequently, the total needs for the first quarter are 16,000 cases. However, since the company already has 2,000 cases in beginning inventory, only 14,000 cases need to be produced in the first quarter.

Pay particular attention to the Year column to the right of the production budget in Schedule 2. In some cases (e.g., budgeted sales, total needs, and required production), the amount listed for the year is the sum of the quarterly amounts for the item. In other

SCHEDULE 2

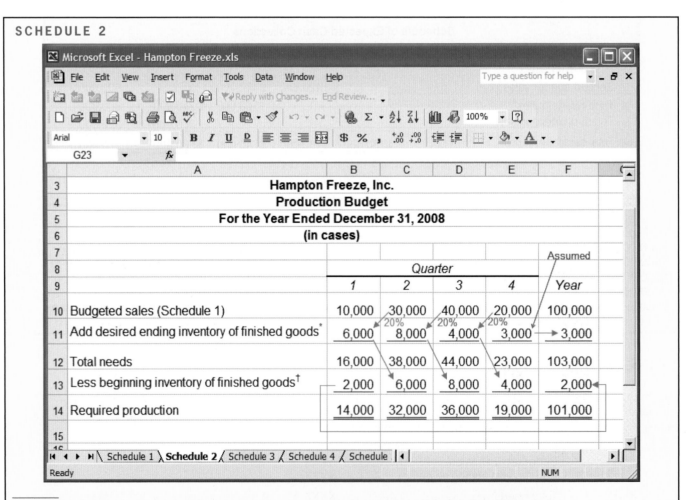

*Twenty percent of the next quarter's sales. The ending inventory of 3,000 cases is assumed.
†The beginning inventory in each quarter is the same as the prior quarter's ending inventory.

cases (e.g., desired ending inventory of finished goods and beginning inventory of finished goods), the amount listed for the year is not simply the sum of the quarterly amounts. From the standpoint of the entire year, the beginning finished goods inventory is the same as the beginning finished goods inventory for the first quarter—it is *not* the sum of the beginning finished goods inventories for all quarters. Similarly, from the standpoint of the entire year, the ending finished goods inventory is the same as the ending finished goods inventory for the fourth quarter—it is *not* the sum of the ending finished goods inventories for all four quarters. It is important to pay attention to such distinctions in all of the schedules that follow.

Inventory Purchases—Merchandising Company

Hampton Freeze prepares a production budget because it is a *manufacturing* company. If it were a *merchandising* company, it would prepare instead a **merchandise purchases budget** showing the amount of goods to be purchased from suppliers during the period. The merchandise purchases budget has the same basic format as the production budget, as shown below:

Budgeted sales.	XXXXX
Add desired ending merchandise inventory	XXXXX
Total needs.	XXXXX
Less beginning merchandise inventory	XXXXX
Required purchases.	XXXXX

A merchandising company would prepare a merchandise purchases budget such as the one above for each item carried in stock. The merchandise purchases budget can be expressed in terms of either units or the purchase cost of those units.

The Direct Materials Budget

A *direct materials budget* is prepared after the production requirements have been computed. The **direct materials budget** details the raw materials that must be purchased to fulfill the production budget and to provide for adequate inventories. The required purchases of raw materials are computed as follows:

LEARNING OBJECTIVE 4
Prepare a direct materials budget, including a schedule of expected cash disbursements for purchases of materials.

Raw materials needed to meet the production schedule	XXXXX
Add desired ending inventory of raw materials	XXXXX
Total raw materials needs	XXXXX
Less beginning inventory of raw materials	XXXXX
Raw materials to be purchased	XXXXX

Schedule 3 contains the direct materials budget for Hampton Freeze. The only raw material included in that budget is high fructose sugar, which is the major ingredient in popsicles other than water. The remaining raw materials are relatively insignificant and are included in variable manufacturing overhead. As with finished goods, management would like to maintain some inventories of raw materials to act as a cushion. In this case, management

SCHEDULE 3

Microsoft Excel - Hampton Freeze.xls

File Edit View Insert Format Tools Data Window Help

Type a question for help

Arial 10 B I U $ % 100%

I35

Hampton Freeze, Inc.
Direct Materials Budget
For the Year Ended December 31, 2008

	A	1	2	3	4	Assumed Year
				Quarter		
9	Required production in cases (Schedule 2)	14,000	32,000	36,000	19,000	101,000
10	Raw materials needed per case (pounds)	15	15	15	15	15
11	Production needs (pounds)	210,000	480,000	540,000	285,000	1,515,000
12	Add desired ending inventory of raw materials[1]	48,000	54,000	28,500	22,500	22,500
13	Total needs	258,000	534,000	568,500	307,500	1,537,500
14	Less beginning inventory of raw materials	21,000	48,000	54,000	28,500	21,000
15	Raw materials to be purchased	237,000	486,000	514,500	279,000	1,516,500
16	Cost of raw materials per pound	$ 0.20	$ 0.20	$ 0.20	$ 0.20	$ 0.20
17	Cost of raw materials to be purchased	$ 47,400	$ 97,200	$ 102,900	$ 55,800	$ 303,300
18						
19	Percentage of purchases paid for in the period of the purchase			50%		
20	Percentage of purchases paid for in the period after purchase			50%		
21		50%	50%			
22	**Schedule of Expected Cash Disbursements for Materials**					
23						
24	Accounts payable, beginning balance[2]	$ 25,800				$ 25,800
25	First-quarter purchases[3]	23,700	$ 23,700			47,400
26	Second-quarter purchases[4]		48,600	$ 48,600		97,200
27	Third-quarter purchases[5]			51,450	$ 51,450	102,900
28	Fourth-quarter purchases[6]	-	-	-	27,900	27,900
29	Total cash disbursements for materials	$ 49,500	$ 72,300	$ 100,050	$ 79,350	$ 301,200

Schedule 1 / Schedule 2 \ **Schedule 3** / Schedule 4 / Schedule 5 / Sch

---

[1]Ten percent of the next quarter's production needs. For example, the second-quarter production needs are 480,000 pounds. Therefore, the desired ending inventory for the first quarter would be 10% × 480,000 pounds = 48,000 pounds. The ending inventory of 22,500 pounds for the fourth quarter is assumed.

[2]Cash payments for last year's fourth-quarter material purchases. See the beginning-of-year balance sheet on page 394.

[3]$47,400 × 50%; $47,400 × 50%.

[4]$97,200 × 50%; $97,200 × 50%.

[5]$102,900 × 50%; $102,900 × 50%.

[6]$55,800 × 50%. Unpaid fourth-quarter purchases appear as accounts payable on the company's end-of-year balance sheet.

would like to maintain ending inventories of sugar equal to 10% of the following quarter's production needs.

The first line in the direct materials budget contains the required production for each quarter, which is taken directly from the production budget (Schedule 2). Looking at the first quarter, since the production schedule calls for production of 14,000 cases of popsicles and each case requires 15 pounds of sugar, the total production needs are 210,000 pounds of sugar (14,000 cases × 15 pounds per case). In addition, management wants to have ending inventories of 48,000 pounds of sugar, which is 10% of the following quarter's needs of 480,000 pounds. Consequently, the total needs are 258,000 pounds (210,000 pounds for the current quarter's production plus 48,000 pounds for the desired ending inventory). However, since the company already has 21,000 pounds in beginning inventory, only 237,000 pounds of sugar (258,000 pounds − 21,000 pounds) will need to be purchased. Finally, the cost of the raw materials purchases is determined by multiplying the amount of raw material to be purchased by its unit cost. In this case, since 237,000 pounds of sugar will need to be purchased during the first quarter and sugar costs $0.20 per pound, the total cost will be $47,400 (237,000 pounds × $0.20 per pound).

As with the production budget, the amounts listed under the Year column are not always the sum of the quarterly amounts. The desired ending raw materials inventory for the year is the same as the desired ending raw materials inventory for the fourth quarter. Likewise, the beginning raw materials inventory for the year is the same as the beginning raw materials inventory for the first quarter.

The direct materials budget (or the merchandise purchases budget for a merchandising company) is usually accompanied by a schedule of expected cash disbursements for raw materials (or merchandise purchases). This schedule is needed to prepare the overall cash budget. Disbursements for raw materials (or merchandise purchases) consist of payments for purchases on account in prior periods plus any payments for purchases in the current budget period. Schedule 3 contains such a schedule of cash disbursements for Hampton Freeze.

Ordinarily, companies do not immediately pay their suppliers. At Hampton Freeze, the policy is to pay for 50% of purchases in the quarter in which the purchase is made and 50% in the following quarter, so while the company intends to purchase $47,400 worth of sugar in the first quarter, the company will only pay for half, $23,700, in the first quarter and the other half will be paid in the second quarter. The company will also pay $25,800 in the first quarter for sugar that was purchased on account in the previous quarter, but not yet paid for. This is the beginning balance in the accounts payable. Therefore, the total cash disbursements for sugar in the first quarter are $49,500—the $25,800 payment for sugar acquired in the previous quarter plus the $23,700 payment for sugar acquired during the first quarter.

The Direct Labor Budget

LEARNING OBJECTIVE 5
Prepare a direct labor budget.

The **direct labor budget** shows the direct labor-hours required to satisfy the production budget. By knowing in advance how much labor time will be needed throughout the budget year, the company can develop plans to adjust the labor force as the situation requires. Companies that neglect to budget run the risk of facing labor shortages or having to hire and lay off workers at awkward times. Erratic labor policies lead to insecurity, low morale, and inefficiency.

The direct labor budget for Hampton Freeze is shown in Schedule 4. The first line in the direct labor budget consists of the required production for each quarter, which is taken directly from the production budget (Schedule 2). The direct labor requirement for each quarter is computed by multiplying the number of units to be produced in that quarter by the number of direct labor-hours required to make a unit. For example, 14,000 cases are to be produced in the first quarter and each case requires 0.40 direct labor-hour, so a total of 5,600 direct labor-hours (14,000 cases × 0.40 direct labor-hour per case) will be required in the first quarter. The direct labor requirements can then be translated into budgeted direct labor costs. How this is done will depend on the company's labor policy. In Schedule 4, Hampton Freeze has assumed that the direct labor force will be adjusted as the work requirements change from quarter to quarter. In that case, the direct labor cost is computed by simply multiplying the direct labor-hour requirements by the direct labor rate per hour. For example, the direct labor cost in the first quarter is $84,000 (5,600 direct labor-hours × $15 per direct labor-hour).

SCHEDULE 4

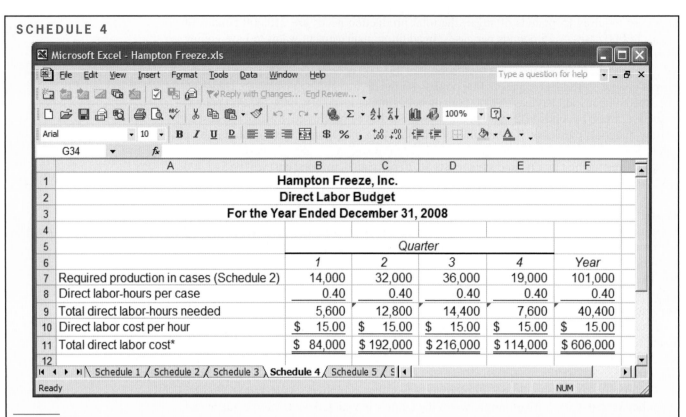

*This schedule assumes that the direct labor workforce will be fully adjusted to the total direct labor-hours needed each quarter.

However, many companies have employment policies or contracts that prevent them from laying off and rehiring workers as needed. Suppose, for example, that Hampton Freeze has 25 workers who are classified as direct labor, but each of them is guaranteed at least 480 hours of pay each quarter at a rate of $15 per hour. In that case, the minimum direct labor cost for a quarter would be as follows:

25 workers × 480 hours per worker × $15 per hour = $180,000

Note that in this case the direct labor costs for the first and fourth quarters would have to be increased to $180,000.

The Manufacturing Overhead Budget

LEARNING OBJECTIVE 6
Prepare a manufacturing overhead budget.

The **manufacturing overhead budget** lists all costs of production other than direct materials and direct labor. Schedule 5 shows the manufacturing overhead budget for Hampton Freeze. At Hampton Freeze, manufacturing overhead is separated into variable and fixed components. The variable component is $4 per direct labor-hour and the fixed component is $60,600 per quarter. Because the variable component of manufacturing overhead depends on direct labor, the first line in the manufacturing overhead budget consists of the budgeted direct labor-hours from the direct labor budget (Schedule 4). The budgeted direct labor-hours in each quarter are multiplied by the variable rate to determine the variable component of manufacturing overhead. For example, the variable manufacturing overhead for the first quarter is $22,400 (5,600 direct labor-hours × $4.00 per direct labor-hour). This is added to the fixed manufacturing overhead for the quarter to determine the total manufacturing overhead for the quarter of $83,000 ($22,400 + $60,600).

SCHEDULE 5

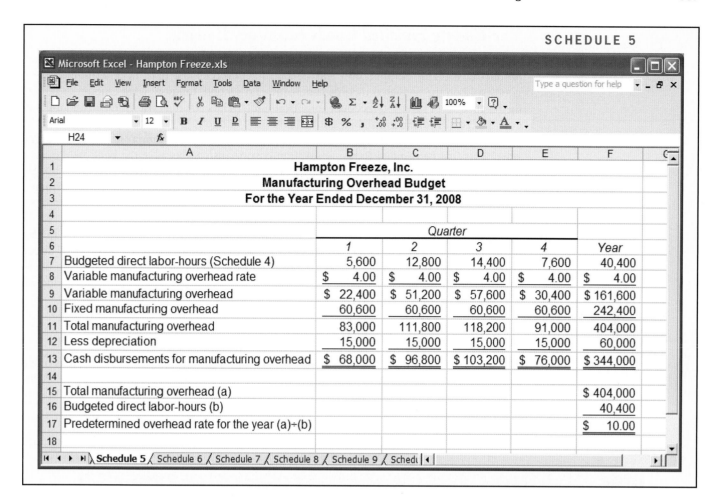

	A	B	C	D	E	F
1		Hampton Freeze, Inc.				
2		Manufacturing Overhead Budget				
3		For the Year Ended December 31, 2008				
4						
5			Quarter			
6		1	2	3	4	Year
7	Budgeted direct labor-hours (Schedule 4)	5,600	12,800	14,400	7,600	40,400
8	Variable manufacturing overhead rate	$ 4.00	$ 4.00	$ 4.00	$ 4.00	$ 4.00
9	Variable manufacturing overhead	$ 22,400	$ 51,200	$ 57,600	$ 30,400	$ 161,600
10	Fixed manufacturing overhead	60,600	60,600	60,600	60,600	242,400
11	Total manufacturing overhead	83,000	111,800	118,200	91,000	404,000
12	Less depreciation	15,000	15,000	15,000	15,000	60,000
13	Cash disbursements for manufacturing overhead	$ 68,000	$ 96,800	$ 103,200	$ 76,000	$ 344,000
14						
15	Total manufacturing overhead (a)					$ 404,000
16	Budgeted direct labor-hours (b)					40,400
17	Predetermined overhead rate for the year (a)÷(b)					$ 10.00
18						

A few words about fixed costs and the budgeting process are in order. In most cases, fixed costs are the costs of supplying capacity to make products, process purchase orders, handle customer calls, and so on. The amount of capacity that will be required depends on the expected level of activity for the period. If the expected level of activity is greater than the company's current capacity, then fixed costs may have to be increased. Or, if the expected level is appreciably below the company's current capacity, then it may be desirable to decrease fixed costs if possible. However, once the level of the fixed costs has been determined in the budget, the costs really are fixed. The time to adjust fixed costs is during the budgeting process. An activity-based costing system can help to determine the appropriate level of fixed costs at budget time by answering questions like, "How many clerks will we need to hire to process the anticipated number of purchase orders next year?" For simplicity, in all of the budgeting examples in this book assume that the appropriate levels of fixed costs have already been determined.

The last line of Schedule 5 for Hampton Freeze shows the budgeted cash disbursements for manufacturing overhead. Since some of the overhead costs are not cash outflows, the total budgeted manufacturing overhead costs must be adjusted to determine the cash disbursements for manufacturing overhead. At Hampton Freeze, the only significant noncash manufacturing overhead cost is depreciation, which is $15,000 per quarter. These noncash depreciation charges are deducted from the total budgeted manufacturing overhead to determine the expected cash disbursements. Hampton Freeze pays all overhead costs involving cash disbursements in the quarter incurred. Note that the company's predetermined overhead rate for the year is $10 per direct labor-hour, which is determined by dividing the total budgeted manufacturing overhead for the year by the total budgeted direct labor-hours for the year.

The Ending Finished Goods Inventory Budget

After completing Schedules 1–5, Larry Giano had all of the data he needed to compute unit product costs. This computation was needed for two reasons: first, to determine cost of goods sold on the budgeted income statement; and second, to know what amount to put on the balance sheet inventory account for unsold units. The carrying cost of the unsold units is computed on the **ending finished goods inventory budget.**

Larry Giano considered using variable costing to prepare Hampton Freeze's budget statements, but he decided to use absorption costing instead because the bank would very likely require absorption costing. He also knew that it would be easy to convert the absorption costing financial statements to a variable costing basis later. At this point, the primary concern was to determine what financing, if any, would be required in 2008 and then to arrange for that financing from the bank.

The unit product cost computations are shown in Schedule 6. For Hampton Freeze, the absorption costing unit product cost is $13 per case of popsicles—consisting of $3 of direct materials, $6 of direct labor, and $4 of manufacturing overhead. The manufacturing overhead is applied to units of product at the rate of $10 per direct labor-hour. The budgeted carrying cost of the ending inventory is $39,000.

> **LEARNING OBJECTIVE 7**
> Prepare a selling and administrative expense budget.

The Selling and Administrative Expense Budget

The **selling and administrative expense budget** lists the budgeted expenses for areas other than manufacturing. In large organizations, this budget would be a compilation of many smaller, individual budgets submitted by department heads and other persons responsible for

SCHEDULE 6

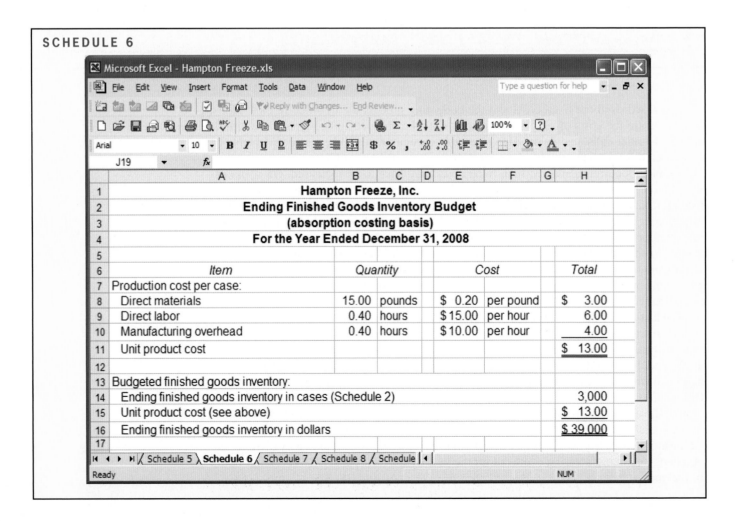

Item	Quantity		Cost		Total
Hampton Freeze, Inc.					
Ending Finished Goods Inventory Budget					
(absorption costing basis)					
For the Year Ended December 31, 2008					
Production cost per case:					
Direct materials	15.00	pounds	$ 0.20	per pound	$ 3.00
Direct labor	0.40	hours	$15.00	per hour	6.00
Manufacturing overhead	0.40	hours	$10.00	per hour	4.00
Unit product cost					$ 13.00
Budgeted finished goods inventory:					
Ending finished goods inventory in cases (Schedule 2)					3,000
Unit product cost (see above)					$ 13.00
Ending finished goods inventory in dollars					$ 39,000

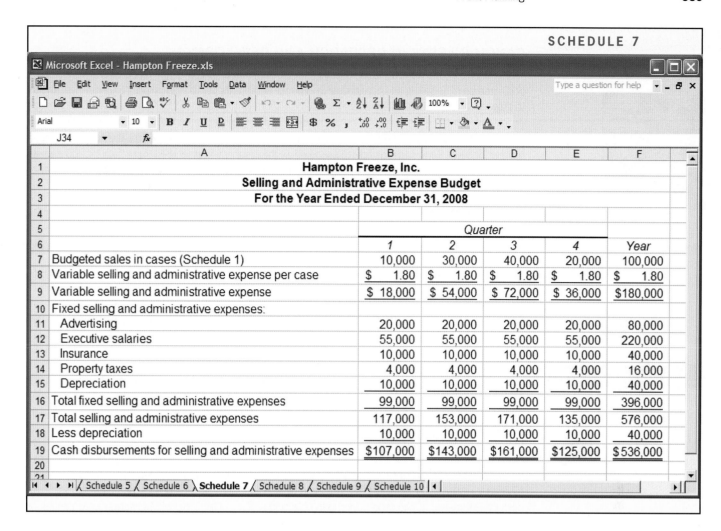

SCHEDULE 7

| | Quarter | | | | |
A	1	2	3	4	Year
Hampton Freeze, Inc.					
Selling and Administrative Expense Budget					
For the Year Ended December 31, 2008					
7 Budgeted sales in cases (Schedule 1)	10,000	30,000	40,000	20,000	100,000
8 Variable selling and administrative expense per case	$ 1.80	$ 1.80	$ 1.80	$ 1.80	$ 1.80
9 Variable selling and administrative expense	$ 18,000	$ 54,000	$ 72,000	$ 36,000	$180,000
10 Fixed selling and administrative expenses:					
11 Advertising	20,000	20,000	20,000	20,000	80,000
12 Executive salaries	55,000	55,000	55,000	55,000	220,000
13 Insurance	10,000	10,000	10,000	10,000	40,000
14 Property taxes	4,000	4,000	4,000	4,000	16,000
15 Depreciation	10,000	10,000	10,000	10,000	40,000
16 Total fixed selling and administrative expenses	99,000	99,000	99,000	99,000	396,000
17 Total selling and administrative expenses	117,000	153,000	171,000	135,000	576,000
18 Less depreciation	10,000	10,000	10,000	10,000	40,000
19 Cash disbursements for selling and administrative expenses	$107,000	$143,000	$161,000	$125,000	$536,000

selling and administrative expenses. For example, the marketing manager would submit a budget detailing the advertising expenses for each budget period.

Schedule 7 contains the selling and administrative expense budget for Hampton Freeze. Like the manufacturing overhead budget, the selling and administrative expense budget is divided into variable and fixed cost components. In the case of Hampton Freeze, the variable selling and administrative expense is $1.80 per case. Consequently, budgeted sales in cases for each quarter are entered at the top of the schedule. These data are taken from the sales budget (Schedule 1). The budgeted variable selling and administrative expenses are determined by multiplying the budgeted cases sold by the variable selling and administrative expense per case. For example, the budgeted variable selling and administrative expense for the first quarter is $18,000 (10,000 cases × $1.80 per case). The fixed selling and administrative expenses (all given data) are then added to the variable selling and administrative expenses to arrive at the total budgeted selling and administrative expenses. Finally, to determine the cash disbursements for selling and administrative items, the total budgeted selling and administrative expense is adjusted by subtracting any noncash selling and administrative expenses (in this case, just depreciation).[1]

---

[1] Other adjustments might need to be made for differences between cash flows on the one hand and revenues and expenses on the other hand. For example, if property taxes are paid twice a year in installments of $8,000 each, the expense for property tax would have to be "backed out" of the total budgeted selling and administrative expenses and the cash installment payments added to the appropriate quarters to determine the cash disbursements. Similar adjustments might also need to be made in the manufacturing overhead budget. We generally ignore these complications in this chapter.

CANON INVESTS IN RESEARCH AND DEVELOPMENT

When Canon Inc., the world's leading digital camera manufacturer, prepares the research and development (R&D) portion of its selling and administrative expense budget, the focus is on making long-run investments to grow sales rather than cutting costs to maximize short-run profits. In 2005, Canon spent 8% of its sales on R&D while many of its competitors spent 6% to 7.5% of their sales on R&D. Canon's CEO Fujio Mitarai described his company's R&D philosophy by saying "we have to plant the seeds for the next decade and beyond." Indeed, Canon's seeds have blossomed as the company has secured more than 17,000 patents since 1995—second only to IBM. Canon's commitment to R&D helps explain why its digital cameras are delivering healthy earnings at a time when many of its competitors are losing money.

Source: Ian Rowley, Hiroko Tashiro, and Louise Lee, "Canon: Combat-Ready," *BusinessWeek*, September 5, 2005, pp. 48–49.

The Cash Budget

As illustrated in Exhibit 9–2, the cash budget combines much of the data developed in the preceding steps. It is a good idea to review Exhibit 9–2 to get the big picture firmly in your mind before moving on.

CONCENTRATING ON THE CASH FLOW

Burlington Northern Santa Fe (BNSF) operates the second largest railroad in the United States. The company's senior vice president, CFO, and treasurer is Tom Hunt, who reports that "As a general theme, we've become very cash-flow-oriented." After the merger of the Burlington Northern and Santa Fe railroads, the company went through a number of years of heavy investments and negative cash flows. To keep on top of the company's cash position, Hunt has a cash forecast prepared every month. "Everything falls like dominoes from free cash flow," Hunt says. "It provides us with alternatives. Right now, the alternative of choice is buying back our own stock . . . [b]ut it could be increasing dividends or making acquisitions. All those things are not even on the radar screen if you don't have free cash flow."

Source: Randy Myers, "Cash Crop: The 2000 Working Capital Survey," *CFO*, August 2000, pp. 59–82.

The cash budget is composed of four major sections:

1. The receipts section.
2. The disbursements section
3. The cash excess or deficiency section.
4. The financing section.

The receipts section lists all of the cash inflows, except from financing, expected during the budget period. Generally, the major source of receipts are from sales.

The disbursements section summarizes all cash payments that are planned for the budget period. These payments include raw materials purchases, direct labor payments, manufacturing overhead costs, and so on, as contained in their respective budgets. In addition, other cash disbursements such as equipment purchases and dividends are listed.

The cash excess or deficiency section is computed as follows:

Topic Tackler

PLUS

9–2

Cash balance, beginning	XXXX
Add receipts	XXXX
Total cash available	XXXX
Less disbursements	XXXX
Excess (deficiency) of cash available over disbursements	XXXX

SCHEDULE 8

Microsoft Excel - Hampton Freeze.xls

File   Edit   View   Insert   Format   Tools   Data   Window   Help

Arial   10   B I U

L36

	A	B	C	D	E	F	G
1			Hampton Freeze, Inc.				
2			Cash Budget				
3			For the Year Ended December 31, 2008				
4							
5			Quarter				
6		Schedule	1	2	3	4	Year
7	Cash balance, beginning		$42,500	$36,000	$ 33,900	$165,650	$ 42,500
8	Add receipts:						
9	Collections from customers	1	230,000	480,000	740,000	520,000	1,970,000
10	Total cash available		272,500	516,000	773,900	685,650	2,012,500
11	Less disbursements:						
12	Direct materials	3	49,500	72,300	100,050	79,350	301,200
13	Direct labor	4	84,000	192,000	216,000	114,000	606,000
14	Manufacturing overhead	5	68,000	96,800	103,200	76,000	344,000
15	Selling and administrative	7	107,000	143,000	161,000	125,000	536,000
16	Equipment purchases		50,000	40,000	20,000	20,000	130,000
17	Dividends		8,000	8,000	8,000	8,000	32,000
18	Total disbursements		366,500	552,100	608,250	422,350	1,949,200
19	Excess (deficiency) of cash available over disbursements		(94,000)	(36,100)	165,650	263,300	63,300
20	Financing:						
21	Borrowings (at the beginnings of quarters)		130,000	70,000	-	-	200,000
22	Repayments (at end of the year)		-	-	-	(200,000)	(200,000)
23	Interest		-	-	-	(21,900)	(21,900)
24	Total financing		130,000	70,000	-	(221,900)	(21,900)
25	Cash balance, ending		$36,000	$33,900	$165,650	$ 41,400	$ 41,400
26							
27							

Schedule 5 / Schedule 6 / Schedule 7 \ Schedule 8 / Schedule 9 / Schedule 10

If a cash deficiency exists during any budget period, the company will need to borrow funds. If there is a cash excess during any budget period, funds borrowed in previous periods can be repaid or the excess funds can be invested.

The financing section details the borrowings and repayments projected to take place during the budget period. It also lists interest payments that will be due on money borrowed.[2]

The cash balances at both the beginning and end of the year may be adequate even though a serious cash deficit occurs at some point during the year. Consequently, the cash budget should be broken down into time periods that are short enough to capture major fluctuations in cash balances. While a monthly cash budget is most common, some organizations budget cash on a weekly or even daily basis. Larry Giano has prepared a quarterly cash budget for Hampton Freeze that can be further refined as necessary. This budget appears in Schedule 8. The cash budget builds on the earlier schedules and on additional data that are provided below:

- The beginning cash balance is $42,500.
- Management plans to spend $130,000 during the year on equipment purchases: $50,000 in the first quarter; $40,000 in the second quarter; $20,000 in the third quarter; and $20,000 in the fourth quarter.
- The board of directors has approved cash dividends of $8,000 per quarter.

---

[2] The format for the statement of cash flows, which is discussed in Chapter 15, may also be used for the cash budget.

- Management would like to have a cash balance of at least $30,000 at the beginning of each quarter for contingencies.
- Hampton Freeze has an agreement with a local bank that allows the company to borrow in increments of $10,000 at the beginning of each quarter, up to a total loan balance of $250,000. The interest rate on these loans is 1% per month and for simplicity we will assume that interest is not compounded. The company would, as far as it is able, repay the loan plus accumulated interest at the end of the year.

The cash budget is prepared one quarter at a time, starting with the first quarter. Larry began the cash budget by entering the beginning balance of cash for the first quarter of $42,500—a number that is given on the prior page. Receipts—in this case, just the $230,000 in cash collections from customers—are added to the beginning balance to arrive at the total cash available of $272,500. Since the total disbursements are $366,500 and the total cash available is only $272,500, there is a shortfall of $94,000. Since management would like to have a beginning cash balance of at least $30,000 for the second quarter, the company will need to borrow at least $124,000.

Required Borrowings at the Beginning of the First Quarter	
Desired ending cash balance.	$ 30,000
Plus deficiency of cash available over disbursements	94,000
Minimum required borrowings	$124,000

Recall that the bank requires that loans be made in increments of $10,000. Because Hampton Freeze needs to borrow at least $124,000, it will have to borrow $130,000.

The second quarter of the cash budget is handled similarly. Note that the ending cash balance for the first quarter is brought forward as the beginning cash balance for the second quarter. Also note that additional borrowing is required in the second quarter because of the continued cash shortfall.

Required Borrowings at the Beginning of the Second Quarter	
Desired ending cash balance.	$30,000
Plus deficiency of cash available over disbursements	36,100
Minimum required borrowings	$66,100

Again, recall that the bank requires that loans be made in increments of $10,000. Because Hampton Freeze needs to borrow at least $66,100 at the beginning of the second quarter, the company will have to borrow $70,000 from the bank.

In the third quarter, the cash flow situation improves dramatically and the excess of cash available over disbursements is $165,650. Therefore, the company will end the quarter with ample cash and no further borrowing is necessary.

At the end of the fourth quarter, the loan and accumulated interest must be repaid. The accumulated interest can be computed as follows:

Interest on $130,000 borrowed at the beginning of the first quarter:	
$130,000 × 0.01 per month × 12 months*.	$15,600
Interest on $70,000 borrowed at the beginning of the second quarter:	
$70,000 × 0.01 per month × 9 months*.	6,300
Total interest accrued to the end of the fourth quarter	$21,900

*Simple, rather than compounded, interest is assumed for simplicity.

Note that the loan repayment of $200,000 ($130,000 + $70,000) appears in the financing section for the fourth quarter along with the interest payment of $21,900 computed above.

As with the production and raw materials budgets, the amounts under the Year column in the cash budget are not always the sum of the amounts for the four quarters. In particular, the beginning cash balance for the year is the same as the beginning cash balance for the first quarter and the ending cash balance for the year is the same as the ending cash balance for the fourth quarter. Also note the beginning cash balance in any quarter is the same as the ending cash balance for the previous quarter.

IN BUSINESS

CASH CRISIS AT A START-UP COMPANY

Good Home Co., headquartered in New York City, sells home cleaning and laundry products through merchandisers such as Restoration Hardware and Nordstrom. In 2001, the company's sales were $2.1 million. Then in September 2002, the company's founder Christine Dimmick appeared on the cable shopping network QVC and in a few hours she sold more than $300,000 worth of merchandise. However, euphoria turned to panic when Christine realized that she needed $200,000 in short-term financing to fill those orders. When attempts to renegotiate payment terms with suppliers failed, Christine realized that she needed to hire a finance professional. Jerry Charlup, who was hired as Good Home's part-time CFO, spent $6,000 to create a cash flow forecasting system using Excel. As Good Home's annual sales have grown to $4 million, Charlup says the new forecasting system is giving the company "a far clearer fix on how much operating capital it needs at any given time."

Source: Susan Hansen, "The Rent-To-Own CFO Program," *Inc.* magazine, February 2004, pp. 28–29.

The Budgeted Income Statement

A budgeted income statement can be prepared from the data developed in Schedules 1–8. *The budgeted income statement is one of the key schedules in the budget process.* It shows the company's planned profit and serves as a benchmark against which subsequent company performance can be measured.

LEARNING OBJECTIVE 9
Prepare a budgeted income statement.

Schedule 9 contains the budgeted income statement for Hampton Freeze.

SCHEDULE 9

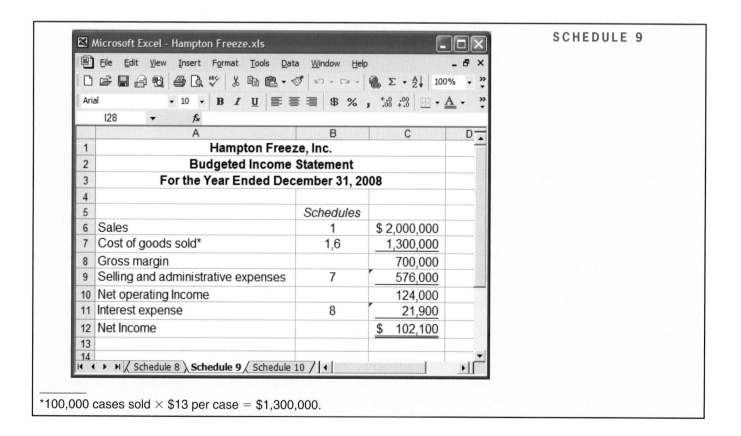

Hampton Freeze, Inc.
Budgeted Income Statement
For the Year Ended December 31, 2008

	Schedules	
Sales	1	$ 2,000,000
Cost of goods sold*	1,6	1,300,000
Gross margin		700,000
Selling and administrative expenses	7	576,000
Net operating Income		124,000
Interest expense	8	21,900
Net Income		$ 102,100

*100,000 cases sold × $13 per case = $1,300,000.

The Budgeted Balance Sheet

The budgeted balance sheet is developed using data from the balance sheet from the beginning of the budget period and data contained in the various schedules. Hampton Freeze's budgeted balance sheet is presented in Schedule 10. Some of the data on the budgeted balance sheet have been taken from the company's previous end-of-year balance sheet for 2007 which appears below:

Hampton Freeze, Inc.
Balance Sheet
December 31, 2007

Assets

Current assets:

Cash	$ 42,500	
Accounts receivable	90,000	
Raw materials inventory (21,000 pounds)	4,200	
Finished goods inventory (2,000 cases)	26,000	
Total current assets.		$162,700

Plant and equipment:

Land	80,000	
Buildings and equipment.	700,000	
Accumulated depreciation.	(292,000)	
Plant and equipment, net		488,000
Total assets.		$650,700

Liabilities and Stockholders' Equity

Current liabilities:

Accounts payable (raw materials)		$ 25,800

Stockholders' equity:

Common stock, no par	$175,000	
Retained earnings.	449,900	
Total stockholders' equity		624,900
Total liabilities and stockholders' equity.		$650,700

After completing the master budget, Larry Giano took the documents to Tom Wills, chief executive officer of Hampton Freeze, for his review.

Larry: Here's the budget. Overall, the net income is excellent, and the net cash flow for the entire year is positive.

Tom: Yes, but I see on this cash budget that we have the same problem with negative cash flows in the first and second quarters that we had last year.

Larry: That's true. I don't see any way around that problem. However, there is no doubt in my mind that if you take this budget to the bank today, they'll approve an open line of credit that will allow you to borrow enough to make it through the first two quarters without any problem.

Tom: Are you sure? They didn't seem very happy to see me last year when I came in for an emergency loan.

Larry: Did you repay the loan on time?

Tom: Sure.

Larry: I don't see any problem. You won't be asking for an emergency loan this time. The bank will have plenty of warning. And with this budget, you have a solid plan that shows when and how you are going to pay off the loan. Trust me, they'll go for it.

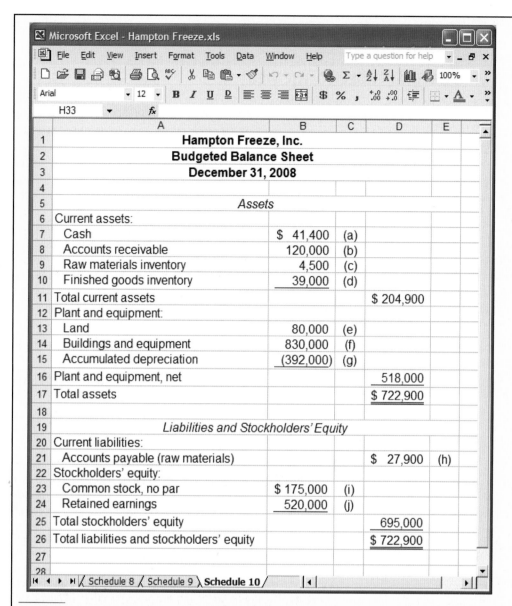

Hampton Freeze, Inc.
Budgeted Balance Sheet
December 31, 2008

A	B	C	D	E
Assets				
Current assets:				
Cash	$ 41,400	(a)		
Accounts receivable	120,000	(b)		
Raw materials inventory	4,500	(c)		
Finished goods inventory	39,000	(d)		
Total current assets			$ 204,900	
Plant and equipment:				
Land	80,000	(e)		
Buildings and equipment	830,000	(f)		
Accumulated depreciation	(392,000)	(g)		
Plant and equipment, net			518,000	
Total assets			$ 722,900	
Liabilities and Stockholders' Equity				
Current liabilities:				
Accounts payable (raw materials)			$ 27,900	(h)
Stockholders' equity:				
Common stock, no par	$ 175,000	(i)		
Retained earnings	520,000	(j)		
Total stockholders' equity			695,000	
Total liabilities and stockholders' equity			$ 722,900	

Schedule 8 / Schedule 9 / **Schedule 10**

Explanation of December 31, 2008, balance sheet figures:
(a) The ending cash balance, as projected by the cash budget in Schedule 8.
(b) Thirty percent of fourth-quarter sales, from Schedule 1 ($400,000 × 30% = $120,000).
(c) From Schedule 3, the ending raw materials inventory will be 22,500 pounds. This material costs $0.20 per pound. Therefore, the ending inventory in dollars will be 22,500 pounds × $0.20 per pound = $4,500.
(d) From Schedule 6.
(e) From the December 31, 2007, balance sheet (no change).
(f) The December 31, 2007, balance sheet indicated a balance of $700,000. During 2008, $130,000 of additional equipment will be purchased (see Schedule 8), bringing the December 31, 2008, balance to $830,000.
(g) The December 31, 2007, balance sheet indicated a balance of $292,000. During 2008, $100,000 of depreciation will be taken ($60,000 on Schedule 5 and $40,000 on Schedule 7), bringing the December 31, 2008, balance to $392,000.
(h) One-half of the fourth-quarter raw materials purchases, from Schedule 3.
(i) From the December 31, 2007, balance sheet (no change).
(j)

December 31, 2007, balance	$449,900
Add net income, from Schedule 9	102,100
	552,000
Deduct dividends paid, from Schedule 8	32,000
December 31, 2008, balance	$520,000

MOVING BEYOND EXCEL TO THE WEB

While research shows that two-thirds of U.S. companies still rely on Microsoft Excel for their budgeting process, some companies are evolving to a more technologically advanced approach. For example, Hendrick Motorsports has vaulted to the top of the NASCAR racing circuit thanks in part to its new budgeting process. Scott Lampe, Hendrick's CFO, discarded Excel in favor of Forecaster, a web-based budgeting program. He commented "with a spreadsheet, you can build the model the way you want it . . . The problem is, only you understand that model. Then you have to explain it to everyone, one at a time." The web-based approach enables Lampe to involve his crew chiefs, chassis guys, and engine guys in the budgeting process.

The Facilities & Operations (F&O) Business Office of the Battelle, Pacific Northwest National Laboratory has over 130 budget activities—each of which requires the preparation of an annual budget. In 2001, F&O replaced its spreadsheet-driven budget with a web-based approach. The new system enables F&O "management and their support staff to directly input their business plan and budget requests, eliminating the need for central business planning and budgeting staff to upload the numerous budget requests and subsequent changes." The web-based budgeting system saves F&O personnel more than 500 hours that were previously spent preparing Excel spreadsheets and uploading data.

Source: John Goff, "In The Fast Lane," *CFO*, December 2004, pp. 53–58; Peter T. Smith, Craig A. Goranson, and Mary F. Astley, "Intranet Budgeting Does the Trick," *Strategic Finance*, May 2003, pp. 30–33.

Summary

This chapter describes the budgeting process and shows how the various operating budgets relate to each other. The sales budget is the foundation for profit planning. Once the sales budget has been set, the production budget and the selling and administrative expense budget can be prepared since they depend on how many units are to be sold. The production budget determines how many units are to be produced, so after it is prepared, the various manufacturing cost budgets can be prepared. All of these budgets feed into the cash budget and the budgeted income statement and balance sheet. The parts of the master budget are connected in many ways. For example, the schedule of expected cash collections, which is completed in connection with the sales budget, provides data for both the cash budget and the budgeted balance sheet.

The material in this chapter is just an introduction to budgeting and profit planning. In later chapters, we will see how budgets are used to control day-to-day operations and how they are used in performance evaluation.

Review Problem: Budget Schedules

Mynor Corporation manufactures and sells a seasonal product that has peak sales in the third quarter. The following information concerns operations for Year 2—the coming year—and for the first two quarters of Year 3:

a. The company's single product sells for $8 per unit. Budgeted sales in units for the next six quarters are as follows (all sales are on credit):

	Year 2 Quarter				Year 3 Quarter	
	1	2	3	4	1	2
Budgeted unit sales	40,000	60,000	100,000	50,000	70,000	80,000

b. Sales are collected in the following pattern: 75% in the quarter the sales are made, and the remaining 25% in the following quarter. On January 1, Year 2, the company's balance sheet showed $65,000 in accounts receivable, all of which will be collected in the first quarter of the year. Bad debts are negligible and can be ignored.

c. The company desires an ending finished goods inventory at the end of each quarter equal to 30% of the budgeted unit sales for the next quarter. On December 31, Year 1, the company had 12,000 units on hand.

d. Five pounds of raw materials are required to complete one unit of product. The company requires ending raw materials inventory at the end of each quarter equal to 10% of the following quarter's production needs. On December 31, Year 1, the company had 23,000 pounds of raw materials on hand.

e. The raw material costs $0.80 per pound. Raw material purchases are paid for in the following pattern: 60% paid in the quarter the purchases are made, and the remaining 40% paid in the following quarter. On January 1, Year 2, the company's balance sheet showed $81,500 in accounts payable for raw material purchases, all of which will be paid for in the first quarter of the year.

Required:

Prepare the following budgets and schedules for the year, showing both quarterly and total figures:

1. A sales budget and a schedule of expected cash collections.
2. A production budget.
3. A direct materials budget and a schedule of expected cash payments for purchases of materials.

Solution to Review Problem

1. The sales budget is prepared as follows:

	Year 2 Quarter				
	1	2	3	4	Year
Budgeted unit sales........	40,000	60,000	100,000	50,000	250,000
Selling price per unit	× $8	× $8	× $8	× $8	× $8
Total sales	$320,000	$480,000	$800,000	$400,000	$2,000,000

Based on the budgeted sales above, the schedule of expected cash collections is prepared as follows:

	Year 2 Quarter				
	1	2	3	4	Year
Accounts receivable, beginning balance	$ 65,000				$ 65,000
First-quarter sales ($320,000 × 75%, 25%)	240,000	$ 80,000			320,000
Second-quarter sales ($480,000 × 75%, 25%)........		360,000	$120,000		480,000
Third-quarter sales ($800,000 × 75%, 25%)..........			600,000	$200,000	800,000
Fourth-quarter sales ($400,000 × 75%)				300,000	300,000
Total cash collections.....................	$305,000	$440,000	$720,000	$500,000	$1,965,000

2. Based on the sales budget in units, the production budget is prepared as follows:

	Year 2 Quarter					Year 3 Quarter	
	1	2	3	4	Year	1	2
Budgeted unit sales	40,000	60,000	100,000	50,000	250,000	70,000	80,000
Add desired ending finished goods inventory*........	18,000	30,000	15,000	21,000†	21,000	24,000	
Total needs..................................	58,000	90,000	115,000	71,000	271,000	94,000	
Less beginning finished goods inventory	12,000	18,000	30,000	15,000	12,000	21,000	
Required production..........................	46,000	72,000	85,000	56,000	259,000	73,000	

*30% of the following quarter's budgeted sales in units.
†30% of the budgeted Year 3 first-quarter sales.

3. Based on the production budget, raw materials will need to be purchased during the year as follows:

	Year 2 Quarter					Year 3 Quarter
	1	2	3	4	Year 2	1
Required production (units)............................	46,000	72,000	85,000	56,000	259,000	73,000
Raw materials needed per unit (pounds)...................	× 5	× 5	× 5	× 5	× 5	× 5
Production needs (pounds)............................	230,000	360,000	425,000	280,000	1,295,000	365,000
Add desired ending inventory of raw materials (pounds)*........	36,000	42,500	28,000	36,500†	36,500	
Total needs (pounds)	266,000	402,500	453,000	316,500	1,331,500	
Less beginning inventory of raw materials (pounds)	23,000	36,000	42,500	28,000	23,000	
Raw materials to be purchased (pounds)	243,000	366,500	410,500	288,500	1,308,500	

*10% of the following quarter's production needs in pounds.
†10% of the Year 3 first-quarter production needs in pounds.

Based on the raw material purchases above, expected cash payments are computed as follows:

	Year 2 Quarter				Year 2
	1	2	3	4	
Cost of raw materials to be purchased at $0.80 per pound........	$194,400	$293,200	$328,400	$230,800	$1,046,800
Accounts payable, beginning balance	$ 81,500				$ 81,500
First-quarter purchases ($194,400 × 60%, 40%)	116,640	$ 77,760			194,400
Second-quarter purchases ($293,200 × 60%, 40%)		175,920	$117,280		293,200
Third-quarter purchases ($328,400 × 60%, 40%)			197,040	$131,360	328,400
Fourth-quarter purchases ($230,800 × 60%)				138,480	138,480
Total cash disbursements	$198,140	$253,680	$314,320	$269,840	$1,035,980

Glossary

Budget A quantitative plan for acquiring and using resources over a specified time period. (p. 372)

Budget committee A group of key managers who are responsible for overall budgeting policy and for coordinating the preparation of the budget. (p. 377)

Cash budget A detailed plan showing how cash resources will be acquired and used over a specific time period. (p. 378)

Continuous budget A 12-month budget that rolls forward one month as the current month is completed. (p. 373)

Control Those steps taken by management to increase the likelihood that all parts of the organization are working together to achieve the goals set down at the planning stage. (p. 372)

Direct labor budget A detailed plan that shows the direct labor-hours required to fulfill the production budget. (p. 385)

Direct materials budget A detailed plan showing the amount of raw materials that must be purchased to fulfill the production budget and to provide for adequate inventories. (p. 383)

Ending finished goods inventory budget A budget showing the dollar amount of unsold finished goods inventory that will appear on the ending balance sheet. (p. 388)

Manufacturing overhead budget A detailed plan showing the production costs, other than direct materials and direct labor, that will be incurred over a specified time period. (p. 386)

Master budget A summary of a company's plans that sets specific targets for sales, production, and financing activities and that generally culminates in a cash budget, budgeted income statement, and budgeted balance sheet. (p. 372)

Merchandise purchases budget A detailed plan used by a merchandising company that shows the amount of goods that must be purchased from suppliers during the period. (p. 383)

Participative budget See *Self-imposed budget*. (p. 374)

Perpetual budget See *Continuous budget*. (p. 373)

Planning Developing goals and preparing budgets to achieve those goals. (p. 372)

Production budget A detailed plan showing the number of units that must be produced during a period in order to satisfy both sales and inventory needs. (p. 381)

Responsibility accounting A system of accountability in which managers are held responsible for those items of revenue and cost—and only those items—over which they can exert significant control. The managers are held responsible for differences between budgeted and actual results. (p. 372)

Sales budget A detailed schedule showing expected sales expressed in both dollars and units. (p. 377)

Self-imposed budget A method of preparing budgets in which managers prepare their own budgets. These budgets are then reviewed by higher-level managers, and any issues are resolved by mutual agreement. (p. 374)

Selling and administrative expense budget A detailed schedule of planned expenses that will be incurred in areas other than manufacturing during a budget period. (p. 388)

Questions

9-1 What is a budget? What is budgetary control?

9-2 Discuss some of the major benefits to be gained from budgeting.

9-3 What is meant by the term *responsibility accounting?*

9-4 What is a master budget? Briefly describe its contents.

9-5 Why is the sales forecast the starting point in budgeting?

9-6 "As a practical matter, planning and control mean exactly the same thing." Do you agree? Explain.

9-7 Describe the flow of budget data in an organization. Who are the participants in the budgeting process, and how do they participate?

9-8 What is a self-imposed budget? What are the major advantages of self-imposed budgets? What caution must be exercised in their use?

9-9 How can budgeting assist a company in planning its workforce staffing levels?

9-10 "The principal purpose of the cash budget is to see how much cash the company will have in the bank at the end of the year." Do you agree? Explain.

Exercises

EXERCISE 9-1 Schedule of Expected Cash Collections [LO2]

Silver Company makes a product that is very popular as a Mother's Day gift. Thus, peak sales occur in May of each year. These peak sales are shown in the company's sales budget for the second quarter given below (all sales are on account):

	April	May	June	Total
Budgeted sales...	$300,000	$500,000	$200,000	$1,000,000

From past experience, the company has learned that 20% of a month's sales are collected in the month of sale, another 70% are collected in the month following sale, and the remaining 10% are collected in the second month following sale. Bad debts are negligible and can be ignored. February sales totaled $230,000, and March sales totaled $260,000.

Required:

1. Prepare a schedule of expected cash collections from sales, by month and in total, for the second quarter.

2. Assume that the company will prepare a budgeted balance sheet as of June 30. Compute the accounts receivable as of that date.

EXERCISE 9-2 Production Budget [LO3]

Down Under Products, Ltd., of Australia has budgeted sales of its popular boomerang for the next four months as follows:

	Sales in Units
April	50,000
May	75,000
June.	90,000
July.	80,000

The company is now in the process of preparing a production budget for the second quarter. Past experience has shown that end-of-month inventory levels must equal 10% of the following month's sales. The inventory at the end of March was 5,000 units.

Required:

Prepare a production budget for the second quarter; in your budget, show the number of units to be produced each month and for the quarter in total.

EXERCISE 9-3 Direct Materials Budget [LO4]

Three grams of musk oil are required for each bottle of Mink Caress, a very popular perfume made by a small company in western Siberia. The cost of the musk oil is 150 roubles per kilogram. (Siberia is located in Russia, whose currency is the rouble.) Budgeted production of Mink Caress is given below by quarters for Year 2 and for the first quarter of Year 3.

	Year 2 Quarter				Year 3 Quarter
	First	Second	Third	Fourth	First
Budgeted production, in bottles.	60,000	90,000	150,000	100,000	70,000

Musk oil has become so popular as a perfume ingredient that it has become necessary to carry large inventories as a precaution against stock-outs. For this reason, the inventory of musk oil at the end of a quarter must be equal to 20% of the following quarter's production needs. Some 36,000 grams of musk oil will be on hand to start the first quarter of Year 2.

Required:

Prepare a direct materials budget for musk oil, by quarter and in total, for Year 2. At the bottom of your budget, show the amount of purchases in roubles for each quarter and for the year in total.

EXERCISE 9-4 Direct Labor Budget [LO5]

The production department of Rordan Corporation has submitted the following forecast of units to be produced by quarter for the upcoming fiscal year.

	1st Quarter	2nd Quarter	3rd Quarter	4th Quarter
Units to be produced.	8,000	6,500	7,000	7,500

Each unit requires 0.35 direct labor-hours, and direct laborers are paid $12.00 per hour.

Required:

1. Construct the company's direct labor budget for the upcoming fiscal year, assuming that the direct labor work force is adjusted each quarter to match the number of hours required to produce the forecasted number of units produced.
2. Construct the company's direct labor budget for the upcoming fiscal year, assuming that the direct labor work force is not adjusted each quarter. Instead, assume that the company's direct labor work force consists of permanent employees who are guaranteed to be paid for at least 2,600 hours of work each quarter. If the number of required direct labor-hours is less than this number, the workers are paid for 2,600 hours anyway. Any hours worked in excess of 2,600 hours in a quarter are paid at the rate of 1.5 times the normal hourly rate for direct labor.

EXERCISE 9-5 Manufacturing Overhead Budget [LO6]

The direct labor budget of Yuvwell Corporation for the upcoming fiscal year contains the following details concerning budgeted direct labor-hours.

	1st Quarter	2nd Quarter	3rd Quarter	4th Quarter
Budgeted direct labor-hours	8,000	8,200	8,500	7,800

The company's variable manufacturing overhead rate is $3.25 per direct labor-hour and the company's fixed manufacturing overhead is $48,000 per quarter. The only noncash item included in the fixed manufacturing overhead is depreciation, which is $16,000 per quarter.

Required:
1. Construct the company's manufacturing overhead budget for the upcoming fiscal year.
2. Compute the company's manufacturing overhead rate (including both variable and fixed manufacturing overhead) for the upcoming fiscal year. Round off to the nearest whole cent.

EXERCISE 9-6 Selling and Administrative Expense Budget [LO7]

The budgeted unit sales of Weller Company for the upcoming fiscal year are provided below:

	1st Quarter	2nd Quarter	3rd Quarter	4th Quarter
Budgeted unit sales........	15,000	16,000	14,000	13,000

The company's variable selling and administrative expense per unit is $2.50. Fixed selling and administrative expenses include advertising expenses of $8,000 per quarter, executive salaries of $35,000 per quarter, and depreciation of $20,000 per quarter. In addition, the company will make insurance payments of $5,000 in the first quarter and $5,000 in the third quarter. Finally, property taxes of $8,000 will be paid in the second quarter.

Required:
Prepare the company's selling and administrative expense budget for the upcoming fiscal year.

EXERCISE 9-7 Cash Budget Analysis [LO8]

A cash budget, by quarters, is given below for a retail company. (000 omitted). The company requires a minimum cash balance of at least $5,000 to start each quarter.

	Quarter				
	1	2	3	4	Year
Cash balance, beginning	$ 6	$?	$?	$?	$?
Add collections from customers...........	?	?	96	?	323
Total cash available	71	?	?	?	?
Less disbursements:					
Purchases of inventory.................	35	45	?	35	?
Operating expenses....................	?	30	30	?	113
Equipment purchases..................	8	8	10	?	36
Dividends...........................	2	2	2	2	?
Total disbursements.....................	?	85	?	?	?
Excess (deficiency) of cash available over disbursements	(2)	?	11	?	?
Financing:					
Borrowings.........................	?	15	—	—	?
Repayments (including interest)*.........	—	—	(?)	(17)	(?)
Total financing	?	?	?	?	?
Cash balance, ending	$?	$?	$?	$?	$?

*Interest will total $1,000 for the year.

Required:
Fill in the missing amounts in the above table.

Problems

PROBLEM 9-8 Evaluating a Company's Budget Procedures [LO1]

Springfield Corporation operates on a calendar-year basis. It begins the annual budgeting process in late August, when the president establishes targets for total sales dollars and net operating income before taxes for the next year.

The sales target is given to the Marketing Department, where the marketing manager formulates a sales budget by product line in both units and dollars. From this budget, sales quotas by product line in units and dollars are established for each of the corporation's sales districts.

The marketing manager also estimates the cost of the marketing activities required to support the target sales volume and prepares a tentative marketing expense budget.

The executive vice president uses the sales and profit targets, the sales budget by product line, and the tentative marketing expense budget to determine the dollar amounts that can be devoted to manufacturing and corporate office expense. The executive vice president prepares the budget for corporate expenses, and then forwards to the Production Department the product-line sales budget in units and the total dollar amount that can be devoted to manufacturing.

The production manager meets with the factory managers to develop a manufacturing plan that will produce the required units when needed within the cost constraints set by the executive vice president. The budgeting process usually comes to a halt at this point because the Production Department does not consider the financial resources allocated to it to be adequate.

When this standstill occurs, the vice president of finance, the executive vice president, the marketing manager, and the production manager meet to determine the final budgets for each of the areas. This normally results in a modest increase in the total amount available for manufacturing costs, while the marketing expense and corporate office expense budgets are cut. The total sales and net operating income figures proposed by the president are seldom changed. Although the participants are seldom pleased with the compromise, these budgets are final. Each executive then develops a new detailed budget for the operations in his or her area.

None of the areas has achieved its budget in recent years. Sales often run below the target. When budgeted sales are not achieved, each area is expected to cut costs so that the president's profit target can still be met. However, the profit target is seldom met because costs are not cut enough. In fact, costs often run above the original budget in all functional areas. The president is disturbed that Springfield has not been able to meet the sales and profit targets. He hired a consultant with considerable relevant industry experience. The consultant reviewed the budgets for the past four years. He concluded that the product-line sales budgets were reasonable and that the cost and expense budgets were adequate for the budgeted sales and production levels.

Required:

1. Discuss how the budgeting process as employed by Springfield Corporation contributes to the failure to achieve the president's sales and profit targets.
2. Suggest how Springfield Corporation's budgeting process could be revised to correct the problem.
3. Should the functional areas be expected to cut their costs when sales volume falls below budget? Explain your answer.

(CMA, adapted)

PROBLEM 9-9 Schedules of Expected Cash Collections and Disbursements [LO2, LO4, LO8]

You have been asked to prepare a December cash budget for Ashton Company, a distributor of exercise equipment. The following information is available about the company's operations:

a. The cash balance on December 1 is $40,000.

b. Actual sales for October and November and expected sales for December are as follows:

	October	November	December
Cash sales...........	$65,000	$70,000	$83,000
Sales on account........	$400,000	$525,000	$600,000

Sales on account are collected over a three-month period as follows: 20% collected in the month of sale, 60% collected in the month following sale, and 18% collected in the second month following sale. The remaining 2% is uncollectible.

c. Purchases of inventory will total $280,000 for December. Thirty percent of a month's inventory purchases are paid during the month of purchase. The accounts payable remaining from November's inventory purchases total $161,000, all of which will be paid in December.

d.   Selling and administrative expenses are budgeted at $430,000 for December. Of this amount, $50,000 is for depreciation.
e.   A new web server for the Marketing Department costing $76,000 will be purchased for cash during December, and dividends totaling $9,000 will be paid during the month.
f.   The company maintains a minimum cash balance of $20,000. An open line of credit is available from the company's bank to bolster the cash position as needed.

Required:
1.   Prepare a schedule of expected cash collections for December.
2.   Prepare a schedule of expected cash disbursements for merchandise purchases for December.
3.   Prepare a cash budget for December. Indicate in the financing section any borrowing that will be needed during the month.

PROBLEM 9-10 Behavioral Aspects of Budgeting; Ethics and the Manager [LO1]

Norton Company, a manufacturer of infant furniture and carriages, is in the initial stages of preparing the annual budget for next year. Scott Ford has recently joined Norton's accounting staff and is interested to learn as much as possible about the company's budgeting process. During a recent lunch with Marge Atkins, sales manager, and Pete Granger, production manager, Ford initiated the following conversation.

Ford: Since I'm new around here and am going to be involved with the preparation of the annual budget, I'd be interested to learn how the two of you estimate sales and production numbers.
Atkins: We start out very methodically by looking at recent history, discussing what we know about current accounts, potential customers, and the general state of consumer spending. Then, we add that usual dose of intuition to come up with the best forecast we can.
Granger: I usually take the sales projections as the basis for my projections. Of course, we have to make an estimate of what this year's ending inventories will be, which is sometimes difficult.
Ford: Why does that present a problem? There must have been an estimate of ending inventories in the budget for the current year.
Granger: Those numbers aren't always reliable since Marge makes some adjustments to the sales numbers before passing them on to me.
Ford: What kind of adjustments?
Atkins: Well, we don't want to fall short of the sales projections so we generally give ourselves a little breathing room by lowering the initial sales projection anywhere from 5% to 10%.
Granger: So, you can see why this year's budget is not a very reliable starting point. We always have to adjust the projected production rates as the year progresses and, of course, this changes the ending inventory estimates. By the way, we make similar adjustments to expenses by adding at least 10% to the estimates; I think everyone around here does the same thing.

Required:
1.   Marge Atkins and Pete Granger have described the use of what is sometimes called *budgetary slack*.
     a.   Explain why Atkins and Granger behave in this manner and describe the benefits they expect to realize from the use of budgetary slack.
     b.   Explain how the use of budgetary slack can adversely affect Atkins and Granger.
2.   As a management accountant, Scott Ford believes that the behavior described by Marge Atkins and Pete Granger may be unethical. By referring to the IMA's Statement of Ethical Professional Practice in Chapter 1, explain why the use of budgetary slack may be unethical.

(CMA, adapted)

PROBLEM 9-11 Production and Direct Materials Budgets [LO3, LO4]

Pearl Products Limited of Shenzhen, China, manufactures and distributes toys throughout South East Asia. Three cubic centimeters (cc) of solvent H300 are required to manufacture each unit of Supermix, one of the company's products. The company is now planning raw materials needs for the third quarter, the quarter in which peak sales of Supermix occur. To keep production and sales moving smoothly, the company has the following inventory requirements:
a.   The finished goods inventory on hand at the end of each month must be equal to 3,000 units of Supermix plus 20% of the next month's sales. The finished goods inventory on June 30 is budgeted to be 10,000 units.
b.   The raw materials inventory on hand at the end of each month must be equal to one-half of the following month's production needs for raw materials. The raw materials inventory on June 30 is budgeted to be 54,000 cc of solvent H300.

c.   The company maintains no work in process inventories.
   A sales budget for Supermix for the last six months of the year follows.

	Budgeted Sales in Units
July.	35,000
August	40,000
September.	50,000
October	30,000
November.	20,000
December	10,000

Required:
1.   Prepare a production budget for Supermix for the months July, August, September, and October.
2.   Examine the production budget that you prepared. Why will the company produce more units than it sells in July and August, and less than it sells in September and October?
3.   Prepare a direct materials budget showing the quantity of solvent H300 to be purchased for July, August, and September and for the quarter in total.

PROBLEM 9-12 Direct Materials and Direct Labor Budgets [LO4, LO5]
The production department of Zan Corporation has submitted the following forecast of units to be produced by quarter for the upcoming fiscal year.

	1st Quarter	2nd Quarter	3rd Quarter	4th Quarter
Units to be produced.	5,000	8,000	7,000	6,000

In addition, the beginning raw materials inventory for the 1st Quarter is budgeted to be 6,000 grams and the beginning accounts payable for the 1st Quarter is budgeted to be $2,880.
   Each unit requires 8 grams of raw material that costs $1.20 per gram. Management desires to end each quarter with an inventory of raw materials equal to 25% of the following quarter's production needs. The desired ending inventory for the 4th Quarter is 8,000 grams. Management plans to pay for 60% of raw material purchases in the quarter acquired and 40% in the following quarter. Each unit requires 0.20 direct labor-hour and direct laborers are paid $11.50 per hour.

Required:
1.   Prepare the company's direct materials budget and schedule of expected cash disbursements for materials for the upcoming fiscal year.
2.   Prepare the company's direct labor budget for the upcoming fiscal year, assuming that the direct labor workforce is adjusted each quarter to match the number of hours required to produce the forecasted number of units produced.

PROBLEM 9-13 Direct Labor and Manufacturing Overhead Budgets [LO5, LO6]
The Production Department of Hruska Corporation has submitted the following forecast of units to be produced by quarter for the upcoming fiscal year.

	1st Quarter	2nd Quarter	3rd Quarter	4th Quarter
Units to be produced.	12,000	10,000	13,000	14,000

Each unit requires 0.2 direct labor-hour and direct laborers are paid $12.00 per hour.
   In addition, the variable manufacturing overhead rate is $1.75 per direct labor-hour. The fixed manufacturing overhead is $86,000 per quarter. The only noncash element of manufacturing overhead is depreciation, which is $23,000 per quarter.

Required:
1.   Prepare the company's direct labor budget for the upcoming fiscal year, assuming that the direct labor work force is adjusted each quarter to match the number of hours required to produce the forecasted number of units produced.
2.   Prepare the company's manufacturing overhead budget.

PROBLEM 9-14 Schedule of Expected Cash Collections; Cash Budget [LO2, LO8]

Herbal Care Corp., a distributor of herb-based sunscreens, is ready to begin its third quarter, in which peak sales occur. The company has requested a $40,000, 90-day loan from its bank to help meet cash requirements during the quarter. Since Herbal Care has experienced difficulty in paying off its loans in the past, the loan officer at the bank has asked the company to prepare a cash budget for the quarter. In response to this request, the following data have been assembled:

a. On July 1, the beginning of the third quarter, the company will have a cash balance of $44,500.

b. Actual sales for the last two months and budgeted sales for the third quarter follow (all sales are on account):

May (actual)................	$250,000
June (actual)	$300,000
July (budgeted)	$400,000
August (budgeted)...........	$600,000
September (budgeted)........	$320,000

Past experience shows that 25% of a month's sales are collected in the month of sale, 70% in the month following sale, and 3% in the second month following sale. The remainder is uncollectible.

c. Budgeted merchandise purchases and budgeted expenses for the third quarter are given below:

	July	August	September
Merchandise purchases........	$240,000	$350,000	$175,000
Salaries and wages	$45,000	$50,000	$40,000
Advertising...................	$130,000	$145,000	$80,000
Rent payments...............	$9,000	$9,000	$9,000
Depreciation.................	$10,000	$10,000	$10,000

Merchandise purchases are paid in full during the month following purchase. Accounts payable for merchandise purchases on June 30, which will be paid during July, total $180,000.

d. Equipment costing $10,000 will be purchased for cash during July.

e. In preparing the cash budget, assume that the $40,000 loan will be made in July and repaid in September. Interest on the loan will total $1,200.

Required:

1. Prepare a schedule of expected cash collections for July, August, and September and for the quarter in total.

2. Prepare a cash budget, by month and in total, for the third quarter.

3. If the company needs a minimum cash balance of $20,000 to start each month, can the loan be repaid as planned? Explain.

PROBLEM 9-15 Cash Budget; Income Statement; Balance Sheet [LO2, LO4, LO8, LO9, LO10]

Minden Company is a wholesale distributor of premium European chocolates. The company's balance sheet as of April 30 is given below:

Minden Company Balance Sheet April 30	
Assets	
Cash	$ 9,000
Accounts receivable	54,000
Inventory	30,000
Buildings and equipment, net of depreciation........	207,000
Total assets	$300,000
Liabilities and Stockholders' Equity	
Accounts payable	$ 63,000
Note payable	14,500
Capital stock, no par	180,000
Retained earnings............................	42,500
Total liabilities and stockholders' equity.............	$300,000

The company is in the process of preparing budget data for May. A number of budget items have already been prepared, as stated below:

a.   Sales are budgeted at $200,000 for May. Of these sales, $60,000 will be for cash; the remainder will be credit sales. One-half of a month's credit sales are collected in the month the sales are made, and the remainder is collected in the following month. All of the April 30 accounts receivable will be collected in May.

b.   Purchases of inventory are expected to total $120,000 during May. These purchases will all be on account. Forty percent of all purchases are paid for in the month of purchase; the remainder are paid in the following month. All of the April 30 accounts payable to suppliers will be paid during May.

c.   The May 31 inventory balance is budgeted at $40,000.

d.   Operating expenses for May are budgeted at $72,000, exclusive of depreciation. These expenses will be paid in cash. Depreciation is budgeted at $2,000 for the month.

e.   The note payable on the April 30 balance sheet will be paid during May, with $100 in interest. (All of the interest relates to May.)

f.   New refrigerating equipment costing $6,500 will be purchased for cash during May.

g.   During May, the company will borrow $20,000 from its bank by giving a new note payable to the bank for that amount. The new note will be due in one year.

Required:

1.   Prepare a cash budget for May. Support your budget with a schedule of expected cash collections from sales and a schedule of expected cash disbursements for merchandise purchases.

2.   Prepare a budgeted income statement for May. Use the absorption costing income statement format as shown in Schedule 9.

3.   Prepare a budgeted balance sheet as of May 31.

PROBLEM 9-16 Integration of Sales, Production, and Direct Materials Budgets [LO2, LO3, LO4]
Milo Company manufactures beach umbrellas. The company is preparing detailed budgets for the third quarter and has assembled the following information to assist in the budget preparation:

a.   The Marketing Department has estimated sales as follows for the remainder of the year (in units):

July.	30,000	October.	20,000
August	70,000	November.	10,000
September.	50,000	December.	10,000

The selling price of the beach umbrellas is $12 per unit.

b.   All sales are on account. Based on past experience, sales are collected in the following pattern:

> 30% in the month of sale
> 65% in the month following sale
> 5% uncollectible

Sales for June totaled $300,000.

c.   The company maintains finished goods inventories equal to 15% of the following month's sales. This requirement will be met at the end of June.

d.   Each beach umbrella requires 4 feet of Gilden, a material that is sometimes hard to acquire. Therefore, the company requires that the ending inventory of Gilden be equal to 50% of the following month's production needs. The inventory of Gilden on hand at the beginning and end of the quarter will be:

June 30	72,000 feet
September 30.	? feet

e.   Gilden costs $0.80 per foot. One-half of a month's purchases of Gilden is paid for in the month of purchase; the remainder is paid for in the following month. The accounts payable on July 1 for purchases of Gilden during June will be $76,000.

Required:

1.   Prepare a sales budget, by month and in total, for the third quarter. (Show your budget in both units and dollars.) Also prepare a schedule of expected cash collections, by month and in total, for the third quarter.

2. Prepare a production budget for each of the months July through October.
3. Prepare a direct materials budget for Gilden, by month and in total, for the third quarter. Also prepare a schedule of expected cash disbursements for Gilden, by month and in total, for the third quarter.

PROBLEM 9-17 Completing a Master Budget [LO2, LO4, LO7, LO8, LO9, LO10]

Hillyard Company, an office supplies specialty store, prepares its master budget on a quarterly basis. The following data have been assembled to assist in preparing the master budget for the first quarter:

a. As of December 31 (the end of the prior quarter), the company's balance sheet showed the following account balances:

Cash.	$ 48,000	
Accounts receivable	224,000	
Inventory	60,000	
Buildings and equipment (net).	370,000	
Accounts payable.		$ 93,000
Capital stock.		500,000
Retained earnings		109,000
	$702,000	$702,000

b. Actual sales for December and budgeted sales for the next four months are as follows:

December (actual)	$280,000
January	$400,000
February	$600,000
March.	$300,000
April	$200,000

c. Sales are 20% for cash and 80% on credit. All payments on credit sales are collected in the month following sale. The accounts receivable at December 31 are a result of December credit sales.
d. The company's gross margin is 40% of sales. (In other words, cost of goods sold is 60% of sales.)
e. Monthly expenses are budgeted as follows: salaries and wages, $27,000 per month: advertising, $70,000 per month; shipping, 5% of sales; other expenses, 3% of sales. Depreciation, including depreciation on new assets acquired during the quarter, will be $42,000 for the quarter.
f. Each month's ending inventory should equal 25% of the following month's cost of goods sold.
g. One-half of a month's inventory purchases is paid for in the month of purchase; the other half is paid in the following month.
h. During February, the company will purchase a new copy machine for $1,700 cash. During March, other equipment will be purchased for cash at a cost of $84,500.
i. During January, the company will declare and pay $45,000 in cash dividends.
j. The company must maintain a minimum cash balance of $30,000. An open line of credit is available at a local bank for any borrowing that may be needed during the quarter. All borrowing is done at the beginning of a month, and all repayments are made at the end of a month. Borrowings and repayments of principal must be in multiples of $1,000. Interest is paid only at the time of payment of principal. The annual interest rate is 12%. (Figure interest on whole months, e.g., $\frac{1}{12}$, $\frac{2}{12}$.)

Required:
Using the data above, complete the following statements and schedules for the first quarter:
1. Schedule of expected cash collections:

	January	February	March	Quarter
Cash sales.	$ 80,000			
Credit sales	224,000			
Total collections	$304,000			

2. *a.* Merchandise purchases budget:

	January	February	March	Quarter
Budgeted cost of goods sold	$240,000*	$360,000		
Add desired ending inventory.	90,000†			
Total needs.	330,000			
Less beginning inventory	60,000			
Required purchases.	$270,000			

*$400,000 sales × 60% cost ratio = $240,000.
†$360,000 × 25% = $90,000.

b. Schedule of expected cash disbursements for merchandise purchases:

	January	February	March	Quarter
For December purchases.	$ 93,000			$ 93,000
For January purchases.	135,000	135,000		270,000
For February purchases.				
For March purchases				
Total cash disbursements for purchases	$228,000			

3. Schedule of expected cash disbursements for operating expenses:

	January	February	March	Quarter
Salaries and wages	$ 27,000			
Advertising.	70,000			
Shipping.	20,000			
Other expenses	12,000			
Total cash disbursements for operating expenses	$129,000			

4. Cash budget:

	January	February	March	Quarter
Cash balance, beginning	$ 48,000			
Add cash collections	304,000			
Total cash available	352,000			
Less cash disbursements:				
For inventory purchases	228,000			
For operating expenses	129,000			
For equipment purchases.	—			
For dividends	45,000			
Total cash disbursements.	402,000			
Excess (deficiency) of cash	(50,000)			
Financing				
Etc.				

5. Prepare an absorption costing income statement for the quarter ending March 31 as shown in Schedule 9 in the chapter.

6. Prepare a balance sheet as of March 31.

PROBLEM 9-18 Cash Budget with Supporting Schedules [LO2, LO4, LO7, LO8]

Westex Products is a wholesale distributor of industrial cleaning products. When the treasurer of Westex Products approached the company's bank late in the current year seeking short-term financing, he was told that money was very tight and that any borrowing over the next year would have to be supported by a detailed statement of cash collections and disbursements. The treasurer also was told that it would be very helpful to the bank if borrowers would indicate the quarters in which they would be needing funds, as well as the amounts that would be needed, and the quarters in which repayments could be made.

Since the treasurer is unsure as to the particular quarters in which bank financing will be needed, he has assembled the following information to assist in preparing a detailed cash budget:

a. Budgeted sales and merchandise purchases for next year, as well as actual sales and purchases for the last quarter of the current year, are:

	Sales	Merchandise Purchases	
Current year:			
Fourth quarter actual	$200,000	$126,000	
Next year:			
First quarter estimated	$300,000	$186,000	
Second quarter estimated	$400,000	$246,000	
Third quarter estimated	$500,000	$305,000	
Fourth quarter estimated	$200,000	$126,000	

b. The company normally collects 65% of a quarter's sales before the quarter ends and another 33% in the following quarter. The remainder is uncollectible. This pattern of collections is now being experienced in the current year's fourth-quarter actual data.
c. Eighty percent of a quarter's merchandise purchases are paid for within the quarter. The remainder is paid for in the following quarter.
d. Operating expenses for next year are budgeted at $50,000 per quarter plus 15% of sales. Of the fixed amount, $20,000 each quarter is depreciation.
e. The company will pay $10,000 in dividends each quarter.
f. Equipment purchases of $75,000 will be made in the second quarter, and purchases of $48,000 will be made in the third quarter. These purchases will be for cash.
g. The Cash account contained $10,000 at the end of the current year. The treasurer feels that this represents a minimum balance that must be maintained.
h. Any borrowing will take place at the beginning of a quarter, and any repayments will be made at the end of a quarter at an annual interest rate of 10%. Interest is paid only when principal is repaid. All borrowings and all repayments of principal must be in round $1,000 amounts. Interest payments can be in any amount. (Compute interest on whole months, e.g., $1/12$, $2/12$.)
i. At present, the company has no loans outstanding.

Required:
1. Prepare the following, by quarter and in total, for next year:
    a. A schedule of expected cash collections.
    b. A schedule of expected cash disbursements for merchandise purchases.
2. Compute the expected cash disbursements for operating expenses, by quarter and in total, for next year.
3. Prepare a cash budget, by quarter and in total, for next year.

PROBLEM 9-19 Cash Budget with Supporting Schedules [LO2, LO4, LO8]

Garden Sales, Inc., sells garden supplies. Management is planning its cash needs for the second quarter. The company usually has to borrow money during this quarter to support peak sales of lawn care equipment, which occur during May. The following information has been assembled to assist in preparing a cash budget for the quarter:

a.   Budgeted monthly absorption costing income statements for April–July are as follows:

	April	May	June	July
Sales	$600,000	$900,000	$500,000	$400,000
Cost of goods sold	420,000	630,000	350,000	280,000
Gross margin	180,000	270,000	150,000	120,000
Selling and administrative expenses:				
Selling expense	79,000	120,000	62,000	51,000
Administrative expense*	45,000	52,000	41,000	38,000
Total expenses	124,000	172,000	103,000	89,000
Net operating income	$ 56,000	$ 98,000	$ 47,000	$ 31,000

*Includes $20,000 depreciation each month.

b.   Sales are 20% for cash and 80% on account.
c.   Sales on account are collected over a three-month period with 10% collected in the month of sale; 70% collected in the first month following the month of sale; and the remaining 20% collected in the second month following the month of sale. February's sales totaled $200,000, and March's sales totaled $300,000.
d.   Inventory purchases are paid for within 15 days. Therefore, 50% of a month's inventory purchases are paid for in the month of purchase. The remaining 50% is paid in the following month. Accounts payable at March 31 for inventory purchases during March total $126,000.
e.   Each month's ending inventory must equal 20% of the cost of the merchandise to be sold in the following month. The merchandise inventory at March 31 is $84,000.
f.   Dividends of $49,000 will be declared and paid in April.
g.   Land costing $16,000 will be purchased for cash in May.
h.   The cash balance at March 31 is $52,000; the company must maintain a cash balance of at least $40,000 at the end of each month.
i.   The company can borrow from its bank as needed to bolster the Cash account. Borrowings and repayments must be in increments of $1,000. All borrowings take place at the beginning of a month, and all repayments are made at the end of a month. The annual interest rate is 12%. Compute interest on whole months ($\frac{1}{12}$, $\frac{2}{12}$, and so forth).

Required:
1.   Prepare a schedule of expected cash collections for April, May, and June, and for the quarter in total.
2.   Prepare the following for merchandise inventory:
    a.   A merchandise purchases budget for April, May, and June.
    b.   A schedule of expected cash disbursements for merchandise purchases for April, May, and June, and for the quarter in total.
3.   Prepare a cash budget for April, May, and June as well as in total for the quarter.

PROBLEM 9-20 Integrated Operating Budgets [LO3, LO4, LO5, LO6]
The West Division of Vader Corporation produces an intricate component part used in Vader's major product line. The divisional manager has recently been concerned about a lack of coordination between purchasing and production personnel and believes that a monthly budgeting system would be better than the present system.

The manager of the West Division has decided to develop budget information for the third quarter of the current year as a trial before the budget system is implemented for an entire fiscal year. In response to the manager's request for data that could be used to develop budget information, the controller of the West Division accumulated the following data:

Sales.   Sales through June 30, the first six months of the current year, were 24,000 units. Actual sales in units for May and June and estimated unit sales for the next five months are detailed as follows:

May (actual)	4,000
June (actual)	4,000
July (estimated)	5,000
August (estimated).	6,000
September (estimated)	7,000
October (estimated).	7,500
November (estimated)	8,000

The West Division expects to sell 65,000 units during the year ending December 31.

Direct Material. Data regarding the direct materials used in the component are shown in the following schedule. Each month's ending direct materials inventory should equal 50% of the next month's production needs.

Direct Material	Units of Direct Materials per Finished Component	Cost per Unit	Inventory Level June 30
No. 101.	6 ounces	$2.40	35,000 ounces
No. 211.	4 pounds	$5.00	30,000 pounds

Direct Labor. Each component must pass through three processes to be completed. Data regarding the direct labor are as follows:

Process	Direct Labor-Hours per Finished Component	Cost per Direct Labor-Hour
Forming	0.40	$16.00
Assembly	1.00	$11.00
Finishing	0.10	$15.00

Manufacturing Overhead. The West Division produced 27,000 components and incurred the variable overhead costs shown below during the six-month period ended June 30. The controller of the West Division believes that the variable overhead costs will be incurred at the same rate during the last six months of the year.

Supplies	$ 59,400
Electricity	27,000
Indirect labor.	54,000
Other	8,100
Total variable overhead.	$148,500

The actual fixed manufacturing overhead costs incurred during the first six months amounted to $93,500. Fixed manufacturing overhead costs are budgeted for the entire year as follows:

Supervision	$ 60,000
Taxes	7,200
Depreciation.	86,400
Other	32,400
Total fixed manufacturing overhead.	$186,000

Finished Goods Inventory. The desired monthly ending finished goods inventory in units is 80% of the next month's estimated sales. There are 4,000 finished units in inventory on June 30.

Required:

1. Prepare a production budget for the West Division for the third quarter ending September 30. Show computations by month and in total for the quarter.
2. Prepare a direct materials budget for each type of material for the third quarter ending September 30. Again show computations by month and in total for the quarter.
3. Prepare a direct labor budget for the third quarter ending September 30. This time it is *not* necessary to show monthly figures; show quarterly totals only. Assume that the workforce is adjusted as work requirements change.
4. Assume that the company plans to produce a total of 65,000 units for the year. Prepare a manufacturing overhead budget for the six-month period ending December 31. (Do not compute a predetermined overhead rate.) Again, it is *not* necessary to show monthly figures.

(CMA, adapted)

PROBLEM 9-21 Completing a Master Budget [LO2, LO4, LO7, LO8, LO9, LO10]

The following data relate to the operations of Shilow Company, a wholesale distributor of consumer goods:

Current assets as of March 31:	
Cash........................	$8,000
Accounts receivable	$20,000
Inventory....................	$36,000
Buildings and equipment, net	$120,000
Accounts payable	$21,750
Capital stock...................	$150,000
Retained earnings	$12,250

a. The gross margin is 25% of sales. (In other words, cost of goods sold is 75% of sales.)
b. Actual and budgeted sales data are as follows:

March (actual).........	$50,000
April	$60,000
May................	$72,000
June	$90,000
July................	$48,000

c. Sales are 60% for cash and 40% on credit. Credit sales are collected in the month following sale. The accounts receivable at March 31 are a result of March credit sales.
d. Each month's ending inventory should equal 80% of the following month's budgeted cost of goods sold.
e. One-half of a month's inventory purchases is paid for in the month of purchase; the other half is paid for in the following month. The accounts payable at March 31 are the result of March purchases of inventory.
f. Monthly expenses are as follows: commissions, 12% of sales; rent, $2,500 per month; other expenses (excluding depreciation), 6% of sales. Assume that these expenses are paid monthly. Depreciation is $900 per month (includes depreciation on new assets).
g. Equipment costing $1,500 will be purchased for cash in April.
h. The company must maintain a minimum cash balance of $4,000. An open line of credit is available at a local bank. All borrowing is done at the beginning of a month, and all repayments are made at the end of a month; borrowing must be in multiples of $1,000. The annual interest rate is 12%. Interest is paid only at the time of repayment of principal; figure interest on whole months ($\frac{1}{12}$, $\frac{2}{12}$, and so forth).

Required:

Using the preceding data:

1. Complete the following schedule:

Schedule of Expected Cash Collections	April	May	June	Quarter
Cash sales............	$36,000			
Credit sales	20,000			
Total collections........	$56,000			

2. Complete the following:

Merchandise Purchases Budget	April	May	June	Quarter
Budgeted cost of goods sold	$45,000*	$54,000		
Add desired ending inventory........	43,200†			
Total needs.....................	88,200			
Less beginning inventory	36,000			
Required purchases...............	$52,200			

*For April sales: $60,000 sales × 75% cost ratio = $45,000.
†$54,000 × 80% = $43,200

Schedule of Expected Cash Disbursements—Merchandise Purchases	April	May	June	Quarter
March purchases	$21,750			$21,750
April purchases	26,100	$26,100		52,200
May purchases............				
June purchases				
Total disbursements........	$47,850			

3. Complete the following schedule:

Schedule of Expected Cash Disbursements—Selling and Administrative Expenses	April	May	June	Quarter
Commissions...............	$ 7,200			
Rent.....................	2,500			
Other expenses	3,600			
Total disbursements..........	$13,300			

4. Complete the following cash budget:

Cash Budget	April	May	June	Quarter
Cash balance, beginning..........	$ 8,000			
Add cash collections	56,000			
Total cash available	64,000			
Less cash disbursements:				
For inventory	47,850			
For expenses	13,300			
For equipment	1,500			
Total cash disbursements	62,650			
Excess (deficiency) of cash........	1,350			
Financing				
Etc.				

5. Prepare an absorption costing income statement, similar to the one shown in Schedule 9 in the text, for the quarter ended June 30.
6. Prepare a balance sheet as of June 30.

Cases

CASE 9-22 Evaluating a Company's Budget Procedures [LO1]

Tom Emory and Jim Morris strolled back to their plant from the administrative offices of Ferguson & Son Mfg. Company. Tom is manager of the machine shop in the company's factory; Jim is the manager of the equipment maintenance department.

The men had just attended the monthly performance evaluation meeting for plant department heads. These meetings had been held on the third Tuesday of each month since Robert Ferguson, Jr., the president's son, had become plant manager a year earlier.

As they were walking, Tom Emory spoke: "Boy, I hate those meetings! I never know whether my department's accounting reports will show good or bad performance. I'm beginning to expect the worst. If the accountants say I saved the company a dollar, I'm called 'Sir,' but if I spend even a little too much—boy, do I get in trouble. I don't know if I can hold on until I retire."

Tom had just been given the worst evaluation he had ever received in his long career with Ferguson & Son. He was the most respected of the experienced machinists in the company. He had been with Ferguson & Son for many years and was promoted to supervisor of the machine shop when the company expanded and moved to its present location. The president (Robert Ferguson, Sr.) had often stated that the company's success was due to the high quality of the work of machinists like Tom. As supervisor, Tom stressed the importance of craftsmanship and told his workers that he wanted no sloppy work coming from his department.

When Robert Ferguson, Jr., became the plant manager, he directed that monthly performance comparisons be made between actual and budgeted costs for each department. The departmental budgets were intended to encourage the supervisors to reduce inefficiencies and to seek cost reduction opportunities. The company controller was instructed to have his staff "tighten" the budget slightly whenever a department attained its budget in a given month; this was done to reinforce the plant manager's desire to reduce costs. The young plant manager often stressed the importance of continued progress toward attaining the budget; he also made it known that he kept a file of these performance reports for future reference when he succeeded his father.

Tom Emory's conversation with Jim Morris continued as follows:

Emory: I really don't understand. We've worked so hard to meet the budget, and the minute we do so they tighten it on us. We can't work any faster and still maintain quality. I think my men are ready to quit trying. Besides, those reports don't tell the whole story. We always seem to be interrupting the big jobs for all those small rush orders. All that setup and machine adjustment time is killing us. And quite frankly, Jim, you were no help. When our hydraulic press broke down last month, your people were nowhere to be found. We had to take it apart ourselves and got stuck with all that idle time.

Morris: I'm sorry about that, Tom, but you know my department has had trouble making budget, too. We were running well behind at the time of that problem, and if we'd spent a day on that old machine, we would never have made it up. Instead we made the scheduled inspections of the forklift trucks because we knew we could do those in less than the budgeted time.

Emory: Well, Jim, at least you have some options. I'm locked into what the scheduling department assigns to me and you know they're being harassed by sales for those special orders. Incidentally, why didn't your report show all the supplies you guys wasted last month when you were working in Bill's department?

Morris: We're not out of the woods on that deal yet. We charged the maximum we could to other work and haven't even reported some of it yet.

Emory: Well, I'm glad you have a way of getting out of the pressure. The accountants seem to know everything that's happening in my department, sometimes even before I do. I thought all that budget and accounting stuff was supposed to help, but it just gets me into trouble. It's all a big pain. I'm trying to put out quality work; they're trying to save pennies.

Required:

1. Identify the problems that appear to exist in Ferguson & Son Mfg. Company's budgetary control system and explain how the problems are likely to reduce the effectiveness of the system.
2. Explain how Ferguson & Son Mfg. Company's budgetary control system could be revised to improve its effectiveness.

(CMA, adapted)

CASE 9-23 Master Budget with Supporting Schedules [LO2, LO4, LO8, LO9, LO10]

You have just been hired as a new management trainee by Earrings Unlimited, a distributor of earrings to various retail outlets located in shopping malls across the country. In the past, the company has done very little in the way of budgeting and at certain times of the year has experienced a shortage of cash.

Since you are well trained in budgeting, you have decided to prepare comprehensive budgets for the upcoming second quarter in order to show management the benefits that can be gained from an integrated budgeting program. To this end, you have worked with accounting and other areas to gather the information assembled below.

The company sells many styles of earrings, but all are sold for the same price—$10 per pair. Actual sales of earrings for the last three months and budgeted sales for the next six months follow (in pairs of earrings):

January (actual)	20,000	June	50,000
February (actual)	26,000	July	30,000
March (actual)	40,000	August	28,000
April	65,000	September	25,000
May	100,000		

The concentration of sales before and during May is due to Mother's Day. Sufficient inventory should be on hand at the end of each month to supply 40% of the earrings sold in the following month.

Suppliers are paid $4 for a pair of earrings. One-half of a month's purchases is paid for in the month of purchase; the other half is paid for in the following month. All sales are on credit, with no discount, and payable within 15 days. The company has found, however, that only 20% of a month's sales are collected in the month of sale. An additional 70% is collected in the following month, and the remaining 10% is collected in the second month following sale. Bad debts have been negligible.

Monthly operating expenses for the company are given below:

Variable:	
Sales commissions	4% of sales
Fixed:	
Advertising	$200,000
Rent	$18,000
Salaries	$106,000
Utilities	$7,000
Insurance	$3,000
Depreciation	$14,000

Insurance is paid on an annual basis, in November of each year.

The company plans to purchase $16,000 in new equipment during May and $40,000 in new equipment during June; both purchases will be for cash. The company declares dividends of $15,000 each quarter, payable in the first month of the following quarter.

A listing of the company's ledger accounts as of March 31 is given below:

Assets	
Cash	$ 74,000
Accounts receivable ($26,000 February sales; $320,000 March sales)	346,000
Inventory	104,000
Prepaid insurance	21,000
Property and equipment (net)	950,000
Total assets	$1,495,000

Liabilities and Stockholders' Equity	
Accounts payable	$ 100,000
Dividends payable	15,000
Capital stock	800,000
Retained earnings	580,000
Total liabilities and stockholders' equity	$1,495,000

The company maintains a minimum cash balance of $50,000. All borrowing is done at the beginning of a month; any repayments are made at the end of a month.

The annual interest rate is 12%. Interest is computed and paid at the end of each quarter on all loans outstanding during the quarter.

Required:

Prepare a master budget for the three-month period ending June 30. Include the following detailed budgets:

1. *a.*　A sales budget, by month and in total.
   b.　A schedule of expected cash collections from sales, by month and in total.
   c.　A merchandise purchases budget in units and in dollars. Show the budget by month and in total.
   d.　A schedule of expected cash disbursements for merchandise purchases, by month and in total.
2. A cash budget. Show the budget by month and in total. Determine any borrowing that would be needed to maintain the minimum cash balance of $50,000.
3. A budgeted income statement for the three-month period ending June 30. Use the contribution approach.
4. A budgeted balance sheet as of June 30.

RESEARCH AND APPLICATION 9-24　[LO1]

The questions in this exercise give you an appreciation for the complexity of budgeting in a large multinational corporation. To answer the questions, you will need to download the Procter & Gamble (P&G) 2005 Annual Report at www.pg.com/investors/sectionmain.jhtml and briefly refer to "Item 2: Properties" in P&G's 2005 10-K at www.pginvestor.com/phoenix.zhtml?c=104574&p=irol-sec#3673889. You will also need to briefly refer to Federated Department Stores' 2004 10-K at www.fds.com/ir/ann.asp. Although you may not be familiar with Federated Department Stores, you are probably familiar with its flagship brands—Macy's and Bloomingdale's. You do not need to print any documents to answer the questions.

Required:

1. What is P&G's strategy for success in the marketplace? Does the company rely primarily on a customer intimacy, operational excellence, or product leadership customer value proposition? What evidence supports your conclusion?
2. What business risks does P&G face that may threaten its ability to satisfy stockholder expectations? What are some examples of control activities that the company could use to reduce these risks? (Hint: Focus on page 28 of the annual report).
3. What were P&G's quarterly net sales for the fiscal year ended June 30, 2005? What were Federated Department Stores' quarterly net sales for 2004? (Hint: see page 79 of its 10-K.) How does P&G's quarterly sales trend compare to Federated Department Stores' quarterly sales trend? Which of the two quarterly sales trends is likely to cause greater cash budgeting concerns? Why?
4. Describe the scope of P&G's business in three respects—physical facilities, products, and customers. More specifically, how many manufacturing facilities does P&G operate globally? What are P&G's three Global Business Units (GBUs)? Which of P&G's 17 "billion dollar brands" are included in each of these GBU's? How many brands does P&G offer in total and in how many countries do they sell these brands? How many countries does P&G's Market Development Organization operate in?
5. Describe five uncertainties that complicate P&G's efforts to accurately forecast its sales and expenses.
6. Although not specifically discussed in P&G's annual report, how could an Enterprise System as described in Chapter 1 help a globally dispersed, highly complex company such as P&G improve its budgeting process?
7. P&G's annual report briefly discusses the acquisition of Gillette (see pages 10–11). It acknowledges that Gillette has some different cultural norms in terms of how it defines accountability and communicates internally. Although not discussed in the annual report, how could differences in two organization's budgeting practices be responsible for these types of divergent cultural norms?

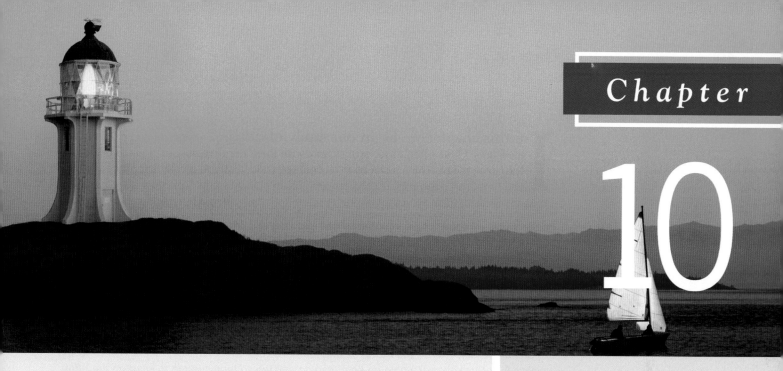

Standard Costs and the Balanced Scorecard

Managing Materials and Labor

Schneider Electric's Oxford, Ohio, plant manufactures *busways* that transport electricity from its point of entry into a building to remote locations throughout the building. The plant's managers pay close attention to direct material costs because they are more than half of the plant's total manufacturing costs. To help control scrap rates for direct material inputs such as copper, steel, and aluminum, the accounting department prepares direct materials quantity variances. These variances compare the standard quantity of direct materials that should have been used to make a product (according to computations by the plant's engineers) to the amount of direct materials that were actually used. Keeping a close eye on these differences helps to identify and deal with the causes of excessive scrap, such as an inadequately trained machine operator, poor quality raw material inputs, or a malfunctioning machine.

Because direct labor is also a significant component of the plant's total manufacturing costs, the management team daily monitors the direct labor efficiency variance. This variance compares the standard amount of labor time allowed to make a product to the actual amount of labor time used. When idle workers cause an unfavorable labor efficiency variance, managers temporarily move workers from departments with slack to departments with a backlog of work to be done. ■

Source: Author's conversation with Doug Taylor, plant controller, Schneider Electric's Oxford, Ohio, plant.

Learning Objectives

After studying Chapter 10, you should be able to:

LO1 Explain how direct materials standards and direct labor standards are set.

LO2 Compute the direct materials price and quantity variances and explain their significance.

LO3 Compute the direct labor rate and efficiency variances and explain their significance.

LO4 Compute the variable manufacturing overhead spending and efficiency variances.

LO5 Understand how a balanced scorecard fits together and how it supports a company's strategy.

LO6 Compute delivery cycle time, throughput time, and manufacturing cycle efficiency (MCE).

LO7 (Appendix 10A) Prepare journal entries to record standard costs and variances.

In this chapter we begin our study of management control and performance measures. Quite often, these terms carry with them negative connotations. Indeed, performance measurements can be used counterproductively to create fear, to cast blame, and to punish. However, if used properly, as explained in the following quotation, performance measurement serves a vital function in both daily life and in organizations:

Imagine you want to improve your basketball shooting skill. You know that practice will help, so you [go] to the basketball court. There you start shooting toward the hoop, but as soon as the ball gets close to the rim your vision goes blurry for a second, so that you cannot observe where the ball ended up in relation to the target (left, right, in front, too far back, inside the hoop?). It would be pretty difficult to improve under those conditions. . . . (And by the way, how long would [shooting baskets] sustain your interest if you couldn't observe the outcome of your efforts?)

Or imagine someone engaging in a weight loss program. A normal step in such programs is to purchase a scale to be able to track one's progress: Is this program working? Am I losing weight? A positive answer would be encouraging and would motivate me to keep up the effort, while a negative answer might lead me to reflect on the process: Am I working on the right diet and exercise program? Am I doing everything I am supposed to?, etc. Suppose you don't want to set up a sophisticated measurement system and decide to forgo the scale. You would still have some idea of how well you are doing from simple methods such as clothes feeling looser, a belt that fastens at a different hole, or simply via observation in a mirror! Now, imagine trying to sustain a weight loss program without any feedback on how well you are doing.

In these . . . examples, availability of quantitative measures of performance can yield two types of benefits: First, performance feedback can help improve the "production process" through a better understanding of what works and what doesn't; e.g., shooting this way works better than shooting that way. Secondly, feedback on performance can sustain motivation and effort, because it is encouraging and/or because it suggests that more effort is required for the goal to be met.[1]

In the same way, performance measurement can be helpful in an organization. It can provide feedback concerning what works and what does not work, and it can help motivate people to sustain their efforts.

IN BUSINESS

FOCUSING ON THE NUMBERS

Joe Knight is the CEO of Setpoint, a company that designs and builds factory-automation equipment. Knight uses a large whiteboard, with about 20 rows and 10 columns, to focus worker attention on key factors involved in managing projects. A visitor to the plant, Steve Petersen, asked Knight to explain the board, but Knight instead motioned one of his workers to come over. The young man, with a baseball cap turned backward on his head, proceeded to walk the visitor through the board, explaining the calculation of gross margin and other key indicators on the board.

"'I was just amazed,' Petersen recalls. 'He knew that board inside and out. He knew every number on it. He knew exactly where the company was and where they had to focus their attention. There was no hesitation . . . . I was so impressed . . . that the people on the shop floor had it down like that. It was their scoreboard. It was the way they could tell if they were winning or losing. I talked to several of them, and I just couldn't get over the positive attitude they had and their understanding of the numbers.'"

Source: Bo Burlinghan, "What's Your Culture Worth?," *Inc.* magazine, September 2001, pp. 124–133.

---

[1] Soumitra Dutta and Jean-François Manzoni, *Process Reengineering, Organizational Change and Performance Improvement* (New York: McGraw-Hill), Chapter IV.

Our study of performance measurement begins with the lowest levels in the organization. We work our way up the organizational ladder in subsequent chapters. In this chapter we see how various measures are used to control operations and to evaluate performance. Even though we are starting with the lowest levels in the organization, keep in mind that performance measures should be derived from the organization's overall strategy. For example, a company like Sony that bases its strategy on rapid introduction of innovative consumer products should use different performance measures than a company like Federal Express where on-time delivery, customer convenience, and low cost are key competitive advantages. Sony may want to keep close track of the percentage of revenues from products introduced within the last year; whereas Federal Express may want to closely monitor the percentage of packages delivered on time. Later in this chapter when we discuss the *balanced scorecard,* we will have more to say concerning the role of strategy in the selection of performance measures. But first we will see how *standard costs* are used by managers to help control costs.

Companies in highly competitive industries like Federal Express, Southwest Airlines, Dell, and Toyota must be able to provide high-quality goods and services at low cost. If they do not, their customers will buy from more efficient competitors. Stated in the starkest terms, managers must obtain inputs such as raw materials and electricity at the lowest possible prices and must use them as effectively as possible—while maintaining or increasing the quality of what they sell. If inputs are purchased at prices that are too high or more input is used than is really necessary, higher costs will result.

How do managers control the prices that are paid for inputs and the quantities that are used? They could examine every transaction in detail, but this obviously would be an inefficient use of management time. For many companies, the answer to this control problem lies at least partially in *standard costs.*

Standard Costs—Management by Exception

A *standard* is a benchmark or "norm" for measuring performance. Standards are found everywhere. Your doctor evaluates your weight using standards for individuals of your age, height, and gender. The food we eat in restaurants is prepared under specified standards of cleanliness. The buildings we live in conform to standards set in building codes. Standards are also widely used in managerial accounting where they relate to the *quantity* and *cost* (or acquisition price) of inputs used in manufacturing goods or providing services.

Quantity and cost standards are set for each major input such as raw materials and labor time. *Quantity standards* specify how much of an input should be used to make a product or provide a service. *Cost (price) standards* specify how much should be paid for each unit of the input. Actual quantities and actual costs of inputs are compared to these standards. If either the quantity or the cost of inputs departs significantly from the standards, managers investigate the discrepancy to find the cause of the problem and eliminate it. This process is called **management by exception.**

In our daily lives, we operate in a management by exception mode most of the time. Consider what happens when you sit down in the driver's seat of your car. You put the key in the ignition, you turn the key, and your car starts. Your expectation (standard) that the car will start is met; you do not have to open the car hood and check the battery, the connecting cables, the fuel lines, and so on. If you turn the key and the car does not start, then you have a discrepancy (variance). Your expectations are not met, and you need to investigate why. Note that even if the car starts after a second try, it still would be wise to investigate. The fact that the expectation was not met should be viewed as an opportunity to uncover the cause of the problem rather than as simply an annoyance. If the underlying cause is not discovered and corrected, the problem may recur and become much worse.

EXHIBIT 10–1
The Variance Analysis Cycle

This basic approach to identifying and solving problems is the essence of the *variance analysis cycle,* which is illustrated in Exhibit 10–1. The cycle begins with the preparation of standard cost performance reports in the accounting department. These reports highlight the *variances,* which are the differences between actual results and what should have occurred according to the standards. The variances raise questions. Why did this variance occur? Why is this variance larger than it was last period? The significant variances are investigated to discover their root causes. Corrective actions are taken. And then next period's operations are carried out. The cycle begins again with the preparation of a new standard cost performance report for the latest period. The emphasis should be on highlighting problems, finding their root causes, and then taking corrective action. The goal is to improve operations—not to assign blame.

Who Uses Standard Costs?

Manufacturing, service, food, and not-for-profit organizations all make use of standards to some extent. Auto service centers like Firestone and Sears, for example, often set specific labor time standards for the completion of certain tasks, such as installing a carburetor or doing a valve job, and then measure actual performance against these standards. Fast-food outlets such as McDonald's have exacting standards for the quantity of meat going into a sandwich, as well as standards for the cost of the meat. Hospitals have standard costs for food, laundry, and other items, as well as standard time allowances for certain routine activities, such as laboratory tests. In short, you are likely to run into standard costs in virtually any line of business.

IN BUSINESS

STANDARD COSTING AT PARKER BRASS

The Brass Products Division at Parker Hannifin Corporation, known as Parker Brass, is a world-class manufacturer of tube and brass fittings, valves, hose and hose fittings. Management at the company uses variances from its standard costing system to target problem areas for improvement. If a production variance exceeds 5% of sales, the responsible manager is required to explain the variance and to propose a plan of action to correct the detected problems. In the past, variances were reported at the end of the month—often several weeks after a particular job had been completed. Now, a variance report is generated the day after a job is completed and summary variance reports are prepared weekly. These more frequent reports help managers take more timely corrective action.

Source: David Johnsen and Parvez Sopariwala, "Standard Costing Is Alive and Well at Parker Brass," *Management Accounting Quarterly,* Winter 2000, pp. 12–20.

Manufacturing companies often have highly developed standard costing systems in which standards for direct materials, direct labor, and overhead are created for each product. A **standard cost card** shows the standard quantities and costs of the inputs required to produce a unit of a specific product. In the following section, we provide a detailed example of setting standard costs and preparing a standard cost card.

Setting Standard Costs

Setting price and quantity standards ideally combines the expertise of everyone who has responsibility for purchasing and using inputs. In a manufacturing setting, this might include accountants, purchasing managers, engineers, production supervisors, line managers, and production workers. Past records of purchase prices and input usage can be helpful in setting standards. However, the standards should be designed to encourage efficient *future* operations, not just a repetition of *past* operations that may or may not have been efficient.

Ideal versus Practical Standards

Should standards be attainable all of the time, part of the time, or almost none of the time? Opinions vary, but standards tend to fall into one of two categories—either ideal or practical.

Ideal standards can be attained only under the best circumstances. They allow for no machine breakdowns or other work interruptions, and they call for a level of effort that can be attained only by the most skilled and efficient employees working at peak effort 100% of the time. Some managers feel that such standards spur continual improvement. These managers argue that even though employees know they will rarely meet the standard, it is a constant reminder of the need for ever-increasing efficiency and effort. Few organizations use ideal standards. Most managers feel that ideal standards tend to discourage even the most diligent workers. Moreover, variances from ideal standards are difficult to interpret. Large variances from the ideal are normal and it is therefore difficult to "manage by exception."

Practical standards are standards that are "tight but attainable." They allow for normal machine downtime and employee rest periods, and they can be attained through reasonable, though highly efficient, efforts by the average worker. Variances from practical standards typically signal a need for management attention because they represent deviations that fall outside of normal operating conditions. Furthermore, practical standards can serve multiple purposes. In addition to signaling abnormal conditions, they can also be used in forecasting cash flows and in planning inventory. By contrast, ideal standards cannot be used for these purposes because they do not allow for normal inefficiencies and result in unrealistic forecasts.

Throughout the remainder of this chapter, we will assume that practical rather than ideal standards are in use.

The Colonial Pewter Company was organized a year ago. The company's only product is a reproduction of an 18th century pewter bookend. The bookend is made largely by hand, using traditional metalworking tools. Consequently, the manufacturing process is labor intensive and requires a high level of skill.

Colonial Pewter has recently expanded its workforce to take advantage of unexpected demand for the bookends as gifts. The company started with a small cadre of experienced pewter workers but has had to hire less experienced workers as a result of the expansion. The president of the company, J. D. Wriston, has called a meeting to discuss production problems. Attending the meeting are Tom Kuchel, the production manager; Janet Warner, the purchasing manager; and Terry Sherman, the corporate controller.

**MANAGERIAL
ACCOUNTING
IN ACTION**
The Issue

J. D.: I've got a feeling that we aren't getting the production we should out of our new people.

Tom: Give us a chance. Some of the new people have been with the company for less than a month.

Janet: Let me add that production seems to be wasting an awful lot of material—particularly pewter. That stuff is very expensive.

Tom: What about the shipment of defective pewter that you bought a couple of months ago—the one with the iron contamination? That caused us major problems.

Janet: That's ancient history. How was I to know it was off-grade? Besides, it was a great deal.

J. D.: Calm down everybody. Let's get the facts before we start sinking our fangs into each other.

Tom: I agree. The more facts the better.

J. D.: Okay, Terry, it's your turn. Facts are the controller's department.

Terry: I'm afraid I can't provide the answers off the top of my head, but it won't take me too long to set up a system that can routinely answer questions relating to worker productivity, material waste, and input prices.

J. D.: How long is "not too long"?

Terry: I will need all of your cooperation, but how about a week from today?

J. D.: That's okay with me. What about everyone else?

Tom: Sure.

Janet: Fine with me.

J. D.: Let's mark it on our calendars.

Setting Direct Materials Standards

LEARNING OBJECTIVE 1
Explain how direct materials standards and direct labor standards are set.

Terry Sherman's first task was to prepare price and quantity standards for the company's only significant raw material, pewter ingots. The **standard price per unit** for direct materials should reflect the final, delivered cost of the materials, net of any discounts taken. After consulting with purchasing manager Janet Warner, Terry prepared the following documentation for the standard price of a pound of pewter in ingot form:

Purchase price, top-grade pewter ingots, in 40-pound ingots	$3.85
Freight, by truck, from the supplier's warehouse	0.24
Less purchase discount	(0.09)
Standard price per pound	$4.00

Notice that the standard price reflects a particular grade of material (top grade), purchased in particular lot sizes (40-pound ingots), and delivered by a particular type of carrier (truck). Allowances have also been made for discounts. If everything proceeds according to these expectations, the net cost of a pound of pewter should be $4.00.

The **standard quantity per unit** for direct materials should reflect the amount of material required for each unit of finished product, as well as an allowance for unavoidable waste, spoilage, and other normal inefficiencies. After consulting with the production manager, Tom Kuchel, Terry Sherman prepared the following documentation for the standard quantity of pewter in a pair of bookends:

Material requirements as specified in the bill of materials for a pair of bookends, in pounds	2.7
Allowance for waste and spoilage, in pounds	0.2
Allowance for rejects, in pounds	0.1
Standard quantity per pair of bookends, in pounds	3.0

As discussed in Chapter 3, the bill of materials details the quantity of each type of material that should be used in a product. As shown above, the material requirements listed on the bill of materials should be adjusted for waste and other factors when determining the standard quantity per unit of product. "Waste and spoilage" refers to materials that are wasted as a normal part of the production process or that spoil before they are used. "Rejects" refers to the direct material contained in defective units that must be scrapped.

Although allowances for waste, spoilage, and rejects are often built into standards, this practice is often criticized because it contradicts the zero defects goal that underlies improvement programs such as Six Sigma. If allowances for waste, spoilage, and rejects are built into the standard cost, those allowances should be periodically reviewed and reduced over time to reflect improved processes, better training, and better equipment.

Once the price and quantity standards have been set, the standard cost of material per unit of the finished product can be computed as follows:

$$3.0 \text{ pounds per unit} \times \$4.00 \text{ per pound} = \$12.00 \text{ per unit}$$

This $12.00 cost will appear on the product's standard cost card.

Setting Direct Labor Standards

Direct labor price and quantity standards are usually expressed in terms of a labor rate and labor-hours. The **standard rate per hour** for direct labor includes wages, employment taxes, and fringe benefits. Using wage records and in consultation with the production manager, Terry Sherman determined the standard rate per direct labor-hour at the Colonial Pewter Company as follows:

Basic wage rate per hour	$10.00
Employment taxes at 10% of the basic rate	1.00
Fringe benefits at 30% of the basic rate	3.00
Standard rate per direct labor-hour	$14.00

Many companies prepare a single standard rate per hour for all employees in a department. This standard rate reflects the expected "mix" of workers, even though the actual wage rates may vary somewhat from individual to individual due to differing skills or seniority. According to the standard computed above, the direct labor rate for Colonial Pewter should average $14 per hour.

The standard direct labor time required to complete a unit of product (called the **standard hours per unit**) is perhaps the single most difficult standard to determine. One approach is to break down each task into elemental body movements (such as reaching, pushing, and turning over). Published tables of standard times for such movements can be used to estimate the total time required to complete the task. Another approach is for an industrial engineer to do a time and motion study, actually clocking the time required for each task. As stated earlier, the standard time should include allowances for breaks, personal needs of employees, cleanup, and machine downtime.

After consulting with the production manager, Terry Sherman prepared the following documentation for the standard direct labor hours per unit:

Basic labor time per unit, in hours	1.9
Allowance for breaks and personal needs	0.1
Allowance for cleanup and machine downtime	0.3
Allowance for rejects	0.2
Standard direct labor-hours per unit of product	2.5

EXHIBIT 10–2
Standard Cost Card—
Variable Manufacturing
Costs

Inputs	(1) Standard Quantity or Hours	(2) Standard Price or Rate	Standard Cost (1) × (2)
Direct materials....................	3.0 pounds	$4.00 per pound	$12.00
Direct labor.......................	2.5 hours	$14.00 per hour	35.00
Variable manufacturing overhead.......	2.5 hours	$3.00 per hour	7.50
Total standard cost per unit...........			$54.50

Once the rate and time standards have been set, the standard direct labor cost per unit of product can be computed as follows:

2.5 direct labor-hours per unit × $14 per direct labor-hour = $35 per unit

This $35 per unit standard direct labor cost appears along with direct materials on the standard cost card for a pair of pewter bookends.

Setting Variable Manufacturing Overhead Standards

As with direct labor, the price and quantity standards for variable manufacturing overhead are usually expressed in terms of rate and hours. The rate represents *the variable portion of the predetermined overhead rate* discussed in Chapter 3; the hours relate to the activity base that is used to apply overhead to units of product (usually machine-hours or direct labor-hours, as we learned in Chapter 3). At Colonial Pewter, the variable portion of the predetermined overhead rate is $3 per direct labor-hour. Therefore, the standard variable manufacturing overhead cost per unit is computed as follows:

2.5 direct labor-hours per unit × $3 per direct labor-hour = $7.50 per unit

This $7.50 per unit cost for variable manufacturing overhead appears along with direct materials and direct labor on the standard cost card in Exhibit 10–2. Observe that the **standard cost per unit** for variable manufacturing overhead is computed the same way as for direct materials or direct labor—the standard quantity allowed per unit of the output is multiplied by the standard price. In this case, the standard quantity is expressed as 2.5 direct labor-hours per unit and the standard price (or rate) is expressed as $3 per direct labor-hour.

Are Standards the Same as Budgets?

Standards and budgets are very similar. The major distinction between the two terms is that a standard is a *unit* amount, whereas a budget is a *total* amount. The standard cost for direct materials at Colonial Pewter is $12 per pair of bookends. If 1,000 pairs of bookends are to be made, then the budgeted cost of direct materials would be $12,000. In effect, *a standard can be viewed as the budgeted cost for one unit of product.*

A General Model for Variance Analysis

Why are standards separated into two categories—price and quantity? Different managers are usually responsible for buying and for using inputs. For example, in the case of a raw material, a purchasing manager is responsible for its price. However, the production manager is responsible for the amount of the raw material actually used to make products. As we shall see, setting up separate standards for price and quantity allows us to better separate the responsibilities of these two managers. It also allows us to prepare more timely reports. The purchasing manager's tasks are completed when the material is delivered for use in the factory. A performance report for the purchasing manager can be prepared at that point. However, the production manager's responsibilities have just begun at that point. A performance

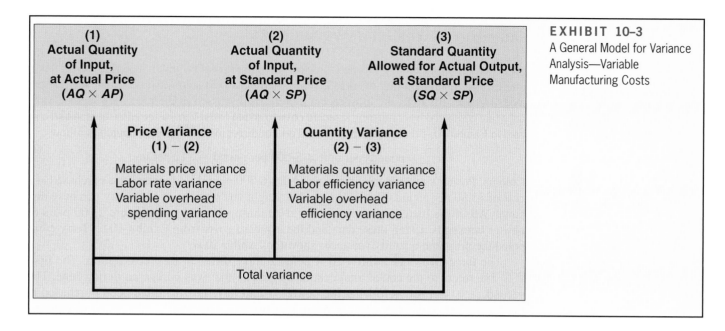

EXHIBIT 10–3
A General Model for Variance Analysis—Variable Manufacturing Costs

report for the production manager must be delayed until production is completed and it is known how much raw material was used in the final product. Therefore, it is important to clearly distinguish between deviations from price standards (the responsibility of the purchasing manager) and deviations from quantity standards (the responsibility of the production manager). Differences between *standard* prices and *actual* prices and between *standard* quantities and *actual* quantities are called **variances.** The act of computing and interpreting variances is called *variance analysis.*

Price and Quantity Variances

Exhibit 10–3 presents a general model for computing standard cost variances for variable costs. This model isolates price variances from quantity variances and shows how each of these variances is computed.[2] We will be using this model throughout the chapter to compute variances for direct materials, direct labor, and variable manufacturing overhead.

Three things should be noted from Exhibit 10–3. First, a price variance and a quantity variance can be computed for each of the three variable cost elements—direct materials, direct labor, and variable manufacturing overhead—even though the variances have different names. For example, a price variance is called a *materials price variance* in the case of direct materials but a *labor rate variance* in the case of direct labor and an *overhead spending variance* in the case of variable manufacturing overhead.

Second, the price variance—regardless of what it is called—is computed in exactly the same way regardless of whether one is dealing with direct materials, direct labor, or variable manufacturing overhead. The same is true of the quantity variance.

Third, the input is the actual quantity of direct materials, direct labor, and variable manufacturing overhead purchased or used; the output is the good production of the period, expressed in terms of the *standard quantity* (or the *standard hours) allowed for the actual output* (see column 3 in Exhibit 10–3). The **standard quantity allowed** or **standard hours allowed** means the amount of an input *that should have been used* to produce the actual output of the period. This could be more or less than the actual amount of the input, depending on the efficiency or inefficiency of operations. The standard quantity allowed is computed by multiplying the actual output in units by the standard input allowed per unit of output.

With this general model as the foundation, we will now calculate Colonial Pewter's price and quantity variances.

---

[2] Variance analysis of fixed costs will be discussed in the next chapter.

Using Standard Costs—Direct Materials Variances

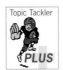

After determining Colonial Pewter Company's standard costs for direct materials, direct labor, and variable manufacturing overhead, Terry Sherman's next step was to compute the company's variances for June, the most recent month. As discussed in the preceding section, variances are computed by comparing standard costs to actual costs. Terry referred to the standard cost card in Exhibit 10–2 that shows the standard cost of direct materials was computed as follows:

$$3.0 \text{ pounds per unit} \times \$4.00 \text{ per pound} = \$12 \text{ per unit}$$

Colonial Pewter's records for June showed that 6,500 pounds of pewter were purchased at a cost of $3.80 per pound. This cost included freight and was net of a quantity purchase discount. All of the material purchased was used during June to manufacture 2,000 pairs of pewter bookends. Using these data and the standard costs from Exhibit 10–2, Terry computed the price and quantity variances shown in Exhibit 10–4.

The three arrows in Exhibit 10–4 point to three different total cost figures. The first, $24,700, refers to the actual total cost of the pewter that was purchased during June. The second, $26,000, refers to what the pewter would have cost if it had been purchased at the standard price of $4.00 a pound rather than the actual price of $3.80 a pound. The difference between these two figures, $1,300 ($26,000 − $24,700), is the price variance. It exists because the actual purchase price was $0.20 per pound less than the standard purchase price. Since 6,500 pounds were purchased, the total amount of the variance is $1,300 ($0.20 per pound × 6,500 pounds). This variance is labeled favorable (denoted by F), since the actual purchase price was less than the standard purchase price. A price variance is labeled unfavorable (denoted by U) if the actual purchase price exceeds the standard purchase price.

The third arrow in Exhibit 10–4 points to $24,000—the cost if the pewter had been purchased at the standard price *and* only the standard quantity allowed per unit had been used. The standards call for 3 pounds of pewter per unit. Since 2,000 units were produced, 6,000 pounds of pewter should have been used. This is referred to as the standard quantity allowed for the actual output. If this 6,000 pounds of pewter had been purchased at the standard price of $4.00 per pound, the company would have spent $24,000. The difference between this figure, $24,000, and the figure at the end of the middle arrow in Exhibit 10–4, $26,000, is the quantity variance of $2,000.

To understand this quantity variance, note that the actual amount of pewter used in production was 6,500 pounds. However, the standard amount of pewter allowed for the actual

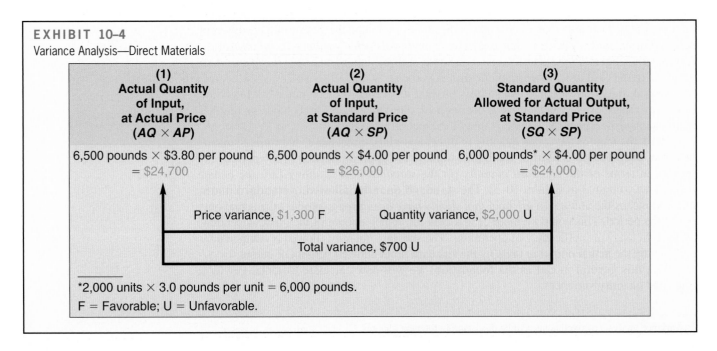

EXHIBIT 10–4
Variance Analysis—Direct Materials

(1) **Actual Quantity of Input, at Actual Price (AQ × AP)**	(2) **Actual Quantity of Input, at Standard Price (AQ × SP)**	(3) **Standard Quantity Allowed for Actual Output, at Standard Price (SQ × SP)**
6,500 pounds × $3.80 per pound = $24,700	6,500 pounds × $4.00 per pound = $26,000	6,000 pounds* × $4.00 per pound = $24,000

Price variance, $1,300 F   Quantity variance, $2,000 U

Total variance, $700 U

*2,000 units × 3.0 pounds per unit = 6,000 pounds.
F = Favorable; U = Unfavorable.

output is 6,000 pounds. Therefore, too much pewter was used to produce the actual output—by a total of 500 pounds. To express this in dollar terms, the 500 pounds is multiplied by the standard price of $4.00 per pound to yield the quantity variance of $2,000. Why is the standard price, rather than the actual price, of the pewter used in this calculation? The production manager is ordinarily responsible for the quantity variance. If the actual price were used in the calculation of the quantity variance, the production manager would be held responsible for the efficiency or inefficiency of the purchasing manager. Apart from being unfair, fruitless arguments between the production manager and purchasing manager would occur every time the actual price of an input was above its standard price. To avoid these arguments, the standard price is used when computing the quantity variance.

The quantity variance in Exhibit 10–4 is labeled unfavorable (denoted by U). This is because more pewter was used to produce the actual output than the standard allows. A quantity variance is labeled favorable (F) if the actual quantity is less than the standard quantity.

The computations in Exhibit 10–4 reflect the fact that all of the material purchased during June was also used during June. How are the variances computed if the amount of material purchased differs from the amount that is used? To illustrate, assume that during June the company purchased 6,500 pounds of materials, as before, but that it used only 5,000 pounds of material during the month and produced only 1,600 units. In this case, the price variance and quantity variance would be computed as shown in Exhibit 10–5.

Most companies compute the materials price variance when materials are *purchased* rather than when they are used in production. There are two reasons for this practice. First, delaying the computation of the price variance until the materials are used would result in less timely variance reports. Second, computing the price variance when the materials are purchased allows materials to be carried in the inventory accounts at their standard cost. This greatly simplifies bookkeeping. (See Appendix 10A at the end of the chapter for an explanation of how the bookkeeping works in a standard costing system.)

Note from the exhibit that the price variance is computed on the entire amount of material purchased (6,500 pounds), as before, whereas the quantity variance is computed only on

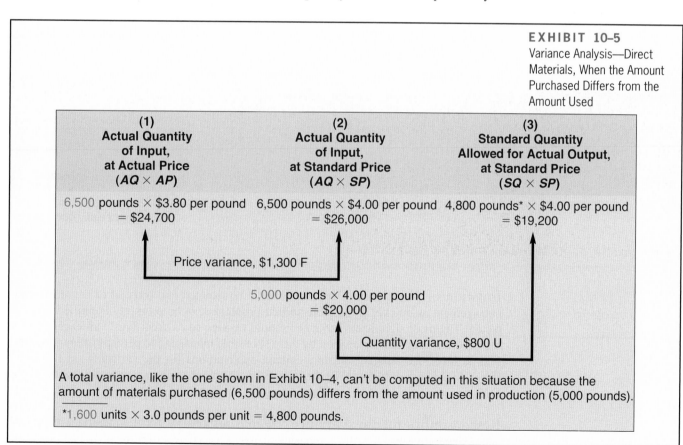

EXHIBIT 10–5
Variance Analysis—Direct Materials, When the Amount Purchased Differs from the Amount Used

the portion of this material used in production during the month (5,000 pounds). What about the other 1,500 pounds of material that were purchased during the period, but that have not yet been used? When those materials are used in future periods, a quantity variance will be computed. However, a price variance will not be computed when the materials are finally used because the price variance was computed when the materials were purchased. The situation illustrated in Exhibit 10–5 is common for companies that purchase materials well in advance of when they are used in production.

Materials Price Variance—A Closer Look

A **materials price variance** measures the difference between what is paid for a given quantity of materials and what should have been paid according to the standard. From Exhibit 10–4, this difference can be expressed by the following formula:

$$\text{Materials price variance} = (AQ \times AP) - (AQ \times SP)$$

	Actual quantity	Actual price	Standard price

The formula can be factored as follows:

$$\text{Materials price variance} = AQ(AP - SP)$$

Using the data from Exhibit 10–4 in this formula, we have the following:

$$6{,}500 \text{ pounds } (\$3.80 \text{ per pound} - \$4.00 \text{ per pound}) = \$1{,}300 \text{ F}$$

Notice that the answer is the same as that shown in Exhibit 10–4. Also note that when using this formula approach, a negative variance is always labeled as favorable (F) and a positive variance is always labeled as unfavorable (U). This will be true of all variance formulas in this and later chapters.

Variance reports are often presented in the form of a table. An excerpt from Colonial Pewter's variance report is shown below along with the purchasing manager's explanation for the materials price variance.

Colonial Pewter Company Performance Report—Purchasing Department						
	(1)	(2)	(3)	(4) Difference in Price	Total Price Variance	
Item Purchased	Quantity Purchased	Actual Price	Standard Price	(2) − (3)	(1) × (4)	Explanation
Pewter	6,500 pounds	$3.80	$4.00	$0.20	$1,300 F	Bargained for an especially good price.

F = Favorable; U = Unfavorable.

Isolation of Variances   Variances should be isolated and brought to the attention of management as quickly as possible so that problems can be promptly identified and corrected. The most significant variances should be viewed as "red flags"; an exception has occurred that requires explanation by the responsible manager and perhaps follow-up effort. The performance report itself may contain explanations for the variances, as illustrated above. In the case of Colonial Pewter Company, the purchasing manager said that the favorable price variance resulted from bargaining for an especially good price.

Responsibility for the Variance   Who is responsible for the materials price variance? Generally speaking, the purchasing manager has control over the price paid for goods and is therefore responsible for the materials price variance. Many factors influence the prices paid for goods including how many units are ordered, how the order is delivered, whether the order is a rush order, and the quality of materials purchased. If any of these factors deviates from what was assumed when the standards were set, a price variance can result. For example, purchasing second-grade materials rather than top-grade materials may result in a favorable price variance, since the lower-grade materials may be less costly. However, we should keep in mind that the lower-grade materials may be less suitable for production.

However, someone other than the purchasing manager could be responsible for a materials price variance. Production may be scheduled in such a way, for example, that the purchasing manager must request express delivery. In these cases, the production manager should be held responsible for the resulting price variances.

A word of caution is in order. Variance analysis should not be used to assign blame. The emphasis should be on *supporting* the line managers and *assisting* them in meeting the goals that they have participated in setting for the company. In short, the emphasis should be positive rather than negative. Excessive dwelling on what has already happened, particularly in terms of trying to find someone to blame, can destroy morale and kill any cooperative spirit.

Materials Quantity Variance—A Closer Look

The **materials quantity variance** measures the difference between the quantity of materials used in production and the quantity that should have been used according to the standard. Although the variance is concerned with the physical usage of materials, as shown in Exhibit 10–4, it is generally stated in dollar terms to help gauge its importance. The formula for the materials quantity variance is as follows:

$$\text{Materials quantity variance} = (AQ \times SP) - (SQ \times SP)$$

Actual quantity   Standard price   Standard quantity allowed for actual output

Again, the formula can be factored as follows:

$$\text{Materials quantity variance} = SP(AQ - SQ)$$

Using the data from Exhibit 10–4 in the formula, we have the following:

$$\$4.00 \text{ per pound } (6,500 \text{ pounds } - 6,000 \text{ pounds*}) = \$2,000 \text{ U}$$

*2,000 units $\times$ 3.0 pounds per unit = 6,000 pounds.

The answer, of course, is the same as that shown in Exhibit 10–4.

The data might appear as follows if a formal performance report were prepared:

	Colonial Pewter Company					
	Performance Report—Production Department					
	(1)	(2)	(3)	(4)		
Type of Materials	Standard Price	Actual Quantity	Standard Quantity Allowed	Difference in Quantity (2) − (3)	Total Quantity Variance (1) × (4)	Explanation
Pewter	$4.00	6,500 pounds	6,000 pounds	500 pounds	$2,000 U	Low-quality materials unsuitable for production.

F = Favorable; U = Unfavorable.

The materials quantity variance is best isolated when materials are used in production. Materials are drawn for the number of units to be produced, according to the standard bill of materials for each unit. Any additional materials are usually drawn with an excess materials requisition slip, which is different in color from the normal requisition slips. This procedure calls attention to the excessive usage of materials *while production is still in process* and provides an opportunity to correct any developing problem.

Excessive materials usage can result from many factors, including faulty machines, inferior materials quality, untrained workers, and poor supervision. Generally speaking, it is the responsibility of the production department to see that material usage is kept in line with standards. There may be times, however, when the *purchasing* department is responsible for an unfavorable materials quantity variance. For example, if the purchasing department buys inferior materials at a lower price, the materials may be unsuitable for use and may result in excessive waste. Thus, purchasing rather than production would be responsible for the quantity variance. At Colonial Pewter, the production manager, Tom Kuchel, claimed on the Production Department's Performance Report that low-quality materials were the cause of the unfavorable materials quantity variance for June.

IN BUSINESS

WHAT HAPPENED TO THE RAISINS?

Management at an unnamed breakfast cereal company became concerned about the apparent waste of raisins in one of its products. A box of the product was supposed to contain 10 ounces of cereal and 2 ounces of raisins. However, the production process had been using an average of 2.5 ounces of raisins per box. To correct the problem, a bonus was offered to employees if the consumption of raisins dropped to 2.1 ounces per box or less—which would allow for about 5% waste. Within a month, the target was hit and bonuses were distributed. However, another problem began to appear. Market studies indicated that customers had become dissatisfied with the amount of raisins in the product. Workers had hit the 2.1-ounce per box target by drastically reducing the amount of raisins in rush orders. Boxes of the completed product are ordinarily weighed and if the weight is less than 12 ounces, the box is rejected. However, rush orders aren't weighed since that would slow down the production process. Consequently, workers were reducing the raisins in rush orders so as to hit the overall target of 2.1 ounces of raisins per box. This resulted in substandard boxes of cereal in rush orders and customer complaints. Clearly, managers need to be very careful when they set targets and standards. They may not get what they bargained for. Subsequent investigation by an internal auditor revealed that, due to statistical fluctuations, an average of about 2.5 ounces of raisins must be used to ensure that every box contains at least 2 ounces of raisins.

Source: Harper A. Roehm and Joseph R. Castellano, "The Danger of Relying on Accounting Numbers Alone," *Management Accounting Quarterly,* Fall 1999, pp. 4–9.

Using Standard Costs—Direct Labor Variances

LEARNING OBJECTIVE 3
Compute the direct labor rate and efficiency variances and explain their significance.

Terry Sherman's next step in determining Colonial Pewter's variances for June was to compute the direct labor variances for the month. Recall from Exhibit 10–2 that the standard direct labor cost per unit of product is $35, computed as follows:

$$2.5 \text{ hours per unit} \times \$14.00 \text{ per hour} = \$35 \text{ per unit}$$

During June, the company paid its direct labor workers $74,250, including employment taxes and fringe benefits, for 5,400 hours of work. This was an average of $13.75 per hour.

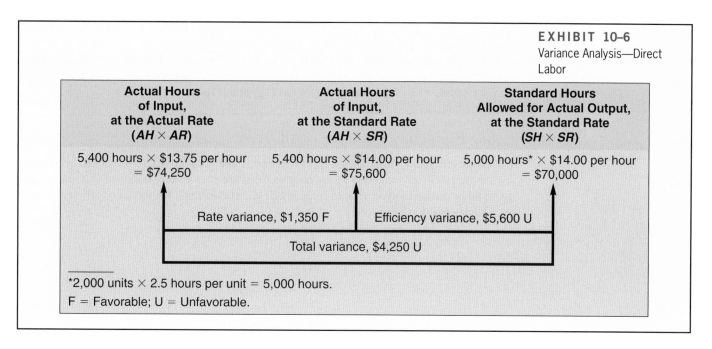

EXHIBIT 10–6
Variance Analysis—Direct Labor

Actual Hours of Input, at the Actual Rate (**AH × AR**)	Actual Hours of Input, at the Standard Rate (**AH × SR**)	Standard Hours Allowed for Actual Output, at the Standard Rate (**SH × SR**)
5,400 hours × $13.75 per hour = $74,250	5,400 hours × $14.00 per hour = $75,600	5,000 hours* × $14.00 per hour = $70,000

Rate variance, $1,350 F   Efficiency variance, $5,600 U

Total variance, $4,250 U

*2,000 units × 2.5 hours per unit = 5,000 hours.
F = Favorable; U = Unfavorable.

Using these data and the standard costs from Exhibit 10–2, Terry computed the direct labor rate and efficiency variances that appear in Exhibit 10–6.

Notice that the column headings in Exhibit 10–6 are the same as those used in the prior two exhibits, except that in Exhibit 10–6 the terms *hours* and *rate* are used in place of the terms *quantity* and *price*.

Labor Rate Variance—A Closer Look

As explained earlier, the price variance for direct labor is commonly termed a **labor rate variance.** This variance measures any deviation from standard in the average hourly rate paid to direct labor workers. The formula for the labor rate variance is expressed as follows:

$$\text{Labor rate variance} = (AH \times AR) - (AH \times SR)$$

Actual hours	Actual rate	Standard rate

The formula can be factored as follows:

$$\text{Labor rate variance} = AH(AR - SR)$$

Using the data from Exhibit 10–6 in the formula, the labor rate variance can be computed as follows:

$$5,400 \text{ hours } (\$13.75 \text{ per hour} - \$14.00 \text{ per hour}) = \$1,350 \text{ F}$$

In most companies, the wage rates paid to workers are quite predictable. Nevertheless, rate variances can arise because of the way labor is used. Skilled workers with high hourly rates of pay may be given duties that require little skill and call for lower hourly rates of pay. This will result in an unfavorable labor rate variance, since the actual hourly rate of pay will exceed the standard rate specified for the particular task. In contrast, a favorable rate variance would result when workers who are paid at a rate lower than specified in the standard are assigned to the task. However, the lower-paid workers may not be as efficient. Finally,

Topic Tackler
PLUS
10–2

overtime work at premium rates will result in an unfavorable rate variance if the overtime premium is charged to the direct labor account.

Who is responsible for controlling the labor rate variance? Since labor rate variances generally arise as a result of how labor is used, production supervisors are usually responsible for seeing that labor rate variances are kept under control.

Labor Efficiency Variance—A Closer Look

The **labor efficiency variance** attempts to measure the productivity of direct labor. No variance is more closely watched by management, since it is widely believed that increasing direct labor productivity is vital to reducing costs. The formula for the labor efficiency variance is expressed as follows:

$$\text{Labor efficiency variance} = (AH \times SR) - (SH \times SR)$$

| Actual | Standard | Standard hours |
| hours | rate | allowed for actual output |

The formula can be factored as follows:

$$\text{Labor efficiency variance} = SR(AH - SH)$$

Using the data from Exhibit 10–6 in the formula, we have the following:

$$\$14.00 \text{ per hour } (5,400 \text{ hours} - 5,000 \text{ hours*}) = \$5,600 \text{ U}$$

*2,000 units × 2.5 hours per unit = 5,000 hours.

Possible causes of an unfavorable labor efficiency variance include poorly trained or motivated workers; poor quality materials, requiring more labor time; faulty equipment, causing breakdowns and work interruptions; poor supervision of workers; and inaccurate standards. The managers in charge of production would usually be responsible for control of the labor efficiency variance. However, the purchasing manager could be held responsible if the purchase of poor-quality materials resulted in excessive labor processing time.

Another important cause of an unfavorable labor efficiency variance may be insufficient demand for the company's products. Managers in some companies argue that it is difficult, and perhaps unwise, to constantly adjust the workforce in response to changes in the amount of work that needs to be done. In such companies, the direct labor workforce is essentially fixed in the short run. If demand is insufficient to keep everyone busy, workers are not laid off. In this case, if demand falls below the level needed to keep everyone busy, an unfavorable labor efficiency variance will often be recorded.

If customer orders are insufficient to keep the workers busy, the work center manager has two options—either accept an unfavorable labor efficiency variance or build inventory.[3] A central lesson of Lean Production is that building inventory with no immediate prospect of sale is a bad idea. Excessive inventory—particularly work in process inventory—leads to high defect rates, obsolete goods, and inefficient operations. As a consequence, when the workforce is basically fixed in the short term, managers must be cautious about how labor efficiency variances are used. Some experts advocate eliminating labor efficiency variances in such situations—at least for the purposes of motivating and controlling workers on the shop floor.

---

[3] For further discussion, see Eliyahu M. Goldratt and Jeff Cox, *The Goal,* 2nd rev. ed. (Croton-on-Hudson, NY: North River Press).

DOES DIRECT LABOR VARIANCE REPORTING INCREASE PRODUCTIVITY?

Professors Rajiv Banker, Sarv Devaraj, Roger Schroeder, and Kingshuk Sinha studied the direct labor variance reporting practices at 18 plants of a Fortune 500 manufacturing company. Seven of the plants eliminated direct labor variance reporting and the other 11 plants did not. The group of seven plants that eliminated direct labor variance reporting experienced an 11% decline in labor productivity, which was significantly greater than the decline experienced by the other 11 plants. The authors estimated that the annual loss due to the decline in labor productivity across the seven plants of $1,996,000 was only partially offset by the $200,000 saved by eliminating the need to track direct labor variances.

While these findings suggest that direct labor variance reporting is a useful tool for monitoring direct labor workers, advocates of Lean Production would argue otherwise. They would claim that direct labor variance reporting is a non-value-added activity that encourages excessive production and demoralizes direct labor workers. The two points of view provide an interesting opportunity to debate the appropriate role of management accounting within organizations.

Source: Rajiv Banker, Sarv Devaraj, Roger Schroeder, and Kingshuk Sinha, "Performance Impact of the Elimination of Direct Labor Variance Reporting: A Field Study," *Journal of Accounting Research*, September 2002, pp. 1013–1036.

Using Standard Costs—Variable Manufacturing Overhead Variances

The final step in Terry Sherman's analysis of Colonial Pewter's variances for June was to compute the variable manufacturing overhead variances. The variable portion of manufacturing overhead can be analyzed using the same basic formulas that are used to analyze direct materials and direct labor. Recall from Exhibit 10–2 that the standard variable manufacturing overhead is $7.50 per unit of product, computed as follows:

LEARNING OBJECTIVE 4
Compute the variable manufacturing overhead spending and efficiency variances.

$$2.5 \text{ hours per unit} \times \$3.00 \text{ per hour} = \$7.50 \text{ per unit}$$

Colonial Pewter's cost records showed that the total actual variable manufacturing overhead cost for June was $15,390. Recall from the earlier discussion of the direct labor variances that 5,400 hours of direct labor time were recorded during the month and that the company produced 2,000 pairs of bookends. Terry's analysis of this overhead data appears in Exhibit 10–7.

EXHIBIT 10–7
Variance Analysis—Variable
Manufacturing Overhead

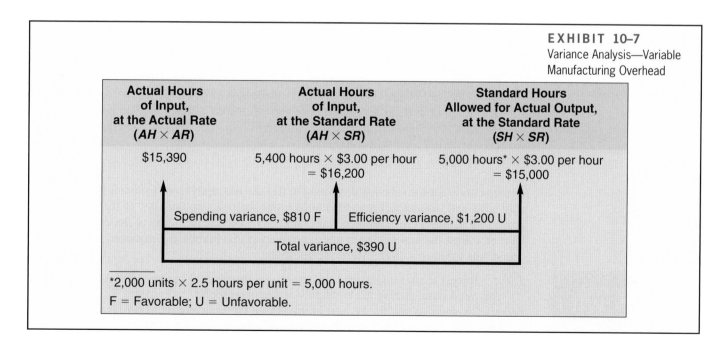

Actual Hours of Input, at the Actual Rate (*AH* × *AR*)	Actual Hours of Input, at the Standard Rate (*AH* × *SR*)	Standard Hours Allowed for Actual Output, at the Standard Rate (*SH* × *SR*)
$15,390	5,400 hours × $3.00 per hour = $16,200	5,000 hours* × $3.00 per hour = $15,000

Spending variance, $810 F   Efficiency variance, $1,200 U

Total variance, $390 U

*2,000 units × 2.5 hours per unit = 5,000 hours.
F = Favorable; U = Unfavorable.

Notice the similarities between Exhibits 10–6 and 10–7. These similarities arise from the fact that direct labor-hours are being used as the base for allocating overhead cost to units of product; thus, the same hourly figures appear in Exhibit 10–7 for variable manufacturing overhead as in Exhibit 10–6 for direct labor. The main difference between the two exhibits is in the standard hourly rate being used, which in this company is much lower for variable manufacturing overhead than for direct labor.

Manufacturing Overhead Variances—A Closer Look

The formula for the **variable overhead spending variance** is expressed as follows:

Variable overhead spending variance = $(AH \times AR) - (AH \times SR)$

Actual hours   Actual rate   Standard rate

This formula can be factored as follows:

Variable overhead spending variance = $AH(AR - SR)$

Using the data from Exhibit 10–7 in the formula, the variable overhead spending variance can be computed as follows:

5,400 hours ($2.85 per hour* − $3.00 per hour) = $810 F

*$15,390 ÷ 5,400 hours = $2.85 per hour.

The formula for the **variable overhead efficiency variance** is expressed as follows:

Variable overhead efficiency variance = $(AH \times SR) - (SH \times SR)$

Actual hours   Standard rate   Standard hours allowed for actual output

This formula can be factored as follows:

Variable overhead efficiency variance = $SR(AH - SH)$

Again using the data from Exhibit 10–7, the variance can be computed as follows:

$3.00 per hour (5,400 hours − 5,000 hours*) = $1,200 U

*2,000 units × 2.5 hours per unit = 5,000 hours.

We will reserve further discussion of the variable overhead spending and efficiency variances until the next chapter, where overhead analysis is discussed in depth.

Before proceeding further, we suggest that you pause at this point and go back and review the data contained in Exhibits 10–2 through 10–7. These exhibits and the accompanying text discussion provide a comprehensive, integrated illustration of standard setting and variance analysis.

MANAGERIAL ACCOUNTING IN ACTION

The Wrap-up

In preparation for the scheduled meeting to discuss her analysis of Colonial Pewter's standard costs and variances, Terry distributed Exhibits 10–2 through 10–7 to the management group of Colonial Pewter. This included J. D. Wriston, the president of the company; Tom Kuchel, the production manager; and Janet Warner, the purchasing manager. J. D. Wriston opened the meeting with the following question:

J. D.:   Terry, I think I understand the report you distributed, but just to make sure, would you mind summarizing the highlights of what you found?

Terry: As you can see, the biggest problems are the unfavorable materials quantity variance of $2,000 and the unfavorable labor efficiency variance of $5,600.

J. D.:   Tom, you're the production boss. What do you think is causing the unfavorable labor efficiency variance?

Tom: It has to be the new production workers. Our experienced workers shouldn't have much problem meeting the standard of 2.5 hours per unit. We all knew that there would be some inefficiency for a while as we brought new people on board. My plan for overcoming the problem is to pair up each of the new guys with one of our old-timers and have them work together for a while. It would slow down our older guys a bit, but I'll bet the unfavorable variance disappears and our new workers would learn a lot.

J. D.:   Sounds good. Now, what about that $2,000 unfavorable materials quantity variance?

Terry: Tom, are the new workers generating a lot of scrap?

Tom: Yeah, I guess so.

J. D.:   I think that could be part of the problem. Can you do anything about it?

Tom: I can watch the scrap closely for a few days to see where it's being generated. If it is the new workers, I can have the old-timers work with them on the problem when I team them up.

J. D.:   Janet, the favorable materials price variance of $1,300 isn't helping us if it is contributing to the unfavorable materials quantity and labor efficiency variances. Let's make sure that our raw material purchases conform to our quality standards.

Janet: Fair enough.

J. D.:   Good. Let's reconvene in a few weeks to see what has happened. Hopefully, we can get those unfavorable variances under control.

Variance Analysis and Management by Exception

Variance analysis and performance reports are important elements of *management by exception*, which is an approach that emphasizes focusing on those areas of responsibility where goals and expectations are not being met.

The budgets and standards discussed in this chapter and in the preceding chapter reflect management's plans. If all goes according to plan, there will be little difference between actual results and the results that would be expected according to the budgets and standards. If this happens, managers can concentrate on other issues. However, if actual results do not conform to the budget and to standards, the performance reporting system sends a signal to managers that an "exception" has occurred. This signal is in the form of a variance from the budget or standards.

However, are all variances worth investigating? The answer is no. Differences between actual results and what was expected will almost always occur. If every variance were investigated, management would waste a great deal of time tracking down nickel-and-dime differences. Variances may occur for a variety of reasons—only some of which are significant and worthy of management's attention. For example, hotter-than-normal weather in the summer may result in higher-than-expected electrical bills for air conditioning. Or, workers may work slightly faster or slower on a particular day. Because of unpredictable random factors, one can expect that virtually every cost category will produce a variance of some kind.

How should managers decide which variances are worth investigating? One clue is the size of the variance. A variance of $5 is probably not big enough to warrant attention, whereas a variance of $5,000 might well be worth tracking down. Another clue is the size of the variance relative to the amount of spending. A variance that is only 0.1% of spending on an item is likely to be well within the bounds one would normally expect due to random factors. On the other hand, a variance of 10% of spending is much more likely to be a signal that something is wrong.

A more dependable approach is to plot variance data on a statistical control chart, such as illustrated in Exhibit 10–8 (page 436). The basic idea underlying a statistical

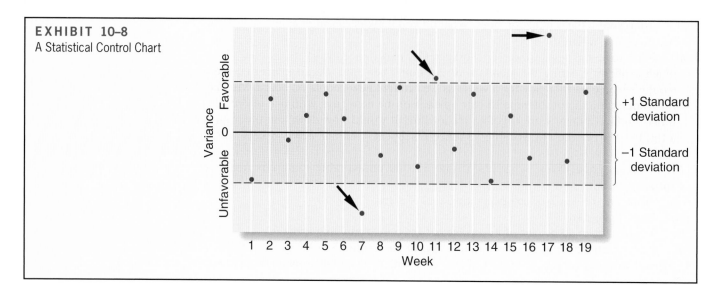

EXHIBIT 10–8
A Statistical Control Chart

control chart is that some random fluctuations in variances from period to period are normal. A variance should only be investigated when it is unusual relative to that normal level of random fluctuation. Typically, the standard deviation of the variances is used as the measure of the normal level of fluctuations. A rule of thumb is adopted such as "investigate all variances that are more than X standard deviations from zero." In the control chart in Exhibit 10–8, X is 1.0. That is, the rule of thumb in this company is to investigate all variances that are more than one standard deviation in either direction (favorable or unfavorable) from zero. This means that the variances in weeks 7, 11, and 17 would have been investigated, but none of the others.

What value of X should be chosen? The bigger the value of X, the wider the band of acceptable variances that would not be investigated. Thus, the bigger the value of X, the less time will be spent tracking down variances, but the more likely it is that a real out-of-control situation will be overlooked. Ordinarily, if X is selected to be 1.0, roughly 30% of all variances will trigger an investigation even though there is no real problem. If X is set at 1.5, the figure drops to about 13%. If X is set at 2.0, the figure drops all the way to about 5%. Don't forget, however, that selecting a big value of X will result not only in fewer false alarms but also a higher probability that a real problem will be overlooked.

In addition to watching for unusually large variances, the pattern of the variances should be monitored. For example, a run of steadily mounting variances should trigger an investigation even though none of the variances is large enough by itself to warrant investigation.

International Uses of Standard Costs

Standard costs are used by companies throughout the world. One study found that three-fourths of the companies surveyed in the United Kingdom, two-thirds of the companies surveyed in Canada, and 40% of the companies surveyed in Japan used standard cost systems.[4]

Standard costs were first introduced in Japan after World War II, with Nippon Electronics Company (NEC) being one of the first Japanese companies to adopt standard costs for all of its products. Many other Japanese companies followed NEC's lead and developed standard

---

[4]   Shin'ichi Inoue, "Comparative Studies of Recent Development of Cost Management Problems in U.S.A., U.K., Canada, and Japan," Research Paper No. 29, Kagawa University, p. 17. The study included 95 United States companies, 52 United Kingdom companies, 82 Canadian companies, and 646 Japanese companies.

	United States	United Kingdom	Canada	Japan
Cost management	1*	2	2	1
Budgetary planning and control†	2	3	1	3
Pricing decisions	3	1	3	2
Financial statement preparation	4	4	4	4

*The numbers 1 through 4 denote importance of use, from greatest to least.
†Includes management planning.
Source: Compiled from data in a study by Shin'ichi Inoue, "Comparative Studies of Recent Development of Cost Management Problems in U.S.A., U.K., Canada, and Japan," Research Paper No. 29, Kagawa University, p. 20.

EXHIBIT 10–9
Uses of Standard Costs in Four Countries

cost systems. The ways in which these standard costs are used in Japan—and also in the other countries cited above—are shown in Exhibit 10–9.

Over time, the pattern of use shown in Exhibit 10–9 may change, but at present managers can expect to encounter standard costs in most industrialized nations. Moreover, the most important uses are for cost management and budgetary planning purposes.

Evaluation of Controls Based on Standard Costs

Advantages of Standard Costs

Standard cost systems have a number of advantages.

1. Standard costs are a key element in a management by exception approach. If costs conform to the standards, managers can focus on other issues. When costs are significantly outside the standards, managers are alerted that problems may exist that require attention. This approach helps managers focus on important issues.
2. Standards that are viewed as reasonable by employees can promote economy and efficiency. They provide benchmarks that individuals can use to judge their own performance.
3. Standard costs can greatly simplify bookkeeping. Instead of recording actual costs for each job, the standard costs for direct materials, direct labor, and overhead can be charged to jobs.
4. Standard costs fit naturally in an integrated system of "responsibility accounting." The standards establish what costs should be, who should be responsible for them, and whether actual costs are under control.

Potential Problems with the Use of Standard Costs

The improper use of standard costs can present a number of potential problems.

1. Standard cost variance reports are usually prepared on a monthly basis and often are released days or even weeks after the end of the month. As a consequence, the information in the reports may be so outdated that it is almost useless. Timely, frequent reports that are approximately correct are better than infrequent reports that are very precise but out of date by the time they are released. Some companies are now reporting variances and other key operating data daily or even more frequently.
2. If managers are insensitive and use variance reports as a club, morale will suffer. Employees should receive positive reinforcement for work well done. Management by exception, by its nature, tends to focus on the negative. If variances are used as a club, subordinates may be tempted to cover up unfavorable variances or take actions that are not in the best interests of the company to make sure the variances are favorable. For

example, workers may put on a crash effort to increase output at the end of the month to avoid an unfavorable labor efficiency variance. In the rush to produce more output, quality may suffer.

3. Labor quantity standards and efficiency variances make two important assumptions. First, they assume that the production process is labor-paced; if labor works faster, output will go up. However, output in many companies is not determined by how fast labor works; rather, it is determined by the processing speed of machines. Second, the computations assume that labor is a variable cost. However, direct labor may be essentially fixed. If labor is fixed, then an undue emphasis on labor efficiency variances creates pressure to build excess inventories.

4. In some cases, a "favorable" variance can be as bad or worse than an "unfavorable" variance. For example, McDonald's has a standard for the amount of hamburger meat that should be in a Big Mac. A "favorable" variance would mean that less meat was used than the standard specifies. The result is a substandard Big Mac and possibly a dissatisfied customer.

5. Too much emphasis on meeting the standards may overshadow other important objectives such as maintaining and improving quality, on-time delivery, and customer satisfaction. This tendency can be reduced by using supplemental performance measures that focus on these other objectives.

6. Just meeting standards may not be sufficient; continual improvement may be necessary to survive in a competitive environment. For this reason, some companies focus on the trends in the standard cost variances—aiming for continual improvement rather than just meeting the standards. In other companies, engineered standards are replaced either by a rolling average of actual costs, which is expected to decline, or by very challenging target costs.

In sum, managers should exercise considerable care when using a standard cost system. It is particularly important that managers go out of their way to focus on the positive, rather than just on the negative, and to be aware of possible unintended consequences.

Nevertheless, standard costs are found in the vast majority of manufacturing companies and in many service companies, although their use is changing. For evaluating performance, standard cost variances are often complemented by a performance measurement system called the *balanced scorecard,* which is discussed in the next section. The balanced scorecard concept has been eagerly embraced by a wide variety of organizations including Analog Devices, KPMG, Tenneco, Allstate, AT&T, Elf Atochem, Conair-Franklin, CIGNA Corporation, London Life Insurance Co., Southern Gardens Citrus Processing, Duke Children's Hospital, JP Morgan Chase, 3COM, Rockwater, Apple Computer, Advanced Micro Devices (AMD), FMC, the Bank of Montreal, the Massachusetts Special Olympics, United Way of Southeastern New England, Boston Lyric Opera, Bridgeport Hospital and Healthcare Services, Housing Authority of Fiji, and Verizon Communications. It has been estimated that about half of all Fortune 1000 companies have implemented a balanced scorecard.

Balanced Scorecard

LEARNING OBJECTIVE 5
Understand how a balanced scorecard fits together and how it supports a company's strategy.

A **balanced scorecard** consists of an integrated set of performance measures that are derived from and support the company's strategy throughout the organization. A strategy is essentially a theory about how to achieve the organization's goals. For example, Southwest Airlines' strategy is to offer an *operational excellence* customer value proposition that has three key components—low ticket prices, convenience, and reliability. The company operates only one type of aircraft, the Boeing 737, to reduce maintenance and training costs and simplify scheduling. It further reduces costs by not offering meals, seat assignments, or baggage transfers and by booking a large portion of its passenger revenue over the Internet. Southwest also uses point-to-point flights rather than the hub-and-spoke approach of its larger competitors, thereby providing customers convenient, nonstop service to their final destination. Since Southwest serves many less-congested airports such as Chicago Midway, Burbank, Manchester, Oakland, and Providence, it offers quicker passenger check-ins and reliable departures, while maintaining high asset utilization (i.e., the company's average gate turnaround time of 25 minutes enables it to function with fewer planes and gates). Overall, the company's strategy has worked. At a time when Southwest Airlines' larger competitors are struggling, it continues to earn substantial profits.

Under the balanced scorecard approach, top management translates its strategy into performance measures that employees can understand and influence. For example, the amount of time passengers have to wait in line to have their baggage checked might be a performance measure for the supervisor in charge of the Southwest Airlines check-in counter at the Burbank airport. This performance measure is easily understood by the supervisor, and can be improved by the supervisor's actions.

IN BUSINESS

WHY DO COMPANIES FAIL TO EXECUTE THEIR STRATEGIES?

Robert Paladino served as the vice president and global leader of the Telecommunications and Utility Practice for the Balanced Scorecard Collaborative—a consulting organization that works with companies to implement balanced scorecards. He offers four reasons why nine out of ten organizations fail to execute their business strategies.

First, only 5% of a company's workforce understands their organization's strategy. Paladino commented "if employees don't understand the strategic objectives, then they could be focused on closing the wrong performance gaps." Second, 85% of management teams spend less than one hour per month discussing strategy. Managers cannot effectively implement strategies if they do not spend enough time talking about them. Third, 60% of organizations do not link their budgets to strategy. The inevitable result is that companies pursue "financial strategies that differ from or, worse, may be in conflict with their business and customer quality strategies." Finally, only 25% of managers have their incentives linked to strategy. Thus, most managers are working to maximize their compensation by improving strategically misguided metrics.

Paladino says the balanced scorecard overcomes these four barriers because it helps employees focus their actions on executing organizational strategies.

Source: Robert E. Paladino, "Balanced Forecasts Drive Value," *Strategic Finance*, January 2005, pp. 37–42.

Common Characteristics of Balanced Scorecards

Performance measures used in the balanced scorecard approach tend to fall into the four groups illustrated in Exhibit 10–10 (page 440): financial, customer, internal business processes, and learning and growth. Internal business processes are what the company does in an attempt to satisfy customers. For example, in a manufacturing company, assembling a product is an internal business process. In an airline, handling baggage is an internal business process. The idea underlying these groupings (as indicated by the vertical arrows in Exhibit 10–10) is that learning is necessary to improve internal business processes; improving business processes is necessary to improve customer satisfaction; and improving customer satisfaction is necessary to improve financial results.

Note that the emphasis in Exhibit 10–10 is on *improvement*—not on just attaining some specific objective such as profits of $10 million. In the balanced scorecard approach, continual improvement is encouraged. If an organization does not continually improve, it will eventually lose out to competitors that do.

Financial performance measures appear at the top of Exhibit 10–10. Ultimately, most companies exist to provide financial rewards to owners. There are exceptions. Some companies—for example, The Body Shop—may have loftier goals such as providing environmentally friendly

EXHIBIT 10–10
From Strategy to
Performance Measures:
The Balanced Scorecard

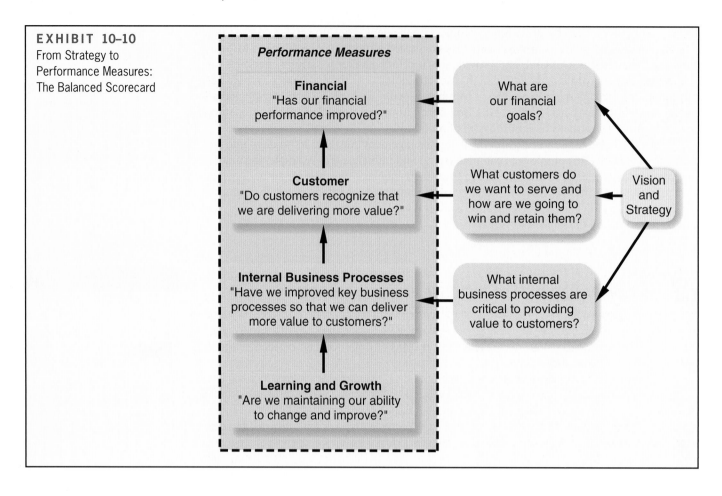

products to consumers. However, even nonprofit organizations must generate enough financial resources to stay in operation.

However, for several reasons, financial performance measures are not sufficient in themselves—they should be integrated with nonfinancial measures in a well-designed balanced scorecard. First, financial measures are lag indicators that report on the results of past actions. In contrast, nonfinancial measures of key success drivers such as customer satisfaction are leading indicators of future financial performance. Second, top managers are ordinarily responsible for the financial performance measures—not lower-level managers. The supervisor in charge of checking in passengers can be held responsible for how long passengers have to wait in line. However, this supervisor cannot reasonably be held responsible for the entire company's profit. That is the responsibility of the airline's top managers. We will have more to say about financial performance measures in later chapters.

Exhibit 10–11 lists some examples of performance measures that can be found on the balanced scorecards of companies. However, few companies, if any, would use all of these performance measures, and almost all companies would add other performance measures. Managers should carefully select performance measures for their own company's balanced scorecard, keeping the following points in mind. First and foremost, the performance measures should be consistent with, and follow from, the company's strategy. If the performance measures are not consistent with the company's strategy, people will find themselves working at cross-purposes. Second, the performance measures should be understandable and controllable to a significant extent by those being evaluated. Third, the scorecard should not have too many performance measures. This can lead to a lack of focus and confusion.

While the entire organization will have an overall balanced scorecard, each responsible individual will have his or her own personal scorecard as well. This scorecard should

EXHIBIT 10–11
Examples of Performance
Measures for Balanced
Scorecards

Customer Perspective

Performance Measure	Desired Change
Customer satisfaction as measured by survey results	+
Number of customer complaints	−
Market share	+
Product returns as a percentage of sales	−
Percentage of customers retained from last period	+
Number of new customers	+

Internal Business Processes Perspective

Performance Measure	Desired Change
Percentage of sales from new products	+
Time to introduce new products to market	−
Percentage of customer calls answered within 20 seconds	+
On-time deliveries as a percentage of all deliveries	+
Work in process inventory as a percentage of sales	−
Unfavorable standard cost variances	−
Defect-free units as a percentage of completed units	+
Delivery cycle time*	−
Throughput time*	−
Manufacturing cycle efficiency*	+
Quality costs[†]	−
Setup time	−
Time from call by customer to repair of product	−
Percent of customer complaints settled on first contact	+
Time to settle a customer claim	−

Learning and Growth Perspective

Performance Measure	Desired Change
Suggestions per employee	+
Value-added per employee[‡]	+
Employee turnover	−
Hours of in-house training per employee	+

*Explained later in this chapter.
[†]See Appendix 2B, Cost of Quality.
[‡]Value-added is revenue less externally purchased materials, supplies, and services.

consist of items the individual can personally influence that relate directly to the performance measures on the overall balanced scorecard. The performance measures on this personal scorecard should not be overly influenced by actions taken by others in the company or by events that are outside of the individual's control. And, focusing on the performance measure should not lead an individual to take actions that are counter to the organization's objectives.

With those broad principles in mind, we will now take a look at how a company's strategy affects its balanced scorecard.

LOSING SIGHT OF THE CUSTOMER

Understanding customer needs sounds simple enough, but it is surprising how often companies lose sight of what their customers want. For example, Waste Management, one of the largest trash haulers in the United States, assumed that its customers were most interested in receiving low prices. However, when the company actually surveyed its customers, it found out that they were more concerned about billing errors and missed garbage pickups. Waste Management responded to this feedback by upgrading its billing program—as a result customers are paying their bills in an average of 47 days instead of 71. Not only are customers happier with fewer billing errors, but shaving 24 days off the accounts receivable collection cycle is worth $30 million per day to the company!

Waste Management also addressed the issue of missed garbage pickups by initiating a program called Haul or Call. When a garbage truck driver sees an impediment blocking a garbage bin, his home office calls the customer to see when they can reschedule a pickup. Customers have been so impressed with this level of service that their defection rate has dropped from 12% to 8.6% in less than one year.

Waste Management has found that the key to improving bottom-line results is gathering information from its customers about the underlying drivers of financial performance.

Source: Julie Creswell, "Scandal Hits—Now What?" *Fortune*, July 7, 2003, pp. 127–130.

IN DENIAL

Larry Bossidy, the long-time CEO of Allied Signal, reports that "When I took over at Allied Signal . . . I got two different pictures from our people and our customers. While our people were saying that we were delivering an order-fill rate of 98%, our customers thought we were at 60%. The irony was, instead of trying to address the customers' complaints, we seemed to think we had to show that we were right and they were wrong." Note the two messages contained in this short quotation. First, make sure you measure the right thing. Apparently, the internal measure of order-fill rates that had been used at Allied Signal was deficient—it did not capture customer perceptions, which are of paramount importance. Second, if customers are unhappy, don't tell them they are wrong. Try to figure out why they are unhappy.

Source: Larry Bossidy and Ram Charan, "How Did Honeywell Chairman Larry Bossidy Turn the Company Around? By His Maniacal Focus on Just One Thing: Execution," *Fortune*, June 10, 2002, pp. 149–152.

A Company's Strategy and the Balanced Scorecard

Returning to the performance measures in Exhibit 10–10, each company must decide which customers to target and what internal business processes are crucial to attracting and retaining those customers. Different companies, having different strategies, will target different customers with different kinds of products and services. Take the automobile industry as an example. BMW stresses engineering and handling; Volvo, safety; Jaguar, luxury detailing; Corvette, racy styling; and Toyota, reliability. Because of these differences in emphases, a one-size-fits-all approach to performance measurement won't work even within this one industry. Performance measures must be tailored to the specific strategy of each company.

Suppose, for example, that Jaguar's strategy is to offer distinctive, richly finished luxury automobiles to wealthy individuals who prize handcrafted, individualized products. To deliver this customer intimacy value proposition to its wealthy target customers, Jaguar might create such a large number of options for details, such as leather seats, interior and exterior color combinations, and wooden dashboards, that each car becomes virtually one of a kind. For example, instead of just offering tan or blue leather seats in standard cowhide, the company may offer customers the choice of an almost infinite palette of colors in any of a number of different exotic leathers. For such a system to work effectively, Jaguar would have to be able to deliver a completely customized car within a reasonable amount of time—and without incurring more cost for this customization than the customer is willing to pay. Exhibit 10–12 suggests how Jaguar might reflect this strategy in its balanced scorecard.

If the balanced scorecard is correctly constructed, the performance measures should be linked together on a cause-and-effect basis. Each link can then be read as a hypothesis in the form "If we improve this performance measure, then this other performance measure should also improve." Starting from the bottom of Exhibit 10–12, we can read the links between performance measures as follows. If employees acquire the skills to install new options more effectively, then the company can offer more options and the options can be installed in less time. If more options are available and they are installed in less time, then customer surveys should show greater satisfaction with the range of options available. If customer satisfaction improves, then the number of cars sold should increase. In addition, if customer satisfaction improves, the company should be able to maintain or increase its selling prices, and if the time to install options decreases, the costs of installing the options should decrease. Together, this should result in an increase in the contribution margin

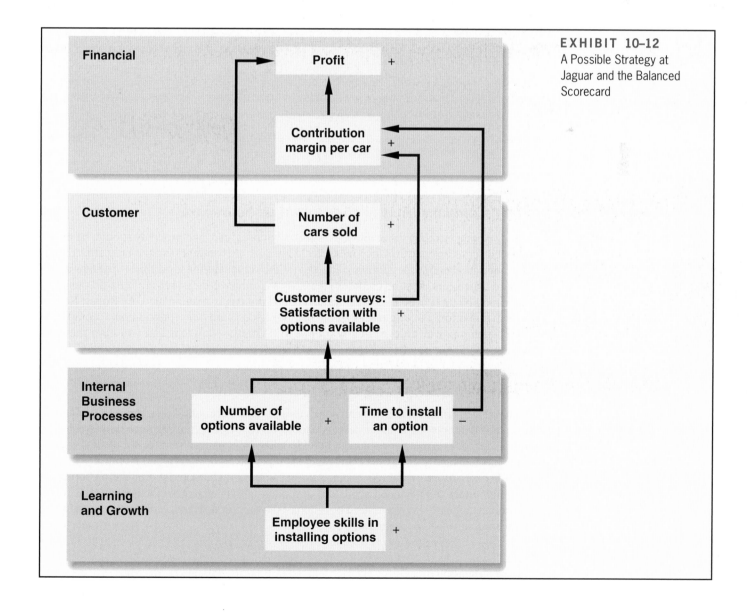

EXHIBIT 10–12
A Possible Strategy at Jaguar and the Balanced Scorecard

per car. If the contribution margin per car increases and more cars are sold, the result should be an increase in profits.

In essence, the balanced scorecard lays out a theory of how the company can take concrete actions to attain its desired outcomes (financial, in this case). While the strategy laid out in Exhibit 10–12 seems plausible, it should be regarded as only a theory. For example, if the company succeeds in increasing the number of options available and in decreasing the time required to install options and yet there is no increase in customer satisfaction, the number of cars sold, the contribution margin per car, or profits, the strategy would have to be reconsidered. One of the advantages of the balanced scorecard is that it continually tests the theories underlying management's strategy. If a strategy is not working, it should become evident when some of the predicted effects (i.e., more car sales) don't occur. Without this feedback, the organization may drift on indefinitely with an ineffective strategy based on faulty assumptions.

IN BUSINESS

CAUSE-AND-EFFECT IS THE KEY

Professors Christopher D. Ittner and David F. Larcker surveyed 157 companies and found that only 23% consistently verified the hypothesized cause-and-effect linkages embedded in their balanced scorecards. These companies earned a 5.14% higher return on common stockholders' equity than the 77% of companies that did not verify their cause-and-effect linkages.

The authors found that most companies do not verify cause-and-effect linkages because they erroneously believe that they are self-evident. For example, one fast-food chain chose employee turnover as a performance measure believing that its positive effects on profits were obvious. However, the professors' research revealed that the fast-food chain's profitability was only influenced by turnover among its supervisors, not lower-level employees. A broad measure of employee turnover did not help explain differences in profitability across restaurants.

Source: Christopher D. Ittner and David F. Larcker, "Coming Up Short on Nonfinancial Performance Measurement," *Harvard Business Review,* November 2003, pp. 88–95.

Tying Compensation to the Balanced Scorecard

Incentive compensation for employees, such as bonuses, can, and probably should, be tied to balanced scorecard performance measures. However, this should be done only after the organization has been successfully managed with the scorecard for some time—perhaps a year or more. Managers must be confident that the performance measures are reliable, sensible, understood by those who are being evaluated, and not easily manipulated. As Robert Kaplan and David Norton, the originators of the balanced scorecard concept point out, "compensation is such a powerful lever that you have to be pretty confident that you have the right measures and have good data for the measures before making the link."[5]

Advantages of Timely and Graphic Feedback

Whatever performance measures are used, they should be reported on a frequent and timely basis. For example, data about defects should be reported to the responsible managers at least once a day so that action can be quickly taken if an unusual number of defects occurs. In the most advanced companies, any defect is reported *immediately,* and its cause is tracked down before any more defects occur. Another common characteristic of the performance measures under the balanced scorecard approach is that managers focus on *trends* in the performance measures over time. The emphasis is on progress and *improvement* rather than on meeting any specific standard.

---

[5] Lori Calabro, "On Balance: A CFO Interview," *CFO,* February 2001, pp. 73–78.

For tracking trends and improvement over time, graphic displays are often far more informative than rows or columns of numbers. Consider, for example, the problem of passengers who reserve seats but do not show up to buy their tickets. Because of these "no-show" passengers, airlines routinely overbook popular flights. The airlines gamble that the number of overbooked passengers will be offset by the number of no-shows. Sometimes airlines lose this gamble. This results in the airline incurring substantial additional costs to either pay passengers to relinquish their reservations or to house and feed excess passengers until suitable replacement flights can be found. Because of these costs (and the ill will created among passengers), airlines carefully monitor the percentage of overbooked seats that actually turn out to be a problem and result in a passenger being bumped from a flight. Suppose, for example, that an airline has recorded the following data over the last 20 weeks:

Bumped passengers per hundred overbooked seats		Bumped passengers per hundred overbooked seats	
Week 1	7.1	Week 11	6.4
Week 2	6.5	Week 12	6.3
Week 3	6.7	Week 13	6.7
Week 4	7.2	Week 14	5.8
Week 5	7.0	Week 15	6.6
Week 6	7.3	Week 16	6.6
Week 7	6.7	Week 17	6.9
Week 8	6.5	Week 18	7.1
Week 9	6.2	Week 19	7.4
Week 10	5.8	Week 20	7.8

These data are plotted in Exhibit 10–13. Note how much easier it is to spot trends and unusual points when the data are plotted than when they are displayed in the form of a table. In particular, the worrisome increase in bumped passengers over the final seven weeks is very evident in the plotted data.

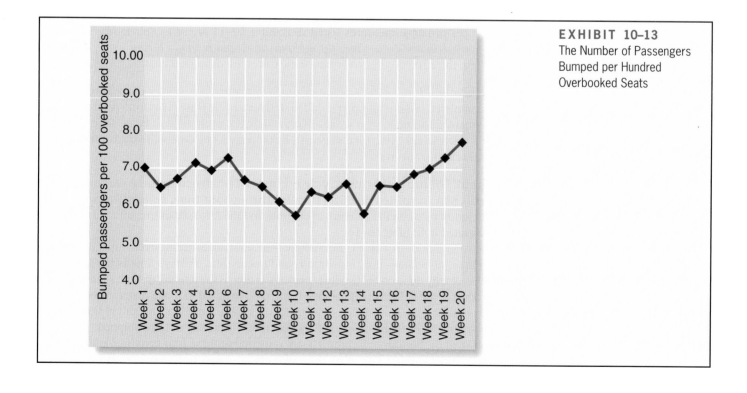

EXHIBIT 10–13
The Number of Passengers Bumped per Hundred Overbooked Seats

A PICTURE IS WORTH A THOUSAND NUMBERS

Graphics are routinely integrated in Balanced Scorecard reports, with data often displayed on a "dashboard" with representations of gauges and digital readouts. At Beverage Can Americas Co. in Chicago, a division of London-based Rexam Plc., executive dashboards and scorecards are being rolled out to thousands of employees. "Each worker sees a handful of metrics that pertain to his or her job, which are represented as green, yellow, or red icons depending on whether they are satisfactory, borderline, or subpar."

Source: Scott Leibs, "Now You See It," *CFO*, July 2002, pp. 61–66.

CORPORATE GOVERNANCE AND THE BALANCED SCORECARD

Historically, the board of directors of First Commonwealth Financial Corporation of Pennsylvania had only been given access to financial measures that were required for regulatory purposes. In the aftermath of corporate scandals such as Enron, Tyco, and WorldCom, the board decided to improve its oversight of the corporation by creating a balanced scorecard that not only helped ensure regulatory compliance but that also included forward-looking information about the company's strategy execution.

The board's scorecard had four main perspectives—learning and growth, internal, stakeholder, and financial. The internal perspective included three main processes—performance oversight, executive enhancement, and compliance and communication. For performance oversight, the board created measures related to approving strategies and overseeing execution and approving and monitoring funding for strategic initiatives. The executive enhancement measures focused on evaluating and rewarding executive performance and overseeing succession planning for key positions. The compliance and communication measures related to ensuring clear and reliable corporate disclosures and actively monitoring risk and regulatory compliance.

Source: Robert S. Kaplan and Michael Nagel, "First Commonwealth Financial Corporation," *Harvard Business School Publishing*, 2003, pp. 1–30.

LEARNING OBJECTIVE 6
Compute delivery cycle time, throughput time, and manufacturing cycle efficiency (MCE).

Some Measures of Internal Business Process Performance

Most of the performance measures listed in Exhibit 10–11 are self-explanatory. However, three are not—*delivery cycle time, throughput time,* and *manufacturing cycle efficiency (MCE).* These three important performance measures are discussed next.

Delivery Cycle Time   The amount of time from when a customer order is received to when the completed order is shipped is called **delivery cycle time.** This time is clearly a key concern to many customers, who would like the delivery cycle time to be as short as possible. Cutting the delivery cycle time may give a company a key competitive advantage—and may be necessary for survival.

Throughput (Manufacturing Cycle) Time   The amount of time required to turn raw materials into completed products is called **throughput time,** or *manufacturing cycle time.* The relation between the delivery cycle time and the throughput (manufacturing cycle) time is illustrated in Exhibit 10–14.

As shown in Exhibit 10–14, the throughput time, or manufacturing cycle time, is made up of process time, inspection time, move time, and queue time. *Process time* is the amount of time work is actually done on the product. *Inspection time* is the amount of time spent ensuring that the product is not defective. *Move time* is the time required to move materials or partially completed products from workstation to workstation. *Queue time* is the amount of time a product spends waiting to be worked on, to be moved, to be inspected, or to be shipped.

As shown at the bottom of Exhibit 10–14, only one of these four activities adds value to the product—process time. The other three activities—inspecting, moving, and queuing—add no value and should be eliminated as much as possible.

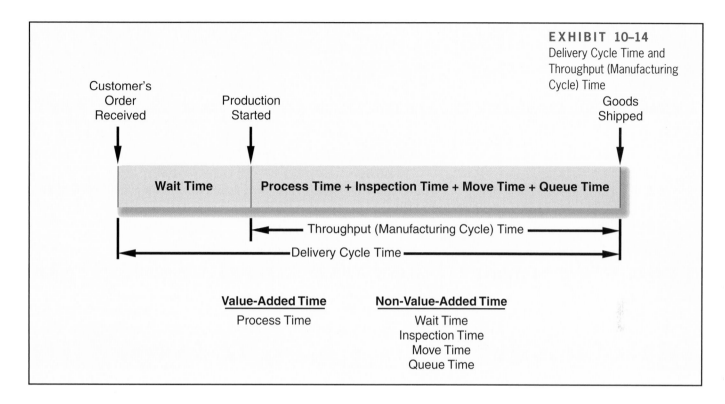

Manufacturing Cycle Efficiency (MCE)   Through concerted efforts to eliminate the *non-value-added* activities of inspecting, moving, and queuing, some companies have reduced their throughput time to only a fraction of previous levels. In turn, this has helped to reduce the delivery cycle time from months to only weeks or hours. Throughput time, which is considered to be a key measure in delivery performance, can be put into better perspective by computing the **manufacturing cycle efficiency (MCE).** The MCE is computed by relating the value-added time to the throughput time. The formula is:

$$MCE = \frac{\text{Value-added time (Process time)}}{\text{Throughput (manufacturing cycle) time}}$$

Any non-value-added time results in an MCE of less than 1. An MCE of 0.5, for example, would mean that half of the total production time consists of inspection, moving, and similar non-value-added activities. In many manufacturing companies, the MCE is less than 0.1 (10%), which means that 90% of the time a unit is in process is spent on activities that do not add value to the product. Monitoring the MCE helps companies to reduce non-value-added activities and thus get products into the hands of customers more quickly and at a lower cost.

Example   To provide an example of these measures, consider the following data for Novex Company:

Novex Company keeps careful track of the time to complete customer orders. During the most recent quarter, the following average times were recorded for each unit or order:

	Days
Wait time	17.0
Inspection time	0.4
Process time	2.0
Move time	0.6
Queue time	5.0

Goods are shipped as soon as production is completed.

Required:
1. Compute the throughput time.
2. Compute the manufacturing cycle efficiency (MCE).
3. What percentage of the production time is spent in non-value-added activities?
4. Compute the delivery cycle time.

Solution

1. Throughput time = Process time + Inspection time + Move time + Queue time
    = 2.0 days + 0.4 days + 0.6 days + 5.0 days
    = 8.0 days

2. Only process time represents value-added time; therefore, the computation of the MCE would be as follows:

$$\text{MCE} = \frac{\text{Value-added time}}{\text{Throughput time}} = \frac{2.0 \text{ days}}{8.0 \text{ days}}$$

$$= 0.25$$

    Thus, once put into production, a typical unit is actually being worked on only 25% of the time.

3. Since the MCE is 25%, 75% (100% − 25%) of total production time is spent in non-value-added activities.

4. Delivery cycle time = Wait time + Throughput time
    = 17.0 days + 8.0 days
    = 25.0 days

Some Final Observations Concerning the Balanced Scorecard   We would like to emphasize a few points concerning the balanced scorecard. First, the balanced scorecard should be tailored to the company's strategy; each company's balanced scorecard should be unique. The examples given in this chapter are just that—examples. They should not be interpreted as general templates to be fitted to each company. Second, the balanced scorecard reflects a particular strategy, or theory, about how a company can further its objectives by taking specific actions. The theory should be viewed as tentative and subject to change if the actions do not in fact result in improvements in the company's financial and other goals. If the theory (i.e., strategy) changes, then the performance measures on the balanced scorecard should also change. The balanced scorecard should be viewed as a dynamic system that evolves as the company's strategy evolves.

IN BUSINESS

DELIVERY CYCLE TIMES IN THE DARK AGES

Have you ever ordered a new magazine and counted how many days it took for the first issue to arrive? Chances are that your delivery cycle time was somewhere between four to six weeks—a glacial pace in today's Internet environment. One of the root causes of the problem is fragmented organizational structures where circulation, fulfillment, production, manufacturing, and distribution focus on their departmental agendas instead of the customer. Most circulation directors agree that removing non-value-added time from the process of responding to customer orders would certainly have its benefits. For example, customers who receive their first issue of the magazine sooner are likely to pay their bill sooner. Furthermore, they are less likely to cancel their subscription or issue complaints that are costly to resolve.

One way to reduce the problem is for publishers to mail the first issue to customers using first class mail rather than periodical mail. This would shave six to seven days off of their delivery cycle time, but it would also cost an extra 80 to 90 cents for each first issue mailed. Do you think the time saved is worth the money spent?

Source: William B. Dugan, "Thanks for Ordering our Magazine . . . Now Don't Expect to See It for Five Weeks," *Circulation Management*, May 1, 2004, pp. 24–29.

Summary

A standard is a benchmark or "norm" for measuring performance. Standards are set for both the cost and the quantity of inputs needed to manufacture goods or to provide services. Quantity standards indicate how much of an input, such as labor time or raw materials, should be used to make a product or provide a service. Cost standards indicate what the cost of the input should be.

Standards are normally set so that they can be attained by reasonable, though highly efficient, efforts. Such "practical" standards are believed to positively motivate employees.

When standards are compared to actual performance, the difference is referred to as a *variance*. Variances are computed and reported to management on a regular basis for both the price and the quantity elements of direct materials, direct labor, and overhead. Price variances are computed by taking the difference between actual and standard prices and multiplying the result by the amount of input purchased. Quantity variances are computed by taking the difference between the actual amount of the input used and the amount of input that is allowed for the actual output, and then multiplying the result by the standard price of the input.

Not all variances require management time or attention. Only unusual or particularly significant variances should be investigated—otherwise a great deal of time would be spent investigating unimportant matters. Additionally, it should be emphasized that the point of the investigation should not be to find someone to blame. The point of the investigation is to pinpoint the problem so that it can be fixed and operations improved.

Traditional standard cost variance reports are often supplemented with other performance measures. Overemphasis on standard cost variances may lead to problems in other critical areas such as product quality, inventory levels, and on-time delivery.

A balanced scorecard consists of an integrated system of performance measures that are derived from and support the company's strategy. Different companies will have different balanced scorecards because they have different strategies. A well-constructed balanced scorecard provides a means for guiding the company and also provides feedback concerning the effectiveness of the company's strategy.

Review Problem: Standard Costs

Xavier Company produces a single product. Variable manufacturing overhead is applied to products on the basis of direct labor-hours. The standard costs for one unit of product are as follows:

Direct material: 6 ounces at $0.50 per ounce	$3
Direct labor: 1.8 hours at $10 per hour	18
Variable manufacturing overhead: 1.8 hours at $5 per hour	9
Total standard variable cost per unit	$30

During June, 2,000 units were produced. The costs associated with June's operations were as follows:

Material purchased: 18,000 ounces at $0.60 per ounce	$10,800
Material used in production: 14,000 ounces	—
Direct labor: 4,000 hours at $9.75 per hour	$39,000
Variable manufacturing overhead costs incurred	$20,800

Required:

Compute the direct materials, direct labor, and variable manufacturing overhead variances.

Solution to the Review Problem

Direct Materials Variances

Actual Quantity of Input, at Actual Price ($AQ \times AP$)	Actual Quantity of Input, at Standard Price ($AQ \times SP$)	Standard Quantity Allowed for Actual Output, at Standard Price ($SQ \times SP$)
18,000 ounces × $0.60 per ounce = $10,800	18,000 ounces × $0.50 per ounce = $9,000	12,000 ounces* × $0.50 per ounce = $6,000

Price variance, $1,800 U

14,000 ounces × $0.50 per ounce = $7,000

Quantity variance, $1,000 U

———

*2,000 units × 6 ounces per unit = 12,000 ounces.

Using the formulas in the chapter, the same variances would be computed as follows:

$$\text{Materials price variance} = AQ(AP - SP)$$

$$18{,}000 \text{ ounces } (\$0.60 \text{ per ounce} - \$0.50 \text{ per ounce}) = \$1{,}800 \text{ U}$$

$$\text{Materials quantity variance} = SP(AQ - SQ)$$

$$\$0.50 \text{ per ounce } (14{,}000 \text{ ounces} - 12{,}000 \text{ ounces}) = \$1{,}000 \text{ U}$$

Direct Labor Variances

Actual Hours of Input, at the Actual Rate ($AH \times AR$)	Actual Hours of Input, at the Standard Rate ($AH \times SR$)	Standard Hours Allowed for Actual Output, at the Standard Rate ($SH \times SR$)
4,000 hours × $9.75 per hour = $39,000	4,000 hours × $10.00 per hour = $40,000	3,600 hours* × $10.00 per hour = $36,000

Rate variance, $1,000 F   Efficiency variance, $4,000 U

Total variance, $3,000 U

———

*2,000 units × 1.8 hours per unit = 3,600 hours.

Using the formulas in the chapter, the same variances would be computed as:

$$\text{Labor rate variance} = AH(AR - SR)$$

$$4{,}000 \text{ hours } (\$9.75 \text{ per hour} - \$10.00 \text{ per hour}) = \$1{,}000 \text{ F}$$

$$\text{Labor efficiency variance} = SR(AH - SH)$$

$$\$10.00 \text{ per hour } (4{,}000 \text{ hours} - 3{,}600 \text{ hours}) = \$4{,}000 \text{ U}$$

Variable Manufacturing Overhead Variances

Actual Hours of Input, at the Actual Rate (*AH* × *AR*)	Actual Hours of Input, at the Standard Rate (*AH* × *SR*)	Standard Hours Allowed for Actual Output, at the Standard Rate (*SH* × *SR*)
	4,000 hours × $\dfrac{\$5.00}{\text{per hour}}$	3,600 hours* × $\dfrac{\$5.00}{\text{per hour}}$
$20,800	= $20,000	= $18,000

Spending variance, $800 U   Efficiency variance, $2,000 U

Total variance, $2,800 U

*2,000 units × 1.8 hours per unit = 3,600 hours.

Using the formulas in the chapter, the same variances would be computed as follows:

$$\text{Variable overhead spending variance} = AH(AR - SR)$$

$$4{,}000 \text{ hours } (\$5.20 \text{ per hour*} - \$5.00 \text{ per hour}) = \$800 \text{ U}$$

$$\text{*}\$20{,}800 \div 4{,}000 \text{ hours} = \$5.20 \text{ per hour.}$$

$$\text{Variable overhead efficiency variance} = SR(AH - SH)$$

$$\$5.00 \text{ per hour } (4{,}000 \text{ hours} - 3{,}600 \text{ hours}) = \$2{,}000 \text{ U}$$

Glossary

Balanced scorecard An integrated set of performance measures that are derived from and support the organization's strategy. (p. 438)

Delivery cycle time The elapsed time from receipt of a customer order to when the completed goods are shipped to the customer. (p. 446)

Ideal standards Standards that assume peak efficiency at all times. (p. 421)

Labor efficiency variance The difference between the actual hours taken to complete a task and the standard hours allowed for the actual output, multiplied by the standard hourly labor rate. (p. 432)

Labor rate variance The difference between the actual hourly labor rate and the standard rate, multiplied by the number of hours worked during the period. (p. 431)

Management by exception A management system in which standards are set for various activities, with actual results compared to these standards. Significant deviations from standards are flagged as exceptions. (p. 419)

Manufacturing cycle efficiency (MCE) Process (value-added) time as a percentage of throughput time. (p. 447)

Materials price variance The difference between the actual unit price paid for an item and the standard price, multiplied by the quantity purchased. (p. 428)

Materials quantity variance The difference between the actual quantity of materials used in production and the standard quantity allowed for the actual output, multiplied by the standard price per unit of materials. (p. 429)

Practical standards Standards that allow for normal machine downtime and other work interruptions and that can be attained through reasonable, though highly efficient, efforts by the average worker. (p. 421)

Standard cost card A detailed listing of the standard amounts of inputs and their costs that are required to produce a unit of a specific product. (p. 421)

Standard cost per unit The standard quantity allowed of an input per unit of a specific product, multiplied by the standard price of the input. (p. 424)

Standard hours allowed The time that should have been taken to complete the period's output. It is computed by multiplying the actual number of units produced by the standard hours per unit. (p. 425)

Standard hours per unit The amount of direct labor time that should be required to complete a single unit of product, including allowances for breaks, machine downtime, cleanup, rejects, and other normal inefficiencies. (p. 423)

Standard price per unit The price that should be paid for an input. The price should be net of discounts and should include any shipping costs. (p. 422)

Standard quantity allowed The amount of an input that should have been used to complete the period's actual output. It is computed by multiplying the actual number of units produced by the standard quantity per unit. (p. 425)

Standard quantity per unit The amount of an input that should be required to complete a single unit of product, including allowances for normal waste, spoilage, rejects, and other normal inefficiencies. (p. 422)

Standard rate per hour The labor rate that should be incurred per hour of labor time, including employment taxes and fringe benefits. (p. 423)

Throughput time The amount of time required to turn raw materials into completed products. (p. 446)

Variable overhead efficiency variance The difference between the actual level of activity (direct labor-hours, machine-hours, or some other base) and the standard activity allowed, multiplied by the variable part of the predetermined overhead rate. (p. 434)

Variable overhead spending variance The difference between the actual variable overhead cost incurred during a period and the standard cost that should have been incurred based on the actual activity of the period. (p. 434)

Variances The differences between standard prices and actual prices and between standard quantities and actual quantities. (p. 425)

Appendix 10A: Journal Entries to Record Variances

LEARNING OBJECTIVE 7
Prepare journal entries to record standard costs and variances.

Although standard costs and variances can be computed and used by management without being formally entered into the accounting records, many organizations prefer to make formal journal entries. Formal entry tends to give variances a greater emphasis than informal, off-the-record computations. This emphasis signals management's desire to keep costs within the limits that have been set. In addition, formal use of standard costs simplifies the bookkeeping process enormously. Inventories and cost of goods sold can be valued at their standard costs—eliminating the need to keep track of the actual cost of each unit.

Direct Materials Variances

To illustrate the journal entries needed to record standard cost variances, we will return to the data contained in the review problem at the end of the chapter. The entry to record the purchase of direct materials would be as follows:

Raw Materials (18,000 ounces at $0.50 per ounce)............	9,000	
Materials Price Variance (18,000 ounces at $0.10 per ounce U).......................................	1,800	
Accounts Payable (18,000 ounces at $0.60 per ounce)......		10,800

Notice that the price variance is recognized when purchases are made, rather than when materials are actually used in production and that the materials are carried in the inventory account at standard cost. As direct materials are later drawn from inventory and used in production, the quantity variance is isolated as follows:

Work in Process (12,000 ounces at $0.50 per ounce)...........	6,000	
Materials Quantity Variance (2,000 ounces U at $0.50 per ounce)..	1,000	
Raw Materials (14,000 ounces at $0.50 per ounce).........		7,000

Thus, direct materials are added to the Work in Process account at the standard cost of the materials that should have been used to produce the actual output.

Notice that both the price variance and the quantity variance above are unfavorable and are debit entries. If either of these variances had been favorable, it would have appeared as a credit entry.

Direct Labor Variances

Referring again to the cost data in the review problem at the end of the chapter, the journal entry to record the incurrence of direct labor cost would be:

Work in Process (3,600 hours at $10.00 per hour).	36,000	
Labor Efficiency Variance (400 hours U at $10.00 per hour)	4,000	
Labor Rate Variance (4,000 hours at $0.25 per hour F)		1,000
Wages Payable (4,000 hours at $9.75 per hour)		39,000

Thus, as with direct materials, direct labor costs enter into the Work in Process account at standard, both in terms of the rate and in terms of the hours allowed for the actual production of the period. Note that the unfavorable labor efficiency variance is a debit entry whereas the favorable labor rate variance is a credit entry.

Variable Manufacturing Overhead Variances

Variable manufacturing overhead variances usually are not recorded in the accounts separately but rather are determined as part of the general analysis of overhead, which is discussed in the next chapter.

Cost Flows in a Standard Cost System

The flow of costs through the company's accounts are illustrated in Exhibit 10A–1. Note that entries into the various inventory accounts are made at standard cost—not actual cost. The differences between actual and standard costs are entered into special accounts that accumulate the various standard cost variances. Ordinarily, these standard cost variance accounts are closed out to Cost of Goods Sold at the end of the period. Unfavorable variances increase Cost of Goods Sold, and favorable variances decrease Cost of Goods Sold.

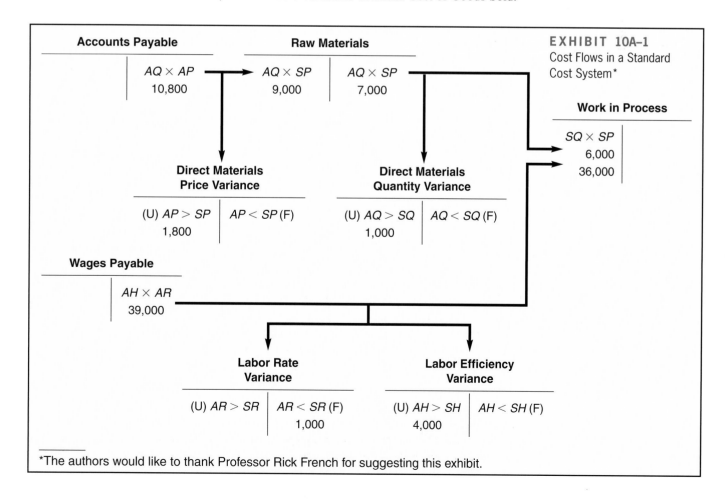

EXHIBIT 10A–1
Cost Flows in a Standard Cost System*

*The authors would like to thank Professor Rick French for suggesting this exhibit.

Questions

10-1   What is a quantity standard? What is a price standard?

10-2   Distinguish between ideal and practical standards.

10-3   If employees are chronically unable to meet a standard, what effect would you expect this to have on their productivity?

10-4   What is the difference between a standard and a budget?

10-5   What is meant by the term *variance?*

10-6   What is meant by the term *management by exception?*

10-7   Why are separate price and quantity variances computed?

10-8   Who is generally responsible for the materials price variance? The materials quantity variance? The labor efficiency variance?

10-9   The materials price variance can be computed at what two different points in time? Which point is better? Why?

10-10 If the materials price variance is favorable but the materials quantity variance is unfavorable, what might this indicate?

10-11 Should standards be used to identify who to blame for problems?

10-12 "Our workers are all under labor contracts; therefore, our labor rate variance is bound to be zero." Discuss.

10-13 What effect, if any, would you expect poor-quality materials to have on direct labor variances?

10-14 If variable manufacturing overhead is applied to production on the basis of direct labor-hours and the direct labor efficiency variance is unfavorable, will the variable overhead efficiency variance be favorable or unfavorable, or could it be either? Explain.

10-15 What is a statistical control chart, and how is it used?

10-16 Why can undue emphasis on labor efficiency variances lead to excess work in process inventories?

10-17 Why do the measures used in a balanced scorecard differ from company to company?

10-18 Why does the balanced scorecard include financial performance measures as well as measures of how well internal business processes are doing?

10-19 What is the difference between delivery cycle time and throughput time? What four elements make up throughput time? Into what two classes can these four elements be placed?

10-20 If a company has a manufacturing cycle efficiency (MCE) of less than 1, what does it mean? How would you interpret an MCE of 0.40?

10-21 (Appendix 10A) What are the advantages of making formal journal entries in the accounting records for variances?

Exercises

EXERCISE 10-1 Setting Standards; Preparing a Standard Cost Card [LO1]

Martin Company manufactures a powerful cleaning solvent. The main ingredient in the solvent is a raw material called Echol. Information concerning the purchase and use of Echol follows:

> *Purchase of Echol* Echol is purchased in 15-gallon containers at a cost of $115 per container. A discount of 2% is offered by the supplier for payment within 10 days, and Martin Company takes all discounts. Shipping costs, which Martin Company must pay, amount to $130 for an average shipment of 100 15-gallon containers of Echol.

> *Use of Echol* The bill of materials calls for 7.6 quarts of Echol per bottle of cleaning solvent. (Each gallon contains four quarts.) About 5% of all Echol used is lost through spillage or evaporation (the 7.6 quarts above is the *actual* content per bottle). In addition, statistical analysis has shown that every 41st bottle is rejected at final inspection because of contamination.

Required:

1. Compute the standard purchase price for one quart of Echol.
2. Compute the standard quantity of Echol (in quarts) per salable bottle of cleaning solvent.
3. Using the data from (1) and (2) above, prepare a standard cost card showing the standard cost of Echol per bottle of cleaning solvent.

EXERCISE 10-2 Direct Materials Variances [LO2]

Bandar Industries Berhad of Malaysia manufactures sporting equipment. One of the company's products, a football helmet for the North American market, requires a special plastic. During the quarter ending June 30, the company manufactured 35,000 helmets, using 22,500 kilograms of plastic. The plastic cost the company RM 171,000. (The currency in Malaysia is the ringgit, which is denoted here by RM.)

According to the standard cost card, each helmet should require 0.6 kilograms of plastic, at a cost of RM 8 per kilogram.

Required:

1. What cost for plastic should have been incurred to make 35,000 helmets? How much greater or less is this than the cost that was incurred?
2. Break down the difference computed in (1) above into a materials price variance and a materials quantity variance.

EXERCISE 10-3 Direct Labor Variances [LO3]

SkyChefs, Inc., prepares in-flight meals for a number of major airlines. One of the company's products is grilled salmon in dill sauce with baby new potatoes and spring vegetables. During the most recent week, the company prepared 4,000 of these meals using 960 direct labor-hours. The company paid these direct labor workers a total of $9,600 for this work, or $10.00 per hour.

According to the standard cost card for this meal, it should require 0.25 direct labor-hours at a cost of $9.75 per hour.

Required:

1. What direct labor cost should have been incurred to prepare 4,000 meals? How much does this differ from the actual direct labor cost?
2. Break down the difference computed in (1) above into a labor rate variance and a labor efficiency variance.

EXERCISE 10-4 Variable Overhead Variances [LO4]

Logistics Solutions provides order fulfillment services for dot.com merchants. The company maintains warehouses that stock items carried by its dot.com clients. When a client receives an order from a customer, the order is forwarded to Logistics Solutions, which pulls the item from storage, packs it, and ships it to the customer. The company uses a predetermined variable overhead rate based on direct labor-hours.

In the most recent month, 120,000 items were shipped to customers using 2,300 direct labor-hours. The company incurred a total of $7,360 in variable overhead costs.

According to the company's standards, 0.02 direct labor-hours are required to fulfill an order for one item and the variable overhead rate is $3.25 per direct labor-hour.

Required:

1. What variable overhead cost should have been incurred to fill the orders for the 120,000 items? How much does this differ from the actual variable overhead cost?
2. Break down the difference computed in (1) above into a variable overhead spending variance and a variable overhead efficiency variance.

EXERCISE 10-5 Creating a Balanced Scorecard [LO5]

Historically, the Mason Paper Company (MPC) has manufactured commodity grade papers for use in computer printers and photocopiers. MPC has reported net operating losses for the last two years due to intense price pressure from much larger competitors. The MPC management team—including Kristen Townsend (CEO), Mike Martinez (vice president of Manufacturing), Tom Andrews (vice president of Marketing), and Wendy Chen (CFO)—is contemplating a change in strategy to save the company from impending bankruptcy. Excerpts from a recent management team meeting are shown below:

Townsend: As we all know, the commodity paper manufacturing business is all about economies of scale. The largest competitors with the lowest cost per unit win. The limited capacity of our older machines prohibits us from competing in the high-volume commodity paper grades. Furthermore, expanding our capacity by acquiring a new paper-making machine is out of the question given the extraordinarily high price tag. Therefore, I propose that we abandon cost reduction as a strategic goal and instead pursue manufacturing flexibility as the key to our future success.

Chen: Manufacturing flexibility? What does that mean?

Martinez: It means we have to abandon our "crank out as many tons of paper as possible" mentality. Instead, we need to pursue the low-volume business opportunities that exist in the nonstandard, specialized paper grades. To succeed in this regard, we'll need to improve our flexibility in three ways. First, we must improve our ability to switch between paper grades. Right now, we require an average of four hours to change over to another paper grade. Timely customer deliveries are a function of changeover performance. Second, we need to expand the range of paper grades that we can manufacture. Currently, we can only manufacture three paper grades. Our customers must perceive that we are a "one-stop shop" that can meet all of their paper grade needs. Third, we will need to improve our yields (e.g., tons of acceptable output relative to total tons processed) in the nonstandard paper grades. I am certain that our percentage of waste within these grades will be unacceptably high unless we do something to improve our processes. Our variable costs will go through the roof if we cannot increase our yields!

Chen: Wait just a minute! These changes are going to destroy our equipment utilization numbers!

Andrews: You're right Wendy; however, equipment utilization is not the name of the game when it comes to competing in terms of flexibility. Our customers don't care about our equipment utilization. Instead, as Mike just alluded to, they want just-in-time delivery of smaller quantities of a full range of paper grades. If we can shrink the elapsed time from order placement to order delivery and expand our product offerings, it will increase sales from current customers and bring in new customers. Furthermore, we will be able to charge a premium price because of the limited competition within this niche from our cost-focused larger competitors. Our contribution margin per ton should drastically improve!

Martinez: Of course, executing the change in strategy will not be easy. We'll need to make a substantial investment in training. It is imperative that we do not shortchange our commitment to training because ultimately it is our people who create our flexible manufacturing capabilities.

Chen: If we adopt this new strategy, it is definitely going to impact how we measure performance. We'll need to create measures that motivate our employees to make decisions that support our flexibility goals.

Townsend: Wendy, you hit the nail right on the head. For our next meeting, could you pull together some potential measures that support our new strategy?

Later that same day, Wendy shared the essence of the above conversation with the employees of her Finance Department. She indicated that she would welcome suggested performance measures from anyone within the department. As an employee in the Finance Department, you have decided to pursue this opportunity to enhance your career prospects within the organization.

Required:
1. Contrast MPC's previous manufacturing strategy with its new manufacturing strategy.
2. Generally speaking, why would a company that changes its strategic goals need to change its performance measurement system as well? What are some examples of measures that would have been appropriate for MPC prior to its change in strategy? Why would those measures fail to support MPC's new strategy?
3. Using Exhibit 10–12 as a guide, construct a balanced scorecard that would support MPC's new manufacturing strategy. Use arrows to show the causal links between the performance measures and show whether the performance measure should increase or decrease over time. Feel free to create measures that may not be specifically mentioned in the chapter, but nonetheless make sense given the strategic goals of the company.
4. What hypotheses are built into MPC's balanced scorecard? Which of these hypotheses do you believe are most questionable and why?

EXERCISE 10-6 Measures of Internal Business Process Performance [LO6]

Management of Mittel Rhein AG of Köln, Germany, would like to reduce the amount of time between when a customer places an order and when the order is shipped. For the first quarter of operations during the current year the following data were reported:

Inspection time...............................	0.3 days
Wait time (from order to start of production)........	14.0 days
Process time	2.7 days
Move time...................................	1.0 days
Queue time..................................	5.0 days

Required:
1. Compute the throughput time.
2. Compute the manufacturing cycle efficiency (MCE) for the quarter.
3. What percentage of the throughput time was spent in non-value-added activities?
4. Compute the delivery cycle time.
5. If by using Lean Production all queue time during production is eliminated, what will be the new MCE?

EXERCISE 10-7 (Appendix 10A) Recording Variances in the General Ledger [LO7]

Bliny Corporation makes a product with the following standard costs for direct material and direct labor:

> Direct material: 2.00 meters at $3.25 per meter $6.50
> Direct labor: 0.40 hours at $12.00 per hour $4.80

During the most recent month, 5,000 units were produced. The costs associated with the month's production of this product were as follows:

> Material purchased: 12,000 meters at $3.15 per meter $37,800
> Material used in production: 10,500 meters . . . . —
> Direct labor: 1,975 hours at $12.20 per hour $24,095

The standard cost variances for direct material and direct labor are:

> Materials price variance: 12,000 meters at $0.10 per meter F . . . . $1,200 F
> Materials quantity variance: 500 meters at $3.25 per meter U . . . . $1,625 U
> Labor rate variance: 1,975 hours at $0.20 per hour U . . . . $395 U
> Labor efficiency variance: 25 hours at $12.00 per hour F . . . . $300 F

Required:

1. Prepare the journal entry to record the purchase of materials on account for the month.
2. Prepare the journal entry to record the use of materials for the month.
3. Prepare the journal entry to record the incurrence of direct labor cost for the month.

EXERCISE 10-8 Setting Standards (LO1)

Victoria Chocolates, Ltd., makes premium handcrafted chocolate confections in London. The owner of the company is setting up a standard cost system and has collected the following data for one of the company's products, the Empire Truffle. This product is made with the finest white chocolate and various fillings. The data below pertain only to the white chocolate used in the product (the currency is stated in pounds denoted here as £):

> Material requirements, kilograms of white chocolate per dozen truffles . . . . . . 0.70 kilograms
> Allowance for waste, kilograms of white chocolate per dozen truffles . . . . 0.03 kilograms
> Allowance for rejects, kilograms of white chocolate per dozen truffles . . . . 0.02 kilograms
> Purchase price, finest grade white chocolate . . . . £7.50 per kilogram
> Purchase discount . . . . 8% of purchase price
> Shipping cost from the supplier in Belgium . . . . £0.30 per kilogram
> Receiving and handling cost . . . . £0.04 per kilogram

Required:

1. Determine the standard price of a kilogram of white chocolate.
2. Determine the standard quantity of white chocolate for a dozen truffles.
3. Determine the standard cost of the white chocolate in a dozen truffles.

EXERCISE 10-9 Direct Materials and Direct Labor Variances [LO2, LO3]

Dawson Toys, Ltd., produces a toy called the Maze. The company has recently established a standard cost system to help control costs and has established the following standards for the Maze toy:

> Direct materials: 6 microns per toy at $0.50 per micron
> Direct labor: 1.3 hours per toy at $8 per hour

During July, the company produced 3,000 Maze toys. Production data for the month on the toy follow:

Direct materials: 25,000 microns were purchased at a cost of $0.48 per micron. 5,000 of these microns were still in inventory at the end of the month.

Direct labor: 4,000 direct labor-hours were worked at a cost of $36,000.

Required:
1. Compute the following variances for July:
   a. Direct materials price and quantity variances.
   b. Direct labor rate and efficiency variances.
2. Prepare a brief explanation of the possible causes of each variance.

EXERCISE 10-10 Direct Materials and Direct Labor Variances [LO2, LO3]

Huron Company produces a commercial cleaning compound known as Zoom. The direct materials and direct labor standards for one unit of Zoom are given below:

	Standard Quantity or Hours	Standard Price or Rate	Standard Cost
Direct materials........	4.6 pounds	$2.50 per pound	$11.50
Direct labor...........	0.2 hours	$12.00 per hour	$2.40

During the most recent month, the following activity was recorded:
a. Twenty thousand pounds of material were purchased at a cost of $2.35 per pound.
b. All of the material purchased was used to produce 4,000 units of Zoom.
c. 750 hours of direct labor time were recorded at a total labor cost of $10,425.

Required:
1. Compute the direct materials price and quantity variances for the month.
2. Compute the direct labor rate and efficiency variances for the month.

EXERCISE 10-11 Direct Materials Variances [LO2]

Refer to the data in Exercise 10–10. Assume that instead of producing 4,000 units during the month, the company produced only 3,000 units, using 14,750 pounds of material. (The rest of the material purchased remained in raw materials inventory.)

Required:
Compute the direct materials price and quantity variances for the month.

EXERCISE 10-12 Direct Labor and Variable Manufacturing Overhead Variances [LO3, LO4]

Erie Company manufactures a small CD player called the Jogging Mate. The company uses standards to control its costs. The labor standards that have been set for one Jogging Mate CD player are as follows:

Standard Hours	Standard Rate per Hour	Standard Cost
18 minutes	$12.00	$3.60

During August, 5,750 hours of direct labor time were needed to make 20,000 units of the Jogging Mate. The direct labor cost totaled $73,600 for the month.

Required:
1. What direct labor cost should have been incurred to make 20,000 units of the Jogging Mate? By how much does this differ from the cost that was incurred?
2. Break down the difference in cost from (1) above into a labor rate variance and a labor efficiency variance.
3. The budgeted variable manufacturing overhead rate is $4 per direct labor-hour. During August, the company incurred $21,850 in variable manufacturing overhead cost. Compute the variable overhead spending and efficiency variances for the month.

EXERCISE 10-13 Creating a Balanced Scorecard [LO5]

Ariel Tax Services prepares tax returns for individual and corporate clients. As the company has gradually expanded to 10 offices, the founder Max Jacobs has begun to feel as though he is losing control of operations. In response to this concern, he has decided to implement a performance measurement system that will help control current operations and facilitate his growth plans of expanding to 20 offices.

Jacobs describes the keys to the success of his business as follows:

"Our only real asset is our people. We must keep our employees highly motivated and we must continually replenish our human capital by hiring the 'cream of the crop.' Interestingly, employee morale and recruiting success are both driven by the same two factors—compensation and career advancement. In other words, providing superior compensation relative to the industry average coupled with fast-track career advancement opportunities keeps morale high and makes us a very attractive place to work. It drives a high rate of job offer acceptances relative to job offers tendered.

"Hiring highly qualified people and keeping them energized ensures operational success, which in our business is a function of productivity, efficiency, and effectiveness. Productivity boils down to employees being billable rather idle. Efficiency relates to the time required to complete a tax return. Finally, effectiveness is critical to our business in the sense that we cannot tolerate errors. Completing a tax return quickly is meaningless if the return contains errors.

"Our growth plans hinge upon acquiring new customers through word-of-mouth from satisfied repeat customers. We believe that our customers come back year after year because they value error-free, timely, and courteous tax return preparation. Common courtesy is an important aspect of our business! We call it service quality, and it all ties back to employee morale in the sense that happy employees treat their clients with care and concern.

"While sales growth is obviously important to our future plans, growth without a corresponding increase in profitability is useless. Therefore, we understand that increasing our profit margin is a function of cost-efficiency as well as sales growth. Given that payroll is our biggest expense, we must maintain an optimal balance between staffing levels and the revenue being generated. As I alluded to earlier, the key to maintaining this balance is employee productivity. If we can achieve cost-efficient sales growth, we should eventually have 20 profitable offices!"

Required:
1. Create a balanced scorecard for Ariel Tax Services. Link your scorecard measures using the framework from Exhibit 10–12. Indicate whether each measure is expected to increase or decrease. Feel free to create measures that may not be specifically mentioned in the chapter, but make sense given the strategic goals of the company.
2. What hypotheses are built into the balanced scorecard for Ariel Tax Services? Which of these hypotheses do you believe are most questionable and why?
3. Discuss the potential advantages and disadvantages of implementing an internal business process measure called *total dollar amount of tax refunds generated*. Would you recommend using this measure in Ariel's balanced scorecard?
4. Would it be beneficial to attempt to measure each office's individual performance with respect to the scorecard measures that you created? Why or why not?

EXERCISE 10-14 Working Backwards from Labor Variances [LO3]
The auto repair shop of Quality Motor Company uses standards to control the labor time and labor cost in the shop. The standard labor cost for a motor tune-up is given below:

Job	Standard Hours	Standard Rate	Standard Cost
Motor tune-up........	2.5	$9	$22.50

The record showing the time spent in the shop last week on motor tune-ups has been misplaced. However, the shop supervisor recalls that 50 tune-ups were completed during the week, and the controller recalls the following variance data relating to tune-ups:

Labor rate variance........	$87 F
Total labor variance........	$93 U

Required:
1. Determine the number of actual labor-hours spent on tune-ups during the week.
2. Determine the actual hourly rate of pay for tune-ups last week.
(Hint: A useful way to proceed would be to work from known to unknown data either by using the variance formulas or by using the columnar format shown in Exhibit 10–6.)

EXERCISE 10-15 (Appendix 10A) Direct Materials and Direct Labor Variances; Journal Entries
[LO2, LO3, LO7]

Genola Fashions began production of a new product on June 1. The company uses a standard cost system and has established the following standards for one unit of the new product:

	Standard Quantity or Hours	Standard Price or Rate	Standard Cost
Direct materials.	2.5 yards	$14 per yard	$35.00
Direct labor.	1.6 hours	$8 per hour	$12.80

During June, the following activity was recorded regarding the new product:

a. Purchasing acquired 10,000 yards of material at a cost of $13.80 per yard.
b. Production used 8,000 yards of the material to manufacture 3,000 units of the new product.
c. Production reported that 5,000 direct labor-hours were worked on the new product at a cost of $43,000.

Required:
1. For direct materials:
    a. Compute the direct materials price and quantity variances.
    b. Prepare journal entries to record the purchase of materials and the use of materials in production.
2. For direct labor:
    a. Compute the direct labor rate and efficiency variances.
    b. Prepare a journal entry to record the incurrence of direct labor cost for the month.
3. Post the entries you have prepared to the following T-accounts:

Raw Materials	
	? ?
Bal. ?	

Work in Process	
Materials used ?	
Labor cost ?	

Accounts Payable	
	138,000

Wages Payable	
	43,000

Materials Price Variance	

Materials Quantity Variance	

Labor Rate Variance	

Labor Efficiency Variance	

Problems

PROBLEM 10-16 Comprehensive Variance Analysis [LO2, LO3, LO4]

Miller Toy Company manufactures a plastic swimming pool at its Westwood Plant. The plant has been experiencing problems as shown by its June contribution format income statement below:

	Budgeted	Actual
Sales (15,000 pools)...............	$450,000	$450,000
Variable expenses:		
Variable cost of goods sold*........	180,000	196,290
Variable selling expenses	20,000	20,000
Total variable expenses	200,000	216,290
Contribution margin	250,000	233,710
Fixed expenses:		
Manufacturing overhead...........	130,000	130,000
Selling and administrative.........	84,000	84,000
Total fixed expenses...............	214,000	214,000
Net operating income	$ 36,000	$ 19,710

*Contains direct materials, direct labor, and variable manufacturing overhead.

Janet Dunn, who has just been appointed general manager of the Westwood Plant, has been given instructions to "get things under control." Upon reviewing the plant's income statement, Ms. Dunn has concluded that the major problem lies in the variable cost of goods sold. She has been provided with the following standard cost per swimming pool:

	Standard Quantity or Hours	Standard Price or Rate	Standard Cost
Direct materials	3.0 pounds	$2.00 per pound	$ 6.00
Direct labor........................	0.8 hours	$6.00 per hour	4.80
Variable manufacturing overhead........	0.4 hours*	$3.00 per hour	1.20
Total standard variable cost			$12.00

*Based on machine-hours.

Ms. Dunn has determined that during June the plant produced 15,000 pools and incurred the following costs:
a. Purchased 60,000 pounds of materials at a cost of $1.95 per pound.
b. Used 49,200 pounds of materials in production. (Finished goods and work in process inventories are insignificant and can be ignored.)
c. Worked 11,800 direct labor-hours at a cost of $7.00 per hour.
d. Incurred variable manufacturing overhead cost totaling $18,290 for the month. A total of 5,900 machine-hours was recorded.

It is the company's policy to close all variances to cost of goods sold on a monthly basis.

Required:
1. Compute the following variances for June:
   a. Direct materials price and quantity variances.
   b. Direct labor rate and efficiency variances.
   c. Variable overhead spending and efficiency variances.
2. Summarize the variances that you computed in (1) above by showing the net overall favorable or unfavorable variance for the month. What impact did this figure have on the company's income statement?
3. Pick out the two most significant variances that you computed in (1) above. Explain to Ms. Dunn possible causes of these variances.

PROBLEM 10-17 Variance Analysis in a Hospital [LO2, LO3, LO4]
John Fleming, chief administrator for Valley View Hospital, is concerned about the costs for tests in the hospital's lab. Charges for lab tests are consistently higher at Valley View than at other hospitals and have resulted in many complaints. Also, because of strict regulations on amounts reimbursed for lab tests, payments received from insurance companies and governmental units have not been high enough to cover lab costs.

Mr. Fleming has asked you to evaluate costs in the hospital's lab for the past month. The following information is available:

a. Two types of tests are performed in the lab—blood tests and smears. During the past month, 1,800 blood tests and 2,400 smears were performed in the lab.

b. Small glass plates are used in both types of tests. During the past month, the hospital purchased 12,000 plates at a cost of $28,200. This cost is net of a 6% quantity discount. 1,500 of these plates were unused at the end of the month; no plates were on hand at the beginning of the month.

c. During the past month, 1,150 hours of labor time were recorded in the lab at a cost of $13,800.

d. The lab's variable overhead cost last month totaled $7,820.

Valley View Hospital has never used standard costs. By searching industry literature, however, you have determined the following nationwide averages for hospital labs:

Plates: Two plates are required per lab test. These plates cost $2.50 each and are disposed of after the test is completed.

Labor: Each blood test should require 0.3 hours to complete, and each smear should require 0.15 hours to complete. The average cost of this lab time is $14 per hour.

Overhead: Overhead cost is based on direct labor-hours. The average rate for variable overhead is $6 per hour.

Required:

1. Compute a materials price variance for the plates purchased last month and a materials quantity variance for the plates used last month.

2. For labor cost in the lab:
    a. Compute a labor rate variance and a labor efficiency variance.
    b. In most hospitals, one-half of the workers in the lab are senior technicians and one-half are assistants. In an effort to reduce costs, Valley View Hospital employs only one-fourth senior technicians and three-fourths assistants. Would you recommend that this policy be continued? Explain.

3. Compute the variable overhead spending and efficiency variances. Is there any relation between the variable overhead efficiency variance and the labor efficiency variance? Explain.

PROBLEM 10-18 (Appendix 10A) Comprehensive Variance Analysis; Journal Entries
[LO2, LO3, LO4, LO7]
Trueform Products, Inc., produces a broad line of sports equipment and uses a standard cost system for control purposes. Last year the company produced 8,000 varsity footballs. The standard costs associated with this football, along with the actual costs incurred last year, are given below (per football):

	Standard Cost	Actual Cost
Direct materials:		
Standard: 3.7 feet at $5.00 per foot	$18.50	
Actual: 4.0 feet at $4.80 per foot.		$19.20
Direct labor:		
Standard: 0.9 hour at $7.50 per hour	6.75	
Actual: 0.8 hour at $8.00 per hour		6.40
Variable manufacturing overhead:		
Standard: 0.9 hour at $2.50 per hour	2.25	
Actual: 0.8 hour at $2.75 per hour		2.20
Total cost per football	$27.50	$27.80

The president was elated when he saw that actual costs exceeded standard costs by only $0.30 per football. He stated, "I was afraid that our unit cost might get out of hand when we gave out those raises last year in order to stimulate output. But it's obvious our costs are well under control."

There was no inventory of materials on hand to start the year. During the year, 32,000 feet of materials were purchased and used in production.

Required:

1. For direct materials:
    a. Compute the price and quantity variances for the year.
    b. Prepare journal entries to record all activity relating to direct materials for the year.

2. For direct labor:
   a. Compute the rate and efficiency variances.
   b. Prepare a journal entry to record the incurrence of direct labor cost for the year.
3. Compute the variable overhead spending and efficiency variances.
4. Was the president correct in his statement that "our costs are well under control"? Explain.
5. State possible causes of each variance that you have computed.

PROBLEM 10-19 Basic Variance Analysis [LO2, LO3, LO4]

Becton Labs, Inc., produces various chemical compounds for industrial use. One compound, called Fludex, is prepared using an elaborate distilling process. The company has developed standard costs for one unit of Fludex, as follows:

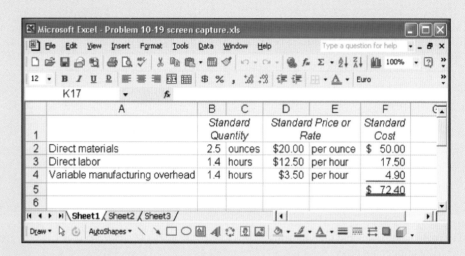

	Standard Quantity		Standard Price or Rate		Standard Cost
Direct materials	2.5	ounces	$20.00	per ounce	$ 50.00
Direct labor	1.4	hours	$12.50	per hour	17.50
Variable manufacturing overhead	1.4	hours	$3.50	per hour	4.90
					$ 72.40

During November, the following activity was recorded by the company relative to production of Fludex:

a. Materials purchased, 12,000 ounces at a cost of $225,000.
b. There was no beginning inventory of materials; however, at the end of the month, 2,500 ounces of material remained in ending inventory.
c. The company employs 35 lab technicians to work on the production of Fludex. During November, each worked an average of 160 hours at an average rate of $12 per hour.
d. Variable manufacturing overhead is assigned to Fludex on the basis of direct labor-hours. Variable manufacturing overhead costs during November totaled $18,200.
e. During November, 3,750 good units of Fludex were produced.

The company's management is anxious to determine the efficiency of the Fludex production activities.

Required:
1. For direct materials used in the production of Fludex:
   a. Compute the price and quantity variances.
   b. The materials were purchased from a new supplier who is anxious to enter into a long-term purchase contract. Would you recommend that the company sign the contract? Explain.
2. For labor employed in the production of Fludex:
   a. Compute the rate and efficiency variances.
   b. In the past, the 35 technicians employed in the production of Fludex consisted of 20 senior technicians and 15 assistants. During November, the company experimented with fewer senior technicians and more assistants in order to save costs. Would you recommend that the new labor mix be continued? Explain.
3. Compute the variable overhead spending and efficiency variances. What relation can you see between this efficiency variance and the labor efficiency variance?

PROBLEM 10-20 Measures of Internal Business Process Performance [LO6]

DataSpan, Inc., automated its plant at the start of the current year and installed a flexible manufacturing system. The company is also evaluating its suppliers and moving toward a just-in-time (JIT) inventory system. Many adjustment problems have been encountered, including problems relating to performance measurement. After much study, the company has decided to use the performance measures below as part of its balanced scorecard, and it has gathered data relating to these measures for the first four months of operations.

	Month			
	1	2	3	4
Throughput time	?	?	?	?
Delivery cycle time	?	?	?	?
Manufacturing cycle efficiency	?	?	?	?
Percentage of on-time deliveries	91%	86%	83%	79%
Total sales (units)	3,210	3,072	2,915	2,806

Management has asked for your help in computing throughput time, delivery cycle time, and MCE. The following average times have been logged over the last four months:

	Average per Month (in days)			
	1	2	3	4
Move time per unit, in days.	0.4	0.3	0.4	0.4
Process time per unit, in days	2.1	2.0	1.9	1.8
Wait time per order before start				
of production, in days	16.0	17.5	19.0	20.5
Queue time per unit, in days	4.3	5.0	5.8	6.7
Inspection time per unit, in days	0.6	0.7	0.7	0.6

Required:
1. For each month, compute the following:
   a. The throughput time.
   b. The manufacturing cycle efficiency (MCE).
   c. The delivery cycle time.
2. Using the performance measures given in the problem and those you computed in (1) above, identify whether the trend over the four months is generally favorable, generally unfavorable, or mixed. What areas apparently require improvement and how might they be improved?
3. Refer to the move time, process time, and so forth, given above for month 4.
   a. Assume that in month 5 the move time, process time, and so forth, are the same as for month 4, except that through the implementation of Lean Production, the company is able to completely eliminate the queue time during production. Compute the new throughput time and MCE.
   b. Assume that in month 6 the move time, process time, and so forth, are the same as for month 4, except that the company is able to completely eliminate both the queue time during production and the inspection time. Compute the new throughput time and MCE.

PROBLEM 10-21 Perverse Effects of Some Performance Measures [LO5]
There is often more than one way to improve a performance measure. Unfortunately, some of the actions taken by managers to make their performance look better may actually harm the organization. For example, suppose the marketing department is held responsible only for increasing the performance measure "total revenues." Increases in total revenues may be achieved by working harder and smarter, but they can also usually be achieved by simply cutting prices. The increase in volume from cutting prices almost always results in greater total revenues; however, it does not always lead to greater total profits. Those who design performance measurement systems need to keep in mind that managers who are under pressure to perform may take actions to improve performance measures that have negative consequences elsewhere.

Required:
For each of the following situations, describe actions that managers might take to show improvement in the performance measure but which do not actually lead to improvement in the organization's overall performance.
1. Concerned with the slow rate at which new products are brought to market, top management of a consumer electronics company introduces a new performance measure—speed-to-market. The research and development department is given responsibility for this performance measure, which measures the average amount of time a product is in development before it is released to the market for sale.

2. The CEO of a telephone company has been under public pressure from city officials to fix the large number of public pay phones that do not work. The company's repair people complain that the problem is vandalism and damage caused by theft of coins from coin boxes—particularly in high-crime areas in the city. The CEO says she wants the problem solved and has pledged to city officials that there will be substantial improvement by the end of the year. To ensure that this is done, she makes the managers in charge of installing and maintaining pay phones responsible for increasing the percentage of public pay phones that are fully functional.

3. A manufacturing company has been plagued by the chronic failure to ship orders to customers by the promised date. To solve this problem, the production manager has been given the responsibility of increasing the percentage of orders shipped on time. When a customer calls in an order, the production manager and the customer agree to a delivery date. If the order is not completed by that date, it is counted as a late shipment.

4. Concerned with the productivity of employees, the board of directors of a large multinational corporation has dictated that the manager of each subsidiary will be held responsible for increasing the revenue per employee of his or her subsidiary.

PROBLEM 10-22 Setting Standards [LO1]

Danson Company is a chemical manufacturer that supplies various products to industrial users. The company plans to introduce a new chemical solution, called Nysap, for which it needs to develop a standard product cost. The following information is available on the production of Nysap:

a. Nysap is made by combining a chemical compound (nyclyn) and a solution (salex), and boiling the mixture. A 20% loss in volume occurs for both the salex and the nyclyn during boiling. After boiling, the mixture consists of 9.6 liters of salex and 12 kilograms of nyclyn per 10-liter batch of Nysap.

b. After the boiling process is complete, the solution is cooled slightly before 5 kilograms of protet are added per 10-liter batch of Nysap. The addition of the protet does not affect the total liquid volume. The resulting solution is then bottled in 10-liter containers.

c. The finished product is highly unstable, and one 10-liter batch out of five is rejected at final inspection. Rejected batches have no commercial value and are thrown out.

d. It takes a worker 35 minutes to process one 10-liter batch of Nysap. Employees work an eight-hour day, including one hour per day for rest breaks and cleanup.

Required:

1. Determine the standard quantity for each of the raw materials needed to produce an acceptable 10-liter batch of Nysap.

2. Determine the standard labor time allowed to produce an acceptable 10-liter batch of Nysap.

3. Assuming the following purchase prices and costs, prepare a standard cost card for direct materials and direct labor for one acceptable 10-liter batch of Nysap:

Salex	$1.50 per liter
Nyclyn	$2.80 per kilogram
Protet	$3.00 per kilogram
Direct labor cost	$9.00 per hour

(CMA, adapted)

PROBLEM 10-23 Creating Balanced Scorecards that Support Different Strategies [LO5]

The Midwest Consulting Group (MCG) helps companies build balanced scorecards. As part of its marketing efforts, MCG conducts an annual balanced scorecard workshop for prospective clients. As MCG's newest employee, your boss has asked you to participate in this year's workshop by explaining to attendees how a company's strategy determines the measures that are appropriate for its balanced scorecard. Your boss has provided you with the excerpts below from the annual reports of two current MCG clients. She has asked you to use these excerpts as a basis for facilitating your portion of the workshop.

Excerpt from Applied Pharmaceuticals' annual report:

The keys to our business are consistent and timely new product introductions and manufacturing process integrity. The new product introduction side of the equation is a function of research and development (R&D) yield (e.g., the number of marketable drug compounds created relative to the total number of potential compounds pursued). We seek to optimize our R&D yield and first-to-market capability by investing in state-of-the-art technology, hiring the highest possible percentage of the "best and the brightest" engineers that we pursue, and providing world-class training to those engineers. Manufacturing process integrity is all about establishing world-class quality specifications and then relentlessly engaging in prevention and appraisal activities to minimize defect rates. Our customers must have an awareness of and respect for our brand image of being "first to market and first in quality." If we deliver on this pledge to our customers, then our financial goal of increasing our return on stockholders' equity should take care of itself.

Excerpt from Destination Resorts International's annual report:

Our business succeeds or fails based on the quality of the service that our front-line employees provide to customers. Therefore, it is imperative that we strive to maintain high employee morale and minimize employee turnover. In addition, it is critical that we train our employees to use technology to create one seamless worldwide experience for our repeat customers. Once an employee enters a customer preference (e.g., provide two extra pillows in the room, deliver fresh brewed coffee to the room at 8:00 A.M., etc.) into our database, our worldwide workforce strives to ensure that a customer will never need to repeat it at any of our destination resorts. If we properly train and retain a motivated workforce, we should see continuous improvement in our percentage of error-free repeat customer check-ins, the time taken to resolve customer complaints, and our independently assessed room cleanliness. This in turn should drive improvement in our customer retention, which is the key to meeting our revenue growth goals.

Required:

1. Based on the excerpts above, compare and contrast the strategies of Applied Pharmaceuticals and Destination Resorts International.

2. Select balanced scorecard measures for each company and link the scorecard measures using the framework from Exhibit 10–12. Use arrows to show the causal links between the performance measures and show whether the performance measure should increase or decrease over time. Feel free to create measures that may not be specifically mentioned in the chapter, but nonetheless make sense given the strategic goals of each company.

3. What hypotheses are built into each balanced scorecard? Why do the hypotheses differ between the two companies?

PROBLEM 10-24 Internal Business Process Performance Measures [LO6]
Tombro Industries is in the process of automating one of its plants and developing a flexible manufacturing system. The company is finding it necessary to make many changes in operating procedures. Progress has been slow, particularly in trying to develop new performance measures for the factory.

In an effort to evaluate performance and determine where improvements can be made, management has gathered the following data relating to activities over the last four months:

	Month			
	1	2	3	4
Quality control measures:				
Number of defects	185	163	124	91
Number of warranty claims	46	39	30	27
Number of customer complaints	102	96	79	58
Material control measures:				
Purchase order lead time	8 days	7 days	5 days	4 days
Scrap as a percent of total cost	1%	1%	2%	3%
Machine performance measures:				
Machine downtime as a percentage of availability	3%	4%	4%	6%
Use as a percentage of availability	95%	92%	89%	85%
Setup time (hours)	8	10	11	12
Delivery performance measures:				
Throughput time	?	?	?	?
Manufacturing cycle efficiency (MCE)	?	?	?	?
Delivery cycle time	?	?	?	?
Percentage of on-time deliveries	96%	95%	92%	89%

The president has read in industry journals that throughput time, MCE, and delivery cycle time are important measures of performance, but no one is sure how they are computed. You have been asked to assist the company, and you have gathered the following data relating to these measures:

	Average per Month (in days)			
	1	2	3	4
Wait time per order before start of production....................	9.0	11.5	12.0	14.0
Inspection time per unit	0.8	0.7	0.7	0.7
Process time per unit................	2.1	2.0	1.9	1.8
Queue time per unit.................	2.8	4.4	6.0	7.0
Move time per unit	0.3	0.4	0.4	0.5

As part of its modernization process, the company is also moving toward a just-in-time (JIT) inventory system. Over the next year, the company hopes to have the bulk of its raw materials and parts on a JIT basis.

Required:
1. For each month, compute the following performance measures:
   a. Throughput time.
   b. Manufacturing cycle efficiency (MCE).
   c. Delivery cycle time.
2. Using the performance measures given in the main body of the problem and the performance measures computed in (1) above, do the following:
   a. Identify areas where the company seems to be improving.
   b. Identify areas where the company seems to be deteriorating.
3. Refer to the inspection time, process time, and so forth, given above for month 4.
   a. Assume that in month 5 the inspection time, process time, and so forth, are the same as for month 4, except that the company is able to completely eliminate the queue time during production. Compute the new throughput time and MCE.
   b. Assume that in month 6 the inspection time, process time, and so forth, are the same as in month 4, except that the company is able to eliminate both the queue time during production and the inspection time. Compute the new throughput time and MCE.

PROBLEM 10-25 Building a Balanced Scorecard [LO5]

Lost Peak ski resort was for many years a small, family-owned resort serving day skiers from nearby towns. Lost Peak was recently acquired by Western Resorts, a major ski resort operator. The new owners have plans to upgrade the resort into a destination resort for vacationers. As part of this plan, the new owners would like to make major improvements in the Powder 8 Lodge, the resort's on-the-hill cafeteria. The menu at the lodge is very limited—hamburgers, hot dogs, chili, tuna fish sandwiches, pizzas, french fries, and packaged snacks. With little competition, the previous owners of the resort had felt no urgency to upgrade the food service at the lodge. If skiers want lunch on the mountain, the only alternatives are the Powder 8 Lodge or a brown bag lunch brought from home.

As part of the deal when acquiring Lost Peak, Western Resorts agreed to retain all of the current employees of the resort. The manager of the lodge, while hardworking and enthusiastic, has very little experience in the restaurant business. The manager is responsible for selecting the menu, finding and training employees, and overseeing daily operations. The kitchen staff prepare food and wash dishes. The dining room staff take orders, serve as cashiers, and clean the dining room area.

Shortly after taking over Lost Peak, management of Western Resorts held a day-long meeting with all of the employees of the Powder 8 Lodge to discuss the future of the ski resort and the new management's plans for the lodge. At the end of this meeting, management and lodge employees created a balanced scorecard for the lodge that would help guide operations for the coming ski season. Almost everyone who participated in the meeting seemed to be enthusiastic about the scorecard and management's plans for the lodge.

The following performance measures were included on the balanced scorecard for the Powder 8 Lodge:
a. Weekly Powder 8 Lodge sales
b. Weekly Powder 8 Lodge profit
c. Number of menu items
d. Dining area cleanliness as rated by a representative from Western Resorts management
e. Customer satisfaction with menu choices as measured by customer surveys

f. Customer satisfaction with service as measured by customer surveys
g. Average time to take an order
h. Average time to prepare an order
i. Percentage of kitchen staff completing basic cooking course at the local community college
j. Percentage of dining room staff completing basic hospitality course at the local community college

Western Resorts will pay for the costs of staff attending courses at the local community college.

Required:

1. Using the above performance measures, construct a balanced scorecard for the Powder 8 Lodge. Use Exhibit 10–12 as a guide. Use arrows to show causal links and indicate with a + or − whether the performance measure should increase or decrease.
2. What hypotheses are built into the balanced scorecard for the Powder 8 Lodge? Which of these hypotheses do you believe are most questionable? Why?
3. How will management know if one of the hypotheses underlying the balanced scorecard is false?

PROBLEM 10-26 Developing Standard Costs [LO1]

ColdKing Company is a small producer of fruit-flavored frozen desserts. For many years, ColdKing's products have had strong regional sales on the basis of brand recognition; however, other companies have begun marketing similar products in the area, and price competition has become increasingly intense. John Wakefield, the company's controller, is planning to implement a standard cost system for ColdKing and has gathered considerable information from his co-workers on production and material requirements for ColdKing's products. Wakefield believes that the use of standard costing will allow ColdKing to improve cost control and make better pricing decisions.

ColdKing's most popular product is raspberry sherbet. The sherbet is produced in 10-gallon batches, and each batch requires 6 quarts of good raspberries. The fresh raspberries are sorted by hand before they enter the production process. Because of imperfections in the raspberries and normal spoilage, 1 quart of berries is discarded for every 4 quarts of acceptable berries. Three minutes is the standard direct labor time for the sorting that is required to obtain 1 quart of acceptable raspberries. The acceptable raspberries are then blended with the other ingredients; blending requires 12 minutes of direct labor time per batch. After blending, the sherbet is packaged in quart containers. Wakefield has gathered the following pricing information:

a. ColdKing purchases raspberries at a cost of $0.80 per quart. All other ingredients cost a total of $0.45 per gallon of sherbet.
b. Direct labor is paid at the rate of $9.00 per hour.
c. The total cost of direct material and direct labor required to package the sherbet is $0.38 per quart.

Required:

1. Develop the standard cost for the direct cost components (materials, labor, and packaging) of a 10-gallon batch of raspberry sherbet. The standard cost should identify the standard quantity, standard rate, and standard cost per batch for each direct cost component of a batch of raspberry sherbet.
2. As part of the implementation of a standard cost system at ColdKing, John Wakefield plans to train those responsible for maintaining the standards on how to use variance analysis. Wakefield is particularly concerned with the causes of unfavorable variances.
    a. Discuss possible causes of unfavorable materials price variances and identify the individual(s) who should be held responsible for these variances.
    b. Discuss possible causes of unfavorable labor efficiency variances and identify the individual(s) who should be held responsible for these variances.

(CMA, adapted)

PROBLEM 10-27 Direct Materials and Direct Labor Variances; Computations from Incomplete Data [LO1, LO2, LO3]

Sharp Company manufactures a product for which the following standards have been set:

	Standard Quantity or Hours	Standard Price or Rate	Standard Cost
Direct materials.	3 feet	$5 per foot	$15
Direct labor.	? hours	? per hour	?

During March, the company purchased direct materials at a cost of $55,650, all of which were used in the production of 3,200 units of product. In addition, 4,900 hours of direct labor time were worked on the product during the month. The cost of this labor time was $36,750. The following variances have been computed for the month:

Materials quantity variance	$4,500 U
Total labor variance	$1,650 F
Labor efficiency variance	$800 U

Required:
1. For direct materials:
   - a. Compute the actual cost per foot for materials for March.
   - b. Compute the materials price variance and a total variance for materials.
2. For direct labor:
   - a. Compute the standard direct labor rate per hour.
   - b. Compute the standard hours allowed for the month's production.
   - c. Compute the standard hours allowed per unit of product.

(Hint: In completing the problem, it may be helpful to move from known to unknown data either by using the columnar format shown in Exhibits 10–4 and 10–6 or by using the variance formulas.)

PROBLEM 10-28 (Appendix 10A) Comprehensive Variance Analysis with Incomplete Data; Journal Entries [LO2, LO3, LO4, LO7]

Maple Products, Ltd., manufactures a super-strong hockey stick. The standard cost of one hockey stick is:

	Standard Quantity or Hours	Standard Price or Rate	Standard Cost
Direct materials	? feet	$3.00 per foot	$?
Direct labor.	2 hours	? per hour	?
Variable manufacturing overhead.	? hours	$1.30 per hour	?
Total standard cost.			$27.00

Last year, 8,000 hockey sticks were produced and sold. Selected cost data relating to last year's operations follow:

	Dr.	Cr.
Accounts payable—direct materials purchased (60,000 feet)		$174,000
Wages payable (? hours)		$79,200*
Work in process—direct materials	$115,200	
Direct labor rate variance		$3,300
Variable overhead efficiency variance	$650	

*Relates to the actual direct labor cost for the year.

The following additional information is available for last year's operations:
a. No materials were on hand at the start of last year. Some of the materials purchased during the year were still on hand in the warehouse at the end of the year.
b. The variable manufacturing overhead rate is based on direct labor-hours. Total actual variable manufacturing overhead cost for last year was $19,800.
c. Actual direct materials usage for last year exceeded the standard by 0.2 feet per stick.

Required:
1. For direct materials:
   - a. Compute the price and quantity variances for last year.
   - b. Prepare journal entries to record all activities relating to direct materials for last year.

2. For direct labor:
   a. Verify the rate variance given above and compute the efficiency variance for last year.
   b. Prepare a journal entry to record activity relating to direct labor for last year.
3. Compute the variable overhead spending variance for last year and verify the variable overhead efficiency variance given above.
4. State possible causes of each variance that you have computed.
5. Prepare a standard cost card for one hockey stick.

PROBLEM 10-29 Comprehensive Variance Analysis [LO2, LO3, LO4]

Marvel Parts, Inc., manufactures auto accessories. One of the company's products is a set of seat covers that can be adjusted to fit nearly any small car. The company has a standard cost system in use for all of its products. According to the standards that have been set for the seat covers, the factory should work 2,850 hours each month to produce 1,900 sets of covers. The standard costs associated with this level of production are:

	Total	Per Set of Covers
Direct materials	$42,560	$22.40
Direct labor	$17,100	9.00
Variable manufacturing overhead		
(based on direct labor-hours)	$6,840	3.60
		$35.00

During August, the factory worked only 2,800 direct labor-hours and produced 2,000 sets of covers. The following actual costs were recorded during the month:

	Total	Per Set of Covers
Direct materials (12,000 yards)	$45,600	$22.80
Direct labor	$18,200	9.10
Variable manufacturing overhead	$7,000	3.50
		$35.40

At standard, each set of covers should require 5.6 yards of material. All of the materials purchased during the month were used in production.

Required:

Compute the following variances for August:
1. The materials price and quantity variances.
2. The labor rate and efficiency variances.
3. The variable overhead spending and efficiency variances.

PROBLEM 10-30 Comprehensive Variance Analysis [LO1, LO2, LO3, LO4]

Highland Company produces a lightweight backpack that is popular with college students. Standard variable costs relating to a single backpack are given below:

	Standard Quantity or Hours	Standard Price or Rate	Standard Cost
Direct materials	?	$6 per yard	$?
Direct labor	?	?	?
Variable manufacturing overhead	?	$3 per direct labor-hour	?
Total standard cost			$?

Overhead is applied to production on the basis of direct labor-hours. During March, 1,000 back-packs were manufactured and sold. Selected information relating to the month's production is given below:

	Materials Used	Direct Labor	Variable Manufacturing Overhead
Total standard cost allowed*	$16,800	$10,500	$4,200
Actual costs incurred	$15,000	?	$3,600
Materials price variance...................	?		
Materials quantity variance	$ 1,200 U		
Labor rate variance		?	
Labor efficiency variance.................		?	
Variable overhead spending variance			?
Variable overhead efficiency variance.......			?

*For the month's production.

The following additional information is available for March's production:

Actual direct labor-hours	1,500
Standard overhead rate per direct labor-hour........	$3.00
Standard price of one yard of materials	$6.00
Difference between standard and actual cost per backpack produced during March............	$0.15 F

Required:
1. What is the standard cost of a single backpack?
2. What was the actual cost per backpack produced during March?
3. How many yards of material are required at standard per backpack?
4. What was the materials price variance for March?
5. What is the standard direct labor rate per hour?
6. What was the labor rate variance for March? The labor efficiency variance?
7. What was the variable overhead spending variance for March? The variable overhead efficiency variance?
8. Prepare a standard cost card for one backpack.

Cases

CASE 10-31 Ethics and the Manager; Rigging Standards [LO1]

Stacy Cummins, the newly hired controller at Merced Home Products, Inc., was disturbed by what she had discovered about the standard costs at the Home Security Division. In looking over the past several years of quarterly earnings reports at the Home Security Division, she noticed that the first-quarter earnings were always poor, the second-quarter earnings were slightly better, the third-quarter earnings were again slightly better, and the fourth quarter always ended with a spectacular performance in which the Home Security Division managed to meet or exceed its target profit for the year. She also was concerned to find letters from the company's external auditors to top management warning about an unusual use of standard costs at the Home Security Division.

When Ms. Cummins ran across these letters, she asked the assistant controller, Gary Farber, if he knew what was going on at the Home Security Division. Gary said that it was common knowledge in the company that the vice president in charge of the Home Security Division, Preston Lansing, had rigged the standards at his division in order to produce the same quarterly earnings pattern every year. According to company policy, variances are taken directly to the income statement as an adjustment to cost of goods sold.

Favorable variances have the effect of increasing net operating income, and unfavorable variances have the effect of decreasing net operating income. Lansing had rigged the standards so that there were always large favorable variances. Company policy was a little vague about when these variances have to be reported on the divisional income statements. While the intent was clearly to recognize variances on the income statement in the period in which they arise, nothing in the company's accounting manuals actually explicitly required this. So for many years Lansing had followed a practice of saving up the favorable variances and using them to create a nice smooth pattern of earnings growth in the first three quarters, followed by a big "Christmas present" of an extremely good fourth quarter. (Financial reporting regulations forbid carrying variances forward from one year to the next on the annual audited financial statements, so all of the variances must appear on the divisional income statement by the end of the year.)

Ms. Cummins was concerned about these revelations and attempted to bring up the subject with the president of Merced Home Products but was told that "we all know what Lansing's doing, but as long as he continues to turn in such good reports, don't bother him." When Ms. Cummins asked if the board of directors was aware of the situation, the president somewhat testily replied, "Of course they are aware."

Required:
1. How did Preston Lansing probably "rig" the standard costs—are the standards set too high or too low? Explain.
2. Should Preston Lansing be permitted to continue his practice of managing reported earnings?
3. What should Stacy Cummins do in this situation?

CASE 10-32 Balanced Scorecard [LO5]
Haglund Department Store is located in the downtown area of a small city. While the store had been profitable for many years, it is facing increasing competition from large national chains that have set up stores on the outskirts of the city. Recently the downtown area has been undergoing revitalization, and the owners of Haglund Department Store are somewhat optimistic that profitability can be restored.

In an attempt to accelerate the return to profitability, management of Haglund Department Store is in the process of designing a balanced scorecard for the company. Management believes the company should focus on two key problems. First, customers are taking longer and longer to pay the bills they incur using the department store's charge card, and the company has far more bad debts than are normal for the industry. If this problem were solved, the company would have more cash to make much needed renovations. Investigation has revealed that much of the problem with late payments and unpaid bills results from customers disputing incorrect charges on their bills. These incorrect charges usually occur because salesclerks incorrectly enter data on the charge account slip. Second, the company has been incurring large losses on unsold seasonal apparel. Such items are ordinarily resold at a loss to discount stores that specialize in such distress items.

The meeting in which the balanced scorecard approach was discussed was disorganized and ineffectively led—possibly because no one other than one of the vice presidents had read anything about how to build a balanced scorecard. Nevertheless, a number of potential performance measures were suggested by various managers. These potential performance measures are:
a. Percentage of charge account bills containing errors.
b. Percentage of salesclerks trained to correctly enter data on charge account slips.
c. Average age of accounts receivables.
d. Profit per employee.
e. Customer satisfaction with accuracy of charge account bills from monthly customer survey.
f. Total sales revenue.
g. Sales per employee.
h. Travel expenses for buyers for trips to fashion shows.
i. Unsold inventory at the end of the season as a percentage of total cost of sales.
j. Courtesy shown by junior staff members to senior staff members based on surveys of senior staff.
k. Percentage of suppliers making just-in-time deliveries.
l. Sales per square foot of floor space.
m. Written-off accounts receivable (bad debts) as a percentage of sales.
n. Quality of food in the staff cafeteria based on staff surveys.
o. Percentage of employees who have attended the city's cultural diversity workshop.
p. Total profit.

Required:
1. As someone with more knowledge of the balanced scorecard than almost anyone else in the company, you have been asked to build an integrated balanced scorecard. In your scorecard, use only performance measures listed previously. You do not have to use all of the performance measures suggested by the managers, but you should build a balanced scorecard that reveals a strategy for dealing with the problems with accounts receivable and with unsold merchandise. Construct the

balanced scorecard following the format used in Exhibit 10–12. Do not be concerned with whether a specific performance measure falls within the learning and growth, internal business process, customer, or financial perspective. However, use arrows to show the causal links between performance measures within your balanced scorecard and explain whether the performance measures should show increases or decreases.

2. Assume that the company adopts your balanced scorecard. After operating for a year, some performance measures show improvements, but not others. What should management do next?

3. *a.* Suppose that customers express greater satisfaction with the accuracy of their charge account bills but the performance measures for the average age of accounts receivable and for bad debts do not improve. Explain why this might happen.

   b. Suppose that the performance measures for the average age of accounts receivable, bad debts, and unsold inventory improve, but total profits do not. Explain why this might happen. Assume in your answer that the explanation lies within the company.

RESEARCH AND APPLICATION 10-33 [LO5]

The questions in this exercise are based on the Nordstrom, Inc., 2004 annual report at http://phx. corporate-ir.net/phoenix.zhtml?c=93295&p=irol-reportsAnnual. You do not need to print the annual report in order to answer the questions.

Required:

1. What is Nordstrom's strategy for success in the marketplace? Does the company rely primarily on a customer intimacy, operational excellence, or product leadership customer value proposition? What evidence supports your conclusion?

2. Page 3 of the annual report summarizes six measures that Nordstrom collectively refers to as its scorecard. Do these measures constitute a balanced scorecard? Why or why not?

3. Identify four measures that Nordstrom could include in the financial perspective of a balanced scorecard. How do the measures that you have chosen differ from one another? Ideally, should each measure increase or decrease over time?

4. Identify four measures that Nordstrom could include in the customer perspective of a balanced scorecard. Feel free to create measures that are not explicitly mentioned in the annual report. What statements in the annual report motivated your choices? Ideally, should each of your measures increase or decrease over time?

5. Identify four measures that Nordstrom could include in the internal business process perspective of a balanced scorecard. Feel free to create measures that are not explicitly mentioned in the annual report. What statements in the annual report motivated your choices? Ideally, should each of your measures increase or decrease over time?

6. Identify four measures that Nordstrom could include in the learning and growth perspective of a balanced scorecard. Feel free to create measures that are not explicitly mentioned in the annual report. What statements in the annual report motivated your choices? Ideally, should each of your measures increase or decrease over time?

7. Create four hypothesis statements (in "if-then" form) that demonstrate four of the causal links between measures that you have chosen.

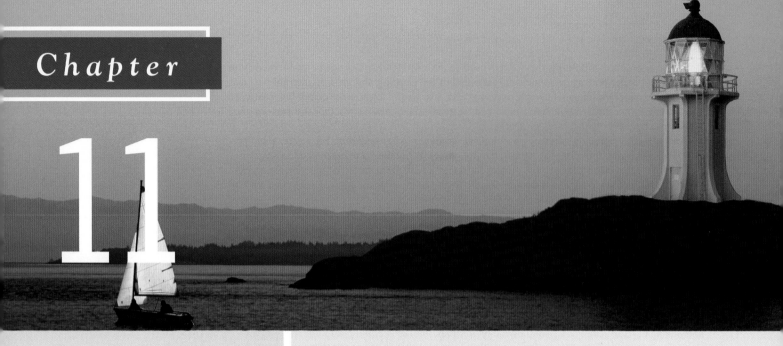

Chapter 11

Learning Objectives

After studying Chapter 11, you should be able to:

LO1 Prepare a flexible budget and explain the advantages of the flexible budget approach over the static budget approach.

LO2 Prepare a performance report for both variable and fixed overhead costs using the flexible budget approach.

LO3 Use a flexible budget to prepare a variable overhead performance report containing only a spending variance.

LO4 Use a flexible budget to prepare a variable overhead performance report containing both a spending and an efficiency variance.

LO5 Compute the predetermined overhead rate and apply overhead to products in a standard cost system.

LO6 Compute and interpret the fixed overhead budget and volume variances.

Flexible Budgets and Overhead Analysis

Controlling Costs—Rain or Shine

Totes»Isotoner Corporation is the world's largest marketer of umbrellas, gloves, rainwear, and other weather-related accessories. One of the company's costs is a "flex advertising" fee that it pays to department stores based on the stores' sales of totes»Isotoner products. The company prepares a management report that compares actual flex advertising costs *as a percentage of actual sales* to budgeted flex advertising costs *as a percentage of budgeted sales*. This is done because management expects a variable cost, such as flex advertising, to stay constant on a per sales dollar basis.

The company purposely does not compare its actual and budgeted *total dollar amounts* of flex advertising expense because it provides misleading feedback about managerial performance. For example, if actual sales exceed budgeted sales, a highly efficient manager could be naively penalized for incurring actual variable costs that exceed budgeted variable costs. Conversely, if actual sales are less than budgeted sales, an inefficient manager could be naively rewarded for incurring actual variable costs that are less than budgeted variable costs.

When it comes to fixed costs, totes»Isotoner monitors total dollar amounts rather than percentages. For example, the Information Technology (IT) Department incurs numerous costs that are not affected by sales variation within the relevant range. If percentages were used to manage these costs, an increase in sales would decrease the IT Department's total fixed costs as a percentage of sales, thereby sending misleading signals about managerial efficiency.

In addition to cost information, totes»Isotoner uses other non-financial performance measures to ensure its employees do not fixate on minimizing costs to the detriment of customers. ■

Source: Author's conversation with Donna Deye, senior vice president and CFO, totes»Isotoner Corporation.

Overhead is a major cost, if not *the* major cost, in many organizations. For example, it costs Microsoft very little to make copies of its software for sale to customers; almost all of Microsoft's costs are in research and development and marketing—elements of overhead. Or consider Disney World. The only direct cost of serving a particular guest is the cost of the food the guest consumes at the park; virtually all of the other costs of running the amusement park are overhead. Even Boeing, a manufacturer, has huge amounts of overhead in the form of engineering salaries, buildings, insurance, administrative salaries, and marketing costs. Not surprisingly, controlling overhead costs is a major preoccupation of managers.

FOCUS ON OVERHEAD COSTS

Overhead costs now account for as much as 66% of the costs incurred by companies in service industries and up to 37% of the total costs of manufacturers. Consequently, overhead reduction is a recurring theme in many organizations. However, the extent of the reductions must be considered in light of competitive pressures to improve services and product quality. Managers must avoid cutting costs that add value to the organization.

Source: Nick Develin, "Unlocking Overhead Value," *Management Accounting*, December 1999, pp. 22–34.

Since overhead is usually made up of many separate costs, including everything from disposable coffee cups in the visitors' waiting area to the president's salary, it is more difficult to control than direct materials and direct labor. Overhead control is further complicated by the fact that overhead costs can be variable, fixed, or a mixture of variable and fixed. However, these complications can be largely overcome by using flexible budgets. In this chapter, we learn how to prepare flexible budgets and how they can be used to control costs. We also expand the study of overhead variances that we started in Chapter 10.

Let's start with a simple example. Imagine that you work as a baggage handler for an airline. Your boss has said that you should be able to unload 20 pieces of luggage from an airplane per minute. Flight 2707 from Boston carries *on average* 300 pieces of luggage. Today flight 2707 is scheduled to arrive from Boston and your boss has decided that you should be able to unload the luggage on the flight in 15 minutes (300 pieces of luggage ÷ 20 pieces per minute). However, it takes you 20 minutes instead of 15 minutes to unload the luggage and consequently your boss yells at you. But, the flight actually contained 460 pieces of luggage. How would you feel? You might do some quick math as follows. Since there were 460 pieces of luggage on this flight and you are expected to unload 20 pieces per minute, then you should have been expected to unload the luggage on this flight in 23 minutes (460 pieces of luggage ÷ 20 pieces per minute). You did it in just 20 minutes instead of 23 minutes. Therefore, you should be getting a pat on the back, not yelled at! Notice, your natural inclination was to "flex" the budget of 15 minutes, which was based on 300 pieces of luggage, to reflect what the budget should be for 460 pieces of luggage—23 minutes. Now, let's proceed by applying dollars and cents to this concept.

Flexible Budgets

Characteristics of a Flexible Budget

The budgets that we studied in Chapter 9 were *static budgets*. A **static budget** is prepared at the beginning of the budgeting period and is valid for only the planned level of activity. A static budget is suitable for planning but is inappropriate for evaluating how well costs are controlled. If the actual level of activity differs from what was planned, it would be misleading to compare actual costs to the static budget. If activity is higher than expected, variable costs should be higher than expected; and if activity is lower than expected, variable costs should be lower than expected.

Flexible budgets take into account how changes in activity affect costs. A **flexible budget** makes it easy to estimate what costs should be for any level of activity within a specified range. When a flexible budget is used in performance evaluation, actual costs are compared to what the *costs should have been for the actual level of activity during the period* rather than to the budgeted costs from the original budget. This is a very important distinction— particularly for variable costs. If adjustments for the level of activity are not made, it is very difficult to interpret discrepancies between budgeted and actual costs.

WHY DO COMPANIES NEED FLEXIBLE BUDGETS?

The difficulty of accurately predicting future financial performance can be readily understood by reading the annual report of any publicly traded company. For example Nucor Corporation, a steel manufacturer headquartered in Charlotte, North Carolina, cites numerous reasons why its actual results may differ from expectations, including the following: (1) the supply and cost of raw materials, electricity, and natural gas may change unexpectedly; (2) the market demand for steel products may change; (3) competitive pressures from imports and substitute materials may intensify; (4) uncertainties regarding the global economy may affect customer demand; (5) changes to U.S. and foreign trade policy may alter current importing and exporting practices; and (6) new government regulations could significantly increase environmental compliance costs. Each of these factors could cause static budget revenues and/or costs to differ from actual results.

Source: Nucor Corporation 2004 annual report, p. 3.

Deficiencies of the Static Budget

To illustrate the difference between a static budget and a flexible budget, consider the case of Rick's Hairstyling, an upscale hairstyling salon located in Beverly Hills that is owned and managed by Rick Manzi. The salon has very loyal customers—many of whom are associated with the film industry. Recently Rick has been attempting to get better control of his overhead, and at the urging of his accounting and business adviser Victoria Kho, he has begun to prepare monthly budgets. Victoria Kho is an accountant in independent practice who specializes in small service-oriented businesses like Rick's Hairstyling.

At the end of February, Rick carefully prepared the March budget for overhead items that appears in Exhibit 11–1. Rick believes that the number of customers served in a month

EXHIBIT 11–1

Rick's Hairstyling Static Budget For the Month Ended March 31	
Budgeted number of client-visits	5,000
Budgeted variable overhead costs:	
Hairstyling supplies (@$1.20 per client-visit)	$ 6,000
Client gratuities (@$4.00 per client-visit)	20,000
Electricity (@$0.20 per client-visit)	1,000
Total variable overhead cost....................	27,000
Budgeted fixed overhead costs:	
Support staff wages and salaries..............	8,000
Rent.....................................	12,000
Insurance	1,000
Utilities other than electricity...................	500
Total fixed overhead cost	21,500
Total budgeted overhead cost	$48,500

is the best way to measure the overall level of activity in his salon. He refers to these visits as client-visits. A customer who comes into the salon and has his or her hair styled is counted as one client-visit. After some discussion with Victoria Kho, Rick identified three major categories of variable overhead costs—hairstyling supplies, client gratuities, and electricity—and four major categories of fixed costs—support staff wages and salaries, rent, insurance, and utilities other than electricity. Client gratuities consist of flowers, candies, and glasses of champagne that Rick gives to his customers while they are in the salon. Rick considers electricity to be a variable cost because almost all of the electricity in the salon is consumed by running blow-dryers, curling irons, and other hairstyling equipment.

To develop the budget for variable overhead, Rick estimated that the average cost per client-visit should be $1.20 for hairstyling supplies, $4.00 for client gratuities, and $0.20 for electricity. Based on his estimate of 5,000 client-visits in March, Rick budgeted for $6,000 ($1.20 per client-visit × 5,000 client-visits) in hairstyling supplies, $20,000 ($4.00 per client-visit × 5,000 client-visits) in client gratuities, and $1,000 ($0.20 per client-visit × 5,000 client-visits) in electricity.

The budget for fixed overhead items was based on Rick's records of how much he had spent on these items in the past. The budget included $8,000 for support staff wages and salaries, $12,000 for rent, $1,000 for insurance, and $500 for utilities other than electricity.

At the end of March, Rick prepared a report comparing actual to budgeted costs. That report appears in Exhibit 11–2. The problem with that report, as Rick immediately realized, is that it compares costs at one level of activity (5,200 client-visits) to costs at a different level of activity (5,000 client-visits). Since Rick had 200 more client-visits than expected, some of his costs *should* be higher than budgeted. The static budget performance report confuses control over activity and control over costs. From Rick's standpoint, the increase in activity was good and should be counted as a favorable variance, but the increase in activity has an apparently negative impact on the costs in the report. Rick knew that something would have to be done to make the report more meaningful, but he was unsure of what to do. So he made an appointment to meet with Victoria Kho to discuss the next step.

Victoria: How is the budgeting going?

Rick: Pretty well. I didn't have any trouble putting together the overhead budget for March. I also prepared a report comparing the actual costs for March to the budgeted costs, but that report isn't giving me what I really want to know.

MANAGERIAL ACCOUNTING IN ACTION

RICK'S hairstyling salon

The Issue

EXHIBIT 11–2

Rick's Hairstyling Static Budget Performance Report For the Month Ended March 31			
	Actual	Budgeted	Variance
Client-visits........................	5,200	5,000	200 F
Variable overhead costs:			
Hairstyling supplies..................	$ 6,400	$ 6,000	$ 400 U*
Client gratuities....................	22,300	20,000	2,300 U*
Electricity	1,020	1,000	20 U*
Total variable overhead cost............	29,720	27,000	2,720 U*
Fixed overhead costs:			
Support staff wages and salaries........	8,100	8,000	100 U
Rent	12,000	12,000	0
Insurance	1,000	1,000	0
Utilities other than electricity...........	470	500	30 F
Total fixed overhead cost	21,570	21,500	70 U
Total overhead cost	$51,290	$48,500	$2,790 U*

*The cost variances for variable costs and for total overhead are useless for evaluating how well costs were controlled since they have been derived by comparing actual costs at one level of activity to budgeted costs at a different level of activity.

Victoria: Because your actual level of activity didn't match your budgeted activity?

Rick: Right. I know the level of activity shouldn't affect my fixed costs, but we had a lot more client-visits than I had expected and that had to affect my variable costs.

Victoria: So you want to know whether the actual costs are justified by the actual level of activity you had in March?

Rick: Precisely.

Victoria: If you leave your reports and data with me, I can work on it later today, and by tomorrow I'll have a report to show to you.

How a Flexible Budget Works

A flexible budget approach recognizes that a budget can be adjusted to show what costs *should be* for the actual level of activity. To illustrate how flexible budgets work, Victoria prepared the report in Exhibit 11–3. It shows how overhead costs should be expected to change, depending on the monthly level of activity. Within the activity range of 4,900 to 5,200 client-visits, the fixed costs are expected to remain the same. For the variable overhead costs, Victoria multiplied Rick's per-client costs ($1.20 for hairstyling supplies, $4.00 for client gratuities, and $0.20 for electricity) by the appropriate number of client-visits in each column. For example, the $1.20 cost of hairstyling supplies was multiplied by 4,900 client-visits to give the total cost of $5,880 for hairstyling supplies at that level of activity.

Topic Tackler

PLUS

11–1

Using the Flexible Budgeting Concept in Performance Evaluation

LEARNING OBJECTIVE 2
Prepare a performance report for both variable and fixed overhead costs using the flexible budget approach.

To get a better idea of how well Rick controlled his variable overhead costs in March, Victoria applied the flexible budgeting concept to create a budget based on the *actual* number of client-visits for the month (Exhibit 11–4). This new budget is prepared by multiplying the actual level of activity by the cost formula for each of the variable cost categories. For example, using the $1.20 per client-visit for hairstyling supplies, the total cost for this item *should be* $6,240 for 5,200 client-visits ($1.20 per client-visit × 5,200 client-visits). Since

EXHIBIT 11–3
Illustration of the Flexible Budgeting Concept

		Activity (in client-visits)			
Rick's Hairstyling — Flexible Budget — For the Month Ended March 31					
Budgeted number of client-visits	5,000				
Overhead Costs	Cost Formula (per client-visit)	4,900	5,000	5,100	5,200
Variable overhead costs:					
Hairstyling supplies	$1.20	$ 5,880	$ 6,000	$ 6,120	$ 6,240
Client gratuities	4.00	19,600	20,000	20,400	20,800
Electricity (variable)	0.20	980	1,000	1,020	1,040
Total variable overhead cost	$5.40	26,460	27,000	27,540	28,080
Fixed overhead costs:					
Support staff wages and salaries		8,000	8,000	8,000	8,000
Rent		12,000	12,000	12,000	12,000
Insurance		1,000	1,000	1,000	1,000
Utilities other than electricity		500	500	500	500
Total fixed overhead cost		21,500	21,500	21,500	21,500
Total overhead cost		$47,960	$48,500	$49,040	$49,580

EXHIBIT 11–4

	Rick's Hairstyling Flexible Budget Performance Report For the Month Ended March 31			
Budgeted number of client-visits	5,000			
Actual number of client-visits	5,200			
Overhead Costs	Cost Formula (per client-visit)	Actual Costs Incurred for 5,200 Client-Visits	Flexible Budget Based on 5,200 Client-Visits	Variance
Variable overhead costs:				
Hairstyling supplies	$1.20	$ 6,400	$ 6,240	$ 160 U
Client gratuities	4.00	22,300	20,800	1,500 U
Electricity (variable)	0.20	1,020	1,040	20 F
Total variable overhead cost	$5.40	29,720	28,080	1,640 U
Fixed overhead costs:				
Support staff wages and salaries		8,100	8,000	100 U
Rent		12,000	12,000	0
Insurance		1,000	1,000	0
Utilities other than electricity		470	500	30 F
Total fixed overhead cost		21,570	21,500	70 U
Total overhead cost		$51,290	$49,580	$1,710 U

the actual cost for hairstyling supplies was $6,400, the unfavorable variance is $160. This differs from the $400 unfavorable variance shown for hairstyling supplies in Exhibit 11–2. The difference arises because Exhibit 11–2 uses a static budget approach that compares actual costs at one level of activity to budgeted costs at a different level of activity. This is like comparing apples to oranges. Because actual activity was higher by 200 client-visits than budgeted activity, the total cost of hairstyling supplies *should* have been $240 ($1.20 per client-visit × 200 client-visits) higher than budgeted. As a result, $240 of the $400 "unfavorable" variance in the static budget performance report in Exhibit 11–2 is spurious.

The flexible budget performance report in Exhibit 11–4 provides a more valid assessment of performance because actual costs are compared to what costs should have been at the actual level of activity. In other words, apples are compared to apples. When this is done, we see that the hairstyling supplies variance is $160 unfavorable rather than $400 unfavorable as it was in the original static budget performance report. In some cases, as with electricity in Rick's report, an unfavorable static budget variance may be transformed into a favorable variance when an increase in activity is properly taken into account.

The following discussion took place the next day at Rick's salon.

Victoria: Let me show you what I've got. [Victoria shows the report contained in Exhibit 11–4.] For the variable costs all I did was multiply the costs per client-visit by the number of client-visits you actually had in March. That allowed me to come up with a better benchmark for what the variable costs should have been.

Rick: That's what you labeled the "flexible budget based on 5,200 client-visits"?

Victoria: That's right. Your original budget was based on 5,000 client-visits, so it understated what the variable overhead costs should be when you actually serve 5,200 customers.

Rick: That's clear enough. These variances aren't quite as shocking as the variances on my first report.

Victoria: Yes, but you still have an unfavorable variance of $1,500 for client gratuities.

Rick: I know how that happened. In March there was a big Democratic Party fundraising dinner that I forgot about when I prepared the March budget.

MANAGERIAL ACCOUNTING IN ACTION

The Wrap-Up

Rick: To fit all of our regular clients in, we had to push them through here pretty fast. Everyone still got top-rate service, but I felt bad about not being able to spend as much time with each customer. I wanted to give my customers a little extra something to compensate them for the less personal service, so I ordered a lot of flowers which I gave away by the bunch.

Victoria: With the prices you charge, Rick, I am sure the gesture was appreciated.

Rick: One thing bothers me about the report. Why are some of my actual fixed costs different from what I budgeted? Doesn't fixed mean that they are not supposed to change?

Victoria: We call these costs *fixed* because they shouldn't be affected by *changes in the level of activity.* However, that doesn't mean that they can't change for other reasons. For example, your utilities bill, which includes natural gas for heating, varies with the weather.

Rick: I can see that. March was warmer than normal, so my utilities bill was lower than I had expected.

Victoria: The use of the term *fixed* also suggests to people that the cost can't be controlled, but that isn't true. It is often easier to control fixed costs than variable costs. For example, it would be fairly easy for you to change your insurance bill by adjusting the amount of insurance you carry. It would be much more difficult for you to reduce the electricity bill—a variable cost that is a necessary part of serving customers.

Rick: I think I understand, but it *is* confusing.

Victoria: Just remember that a cost is called variable if it is proportional to activity; it is called fixed if it does not depend on the level of activity. However, fixed costs can change for reasons unrelated to changes in the level of activity. And controllability has little to do with whether a cost is variable or fixed. Fixed costs are often more controllable than variable costs.

IN BUSINESS

FOCUS ON OPPORTUNITIES

The late management guru Peter F. Drucker cautioned managers that "almost without exception, the first page of the [monthly] report presents the areas in which results fall below expectations or in which expenditures exceed the budget. It focuses on problems. Problems cannot be ignored. But . . . enterprises have to focus on opportunities. That requires a small but fundamental procedural change: a new first page to the monthly report, one that precedes the page that shows the problems. The new page should focus on where results are better than expected. As much time should be spent on that new first page as traditionally was spent on the problem page."

Source: Peter F. Drucker, "Change Leaders," *Inc.* magazine, June 1999, pp. 65–72.

Using the flexible budget approach, Rick Manzi now has a better way of assessing whether overhead costs are under control. The analysis is not so simple, however, in companies that provide a variety of products and services. The number of units produced or customers served may not be an adequate measure of overall activity. For example, does it make sense to count a Sony CD player, worth less than $50, as equivalent to a large-screen Sony HD-TV? If the number of units produced is used as a measure of overall activity, then the CD player and the large-screen HD-TV would be counted as equivalent. Clearly, the number of units produced (or customers served) may not be appropriate as an overall measure of activity when the organization has a variety of products or services; a common denominator may be needed.

The Measure of Activity—A Critical Choice

What should be used as the measure of activity when a company produces a variety of products and services? At least three factors are important in selecting an activity base for an overhead flexible budget:

1. Changes in the activity base should cause, or at least be highly correlated with, changes in the variable overhead costs in the flexible budget. Ideally, the variable overhead costs

in the flexible budget should vary in direct proportion to changes in the activity base. For example, in a carpentry shop specializing in handmade wood furniture, the costs of miscellaneous supplies such as glue, wooden dowels, and sandpaper should vary with the number of direct labor-hours. Direct labor-hours would therefore be a good measure of activity to use in a flexible budget for the costs of such supplies.

2. The activity base should not be expressed in dollars or some other currency. For example, direct labor cost is usually a poor choice for an activity base in flexible budgets because changes in wage rates affect the activity base but do not usually result in a proportionate change in overhead. For example, we would not ordinarily expect to see a 5% increase in the consumption of glue in a carpentry shop if the workers receive a 5% increase in pay. Therefore, it is best to use physical rather than financial measures of activity in flexible budgets.

3. The activity base should be simple and easily understood, otherwise it will result in confusion and misunderstanding. It is difficult to control costs if people don't understand the reports or do not accept them as valid.

Variable Overhead Variances—A Closer Look

When the flexible budget is based on *hours* of activity (such as direct labor-hours) rather than on units of product or number of customers served, the flexible budget on the performance report can be based on either the actual hours used *or* the standard hours allowed for the actual output. Which should be used?

Topic Tackler

PLUS

11–2

Actual versus Standard Hours

To explain these two options, we will use an example involving MicroDrive Corporation, a manufacturer of precision computer disk-drive motors for military applications. Data concerning the company's variable manufacturing overhead costs are shown in Exhibit 11–5.

MicroDrive uses machine-hours as the activity base in its flexible budget because its managers believe most of the company's overhead costs are driven by machine-hours. At the beginning of the year, MicroDrive estimated that it would produce 25,000 motors. Since the company's standard allowance is 2 machine-hours per motor, the budgeted level of activity for the year was 50,000 machine-hours. During the year the company actually produced 20,000 motors that *should* have been produced in 40,000 machine-hours (40,000 machine-hours = 2 machine-hours allowed per motor × 20,000 motors); however, the company actually used 42,000 machine-hours to makes these motors.

Budgeted production	25,000 motors
Actual production	20,000 motors
Standard machine-hours per motor	2 machine-hours per motor
Budgeted machine-hours (2 × 25,000)	50,000 machine-hours
Standard machine-hours allowed for the actual output (2 × 20,000)	40,000 machine-hours
Actual machine-hours	42,000 machine-hours
Variable overhead costs per machine-hour:	
Indirect labor	$0.80 per machine-hour
Lubricants	$0.30 per machine-hour
Power	$0.40 per machine-hour
Actual total variable overhead costs:	
Indirect labor	$36,000
Lubricants	11,000
Power	24,000
Total actual variable overhead cost	$71,000

EXHIBIT 11–5
MicroDrive Corporation Data

In preparing an overhead performance report for the year, MicroDrive could use the 42,000 machine-hours actually worked during the year *or* the 40,000 machine-hours that should have been worked according to the standard. If the actual hours are used, only a spending variance will be computed. If the standard hours are used, both a spending *and* an efficiency variance will be computed. Both of these approaches are illustrated in the following sections.

Spending Variance Alone

LEARNING OBJECTIVE 3
Use a flexible budget to prepare a variable overhead performance report containing only a spending variance.

If MicroDrive Corporation bases its overhead performance report on the 42,000 machine-hours actually worked during the year, then the performance report will show only a spending variance for variable overhead. Exhibit 11–6 shows a performance report prepared in this way.

The formula for the spending variance was introduced in the preceding chapter. That formula is:

Or, in factored form:

$$\frac{\text{Variable overhead}}{\text{spending variance}} = AH(AR - SR)$$

The report in Exhibit 11–6 is structured around the first, or unfactored, format.

EXHIBIT 11–6

MicroDrive Corporation
Variable Overhead Performance Report
For the Year Ended December 31

> Budget allowances are based on 42,000 machine-hours actually worked.

> Comparing the flexible budget to actual overhead cost yields only a spending variance.

Budgeted machine-hours	50,000
Actual machine-hours	42,000
Standard machine-hours allowed	40,000

Overhead Costs	Cost Formula (per machine-hour)	Actual Costs Incurred 42,000 Machine-Hours ($AH \times AR$)	Flexible Budget Based on 42,000 Machine-Hours ($AH \times SR$)	Spending Variance
Variable overhead costs:				
Indirect labor	$0.80	$36,000	$33,600*	$2,400 U
Lubricants	0.30	11,000	12,600	1,600 F
Power	0.40	24,000	16,800	7,200 U
Total variable overhead cost	$1.50	$71,000	$63,000	$8,000 U

*42,000 machine-hours $\times$ $0.80 per machine-hour = $33,600. Other budget allowances are computed in the same way.

Interpreting the Spending Variance   The variable overhead spending variance is useful only to the extent that the cost driver for variable overhead really is the actual hours worked. Then the flexible budget based on the actual hours worked is a valid benchmark that tells us how much *should* have been spent in total on variable overhead items during the period. The actual overhead costs are larger than this benchmark, resulting in an unfavorable variance, if either (1) the variable overhead items cost more to purchase than the standards allow or (2) more variable overhead items were used than the standards allow. So the spending variance includes both price and quantity variances.

Both Spending and Efficiency Variances

If management of MicroDrive Corporation wants to compute variable overhead spending and efficiency variances, then it should compute budget allowances for *both* the 40,000 machine-hour and the 42,000 machine-hour levels of activity. Exhibit 11–7 shows a performance report prepared in this way.

Note that the spending variance in Exhibit 11–7 is the same as the spending variance shown in Exhibit 11–6. The performance report in Exhibit 11–7 has simply been expanded to also include an efficiency variance. Together, the spending and efficiency variances make up the total variance.

Interpreting the Efficiency Variance   Like the variable overhead spending variance, the variable overhead efficiency variance is useful only to the extent that the cost

> **LEARNING OBJECTIVE 4**
> Use a flexible budget to prepare a variable overhead performance report containing both a spending and an efficiency variance.

EXHIBIT 11–7

MicroDrive Corporation
Variable Overhead Performance Report
For the Year Ended December 31

Budget allowances are based on 40,000 machine-hours—the time it *should have taken* to produce the year's actual output of 20,000 motors—as well as on the 42,000 *actual* machine-hours worked.

This approach yields both a spending and an efficiency variance.

Budgeted machine-hours	50,000		
Actual machine-hours	42,000		
Standard machine-hours allowed	40,000		

	Cost Formula (per machine-hour)	(1) Actual Costs Incurred 42,000 Machine-Hours (AH × AR)	(2) Flexible Budget Based on 42,000 Machine-Hours (AH × SR)	(3) Flexible Budget Based on 40,000 Machine-Hours (SH × SR)	Total Variance (1) − (3)	Spending Variance (1) − (2)	Efficiency Variance (2) − (3)
Overhead Costs							
Variable overhead costs:							
Indirect labor	$0.80	$36,000	$33,600*	$32,000	$ 4,000 U	$2,400 U	$1,600 U
Lubricants	0.30	11,000	12,600	12,000	1,000 F	1,600 F	600 U
Power	0.40	24,000	16,800	16,000	8,000 U	7,200 U	800 U
Total variable overhead cost	$1.50	$71,000	$63,000	$60,000	$11,000 U	$8,000 U	$3,000 U

*42,000 machine-hours × $0.80 per machine-hour = $33,600. Other budget allowances are computed in the same way.

driver for variable overhead really is the actual hours worked. Then any increase in hours actually worked should result in additional variable overhead costs. Consequently, if too many hours are used to create the actual output, this is presumed to result in an increase in variable overhead. The variable overhead efficiency variance is an estimate of the effect on variable overhead costs of inefficiency in the use of the base (i.e., hours). In a sense, the term *variable overhead efficiency variance* is a misnomer. It seems to suggest that it measures the efficiency with which variable overhead resources are used. It does not. It is an estimate of the indirect effect on variable overhead costs of inefficiency in the use of the activity base.

Recall from the preceding chapter that the variable overhead efficiency variance is a function of the difference between the actual hours incurred and the hours that should have been used to produce the period's output:

Or, in factored form:

$$\text{Variable overhead efficiency variance} = SR(AH - SH)$$

If more hours are worked than are allowed at standard, then the overhead efficiency variance will be unfavorable. However, as discussed above, the inefficiency is not in the use of overhead *but rather in the use of the base itself.*

This point can be illustrated by looking again at Exhibit 11–7. Two thousand more machine-hours were used during the period than should have been used to produce the period's output. Each of these hours presumably required the incurrence of $1.50 of variable overhead cost, resulting in an unfavorable variance of $3,000 (2,000 machine-hours × $1.50 per machine-hour = $3,000). Although this $3,000 variance is called an overhead efficiency variance, it could better be called a machine-hours efficiency variance, since it results from using too many machine-hours rather than from inefficient use of overhead resources.

Control of the Efficiency Variance   Who is responsible for control of the overhead efficiency variance? Since the variance reflects efficiency in the utilization of the base underlying the flexible budget, whoever is responsible for control of this base is responsible for control of the variance. If the base is direct labor-hours, then the supervisor responsible for the use of labor time is responsible for any overhead efficiency variance.

Activity-Based Costing and the Flexible Budget

It is unlikely that all of the variable overhead in a complex organization is driven by a single factor such as the number of units produced or the number of labor-hours or machine-hours. The flexible budgeting approach can be easily adapted to accommodate a number of cost drivers. The cost formula for each variable cost element can depend on its own cost driver rather than on a single organization-wide measure of activity. For example, in a medical clinic the variable overhead cost of providing clinic staff with latex gloves might be driven by the number of patient-visits whereas the variable overhead cost of sterile wiping pads to prepare injection sites might be driven by the number of injections administered. In the flexible budget, the cost formula for latex gloves would be stated in terms of patient-visits whereas the cost formula for sterile wiping pads would be stated in terms of injections administered.

Overhead Rates and Fixed Overhead Analysis

As we shall see, fixed overhead variances are fundamentally different from variable overhead variances. To understand fixed overhead variances, we will need to review how predetermined overhead rates are established and used.

Flexible Budgets and Overhead Rates

Fixed costs come in large chunks that by definition do not vary with changes in the level of activity within the relevant range. This creates a problem in product costing, since the average fixed cost per unit will vary with the level of activity. Consider the data in the following table:

Month	(1) Total Fixed Overhead Cost	(2) Number of Units Produced	Average Fixed Cost per Unit (1) ÷ (2)
January.........	$6,000	1,000	$6.00
February.......	$6,000	1,500	$4.00
March	$6,000	800	$7.50

Notice that the large number of units produced in February results in a low unit cost ($4.00), whereas the smaller number of units produced in March results in a higher unit cost ($7.50). This occurs because the fixed cost is spread across more units in February than in March. One of the major reasons for using a predetermined overhead rate is to avoid such fluctuations in unit costs. A predetermined overhead rate can be set for an entire year, resulting in the same unit cost being recorded in the accounting system throughout the year.

Throughout the remainder of this chapter, we will be analyzing the fixed overhead costs of MicroDrive Corporation. To assist us in that task, the flexible budget of the company—including fixed costs—is displayed in Exhibit 11–8. Note that the total fixed overhead costs amount to $300,000 within the range of activity in the flexible budget.

EXHIBIT 11–8

MicroDrive Corporation Flexible Budgets at Various Levels of Activity					
Overhead Costs	Cost Formula (per machine- hour)	Activity (in machine-hours)			
		40,000	45,000	50,000	55,000
Variable overhead costs:					
Indirect labor	$0.80	$ 32,000	$ 36,000	$ 40,000	$ 44,000
Lubricants	0.30	12,000	13,500	15,000	16,500
Power	0.40	16,000	18,000	20,000	22,000
Total variable overhead cost ..	$1.50	60,000	67,500	75,000	82,500
Fixed overhead costs:					
Depreciation............		100,000	100,000	100,000	100,000
Supervisory salaries		160,000	160,000	160,000	160,000
Insurance		40,000	40,000	40,000	40,000
Total fixed overhead cost		300,000	300,000	300,000	300,000
Total overhead cost		$360,000	$367,500	$375,000	$382,500

Denominator Activity   The formula that we used in Chapter 3 to compute the predetermined overhead rate was:

$$\frac{\text{Predetermined}}{\text{overhead rate}} = \frac{\text{Estimated total manufacturing overhead cost}}{\text{Estimated total amount of the base (MH, DLH, etc.)}}$$

The estimated total amount of the base in the formula for the predetermined overhead rate is called the **denominator activity.** Recall from our discussion in Chapter 3 that once an estimated activity level (denominator activity) has been chosen, it remains unchanged throughout the year, even if the actual level of activity differs from what was estimated. The reason for not changing the denominator is to keep the amount of overhead applied to each unit of product the same regardless of when it is produced during the year.

IN BUSINESS

KNOW YOUR COSTS

Understanding the difference between fixed and variable costs can be critical. Kennard T. Wing, of OMG Center for Collaborative Learning, reports that a large health care system made the mistake of classifying all of its costs as variable. As a consequence, when volume dropped, managers felt that costs should be cut proportionately and more than 1,000 people were laid off—even though "the workload of most of them had no direct relation to patient volume. The result was that morale of the survivors plummeted and within a year the system was scrambling to replace not only those it had let go, but many others who had quit. The point is, the accounting systems we design and implement really do affect management decisions in significant ways. A system built on a bad model of the business will either not be used or, if used, will lead to bad decisions."

Source: Kennard T. Wing, "Using Enhanced Cost Models in Variance Analysis for Better Control and Decision Making," *Management Accounting Quarterly*, Winter 2000, pp. 27–35.

Computing the Overhead Rate   When we discussed predetermined overhead rates in Chapter 3, we didn't explain how the estimated total manufacturing cost was determined. This figure can be derived using a flexible budget. The flexible budget can be used to determine the total amount of overhead cost that should be incurred at the denominator level of activity. The predetermined overhead rate can then be computed using the following variation on the basic formula for the predetermined overhead rate:

$$\frac{\text{Predetermined}}{\text{overhead rate}} = \frac{\substack{\text{Overhead from the flexible budget} \\ \text{at the denominator level of activity}}}{\text{Denominator level of activity}}$$

To illustrate, refer to MicroDrive Corporation's flexible budget for manufacturing overhead in Exhibit 11–8. Suppose that the budgeted activity level for the year is 50,000 machine-hours and that this will be used as the denominator activity in the formula for the predetermined overhead rate. The numerator in the formula is the estimated total overhead cost of $375,000 when the activity level is 50,000 machine-hours. This amount is taken from the flexible budget in Exhibit 11–8. Thus, the predetermined overhead rate for MicroDrive Corporation is computed as follows:

$$\frac{\text{Predetermined}}{\text{overhead rate}} = \frac{\$375,000}{50,000 \text{ MHs}} = \$7.50 \text{ per machine-hour (MH)}$$

Or the company can break its predetermined overhead rate down into its variable and fixed components:

$$\text{Variable component: } \frac{\$75,000}{50,000 \text{ MHs}} = \$1.50 \text{ per MH}$$

$$\text{Fixed component: } \frac{\$300,000}{50,000 \text{ MHs}} = \$6.00 \text{ per MH}$$

For every standard machine-hour recorded, work in process will be charged with $7.50 of overhead, of which $1.50 will be variable overhead and $6.00 will be fixed overhead. Since a disk-drive motor should take two machine-hours to complete, its cost will include $3.00 of variable overhead and $12.00 of fixed overhead, as shown on the following standard cost card:

Standard Cost Card—Per Motor	
Direct materials (assumed)	$14.00
Direct labor (assumed)	6.00
Variable overhead (2 MHs at $1.50 per MH)	3.00
Fixed overhead (2 MHs at $6.00 per MH)	12.00
Total standard cost per motor	$35.00

In sum, the flexible budget provides the estimated overhead cost needed to compute the predetermined overhead rate. Thus, the flexible budget plays a key role in determining the amount of fixed and variable overhead cost that will be charged to units of product.

Overhead Application in a Standard Cost System

To understand fixed overhead variances, we first have to understand how overhead is applied to work in process in a standard cost system. Recall that in Chapter 3 we applied overhead to work in process on the basis of the actual level of activity. This procedure was correct, since at the time we were dealing with a normal cost system.[1] However, we are now dealing with a standard cost system. In such a system, overhead is applied to work in process on the basis of the *standard hours allowed for the actual output of the period* rather than on the basis of the actual number of hours worked. Exhibit 11–9 illustrates this point. In a standard cost system, every unit of product is charged with the same amount of overhead cost, regardless of how much time the unit actually requires for processing.

The Fixed Overhead Variances

To illustrate the computation of fixed overhead variances, we will refer again to the data for MicroDrive Corporation.

LEARNING OBJECTIVE 6
Compute and interpret the fixed overhead budget and volume variances.

Denominator activity in machine-hours	50,000
Budgeted fixed overhead costs	$300,000
Fixed portion of the predetermined overhead rate (computed earlier)	$6 per machine-hour

Normal Cost System		Standard Cost System	
Manufacturing Overhead		Manufacturing Overhead	
Actual overhead costs incurred.	Applied overhead costs: Actual hours × Predetermined overhead rate.	Actual overhead costs incurred.	Applied overhead costs: Standard hours allowed for actual output × Predetermined overhead rate.
Underapplied or overapplied overhead		Underapplied or overapplied overhead	

EXHIBIT 11–9
Applied Overhead Costs: Normal Cost System versus Standard Cost System

[1] Normal cost systems are discussed on page 98 in Chapter 3.

Let's assume that the following actual operating results were recorded for the year:

Actual machine-hours	42,000
Standard machine-hours allowed*	40,000
Actual fixed overhead costs:	
Depreciation	$100,000
Supervisory salaries	172,000
Insurance	36,000
Total actual fixed overhead cost	$308,000

*For the actual production of the year.

From these data, two variances are computed for fixed overhead—a *budget variance* and a *volume variance.* The variances are shown in Exhibit 11–10.

Notice from the exhibit that overhead has been applied to work in process on the basis of 40,000 standard hours allowed for the actual output of the year rather than on the basis of 42,000 actual hours worked. This keeps unit costs from being affected by variations in efficiency.

The Budget Variance—A Closer Look

The **budget variance** is the difference between the actual fixed overhead costs incurred during the period and the original budgeted fixed overhead costs for the period. It can be computed as shown in Exhibit 11–10 or by using the following formula:

$$\frac{\text{Budget}}{\text{variance}} = \frac{\text{Actual fixed}}{\text{overhead cost}} - \frac{\text{Budgeted fixed}}{\text{overhead cost}}$$

Applying this formula to MicroDrive Corporation, the budget variance would be computed as follows:

$$\$308,000 - \$300,000 = \$8,000\ U$$

The variances computed for the fixed costs at Rick's Hairstyling in Exhibit 11–4 are all budget variances, since they represent the difference between the actual fixed overhead cost and the budgeted fixed overhead cost.

An expanded overhead performance report for MicroDrive Corporation appears in Exhibit 11–11. This report includes the budget variances for fixed overhead as well as the spending variances for variable overhead from Exhibit 11–6.

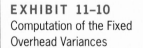

EXHIBIT 11–10
Computation of the Fixed Overhead Variances

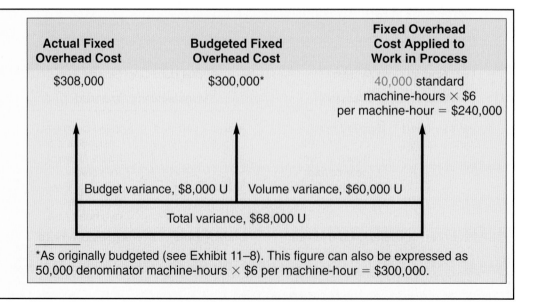

Actual Fixed Overhead Cost	Budgeted Fixed Overhead Cost	Fixed Overhead Cost Applied to Work in Process
$308,000	$300,000*	40,000 standard machine-hours × $6 per machine-hour = $240,000

Budget variance, $8,000 U | Volume variance, $60,000 U

Total variance, $68,000 U

*As originally budgeted (see Exhibit 11–8). This figure can also be expressed as 50,000 denominator machine-hours × $6 per machine-hour = $300,000.

EXHIBIT 11–11
Fixed Overhead Costs on the
Overhead Performance Report

MicroDrive Corporation
Overhead Performance Report
For the Year Ended December 31

Budgeted machine-hours 50,000
Actual machine-hours 42,000
Standard machine-hours allowed 40,000

	Cost Formula (per machine-hour)	Actual Costs 42,000 Machine-Hours	Flexible Budget Based on 42,000 Machine-Hours	Spending or Budget Variance
Overhead Costs				
Variable overhead costs:				
Indirect labor	$0.80	$ 36,000	$ 33,600	$ 2,400 U
Lubricants	0.30	11,000	12,600	1,600 F
Power	0.40	24,000	16,800	7,200 U
Total variable overhead cost	$1.50	71,000	63,000	8,000 U
Fixed overhead costs:				
Depreciation		100,000	100,000	0
Supervisory salaries		172,000	160,000	12,000 U
Insurance		36,000	40,000	4,000 F
Total fixed overhead cost		308,000	300,000	8,000 U
Total overhead cost		$379,000	$363,000	$16,000 U

The budget variances for fixed overhead can be very useful, since they represent the difference between how much *should* have been spent (according to the original budget) and how much was actually spent. For example, Exhibit 11–11 shows that supervisory salaries has a $12,000 unfavorable variance. This large variance should be explained. Was it due to an increase in salaries? Was it due to overtime? Was another supervisor hired? If so, why was another supervisor hired?

The Volume Variance—A Closer Look

The **volume variance** measures utilization of facilities. The variance arises whenever the standard hours allowed for the actual output of a period are different from the denominator activity level that was planned when the period began. It can be computed as shown in Exhibit 11–10 or by using the following formula:

$$\text{Volume variance} = \text{Fixed component of the predetermined overhead rate} \times \left(\text{Denominator hours} - \text{Standard hours allowed} \right)$$

Applying this formula to MicroDrive Corporation, the volume variance would be computed as follows:

$$\$6 \text{ per MH } (50,000 \text{ MHs} - 40,000 \text{ MHs}) = \$60,000 \text{ U}$$

Note that this computation agrees with the volume variance shown in Exhibit 11–10. As stated earlier, the volume variance is a measure of facility utilization. Or, to be more precise, it is a measure of how much actual output departed from the planned output that determined the denominator level of activity. An unfavorable variance, as above, means that the company's actual output was *less* than planned. A favorable variance would mean that the company's actual output was *greater* than planned.

It is important to note that the volume variance does not measure overspending or underspending. A company normally would incur the same dollar amount of fixed overhead cost regardless of whether the period's activity was above or below the planned (denominator) level. In short, the volume variance is an activity-related variance. It is explainable only by activity and is controllable only through activity.

To summarize:

1. If the denominator activity and the standard hours allowed for the actual output of the period are the same, the volume variance is zero.
2. If the denominator activity is greater than the standard hours allowed for the actual output of the period, then the volume variance is unfavorable. This indicates that facilities were utilized less than was planned.
3. If the denominator activity is less than the standard hours allowed for the actual output of the period, then the volume variance is favorable. This indicates that facilities were utilized more than was planned.

Graphic Analysis of Fixed Overhead Variances

Exhibit 11–12 shows a graphic analysis that offers insights into the fixed overhead budget and volume variances. As shown in the graph, fixed overhead cost is applied to work in process at the predetermined rate of $6 for each standard hour of activity. (The applied-cost line is the upward-sloping line on the graph.) Since a denominator level of 50,000 machine-hours was used in computing the $6 rate, the applied-cost line crosses the budget-cost line at exactly 50,000 machine-hours. If the denominator hours and the standard hours allowed for the actual output are the same, there is no volume variance. It is only when the standard hours differ from the denominator hours that a volume variance arises.

In MicroDrive's case, the standard hours allowed for the actual output (40,000 hours) are less than the denominator hours (50,000 hours). The result is an unfavorable volume

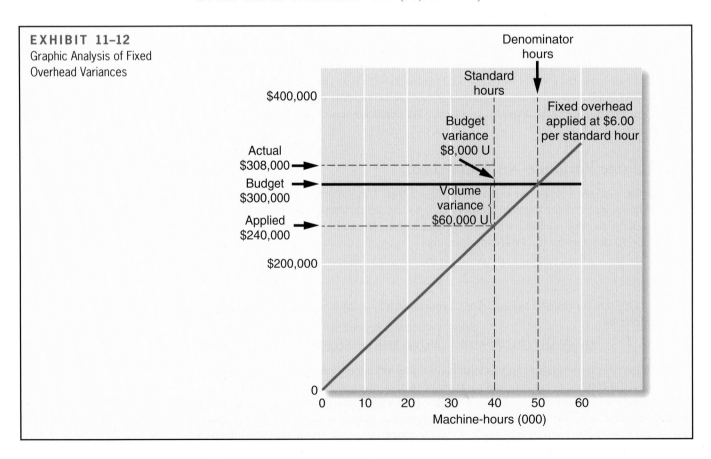

EXHIBIT 11–12
Graphic Analysis of Fixed Overhead Variances

variance because less cost was applied to production than was originally budgeted. If the situation had been reversed and the standard hours allowed for the actual output had exceeded the denominator hours, then the volume variance on the graph would have been favorable.

Cautions in Fixed Overhead Analysis

A volume variance for fixed overhead arises because when applying the costs to work in process, we act *as if* the fixed costs are variable. The graph in Exhibit 11–12 illustrates this point. Notice from the graph that fixed overhead costs are applied to work in process at a rate of $6 per hour *as if* they are variable. Treating these costs as if they are variable is necessary for product costing purposes, but some real dangers lurk here. Managers can easily be misled into thinking that fixed costs are *in fact* variable.

Keep clearly in mind that fixed overhead costs come in large chunks. Expressing fixed costs on a unit or per hour basis, though necessary for product costing for external reports, is artificial. Increases or decreases in activity in fact have no effect on total fixed costs within the relevant range of activity. Even though fixed costs are expressed on a unit or per hour basis, they are *not* proportional to activity. In a sense, the volume variance is the error that occurs as a result of treating fixed costs as variable costs in the costing system.

Overhead Variances and Underapplied or Overapplied Overhead Cost

Four variances relating to overhead cost have been computed for MicroDrive Corporation in this chapter. These four variances are as follows:

Variable overhead spending variance (p. 482)	$ 8,000 U
Variable overhead efficiency variance (p. 483)	3,000 U
Fixed overhead budget variance (p. 488)	8,000 U
Fixed overhead volume variance (p. 488)	60,000 U
Total overhead variance	$79,000 U

Recall from Chapter 3 that underapplied or overapplied overhead is the difference between the amount of overhead applied to products and the actual overhead costs incurred during a period. Basically, the overhead variances we have computed in this chapter break the underapplied or overapplied overhead down into variances that can be used by managers for control purposes. *The sum of the overhead variances equals the underapplied or overapplied overhead cost for a period.*

Furthermore, in a standard cost system, unfavorable variances are equivalent to underapplied overhead and favorable variances are equivalent to overapplied overhead. Unfavorable variances occur because more was spent on overhead than the standards allow. Underapplied overhead occurs when more was spent on overhead than was applied to products during the period. But in a standard costing system, the standard amount of overhead allowed is exactly the same as the amount of overhead applied to products. Therefore, in a standard costing system, unfavorable variances and underapplied overhead are the same thing, as are favorable variances and overapplied overhead.

For MicroDrive Corporation, the total overhead variance is $79,000 unfavorable. Therefore, its overhead cost is underapplied by $79,000 for the year. To solidify this point in your mind, *carefully study the review problem at the end of the chapter!* This review problem provides a comprehensive summary of overhead analysis, including the computation of underapplied or overapplied overhead cost in a standard cost system.

OVERHEAD ACCOUNTS: FERTILE GROUND FOR FRAUD

Particularly in small companies, the controller may be the only person who understands concepts such as overhead variances and overapplied and underapplied overhead. Furthermore, a small company controller may be able to both authorize cash disbursements and account for them. Since small, closely held companies often do not hire external auditors, these circumstances create an ideal environment for fraud.

Such was the case in a small manufacturing company with 100 employees and $30 million in annual sales. The controller embezzled nearly $1 million from the company over three years by writing checks to himself. The consultant who uncovered the fraud was tipped off by the unusually high overhead variances that resulted from the controller recording fictitious expenses in the overhead accounts to offset his fraudulent cash withdrawals. After the fraud was exposed, the company implemented various controls to reduce the risk of future problems. These controls included hiring an internal auditor and requiring periodic review of overhead variances to identify and explain significant discrepancies.

Source: John B. MacArthur, Bobby E. Waldrup, and Gary R. Fane, "Caution: Fraud Overhead," *Strategic Finance*, October 2004, pp. 28–32.

Summary

When analyzing overhead costs, it is essential to distinguish between variable overhead and fixed overhead. Total variable overhead costs vary in total in proportion to changes in activity whereas total fixed costs do not change within the relevant range. This distinction is important when constructing flexible budgets and when computing overhead variances.

A flexible budget shows what costs should be for various levels of activity. The flexible budget amount for a specific level of activity is determined differently depending on whether a cost is variable or fixed. If a cost is variable, the flexible budget amount is computed by multiplying the cost per unit of activity by the level of activity specified for the flexible budget. If a cost is fixed, the original total budgeted fixed cost is used as the flexible budget amount.

The two variances for variable overhead discussed in the chapter are the variable overhead spending and variable overhead efficiency variances. These variances were also covered in the previous chapter.

Two variances for fixed overhead are covered in the chapter. One—the budget variance—is quite simple; the other is considerably more complex. The budget variance is the difference between the actual total fixed overhead cost incurred and the total amount of fixed overhead cost that was originally budgeted. The volume variance is the difference between the amount of fixed overhead cost applied to inventory and the total amount of fixed overhead cost that was originally budgeted. The budget variance is a straightforward measure of the degree to which fixed overhead spending was under control. The volume variance is a consequence of treating a fixed cost as if it were variable and is more difficult to interpret meaningfully.

The sum of all four overhead variances equals the overhead overapplied or underapplied for the period. Unfavorable variances are equivalent to underapplied overhead and favorable variances are equivalent to overapplied overhead.

Review Problem: Overhead Analysis

(This problem provides a comprehensive review of Chapter 11, including the computation of underapplied or overapplied overhead and its breakdown into the four overhead variances.)

Data for the manufacturing overhead of Aspen Company are as follows:

Overhead Costs	Cost Formula (per machine-hour)	Machine-Hours		
		5,000	6,000	7,000
Variable overhead costs:				
Supplies	$0.20	$ 1,000	$ 1,200	$ 1,400
Indirect labor.	0.30	1,500	1,800	2,100
Total variable overhead cost.	$0.50	2,500	3,000	3,500
Fixed overhead costs:				
Depreciation		4,000	4,000	4,000
Supervision.		5,000	5,000	5,000
Total fixed overhead cost		9,000	9,000	9,000
Total overhead cost		$11,500	$12,000	$12,500

Five hours of machine time are required per unit of product. The company has set its denominator activity for the coming period at 6,000 machine-hours (or 1,200 units). The predetermined overhead rate is computed as follows:

$$\text{Total: } \frac{\$12,000}{6,000 \text{ MHs}} = \$2.00 \text{ per machine-hour}$$

$$\text{Variable component: } \frac{\$3,000}{6,000 \text{ MHs}} = \$0.50 \text{ per machine-hour}$$

$$\text{Fixed component: } \frac{\$9,000}{6,000 \text{ MHs}} = \$1.50 \text{ per machine-hour}$$

Assume the following *actual* results for the period:

Number of units produced	1,300 units
Actual machine-hours	6,800 machine-hours
Standard machine-hours allowed*	6,500 machine-hours
Actual variable overhead cost	$4,200
Actual fixed overhead cost	$9,400

*1,300 units × 5 machine-hours per unit.

Therefore, the company's Manufacturing Overhead account would appear as follows at the end of the period:

Manufacturing Overhead

Actual overhead costs	13,600*	13,000†	Applied overhead costs
Underapplied overhead	600		

*$4,200 variable + $9,400 fixed = $13,600.
†6,500 standard machine-hours × $2 per machine-hour = $13,000. In a standard cost system, overhead is applied on the basis of standard hours, not actual hours.

Required:
Analyze the $600 underapplied overhead in terms of:
1. The variable overhead spending variance.
2. The variable overhead efficiency variance.
3. The fixed overhead budget variance.
4. The fixed overhead volume variance.

Solution to Review Problem

Variable Overhead Variances

These same variances can be computed as follows:

Variable overhead spending variance:

$$\text{Spending variance} = (AH \times AR) - (AH \times SR)$$

$$= \text{Total actual variable overhead} - (AH \times SR)$$

$$\$4,200 - (6,800 \text{ machine-hours} \times \$0.50 \text{ per machine-hour}) = \$800 \text{ U}$$

Variable overhead efficiency variance:

$$\text{Efficiency variance} = SR(AH - SH)$$

$$\$0.50 \text{ per machine-hour} (6,800 \text{ machine-hours} - 6,500 \text{ machine-hours}) = \$150 \text{ U}$$

Fixed Overhead Variances

*Can be expressed as: 6,000 denominator machine-hours × $1.50 per machine-hour = $9,000.

These same variances can be computed as follows:

Fixed overhead budget variance:

$$\text{Budget variance} = \text{Actual fixed overhead cost} - \text{Budgeted fixed overhead cost}$$

$$\$9,400 - \$9,000 = \$400 \text{ U}$$

Fixed overhead volume variance:

$$\text{Volume variance} = \text{Fixed portion of the predetermined overhead rate} \times (\text{Denominator hours} - \text{Standard hours})$$

$$\$1.50 \text{ per machine-hour} (6,000 \text{ machine-hours} - 6,500 \text{ machine-hours}) = \$750 \text{ F}$$

Summary of Variances

The four overhead variances are summarized below:

Variable overhead:	
Spending variance	$800 U
Efficiency variance	150 U
Fixed overhead:	
Budget variance	400 U
Volume variance	750 F
Underapplied overhead	$600

Notice that the sum of the variances agrees with the underapplied balance in the company's Manufacturing Overhead account.

Glossary

Budget variance The difference between the actual fixed overhead costs incurred and the budgeted fixed overhead costs in the flexible budget. (p. 488)

Denominator activity The level of activity used to compute the predetermined overhead rate. (p. 486)

Flexible budget A budget that can be used to estimate what costs should be for any level of activity within a specified range. (p. 476)

Static budget A budget created at the beginning of the budgeting period that is valid only for the planned level of activity. (p. 475)

Volume variance The variance that arises whenever the standard hours allowed for the actual output of a period are different from the denominator activity level that was used to compute the predetermined overhead rate. It is computed by multiplying the fixed component of the predetermined overhead rate by the difference between the denominator hours and the standard hours allowed for the actual output. (p. 489)

Questions

11-1 What is a static budget?

11-2 What is a flexible budget and how does it differ from a static budget?

11-3 Name three criteria that should be considered in choosing an activity base on which to construct a flexible budget.

11-4 In a performance report for variable overhead, what variance(s) will be produced if the flexible budget is based on actual hours worked? On both actual hours worked and standard hours allowed?

11-5 What is meant by the term *standard hours allowed?*

11-6 How does the variable manufacturing overhead spending variance differ from the materials price variance?

11-7 Why is the term *overhead efficiency variance* potentially misleading?

11-8 What is meant by the term *denominator level of activity?*

11-9 Why do we apply overhead to work in process on the basis of standard hours allowed in Chapter 11 when we applied it on the basis of actual hours in Chapter 3? What is the difference in costing systems between the two chapters?

11-10 In a standard cost system, what two variances are computed for fixed manufacturing overhead?

11-11 What does the fixed overhead budget variance measure?

11-12 Under what circumstances would you expect the volume variance to be favorable? Unfavorable? Does the variance measure deviations in spending for fixed overhead items? Explain.

11-13 What is the danger in expressing fixed costs on a per unit basis?

11-14 Underapplied or overapplied overhead can be broken down into what four variances?

11-15 If factory overhead is overapplied for August, would you expect the total of the overhead variances to be favorable or unfavorable?

Exercises

EXERCISE 11-1 Prepare a Flexible Budget [LO1]

The cost formulas for Emory Company's manufacturing overhead costs are given below. These cost formulas cover a relevant range of 15,000 to 25,000 machine-hours each year.

Overhead Costs	Cost Formula
Utilities	$0.30 per machine-hour
Indirect labor.	$52,000 plus $1.40 per machine-hour
Supplies	$0.20 per machine-hour
Maintenance.	$18,000 plus $0.10 per machine-hour
Depreciation	$90,000

Required:

Prepare a flexible budget in increments of 5,000 machine-hours. Include all costs in your flexible budget.

EXERCISE 11-2 Preparing a Flexible Budget Performance Report [LO2]

Orcas Boat Charter Service rents live-aboard boats for cruising in the San Juan Islands of Washington State. The company bases its overhead cost budgets on the following data:

Variable overhead costs:	
Cleaning	$60.50 per charter
Maintenance	$35.25 per charter
Port fees	$15.75 per charter
Fixed overhead costs:	
Salaries and wages	$9,150 per month
Depreciation	$12,100 per month
Utilities	$860 per month
Moorage	$4,980 per month

Each time a boat is chartered, whether it is for one day or a week, certain costs must be incurred. Those costs are listed above under the variable overhead costs. For example, each time a boat returns from a charter, it must be thoroughly cleaned, which costs on average $60.50.

In July, the following actual costs were incurred for 160 charters:

Cleaning	$9,440
Maintenance	$5,980
Port fees	$2,670
Salaries and wages	$9,200
Depreciation	$12,800
Utilities	$835
Moorage	$5,360

Due to an unanticipated surge in demand for charters, the company purchased a new boat in July to add to its charter fleet.

Required:

1. Construct a Flexible Budget Performance Report for Orcas Boat Charter Service for July, following the format in Exhibit 11–4.
2. What is apparently the major cause of the overall variance for the month? Explain.

EXERCISE 11-3 Variable Overhead Performance Report with Just a Spending Variance [LO3]

Yung Corporation bases its variable overhead performance report on the actual direct labor-hours of the period. Data concerning the most recent year that ended on December 31 appear below:

Budgeted direct labor-hours	38,000
Actual direct labor-hours	34,000
Standard direct labor-hours allowed	35,000

Cost formula (per direct labor-hour):

Indirect labor	$0.60
Supplies.............................	$0.10
Electricity	$0.05

Actual costs incurred:

Indirect labor	$21,200
Supplies.............................	$3,200
Electricity	$1,600

Required:

Prepare a variable overhead performance report using the format in Exhibit 11–6. Compute just the variable overhead spending variances (do not compute the variable overhead efficiency variances).

EXERCISE 11-4 Variable Overhead Performance Report with Both Spending and Efficiency Variances [LO4]

Refer to the data for Yung Corporation in Exercise 11-3. Management would like to compute both spending and efficiency variances for variable overheads in the company's variable overhead performance report.

Required:

Prepare a variable overhead performance report using the format in Exhibit 11–7. Compute both the variable overhead spending variances and the overhead efficiency variances.

EXERCISE 11-5 Applying Overhead in a Standard Costing System [LO5]

Privack Corporation has a standard cost system in which it applies overhead to products based on the standard direct labor-hours allowed for the actual output of the period. Data concerning the most recent year appear below:

Variable overhead cost per direct labor-hour	$2.00
Total fixed overhead cost per year	$250,000
Budgeted standard direct labor-hours (denominator level of activity)	40,000
Actual direct labor-hours	39,000
Standard direct labor-hours allowed for the actual output	38,000

Required:

1. Compute the predetermined overhead rate for the year.
2. Determine the amount of overhead that would be applied to the output of the period.

EXERCISE 11-6 Fixed Overhead Variances [LO6]

Primara Corporation has a standard cost system in which it applies overhead to products based on the standard direct labor-hours allowed for the actual output of the period. Data concerning the most recent year appear below:

Total budgeted fixed overhead cost for the year	$250,000
Actual fixed overhead cost for the year...............................	$254,000
Budgeted standard direct labor-hours (denominator level of activity)........	25,000
Actual direct labor-hours	27,000
Standard direct labor-hours allowed for the actual output................	26,000

Required:

1. Compute the fixed portion of the predetermined overhead rate for the year.
2. Compute the fixed overhead budget variance and volume variance.

EXERCISE 11-7 Preparing a Flexible Budget [LO1]

An incomplete flexible budget is given below for Lavage Rapide, a Swiss company that owns and operates a large automatic carwash facility near Geneva. The Swiss currency is the Swiss franc, which is denoted by SFr.

	Cost Formula (per car)	Activity (cars)		
Overhead Costs		8,000	9,000	10,000
Variable overhead costs:				
Cleaning supplies	?	?	7,200 SFr	?
Electricity	?	?	2,700	?
Maintenance	?	?	1,800	?
Total variable overhead cost	?	?	?	
Fixed overhead costs:				
Operator wages		?	9,000	?
Depreciation		?	6,000	?
Rent		?	8,000	?
Total fixed overhead cost		?	?	
Total overhead cost		?	? SFr	

Lavage Rapide / Flexible Budget / For the Month Ended August 31

Required:

Fill in the missing data in the flexible budget.

EXERCISE 11-8 Using a Flexible Budget [LO1]

Refer to the data in Exercise 11-7. Lavage Rapide's owner-manager would like to prepare a budget for August assuming an activity level of 8,800 cars.

Required:

Prepare a static budget for August. Use Exhibit 11–1 in the chapter as your guide.

EXERCISE 11-9 Flexible Budget Performance Report [LO2]

Refer to the data in Exercise 11-7. Lavage Rapide's actual level of activity during August was 8,900 cars, although the owner had constructed his static budget for the month assuming the level of activity would be 8,800 cars. The actual overhead costs incurred during August are given below:

	Actual Costs Incurred for 8,900 Cars
Variable overhead costs:	
Cleaning supplies	7,080 SFr
Electricity	2,460 SFr
Maintenance	1,550 SFr
Fixed overhead costs:	
Operator wages	9,100 SFr
Depreciation	7,200 SFr
Rent	8,000 SFr

Required:

Prepare a flexible budget performance report for both the variable and fixed overhead costs for August. Use Exhibit 11–4 in the chapter as your guide.

EXERCISE 11-10 Variable Overhead Performance Report [LO3]

The variable portion of Murray Company's flexible budget for manufacturing overhead is given below:

Overhead Costs	Cost Formula (per machine-hour)	Machine-Hours		
		10,000	12,000	14,000
Supplies	$0.20	$ 2,000	$ 2,000	$ 2,800
Maintenance.	0.80	8,000	9,600	11,200
Utilities	0.10	1,000	1,200	1,400
Rework	0.40	4,000	4,800	5,600
Total variable overhead cost	$1.50	$15,000	$18,000	$21,000

During a recent period, the company recorded 11,500 machine-hours of activity. The variable overhead costs incurred were:

Supplies	$2,400
Maintenance.	$8,000
Utilities	$1,100
Rework.	$5,300

The budgeted activity for the period had been 12,000 machine-hours.

Required:

1. Prepare a variable overhead performance report for the period. Indicate whether variances are favorable (F) or unfavorable (U). Show only a spending variance on your report.
2. Discuss the significance of the variances. Might some variances be the result of others? Explain.

EXERCISE 11-11 Predetermined Overhead Rate; Overhead Variances [LO4, LO5, LO6]
Norwall Company's flexible budget for manufacturing overhead (in condensed form) is given below:

Overhead Costs	Cost Formula (per machine-hour)	Machine-Hours		
		50,000	60,000	70,000
Variable cost	$3	$150,000	$180,000	$210,000
Fixed cost.		300,000	300,000	300,000
Total overhead cost		$450,000	$480,000	$510,000

The following information is available for a recent period:
a. The denominator activity of 60,000 machine-hours was chosen to compute the predetermined overhead rate.
b. At the 60,000 standard machine-hours level of activity, the company should produce 40,000 units of product.
c. The company's actual operating results were:

Number of units produced	42,000
Actual machine-hours	64,000
Actual variable overhead costs	$185,600
Actual fixed overhead costs	$302,400

Required:

1. Compute the predetermined overhead rate and break it down into variable and fixed cost elements.
2. What were the standard hours allowed for the year's actual output?
3. Compute the variable overhead spending and efficiency variances and the fixed overhead budget and volume variances.

EXERCISE 11-12 Using Fixed Overhead Variances [LO6]

The standard cost card for the single product manufactured by Cutter, Inc., is given below:

Standard Cost Card—Per Unit	
Direct materials, 3 yards at $6 per yard	$ 18
Direct labor, 4 hours at $15.50 per direct labor-hour.	62
Variable overhead, 4 direct labor-hours at $1.50 per direct labor-hour	6
Fixed overhead, 4 direct labor-hours at $5 per direct labor-hour.	20
Total standard cost per unit.	$106

Manufacturing overhead is applied to production on the basis of standard direct labor-hours. During the year, the company worked 37,000 hours and manufactured 9,500 units of product. Selected data relating to the company's fixed manufacturing overhead cost for the year are shown below:

Actual Fixed Overhead Cost	Flexible Budget Fixed Overhead Cost	Fixed Overhead Cost Applied to Work in Process
$198,700	?	__?__ hours × $__?__ per hour = $__?__

Budget variance, $__?__   Volume variance, $10,000 U

Required:

1. What were the standard hours allowed for the year's production?
2. What was the amount of budgeted fixed overhead cost for the year?
3. What was the budget variance for the year?
4. What denominator activity level did the company use in setting the predetermined overhead rate for the year?

EXERCISE 11-13 Variable Overhead Performance Report with Both Spending and Efficiency Variances [LO4]

The check-clearing office of Columbia National Bank is responsible for processing all checks that come to the bank for payment. Managers at the bank believe that variable overhead costs are essentially proportional to the number of labor-hours worked in the office, so labor-hours are used as the activity base when preparing variable overhead budgets and performance reports. Data for September, the most recent month, appear below:

Budgeted labor-hours	3,080
Actual labor-hours	3,100
Standard labor-hours allowed for the actual number of checks processed	3,200

	Cost Formula (per labor-hour)	Actual Costs Incurred in October
Variable overhead costs:		
Office supplies	$0.10	$ 365
Staff coffee lounge	0.20	520
Indirect labor	0.90	2,710
Total variable overhead cost	$1.20	$3,595

Required:

Prepare a variable overhead performance report for September for the check-clearing office that includes both spending and efficiency variances. Use Exhibit 11–7 as a guide.

EXERCISE 11-14 Relations Among Fixed Overhead Variances [LO5, LO6]

Selected information relating to Yost Company's operations for the most recent year is given below:

Activity:	
Denominator activity (machine-hours)	45,000
Standard machine-hours allowed per unit.	3
Number of units produced.	14,000
Costs:	
Actual fixed overhead costs incurred	$267,000
Budget variance	$3,000 F

The company applies overhead cost to products on the basis of standard machine-hours.

Required:
1. What were the standard machine-hours allowed for the period's production?
2. What was the fixed portion of the predetermined overhead rate?
3. What was the volume variance?

EXERCISE 11-15 Predetermined Overhead Rate [LO5]

Operating at a normal level of 30,000 direct labor-hours, Lasser Company produces 10,000 units of product each period. The direct labor wage rate is $12 per hour. Two and one-half yards of direct materials go into each unit of product; the material costs $8.60 per yard. The flexible budget used to plan and control manufacturing overhead costs is given below (in condensed form):

Overhead Costs	Cost Formula (per direct labor-hour)	Direct Labor-Hours		
		20,000	30,000	40,000
Variable cost	$1.90	$ 38,000	$ 57,000	$ 76,000
Fixed cost		168,000	168,000	168,000
Total overhead cost		$206,000	$225,000	$244,400

Required:
1. Using 30,000 direct labor-hours as the denominator activity, compute the predetermined overhead rate and break it down into variable and fixed elements.
2. Complete the standard cost card below for one unit of product:

Direct materials, 2.5 pounds at $8.60 per yard	$21.50
Direct labor, ?..........................	?
Variable overhead, ?..........................	?
Fixed overhead, ?..........................	?
Total standard cost per unit	$?

EXERCISE 11-16 Fixed Overhead Variances [LO6]

Selected operating information on three different companies for a recent year is given below:

	Company		
	A	B	C
Full-capacity direct machine-hours........	10,000	18,000	20,000
Budgeted machine-hours*	9,000	17,000	20,000
Actual machine-hours	9,000	17,800	19,000
Standard machine-hours allowed for actual production.	9,500	16,000	20,000

*Denominator activity for computing the predetermined overhead rate.

Required:
For each company, state whether the volume variance would be favorable or unfavorable; also, explain in each case *why* the volume variance would be favorable or unfavorable.

Problems

PROBLEM 11-17 Preparing an Overhead Performance Report [LO2]

Several years ago, Westmont Company developed a comprehensive budgeting system for profit planning and control purposes. The line supervisors have been very happy with the system and with the reports being prepared on their performance, but both middle and upper management have expressed considerable dissatisfaction with the information being generated by the system. A typical manufacturing overhead performance report for a recent period follows:

	Westmont Company Overhead Performance Report—Assembly Department For the Quarter Ended March 31		
	Actual	Budget	Variance
Machine-hours	35,000	40,000	
Variable overhead			
Indirect materials	$ 29,700	$ 32,000	$2,300 F
Rework	7,900	8,000	100 F
Utilities	51,800	56,000	4,200 F
Machine setup	11,600	12,000	400 F
Total variable overhead cost.	101,000	108,000	7,000 F
Fixed overhead			
Maintenance.	79,200	80,000	800 F
Inspection.	60,000	60,000	0
Total fixed overhead cost	139,200	140,000	800 F
Total overhead cost	$240,200	$248,000	$7,800 F

After receiving a copy of this overhead performance report, the supervisor of the Assembly Department stated, "These reports are super. It makes me feel really good to see how well things are going in my department. I can't understand why those people upstairs complain so much."

The budget data above are for the original planned level of activity for the quarter.

Required:

1. The company's vice president is uneasy about the performance reports being prepared and would like you to evaluate their usefulness to the company.
2. What changes, if any, should be made in the overhead performance report to give better insight into how well the supervisor is controlling costs?
3. Prepare a new overhead performance report for the quarter, incorporating any changes you suggested in (2) above. Include both the variable and the fixed costs in your report.

PROBLEM 11-18 Comprehensive Standard Cost Variances [LO4, LO6]

"Wonderful! Not only did our salespeople do a good job in meeting the sales budget this year, but our production people did a good job in controlling costs as well," said Kim Clark, president of Martell Company. "Our $18,300 overall manufacturing cost variance is only 1.2% of the $1,536,000 standard cost of products made during the year. That's well within the 3% parameter set by management for acceptable variances. It looks like everyone will be in line for a bonus this year."

The company produces and sells a single product. The standard cost card for the product follows:

Standard Cost Card—Per Unit	
Direct materials, 2 feet at $8.45 per foot	$16.90
Direct labor, 1.4 direct labor-hours at $16 per direct labor-hour	22.40
Variable overhead, 1.4 direct labor-hours at $2.50 per direct labor-hour.	3.50
Fixed overhead, 1.4 direct labor-hours at $6 per direct labor-hour	8.40
Standard cost per unit	$51.20

The following additional information is available for the year just completed:

a. The company manufactured 30,000 units of product during the year.

b. A total of 64,000 feet of material was purchased during the year at a cost of $8.55 per foot. All of this material was used to manufacture the 30,000 units. There were no beginning or ending inventories for the year.

c. The company worked 43,500 direct labor-hours during the year at a direct labor cost of $15.80 per hour.

d. Overhead cost is applied to products on the basis of standard direct labor-hours. Data relating to manufacturing overhead costs follow:

Denominator activity level (direct labor-hours)	35,000
Budgeted fixed overhead costs (from the flexible budget).	$210,000
Actual variable overhead costs.	$108,000
Actual fixed overhead costs	$211,800

Required:

1. Compute the direct materials price and quantity variances for the year.
2. Compute the direct labor rate and efficiency variances for the year.
3. For manufacturing overhead, compute the following:
   a. The variable overhead spending and efficiency variances for the year.
   b. The fixed overhead budget and volume variances for the year.
4. Total the variances you have computed, and compare the net amount with the $18,300 mentioned by the president. Do you agree that bonuses should be given to everyone for good cost control during the year? Explain.

PROBLEM 11-19 Applying Overhead; Overhead Variances [LO4, LO5, LO6]

Chilczuk, S.A., of Gdansk, Poland, is a major producer of classic Polish sausage. The company uses a standard cost system to help control costs. Manufacturing overhead is applied to production on the basis of standard direct labor-hours. According to the company's flexible budget, the following manufacturing overhead costs should be incurred at an activity level of 35,000 labor-hours (the denominator activity level chosen for the year):

Variable manufacturing overhead cost.	PZ 87,500
Fixed manufacturing overhead cost.	210,000
Total manufacturing overhead cost	PZ297,500

The currency in Poland is the zloty, which is denoted here by PZ.

During the most recent year, the following operating results were recorded:

Actual labor-hours worked	30,000
Standard labor-hours allowed for output	32,000
Actual variable manufacturing overhead cost incurred.	PZ78,000
Actual fixed manufacturing overhead cost incurred	PZ209,400

At the end of the year, the company's Manufacturing Overhead account contained the following data:

Manufacturing Overhead

Actual costs	287,400	Applied costs	272,000
	15,400		

Management would like to determine the cause of the PZ15,400 underapplied overhead.

Required:

1. Compute the predetermined overhead rate for the year. Break it down into variable and fixed cost elements.
2. Show how the PZ272,000 "Applied costs" in the Manufacturing Overhead account was computed.
3. Analyze the PZ15,400 underapplied overhead figure in terms of the variable overhead spending and efficiency variances and the fixed overhead budget and volume variances.
4. Explain the meaning of each variance that you computed in (3) above.

PROBLEM 11-20 Applying the Flexible Budget Approach [LO2]

The St. Lucia Blood Bank, a private charity partly supported by government grants, is located on the Caribbean island of St. Lucia. The Blood Bank has just finished its operations for September, which was a particularly busy month due to a powerful hurricane that hit neighboring islands causing many injuries. The hurricane largely bypassed St. Lucia, but residents of St. Lucia willingly donated their blood to help people on other islands. As a consequence, the blood bank collected and processed over 20% more blood than had been originally planned for the month.

A report prepared by a government official comparing actual costs to budgeted costs for the Blood Bank appears below. (The currency on St. Lucia is the East Caribbean dollar.) Continued support from the government depends on the Blood Bank's ability to demonstrate control over its costs.

St. Lucia Blood Bank Cost Control Report For the Month Ended September 30			
	Actual	Budget	Variance
Liters of blood collected	620	500	120
Variable costs:			
Medical supplies	$ 9,350	$ 7,500	$1,850 U
Lab tests	6,180	6,000	180 U
Refreshments for donors	1,340	1,000	340 U
Administrative supplies	400	250	150 U
Total variable cost	17,270	14,750	2,520 U
Fixed costs:			
Staff salaries	10,000	10,000	0
Equipment depreciation	2,800	2,500	300 U
Rent	1,000	1,000	0
Utilities	570	500	70 U
Total fixed cost	14,370	14,000	370 U
Total cost	$31,640	$28,750	$2,890 U

The managing director of the Blood Bank was very unhappy with this report, claiming that his costs were higher than expected due to the emergency on the neighboring islands. He also pointed out that the additional costs had been fully covered by payments from grateful recipients on the other islands. The government official who prepared the report countered that all of the figures had been submitted by the Blood Bank to the government; he was just pointing out that actual costs were a lot higher than promised in the budget.

Required:

1. Prepare a new performance report for September using the flexible budget approach. (Note: Even though some of these costs might be classified as direct costs rather than as overhead, the flexible budget approach can still be used to prepare a flexible budget performance report.)

2. Do you think any of the variances in the report you prepared should be investigated? Why?

PROBLEM 11-21 Comprehensive Standard Cost Variances [LO4, LO5, LO6]

Flandro Company uses a standard cost system and sets predetermined overhead rates on the basis of direct labor-hours. The following data are taken from the company's budget for the current year:

Denominator activity (direct labor-hours)	5,000
Variable manufacturing overhead cost	$25,000
Fixed manufacturing overhead cost	$59,000

The standard cost card for the company's only product is given below:

Direct materials, 3 yards at $4.40 per yard	$13.20
Direct labor, 1 direct labor-hour at $12 per direct labor-hour	12.00
Manufacturing overhead, 140% of direct labor cost	16.80
Standard cost per unit	$42.00

During the year, the company produced 6,000 units of product and incurred the following costs:

Materials purchased, 24,000 yards at $4.80 per yard	$115,200
Materials used in production (in yards)	18,500
Direct labor cost incurred, 5,800 direct labor-hours at $13 per direct labor-hour	$75,400
Variable manufacturing overhead cost incurred	$29,580
Fixed manufacturing overhead cost incurred	$60,400

Required:
1. Redo the standard cost card in a clearer, more usable format by detailing the variable and fixed overhead cost elements.
2. Prepare an analysis of the variances for materials and labor for the year.
3. Prepare an analysis of the variances for variable and fixed overhead for the year.
4. What effect, if any, does the choice of a denominator activity level have on unit standard costs? Is the volume variance a controllable variance from a spending point of view? Explain.

PROBLEM 11-22 Flexible Budget and Overhead Analysis [LO1, LO4, LO5, LO6]

Harper Company assembles all of its products in the Assembly Department. Budgeted costs for the operation of this department for the year have been set as follows:

Variable costs:	
Direct materials	$ 900,000
Direct labor	675,000
Utilities	45,000
Indirect labor	67,500
Supplies	22,500
Total variable cost	1,710,000
Fixed costs:	
Insurance	8,000
Supervisory salaries	90,000
Depreciation	160,000
Equipment rental	42,000
Total fixed cost	300,000
Total budgeted cost	$2,010,000
Budgeted direct labor-hours	75,000

Since the assembly work is done mostly by hand, operating activity in this department is best measured by direct labor-hours. The cost formulas used to develop the budgeted costs above are valid over a relevant range of 60,000 to 90,000 direct labor-hours per year.

Required:
1. Prepare a manufacturing overhead flexible budget for the Assembly Department using increments of 15,000 hours. (The company does not include direct materials and direct labor costs in the flexible budget.)
2. Assume that the company computes predetermined overhead rates by department. Compute the rates, variable and fixed, that will be used to apply Assembly Department overhead costs to production.
3. Suppose that during the year the following actual activity and costs are recorded by the Assembly Department:

Actual direct labor-hours worked	73,000
Standard direct labor-hours allowed for the output of the year	70,000
Actual variable manufacturing overhead cost incurred	$124,100
Actual fixed manufacturing overhead cost incurred	$301,600

   a. A T-account for manufacturing overhead costs in the Assembly Department for the year is given below. Determine the amount of applied overhead cost for the year, and compute the underapplied or overapplied overhead.

Manufacturing Overhead

Actual costs	425,700	

b.   Analyze the under- or overapplied overhead in terms of the variable overhead spending and efficiency variances and the fixed overhead budget and volume variances.

PROBLEM 11-23 Comprehensive Problem; Flexible Budget; Overhead Performance Report [LO1, LO2, LO3, LO4]

Gant Products, Inc., has recently introduced budgeting as an integral part of its corporate planning process. The company's first effort at constructing a flexible budget for manufacturing overhead is shown below:

Percentage of Capacity	80%	100%
Machine-hours	4,800	6,000
Maintenance	$1,480	$ 1,600
Supplies	1,920	2,400
Utilities	1,940	2,300
Supervision	3,000	3,000
Machine setup	960	1,200
Total manufacturing overhead cost	$9,300	$10,500

The budgets above are relevant over a range of 80% to 100% of capacity. The managers who will be working under these budgets have control over both fixed and variable costs. The company applies manufacturing overhead to products on the basis of standard machine-hours.

Required:

1.   Redo the company's flexible budget, presenting it in better format. Show the budget at 80%, 90%, and 100% levels of capacity. (Use the high-low method to separate fixed and variable costs.)
2.   Express the flexible budget prepared in (1) above using a single cost formula for all overhead costs.
3.   The company operated at 95% of machine-hour capacity during April. Five thousand six hundred standard machine-hours were allowed for the output of the month. Actual overhead costs incurred were:

Maintenance	$ 2,083
Supplies	3,420
Utilities	2,666
Supervision	3,000
Machine setup	855
Total overhead cost	$12,024

The fixed costs had no budget variances. Prepare an overhead performance report for April. Structure your report so that it shows only a spending variance for overhead. You may assume that the master budget for April called for an activity level during the month of 6,000 machine-hours.

4.   Upon receiving the performance report you have prepared, the production manager commented, "I have two observations to make. First, I think there's an error on your report. You show an unfavorable spending variance for supplies, yet I know that we paid exactly the budgeted price for all the supplies we used last month. Pat Stevens, the purchasing agent, made a comment to me that our supplies prices haven't changed in over a year. Second, I wish you would modify your report to include an efficiency variance for overhead. The reason is that waste has been a problem in the factory for years and the efficiency variance would help us get overhead waste under control."

a.   Explain the probable cause of the unfavorable spending variance for supplies.
b.   Compute an efficiency variance for *total* variable overhead and explain to the production manager why it would or would not contain elements of overhead waste.

PROBLEM 11-24 Applying Overhead; Overhead Variances [LO4, LO5, LO6]

Lane Company manufactures a single product that requires a great deal of hand labor. Overhead cost is applied on the basis of standard direct labor-hours. The company's condensed flexible budget for manufacturing overhead is given below:

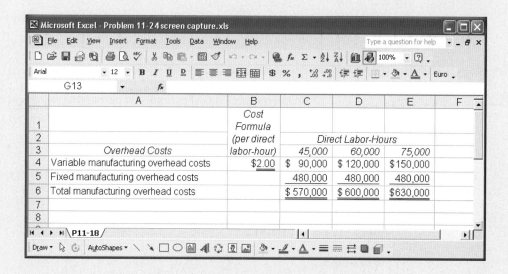

The company's product requires 3 pounds of material that has a standard cost of $7 per pound and 1.5 hours of direct labor time that has a standard rate of $12 per hour.

The company planned to operate at a denominator activity level of 60,000 direct labor-hours and to produce 40,000 units of product during the most recent year. Actual activity and costs for the year were as follows:

Number of units produced	42,000
Actual direct labor-hours worked	65,000
Actual variable manufacturing overhead cost incurred.	$123,500
Actual fixed manufacturing overhead cost incurred	$483,000

Required:
1. Compute the predetermined overhead rate for the year. Break the rate down into variable and fixed components.
2. Prepare a standard cost card for the company's product; show the details for all manufacturing costs on your standard cost card.
3. *a.* Compute the standard direct labor-hours allowed for the year's production.
   b. Complete the following Manufacturing Overhead T-account for the year:

Manufacturing Overhead

?	?
?	?

4. Determine the reason for any under- or overapplied overhead from (3) above by computing the variable overhead spending and efficiency variances and the fixed overhead budget and volume variances.
5. Suppose the company had chosen 65,000 direct labor-hours as the denominator activity rather than 60,000 hours. State which, if any, of the variances computed in (4) above would have changed, and explain how the variance(s) would have changed. No computations are necessary.

PROBLEM 11-25 Flexible Budget and Overhead Performance Report [LO1, LO2, LO4]
You have just been hired by FAB Company, the manufacturer of a revolutionary new garage door opening device. John Foster, the president, has asked that you review the company's costing system and "do what you can to help us get better control of our manufacturing overhead costs." You find that the company has never used a flexible budget, and you suggest that preparing such a budget would be an excellent first step in overhead planning and control.

After much effort and analysis, you are able to determine the following cost formulas for the company's normal operating range of 20,000 to 30,000 machine-hours each month:

Overhead Costs	Cost Formula
Utilities	$0.90 per machine-hour
Maintenance	$1.60 per machine-hour plus $40,000 per month
Machine setup	$0.30 per machine-hour
Indirect labor	$0.70 per machine-hour plus $130,000 per month
Depreciation.	$70,000 per month

To show the president how the flexible budget concept works, you have gathered the following actual manufacturing overhead cost data for the most recent month, March, in which the company worked 26,000 machine-hours and produced 15,000 units:

Utilities	$ 24,200
Maintenance.	78,100
Machine setup	8,400
Indirect labor	149,600
Depreciation.	71,500
Total manufacturing overhead cost.	$331,800

The only variance in the fixed costs for the month was with depreciation, which increased as a result of purchasing new equipment.

The company had originally planned to work 30,000 machine-hours during March.

Required:
1. Prepare a flexible budget for the company in increments of 5,000 hours. Include both variable and fixed costs in your budget.
2. Prepare an overhead performance report for the company for March. Include both variable and fixed costs in the report (in separate sections). Show only a spending variance on the report.
3. What additional information would you need to compute an overhead efficiency variance for the company?

PROBLEM 11-26 Evaluating an Overhead Performance Report [LO2, LO4]
Frank Western, supervisor of the Machining Department for Freemont Company, was visibly upset after being reprimanded for his department's poor performance over the prior month. The department's performance report is given below:

Freemont Company Overhead Performance Report—Machining Department	Cost Formula (per machine-hour)	Actual	Budget	Variance
Machine-hours		38,000	35,000	
Variable overhead costs:				
Utilities	$0.40	$ 15,700	$ 14,000	$ 1,700 U
Indirect labor.	2.30	86,500	80,500	6,000 U
Supplies	0.60	26,000	21,000	5,000 U
Maintenance.	1.20	44,900	42,000	2,900 U
Total variable overhead cost.	$4.50	173,100	157,500	15,600 U
Fixed overhead costs:				
Supervision.		38,000	38,000	0
Maintenance.		92,400	92,000	400 U
Depreciation		80,000	80,000	0
Total fixed overhead cost		210,400	210,000	400 U
Total overhead cost		$383,500	$367,500	$16,000 U

"I just can't understand all the red ink," said Western to Sarah Mason, supervisor of another department. "When the boss called me in, I thought he was going to give me a pat on the back because I know for a fact that my department worked more efficiently last month than it has ever worked before. Instead, he tore me apart. I thought for a minute that it might be over the supplies that were stolen out of our warehouse last month. But they only amounted to a couple of thousand dollars, and just look at this report. *Everything* is unfavorable."

The budget for the Machining Department had called for production of 14,000 units last month, which is equal to a budgeted activity level of 35,000 machine-hours (at a standard time of 2.5 machine-hours per unit). Actual production in the Machining Department for the month was 16,000 units.

Required:

1. Evaluate the overhead performance report given above and explain why the variances are all unfavorable.
2. Prepare a new overhead performance report that will help Mr. Western's superiors assess efficiency and cost control in the Machining Department. (Hint: Exhibit 11–7 may be helpful in structuring your report; however, the report you prepare should include both variable and fixed costs.)
3. Would the supplies stolen out of the warehouse be included as part of the variable overhead spending variance or as part of the variable overhead efficiency variance for the month? Explain.

PROBLEM 11-27 Selection of a Denominator; Overhead Analysis; Standard Cost Card [LO4, LO5, LO6]

Morton Company's condensed flexible budget for manufacturing overhead is given below:

Overhead Costs	Cost Formula (per DLH)	Direct Labor-Hours		
		20,000	30,000	40,000
Variable manufacturing overhead cost........	$4.50	$ 90,000	$135,000	$180,000
Fixed manufacturing overhead cost..........		270,000	270,000	270,000
Total manufacturing overhead cost		$360,000	$405,000	$450,000

The company manufactures a single product that requires two direct labor-hours to complete. The direct labor wage rate is $15 per hour. Four feet of raw material are required for each unit of product; the standard cost of the material is $8.75 per foot.

Although normal activity is 30,000 direct labor-hours each year, the company expects to operate at a 40,000-hour level of activity this year.

Required:

1. Assume that the company chooses 30,000 direct labor-hours as the denominator level of activity. Compute the predetermined overhead rate, breaking it down into variable and fixed cost elements.
2. Assume that the company chooses 40,000 direct labor-hours as the denominator level of activity. Repeat the computations in (1) above.
3. Complete two standard cost cards as outlined below.

Denominator Activity: 30,000 DLHs	
Direct materials, 4 feet at $8.75 per foot	$35.00
Direct labor, ?	?
Variable overhead, ?	?
Fixed overhead, ?	?
Standard cost per unit	$?

Denominator Activity: 40,000 DLHs	
Direct materials, $4 feet at $8.75 per foot	$35.00
Direct labor, ?	?
Variable overhead, ?	?
Fixed overhead, ?	?
Standard cost per unit	$?

4.   Assume that the company actually produces 18,000 units and works 38,000 direct labor-hours during the year. Actual manufacturing overhead costs for the year are:

Variable manufacturing overhead cost........	$174,800
Fixed manufacturing overhead cost..........	271,600
Total manufacturing overhead cost	$446,400

   a.   Compute the standard direct labor-hours allowed for this year's production.
   b.   Compute the missing items from the Manufacturing Overhead account below. Assume that the company uses 30,000 direct labor-hours (normal activity) as the denominator activity figure in computing overhead rates, as you have done in (1) above.

Manufacturing Overhead

Actual costs	446,400	?
?		?

   c.   Determine the cause of the under- or overapplied overhead for the year by computing the variable overhead spending and efficiency variances and the fixed overhead budget and volume variances.
5.   Looking at the variances you have computed, what appears to be the major disadvantage of using normal activity rather than expected actual activity as a denominator in computing the predetermined overhead rate? What advantages can you see to offset this disadvantage?

PROBLEM 11-28 Variable Overhead Performance Report [LO4]
The cost formulas for variable overhead costs in a machine shop are given below:

Variable Overhead Cost	Cost Formula (per machine-hour)
Power................	$0.30
Setup time	0.20
Polishing wheels........	0.16
Maintenance...........	0.18
Total	$0.84

   During August, the machine shop was scheduled to work 11,250 machine-hours and to produce 4,500 units of product. The standard machine time per unit of product is 2.5 hours. A strike near the end of the month forced a cutback in production. Actual results for the month were:

Actual machine-hours worked..........	9,250
Actual number of units produced........	3,600

Actual costs for the month were:

Variable Overhead Cost	Total Actual Costs	Per Machine-Hour
Power.....................	$2,405	$0.26
Setup time	2,035	0.22
Polishing wheels	1,110	0.12
Maintenance	925	0.10
Total	$6,475	$0.70

Required:

Prepare an overhead performance report for the machine shop for August. Use column headings in your report as shown below:

Overhead Item	Cost Formula (per MH)	Actual Costs Incurred, 9,250 MHs	Budget Based on ? MHs	Budget Based on ? MHs	Total Variance	Breakdown of the Total Variance	
						Spending Variance	Efficiency Variance

Cases

CASE 11-29 Activity-Based Costing and the Flexible Budget Approach [LO2]

The Little Theatre is a nonprofit organization devoted to staging plays for children in Manchester, England. The theater has a very small full-time professional administrative staff. Through a special arrangement with the actors' union, actors and directors rehearse without pay and are paid only for actual performances.

The costs of 2008's operations appear below. (The currency in England is the pound, denoted £.) During 2008, The Little Theatre had six different productions—each of which was performed 18 times. For example, one of the productions was Peter the Rabbit, which had the usual six-week run with three performances on each weekend.

The Little Theatre Cost Report For the Year Ended 31 December 2008	
Number of productions.	6
Number of performances of each production.	18
Total number of performances	108
Actual costs incurred:	
Actors' and directors' wages.	£216,000
Stagehands' wages	32,400
Ticket booth personnel and ushers' wages.	16,200
Scenery, costumes, and props.	108,000
Theater hall rent	54,000
Printed programs	27,000
Publicity	12,000
Administrative expenses.	43,200
Total actual cost incurred	£508,800

Some of the costs vary with the number of productions, some with the number of performances, and some are relatively fixed and depend on neither the number of productions nor the number of performances. The costs of scenery, costumes, props, and publicity vary with the number of productions. It doesn't make any difference how many times Peter the Rabbit is performed, the cost of the scenery is the same. Likewise, the cost of publicizing a play with posters and radio commercials is the same whether there are 10, 20, or 30 performances of the play. On the other hand, the wages of the actors, directors, stagehands, ticket booth personnel, and ushers vary with the number of performances. The greater the number of performances, the higher the wage costs will be. Similarly, the costs of renting the hall and printing the programs will vary with the number of performances. Administrative expenses are more difficult to pin down, but the best estimate is that approximately 75% of these costs are fixed, 15% depend on the number of productions staged, and the remaining 10% depend on the number of performances.

At the end of 2008, the board of directors of the theater authorized expanding the theater's program in 2009 to seven productions, with 24 performances each. Not surprisingly, actual costs for 2009 were considerably higher than the costs for 2008. (Grants from donors and ticket sales were also correspondingly higher.) Data concerning 2009's operations appear below:

The Little Theatre Cost Report For the Year Ended 31 December 2009	
Number of productions.	7
Number of performances of each production.	24
Total number of performances	168
Actual costs incurred:	
Actors' and directors' wages.	£341,800
Stagehands' wages	49,700
Ticket booth personnel and ushers' wages.	25,900
Scenery, costumes, and props	130,600
Theater hall rent	78,000
Printed programs	38,300
Publicity	15,100
Administrative expenses.	47,500
Total actual cost incurred	£726,900

Even though many of the costs above may be considered direct costs rather than overhead, the flexible budget approach covered in the chapter can still be used to evaluate how well these costs are controlled. The principles are the same whether a cost is a direct cost or is overhead.

Required:

1. Use the actual results from 2008 to estimate the cost formulas for the flexible budget for The Little Theatre. Keep in mind that the theater has two measures of activity—the number of productions and the number of performances.

2. Prepare a performance report for 2009 using the flexible budget approach and both measures of activity. Assume there was no inflation. (Note: To evaluate administrative expenses, first determine the flexible budget amounts for the three elements of administrative expenses. Then compare the total of the three elements to the actual administrative expense of £47,500.)

3. If you were on the board of directors of the theater, would you be pleased with how well costs were controlled during 2009? Why or why not?

4. The cost formulas provide figures for the average cost per production and average cost per performance. How accurate do you think these figures would be for predicting the cost of a new production or of an additional performance of a particular production?

CASE 11-30 Preparing a Performance Report Using Activity-Based Costing [LO2]

Boyne University offers an extensive continuing education program in many cities throughout the state. For the convenience of its faculty and administrative staff and to save costs, the university employs a supervisor to operate a motor pool. The motor pool operated with 20 vehicles until February, when an additional automobile was acquired. The motor pool furnishes gasoline, oil, and other supplies for its automobiles. A mechanic does routine maintenance and minor repairs. Major repairs are done at a nearby commercial garage.

Each year, the supervisor prepares an operating budget that informs the university administration of the funds needed for operating the motor pool. Depreciation (straight line) on the automobiles is recorded in the budget in order to determine the cost per mile of operating the vehicles.

The following schedule presents the operating budget for the current year, which has been approved by the university. The schedule also shows actual operating costs for March of the current year compared to one-twelfth of the annual operating budget.

University Motor Pool Budget Report for March				
	Annual Operating Budget	Monthly Budget*	March Actual	(Over) Under Budget
Gasoline..........................	$ 42,000	$ 3,500	$ 4,300	$(800)
Oil, minor repairs, parts.............	3,600	300	380	(80)
Outside repairs...................	2,700	225	50	175
Insurance.......................	6,000	500	525	(25)
Salaries and benefits..............	30,000	2,500	2,500	0
Depreciation of vehicles............	26,400	2,200	2,310	(110)
Total cost	$110,700	$ 9,225	$10,065	$(840)
Total miles	600,000	50,000	63,000	
Cost per mile	$ 0.1845	$0.1845	$0.1598	
Number of automobiles in use........	20	20	21	

*Annual operating budget ÷ 12 months.

The annual operating budget was constructed on the following assumptions:
a. Twenty automobiles in the motor pool.
b. Thirty thousand miles driven per year per automobile.
c. Twenty-five miles per gallon per automobile.
d. $1.75 per gallon of gasoline.
e. $0.006 cost per mile for oil, minor repairs, and parts.
f. $135 cost per automobile per year for outside repairs.
g. $300 cost per automobile per year for insurance.

The supervisor of the motor pool is unhappy with the monthly report comparing budget and actual costs for March, claiming it presents an unfair picture of performance. A previous employer used flexible budgeting to compare actual costs to budgeted amounts.

Required:

1. Prepare a new performance report for March showing budgeted costs, actual costs, and variances. In preparing your report, use flexible budgeting techniques to compute the monthly budget figures.

2. What are the deficiencies in the performance report presented above? How does the report that you prepared in (1) above overcome these deficiencies?

(CMA, adapted)

CASE 11-31 Ethics and the Manager [LO2]

Tom Kemper is the controller of the Wichita manufacturing facility of Prudhom Enterprises, Incorporated. Among the many reports that must be filed with corporate headquarters is the annual overhead performance report. The report covers the year ended December 31, and is due at corporate headquarters shortly after the beginning of the New Year. Kemper does not like putting work off to the last minute, so just before Christmas he put together a preliminary draft of the overhead performance report. Some adjustments would later be required for transactions that occur between Christmas and New Year's Day, but there are generally very few of these. A copy of the preliminary draft report, which Kemper completed on December 21, follows:

Melissa Ilianovitch, the general manager at the Wichita facility, asked to see a copy of the preliminary draft report at 4:45 p.m. on December 23. Kemper carried a copy of the report to her office where the following discussion took place:

Ilianovitch: Ouch! Almost all of the variances on the report are unfavorable. The only thing that looks good at all are the favorable variances for supervisory salaries and for industrial engineering. How did we have an unfavorable variance for depreciation?

Kemper: Do you remember that milling machine that broke down because the wrong lubricant was used by the machine operator?

Ilianovitch: Only vaguely.

Kemper: It turned out we couldn't fix it. We had to scrap the machine and buy a new one.

Ilianovitch: This report doesn't look good. I was raked over the coals last year when we had just a few unfavorable variances.

Wichita Manufacturing Facility Overhead Performance Report December 21 Preliminary Draft				
Budgeted machine-hours........ 200,000				
Actual machine-hours 180,000				
Overhead Costs	Cost Formula (per machine-hour)	Actual Costs for 180,000 Machine-Hours	Budget Based on 180,000 Machine-Hours	Spending or Budget Variance
Variable overhead costs:				
Power	$0.10	$ 19,750	$ 18,000	$ 1,750 U
Supplies	0.25	47,000	45,000	2,000 U
Abrasives	0.30	58,000	54,000	4,000 U
Total variable overhead cost	$0.65	124,750	117,000	7,750 U
Fixed overhead costs:				
Depreciation		345,000	332,000	13,000 U
Supervisory salaries		273,000	275,000	2,000 F
Insurance		37,000	37,000	0
Industrial engineering		189,000	210,000	21,000 F
Factory building lease		60,000	60,000	0
Total fixed overhead cost		904,000	914,000	10,000 F
Total overhead cost		$1,028,750	$1,031,000	$ 2,250 F

Kemper: I'm afraid the final report is going to look even worse.

Ilianovitch: Oh?

Kemper: The line item for industrial engineering on the report is for work we hired Ferguson Engineering to do for us on a contract basis. The original contract was for $210,000, but we asked them to do some additional work that was not in the contract. Under the terms of the contract, we have to reimburse Ferguson Engineering for the costs of the additional work. The $189,000 in actual costs that appear on the preliminary draft report reflects only their billings up through December 21. The last bill they had sent us was on November 28, and they completed the project just last week. Yesterday I got a call from Laura Sunder over at Ferguson and she said they would be sending us a final bill for the project before the end of the year. The total bill, including the reimbursements for the additional work, is going to be . . .

Ilianovitch: I am not sure I want to hear this.

Kemper: $225,000

Ilianovitch: Ouch! Ouch! Ouch!

Kemper: The additional work we asked them to do added $15,000 to the cost of the project.

Ilianovitch: No way can I turn in a performance report with an overall unfavorable variance. They'll kill me at corporate headquarters. Call up Laura at Ferguson and ask her not to send the bill until after the first of the year. We have to have that $21,000 favorable variance for industrial engineering on the performance report.

Required:

What should Tom Kemper do? Explain.

12

Segment Reporting and Decentralization

Centralizing Communications

Ingersoll-Rand, a global conglomerate that traces its roots to the early 1870s, has about 46,000 employees. The company has received numerous recognitions and awards, including being named the *Industryweek* Best Managed Company for several years in a row. Even so, the company decided that it needed to restructure its organization to effectively compete in the current economic environment.

Previously comprising 8 autonomous companies, Ingersoll-Rand now operates as 13 separate business units. To improve communications, its computer systems were integrated to provide information to managers and headquarters in real time. The company continues to operate in a decentralized fashion. Even though many of its functions have been centralized, such as purchasing, payroll, and accounts receivable and payable, decision making is still spread throughout the organization. For example, factory managers continue to be responsible for deciding what must be purchased. However, instead of directly issuing purchase orders to vendors, requisitions are communicated to headquarters, which then issues the purchase orders. As a result of this centralized approach to purchasing, the company has been able to negotiate better discounts with suppliers.

Analysts estimate the cost of the restructuring at $50 million. Don Janson, director of common administrative resources implementations at Ingersoll-Rand, predicts that the changes will pay for themselves within three years.

Sources: Ingersoll-Rand Company website; and Steve Konicki, "A Company Merges Its Many Units—Successfully," *Informationweek*, May 8, 2000, pp. 174–178. ■

After studying Chapter 12, you should be able to:

LO1 Prepare a segmented income statement using the contribution format, and explain the difference between traceable fixed costs and common fixed costs.

LO2 Compute return on investment (ROI) and show how changes in sales, expenses, and assets affect ROI.

LO3 Compute residual income and understand its strengths and weaknesses.

LO4 (Appendix 12A) Determine the range, if any, within which a negotiated transfer price should fall.

LO5 (Appendix 12B) Charge operating departments for services provided by service departments.

It is impossible for the top manager to make decisions about everything except in very small organizations. For example, the CEO of the Hyatt Hotel chain cannot be expected to decide whether a particular hotel guest at the Hyatt Hotel on Maui should be allowed to check out later than the normal checkout time. It makes sense for the CEO to authorize employees at Maui to make this decision. As in this example, managers in large organizations have to delegate some decisions to those who are at lower levels in the organization.

Decentralization in Organizations

In a **decentralized organization,** decision-making authority is spread throughout the organization rather than being confined to a few top executives. All large organizations are decentralized to some extent out of necessity. At one extreme, a strongly decentralized organization empowers even the lowest-level managers and employees to make decisions. At the other extreme, a strongly centralized organization provides lower-level managers with little freedom to make decisions. Most organizations fall somewhere between these two extremes.

Advantages and Disadvantages of Decentralization

The major advantages of decentralization include:

1. By delegating day-to-day problem solving to lower-level managers, top management can concentrate on bigger issues such as overall strategy.
2. Empowering lower-level managers to make decisions puts the decision-making authority in the hands of those who tend to have the most detailed and up-to-date information about day-to-day operations.
3. By eliminating layers of decision making and approvals, organizations can respond more quickly to customers and to changes in the operating environment.
4. Granting decision-making authority helps train lower-level managers for higher-level positions.
5. Empowering lower-level managers to make decisions can increase their motivation and job satisfaction.

The major disadvantages of decentralization include:

1. Lower-level managers may make decisions without fully understanding the big picture.
2. If lower-level managers make their own decisions, coordination may be lacking.
3. Lower-level managers may have objectives that clash with the objectives of the entire organization.[1] For example, a manager may be more interested in increasing the size of his or her department, leading to more power and prestige, than in increasing the department's effectiveness.

---

[1]   Similar problems exist with top-level managers as well. The shareholders of the company delegate their decision-making authority to the top managers. Unfortunately, top managers may abuse that trust by rewarding themselves and their friends too generously, spending too much company money on palatial offices, and so on. The issue of how to ensure that top managers act in the best interests of the company's owners continues to puzzle experts. To a large extent, the owners rely on performance evaluation using return on investment and residual income measures as discussed later in the chapter and on bonuses and stock options. The stock market is also an important disciplining mechanism. If top managers squander the company's resources, the price of the company's stock will almost surely fall—resulting in a loss of prestige, bonuses, and possibly a job. And, of course, particularly outrageous self-dealing may land a CEO in court, as recent events have demonstrated.

4. Spreading innovative ideas may be difficult in a decentralized organization. Someone in one part of the organization may have a terrific idea that would benefit other parts of the organization, but without strong central direction the idea may not be shared with, and adopted by, other parts of the organization. This problem can be reduced by effective use of intranet systems that make it easier for information to be shared across departments.

DECENTRALIZATION: A DELICATE BALANCE

Decentralization has its advantages and disadvantages. Bed Bath & Beyond, a specialty retailer, benefits from allowing its local store managers to choose 70% of their store's merchandise based on local customer tastes. For example, the company's Manhattan stores stock wall paint, but its suburban stores do not because home improvement giants in the suburbs, such as Home Depot, meet this customer need.

On the other hand, Nestle, the Swiss consumer food products company, has been working to overcome glaring inefficiencies resulting from its decentralized management structure. For example, in Switzerland "each candy and ice cream factory was ordering its own sugar. Moreover, different factories were using different names for the identical grade of sugar, making it almost impossible for bosses at headquarters to track costs." Nestle hopes to significantly reduce costs and simplify recordkeeping by centralizing its raw materials purchases.

Sources: Nanette Byrnes, "What's Beyond for Bed Bath & Beyond?" *BusinessWeek*, January 19, 2004, pp. 44–50; and Carol Matlack, "Nestle Is Starting to Slim Down at Last," *BusinessWeek*, October 27, 2003, pp. 56–57.

Responsibility Accounting

Decentralized organizations need *responsibility accounting systems* that link lower-level managers' decision-making authority with accountability for the outcomes of those decisions. The term **responsibility center** is used for any part of an organization whose manager has control over and is accountable for cost, profit, or investments. The three primary types of responsibility centers are *cost centers, profit centers,* and *investment centers.*[2]

Cost, Profit, and Investment Centers

Cost Center   The manager of a **cost center** has control over costs, but not over revenue or the use of investment funds. Service departments such as accounting, finance, general administration, legal, and personnel are usually classified as cost centers. In addition, manufacturing facilities are often considered to be cost centers. The managers of cost centers are expected to minimize costs while providing the level of products and services demanded by other parts of the organization. For example, the manager of a manufacturing facility would be evaluated at least in part by comparing actual costs to how much costs should have been for the actual level of output during the period. Standard cost variances and flexible budget variances, such as those discussed in Chapters 10 and 11, are often used to evaluate cost center performance.

Profit Center   The manager of a **profit center** has control over both costs and revenue, but not over the use of investment funds. For example, the manager in charge of a Six Flags amusement park would be responsible for both the revenues and costs, and hence the profits, of the amusement park, but may not have control over major investments in the park. Profit center managers are often evaluated by comparing actual profit to targeted or budgeted profit.

---

[2] Some companies classify business segments that are responsible mainly for generating revenue, such as an insurance sales office, as *revenue centers.* Other companies would consider this to be just another type of profit center, since costs of some kind (salaries, rent, utilities) are usually deducted from the revenues in the segment's income statement.

RESPONSIBILITY ACCOUNTING: A CHINESE PERSPECTIVE

For years Han Dan Iron and Steel Company was under Chinese government control. During this period, the company's management accounting system focused on complying with government mandates rather than responding to the market. As a market-oriented economy began to emerge, the company realized that its management accounting system was obsolete. Managers were preoccupied with meeting production quotas imposed by the government rather than controlling costs and meeting profit targets or encouraging productivity improvements. To remedy this situation, the company implemented what it called a *responsibility cost control system* that (1) set cost and profit targets, (2) assigned target costs to responsibility center managers, (3) evaluated the performance of responsibility center managers based on their ability to meet the targets, and (4) provided incentives to improve productivity.

Source: Z. Jun Lin and Zengbiao Yu, "Responsibility Cost Control System in China: A Case of Management Accounting Application," *Management Accounting Research*, December 2002, pp. 447–467.

Investment Center   The manager of an **investment center** has control over cost, revenue, and investments in operating assets. For example, the vice president of the Truck Division at General Motors would have a great deal of discretion over investments in the division. This vice president would be responsible for initiating investment proposals, such as funding research into more fuel-efficient engines for sport-utility vehicles. Once the proposal has been approved by General Motor's top-level managers and board of directors, the vice president of the Truck Division would then be responsible for making sure that the investment pays off. Investment center managers are usually evaluated using return on investment (ROI) or residual income measures, as discussed later in the chapter.

EXTREME INCENTIVES

In 2003, Tyco International, Ltd., was rocked by a series of scandals including disclosure of $2 billion of accounting-related problems, investigations by the Securities and Exchange Commission, and a criminal trial of its ex-CEO, Dennis Kozlowski, on charges of more than $600 million in unauthorized compensation and fraudulent stock sales. Was any of this foreseeable? Well, in a word, yes.

BusinessWeek reported in 1999 that the CEO of Tyco International, Ltd., was putting unrelenting pressure on his managers to deliver growth. "Each year, [the CEO] sets targets for how much each manager must increase his or her unit's earnings in the coming year. The targets are coupled with a powerful incentive system. If they meet or exceed these targets, managers are promised a bonus that can be many times their salary. But if they fall even a bit short, the bonus plummets." This sounds good, but "to many accounting experts, the sort of all-or-nothing bonus structure set up at Tyco is a warning light. If top executives set profit targets too high or turn a blind eye to how managers achieve them, the incentive for managers to cut corners is enormous. Indeed, a blue-ribbon panel of accounting experts who were trying to improve corporate auditing standards several years ago . . . identified just such extreme incentives as a red flag. 'If you're right under the target, there's a tremendous economic interest to accelerate earnings,' says David F. Larcker, a professor of accounting at the Wharton School. 'If you're right over it, there is an incentive to push earnings into the next period.'"

Sources: *Reuters*, "Tyco Says to Restate Several Years of Results," June 16, 2003; Jeanne King, *Reuters*, "New York Trial of ex-Tyco CEO Koslowski Can Proceed," June 23, 2003; and, William C. Symonds, Diane Brady, Geoffrey Smith, and Lorraine Woellert, "Tyco: Aggressive or Out of Line?" *BusinessWeek*, November 1, 1999, pp. 160–165.

An Organizational View of Responsibility Centers

Superior Foods Corporation, a company that manufactures and distributes snack foods and beverages, provides an example of the various kinds of responsibility centers. Exhibit 12–1 shows a

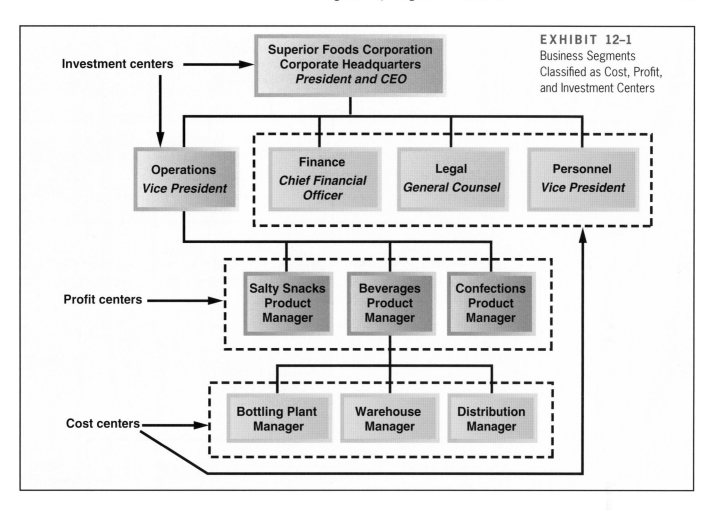

EXHIBIT 12–1
Business Segments Classified as Cost, Profit, and Investment Centers

partial organization chart for Superior Foods that displays its cost, profit, and investment centers. The departments and work centers that do not generate significant revenues by themselves are classified as cost centers. These are staff departments—such as finance, legal, and personnel—and operating units—such as the bottling plant, warehouse, and beverage distribution center. The profit centers generate revenues, and they include the salty snacks, beverages, and confections product families. The vice president of operations oversees the allocation of investment funds across the product families and is responsible for the profits of those product families. And finally, corporate headquarters is an investment center, since it is responsible for all revenues, costs, and investments.

Decentralization and Segment Reporting

Effective decentralization requires *segmented reporting*. In addition to the companywide income statement, reports are needed for individual segments of the organization. A **segment** is a part or activity of an organization about which managers would like cost, revenue, or profit data. Cost, profit, and investment centers are segments as are sales territories, individual stores, service centers, manufacturing plants, marketing departments, individual customers, and product lines. A company's operations can be segmented in many ways. For example, Exhibit 12–2 (page 520) shows several ways in which Superior Foods could segment its business. The top half of the exhibit shows Superior segmenting its $500 million in revenue by geographical region, and the bottom half shows Superior segmenting its total

LEARNING OBJECTIVE 1
Prepare a segmented income statement using the contribution format, and explain the difference between traceable fixed costs and common fixed costs.

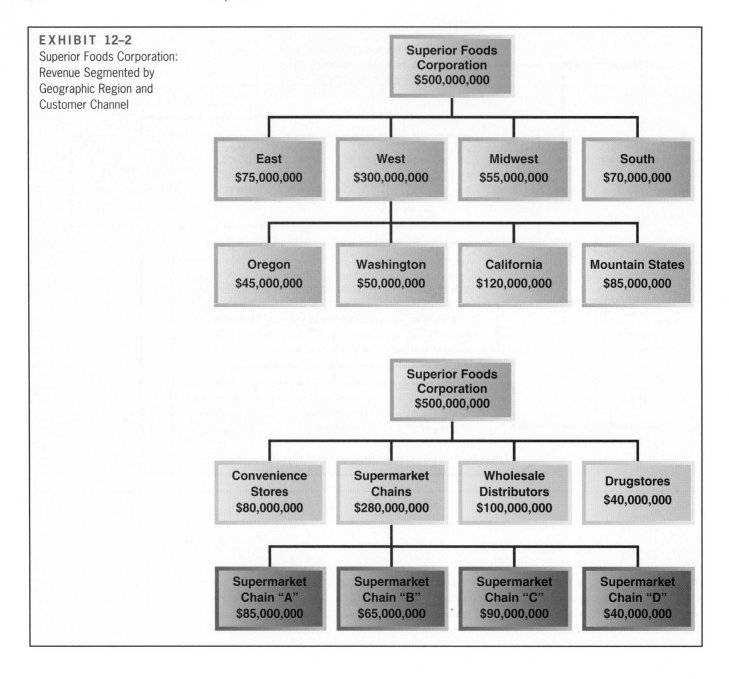

revenue by customer channel. With the appropriate database and software, managers could easily drill even further down into the organization. For example, the sales in California could be segmented by product family, then by product line. This drill-down capability helps managers to identify the sources of strong or weak overall financial performance. In this chapter, we learn how to construct income statements for business segments. These segmented income statements are useful in analyzing the profitability of segments and in measuring the performance of segment managers.

Building a Segmented Income Statement

Several important principles are involved in constructing a useful segmented income statement. These principles are illustrated in the following example.

SoftSolutions, Inc., is a rapidly growing computer software company founded by Lori Saffer, who had previously worked in a large software company, and Marjorie Matsuo, who had previously worked in the hotel industry as a general manager. They formed the company to develop and market user-friendly accounting and operations software designed specifically for hotels. They quit their jobs, pooled their savings, hired several programmers, and got down to work.

MANAGERIAL
ACCOUNTING
IN ACTION
The Issue

The first sale was by far the most difficult. No hotel wanted to be the first to use an untested product from an unknown company. After overcoming this obstacle with persistence, good luck, dedication to customer service, and a very low introductory price, the company's sales grew.

The company quickly developed similar business software for other specialized markets and then branched out into clip art and computer games. Within four years of its founding, the organization had grown to the point where Saffer and Matsuo were no longer able to personally direct all of the company's activities. Decentralization had become a necessity.

Accordingly, the company was split into two divisions—Business Products and Consumer Products. By mutual consent, Matsuo took the title president and Saffer took the title vice president of the Business Products Division. Chris Worden, a programmer who had spearheaded the drive into the clip art and computer games markets, was designated vice president of the Consumer Products Division.

Almost immediately, the issue arose of how best to evaluate the performance of the divisions. Matsuo called a meeting to consider this issue and asked Saffer, Worden, and the controller, Bill Carson, to attend. The following discussion took place at that meeting:

Marjorie: We need to find a better way to measure the performance of our divisions.

Chris: I agree. Consumer Products has been setting the pace in this company for the last two years, and we should be getting more recognition.

Lori: Chris, we are delighted with the success of the Consumer Products Division.

Chris: I know. But it is hard to figure out just how successful we are with the present accounting reports. All we have are sales and cost of goods sold figures for the division.

Bill: What's the matter with those figures? They are prepared using generally accepted accounting principles.

Chris: The sales figures are fine. However, cost of goods sold includes some costs that really aren't the costs of our division, and it excludes some costs that are. Let's take a simple example. Everything we sell in the Consumer Products Division has to pass through the automatic bar-coding machine, which applies a unique bar code to the product.

Lori: That's true for items from the Business Products Division as well as for items from the Consumer Products Division.

Chris: That's precisely the point. Whether an item comes from the Business Products Division or the Consumer Products Division, it must pass through the automatic bar-coding machine after the software has been packaged. How much of the cost of the automatic bar coder would be saved if we didn't have any consumer products?

Marjorie: Since we have only one automatic bar coder and we would need it anyway to code the business products, I guess none of the cost would be saved.

Chris: That's right. And since none of the cost could be saved even if the entire Consumer Products Division were eliminated, how can we logically say that some of the cost of the automatic bar coder is a cost of the Consumer Products Division?

Lori: Just a minute, Chris, are you saying that my Business Products Division should be charged with the entire cost of the automatic bar coder?

Chris: No, that's not what I am saying.

Marjorie: But Chris, I don't see how we can have sensible performance reports without making someone responsible for costs like the cost of the automatic bar coder. Bill, as our accounting expert, what do you think?

Bill: I have some ideas for handling issues like the automatic bar coder. The best approach would probably be for me to put together a draft performance report. We can discuss it at the next meeting when everyone has something concrete to look at.

Marjorie: Okay, let's see what you come up with.

Bill Carson, the controller of SoftSolutions, realized that segmented income statements would be required to more appropriately evaluate the performance of the two divisions. To construct the segmented reports, he would have to carefully segregate costs that are attributable to the segments from costs that are not. Since most of the disputes over costs would be about fixed costs such as the automatic bar-coding machine, he knew he would also have to separate fixed from variable costs. The conventional absorption costing income statement prepared for the entire company commingles variable and fixed manufacturing costs in the cost of goods sold.

Largely for these reasons, Bill Carson decided to use the contribution format income statement based on variable costing that was discussed in earlier chapters. Recall that when the contribution format is used: (1) the cost of goods sold consists only of the variable manufacturing costs; (2) variable and fixed costs are listed in separate sections; and (3) a contribution margin is computed. When such a statement is segmented as in this chapter, fixed costs are broken down further into what are called traceable and common costs as discussed later. This breakdown allows a *segment margin* to be computed for each segment of the company. The segment margin is a valuable tool for assessing the long-run profitability of a segment and is also a much better tool for evaluating performance than absorption costing reports.

Levels of Segmented Statements

A portion of the segmented report Bill Carson prepared is shown in Exhibit 12–3. The contribution format income statement for the entire company appears at the very top of the exhibit under the column labeled Total Company. Immediately to the right of this column are two columns—one for each of the two divisions. We can see that the Business Products Division's segment margin is $60,000 and the Consumer Products Division's is $40,000. These segment margins show the company's divisional managers how much each of their divisions is contributing to the company's profits.

However, segmented income statements can be prepared for activities at many levels in a company. To provide more information to the company's divisional managers, Bill Carson has further segmented the divisions according to their major product lines. In the case of the Consumer Products Division, the product lines are clip art and computer games. Going even further, Bill Carson has segmented each of the product lines according to how they are sold—in retail computer stores or over the Internet. In Exhibit 12–3, this further segmentation is illustrated for the computer games product line. Notice that as we go from one segmented statement to another, we look at smaller and smaller pieces of the company. While not shown in Exhibit 12–3, Bill Carson also prepared segmented income statements for the major product lines in the Business Products Division.

IN BUSINESS

COMPUTING SEGMENT MARGINS HELPS AN ENTREPRENEUR

In 2001, Victoria Pappas Collection, a small company specializing in women's sportswear, reported a net loss of $280,000 on sales of $1 million. When the company's founder, Vickie Giannukos, segmented her company's income statement into the six markets that she was serving, the results were revealing. The Dallas and Atlanta markets generated $825,000 of sales and incurred $90,000 of traceable fixed costs. The other four markets combined produced $175,000 of sales and also incurred $90,000 of traceable fixed costs. Given her average contribution margin ratio of 38%, the Dallas and Atlanta markets earned a segment margin of $223,500 [($825,000 × 38%) − $90,000] while the other four markets combined incurred a loss of $23,500 [($175,000 × 38%) − $90,000].

Vicky had made a common mistake—she chased every possible dollar of sales without knowing if her efforts were profitable. Based on her segmented income statements, she discontinued operations in three cities and hired a new sales representative in Los Angeles. She decided to focus on growing sales in Dallas and Atlanta while deferring expansion into new markets until it could be done profitably.

Source: Norm Brodsky, "The Thin Red Line," *Inc.* magazine, January 2004, pp. 49–52.

Segments Defined as Divisions

		Divisions	
	Total Company	Business Products Division	Consumer Products Division
Sales	$500,000	$300,000	$200,000
Variable expenses:			
Variable cost of goods sold	180,000	120,000	60,000
Other variable expenses	50,000	30,000	20,000
Total variable expenses	230,000	150,000	80,000
Contribution margin	270,000	150,000	120,000
Traceable fixed expenses	170,000	90,000	80,000*
Divisional segment margin	100,000	$ 60,000	$ 40,000
Common fixed expenses not traceable to individual divisions	85,000		
Net operating income	$ 15,000		

Segments Defined as Product Lines of the Consumer Products Division

		Product Line	
	Consumer Products Division	Clip Art	Computer Games
Sales	$200,000	$ 75,000	$125,000
Variable expenses:			
Variable cost of goods sold	60,000	20,000	40,000
Other variable expenses	20,000	5,000	15,000
Total variable expenses	80,000	25,000	55,000
Contribution margin	120,000	50,000	70,000
Traceable fixed expenses	70,000	30,000	40,000
Product-line segment margin	50,000	$ 20,000	$ 30,000
Common fixed expenses not traceable to individual product lines	10,000		
Divisional segment margin	$ 40,000		

Segments Defined as Sales Channels for One Product Line, Computer Games, of the Consumer Products Division

		Sales Channels	
	Computer Games	On-Line Sales	Retail Stores
Sales	$125,000	$100,000	$ 25,000
Variable expenses:			
Variable cost of goods sold	40,000	32,000	8,000
Other variable expenses	15,000	5,000	10,000
Total variable expenses	55,000	37,000	18,000
Contribution margin	70,000	63,000	7,000
Traceable fixed expenses	25,000	15,000	10,000
Sales-channel segment margin	45,000	$ 48,000	$ (3,000)
Common fixed expenses not traceable to individual sales channels	15,000		
Product-line segment margin	$ 30,000		

*Notice that this $80,000 in traceable fixed expenses is divided into two parts when the Consumer Products Division is broken down into product lines—$70,000 traceable and $10,000 common. The reasons for this are discussed later in the section "Traceable Costs Can Become Common Costs."

EXHIBIT 12–3
SoftSolutions, Inc.—Segmented Income Statements in the Contribution Format

Sales and Contribution Margin

To prepare a segmented income statement, variable expenses are deducted from sales to yield the contribution margin for the segment. The contribution margin tells us what happens to profits as volume changes—holding a segment's capacity and fixed costs constant. The contribution margin is especially useful in decisions involving temporary uses of capacity such as special orders. These types of decisions often involve only variable costs and revenues—the two components of contribution margin. Such decisions will be discussed in detail in Chapter 13.

Traceable and Common Fixed Costs

The most puzzling aspect of Exhibit 12–3 is probably the treatment of fixed costs. The report has two kinds of fixed costs—traceable and common. Only the *traceable fixed costs* are charged to particular segments. If a cost is not traceable to a segment, then it is not assigned to the segment.

A **traceable fixed cost** of a segment is a fixed cost that is incurred because of the existence of the segment—if the segment had never existed, the fixed cost would not have been incurred; and if the segment were eliminated, the fixed cost would disappear. Examples of traceable fixed costs include the following:

- The salary of the Fritos product manager at PepsiCo is a *traceable* fixed cost of the Fritos business segment of PepsiCo.
- The maintenance cost for the building in which Boeing 747s are assembled is a *traceable* fixed cost of the 747 business segment of Boeing.
- The liability insurance at Disney World is a *traceable* fixed cost of the Disney World business segment of the Disney Corporation.

A **common fixed cost** is a fixed cost that supports the operations of more than one segment, but is not traceable in whole or in part to any one segment. Even if a segment were entirely eliminated, there would be no change in a true common fixed cost. For example:

- The salary of the CEO of General Motors is a *common* fixed cost of the various divisions of General Motors.
- The cost of heating a Safeway or Kroger grocery store is a *common* fixed cost of the store's various departments—groceries, produce, bakery, meat, etc.
- The cost of the automatic bar-coding machine at SoftSolutions is a *common* fixed cost of the Consumer Products Division and of the Business Products Division.
- The cost of the receptionist's salary at an office shared by a number of doctors is a *common* fixed cost of the doctors. The cost is traceable to the office, but not to individual doctors.

Identifying Traceable Fixed Costs
The distinction between traceable and common fixed costs is crucial in segment reporting, since traceable fixed costs are charged to segments and common fixed costs are not. In an actual situation, it is sometimes hard to determine whether a cost should be classified as traceable or common.

The general guideline is to treat as traceable costs *only those costs that would disappear over time if the segment itself disappeared.* For example, if the Consumer Products Division were sold or discontinued, it would no longer be necessary to pay the division manager's salary. Therefore the division manager's salary should be classified as a traceable fixed cost of the division. On the other hand, the president of the company undoubtedly would continue to be paid even if the Consumer Products Division were dropped. In fact, he or she might even be paid more if dropping the division was a good idea. Therefore, the president's salary is common to both divisions and should not be charged to either division.

When assigning costs to segments, the key point is to resist the temptation to allocate costs (such as depreciation of corporate facilities) that are clearly common and that will continue regardless of whether the segment exists or not. *Any allocation of common costs to segments reduces the value of the segment margin as a measure of long-run segment profitability and segment performance.*

Activity-Based Costing   Some costs are easy to identify as traceable costs. For example, the cost of advertising Crest toothpaste on television is clearly traceable to Crest. A more difficult situation arises when a building, machine, or other resource is shared by two or more segments. For example, assume that a multiproduct company leases warehouse space that is used for storing the full range of its products. Would the lease cost of the warehouse be a traceable or a common cost of the products? Managers familiar with activity-based costing might argue that the lease cost is traceable and should be assigned to the products according to how much space the products use in the warehouse. In like manner, these managers would argue that order processing costs, sales support costs, and other selling and administrative expenses should also be charged to segments according to the segments' consumption of selling and administrative resources.

To illustrate, consider Holt Corporation, a company that manufactures concrete pipe for industrial uses. The company has three products—9-inch pipe, 12-inch pipe, and 18-inch pipe. Space is rented in a large warehouse on a yearly basis as needed. The rental cost of this space is $4 per square foot per year. The 9-inch pipe occupies 1,000 square feet of space, the 12-inch pipe occupies 4,000 square feet, and the 18-inch pipe occupies 5,000 square feet. The company also has an order processing department that incurred $150,000 in order processing costs last year. Management believes that order processing costs are driven by the number of orders placed by customers. Last year 2,500 orders were placed, of which 1,200 were for 9-inch pipe, 800 were for 12-inch pipe, and 500 were for 18-inch pipe. Given these data, the following costs would be assigned to each product using the activity-based costing approach:

```
Warehouse space cost:
  9-inch pipe: $4 per square foot × 1,000 square feet . . . . . . .   $  4,000
  12-inch pipe: $4 per square foot × 4,000 square feet . . . . . .     16,000
  18-inch pipe: $4 per square foot × 5,000 square feet . . . . . .     20,000
  Total cost assigned . . . . . . . . . . . . . . . . . . . . . . .   $ 40,000

Order processing costs:
  $150,000 ÷ 2,500 orders = $60 per order
  9-inch pipe: $60 per order × 1,200 orders . . . . . . . . . . . .   $ 72,000
  12-inch pipe: $60 per order × 800 orders  . . . . . . . . . . . .     48,000
  18-inch pipe: $60 per order × 500 orders  . . . . . . . . . . . .     30,000
  Total cost assigned  . . . . . . . . . . . . . . . . . . . . . .   $150,000
```

This method of assigning costs combines the strength of activity-based costing with the power of the contribution approach and greatly enhances the manager's ability to measure the profitability and performance of segments. However, managers must still ask themselves if the costs would in fact disappear over time if the segment itself disappeared. In the case of Holt Corporation, it is clear that the $20,000 in warehousing costs for the 18-inch pipe would be eliminated if 18-inch pipes were no longer being produced. The company would simply rent less warehouse space the following year. However, suppose the company owns the warehouse. Then it is not so clear that $20,000 of warehousing cost would really disappear if the 18-inch pipes were discontinued. The company might be able to sublease the space, or use it for other products, but then again the space might simply be empty while the warehousing costs continue to be incurred.

Traceable Costs Can Become Common Costs

Fixed costs that are traceable to one segment may be a common cost of another segment. For example, an airline might want a segmented income statement that shows the segment margin for a particular flight from Los Angeles to Paris further broken down into first-class, business-class, and economy-class segment margins. The airline must pay a substantial landing fee at Charles DeGaulle airport in Paris. This fixed landing fee is a traceable cost of the flight, but it is a common cost of the first-class, business-class, and economy-class segments. Even if the first-class cabin is empty, the entire landing fee must be paid. So the landing fee is not a traceable cost of the first-class cabin. But on the other hand, paying the fee is necessary in order to have any first-class, business-class, or economy-class passengers. So the landing fee is a common cost of these three classes.

The dual nature of some fixed costs can be seen in Exhibit 12–4. Notice from the diagram that when segments are defined as divisions, the Consumer Products Division has $80,000 in traceable fixed expenses. However, when we drill down to the product lines, only $70,000 of the $80,000 cost that was traceable to the Consumer Products Division is traceable to the product lines. The other $10,000 becomes a common cost of the two product lines of the Consumer Products Division.

Why would $10,000 of traceable fixed cost become a common cost when the division is divided into product lines? The $10,000 is the monthly salary of the manager of the Consumer Products Division. This salary is a traceable cost of the division as a whole, but it is a common cost of the division's product lines. The manager's salary is a necessary cost of having the two product lines, but even if one of the product lines were discontinued entirely, the manager's salary would probably not be cut. Therefore, none of the manager's salary can really be traced to the individual products.

The $70,000 traceable fixed cost of the product lines consists of the costs of product specific advertising. A total of $30,000 was spent on advertising clip art and $40,000 was spent on advertising computer games. These costs can clearly be traced to the individual product lines.

Segment Margin

Observe from Exhibit 12–3 that the **segment margin** is obtained by deducting the traceable fixed costs of a segment from the segment's contribution margin. It represents the margin available after a segment has covered all of its own costs. *The segment margin is the best gauge of the long-run profitability of a segment* because it includes only those costs that are caused by the segment. If a segment can't cover its own costs, then that segment probably should be dropped (unless it has important side effects on other segments). Notice from Exhibit 12–3, for example, that the Retail Stores sales channel has a negative segment margin. This means that the segment is not generating enough revenue to cover its own costs. Retention or elimination of product lines and other segments is covered in more depth in Chapter 13.

EXHIBIT 12–4
Reclassification of Traceable Fixed Expenses from Exhibit 12–3

		Segment	
		Business	Consumer
	Total	Products	Products
	Company	Division	Division
Contribution margin	$270,000	$150,000	$120,000
Traceable fixed expenses	170,000	90,000	80,000

		Segment	
	Consumer		
	Products	Clip	Computer
	Division	Art	Games
Contribution margin	$120,000	$50,000	$70,000
Traceable fixed expenses	70,000	30,000	40,000
Product-line segment margin	50,000	$20,000	$30,000
Common fixed expenses	10,000		
Divisional segment margin	$ 40,000		

From a decision-making point of view, the segment margin is most useful in major decisions that affect capacity such as dropping a segment. By contrast, as we noted earlier, the contribution margin is most useful in decisions involving short-run changes in volume, such as pricing special orders that involve temporary use of existing capacity.

SEGMENT INFORMATION MAKES PROFITS RISE

Great Harvest bakeries use freshly milled Montana whole wheat to make soft-crust specialty breads. The company was founded by Pete and Laura Wakeman and is headquartered in Dillon, Montana. Great Harvest encourages each of its over 100 franchised bakeries to experiment with new approaches to business management, customer service, and marketing and uses several methods to spread the best innovations throughout the system. Staffers at the headquarters in Dillon "provide franchisees with a **top 10 list** of the 10 best-performing bakeries in 14 statistical and financial categories. . . . Got a problem controlling labor expenses at your store? Call up the bakery owners who've got that figured out and get their advice." In addition, bakery owners who join the Numbers Club agree to open their books to the other owners in the club. "Franchisees can spot other owners whose situations might be similar to theirs (same size bakery and market, say, or the same level of owner's labor)—and who appear to have found better solutions to problems. They can identify the perfectly useful peer—and call him or her up."

Source: Michael Hopkins, "Zen and the Art of the Self-Managing Company," *Inc.* magazine, November 2000, pp. 54–63.

Shortly after Bill Carson, the SoftSolutions, Inc., controller, completed the segmented income statement, he sent copies to the other managers and called a meeting in which the report could be explained—Marjorie Matsuo, Lori Saffer, and Chris Worden were all in attendance.

**MANAGERIAL
ACCOUNTING
IN ACTION**
The Wrap-up

Soft Solutions Inc.

Lori: I think these segmented income statements are fairly self-explanatory. However, there is one thing I wonder about.

Bill: What's that?

Lori: What is this common fixed expense of $85,000 listed under the total company? And who is going to be responsible for it if neither Chris nor I have responsibility?

Bill: The $85,000 of common fixed expenses represents expenses like administrative salaries and the costs of common production equipment such as the automatic bar-coding machine. Marjorie, do you want to respond to the question about responsibility for these expenses?

Marjorie: Sure. Since I'm the president of the company, I'm responsible for those costs. Some things can be delegated, others cannot be. It wouldn't make any sense for either you or Chris to make strategic decisions about the bar coder because it affects both of you. That's an important part of my job—making decisions about resources that affect all parts of the organization. This report makes it much clearer who is responsible for what. I like it.

Chris: So do I—my division's segment margin is higher than the net operating income for the entire company.

Marjorie: Don't get carried away, Chris. Let's not misinterpret what this report means. The segment margins *have* to be big to cover the common costs of the company. We can't let the big segment margins lull us into a sense of complacency. If we use these reports, we all have to agree that our objective is to increase all of our segment margins over time.

Lori: I'm willing to give it a try.

Chris: The reports make sense to me.

Marjorie: So be it. Then the first item of business would appear to be a review of the Retail Stores channel for selling computer games, where we appear to be losing money. Chris, could you brief us on this at our next meeting?

Chris: Yes. I have been suspecting for some time that our retail sales strategy could be improved.

Marjorie: We look forward to hearing your analysis.

WHAT'S IN A SEGMENT?

Continental Airlines could figure out the profitability of a specific route on a monthly basis—for example, Houston to Los Angeles—but management did not know the profitability of a particular flight on that route. The company's new chief financial officer (CFO), Larry Kellner, placed top priority on developing a flight profitability system that would break out the profit (or loss) for each individual flight. Once completed, the flight profitability system revealed such money-losing flights as two December flights that left Houston for London within a four-hour period with only about 30 passengers each. "If those flights are blurred in with the whole month of December, they just don't jump off the page," says Kellner. With the data on the profitability of individual flights, Continental was able to design more appropriate schedules.

Source: Tim Reason, "Making Continental Airlines' Turnaround Permanent Meant Installing Some High-Flying IT Systems," *CFO*, October 2000, pp. 61–64.

Segmented Financial Information in External Reports

The Financial Accounting Standards Board (FASB) now requires that companies in the United States include segmented financial and other data in their annual reports and that the segmented reports prepared for external users *must use the same methods and definitions that the companies use in internal segmented reports that are prepared to aid in making operating decisions.* This is a very unusual requirement. Companies are not ordinarily required to report the same data to external users that are reported internally for decision-making purposes. This may seem like a reasonable requirement for the FASB to make, but it has some serious drawbacks. First, segmented data are often highly sensitive and companies are reluctant to release such data to the public for the simple reason that their competitors will then have access to the data. Second, segmented statements prepared in accordance with GAAP do not distinguish between fixed and variable costs and between traceable and common costs. Indeed, the segmented income statements illustrated earlier in this chapter do not conform to GAAP for that reason. To avoid the complications of reconciling non-GAAP segment earnings with GAAP consolidated earnings, it is likely that at least some managers will choose to construct their segmented financial statements in a manner that conforms with GAAP. This will result in more occurrences of the problems discussed in the following section.

Hindrances to Proper Cost Assignment

Costs must be properly assigned to segments. All of the costs attributable to a segment—and only those costs—should be assigned to the segment. Unfortunately, companies often make mistakes when assigning costs to segments. They omit some costs, inappropriately assign traceable fixed costs, and arbitrarily allocate common fixed costs.

Omission of Costs

The costs assigned to a segment should include all costs attributable to that segment from the company's entire value chain as discussed in Chapter 1. All of these functions, from research and development, through product design, manufacturing, marketing, distribution, and customer service, are required to bring a product or service to the customer and generate revenues.

However, as discussed in Chapters 2, 3, and 7, only manufacturing costs are included in product costs under absorption costing, which is widely regarded as required for external financial reporting. To avoid having to maintain two costing systems and to provide consistency between internal and external reports, many companies also use absorption costing for their internal reports such as segmented income statements. As a result, such companies omit from their profitability analysis part or all of the "upstream" costs in the value chain, which consist of research and development and product design, and the "downstream" costs, which consist of marketing, distribution, and customer service. Yet these nonmanufacturing costs are just as essential in determining product profitability as are the manufacturing costs. These upstream and downstream costs, which are usually included in selling and administrative expenses on the income statement, can represent half or more of the total costs of an organization. If either the upstream or downstream costs are omitted in profitability analysis, then the product is undercosted and management may unwittingly develop and maintain products that in the long run result in losses.

Inappropriate Methods for Assigning Traceable Costs among Segments

In addition to omitting costs, many companies do not correctly handle traceable fixed expenses on segmented income statements. First, they may not trace fixed expenses to segments even when it is feasible to do so. Second, they may use inappropriate allocation bases to allocate traceable fixed expenses to segments.

Failure to Trace Costs Directly
Costs that can be traced directly to a specific segment should be charged directly to that segment and should not be allocated to other segments. For example, the rent for a branch office of an insurance company should be charged directly to the branch office rather than included in a companywide overhead pool and then spread throughout the company.

Inappropriate Allocation Base
Some companies use arbitrary allocation bases to allocate costs to segments. For example, some companies allocate selling and administrative expenses on the basis of sales revenues. Thus, if a segment generates 20% of total company sales, it would be allocated 20% of the company's selling and administrative expenses as its "fair share." This same basic procedure is followed if cost of goods sold or some other measure is used as the allocation base.

Costs should be allocated to segments for internal decision-making purposes only when the allocation base actually drives the cost being allocated (or is very highly correlated with the real cost driver). For example, sales should be used to allocate selling and administrative expenses only if a 10% increase in sales will result in a 10% increase in selling and administrative expenses. To the extent that selling and administrative expenses are not driven by sales volume, these expenses will be improperly allocated—with a disproportionately high percentage of the selling and administrative expenses assigned to the segments with the largest sales.

Arbitrarily Dividing Common Costs among Segments

The third business practice that leads to distorted segment costs is the practice of assigning nontraceable costs to segments. For example, some companies allocate the common costs of the corporate headquarters building to products on segment reports. However, in a multi-product company, no single product is likely to be responsible for any significant amount of this cost. Even if a product were eliminated entirely, there would usually be no significant effect on any of the costs of the corporate headquarters building. In short, there is no cause-and-effect relation between the cost of the corporate headquarters building and the existence of any one product. As a consequence, any allocation of the cost of the corporate headquarters building to the products must be arbitrary.

Common costs like the costs of the corporate headquarters building are necessary, of course, to have a functioning organization. The practice of arbitrarily allocating common costs to segments is often justified on the grounds that "someone" has to "cover the common costs." While it is undeniably true that the common costs must be covered, arbitrarily allocating common costs to segments does not ensure that this will happen. In fact, adding a share of common costs to the real costs of a segment may make an otherwise profitable segment appear to be unprofitable. If a manager eliminates the apparently unprofitable segment, the real traceable costs of the segment will be saved, but its revenues will be lost. And what happens to the common fixed costs that were allocated to the segment? They don't disappear; they are reallocated to the remaining segments of the company. That makes all of the remaining segments appear to be less profitable—possibly resulting in dropping other segments. The net effect will be to reduce the overall profits of the company and make it even more difficult to "cover the common costs."

Additionally, common fixed costs are not manageable by the manager to whom they are arbitrarily allocated; they are the responsibility of higher-level managers. Allocating common fixed costs to responsibility centers is counterproductive in a responsibility accounting system. When common fixed costs are allocated to managers, they are held responsible for those costs even though they cannot control them.

In sum, the way many companies handle segment reporting results in cost distortion. This distortion results from three practices—the failure to trace costs directly to a specific segment when it is feasible to do so, the use of inappropriate bases for allocating costs, and the allocation of common costs to segments. These practices are widespread. One study found that 60% of the companies surveyed made no attempt to assign selling and administrative costs to segments on a cause-and-effect basis.[3]

IN BUSINESS

THE BIG GOUGE?

The Big Dig in Boston is a $14 billion-plus project to bury major roads underground in downtown Boston. Two companies—Bechtel and Parsons Brinckerhoff (PB)—manage the 20-year project, which is $1.6 billion over budget. The two companies will likely collect in excess of $120 million in fixed fees for their work on the project—not including reimbursements for overhead costs. Bechtel and PB have many projects underway at any one time and many common fixed costs. These common fixed costs are not actually caused by the Big Dig project and yet portions of these costs have been claimed as reimbursable expenses. "Bechtel and PB say they don't collect a penny more for overhead than they are entitled to." A Bechtel spokesman says, "Our allocation of overhead [on the Big Dig] is rigorously audited . . . " This is undoubtedly true; in practice, fixed common costs are routinely (and arbitrarily) allocated to segments for cost reimbursement and other purposes. Managers at Bechtel, PB, and other companies argue that someone must pay for these costs. While this too is true, who actually pays for these costs will depend on how the common fixed costs are arbitrarily allocated among segments. Massachusetts has lodged a number of complaints concerning Bechtel's cost recovery claims. Such complaints are almost inevitable when common fixed costs are allocated to segments. It might be better to simply set an all-inclusive fixed fee up front with no cost recovery and hence no issues concerning what costs are really attributable to the project.

Source: Nathan Vardi, "Desert Storm," *Forbes*, June 23, 2003, pp. 63–66.

Evaluating Investment Center Performance—Return on Investment

Thus far, the chapter has focused on how to properly assign costs to responsibility centers and how to construct segmented income statements. These are vital steps when evaluating cost and profit centers. However, evaluating an investment center's performance requires more than accurate cost and segment margin reporting. In addition, an investment center is responsible for earning an adequate return on investment. This section and the next section

---

[3]   James R. Emore and Joseph A. Ness, "The Slow Pace of Meaningful Change in Cost Systems," *Journal of Cost Management* 4, no. 4, p. 39.

of the chapter present two methods for evaluating this aspect of an investment center's performance. The first method, covered in this section, is called *return on investment (ROI)*. The second method, covered in the next section, is called *residual income.*

The Return on Investment (ROI) Formula

Return on investment (ROI) is defined as net operating income divided by average operating assets:

$$\text{ROI} = \frac{\text{Net operating income}}{\text{Average operating assets}}$$

The higher a business segment's return on investment (ROI), the greater the profit earned per dollar invested in the segment's operating assets.

Net Operating Income and Operating Assets Defined

Topic Tackler

PLUS

12–1

Note that *net operating income,* rather than net income, is used in the ROI formula. **Net operating income** is income before interest and taxes and is sometimes referred to as EBIT (earnings before interest and taxes). Net operating income is used in the formula because the base (i.e., denominator) consists of *operating assets.* To be consistent, we use net operating income in the numerator.

Operating assets include cash, accounts receivable, inventory, plant and equipment, and all other assets held for operating purposes. Examples of assets that are not included in operating assets (i.e., examples of nonoperating assets) include land held for future use, an investment in another company, or a building rented to someone else. These assets are not held for operating purposes and therefore are excluded from operating assets. The operating assets base used in the formula is typically computed as the average of the operating assets between the beginning and the end of the year.

Most companies use the net book value (i.e., acquisition cost less accumulated depreciation) of depreciable assets to calculate average operating assets. This approach has drawbacks. An asset's net book value decreases over time as the accumulated depreciation increases. This decreases the denominator in the ROI calculation, thus increasing ROI. Consequently, ROI mechanically increases over time. Moreover, replacing old depreciated equipment with new equipment increases the book value of depreciable assets and decreases ROI. Hence, using net book value in the calculation of average operating assets results in a predictable pattern of increasing ROI over time as accumulated depreciation grows and discourages replacing old equipment with new, updated equipment. An alternative to using net book value is the gross cost of the asset, which ignores accumulated depreciation. Gross cost stays constant over time because depreciation is ignored; therefore, ROI does not grow automatically over time, and replacing a fully depreciated asset with a comparably priced new asset will not adversely affect ROI.

Nevertheless, most companies use the net book value approach to computing average operating assets because it is consistent with their financial reporting practices of recording the net book value of assets on the balance sheet and including depreciation as an operating expense on the income statement. In this text, we will use the net book value approach unless a specific exercise or problem directs otherwise.

Understanding ROI

The equation for ROI, net operating income divided by average operating assets, does not provide much help to managers interested in taking actions to improve their ROI. It only offers two levers for improving performance—net operating income and average operating assets. Fortunately, ROI can also be expressed as follows:

$$\text{ROI} = \text{Margin} \times \text{Turnover}$$

where

$$\text{Margin} = \frac{\text{Net operating income}}{\text{Sales}}$$

and

$$\text{Turnover} = \frac{\text{Sales}}{\text{Average operating assets}}$$

Note that the sales terms in the margin and turnover formulas cancel out when they are multiplied together, yielding the original formula for ROI stated in terms of net operating income and average operating assets. So either formula for ROI will give the same answer. However, the margin and turnover formulation provides some additional insights.

From a manager's perspective, **margin** and **turnover** are very important concepts. Margin is ordinarily improved by increasing sales or reducing operating expenses, including cost of goods sold and selling and administrative expenses. The lower the operating expenses per dollar of sales, the higher the margin earned. Some managers tend to focus too much on margin and ignore turnover. However, turnover incorporates a crucial area of a manager's responsibility—the investment in operating assets. Excessive funds tied up in operating assets (e.g., cash, accounts receivable, inventories, plant and equipment, and other assets) depress turnover and lower ROI. In fact, inefficient use of operating assets can be just as much of a drag on profitability as excessive operating expenses, which depress margin.

E.I. du Pont de Nemours and Company (better know as DuPont) pioneered the use of ROI and recognized the importance of looking at both margin and turnover in assessing a manager's performance. ROI is now widely used as the key measure of investment center performance. ROI reflects in a single figure many aspects of the manager's responsibilities. It can be compared to the returns of other investment centers in the organization, the returns of other companies in the industry, and to the past returns of the investment center itself.

DuPont also developed the diagram that appears in Exhibit 12–5. This exhibit helps managers understand how they can improve ROI. Any increase in ROI must involve at least one of the following:

1. Increased sales
2. Reduced operating expenses
3. Reduced operating assets

Many actions involve combinations of changes in sales, expenses, and operating assets. For example, a manager may make an investment in (i.e., increase) operating assets to reduce operating expenses or increase sales. Whether the net effect is favorable or not is judged in terms of its overall impact on ROI.

IN BUSINESS

J. CREW PULLS THE ROI LEVERS

J. Crew has adopted an interesting strategy for improving its ROI. The company has started selling "super-premium products—such as $1,500 cashmere coats and $1,500 beaded tunics—in limited editions, sometimes no more than 100 pieces nationwide." The intentional creation of scarcity causes many items to sell out within weeks as shoppers snatch them up before they are gone for good.

This strategy is helping boost J. Crew's ROI in two ways. First, the company earns higher margins on premium-priced products where customer demand dramatically exceeds supply. Second, the company is slashing its inventories because such small quantities of each item are purchased from suppliers. While J. Crew sacrifices some sales from customers who would have purchased sold out items, the overall effect on profits has been favorable. "Tighter inventories mean that J. Crew is no longer putting reams of clothes on sale, a move that kills profit margins and trains shoppers to wait for discounts. At one point . . . half of J. Crew's clothing sold at a discount. Today only a small percentage of it does."

Source: Julia Boorstin, "Mickey Drexler's Second Coming," *Fortune*, May 2, 2005, pp. 101–104.

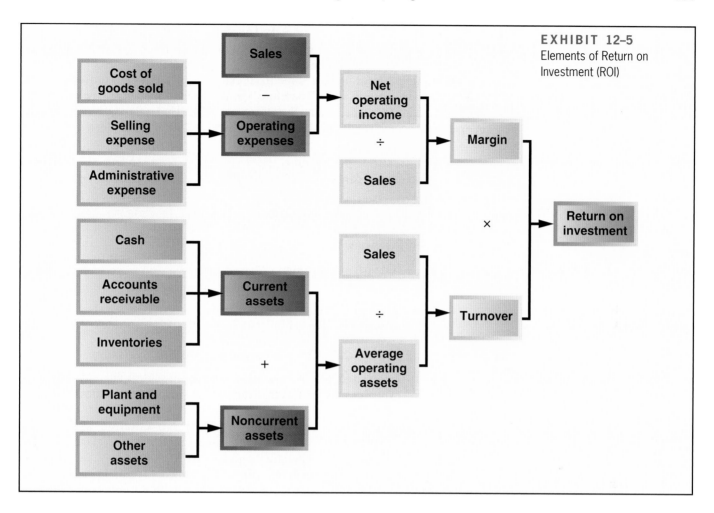

EXHIBIT 12–5
Elements of Return on Investment (ROI)

To illustrate how ROI is impacted by various actions, we will use the Monthaven outlet of the Burger Grill chain as an example. Burger Grill is a small chain of upscale casual restaurants that has been rapidly adding outlets via franchising. The Monthaven franchise is owned by a group of local surgeons who have little time to devote to management and little expertise in business matters. Therefore, they delegate operating decisions—including decisions concerning investments in operating assets such as inventories—to a professional manager they have hired. The manager is evaluated largely based on the ROI the franchise generates.

The following data represent the results of operations for the most recent month:

Sales	$100,000
Operating expenses	$90,000
Net operating income	$10,000
Average operating assets	$50,000

The return on investment (ROI) for the month is computed as follows:

$$\text{ROI} = \frac{\text{Net operating income}}{\text{Sales}} \times \frac{\text{Sales}}{\text{Average operating assets}}$$

$$= \frac{\$10,000}{\$100,000} \times \frac{\$100,000}{\$50,000}$$

$$= 10\% \times 2 = 20\%$$

Example 1: Increased Sales without Any Increase in Operating Assets   Assume that the manager of the Monthaven Burger Grill can increase sales by 10% without any increase in operating assets. The increase in sales will require additional operating expenses. However, operating expenses include some fixed expenses, which would probably not be affected by a 10% increase in sales. Therefore, the increase in operating expenses would probably be less than 10%; let's assume the increase is 7.8%. Under those assumptions, the new net operating income would be $12,980, an increase of 29.8%, determined as follows:

Sales (1.10 × $100,000)	$110,000
Operating expenses (1.078 × $90,000)	97,020
Net operating income	$ 12,980

In this case, the new ROI would be:

$$\text{ROI} = \frac{\text{Net operating income}}{\text{Sales}} \times \frac{\text{Sales}}{\text{Average operating assets}}$$

$$= \frac{\$12,980}{\$110,000} \times \frac{\$110,000}{\$50,000}$$

$$= 11.8\% \times 2.2 = 25.96\% \text{ (as compared to 20\% originally)}$$

Note that the key to improved ROI in the case of an increase in sales is that the percentage increase in operating expenses must be less than the percentage increase in sales.

Example 2: Decreased Operating Expenses with No Change in Sales or Operating Assets   Assume that by improving business processes, the manager of the Monthaven Burger Grill can reduce operating expenses by $1,000 without any effect on sales or operating assets. This reduction in operating expenses would result in increasing net operating income by $1,000, from $10,000 to $11,000. The new ROI would be:

$$\text{ROI} = \frac{\text{Net operating income}}{\text{Sales}} \times \frac{\text{Sales}}{\text{Average operating assets}}$$

$$= \frac{\$11,000}{\$100,000} \times \frac{\$100,000}{\$50,000}$$

$$= 11\% \times 2 = 22\% \text{ (as compared to 20\% originally)}$$

When margins or profits are being squeezed, the first line of attack is often to cut costs. Discretionary fixed costs are particularly vulnerable to cuts. However, managers must be careful not to cut too much or in the wrong place. Inappropriate cost cutting can lead to decreased sales, increased costs elsewhere, and a drop in morale.

Example 3: Decreased Operating Assets with No Change in Sales or Operating Expenses   Assume that the manager of the Monthaven Burger Grill uses lean production techniques to reduce inventories by $10,000. This might actually have a positive effect on sales (through fresher ingredients) and on operating expenses (through reduced inventory spoilage), but for the sake of illustration, suppose the reduction in inventories has no effect on sales or operating expenses. The reduction in inventories will reduce average operating assets by $10,000, from $50,000 down to $40,000. The new ROI would be:

$$\text{ROI} = \frac{\text{Net operating income}}{\text{Sales}} \times \frac{\text{Sales}}{\text{Average operating assets}}$$

$$= \frac{\$10,000}{\$100,000} \times \frac{\$100,000}{\$40,000}$$

$$= 10\% \times 2.5 = 25\% \text{ (as compared to 20\% originally)}$$

In this example, Lean Production was used to reduce operating assets. Another common tactic for reducing operating assets is to speed up the collection of accounts receivable. For example, many companies encourage customers to pay electronically rather than by mail.

JIT AND ROI IMPROVEMENT

A study of companies that adopted just-in-time (JIT) in comparison to a control group that did not adopt JIT, found that the JIT adopters improved their ROIs more. The JIT adopters' success resulted from improvements in both profit margins and asset turnover. The elimination of inventories in JIT reduces total assets, but more important, it leads to process improvements as production problems are exposed. When production problems and non-value-added activities are eliminated, costs go down.

Source: Michael R. Kinney and William F. Wempe, "Further Evidence on the Extent and Origins of JIT's Profitability Effects," *The Accounting Review*, January 2002, pp. 203–225.

Example 4: Invest in Operating Assets to Increase Sales   Assume that the manager of the Monthaven Burger Grill invests $2,000 in a state-of-the-art soft-serve ice cream machine that can dispense a number of different flavors. This new machine will boost sales by $4,000, but will require additional operating expenses of $1,000. Thus, net operating income will increase by $3,000, to $13,000. The new ROI will be:

$$\text{ROI} = \frac{\text{Net operating income}}{\text{Sales}} \times \frac{\text{Sales}}{\text{Average operating assets}}$$

$$= \frac{\$13,000}{\$104,000} \times \frac{\$104,000}{\$52,000}$$

$$= 12.5\% \times 2 = 25\% \text{ (as compared to 20\% originally)}$$

In this particular example, the investment had no effect on turnover, which remained at 2, so there had to be an increase in margin in order to improve the ROI.

MCDONALD CHIC

McDonald's France has been spending lavishly to remodel its restaurants to blend with local architecture and to make their interiors less uniform and sterile. For example, some outlets in the Alps have wood-and-stone interiors similar to those of alpine chalets. The idea is to defuse the negative feelings many of the French people have toward McDonald's as a symbol of American culture and, perhaps more importantly, to try to entice customers to linger over their meals and spend more. This investment in operating assets has apparently been successful—even though a Big Mac costs about the same in Paris as in New York, the average French customer spends about $9 per visit versus only about $4 in the U.S.

Source: Carol Matlack and Pallavi Gogoi, "What's This? The French Love McDonald's?" *BusinessWeek*, January 13, 2003, p. 50.

ROI and the Balanced Scorecard

The DuPont scheme, which is illustrated in Exhibit 12–5, provides managers with *some* guidance about how to increase ROI. Generally speaking, ROI can be increased by increasing sales, decreasing costs, and/or decreasing investments in operating assets. However, it may not be obvious to managers *how* they are supposed to increase sales, decrease costs, and decrease investments in a way that is consistent with the company's strategy. For example, a manager who is given inadequate guidance may cut back on investments that are critical to implementing the company's strategy.

For that reason, as discussed in Chapter 10, managers should be evaluated using a balanced scorecard approach. ROI, or residual income (discussed below), is typically included as one of the financial performance measures on a company's balanced scorecard. However, this measure is supplemented by other measures that indicate *how* the company intends to improve its financial performance. A well-constructed balanced scorecard should answer questions like: "What internal business processes should be improved?" and "Which customers should be targeted and how will they be attracted and retained at a profit?" In short, a well-constructed balanced scorecard provides managers with a road map that indicates how the company intends to increase its ROI. In the absence of such a road map of the company's strategy, managers may have difficulty understanding what they are supposed to do to increase ROI and they may work at cross-purposes rather than in harmony with the overall strategy of the company.

Criticisms of ROI

Although ROI is widely used in evaluating performance, it is subject to the following criticisms:

1. Just telling managers to increase ROI may not be enough. Managers may not know how to increase ROI; they may increase ROI in a way that is inconsistent with the company's strategy; or they may take actions that increase ROI in the short run but harm the company in the long run (such as cutting back on research and development). This is why ROI is best used as part of a balanced scorecard. A balanced scorecard can provide concrete guidance to managers, making it more likely that their actions are consistent with the company's strategy and reducing the likelihood that they will boost short-run performance at the expense of long-term performance.
2. A manager who takes over a business segment typically inherits many committed costs over which the manager has no control. These committed costs may be relevant in assessing the performance of the business segment as an investment but they make it difficult to fairly assess the performance of the manager.
3. As discussed in the next section, a manager who is evaluated based on ROI may reject investment opportunities that are profitable for the whole company but that would have a negative impact on the manager's performance evaluation.

IN BUSINESS

LET THE BUYER BEWARE

Those who sell products and services to businesses are well aware that many potential customers look very carefully at the impact the purchase would have on ROI before making a purchase. Unfortunately, some salespersons make extravagant ROI claims. For example, businesspeople complain that software salespersons routinely exaggerate the impact that new software will have on ROI. Some of the tricks used by salespersons include: inflating the salaries of workers who are made redundant by productivity gains; omitting costs such as training costs and implementation costs; inflating expected sales increases; and using former clients as examples of ROI gains when the clients were given the software for free or for nominal cost. The message? Be skeptical of salespersons' claims with respect to ROI gains from purchasing their products and services.

Source: Scott Leibs, "All Hail the ROI," *CFO*, April 2002, pp. 27–28.

Residual income is another approach to measuring an investment center's performance. **Residual income** is the net operating income that an investment center earns above the minimum required return on its operating assets. In equation form, residual income is calculated as follows:

LEARNING OBJECTIVE 3
Compute residual income and understand its strengths and weaknesses.

$$\begin{array}{c}\text{Residual}\\\text{income}\end{array} = \begin{array}{c}\text{Net operating}\\\text{income}\end{array} - \left(\begin{array}{c}\text{Average operating}\\\text{assets}\end{array} \times \begin{array}{c}\text{Minimum required}\\\text{rate of return}\end{array}\right)$$

Economic Value Added (EVA®) is an adaptation of residual income that has been adopted by many companies.[4] Under EVA, companies often modify their accounting principles in various ways. For example, funds used for research and development are often treated as investments rather than as expenses.[5] These complications are best dealt with in a more advanced course; in this text we will not draw any distinction between residual income and EVA.

When residual income or EVA is used to measure performance, the objective is to maximize the total amount of residual income or EVA, not to maximize ROI. This is an important distinction. If the objective were to maximize ROI, then every company should divest all of its products except the single product with the highest ROI.

12–2

A wide variety of organizations have embraced some version of residual income or EVA, including Bausch & Lomb, Best Buy, Boise Cascade, Coca-Cola, Dun and Bradstreet, Eli Lilly, Federated Mogul, Georgia-Pacific, Guidant Corporation, Hershey Foods, Husky Injection Molding, J.C. Penney, Kansas City Power & Light, Olin, Quaker Oats, Silicon Valley Bank, Sprint, Toys R Us, Tupperware, and the United States Postal Service. In addition, financial institutions such as Credit Suisse First Boston now use EVA—and its allied concept, market value added—to evaluate potential investments in other companies.

For purposes of illustration, consider the following data for an investment center—the Ketchikan Division of Alaskan Marine Services Corporation.

Alaskan Marine Services Corporation Ketchikan Division Basic Data for Performance Evaluation	
Average operating assets	$100,000
Net operating income	$20,000
Minimum required rate of return	15%

Alaskan Marine Services Corporation has long had a policy of using ROI to evaluate its investment center managers, but it is considering switching to residual income. The controller of the company, who is in favor of the change to residual income, has provided the table on the following page that shows how the performance of the division would be evaluated under each of the two methods:

---

[4] The basic idea underlying residual income and economic value added has been around for over 100 years. In recent years, economic value added has been popularized and trademarked by the consulting firm Stern, Stewart & Co.

[5] Over 100 different adjustments could be made for deferred taxes, LIFO reserves, provisions for future liabilities, mergers and acquisitions, gains or losses due to changes in accounting rules, operating leases, and other accounts, but most companies make only a few. For further details, see John O'Hanlon and Ken Peasnell, "Wall Street's Contribution to Management Accounting: the Stern Stewart EVA® Financial Management System," *Management Accounting Research* 9, 1998, pp. 421–444.

Alaskan Marine Services Corporation Ketchikan Division	Alternative Performance Measures	
	ROI	Residual Income
Average operating assets (a)	$100,000	$100,000
Net operating income (b)	$ 20,000	$ 20,000
ROI, (b) ÷ (a)	20%	
Minimum required return (15% × $100,000)		15,000
Residual income		$ 5,000

The reasoning underlying the residual income calculation is straightforward. The company is able to earn a rate of return of at least 15% on its investments. Since the company has invested $100,000 in the Ketchikan Division in the form of operating assets, the company should be able to earn at least $15,000 (15% × $100,000) on this investment. Because the Ketchikan Division's net operating income is $20,000, the residual income above and beyond the minimum required return is $5,000. If residual income is adopted as the performance measure to replace ROI, the manager of the Ketchikan Division would be evaluated based on the growth in residual income from year to year.

Motivation and Residual Income

One of the primary reasons why the controller of Alaskan Marine Services Corporation would like to switch from ROI to residual income relates to how managers view new investments under the two performance measurement schemes. The residual income approach encourages managers to make investments that are profitable for the entire company but that would be rejected by managers who are evaluated using the ROI formula.

To illustrate this problem with ROI, suppose that the manager of the Ketchikan Division is considering purchasing a computerized diagnostic machine to aid in servicing marine diesel engines. The machine would cost $25,000 and is expected to generate additional operating income of $4,500 a year. From the standpoint of the company, this would be a good investment because it promises a rate of return of 18% ($4,500 ÷ $25,000), which exceeds the company's minimum required rate of return of 15%.

If the manager of the Ketchikan Division is evaluated based on residual income, she would be in favor of the investment in the diagnostic machine as shown below:

Alaskan Marine Services Corporation Ketchikan Division Performance Evaluated Using Residual Income	Present	New Project	Overall
Average operating assets	$100,000	$25,000	$125,000
Net operating income	$ 20,000	$ 4,500	$ 24,500
Minimum required return	15,000	3,750*	18,750
Residual income	$ 5,000	$ 750	$ 5,750

*$25,000 × 15% = $3,750.

Since the project would increase the residual income of the Ketchikan Division by $750, the manager would choose to invest in the new diagnostic machine.

Now suppose that the manager of the Ketchikan Division is evaluated based on ROI. The effect of the diagnostic machine on the division's ROI is computed below:

Alaskan Marine Services Corporation Ketchikan Division Performance Evaluated Using ROI			
	Present	New Project	Overall
Average operating assets (a)	$100,000	$25,000	$125,000
Net operating income (b)	$20,000	$4,500	$24,500
ROI, (b) ÷ (a)	20%	18%	19.6%

The new project reduces the division's ROI from 20% to 19.6%. This happens because the 18% rate of return on the new diagnostic machine, while above the company's 15% minimum required rate of return, is below the division's current ROI of 20%. Therefore, the new diagnostic machine would decrease the division's ROI even though it would be a good investment from the standpoint of the company as a whole. If the manager of the division is evaluated based on ROI, she will be reluctant to even propose such an investment.

Generally, a manager who is evaluated based on ROI will reject any project whose rate of return is below the division's current ROI even if the rate of return on the project is above the company's minimum required rate of return. In contrast, managers who are evaluated using residual income will pursue any project whose rate of return is above the minimum required rate of return because it will increase their residual income. Because it is in the best interests of the company as a whole to accept any project whose rate of return is above the minimum required rate of return, managers who are evaluated based on residual income will tend to make better decisions concerning investment projects than managers who are evaluated based on ROI.

Divisional Comparison and Residual Income

The residual income approach has one major disadvantage. It can't be used to compare the performance of divisions of different sizes. Larger divisions often have more residual income than smaller divisions, not necessarily because they are better managed but simply because they are bigger.

As an example, consider the following residual income computations for the Wholesale Division and the Retail Division of Sisal Marketing Corporation:

	Wholesale Division	Retail Division
Average operating assets (a)	$1,000,000	$250,000
Net operating income	$ 120,000	$ 40,000
Minimum required return: 10% × (a)	100,000	25,000
Residual income	$ 20,000	$ 15,000

Observe that the Wholesale Division has slightly more residual income than the Retail Division, but that the Wholesale Division has $1,000,000 in operating assets as compared to only $250,000 in operating assets for the Retail Division. Thus, the Wholesale Division's greater residual income is probably due to its larger size rather than the quality of its management. In fact, it appears that the smaller division may be better managed, since it has been able to generate nearly as much residual income with only one-fourth as much in operating assets. When comparing investment centers, it is probably better to focus on the percentage change in residual income from year to year rather than on the absolute amount of the residual income.

HEADS I WIN, TAILS YOU LOSE

A number of companies, including AT&T, Armstrong Holdings, and Baldwin Technology, have stopped using residual income measures of performance after trying them. Why? Reasons differ, but "bonus evaporation is often seen as the Achilles' heel of value-based metrics [like residual income and EVA]— and a major cause of plans being dropped." Managers tend to love residual income and EVA when their bonuses are big, but clamor for changes in performance measures when bonuses shrink.

Source: Bill Richard and Alix Nyberg, "Do EVA and Other Value Metrics Still Offer a Good Mirror of Company Performance?" *CFO*, March 2001, pp. 56–64.

Summary

For purposes of evaluating performance, business units are classified as cost centers, profit centers, and investment centers. Cost centers are commonly evaluated using standard cost and flexible budget variances as discussed in prior chapters. Profit centers and investment centers are evaluated using the techniques discussed in this chapter.

Segmented income statements provide information for evaluating the profitability and performance of divisions, product lines, sales territories, and other segments of a company. Under the contribution approach covered in this chapter, variable costs and fixed costs are clearly distinguished from each other and only those costs that are traceable to a segment are assigned to the segment. A cost is considered traceable to a segment only if the cost is caused by the segment and could be avoided by eliminating the segment. Fixed common costs are not allocated to segments. The segment margin consists of revenues, less variable expenses, less traceable fixed expenses of the segment.

Return on investment (ROI) and residual income and its cousin EVA are widely used to evaluate the performance of investment centers. ROI suffers from the underinvestment problem—managers are reluctant to invest in projects that would decrease their ROI but whose returns exceed the company's required rate of return. The residual income and EVA approaches solve this problem by giving managers full credit for any returns in excess of the company's required rate of return.

Review Problem 1: Segmented Statements

The business staff of the law firm Frampton, Davis & Smythe has constructed the following report which breaks down the firm's overall results for last month into two main business segments—family law and commercial law:

	Total	Family Law	Commercial Law
Revenues from clients	$1,000,000	$400,000	$600,000
Variable expenses	220,000	100,000	120,000
Contribution margin	780,000	300,000	480,000
Traceable fixed expenses	670,000	280,000	390,000
Segment margin	110,000	20,000	90,000
Common fixed expenses	60,000	24,000	36,000
Net operating income	$ 50,000	$ (4,000)	$ 54,000

However, this report is not quite correct. The common fixed expenses such as the managing partner's salary, general administrative expenses, and general firm advertising have been allocated to the two segments based on revenues from clients.

Required:

1. Redo the segment report, eliminating the allocation of common fixed expenses. Would the firm be better off financially if the family law segment were dropped? (Note: Many of the firm's commercial law clients also use the firm for their family law requirements such as drawing up wills.)

2. The firm's advertising agency has proposed an ad campaign targeted at boosting the revenues of the family law segment. The ad campaign would cost $20,000, and the advertising agency claims that it would increase family law revenues by $100,000. The managing partner of Frampton, Davis & Smythe believes this increase in business could be accommodated without any increase in fixed expenses. What effect would this ad campaign have on the family law segment margin and on the firm's overall net operating income?

Solution to Review Problem 1

1. The corrected segmented income statement appears below:

	Total	Family Law	Commercial Law
Revenues from clients	$1,000,000	$400,000	$600,000
Variable expenses	220,000	100,000	120,000
Contribution margin	780,000	300,000	480,000
Traceable fixed expenses	670,000	280,000	390,000
Segment margin	110,000	$ 20,000	$ 90,000
Common fixed expenses	60,000		
Net operating income	$ 50,000		

No, the firm would not be financially better off if the family law practice were dropped. The family law segment is covering all of its own costs and is contributing $20,000 per month to covering the common fixed expenses of the firm. While the segment margin for family law is much lower than for commercial law, it is still profitable. Moreover, family law may be a service that the firm must provide to its commercial clients in order to remain competitive.

2. The ad campaign would increase the family law segment margin by $55,000 as follows:

Increased revenues from clients	$100,000
Family law contribution margin ratio ($300,000 ÷ $400,000)	× 75%
Incremental contribution margin	$ 75,000
Less cost of the ad campaign	20,000
Increased segment margin.	$ 55,000

Since there would be no increase in fixed expenses (including common fixed expenses), the increase in overall net operating income is also $55,000.

Review Problem 2: Return on Investment (ROI) and Residual Income

The Magnetic Imaging Division of Medical Diagnostics, Inc., has reported the following results for last year's operations:

Sales	$25 million
Net operating income	$3 million
Average operating assets	$10 million

Required:

1. Compute the Magnetic Imaging Division's margin, turnover, and ROI.
2. Top management of Medical Diagnostics, Inc., has set a minimum required rate of return on average operating assets of 25%. What is the Magnetic Imaging Division's residual income for the year?

Solution to Review Problem 2

1. The required calculations follow:

$$\text{Margin} = \frac{\text{Net operating income}}{\text{Sales}}$$

$$= \frac{\$3,000,000}{\$25,000,000}$$

$$= 12\%$$

$$\text{Turnover} = \frac{\text{Sales}}{\text{Average operating assets}}$$

$$= \frac{\$25,000,000}{\$10,000,000}$$

$$= 2.5\%$$

$$\text{ROI} = \text{Margin} \times \text{Turnover}$$

$$= 12\% \times 2.5$$

$$= 30\%$$

2. The Magnetic Imaging Division's residual income is computed as follows:

Average operating assets	$10,000,000
Net operating income	$ 3,000,000
Minimum required return (25% × $10,000,000)	2,500,000
Residual income	$ 500,000

Glossary

Common fixed cost A fixed cost that supports more than one business segment, but is not traceable in whole or in part to any one of the business segments. (p. 524)

Cost center A business segment whose manager has control over cost but has no control over revenue or investments in operating assets. (p. 517)

Decentralized organization An organization in which decision-making authority is not confined to a few top executives but rather is spread throughout the organization. (p. 516)

Economic Value Added (EVA) A concept similar to residual income in which a variety of adjustments may be made to GAAP financial statements for performance evaluation purposes. (p. 537)

Investment center A business segment whose manager has control over cost, revenue, and investments in operating assets. (p. 518)

Margin Net operating income divided by sales. (p. 532)

Net operating income Income before interest and income taxes have been deducted. (p. 531)

Operating assets Cash, accounts receivable, inventory, plant and equipment, and all other assets held for operating purposes. (p. 531)

Profit center A business segment whose manager has control over cost and revenue but has no control over investments in operating assets. (p. 517)

Residual income The net operating income that an investment center earns above the minimum required return on its operating assets. (p. 537)

Responsibility center Any business segment whose manager has control over costs, revenues, or investments in operating assets. (p. 517)

Return on investment (ROI) Net operating income divided by average operating assets. It also equals margin multiplied by turnover. (p. 531)

Segment Any part or activity of an organization about which managers seek cost, revenue, or profit data. (p. 519)

Segment margin A segment's contribution margin less its traceable fixed costs. It represents the margin available after a segment has covered all of its own traceable costs. (p. 526)

Traceable fixed cost A fixed cost that is incurred because of the existence of a particular business segment and that would be eliminated if the segment were eliminated. (p. 524)

Turnover Sales divided by average operating assets. (p. 532)

Appendix 12A: Transfer Pricing

Divisions in a company often supply goods and services to other divisions within the same company. For example, the truck division of Toyota supplies trucks to other Toyota divisions to use in their operations. When the divisions are evaluated based on their profit, return on investment, or residual income, a price must be established for such a transfer—otherwise, the division that produces the good or service will receive no credit. The price in such a situation is called a *transfer price*. A **transfer price** is the price charged when one segment of a company provides goods or services to another segment of the same company. For example, most companies in the oil industry, such as Shell, have petroleum refining and retail sales divisions that are evaluated on the basis of ROI or residual income. The petroleum refining division processes crude oil into gasoline, kerosene, lubricants, and other end products. The retail sales division takes gasoline and other products from the refining division and sells them through the company's chain of service stations. Each product has a price for transfers within the company. Suppose the transfer price for gasoline is $0.80 a gallon. Then the refining division gets credit for $0.80 a gallon of revenue on its segment report and the retailing division must deduct $0.80 a gallon as an expense on its segment report. Clearly, the refining division would like the transfer price to be as high as possible, whereas the retailing division would like the transfer price to be as low as possible. However, the transaction has no direct effect on the entire company's reported profit. It is like taking money out of one pocket and putting it into the other.

Managers are intensely interested in how transfer prices are set because they can have a dramatic effect on the reported profitability of their divisions. Three common approaches are used to set transfer prices:

1. Allow the managers involved in the transfer to negotiate their own transfer price.
2. Set transfer prices at cost using either variable cost or full (absorption) cost.
3. Set transfer prices at the market price.

We will consider each of these transfer pricing methods in turn, beginning with negotiated transfer prices. Throughout the discussion, keep in mind that *the fundamental objective in setting transfer prices is to motivate the managers to act in the best interests of the overall company.* In contrast, **suboptimization** occurs when managers do not act in the best interests of the overall company or even in the best interests of their own division.

Negotiated Transfer Prices

A **negotiated transfer price** results from discussions between the selling and buying divisions. Negotiated transfer prices have several important advantages. First, this approach preserves the autonomy of the divisions and is consistent with the spirit of decentralization. Second, the managers of the divisions are likely to have much better information about the potential costs and benefits of the transfer than others in the company.

When negotiated transfer prices are used, the managers who are involved in a proposed transfer within the company meet to discuss the terms and conditions of the transfer. They may decide not to go through with the transfer, but if they do, they must agree to a transfer price. Generally speaking, we cannot predict the exact transfer price they will agree to. However, we can confidently predict two things: (1) the selling division will agree to the transfer only if its profits increase as a result of the transfer, and (2) the buying division will agree to the transfer only if its profits also increase as a result of the transfer. This may seem obvious, but it is an important point.

Clearly, if the transfer price is below the selling division's cost, the selling division will incur a loss on the transaction and it will refuse to agree to the transfer. Likewise, if the transfer price is set too high, it will be impossible for the buying division to make any profit on the transferred item. For any given proposed transfer, the transfer price has both a lower limit (determined by the selling division) and an upper limit (determined by the buying division). The actual transfer price agreed to by the two division managers can fall anywhere between those two limits. These limits determine the **range of acceptable**

LEARNING OBJECTIVE 4
Determine the range, if any, within which a negotiated transfer price should fall.

transfer prices—the range of transfer prices within which the profits of both divisions participating in a transfer would increase.

An example will help us to understand negotiated transfer prices. Harris & Louder, Ltd., owns fast-food restaurants and snack food and beverage manufacturers in the United Kingdom. One of the restaurants, Pizza Maven, serves a variety of beverages along with pizzas. One of the beverages is ginger beer, which is served on tap. Harris & Louder has just purchased a new division, Imperial Beverages, that produces ginger beer. The managing director of Imperial Beverages has approached the managing director of Pizza Maven about purchasing Imperial Beverages ginger beer for sale at Pizza Maven restaurants rather than its usual brand of ginger beer. Managers at Pizza Maven agree that the quality of Imperial Beverages' ginger beer is comparable to the quality of their regular brand. It is just a question of price. The basic facts are as follows (the currency in this example is pounds, denoted here as £):

Imperial Beverages:	
Ginger beer production capacity per month.	10,000 barrels
Variable cost per barrel of ginger beer.	£8 per barrel
Fixed costs per month.	£70,000
Selling price of Imperial Beverages ginger beer on the outside market	£20 per barrel
Pizza Maven:	
Purchase price of regular brand of ginger beer	£18 per barrel
Monthly consumption of ginger beer	2,000 barrels

The Selling Division's Lowest Acceptable Transfer Price The selling division, Imperial Beverages, will be interested in a proposed transfer only if its profit increases. Clearly, the transfer price must not fall below the variable cost per barrel of £8. In addition, if Imperial Beverages has insufficient capacity to fill the Pizza Maven order while supplying its regular customers, then it would have to sacrifice some of its regular sales. Imperial Beverages would expect to be compensated for the contribution margin on these lost sales. In sum, if the transfer has no effect on fixed costs, then from the selling division's standpoint, the transfer price must cover both the variable costs of producing the transferred units and any opportunity costs from lost sales.

Seller's perspective:

$$\text{Transfer price} \geq \frac{\text{Variable cost}}{\text{per unit}} + \frac{\text{Total contribution margin on lost sales}}{\text{Number of units transferred}}$$

The Buying Division's Highest Acceptable Transfer Price The buying division, Pizza Maven, will be interested in a transfer only if its profit increases. In cases like this where a buying division has an outside supplier, the buying division's decision is simple. Buy from the inside supplier if the price is less than the price offered by the outside supplier.

Purchaser's perspective:

$$\text{Transfer price} \leq \text{Cost of buying from outside supplier}$$

Or, if an outside supplier does not exist:

$$\text{Transfer price} \leq \text{Profit to be earned per unit sold (not including the transfer price)}$$

We will consider several different hypothetical situations and see what the range of acceptable transfer prices would be in each situation.

Selling Division with Idle Capacity   Suppose that Imperial Beverages has sufficient idle capacity to satisfy the demand for ginger beer from Pizza Maven without sacrificing sales of ginger beer to its regular customers. To be specific, let's suppose that Imperial Beverages is selling only 7,000 barrels of ginger beer a month on the outside market. That leaves unused capacity of 3,000 barrels a month—more than enough to satisfy Pizza Maven's requirement of 2,000 barrels a month. What range of transfer prices, if any, would make both divisions better off with the transfer of 2,000 barrels a month?

1.   The selling division, Imperial Beverages, will be interested in the transfer only if:

$$\text{Transfer price} \geq \frac{\text{Variable cost}}{\text{per unit}} + \frac{\text{Total contribution margin on lost sales}}{\text{Number of units transferred}}$$

Since Imperial Beverages has ample idle capacity, there are no lost outside sales. And since the variable cost per unit is £8, the lowest acceptable transfer price for the selling division is £8.

$$\text{Transfer price} \geq £8 + \frac{£0}{2,000} = £8$$

2.   The buying division, Pizza Maven, can buy similar ginger beer from an outside vendor for £18. Therefore, Pizza Maven would be unwilling to pay more than £18 per barrel for Imperial Beverages' ginger beer.

$$\text{Transfer price} \leq \text{Cost of buying from outside supplier} = £18$$

3.   Combining the requirements of both the selling division and the buying division, the acceptable range of transfer prices in this situation is:

$$£8 \leq \text{Transfer price} \leq £18$$

Assuming that the managers understand their own businesses and that they are cooperative, they should be able to agree on a transfer price within this range.

Selling Division with No Idle Capacity   Suppose that Imperial Beverages has *no* idle capacity; it is selling 10,000 barrels of ginger beer a month on the outside market at £20 per barrel. To fill the order from Pizza Maven, Imperial Beverages would have to divert 2,000 barrels from its regular customers. What range of transfer prices, if any, would make both divisions better off transferring the 2,000 barrels within the company?

1.   The selling division, Imperial Beverages, will be interested in the transfer only if:

$$\text{Transfer price} \geq \frac{\text{Variable cost}}{\text{per unit}} + \frac{\text{Total contribution margin on lost sales}}{\text{Number of units transferred}}$$

Since Imperial Beverages has no idle capacity, there *are* lost outside sales. The contribution margin per barrel on these outside sales is £12 (£20 − £8).

$$\text{Transfer price} \geq £8 + \frac{(£20 - £8) \times 2,000}{2,000} = £8 + (£20 - £8) = £20$$

Thus, as far as the selling division is concerned, the transfer price must at least cover the revenue on the lost sales, which is £20 per barrel. This makes sense since the cost of producing the 2,000 barrels is the same whether they are sold on the inside market or on the outside. The only difference is that the selling division loses the revenue of £20 per barrel if it transfers the barrels to Pizza Maven.

2.   As before, the buying division, Pizza Maven, would be unwilling to pay more than the £18 per barrel it is already paying for similar ginger beer from its regular supplier.

$$\text{Transfer price} \leq \text{Cost of buying from outside supplier} = £18$$

3.   Therefore, the selling division would insist on a transfer price of at least £20. But the buying division would refuse any transfer price above £18. It is impossible to satisfy

both division managers simultaneously; there can be no agreement on a transfer price and no transfer will take place. Is this good? The answer is yes. From the standpoint of the entire company, the transfer doesn't make sense. Why give up sales of £20 to save costs of £18?

Basically, the transfer price is a mechanism for dividing between the two divisions any profit the entire company earns as a result of the transfer. If the company as a whole loses money on the transfer, there will be no profit to divide up, and it will be impossible for the two divisions to come to an agreement. On the other hand, if the company as a whole makes money on the transfer, there will be a profit to share, and it will always be possible for the two divisions to find a mutually agreeable transfer price that increases the profits of both divisions. If the pie is bigger, it is always possible to divide it up in such a way that everyone has a bigger piece.

Selling Division Has Some Idle Capacity

Suppose now that Imperial Beverages is selling 9,000 barrels of ginger beer a month on the outside market. Pizza Maven can only sell one kind of ginger beer on tap. It cannot buy 1,000 barrels from Imperial Beverages and 1,000 barrels from its regular supplier; it must buy all of its ginger beer from one source.

To fill the entire 2,000-barrel a month order from Pizza Maven, Imperial Beverages would have to divert 1,000 barrels from its regular customers who are paying £20 per barrel. The other 1,000 barrels can be made using idle capacity. What range of transfer prices, if any, would make both divisions better off transferring the 2,000 barrels within the company?

1. As before, the selling division, Imperial Beverages, will insist on a transfer price that at least covers its variable cost and opportunity cost:

$$\text{Transfer price} \geq \frac{\text{Variable cost}}{\text{per unit}} + \frac{\text{Total contribution margin on lost sales}}{\text{Number of units transferred}}$$

   Since Imperial Beverages does not have enough idle capacity to fill the entire order for 2,000 barrels, there *are* lost outside sales. The contribution margin per barrel on the 1,000 barrels of lost outside sales is £12 (£20 − £8).

$$\text{Transfer price} \geq £8 + \frac{(£20 - £8) \times 1,000}{2,000} = £8 + £6 = £14$$

   Thus, as far as the selling division is concerned, the transfer price must cover the variable cost of £8 plus the average opportunity cost of lost sales of £6.

2. As before, the buying division, Pizza Maven, would be unwilling to pay more than the £18 per barrel it pays its regular supplier.

$$\text{Transfer price} \leq \text{Cost of buying from outside suppliers} = £18$$

3. Combining the requirements for both the selling and buying divisions, the range of acceptable transfer prices is:

$$£14 \leq \text{Transfer price} \leq £18$$

   Again, assuming that the managers understand their own businesses and that they are cooperative, they should be able to agree on a transfer price within this range.

No Outside Supplier

If Pizza Maven has no outside supplier for the ginger beer, the highest price the buying division would be willing to pay depends on how much the buying division expects to make on the transferred units—excluding the transfer price. If, for example, Pizza Maven expects to earn £30 per barrel of ginger beer after paying its own expenses, then it should be willing to pay up to £30 per barrel to Imperial Beverages. Remember, however, that this assumes Pizza Maven cannot buy ginger beer from other sources.

Evaluation of Negotiated Transfer Prices

As discussed earlier, if a transfer within the company would result in higher overall profits for the company, there is always a range of transfer prices within which both the selling and buying division would also have higher profits if they agree to the transfer. Therefore, if the managers understand their own businesses and are cooperative, then they should always be able to agree on a transfer price if it is in the best interests of the company that they do so.

Unfortunately, not all managers understand their own businesses and not all managers are cooperative. As a result, negotiations often break down even when it would be in the managers' own best interests to come to an agreement. Sometimes that is the fault of the way managers are evaluated. If managers are pitted against each other rather than against their own past performance or reasonable benchmarks, a noncooperative atmosphere is almost guaranteed. Nevertheless, even with the best performance evaluation system, some people by nature are not cooperative.

Given the disputes that often accompany the negotiation process, most companies rely on some other means of setting transfer prices. Unfortunately, as we will see below, all of the alternatives to negotiated transfer prices have their own serious drawbacks.

Transfers at the Cost to the Selling Division

Many companies set transfer prices at either the variable cost or full (absorption) cost incurred by the selling division. Although the cost approach to setting transfer prices is relatively simple to apply, it has some major defects.

First, the use of cost—particularly full cost—as a transfer price can lead to bad decisions and thus suboptimization. Return to the example involving the ginger beer. The full cost of ginger beer can never be less than £15 per barrel (£8 per barrel variable cost + £7 per barrel fixed cost at capacity). What if the cost of buying the ginger beer from an outside supplier is less than £15—for example, £14 per barrel? If the transfer price were set at full cost, then Pizza Maven would never want to buy ginger beer from Imperial Beverages, since it could buy its ginger beer from an outside supplier at a lower price. However, from the standpoint of the company as a whole, ginger beer should be transferred from Imperial Beverages to Pizza Maven whenever Imperial Beverages has idle capacity. Why? Because when Imperial Beverages has idle capacity, it only costs the company £8 in variable cost to produce a barrel of ginger beer, but it costs £14 per barrel to buy from outside suppliers.

Second, if cost is used as the transfer price, the selling division will never show a profit on any internal transfer. The only division that shows a profit is the division that makes the final sale to an outside party.

Third, cost-based prices do not provide incentives to control costs. If the actual costs of one division are simply passed on to the next, there is little incentive for anyone to work to reduce costs. This problem can be overcome by using standard costs rather than actual costs for transfer prices.

Despite these shortcomings, cost-based transfer prices are commonly used in practice. Advocates argue that they are easily understood and convenient to use.

Transfers at Market Price

Some form of competitive **market price** (i.e., the price charged for an item on the open market) is often regarded as the best approach to the transfer pricing problem—particularly if transfer price negotiations routinely become bogged down.

The market price approach is designed for situations in which there is an *outside market* for the transferred product or service; the product or service is sold in its present form to outside customers. If the selling division has no idle capacity, the market price is the perfect choice for the transfer price. This is because, from the company's perspective, the real cost of the transfer is the opportunity cost of the lost revenue on the outside sale. Whether the item is transferred internally or sold on the outside market, the production costs are exactly the same. If the market price is used as the transfer price, the selling division manager will not lose anything by making the transfer, and the buying division manager will get the correct signal about how much it really costs the company for the transfer to take place.

While the market price works beautifully when the selling division has no idle capacity, difficulties occur when the selling division has idle capacity. Recalling once again the ginger beer example, the outside market price for the ginger beer produced by Imperial Beverages is £20 per barrel. However, Pizza Maven can purchase all of the ginger beer it wants from outside suppliers for £18 per barrel. Why would Pizza Maven ever buy from Imperial Beverages if Pizza Maven is forced to pay Imperial Beverages' market price? In some market price-based transfer pricing schemes, the transfer price would be lowered to £18, the outside vendor's market price, and Pizza Maven would be directed to buy from Imperial Beverages as long as Imperial Beverages is willing to sell. This scheme can work reasonably well, but a drawback is that managers at Pizza Maven will regard the cost of ginger beer as £18 rather than the £8, which is the real cost to the company when the selling division has idle capacity. Consequently, the managers of Pizza Maven will make pricing and other decisions based on an incorrect cost.

Unfortunately, none of the possible solutions to the transfer pricing problem are perfect—not even market-based transfer prices.

Divisional Autonomy and Suboptimization

The principles of decentralization suggest that companies should grant managers autonomy to set transfer prices and to decide whether to sell internally or externally. It may be very difficult for top managers to accept this principle when their subordinate managers are about to make a suboptimal decision. However, if top management intervenes, the purposes of decentralization are defeated. Furthermore, to impose the correct transfer price, top managers would have to know details about the buying and selling divisions' outside market, variable costs, and capacity utilization. The whole premise of decentralization is that local managers have access to better information for operational decisions than top managers at corporate headquarters.

Of course, if a division manager consistently makes suboptimal decisions, the performance of the division will suffer. The offending manager's compensation will be adversely affected and promotion will become less likely. Thus, a performance evaluation system based on divisional profits, ROI, or residual income provides some built-in checks and balances. Nevertheless, if top managers wish to create a culture of autonomy and independent profit responsibility, they must allow their subordinate managers to control their own destiny—even to the extent of granting their managers the right to make mistakes.

International Aspects of Transfer Pricing

The objectives of transfer pricing change when a multinational corporation is involved and the goods and services being transferred cross international borders. The objectives of international transfer pricing, as compared to domestic transfer pricing, are summarized in Exhibit 12A–1.[1]

As shown in the exhibit, the objectives of international transfer pricing focus on minimizing taxes, duties, and foreign exchange risks, along with enhancing a company's competitive

EXHIBIT 12A–1
Domestic and International Transfer Pricing Objectives

Transfer pricing objectives

Domestic
Greater divisional autonomy
Greater motivation for managers
Better performance evaluation
Better goal congruence

International
Less taxes, duties, and tariffs
Less foreign exchange risks
Better competitive position
Better governmental relations

---

[1] The exhibit is adapted from Wagdy M. Abdallah, "Guidelines for CEOs in Transfer Pricing Policies," *Management Accounting* 70, no. 3, p. 61.

position and improving its relations with foreign governments. Although domestic objectives such as managerial motivation and divisional autonomy are always important, they often become secondary when international transfers are involved. Companies will focus instead on charging a transfer price that reduces its total tax bill or that strengthens a foreign subsidiary.

For example, charging a low transfer price for parts shipped to a foreign subsidiary may reduce customs duty payments as the parts cross international borders, or it may help the subsidiary to compete in foreign markets by keeping the subsidiary's costs low. On the other hand, charging a high transfer price may help a multinational corporation draw profits out of a country that has stringent controls on foreign remittances, or it may allow a multinational corporation to shift income from a country that has high income tax rates to a country that has low rates.

Review Problem 3: Transfer Pricing

Situation A

Collyer Products, Inc., has a Valve Division that manufactures and sells a standard valve:

Capacity in units	100,000
Selling price to outside customers	$30
Variable costs per unit	$16
Fixed costs per unit (based on capacity)	$9

The company has a Pump Division that could use this valve in one of its pumps. The Pump Division is currently purchasing 10,000 valves per year from an overseas supplier at a cost of $29 per valve.

Required:
1. Assume that the Valve Division has ample idle capacity to handle all of the Pump Division's needs. What is the acceptable range, if any, for the transfer price between the two divisions?
2. Assume that the Valve Division is selling all of the valves that it can produce to outside customers. What is the acceptable range, if any, for the transfer price between the two divisions?
3. Assume again that the Valve Division is selling all of the valves that it can produce to outside customers. Also assume that $3 in variable expenses can be avoided on transfers within the company, due to reduced selling costs. What is the acceptable range, if any, for the transfer price between the two divisions?

Solution to Situation A

1. Since the Valve Division has idle capacity, it does not have to give up any outside sales to take on the Pump Division's business. Applying the formula for the lowest acceptable transfer price from the viewpoint of the selling division, we get:

$$\text{Transfer price} \geq \frac{\text{Variable cost}}{\text{per unit}} + \frac{\text{Total contribution margin on lost sales}}{\text{Number of units transferred}}$$

$$\text{Transfer price} \geq \$16 + \frac{\$0}{10,000} = \$16$$

The Pump Division would be unwilling to pay more than $29, the price it is currently paying an outside supplier for its valves. Therefore, the transfer price must fall within the range:

$$\$16 \leq \text{Transfer price} \leq \$29$$

2. Since the Valve Division is selling all of the valves that it can produce on the outside market, it would have to give up some of these outside sales to take on the Pump Division's business. Thus, the Valve Division has an opportunity cost, which is the total contribution margin on lost sales:

$$\text{Transfer price} \geq \frac{\text{Variable cost}}{\text{per unit}} + \frac{\text{Total contribution margin on lost sales}}{\text{Number of units transferred}}$$

$$\text{Transfer price} \geq \$16 + \frac{(\$30 - \$16) \times 10,000}{10,000} = \$16 + \$14 = \$30$$

Since the Pump Division can purchase valves from an outside supplier at only $29 per unit, no transfers will be made between the two divisions.

3. Applying the formula for the lowest acceptable transfer price from the viewpoint of the selling division, we get:

$$\text{Transfer price} \geq \frac{\text{Variable cost}}{\text{per unit}} + \frac{\text{Total contribution margin on lost sales}}{\text{Number of units transferred}}$$

$$\text{Transfer price} \geq (\$16 - \$3) + \frac{(\$30 - \$16) \times 10{,}000}{10{,}000} = \$13 + \$14 = \$27$$

In this case, the transfer price must fall within the range:

$$\$27 \leq \text{Transfer price} \leq \$29$$

Situation B

Refer to the original data in situation A above. Assume that the Pump Division needs 20,000 special high-pressure valves per year. The Valve Division's variable costs to manufacture and ship the special valve would be $20 per unit. To produce these special valves, the Valve Division would have to reduce its production and sales of regular valves from 100,000 units per year to 70,000 units per year.

Required:
As far as the Valve Division is concerned, what is the lowest acceptable transfer price?

Solution to Situation B

To produce the 20,000 special valves, the Valve Division will have to give up sales of 30,000 regular valves to outside customers. Applying the formula for the lowest acceptable transfer price from the viewpoint of the selling division, we get:

$$\text{Transfer price} \geq \frac{\text{Variable cost}}{\text{per unit}} + \frac{\text{Total contribution margin on lost sales}}{\text{Number of units transferred}}$$

$$\text{Transfer price} \geq \$20 + \frac{(\$30 - \$16) \times 30{,}000}{20{,}000} = \$20 + \$21 = \$41$$

Glossary (Appendix 12A)

Market price The price charged for an item on the open market. (p. 547)
Negotiated transfer price A transfer price agreed on between buying and selling divisions. (p. 543)
Range of acceptable transfer prices The range of transfer prices within which the profits of both the selling division and the buying division would increase as a result of a transfer. (p. 543)
Suboptimization An overall level of profits that is less than a segment or a company is capable of earning. (p. 543)
Transfer price The price charged when one division or segment provides goods or services to another division or segment of an organization. (p. 543)

Appendix 12B: Service Department Charges

LEARNING OBJECTIVE 5
Charge operating departments for services provided by service departments.

Most large organizations have both *operating departments* and *service departments*. The central purposes of the organization are carried out in the **operating departments.** In contrast, **service departments** do not directly engage in operating activities. Instead, they provide services or assistance to the operating departments. Examples of operating departments include the Surgery Department at Mt. Sinai Hospital, the Geography Department at the University of Washington, the Marketing Department at Allstate Insurance Company, and production departments at manufacturers such as Mitsubishi, Hewlett-Packard, and Michelin.

Examples of service departments include Cafeteria, Internal Auditing, Human Resources, Cost Accounting, and Purchasing.

Service department costs are charged to operating departments for a variety of reasons including:

- To encourage operating departments to make wise use of service department resources. If the services were provided for free, operating managers would be inclined to waste these resources.

- To provide operating departments with more complete cost data for making decisions. Actions taken by operating departments have impacts on service department costs. For example, hiring another employee will increase costs in the human resources department. Such service department costs should be charged to the operating departments, otherwise the operating departments will not take them into account when making decisions.

- To help measure the profitability of operating departments. Charging service department costs to operating departments provides a more complete accounting of the costs incurred as a consequence of activities in the operating departments.

- To create an incentive for service departments to operate efficiently. Charging service department costs to operating departments provides a system of checks and balances in the sense that cost-conscious operating departments will take an active interest in keeping service department costs low.

In Appendix 12A, we discussed *transfer prices* that are charged within an organization when one part of an organization provides a product to another part of the organization. The service department charges considered in this appendix can be viewed as a transfer price that is charged for services provided by service departments to operating departments.

Charging Costs by Behavior

Whenever possible, variable and fixed service department costs should be charged to operating departments separately to provide more useful data for planning and control of departmental operations.

Variable Costs

Variable costs vary in total in proportion to changes in the level of service provided. For example, the cost of food in a cafeteria is a variable cost that varies in proportion to the number of persons using the cafeteria or the number of meals served.

As a general rule, a variable cost should be charged to consuming departments according to whatever activity causes the incurrence of the cost. For example, variable costs of a maintenance department that are caused by the number of machine-hours worked in the operating departments should be charged to the operating departments using machine-hours as the charge-out base. This will ensure that these costs are properly traced to departments, products, and customers.

Fixed Costs

The fixed costs of service departments represent the costs of making capacity available for use. These costs should be charged to consuming departments in *predetermined lump-sum amounts*. By predetermined lump-sum amounts we mean that the total amount charged to each consuming department is determined in advance and, once determined, does not change. The lump-sum amount charged to a department can be based either on the department's peak-period or long-run average servicing needs. The logic behind lump-sum charges of this type is as follows:

When a service department is first established, its capacity will be determined by the needs of the departments that it will serve. This capacity may reflect the peak-period needs of the other departments, or it may reflect their long-run average or "normal" servicing needs. Depending on how much servicing capacity is provided for, it will be necessary to make a commitment of resources, which will be reflected in the service department's fixed costs. These fixed costs should be borne by the consuming departments in proportion to the amount of capacity each consuming department requires. That is, if available capacity in the service department has been provided to meet the peak-period needs of consuming departments, then the fixed costs of the service department should be charged in predetermined lump-sum amounts to consuming departments on that basis. If available capacity has been provided only to meet "normal" or long-run average needs, then the fixed costs should be charged on that basis.

Once set, charges should not vary from period to period, since they represent the cost of having a certain level of service capacity available and on line for each consuming department. The fact that a consuming department does not need the peak level or even the "normal" level of service every period is immaterial; the capacity to deliver this level of service must be available. The consuming departments should bear the cost of that availability.

To illustrate this idea, assume that Novak Company has just organized a Maintenance Department to service all machines in the Cutting, Assembly, and Finishing Departments. In determining the capacity of the newly organized Maintenance Department, the various operating departments estimated that they would have the following peak-period needs for maintenance:

Department	Peak-Period Maintenance Needs in Terms of Number of Hours of Maintenance Work Required	Percent of Total Hours
Cutting	900	30%
Assembly	1,800	60
Finishing	300	10
	3,000	100%

Therefore, 30% of the Maintenance Department fixed costs should be charged to the Cutting Department, 60% to the Assembly Department, and 10% to the Finishing Department. These lump-sum charges *will not change* from period to period unless peak-period servicing needs change.

Should Actual or Budgeted Costs Be Charged?

Should the *actual* or *budgeted* costs of a service department be charged to operating departments? The answer is that budgeted costs should be charged because allocating actual costs would burden the operating departments with any inefficiencies in the service department. In other words, if actual costs are charged, any lack of cost control on the part of the service department is simply buried in the charges to other departments.

Any variance over budgeted costs is the responsibility of the service department and that variance should be retained in the service department. Operating department managers justifiably complain bitterly if they are forced to absorb service department inefficiencies.

In effect, management says, "You will be charged X dollars for every unit of service that you consume or capacity that you require. You can consume as much or as little as you desire; the total charge you bear will vary proportionately." The purpose of making such charges is to ensure that the managers of the operating departments are fully aware of all of the costs of their actions—including costs that are incurred in service departments. This helps operating department managers make appropriate trade-offs when deciding, for example, whether to purchase a service from an external provider or to obtain it from a service department inside the company.

Guidelines for Service Department Charges

The following guidelines summarize how service department costs should be charged out to other departments:

- Variable and fixed service department costs should be charged separately.
- Variable service department costs should be charged using a predetermined rate applied to the actual services consumed.
- Fixed costs represent the costs of having service capacity available. These costs should be charged in lump sums to each department in proportion to their peak-period needs or long-run average needs. The lump-sum amounts should be based on budgeted fixed costs, not actual fixed costs.

Implementing the Guidelines

Seaboard Airlines has two operating divisions: a Freight Division and a Passenger Division. The company has a Maintenance Department that provides servicing to both divisions. Variable servicing costs are budgeted at $10 per flight-hour. The department's fixed costs are budgeted at $750,000 for the year. The fixed costs of the Maintenance Department are budgeted based on the peak-period demand, which occurs during the Thanksgiving to New Year's holiday period. The airline wants to make sure that none of its aircraft are grounded during this key period due to unavailability of maintenance facilities. Approximately 40% of the maintenance during this period is performed on the Freight Division's equipment, and 60% is performed on the Passenger Division's equipment. These figures and the budgeted flight-hours for the coming year are as follows:

	Percent of Peak Period Capacity Required	Budgeted Flight-Hours
Freight Division..........	40%	9,000
Passenger Division.......	60	15,000
Total	100%	24,000

Year-end records show that actual variable and fixed costs in the aircraft Maintenance Department for the year were $260,000 and $780,000, respectively. One division logged more flight-hours during the year than planned, and the other division logged fewer flight-hours than planned, as shown below:

	Flight-Hours	
	Budgeted (see above)	Actual
Freight Division	9,000	8,000
Passenger Division	15,000	17,000
Total flight-hours	24,000	25,000

The amount of Maintenance Department cost charged to each division for the year would be as follows:

				Actual activity		Division	
						Freight	Passenger
Budgeted variable rate	Variable cost charges:						
	$10 per flight-hour	×	8,000 flight-hours	...		$ 80,000	
	$10 per flight-hour	×	17,000 flight-hours	...			$170,000
	Fixed cost charges:						
Peak-period capacity required	40%	×	$750,000	....		300,000	
	60%	×	$750,000	....			450,000
	Total charges	....				$380,000	$620,000
			Budgeted fixed cost				

Notice that variable servicing costs are charged to the operating divisions based on the budgeted rate ($10 per hour) and the *actual activity* for the year. In contrast, the charges for fixed costs are based entirely on budgeted data. Also note that the two operating divisions are *not* charged for the actual costs of the service department, which may be influenced by inefficiency in the service department and may be beyond the control of the managers of the operating divisions. Instead, the service department is held responsible for the actual costs not charged to other departments as shown below:

	Variable	Fixed
Total actual costs incurred	$260,000	$780,000
Total charges (above)	250,000*	750,000
Spending variance—responsibility of the Maintenance Department	$ 10,000	$ 30,000

*$10 per flight-hour × 25,000 actual flight-hours = $250,000.

Some Cautions in Allocating Service Department Costs

Pitfalls in Allocating Fixed Costs

Rather than charge fixed costs to using departments in predetermined lump-sum amounts, some companies allocate them using a *variable* allocation base that fluctuates from period to period. This practice can distort decisions and create serious inequities between departments. The inequities arise from the fact that the fixed costs allocated to one department are heavily influenced by what happens in *other* departments.

To illustrate, assume that Kolby Products has an auto service center that provides maintenance work on the fleet of autos used in the company's two sales territories. The auto service center costs are all fixed. Contrary to good practice, the company allocates these fixed costs to the sales territories on the basis of actual miles driven (a variable allocation base). Selected cost data for the last two years follow:

	Year 1	Year 2
Auto service center costs (all fixed) (a)	$120,000	$120,000
Western sales territory—miles driven	1,500,000	1,500,000
Eastern sales territory—miles driven	1,500,000	900,000
Total miles driven (b)	3,000,000	2,400,000
Allocation rate per mile, (a) ÷ (b)	$0.04	$0.05

Notice that the Western sales territory maintained an activity level of 1,500,000 miles driven in both years. On the other hand, activity in the Eastern sales territory dropped from 1,500,000 miles in Year 1 to only 900,000 miles in Year 2. The auto service center costs that would be allocated to the two sales territories over the two-year span using actual miles driven as the allocation base are as follows:

Year 1:
Western sales territory: 1,500,000 miles at $0.04 per mile	$ 60,000
Eastern sales territory: 1,500,000 miles $0.04 per mile	60,000
Total cost allocated	$120,000

Year 2:
Western sales territory: 1,500,000 miles at $0.05 per mile	$ 75,000
Eastern sales territory: 900,000 miles $0.05 per mile	45,000
Total cost allocated	$120,000

In Year 1, the two sales territories share the service department costs equally. In Year 2, however, the bulk of the service department costs are allocated to the Western sales territory. This is not because of any increase in activity in the Western sales territory; rather, it is because of the *decrease* in activity in the Eastern sales territory. Even though the Western sales territory maintained the same level of activity in both years, it is penalized with a heavier cost allocation in Year 2 because of what happened in *another* part of the company.

This kind of inequity is almost inevitable when a variable allocation base is used to allocate fixed costs. The manager of the Western sales territory undoubtedly will be upset about the additional costs forced on his territory, but he will feel powerless to do anything about it. The result will be a loss of confidence in the system and considerable ill will.

Beware of Sales Dollars as an Allocation Base

Sales dollars is a popular base for allocating or charging service department costs. One reason is that a sales dollars base is simple, straightforward, and easy to work with. Another reason is that people tend to view sales dollars as a measure of ability to pay, and, hence, as a measure of how readily costs can be absorbed from other parts of the organization.

Unfortunately, sales dollars are often a very poor base for allocating or charging costs, for the reason that sales dollars vary from period to period, whereas the costs are often largely *fixed*. As discussed earlier, if a variable allocation base is used to allocate fixed costs, the costs allocated to one department will depend in large part on what happens in *other* departments. A letup in sales effort in one department will shift allocated costs from that department to other, more successful departments. In effect, the departments putting forth the best sales efforts are penalized in the form of higher allocations. The result is often bitterness and resentment on the part of the managers of the better departments.

Consider the following situation encountered by one of the authors:

A large men's clothing store has one service department and three sales departments—Suits, Shoes, and Accessories. The service department's costs total $60,000 per period and are allocated to the three sales departments according to sales dollars. A recent period showed the following allocation:

	Departments			
	Suits	Shoes	Accessories	Total
Sales by department	$260,000	$40,000	$100,000	$400,000
Percentage of total sales	65%	10%	25%	100%
Allocation of service department costs, based on percentage of total sales	$39,000	$6,000	$15,000	$60,000

In the following period, the manager of the Suits Department launched a very successful program to expand sales by $100,000 in his department. Sales in the other two departments remained unchanged. Total service department costs also remained unchanged, but the allocation of these costs changed substantially, as shown below:

	Departments			
	Suits	Shoes	Accessories	Total
Sales by department	$360,000	$40,000	$100,000	$500,000
Percentage of total sales	72%	8%	20%	100%
Allocation of service department costs, based on percentage of total sales	$43,200	$4,800	$12,000	$60,000
Increase (or decrease) from prior allocation	$4,200	$(1,200)	$(3,000)	$0

The manager of the Suits Department complained that as a result of his successful effort to expand sales in his department, he was being forced to carry a larger share of the service department costs. On the other hand, the managers of the departments that showed no improvement in sales were relieved of a portion of the costs that they had been carrying. Yet there had been no change in the amount of services provided for any department.

The manager of the Suits Department viewed the increased service department cost allocation to his department as a penalty for his outstanding performance, and he wondered whether his efforts had really been worthwhile in the eyes of top management.

Sales dollars should be used as a base for allocating or charging costs only in those cases where service department costs are driven by sales. In those situations where service department costs are fixed, they should be charged according to the three guidelines discussed earlier in the chapter.

Glossary (Appendix 12B)

Operating department A department in which the central purposes of the organization are carried out. (p. 550)

Service department A department that does not directly engage in operating activities; rather, it provides services or assistance to the operating departments. (p. 550)

Questions

12-1   What is meant by the term *decentralization?*
12-2   What benefits result from decentralization?
12-3   Distinguish between a cost center, a profit center, and an investment center.
12-4   What is a segment of an organization? Give several examples of segments.
12-5   What costs are assigned to a segment under the contribution approach?
12-6   Distinguish between a traceable cost and a common cost. Give several examples of each.
12-7   Explain how the segment margin differs from the contribution margin.
12-8   Why aren't common costs allocated to segments under the contribution approach?
12-9   How is it possible for a cost that is traceable to a segment to become a common cost if the segment is divided into further segments?
12-10 What is meant by the terms *margin* and *turnover* in ROI calculations?
12-11 What is meant by residual income?
12-12 In what way can the use of ROI as a performance measure for investment centers lead to bad decisions? How does the residual income approach overcome this problem?
12-13 (Appendix 12A) What is meant by the term *transfer price,* and why are transfer prices needed?
12-14 (Appendix 12A) From the standpoint of a selling division that has idle capacity, what is the lowest acceptable transfer price for an item?
12-15 (Appendix 12A) From the standpoint of a selling division that has *no* idle capacity, what is the lowest acceptable transfer price for an item?
12-16 (Appendix 12A) What are the advantages and disadvantages of cost-based transfer prices?
12-17 (Appendix 12A) If a market price for a product can be determined, why isn't it always the best transfer price?
12-18 (Appendix 12B) How should the variable costs of a service department be charged to operating departments?
12-19 (Appendix 12B) How should the fixed costs of a service department be charged to operating departments?

 ## Exercises

EXERCISE 12-1 Basic Segmented Income Statement [LO1]

Royal Lawncare Company produces and sells two packaged products, Weedban and Greengrow. Revenue and cost information relating to the products follow:

	Product	
	Weedban	Greengrow
Selling price per unit	$6.00	$7.50
Variable expenses per unit	$2.40	$5.25
Traceable fixed expenses per year	$45,000	$21,000

Common fixed expenses in the company total $33,000 annually. Last year the company produced and sold 15,000 units of Weedban and 28,000 units of Greengrow.

Required:
Prepare a contribution format income statement segmented by product lines.

EXERCISE 12-2 Compute the Return on Investment (ROI) [LO2]

Alyeska Services Company, a division of a major oil company, provides various services to the operators of the North Slope oil field in Alaska. Data concerning the most recent year appear below:

Sales	$7,500,000
Net operating income	$600,000
Average operating assets	$5,000,000

Required:
1. Compute the margin for Alyeska Services Company.
2. Compute the turnover for Alyeska Services Company.
3. Compute the return on investment (ROI) for Alyeska Services Company.

EXERCISE 12-3 Residual Income [LO3]

Juniper Design Ltd. of Manchester, England, is a company specializing in providing design services to residential developers. Last year the company had net operating income of £600,000 on sales of £3,000,000. The company's average operating assets for the year were £2,800,000 and its minimum required rate of return was 18%. (The currency used in England is the pound sterling, denoted by £.)

Required:
Compute the company's residual income for the year.

EXERCISE 12-4 (Appendix 12A) Transfer Pricing Situations [LO4]

In each of the cases below, assume that Division X has a product that can be sold either to outside customers or to Division Y of the same company for use in its production process. The managers of the divisions are evaluated based on their divisional profits.

	Case	
	A	B
Division X:		
Capacity in units	200,000	200,000
Number of units being sold to outside customers	200,000	160,000
Selling price per unit to outside customers	$90	$75
Variable costs per unit	$70	$60
Fixed costs per unit (based on capacity)	$13	$8
Division Y:		
Number of units needed for production	40,000	40,000
Purchase price per unit now being paid to an outside supplier	$86	$74

Required:
1. Refer to the data in case A above. Assume in this case that $3 per unit in variable selling costs can be avoided on intracompany sales. If the managers are free to negotiate and make decisions on their own, will a transfer take place? If so, within what range will the transfer price fall? Explain.
2. Refer to the data in case B above. In this case there will be no savings in variable selling costs on intracompany sales. If the managers are free to negotiate and make decisions on their own, will a transfer take place? If so, within what range will the transfer price fall? Explain.

EXERCISE 12-5 (Appendix 12B) Service Department Charges [LO5]

Hannibal Steel Company has a Transport Services Department that provides trucks to haul ore from the company's mine to its two steel mills—the Northern Plant and the Southern Plant. Budgeted costs for the Transport Services Department total $350,000 per year, consisting of $0.25 per ton variable cost and $300,000 fixed cost. The level of fixed cost is determined by peak-period requirements. During the peak period, the Northern Plant requires 70% of the Transport Services Department's capacity and the Southern Plant requires 30%.

During the year, the Transport Services Department actually hauled the following amounts of ore for the two plants: Northern Plant, 130,000 tons; Southern Plant, 50,000 tons. The Transport Services Department incurred $364,000 in cost during the year, of which $54,000 was variable cost and $310,000 was fixed cost.

Management wants end-of-year service department cost allocations in order to compare actual performance to planned performance.

Required:
1. Determine how much of the $54,000 in variable cost should be allocated to each plant.
2. Determine how much of the $310,000 in fixed cost should be allocated to each plant.
3. Will any of the $364,000 in the Transport Services Department cost not be allocated to the plants? Explain.

EXERCISE 12-6 Segmented Income Statement [LO1]

Wingate Company, a wholesale distributor of DVDs, has been experiencing losses for some time, as shown by its most recent monthly contribution format income statement, which follows:

Sales	$1,000,000
Less Variable expenses	390,000
Contribution margin	610,000
Less fixed expenses	625,000
Net operating income (loss)	$ (15,000)

In an effort to isolate the problem, the president has asked for an income statement segmented by division. Accordingly, the Accounting Department has developed the following information:

	Division		
	East	Central	West
Sales	$250,000	$400,000	$350,000
Variable expenses as a percentage of sales	52%	30%	40%
Traceable fixed expenses	$160,000	$200,000	$175,000

Required:

1. Prepare a contribution format income statement segmented by divisions, as desired by the president.
2. As a result of a marketing study, the president believes that sales in the West Division could be increased by 20% if monthly advertising in that division were increased by $15,000. Would you recommend the increased advertising? Show computations to support your answer.

EXERCISE 12-7 Computing and Interpreting Return on Investment (ROI) [LO2]

Selected operating data for two divisions of Outback Brewing, Ltd., of Australia are given below:

	Division	
	Queensland	New South Wales
Sales	$4,000,000	$7,000,000
Average operating assets	$2,000,000	$2,000,000
Net operating income	$360,000	$420,000
Property, plant, and equipment	$950,000	$800,000

Required:

1. Compute the rate of return for each division using the return on investment (ROI) formula stated in terms of margin and turnover.
2. Which divisional manager seems to be doing the better job? Why?

EXERCISE 12-8 Evaluating New Investments Using Return on Investment (ROI) and Residual Income [LO2, LO3]

Selected sales and operating data for three divisions of different structural engineering firms are given below:

	Division A	Division B	Division C
Sales	$12,000,000	$14,000,000	$25,000,000
Average operating assets	$3,000,000	$7,000,000	$5,000,000
Net operating income	$600,000	$560,000	$800,000
Minimum required rate of return	14%	10%	16%

Required:
1. Compute the return on investment (ROI) for each division, using the formula stated in terms of margin and turnover.
2. Compute the residual income for each division.
3. Assume that each division is presented with an investment opportunity that would yield a 15% rate of return.
   a. If performance is being measured by ROI, which division or divisions will probably accept the opportunity? Reject? Why?
   b. If performance is being measured by residual income, which division or divisions will probably accept the opportunity? Reject? Why?

EXERCISE 12-9 (Appendix 12A) Transfer Pricing from the Viewpoint of the Entire Company [LO4]
Division A manufactures electronic circuit boards. The boards can be sold either to Division B of the same company or to outside customers. Last year, the following activity occurred in Division A:

Selling price per circuit board	$125
Variable cost per circuit board.	$90
Number of circuit boards:	
Produced during the year	20,000
Sold to outside customers.	16,000
Sold to Division B	4,000

Sales to Division B were at the same price as sales to outside customers. The circuit boards purchased by Division B were used in an electronic instrument manufactured by that division (one board per instrument). Division B incurred $100 in additional cost per instrument and then sold the instruments for $300 each.

Required:
1. Prepare income statements for Division A, Division B, and the company as a whole.
2. Assume that Division A's manufacturing capacity is 20,000 circuit boards. Next year, Division B wants to purchase 5,000 circuit boards from Division A rather than 4,000. (Circuit boards of this type are not available from outside sources.) From the standpoint of the company as a whole, should Division A sell the 1,000 additional circuit boards to Division B or continue to sell them to outside customers? Explain.

EXERCISE 12-10 (Appendix 12B) Service Department Charges [LO5]
Reed Corporation operates a Medical Services Department for its employees. Charges to the company's operating departments for the variable costs of the Medical Services Department are based on the actual number of employees in each department. Charges for the fixed costs of the Medical Services Department are based on the long-run average number of employees in each operating department.

Variable Medical Services Department costs are budgeted at $60 per employee. Fixed Medical Services Department costs are budgeted at $600,000 per year. Actual Medical Services Department costs for the most recent year were $105,400 for variable costs and $605,000 for fixed costs. Data concerning employees in the three operating departments follow:

	Cutting	Milling	Assembly
Budgeted number of employees	600	300	900
Actual number of employees for the most recent year	500	400	800
Long-run average number of employees	600	400	1,000

Required:
1. Determine the Medical Services Department charges for the year to each of the operating departments—Cutting, Milling, and Assembly.
2. How much, if any, of the actual Medical Services Department costs for the year should not be allocated to the operating departments?

EXERCISE 12-11 Working with a Segmented Income Statement [LO1]

Raner, Harris, & Chan is a consulting firm that specializes in information systems for medical and dental clinics. The firm has two offices—one in Chicago and one in Minneapolis. The firm classifies the direct costs of consulting jobs as variable costs. A segmented contribution format income statement for the company's most recent year is given below:

| | Total Company | | Office | | | |
			Chicago		Minneapolis	
Sales	$450,000	100.0%	$150,000	100%	$300,000	100%
Variable expenses	225,000	50%	45,000	30%	180,000	60%
Contribution margin	225,000	50%	105,000	70%	120,000	40%
Traceable fixed expenses	126,000	28%	78,000	52%	48,000	16%
Office segment margin	99,000	22%	$ 27,000	18%	$ 72,000	24%
Common fixed expenses not traceable to offices	63,000	14%				
Net operating income	$ 36,000	8%				

Required:

1. By how much would the company's net operating income increase if Minneapolis increased its sales by $75,000 per year? Assume no change in cost behavior patterns.
2. Refer to the original data. Assume that sales in Chicago increase by $50,000 next year and that sales in Minneapolis remain unchanged. Assume no change in fixed costs.
   a. Prepare a new segmented income statement for the company using the format shown previously. Show both amounts and percentages.
   b. Observe from the income statement you have prepared that the contribution margin ratio for Chicago has remained unchanged at 70% (the same as in the previous data) but that the segment margin ratio has changed. How do you explain the change in the segment margin ratio?

EXERCISE 12-12 Working with a Segmented Income Statement [LO1]

Refer to the data in Exercise 12–11. Assume that Minneapolis' sales by major market are:

| | Minneapolis | | Market | | | |
			Medical		Dental	
Sales	$300,000	100%	$200,000	100%	$100,000	100%
Variable expenses	180,000	60%	128,000	65%	52,000	52%
Contribution margin	120,000	40%	72,000	36%	48,000	48%
Traceable fixed expenses	33,000	11%	12,000	6%	21,000	21%
Market segment margin	87,000	29%	$ 60,000	30%	$ 27,000	27%
Common fixed expenses not traceable to markets	15,000	5%				
Office segment margin	$ 72,000	24%				

The company would like to initiate an intensive advertising campaign in one of the two market segments during the next month. The campaign would cost $5,000. Marketing studies indicate that such a campaign would increase sales in the Medical market by $40,000 or increase sales in the Dental market by $35,000.

Required:

1. In which of the markets would you recommend that the company focus its advertising campaign? Show computations to support your answer.
2. In Exercise 12–11, Minneapolis shows $48,000 in traceable fixed expenses. What happened to the $48,000 in this exercise?

EXERCISE 12-13 Contrasting Return on Investment (ROI) and Residual Income [LO2, LO3]
Meiji Isetan Corp. of Japan has two regional divisions with headquarters in Osaka and Yokohama. Selected data on the two divisions follow (in millions of yen, denoted by ¥):

	Division	
	Osaka	Yokohama
Sales	¥3,000,000	¥9,000,000
Net operating income...........	¥210,000	¥720,000
Average operating assets	¥1,000,000	¥4,000,000

Required:
1. Compute the return on investment (ROI) for each division.
2. Assume that the company evaluates performance using residual income and that the minimum required rate of return for any division is 15%. Compute the residual income for each division.
3. Is Yokohama's greater amount of residual income an indication that it is better managed? Explain.

EXERCISE 12-14 Effects of Changes in Sales, Expenses, and Assets on ROI [LO2]
CommercialServices.com Corporation provides business-to-business services on the Internet. Data concerning the most recent year appear below:

Sales	$3,000,000
Net operating income...........	$150,000
Average operating assets........	$750,000

Required:
Consider each question below independently. Carry out all computations to two decimal places.
1. Compute the company's return on investment (ROI).
2. The entrepreneur who founded the company is convinced that sales will increase next year by 50% and that net operating income will increase by 200%, with no increase in average operating assets. What would be the company's ROI?
3. The chief financial officer of the company believes a more realistic scenario would be a $1,000,000 increase in sales, requiring a $250,000 increase in average operating assets, with a resulting $200,000 increase in net operating income. What would be the company's ROI in this scenario?

EXERCISE 12-15 Return on Investment (ROI) and Residual Income Relations [LO2, LO3]
A family friend has asked your help in analyzing the operations of three anonymous companies operating in the same service sector industry. Supply the missing data in the table below:

	Company		
	A	B	C
Sales	$9,000,000	$7,000,000	$4,500,000
Net operating income	$?	$ 280,000	$?
Average operating assets	$3,000,000	?	$1,800,000
Return on investment (ROI)	18%	14%	?
Minimum required rate of return:			
Percentage	16%	?	15%
Dollar amount	$?	$ 320,000	$?
Residual income..................	$?	$?	$ 90,000

EXERCISE 12-16 (Appendix 12A) Transfer Pricing Basics [LO4]
Sako Company's Audio Division produces a speaker that is used by manufacturers of various audio products. Sales and cost data on the speaker follow:

Selling price per unit on the outside market	$60
Variable costs per unit	$42
Fixed costs per unit (based on capacity)	$8
Capacity in units	25,000

Sako Company has a Hi-Fi Division that could use this speaker in one of its products. The Hi-Fi Division will need 5,000 speakers per year. It has received a quote of $57 per speaker from another manufacturer. Sako Company evaluates division managers on the basis of divisional profits.

Required:

1. Assume that the Audio Division is now selling only 20,000 speakers per year to outside customers.
    a. From the standpoint of the Audio Division, what is the lowest acceptable transfer price for speakers sold to the Hi-Fi Division?
    b. From the standpoint of the Hi-Fi Division, what is the highest acceptable transfer price for speakers acquired from the Audio Division?
    c. If left free to negotiate without interference, would you expect the division managers to voluntarily agree to the transfer of 5,000 speakers from the Audio Division to the Hi-Fi Division? Why or why not?
    d. From the standpoint of the entire company, should the transfer take place? Why or why not?
2. Assume that the Audio Division is selling all of the speakers it can produce to outside customers.
    a. From the standpoint of the Audio Division, what is the lowest acceptable transfer price for speakers sold to the Hi-Fi Division?
    b. From the standpoint of the Hi-Fi Division, what is the highest acceptable transfer price for speakers acquired from the Audio Division?
    c. If left free to negotiate without interference, would you expect the division managers to voluntarily agree to the transfer of 5,000 speakers from the Audio Division to the Hi-Fi Division? Why or why not?
    d. From the standpoint of the entire company, should the transfer take place? Why or why not?

EXERCISE 12-17 Sales Dollars as an Allocation Base for Fixed Costs [LO5]

Konig Enterprises, Ltd., owns and operates three restaurants in Vancouver, B.C. The company allocates its fixed administrative expenses to the three restaurants on the basis of sales dollars. During 2008, the fixed administrative expenses totaled $2,000,000. These expenses were allocated as follows:

	Restaurants			
	Rick's Harborside	Imperial Garden	Ginger Wok	Total
Total sales—2008.............	$16,000,000	$15,000,000	$9,000,000	$40,000,000
Percentage of total sales........	40%	37.5%	22.5%	100%
Allocation (based on the above percentages)	$800,000	$750,000	$450,000	$2,000,000

During 2009, the following year, the Imperial Garden restaurant increased its sales by $10 million. The sales levels in the other two restaurants remained unchanged. The company's 2009 sales data were as follows:

	Restaurants			
	Rick's Harborside	Imperial Garden	Ginger Wok	Total
Total sales—2009.............	$16,000,000	$25,000,000	$9,000,000	$50,000,000
Percentage of total sales........	32%	50%	18%	100%

Fixed administrative expenses remained unchanged at $2,000,000 during 2009.

Required:

1. Using sales dollars as an allocation base, show the allocation of the fixed administrative expenses among the three restaurants for 2009.
2. Compare your allocation from (1) above to the allocation for 2008. As the manager of the Imperial Garden, how would you feel about the allocation that has been charged to you for 2009?
3. Comment on the usefulness of sales dollars as an allocation base.

EXERCISE 12-18 Return on Investment (ROI) Relations [LO2]
Provide the missing data in the following table for a distributor of martial arts products:

	Division		
	Alpha	Bravo	Charlie
Sales	$?	$11,500,000	$?
Net operating income	$?	$ 920,000	$210,000
Average operating assets	$800,000	$?	$?
Margin	4%	?	7%
Turnover	5	?	?
Return on investment (ROI)	?	20%	14%

EXERCISE 12-19 Cost-Volume Profit Analysis and Return on Investment (ROI) [LO2]
Posters.com is a small Internet retailer of high-quality posters. The company has $1,000,000 in operating assets and fixed expenses of $150,000 per year. With this level of operating assets and fixed expenses, the company can support sales of up to $3,000,000 per year. The company's contribution margin ratio is 25%, which means that an additional dollar of sales results in additional contribution margin, and net operating income, of 25 cents.

Required:

1. Complete the following table showing the relationship between sales and return on investment (ROI).

Sales	Net Operating Income	Average Operating Assets	ROI
$2,500,000	$475,000	$1,000,000	?
$2,600,000	$?	$1,000,000	?
$2,700,000	$?	$1,000,000	?
$2,800,000	$?	$1,000,000	?
$2,900,000	$?	$1,000,000	?
$3,000,000	$?	$1,000,000	?

2. What happens to the company's return on investment (ROI) as sales increase? Explain.

EXERCISE 12-20 Effects of Changes in Profits and Assets on Return on Investment (ROI) [LO2]
Pecs Alley is a regional chain of health clubs. The managers of the clubs, who have authority to make investments as needed, are evaluated based largely on return on investment (ROI). The Springfield Club reported the following results for the past year:

Sales	$1,400,000
Net operating income	$70,000
Average operating assets........	$350,000

Required:
The following questions are to be considered independently. Carry out all computations to two decimal places.

1. Compute the club's return on investment (ROI).

2. Assume that the manager of the club is able to increase sales by $70,000 and that, as a result, net operating income increases by $18,200. Further assume that this is possible without any increase in operating assets. What would be the club's return on investment (ROI)?
3. Assume that the manager of the club is able to reduce expenses by $14,000 without any change in sales or operating assets. What would be the club's return on investment (ROI)?
4. Assume that the manager of the club is able to reduce operating assets by $70,000 without any change in sales or net operating income. What would be the club's return on investment (ROI)?

Problems

PROBLEM 12-21 Restructuring a Segmented Income Statement [LO1]

Losses have been incurred at Millard Corporation for some time. In an effort to isolate the problem and improve the company's performance, management has requested that the monthly income statement be segmented by sales region. The company's first effort at preparing a segmented statement is given below. This statement is for May, the most recent month of activity.

	Sales Region		
	West	Central	East
Sales	$450,000	$800,000	$750,000
Regional expenses (traceable):			
Cost of goods sold	162,900	280,000	376,500
Advertising	108,000	200,000	210,000
Salaries	90,000	88,000	135,000
Utilities	13,500	12,000	15,000
Depreciation......................	27,000	28,000	30,000
Shipping expense..................	17,100	32,000	28,500
Total regional expenses...............	418,500	640,000	795,000
Regional income (loss) before			
corporate expenses	31,500	160,000	(45,000)
Corporate expenses:			
Advertising (general)	18,000	32,000	30,000
General administrative expense........	50,000	50,000	50,000
Total corporate expenses..............	68,000	82,000	80,000
Net operating income (loss).............	$ (36,500)	$ 78,000	$(125,000)

Cost of goods sold and shipping expense are both variable; other costs are all fixed. Millard Corporation is a wholesale distributor of office products. It purchases office products from manufacturers and distributes them in the three regions given above. The three regions are about the same size, and each has its own manager and sales staff. The products that the company distributes vary widely in profitability.

Required:
1. List any disadvantages or weaknesses that you see to the statement format illustrated previously.
2. Explain the basis that is apparently being used to allocate the corporate expenses to the regions. Do you agree with these allocations? Explain.
3. Prepare a new segmented contribution format income statement for May. Show a Total column as well as data for each region. Include percentages on your statement for all columns. Carry percentages to one decimal place.
4. Analyze the statement that you prepared in part (3) shown previously. What points that might help to improve the company's performance would you bring to management's attention?

PROBLEM 12-22 Comparison of Performance Using Return on Investment (ROI) [LO2]
Comparative data on three companies in the same service industry are given below:

	Company		
	A	B	C
Sales	$600,000	$500,000	$?
Net operating income...........	$ 84,000	$ 70,000	$?
Average operating assets	$300,000	?	$1,000,000
Margin	?	?	3.5%
Turnover....................	?	?	2
(ROI)	?	7%	?

Required:
1. What advantages are there to breaking down the ROI computation into two separate elements, margin and turnover?
2. Fill in the missing information above, and comment on the relative performance of the three companies in as much detail as the data permit. Make *specific recommendations* about how to improve the return on investment.

(Adapted from National Association of Accountants, *Research Report No. 35,* p. 34)

PROBLEM 12-23 Return on Investment (ROI) and Residual Income [LO2, LO3]
"I know headquarters wants us to add that new product line," said Dell Havasi, manager of Billings Company's Office Products Division. "But I want to see the numbers before I make any move. Our division's return on investment (ROI) has led the company for three years, and I don't want any letdown."

Billings Company is a decentralized wholesaler with five autonomous divisions. The divisions are evaluated on the basis of ROI, with year-end bonuses given to the divisional managers who have the highest ROIs. Operating results for the company's Office Products Division for the most recent year are given below:

Sales	$10,000,000
Variable expenses	6,000,000
Contribution margin	4,000,000
Fixed expenses	3,200,000
Net operating income............	$ 800,000
Divisional operating assets........	$ 4,000,000

The company had an overall return on investment (ROI) of 15% last year (considering all divisions). The Office Products Division has an opportunity to add a new product line that would require an additional investment in operating assets of $1,000,000. The cost and revenue characteristics of the new product line per year would be:

Sales	$2,000,000
Variable expenses	60% of sales
Fixed expenses..........	$640,000

Required:
1. Compute the Office Products Division's ROI for the most recent year; also compute the ROI as it would appear if the new product line is added.
2. If you were in Dell Havasi's position, would you accept or reject the new product line? Explain.
3. Why do you suppose headquarters is anxious for the Office Products Division to add the new product line?
4. Suppose that the company's minimum required rate of return on operating assets is 12% and that performance is evaluated using residual income.
    a. Compute the Office Products Division's residual income for the most recent year; also compute the residual income as it would appear if the new product line is added.
    b. Under these circumstances, if you were in Dell Havasi's position, would you accept or reject the new product line? Explain.

PROBLEM 12-24 (Appendix 12A) Basic Transfer Pricing [LO4]

Alpha and Beta are divisions within the same company. The managers of both divisions are evaluated based on their own division's return on investment (ROI). Assume the following information relative to the two divisions:

	Case			
	1	2	3	4
Alpha Division:				
Capacity in units	80,000	400,000	150,000	300,000
Number of units now being sold to				
outside customers	80,000	400,000	100,000	300,000
Selling price per unit to outside customers	$30	$90	$75	$50
Variable costs per unit	$18	$65	$40	$26
Fixed costs per unit (based on capacity)	$6	$15	$20	$9
Beta Division:				
Number of units needed annually	5,000	30,000	20,000	120,000
Purchase price now being paid to an				
outside supplier	$27	$89	$75*	—

*Before any quantity discount.

Managers are free to decide if they will participate in any internal transfers. All transfer prices are negotiated.

Required:

1. Refer to case 1 shown previously. Alpha Division can avoid $2 per unit in commissions on any sales to Beta Division. Will the managers agree to a transfer and if so, within what range will the transfer price be? Explain.
2. Refer to case 2 shown previously. A study indicates that Alpha Division can avoid $5 per unit in shipping costs on any sales to Beta Division.
    a. Would you expect any disagreement between the two divisional managers over what the transfer price should be? Explain.
    b. Assume that Alpha Division offers to sell 30,000 units to Beta Division for $88 per unit and that Beta Division refuses this price. What will be the loss in potential profits for the company as a whole?
3. Refer to case 3 shown previously. Assume that Beta Division is now receiving an 8% quantity discount from the outside supplier.
    a. Will the managers agree to a transfer? If so, what is the range within which the transfer price would be?
    b. Assume that Beta Division offers to purchase 20,000 units from Alpha Division at $60 per unit. If Alpha Division accepts this price, would you expect its ROI to increase, decrease, or remain unchanged? Why?
4. Refer to case 4 shown previously. Assume that Beta Division wants Alpha Division to provide it with 120,000 units of a *different* product from the one that Alpha Division is now producing. The new product would require $21 per unit in variable costs and would require that Alpha Division cut back production of its present product by 45,000 units annually. What is the lowest acceptable transfer price from Alpha Division's perspective?

PROBLEM 12-25 (Appendix 12B) Service Department Charges [LO5]

Sharp Motor Company has two operating divisions—an Auto Division and a Truck Division. The company has a cafeteria that serves the employees of both divisions. The costs of operating the cafeteria are budgeted at $40,000 per month plus $3 per meal served. The company pays all the cost of the meals.

The fixed costs of the cafeteria are determined by peak-period requirements. The Auto Division is responsible for 65% of the peak-period requirements, and the Truck Division is responsible for the other 35%.

For June, the Auto Division has estimated that it will need 35,000 meals served, and the Truck Division has estimated that it will need 20,000 meals served.

Required:

1. At the beginning of June, how much cafeteria cost should be allocated to each division for planning purposes?
2. Assume that it is now the end of June. Cost records in the cafeteria show that actual fixed costs for the month totaled $42,000 and that actual meal costs totaled $128,000. Due to unexpected layoffs of employees during the month, only 20,000 meals were served to the Auto Division. Another 20,000 meals were served to the Truck Division, as planned. How much of the actual cafeteria costs for the month should be allocated to each division? (Management uses these end-of-month allocations to compare actual performance with planned performance.)
3. Refer to the data in (2) above. Assume that the company follows the practice of allocating *all* cafeteria costs to the divisions in proportion to the number of meals served to each division during the month. On this basis, how much cost would be allocated to each division for June?
4. What criticisms can you make of the allocation method used in (3) above?
5. If managers of operating departments know that fixed service costs are going to be allocated on the basis of peak-period requirements, what will be their probable strategy as they report their estimate of peak-period requirements to the company's budget committee? As a member of top management, what would you do to neutralize such strategies?

PROBLEM 12-26 Segment Reporting and Decision-Making [LO1]
Vulcan Company's contribution format income statement for June is given below:

Vulcan Company Income Statement For the Month Ended June 30	
Sales	$750,000
Variable expenses	336,000
Contribution margin	414,000
Fixed expenses	378,000
Net operating income	$ 36,000

Management is disappointed with the company's performance and is wondering what can be done to improve profits. By examining sales and cost records, you have determined the following:

a. The company is divided into two sales territories—Northern and Southern. The Northern territory recorded $300,000 in sales and $156,000 in variable expenses during June; the remaining sales and variable expenses were recorded in the Southern territory. Fixed expenses of $120,000 and $108,000 are traceable to the Northern and Southern territories, respectively. The rest of the fixed expenses are common to the two territories.

b. The company is the exclusive distributor for two products—Paks and Tibs. Sales of Paks and Tibs totaled $50,000 and $250,000, respectively, in the Northern territory during June. Variable expenses are 22% of the selling price for Paks and 58% for Tibs. Cost records show that $30,000 of the Northern territory's fixed expenses are traceable to Paks and $40,000 to Tibs, with the remainder common to the two products.

Required:

1. Prepare contribution format segmented income statements first showing the total company broken down between sales territories and then showing the Northern territory broken down by product line. Show both Amount and Percent columns for the company in total and for each segment.
2. Look at the statement you have prepared showing the total company segmented by sales territory. What insights revealed by this statement should be brought to the attention of management?
3. Look at the statement you have prepared showing the Northern territory segmented by product lines. What insights revealed by this statement should be brought to the attention of management?

PROBLEM 12-27 Return on Investment (ROI) and Residual Income [LO2, LO3]
Financial data for Joel de Paris, Inc., for last year follow:

Joel de Paris, Inc. Balance Sheet	Ending Balance	Beginning Balance
Assets		
Cash	$ 120,000	$ 140,000
Accounts receivable	530,000	450,000
Inventory	380,000	320,000
Plant and equipment, net	620,000	680,000
Investment in Buisson, S.A.	280,000	250,000
Land (undeveloped)	170,000	180,000
Total assets	$2,100,000	$2,020,000
Liabilities and Stockholders' Equity		
Accounts payable	$ 310,000	$ 360,000
Long-term debt	1,500,000	1,500,000
Stockholders' equity	290,000	160,000
Total liabilities and stockholders' equity	$2,100,000	$2,020,000

Joel de Paris, Inc. Income Statement		
Sales		$4,050,000
Selling and administrative expenses		3,645,000
Net operating income		405,000
Interest and taxes:		
Interest expense	$150,000	
Tax expense	110,000	260,000
Net income		$ 145,000

The company paid dividends of $15,000 last year. The "Investment in Buisson, S.A.," on the balance sheet represents an investment in the stock of another company.

Required:
1. Compute the company's margin, turnover, and return on investment (ROI) for last year.
2. The board of directors of Joel de Paris, Inc., has set a minimum required return of 15%. What was the company's residual income last year?

PROBLEM 12-28 (Appendix 12A) Transfer Price with an Outside Market [LO4]
Hrubec Products, Inc., operates a Pulp Division that manufactures wood pulp for use in the production of various paper goods. Revenue and costs associated with a ton of pulp follow:

Selling price		$70
Expenses:		
Variable	$42	
Fixed (based on a capacity of 50,000 tons per year)	18	60
Net operating income		$10

Hrubec Products has just acquired a small company that manufactures paper cartons. This company will be treated as a division of Hrubec with full profit responsibility. The newly formed Carton Division is currently purchasing 5,000 tons of pulp per year from a supplier at a cost of $70 per ton, less a 10% quantity discount. Hrubec's president is anxious for the Carton Division to begin purchasing its pulp from the Pulp Division if an acceptable transfer price can be worked out.

Required:

For (1) and (2) below, assume that the Pulp Division can sell all of its pulp to outside customers for $70 per ton.

1. Are the managers of the Carton and Pulp Divisions likely to voluntarily agree to a transfer price for 5,000 tons of pulp next year? Why or why not?
2. If the Pulp Division meets the price that the Carton Division is currently paying to its supplier and sells 5,000 tons of pulp to the Carton Division each year, what will be the effect on the profits of the Pulp Division, the Carton Division, and the company as a whole?

    For (3)–(6) below, assume that the Pulp Division is currently selling only 30,000 tons of pulp each year to outside customers at the stated $70 price.

3. Are the managers of the Carton and Pulp Divisions likely to voluntarily agree to a transfer price for 5,000 tons of pulp next year? Why or why not?
4. Suppose that the Carton Division's outside supplier drops its price (net of the quantity discount) to only $59 per ton. Should the Pulp Division meet this price? Explain. If the Pulp Division does *not* meet the $59 price, what will be the effect on the profits of the company as a whole?
5. Refer to (4) above. If the Pulp Division refuses to meet the $59 price, should the Carton Division be required to purchase from the Pulp Division at a higher price for the good of the company as a whole?
6. Refer to (4) above. Assume that due to inflexible management policies, the Carton Division is required to purchase 5,000 tons of pulp each year from the Pulp Division at $70 per ton. What will be the effect on the profits of the company as a whole?

PROBLEM 12-29 Basic Segment Reporting; Activity-Based Cost Assignment [LO1]

Diversified Products, Inc., has recently acquired a small publishing company that Diversified Products intends to operate as one of its investment centers. The newly acquired company has three books that it offers for sale—a cookbook, a travel guide, and a handy speller. Each book sells for $10. The publishing company's most recent monthly income statement is given below:

	Total Company		Product Line Cookbook	Travel Guide	Handy Speller
Sales	$300,000	100%	$90,000	$150,000	$60,000
Expenses:					
Printing costs	102,000	34%	27,000	63,000	12,000
Advertising	36,000	12%	13,500	19,500	3,000
General sales	18,000	6%	5,400	9,000	3,600
Salaries	33,000	11%	18,000	9,000	6,000
Equipment depreciation	9,000	3%	3,000	3,000	3,000
Sales commissions	30,000	10%	9,000	15,000	6,000
General administration	42,000	14%	14,000	14,000	14,000
Warehouse rent	12,000	4%	3,600	6,000	2,400
Depreciation—office facilities	3,000	1%	1,000	1,000	1,000
Total expenses	285,000	95%	94,500	139,500	51,000
Net operating income (loss)	$ 15,000	5%	$ (4,500)	$ 10,500	$ 9,000

The following additional information is available about the company:

a. Only printing costs and sales commissions are variable; all other costs are fixed. The printing costs (which include materials, labor, and variable overhead) are traceable to the three product lines as shown in the statement above. Sales commissions are 10% of sales for any product.
b. The same equipment is used to produce all three books, so the equipment depreciation cost has been allocated equally among the three product lines. An analysis of the company's activities indicates that the equipment is used 30% of the time to produce cookbooks, 50% of the time to produce travel guides, and 20% of the time to produce handy spellers.
c. The warehouse is used to store finished units of product, so the rental cost has been allocated to the product lines on the basis of sales dollars. The warehouse rental cost is $3 per square foot per year. The warehouse contains 48,000 square feet of space, of which 7,200 square feet is used by the cookbook line, 24,000 square feet by the travel guide line, and 16,800 square feet by the handy speller line.

d. The general sales cost above includes the salary of the sales manager and other sales costs not traceable to any specific product line. This cost has been allocated to the product lines on the basis of sales dollars.

e. The general administration cost and depreciation of office facilities both relate to overall administration of the company as a whole. These costs have been allocated equally to the three product lines.

f. All other costs are traceable to the three product lines in the amounts shown on the statement above.

The management of Diversified Products, Inc., is anxious to improve the new investment center's 5% return on sales.

Required:

1. Prepare a new contribution format segmented income statement for the month. Show both an Amount column and a Percent column for the company as a whole and for each product line. Adjust allocations of equipment depreciation and of warehouse rent as indicated by the additional information provided.

2. After seeing the income statement in the main body of the problem, management has decided to eliminate the cookbook, since it is not returning a profit, and to focus all available resources on promoting the travel guide.

    a. Based on the statement you have prepared, do you agree with the decision to eliminate the cookbook? Explain.

    b. Based on the statement you have prepared, do you agree with the decision to focus all available resources on promoting the travel guide? Explain. (You may assume that an ample market is available for all three product lines.)

PROBLEM 12-30 Return on Investment (ROI) Analysis [LO2]

The contribution format income statement for Huerra Company for last year is given below:

		Total	Unit	
2	Sales	$4,000,000	$80.00	
3	Variable expenses	2,800,000	56.00	
4	Contribution margin	1,200,000	24.00	
5	Fixed expenses	840,000	16.80	
6	Net operating income	360,000	7.20	
7	Income taxes @ 30%	108,000	2.16	
8	Net income	$ 252,000	$ 5.04	

The company had average operating assets of $2,000,000 during the year.

Required:

1. Compute the company's return on investment (ROI) for the period using the ROI formula stated in terms of margin and turnover.

    For each of the following questions, indicate whether the margin and turnover will increase, decrease, or remain unchanged as a result of the events described, and then compute the new ROI figure. Consider each question separately, starting in each case from the data used to compute the original ROI in (1) above.

2. Using just-in-time (JIT), the company is able to reduce the average level of inventory by $400,000. (The released funds are used to pay off short-term creditors.)

3. The company achieves a cost savings of $32,000 per year by using less costly materials.

4. The company issues bonds and uses the proceeds to purchase $500,000 in machinery and equipment at the beginning of the period. Interest on the bonds is $60,000 per year. Sales remain unchanged. The new, more efficient equipment reduces production costs by $20,000 per year.

5. As a result of a more intense effort by salespeople, sales are increased by 20%; operating assets remain unchanged.

6. Obsolete inventory carried on the books at a cost of $40,000 is scrapped and written off as a loss.

7. The company uses $200,000 of cash (received on accounts receivable) to repurchase and retire some of its common stock.

PROBLEM 12-31 (Appendix 12A) Market-Based Transfer Price [LO4]

Stavos Company's Cabinet Division manufactures a standard cabinet for television sets. The cost per cabinet is:

Variable cost per cabinet	$70
Fixed cost per cabinet	30*
Total cost per cabinet	$100

*Based on a capacity of 10,000 cabinets per year.

Part of the Cabinet Division's output is sold to outside manufacturers of television sets and part is sold to Stavos Company's Quark Division, which produces a TV set under its own name. The Cabinet Division charges $140 per cabinet for all sales.

The costs, revenue, and net operating income associated with the Quark Division's TV set is given below:

Selling price per TV set.		$480
Variable costs per TV set:		
Cost of the cabinet	$140	
Variable cost of electronic parts.	210	
Total variable costs		350
Contribution margin		130
Fixed costs per TV set		80*
Net operating income per TV set		$ 50

*Based on a capacity of 3,000 sets per year.

The Quark Division has an order from an overseas source for 1,000 TV sets. The overseas source wants to pay only $340 per set.

Required:

1. Assume that the Quark Division has enough idle capacity to fill the 1,000-set order. Is the division likely to accept the $340 price or to reject it? Explain.
2. Assume that both the Cabinet Division and the Quark Division have idle capacity. Under these conditions, would it be advantageous for the company as a whole if the Quark Division rejects the $340 price? Show computations to support your answer.
3. Assume that the Quark Division has idle capacity but that the Cabinet Division is operating at capacity and could sell all of its cabinets to outside manufacturers. Compute the profit impact to the Quark Division of accepting the 1,000-set order at the $340 unit price.
4. What conclusions do you draw concerning the use of market price as a transfer price in intracompany transactions?

PROBLEM 12-32 (Appendix 12B) Service Department Charges [LO5]

Tasman Products, Ltd., of Australia has a Maintenance Department that services the equipment in the company's Forming Department and Assembly Department. The cost of this servicing is allocated to the operating departments on the basis of machine-hours. Cost and other data relating to the Maintenance Department and to the other two departments for the most recent year are presented below. (The currency in Australia is the Australian dollar.)

Data for the Maintenance Department follow:

	Budget	Actual
Variable costs for lubricants	$96,000*	$110,000
Fixed costs	$150,000	$153,000

*Budgeted at $0.40 per machine-hour.

Data for the Forming and Assembly departments follow:

	Percentage of Peak-Period Capacity Required	Machine-Hours Budget	Machine-Hours Actual
Forming Department	70%	160,000	190,000
Assembly Department........	30%	80,000	70,000
Total.....................	100%	240,000	260,000

The company allocates variable and fixed costs separately. The level of fixed costs in the Maintenance Department is determined by peak-period requirements.

Required:
1. Assume that it is the beginning of the year. How much of the budgeted Maintenance Department cost would be allocated to each department?
2. Assume that it is now the end of the year. Management would like data to assist in comparing actual performance to planned performance in the Maintenance Department and in the other departments.
    a. How much of the actual Maintenance Department costs should be allocated to the Forming Department and to the Assembly Department? Show all computations.
    b. Should any portion of the actual Maintenance Department costs not be allocated to the other departments? If all costs should be allocated, explain why; if a portion should not be allocated, compute the amount and explain why it should not be allocated.

PROBLEM 12-33 Multiple Segmented Income Statements [LO1]

Companhia Bradesco, S.A., of Brazil, an industrial supply store chain, has two divisions. The company's contribution format income statement segmented by divisions for last year is given below (the currency in Brazil is the real, denoted here by R):

	Total Company	Division Plastics	Division Glass
Sales	R1,500,000	R900,000	R600,000
Less variable expenses	700,000	400,000	300,000
Contribution margin	800,000	500,000	300,000
Less traceable fixed expenses:			
Advertising	300,000	180,000	120,000
Depreciation	140,000	92,000	48,000
Administration...................	220,000	118,000	102,000
Total	660,000	390,000	270,000
Divisional segment margin	140,000	R110,000	R 30,000
Less common fixed expenses	100,000		
Net operating income	R 40,000		

Top management doesn't understand why the Glass Division has such a low segment margin when its sales are only one-third less than sales in the Plastics Division. Accordingly, management has directed that the Glass Division be further segmented into product lines. The following information is available on the product lines in the Glass Division:

	Glass Division Product Lines Flat Glass	Auto Glass	Specialty Glass
Sales	R200,000	R300,000	R100,000
Traceable fixed expenses:			
Advertising..................	R30,000	R42,000	R48,000
Depreciation.................	R10,000	R24,000	R14,000
Administration	R14,000	R21,000	R7,000
Variable expenses as a percentage of sales...........	65%	40%	50%

Analysis shows that R60,000 of the Glass Division's administration expenses are common to the product lines.

Required:

1. Prepare a contribution format segmented income statement for the Glass Division with segments defined as product lines.
2. Management is surprised by Specialty Glass's poor showing and would like to have the product line segmented by market. The following information is available about the two markets in which Specialty Glass is sold:

	Specialty Glass Markets	
	Domestic	Foreign
Sales	R60,000	R40,000
Traceable fixed expenses:		
Advertising	R18,000	R30,000
Variable expenses as a		
percentage of sales...........	50%	50%

All of Specialty Glass's depreciation and administration expenses are common to the markets in which the product is sold. Prepare a contribution format segmented income statement for Specialty Glass with segments defined as markets. Show both Amount and Percent columns.

3. Refer to the statement prepared in (1) above. The sales manager wants to run a special promotional campaign on one of the products over the next month. A market study indicates that such a campaign would increase sales of Flat Glass by R40,000 or sales of Auto Glass by R30,000. The campaign would cost R8,000. Show computations to determine which product line should be chosen.

Cases

CASE 12-34 Service Organization; Segment Reporting [LO1]

Music Teachers, Inc., is an educational association for music teachers that has 20,000 members. The association operates from a central headquarters but has local membership chapters throughout the United States. Monthly meetings are held by the local chapters to discuss recent developments on topics of interest to music teachers. The association's journal, *Teachers' Forum,* is issued monthly with features about recent developments in the field. The association publishes books and reports and also sponsors professional courses that qualify for continuing professional education credit. The association's statement of revenues and expenses for the current year is presented below.

Music Teachers, Inc. Statement of Revenues and Expenses For the Year Ended November 30	
Revenues.......................................	$3,275,000
Expenses:	
Salaries	920,000
Personnel costs	230,000
Occupancy costs	280,000
Reimbursement of member costs to local chapters	600,000
Other membership services	500,000
Printing and paper	320,000
Postage and shipping.............................	176,000
Instructors' fees	80,000
General and administrative.........................	38,000
Total expenses.................................	3,144,000
Excess of revenues over expenses	$ 131,000

The board of directors of Music Teachers, Inc., has requested that a segmented income statement be prepared showing the contribution of each profit center to the association. The association has four profit centers: Membership Division, Magazine Subscriptions Division, Books and Reports Division, and Continuing Education Division. Mike Doyle has been assigned responsibility for preparing the segmented income statement, and he has gathered the following data prior to its preparation.

a. Membership dues are $100 per year, of which $20 is considered to cover a one-year subscription to the association's journal. Other benefits include membership in the association and chapter affiliation. The portion of the dues covering the magazine subscription ($20) should be assigned to the Magazine Subscription Division.

b. One-year subscriptions to *Teachers' Forum* were sold to nonmembers and libraries at $30 per subscription. A total of 2,500 of these subscriptions were sold last year. In addition to subscriptions, the magazine generated $100,000 in advertising revenues. The costs per magazine subscription were $7 for printing and paper and $4 for postage and shipping.

c. A total of 28,000 technical reports and professional texts were sold by the Books and Reports Division at an average unit selling price of $25. Average costs per publication were $4 for printing and paper and $2 for postage and shipping.

d. The association offers a variety of continuing education courses to both members and nonmembers. The one-day courses had a tuition cost of $75 each and were attended by 2,400 students. A total of 1,760 students took two-day courses at a tuition cost of $125 for each student. Outside instructors were paid to teach some courses.

e. Salary costs and space occupied by division follow:

	Salaries	Space Occupied (square feet)
Membership	$210,000	2,000
Magazine Subscriptions.	150,000	2,000
Books and Reports	300,000	3,000
Continuing Education.	180,000	2,000
Corporate staff	80,000	1,000
Total	$920,000	10,000

Personnel costs are 25% of salaries in the separate divisions as well as for the corporate staff. The $280,000 in occupancy costs includes $50,000 in rental cost for a warehouse used by the Books and Reports Division for storage purposes.

f. Printing and paper costs other than for magazine subscriptions and for books and reports relate to the Continuing Education Division.

g. General and administrative expenses include costs relating to overall administration of the association as a whole. The company's corporate staff does some mailing of materials for general administrative purposes.

The expenses that can be traced or assigned to the corporate staff, as well as any other expenses that are not traceable to the profit centers, will be treated as common costs. It is not necessary to distinguish between variable and fixed costs.

Required:

1. Prepare a contribution format segmented income statement for Music Teachers, Inc. This statement should show the segment margin for each division as well as results for the association as a whole.

2. Give arguments for and against allocating *all* costs of the association to the four divisions.

(CMA, adapted)

CASE 12-35 (Appendix 12A) Transfer Pricing; Divisional Performance [LO4]

Weller Industries is a decentralized organization with six divisions. The company's Electrical Division produces a variety of electrical items, including an X52 electrical fitting. The Electrical Division (which is operating at capacity) sells this fitting to its regular customers for $7.50 each; the fitting has a variable manufacturing cost of $4.25.

The company's Brake Division has asked the Electrical Division to supply it with a large quantity of X52 fittings for only $5 each. The Brake Division, which is operating at 50% of capacity, will put the fitting into a brake unit that it will produce and sell to a large commercial airline manufacturer. The cost of the brake unit being built by the Brake Division follows:

Purchased parts (from outside vendors).........	$22.50
Electrical fitting X52	5.00
Other variable costs	14.00
Fixed overhead and administration............	8.00
Total cost per brake unit	$49.50

Although the $5 price for the X52 fitting represents a substantial discount from the regular $7.50 price, the manager of the Brake Division believes that the price concession is necessary if his division is to get the contract for the airplane brake units. He has heard "through the grapevine" that the airplane manufacturer plans to reject his bid if it is more than $50 per brake unit. Thus, if the Brake Division is forced to pay the regular $7.50 price for the X52 fitting, it will either not get the contract or it will suffer a substantial loss at a time when it is already operating at only 50% of capacity. The manager of the Brake Division argues that the price concession is imperative to the well-being of both his division and the company as a whole.

Weller Industries uses return on investment (ROI) to measure divisional performance.

Required:
1. Assume that you are the manager of the Electrical Division. Would you recommend that your division supply the X52 fitting to the Brake Division for $5 each as requested? Why or why not? Show all computations.
2. Would it be profitable for the company as a whole for the Electrical Division to supply the fittings to the Brake Division if the airplane brakes can be sold for $50? Show all computations, and explain your answer.
3. In principle, should it be possible for the two managers to agree to a transfer price in this particular situation? If so, within what range would that transfer price lie?
4. Discuss the organizational and manager behavior problems, if any, inherent in this situation. What would you advise the company's president to do in this situation?

(CMA, adapted)

RESEARCH AND APPLICATION 12–36 [LO1, LO2, LO3]

The questions in this exercise are based on FedEx Corporation. To answer the questions, you will need to download FedEx's 2005 10-K at http://ir.fedex.com/finance/edgar.cfm. You do not need to print the 10-K to answer the questions.

Required:
1. What is FedEx's strategy for success in the marketplace? Does the company rely primarily on a customer intimacy, operational excellence, or product leadership customer value proposition? What evidence supports your conclusion?
2. What are FedEx's four main business segments? Provide two examples of traceable fixed costs for each of FedEx's four business segments. Provide two examples of common costs that are not traceable to the four business segments.
3. Identify one example of a cost center, a profit center, and an investment center for FedEx.
4. Provide three examples of fixed costs that can be traceable or common depending on how FedEx defines its business segments.
5. Compute the margin, turnover, and return on investment (ROI) in 2005 for each of FedEx's four business segments. (Hint: page 99 reports total segment assets for each business segment).
6. Assume that FedEx established a minimum required rate of return of 15% for each of its business segments. Compute the residual income earned in 2005 in each of FedEx's four segments.
7. Assume that the senior managers of FedEx Express and FedEx Ground each have an investment opportunity that would require $20 million of additional operating assets and that would increase operating income by $4 million. If FedEx evaluates all of its senior managers using ROI, would the managers of both segments pursue the investment opportunity? If FedEx evaluates all of its senior managers using residual income, would the managers of both segments pursue the investment opportunity?

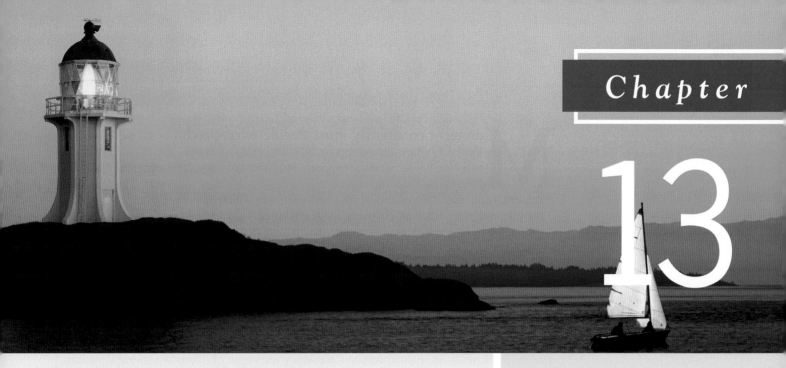

Relevant Costs for Decision Making

Massaging the Numbers

Building and expanding convention centers appears to be an obsession with politicians. Indeed, billions of dollars are being spent to build or expand convention centers in 44 cities across the United States—adding more than 7 million square feet of convention space to the 64 million square feet that already exists. Given that trade show attendance across the country has been steadily declining, how do politicians justify these enormous investments? Politicians frequently rely on consultants who produce studies that purport to show the convention center will have a favorable economic impact on the area.

These economic impact studies are bogus in two respects. First, a large portion of the so-called favorable economic impact that is cited by consultants would be realized by a city even if it did not invest in a new or expanded convention center. For example, Portland, Oregon, voters overwhelmingly opposed spending $82 million to expand their city's convention center. Nonetheless, local politicians proceeded with the project. After completing the expansion, more than 70% of the people spending money at trade shows in Portland were from the Portland area. How much of the money spent by these locals would have been spent in Portland anyway if the convention center had not been expanded? We don't know, but in all likelihood much of this money would have been spent at the zoo, the art museum, the theater, local restaurants, and so on. This portion of the "favorable" economic impact cited by consultants and used by politicians to justify expanding convention centers should be ignored. Second, since the supply of convention centers throughout the United States substantially exceeds demand, convention centers must offer substantial economic incentives, such as waiving rental fees, to attract trade shows. The cost of these concessions, although often excluded from consultants' projections, further erodes the genuine economic viability of building or expanding a convention center. ■

Source: Victoria Murphy, "The Answer Is Always Yes," *Forbes*, February 28, 2005, pp. 82–84.

BUSINESS FOCUS

Learning Objectives

After studying Chapter 13, you should be able to:

LO1 Identify relevant and irrelevant costs and benefits in a decision.

LO2 Prepare an analysis showing whether a product line or other business segment should be dropped or retained.

LO3 Prepare a make or buy analysis.

LO4 Prepare an analysis showing whether a special order should be accepted.

LO5 Determine the most profitable use of a constrained resource and the value of obtaining more of the constrained resource.

LO6 Prepare an analysis showing whether joint products should be sold at the split-off point or processed further.

Managers constantly must decide what products to sell, whether to make or buy component parts, what prices to charge, what channels of distribution to use, whether to accept special orders at special prices, and so forth. Making such decisions is often a difficult task that is complicated by numerous alternatives and massive amounts of data, only some of which may be relevant.

Every decision involves choosing from among at least two alternatives. In making a decision, the costs and benefits of one alternative must be compared to the costs and benefits of other alternatives. Costs that differ between alternatives are called **relevant costs.** Distinguishing between relevant and irrelevant costs and benefits is critical for two reasons. First, irrelevant data can be ignored—saving decision makers tremendous amounts of time and effort. Second, bad decisions can easily result from erroneously including irrelevant costs and benefits when analyzing alternatives. To be successful in decision making, managers must be able to tell the difference between relevant and irrelevant data and must be able to correctly use the relevant data in analyzing alternatives. The purpose of this chapter is to develop these skills by illustrating their use in a wide range of decision-making situations. These decision-making skills are as important in your personal life as they are to managers. After completing your study of this chapter, you should be able to think more clearly about decisions in many facets of your life.

Cost Concepts for Decision Making

LEARNING OBJECTIVE 1
Identify relevant and irrelevant costs and benefits in a decision.

Four cost terms discussed in Chapter 2 are particularly applicable to this chapter. These terms are *differential costs, incremental costs, opportunity costs,* and *sunk costs.* You may find it helpful to turn back to Chapter 2 and refresh your memory concerning these terms before reading on.

Identifying Relevant Costs and Benefits

Only those costs and benefits that differ in total between alternatives are relevant in a decision. If the total amount of a cost will be the same regardless of the alternative selected, then the decision has no effect on the cost and it can be ignored. For example, if you are trying to decide whether to go to a movie or to rent a videotape for the evening, the rent on your apartment is irrelevant. Whether you go to a movie or rent a videotape, the rent on your apartment will be exactly the same and is therefore irrelevant to the decision. On the other hand, the cost of the movie ticket and the cost of renting the videotape would be relevant in the decision because they are *avoidable costs.*

An **avoidable cost** is a cost that can be eliminated in whole or in part by choosing one alternative over another. By choosing the alternative of going to the movie, the cost of renting the videotape can be avoided. By choosing the alternative of renting the videotape, the cost of the movie ticket can be avoided. Therefore, the cost of the movie ticket and the cost of renting the videotape are both avoidable costs. On the other hand, the rent on the apartment is not an avoidable cost of either alternative. You would continue to rent your apartment under either alternative. Avoidable costs are relevant costs. Unavoidable costs are irrelevant costs.

Two broad categories of costs are never relevant in decisions. These irrelevant costs are:

1. Sunk costs.
2. Future costs that do not differ between the alternatives.

As we learned in Chapter 2, a **sunk cost** is a cost that has already been incurred and cannot be avoided regardless of what a manager decides to do. For example, suppose a used car dealer purchased a five-year-old Toyota Camry for $12,000. The amount paid for the Camry is a sunk cost because it has already been incurred and the transaction cannot be undone. Sunk costs are always the same no matter what alternatives are being considered; therefore, they are irrelevant and should be ignored when making decisions. Future costs that do not differ between alternatives should also be ignored when making decisions. Continuing with the example discussed earlier, suppose you intend to order a pizza after you go to the movie theater or you rent a video. In that case, if you are going to buy the same pizza regardless of your choice of entertainment, its cost is irrelevant to the choice of whether you go to the movie theater or rent a video. Notice, the cost of the pizza is not a sunk cost because it has not yet been incurred. Nonetheless, the cost of the pizza is irrelevant to the entertainment decision because it is a future cost that does not differ between the alternatives.

The term **differential cost** was also introduced in Chapter 2. In managerial accounting, the terms *avoidable cost, differential cost, incremental cost,* and *relevant cost* are often used interchangeably. To identify the costs that are avoidable in a particular decision situation and are therefore relevant, these steps should be followed:

1. Eliminate costs and benefits that do not differ between alternatives. These irrelevant costs consist of (a) sunk costs and (b) future costs that do not differ between alternatives.
2. Use the remaining costs and benefits that do differ between alternatives in making the decision. The costs that remain are the differential, or avoidable, costs.

THE RELEVANT COST OF EXECUTIVE PERKS

The Securities and Exchange Commission is concerned about CEOs who use company-owned airplanes for personal travel. For example, consider a CEO who uses his employers' Gulfstream V luxury airplane to transport his family on a 2,000 mile roundtrip vacation from New York City to Orlando, Florida. The standard practice among companies with personal travel reimbursement policies would be to charge their CEO $1,500 for this flight based on a per-mile reimbursement rate established by the Internal Revenue Service (the IRS rates are meant to approximate the per-mile cost of a first-class ticket on a commercial airline). However, critics argue that using IRS reimbursement rates grossly understates the flight costs that are borne by shareholders. Some of these critics claim that the $11,000 incremental cost of the flight, including fuel, landing fees, and crew hotel charges, should be reimbursed by the CEO. Still others argue that even basing reimbursements on incremental costs understates the true cost of a flight because it excludes fixed costs such as the cost of the airplane, crew salaries, and insurance. These costs are relevant because the excessive amount of personal travel by corporate executives essentially requires their employers to purchase, insure, and staff additional airplanes. This latter group of critics argues that the relevant cost of the trip from New York City to Orlando is $43,000—the market price that would have to be paid to charter a comparable size airplane for this flight. What do you think should be the relevant cost of this flight? Should shareholders expect their CEO to reimburse $0 (as is the practice at some companies), $1,500, $11,000, or $43,000? Or, should all companies disallow personal use of corporate assets?

Source: Mark Maremont, "Amid Crackdown, the Jet Perk Suddenly Looks a Lot Pricier," *The Wall Street Journal,* May 25, 2005, pp. A1 and A8.

Different Costs for Different Purposes

We need to recognize a fundamental concept of managerial accounting from the outset of our discussion—costs that are relevant in one decision situation are not necessarily relevant in another. This means that *managers need different costs for different purposes.* For one purpose, a particular group of costs may be relevant; for another purpose, an entirely different group of costs may be relevant. Thus, *each* decision situation must be carefully analyzed to isolate the relevant costs. Otherwise, irrelevant data may cloud the situation and lead to a bad decision.

The concept of "different costs for different purposes" is basic to managerial accounting; we shall frequently see its application in the pages that follow.

An Example of Identifying Relevant Costs and Benefits

Cynthia is currently a student in an MBA program in Boston and would like to visit a friend in New York City over the weekend. She is trying to decide whether to drive or take the train. Because she is on a tight budget, she wants to carefully consider the costs of the two alternatives. If one alternative is far less expensive than the other, that may be decisive in her choice. By car, the distance between her apartment in Boston and her friend's apartment in New York City is 230 miles. Cynthia has compiled the following list of items to consider:

Automobile Costs		
Item	Annual Cost of Fixed Items	Cost per Mile (based on 10,000 miles per year)
(a) Annual straight-line depreciation on car [($24,000 original cost − $10,000 estimated resale value in 5 years)/5 years]	$2,800	$0.280
(b) Cost of gasoline ($1.60 per gallon ÷ 32 miles per gallon)		0.050
(c) Annual cost of auto insurance and license	$1,380	0.138
(d) Maintenance and repairs		0.065
(e) Parking fees at school ($45 per month × 8 months)	$360	0.036
(f) Total average cost per mile		$0.569

Additional Data	
Item	
(g) Reduction in the resale value of car due solely to wear and tear	$0.026 per mile
(h) Cost of round-trip Amtrak ticket from Boston to New York City	$104
(i) Benefit of relaxing and being able to study during the train ride rather than having to drive	?
(j) Cost of putting the dog in a kennel while gone	$40
(k) Benefit of having a car available in New York City	?
(l) Hassle of parking the car in New York City	?
(m) Cost of parking the car in New York City	$25 per day

Which costs and benefits are relevant in this decision? Remember, only those costs and benefits that differ between alternatives are relevant. Everything else is irrelevant and can be ignored.

Start at the top of the list with item (a): the original cost of the car is a sunk cost. This cost has already been incurred and therefore can never differ between alternatives. Consequently, it is irrelevant and should be ignored. The same is true of the accounting depreciation of $2,800 per year, which simply spreads the sunk cost across five years.

Item (b), the cost of gasoline consumed by driving to New York City, is a relevant cost. If Cynthia takes the train, this cost would not be incurred. Hence, the cost differs between alternatives and is therefore relevant.

Item (c), the annual cost of auto insurance and license, is not relevant. Whether Cynthia takes the train or drives on this particular trip, her annual auto insurance premium and her auto license fee will remain the same.[1]

---

[1]　If Cynthia has an accident while driving to New York City or back, this might affect her insurance premium when the policy is renewed. The increase in the insurance premium would be a relevant cost of this particular trip, but the normal amount of the insurance premium is not relevant in any case.

Item (d), the cost of maintenance and repairs, is relevant. While maintenance and repair costs have a large random component, over the long run they should be more or less proportional to the number of miles the car is driven. Thus, the average cost of $0.065 per mile is a reasonable estimate to use.

Item (e), the monthly fee that Cynthia pays to park at her school during the academic year is not relevant. Regardless of which alternative she selects—driving or taking the train—she will still need to pay for parking at school.

Item (f) is the total average cost of $0.569 per mile. As discussed above, some elements of this total are relevant, but some are not relevant. Since it contains some irrelevant costs, it would be incorrect to estimate the cost of driving to New York City and back by simply multiplying the $0.569 by 460 miles (230 miles each way × 2). This erroneous approach would yield a cost of driving of $261.74. Unfortunately, such mistakes are often made in both personal life and in business. Since the total cost is stated on a per-mile basis, people are easily misled. Often people think that if the cost is stated as $0.569 per mile, the cost of driving 100 miles is $56.90. But it is not. Many of the costs included in the $0.569 cost per mile are sunk and/or fixed and will not increase if the car is driven another 100 miles. The $0.569 is an average cost, not an incremental cost. Beware of such unitized costs (i.e., costs stated in terms of a dollar amount per unit, per mile, per direct labor-hour, per machine-hour, and so on)—they are often misleading.

Item (g), the decline in the resale value of the car that occurs as a consequence of driving more miles, is relevant in the decision. Because she uses the car, its resale value declines, which is a real cost of using the car that should be taken into account. Cynthia estimated this cost by accessing the *Kelly Blue Book* website at www.kbb.com. The reduction in resale value of an asset through use or over time is often called *real* or *economic depreciation*. This is different from accounting depreciation, which attempts to match the sunk cost of an asset with the periods that benefit from that cost.

Item (h), the $104 cost of a round-trip ticket on Amtrak, is relevant in this decision. If she drives, she would not have to buy the ticket.

Item (i) is relevant to the decision, even if it is difficult to put a dollar value on relaxing and being able to study while on the train. It is relevant because it is a benefit that is available under one alternative but not under the other.

Item (j), the cost of putting Cynthia's dog in the kennel while she is gone, is irrelevant in this decision. Whether she takes the train or drives to New York City, she will still need to put her dog in a kennel.

Like item (i), items (k) and (l) are relevant to the decision even if it is difficult to measure their dollar impacts.

Item (m), the cost of parking in New York City, is relevant to the decision.

Bringing together all of the relevant data, Cynthia would estimate the relevant costs of driving and taking the train as follows:

Relevant financial cost of driving to New York City:

Gasoline (460 miles at $0.050 per mile)	$ 23.00
Maintenance and repairs (460 miles @ $0.065 per mile)	29.90
Reduction in the resale value of car due solely to wear and tear (460 miles @ $0.026 per mile)	11.96
Cost of parking the car in New York City (2 days @ $25 per day)	50.00
Total	$114.86

Relevant financial cost of taking the train to New York City:

Cost of round-trip Amtrak ticket from Boston to New York City	$104.00

What should Cynthia do? From a purely financial standpoint, it would be cheaper by $10.86 ($114.86 − $104.00) to take the train than to drive. Cynthia has to decide if the convenience of having a car in New York City outweighs the additional cost and the disadvantages of being unable to relax and study on the train and the hassle of finding parking in the city.

In this example, we focused on identifying the relevant costs and benefits—everything else was ignored. In the next example, we include all of the costs and benefits—relevant or not. Nonetheless, we'll still get the correct answer because the irrelevant costs and benefits will cancel out when we compare the alternatives.

Reconciling the Total and Differential Approaches

Oak Harbor Woodworks is considering a new labor-saving machine that rents for $3,000 per year. The machine will be used on the company's butcher block production line. Data concerning the company's annual sales and costs of butcher blocks with and without the new machine are shown below:

	Current Situation	Situation with the New Machine
Units produced and sold	5,000	5,000
Selling price per unit	$40	$40
Direct materials cost per unit	$14	$14
Direct labor cost per unit	$8	$5
Variable overhead cost per unit	$2	$2
Fixed costs, other	$62,000	$62,000
Fixed costs, rental of new machine	—	$3,000

Given the data above, the net operating income for the product under the two alternatives can be computed as shown in Exhibit 13–1.

Note that the net operating income is $12,000 higher with the new machine, so that is the better alternative. Note also that the $12,000 advantage for the new machine can be obtained in two different ways. It is the difference between the $30,000 net operating income with the new machine and the $18,000 net operating income for the current situation. It is also the sum of the differential costs and benefits as shown in the last column of Exhibit 13–1. A positive number in the Differential Costs and Benefits column indicates that the difference between the alternatives favors the new machine; a negative number indicates that the difference favors the current situation. A zero in that column simply means that the total amount for the item is exactly the same for both alternatives. Thus, since the difference in the net operating incomes equals the sum of the differences for the individual items, any cost or benefit that is the same for both alternatives will have no impact on which alternative is preferred. This is the reason that costs and benefits that do not differ between alternatives are irrelevant and can be ignored. If we properly account for them, they will cancel out when we compare the alternatives.

EXHIBIT 13–1
Total and Differential Costs

	Current Situation	Situation with New Machine	Differential Costs and Benefits
Sales (5,000 units @ $40 per unit)	$200,000	$200,000	$ 0
Variable expenses:			
Direct materials (5,000 units @ $14 per unit).	70,000	70,000	0
Direct labor (5,000 units @ $8 and $5 per unit).	40,000	25,000	15,000
Variable overhead (5,000 units @ $2 per unit).	10,000	10,000	0
Total variable expenses.	120,000	105,000	
Contribution margin.	80,000	95,000	
Fixed expenses:			
Other.	62,000	62,000	0
Rent of new machine.	0	3,000	(3,000)
Total fixed expenses	62,000	65,000	
Net operating income	$ 18,000	$ 30,000	$12,000

We could have arrived at the same solution much more quickly by completely ignoring the irrelevant costs and benefits.

- The selling price per unit and the number of units sold do not differ between the alternatives. Therefore, the total sales revenues are exactly the same for the two alternatives as shown in Exhibit 13–1. Since the sales revenues are exactly the same, they have no effect on the difference in net operating income between the two alternatives. That is shown in the last column in Exhibit 13–1, which shows a $0 differential benefit.

- The direct materials cost per unit, the variable overhead cost per unit, and the number of units produced and sold do not differ between the alternatives. Consequently, the total direct materials cost and the total variable overhead cost will be the same for the two alternatives and can be ignored.

- The "other" fixed expenses do not differ between the alternatives, so they can be ignored as well.

Indeed, the only costs that do differ between the alternatives are direct labor costs and the fixed rental cost of the new machine. Hence, the two alternatives can be compared based only on these relevant costs:

Net Advantage of Renting the New Machine	
Decrease in direct labor costs (5,000 units at a cost savings of $3 per unit)	$15,000
Increase in fixed expenses	(3,000)
Net annual cost savings from renting the new machine	$12,000

If we focus on just the relevant costs and benefits, we get exactly the same answer as when we listed all of the costs and benefits—including those that do not differ between the alternatives and hence are irrelevant. We get the same answer because the only costs and benefits that matter in the final comparison of the net operating incomes are those that differ between the two alternatives and hence are not zero in the last column of Exhibit 13–1. Those two relevant costs are both listed in the above analysis showing the net advantage of renting the new machine.

Why Isolate Relevant Costs?

In the preceding example, we used two different approaches to analyze the alternatives. First, we considered all costs, both those that were relevant and those that were not; and second, we considered only the relevant costs. We obtained the same answer under both approaches. It would be natural to ask, "Why bother to isolate relevant costs when total costs will do the job just as well?" Isolating relevant costs is desirable for at least two reasons.

First, only rarely will enough information be available to prepare a detailed income statement for both alternatives. Assume, for example, that you are called on to make a decision relating to a portion of a single business process in a multidepartmental, multiproduct company. Under these circumstances, it would be virtually impossible to prepare an income statement of any type. You would have to rely on your ability to recognize which costs are relevant and which are not in order to assemble the data necessary to make a decision.

Second, mingling irrelevant costs with relevant costs may cause confusion and distract attention from the information that is really critical. Furthermore, the danger always exists that an irrelevant piece of data may be used improperly, resulting in an incorrect decision. The best approach is to ignore irrelevant data and base the decision entirely on relevant data.

Relevant cost analysis, combined with the contribution approach to the income statement, provides a powerful tool for making decisions. We will investigate various uses of this tool in the remaining sections of this chapter.

IN BUSINESS

ENVIRONMENTAL COSTS ADD UP

A decision analysis can be flawed by incorrectly including irrelevant costs such as sunk costs and future costs that do not differ between alternatives. It can also be flawed by omitting future costs that *do* differ between alternatives. This is a problem particularly with environmental costs because they have dramatically increased in recent years and are often overlooked by managers.

Consider the environmental complications posed by a decision of whether to install a solvent-based or powder-based system for spray-painting parts. In a solvent painting system, parts are sprayed as they move along a conveyor. The paint that misses the part is swept away by a wall of water, called a water curtain. The excess paint accumulates in a pit as sludge that must be removed each month. Environmental regulations classify this sludge as hazardous waste. As a result, a permit must be obtained to produce the waste and meticulous records must be maintained of how the waste is transported, stored, and disposed of. The annual costs of complying with these regulations can easily exceed $140,000 in total for a painting facility that initially costs only $400,000 to build. The costs of complying with environmental regulations include the following:

- The waste sludge must be hauled to a special disposal site. The typical disposal fee is about $300 per barrel, or $55,000 per year for a modest solvent-based painting system.
- Workers must be specially trained to handle the paint sludge.
- The company must carry special insurance.
- The company must pay substantial fees to the state for releasing pollutants (i.e., the solvent) into the air.
- The water in the water curtain must be specially treated to remove contaminants. This can cost tens of thousands of dollars per year.

In contrast, a powder-based painting system avoids almost all of these environmental costs. Excess powder used in the painting process can be recovered and reused without creating a hazardous waste. Additionally, the powder-based system does not release contaminants into the atmosphere. Therefore, even though the cost of building a powder-based system may be higher than the cost of building a solvent-based system, over the long run the costs of the powder-based system may be far lower due to the high environmental costs of a solvent-based system. Managers need to be aware of such environmental costs and take them fully into account when making decisions.

Source: Germain Böer, Margaret Curtin, and Louis Hoyt, "Environmental Cost Management," *Management Accounting*, September 1998, pp. 28–38.

Adding and Dropping Product Lines and Other Segments

Decisions relating to whether product lines or other segments of a company should be dropped and new ones added are among the most difficult that a manager has to make. In such decisions, many qualitative and quantitative factors must be considered. Ultimately, however, any final decision to drop a business segment or to add a new one is going to hinge primarily on the impact the decision will have on net operating income. To assess this impact, costs must be carefully analyzed.

LEARNING OBJECTIVE 2
Prepare an analysis showing whether a product line or other business segment should be dropped or retained.

An Illustration of Cost Analysis

Exhibit 13–2 provides sales and cost information for the preceding month for the Discount Drug Company and its three major product lines—drugs, cosmetics, and housewares. A quick review of this exhibit suggests that dropping the housewares segment would increase the company's overall net operating income by $8,000. However, this would be a flawed conclusion because the data in Exhibit 13–2 do not distinguish between fixed expenses that can be avoided if a product line is dropped and common fixed expenses that cannot be avoided by dropping any particular product line.

In this scenario, the two alternatives under consideration are keeping the housewares product line and dropping the housewares product line. Therefore, only those costs that differ between these two alternatives (i.e., that can be avoided by dropping the housewares product line) are relevant. In deciding whether to drop housewares, it is crucial to identify which costs can be avoided, and hence are relevant to the decision, and which costs cannot be avoided, and hence are irrelevant. The decision should be analyzed as follows.

If the housewares line is dropped, then the company will lose $20,000 per month in contribution margin, but by dropping the line it may be possible to avoid some fixed costs such as salaries or advertising costs. If dropping the housewares line enables the company to avoid more in fixed costs than it loses in contribution margin, then its overall net operating income will improve by eliminating the product line. On the other hand, if the company is not able to avoid as much in fixed costs as it loses in contribution margin, then the housewares line should be kept. In short, the manager should ask, "What costs can I avoid if I drop this product line?"

As we have seen from our earlier discussion, not all costs are avoidable. For example, some of the costs associated with a product line may be sunk costs. Other costs may be allocated fixed costs that will not differ in total regardless of whether the product line is dropped or retained.

Topic Tackler

PLUS

13–1

EXHIBIT 13–2
Discount Drug Company Product Lines

		Product Line		
	Total	Drugs	Cosmetics	House-wares
Sales	$250,000	$125,000	$75,000	$50,000
Variable expenses	105,000	50,000	25,000	30,000
Contribution margin	145,000	75,000	50,000	20,000
Fixed expenses:				
Salaries	50,000	29,500	12,500	8,000
Advertising	15,000	1,000	7,500	6,500
Utilities	2,000	500	500	1,000
Depreciation—fixtures	5,000	1,000	2,000	2,000
Rent	20,000	10,000	6,000	4,000
Insurance	3,000	2,000	500	500
General administrative	30,000	15,000	9,000	6,000
Total fixed expenses.	125,000	59,000	38,000	28,000
Net operating income (loss)	$ 20,000	$ 16,000	$12,000	$ (8,000)

To show how to proceed in a product-line analysis, suppose that Discount Drug Company has analyzed the fixed costs being charged to the three product lines and has determined the following:

1. The salaries expense represents salaries paid to employees working directly on the product. All of the employees working in housewares would be discharged if the product line is dropped.
2. The advertising expense represents advertisements that are specific to each product line and are avoidable if the line is dropped.
3. The utilities expense represents utilities costs for the entire company. The amount charged to each product line is an allocation based on space occupied and is not avoidable if the product line is dropped.
4. The depreciation expense represents depreciation on fixtures used to display the various product lines. Although the fixtures are nearly new, they are custom-built and will have no resale value if the housewares line is dropped.
5. The rent expense represents rent on the entire building housing the company; it is allocated to the product lines on the basis of sales dollars. The monthly rent of $20,000 is fixed under a long-term lease agreement.
6. The insurance expense is for insurance carried on inventories within each of the three product lines. If housewares is dropped, the related inventories will be liquidated and the insurance premiums will decrease accordingly.
7. The general administrative expense represents the costs of accounting, purchasing, and general management, which are allocated to the product lines on the basis of sales dollars. These costs will not change if the housewares line is dropped.

With this information, management can determine that $15,000 of the fixed expenses associated with the housewares product line are avoidable and $13,000 are not:

Fixed Expenses	Total Cost Assigned to Housewares	Not Avoidable*	Avoidable
Salaries	$ 8,000		$ 8,000
Advertising	6,500		6,500
Utilities	1,000	$ 1,000	
Depreciation—fixtures	2,000	2,000	
Rent	4,000	4,000	
Insurance	500		500
General administrative	6,000	6,000	
Total	$28,000	$13,000	$15,000

*These fixed costs represent either sunk costs or future costs that will not change whether the housewares line is retained or discontinued.

As stated earlier, if the housewares product line were dropped, the company would lose the product's contribution margin of $20,000, but would save its associated avoidable fixed expenses. We now know that those avoidable fixed expenses total $15,000. Therefore, dropping the housewares product line would result in a $5,000 *reduction* in net operating income as shown below:

Contribution margin lost if the housewares line is discontinued (see Exhibit 13–2)	$(20,000)
Less fixed costs that can be avoided if the housewares line is discontinued (see above)	15,000
Decrease in overall company net operating income	$ (5,000)

In this case, the fixed costs that can be avoided by dropping the housewares product line ($15,000) are less than the contribution margin that will be lost ($20,000). Therefore, based on the data given, the housewares line should not be discontinued unless a more profitable use can be found for the floor and counter space that it is occupying.

A Comparative Format

This decision can also be approached by preparing comparative income statements showing the effects of either keeping or dropping the product line. Exhibit 13–3 contains such an analysis for the Discount Drug Company. As shown in the last column of the exhibit, if the housewares line is dropped, then overall company net operating income will decrease by $5,000 each period. This is the same answer, of course, as we obtained when we focused just on the lost contribution margin and avoidable fixed costs.

Beware of Allocated Fixed Costs

Go back to Exhibit 13–2. Does this exhibit suggest that the housewares product line should be kept—as we have just concluded? No, it does not. Exhibit 13–2 suggests that the housewares product line is losing money. Why keep a product line that is showing a loss? The explanation for this apparent inconsistency lies in part with the common fixed costs that are being allocated to the product lines. As we observed in Chapter 12, one of the great dangers in allocating common fixed costs is that such allocations can make a product line (or other segment of a business) look less profitable than it really is. In this instance, allocating the common fixed costs among all product lines makes the housewares product line appear to be unprofitable. However, as we have shown above, dropping the product line would result in a decrease in the company's overall net operating income. This point can be seen clearly if we redo Exhibit 13–2 by eliminating the allocation of the common fixed costs. Exhibit 13–4 (page 588) uses the segmented approach from Chapter 12 to estimate the profitability of the product lines.

Exhibit 13–4 gives us a much different perspective of the housewares line than does Exhibit 13–2. As shown in Exhibit 13–4, the housewares line is covering all of its own traceable fixed costs and generating a $3,000 segment margin toward covering the common fixed costs of the company. Unless another product line can be found that will generate a segment margin greater than $3,000, the company would be better off keeping the housewares line.

EXHIBIT 13–3
A Comparative Format for Product-Line Analysis

	Keep Housewares	Drop Housewares	Difference: Net Operating Income Increase (or Decrease)
Sales	$50,000	$ 0	$(50,000)
Variable expenses	30,000	0	30,000
Contribution margin	20,000	0	(20,000)
Fixed expenses:			
Salaries	8,000	0	8,000
Advertising	6,500	0	6,500
Utilities	1,000	1,000	0
Depreciation—fixtures	2,000	2,000	0
Rent	4,000	4,000	0
Insurance	500	0	500
General administrative	6,000	6,000	0
Total fixed expenses	28,000	13,000	15,000
Net operating income (loss)	$ (8,000)	$(13,000)	$ (5,000)

EXHIBIT 13–4
Discount Drug Company
Product Lines—Recast in
Contribution Format (from
Exhibit 13–2)

		Product Line		
	Total	Drugs	Cosmetics	House-wares
Sales	$250,000	$125,000	$75,000	$50,000
Variable expenses	105,000	50,000	25,000	30,000
Contribution margin	145,000	75,000	50,000	20,000
Traceable fixed expenses:				
Salaries	50,000	29,500	12,500	8,000
Advertising	15,000	1,000	7,500	6,500
Depreciation—fixtures	5,000	1,000	2,000	2,000
Insurance	3,000	2,000	500	500
Total traceable fixed expenses	73,000	33,500	22,500	17,000
Product-line segment margin	72,000	$ 41,500	$27,500	$ 3,000*
Common fixed expenses:				
Utilities	2,000			
Rent	20,000			
General administrative	30,000			
Total common fixed expenses	52,000			
Net operating income	$ 20,000			

*If the housewares line is dropped, this $3,000 in segment margin will be lost to the company. In addition, we have seen that the $2,000 depreciation on the fixtures is a sunk cost that cannot be avoided. The sum of these two figures ($3,000 + $2,000 = $5,000) would be the decrease in the company's overall profits if the housewares line were discontinued. Of course, the company may later choose to drop the product if circumstances change—such as a pending decision to replace the fixtures.

By keeping the line, the company's overall net operating income will be higher than if the product line were dropped.

Additionally, managers may choose to retain an unprofitable product line if the line helps sell other products or if it serves as a "magnet" to attract customers. Bread, for example, may not be an especially profitable line in some food stores, but customers expect it to be available, and many of them would undoubtedly shift their buying elsewhere if a particular store decided to stop carrying it.

The Make or Buy Decision

LEARNING OBJECTIVE 3
Prepare a make or buy
analysis.

Providing a product or service to a customer involves many steps. For example, consider all of the steps that are necessary to develop and sell a product such as tax preparation software in retail stores. First the software must be developed, which involves highly skilled software engineers and a great deal of project management effort. Then the product must be put into a form that can be delivered to customers. This involves burning the application onto a blank CD or DVD, applying a label, and packaging the result in an attractive box. Then the product must be distributed to retail stores. Then the product must be sold. And finally, help lines and other forms of after-sale service may have to be provided. And we should not forget that the blank CD or DVD, the label, and the box must of course be made by someone before any of this can happen. All of these activities, from development, to production, to after-sales service are called a *value chain.*

Separate companies may carry out each of the activities in the value chain or a single company may carry out several. When a company is involved in more than one activity in the entire value chain, it is **vertically integrated.** Vertical integration is very common.

Some companies control all of the activities in the value chain from producing basic raw materials right up to the final distribution of finished goods and provision of after-sales service. Other companies are content to integrate on a smaller scale by purchasing many of the parts and materials that go into their finished products. A decision to carry out one of the activities in the value chain internally, rather than to buy externally from a supplier, is called a **make or buy decision.** Quite often these decisions involve whether to buy a particular part or to make it internally. Make or buy decisions also involve decisions concerning whether to outsource development tasks, after-sales service, or other activities.

Topic Tackler

PLUS

13–2

EMPLOYEE HEALTH BENEFITS—MAKE OR BUY?

With health care insurance premiums rising by over 10% per year, companies have been searching for ways to reduce the costs of providing health care to their employees. Some companies have adopted the unconventional approach of providing health care services in-house. Quad/Graphics, a printing company with 14,000 employees, hired its own doctors and nurses to provide primary health care on-site. By "making" its own health care for employees rather than "buying" it through the purchase of insurance, the company claims that its health care costs have risen just 6% annually and that their spending on health care is now 17% less than the industry average.

Source: Kimberly Weisul, "There's a Doctor in the House," *BusinessWeek*, December 16, 2002, p. 8

Strategic Aspects of the Make or Buy Decision

Vertical integration provides certain advantages. An integrated company is less dependent on its suppliers and may be able to ensure a smoother flow of parts and materials for production than a nonintegrated company. For example, a strike against a major parts supplier can interrupt the operations of a nonintegrated company for many months, whereas an integrated company that is producing its own parts would be able to continue operations. Also, some companies feel that they can control quality better by producing their own parts and materials, rather than by relying on the quality control standards of outside suppliers. In addition, an integrated company realizes profits from the parts and materials that it is "making" rather than "buying," as well as profits from its regular operations.

The advantages of vertical integration are counterbalanced by the advantages of using external suppliers. By pooling demand from a number of companies, a supplier may be able to enjoy economies of scale. These economies of scale can result in higher quality and lower costs than would be possible if the company were to attempt to make the parts or provide the service on its own. A company must be careful, however, to retain control over activities that are essential to maintaining its competitive position. For example, Hewlett-Packard controls the software for laser printers that it makes in cooperation with Canon Inc. of Japan. The present trend appears to be toward less vertical integration, with companies like Sun Microsystems and Hewlett-Packard concentrating on hardware and software design and relying on outside suppliers for almost everything else in the value chain. These factors suggest that the make or buy decision should be weighed very carefully.

An Example of Make or Buy

To provide an illustration of a make or buy decision, consider Mountain Goat Cycles. The company is now producing the heavy-duty gear shifters used in its most popular line of mountain bikes. The company's Accounting Department reports the following costs of producing 8,000 units of the shifter internally each year:

	Per Unit	8,000 Units
Direct materials	$ 6	$ 48,000
Direct labor	4	32,000
Variable overhead	1	8,000
Supervisor's salary	3	24,000
Depreciation of special equipment	2	16,000
Allocated general overhead	5	40,000
Total cost	$21	$168,000

An outside supplier has offered to sell 8,000 shifters a year to Mountain Goat Cycles at a price of only $19 each. Should the company stop producing the shifters internally and buy them from the outside supplier? As always, the focus should be on the relevant costs—those that differ between the alternatives. And the costs that differ between the alternatives consist of the costs that could be avoided by purchasing the shifters from the outside supplier. If the costs that can be avoided by purchasing the shifters from the outside supplier total less than $19, then the company should continue to manufacture its own shifters and reject the outside supplier's offer. On the other hand, if the costs that can be avoided by purchasing the shifters from the outside supplier total more than $19, the outside supplier's offer should be accepted.

Note that depreciation of special equipment is listed as one of the costs of producing the shifters internally. Since the equipment has already been purchased, this depreciation is a sunk cost and is therefore irrelevant. If the equipment could be sold, its salvage value would be relevant. Or if the machine could be used to make other products, this could be relevant as well. However, we will assume that the equipment has no salvage value and that it has no other use except making the heavy-duty gear shifters.

Also note that the company is allocating a portion of its general overhead costs to the shifters. Any portion of this general overhead cost that would actually be eliminated if the gear shifters were purchased rather than made would be relevant in the analysis. However, it is likely that the general overhead costs allocated to the gear shifters are in fact common to all items produced in the factory and would continue unchanged even if the shifters were purchased from the outside. Such allocated common costs are not relevant costs (since they do not differ between the make or buy alternatives) and should be eliminated from the analysis along with the sunk costs.

The variable costs of producing the shifters can be avoided by buying the shifters from the outside supplier so they are relevant costs. We will assume in this case that the variable costs include direct materials, direct labor, and variable overhead. The supervisor's salary is also relevant if it could be avoided by buying the shifters. Exhibit 13–5 contains the relevant

EXHIBIT 13–5
Mountain Goat Cycles Make or Buy Analysis

	Total Relevant Costs—8,000 units	
	Make	Buy
Direct materials (8,000 units @ $6 per unit).	$ 48,000	
Direct labor (8,000 units @ $4 per unit)	32,000	
Variable overhead (8,000 units @ $1 per unit).	8,000	
Supervisor's salary.	24,000	
Depreciation of special equipment (not relevant)		
Allocated general overhead (not relevant)		
Outside purchase price		$152,000
Total cost	$112,000	$152,000
Difference in favor of continuing to make	$40,000	

cost analysis of the make or buy decision assuming that the supervisor's salary can indeed be avoided.

Since it costs $40,000 less to make the shifters internally than to buy them from the outside supplier, Mountain Goat Cycles should reject the outside supplier's offer. However, the company may wish to consider one additional factor before coming to a final decision—the opportunity cost of the space now being used to produce the shifters.

OUTSOURCING R&D

A few years ago many experts felt that U.S. companies were unlikely to outsource their research and development (R&D) activities to lower labor cost Asian countries. However, these experts were wrong. Companies such as Procter & Gamble, Boeing, Dell, Eli Lilly, and Motorola are increasingly relying on Asian business partners to meet their R&D needs. In fact, research shows that U.S. technology companies outsource 70% of their personal digital assistant (PDA) designs, 65% of their notebook personal computer designs, and 30% of their digital camera designs.

Allen J. Delattre, head of Accenture's high-tech consulting practice, says "R&D is the single remaining controllable expense to work on. Companies either will have to cut costs or increase R&D productivity." In light of this stark reality, most Western companies are creating a global model of innovation that leverages the skills of Indian software developers, Taiwanese engineers, and Chinese factories. The lower labor rates available in these countries coupled with their strong technology orientation makes "buying" R&D capability from overseas more attractive to U.S. companies than relying solely on their domestic workforce to "make" R&D breakthroughs.

Source: Pete Engardio and Bruce Einhorn, "Outsourcing Innovation," *BusinessWeek*, March 21, 2005, pp. 82–94.

Opportunity Cost

If the space now being used to produce the shifters *would otherwise be idle,* then Mountain Goat Cycles should continue to produce its own shifters and the supplier's offer should be rejected, as stated above. Idle space that has no alternative use has an opportunity cost of zero.

But what if the space now being used to produce shifters could be used for some other purpose? In that case, the space would have an opportunity cost equal to the segment margin that could be derived from the best alternative use of the space.

To illustrate, assume that the space now being used to produce shifters could be used to produce a new cross-country bike that would generate a segment margin of $60,000 per year. Under these conditions, Mountain Goat Cycles should accept the supplier's offer and use the available space to produce the new product line:

	Make	Buy
Total annual cost (see Exhibit 13–5)	$112,000	$152,000
Opportunity cost—segment margin forgone on a potential new product line	60,000	
Total cost	$172,000	$152,000
Difference in favor of purchasing from the outside supplier.		$20,000

Opportunity costs are not recorded in the organization's general ledger because they do not represent actual dollar outlays. Rather, they represent economic benefits that are *forgone* as a result of pursuing some course of action. The opportunity cost for Mountain Goat Cycles is sufficiently large in this case to change the decision.

TOUGH CHOICES

Brad and Carole Karafil own and operate White Grizzly Adventures, a snowcat skiing and snowboarding company in Meadow Creek, British Columbia. While rare, it does sometimes happen that the company is unable to operate due to bad weather. Guests are housed and fed, but no one can ski. The contract signed by each guest stipulates that no refund is given in the case of an unavoidable cancellation that is beyond the control of the operators. So technically, Brad and Carole are not obligated to provide any refund if they must cancel operations due to bad weather. However, 70% of their guests are repeat customers and a guest who has paid roughly $300 a day to ski is likely to be unhappy if skiing is cancelled even though it is no fault of White Grizzly.

What costs, if any, are saved if skiing is cancelled and the snowcat does not operate? Not much. Guests are still housed and fed and the guides, who are independent contractors, are still paid. Some snowcat operating costs are avoided, but little else. Therefore, there would be little cost savings to pass on to guests.

Brad and Carole could issue a credit to be used for one day of skiing at another time. If a customer with such a credit occupied a seat on a snowcat that would otherwise be empty, the only significant cost to Brad and Carole would be the cost of feeding the customer. However, an empty seat basically doesn't exist—the demand for seats far exceeds the supply and the schedule is generally fully booked far in advance of the ski season. Consequently, the real cost of issuing a credit for one day of skiing is high. Brad and Carole would be giving up $300 from a paying customer for every guest they issue a credit voucher to. Issuing a credit voucher involves an opportunity cost of $300 in forgone sales revenues.

What would you do if you had to cancel skiing due to bad weather? Would you issue a refund or a credit voucher, losing money in the process, or would you risk losing customers? It's a tough choice.

Source: Brad and Carole Karafil, owners and operators of White Grizzly Adventures, www.whitegrizzly.com.

Special Orders

LEARNING OBJECTIVE 4
Prepare an analysis showing whether a special order should be accepted.

Managers must often evaluate whether a *special order* should be accepted, and if the order is accepted, the price that should be charged. A **special order** is a one-time order that is not considered part of the company's normal ongoing business. To illustrate, Mountain Goat Cycles has just received a request from the Seattle Police Department to produce 100 specially modified mountain bikes at a price of $279 each. The bikes would be used to patrol some of the more densely populated residential sections of the city. Mountain Goat Cycles can easily modify its City Cruiser model to fit the specifications of the Seattle Police. The normal selling price of the City Cruiser bike is $349, and its unit product cost is $282 as shown below:

Direct materials	$186
Direct labor.	45
Manufacturing overhead	51
Unit product cost	$282

The variable portion of the above manufacturing overhead is $6 per unit. The order would have no effect on the company's total fixed manufacturing overhead costs.

The modifications requested by the Seattle Police Department consist of welded brackets to hold radios, nightsticks, and other gear. These modifications would require $17 in incremental variable costs. In addition, the company would have to pay a graphics design studio $1,200 to design and cut stencils that would be used for spray painting the Seattle Police Department's logo and other identifying marks on the bikes.

This order should have no effect on the company's other sales. The production manager says that she can handle the special order without disrupting any of the company's regular scheduled production.

What effect would accepting this order have on the company's net operating income?

Only the incremental costs and benefits are relevant. Since the existing fixed manufacturing overhead costs would not be affected by the order, they are not relevant. The incremental net operating income can be computed as follows:

	Per Unit	Total 100 Bikes
Incremental revenue	$279	$27,900
Less incremental costs:		
Variable costs:		
Direct materials	186	18,600
Direct labor	45	4,500
Variable manufacturing overhead	6	600
Special modifications	17	1,700
Total variable cost	$254	25,400
Fixed cost:		
Purchase of stencils		1,200
Total incremental cost		26,600
Incremental net operating income		$ 1,300

Therefore, even though the $279 price on the special order is below the normal $282 unit product cost and the order would require additional costs, the order would increase net operating income. In general, a special order is profitable if the incremental revenue from the special order exceeds the incremental costs of the order. However, it is important to make sure that there is indeed idle capacity and that the special order does not cut into normal unit sales or undercut prices on normal sales. For example, if the company was operating at capacity, opportunity costs would have to be taken into account as well as the incremental costs that have already been detailed above.

IN BUSINESS

FLY THE FRIENDLY AISLES

Shoppers at Safeway can now earn United Airlines frequent flier miles when they buy their groceries. Airlines charge marketing partners such as Safeway about 2¢ per mile. Since airlines typically require 25,000 frequent flier miles for a domestic round-trip ticket, United is earning about $500 per frequent-flier ticket issued to Safeway customers. This income to United is higher than many discounted fares. Moreover, United carefully manages its frequent flier program so that few frequent flier passengers displace regular fare-paying customers. The only incremental costs of adding a frequent flier passenger to a flight may be food, a little extra fuel, and some administrative costs. All of the other costs of the flight would be incurred anyway. Thus, the miles that United sells to Safeway are almost pure profit.

Source: Wendy Zellner, *BusinessWeek*, March 6, 2000, pp. 152–154.

Utilization of a Constrained Resource

Managers routinely face the problem of deciding how constrained resources are going to be used. A department store, for example, has a limited amount of floor space and therefore cannot stock every product that may be available. A manufacturer has a limited number of machine-hours and a limited number of direct labor-hours at its disposal. When a limited resource of some type restricts the company's ability to satisfy demand, the company has a **constraint.** Since the company cannot fully satisfy demand, managers must decide which products or services should be cut back. In other words, managers must decide which products or services make the best use of the constrained resource. Fixed costs are usually unaffected by such choices, so the course of action that will maximize the company's total contribution margin should ordinarily be selected.

Contribution Margin per Unit of the Constrained Resource

If some products must be cut back because of a constraint, the key to maximizing the total contribution margin may seem obvious—favor the products with the highest unit contribution margins. Unfortunately, that is not quite correct. Rather, the correct solution is to favor the products that provide the highest *contribution margin per unit of the constrained resource.* To illustrate, in addition to its other products, Mountain Goat Cycles makes saddlebags for bicycles called *panniers.* These panniers come in two models—a touring model and a mountain model. Cost and revenue data for the two models of panniers follow:

	Mountain Pannier	Touring Pannier
Selling price per unit	$25	$30
Variable cost per unit	10	18
Contribution margin per unit	$15	$12
Contribution margin (CM) ratio	60%	40%

The mountain pannier appears to be much more profitable than the touring pannier. It has a $15 per unit contribution margin as compared to only $12 per unit for the touring model, and it has a 60% CM ratio as compared to only 40% for the touring model.

But now let us add one more piece of information—the plant that makes the panniers is operating at capacity. This does not mean that every machine and every person in the plant is working at the maximum possible rate. Because machines have different capacities, some machines will be operating at less than 100% of capacity. However, if the plant as a whole cannot produce any more units, some machine or process must be operating at capacity. The machine or process that is limiting overall output is called the **bottleneck**—it is the constraint.

At Mountain Goat Cycles, the bottleneck (i.e., constraint) is a stitching machine. The mountain pannier requires two minutes of stitching time per unit, and the touring pannier requires one minute of stitching time per unit. By definition, since the stitching machine is a bottleneck, the stitching machine does not have enough capacity to satisfy the existing demand for mountain panniers and touring panniers Therefore, some orders for the products will have to be turned down. Naturally, managers will want to know which product is less profitable. To answer this question, they should focus on the contribution margin per unit of the constrained resource. This figure is computed by dividing a product's contribution margin per unit by the amount of the constrained resource required to make a unit of that product. These calculations are carried out below for the mountain and touring panniers:

	Mountain Pannier	Touring Pannier
Contribution margin per unit (a)	$15.00	$12.00
Stitching machine time required to produce one unit (b)	2 minutes	1 minute
Contribution margin per unit of the constrained resource, (a) ÷ (b)	$7.50 per minute	$12.00 per minute

It is now easy to decide which product is less profitable and should be deemphasized. Each minute on the stitching machine that is devoted to the touring pannier results in an increase of $12.00 in contribution margin and profits. The comparable figure for the mountain pannier is only $7.50 per minute. Therefore, the touring model should be emphasized. Even though the mountain model has the larger contribution margin per unit and the larger CM ratio, the touring model provides the larger contribution margin in relation to the constrained resource.

To verify that the touring model is indeed the more profitable product, suppose an hour of additional stitching time is available and that unfilled orders exist for both products. The additional hour on the stitching machine could be used to make either 30 mountain panniers (60 minutes ÷ 2 minutes per mountain pannier) or 60 touring panniers (60 minutes ÷ 1 minute per touring pannier), with the following profit implications:

	Mountain Pannier	Touring Pannier
Contribution margin per unit	$ 15	$ 12
Additional units that can be processed in one hour	× 30	× 60
Additional contribution margin	$450	$720

Since the additional contribution margin would be $720 for the touring panniers and only $450 for the mountain panniers, the touring panniers make the most profitable use of the company's constrained resource—the stitching machine.

This example clearly shows that looking at unit contribution margins alone is not enough; the contribution margin must be viewed in relation to the amount of the constrained resource each product requires.

IN BUSINESS

THEORY OF CONSTRAINTS SOFTWARE

Indalex Aluminum Solutions Group is the largest producer of soft alloy extrusions in North America. The company has installed a new generation of business intelligence software created by pVelocity, Inc., of Toronto, Canada. The software "provides decision makers across our entire manufacturing enterprise with time-based financial metrics using TOC concepts to identify bottlenecks." And, it "shifts the focus of a manufacturing company from traditional cost accounting measurements to measuring the generation of dollars per unit of time." For example, instead of emphasizing products with the largest gross margins or contribution margins, the software helps managers to identify and emphasize the products that maximize the contribution margin per unit of the constrained resource.

Source: Mike Alger, "Managing a Business as a Portfolio of Customers," *Strategic Finance*, June 2003, pp. 54–57.

Managing Constraints

Effectively managing an organization's constraints is a key to increased profits. Effective management of a bottleneck constraint involves selecting the most profitable product mix and finding ways to increase the capacity of the bottleneck operation. As discussed above, if the constraint is a bottleneck in the production process, the most profitable product mix consists of the products with the highest contribution margin per unit of the constrained resource. In addition, as discussed below, increasing the capacity of the bottleneck operation should lead to increased production and sales. Such efforts will often pay off in an almost immediate increase in profits.

It is often possible for a manager to increase the capacity of the bottleneck, which is called **relaxing (or elevating) the constraint.** For example, the stitching machine operator could be asked to work overtime. This would result in more available stitching time and hence the production of more finished goods that can be sold. The benefits from relaxing the constraint are often enormous and can be easily quantified. The manager should first ask, "What would I do with additional capacity at the bottleneck if it were available?" In our example, if unfilled orders exist for both the touring and mountain panniers, the additional capacity would be used to process more touring panniers, since they earn a contribution margin of $12 per minute, or $720 per hour. Given that the overtime pay for the operator is likely to be much less than $720 per hour, running the stitching machine on overtime would be an excellent way to increase the company's profits while at the same time satisfying more customers.

To reinforce this concept, suppose that there are only unfilled orders for the mountain pannier. How much would it be worth to the company to run the stitching machine overtime in this situation? Since the additional capacity would be used to make the mountain pannier, the value of that additional capacity would drop to $7.50 per minute or $450 per hour. Nevertheless, the value of relaxing the constraint would still be quite high.

These calculations indicate that managers should pay great attention to the bottleneck operation. If a bottleneck machine breaks down or is ineffectively utilized, the losses to the company can be quite large. In our example, for every minute the stitching machine is down due to breakdowns or setups, the company loses between $7.50 and $12.00.[2] The losses on an hourly basis are between $450 and $720! In contrast, there is no such loss of contribution margin if time is lost on a machine that is not a bottleneck—such machines have excess capacity anyway.

The implications are clear. Managers should focus much of their attention on managing the bottleneck. As we have discussed, managers should emphasize products that most profitably utilize the constrained resource. They should also make sure that products are processed smoothly through the bottleneck, with minimal lost time due to breakdowns and setups. And they should try to find ways to increase the capacity at the bottleneck.

The capacity of a bottleneck can be effectively increased in a number of ways, including:

- Working overtime on the bottleneck.
- Subcontracting some of the processing that would be done at the bottleneck.
- Investing in additional machines at the bottleneck.
- Shifting workers from processes that are not bottlenecks to the process that is the bottleneck.
- Focusing business process improvement efforts such as Six Sigma on the bottleneck.
- Reducing defective units. Each defective unit that is processed through the bottleneck and subsequently scrapped takes the place of a good unit that could have been sold.

The last three methods of increasing the capacity of the bottleneck are particularly attractive because they are essentially free and may even yield additional cost savings.

---

[2] Setups are required when production switches from one product to another. For example, consider a company that makes automobile side panels. The panels are painted before shipping them to an automobile manufacturer for final assembly. The customer might require 100 blue panels, 50 black panels, and 20 yellow panels. Each time the color is changed, the painting equipment must be purged of the old paint color, cleaned with solvents, and refilled with the new paint color. This takes time. In fact, some equipment may require such lengthy and frequent setups that it is unavailable for actual production more often than not.

The methods and ideas discussed in this section are all part of the Theory of Constraints, which was introduced in Chapter 1. A number of organizations have successfully used the Theory of Constraints to improve their performance, including Avery Dennison, Bethlehem Steel, Binney & Smith, Boeing, Champion International, Ford Motor Company, General Motors, ITT, Monster Cable, National Semiconductor, Pratt and Whitney Canada, Pretoria Academic Hospital, Procter and Gamble, Texas Instruments, United Airlines, United Electrical Controls, the United States Air Force Logistics Command, and the United States Navy Transportation Corps.

IN BUSINESS

ELEVATING A CONSTRAINT

The Odessa Texas Police Department was having trouble hiring new employees. Its eight-step hiring process was taking 117 days to complete and the best-qualified job applicants were accepting other employment offers before the Odessa Police Department could finish evaluating their candidacy. The constraint in the eight-step hiring process was the background investigation that required an average of 104 days. The other seven steps—filling out an application and completing a written exam, an oral interview, a polygraph exam, a medical exam, a psychological exam, and a drug screen—took a combined total of only 13 days. The Odessa Police Department elevated its constraint by hiring additional background checkers. This resulted in slashing its application processing time from 117 days to 16 days.

Source: Lloyd J. Taylor III, Brian J. Moersch, and Geralyn McClure Franklin, "Applying the Theory of Constraints to a Public Safety Hiring Process," *Public Personnel Management*, Fall 2003, pp. 367–382.

The Problem of Multiple Constraints

What does a company do if it has more than one potential constraint? For example, a company may have limited raw materials, limited direct labor-hours available, limited floor space, and limited advertising dollars to spend on product promotion. How would it determine the right combination of products to produce? The proper combination or "mix" of products can be found by use of a quantitative method known as *linear programming,* which is covered in quantitative methods and operations management courses.

Joint Product Costs and the Contribution Approach

In some industries, a number of end products are produced from a single raw material input. For example, in the petroleum refining industry a large number of products are extracted from crude oil, including gasoline, jet fuel, home heating oil, lubricants, asphalt, and various organic chemicals. Another example is provided by the Santa Maria Wool Cooperative of New Mexico. The company buys raw wool from local sheepherders, separates the wool into three grades—coarse, fine, and superfine—and then dyes the wool using traditional methods that rely on pigments from local materials. Exhibit 13–6 on page 598 contains a diagram of the production process.

At Santa Maria Wool Cooperative, coarse wool, fine wool, and superfine wool are produced from one input—raw wool. Two or more products that are produced from a common input are known as **joint products.** The **split-off point** is the point in the manufacturing process at which the joint products can be recognized as separate products. This does not occur at Santa Maria Cooperative until the raw wool has gone through the separating process. The term **joint cost** is used to describe the costs incurred up to the split-off point. At Santa Maria Wool Cooperative, the joint costs are the $200,000 cost of the raw wool and the $40,000 cost of separating the wool. The undyed wool is called an *intermediate product*

LEARNING OBJECTIVE 6
Prepare an analysis showing whether joint products should be sold at the split-off point or processed further.

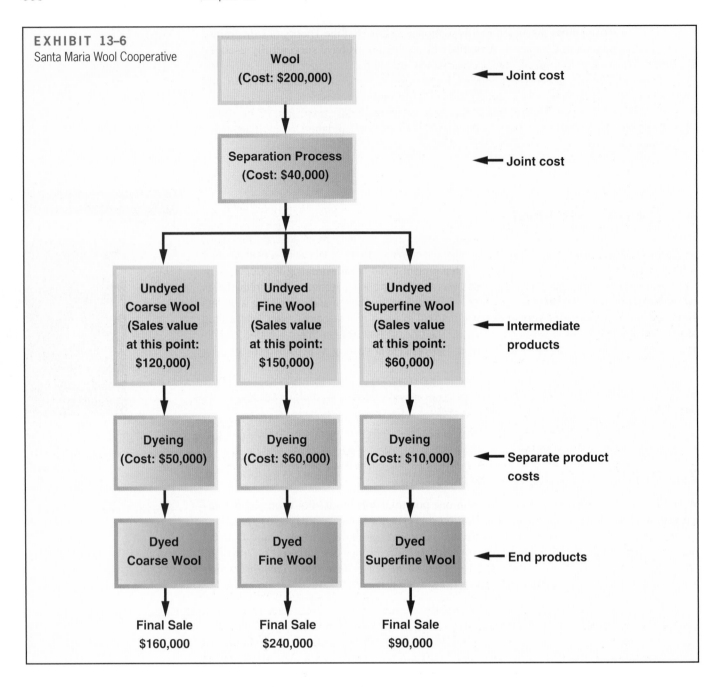

EXHIBIT 13–6
Santa Maria Wool Cooperative

Wool
(Cost: $200,000) ← Joint cost

Separation Process
(Cost: $40,000) ← Joint cost

Undyed
Coarse Wool
(Sales value
at this point:
$120,000)

Undyed
Fine Wool
(Sales value
at this point:
$150,000)

Undyed
Superfine Wool
(Sales value
at this point:
$60,000) ← Intermediate products

Dyeing
(Cost: $50,000)

Dyeing
(Cost: $60,000)

Dyeing
(Cost: $10,000) ← Separate product costs

Dyed
Coarse Wool

Dyed
Fine Wool

Dyed
Superfine Wool ← End products

Final Sale
$160,000

Final Sale
$240,000

Final Sale
$90,000

because it is not finished at this point. Nevertheless, a market does exist for undyed wool—although at a significantly lower price than finished, dyed wool.

The Pitfalls of Allocation

Joint costs are common costs that are incurred to simultaneously produce a variety of end products. These joint costs are traditionally allocated among the different products at the split-off point. A typical approach is to allocate the joint costs according to the relative sales value of the end products.

Although allocation of joint product costs is needed for some purposes, such as balance sheet inventory valuation, allocations of this kind are extremely misleading for decision making. The In Business box "Getting It All Wrong" on page 599 illustrates an incorrect decision that resulted from using such an allocated joint cost. You should stop now and read that box before proceeding further.

GETTING IT ALL WRONG

A company located on the Gulf of Mexico produces soap products. Its six main soap product lines are produced from common inputs. Joint product costs up to the split-off point constitute the bulk of the production costs for all six product lines. These joint product costs are allocated to the six product lines on the basis of the relative sales value of each line at the split-off point.

A waste product results from the production of the six main product lines. The company loaded the waste onto barges and dumped it into the Gulf of Mexico, since the waste was thought to have no commercial value. The dumping was stopped, however, when the company's research division discovered that with some further processing the waste could be sold as a fertilizer ingredient. The further processing costs $175,000 per year. The waste was then sold to fertilizer manufacturers for $300,000.

The accountants responsible for allocating manufacturing costs included the sales value of the waste product along with the sales value of the six main product lines in their allocation of the joint product costs at the split-off point. This allocation resulted in the waste product being allocated $150,000 in joint product cost. This $150,000 allocation, when added to the further processing costs of $175,000 for the waste, made it appear that the waste product was unprofitable—as shown in the table below. When presented with this analysis, the company's management decided that further processing of the waste should be stopped. The company went back to dumping the waste in the Gulf.

Sales value of the waste product after further processing	$300,000
Less costs assignable to the waste product	325,000
Net loss	$ (25,000)

Sell or Process Further Decisions

Joint costs are irrelevant in decisions regarding what to do with a product from the split-off point forward. Once the split-off point is reached, the joint costs have already been incurred and nothing can be done to avoid them. Furthermore, even if the product were disposed of in a landfill without any further processing, all of the joint costs must be incurred to obtain the other products that come out of the joint process. None of the joint costs are avoidable by disposing of any one of the products that emerge from the split-off point. Therefore, none of the joint costs are economically attributable to any one of the intermediate or end products. The joint costs are a common cost of all of the intermediate and end products and should not be allocated to them for purposes of making decisions about the individual products. In the case of the soap company in the accompanying In Business box "Getting It All Wrong," the $150,000 in allocated joint costs should not have been permitted to influence what was done with the waste product from the split-off point forward. Even ignoring the negative environmental impact of dumping the waste in the Gulf of Mexico, a correct analysis would have shown that the company was making money by further processing the waste into a fertilizer ingredient. The analysis should have been done as follows:

	Dump in Gulf	Process Further
Sales value of fertilizer ingredient	0	$300,000
Additional processing costs	0	175,000
Contribution margin	0	$125,000
Advantage of processing further	$125,000	

Decisions of this type are known as **sell or process further decisions.** It is profitable to continue processing a joint product after the split-off point *so long as the incremental revenue from such processing exceeds the incremental processing cost incurred after the split-off point.* Joint costs that have already been incurred up to the split-off point are always irrelevant in decisions concerning what to do from the split-off point forward.

To provide a detailed example of the sell or process further decision, return to the data for Santa Maria Wool Cooperative in Exhibit 13–6. We can answer several important questions using this data. First, is the company making money if it runs the entire process from beginning to end? Assuming there are no costs other than those displayed in Exhibit 13–6, the company is indeed making money as follows:

Analysis of the profitability of the overall operation:		
Combined final sales value		
($160,000 + $240,000 + $90,000)		$490,000
Less costs of producing the end products:		
Cost of wool	$200,000	
Cost of separating wool	40,000	
Combined costs of dyeing		
($50,000 + $60,000 + $10,000)	120,000	360,000
Profit		$130,000

Note that the joint costs of buying the wool and separating the wool *are* relevant when considering the profitability of the entire operation. This is because these joint costs *could* be avoided if the entire operation were shut down. However, these joint costs are *not* relevant when considering the profitability of any one product. As long as the process is being run to make the other products, no additional joint costs are incurred to make the specific product in question.

Even though the company is making money overall, it may be losing money on one or more of the products. If the company buys wool and runs the separation process, it will get all three intermediate products. Nothing can be done about that. However, each of these products can be sold *as is* without further processing. It may be that the company would be better off selling one or more of the products prior to dyeing to avoid the dyeing costs. The appropriate way to make this choice is to compare the incremental revenues to the incremental costs from further processing as follows:

Analysis of sell or process further:	Coarse Wool	Fine Wool	Superfine Wool
Final sales value after further processing	$160,000	$240,000	$90,000
Less sales value at the split-off point	120,000	150,000	60,000
Incremental revenue from further processing	40,000	90,000	30,000
Less cost of further processing (dyeing)	50,000	60,000	10,000
Profit (loss) from further processing	$ (10,000)	$ 30,000	$20,000

As this analysis shows, the company would be better off selling the undyed coarse wool as is rather than processing it further. The other two products should be processed further and dyed before selling them.

Note that the joint costs of the wool ($200,000) and of the wool separation process ($40,000) play no role in the decision to sell or further process the intermediate products. These joint costs are relevant in a decision of whether to buy wool and to run the wool separation process, but they are not relevant in decisions about what to do with the intermediate products once they have been separated.

Activity-Based Costing and Relevant Costs

As discussed in Chapter 8, activity-based costing can be used to help identify potentially relevant costs for decision-making purposes. Activity-based costing improves the traceability of costs by focusing on the activities caused by a product or other segment. However, managers should exercise caution against reading more into this "traceability" than really exists. People have a tendency to assume that if a cost is traceable to a segment, then the cost is automatically an avoidable cost. That is not true. As emphasized in Chapter 8, the costs provided by a well-designed activity-based costing system are only *potentially* relevant. Before making a decision, managers must still decide which of the potentially relevant costs are actually avoidable. Only those costs that are avoidable are relevant and the others should be ignored.

To illustrate, refer again to the data relating to the housewares line in Exhibit 13–4. The $2,000 fixtures depreciation is a traceable cost of the housewares lines because it directly relates to activities in that department. We found, however, that the $2,000 is not avoidable if the housewares line is dropped. The key lesson here is that the method used to assign a cost to a product or other segment does not change the basic nature of the cost. A sunk cost such as depreciation of old equipment is still a sunk cost regardless of whether it is traced directly to a particular segment on an activity basis, allocated to all segments on the basis of labor-hours, or treated in some other way in the costing process. Regardless of the method used to assign costs to products or other segments, the principles discussed in this chapter must be applied to determine the costs that are avoidable in each situation.

Summary

Everything in this chapter consists of applications of one simple but powerful idea. Only those costs and benefits that differ between alternatives are relevant in a decision. All other costs and benefits are irrelevant and should be ignored. In particular, sunk costs are irrelevant as are future costs that do not differ between alternatives.

This simple idea was applied in a variety of situations including decisions that involve making or buying a component, adding or dropping a product line, accepting or rejecting a special order, processing a joint product further, and using a constrained resource. This list includes only a small sample of the possible applications of the relevant cost concept. Indeed, any decision involving costs hinges on the proper identification and analysis of the costs that are relevant. We will continue to focus on the concept of relevant costs in the following chapter where long-run investment decisions are considered.

Review Problem: Relevant Costs

Charter Sports Equipment manufactures round, rectangular, and octagonal trampolines. Sales and expense data for the past month follow:

| | Total | Trampoline | | |
		Round	Rectangular	Octagonal
Sales	$1,000,000	$140,000	$500,000	$360,000
Variable expenses	410,000	60,000	200,000	150,000
Contribution margin	590,000	80,000	300,000	210,000
Fixed expenses:				
Advertising—traceable	216,000	41,000	110,000	65,000
Depreciation of special equipment	95,000	20,000	40,000	35,000
Line supervisors' salaries	19,000	6,000	7,000	6,000
General factory overhead*	200,000	28,000	100,000	72,000
Total fixed expenses.	530,000	95,000	257,000	178,000
Net operating income (loss)	$ 60,000	$ (15,000)	$ 43,000	$ 32,000

*A common fixed cost that is allocated on the basis of sales dollars.

Management is concerned about the continued losses shown by the round trampolines and wants a recommendation as to whether or not the line should be discontinued. The special equipment used to produce the trampolines has no resale value. If the round trampoline model is dropped, the two line supervisors assigned to the model would be discharged.

Required:
1. Should production and sale of the round trampolines be discontinued? The company has no other use for the capacity now being used to produce the round trampolines. Show computations to support your answer.
2. Recast the above data in a format that would be more useful to management in assessing the profitability of the various product lines.

Solution to Review Problem

1. No, production and sale of the round trampolines should not be discontinued. Computations to support this answer follow:

Contribution margin lost if the round trampolines are discontinued		$(80,000)
Less fixed costs that can be avoided:		
Advertising—traceable	$41,000	
Line supervisors' salaries	6,000	47,000
Decrease in net operating income for the company as a whole		$(33,000)

The depreciation of the special equipment represents a sunk cost, and therefore it is not relevant to the decision. The general factory overhead is allocated and will presumably continue regardless of whether or not the round trampolines are discontinued; thus, it is not relevant.

2. If management wants a clearer picture of the profitability of the segments, the general factory overhead should not be allocated. It is a common cost and therefore should be deducted from the total product-line segment margin, as shown in Chapter 12. A more useful income statement format would be as follows:

		Trampoline		
	Total	Round	Rectangular	Octagonal
Sales	$1,000,000	$140,000	$500,000	$360,000
Variable expenses	410,000	60,000	200,000	150,000
Contribution margin	590,000	80,000	300,000	210,000
Traceable fixed expenses:				
Advertising—traceable	216,000	41,000	110,000	65,000
Depreciation of special equipment	95,000	20,000	40,000	35,000
Line supervisors' salaries	19,000	6,000	7,000	6,000
Total traceable fixed expenses	330,000	67,000	157,000	106,000
Product-line segment margin	260,000	$ 13,000	$143,000	$104,000
Common fixed expenses	200,000			
Net operating income (loss)	$ 60,000			

Glossary

Avoidable cost A cost that can be eliminated (in whole or in part) by choosing one alternative over another in a decision. This term is synonymous with *relevant cost* and *differential cost*. (p. 578)

Bottleneck A machine or some other part of a process that limits the total output of the entire system. (p. 594)

Constraint A limitation under which a company must operate, such as limited available machine time or raw materials, that restricts the company's ability to satisfy demand. (p. 594)

Differential cost Any cost that differs between alternatives in a decision-making situation. This term is synonymous with *avoidable cost* and *relevant cost.* (p. 579)

Joint costs Costs that are incurred up to the split-off point in a process that produces joint products. (p. 597)

Joint products Two or more products that are produced from a common input. (p. 597)

Make or buy decision A decision concerning whether an item should be produced internally or purchased from an outside supplier. (p. 589)

Relaxing (or elevating) the constraint An action that increases the amount of a constrained resource. Equivalently, an action that increases the capacity of the bottleneck. (p. 596)

Relevant cost A cost that differs between alternatives in a decision. This term is synonymous with *avoidable cost* and *differential cost.* (p. 578)

Sell or process further decision A decision as to whether a joint product should be sold at the split-off point or sold after further processing. (p. 600)

Special order A one-time order that is not considered part of the company's normal ongoing business. (p. 592)

Split-off point That point in the manufacturing process where some or all of the joint products can be recognized as individual products. (p. 597)

Sunk cost Any cost that has already been incurred and that cannot be changed by any decision made now or in the future. (p. 578)

Vertical integration The involvement by a company in more than one of the activities in the entire value chain from development through production, distribution, sales, and after-sales service. (p. 598)

Questions

13-1 What is a *relevant cost?*

13-2 Define the following terms: *incremental cost, opportunity cost,* and *sunk cost.*

13-3 Are variable costs always relevant costs? Explain.

13-4 "Sunk costs are easy to spot—they're simply the fixed costs associated with a decision." Do you agree? Explain.

13-5 "Variable costs and differential costs mean the same thing." Do you agree? Explain.

13-6 "All future costs are relevant in decision making." Do you agree? Why?

13-7 Prentice Company is considering dropping one of its product lines. What costs of the product line would be relevant to this decision? Irrelevant?

13-8 "If a product line is generating a loss, then it should be discontinued." Do you agree? Explain.

13-9 What is the danger in allocating common fixed costs among product lines or other segments of an organization?

13-10 How does opportunity cost enter into the make or buy decision?

13-11 Give at least four examples of possible constraints.

13-12 How will relating product contribution margins to the amount of the constrained resource they consume help a company maximize its profits?

13-13 Define the following terms: *joint products, joint costs,* and *split-off point.*

13-14 From a decision-making point of view, should joint costs be allocated among joint products?

13-15 What guideline should be used in determining whether a joint product should be sold at the split-off point or processed further?

13-16 Airlines sometimes offer reduced rates during certain times of the week to members of a businessperson's family if they accompany him or her on trips. How does the concept of relevant costs enter into the decision by the airline to offer reduced rates of this type?

Exercises

EXERCISE 13-1 Identifying Relevant Costs [LO1]

A number of costs are listed below that may be relevant in decisions faced by the management of Svahn, AB, a Swedish manufacturer of sailing yachts:

Item	Case 1 Relevant	Case 1 Not Relevant	Case 2 Relevant	Case 2 Not Relevant
a. Sales revenue..........................				
b. Direct materials.........................				
c. Direct labor............................				
d. Variable manufacturing overhead				
e. Depreciation—Model B100 machine				
f. Book value—Model B100 machine				
g. Disposal value—Model B100 machine.........				
h. Market value—Model B300 machine (cost)				
i. Fixed manufacturing overhead (general)				
j. Variable selling expense...................				
k. Fixed selling expense.....................				
l. General administrative overhead				

Required:

Copy the information above onto your answer sheet and place an X in the appropriate column to indicate whether each item is relevant or not relevant in the following situations. Requirement 1 relates to Case 1 above, and requirement 2 relates to Case 2.

1. The company chronically has no idle capacity and the old Model B100 machine is the company's constraint. Management is considering purchasing a Model B300 machine to use in addition to the company's present Model B100 machine. The old Model B100 machine will continue to be used to capacity as before, with the new Model B300 machine being used to expand production. This will increase the company's production and sales. The increase in volume will be large enough to require increases in fixed selling expenses and in general administrative overhead, but not in the fixed manufacturing overhead.

2. The old Model B100 machine is not the company's constraint, but management is considering replacing it with a new Model B300 machine because of the potential savings in direct materials with the new machine. The Model B100 machine would be sold. This change will have no effect on production or sales, other than some savings in direct materials costs due to less waste.

EXERCISE 13-2 Dropping or Retaining a Segment [LO2]

The Regal Cycle Company manufactures three types of bicycles—a dirt bike, a mountain bike, and a racing bike. Data on sales and expenses for the past quarter follow:

	Total	Dirt Bikes	Mountain Bikes	Racing Bikes
Sales	$300,000	$90,000	$150,000	$60,000
Variable manufacturing and selling expenses	120,000	27,000	60,000	33,000
Contribution margin	180,000	63,000	90,000	27,000
Fixed expenses:				
Advertising, traceable...........	30,000	10,000	14,000	6,000
Depreciation of special equipment.................	23,000	6,000	9,000	8,000
Salaries of product-line managers	35,000	12,000	13,000	10,000
Allocated common fixed expenses*.................	60,000	18,000	30,000	12,000
Total fixed expenses.............	148,000	46,000	66,000	36,000
Net operating income (loss)........	$ 32,000	$17,000	$ 24,000	$(9,000)

*Allocated on the basis of sales dollars.

Management is concerned about the continued losses shown by the racing bikes and wants a recommendation as to whether or not the line should be discontinued. The special equipment used to produce racing bikes has no resale value and does not wear out.

Required:

1. Should production and sale of the racing bikes be discontinued? Explain. Show computations to support your answer.
2. Recast the above data in a format that would be more usable to management in assessing the long-run profitability of the various product lines.

EXERCISE 13-3 Make or Buy a Component [LO3]

Troy Engines, Ltd., manufactures a variety of engines for use in heavy equipment. The company has always produced all of the necessary parts for its engines, including all of the carburetors. An outside supplier has offered to sell one type of carburetor to Troy Engines, Ltd., for a cost of $35 per unit. To evaluate this offer, Troy Engines, Ltd., has gathered the following information relating to its own cost of producing the carburetor internally:

	Per Unit	15,000 Units per Year
Direct materials	$14	$210,000
Direct labor	10	150,000
Variable manufacturing overhead	3	45,000
Fixed manufacturing overhead, traceable	6*	90,000
Fixed manufacturing overhead, allocated	9	135,000
Total cost	$42	$630,000

*One-third supervisory salaries; two-thirds depreciation of special equipment (no resale value).

Required:

1. Assuming that the company has no alternative use for the facilities that are now being used to produce the carburetors, should the outside supplier's offer be accepted? Show all computations.
2. Suppose that if the carburetors were purchased, Troy Engines, Ltd., could use the freed capacity to launch a new product. The segment margin of the new product would be $150,000 per year. Should Troy Engines, Ltd., accept the offer to buy the carburetors for $35 per unit? Show all computations.

EXERCISE 13-4 Evaluating a Special Order [LO4]

Imperial Jewelers is considering a special order for 20 handcrafted gold bracelets to be given as gifts to members of a wedding party. The normal selling price of a gold bracelet is $189.95 and its unit product cost is $149.00 as shown below:

Direct materials	$ 84.00
Direct labor	45.00
Manufacturing overhead	20.00
Unit product cost	$149.00

Most of the manufacturing overhead is fixed and unaffected by variations in how much jewelry is produced in any given period. However, $4.00 of the overhead is variable with respect to the number of bracelets produced. The customer who is interested in the special bracelet order would like special filigree applied to the bracelets. This filigree would require additional materials costing $2.00 per bracelet and would also require acquisition of a special tool costing $250 that would have no other use once the special order is completed. This order would have no effect on the company's regular sales and the order could be fulfilled using the company's existing capacity without affecting any other order.

Required:

What effect would accepting this order have on the company's net operating income if a special price of $169.95 per bracelet is offered for this order? Should the special order be accepted at this price?

EXERCISE 13-5 Utilization of a Constrained Resource [LO5]

Barlow Company manufactures three products: A, B, and C. The selling price, variable costs, and contribution margin for one unit of each product follow:

	Product		
	A	B	C
Selling price	$180	$270	$240
Less variable expenses:			
Direct materials.	24	72	32
Other variable expenses	102	90	148
Total variable expenses	126	162	180
Contribution margin	$ 54	$108	$ 60
Contribution margin ratio	30%	40%	25%

The same raw material is used in all three products. Barlow Company has only 5,000 pounds of raw material on hand and will not be able to obtain any more of it for several weeks due to a strike in its supplier's plant. Management is trying to decide which product(s) to concentrate on next week in filling its backlog of orders. The material costs $8 per pound.

Required:

1. Compute the amount of contribution margin that will be obtained per pound of material used in each product.
2. Which orders would you recommend that the company work on next week—the orders for product A, product B, or product C? Show computations.
3. A foreign supplier could furnish Barlow with additional stocks of the raw material at a substantial premium over the usual price. If there is unfilled demand for all three products, what is the highest price that Barlow Company should be willing to pay for an additional pound of materials? Explain.

EXERCISE 13-6 Sell or Process Further [LO6]

Dorsey Company manufactures three products from a common input in a joint processing operation. Joint processing costs up to the split-off point total $350,000 per quarter. The company allocates these costs to the joint products on the basis of their relative sales value at the split-off point. Unit selling prices and total output at the split-off point are as follows:

Product	Selling Price	Quarterly Output
A	$16 per pound	15,000 pounds
B	$8 per pound	20,000 pounds
C	$ 25 per gallon	4,000 gallons

Each product can be processed further after the split-off point. Additional processing requires no special facilities. The additional processing costs (per quarter) and unit selling prices after further processing are given below:

Product	Additional Processing Costs	Selling Price
A	$63,000	$20 per pound
B	$80,000	$13 per pound
C	$36,000	$32 per gallon

Required:

Which product or products should be sold at the split-off point and which product or products should be processed further? Show computations.

EXERCISE 13-7 Identification of Relevant Costs [LO1]

Bill has just returned from a duck hunting trip. He has brought home eight ducks. Bill's friend, John, disapproves of duck hunting, and to discourage Bill from further hunting, John has presented him with the following cost estimate per duck:

Camper and equipment:	
Cost, $12,000; usable for eight seasons; 10 hunting trips per season	$150
Travel expense (pickup truck):	
100 miles at $0.31 per mile (gas, oil, and tires—$0.21 per mile; depreciation	
and insurance—$0.10 per mile)	31
Shotgun shells (two boxes).	20
Boat:	
Cost, $2,320, usable for eight seasons; 10 hunting trips per season	29
Hunting license:	
Cost, $30 for the season; 10 hunting trips per season	3
Money lost playing poker:	
Loss, $24 (Bill plays poker every weekend)	24
Bottle of whiskey:	
Cost, $15 (used to ward off the cold).	15
Total cost	$272
Cost per duck ($272 ÷ 8 ducks)	$ 34

Required:
1. Assuming that the duck hunting trip Bill has just completed is typical, what costs are relevant to a decision as to whether Bill should go duck hunting again this season?
2. Suppose that Bill gets lucky on his next hunting trip and shoots 10 ducks in the amount of time it took him to shoot 8 ducks on his last trip. How much would it have cost him to shoot the last two ducks? Explain.
3. Which costs are relevant in a decision of whether Bill should give up hunting? Explain.

EXERCISE 13-8 Dropping or Retaining a Segment [LO2]

Bed & Bath, a retailing company, has two departments, Hardware and Linens. A recent monthly contribution format income statement for the company follows:

	Total	Department Hardware	Linens
Sales	$4,000,000	$3,000,000	$1,000,000
Variable expenses	1,300,000	900,000	400,000
Contribution margin	2,700,000	2,100,000	600,000
Fixed expenses	2,200,000	1,400,000	800,000
Net operating income (loss)	$ 500,000	$ 700,000	$ (200,000)

A study indicates that $340,000 of the fixed expenses being charged to Linens are sunk costs or allocated costs that will continue even if the Linens Department is dropped. In addition, the elimination of the Linens Department will result in a 10% decrease in the sales of the Hardware Department.

Required:
If the Linens Department is dropped, what will be the effect on the net operating income of the company as a whole?

EXERCISE 13-9 Make or Buy a Component [LO3]

For many years Futura Company has purchased the starters that it installs in its standard line of farm tractors. Due to a reduction in output, the company has idle capacity that could be used to produce the starters. The chief engineer has recommended against this move, however, pointing out that the cost to produce the starters would be greater than the current $8.40 per unit purchase price:

	Per Unit	Total
Direct materials	$3.10	
Direct labor	2.70	
Supervision	1.50	$60,000
Depreciation	1.00	40,000
Variable manufacturing overhead	0.60	
Rent	0.30	12,000
Total production cost	$9.20	

A supervisor would have to be hired to oversee production of the starters. However, the company has sufficient idle tools and machinery that no new equipment would have to be purchased. The rent charge above is based on space utilized in the plant. The total rent on the plant is $80,000 per period. Depreciation is due to obsolescence rather than wear and tear.

Required:

Prepare computations showing how much profits will increase or decrease as a result of making the starters rather than purchasing them.

EXERCISE 13-10 Special Order [LO4]

Delta Company produces a single product. The cost of producing and selling a single unit of this product at the company's normal activity level of 60,000 units per year is:

Direct materials	$5.10
Direct labor	$3.80
Variable manufacturing overhead	$1.00
Fixed manufacturing overhead	$4.20
Variable selling and administrative expense	$1.50
Fixed selling and administrative expense	$2.40

The normal selling price is $21 per unit. The company's capacity is 75,000 units per year. An order has been received from a mail-order house for 15,000 units at a special price of $14 per unit. This order would not affect regular sales.

Required:

1. If the order is accepted, by how much will annual profits be increased or decreased? (The order will not change the company's total fixed costs.)
2. Assume the company has 1,000 units of this product left over from last year that are vastly inferior to the current model. The units must be sold through regular channels at reduced prices. What unit cost figure is relevant for establishing a minimum selling price for these units? Explain.

EXERCISE 13-11 Utilization of a Constrained Resource [LO5]

Benoit Company produces three products, A, B, and C. Data concerning the three products follow (per unit):

	Product		
	A	B	C
Selling price	$80	$56	$70
Less variable expenses:			
Direct materials.	24	15	9
Other variable expenses	24	27	40
Total variable expenses	48	42	49
Contribution margin	$32	$14	$21
Contribution margin ratio	40%	25%	30%

Demand for the company's products is very strong, with far more orders each month than the company has raw materials available to produce. The same material is used in each product. The material costs $3 per pound with a maximum of 5,000 pounds available each month.

Required:
Which orders would you advise the company to accept first, those for A, for B, or for C? Which orders second? Third?

EXERCISE 13-12 Sell or Process Further [LO6]
Wexpro, Inc., produces several products from processing 1 ton of clypton, a rare mineral. Material and processing costs total $60,000 per ton, one-fourth of which is allocated to product X. Seven thousand units of product X are produced from each ton of clypton. The units can either be sold at the split-off point for $9 each, or processed further at a total cost of $9,500 and then sold for $12 each.

Required:
Should product X be processed further or sold at the split-off point?

EXERCISE 13-13 Identification of Relevant Costs [LO1]
Hollings Company sells and delivers office furniture in the Rocky Mountain area.

The costs associated with the acquisition and annual operation of a delivery truck are given below:

Insurance	$1,600
Licenses.	$250
Taxes (vehicle)	$150
Garage rent for parking (per truck).	$1,200
Depreciation ($9,000 ÷ 5 years)	$1,800*
Gasoline, oil, tires, and repairs.	$0.07 per mile

*Based on obsolescence rather than on wear and tear.

Required:
1. Assume that Hollings Company has purchased one truck that has been driven 50,000 miles during the first year. Compute the average cost per mile of owning and operating the truck.
2. At the beginning of the second year, Hollings Company is unsure whether to use the truck or leave it parked in the garage and have all hauling done commercially. (The state requires the payment of vehicle taxes even if the vehicle isn't used.) What costs from the previous list are relevant to this decision? Explain.
3. Assume that the company decides to use the truck during the second year. Near year-end an order is received from a customer over 1,000 miles away. What costs from the previous list are relevant in a decision between using the truck to make the delivery and having the delivery done commercially? Explain.
4. Occasionally, the company could use two trucks at the same time. For this reason, some thought is being given to purchasing a second truck. The total miles driven would be the same as if only one truck were owned. What costs from the previous list are relevant to a decision over whether to purchase the second truck? Explain.

EXERCISE 13-14 Dropping or Retaining a Segment [LO2]

Thalassines Kataskeves, S.A., of Greece makes marine equipment. The company has been experiencing losses on its bilge pump product line for several years. The most recent quarterly contribution format income statement for the bilge pump product line follows:

Thalassines Kataskeves, S.A. Income Statement—Bilge Pump For the Quarter Ended March 31		
Sales		€850,000
Less variable expenses:		
Variable manufacturing expenses	€330,000	
Sales commissions	42,000	
Shipping	18,000	
Total variable expenses		390,000
Contribution margin		460,000
Less fixed expenses:		
Advertising	270,000	
Depreciation of equipment (no resale value)	80,000	
General factory overhead	105,000*	
Salary of product-line manager	32,000	
Insurance on inventories	8,000	
Purchasing department expenses	45,000†	
Total fixed expenses		540,000
Net operating loss		€(80,000)

*Common costs allocated on the basis of machine-hours.
†Common costs allocated on the basis of sales dollars.

The currency in Greece is the euro, denoted here by €. Discontinuing the bilge pump product line would not affect sales of other product lines and would have no effect on the company's total general factory overhead or total Purchasing Department expenses.

Required:

Would you recommend that the bilge pump product line be discontinued? Support your answer with appropriate computations.

EXERCISE 13-15 Make or Buy a Component [LO3]

Han Products manufactures 30,000 units of part S-6 each year for use on its production line. At this level of activity, the cost per unit for part S-6 is as follows:

Direct materials	$ 3.60
Direct labor	10.00
Variable manufacturing overhead	2.40
Fixed manufacturing overhead	9.00
Total cost per part	$25.00

An outside supplier has offered to sell 30,000 units of part S-6 each year to Han Products for $21 per part. If Han Products accepts this offer, the facilities now being used to manufacture part S-6 could be rented to another company at an annual rental of $80,000. However, Han Products has determined that two-thirds of the fixed manufacturing overhead being applied to part S-6 would continue even if part S-6 were purchased from the outside supplier.

Required:

Prepare computations showing how much profits will increase or decrease if the outside supplier's offer is accepted.

PROBLEM 13-16 Dropping or Retaining a Flight [LO2]

Profits have been decreasing for several years at Pegasus Airlines. In an effort to improve the company's performance, consideration is being given to dropping several flights that appear to be unprofitable.

A typical income statement for one such flight (flight 482) is given below (per flight):

Ticket revenue (175 seats × 40% occupancy × $200 ticket price).............	$14,000	100.0%
Variable expenses ($15 per person)............	1,050	7.5
Contribution margin	12,950	92.5%
Flight expenses:		
Salaries, flight crew......................	1,800	
Flight promotion	750	
Depreciation of aircraft	1,550	
Fuel for aircraft	5,800	
Liability insurance	4,200	
Salaries, flight assistants	1,500	
Baggage loading and flight preparation........	1,700	
Overnight costs for flight crew and		
assistants at destination	300	
Total flight expenses.......................	17,600	
Net operating loss	$ (4,650)	

The following additional information is available about flight 482:

a. Members of the flight crew are paid fixed annual salaries, whereas the flight assistants are paid by the flight.

b. One-third of the liability insurance is a special charge assessed against flight 482 because in the opinion of the insurance company, the destination of the flight is in a "high-risk" area. The remaining two-thirds would be unaffected by a decision to drop flight 482.

c. The baggage loading and flight preparation expense is an allocation of ground crews' salaries and depreciation of ground equipment. Dropping flight 482 would have no effect on the company's total baggage loading and flight preparation expenses.

d. If flight 482 is dropped, Pegasus Airlines has no authorization at present to replace it with another flight.

e. Aircraft depreciation is due entirely to obsolescence. Depreciation due to wear and tear is negligible.

f. Dropping flight 482 would not allow Pegasus Airlines to reduce the number of aircraft in its fleet or the number of flight crew on its payroll.

Required:

1. Prepare an analysis showing what impact dropping flight 482 would have on the airline's profits.

2. The airline's scheduling officer has been criticized because only about 50% of the seats on Pegasus' flights are being filled compared to an industry average of 60%. The scheduling officer has explained that Pegasus' average seat occupancy could be improved considerably by eliminating about 10% of its flights, but that doing so would reduce profits. Explain how this could happen.

PROBLEM 13-17 Sell or Process Further [LO6]

(Prepared from a situation suggested by Professor John W. Hardy.) Lone Star Meat Packers is a major processor of beef and other meat products. The company has a large amount of T-bone steak on hand, and it is trying to decide whether to sell the T-bone steaks as they are initially cut or to process them further into filet mignon and the New York cut.

If the T-bone steaks are sold as initially cut, the company figures that a 1-pound T-bone steak would yield the following profit:

Selling price ($2.25 per pound)	$2.25
Less joint costs incurred up to the split-off point where T-bone steak can be identified as a separate product........	1.80
Profit per pound	$0.45

As mentioned above, instead of being sold as initially cut, the T-bone steaks could be further processed into filet mignon and New York cut steaks. Cutting one side of a T-bone steak provides the filet mignon, and cutting the other side provides the New York cut. One 16-ounce T-bone steak cut in this way will yield one 6-ounce filet mignon and one 8-ounce New York cut; the remaining ounces are waste. The cost of processing the T-bone steaks into these cuts is $0.25 per pound. The filet mignon can be sold for $4.00 per pound, and the New York cut can be sold for $2.80 per pound.

Required:

1. Determine the profit per pound from processing the T-bone steaks into filet mignon and New York cut steaks.

2. Would you recommend that the T-bone steaks be sold as initially cut or processed further? Why?

PROBLEM 13-18 Close or Retain a Store [LO2]

Superior Markets, Inc., operates three stores in a large metropolitan area. A segmented absorption costing income statement for the company for the last quarter is given below:

Superior Markets, Inc. Income Statement For the Quarter Ended September 30				
	Total	North Store	South Store	East Store
Sales..........................	$3,000,000	$720,000	$1,200,000	$1,080,000
Cost of goods sold	1,657,200	403,200	660,000	594,000
Gross margin	1,342,800	316,800	540,000	486,000
Selling and administrative expenses:				
Selling expenses..................	817,000	231,400	315,000	270,600
Administrative expenses:..........	383,000	106,000	150,900	126,100
Total expenses	1,200,000	337,400	465,900	396,700
Net operating income (loss)	$ 142,800	$(20,600)	$ 74,100	$ 89,300

The North Store has consistently shown losses over the past two years. For this reason, management is giving consideration to closing the store. The company has retained you to make a recommendation as to whether the store should be closed or kept open. The following additional information is available for your use:

a. The breakdown of the selling and administrative expenses is as follows:

	Total	North Store	South Store	East Store
Selling expenses:				
Sales salaries....................	$239,000	$ 70,000	$ 89,000	$ 80,000
Direct advertising.................	187,000	51,000	72,000	64,000
General advertising*	45,000	10,800	18,000	16,200
Store rent.......................	300,000	85,000	120,000	95,000
Depreciation of store fixtures........	16,000	4,600	6,000	5,400
Delivery salaries..................	21,000	7,000	7,000	7,000
Depreciation of delivery				
equipment....................	9,000	3,000	3,000	3,000
Total selling expenses	$817,000	$231,400	$315,000	$270,600

*Allocated on the basis of sales dollars.

	Total	North Store	South Store	East Store
Administrative expenses:				
Store management salaries	$ 70,000	$ 21,000	$ 30,000	$ 19,000
General office salaries*	50,000	12,000	20,000	18,000
Insurance on fixtures and inventory.	25,000	7,500	9,000	8,500
Utilities	106,000	31,000	40,000	35,000
Employment taxes	57,000	16,500	21,900	18,600
General office—other*	75,000	18,000	30,000	27,000
Total administrative expenses	$383,000	$106,000	$150,900	$126,100

*Allocated on the basis of sales dollars.

b.   The lease on the building housing the North Store can be broken with no penalty.
c.   The fixtures being used in the North Store would be transferred to the other two stores if the North Store were closed.
d.   The general manager of the North Store would be retained and transferred to another position in the company if the North Store were closed. She would be filling a position that would otherwise be filled by hiring a new employee at a salary of $11,000 per quarter. The general manager of the North Store would be retained at her normal salary of $12,000 per quarter. All other employees in the store would be discharged.
e.   The company has one delivery crew that serves all three stores. One delivery person could be discharged if the North Store were closed. This person's salary is $4,000 per quarter. The delivery equipment would be distributed to the other stores. The equipment does not wear out through use, but does eventually become obsolete.
f.   The company's employment taxes are 15% of salaries.
g.   One-third of the insurance in the North Store is on the store's fixtures.
h.   The "General office salaries" and "General office—other" relate to the overall management of Superior Markets, Inc. If the North Store were closed, one person in the general office could be discharged because of the decrease in overall workload. This person's compensation is $6,000 per quarter.

Required:
1.   Prepare a schedule showing the change in revenues and expenses and the impact on the company's overall net operating income that would result if the North Store were closed.
2.   Assuming that the store space can't be subleased, what recommendation would you make to the management of Superior Markets, Inc.?
3.   Disregard requirement 2. Assume that if the North Store were closed, at least one-fourth of its sales would transfer to the East Store, due to strong customer loyalty to Superior Markets. The East Store has ample capacity to handle the increased sales. You may assume that the increased sales in the East Store would yield the same gross margin percentage as present sales in that store. What effect would these factors have on your recommendation concerning the North Store? Show all computations to support your answer.

PROBLEM 13-19 Make or Buy Decision [LO3]

Silven Industries, which manufactures and sells a highly successful line of summer lotions and insect repellents, has decided to diversify in order to stabilize sales throughout the year. A natural area for the company to consider is the production of winter lotions and creams to prevent dry and chapped skin.

After considerable research, a winter products line has been developed. However, Silven's president has decided to introduce only one of the new products for this coming winter. If the product is a success, further expansion in future years will be initiated.

The product selected (called Chap-Off) is a lip balm that will be sold in a lipstick-type tube. The product will be sold to wholesalers in boxes of 24 tubes for $8 per box. Because of excess capacity, no additional fixed manufacturing overhead costs will be incurred to produce the product. However, a $90,000 charge for fixed manufacturing overhead will be absorbed by the product under the company's absorption costing system.

Using the estimated sales and production of 100,000 boxes of Chap-Off, the Accounting Department has developed the following cost per box:

Direct material	$3.60
Direct labor	2.00
Manufacturing overhead	1.40
Total cost	$7.00

The costs above include costs for producing both the lip balm and the tube that contains it. As an alternative to making the tubes, Silven has approached a supplier to discuss the possibility of purchasing the tubes for Chap-Off. The purchase price of the empty tubes from the supplier would be $1.35 per box of 24 tubes. If Silven Industries accepts the purchase proposal, direct labor and variable manufacturing overhead costs per box of Chap-Off would be reduced by 10% and direct materials costs would be reduced by 25%.

Required:
1. Should Silven Industries make or buy the tubes? Show calculations to support your answer.
2. What would be the maximum purchase price acceptable to Silven Industries? Explain.
3. Instead of sales of 100,000 boxes, revised estimates show a sales volume of 120,000 boxes. At this new volume, additional equipment must be acquired to manufacture the tubes at an annual rental of $40,000. Assuming that the outside supplier will not accept an order for less than 100,000 boxes, should Silven Industries make or buy the tubes? Show computations to support your answer.
4. Refer to the data in (3) above. Assume that the outside supplier will accept an order of any size for the tubes at $1.35 per box. How, if at all, would this change your answer? Show computations.
5. What qualitative factors should Silven Industries consider in determining whether they should make or buy the tubes?

(CMA, adapted)

PROBLEM 13-20 Accept or Reject a Special Order [LO4]
Polaski Company manufactures and sells a single product called a Ret. Operating at capacity, the company can produce and sell 30,000 Rets per year. Costs associated with this level of production and sales are given below:

	Unit	Total
Direct materials	$15	$ 450,000
Direct labor.	8	240,000
Variable manufacturing overhead.	3	90,000
Fixed manufacturing overhead.	9	270,000
Variable selling expense.	4	120,000
Fixed selling expense.	6	180,000
Total cost	$45	$1,350,000

The Rets normally sell for $50 each. Fixed manufacturing overhead is constant at $270,000 per year within the range of 25,000 through 30,000 Rets per year.

Required:
1. Assume that due to a recession, Polaski Company expects to sell only 25,000 Rets through regular channels next year. A large retail chain has offered to purchase 5,000 Rets if Polaski is willing to accept a 16% discount off the regular price. There would be no sales commissions on this order; thus, variable selling expenses would be slashed by 75%. However, Polaski Company would have to purchase a special machine to engrave the retail chain's name on the 5,000 units. This machine would cost $10,000. Polaski Company has no assurance that the retail chain will purchase additional units in the future. Determine the impact on profits next year if this special order is accepted.
2. Refer to the original data. Assume again that Polaski Company expects to sell only 25,000 Rets through regular channels next year. The U.S. Army would like to make a one-time-only purchase of 5,000 Rets. The Army would pay a fixed fee of $1.80 per Ret, and it would reimburse Polaski Company for all costs of production (variable and fixed) associated with the units. Since the army would pick up the Rets with its own trucks, there would be no variable selling expenses associated with this order. If Polaski Company accepts the order, by how much will profits increase or decrease for the year?
3. Assume the same situation as that described in (2) above, except that the company expects to sell 30,000 Rets through regular channels next year. Thus, accepting the U.S. Army's order would require giving up regular sales of 5,000 Rets. If the Army's order is accepted, by how much will profits increase or decrease from what they would be if the 5,000 Rets were sold through regular channels?

PROBLEM 13-21 Shutting Down or Continuing to Operate a Plant [LO2]

(Note: This type of decision is similar to dropping a product line.)

Birch Company normally produces and sells 30,000 units of RG-6 each month. RG-6 is a small electrical relay used as a component part in the automotive industry. The selling price is $22 per unit, variable costs are $14 per unit, fixed manufacturing overhead costs total $150,000 per month, and fixed selling costs total $30,000 per month.

Employment-contract strikes in the companies that purchase the bulk of the RG-6 units have caused Birch Company's sales to temporarily drop to only 8,000 units per month. Birch Company estimates that the strikes will last for two months, after which time sales of RG-6 should return to normal. Due to the current low level of sales, Birch Company is thinking about closing down its own plant during the strike, which would reduce its fixed manufacturing overhead costs by $45,000 per month and its fixed selling costs by 10%. Start-up costs at the end of the shutdown period would total $8,000. Since Birch Company uses just-in-time (JIT) production methods, no inventories are on hand.

Required:

1. Assuming that the strikes continue for two months, would you recommend that Birch Company close its own plant? Explain. Show computations to support your answer.
2. At what level of sales (in units) for the two-month period should Birch Company be indifferent between closing the plant or keeping it open? Show computations. (Hint: This is a type of break-even analysis, except that the fixed cost portion of your break-even computation should include only those fixed costs that are relevant [i.e., avoidable] over the two-month period.)

PROBLEM 13-22 Relevant Cost Analysis in a Variety of Situations [LO2, LO3, LO4]

Andretti Company has a single product called a Dak. The company normally produces and sells 60,000 Daks each year at a selling price of $32 per unit. The company's unit costs at this level of activity are given below:

Direct materials	$10.00
Direct labor.	4.50
Variable manufacturing overhead.	2.30
Fixed manufacturing overhead.	5.00 ($300,000 total)
Variable selling expenses.	1.20
Fixed selling expenses.	3.50 ($210,000 total)
Total cost per unit.	$26.50

A number of questions relating to the production and sale of Daks follow. Each question is independent.

Required:

1. Assume that Andretti Company has sufficient capacity to produce 90,000 Daks each year without any increase in fixed manufacturing overhead costs. The company could increase its sales by 25% above the present 60,000 units each year if it were willing to increase the fixed selling expenses by $80,000. Would the increased fixed selling expenses be justified?
2. Assume again that Andretti Company has sufficient capacity to produce 90,000 Daks each year. A customer in a foreign market wants to purchase 20,000 Daks. Import duties on the Daks would be $1.70 per unit, and costs for permits and licenses would be $9,000. The only selling costs that would be associated with the order would be $3.20 per unit shipping cost. Compute the per unit break-even price on this order.
3. The company has 1,000 Daks on hand that have some irregularities and are therefore considered to be "seconds." Due to the irregularities, it will be impossible to sell these units at the normal price through regular distribution channels. What unit cost figure is relevant for setting a minimum selling price? Explain.
4. Due to a strike in its supplier's plant, Andretti Company is unable to purchase more material for the production of Daks. The strike is expected to last for two months. Andretti Company has enough material on hand to operate at 30% of normal levels for the two-month period. As an alternative, Andretti could close its plant down entirely for the two months. If the plant were closed, fixed manufacturing overhead costs would continue at 60% of their normal level during the two-month period and the fixed selling expenses would be reduced by 20%. What would be the impact on profits of closing the plant for the two-month period?
5. An outside manufacturer has offered to produce Daks and ship them directly to Andretti's customers. If Andretti Company accepts this offer, the facilities that it uses to produce Daks would be idle; however, fixed manufacturing overhead costs would be reduced by 75%. Since the

outside manufacturer would pay for all shipping costs, the variable selling expenses would be only two-thirds of their present amount. Compute the unit cost that is relevant for comparison to the price quoted by the outside manufacturer.

PROBLEM 13-23 Make or Buy Analysis [LO3]
"In my opinion, we ought to stop making our own drums and accept that outside supplier's offer," said Wim Niewindt, managing director of Antilles Refining, N.V., of Aruba. "At a price of 18 florins per drum, we would be paying 5 florins less than it costs us to manufacture the drums in our own plant. (The currency in Aruba is the florin, denoted below by fl.) Since we use 60,000 drums a year, that would be an annual cost savings of 300,000 florins." Antilles Refining's present cost to manufacture one drum is given below (based on 60,000 drums per year):

Direct materials	fl10.35
Direct labor.	6.00
Variable overhead	1.50
Fixed overhead (fl2.80 general company overhead, fl1.60 depreciation and, fl0.75 supervision)	5.15
Total cost per drum.	fl23.00

A decision about whether to make or buy the drums is especially important at this time since the equipment being used to make the drums is completely worn out and must be replaced. The choices facing the company are:

Alternative 1: Rent new equipment and continue to make the drums. The equipment would be rented for fl135,000 per year.

Alternative 2: Purchase the drums from an outside supplier at fl18 per drum.

The new equipment would be more efficient than the equipment that Antilles Refining has been using and, according to the manufacturer, would reduce direct labor and variable overhead costs by 30%. The old equipment has no resale value. Supervision cost (fl45,000 per year) and direct materials cost per drum would not be affected by the new equipment. The new equipment's capacity would be 90,000 drums per year.

The company's total general company overhead would be unaffected by this decision.

Required:

1. To assist the managing director in making a decision, prepare an analysis showing the total cost and the cost per drum for each of the two alternatives given above. Assume that 60,000 drums are needed each year. Which course of action would you recommend to the managing director?

2. Would your recommendation in (1) above be the same if the company's needs were: (a) 75,000 drums per year or (b) 90,000 drums per year? Show computations to support your answer, with costs presented on both a total and a per unit basis.

3. What other factors would you recommend that the company consider before making a decision?

PROBLEM 13-24 Utilization of a Constrained Resource [LO5]
The Walton Toy Company manufactures a line of dolls and a doll dress sewing kit. Demand for the dolls is increasing, and management requests assistance from you in determining an economical sales and production mix for the coming year. The company has provided the following data:

Product	Demand Next Year (units)	Selling Price per Unit	Direct Materials	Direct Labor
Debbie	50,000	$13.50	$4.30	$3.20
Trish	42,000	$5.50	$1.10	$2.00
Sarah	35,000	$21.00	$6.44	$5.60
Mike	40,000	$10.00	$2.00	$4.00
Sewing kit	325,000	$8.00	$3.20	$1.60

The following additional information is available:

a.   The company's plant has a capacity of 130,000 direct labor-hours per year on a single-shift basis. The company's present employees and equipment can produce all five products.

b.   The direct labor rate of $8 per hour is expected to remain unchanged during the coming year.

c.   Fixed costs total $520,000 per year. Variable overhead costs are $2 per direct labor-hour.

d.   All of the company's nonmanufacturing costs are fixed.

e.   The company's finished goods inventory is negligible and can be ignored.

Required:

1.   Determine the contribution margin per direct labor-hour expended on each product.

2.   Prepare a schedule showing the total direct labor-hours that will be required to produce the units estimated to be sold during the coming year.

3.   Examine the data you have computed in (1) and (2) above. How would you allocate the 130,000 direct labor hours of capacity to Walton Toy Company's various products?

4.   What is the highest price, in terms of a rate per hour, that Walton Toy Company should be willing to pay for additional capacity (that is, for added direct labor time)?

5.   Assume again that the company does not want to reduce sales of any product. Identify ways in which the company could obtain the additional output.

(CPA, adapted)

PROBLEM 13-25 Sell or Process Further [LO6]

Come-Clean Corporation produces a variety of cleaning compounds and solutions for both industrial and household use. While most of its products are processed independently, a few are related, such as the company's Grit 337 and its Sparkle silver polish.

Grit 337 is a coarse cleaning powder with many industrial uses. It costs $1.60 a pound to make, and it has a selling price of $2.00 a pound. A small portion of the annual production of Grit 337 is retained in the factory for further processing. It is combined with several other ingredients to form a paste that is marketed as Sparkle silver polish. The silver polish sells for $4.00 per jar.

This further processing requires one-fourth pound of Grit 337 per jar of silver polish. The additional direct costs involved in the processing of a jar of silver polish are:

Other ingredients	$0.65
Direct labor	1.48
Total direct cost	$2.13

Overhead costs associated with the processing of the silver polish are:

Variable manufacturing overhead cost.	25% of direct labor cost
Fixed manufacturing overhead cost (per month):	
Production supervisor.	$3,000
Depreciation of mixing equipment	$1,400

The production supervisor has no duties other than to oversee production of the silver polish. The mixing equipment is special-purpose equipment acquired specifically to produce the silver polish. Its resale value is negligible and it does not wear out through use.

Direct labor is a variable cost at Come-Clean Corporation.

Advertising costs for the silver polish total $4,000 per month. Variable selling costs associated with the silver polish are 7.5% of sales.

Due to a recent decline in the demand for silver polish, the company is wondering whether its continued production is advisable. The sales manager feels that it would be more profitable to sell all of the Grit 337 as a cleaning powder.

Required:

1.   What is the incremental contribution margin per jar from further processing of Grit 337 into silver polish?

2.   What is the minimum number of jars of silver polish that must be sold each month to justify the continued processing of Grit 337 into silver polish? Explain. Show all computations in good form.

(CMA, adapted)

Cases

CASE 13-26 Integrative Case: Relevant Costs; Pricing [LO1, LO4]

Wesco Incorporated's only product is a combination fertilizer-weed killer called GrowNWeed. GrowNWeed is sold nationwide to retail nurseries and garden stores.

Zwinger Nursery plans to sell a similar fertilizer weed killer compound through its regional nursery chain under its own private label. Zwinger does not have manufacturing facilities of its own, so it has asked Wesco (and several other companies) to submit a bid for manufacturing and delivering a 20,000-pound order of the private brand compound to Zwinger. While the chemical composition of the Zwinger compound differs from that of GrowNWeed, the manufacturing processes are very similar.

The Zwinger compound would be produced in 1,000-pound lots. Each lot would require 25 direct labor-hours and the following chemicals:

Chemicals	Quantity in Pounds
AG-5	300
KL-2	200
CW-7	150
DF-6	175

The first three chemicals (AG-5, KL-2, and CW-7) are all used in the production of GrowNWeed. DF-6 was used in another compound that Wesco discontinued several months ago. The supply of DF-6 that Wesco had on hand when the other compound was discontinued was not discarded. Wesco could sell its supply of DF-6 at the prevailing market price less $0.10 per pound selling and handling expenses.

Wesco also has on hand a chemical called BH-3, which was manufactured for use in another product that is no longer produced. BH-3, which cannot be used in GrowNWeed, can be substituted for AG-5 on a one-for-one basis without affecting the quality of the Zwinger compound. The BH-3 in inventory has a salvage value of $600.

Inventory and cost data for the chemicals that can be used to produce the Zwinger compound are shown below:

Raw Material	Pounds in Inventory	Actual Price per Pound When Purchased	Current Market Price per Pound
AG-5	18,000	$1.15	$1.20
KL-2	6,000	$1.10	$1.05
CW-7	7,000	$1.35	$1.35
DF-6	3,000	$0.80	$0.70
BH-3	3,500	$0.90	(Salvage)

The current direct labor wage rate is $14 per hour. The predetermined overhead rate is based on direct labor-hours (DLH). The predetermined overhead rate for the current year, based on a two-shift capacity with no overtime, is as follows:

Variable manufacturing overhead	$ 3.00 per DLH
Fixed manufacturing overhead	10.50 per DLH
Combined predetermined overhead rate	$13.50 per DLH

Wesco's production manager reports that the present equipment and facilities are adequate to manufacture the Zwinger compound. Therefore, the order would have no effect on total fixed manufacturing overhead costs. However, Wesco is within 400 hours of its two-shift capacity this month. Any additional hours beyond the 400 hours must be done in overtime. If need be, the Zwinger compound could be produced on regular time by shifting a portion of GrowNWeed production to overtime. Wesco's direct labor wage rate for overtime is $21 per hour. There is no allowance for any overtime premium in the predetermined overhead rate.

Required:

1. Wesco has decided to submit a bid for the 20,000-pound order of Zwinger's new compound. The order must be delivered by the end of the current month. Zwinger has indicated that this is a one-time order that will not be repeated. Calculate the lowest price that Wesco could bid for the order without reducing its net operating income.

2. Refer to the original data. Assume that Zwinger Nursery plans to place regular orders for 20,000-pound lots of the new compound. Wesco expects the demand for GrowNWeed to remain strong. Therefore, the recurring orders from Zwinger would put Wesco over its two-shift capacity. However, production could be scheduled so that 90% of each Zwinger order could be completed during regular hours. As another option, some GrowNWeed production could be shifted temporarily to overtime so that the Zwinger orders could be produced on regular time. Current market prices are the best available estimates of future market prices.

   Wesco's standard markup policy for new products is 40% of the full manufacturing cost, including fixed manufacturing overhead. Calculate the price that Wesco, Inc., would quote Zwinger Nursery for each 20,000-pound lot of the new compound, assuming that it is to be treated as a new product and this pricing policy is followed.

   (CMA, adapted)

CASE 13-27 Ethics and the Manager; Shut Down or Continue Operations [LO2]

Haley Romeros had just been appointed vice president of the Rocky Mountain Region of the Bank Services Corporation (BSC). The company provides check processing services for small banks. The banks send checks presented for deposit or payment to BSC, which records the data on each check in a computerized database. BSC then sends the data electronically to the nearest Federal Reserve Bank check-clearing center where the appropriate transfers of funds are made between banks. The Rocky Mountain Region has three check processing centers, which are located in Billings, Montana; Great Falls, Montana; and Clayton, Idaho. Prior to her promotion to vice president, Ms. Romeros had been the manager of a check processing center in New Jersey.

Immediately upon assuming her new position, Ms. Romeros requested a complete financial report for the just-ended fiscal year from the region's controller, John Littlebear. Ms. Romeros specified that the financial report should follow the standardized format required by corporate headquarters for all regional performance reports. That report follows:

Financial Performance Rocky Mountain Region				
		Check Processing Centers		
	Total	Billings	Great Falls	Clayton
Sales.	$50,000,000	$20,000,000	$18,000,000	$12,000,000
Operating expenses:				
Direct labor	32,000,000	12,500,000	11,000,000	8,500,000
Variable overhead	850,000	350,000	310,000	190,000
Equipment depreciation	3,900,000	1,300,000	1,400,000	1,200,000
Facility expense	2,800,000	900,000	800,000	1,100,000
Local administrative expense*	450,000	140,000	160,000	150,000
Regional administrative expense†	1,500,000	600,000	540,000	360,000
Corporate administrative expense‡	4,750,000	1,900,000	1,710,000	1,140,000
Total operating expense	46,250,000	17,690,000	15,920,000	12,640,000
Net operating income	$ 3,750,000	$ 2,310,000	$ 2,080,000	$ (640,000)

*Local administrative expenses are the administrative expenses incurred at the check processing centers.
†Regional administrative expenses are allocated to the check processing centers based on sales.
‡Corporate administrative expenses are charged to segments of the company such as the Rocky Mountain Region and the check processing centers at the rate of 9.5% of their sales.

Upon seeing this report, Ms. Romeros summoned John Littlebear for an explanation.

Romeros: What's the story on Clayton? It didn't have a loss the previous year did it?

Littlebear: No, the Clayton facility has had a nice profit every year since it was opened six years ago, but Clayton lost a big contract this year.

Romeros: Why?

Littlebear: One of our national competitors entered the local market and bid very aggressively on the contract. We couldn't afford to meet the bid. Clayton's costs—particularly their facility expenses—are just too high. When Clayton lost the contract, we had to lay off a lot of employees, but we could not reduce the fixed costs of the Clayton facility.

Romeros: Why is Clayton's facility expense so high? It's a smaller facility than either Billings or Great Falls and yet its facility expense is higher.

Littlebear: The problem is that we are able to rent suitable facilities very cheaply at Billings and Great Falls. No such facilities were available at Clayton; we had them built. Unfortunately, there were big cost overruns. The contractor we hired was inexperienced at this kind of work and in fact went bankrupt before the project was completed. After hiring another contractor to finish the work, we were way over budget. The large depreciation charges on the facility didn't matter at first because we didn't have much competition at the time and could charge premium prices.

Romeros: Well we can't do that anymore. The Clayton facility will obviously have to be shut down. Its business can be shifted to the other two check processing centers in the region.

Littlebear: I would advise against that. The $1,200,000 in depreciation at the Clayton facility is misleading. That facility should last indefinitely with proper maintenance. And it has no resale value; there is no other commercial activity around Clayton.

Romeros: What about the other costs at Clayton?

Littlebear: If we shifted Clayton's business over to the other two processing centers in the region, we wouldn't save anything on direct labor or variable overhead costs. We might save $90,000 or so in local administrative expense, but we would not save any regional administrative expense and corporate headquarters would still charge us 9.5% of our sales as corporate administrative expense.

In addition, we would have to rent more space in Billings and Great Falls in order to handle the work transferred from Clayton; that would probably cost us at least $600,000 a year. And don't forget that it will cost us something to move the equipment from Clayton to Billings and Great Falls. And the move will disrupt service to customers.

Romeros: I understand all of that, but a money-losing processing center on my performance report is completely unacceptable.

Littlebear: And if you shut down Clayton, you are going to throw some loyal employees out of work.

Romeros: That's unfortunate, but we have to face hard business realities.

Littlebear: And you would have to write off the investment in the facilities at Clayton.

Romeros: I can explain a write-off to corporate headquarters; hiring an inexperienced contractor to build the Clayton facility was my predecessor's mistake. But they'll have my head at headquarters if I show operating losses every year at one of my processing centers. Clayton has to go. At the next corporate board meeting, I am going to recommend that the Clayton facility be closed.

Required:

1. From the standpoint of the company as a whole, should the Clayton processing center be shut down and its work redistributed to other processing centers in the region? Explain.

2. Do you think Haley Romeros's decision to shut down the Clayton facility is ethical? Explain.

3. What influence should the depreciation on the facilities at Clayton have on prices charged by Clayton for its services?

CASE 13-28 Make or Buy; Utilization of a Constrained Resource [LO1, LO3, LO5]

TufStuff, Inc., sells a wide range of drums, bins, boxes, and other containers that are used in the chemical industry. One of the company's products is a heavy-duty corrosion-resistant metal drum, called the WVD drum, used to store toxic wastes. Production is constrained by the capacity of an automated welding machine that is used to make precision welds. A total of 2,000 hours of welding time is available annually on the machine. Since each drum requires 0.4 hour of welding time, annual production is limited to 5,000 drums. At present, the welding machine is used exclusively to make the WVD drums. The accounting department has provided the following financial data concerning the WVD drums:

		WVD Drums
Selling price per drum		$149.00
Cost per drum:		
Direct materials	$52.10	
Direct labor ($18 per hour)	3.60	
Manufacturing overhead	4.50	
Selling and administrative expense	29.80	90.00
Margin per drum		$ 59.00

Management believes 6,000 WVD drums could be sold each year if the company had sufficient manufacturing capacity. As an alternative to adding another welding machine, management has considered buying additional drums from an outside supplier. Harcor Industries, Inc., a supplier of quality products, would be able to provide up to 4,000 WVD-type drums per year at a price of $138 per drum, which TufStuff would resell to its customers at its normal selling price after appropriate relabeling.

Megan Flores, TufStuff's production manager, has suggested that the company could make better use of the welding machine by manufacturing bike frames, which would require only 0.5 hour of welding time per frame and yet sell for far more than the drums. Megan believes that TufStuff could sell up to 1,600 bike frames per year to bike manufacturers at a price of $239 each. The accounting department has provided the following data concerning the proposed new product:

Bike Frames		
Selling price per frame		$239.00
Cost per frame:		
Direct materials.	$99.40	
Direct labor ($18 per hour)	28.80	
Manufacturing overhead	36.00	
Selling and administrative expense.	47.80	212.00
Margin per frame		$ 27.00

The bike frames could be produced with existing equipment and personnel. Manufacturing overhead is allocated to products on the basis of direct labor-hours. Most of the manufacturing overhead consists of fixed common costs such as rent on the factory building, but some of it is variable. The variable manufacturing overhead has been estimated at $1.35 per WVD drum and $1.90 per bike frame. The variable manufacturing overhead cost would not be incurred on drums acquired from the outside supplier.

Selling and administrative expenses are allocated to products on the basis of revenues. Almost all of the selling and administrative expenses are fixed common costs, but it has been estimated that variable selling and administrative expenses amount to $0.75 per WVD drum whether made or purchased and would be $1.30 per bike frame.

All of the company's employees—direct and indirect—are paid for full 40-hour workweeks and the company has a policy of laying off workers only in major recessions.

Required:
1. Given the margins of the two products as indicated in the reports submitted by the accounting department, does it make sense to consider producing the bike frames? Explain.
2. Compute the contribution margin per unit for:
   a. Purchased WVD drums.
   b. Manufactured WVD drums.
   c. Manufactured bike frames.
3. Determine the number of WVD drums (if any) that should be purchased and the number of WVD drums and/or bike frames (if any) that should be manufactured. What is the increase in net operating income that would result from this plan over current operations?

   As soon as your analysis was shown to the top management team at TufStuff, several managers got into an argument concerning how direct labor costs should be treated when making this decision. One manager argued that direct labor is always treated as a variable cost in textbooks and in practice and has always been considered a variable cost at TufStuff. After all, "direct" means you can directly trace the cost to products. "If direct labor is not a variable cost, what is it?" Another manager argued just as strenuously that direct labor should be considered a fixed cost at TufStuff. No one had been laid off in over a decade, and for all practical purposes, everyone at the plant is on a monthly salary. Everyone classified as direct labor works a regular 40-hour workweek and overtime has not been necessary since the company adopted just-in-time techniques. Whether the welding machine is used to make drums or frames, the total payroll would be exactly the same. There is enough slack, in the form of idle time, to accommodate any increase in total direct labor time that the bike frames would require.
4. Redo requirements (2) and (3) above, making the opposite assumption about direct labor from the one you originally made. In other words, if you treated direct labor as a variable cost, redo the

analysis treating it as a fixed cost. If you treated direct labor as a fixed cost, redo the analysis treating it as a variable cost.

5. What do you think is the correct way to treat direct labor cost in this situation—as variable or as fixed?

CASE 13-29 Sell or Process Further Decision [LO6]

The Scottie Sweater Company produces sweaters under the "Scottie" label. The company buys raw wool and processes it into wool yarn from which the sweaters are woven. One spindle of wool yarn is required to produce one sweater. The costs and revenues associated with the sweaters are given below:

		Per Sweater
Selling price		$30.00
Cost to manufacture:		
Raw materials:		
Buttons, thread, lining	$ 2.00	
Wool yarn	16.00	
Total raw materials	18.00	
Direct labor	5.80	
Manufacturing overhead	8.70	32.50
Manufacturing profit (loss)		$ (2.50)

Originally, all of the wool yarn was used to produce sweaters, but in recent years a market has developed for the wool yarn itself. The yarn is purchased by other companies for use in production of wool blankets and other wool products. Since the development of the market for the wool yarn, a continuing dispute has existed in the Scottie Sweater Company as to whether the yarn should be sold simply as yarn or processed into sweaters. Current cost and revenue data on the yarn are given below:

		Per Spindle of Yarn
Selling price		$20.00
Cost to manufacture:		
Raw materials (raw wool)	$7.00	
Direct labor	3.60	
Manufacturing overhead	5.40	16.00
Manufacturing profit		$ 4.00

The market for sweaters is temporarily depressed, due to unusually warm weather in the western states where the sweaters are sold. This has made it necessary for the company to discount the selling price of the sweaters to $30 from the normal $40 price. Since the market for wool yarn has remained strong, the dispute has again surfaced over whether the yarn should be sold outright rather than processed into sweaters. The sales manager thinks that the production of sweaters should be discontinued; she is upset about having to sell sweaters at a $2.50 loss when the yarn could be sold for a $4.00 profit. However, the production superintendent does not want to close down a large portion of the factory. He argues that the company is in the sweater business, not the yarn business, and that the company should focus on its core strength.

All of the manufacturing overhead costs are fixed and would not be affected even if sweaters were discontinued. Manufacturing overhead is assigned to products on the basis of 150% of direct labor cost. Materials and direct labor costs are variable.

Required:

1. Would you recommend that the wool yarn be sold outright or processed into sweaters? Support your answer with appropriate computations and explain your reasoning.
2. What is the lowest price that the company should accept for a sweater? Support your answer with appropriate computations and explain your reasoning.

CASE 13-30 Plant Closing Decision [LO1, LO2]

QualSupport Corporation manufactures seats for automobiles, vans, trucks, and various recreational vehicles. The company has a number of plants around the world, including the Denver Cover Plant, which makes seat covers.

Ted Vosilo is the plant manager of the Denver Cover Plant, but also serves as the regional production manager for the company. His budget as the regional manager is charged to the Denver Cover Plant.

Vosilo has just heard that QualSupport has received a bid from an outside vendor to supply the equivalent of the entire annual output of the Denver Cover Plant for $35 million. Vosilo was astonished at the low outside bid because the budget for the Denver Cover Plant's operating costs for the upcoming year was set at $52 million. If this bid is accepted, the Denver Cover Plant will be closed down.

The budget for Denver Cover's operating costs for the coming year is presented below. Additional facts regarding the plant's operations are as follows:

a. Due to Denver Cover's commitment to use high-quality fabrics in all of its products, the Purchasing Department was instructed to place blanket purchase orders with major suppliers to ensure the receipt of sufficient materials for the coming year. If these orders are canceled as a consequence of the plant closing, termination charges would amount to 20% of the cost of direct materials.
b. Approximately 400 plant employees will lose their jobs if the plant is closed. This includes all of the direct laborers and supervisors as well as the plumbers, electricians, and other skilled workers classified as indirect plant workers. Some would be able to find new jobs while many others would have difficulty. All employees would have difficulty matching Denver Cover's base pay of $18.80 per hour, which is the highest in the area. A clause in Denver Cover's contract with the union may help some employees; the company must provide employment assistance to its former employees for 12 months after a plant closing. The estimated cost to administer this service would be $1.5 million for the year.
c. Some employees would probably choose early retirement because QualSupport has an excellent pension plan. In fact, $3 million of the annual pension expense would continue whether Denver Cover is open or not.
d. Vosilo and his staff would not be affected by the closing of Denver Cover. They would still be responsible for administering three other area plants.
e. If the Denver Cover Plant were closed, the company would realize about $3.2 million salvage value for the equipment and building. If the plant remains open, there are no plans to make any significant investments in new equipment or buildings. The old equipment is adequate and should last indefinitely.

Denver Cover Plant Annual Budget for Operating Costs		
Materials		$14,000,000
Labor:		
Direct	$13,100,000	
Supervision	900,000	
Indirect plant	4,000,000	18,000,000
Overhead:		
Depreciation—equipment	3,200,000	
Depreciation—building	7,000,000	
Pension expense	5,000,000	
Plant manager and staff	800,000	
Corporate allocation	4,000,000	20,000,000
Total budgeted costs		$52,000,000

Required:

1. Without regard to costs, identify the advantages to QualSupport Corporation of continuing to obtain covers from its own Denver Cover Plant.

2. QualSupport Corporation plans to prepare a financial analysis that will be used in deciding whether or not to close the Denver Cover Plant. Management has asked you to identify:

    a. The annual budgeted costs that are relevant to the decision regarding closing the plant (show the dollar amounts).

    b. The annual budgeted costs that are *not* relevant to the decision regarding closing the plant and explain why they are not relevant (again show the dollar amounts).

    c. Any nonrecurring costs that would arise due to the closing of the plant, and explain how they would affect the decision (again show any dollar amounts).

3. Looking at the data you have prepared in (2) above, should the plant be closed? Show computations and explain your answer.

4. Identify any revenues or costs not specifically mentioned in the problem that QualSupport should consider before making a decision.

(CMA, adapted)

Capital Budgeting Decisions

Capital Investments: A Key to Profitable Growth

Cintas Corporation, headquartered in Cincinnati, Ohio, has experienced 37 years of uninterrupted growth in sales and profits. The company provides highly specialized services to businesses of all types throughout North America, but the backbone of its success is providing corporate identity uniforms to more than five million North American workers. Cintas has 350 uniform rental facilities, 15 manufacturing plants, and seven distribution centers across North America. While these numbers are certain to grow in the future, the challenge for Cintas is choosing among competing capital expansion opportunities.

At Cintas, each capital investment proposal must be accompanied by a financial analysis that estimates the cash inflows and outflows associated with the project. The job of Paul Carmichael, the Controller of Cintas' Rental Division, is to challenge the validity of the assumptions underlying the financial estimates. Is the cost to build the new facility underestimated? Are future revenue growth rates overly optimistic? Is it necessary to build a new facility, or could an existing facility be refurbished or expanded? Asking these types of constructive questions helps Cintas channel its limited investment funds to the growth opportunities that will create the most long-term value for shareholders. ■

Source: Author's conversation with Paul Carmichael, Controller, Rental Division, Cintas Corporation.

Learning Objectives

After studying Chapter 14, you should be able to:

LO1 Evaluate the acceptability of an investment project using the net present value method.

LO2 Evaluate the acceptability of an investment project using the internal rate of return method.

LO3 Evaluate an investment project that has uncertain cash flows.

LO4 Rank investment projects in order of preference.

LO5 Determine the payback period for an investment.

LO6 Compute the simple rate of return for an investment.

LO7 (Appendix 14A) Understand present value concepts and the use of present value tables.

LO8 (Appendix 14C) Include income taxes in a capital budgeting analysis.

Managers are often involved in making decisions that involve an investment today in the hope of realizing future profits. For example, Tri-Con Global Restaurants, Inc. makes an investment when it opens a new Pizza Hut restaurant. L. L. Bean makes an investment when it installs a new computer to handle customer billing. DaimlerChrysler makes an investment when it redesigns a product such as the Jeep Eagle. Merck & Co. invests in medical research. Amazon.com makes an investment when it redesigns its website. All of these investments require committing funds today with the expectation of earning a return on those funds in the future in the form of additional cash inflows or reduced cash outflows.

The term **capital budgeting** is used to describe how managers plan significant investments in projects that have long-term implications such as the purchase of new equipment or the introduction of new products. Most companies have many more potential projects than can actually be funded. Hence, managers must carefully select those projects that promise the greatest future return. How well managers make these capital budgeting decisions is a critical factor in the long-run profitability of the company.

Capital Budgeting—Planning Investments

Typical Capital Budgeting Decisions

Any decision that involves an outlay now in order to obtain a future return is a capital budgeting decision. Typical capital budgeting decisions include:

1. Cost reduction decisions. Should new equipment be purchased to reduce costs?
2. Expansion decisions. Should a new plant, warehouse, or other facility be acquired to increase capacity and sales?
3. Equipment selection decisions. Which of several available machines should be purchased?
4. Lease or buy decisions. Should new equipment be leased or purchased?
5. Equipment replacement decisions. Should old equipment be replaced now or later?

Capital budgeting decisions fall into two broad categories—*screening decisions* and *preference decisions*. **Screening decisions** relate to whether a proposed project is acceptable—whether it passes a preset hurdle. For example, a company may have a policy of accepting projects only if they promise a return of 20% on the investment. The required rate of return is the minimum rate of return a project must yield to be acceptable. **Preference decisions,** by contrast, relate to selecting from among several acceptable alternatives. To illustrate, a company may be considering several different machines to replace an existing machine on the assembly line. The choice of which machine to purchase is a preference decision. In this chapter, we first discuss screening decisions and then move on to preference decisions toward the end of the chapter.

The Time Value of Money

As stated earlier, capital investments usually earn returns that extend over fairly long periods of time. Therefore, it is important to recognize *the time value of money* when evaluating investment proposals. A dollar today is worth more than a dollar a year from now if for no other reason than that you could put a dollar in a bank today and have more than a dollar a year from now. Therefore, projects that promise earlier returns are preferable to those that promise later returns.

Capital budgeting techniques that recognize the time value of money involve *discounting cash flows.* We will spend most of this chapter showing how to use discounted cash flow methods in making capital budgeting decisions. If you are not already familiar with discounting and the use of present value tables, you should read Appendix 14A: The Concept of Present Value at the end of this chapter before proceeding any further.

CHOOSING A CAT

Sometimes a long-term decision does not have to involve present value calculations or any other sophisticated analytical technique. White Grizzly Adventures of Meadow Creek, British Columbia, needs two snowcats for its powder skiing operations—one for shuttling guests to the top of the mountain and one to be held in reserve in case of mechanical problems with the first. Bombardier of Canada sells new snowcats for $250,000 and used, reconditioned snowcats for $150,000. In either case, the snowcats are good for about 5,000 hours of operation before they need to be reconditioned. From White Grizzly's perspective, the choice is clear. Since both new and reconditioned snowcats last about 5,000 hours, but the reconditioned snowcats cost $100,000 less, the reconditioned snowcats are the obvious choice. They may not have all of the latest bells and whistles, but they get the job done at a price a small company can afford.

Bombardier snowcats do not have passenger cabs as standard equipment. To save money, White Grizzly builds its own custom-designed passenger cab for about $15,000, using recycled Ford Escort seats and industrial-strength aluminum for the frame and siding. If purchased at retail, a passenger cab would cost about twice as much and would not be as well-suited for snowcat skiing.

Source: Brad & Carole Karafil, owners and operators of White Grizzly Adventures, www.whitegrizzly.com.

Discounted Cash Flows—The Net Present Value Method

Two approaches to making capital budgeting decisions use discounted cash flows. One is the *net present value method,* and the other is the *internal rate of return method.* The net present value method is discussed in this section; the internal rate of return method is discussed in the following section.

The Net Present Value Method Illustrated

Under the net present value method, the present value of a project's cash inflows is compared to the present value of the project's cash outflows. The difference between the present value of these cash flows, called the **net present value,** determines whether or not the project is an acceptable investment. To illustrate, consider the following data:

Example A: Harper Company is contemplating the purchase of a machine capable of performing certain operations that are now performed manually. The machine will cost $50,000, and it will last for five years. At the end of the five-year period, the machine will have a zero scrap value. Use of the machine will reduce labor costs by $18,000 per year. Harper Company requires a minimum pretax return of 20% on all investment projects.[1]

Should the machine be purchased? Harper Company must determine whether a cash investment now of $50,000 can be justified if it will result in an $18,000 reduction in cost in each of the next five years. It may appear that the answer is obvious since the total cost savings is $90,000 ($18,000 per year × 5 years). However, the company can earn a 20% return by investing its money elsewhere. It is not enough that the cost reductions cover just the original cost of the machine; they must also yield a return of at least 20% or the company would be better off investing the money elsewhere.

---

[1] For simplicity, we ignore inflation and taxes. The impact of income taxes on capital budgeting decisions is discussed in Appendix 14C.

EXHIBIT 14–1
Net Present Value Analysis of a Proposed Project

Topic Tackler

PLUS

14–1

Initial cost			$50,000	
Life of the project			5 years	
Annual cost savings			$18,000	
Salvage value			$0	
Required rate of return			20%	

Item	Year(s)	Amount of Cash Flow	20% Factor	Present Value of Cash Flows
Annual cost savings	1–5	$ 18,000	2.991*	$53,838
Initial investment	Now	$(50,000)	1.000	(50,000)
Net present value				$ 3,838

*From Exhibit 14B–2 in Appendix 14B at the end of this chapter.

To determine whether the investment is desirable, the stream of annual $18,000 cost savings should be discounted to its present value and then compared to the cost of the new machine. Harper Company's minimum required return of 20% should be used as the *discount rate* in the discounting process. Exhibit 14–1 illustrates the computation of the net present value of this proposed project. The annual cost savings of $18,000 is multiplied by 2.991, the present value factor of a five-year annuity at the discount rate of 20%, to obtain $53,838.[2] This is the present value of the annual cost savings. The present value of the initial investment is computed by multiplying the investment amount of $50,000 by 1.000, the present value factor for any cash flow that occurs immediately.

According to the analysis, Harper Company should purchase the new machine. The present value of the cost savings is $53,838, whereas the present value of the required investment (cost of the machine) is only $50,000. Deducting the present value of the required investment from the present value of the cost savings yields the *net present value* of $3,838. Whenever the net present value is zero or greater, as in our example, an investment project is acceptable. Whenever the net present value is negative (the present value of the cash outflows exceeds the present value of the cash inflows), an investment project is not acceptable. In sum:

If the Net Present Value Is . . .	Then the Project Is . . .
Positive	Acceptable, since it promises a return greater than the required rate of return.
Zero	Acceptable, since it promises a return equal to the required rate of return.
Negative	Not acceptable, since it promises a return less than the required rate of return.

There is another way to interpret the net present value. Harper Company could spend up to $53,838 for the new machine and still obtain the minimum required 20% rate of return. The net present value of $3,838, therefore, shows the amount of "cushion" or "margin of error." One way to look at this is that the company could underestimate the cost of the new machine by up to $3,838, or overestimate the net present value of the future cash savings by up to $3,838, and the project would still be financially attractive.

---

[2] Unless otherwise stated, for the sake of simplicity we will assume in this chapter that all cash flows other than the initial investment occur at the ends of years.

Emphasis on Cash Flows

Accounting net income is based on accruals that ignore when cash flows occur. However, in capital budgeting, the timing of cash flows is critical. The present value of a cash flow depends on when it occurs. For that reason, cash flow rather than accounting net income is the focus in capital budgeting.[3] Examples of cash outflows and cash inflows that are often relevant to capital investment decisions are described below.

Typical Cash Outflows   Most projects have at least three types of cash outflows. First, they often require an immediate cash outflow in the form of an initial investment in equipment, other assets, and installation costs. Any salvage value realized from the sale of old equipment can be recognized as a reduction in the initial investment or as a cash inflow. Second, some projects require a company to expand its working capital. **Working capital** is current assets (e.g., cash, accounts receivable, and inventory) less current liabilities. When a company takes on a new project, the balances in the current asset accounts often increase. For example, opening a new Nordstrom's department store requires additional cash in sales registers and more inventory. These additional working capital needs are treated as part of the initial investment in a project. Third, many projects require periodic outlays for repairs and maintenance and additional operating costs.

Typical Cash Inflows   Most projects also have at least three types of cash inflows. First, a project will normally increase revenues or reduce costs. Either way, the amount involved should be treated as a cash inflow for capital budgeting purposes. Notice that from a cash flow standpoint, a reduction in costs is equivalent to an increase in revenues. Second, cash inflows are also frequently realized from selling equipment for its salvage value when a project ends, although the company may actually have to pay to dispose of some low-value or hazardous items. Third, any working capital that was tied up in the project can be released for use elsewhere at the end of the project and should be treated as a cash inflow at that time. Working capital is released, for example, when a company sells off its inventory or collects its accounts receivable.

IN BUSINESS

BEST BUY'S BIG GAMBLE

Best Buy is overhauling hundreds of its stores in an effort to tailor merchandise offerings and employee skills to meet the needs of each store's target customers. The cost to revamp one department of one store can easily exceed $600,000 for lighting and fixtures plus additional costs for employee training. While these initial cash outflows are readily quantifiable, the future cash inflows that they will generate are highly uncertain.

The first few dozen stores overhauled by Best Buy recorded sales growth that was three times greater than non-renovated stores. Best Buy reacted to these initial results by hastily renovating 154 more stores over the next three months. Shortly after completing these expensive renovations, the company had the misfortune of informing Wall Street that the newly revamped stores' growth rates were only slightly higher than non-renovated stores. This disappointing news apparently caused the market value of Best Buy's common stock to plummet by almost $3 billion in one day. Clearly, Wall Street analysts had serious concerns about the future cash flow generating ability of this capital investment project. Despite the "bump in the road," Best Buy remains committed to its course of action; however, the company has decided to slow down the pace of its implementation.

Source: Matthew Boyle, "Best Buy's Giant Gamble," *Fortune*, April, 3, 2006, pp. 69–75.

---

[3]   Under certain conditions, capital budgeting decisions can be correctly made by discounting appropriately defined accounting net income. However, this approach requires advanced techniques that are beyond the scope of this book.

In summary, the following types of cash flows are common in business investment projects:

> Cash outflows:
>   Initial investment (including installation costs).
>   Increased working capital needs.
>   Repairs and maintenance.
>   Incremental operating costs.
> Cash inflows:
>   Incremental revenues.
>   Reduction in costs.
>   Salvage value.
>   Release of working capital.

Recovery of the Original Investment

The net present value method automatically provides for return of the original investment. Whenever the net present value of a project is positive, the project will recover the original cost of the investment plus sufficient excess cash inflows to compensate for tying up funds in the project. To demonstrate this point, consider the following situation:

Example B: Carver Hospital is considering the purchase of an attachment for its X-ray machine that will cost $3,170. The attachment will be usable for four years, after which time it will have no salvage value. It will increase net cash inflows by $1,000 per year in the X-ray department. The hospital's board of directors requires a rate of return of at least 10% on such investments in equipment.

A net present value analysis of the desirability of purchasing the X-ray attachment is presented in Exhibit 14–2. Notice that the attachment promises exactly a 10% return on the original investment, since the net present value is zero at a 10% discount rate.

Each annual $1,000 cash inflow arising from use of the attachment is made up of two parts. One part represents a recovery of a portion *of* the original $3,170 paid for the attachment, and the other part represents a return *on* this investment. The breakdown of each year's $1,000 cash inflow between recovery *of* investment and return *on* investment is shown in Exhibit 14–3.

The first year's $1,000 cash inflow consists of a return *on* investment of $317 (a 10% return *on* the $3,170 original investment), plus a $683 return *of* that investment. Since the amount of the unrecovered investment decreases each year, the dollar amount of the return on investment also decreases each year. By the end of the fourth year, all $3,170 of the original investment has been recovered.

EXHIBIT 14–2
Carver Hospital—Net Present Value Analysis of X-Ray Attachment

Initial cost	$3,170
Life of the project	4 years
Annual net cash inflow	$1,000
Salvage value	$0
Required rate of return	10%

Item	Year(s)	Amount of Cash Flow	10% Factor	Present Value of Cash Flows
Annual net cash inflow	1–4	$ 1,000	3.170*	$3,170
Initial investment	Now	$(3,170)	1.000	(3,170)
Net present value				$ 0

*From Exhibit 14B–2 in Appendix 14B.

EXHIBIT 14-3
Carver Hospital—Breakdown of Annual Cash Inflows

Year	(1) Investment Outstanding during the Year	(2) Cash Inflow	(3) Return on Investment (1) × 10%	(4) Recovery of Investment during the Year (2) − (3)	(5) Unrecovered Investment at the End of the Year (1) − (4)
1	$3,170	$1,000	$317	$ 683	$2,487
2	$2,487	$1,000	$249	751	$1,736
3	$1,736	$1,000	$173	827	$909
4	$909	$1,000	$91	909	$0
Total investment recovered				$3,170	

Simplifying Assumptions

Two simplifying assumptions are usually made in net present value analysis.

The first assumption is that all cash flows other than the initial investment occur at the end of periods. This is somewhat unrealistic in that cash flows typically occur *throughout* a period rather than just at its end. The purpose of this assumption is to simplify computations.

The second assumption is that all cash flows generated by an investment project are immediately reinvested at a rate of return equal to the discount rate. Unless these conditions are met, the net present value computed for the project will not be accurate. We used a discount rate of 10% for Carver Hospital in Exhibit 14–2. Unless the cash flows in each period are immediately reinvested at a 10% return, the net present value computed for the X-ray attachment will be misstated.

Choosing a Discount Rate

A positive net present value indicates that the project's return exceeds the discount rate. A negative net present value indicates that the project's return is less than the discount rate. Therefore, if the company's minimum required rate of return is used as the discount rate, a project with a positive net present value has a return that exceeds the minimum required rate of return and is acceptable. Contrarily, a project with a negative net present value has a return that is less than the minimum required rate of return and is unacceptable.

What is a company's minimum required rate of return? The company's *cost of capital* is usually regarded as the minimum required rate of return. The **cost of capital** is the average rate of return the company must pay to its long-term creditors and its shareholders for the use of their funds. If a project's rate of return is less than the cost of capital, the company does not earn enough to compensate its creditors and shareholders. Therefore, any project with a rate of return less than the cost of capital should be rejected.

The cost of capital serves as a *screening device*. When the cost of capital is used as the discount rate in net present value analysis, any project with a negative net present value does not cover the company's cost of capital and should be discarded as unacceptable.

An Extended Example of the Net Present Value Method

Example C provides an extended example of how the net present value method is used to analyze a proposed project. This example helps tie together and reinforce many of the ideas discussed thus far.

Example C: Under a special licensing arrangement, Swinyard Company has an opportunity to market a new product for a five-year period. The product would be purchased from the manufacturer, with Swinyard Company responsible for promotion and distribution costs. The licensing arrangement could be renewed at the end of the five-year period. After careful study, Swinyard Company estimated the following costs and revenues for the new product:

Cost of equipment needed	$60,000
Working capital needed	$100,000
Overhaul of the equipment in four years	$5,000
Salvage value of the equipment in five years	$10,000
Annual revenues and costs:	
Sales revenues	$200,000
Cost of goods sold	$125,000
Out-of-pocket operating costs (for salaries,	
advertising, and other direct costs)	$35,000

At the end of the five-year period, if Swinyard decides not to renew the licensing arrangement the working capital would be released for investment elsewhere. Swinyard Company uses a 14% discount rate. Would you recommend that the new product be introduced?

This example involves a variety of cash inflows and cash outflows. The solution is given in Exhibit 14–4.

Notice how the working capital is handled in this exhibit. It is counted as a cash outflow at the beginning of the project and as a cash inflow when it is released at the end of the project. Also notice how the sales revenues, cost of goods sold, and out-of-pocket costs are handled. **Out-of-pocket costs** are actual cash outlays for salaries, advertising, and other operating expenses.

Since the net present value of the proposal is positive, the new product is acceptable.

EXHIBIT 14–4
The Net Present Value Method—An Extended Example

Sales revenues	$200,000	
Less cost of goods sold	125,000	
Less out-of-pocket costs for		
salaries, advertising, etc.	35,000	
Annual net cash inflows	$ 40,000	

Item	Year(s)	Amount of Cash Flow	14% Factor	Present Value of Cash Flows
Purchase of equipment	Now	$(60,000)	1.000	$ (60,000)
Working capital needed	Now	$(100,000)	1.000	(100,000)
Overhaul of equipment	4	$(5,000)	0.592*	(2,960)
Annual net cash inflows from sales				
of the product line	1–5	$40,000	3.433†	137,320
Salvage value of the equipment	5	$10,000	0.519*	5,190
Working capital released	5	$100,000	0.519*	51,900
Net present value				$ 31,450

*From Exhibit 14B–1 in Appendix 14B.
†From Exhibit 14B–2 in Appendix 14B.

Discounted Cash Flows—The Internal Rate of Return Method

The **internal rate of return** is the rate of return promised by an investment project over its useful life. It is sometimes referred to simply as the *yield* on a project. The internal rate of return is computed by finding the discount rate that equates the present value of a project's cash outflows with the present value of its cash inflows. In other words, the internal rate of return is the discount rate that results in a net present value of zero.

The Internal Rate of Return Method Illustrated

To illustrate the internal rate of return method, consider the following data:

Example D: Glendale School District is considering the purchase of a large tractor-pulled lawn mower. At present, the lawn is mowed using a small hand-pushed gas mower. The large, tractor-pulled mower will cost $16,950 and will have a useful life of 10 years. It will have a negligible scrap value, which can be ignored. The tractor-pulled mower would do the job faster than the old mower, resulting in labor savings of $3,000 per year.

To compute the internal rate of return promised by the new mower, we must find the discount rate that will cause the net present value of the project to be zero. How do we do this? The simplest and most direct approach *when the net cash inflow is the same every year* is to divide the investment in the project by the expected net annual cash inflow. This computation will yield a factor from which the internal rate of return can be determined. The formula is as follows:

$$\text{Factor of the internal rate of return} = \frac{\text{Investment required}}{\text{Net annual cash inflow}} \qquad (1)$$

The factor derived from formula (1) is then located in the present value tables to see what rate of return it represents. Using formula (1) and the data for the Glendale School District's proposed project, we get:

$$\frac{\text{Investment required}}{\text{Net annual cash inflow}} = \frac{\$16,950}{\$3,000} = 5.650$$

Thus, the discount factor that will equate a series of $3,000 cash inflows with a present investment of $16,950 is 5.650. Now we need to find this factor in Exhibit 14B–2 in Appendix 14B to see what rate of return it represents. We should use the 10-period line in Exhibit 14B–2 because the cash flows for the project continue for 10 years. If we scan along the 10-period line, we find that a factor of 5.650 represents a 12% rate of return. Therefore, the internal rate of return promised by the mower project is 12%. We can verify this by computing the project's net present value using a 12% discount rate. This computation is shown in Exhibit 14–5.

Notice from Exhibit 14–5 that using a 12% discount rate equates the present value of the annual cash inflows with the present value of the investment required for the project, leaving a zero net present value. The 12% rate therefore represents the internal rate of return promised by the project.

EXHIBIT 14–5
Evaluation of the Mower Purchase Using a 12% Discount Rate

Initial cost	$16,950
Life of the project	10 years
Annual cost savings	$3,000
Salvage value	$0

Item	Year(s)	Amount of Cash Flow	12% Factor	Present Value of Cash Flows
Annual cost savings	1–10	$3,000	5.650*	$16,950
Initial investment	Now	$(16,950)	1.000	(16,950)
Net present value				$ 0

*From Exhibit 14B–2 in Appendix 14B.

Salvage Value and Other Cash Flows

The technique just demonstrated works if a project's cash flows are identical every year. But what if they are not? For example, what if a project will have some salvage value at the end of its life in addition to the annual cash inflows? Under these circumstances, a trial-and-error process may be used to find the rate of return that will equate the cash inflows with the cash outflows. The trial-and-error process can be carried out by hand; however, computer software programs such as spreadsheets can perform the necessary computations in seconds. In short, erratic or uneven cash flows should not prevent an analyst from determining a project's internal rate of return.

Using the Internal Rate of Return

To evaluate a project, the internal rate of return is compared to the company's minimum required rate of return, which is usually the company's cost of capital. If the internal rate of return is equal to or greater than the required rate of return, then the project is considered to be acceptable. If the internal rate of return is less than the required rate of return, then the project is rejected.

In the case of the Glendale School District example, let us assume that the district has set a minimum required rate of return of 15% on all projects. Since the large mower's internal rate of return is only 12%, the project does not clear the 15% hurdle and should be rejected.

The Cost of Capital as a Screening Tool

As we have seen in preceding examples, the cost of capital often operates as a *screening* device, helping screen out undesirable investment projects. This screening is accomplished in different ways, depending on whether the company is using the internal rate of return method or the net present value method.

When the internal rate of return method is used, the cost of capital is used as the *hurdle rate* that a project must clear for acceptance. If the internal rate of return of a project is not great enough to clear the cost of capital hurdle, then the project is ordinarily rejected. We saw the application of this idea in the Glendale School District example, where the hurdle rate was set at 15%.

When the net present value method is used, the cost of capital is the *discount rate* used to compute the net present value of a proposed project. Any project yielding a negative net present value is rejected unless other factors are significant enough to warrant its acceptance.

The use of the cost of capital as a screening tool is summarized in Exhibit 14–6.

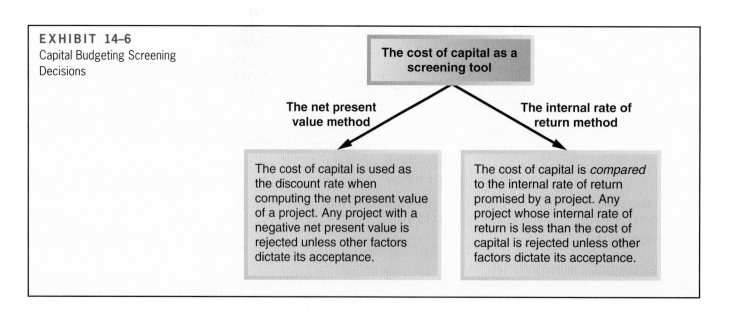

EXHIBIT 14–6
Capital Budgeting Screening Decisions

The cost of capital as a screening tool

The net present value method

The internal rate of return method

The cost of capital is used as the discount rate when computing the net present value of a project. Any project with a negative net present value is rejected unless other factors dictate its acceptance.

The cost of capital is *compared* to the internal rate of return promised by a project. Any project whose internal rate of return is less than the cost of capital is rejected unless other factors dictate its acceptance.

Comparison of the Net Present Value and Internal Rate of Return Methods

The net present value method has several important advantages over the internal rate of return method.

First, the net present value method is often simpler to use than the internal rate of return method. As mentioned earlier, the internal rate of return method may require hunting for the discount rate that results in a net present value of zero. This can be a very laborious trial-and-error process, although it can be automated using a computer.

Second, the internal rate of return method makes a questionable assumption. Both methods assume that cash flows generated by a project during its useful life are immediately reinvested elsewhere. However, the two methods make different assumptions concerning the rate of return that is earned on those cash flows. The net present value method assumes the rate of return is the discount rate, whereas the internal rate of return method assumes the rate of return is the internal rate of return on the project. Specifically, if the internal rate of return of the project is high, this assumption may not be realistic. It is generally more realistic to assume that cash inflows can be reinvested at a rate of return equal to the discount rate—particularly if the discount rate is the company's cost of capital or an opportunity rate of return. For example, if the discount rate is the company's cost of capital, this rate of return can be actually realized by paying off the company's creditors and buying back the company's stock with cash flows from the project. In short, when the net present value method and the internal rate of return method do not agree concerning the attractiveness of a project, it is best to go with the net present value method. Of the two methods, it makes the more realistic assumption about the rate of return that can be earned on cash flows from the project.

Expanding the Net Present Value Method

So far all of our examples have involved an evaluation of a single investment project. In the following section we expand the discussion of the net present value method to include evaluation of two alternative projects. In addition, we integrate relevant cost concepts into the discounted cash flow analysis. We use two approaches to compare competing investment projects—the *total-cost approach* and the *incremental-cost approach*. Each approach is illustrated in the next few pages.

The Total-Cost Approach

The total-cost approach is the most flexible method for comparing competing projects. To illustrate the mechanics of the approach, consider the following data:

Example E: Harper Ferry Company operates a high-speed passenger ferry service across the Mississippi River. One of its ferryboats is in poor condition. This ferry can be renovated at an immediate cost of $200,000. Further repairs and an overhaul of the motor will be needed five years from now at a cost of $80,000. In all, the ferry will be usable for 10 years if this work is done. At the end of 10 years, the ferry will have to be scrapped at a salvage value of $60,000. The scrap value of the ferry right now is $70,000. It will cost $300,000 each year to operate the ferry, and revenues will total $400,000 annually.

As an alternative, Harper Ferry Company can purchase a new ferryboat at a cost of $360,000. The new ferry will have a life of 10 years, but it will require some repairs costing $30,000 at the end of 5 years. At the end of 10 years, the ferry will have a scrap value of $60,000. It will cost $210,000 each year to operate the ferry, and revenues will total $400,000 annually.

Harper Ferry Company requires a return of at least 14% before taxes on all investment projects.

Should the company purchase the new ferry or renovate the old ferry? Exhibit 14–7 (page 636) shows the solution using the total-cost approach.

Two points should be noted from the exhibit. First, *all* cash inflows and *all* cash outflows are included in the solution under each alternative. No effort has been made to isolate those cash flows that are relevant to the decision and those that are not relevant. The inclusion of all cash flows associated with each alternative gives the approach its name—the *total-cost* approach.

EXHIBIT 14–7
The Total-Cost Approach to Project Selection

			New Ferry	Old Ferry
Annual revenues			$400,000	$400,000
Annual cash operating costs			210,000	300,000
Net annual cash inflows			$190,000	$100,000

Item	Year(s)	Amount of Cash Flows	14% Factor*	Present Value of Cash Flows
Buy the new ferry:				
Initial investment	Now	$(360,000)	1.000	$(360,000)
Salvage value of the old ferry	Now	$70,000	1.000	70,000
Repairs in five years	5	$(30,000)	0.519	(15,570)
Net annual cash inflows	1–10	$190,000	5.216	991,040
Salvage value of the new ferry	10	$60,000	0.270	16,200
Net present value				701,670
Keep the old ferry:				
Renovation	Now	$(200,000)	1.000	(200,000)
Repairs in five years	5	$(80,000)	0.519	(41,520)
Net annual cash inflows	1–10	$100,000	5.216	521,600
Salvage value of the old ferry	10	$60,000	0.270	16,200
Net present value				296,280
Net present value in favor of buying the new ferry				$ 405,390

*All present value factors are from Exhibits 14B–1 and 14B–2 in Appendix 14B.

Second, notice that a net present value is computed for each alternative. This is a distinct advantage of the total-cost approach because an unlimited number of alternatives can be compared side by side to determine the best option. For example, another alternative for Harper Ferry Company would be to get out of the ferry business entirely. If management desired, the net present value of this alternative could be computed to compare with the alternatives shown in Exhibit 14–7. Still other alternatives might be open to the company. In the case at hand, given only two alternatives, the data indicate that the most profitable choice is to purchase the new ferry.[4]

IN BUSINESS

DOES IT REALLY NEED TO BE NEW?

Tom Copeland, the director of Corporate Finance Practice at the consulting firm Monitor Group, observes: "If they could afford it, most people would like to drive a new car. Managers are no different . . . [I]n my experience, . . . [managers] routinely spend millions of dollars on new machines years earlier than they need to. In most cases, the overall cost (including the cost of breakdowns) is 30% to 40% lower if a company continues servicing an existing machine for five more years instead of buying a new one. In order to fight impulsive acquisitions of new machinery, companies should require unit managers to run the numbers on all alternative investment options open to them—including maintaining the existing assets or buying used ones."

Source: Tom Copeland, "Cutting Costs Without Drawing Blood," *Harvard Business Review*, September–October 2000, pp. 3–7.

---

[4] The alternative with the highest net present value is not always the best choice, although it is the best choice in this case. For further discussion, see the section Preference Decisions—The Ranking of Investment Projects.

EXHIBIT 14–8
The Incremental-Cost Approach to Project Selection

Item	Year(s)	Amount of Cash Flows	14% Factor*	Present Value of Cash Flows
Incremental investment to buy the new ferry	Now	$(160,000)	1.000	$(160,000)
Salvage value of the old ferry now	Now	$70,000	1.000	70,000
Difference in repairs in five years	5	$50,000	0.519	25,950
Increase in net annual cash inflows	1–10	$90,000	5.216	469,440
Difference in salvage value in 10 years	10	$0	0.270	0
Net present value in favor of buying the new ferry				$ 405,390

*All present value factors are from Exhibits 14B–1 and 14B–2 in Appendix 14B.

The Incremental-Cost Approach

When only two alternatives are being considered, the incremental-cost approach offers a simpler and more direct route to a decision. In the incremental-cost approach, only those costs and revenues that *differ* between the two alternatives are included in the analysis. To illustrate, refer again to the data in Example E relating to Harper Ferry Company. The solution using only differential costs is presented in Exhibit 14–8.[5]

Two things should be noted from the data in this exhibit. First, the net present value in favor of buying the new ferry of $405,390 shown in Exhibit 14–8 agrees with the net present value shown under the total-cost approach in Exhibit 14–7. The two approaches are just different roads to the same destination.

Second, the costs used in Exhibit 14–8 are just the differences between the costs shown for the two alternatives in the prior exhibit. For example, the $160,000 incremental investment required to purchase the new ferry in Exhibit 14–8 is the difference between the $360,000 cost of the new ferry and the $200,000 cost required to renovate the old ferry from Exhibit 14–7. The other figures in Exhibit 14–8 have been computed in the same way.

Least-Cost Decisions

Some decisions do not involve any revenues. For example, a company may be trying to decide whether to buy or lease an executive jet. The choice would be made on the basis of which alternative—buying or leasing—would be least costly. In situations such as these, where no revenues are involved, the most desirable alternative is the one with the *least total cost* from a present value perspective. Hence, these are known as least-cost decisions. To illustrate a least-cost decision, consider the following data:

Example F: Val-Tek Company is considering replacing an old threading machine with a new threading machine that would substantially reduce annual operating costs. Selected data relating to the old and new machines are presented below:

	Old Machine	New Machine
Purchase cost when new	$200,000	$250,000
Salvage value now	$30,000	—
Annual cash operating costs	$150,000	$90,000
Overhaul needed immediately	$40,000	—
Salvage value in six years	$0	$50,000
Remaining life	6 years	6 years

Val-Tek Company uses a 10% discount rate.

---

[5] Technically, the incremental-cost approach is misnamed, since it focuses on differential costs (that is, on both cost increases and decreases) rather than just on incremental costs. As used here, the term *incremental costs* should be interpreted broadly to include both cost increases and cost decreases.

EXHIBIT 14–9
The Total-Cost Approach (Least-Cost Decision)

Item	Year(s)	Amount of Cash Flows	10% Factor*	Present Value of Cash Flows
Buy the new machine:				
Initial investment	Now	$(250,000)	1.000	$(250,000)†
Salvage value of the old machine	Now	$30,000	1.000	30,000†
Annual cash operating costs	1–6	$(90,000)	4.355	(391,950)
Salvage value of the new machine	6	$50,000	0.564	28,200
Present value of net cash outflows				(583,750)
Keep the old machine:				
Overhaul needed now	Now	$(40,000)	1.000	$ (40,000)
Annual cash operating costs	1–6	$(150,000)	4.355	(653,250)
Present value of net cash outflows				(693,250)
Net present value in favor of buying the new machine				$ 109,500

*All factors are from Exhibits 14B–1 and 14B–2 in Appendix 14B.
†These two items could be netted into a single $220,000 incremental-cost figure ($250,000 − $30,000 = $220,000).

Exhibit 14–9 analyzes the alternatives using the total-cost approach. Because this is a least-cost decision, the present values are negative for both alternatives. However, the present value of the alternative of buying the new machine is $109,500 higher than the other alternative. Therefore, buying the new machine is the less costly alternative.

Exhibit 14–10 presents an analysis of the same alternatives using the incremental-cost approach. Once again, the total-cost and incremental-cost approaches arrive at the same answer.

IN BUSINESS

TRADING IN THAT OLD CAR?

Consumer Reports magazine provides the following data concerning the alternatives of keeping a four-year-old Ford Taurus for three years or buying a similar new car to replace it. The illustration assumes the car would be purchased and used in suburban Chicago.

	Keep the Old Taurus	Buy a New Taurus
Annual maintenance	$1,180	$650
Annual insurance	$370	$830
Annual license	$15	$100
Trade-in value in three years	$605	$7,763
Purchase price, including sales tax		$17,150

Consumer Reports is ordinarily extremely careful in its analysis, but in this instance it has omitted one financial item that differs substantially between the alternatives. What is it? To check your answer, go to the textbook website at www.mhhe.com/garrison12e. After accessing the site, click on the link to the Internet Exercises and then the link to this chapter.

Source: "When to Give Up on Your Clunker," *Consumer Reports*, August 2000, pp. 12–16.

EXHIBIT 14–10
The Incremental-Cost Approach (Least-Cost Decision)

Item	Year(s)	Amount of Cash Flows	10% Factor*	Present Value of Cash Flows
Incremental investment required to purchase the new machine	Now	$(210,000)	1.000	$(210,000)†
Salvage value of the old machine	Now	$30,000	1.000	30,000†
Savings in annual cash operating costs	1–6	$60,000	4.355	261,300
Difference in salvage value in six years	6	$50,000	0.564	28,200
Net present value in favor of buying the new machine				$ 109,500

*All factors are from Exhibits 14B–1 and 14B–2 in Appendix 14B.
†These two items could be netted into a single $180,000 incremental-cost figure ($210,000 − $30,000 = $180,000).

Uncertain Cash Flows

Thus far, we have assumed that all future cash flows are known with certainty. However, future cash flows are often uncertain or difficult to estimate. A number of techniques are available for handling this complication. Some of these techniques are quite technical—involving computer simulations or advanced mathematical skills—and are beyond the scope of this book. However, we can provide some very useful information to managers without getting too technical.

An Example

As an example of difficult-to-estimate future cash flows, consider the case of investments in automated equipment. The up-front costs of automated equipment and the tangible benefits, such as reductions in operating costs and waste, tend to be relatively easy to estimate. However, the intangible benefits, such as greater reliability, greater speed, and higher quality, are more difficult to quantify in terms of future cash flows. These intangible benefits certainly impact future cash flows—particularly in terms of increased sales and perhaps higher selling prices—but the cash flow effects are difficult to estimate. What can be done?

A fairly simple procedure can be followed when the intangible benefits are likely to be significant. Suppose, for example, that a company with a 12% discount rate is considering purchasing automated equipment that would have a 10-year useful life. Also suppose that a discounted cash flow analysis of just the tangible costs and benefits shows a negative net present value of $226,000. Clearly, if the intangible benefits are large enough, they could turn this negative net present value into a positive net present value. In this case, the amount of additional cash flow per year from the intangible benefits that would be needed to make the project financially attractive can be computed as follows:

Net present value excluding the intangible benefits (negative)	$(226,000)
Present value factor for an annuity at 12% for 10 periods (from Exhibit 14B–2 in Appendix 14B)	5.650

$$\frac{\text{Negative net present value to be offset, \$226,000}}{\text{Present value factor, 5.650}} = \$40,000$$

Thus, if the intangible benefits of the automated equipment are worth at least $40,000 a year to the company, then the automated equipment should be purchased. If, in the judgment of management, these intangible benefits are not worth $40,000 a year, then the automated equipment should not be purchased.

This technique can be used in other situations in which future cash flows are difficult to estimate. For example, this technique can be used when the salvage value is difficult to estimate. To illustrate, suppose that all of the cash flows from an investment in a supertanker have been estimated—other than its salvage value in 20 years. Using a discount rate of 12%, management has determined that the net present value of all of these cash flows is a negative $1.04 million. This negative net present value would be offset by the salvage value of the supertanker. How large would the salvage value have to be to make this investment attractive?

Net present value excluding salvage value (negative)	$(1,040,000)
Present value factor at 12% for 20 periods (from Exhibit 14B–1 in Appendix 14B)	0.104

$$\frac{\text{Negative net present value to be offset, }\$1,040,000}{\text{Present value factor, }0.104} = \$10,000,000$$

Thus, if the salvage value of the tanker in 20 years is at least $10 million, its net present value would be positive and the investment would be made. However, if management believes the salvage value is unlikely to be as large as $10 million, the investment should not be made.

Real Options

The analysis in this chapter has assumed that an investment cannot be postponed and that, once started, nothing can be done to alter the course of the project. In reality, investments can often be postponed. Postponement is a particularly attractive option when the net present value of a project is modest using current estimates of future cash flows and the future cash flows involve a great deal of uncertainty that may be resolved over time. Similarly, once an investment is made, management can often exploit changes in the business environment and take actions that enhance future cash flows. For example, buying a supertanker provides management with a number of options, some of which may become more attractive as time unfolds. Instead of operating the supertanker itself, the company may decide to lease it to another operator if the rental rates become high enough. Or, if a supertanker shortage develops, management may decide to sell the supertanker and take a gain. In the case of an investment in automated equipment, management may initially buy only the basic model without costly add-ons, but keep the option open to add more capacity and capability later. The ability to delay the start of a project, to expand it if conditions are favorable, to cut losses if they are unfavorable, and to otherwise modify plans as business conditions change adds value to many investments. These advantages can be quantified using what is called *real options* analysis, but the techniques are beyond the scope of this book.

THINKING AHEAD

With an eye on environmental concerns, the board of directors of Royal Dutch/Shell, the Anglo-Dutch energy company, has decided that all big projects must explicitly take into account the likely future costs of abating carbon emissions. Calculations must assume a cost of $5 per ton of carbon dioxide emission in 2005 through 2009, rising to $20 per ton from 2010 onward. A Shell manager explains: "We know that $5 and $20 are surely the wrong price, but everyone else who assumes a carbon price of zero in the future will be more wrong. This is not altruism. We see it as giving us a competitive edge."

Source: "Big Business Bows to Global Warming," *The Economist*, December 2, 2000, p. 81.

Preference Decisions—The Ranking of Investment Projects

Recall that when considering investment opportunities, managers must make two types of decisions—screening decisions and preference decisions. Screening decisions, which come first, pertain to whether or not a proposed investment is acceptable. Preference decisions come *after* screening decisions and attempt to answer the following question: "How do the remaining investment proposals, all of which have been screened and provide an acceptable rate of return, rank in terms of preference? That is, which one(s) would be *best* for the company to accept?"

LEARNING OBJECTIVE 4
Rank investment projects in order of preference.

Sometimes preference decisions are called rationing decisions, or ranking decisions. Limited investment funds must be rationed among many competing alternatives. Hence, the alternatives must be ranked. Either the internal rate of return method or the net present value method can be used in making preference decisions. However, as discussed earlier, if the two methods are in conflict, it is best to use the net present value method, which is more reliable.

Internal Rate of Return Method

When using the internal rate of return method to rank competing investment projects, the preference rule is: *The higher the internal rate of return, the more desirable the project.* An investment project with an internal rate of return of 18% is usually considered preferable to another project that promises a return of only 15%. Internal rate of return is widely used to rank projects.

Net Present Value Method

The net present value of one project cannot be directly compared to the net present value of another project unless the initial investments are equal. For example, assume that a company is considering two competing investments, as shown below:

	Investment	
	A	B
Investment required	$(10,000)	$(5,000)
Present value of cash inflows	11,000	6,000
Net present value	$ 1,000	$ 1,000

Although each project has a net present value of $1,000, the projects are not equally desirable if the funds available for investment are limited. The project requiring an investment of only $5,000 is much more desirable than the project requiring an investment of $10,000. This fact can be highlighted by dividing the net present value of the project by the investment required. The result, shown below in equation form, is called the **project profitability index.**

$$\text{Project profitability index} = \frac{\text{Net present value of the project}}{\text{Investment required}} \qquad (2)$$

The project profitability indexes for the two investments above would be computed as follows:

	Investment	
	A	B
Net present value (a)	$1,000	$1,000
Investment required (b)	$10,000	$5,000
Project profitability index, (a) ÷ (b)	0.10	0.20

When using the project profitability index to rank competing investments projects, the preference rule is: *The higher the project profitability index, the more desirable the project.*[6] Applying this rule to the two investments above, investment B should be chosen over investment A.

The project profitability index is an application of the techniques for utilizing constrained resources discussed in Chapter 13. In this case, the constrained resource is the limited funds available for investment, and the project profitability index is similar to the contribution margin per unit of the constrained resource.

A few details should be clarified with respect to the computation of the project profitability index. The "Investment required" refers to any cash outflows that occur at the beginning of the project, reduced by any salvage value recovered from the sale of old equipment. The "Investment required" also includes any investment in working capital that the project may need.

Other Approaches to Capital Budgeting Decisions

The net present value and internal rate of return methods are widely used as decision-making tools. However, some managers also use the payback method and simple rate of return method to make capital budgeting decisions. Each of these methods will be discussed in turn.

The Payback Method

The payback method focuses on the *payback period*. The **payback period** is the length of time that it takes for a project to recover its initial cost from the cash receipts that it generates. This period is sometimes referred to as "the time that it takes for an investment to pay for itself." The basic premise of the payback method is that the more quickly the cost of an investment can be recovered, the more desirable is the investment.

The payback period is expressed in years. *When the net annual cash inflow is the same every year,* the following formula can be used to compute the payback period:

$$\text{Payback period} = \frac{\text{Investment required}}{\text{Net annual cash inflow}} \tag{3}$$

To illustrate the payback method, consider the following data:

Topic Tackler

PLUS

14–2

Example G: York Company needs a new milling machine. The company is considering two machines: machine A and machine B. Machine A costs $15,000, has a useful life of ten years, and will reduce operating costs by $5,000 per year. Machine B costs only $12,000, will also reduce operating costs by $5,000 per year, but has a useful life of only five years.

Required:
Which machine should be purchased according to the payback method?

$$\text{Machine A payback period} = \frac{\$15,000}{\$5,000} = 3.0 \text{ years}$$

$$\text{Machine B payback period} = \frac{\$12,000}{\$5,000} = 2.4 \text{ years}$$

According to the payback calculations, York Company should purchase machine B because it has a shorter payback period than machine A.

---

[6] Because of the "lumpiness" of projects, the project profitability index ranking may not be perfect. Nevertheless, it is a good starting point. For further details, see the Profitability Analysis Appendix at the end of the book.

ENTREPRENEURIAL INGENUITY AT ITS BEST

Jonathan Pratt owns two Ümani Cafés in Westchester County, New York. He used to pay $200 a month to dispose of the vegetable oil that is used to fry foods in his restaurants. Plus, he bought $700 of gas every month to operate his company's pick-up truck. Then Pratt got an idea. He purchased a diesel-powered Ford F250 on eBay for $11,000 and paid $1,500 to haul the truck from Arizona to New York. Next, he installed an $850 conversion kit on his new truck to enable it to run on vegetable oil. Since he no longer has to pay to dispose of vegetable oil or buy gasoline, Pratt figures that his investment will pay for itself in about 15 months ($13,350 ÷ $900 = 14.83 months). Furthermore, he now has the best smelling car in town—it smells like french fries when he drives down the road.

Source: Jean Chatzky, "Out of the Frying Pan, Into the Ford," *Money*, October, 2004, p. 28.

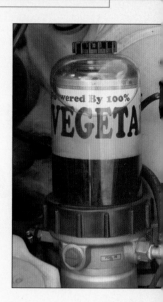

Evaluation of the Payback Method

The payback method is not a true measure of the profitability of an investment. Rather, it simply tells a manager how many years are required to recover the original investment. Unfortunately, a shorter payback period does not always mean that one investment is more desirable than another.

To illustrate, refer back to Example G above. Machine B has a shorter payback period than machine A, but it has a useful life of only 5 years rather than 10 years for machine A. Machine B would have to be purchased twice—once immediately and then again after the fifth year—to provide the same service as just one machine A. Under these circumstances, machine A would probably be a better investment than machine B, even though machine B has a shorter payback period. Unfortunately, the payback method ignores all cash flows that occur after the payback period.

A further criticism of the payback method is that it does not consider the time value of money. A cash inflow to be received several years in the future is weighed the same as a cash inflow received right now. To illustrate, assume that for an investment of $8,000 you can purchase either of the two following streams of cash inflows:

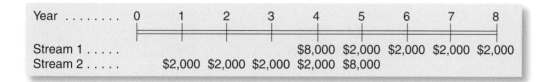

Year	0	1	2	3	4	5	6	7	8
Stream 1					$8,000	$2,000	$2,000	$2,000	$2,000
Stream 2		$2,000	$2,000	$2,000	$2,000	$8,000			

Which stream of cash inflows would you prefer to receive in return for your $8,000 investment? Each stream has a payback period of 4.0 years. Therefore, if payback alone is used to make the decision, the streams would be considered equally desirable. However, from a time value of money perspective, stream 2 is much more desirable than stream 1.

On the other hand, under certain conditions the payback method can be very useful. For one thing, it can help identify which investment proposals are in the "ballpark." That is, it can be used as a screening tool to help answer the question, "Should I consider this proposal further?" If a proposal doesn't provide a payback within some specified period, then there may be no need to consider it further. In addition, the payback period is often of great importance to new companies that are "cash poor." When a company is cash poor, a project with a short payback period but a low rate of return might be preferred over another project with a high rate of return but a long payback period. The reason is that the company may simply need a faster return of its cash investment. And finally, the payback method is sometimes used in industries where products become obsolete very rapidly—such as consumer electronics. Since products may last only a year or two, the payback period on investments must be very short.

IN BUSINESS

CONSERVATION IS NOT SELF-DENIAL

Amory Lovins, the director of the Rocky Mountain Institute in Snowmass, Colorado, is a passionate advocate of energy efficiency as a means of conserving natural resources and reducing pollution. Rather than cutting energy consumption by adopting more austere lifestyles, Lovins believes that energy consumption can be radically cut by using energy more efficiently. This approach has the virtues of combining energy conservation with cash savings and better living standards. He claims that America's annual electric bill of $220 billion could be cut in half by making investments with a payback period of one year or less. To illustrate his point, Lovins designed the institute's headquarters to require no furnace or air conditioning. During the cold winters, daytime solar heat enters the building through a built-in greenhouse, is soaked up by massive stone walls and foundations, and is then released at night. The institute is hardly a chilling, austere structure. Its passive heating system supports a small stand of tropical fruit trees, a mini fish farm, an indoor waterfall, and a hot tub. Lovins claims that the building's efficient design added only $6,000 to its construction costs and the payback period on this investment was only 10 months.

Source: David Stipp, "Can This Man Solve America's Energy Crisis?" *Fortune*, May 13, 2002, pp. 100–110.

An Extended Example of Payback

As shown by formula (3) given earlier, the payback period is computed by dividing the investment in a project by the net annual cash inflows that the project will generate. If new equipment is replacing old equipment, then any salvage value to be received when disposing of the old equipment should be deducted from the cost of the new equipment, and only the *incremental* investment should be used in the payback computation. In addition, any depreciation deducted in arriving at the project's net operating income must be added back to obtain the project's expected net annual cash inflow. To illustrate, consider the following data:

Example H: Goodtime Fun Centers, Inc., operates amusement parks. Some of the vending machines in one of its parks provide very little revenue, so the company is considering removing the machines and installing equipment to dispense soft ice cream. The equipment would cost $80,000 and have an eight-year useful life with no salvage value. Incremental annual revenues and costs associated with the sale of ice cream would be as follows:

Sales	$150,000
Variable expenses	90,000
Contribution margin	60,000
Fixed expenses:	
Salaries.	27,000
Maintenance	3,000
Depreciation	10,000
Total fixed expenses	40,000
Net operating income	$ 20,000

The vending machines can be sold for a $5,000 scrap value. The company will not purchase equipment unless it has a payback period of three years or less. Does the ice cream dispenser pass this hurdle?

EXHIBIT 14–11
Computation of the Payback
Period

Step 1: *Compute the net annual cash inflow.* Since the net annual cash inflow is not given, it must be computed before the payback period can be determined:

Net operating income (given above)	$20,000
Add: Noncash deduction for depreciation	10,000
Net annual cash inflow	$30,000

Step 2: *Compute the payback period.* Using the net annual cash inflow figure from above, the payback period can be determined as follows:

Cost of the new equipment	$80,000
Less salvage value of old equipment	5,000
Investment required	$75,000

$$\text{Payback period} = \frac{\text{Investment required}}{\text{Net annual cash inflow}}$$

$$= \frac{\$75,000}{\$30,000} = 2.5 \text{ years}$$

Exhibit 14–11 computes the payback period for the ice cream dispenser. Several things should be noted. First, depreciation is added back to net operating income to obtain the net annual cash inflow from the new equipment. Depreciation is not a cash outlay; thus, it must be added back to adjust net operating income to a cash basis. Second, the payback computation deducts the salvage value of the old machines from the cost of the new equipment so that only the incremental investment is used in computing the payback period.

Since the proposed equipment has a payback period of less than three years, the company's payback requirement has been met.

IN BUSINESS

COUNTING THE ENVIRONMENTAL COSTS

Companies often grossly underestimate how much they are spending on environmental costs. Many of these costs are buried in broad cost categories such as manufacturing overhead. Kestrel Management Services, LLC, a management consulting firm specializing in environmental matters, found that one chemical facility was spending five times as much on environmental expenses as its cost system reported. At another site, a small manufacturer with $840,000 in pretax profits thought that its annual safety and environmental compliance expenses were about $50,000 but, after digging into the accounts, found that the total was closer to $300,000. Alerted to this high cost, management of the company invested about $125,000 in environmental improvements, anticipating a three- to six-month payback period. By taking steps such as more efficient dust collection, the company improved its product quality, reduced scrap rates, decreased its consumption of city water for cooling, and reduced the expense of discharging wastewater into the city's sewer system. Further analysis revealed that spending $50,000 to improve energy efficiency would reduce annual energy costs by about $45,000. Few of these costs were visible in the company's traditional cost accounting system.

Source: Thomas P. Kunes, "A Green and *Lean* Workplace?" *Strategic Finance,* February 2001, pp. 71–73, 83.

Payback and Uneven Cash Flows

When the cash flows associated with an investment project change from year to year, the simple payback formula that we outlined earlier cannot be used. Consider the following data:

Year	Investment	Cash Inflow
1	$4,000	$1,000
2		$0
3		$2,000
4	$2,000	$1,000
5		$500
6		$3,000
7		$2,000

What is the payback period on this investment? The answer is 5.5 years, but to obtain this figure it is necessary to track the unrecovered investment year by year. The steps involved in this process are shown in Exhibit 14–12. By the middle of the sixth year, sufficient cash inflows will have been realized to recover the entire investment of $6,000 ($4,000 + $2,000).

EXHIBIT 14–12
Payback and Uneven Cash Flows

Year	Investment	Cash Inflow	Unrecovered Investment*
1	$4,000	$1,000	$3,000
2		$0	$3,000
3		$2,000	$1,000
4	$2,000	$1,000	$2,000
5		$500	$1,500
6		$3,000	$0
7		$2,000	$0

*Year X unrecovered investment = Year X-1 unrecovered investment + Year X investment − Year X cash inflow

The Simple Rate of Return Method

The **simple rate of return** method is another capital budgeting technique that does not involve discounting cash flows. The simple rate of return is also known as the accounting rate of return or the unadjusted rate of return.

Unlike the other capital budgeting methods that we have discussed, the simple rate of return method focuses on accounting net operating income rather than cash flows. To obtain the simple rate of return, the annual incremental net operating income generated by a project is divided by the initial investment in the project as shown below.

$$\text{Simple rate of return} = \frac{\text{Annual incremental net operating income}}{\text{Initial investment}} \qquad (4)$$

Two additional points should be made. First, depreciation charges that result from making the investment should be deducted when determining the annual incremental net operating income. Second, the initial investment should be reduced by any salvage value realized from the sale of old equipment.

Example I: Brigham Tea, Inc., is a processor of low-acid tea. The company is contemplating purchasing equipment for an additional processing line. The additional processing line would increase revenues by $90,000 per year. Incremental cash operating expenses would be $40,000 per year. The equipment would cost $180,000 and have a nine-year life with no salvage value.

To apply the formula for the simple rate of return, we must first determine the annual incremental net operating income from the project:

Annual incremental revenues		$90,000
Annual incremental cash operating expenses	$40,000	
Annual depreciation ($180,000 − $0)/9	20,000	
Annual incremental expenses		60,000
Annual incremental net operating income		$30,000

Given that the annual incremental net operating income from the project is $30,000 and the initial investment is $180,000, the simple rate of return is 16.7% as shown below:

$$\text{Simple rate of return} = \frac{\text{Annual incremental net operating income}}{\text{Initial investment}}$$

$$= \frac{\$30,000}{\$180,000}$$

$$= 16.7\%$$

Example J: Midwest Farms, Inc., hires people on a part-time basis to sort eggs. The cost of this hand-sorting process is $30,000 per year. The company is investigating an egg-sorting machine that would cost $90,000 and have a 15-year useful life. The machine would have negligible salvage value, and it would cost $10,000 per year to operate and maintain. The egg-sorting equipment currently being used could be sold now for a scrap value of $2,500.

This project is slightly different from the preceding project because it involves cost reductions with no additional revenues. Nevertheless, the annual incremental net operating income can be computed by treating the annual cost savings as if it were incremental revenues as follows:

Annual incremental cost savings		$30,000
Annual incremental cash operating expenses	$10,000	
Annual depreciation ($90,000 − $0)/15	6,000	
Annual incremental expenses		16,000
Annual incremental net operating income		$14,000

Thus, even though the new equipment would not generate any additional revenues, it would reduce costs by $14,000 a year. This would have the effect of increasing net operating income by $14,000 a year.

Finally, the salvage value of the old equipment offsets the initial cost of the new equipment as follows:

Cost of the new equipment	$90,000
Less salvage value of the old equipment	2,500
Initial investment	$87,500

Given the annual incremental net operating income of $14,000 and the initial investment of $87,500, the simple rate of return is 16.0% computed as follows:

$$\text{Simple rate of return} = \frac{\text{Annual incremental net operating income}}{\text{Initial investment}}$$

$$= \frac{\$14,000}{\$87,500}$$

$$= 16.0\%$$

AN AMAZING RETURN

Ipswitch, Inc., a software developer and seller, has moved much of its business to the Web. Potential customers can download free trial copies of the company's software at www.ipswitch.com. After the trial period, a customer must return to the Web site to purchase and download a permanent copy of the software. The initial investment in setting up a Web site was modest—roughly $190,000. The cost of keeping the Web site up and running and updated with the latest product information is about $1.3 million a year—mainly in the form of salaries and benefits for eight employees. The company estimates that additional revenues brought in by the Web amount to about $13 million per year and that the company saves about $585,000 per year in direct mail advertising costs by using the Web for much of its advertising instead. Assuming that the cost of sales is almost zero for downloaded software, the accounting rate of return on the initial investment in the Web site is 6,466% ([$13,000,000 − $1,300,000 + $585,000] ÷ $190,000)!

Source: Karen N. Kroll, "Many Happy Returns," *Inc.* magazine, November 30, 2001, pp. 150–152.

Criticisms of the Simple Rate of Return

The simple rate of return method ignores the time value of money. It considers a dollar received 10 years from now to be as valuable as a dollar received today. Thus, the simple rate of return method can be misleading if the alternatives have different cash flow patterns. Additionally, many projects do not have constant incremental revenues and expenses over their useful lives. As a result, the simple rate of return will fluctuate from year to year, with the possibility that a project may appear to be desirable in some years and undesirable in others. In contrast, the net present value method provides a single number that summarizes all of the cash flows over the entire useful life of the project.

Postaudit of Investment Projects

After an investment project has been approved and implemented, a *postaudit* should be conducted. A **postaudit** involves checking whether or not expected results are actually realized. This is a key part of the capital budgeting process because it helps keep managers honest in their investment proposals. Any tendency to inflate the benefits or downplay the costs in a proposal should become evident after a few postaudits have been conducted. The postaudit also provides an opportunity to reinforce and possibly expand successful projects and to cut losses on floundering projects.

The same capital budgeting method should be used in the postaudit as was used in the original approval process. That is, if a project was approved on the basis of a net present value analysis, then the same procedure should be used in performing the postaudit. However, the data used in the postaudit analysis should be *actual observed data* rather than estimated data. This gives management an opportunity to make a side-by-side comparison to see how well the project has succeeded. It also helps assure that estimated data received on future proposals will be carefully prepared, since the persons submitting the data knows that their estimates will be compared to actual results in the postaudit process. Actual results that are far out of line with original estimates should be carefully reviewed.

CAPITAL BUDGETING IN PRACTICE

A survey of Fortune 1000 companies—the largest companies in the United States—asked CFOs how often various capital budgeting methods are used in their companies. Some of the results of that survey are displayed below:

Capital Budgeting Tool	Frequency of Use				
	Always	Often	Sometimes	Rarely	Never
Net present value	50%	35%	11%	3%	1%
Internal rate of return..........	45%	32%	15%	6%	2%
Payback	19%	33%	22%	17%	9%
Accounting rate of return	5%	9%	19%	16%	50%

Many companies use more than one method—for example, they may use both the net present value and the internal rate of return methods to evaluate capital budgeting projects. Note that the two discounted cash flow methods—net present value and internal rate of return—are by far the most commonly used in practice.

A similar survey of companies in the United Kingdom yielded the following results:

Capital Budgeting Tool	Frequency of Use			
	Always	Mostly	Often	Rarely
Net present value.............	43%	20%	14%	7%
Internal rate of return..........	48%	20%	10%	5%
Payback	30%	16%	17%	14%
Accounting rate of return	26%	15%	18%	7%

Note that while the results were quite similar for the U.S. and U.K. companies, the U.K. companies were more likely to use the payback and accounting rate of return methods than the U.S. companies.

Sources: Patricia A. Ryan and Glenn P. Ryan, "Capital Budgeting Practices of the Fortune 1000: How Have Things Changed?" *Journal of Business and Management*, Fall 2002, pp. 355–364; and Glen C. Arnold and Panos D. Hatzopoulus, "The Theory-Practice Gap in Capital Budgeting: Evidence from the United Kingdom," *Journal of Business Finance & Accounting* 27(5) & 27(6), June/July 2000, pp. 603–626.

Summary

Investment decisions should take into account the time value of money because a dollar today is more valuable than a dollar received in the future. The net present value and internal rate of return methods both reflect this fact. In the net present value method, future cash flows are discounted to their present value. The difference between the present value of the cash inflows and the present value of the cash outflows is called a project's net present value. If the net present value of a project is negative, the project is rejected. The discount rate in the net present value method is usually based on a minimum required rate of return such as a company's cost of capital.

The internal rate of return is the rate of return that equates the present value of the cash inflows and the present value of the cash outflows, resulting in a zero net present value. If the internal rate of return is less than a company's minimum required rate of return, the project is rejected.

After rejecting projects whose net present values are negative or whose internal rates of return are less than the minimum required rate of return, more projects may remain than can be supported with available funds. The remaining projects can be ranked using either the project profitability index or internal rate of return. The project profitability index is computed by dividing the net present value of the project by the required initial investment.

Some companies prefer to use either the payback method or the simple rate of return to evaluate investment proposals. The payback period is the number of periods that are required to fully recover the initial investment in a project. The simple rate of return is determined by dividing a project's accounting net operating income by the initial investment in the project.

Review Problem 1: Basic Present Value Computations

Each of the following situations is independent. Work out your own solution to each situation, and then check it against the solution provided.

1. John plans to retire in 12 years. Upon retiring, he would like to take an extended vacation, which he expects will cost at least $40,000. What lump-sum amount must he invest now to have $40,000 at the end of 12 years if the rate of return is:
   a. Eight percent?
   b. Twelve percent?
2. The Morgans would like to send their daughter to a music camp at the end of each of the next five years. The camp costs $1,000 a year. What lump-sum amount would have to be invested now to have $1,000 at the end of each year if the rate of return is:
   a. Eight percent?
   b. Twelve percent?
3. You have just received an inheritance from a relative. You can either receive a $200,000 lump-sum amount at the end of 10 years or receive $14,000 at the end of each year for the next 10 years. If your discount rate is 12%, which alternative would you prefer?

Solution to Review Problem 1

1. *a.* The amount that must be invested now would be the present value of the $40,000, using a discount rate of 8%. From Table 14B–1 in Appendix 14B, the factor for a discount rate of 8% for 12 periods is 0.397. Multiplying this discount factor by the $40,000 needed in 12 years will give the amount of the present investment required: $40,000 × 0.397 = $15,880.
   b. We will proceed as we did in (*a*) above, but this time we will use a discount rate of 12%. From Table 14B–1 in Appendix 14B, the factor for a discount rate of 12% for 12 periods is 0.257. Multiplying this discount factor by the $40,000 needed in 12 years will give the amount of the present investment required: $40,000 × 0.257 = $10,280.
   Notice that as the discount rate (desired rate of return) increases, the present value decreases.
2. This part differs from (1) above in that we are now dealing with an annuity rather than with a single future sum. The amount that must be invested now is the present value of the $1,000 needed at the end of each year for five years. Since we are dealing with an annuity, or a series of annual cash flows, we must refer to Exhibit 14B–2 in Appendix 14B for the appropriate discount factor.
   a. From Exhibit 14B–2 in Appendix 14B, the discount factor for 8% for five periods is 3.993. Therefore, the amount that must be invested now to have $1,000 available at the end of each year for five years is $1,000 × 3.993 = $3,993.
   b. From Exhibit 14B–2 in Appendix 14B, the discount factor for 12% for five periods is 3.605. Therefore, the amount that must be invested now to have $1,000 available at the end of each year for five years is $1,000 × 3.605 = $3,605.
   Again, notice that as the discount rate increases, the present value decreases. When the rate of return increases, less must be invested today to yield a given amount in the future.
3. For this part we will need to refer to both Exhibits 14B–1 and 14B–2 in Appendix 14B. From Exhibit 14B–1, we will need to find the discount factor for 12% for 10 periods, then apply it to the $200,000 lump sum to be received in 10 years. From Exhibit 14B–2, we will need to find the discount factor for 12% for 10 periods, then apply it to the series of $14,000 payments to be received over the 10-year period. Whichever alternative has the higher present value is the one that should be selected.

$$\$200,000 \times 0.322 = \$64,400$$

$$\$14,000 \times 5.650 = \$79,100$$

Thus, you should prefer to receive the $14,000 per year for 10 years rather than the $200,000 lump sum. This means that you could invest the $14,000 received at the end of each year at 12% and have *more* than $200,000 at the end of 10 years.

Review Problem 2: Comparison of Capital Budgeting Methods

Lamar Company is considering a project that would have an eight-year life and require a $2,400,000 investment in equipment. At the end of eight years, the project would terminate and the equipment would have no salvage value. The project would provide net operating income each year as follows:

Sales		$3,000,000
Variable expenses		1,800,000
Contribution margin..................		1,200,000
Fixed expenses:		
Advertising, salaries, and other		
fixed out-of-pocket costs	$700,000	
Depreciation	300,000	
Total fixed expenses		1,000,000
Net operating income		$ 200,000

The company's discount rate is 12%.

Required:

1. Compute the net annual cash inflow from the project.
2. Compute the project's net present value. Is the project acceptable?
3. Find the project's internal rate of return to the nearest whole percent.
4. Compute the project's payback period.
5. Compute the project's simple rate of return.

Solution to Review Problem 2

1. The net annual cash inflow can be computed by deducting the cash expenses from sales:

Sales	$3,000,000
Variable expenses	1,800,000
Contribution margin..................	1,200,000
Advertising, salaries, and	
other fixed out-of-pocket costs........	700,000
Net annual cash inflow	$ 500,000

Or the net annual cash inflow can be computed by adding depreciation back to net operating income:

Net operating income......................	$200,000
Add: Noncash deduction for depreciation........	300,000
Net annual cash inflow.....................	$500,000

2. The net present value is computed as follows:

Item	Year(s)	Amount of Cash Flows	12% Factor	Present Value of Cash Flows
Cost of new equipment	Now	$(2,400,000)	1.000	$(2,400,000)
Net annual cash inflow	1–8	$500,000	4.968	2,484,000
Net present value				$ 84,000

Yes, the project is acceptable because it has a positive net present value.

3. The formula for computing the factor of the internal rate of return is:

$$\text{Factor of the internal rate of return} = \frac{\text{Investment required}}{\text{Net annual cash inflow}}$$

$$= \frac{\$2,400,000}{\$500,000} = 4.800$$

Looking in Exhibit 14B–2 in Appendix 14B at the end of the chapter and scanning along the 8-period line, we find that a factor of 4.800 represents a rate of return of about 13%.

4. The formula for the payback period is:

$$\text{Payback period} = \frac{\text{Investment required}}{\text{Net annual cash flow}}$$

$$= \frac{\$2,400,000}{\$500,000}$$

$$= 4.8 \text{ years}$$

5. The formula for the simple rate of return is:

$$\text{Simple rate of return} = \frac{\text{Annual incremental net operating income}}{\text{Initial investment}}$$

$$= \frac{\$200,000}{\$2,400,000}$$

$$= 8.3\%$$

Glossary

Capital budgeting The process of planning significant investments in projects that have long-term implications such as the purchase of new equipment or the introduction of a new product. (p. 626)

Cost of capital The average rate of return a company must pay to its long-term creditors and shareholders for the use of their funds. (p. 631)

Internal rate of return The discount rate at which the net present value of an investment project is zero; the rate of return promised by a project over its useful life. (p. 633)

Net present value The difference between the present value of an investment project's cash inflows and the present value of its cash outflows. (p. 627)

Out-of-pocket costs Actual cash outlays for salaries, advertising, repairs, and similar costs. (p. 632)

Payback period The length of time that it takes for a project to fully recover its initial cost out of the cash receipts that it generates. (p. 642)

Postaudit The follow-up after a project has been approved and implemented to determine whether expected results were actually realized. (p. 648)

Preference decision A decision in which the alternatives must be ranked. (p. 626)

Project profitability index The ratio of the net present value of a project's cash flows to the investment required. (p. 641)

Screening decision A decision as to whether a proposed investment project is acceptable. (p. 626)

Simple rate of return The rate of return computed by dividing a project's annual incremental accounting net operating income by the initial investment required. (p. 646)

Working capital Current assets less current liabilities. (p. 629)

Appendix 14A: The Concept of Present Value

A dollar received today is more valuable than a dollar received a year from now for the simple reason that if you have a dollar today, you can put it in the bank and have more than a dollar a year from now. Since dollars today are worth more than dollars in the future, cash flows that are received at different times must be weighted differently.

The Mathematics of Interest

If a bank pays 5% interest, then a deposit of $100 today will be worth $105 one year from now. This can be expressed as follows:

$$F_1 = P(1 + r) \tag{1}$$

where F_1 = the balance at the end of one period, P = the amount invested now, and r = the rate of interest per period.

In the case where $100 is deposited in a savings account that earns 5% interest, $P = $100 and $r = 0.05$. Under these conditions, $F_1 = $105.

The $100 present outlay is called the **present value** of the $105 amount to be received in one year. It is also known as the *discounted value* of the future $105 receipt. The $100 represents the value in present terms of $105 to be received a year from now when the interest rate is 5%.

Compound Interest What if the $105 is left in the bank for a second year? In that case, by the end of the second year the original $100 deposit will have grown to $110.25:

Original deposit	$100.00
Interest for the first year:	
$100 × 0.05	5.00
Balance at the end of the first year	105.00
Interest for the second year:	
$105 × 0.05	5.25
Balance at the end of the second year	$110.25

Notice that the interest for the second year is $5.25, as compared to only $5.00 for the first year. This difference arises because interest is being paid on interest during the second year. That is, the $5.00 interest earned during the first year has been left in the account and has been added to the original $100 deposit when computing interest for the second year. This is known as **compound interest.** In this case, the compounding is annual. Interest can be compounded on a semiannual, quarterly, monthly, or even more frequent basis. The more frequently compounding is done, the more rapidly the balance will grow.

We can determine the balance in an account after n periods of compounding using the following equation:

$$F_n = P(1 + r)^n \qquad (2)$$

where n = the number of periods of compounding.

If $n = 2$ years and the interest rate is 5% per year, then the balance in two years will be computed as follows:

$$F_2 = \$100(1 + 0.05)^2$$

$$F_2 = \$110.25$$

Present Value and Future Value   Exhibit 14A–1 shows the relationship between present value and future value. As shown in the exhibit, if $100 is deposited in a bank at 5% interest compounded annually, it will grow to $127.63 by the end of five years.

Computation of Present Value

An investment can be viewed in two ways—either in terms of its future value or in terms of its present value. We have seen from our computations above that if we know the present value of a sum (such as our $100 deposit), the future value in n years can be computed by using equation (2). But what if the situation is reversed and we know the *future* value of some amount but we do not know its present value?

For example, assume that you are to receive $200 two years from now. You know that the future value of this sum is $200 because this is the amount that you will be receiving in two years. But what is the sum's present value—what is it worth *right now?* The present value of any sum to be received in the future can be computed by turning equation (2) around and solving for P:

$$P = \frac{F_n}{(1 + r)^n} \qquad (3)$$

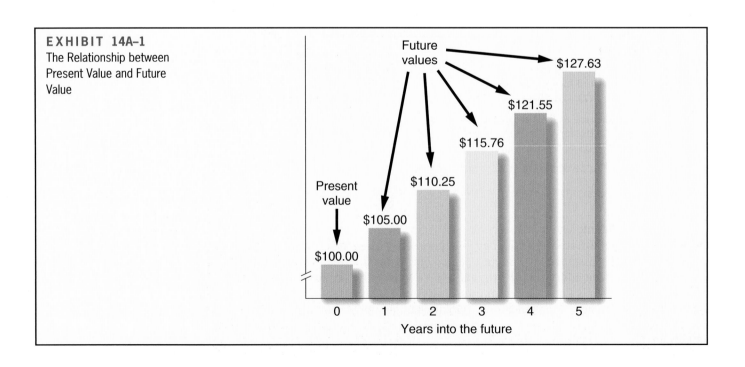

EXHIBIT 14A–1
The Relationship between Present Value and Future Value

In our example, $F_n = \$200$ (the amount to be received in the future), $r = 0.05$ (the annual rate of interest), and $n = 2$ (the number of years in the future that the amount will be received).

$$P = \frac{\$200}{(1 + 0.05)^2}$$

$$P = \frac{\$200}{1.1025}$$

$$P = \$181.40$$

As shown by the computation above, the present value of a $200 amount to be received two years from now is $181.40 if the interest rate is 5%. In effect, $181.40 received *right now* is equivalent to $200 received two years from now.

The process of finding the present value of a future cash flow, which we have just completed, is called **discounting.** We have *discounted* the $200 to its present value of $181.40. The 5% interest that we have used to find this present value is called the **discount rate.** Discounting future sums to their present value is a common practice in business, particularly in capital budgeting decisions.

If you have a power key (y^x) on your calculator, the above calculations are fairly easy. However, some of the present value formulas we will be using are more complex. Fortunately, tables are available in which many of the calculations have already been done. For example, Exhibit 14B–1 in Appendix 14B shows the discounted present value of $1 to be received at various periods in the future at various interest rates. The table indicates that the present value of $1 to be received two periods from now at 5% is 0.907. Since in our example we want to know the present value of $200 rather than just $1, we need to multiply the factor in the table by $200:

$$\$200 \times 0.907 = \$181.40$$

This answer is the same as we obtained earlier using the formula in equation (3).

Present Value of a Series of Cash Flows

Although some investments involve a single sum to be received (or paid) at a single point in the future, other investments involve a *series* of cash flows. A series of identical cash flows is known as an **annuity.** To provide an example, assume that a company has just purchased some government bonds. The bonds will yield interest of $15,000 each year and will be held for five years. What is the present value of the stream of interest receipts from the bonds? As shown in Exhibit 14A–2, if the discount rate is 12%, the present value of this stream is $54,075. The discount factors used in this exhibit were taken from Exhibit 14B–1 in Appendix 14B.

Exhibit 14A–2 illustrates two important points. First, the present value of the $15,000 interest declines the further it is into the future. The present value of $15,000 received a year from now is $13,395, as compared to only $8,505 if received five years from now. This point simply underscores the time value of money.

Year	Factor at 12% (Exhibit 14B–1)	Interest Received	Present Value
1	0.893	$15,000	$13,395
2	0.797	$15,000	11,955
3	0.712	$15,000	10,680
4	0.636	$15,000	9,540
5	0.567	$15,000	8,505
			$54,075

EXHIBIT 14A–2
Present Value of a Series of Cash Receipts

The second point is that the computations used in Exhibit 14A–2 involved unnecessary work. The same present value of $54,075 could have been obtained more easily by referring to Exhibit 14B–2 in Appendix 14B. Exhibit 14B–2 contains the present value of $1 to be received each year over a *series* of years at various interest rates. Exhibit 14B–2 has been derived by simply adding together the factors from Exhibit 14B–1, as follows:

Year	Exhibit 14B–1 Factors at 12%
1	0.893
2	0.797
3	0.712
4	0.636
5	0.567
	3.605

The sum of the five factors above is 3.605. Notice from Exhibit 14B–2 that the factor for $1 to be received each year for five years at 12% is also 3.605. If we use this factor and multiply it by the $15,000 annual cash inflow, then we get the same $54,075 present value that we obtained earlier in Exhibit 14A–2.

$$\$15,000 \times 3.605 = \$54,075$$

Therefore, when computing the present value of a series of equal cash flows that begins at the end of period 1, Exhibit 14B–2 should be used.

To summarize, the present value tables in Appendix 14B should be used as follows:

Exhibit 14B–1: This table should be used to find the present value of a single cash flow (such as a single payment or receipt) occurring in the future.

Exhibit 14B–2: This table should be used to find the present value of a series of identical cash flows beginning at the end of the current period and continuing into the future.

The use of both of these tables is illustrated in various exhibits in the main body of the chapter. *When a present value factor appears in an exhibit, you should take the time to trace it back into either Exhibit 14B–1 or Exhibit 14B–2 to get acquainted with the tables and how they work.* (Review Problem 1 at the end of the chapter is designed for those who would like some practice in present value analysis before attempting the homework exercises and problems.)

Glossary (Appendix 14A)

Annuity A series of identical cash flows. (p. 655)
Compound interest The process of paying interest on interest in an investment. (p. 653)
Discount rate The rate of return that is used to find the present value of a future cash flow. (p. 655)
Discounting The process of finding the present value of a future cash flow. (p. 655)
Present value The value now of an amount that will be received in some future period. (p. 653)

Appendix 14B: Present Value Tables

EXHIBIT 14B-1

Present Value of $1; $\dfrac{1}{(1 + r)^n}$

Periods	4%	5%	6%	7%	8%	9%	10%	11%	12%	13%	14%	15%	16%	17%	18%	19%	20%	21%	22%	23%	24%	25%
1	0.962	0.952	0.943	0.935	0.926	0.917	0.909	0.901	0.893	0.885	0.877	0.870	0.862	0.855	0.847	0.840	0.833	0.826	0.820	0.813	0.806	0.800
2	0.925	0.907	0.890	0.873	0.857	0.842	0.826	0.812	0.797	0.783	0.769	0.756	0.743	0.731	0.718	0.706	0.694	0.683	0.672	0.661	0.650	0.640
3	0.889	0.864	0.840	0.816	0.794	0.772	0.751	0.731	0.712	0.693	0.675	0.658	0.641	0.624	0.609	0.593	0.579	0.564	0.551	0.537	0.524	0.512
4	0.855	0.823	0.792	0.763	0.735	0.708	0.683	0.659	0.636	0.613	0.592	0.572	0.552	0.534	0.516	0.499	0.482	0.467	0.451	0.437	0.423	0.410
5	0.822	0.784	0.747	0.713	0.681	0.650	0.621	0.593	0.567	0.543	0.519	0.497	0.476	0.456	0.437	0.419	0.402	0.386	0.370	0.355	0.341	0.328
6	0.790	0.746	0.705	0.666	0.630	0.596	0.564	0.535	0.507	0.480	0.456	0.432	0.410	0.390	0.370	0.352	0.335	0.319	0.303	0.289	0.275	0.262
7	0.760	0.711	0.665	0.623	0.583	0.547	0.513	0.482	0.452	0.425	0.400	0.376	0.354	0.333	0.314	0.296	0.279	0.263	0.249	0.235	0.222	0.210
8	0.731	0.677	0.627	0.582	0.540	0.502	0.467	0.434	0.404	0.376	0.351	0.327	0.305	0.285	0.266	0.249	0.233	0.218	0.204	0.191	0.179	0.168
9	0.703	0.645	0.592	0.544	0.500	0.460	0.424	0.391	0.361	0.333	0.308	0.284	0.263	0.243	0.225	0.209	0.194	0.180	0.167	0.155	0.144	0.134
10	0.676	0.614	0.558	0.508	0.463	0.422	0.386	0.352	0.322	0.295	0.270	0.247	0.227	0.208	0.191	0.176	0.162	0.149	0.137	0.126	0.116	0.107
11	0.650	0.585	0.527	0.475	0.429	0.388	0.350	0.317	0.287	0.261	0.237	0.215	0.195	0.178	0.162	0.148	0.135	0.123	0.112	0.103	0.094	0.086
12	0.625	0.557	0.497	0.444	0.397	0.356	0.319	0.286	0.257	0.231	0.208	0.187	0.168	0.152	0.137	0.124	0.112	0.102	0.092	0.083	0.076	0.069
13	0.601	0.530	0.469	0.415	0.368	0.326	0.290	0.258	0.229	0.204	0.182	0.163	0.145	0.130	0.116	0.104	0.093	0.084	0.075	0.068	0.061	0.055
14	0.577	0.505	0.442	0.388	0.340	0.299	0.263	0.232	0.205	0.181	0.160	0.141	0.125	0.111	0.099	0.088	0.078	0.069	0.062	0.055	0.049	0.044
15	0.555	0.481	0.417	0.362	0.315	0.275	0.239	0.209	0.183	0.160	0.140	0.123	0.108	0.095	0.084	0.074	0.065	0.057	0.051	0.045	0.040	0.035
16	0.534	0.458	0.394	0.339	0.292	0.252	0.218	0.188	0.163	0.141	0.123	0.107	0.093	0.081	0.071	0.062	0.054	0.047	0.042	0.036	0.032	0.028
17	0.513	0.436	0.371	0.317	0.270	0.231	0.198	0.170	0.146	0.125	0.108	0.093	0.080	0.069	0.060	0.052	0.045	0.039	0.034	0.030	0.026	0.023
18	0.494	0.416	0.350	0.296	0.250	0.212	0.180	0.153	0.130	0.111	0.095	0.081	0.069	0.059	0.051	0.044	0.038	0.032	0.028	0.024	0.021	0.018
19	0.475	0.396	0.331	0.277	0.232	0.194	0.164	0.138	0.116	0.098	0.083	0.070	0.060	0.051	0.043	0.037	0.031	0.027	0.023	0.020	0.017	0.014
20	0.456	0.377	0.312	0.258	0.215	0.178	0.149	0.124	0.104	0.087	0.073	0.061	0.051	0.043	0.037	0.031	0.026	0.022	0.019	0.016	0.014	0.012
21	0.439	0.359	0.294	0.242	0.199	0.164	0.135	0.112	0.093	0.077	0.064	0.053	0.044	0.037	0.031	0.026	0.022	0.018	0.015	0.013	0.011	0.009
22	0.422	0.342	0.278	0.226	0.184	0.150	0.123	0.101	0.083	0.068	0.056	0.046	0.038	0.032	0.026	0.022	0.018	0.015	0.013	0.011	0.009	0.007
23	0.406	0.326	0.262	0.211	0.170	0.138	0.112	0.091	0.074	0.060	0.049	0.040	0.033	0.027	0.022	0.018	0.015	0.012	0.010	0.009	0.007	0.006
24	0.390	0.310	0.247	0.197	0.158	0.126	0.102	0.082	0.066	0.053	0.043	0.035	0.028	0.023	0.019	0.015	0.013	0.010	0.008	0.007	0.006	0.005
25	0.375	0.295	0.233	0.184	0.146	0.116	0.092	0.074	0.059	0.047	0.038	0.030	0.024	0.020	0.016	0.013	0.010	0.009	0.007	0.006	0.005	0.004
26	0.361	0.281	0.220	0.172	0.135	0.106	0.084	0.066	0.053	0.042	0.033	0.026	0.021	0.017	0.014	0.011	0.009	0.007	0.006	0.005	0.004	0.003
27	0.347	0.268	0.207	0.161	0.125	0.098	0.076	0.060	0.047	0.037	0.029	0.023	0.018	0.014	0.011	0.009	0.007	0.006	0.005	0.004	0.003	0.002
28	0.333	0.255	0.196	0.150	0.116	0.090	0.069	0.054	0.042	0.033	0.026	0.020	0.016	0.012	0.010	0.008	0.006	0.005	0.004	0.003	0.002	0.002
29	0.321	0.243	0.185	0.141	0.107	0.082	0.063	0.048	0.037	0.029	0.022	0.017	0.014	0.011	0.008	0.006	0.005	0.004	0.003	0.002	0.002	0.002
30	0.308	0.231	0.174	0.131	0.099	0.075	0.057	0.044	0.033	0.026	0.020	0.015	0.012	0.009	0.007	0.005	0.004	0.003	0.003	0.002	0.002	0.001
40	0.208	0.142	0.097	0.067	0.046	0.032	0.022	0.015	0.011	0.008	0.005	0.004	0.003	0.002	0.001	0.001	0.001	0.000	0.000	0.000	0.000	0.000

EXHIBIT 14B–2

Present Value of an Annuity of $1 in Arrears; $\dfrac{1}{r}\left[1 - \dfrac{1}{(1 + r)^n}\right]$

Periods	4%	5%	6%	7%	8%	9%	10%	11%	12%	13%	14%	15%	16%	17%	18%	19%	20%	21%	22%	23%	24%	25%
1	0.962	0.952	0.943	0.935	0.926	0.917	0.909	0.901	0.893	0.885	0.877	0.870	0.862	0.855	0.847	0.840	0.833	0.826	0.820	0.813	0.806	0.800
2	1.886	1.859	1.833	1.808	1.783	1.759	1.736	1.713	1.690	1.668	1.647	1.626	1.605	1.585	1.566	1.547	1.528	1.509	1.492	1.474	1.457	1.440
3	2.775	2.723	2.673	2.624	2.577	2.531	2.487	2.444	2.402	2.361	2.322	2.283	2.246	2.210	2.174	2.140	2.106	2.074	2.042	2.011	1.981	1.952
4	3.630	3.546	3.465	3.387	3.312	3.240	3.170	3.102	3.037	2.974	2.914	2.855	2.798	2.743	2.690	2.639	2.589	2.540	2.494	2.448	2.404	2.362
5	4.452	4.329	4.212	4.100	3.993	3.890	3.791	3.696	3.605	3.517	3.433	3.352	3.274	3.199	3.127	3.058	2.991	2.926	2.864	2.803	2.745	2.689
6	5.242	5.076	4.917	4.767	4.623	4.486	4.355	4.231	4.111	3.998	3.889	3.784	3.685	3.589	3.498	3.410	3.326	3.245	3.167	3.092	3.020	2.951
7	6.002	5.786	5.582	5.389	5.206	5.033	4.868	4.712	4.564	4.423	4.288	4.160	4.039	3.922	3.812	3.706	3.605	3.508	3.416	3.327	3.242	3.161
8	6.733	6.463	6.210	5.971	5.747	5.535	5.335	5.146	4.968	4.799	4.639	4.487	4.344	4.207	4.078	3.954	3.837	3.726	3.619	3.518	3.421	3.329
9	7.435	7.108	6.802	6.515	6.247	5.995	5.759	5.537	5.328	5.132	4.946	4.772	4.607	4.451	4.303	4.163	4.031	3.905	3.786	3.673	3.566	3.463
10	8.111	7.722	7.360	7.024	6.710	6.418	6.145	5.889	5.650	5.426	5.216	5.019	4.833	4.659	4.494	4.339	4.192	4.054	3.923	3.799	3.682	3.571
11	8.760	8.306	7.887	7.499	7.139	6.805	6.495	6.207	5.938	5.687	5.453	5.234	5.029	4.836	4.656	4.486	4.327	4.177	4.035	3.902	3.776	3.656
12	9.385	8.863	8.384	7.943	7.536	7.161	6.814	6.492	6.194	5.918	5.660	5.421	5.197	4.988	4.793	4.611	4.439	4.278	4.127	3.985	3.851	3.725
13	9.986	9.394	8.853	8.358	7.904	7.487	7.103	6.750	6.424	6.122	5.842	5.583	5.342	5.118	4.910	4.715	4.533	4.362	4.203	4.053	3.912	3.780
14	10.563	9.899	9.295	8.745	8.244	7.786	7.367	6.982	6.628	6.302	6.002	5.724	5.468	5.229	5.008	4.802	4.611	4.432	4.265	4.108	3.962	3.824
15	11.118	10.380	9.712	9.108	8.559	8.061	7.606	7.191	6.811	6.462	6.142	5.847	5.575	5.324	5.092	4.876	4.675	4.489	4.315	4.153	4.001	3.859
16	11.652	10.838	10.106	9.447	8.851	8.313	7.824	7.379	6.974	6.604	6.265	5.954	5.668	5.405	5.162	4.938	4.730	4.536	4.357	4.189	4.033	3.887
17	12.166	11.274	10.477	9.763	9.122	8.544	8.022	7.549	7.120	6.729	6.373	6.047	5.749	5.475	5.222	4.990	4.775	4.576	4.391	4.219	4.059	3.910
18	12.659	11.690	10.828	10.059	9.372	8.756	8.201	7.702	7.250	6.840	6.467	6.128	5.818	5.534	5.273	5.033	4.812	4.608	4.419	4.243	4.080	3.928
19	13.134	12.085	11.158	10.336	9.604	8.950	8.365	7.839	7.366	6.938	6.550	6.198	5.877	5.584	5.316	5.070	4.843	4.635	4.442	4.263	4.097	3.942
20	13.590	12.462	11.470	10.594	9.818	9.129	8.514	7.963	7.469	7.025	6.623	6.259	5.929	5.628	5.353	5.101	4.870	4.657	4.460	4.279	4.110	3.954
21	14.029	12.821	11.764	10.836	10.017	9.292	8.649	8.075	7.562	7.102	6.687	6.312	5.973	5.665	5.384	5.127	4.891	4.675	4.476	4.292	4.121	3.963
22	14.451	13.163	12.042	11.061	10.201	9.442	8.772	8.176	7.645	7.170	6.743	6.359	6.011	5.696	5.410	5.149	4.909	4.690	4.488	4.302	4.130	3.970
23	14.857	13.489	12.303	11.272	10.371	9.580	8.883	8.266	7.718	7.230	6.792	6.399	6.044	5.723	5.432	5.167	4.925	4.703	4.499	4.311	4.137	3.976
24	15.247	13.799	12.550	11.469	10.529	9.707	8.985	8.348	7.784	7.283	6.835	6.434	6.073	5.746	5.451	5.182	4.937	4.713	4.507	4.318	4.143	3.981
25	15.622	14.094	12.783	11.654	10.675	9.823	9.077	8.422	7.843	7.330	6.873	6.464	6.097	5.766	5.467	5.195	4.948	4.721	4.514	4.323	4.147	3.985
26	15.983	14.375	13.003	11.826	10.810	9.929	9.161	8.488	7.896	7.372	6.906	6.491	6.118	5.783	5.480	5.206	4.956	4.728	4.520	4.328	4.151	3.988
27	16.330	14.643	13.211	11.987	10.935	10.027	9.237	8.548	7.943	7.409	6.935	6.514	6.136	5.798	5.492	5.215	4.964	4.734	4.524	4.332	4.154	3.990
28	16.663	14.898	13.406	12.137	11.051	10.116	9.307	8.602	7.984	7.441	6.961	6.534	6.152	5.810	5.502	5.223	4.970	4.739	4.528	4.335	4.157	3.992
29	16.984	15.141	13.591	12.278	11.158	10.198	9.370	8.650	8.022	7.470	6.983	6.551	6.166	5.820	5.510	5.229	4.975	4.743	4.531	4.337	4.159	3.994
30	17.292	15.372	13.765	12.409	11.258	10.274	9.427	8.694	8.055	7.496	7.003	6.566	6.177	5.829	5.517	5.235	4.979	4.746	4.534	4.339	4.160	3.995
40	19.793	17.159	15.046	13.332	11.925	10.757	9.779	8.951	8.244	7.634	7.105	6.642	6.233	5.871	5.548	5.258	4.997	4.760	4.544	4.347	4.166	3.999

Appendix 14C: Income Taxes in Capital Budgeting Decisions

LEARNING OBJECTIVE 8
Include income taxes in a capital budgeting analysis.

We ignored income taxes in this chapter for two reasons. First, many organizations do not pay income taxes. Not-for-profit organizations, such as hospitals and charitable foundations, and governmental agencies are exempt from income taxes. Second, capital budgeting is complex and is best absorbed in small doses. Now that we have a solid foundation in the concepts of present value and discounting, we can explore the effects of income taxes on capital budgeting decisions.

The U.S. income tax code is enormously complex. We only scratch the surface here. To keep the subject within reasonable bounds, we have made many simplifying assumptions about the tax code. Among the most important of these assumptions are: (1) taxable income equals net income as computed for financial reports; and (2) the tax rate is a flat percentage of taxable income. The actual tax code is far more complex than this; indeed, experts acknowledge that no one person knows or can know it all. However, the simplifications that we make throughout this appendix allow us to cover the most important implications of income taxes for capital budgeting without getting bogged down in details.

The Concept of After-Tax Cost

Businesses, like individuals, must pay income taxes. In the case of businesses, the amount of income tax that must be paid is determined by the company's net taxable income. Tax deductible expenses (tax deductions) decrease the company's net taxable income and hence reduce the taxes the company must pay. For this reason, expenses are often stated on an *after-tax* basis. For example, if a company pays rent of $10 million a year but this expense results in a reduction in income taxes of $3 million, the after-tax cost of the rent is $7 million. An expenditure net of its tax effect is known as **after-tax cost.**

To illustrate, assume that a company with a tax rate of 30% is contemplating a training program that costs $60,000. What impact will this have on the company's taxes? To keep matters simple, let's suppose the training program has no immediate effect on sales. How much does the company actually pay for the training program after taking into account the impact of this expense on taxes? The answer is $42,000 as shown in Exhibit 14C–1 (page 660). While the training program costs $60,000 before taxes, it would reduce the company's taxes by $18,000, so its *after-tax* cost would be only $42,000.

The after-tax cost of any tax-deductible cash expense can be determined using the following formula:[1]

$$\begin{array}{c}\text{After-tax cost}\\ \text{(net cash outflow)}\end{array} = (1 - \text{Tax rate}) \times \text{Tax-deductible cash expense} \qquad (1)$$

We can verify the accuracy of this formula by applying it to the $60,000 training program expenditure:

$$(1 - 0.30) \times \$60,000 = \$42,000 \text{ after-tax cost of the training program}$$

This formula is very useful because it provides the actual amount of cash a company must pay after considering tax effects. It is this actual, after-tax, cash outflow that should be used in capital budgeting decisions.

Similar reasoning applies to revenues and other *taxable* cash inflows. Since these cash receipts are taxable, the company must pay out a portion of them in taxes. The **after-tax benefit,** or net cash inflow, realized from a particular cash receipt can be obtained by applying a simple variation of the cash expenditure formula used above:

$$\begin{array}{c}\text{After-tax benefit}\\ \text{(net cash inflow)}\end{array} = (1 - \text{Tax rate}) \times \text{Taxable cash receipt} \qquad (2)$$

---

[1]   This formula assumes that a company is operating at a profit; if it is operating at a loss, the tax situation can be very complex. For simplicity, we assume in all examples, exercises, and problems that the company is operating at a profit.

	Without Training Program	With Training Program
Sales	$850,000	$850,000
Less tax deductible expenses:		
Salaries, insurance, and other	700,000	700,000
New training program		60,000
Total expenses	700,000	760,000
Taxable income	$150,000	$ 90,000
Income taxes (30%)	$ 45,000	$ 27,000

Cost of new training program	$60,000
Less: Reduction in income taxes ($45,000 − $27,000)	18,000
After-tax cost of the new training program	$42,000

We emphasize the term *taxable cash receipts* because not all cash inflows are taxable. For example, the release of working capital at the end of an investment project would not be a taxable cash inflow. It is not counted as income for either financial accounting or income tax reporting purposes since it is simply a recovery of the initial investment.

Depreciation Tax Shield

Depreciation is not a cash flow. For this reason, depreciation was ignored in Chapter 14 in all discounted cash flow computations. However, depreciation does affect the taxes that must be paid and therefore has an indirect effect on a company's cash flows.

To illustrate the effect of depreciation deductions on tax payments, consider a company with annual cash sales of $500,000 and cash operating expenses of $310,000. In addition, the company has a depreciable asset on which the depreciation deduction is $90,000 per year. The tax rate is 30%. As shown in Exhibit 14C–2, the depreciation deduction reduces the company's taxes by $27,000. In effect, the depreciation deduction of $90,000 *shields* $90,000 in revenues from taxation and thereby *reduces* the amount of taxes that the company must pay. Because depreciation deductions shield revenues from taxation, they are generally referred to as a **depreciation tax shield**.[2] The reduction in tax payments made possible by the depreciation tax shield is equal to the amount of the depreciation deduction, multiplied by the tax rate as follows:

$$\text{Tax savings from the depreciation tax shield} = \text{Tax rate} \times \text{Depreciation deduction} \qquad (3)$$

We can verify this formula by applying it to the $90,000 depreciation deduction in our example:

$$0.30 \times \$90,000 = \$27,000 \text{ reduction in tax payments}$$

In this appendix, when we estimate after-tax cash flows for capital budgeting decisions, we will include the tax savings provided by the depreciation tax shield.

To keep matters simple, we will assume in all of our examples and problem materials that depreciation reported for tax purposes is straight-line depreciation, with no deduction for salvage value. In other words, we will assume that the entire original cost of the asset is written

---

[2] The term *depreciation tax shield* may convey the impression that there is something underhanded about depreciation deductions—that companies are getting some sort of a special tax break. However, to use the depreciation deduction, a company must have already acquired a depreciable asset—which typically requires a cash outflow. Essentially, the tax code requires companies to delay recognizing the cash outflow as an expense until depreciation charges are recorded.

	Without Depreciation Deduction	With Depreciation Deduction
Sales	$500,000	$500,000
Cash operating expenses	310,000	310,000
Cash flow from operations	190,000	190,000
Depreciation expense	—	90,000
Taxable income	$190,000	$100,000
Income taxes (30%)	$ 57,000	$ 30,000

$27,000 lower taxes with
the depreciation deduction

Cash flow comparison:		
Cash flow from operations (above)	$190,000	$190,000
Income taxes (above)	57,000	30,000
Net cash flow	$133,000	$160,000

$27,000 greater cash flow with
the depreciation deduction

off evenly over its useful life. Since the net book value of the asset at the end of its useful life will be zero under this depreciation method, we will assume that any proceeds received on disposal of the asset at the end of its useful life will be taxed as ordinary income.

In actuality, the rules for depreciation are more complex than this and most companies take advantage of accelerated depreciation methods allowed under the tax code. These accelerated methods usually result in a reduction in current taxes and an offsetting increase in future taxes. This shifting of part of the tax burden from the current year to future years is advantageous from a present value point of view because a dollar today is worth more than a dollar in the future. A summary of the concepts we have introduced so far is given in Exhibit 14C–3.

Example of Income Taxes and Capital Budgeting

Armed with an understanding of after-tax cost, after-tax revenue, and the depreciation tax shield, we are now prepared to examine a comprehensive example of income taxes and capital budgeting.

Item	Treatment
Tax-deductible cash expense*	Multiply by (1 − Tax rate) to get after-tax cost.
Taxable cash receipt*	Multiply by (1 − Tax rate) to get after-tax cash inflow.
Depreciation deduction	Multiply by the tax rate to get the tax savings from the depreciation tax shield.

*Cash expenses can be deducted from the cash receipts and the difference multiplied by (1 − Tax rate). See the example at the top of Exhibit 14C–4.

Holland Company owns the mineral rights to land that has a deposit of ore. The company is uncertain if it should purchase equipment and open a mine on the property. After careful study, the company assembled the following data.

Cost of equipment needed	$300,000
Working capital needed	$75,000
Estimated annual cash receipts from sales of ore	$250,000
Estimated annual cash expenses for salaries, insurance, utilities, and other cash expenses of mining the ore	$170,000
Cost of road repairs needed in 6 years	$40,000
Salvage value of the equipment in 10 years	$100,000

The ore in the mine would be exhausted after 10 years of mining activity, at which time the mine would be closed. The equipment would then be sold for its salvage value. Holland Company uses the straight-line method, assuming no salvage value, to compute depreciation deductions for tax purposes. The company's after-tax cost of capital is 12% and its tax rate is 30%.

Should Holland Company purchase the equipment and open a mine on the property? The solution to the problem is given in Exhibit 14C–4. We suggest that you go through this solution item by item and note the following points:

Cost of new equipment. The initial investment of $300,000 in the new equipment is included in full with no reductions for taxes. This represents an *investment,* not an expense, so no tax adjustment is made. (Only revenues and expenses are adjusted for the effects of taxes.) However, this investment does affect taxes through the depreciation deductions that are considered below.

Working capital. Observe that the working capital needed for the project is included in full with no reductions for taxes. Like the cost of new equipment, working capital is an investment and not an expense so no tax adjustment is made. Also observe that no tax adjustment is made when the working capital is released at the end of the project's life. The release of working capital is not a taxable cash flow because it is a return of investment funds back to the company.

EXHIBIT 14C–4
Example of Income Taxes and Capital Budgeting

			Per Year			
Cash receipts from sales of ore			$250,000			
Less payments for salaries, insurance, utilities, and other cash expenses			170,000			
Net cash receipts			$ 80,000			

Items and Computations	Year(s)	(1) Amount	(2) Tax Effect*	After-Tax Cash Flows (1) × (2)	12% Factor	Present Value of Cash Flows
Cost of new equipment	Now	$(300,000)	—	$(300,000)	1.000	$(300,000)
Working capital needed	Now	$(75,000)	—	$(75,000)	1.000	(75,000)
Net annual cash receipts (above)	1–10	$80,000	1 − 0.30	$56,000	5.650	316,400
Road repairs	6	$(40,000)	1 − 0.30	$(28,000)	0.507	(14,196)
Annual depreciation deductions	1–10	$30,000	0.30	$9,000	5.650	50,850
Salvage value of equipment	10	$100,000	1 − 0.30	$70,000	0.322	22,540
Release of working capital	10	$75,000	—	$75,000	0.322	24,150
Net present value						$ 24,744

*Taxable cash receipts and tax-deductible cash expenses are multiplied by (1 − Tax rate) to determine the after-tax cash flow. Depreciation deductions are multiplied by the tax rate itself to determine the after-tax cash flow (i.e., tax savings from the depreciation tax shield).

Net annual cash receipts. The net annual cash receipts from sales of ore are adjusted for the effects of income taxes, as discussed earlier in the chapter. Note at the top of Exhibit 14C–4 that the annual cash expenses are deducted from the annual cash receipts to obtain the net cash receipts. This simplifies computations.

Road repairs. Since the road repairs occur just once (in the sixth year), they are treated separately from other expenses. Road repairs would be a tax-deductible cash expense, and therefore they are adjusted for the effects of income taxes, as discussed earlier in the chapter.

Depreciation deductions. The tax savings provided by depreciation deductions is essentially an annuity that is included in the present value computations in the same way as other cash flows.

Salvage value of equipment. Since the company does not consider salvage value when computing depreciation deductions, book value will be zero at the end of the life of an asset. Thus, any salvage value received is taxable as income to the company. The after-tax benefit is determined by multiplying the salvage value by $(1 - \text{Tax rate})$.

Since the net present value of the proposed mining project is positive, the equipment should be purchased and the mine opened. Study Exhibit 14C–4 thoroughly. *Exhibit 14C–4 is the key exhibit!*

Summary (Appendix 14C)

Unless a company is a tax-exempt organization, such as a not-for-profit school or a governmental unit, income taxes should be considered in making capital budgeting decisions. Tax-deductible cash expenditures and taxable cash receipts are placed on an after-tax basis by multiplying them by $(1 - \text{Tax rate})$. Only the after-tax amount should be used in determining the desirability of an investment proposal.

Although depreciation is not a cash outflow, it is a valid deduction for tax purposes and as such affects income tax payments. The depreciation tax shield—computed by multiplying the depreciation deduction by the tax rate itself—also results in savings in income taxes.

Glossary (Appendix 14C)

After-tax benefit The amount of net cash inflow realized from a taxable cash receipt after income tax effects have been considered. The amount is determined by multiplying the taxable cash receipt by $(1 - \text{Tax rate})$. (p. 659)

After-tax cost The amount of net cash outflow resulting from a tax-deductible cash expense after income tax effects have been considered. The amount is determined by multiplying the tax-deductible cash expense by $(1 - \text{Tax rate})$. (p. 659)

Depreciation tax shield A reduction in tax that results from depreciation deductions. The reduction in tax is computed by multiplying the depreciation deduction by the tax rate. (p. 660)

Questions

14-1 What is the difference between capital budgeting screening decisions and capital budgeting preference decisions?

14-2 What is meant by the term *time value of money?*

14-3 What is meant by the term *discounting?*

14-4 Why isn't accounting net income used in the net present value and internal rate of return methods of making capital budgeting decisions?

14-5 Why are discounted cash flow methods of making capital budgeting decisions superior to other methods?

14-6   What is net present value? Can it ever be negative? Explain.

14-7   Identify two simplifying assumptions associated with discounted cash flow methods of making capital budgeting decisions.

14-8   If a company has to pay interest of 14% on long-term debt, then its cost of capital is 14%. Do you agree? Explain.

14-9   What is meant by an investment project's internal rate of return? How is the internal rate of return computed?

14-10 Explain how the cost of capital serves as a screening tool when dealing with (*a*) the net present value method and (*b*) the internal rate of return method.

14-11 As the discount rate increases, the present value of a given future cash flow also increases. Do you agree? Explain.

14-12 Refer to Exhibit 14–4. Is the return on this investment proposal exactly 14%, more than 14%, or less than 14%? Explain.

14-13 How is the project profitability index computed, and what does it measure?

14-14 What is meant by the term *payback period?* How is the payback period determined? How can the payback method be useful?

14-15 What is the major criticism of the payback and simple rate of return methods of making capital budgeting decisions?

14-16 (Appendix 14C) What is meant by after-tax cost and how is the concept used in capital budgeting decisions?

14-17 (Appendix 14C) What is a depreciation tax shield and how does it affect capital budgeting decisions?

14-18 (Appendix 14C) Ludlow Company is considering the introduction of a new product line. Would an increase in the income tax rate tend to make the new investment more or less attractive? Explain.

14-19 (Appendix 14C) Assume that an old piece of equipment is sold at a loss. From a capital budgeting point of view, what two cash inflows will be associated with the sale?

14-20 (Appendix 14C) Assume that a new piece of equipment costs $40,000 and that the tax rate is 30%. Should the new piece of equipment be included in the capital budgeting analysis as a cash outflow of $40,000, or as a cash outflow of $28,000 [$40,000 × (1 − 0.30)]? Explain.

Exercises

EXERCISE 14-1 Net Present Value Method [LO1]

The management of Kunkel Company is considering the purchase of a $40,000 machine that would reduce operating costs by $7,000 per year. At the end of the machine's eight-year useful life, it will have zero scrap value. The company's required rate of return is 12% on all investment projects.

Required:
(Ignore income taxes.)
1. Determine the net present value of the investment in the machine.
2. What is the difference between the total, undiscounted cash inflows and cash outflows over the entire life of the machine?

EXERCISE 14-2 Internal Rate of Return [LO2]

Wendell's Donut Shoppe is investigating the purchase of a new $18,600 donut-making machine. The new machine would permit the company to reduce the amount of part-time help needed, at a cost savings of $3,800 per year. In addition, the new machine would allow the company to produce one new style of donut, resulting in the sale of at least 1,000 dozen more donuts each year. The company realizes a contribution margin of $1.20 per dozen donuts sold. The new machine would have a six-year useful life.

Required:
(Ignore income taxes.)
1. What would be the total annual cash inflows associated with the new machine for capital budgeting purposes?
2. Find the internal rate of return promised by the new machine to the nearest whole percent.
3. In addition to the data given previously, assume that the machine will have a $9,125 salvage value at the end of six years. Under these conditions, compute the internal rate of return to the nearest whole percent. (Hint: You may find it helpful to use the net present value approach; find the discount rate that will cause the net present value to be closest to zero. Use the format shown in Exhibit 14–4.)

EXERCISE 14-3 Uncertain Future Cash Flows [LO3]

Lukow Products is investigating the purchase of a piece of automated equipment that will save $400,000 each year in direct labor and inventory carrying costs. This equipment costs $2,500,000 and is expected to have a 15-year useful life with no salvage value. The company's required rate of return is 20% on all equipment purchases. Management anticipates that this equipment will provide intangible benefits such as greater flexibility and higher quality output.

Required:
(Ignore income taxes.)
What dollar value per year would these intangible benefits have to have to make the equipment an acceptable investment?

EXERCISE 14-4 Preference Ranking [LO4]

Information on four investment proposals is given below:

	Investment Proposal			
	A	B	C	D
Investment required	$(90,000)	$(100,000)	$(70,000)	$(120,000)
Present value of cash inflows	126,000	90,000	105,000	160,000
Net present value	$ 36,000	$ (10,000)	$ 35,000	$ 40,000
Life of the project	5 years	7 years	6 years	6 years

Required:
1. Compute the project profitability index for each investment proposal.
2. Rank the proposals in terms of preference.

EXERCISE 14-5 Payback Method [LO5]

The management of Unter Corporation is considering an investment with the following cash flows:

Year	Investment	Cash Inflow
1.	$15,000	$1,000
2.	$8,000	$2,000
3.		$2,500
4.		$4,000
5.		$5,000
6.		$6,000
7.		$5,000
8.		$4,000
9.		$3,000
10.		$2,000

Required:
1. Determine the payback period of the investment.
2. Would the payback period be affected if the cash inflow in the last year were several times as large?

EXERCISE 14-6 Simple Rate of Return Method [LO6]

The management of Ballard MicroBrew is considering the purchase of an automated bottling machine for $120,000. The machine would replace an old piece of equipment that costs $30,000 per year to operate. The new machine would cost $12,000 per year to operate. The old machine currently in use could be sold now for a scrap value of $40,000. The new machine would have a useful life of 10 years with no salvage value.

Required:
Compute the simple rate of return on the new automated bottling machine.

EXERCISE 14-7 (Appendix 14A) Basic Present Value Concepts [LO7]

Solve each of the following parts independently. (Ignore income taxes.)

1. The Atlantic Medical Clinic can purchase a new computer system that will save $7,000 annually in billing costs. The computer system will last for eight years and have no salvage value. Up to how much should the Atlantic Medical Clinic be willing to pay for the new computer system if the clinic's required rate of return is:
    a. Sixteen percent?
    b. Twenty percent?

2. The Caldwell *Herald* newspaper reported the following story:

    Frank Ormsby of Caldwell is the state's newest millionaire. By choosing the six winning numbers on last week's state lottery, Mr. Ormsby has won the week's grand prize totaling $1.6 million. The State Lottery Commission has indicated that Mr. Ormsby will receive his prize in 20 annual installments of $80,000 each.

    a. If Mr. Ormsby can invest money at a 12% rate of return, what is the present value of his winnings?
    b. Is it correct to say that Mr. Ormsby is the "state's newest millionaire"? Explain your answer.

3. Fraser Company will need a new warehouse in five years. The warehouse will cost $500,000 to build. What lump-sum amount should the company invest now to have the $500,000 available at the end of the five-year period? Assume that the company can invest money at:
    a. Ten percent.
    b. Fourteen percent.

EXERCISE 14-8 (Appendix 14C) After-Tax Costs [LO8]

Solve each of the following parts independently:

a. Neal Company would like to initiate a management development program for its executives. The program would cost $100,000 per year to operate. What would be the after-tax cost of the program if the company's income tax rate is 30%?

b. Smerk's Department Store has rearranged the merchandise display cases on the first floor of its building, placing fast turnover items near the front door. This rearrangement has caused the company's contribution margin (and taxable income) to increase by $40,000 per month. If the company's income tax rate is 30%, what is the after-tax benefit from this rearrangement of facilities?

c. Perfect Press, Inc., has just purchased a new binding machine at a cost of $210,000. For tax purposes, the entire original cost of the machine will be depreciated over seven years using the straight-line method. Determine the yearly tax savings from the depreciation tax shield. Assume that the income tax rate is 30%.

EXERCISE 14-9 Comparison of Projects Using Net Present Value [LO1]

Labeau Products, Ltd., of Perth, Australia, has $35,000 to invest. The company is trying to decide between two alternative uses for the funds as follows:

	Invest in Project X	Invest in Project Y
Investment required..........................	$35,000	$35,000
Annual cash inflows..........................	$9,000	
Single cash inflow at the end of 10 years........		$150,000
Life of the project............................	10 years	10 years

The company's discount rate is 18%.

Required:

(Ignore income taxes.) Which alternative would you recommend that the company accept? Show all computations using net present value. Prepare separate computations for each project.

EXERCISE 14-10 Basic Net Present Value Analysis [LO1]

Kathy Myers frequently purchases stocks and bonds, but she is uncertain how to determine the rate of return that she is earning. For example, three years ago she paid $13,000 for 200 shares of Malti Company's common stock. She received a $420 cash dividend on the stock at the end of each year for three years. At the end of three years, she sold the stock for $16,000. Kathy would like to earn a return of at least 14% on all of her investments. She is not sure whether the Malti Company stock provided a 14% return and would like some help with the necessary computations.

Required:
(Ignore income taxes.) Using the net present value method, determine whether or not the Malti Company stock provided a 14% return. Use the general format illustrated in Exhibit 14–4 and round all computations to the nearest whole dollar.

EXERCISE 14-11 Internal Rate of Return and Net Present Value [LO1, LO2]

Henrie's Drapery Service is investigating the purchase of a new machine for cleaning and blocking drapes. The machine would cost $130,400, including freight and installation. Henrie's has estimated that the new machine would increase the company's cash inflows, net of expenses, by $25,000 per year. The machine would have a 10-year useful life and no salvage value.

Required:
(Ignore income taxes.)
1. Compute the machine's internal rate of return to the nearest whole percent.
2. Compute the machine's net present value. Use a discount rate of 14% and the format shown in Exhibit 14–5. Why do you have a zero net present value?
3. Suppose that the new machine would increase the company's annual cash inflows, net of expenses, by only $22,500 per year. Under these conditions, compute the internal rate of return to the nearest whole percent.

EXERCISE 14-12 Uncertain Future Life [LO3]

The Matchless Dating Service has made an investment in video and recording equipment that costs $106,700. The equipment is expected to generate cash inflows of $20,000 per year.

Required:
How many years will the equipment have to be used in order to provide the company with a 10% return on its investment?

EXERCISE 14-13 Basic Payback Period and Simple Rate of Return Computations [LO5, LO6]

A piece of laborsaving equipment has just come onto the market that Mitsui Electronics, Ltd., could use to reduce costs in one of its plants in Japan. Relevant data relating to the equipment follow (currency is in thousands of yen, denoted by ¥):

Purchase cost of the equipment.........	¥432,000
Annual cost savings that will be provided by the equipment..........	¥90,000
Life of the equipment	12 years

Required:
(Ignore income taxes.)
1. Compute the payback period for the equipment. If the company requires a payback period of four years or less, would the equipment be purchased?
2. Compute the simple rate of return on the equipment. Use straight-line depreciation based on the equipment's useful life. Would the equipment be purchased if the company's required rate of return is 14%?

EXERCISE 14-14 (Appendix 14A) Basic Present Value Concepts [LO7]

Consider each of the following situations independently. (Ignore income taxes.)
1. In three years, when he is discharged from the Air Force, Steve wants to buy an $8,000 power boat. What lump-sum amount must he invest now to have the $8,000 at the end of three years if he can invest money at:
   a. Ten percent?
   b. Fourteen percent?
2. Annual cash inflows that will arise from two competing investment projects are given below:

	Investment	
Year	A	B
1........	$ 3,000	$12,000
2........	6,000	9,000
3........	9,000	6,000
4........	12,000	3,000
	$30,000	$30,000

Each investment project will require the same investment outlay. The discount rate is 18%. Compute the present value of the cash inflows for each investment.

3. Julie has just retired. Her company's retirement program has two options as to how retirement benefits can be received. Under the first option, Julie would receive a lump sum of $150,000 immediately as her full retirement benefit. Under the second option, she would receive $14,000 each year for 20 years plus a lump-sum payment of $60,000 at the end of the 20-year period. If she can invest money at 12%, which option would you recommend that she accept? Use present value analysis.

EXERCISE 14-15 (Appendix 14D) After-Tax Cash Flows in Net Present Value Analysis [LO8]

Dwyer Company is considering two investment projects. Relevant cost and cash flow information on the two projects is given below:

	Project A	Project B
Investment in heavy trucks.	$130,000	
Investment in working capital.		$130,000
Net annual cash inflows.	$25,000	$25,000
Life of the project	9 years*	9 years

*Useful life of the trucks

The trucks will have a $15,000 salvage value in nine years. For tax purposes, the company computes depreciation deductions assuming zero salvage value and uses straight-line depreciation. The trucks will be depreciated over five years. At the end of nine years, the working capital will be released for use elsewhere. The company requires an after-tax return of 12% on all investments. The tax rate is 30%.

Required:
Compute the net present value of each investment project. (Round to the nearest whole dollar.)

EXERCISE 14-16 Working With Net Present Value [LO1]

The Cambro Foundation, a nonprofit organization, is planning to invest $104,950 in a project that will last for three years. The project will provide cash inflows as follows:

Year 1.	$30,000
Year 2.	$40,000
Year 3.	?

Required:
Assuming that the equipment will yield exactly a 12% rate of return, what is the expected cash inflow for Year 3?

EXERCISE 14-17 Basic Net Present Value and Internal Rate of Return Analysis [LO1, LO2]

Consider each part below independently. Ignore income taxes.

1. Preston Company's required rate of return is 14% on all investments. The company can purchase a new machine at a cost of $84,900. The new machine would generate cash inflows of $15,000 per year and have a 12-year useful life with no salvage value. Compute the machine's net present value. (Use the format shown in Exhibit 14–1.) Is the machine an acceptable investment? Explain.

2. The Walton *Daily News* is investigating the purchase of a new auxiliary press that has a projected life of 18 years. It is estimated that the new press will save $30,000 per year in cash operating costs. If the new press costs $217,500, what is its internal rate of return? Is the press an acceptable investment if the company's required rate of return is 16%? Explain.

3. Refer to the data above for the Walton *Daily News*. How much would the annual cash inflows (cost savings) have to be for the new press to provide the required 16% rate of return? Round your answer to the nearest whole dollar.

EXERCISE 14-18 Net Present Value Analysis of Two Alternatives [LO1]
Perit Industries has $100,000 to invest. The company is trying to decide between two alternative uses of the funds. The alternatives are:

	Project A	Project B
Cost of equipment required	$100,000	
Working capital investment required		$100,000
Annual cash inflows	$21,000	$16,000
Salvage value of equipment in six years	$8,000	
Life of the project	6 years	6 years

The working capital needed for project B will be released for investment elsewhere at the end of six years. Perit Industries' discount rate is 14%.

Required:
(Ignore income taxes.) Which investment alternative (if either) would you recommend that the company accept? Show all computations using the net present value format. Prepare separate computations for each project.

EXERCISE 14-19 Payback Period and Simple Rate of Return [LO5, LO6]

Nick's Novelties, Inc., is considering the purchase of electronic pinball machines to place in amusement houses. The machines would cost a total of $300,000, have an eight-year useful life, and have a total salvage value of $20,000. The company estimates that annual revenues and expenses associated with the machines would be as follows:

Revenues		$200,000
Less operating expenses:		
Commissions to amusement houses	$100,000	
Insurance	7,000	
Depreciation	35,000	
Maintenance	18,000	160,000
Net operating income		$ 40,000

Required:
(Ignore income taxes.)
1. Assume that Nick's Novelties, Inc., will not purchase new equipment unless it provides a payback period of five years or less. Would the company purchase the pinball machines?
2. Compute the simple rate of return promised by the pinball machines. If the company requires a simple rate of return of at least 12%, will the pinball machines be purchased?

EXERCISE 14-20 (Appendix 14C) Net Present Value Analysis Including Income Taxes [LO8]
The Midtown Cafeteria employs five people to operate antiquated dishwashing equipment. The cost of wages for these people and for maintenance of the equipment is $85,000 per year. Management is considering the purchase of a single, highly automated dishwashing machine that would cost $140,000 and have a useful life of 12 years. This machine would require the services of only three people to operate at a cost of $48,000 per year. A maintenance contract on the machine would cost an additional $2,000 per year. New water jets would be needed on the machine in six years at a total cost of $15,000.

The old equipment is fully depreciated and has no resale value. The new machine will have a salvage value of $9,000 at the end of its 12-year useful life. For tax purposes, the company computes depreciation deductions assuming zero salvage value and uses straight-line depreciation. The new dishwashing machine would be depreciated over seven years. Management requires a 14% after-tax return on all equipment purchases. The company's tax rate is 30%.

Required:
1. Determine the before-tax net annual cost savings that the new dishwashing machine will provide.
2. Using the data from (1) above and other data from the exercise, compute the new dishwashing machine's net present value. Round all dollar amounts to the nearest whole dollar. Would you recommend that it be purchased?

Problems

PROBLEM 14-21 Net Present Value Analysis; Uncertain Cash Flows [LO1, LO3]

"I'm not sure we should lay out $500,000 for that automated welding machine," said Jim Alder, president of the Superior Equipment Company. "That's a lot of money, and it would cost us $80,000 for software and installation, and another $3,000 every month just to maintain the thing. In addition, the manufacturer admits that it would cost $45,000 more at the end of seven years to replace worn-out parts."

"I admit it's a lot of money," said Franci Rogers, the controller. "But you know the turnover problem we've had with the welding crew. This machine would replace six welders at a cost savings of $108,000 per year. And we would save another $6,500 per year in reduced material waste. When you figure that the automated welder would last for 12 years, I'm sure the return would be greater than our 16% required rate of return."

"I'm still not convinced," countered Mr. Alder. "We can only get $12,000 scrap value out of our old welding equipment if we sell it now, and in 12 years the new machine will only be worth $20,000 for parts. But have your people work up the figures and we'll talk about them at the executive committee meeting tomorrow."

Required:
(Ignore income taxes.)
1. Compute the net annual cost savings promised by the automated welding machine.
2. Using the data from (1) above and other data from the problem, compute the automated welding machine's net present value. (Use the incremental-cost approach.) Would you recommend purchasing the automated welding machine? Explain.
3. Assume that management can identify several intangible benefits associated with the automated welding machine, including greater flexibility in shifting from one type of product to another, improved quality of output, and faster delivery as a result of reduced throughput time. What dollar value per year would management have to attach to these intangible benefits in order to make the new welding machine an acceptable investment?

PROBLEM 14-22 Basic Net Present Value Analysis [LO1]

Windhoek Mines, Ltd., of Namibia, is contemplating the purchase of equipment to exploit a mineral deposit on land to which the company has mineral rights. An engineering and cost analysis has been made, and it is expected that the following cash flows would be associated with opening and operating a mine in the area:

Cost of new equipment and timbers	R275,000
Working capital required.	R100,000
Net annual cash receipts	R120,000*
Cost to construct new roads in three years.	R40,000
Salvage value of equipment in four years	R65,000

*Receipts from sales of ore, less out-of-pocket costs for salaries, utilities, insurance, and so forth.

The currency in Namibia is the rand, denoted here by R.

It is estimated that the mineral deposit would be exhausted after four years of mining. At that point, the working capital would be released for reinvestment elsewhere. The company's required rate of return is 20%.

Required:
(Ignore income taxes.) Determine the net present value of the proposed mining project. Should the project be accepted? Explain.

PROBLEM 14-23 Simple Rate of Return; Payback [LO5, LO6]

Paul Swanson has an opportunity to acquire a franchise from The Yogurt Place, Inc., to dispense frozen yogurt products under The Yogurt Place name. Mr. Swanson has assembled the following information relating to the franchise:
a. A suitable location in a large shopping mall can be rented for $3,500 per month.
b. Remodeling and necessary equipment would cost $270,000. The equipment would have a 15-year life and an $18,000 salvage value. Straight-line depreciation would be used, and the salvage value would be considered in computing depreciation.

c.   Based on similar outlets elsewhere, Mr. Swanson estimates that sales would total $300,000 per year. Ingredients would cost 20% of sales.

d.   Operating costs would include $70,000 per year for salaries, $3,500 per year for insurance, and $27,000 per year for utilities. In addition, Mr. Swanson would have to pay a commission to The Yogurt Place, Inc., of 12.5% of sales.

Required:

(Ignore income taxes.)

1.   Prepare a contribution format income statement that shows the expected net operating income each year from the franchise outlet.

2.   Compute the simple rate of return promised by the outlet. If Mr. Swanson requires a simple rate of return of at least 12%, should he acquire the franchise?

3.   Compute the payback period on the outlet. If Mr. Swanson wants a payback of four years or less, will he acquire the franchise?

PROBLEM 14-24 (Appendix 14C) Basic Net Present Value Analysis Including Income Taxes [LO8]

The Diamond Freight Company has been offered a seven-year contract to haul munitions for the government. Since this contract would represent new business, the company would have to purchase several new heavy-duty trucks at a cost of $350,000 if the contract were accepted. Other data relating to the contract follow:

Net annual cash receipts (before taxes) from the contract.	$105,000
Cost of replacing the motors in the trucks in four years	$45,000
Salvage value of the trucks at termination of the contract	$18,000

With the motors being replaced after four years, the trucks will have a useful life of seven years. To raise money to assist in the purchase of the new trucks, the company will sell several old, fully depreciated trucks for a total selling price of $16,000. The company requires a 16% after-tax return on all equipment purchases. The tax rate is 30%. For tax purposes, the company computes depreciation deductions assuming zero salvage value and using straight-line depreciation. The new trucks would be depreciated over five years.

Required:

Compute the net present value of this investment opportunity. Round all dollar amounts to the nearest whole dollar. Would you recommend that the contract be accepted?

PROBLEM 14-25 Basic Net Present Value Analysis [LO1]

The Sweetwater Candy Company would like to buy a new machine that would automatically "dip" chocolates. The dipping operation is currently done largely by hand. The machine the company is considering costs $120,000. The manufacturer estimates that the machine would be usable for 12 years but would require the replacement of several key parts at the end of the sixth year. These parts would cost $9,000, including installation. After 12 years, the machine could be sold for $7,500.

The company estimates that the cost to operate the machine will be $7,000 per year. The present method of dipping chocolates costs $30,000 per year. In addition to reducing costs, the new machine will increase production by 6,000 boxes of chocolates per year. The company realizes a contribution margin of $1.50 per box. A 20% rate of return is required on all investments.

Required:

(Ignore income taxes.)

1.   What are the net annual cash inflows that will be provided by the new dipping machine?

2.   Compute the new machine's net present value. Use the incremental cost approach and round all dollar amounts to the nearest whole dollar.

PROBLEM 14-26 Preference Ranking of Investment Projects [LO4]

The management of Revco Products is exploring five different investment opportunities. Information on the five projects under study follows:

	Project Number				
	1	2	3	4	5
Investment required..........	$(270,000)	$(450,000)	$(400,000)	$(360,000)	$(480,000)
Present value of cash inflows at a 10% discount rate........	336,140	522,970	379,760	433,400	567,270
Net present value	$ 66,140	$ 72,970	$ (20,240)	$ 73,400	$ 87,270
Life of the project	6 years	3 years	5 years	12 years	6 years
Internal rate of return	18%	19%	8%	14%	16%

The company's required rate of return is 10%; thus, a 10% discount rate has been used in the present value computations above. Limited funds are available for investment, so the company can't accept all of the available projects.

Required:
1. Compute the project profitability index for each investment project.
2. Rank the five projects according to preference, in terms of:
   a. Net present value
   b. Project profitability index
   c. Internal rate of return
3. Which ranking do you prefer? Why?

eXcel

PROBLEM 14-27 Net Present Value Analysis [LO1]
In eight years, Kent Duncan will retire. He is exploring the possibility of opening a self-service car wash. The car wash could be managed in the free time he has available from his regular occupation, and it could be closed easily when he retires. After careful study, Mr. Duncan has determined the following:
a. A building in which a car wash could be installed is available under an eight-year lease at a cost of $1,700 per month.
b. Purchase and installation costs of equipment would total $200,000. In eight years the equipment could be sold for about 10% of its original cost.
c. An investment of an additional $2,000 would be required to cover working capital needs for cleaning supplies, change funds, and so forth. After eight years, this working capital would be released for investment elsewhere.
d. Both a wash and a vacuum service would be offered with a wash costing $2.00 and the vacuum costing $1.00 per use.
e. The only variable costs associated with the operation would be 20 cents per wash for water and 10 cents per use of the vacuum for electricity.
f. In addition to rent, monthly costs of operation would be: cleaning, $450; insurance, $75; and maintenance, $500.
g. Gross receipts from the wash would be about $1,350 per week. According to the experience of other car washes, 60% of the customers using the wash would also use the vacuum.

Mr. Duncan will not open the car wash unless it provides at least a 10% return.

Required:
(Ignore income taxes.)
1. Assuming that the car wash will be open 52 weeks a year, compute the expected net annual cash receipts (gross cash receipts less cash disbursements) from its operation. (Do not include the cost of the equipment, the working capital, or the salvage value in these computations.)
2. Would you advise Mr. Duncan to open the car wash? Show computations using the net present value method of investment analysis. Round all dollar figures to the nearest whole dollar.

PROBLEM 14-28 Simple Rate of Return; Payback; Internal Rate of Return [LO2, LO5, LO6]
The Elberta Fruit Farm of Ontario has always hired transient workers to pick its annual cherry crop. Francie Wright, the farm manager, has just received information on a cherry picking machine that is being purchased by many fruit farms. The machine is a motorized device that shakes the cherry tree, causing the cherries to fall onto plastic tarps that funnel the cherries into bins. Ms. Wright has

gathered the following information to decide whether a cherry picker would be a profitable investment for the Elberta Fruit Farm:

a. Currently, the farm is paying an average of $40,000 per year to transient workers to pick the cherries.

b. The cherry picker would cost $94,500, and it would have an estimated 12-year useful life. The farm uses straight-line depreciation on all assets and considers salvage value in computing depreciation deductions. The estimated salvage value of the cherry picker is $4,500.

c. Annual out-of-pocket costs associated with the cherry picker would be: cost of an operator and an assistant, $14,000; insurance, $200; fuel, $1,800; and a maintenance contract, $3,000.

Required:
(Ignore income taxes.)

1. Determine the annual savings in cash operating costs that would be realized if the cherry picker were purchased.

2. Compute the simple rate of return expected from the cherry picker. (Hint: Note that this is a cost reduction project.) Would the cherry picker be purchased if Elberta Fruit Farm's required rate of return is 16%?

3. Compute the payback period on the cherry picker. The Elberta Fruit Farm will not purchase equipment unless it has a payback period of five years or less. Would the cherry picker be purchased?

4. Compute (to the nearest whole percent) the internal rate of return promised by the cherry picker. Based on this computation, does it appear that the simple rate of return is an accurate guide in investment decisions?

PROBLEM 14-29 Net Present Value; Uncertain Future Cash Flows; Postaudit [LO1, LO3]

Saxon Products, Inc., is investigating the purchase of a robot for use on the company's assembly line. Selected data relating to the robot are provided below:

Cost of the robot.	$1,800,000
Installation and software	$900,000
Annual savings in labor costs	?
Annual savings in inventory carrying costs	$210,000
Monthly increase in power and maintenance costs.	$2,500
Salvage value in 10 years.	$70,000
Useful life	10 years

Engineering studies suggest that use of the robot will result in a savings of 25,000 direct labor-hours each year. The labor rate is $16 per hour. Also, the smoother work flow made possible by the use of automation will allow the company to reduce the amount of inventory on hand by $400,000. This inventory reduction will take place at the end of the first year of operation; the released funds will be available for use elsewhere in the company. Saxon Products has a 20% required rate of return on all purchases of equipment.

Shelly Martins, the controller, has noted that all of Saxon's competitors are automating their plants. She is pessimistic, however, about whether Saxon's management will allow it to automate. In preparing the proposal for the robot, she stated to a colleague, "Let's just hope that reduced labor and inventory costs can justify the purchase of this automated equipment. Otherwise, we'll never get it. You know how the president feels about equipment paying for itself out of reduced costs."

Required:
(Ignore income taxes.)

1. Determine the net *annual* cost savings if the robot is purchased. (Do not include the $400,000 inventory reduction or the salvage value in this computation.)

2. Compute the net present value of the proposed investment in the robot. Based on these data, would you recommend that the robot be purchased? Explain.

3. Assume that the robot is purchased. At the end of the first year, Shelly Martins has found that some items didn't work out as planned. Due to unforeseen problems, software and installation costs were $75,000 more than estimated and direct labor has been reduced by only 22,500 hours per year, rather than by 25,000 hours. Assuming that all other cost data were accurate, does it appear that the company made a wise investment? Show computations using the net present value format as in (2) above. (Hint: It might be helpful to place yourself back at the beginning of the first year with the new data.)

4. Upon seeing your analysis in (3) above, Saxon's president stated, "That robot is the worst investment we've ever made. And now we'll be stuck with it for years."
    a. Explain to the president what benefits other than cost savings might accrue from using the new automated equipment.
    b. Compute for the president the dollar amount of cash inflow that would be needed each year from the benefits in (a) above for the automated equipment to yield a 20% rate of return.

PROBLEM 14-30 Internal Rate of Return; Sensitivity Analysis [LO2]

"In my opinion, a tanning salon would be a natural addition to our spa and very popular with our customers," said Stacey Winder, manager of the Lifeline Spa. "Our figures show that we could remodel the building next door to our spa and install all of the necessary equipment for $330,000. I have contacted tanning salons in other areas, and I am told that the tanning beds will be usable for about nine years. I am also told that a four-bed salon such as we are planning would generate a cash inflow of about $80,000 per year after all expenses."

"It does sound very appealing," replied Kevin Leblanc, the spa's accountant. "Let me push the numbers around a bit and see what kind of a return the salon would generate."

Required:

(Ignore income taxes.)

1. Compute the internal rate of return promised by the tanning salon to the nearest whole percent.
2. Assume that Ms. Winder will not open the salon unless it promises a return of at least 14%. Compute the amount of annual cash inflow that would provide this return on the $330,000 investment.
3. Although nine years is the average life of tanning salon equipment, Ms. Winder has found that this life can vary substantially. Compute the internal rate of return to the nearest whole percent if the life were (a) 6 years and (b) 12 years rather than 9 years. Is there any information provided by these computations that you would be particularly anxious to show Ms. Winder?
4. Ms. Winder has also found that although $80,000 is an average cash inflow from a four-bed salon, some salons vary as much as 20% from this figure. Compute the internal rate of return to the nearest whole percent if the annual cash inflows were (a) 20% less and (b) 20% greater than $80,000.
5. Assume that the $330,000 investment is made and that the salon is opened as planned. Because of concerns about the effects of excessive tanning, however, the salon is not able to attract as many customers as planned. Cash inflows are only $50,000 per year, and after eight years the salon equipment is sold to a competitor for $135,440. Compute the internal rate of return to the nearest whole percent earned on the investment over the eight-year period. (Hint: A useful way to proceed is to find the discount rate that will cause the net present value to be equal to, or near, zero.)

PROBLEM 14-31 Net Present Value Analysis of a Lease or Buy Decision [LO1]

The Riteway Ad Agency provides cars for its sales staff. In the past, the company has always purchased its cars from a dealer and then sold the cars after three years of use. The company's present fleet of cars is three years old and will be sold very shortly. To provide a replacement fleet, the company is considering two alternatives:

Alternative 1: The company can purchase the cars, as in the past, and sell the cars after three years of use. Ten cars will be needed, which can be purchased at a discounted price of $17,000 each. If this alternative is accepted, the following costs will be incurred on the fleet as a whole:

Annual cost of servicing, taxes, and licensing	$3,000
Repairs, first year	$1,500
Repairs, second year	$4,000
Repairs, third year	$6,000

At the end of three years, the fleet could be sold for one-half of the original purchase price.

Alternative 2: The company can lease the cars under a three-year lease contract. The lease cost would be $55,000 per year (the first payment due at the end of Year 1). As part of this lease cost, the owner would provide all servicing and repairs, license the cars, and pay all the taxes. Riteway would be required to make a $10,000 security deposit at the beginning of the lease period, which would be refunded when the cars were returned to the owner at the end of the lease contract.

Required:

(Ignore income taxes.)

1. Riteway Ad Agency has an 18% required rate of return. Use the total-cost approach to determine the present value of the cash flows associated with each alternative. Round all dollar amounts to the nearest whole dollar. Which alternative should the company accept?

2. Using the data in (1) above and other data as needed, explain why it is often less costly for a company to lease equipment and facilities rather than to buy them.

PROBLEM 14-32 Simple Rate of Return; Payback [LO5, LO6]

Sharkey's Fun Center contains a number of electronic games as well as a miniature golf course and various rides located outside the building. Paul Sharkey, the owner, would like to construct a water slide on one portion of his property. Mr. Sharkey has gathered the following information about the slide:

a. Water slide equipment could be purchased and installed at a cost of $330,000. According to the manufacturer, the slide would be usable for 12 years after which it would have no salvage value.

b. Mr. Sharkey would use straight-line depreciation on the slide equipment.

c. To make room for the water slide, several rides would be dismantled and sold. These rides are fully depreciated, but they could be sold for $60,000 to an amusement park in a nearby city.

d. Mr. Sharkey has concluded that about 50,000 more people would use the water slide each year than have been using the rides. The admission price would be $3.60 per person (the same price that the Fun Center has been charging for the old rides).

e. Based on experience at other water slides, Mr. Sharkey estimates that annual incremental operating expenses for the slide would be: salaries, $85,000; insurance, $4,200; utilities, $13,000; and maintenance, $9,800.

Required:

(Ignore income taxes.)

1. Prepare an income statement showing the expected net operating income each year from the water slide.

2. Compute the simple rate of return expected from the water slide. Based on this computation, would the water slide be constructed if Mr. Sharkey requires a simple rate of return of at least 14% on all investments?

3. Compute the payback period for the water slide. If Mr. Sharkey accepts any project with a payback period of five years or less, would the water slide be constructed?

PROBLEM 14-33 Preference Ranking of Investment Projects [LO4]

Oxford Company has limited funds available for investment and must ration the funds among five competing projects. Selected information on the five projects follows:

Project	Investment Required	Net Present Value	Life of the Project (years)	Internal Rate of Return (percent)
A	$160,000	$44,323	7	18%
B	$135,000	$42,000	12	16%
C	$100,000	$35,035	7	20%
D	$175,000	$38,136	3	22%
E	$150,000	$(8,696)	6	8%

The net present values above have been computed using a 10% discount rate. The company wants your assistance in determining which project to accept first, second, and so forth. The company's investment funds are limited.

Required:

1. Compute the project profitability index for each project.

2. In order of preference, rank the five projects in terms of:
    a. Net present value.
    b. Project profitability index.
    c. Internal rate of return.

3. Which ranking do you prefer? Why?

PROBLEM 14-34 Net Present Value Analysis of a New Product [LO1]

Matheson Electronics has just developed a new electronic device which, when mounted on an automobile, will tell the driver how many miles the automobile is traveling per gallon of gasoline.

The company is anxious to begin production of the new device. To this end, marketing and cost studies have been made to determine probable costs and market potential. These studies have provided the following information:

a. New equipment would have to be acquired to produce the device. The equipment would cost $315,000 and have a 12-year useful life. After 12 years, it would have a salvage value of about $15,000.

b. Sales in units over the next 12 years are projected to be as follows:

Year	Sales in Units
1	6,000
2	12,000
3	15,000
4–12	18,000

c. Production and sales of the device would require working capital of $60,000 to finance accounts receivable, inventories, and day-to-day cash needs. This working capital would be released at the end of the project's life.

d. The devices would sell for $35 each; variable costs for production, administration, and sales would be $15 per unit.

e. Fixed costs for salaries, maintenance, property taxes, insurance, and straight-line depreciation on the equipment would total $135,000 per year. (Depreciation is based on cost less salvage value.)

f. To gain rapid entry into the market, the company would have to advertise heavily. The advertising program would be:

Year	Amount of Yearly Advertising
1–2	$180,000
3	$150,000
4–12	$120,000

g. Matheson Electronics' board of directors has specified a required rate of return of 14% on all new products.

Required:
(Ignore income taxes.)

1. Compute the net cash inflow (cash receipts less yearly cash operating expenses) anticipated from sale of the device for each year over the next 12 years.

2. Using the data computed in (1) above and other data provided in the problem, determine the net present value of the proposed investment. Would you recommend that Matheson accept the device as a new product?

PROBLEM 14-35 (Appendix 14C) A Comparison of Investment Alternatives Including
Income Taxes [LO8]

Julia Vanfleet is professor of mathematics. She has received a $225,000 inheritance from her father's estate, and she is anxious to invest it between now and the time she retires in 12 years. Professor Vanfleet is considering two alternatives for investing her inheritance.

Alternative 1. Corporate bonds can be purchased that mature in 12 years and that bear interest at 10%. This interest would be taxable and paid annually.

Alternative 2. A small retail business is available for sale that can be purchased for $225,000. The following information relates to this alternative:

a. Of the purchase price, $80,000 would be for fixtures and other depreciable items. The remainder would be for the company's working capital (inventory, accounts receivable, and cash). The fixtures and other depreciable items would have a remaining useful life of at least 12 years but would be depreciated for tax reporting purposes over eight years using the following allowances published by the Internal Revenue Service:

Year	Percentage of Original Cost Depreciated
1	14.3%
2	24.5%
3	17.5%
4	12.5%
5	8.9%
6	8.9%
7	8.9%
8	4.5%
	100.0%

Salvage value is not taken into account when computing depreciation for tax purposes. At any rate, at the end of 12 years these depreciable items would have a negligible salvage value; however, the working capital would be recovered (either through sale or liquidation of the business) for reinvestment elsewhere.

b. The store building would be leased. At the end of 12 years, if Professor Vanfleet could not find someone to buy the business, it would be necessary to pay $2,000 to the owner of the building to break the lease.

c. Store records indicate that sales have averaged $850,000 per year and out-of-pocket costs (including wages and rent on the building) have averaged $780,000 per year (*not* including income taxes). Management of the store would be entrusted to employees.

d. Professor Vanfleet's tax rate is 40%.

Required:

Advise Professor Vanfleet as to which alternative should be selected. Use the total-cost approach to discounted cash flow in your analysis and a discount rate of 8%. Round all dollar amounts to the nearest whole dollar.

Problem 14-36 Net Present Value; Total and Incremental Approaches [LO1]

Bilboa Freightlines, S.A., of Panama, has a small truck that it uses for intracity deliveries. The truck is worn out and must be either overhauled or replaced with a new truck. The company has assembled the following information. (Panama uses the U.S. dollar as its currency):

Microsoft Excel - Problem 14-36 screen capture.xls

	A	B	C
		Present Truck	*New Truck*
2	Purchase cost new	$21,000	$30,000
3	Remaining book value	$11,500	
4	Overhaul needed now	$7,000	
5	Annual cash operating costs	$10,000	$6,500
6	Salvage value-now	$9,000	
7	Salvage value-eight years from now	$1,000	$4,000

If the company keeps and overhauls its present delivery truck, then the truck will be usable for eight more years. If a new truck is purchased, it will be used for eight years, after which it will be traded in on another truck. The new truck would be diesel-operated, resulting in a substantial reduction in annual operating costs, as shown above.

The company computes depreciation on a straight-line basis. All investment projects are evaluated using a 16% discount rate.

Required:

(Ignore income taxes.)

1. Should Bilboa Freightlines keep the old truck or purchase the new one? Use the total-cost approach to net present value in making your decision. Round to the nearest whole dollar.
2. Redo (1) above, this time using the incremental-cost approach.

PROBLEM 14-37 (Appendix 14C) Net Present Value Analysis Including Income Taxes [LO8]

Reliable Waste Systems provides a solid waste collection service in a large metropolitan area. The company is considering the purchase of several new trucks to replace an equal number of old trucks now in use. The new trucks would cost $650,000, but they would require only one operator per truck (compared to two operators for the trucks now being used), as well as provide other cost savings. A comparison of total annual cash operating costs between the old trucks that would be replaced and the new trucks is provided below:

	Old Trucks	New Trucks
Salaries—operators...................	$170,000	$ 85,000
Fuel	14,000	9,000
Insurance..........................	6,000	11,000
Maintenance	10,000	5,000
Total annual cash operating costs........	$200,000	$110,000

If the new trucks are purchased, the old trucks will be sold to a company in a nearby city for $85,000. These trucks cost $300,000 when they were new and have a current book value of $120,000. If the new trucks are not purchased, the company will take depreciation deductions for tax purposes on the old trucks of $60,000 a year over the next two years.

If the new trucks are not purchased, the old trucks will be used for seven more years and then sold for an estimated $15,000 scrap value. However, to keep the old trucks operating, extensive repairs will be needed in one year that will cost $170,000. These repairs will be expensed for tax purposes in the year incurred.

The new trucks would have a useful life of seven years and would have an estimated $60,000 salvage value at the end of their useful life. The company's tax rate is 30%, and its after-tax cost of capital is 12%. For tax purposes, the company would depreciate the equipment over five years using straight-line depreciation and assuming zero salvage value.

Required:

1. Use the total-cost approach to net present value analysis to determine whether the new trucks should be purchased. Round all dollar amounts to the nearest whole dollar.
2. Repeat the computations in (1) above, this time using the incremental-cost approach to net present value analysis.

Cases

CASE 14-38 Ethics and the Manager

The Fore Corporation is an integrated food processing company that has operations in over two dozen countries. Fore's corporate headquarters is in Chicago, and the company's executives frequently travel to visit Fore's foreign and domestic facilities.

Fore has a fleet of aircraft that consists of two business jets with international range and six smaller turboprop aircraft that are used on shorter flights. Company policy is to assign aircraft to trips on the basis of minimizing cost, but the practice is to assign the aircraft based on the organizational rank of the traveler. Fore offers its aircraft for short-term lease or for charter by other organizations whenever Fore itself does not plan to use the aircraft. Fore surveys the market often in order to keep its lease and charter rates competitive.

William Earle, Fore's vice president of finance, has claimed that a third business jet can be justified financially. However, some people in the controller's office have surmised that the real reason for a third business jet was to upgrade the aircraft used by Earle. Presently, the people outranking Earle keep the two business jets busy with the result that Earle usually flies in smaller turboprop aircraft.

The third business jet would cost $11 million. A capital expenditure of this magnitude requires a formal proposal with projected cash flows and net present value computations using Fore's minimum required rate of return. If Fore's president and the finance committee of the board of directors approve the proposal, it will be submitted to the full board of directors. The board has final approval on capital expenditures exceeding $5 million and has established a firm policy of rejecting any discretionary proposal that has a negative net present value.

Earle asked Rachel Arnett, assistant corporate controller, to prepare a proposal on a third business jet. Arnett gathered the following data:

- Acquisition cost of the aircraft, including instrumentation and interior furnishing.
- Operating cost of the aircraft for company use.
- Projected avoidable commercial airfare and other avoidable costs from company use of the plane.
- Projected value of executive time saved by using the third business jet.
- Projected contribution margin from incremental lease and charter activity.
- Estimated resale value of the aircraft.

When Earle reviewed Arnett's completed proposal and saw the large negative net present value figure, he returned the proposal to Arnett. With a glare, Earle commented, "You must have made an error. The proposal should look better than that."

Feeling some pressure, Arnett went back and checked her computations; she found no errors. However, Earle's message was clear. Arnett discarded her projections that she believed were reasonable and replaced them with figures that had a remote chance of actually occurring but were more favorable to the proposal. For example, she used first-class airfares to refigure the avoidable commercial airfare costs, even though company policy was to fly coach. She found revising the proposal to be distressing.

The revised proposal still had a negative net present value. Earle's anger was evident as he told Arnett to revise the proposal again, and to start with a $100,000 positive net present value and work backwards to compute supporting projections.

Required:
1. Explain whether Rachel Arnett's revision of the proposal was in violation of the IMA's Statement of Ethical Professional Practice.
2. Was William Earle in violation of the IMA's Statement of Ethical Professional Practice by telling Arnett specifically how to revise the proposal? Explain your answer.
3. Identify specific internal controls that Fore Corporation could implement to prevent unethical behavior on the part of the vice president of finance.

(CMA, adapted)

CASE 14-39 Net Present Value Analysis of a Lease or Buy Decision [LO1]

Top-Quality Stores, Inc., owns a nationwide chain of supermarkets. The company is going to open another store soon, and a suitable building site has been located in an attractive and rapidly growing area. In discussing how the company can acquire the desired building and other facilities needed to open the new store, Sam Watkins, the company's vice president in charge of sales, stated, "I know most of our competitors are starting to lease facilities rather than buy, but I just can't see the economics of it. Our development people tell me that we can buy the building site, put a building on it, and get all the store fixtures we need for just $850,000. They also say that property taxes, insurance, and repairs would run $20,000 a year. When you figure that we plan to keep a site for 18 years, that's a total cost of $1,210,000. But then when you realize that the property will be worth at least a half million in 18 years, that's a net cost to us of only $710,000. What would it cost to lease the property?"

"I understand that Beneficial Insurance Company is willing to purchase the building site, construct a building and install fixtures to our specifications, and then lease the facility to us for 18 years at an annual lease payment of $120,000," replied Lisa Coleman, the company's executive vice president.

"That's just my point," said Sam. "At $120,000 a year, it would cost us a cool $2,160,000 over the 18 years. That's three times what it would cost to buy, and what would we have left at the end? Nothing! The building would belong to the insurance company!"

"You're overlooking a few things," replied Lisa. "For one thing, the treasurer's office says that we could only afford to put $350,000 down if we buy the property, and then we would have to pay the other $500,000 off over four years at $175,000 a year. So there would be some interest involved on the purchase side that you haven't figured in."

"But that little bit of interest is nothing compared to over 2 million bucks for leasing," said Sam. "Also, if we lease I understand we would have to put up an $8,000 security deposit that we wouldn't get back until the end. And besides that, we would still have to pay all the yearly repairs and maintenance costs just like we owned the property. No wonder those insurance companies are so rich if they can swing deals like this."

"Well, I'll admit that I don't have all the figures sorted out yet," replied Lisa. "But I do have the operating cost breakdown for the building, which includes $7,500 annually for property taxes, $8,000 for insurance, and $4,500 for repairs and maintenance. If we lease, Beneficial will handle its own insurance costs and of course the owner will have to pay the property taxes. I'll put all this together and see if leasing makes any sense with our required rate of return of 16%. The president wants a presentation and recommendation in the executive committee meeting tomorrow. Let's see, development said the first lease payment would be due now and the remaining ones due in years 1–17. Development also said that this store should generate a net cash inflow that's well above the average for our stores."

Required:
(Ignore income taxes.)
1. Using the net present value approach, determine whether Top-Quality Stores, Inc., should lease or buy the new facility. Assume that you will be making your presentation before the company's executive committee.
2. How will you reply in the meeting if Sam Watkins brings up the issue of the building's future sales value?

CASE 14-40 Comparison of Alternatives Using Net Present Value Analysis [LO1]
Kingsley Products, Ltd., is using a model 400 shaping machine to make one of its products. The company is expecting to have a large increase in demand for the product and is anxious to expand its productive capacity. Two possibilities are under consideration:

Alternative 1. Purchase another model 400 shaping machine to operate along with the currently owned model 400 machine.

Alternative 2. Purchase a model 800 shaping machine and use the currently owned model 400 machine as standby equipment. The model 800 machine is a high-speed unit with double the capacity of the model 400 machine.

The following additional information is available on the two alternatives:
a. Both the model 400 machine and the model 800 machine have a 10-year life from the time they are first used in production. The scrap value of both machines is negligible and can be ignored. Straight-line depreciation is used.
b. The cost of a new model 800 machine is $300,000.
c. The model 400 machine now in use cost $160,000 three years ago. Its present book value is $112,000, and its present market value is $90,000.
d. A new model 400 machine costs $170,000 now. If the company decides not to buy the model 800 machine, then the old model 400 machine will have to be replaced in seven years at a cost of $200,000. The replacement machine will be sold at the end of the tenth year for $140,000.
e. Production over the next 10 years is expected to be:

Year	Production in Units
1	40,000
2	60,000
3	80,000
4–10	90,000

f. The two models of machines are not equally efficient. Comparative variable costs per unit are:

	Model	
	400	800
Direct materials per unit	$0.25	$0.40
Direct labor per unit	0.49	0.16
Supplies and lubricants per unit	0.06	0.04
Total variable cost per unit	$0.80	$0.60

g. The model 400 machine is less costly to maintain than the model 800 machine. Annual repairs and maintenance costs on a model 400 machine are $2,500.

h. Repairs and maintenance costs on a model 800 machine, with a model 400 machine used as standby, would total $3,800 per year.

i. No other costs will change as a result of the decision between the two machines.

j. Kingsley Products has a 20% required rate of return on all investments.

Required:

(Ignore income taxes.)

1. Which alternative should the company choose? Use the net present value approach.

2. Suppose that the cost of labor increases by 10%. Would this make the model 800 machine more or less desirable? Explain. No computations are needed.

3. Suppose that the cost of direct materials doubles. Would this make the model 800 machine more or less desirable? Explain. No computations are needed.

Chapter

15

Learning Objectives

After studying Chapter 15, you should be able to:

LO1 Classify changes in noncash balance sheet accounts as sources or uses of cash.

LO2 Classify transactions as operating, investing, or financing activities.

LO3 Prepare a statement of cash flows using the indirect method to determine the net cash provided by operating activities.

LO4 (Appendix 15A) Use the direct method to determine the net cash provided by operating activities.

"How Well Am I Doing?" Statement of Cash Flows

Focus on Cash

George Pilla is a finance consultant who works with new businesses like AP Engines, a company that provides billing software for Internet Protocol phone and cable service. He has found that the burn rate (the rate at which cash is consumed by a company) is critical. "Running out of cash is the worst thing," says Pilla, "and we are usually working three to six months ahead, trying to figure out when we're going to run out of cash and how we're going to fund [the company]." ■

Source: George Donnelly, "Start Me Up," *CFO*, July 2000, pp. 77–84.

BUSINESS FOCUS

Three major financial statements are required for external reports—an income statement, a balance sheet, and a statement of cash flows. The **statement of cash flows** highlights the major activities that directly and indirectly impact cash flows and hence affect the overall cash balance. Managers focus on cash for a very good reason—without sufficient cash at the right times, a company may miss golden investment opportunities or may even go bankrupt.

The statement of cash flows answers questions that cannot be easily answered by looking at the income statement and balance sheet. Where did Delta Airlines get the cash to pay a dividend of nearly $140 million in a year in which, according to its income statement, it lost more than $1 billion? How was The Walt Disney Company able to invest nearly $800 million to expand and renovate its theme parks despite a loss of more than $500 million on its investment in EuroDisney? Where did Wendy's International, Inc., get $125 million to expand its chain of fast-food restaurants in a year when its net income was only $79 million? The answers to such questions can be found on the statement of cash flows.

The statement of cash flows is a valuable analytical tool for managers as well as for investors and creditors, although managers tend to be more concerned with forecasted statements of cash flows that are prepared as part of the budgeting process. The statement of cash flows can be used to answer crucial questions such as:

1. Is the company generating sufficient positive cash flows from its ongoing operations to remain viable?
2. Will the company be able to repay its debts?
3. Will the company be able to pay its usual dividend?
4. Why do net income and net cash flow differ?
5. To what extent will the company have to borrow money in order to make needed investments?

This chapter focuses on how to prepare the statement of cash flows and on how to use it to assess a company's finances.

PREDICTING CORPORATE FAILURES WITH CASH FLOW INFORMATION

Divesh Sharma and Errol Iselin conducted an experiment using 60 bankers from Queensland, Australia, with an average of more than 11 years of lending experience. The researchers gathered accrual accounting and cash flow data concerning 14 Australian companies, of which 7 had failed (i.e., become insolvent) and 7 had not failed. Without identifying the names of the companies, half of the bankers were presented with accrual accounting information concerning the companies and the other half were presented with cash flow information. Each of the bankers was asked to identify which of the companies had failed and which had not.

Twenty-four of the 30 bankers who were provided cash flow information accurately categorized at least 11 out of 14 companies as failures or nonfailures. Conversely, only 10 of the 30 bankers who were provided accrual accounting information properly categorized at least 11 out of 14 companies. The mean judgment accuracy for the bankers relying on cash flow data was 11.47 out of 14, while the average for the bankers using accrual information was 9.97 out of 14. The authors suggest that the results of their experiment provide "strong and powerful evidence that cash flow information has greater decision usefulness than accrual information for assessing corporate solvency."

Source: Divesh S. Sharma and Errol R. Iselin, "The Decision Usefulness of Reported Cash Flow and Accrual Information in a Behavioural Field Experiment," *Accounting and Business Research* 33, no. 2, 2003, pp. 123–135.

The Basic Approach to a Statement of Cash Flows

LEARNING OBJECTIVE 1
Classify changes in noncash balance sheet accounts as sources or uses of cash.

For the statement of cash flows to be useful to managers and others, it is important that companies use the same definition of cash and follow consistent guidelines for identifying activities that are *sources* of cash and *uses* of cash.

Definition of Cash

In a statement of cash flows, *cash* is broadly defined to include both cash and cash equivalents. **Cash equivalents** consist of short-term, highly liquid investments such as Treasury bills, commercial paper, and money market funds that are made solely for the purpose of generating a return on temporarily idle funds. Instead of simply holding cash, most companies invest their excess cash reserves in these types of interest-bearing assets that can be easily converted into cash. Since such assets are equivalent to cash, they are included with cash in a statement of cash flows.

Constructing the Statement of Cash Flows Using Changes in Noncash Balance Sheet Accounts

A type of statement of cash flows could be constructed by simply summarizing all of the debits and credits to the Cash and Cash Equivalents accounts during a period. However, this approach would overlook all of the transactions that involved an implicit exchange of cash. For example, when a company purchases inventory on credit, cash is implicitly exchanged. In essence, the supplier loans the company cash, which the company then uses to acquire inventory from the supplier. Rather than just looking at the transactions that explicitly involve cash, financial statement users are interested in all of the transactions that implicitly or explicitly involve cash. When inventory is purchased on credit, the Inventory account increases, which is an implicit *use* of cash. At the same time, Accounts Payable increases, which is an implicit *source* of cash. In general, increases in the Inventory account are classified as uses of cash and increases in the Accounts Payable account are classified as sources of cash. This suggests that analyzing changes in balance sheet accounts, such as Inventory and Accounts Payable, will uncover both the explicit and implicit sources and uses of cash. And this is indeed the basic approach taken in the statement of cash flows. The logic underlying this approach is demonstrated in Exhibit 15–1.

EXHIBIT 15–1
Explaining Net Cash Flow by Analysis of the Noncash Balance Sheet Accounts

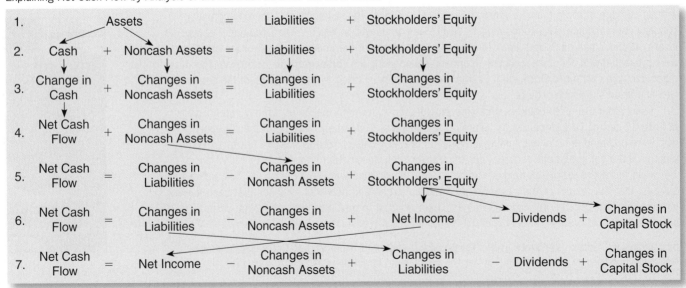

Exhibit 15–1 shows how net cash flow can be explained in terms of net income, dividends, and changes in balance sheet accounts. The first line in the exhibit is the balance sheet equation: Assets = Liabilities + Stockholders' Equity. Assets can be broken down into cash and noncash assets, which is shown in the second line of the exhibit. The third line in the exhibit recognizes that if the account balances are always equal, then *changes* in the account balances must be equal too. The fourth line in the exhibit recognizes that the change in cash is by definition the company's net cash flow. The fifth line involves nothing more than moving Changes in Noncash Assets from the left-hand side of the equation to the right-hand side. This is done because we are attempting to explain net cash flow, so it should be isolated on the left-hand side of the equation. The sixth line breaks down the Changes in Stockholders' Equity into three components—Net Income, Dividends, and Changes in Capital Stock. Net income increases stockholders' equity, while dividends reduce stockholders' equity. The seventh line simply rearranges two terms on the right-hand side of the equation.

WHAT'S UP AT AMAZON?

Amazon.com, the online retailer of books and other merchandise, may have the best chance of eventually succeeding of any Internet retailer. Even so, "[I]t's no news that Amazon has had troubles, but the numbers are worse than many on Wall Street have admitted." Robert Tracy, a CPA and an analyst on the staff of grantsinvestor.com, took a close look at Amazon's financial statements and found that the company was holding its bills longer than it used to, especially at year-end. The cash flow from this increase in accounts payable exceeded the cash flow from all other operating sources combined. "Bulls [i.e., those who are positive about Amazon.com stock] will commend the company on imaginative cash management. Bears [i.e., those who are skeptical about the stock] will accuse it of financial engineering. What is not debatable is that, by stretching out payments into the new year, Amazon has presented a more liquid face to the world than it could otherwise have done."

Source: James Grant, "Diving into Amazon," *Forbes*, January 22, 2001, p. 153.

According to the equation in line 7 in Exhibit 15–1, the net cash flow for a period can be determined by starting with net income, then deducting changes in noncash assets, adding changes in liabilities, deducting dividends paid to stockholders, and finally adding changes in capital stock. It is important to realize that changes in accounts can be either increases (positive) or decreases (negative), and this affects how we should interpret the equation in line 7 in Exhibit 15–1. For example, increases in liabilities are added back to net income, whereas decreases in liabilities are deducted from net income to arrive at the net cash flow. On the other hand, increases in noncash assets are deducted from net income while decreases in noncash assets are added back to net income. Exhibit 15–2 summarizes the appropriate classifications—in terms of sources and uses—of net income, dividends, and changes in the noncash balance sheet accounts.

	Sources	Uses
Net income	Always	
Net loss		Always
Changes in noncash assets	Decreases	Increases
Changes in liabilities*	Increases	Decreases
Changes in capital stock accounts	Increases	Decreases
Dividends paid to stockholders		Always
	Total sources − Total uses = Net cash flow	

*Contra asset accounts, such as the Accumulated Depreciation and Amortization account, follow the rules for liabilities.

EXHIBIT 15–2
Classifications of Sources and Uses of Cash

The classifications in Exhibit 15–2 are intuitive. Positive net income generates cash, whereas a net loss consumes cash. Decreases in noncash assets, such as the sale of inventories or property, are a source of cash. Increases in noncash assets, such as the purchase of inventories or property, are a use of cash. Increases in liabilities, such as taking out a loan, are a source of cash. Decreases in liabilities, such as paying off a loan, are a use of cash. Increases in capital stock accounts, such as the sale of common stock, are a source of cash. And payments of dividends to stockholders use cash.

Constructing a simple statement of cash flows is a straightforward process. Begin with net income (or net loss) and then add to it everything listed as sources in Exhibit 15–2 and subtract from it everything listed as uses. This will be illustrated with an example in the next section.

An Example of a Simplified Statement of Cash Flows

To illustrate the ideas introduced in the preceding section, we will now construct a *simplified* statement of cash flows for Nordstrom, Inc., one of the leading fashion retailers in the United States. This simplified statement does not follow the format required by the Financial Accounting Standards Board for external financial reports, but it is a useful learning aid because it shows where the numbers come from in a statement of cash flows and how they fit together. In later sections, we will show how the same basic data can be used to construct a full-fledged statement of cash flows that would be acceptable for external reports.

Constructing a Simplified Statement of Cash Flows

According to Exhibit 15–2, to construct a statement of cash flows we need the company's net income or loss, the changes in each of its balance sheet accounts, and the dividends paid to stockholders for the year. We can obtain this information from the Nordstrom financial statements that appear in Exhibits 15–3, 15–4, and 15–5. In a few instances, the actual statements have been simplified.

EXHIBIT 15–3

Nordstrom, Inc.* Income Statement (dollars in millions)	
Net sales	$3,638
Cost of goods sold	2,469
Gross margin	1,169
Selling and administrative expenses	941
Net operating income	228
Nonoperating items:	
Gain on sale of store	3
Income before taxes	231
Income taxes	91
Net income	$ 140

*This statement is loosely based on an actual income statement published by Nordstrom. Among other differences, there was no "Gain on sale of store" in the original statement. This "gain" has been included here to illustrate how to handle gains and losses on a statement of cash flows.

EXHIBIT 15–4

Nordstrom, Inc.*
Comparative Balance Sheet
(dollars in millions)

	Ending Balance	Beginning Balance	Change	Source or Use?
Assets				
Current assets:				
Cash and cash equivalents	$ 91	$ 29	+62	
Accounts receivable	637	654	−17	Source
Merchandise inventory	586	537	+49	Use
Total current assets	1,314	1,220		
Property, buildings, and equipment	1,517	1,394	+123	Use
Less accumulated depreciation and amortization	654	561	+93	Source
Net property, buildings, and equipment	863	833		
Total assets	$2,177	$2,053		
Liabilities and Stockholders' Equity				
Current liabilities:				
Accounts payable	$ 264	$ 220	+44	Source
Accrued wages and salaries payable	193	190	+3	Source
Accrued income taxes payable	28	22	+6	Source
Notes payable	40	38	+2	Source
Total current liabilities	525	470		
Long-term debt	439	482	−43	Use
Deferred income taxes	47	49	−2	Use
Total liabilities	1,011	1,001		
Stockholders' equity:				
Common stock	157	155	+2	Source
Retained earnings	1,009	897	+112	†
Total stockholders' equity	1,166	1,052		
Total liabilities and stockholders' equity	$2,177	$2,053		

*This statement differs from the actual statement published by Nordstrom.
†The change in retained earnings of $112 million equals the net income of $140 million less the cash dividends paid to stockholders of $28 million. Net income is classified as a source and dividends as a use.

EXHIBIT 15–5

Nordstrom, Inc.*
Statement of Retained Earnings
(dollars in millions)

Retained earnings, beginning balance	$ 897
Add: Net income	140
	1,037
Deduct: Dividends paid	28
Retained earnings, ending balance	$1,009

*This statement differs in a few details from the actual statement published by Nordstrom.

Note that changes between the beginning and ending balances have been computed for each of the balance sheet accounts in Exhibit 15–4, and each change has been classified as a source or use of cash. For example, the $17 million decrease in accounts receivable has been classified as a source of cash. This is because, as shown in Exhibit 15–2, decreases in non-cash accounts, such as accounts receivable, are classified as sources of cash.

A *simplified* statement of cash flows appears in Exhibit 15–6. This statement was constructed by gathering together all of the entries listed as sources in Exhibit 15–4 and all of the entries listed as uses. The sources exceeded the uses by $62 million. This is the net cash flow for the year and is also, by definition, the change in cash and cash equivalents for the year. (Trace this $62 million back to Exhibit 15–4.)

The Need for a More Detailed Statement

While the simplified statement of cash flows in Exhibit 15–6 is not difficult to construct, it is not acceptable for external financial reports. The FASB requires that the statement of cash flows follow a different format and that a few of the entries be modified. Nevertheless, almost all of the entries on a full-fledged statement of cash flows are the same as the entries on the simplified statement of cash flows—they are just in a different order.

In the following sections, we will discuss the modifications to the simplified statement of cash flows that are necessary to conform to external reporting requirements.

EXHIBIT 15–6

Nordstrom, Inc. Simplified Statement of Cash Flows (dollars in millions)		
Note: This simplified statement is for illustration purposes only. It should *not* be used to complete end-of-chapter homework assignments or for preparing an actual statement of cash flows. See Exhibit 15–11 for the proper format for a statement of cash flows.		
Sources		
Net income	$140	
Decreases in noncash assets:		
Decrease in accounts receivable	17	
Increases in liabilities (and contra asset accounts):		
Increase in accumulated depreciation and amortization	93	
Increase in accounts payable	44	
Increase in accrued wages and salaries	3	
Increase in accrued income taxes	6	
Increase in notes payable	2	
Increases in capital stock accounts:		
Increase in common stock	2	
Total sources		$307
Uses		
Increases in noncash assets:		
Increase in merchandise inventory	49	
Increase in property, buildings, and equipment	123	
Decreases in liabilities:		
Decrease in long-term debt	43	
Decrease in deferred income taxes	2	
Dividends	28	
Total uses		245
Net cash flow		$ 62

PLUGGING THE CASH FLOW LEAK

Modern synthetic fabrics such as polyester fleece and Gore-Tex have almost completely replaced wool in ski clothing. John Fernsell started Ibex Outdoor Clothing in Woodstock, Vermont, to buck this trend. Fernsell's five-person company designs and sells jackets made of high-grade wool from Europe.

Fernsell quickly discovered an unfortunate fact of life about the wool clothing business—he faces a potentially ruinous cash crunch every year. Ibex orders wool from Europe in February but does not pay the mills until June when they ship fabric to the garment makers in California. The garment factories send finished goods to Ibex in July and August, and Ibex pays for them on receipt. Ibex ships to retailers in September and October, but doesn't get paid until November, December, or even January. That means from June to December the company spends like crazy—and takes in virtually nothing. Fernsell tried to get by with a line of credit, but it was insufficient. To survive, he had to ask his suppliers to let him pay late, which was not a long-term solution. To reduce this cash flow problem, Fernsell is introducing a line of wool *summer* clothing so that some cash will be flowing in from May through July, when he must pay his suppliers for the winter clothing.

Source: Daniel Lyons, "Wool Gatherer," *Forbes*, April 16, 2001, p. 310.

Organization of the Full-Fledged Statement of Cash Flows

To make it easier to compare statements of cash flows from different companies, the Financial Accounting Standards Board (FASB) requires that companies follow prescribed rules for preparing the statement of cash flows.

The FASB requires that the statement of cash flows be divided into three sections: *operating activities*, *investing activities*, and *financing activities*. The guidelines for applying these classifications are summarized in Exhibit 15–7 and discussed below.

LEARNING OBJECTIVE 2
Classify transactions as operating, investing, or financing activities.

Operating Activities

Generally, **operating activities** are activities that affect current assets, current liabilities, or net income. Technically, however, the FASB defines operating activities as all the transactions that are not classified as investing or financing activities. Generally speaking, this

---

Operating activities:
- Net income
- Changes in current assets
- Changes in noncurrent assets that affect net income (e.g., depreciation)
- Changes in current liabilities (except for debts to lenders and dividends payable)
- Changes in noncurrent liabilities that affect net income

Investing activities:
- Changes in noncurrent assets that are not included in net income

Financing activities:
- Changes in current liabilities that are debts to lenders rather than obligations to suppliers, employees, or the government
- Changes in noncurrent liabilities that are not included in net income
- Changes in capital stock accounts
- Dividends

EXHIBIT 15–7
Guidelines for Classifying Transactions as Operating, Investing, and Financing Activities

includes all transactions affecting current assets and all transactions affecting current liabilities except for issuing and repaying a note payable. Operating activities also include changes in noncurrent balance sheet accounts that directly affect net income such as Accumulated Depreciation and Amortization.

IN BUSINESS

KEEP AN EYE ON THE CASH FLOW

BusinessWeek advises taking a very close look at the statement of cash flows:

> If you really want to put the quality of a company's earnings to the test, you need to examine the cash flow statement. . . .
>
> To get a feeling for whether a company is playing games with its earnings, compare net income on the income statement with "cash flow from operating activities". . . . "Generally, the closer a ratio of these two numbers is to one, the higher quality the earnings," says David Zion, a Bear Sterns accounting analyst.
>
> Next, compare the rates at which net income and operating cash are growing. If the two normally move in lockstep but cash flow lags, "it's a terrific early warning sign," says Howard Schilit, who heads the Center for Financial Research & Analysis. . . .
>
> [N]egative cash flow from operations isn't always bad. Because of the high costs of building a business, it is perfectly normal—even desirable—for fast-growing companies to consume more cash than they generate. Typically, such companies tide themselves over with bank loans or equity sales. In other words, they run a surplus in "financing" cash flows. Still, if operating cash doesn't pick up, bail out. Eventually, lenders lose patience with companies whose operations hemorrhage cash.

Source: Anne Tergeson, "The Ins and Outs of Cash Flow," *BusinessWeek*, January 22, 2001, p. 102.

Investing Activities

Generally speaking, **investing activities** include transactions that involve acquiring or disposing of noncurrent assets such as acquiring or selling property, plant, and equipment; acquiring or selling securities held for long-term investment, such as bonds and stocks of other companies; and lending money to another entity (such as a subsidiary) and the subsequent collection of the loan. However, as previously discussed, changes in noncurrent assets that directly affect net income, such as depreciation and amortization charges, are classified as operating activities.

Financing Activities

As a general rule, borrowing from creditors or repaying creditors and transactions with the company's owners are classified as **financing activities.** For example, when a company borrows money by issuing a bond, the transaction is classified as a financing activity. However, transactions with creditors that affect net income are classified as operating activities. For example, interest on the company's debt is included in operating activities rather than financing activities because interest is deducted as an expense in computing net income. In contrast, dividend payments to owners do not affect net income and therefore are classified as a financing activity rather than as an operating activity.

Most changes in current liabilities are treated as operating activities unless the transaction involves borrowing money directly from a lender, as with a note payable, or repaying such a debt. Transactions involving accounts payable, wages payable, and taxes payable are included in operating activities rather than financing activities because these transactions occur on a routine basis and involve the company's suppliers, employees, and the government rather than lenders.

MANIPULATIVE CASH FLOW REPORTING

Professor O. Whitfield Broome from the University of Virginia found a common thread that ties together the fraudulent financial reporting at Tyco International, Dynergy, Qwest Communications International, Adelphia Communications Corporation, and WorldCom. Each company misclassified cash flows on the statement of cash flows so as to inflate the net cash provided by operating activities. For example, Tyco paid more than $800 million to purchase customer contracts from dealers. The cash paid for these contracts was reported in the investing activities section of the statement of cash flows. However, when customers made payments to Tyco under these contracts all of the cash received was reported in the operating activities section of the statement of cash flows. As another example, WorldCom recorded a substantial amount of its operating expenses as capital investments. Besides inflating net operating income, this manipulation enabled WorldCom to shift cash outflows from the operating activities section of the statement of cash flows to the investing activities section.

Source: O. Whitfield Broome, "Statement of Cash Flows: Time for Change!" *Financial Analysts Journal*, March/April 2004, pp. 16–22.

Other Issues in Preparing the Statement of Cash Flows

We must consider two additional issues: (1) whether amounts on the statement of cash flows should be presented gross or net; and (2) whether operating activities should be presented using the direct or indirect method.[1]

Cash Flows: Gross or Net?

Both financing and investing activities should be presented in gross amounts rather than in net amounts. To illustrate, suppose that Macy's Department Stores purchases $50 million in property during the year and sells other property for $30 million. Instead of showing the net change of $20 million, the company must show the gross amounts of both the purchases and the sales. The purchases would be recorded as a use of cash, and the sales would be recorded as a source of cash. Similarly, if Alcoa receives $80 million from the issue of long-term bonds and then pays out $30 million to retire other bonds, the two transactions must be reported separately on the statement of cash flows rather than being netted against each other.

The gross method of reporting does *not* extend to operating activities, where debits and credits to an account are netted against each other on the statement of cash flows. For example, if Sears adds $600 million to its accounts receivable as a result of sales during the year and $520 million of accounts receivable are collected, only the net increase of $80 million would be reported on the statement of cash flows.

Operating Activities: Direct or Indirect Method?

The net amount of the cash inflows and outflows resulting from operating activities, which is known formally as the **net cash provided by operating activities,** can be computed by either the *direct* or the *indirect* method.

Under the **direct method,** the income statement is reconstructed on a cash basis from top to bottom. For example, cash collected from customers is listed instead of revenue, and

---

[1] A third complication arises from direct exchange transactions in which noncurrent balance sheet items are swapped. For example, a company might issue common stock in a direct exchange for property. Or creditors might swap their long-term debt for common stock of the company. Direct exchange transactions are not reported on the statement of cash flows; however, they are disclosed in a separate schedule that accompanies the statement. More advanced accounting courses cover this topic in greater detail.

payments to suppliers is listed instead of cost of goods sold. In essence, cash receipts are counted as revenues and cash disbursements are counted as expenses. The difference between the cash receipts and cash disbursements is the net cash provided by operating activities for the period.

Topic Tackler

PLUS

15–2

Under the **indirect method** net income is adjusted to a cash basis. That is, rather than directly computing cash sales, cash expenses, and so forth, these amounts are arrived at *indirectly* by removing from net income any items that do not affect cash flows. The indirect method has an advantage over the direct method because it shows the reasons for any differences between net income and the net cash provided by operating activities. The indirect method is also known as the **reconciliation method.**

Although both the direct and indirect methods will result in exactly the same amount of net cash provided by operating activities, the FASB *recommends* and *encourages* the use of the direct method for external reports. But there is a catch. If the direct method is used, the company must provide a supplementary reconciliation of net income with operating cash flows. In essence, if a company chooses to use the direct method, it must also construct a statement that uses a form of the indirect method. However, if a company chooses to use the indirect method, there is no requirement that it also report the results using the direct method.

Not surprisingly only about 1% of companies use the direct method to construct the statement of cash flows for external reports.[2] The remaining 99% probably use the indirect method because it is simply less work. While there are some good reasons for using the direct method, we use the indirect method in this chapter. The direct method is covered in Appendix 15A at the end of the chapter.

An Example of a Full-Fledged Statement of Cash Flows

LEARNING OBJECTIVE 3
Prepare a statement of cash flows using the indirect method to determine the net cash provided by operating activities.

In this section, we apply the FASB rules to construct a statement of cash flows for Nordstrom that would be acceptable for external reporting. The approach we take is based on an analysis of changes in balance sheet accounts, as in our earlier discussion of the simplified statement of cash flows. Indeed, as you will see, the full-fledged statement of cash flows is for the most part just a reorganized form of the simplified statement that appears in Exhibit 15–6.

The format for the operating activities section of the statement of cash flows is shown in Exhibit 15–8. Notice that net income is adjusted to net cash provided by operating activities by adding sources of cash and deducting uses of cash. For example, consider the effect of an increase in the Accounts Receivable account on the net cash provided by operating activities. Since the Accounts Receivable account is a noncash asset, we know from Exhibit 15–2 that increases in this account are treated as *uses* of cash. In other words, increases in Accounts Receivable are deducted when determining net cash flows.

Eight Basic Steps to Preparing the Statement of Cash Flows

Preparing a statement of cash flows can be confusing and it is easy to overlook important details. For that reason, we recommend that you use a worksheet such as the one in Exhibit 15–9 (page 694) to help prepare the statement of cash flows. To use this worksheet, follow these eight steps:

1. Copy onto the worksheet the title of each account appearing on the comparative balance sheet except for cash and cash equivalents and retained earnings. Contra asset

---

[2] American Institute of Certified Public Accountants, *Accounting Trends and Techniques: 2004* (Jersey City, NJ, 2004), p. 549.

	Add (+) or Deduct (−) to Adjust Net Income
Net income.	$XXX
Adjustments needed to convert net income to a cash basis:	
Depreciation, depletion, and amortization charges	+
Add (deduct) changes in current asset accounts affecting revenue or expense:*	
Increase in the account	−
Decrease in the account	+
Add (deduct) changes in current liability accounts affecting revenue or expense:†	
Increase in the account	+
Decrease in the account	−
Add (deduct) gains or losses on sales of assets:	
Gain on sales of assets	−
Loss on sales of assets	+
Add (deduct) changes in the Deferred Income Taxes account:	
Increase if a liability; decrease if an asset	+
Decrease if a liability; increase if an asset	−
Net cash provided by operating activities	$XXX

*Examples include accounts receivable, accrued receivables, inventory, and prepaid expenses.
†Examples include accounts payable, accrued liabilities, and taxes payable.

EXHIBIT 15–8
General Model: Indirect Method of Determining the "Net Cash Provided by Operating Activities"

accounts such as the Accumulated Depreciation and Amortization account should be listed with the liabilities because they are treated like liabilities on the statement of cash flows.

2. Compute the change from the beginning balance to the ending balance in each balance sheet account. Break down the change in retained earnings into net income and dividends paid to stockholders.

3. Using Exhibit 15–2 as a guide, code each entry on the worksheet as a source or a use of cash.

4. Under the Cash Flow Effect column, write sources as positive numbers and uses as negative numbers.

5. Make any necessary adjustments to reflect gross, rather than net, amounts involved in transactions—including adjustments for gains and losses. Some of these adjustments may require adding new entries to the bottom of the worksheet. The net effect of all such adjusting entries must be zero.

6. Classify each entry on the worksheet as an operating, investing, or financing activity according to the FASB's criteria, as given in Exhibit 15–7.

7. Copy the data from the worksheet to the statement of cash flows section by section, starting with the operating activities section.

8. At the bottom of the statement of cash flows prepare a reconciliation of the beginning and ending balances of cash and cash equivalents. The net change in cash and cash equivalents shown at the bottom of this statement should equal the change in the Cash and Cash Equivalents accounts during the year.

On the following pages we will apply these eight steps to the data contained in the comparative balance sheet for Nordstrom, Inc., found in Exhibit 15–4. *As we discuss each step, refer to Exhibit 15–4 and trace the data from this exhibit into the worksheet in Exhibit 15–9.*

EXHIBIT 15–9

	Nordstrom, Inc. Statement of Cash Flows Worksheet (dollars in millions)					
	(1) Change	(2) Source or Use?	(3) Cash Flow Effect	(4) Adjust- ments	(5) Adjusted Effect (3) + (4)	(6) Classi- fication*
Assets (except cash and cash equivalents)						
Current assets:						
Accounts receivable	−17	Source	$ +17		$ +17	Operating
Merchandise inventory	+49	Use	−49		−49	Operating
Noncurrent assets:						
Property, buildings, and equipment	+123	Use	−123	$−15	−138	Investing
Contra Assets, Liabilities, and Stockholders' Equity						
Contra assets:						
Accumulated depreciation and amortization	+93	Source	+93	+10	+103	Operating
Current liabilities:						
Accounts payable	+44	Source	+44		+44	Operating
Accrued wages and salaries payable	+3	Source	+3		+3	Operating
Accrued income taxes payable	+6	Source	+6		+6	Operating
Notes payable	+2	Source	+2		+2	Financing
Noncurrent liabilities:						
Long-term debt	−43	Use	−43		−43	Financing
Deferred income taxes	−2	Use	−2		−2	Operating
Stockholders' equity:						
Common stock	+2	Source	+2		+2	Financing
Retained earnings:						
Net income	+140	Source	+140		+140	Operating
Dividends	−28	Use	−28		−28	Financing
Additional Entries						
Proceeds from sale of store				+8	+8	Investing
Gain on sale of store				−3	−3	Operating
Total (net cash flow)			$ +62	$ 0	$ +62	

*See Exhibit 15–10 for the reasons for these classifications.

Setting Up the Worksheet (Steps 1–4)

As previously mentioned, step 1 in preparing the worksheet is to simply list all of the relevant account titles from the company's balance sheet. Note that we have done this for Nordstrom, Inc., on the worksheet in Exhibit 15–9. (The titles of Nordstrom's accounts have been taken from the company's comparative balance sheet, which is found in Exhibit 15–4 on page 687.) The only significant differences between Nordstrom's balance sheet accounts and the worksheet listing are that (1) the Accumulated Depreciation and Amortization account has been moved down with the liabilities on the worksheet, (2) the Cash and Cash Equivalents accounts have been omitted, and (3) the change in retained earnings has been broken down into net income and dividends.

As stated in step 2, the change in each account's balance during the year is listed in the first column of the worksheet. We have entered these changes for Nordstrom's accounts onto the worksheet in Exhibit 15–9. (Refer to Nordstrom's comparative balance sheet in Exhibit 15–4 to see how these changes were computed.)

Then, as indicated in step 3, each change on the worksheet is classified as either a source or a use of cash. Whether a change is a source or a use can be determined by referring back to Exhibit 15–2 on page 685, where we first discussed these classifications. For example, Nordstrom's Merchandise Inventory account increased by $49 million during the year. According to Exhibit 15–2, increases in noncash asset accounts are classified as uses of cash, so an entry has been made to that effect in the second column of the worksheet for the Merchandise Inventory account.

So far, nothing is new. All of this was done in Exhibit 15–4 when we constructed the simplified statement of cash flows. Step 4 is mechanical, but it helps prevent careless errors. Sources are coded as positive changes and uses as negative changes in the Cash Flow Effect column on the worksheet.

Adjustments to Reflect Gross, Rather than Net, Amounts (Step 5)

As discussed earlier, the FASB requires that gross, rather than net, amounts be disclosed in the investing and financing sections. This rule requires special treatment of gains and losses. To illustrate, suppose that Nordstrom decided to sell an old store and move its retail operations to a new location. Assume that the original cost of the old store was $15 million, its accumulated depreciation was $10 million, and that it was sold for $8 million in cash. The journal entry to record this transaction appears below:

Cash Proceeds	8,000,000	
Accumulated Depreciation and Amortization	10,000,000	
Property, Buildings, and Equipment		15,000,000
Gain on Sale		3,000,000

The $3 million gain is reflected in the income statement in Exhibit 15–3 on page 686.

We can reconstruct the gross additions to the Property, Buildings, and Equipment account and the gross charges to the Accumulated Depreciation and Amortization account with the help of T-accounts:

Property, Buildings, and Equipment				Accumulated Depreciation and Amortization		
Balance	1,394			Balance	561	
Additions (plug*)	138	Disposal of store	15	Disposal of store	10	Depreciation charges (plug*)	103
Balance	1,517			Balance	654	

*By *plug* we mean the balancing figure in the account.

According to the FASB rules, the gross additions of $138 million to the Property, Buildings, and Equipment account should be disclosed on the statement of cash flows rather than the net change in the account of $123 million ($1,517 million − $1,394 million = $123 million). Likewise, the gross depreciation charges of $103 million should be disclosed rather than the net change in the Accumulated Depreciation and Amortization account of $93 million ($654 million − $561 million = $93 million). And the cash proceeds of $8 million from sale of the building should also be disclosed on the statement of cash flows. All of this is accomplished, while preserving the correct overall net cash flows on the statement, by using the above journal entry to make adjusting entries on the worksheet. The debits are recorded as positive adjustments, and the credits are recorded as negative adjustments. These adjusting entries are recorded under the Adjustments in column 4 in Exhibit 15–9.

It may not be clear why the gain on the sale is *deducted* in the operating activities section of the statement of cash flows. The company's $140 million net income, which is part of the operating activities section, includes the $3 million gain on the sale of the store. But this $3 million gain must be reported in the *investing* activities section of the statement of cash flows as part of the $8 million proceeds from the sale transaction. Therefore, to avoid double counting, the $3 million gain is deducted from net income in the operating activities section of the statement. The adjustments we have made on the worksheet accomplish this. The $3 million gain will be deducted in the operating activities section, and all $8 million of the sale proceeds will be shown as an investing item. As a result, all of the gain will be included in the investing section of the statement of cash flows and none of it will be in the operating activities section. There will be no double-counting of the gain.

In the case of a loss on the sale of an asset, we do the opposite. The loss is added back to net income in the operating activities section of the statement of cash flows. Whatever cash proceeds are received from the sale of the asset are reported in the investing activities section.

Before turning to step 6 in the process of building the statement of cash flows, one small step is required. Add the Adjustments in column (4) to the Cash Flow Effect in column (3) to arrive at the Adjusted Effect in column (5).

Classifying Entries as Operating, Investing, or Financing Activities (Step 6)

In step 6, each entry on the worksheet is classified as an operating, investing, or financing activity using the guidelines in Exhibit 15–7. These classifications are entered directly on the worksheet in Exhibit 15–9 and are explained in Exhibit 15–10. Most of these classifications

EXHIBIT 15–10
Classifications of Entries on Nordstrom's Statement of Cash Flows

Entry	Classification	Reason
• Changes in Accounts Receivable and Merchandise Inventory	Operating activity	Changes in current assets are included in operating activities.
• Change in Property, Buildings, and Equipment	Investing activity	Changes in noncurrent assets that do not directly affect net income are included in investing activities.
• Change in Accumulated Depreciation and Amortization	Operating activity	Depreciation and amortization directly affect net income and are therefore included in operating activities.
• Changes in Accounts Payable, Accrued Wages and Salaries Payable, and Accrued Income Taxes Payable	Operating activity	Changes in current liabilities (except for notes payable) are included in operating activities.
• Change in Notes Payable	Financing activity	Issuing or repaying notes payable is classified as a financing activity.
• Change in Long-Term Debt	Financing activity	Changes in noncurrent liabilities that do not directly affect net income are included in financing activities.
• Change in Deferred Income Taxes	Operating activity	Deferred income taxes result from income tax expense that directly affects net income. Therefore, this entry is included in operating activities.
• Change in Common Stock	Financing activity	Changes in capital stock accounts are always included in financing activities.
• Net income	Operating activity	Net income is always included in operating activities.
• Dividends	Financing activity	Dividends paid to stockholders are always included in financing activities.
• Proceeds from sale of store	Investing activity	The gross amounts received on disposal of noncurrent assets are included in investing activities.
• Gains from sale of store	Operating activity	Gains and losses directly affect net income and are therefore included in operating activities.

are straightforward, but the classification of the change in the Deferred Income Taxes account may require some additional explanation. Because of the way income tax expense is determined for financial reporting purposes, the expense that appears on the income statement often differs from the taxes that are actually owed to the government. Usually, income tax expense overstates the company's actual income tax liability for the year. When this happens, the journal entry to record income taxes includes a credit to Deferred Income Taxes:

Income Tax Expense.	XXX	
Income Taxes Payable		XXX
Deferred Income Taxes (plug)		XXX

Since deferred income taxes arise directly from the computation of an expense, the change in the Deferred Income Taxes account is included in the operating activities section of the statement of cash flows.

In the case of Nordstrom, the Deferred Income Taxes account decreased during the year. Deferred Income Taxes is a liability account for Nordstrom. Since this liability account decreased during the year, the change is counted as a use of cash and is deducted in determining net cash flow for the year.

IN BUSINESS

SEC REQUIRES CATERPILLAR TO RESTATE CASH FLOWS

The Securities and Exchange Commission (SEC) required Caterpillar to restate its cash flows for 2002 and 2003 as follows (amounts are in millions):

	2002	2003
Cash flows as originally reported by Caterpillar:		
Net cash provided by operating activities	$2,366	$2,066
Net cash used for investing activities	(2,708)	(2,793)
Total	($ 342)	($ 727)
Caterpillar's restated cash flows:		
Net cash used for operating activities	($3,962)	($5,611)
Net cash provided by investing activities	3,620	4,884
Total	($ 342)	($ 727)

The restatement resulted in a dramatic drop in Caterpillar's net cash provided by operating activities in both 2002 and 2003, although the overall change in the company's cash and short-term investments remained the same after the restatement. Why do you think the SEC required Caterpillar to report the reclassifications summarized above?

Source: Ghostwriter, "SEC Acts to Curb Cash Flow Shenanigans," *Inc.* magazine, June 2005, p. 26, and Caterpillar's 10-K's for 2002, 2003, and 2004.

The Completed Statement of Cash Flows (Steps 7 and 8)

Once the worksheet is completed, the actual statement of cash flows is easy to complete. Nordstrom's statement of cash flows appears in Exhibit 15–11 (page 698). Trace each item from the worksheet into this statement.

The operating activities section of the statement follows the format laid out in Exhibit 15–8, beginning with net income. The other entries in the operating activities section are adjustments required to convert net income to a cash basis. The sum of all of the entries under the operating activities section is called the "Net cash provided by operating activities."

The investing activities section comes next on the statement of cash flows. The worksheet entries that have been classified as investing activities are listed in this section. The sum of all the entries in this section is called the "Net cash used in investing activities."

The financing activities section of the statement follows the investing activities section. The worksheet entries that have been classified as financing activities are listed in this section. The sum of all of the entries in this section is called the "Net cash used in financing activities."

Finally, for step 8, the bottom of the statement of cash flows contains a reconciliation of the beginning and ending balances of cash and cash equivalents.

Interpretation of the Statement of Cash Flows

The completed statement of cash flows in Exhibit 15–11 provides a very favorable picture of Nordstrom's cash flows. The net cash flow from operations is a healthy $259 million. This positive cash flow permitted the company to make substantial additions to its property, buildings, and equipment and to pay off a sizable portion of its long-term debt. If similar conditions prevail in the future, the company can continue to finance substantial growth from its own cash flows without the necessity of raising debt or selling stock.

When interpreting a statement of cash flows, it is particularly important to examine the net cash provided by operating activities. This figure indicates how successful the company is in generating cash on a continuing basis. A negative cash flow from operations may be a sign of fundamental difficulties. A positive cash flow from operations is necessary to avoid liquidating assets or borrowing money just to sustain day-to-day operations.

EXHIBIT 15–11

Nordstrom, Inc.* Statement of Cash Flows—Indirect Method (dollars in millions)		
Operating Activities		
Net income.		$140
Adjustments to convert net income to a cash basis:		
Depreciation and amortization charges	103	
Decrease in accounts receivable	17	
Increase in merchandise inventory	(49)	
Increase in accounts payable	44	
Increase in accrued wages and salaries payable	3	
Increase in accrued income taxes payable	6	
Decrease in deferred income taxes	(2)	
Gain on sale of store.	(3)	119
Net cash provided by operating activities		259
Investing Activities		
Additions to property, buildings, and equipment	(138)	
Proceeds from sale of store	8	
Net cash used in investing activities		(130)
Financing Activities		
Increase in notes payable	2	
Decrease in long-term debt	(43)	
Increase in common stock	2	
Cash dividends paid	(28)	
Net cash used in financing activities		(67)
Net increase in cash and cash equivalents		62
Cash and cash equivalents at beginning of year		29
Cash and cash equivalents at end of year		$ 91

Reconciliation of the beginning and ending cash balances →

*This statement differs from the actual statement published by Nordstrom.

FREE CASH FLOW: DO THE MATH

Jim Huguet, the manager of the IDEX Great Companies mutual fund, was contemplating investing in an energy company with soaring profits. However, something bothered him about this company. Its profits were growing 27% a year, yet its "free cash flow" was plummeting. How could such a profitable company be bleeding cash? Puzzled, Huguet decided not to invest in this high-flying company—Enron. In light of Enron's stunning financial collapse two years later, it turns out that Huguet's decision to focus on cash flow rather than being swayed by artificial accounting gimmicks saved his investors a bundle of money.

Free cash flow is a measure of the money that a company has left over after paying its bills. Investors often overlook this number because it is not directly reported in a set of financial statements; nonetheless, it is worth investing the time to do the math. To compute a company's free cash flow, begin with its net operating income, then add back its depreciation and amortization and deduct its capital expenditures and dividends paid.

Source: Russell Pearlman, "Go with the Cash Flow," *Smart Money*, October 2004, pp. 86–91.

Depreciation, Depletion, and Amortization

A few pitfalls can trap the unwary when reading a statement of cash flows. Perhaps the most common pitfall is to misinterpret the nature of the depreciation charges on the statement of cash flows. Since depreciation is added back to net income, you might think that you can increase net cash flow by increasing depreciation charges. This is false. In a merchandising company like Nordstrom, increasing the depreciation charge by X dollars would decrease net income by X dollars because of the added expense. Adding back the depreciation charge to net income on the statement of cash flows simply cancels out the reduction in net income caused by the depreciation charge. Referring back to Exhibit 15–2, depreciation, depletion, and amortization charges are added back to net income on the statement of cash flows because they are a decrease in an asset (or an increase in a contra asset)—not because they generate cash.

WHAT'S WRONG WITH THIS PICTURE?

Getty Images is the world's biggest stock photo company—owning the rights to over 70 million images and 30,000 hours of film. The company gets its revenues from licensing the use of these images. The stock market is impressed with the potential in this market—despite losses of $63 million in the first six months of the year, the company's stock was worth $1.8 billion. "What is there for a growth company to talk about if earnings are so rotten? Anything but earnings. . . . Getty Images declared victory in its cash from operations, which it said had swelled to a robust $17.1 million in the second quarter, up from a deficit of $2.6 million in the first. Does that mean Getty collected its bills and whittled down its inventory? Nope. Both receivables and inventory are rising. The cash flow from operations, rather, comes from not paying bills."

Source: Elizabeth MacDonald, "Image Problem," *Forbes*, October 16, 2000, pp. 104–106.

Summary

The statement of cash flows is one of the three major financial statements prepared by organizations. It explains how cash was generated and how it was used during a period. The statement of cash flows is widely used as a tool for assessing the financial health of organizations.

In general, sources of cash include net income, decreases in assets, increases in liabilities, and increases in stockholders' capital accounts. Uses of cash include increases in assets, decreases in liabilities, decreases in stockholders' capital accounts, and dividends. A simplified form of the statement of cash flows can be easily constructed using just these definitions and a comparative balance sheet.

For external reporting purposes, the statement of cash flows must be organized in terms of operating, investing, and financing activities. While some exceptions exist, changes in noncurrent assets are generally included in investing activities and changes in noncurrent liabilities are generally included in financing activities. And, with a few exceptions, operating activities include net income and changes in current assets and current liabilities.

An analyst should pay particularly close attention to the net cash provided by operating activities, since this provides a measure of how successful the company is in generating cash on a continuing basis.

Review Problem

Rockford Company's comparative balance sheet for 2007 and the company's income statement for the year follow:

Rockford Company
Comparative Balance Sheet
December 31, 2007, and 2006
(dollars in millions)

	2007	2006
Assets		
Cash	$ 26	$ 10
Accounts receivable	180	270
Inventory	205	160
Prepaid expenses	17	20
Plant and equipment	430	309
Less accumulated depreciation	(218)	(194)
Long-term investments	60	75
Total assets	$ 700	$ 650
Liabilities and Stockholders' Equity		
Accounts payable	$ 230	$ 310
Accrued liabilities	70	60
Bonds payable	135	40
Deferred income taxes	15	8
Common stock	140	140
Retained earnings	110	92
Total liabilities and stockholders' equity	$ 700	$ 650

Rockford Company
Income Statement
For the Year Ended December 31, 2007
(dollars in millions)

Sales	$1,000
Cost of goods sold	530
Gross margin	470
Selling and administrative expenses	352
Net operating income	118
Nonoperating items:	
Loss on sale of equipment	(4)
Income before taxes	114
Income taxes	48
Net income	$ 66

Notes: Dividends of $48 million were paid in 2007.
The loss on sale of equipment of $4 million reflects a transaction in which equipment with an original cost of $12 million and accumulated depreciation of $5 million was sold for $3 million in cash.

"How Well Am I Doing?" Statement of Cash Flows

701

Required:

Using the indirect method, determine the net cash provided by operating activities for 2007 and construct a statement of cash flows for the year.

Solution to Review Problem

A worksheet for Rockford Company appears below. Using the worksheet, it is a simple matter to construct the statement of cash flows, including the net cash provided by operating activities.

Rockford Company
Statement of Cash Flows Worksheet
For the Year Ended December 31, 2007
(dollars in millions)

	(1) Change	(2) Source or Use?	(3) Cash Flow Effect	(4) Adjustments	(5) Adjusted Effect (3) + (4)	(6) Classification
Assets (except cash and cash equivalents)						
Current assets:						
Accounts receivable	−90	Source	$ +90		$ +90	Operating
Inventory	+45	Use	−45		−45	Operating
Prepaid expenses	−3	Source	+3		+3	Operating
Noncurrent assets:						
Property, buildings, and equipment	+121	Use	−121	$−12	−133	Investing
Long-term investments	−15	Source	+15		+15	Investing
Contra Assets, Liabilities, and Stockholders' Equity						
Contra assets:						
Accumulated depreciation	+24	Source	+24	+5	+29	Operating
Current liabilities:						
Accounts payable	−80	Use	−80		−80	Operating
Accrued liabilities	+10	Source	+10		+10	Operating
Noncurrent liabilities:						
Bonds payable	+95	Source	+95		+95	Financing
Deferred income taxes	+7	Source	+7		+7	Operating
Stockholders' equity:						
Common stock	+0	—	+0		+0	Financing
Retained earnings:						
Net income	+66	Source	+66		+66	Operating
Dividends	−48	Use	−48		−48	Financing
Additional Entries						
Proceeds from sale of equipment				+3	+3	Investing
Loss on sale of equipment				+4	+4	Operating
Total (net cash flow)			$ +16	$ 0	$ +16	

Rockford Company Statement of Cash Flows—Indirect Method For the Year Ended December 31, 2007 (dollars in millions)		
Operating Activities:		
Net income		$ 66
Adjustments to convert net income to a cash basis:		
Depreciation and amortization charges	$ 29	
Decrease in accounts receivable	90	
Increase in inventory	(45)	
Decrease in prepaid expenses	3	
Decrease in accounts payable	(80)	
Increase in accrued liabilities	10	
Increase in deferred income taxes	7	
Loss on sale of equipment	4	18
Net cash provided by operating activities.		84
Investing Activities:		
Additions to property, buildings, and equipment	(133)	
Decrease in long-term investments	15	
Proceeds from sale of equipment	3	
Net cash used in investing activities . . . . (115)		
Financing Activities:		
Increase in bonds payable	95	
Cash dividends paid	(48)	
Net cash provided by financing activities		47
Net increase in cash and cash equivalents		16
Cash and cash equivalents at beginning of year		10

Note that the $16 million increase in cash and cash equivalents agrees with the $16 million increase in the company's Cash account shown in the balance sheet on page 700, and it agrees with the total in column (5) of the worksheet shown on page 701.

Glossary

Cash equivalents Short-term, highly liquid investments such as Treasury bills, commercial paper, and money market funds that are made solely for the purpose of generating a return on temporarily idle funds. (p. 684)

Direct method A method of computing the net cash provided by operating activities in which the income statement is reconstructed on a cash basis from top to bottom. (p. 691)

Financing activities All transactions (other than payment of interest) involving borrowing from creditors or repaying creditors as well as transactions with the company's owners. (p. 690)

Indirect method A method of computing the net cash provided by operating activities that starts with net income and adjusts it to a cash basis. It is also known as the *reconciliation method.* (p. 692)

Investing activities Transactions that involve acquiring or disposing of noncurrent assets. (p. 690)

Net cash provided by operating activities The net result of the cash inflows and outflows arising from day-to-day operations. (p. 691)

Operating activities Generally speaking, activities that affect current assets, current liabilities, or net income. (p. 689)

Reconciliation method See *Indirect method.* (p. 692)

Statement of cash flows A financial statement that highlights the major activities that directly and indirectly impact cash flows and hence affect the overall cash balance. (p. 683)

Appendix 15A: The Direct Method of Determining the Net Cash Provided by Operating Activities

To compute the net cash provided by operating activities under the direct method, we must reconstruct the income statement on a cash basis from top to bottom. Exhibit 15A–1 shows the adjustments that must be made to adjust sales, expenses, and so forth, to a cash basis. To illustrate, we have included in the exhibit the Nordstrom data from the chapter.

Note that the net cash provided by operating activities of $259 million agrees with the amount computed in the chapter by the indirect method. The two amounts agree because the direct and indirect methods are just different roads to the same destination. The investing and financing activities sections of the statement will be exactly the same as shown for the indirect method in Exhibit 15–11. The only difference between the indirect and direct methods is in the operating activities section.

LEARNING OBJECTIVE 4
Use the direct method to determine the net cash provided by operating activities.

Similarities and Differences in the Handling of Data

Although we arrive at the same destination under either the direct or the indirect method, not all data are handled in the same way in the adjustment process. Stop for a moment, flip back

Revenue or Expense Item	Add (+) or Deduct (−) to Adjust to a Cash Basis	Illustration— Nordstrom (in millions)
Sales (as reported)		$3,638
Adjustments to a cash basis:		
Increase in accounts receivable	−	
Decrease in accounts receivable	+	+17
Total		$3,655
Cost of goods sold (as reported)		2,469
Adjustments to a cash basis:		
Increase in merchandise inventory	+	+49
Decrease in merchandise inventory	−	
Increase in accounts payable	−	−44
Decrease in accounts payable	+	
Total		2,474
Selling and administrative expenses (as reported)		941
Adjustments to a cash basis:		
Increase in prepaid expenses	+	
Decrease in prepaid expenses	−	
Increase in accrued liabilities	−	−3
Decrease in accrued liabilities.	+	
Period's depreciation, depletion, and amortization charges	−	−103
Total		835
Income tax expense (as reported)		91
Adjustments to a cash basis:		
Increase in accrued taxes payable	−	−6
Decrease in accrued taxes payable	+	
Increase in deferred income taxes	−	
Decrease in deferred income taxes	+	+2
Total		87
Net cash provided by operating activities		$ 259

EXHIBIT 15A–1
General Model: Direct Method of Determining the Net Cash Provided by Operating Activities

to the general model for the indirect method in Exhibit 15–8 on page 693 and compare the adjustments made in that exhibit to the adjustments made for the direct method in Exhibit 15A–1. The adjustments for accounts that affect revenue are the same in the two methods. In either case, increases in the accounts are deducted and decreases in the accounts are added. The adjustments for accounts that affect expenses, however, are handled in *opposite* ways in the indirect and direct methods. This is because under the indirect method the adjustments are made to *net income,* whereas under the direct method the adjustments are made to the *expense accounts* themselves.

To illustrate this difference, note the handling of prepaid expenses and depreciation in the indirect and direct methods. Under the indirect method (Exhibit 15–8 on page 693), an increase in the Prepaid Expenses account is *deducted* from net income in computing the amount of net cash provided by operating activities. Under the direct method (Exhibit 15A–1), an increase in Prepaid Expenses is *added* to operating expenses. The reason for the difference can be explained as follows: An increase in Prepaid Expenses means that more cash has been paid out for items such as insurance than has been included as expense for the period. Therefore, to adjust net income to a cash basis, we must either deduct this increase from net income (indirect method) or we must add this increase to operating expenses (direct method). Either way, we will end up with the same figure for net cash provided by operating activities. Similarly, depreciation is added to net income under the indirect method to cancel out its effect (Exhibit 15–8), whereas it is deducted from operating expenses under the direct method to cancel out its effect (Exhibit 15A–1). These differences in the handling of data are true for all other expense items in the two methods.

In the matter of gains and losses on sales of assets, no adjustments are needed under the direct method. These gains and losses are simply ignored because they are not part of sales, cost of goods sold, operating expenses, or income taxes. Observe that in Exhibit 15A–1, Nordstrom's $3 million gain on the sale of the store is not listed as an adjustment in the operating activities section.

Special Rules—Direct and Indirect Methods

As stated earlier, when the direct method is used, the FASB requires a reconciliation between net income and the net cash provided by operating activities, as determined by the indirect method. Thus, *when a company elects to use the direct method, it must also present the indirect method* in a separate schedule accompanying the statement of cash flows.

On the other hand, if a company elects to use the indirect method to compute the net cash provided by operating activities, then it must also provide a special breakdown of data. The company must provide a separate disclosure of the amount of interest and the amount of income taxes paid during the year. The FASB requires this separate disclosure so that users can take the data provided by the indirect method and make estimates of what the amounts for sales, income taxes, and so forth, would have been if the direct method had been used instead.

Questions

15-1   What is the purpose of a statement of cash flows?

15-2   What are *cash equivalents,* and why are they included with cash on a statement of cash flows?

15-3   What are the three major sections on a statement of cash flows, and what are the general rules that determine the transactions that should be included in each section?

15-4   Why is interest paid on amounts borrowed from banks and other lenders considered to be an operating activity while the amounts borrowed are financing activities?

15-5   If an asset is sold at a gain, why is the gain deducted from net income when computing the net cash provided by operating activities under the indirect method?

15-6   Why aren't transactions involving accounts payable considered to be financing activities?

15-7   Assume that a company repays a $300,000 loan from its bank and then later in the same year borrows $500,000. What amount(s) would appear on the statement of cash flows?

15-8   How do the direct and the indirect methods differ in their approach to computing the net cash provided by operating activities?

15-9   A business executive once stated, "Depreciation is one of our biggest sources of cash." Do you agree that depreciation is a source of cash? Explain.

15-10   If the balance in Accounts Receivable increases during a period, how will this increase be recognized using the indirect method of computing the net cash provided by operating activities?

15-11   (Appendix 15A) If the balance in Accounts Payable decreases during a period, how will this decrease be recognized using the direct method of computing the net cash provided by operating activities?

15-12   Would a sale of equipment for cash be considered a financing activity or an investing activity? Why?

15-13   (Appendix 15A) A merchandising company showed $250,000 in cost of goods sold on its income statement. The company's beginning inventory was $75,000, and its ending inventory was $60,000. The accounts payable balance was $50,000 at the beginning of the year and $40,000 at the end of the year. Using the direct method, adjust the company's cost of goods sold to a cash basis.

 Exercises

EXERCISE 15-1 Classifying Transactions [LO1, LO2]

Below are transactions that took place in Placid Company during the past year:

a.   Equipment was purchased.
b.   A cash dividend was declared and paid.
c.   Accounts receivable decreased.
d.   Short-term investments were purchased.
e.   Equipment was sold.
f.   Preferred stock was sold to investors.
g.   A stock dividend was declared and issued.
h.   Interest was paid to long-term creditors.
i.   Salaries and wages payable decreased.
j.   Stock of another company was purchased.
k.   Bonds were issued that will be due in 10 years.
l.   Rent was received from subleasing office space, reducing rents receivable.
m.   Common stock was repurchased and retired.

Required:

Prepare an answer sheet with the following headings:

	Activity			Not		
Transaction	Operating	Investing	Financing	Reported	Source	Use
a.						
b.						
etc.						

Enter the transactions above on your answer sheet and indicate how the effects of each transaction would be classified on a statement of cash flows. Place an *X* in the Operating, Investing, or Financing column and an *X* in the Source or Use column as appropriate.

EXERCISE 15-2 Net Cash Provided by Operating Activities (Indirect Method) [LO3]

For the just completed year, Hanna Company had a net income of $35,000. Balances in the company's current asset and current liability accounts at the beginning and end of the year were:

	December 31	
	End of year	Beginning of year
Current assets:		
Cash	$30,000	$40,000
Accounts receivable........	$125,000	$106,000
Inventory	$213,000	$180,000
Prepaid expenses	$6,000	$7,000
Current liabilities:		
Accounts payable..........	$210,000	$195,000
Accrued liabilities	$4,000	$6,000

The Deferred Income Taxes liability account on the balance sheet increased by $4,000 during the year, and depreciation charges were $20,000.

Required:

Using the indirect method, determine the net cash provided by operating activities for the year.

EXERCISE 15-3 (Appendix 15A) Net Cash Provided by Operating Activities (Direct Method) [LO4]

Refer to the data for Hanna Company in Exercise 15-2. The company's income statement for the year appears below:

Sales	$350,000
Cost of goods sold	140,000
Gross margin	210,000
Selling and administrative expenses........	160,000
Income before taxes	50,000
Income taxes	15,000
Net income	$ 35,000

Required:

Using the direct method (and the data from Exercise 15-2), convert the company's income statement to a cash basis.

EXERCISE 15-4 Prepare a Statement of Cash Flows (Indirect Method) [LO2, LO3]

Comparative financial statement data for Carmono Company follow:

	December 31	
	2009	2008
Cash	$ 3	$ 6
Accounts receivable......................	22	24
Inventory	50	40
Plant and equipment	240	200
Accumulated depreciation	(65)	(50)
Total assets	$250	$220
Accounts payable	$ 40	$ 36
Common stock	150	145
Retained earnings	60	39
Total liabilities and stockholders' equity........	$250	$220

For 2009, the company reported net income as follows:

Sales	$275
Cost of goods sold	150
Gross margin	125
Selling and administrative expenses.	90
Net income	$ 35

Dividends of $14 were declared and paid during 2009.

Required:

Using the indirect method, prepare a statement of cash flows for 2009.

EXERCISE 15-5 (Appendix 15A) Net Cash Provided by Operating Activities (Direct Method) [LO4]

Refer to the data for Carmono Company in Exercise 15-4.

Required:

Using the direct method, convert the company's income statement to a cash basis.

EXERCISE 15-6 Net Cash Provided by Operating Activities (Indirect Method) [LO3]

Changes in various accounts and gains and losses on the sale of assets during the year for Argon Company are given below:

Item	Amount
Accounts Receivable.	$90,000 decrease
Accrued Interest Receivable	$4,000 increase
Inventory.	$120,000 increase
Prepaid Expenses.	$3,000 decrease
Accounts Payable	$65,000 decrease
Accrued Liabilities.	$8,000 increase
Deferred Income Taxes Payable	$12,000 increase
Sale of equipment.	$7,000 gain
Sale of long-term investments	$10,000 loss

Required:

Prepare an answer sheet using the following column headings:

Item	Amount	Add	Deduct

For each item, place an X in the Add or Deduct column to indicate whether the dollar amount should be added to or deducted from net income under the indirect method when computing the net cash provided by operating activities for the year.

EXERCISE 15-7 Prepare a Statement of Cash Flows (Indirect Method) [LO2, LO3]

The following changes took place during the year in Pavolik Company's balance sheet accounts:

Cash	$5 D		Accounts Payable	$35 I
Accounts Receivable	$110 I		Accrued Liabilities.	$4 D
Inventory	$70 D		Bonds Payable	$150 I
Prepaid Expenses	$9 I		Deferred Income Taxes.	$8 I
Long-Term Investments	$6 D		Common Stock.	$80 D
Plant and Equipment	$200 I		Retained Earnings	$54 I
Accumulated Depreciation	$(60) I			
Land	$15 D			

D = Decrease; I = Increase.

Long-term investments that had cost the company $6 were sold during the year for $16, and land that had cost $15 was sold for $9. In addition, the company declared and paid $30 in cash dividends during the year. No sales or retirements of plant and equipment took place during the year.

The company's income statement for the year follows:

Sales		$700
Cost of goods sold		400
Gross margin		300
Selling and administrative expenses		184
Net operating income		116
Nonoperating items:		
Gain on sale of investments	$10	
Loss on sale of land	6	4
Income before taxes		120
Income taxes		36
Net income		$ 84

The company's beginning cash balance was $90, and its ending balance was $85.

Required:
1.   Use the indirect method to determine the net cash provided by operating activities for the year.
2.   Prepare a statement of cash flows for the year.

EXERCISE 15-8 (Appendix 15A) Adjust Net Income to a Cash Basis (Direct Method) [LO4]
Refer to the data for Pavolik Company in Exercise 15-7.

Required:
Use the direct method to convert the company's income statement to a cash basis.

Problems

PROBLEM 15-9 Classification of Transactions on a Statement of Cash Flows [LO1, LO2]
Below are a number of transactions that took place in Seneca Company during the past year:
a.   Common stock was sold for cash.
b.   Interest was paid on a note, decreasing Interest Payable.
c.   Bonds were retired.
d.   A long-term loan was made to a subsidiary.
e.   Interest was received on the loan in (d) above, reducing Interest Receivable.
f.   A stock dividend was declared and issued on common stock.
g.   A building was acquired by issuing shares of common stock.
h.   Equipment was sold for cash.
i.   Short-term investments were sold.
j.   Cash dividends were declared and paid.
k.   Preferred stock was converted into common stock.
l.   Deferred Income Taxes, a long-term liability, was reduced.
m.   Dividends were received on stock of another company held as an investment.
n.   Equipment was purchased by giving a long-term note to the seller.

Required:
Prepare an answer sheet with the following column headings:

Transaction	Source, Use, or Neither	Activity			Reported in a Separate Schedule	Not on the Statement
		Operating	Investing	Financing		

Enter the letter of the transaction in the left column and indicate whether the transaction would be a source, use, or neither. Then place an X in the appropriate column to show the proper classification of the transaction on the statement of cash flows, or to show if it would not appear on the statement at all.

PROBLEM 15-10 Prepare a Statement of Cash Flows (Indirect Method) [LO2, LO3]

Comparative financial statements for Weaver Company follow:

Weaver Company Comparative Balance Sheet December 31, 2009 and 2008		
	2009	**2008**
Assets		
Cash	$ 9	$ 15
Accounts receivable	340	240
Inventory	125	175
Prepaid expenses	10	6
Plant and equipment	610	470
Less accumulated depreciation	(93)	(85)
Long-term investments	16	19
Total assets	$1,017	$840
Liabilities and Stockholders' Equity		
Accounts payable	$ 300	$230
Accrued liabilities	60	72
Bonds payable	290	180
Deferred income taxes	40	34
Common stock	210	250
Retained earnings	107	74
Total liabilities and stockholders' equity	$1,017	$840

Weaver Company Income Statement For the Year Ended December 31, 2009		
Sales		$800
Cost of goods sold		500
Gross margin		300
Selling and administrative expenses		213
Net operating income		87
Nonoperating items:		
Gain on sale of investments	$7	
Loss on sale of equipment	4	3
Income before taxes		90
Income taxes		27
Net income		$ 63

During 2009, the company sold some equipment for $20 that had cost $40 and on which there was accumulated depreciation of $16. In addition, the company sold long-term investments for $10 that had cost $3 when purchased several years ago. Cash dividends totaling $30 were paid during 2009.

Required:

1. Using the indirect method, determine the net cash provided by operating activities for 2009.
2. Using the information in (1) above, along with an analysis of the remaining balance sheet accounts, prepare a statement of cash flows for 2009.

PROBLEM 15-11 (Appendix 15A) Prepare a Statement of Cash Flows (Direct Method) [LO2, LO4]

Refer to the financial statement data for Weaver Company in Problem 15-10.

Required:

1. Using the direct method, adjust the company's income statement for 2009 to a cash basis.
2. Using the information obtained in (1) above, along with an analysis of the remaining balance sheet accounts, prepare a statement of cash flows for 2009.

PROBLEM 15-12 Prepare a Statement of Cash Flows (Indirect Method) [LO2, LO3]

Balance sheet accounts for Joyner Company contained the following amounts at the end of Years 1 and 2:

Microsoft Excel - Problem 15-12 screen capture.xls

File Edit View Insert Format Tools Data Window Help

G35

	A	B	C	D
1		Year 2	Year 1	
2	*Debit Balance Accounts*			
3	Cash	$ 4,000	$ 21,000	
4	Accounts Receivable	250,000	170,000	
5	Inventory	310,000	260,000	
6	Prepaid Expenses	7,000	14,000	
7	Loan to Hymas Company	40,000	-	
8	Plant and Equipment	510,000	400,000	
9	Total debits	$1,121,000	$ 865,000	
10				
11	*Credit Balance Accounts*			
12	Accumulated Depreciation	$ 132,000	$ 120,000	
13	Accounts Payable	310,000	250,000	
14	Accrued Liabilities	20,000	30,000	
15	Bonds Payable	190,000	70,000	
16	Deferred Income Taxes	45,000	42,000	
17	Common Stock	300,000	270,000	
18	Retained Earnings	124,000	83,000	
19	Total credits	$1,121,000	$ 865,000	
20				

Sheet1 / Sheet2 / Sheet3 /

The company's income statement for Year 2 follows:

Sales	$900,000
Cost of goods sold	500,000
Gross margin	400,000
Selling and administrative expenses	328,000
Net operating income	72,000
Gain on sale of equipment	8,000
Income before taxes	80,000
Income taxes	24,000
Net income	$ 56,000

Equipment that had cost $40,000 and on which there was accumulated depreciation of $30,000 was sold during Year 2 for $18,000. Cash dividends totaling $15,000 were declared and paid during Year 2.

Required:

1. Using the indirect method, compute the net cash provided by operating activities for Year 2.
2. Prepare a statement of cash flows for Year 2.
3. Briefly explain why cash declined so sharply during the year.

"How Well Am I Doing?" Statement of Cash Flows

711

PROBLEM 15-13 (Appendix 15A) Prepare and Interpret a Statement of Cash Flows (Direct Method) [LO2, LO4]

Refer to the financial statement data for Joyner Company in Problem 15-12. Sam Conway, president of the company, considers $15,000 to be the minimum cash balance for operating purposes. As can be seen from the balance sheet data, only $4,000 in cash was available at the end of the current year. The sharp decline is puzzling to Mr. Conway, particularly since sales and profits are at a record high.

Required:
1. Using the direct method, adjust the company's income statement to a cash basis for Year 2.
2. Using the data from (1) above and other data from the problem as needed, prepare a statement of cash flows for Year 2.
3. Explain why cash declined so sharply during the year.

PROBLEM 15-14 Prepare and Interpret a Statement of Cash Flows (Indirect Method) [LO2, LO3]

Mary Walker, president of Rusco Products, considers $14,000 to be the minimum cash balance for operating purposes. As can be seen from the statements below, only $8,000 in cash was available at the end of 2009. Since the company reported a large net income for the year, and also issued both bonds and common stock, the sharp decline in cash is puzzling to Ms. Walker.

Rusco Products Comparative Balance Sheet July 31, 2009 and 2008		
	2009	2008
Assets		
Current assets:		
Cash	$ 8,000	$ 21,000
Accounts receivable	120,000	80,000
Inventory	140,000	90,000
Prepaid expenses	5,000	9,000
Total current assets	273,000	200,000
Long-term investments	50,000	70,000
Plant and equipment	430,000	300,000
Less accumulated depreciation	60,000	50,000
Net plant and equipment	370,000	250,000
Total assets	$693,000	$520,000
Liabilities and Stockholders' Equity		
Current liabilities:		
Accounts payable	$123,000	$ 60,000
Accrued liabilities	8,000	17,000
Total current liabilities	131,000	77,000
Bonds payable	70,000	
Deferred income taxes	20,000	12,000
Stockholders' equity:		
Preferred stock........................	80,000	96,000
Common stock.........................	286,000	250,000
Retained earnings	106,000	85,000
Total stockholders' equity	472,000	431,000
Total liabilities and stockholders' equity........	$693,000	$520,000

Rusco Products Income Statement For the Year Ended July 31, 2009		
Sales		$500,000
Cost of goods sold		300,000
Gross margin		200,000
Selling and administrative expenses		158,000
Net operating income		42,000
Nonoperating items:		
Gain on sale of investments	$10,000	
Loss on sale of equipment	2,000	8,000
Income before taxes		50,000
Income taxes		20,000
Net income		$ 30,000

The following additional information is available for the year 2009.
a.   Dividends totaling $9,000 were declared and paid in cash.
b.   Equipment was sold during the year for $8,000. The equipment had originally cost $20,000 and had accumulated depreciation of $10,000.
c.   The decrease in the Preferred Stock account is the result of a conversion of preferred stock into an equal dollar amount of common stock.
d.   Long-term investments that had cost $20,000 were sold during the year for $30,000.

Required:
1.   Using the indirect method, compute the net cash provided by operating activities for 2009.
2.   Using the data from (1) above, and other data from the problem as needed, prepare a statement of cash flows for 2009.
3.   Explain the major reasons for the decline in the company's cash position.

PROBLEM 15-15 (Appendix 15A) Prepare and Interpret a Statement of Cash Flows (Direct Method)
[LO2, LO4]
Refer to the financial statements for Rusco Products in Problem 15-14. Since the Cash account decreased so dramatically during 2009, the company's executive committee is anxious to see how the income statement would appear on a cash basis.

Required:
1.   Using the direct method, adjust the company's income statement for 2009 to a cash basis.
2.   Using the data from (1) above, and other data from the problem as needed, prepare a statement of cash flows for 2009.

PROBLEM 15-16 Worksheet; Prepare and Interpret a Statement of Cash Flows (Indirect Method)
[LO2, LO3]
"See, I told you things would work out," said Barry Kresmier, president of Lomax Company. "We expanded sales from $1.6 million to $2.0 million in 2009, nearly doubled our warehouse space, and ended the year with more cash in the bank than we started with. A few more years of expansion like this and we'll be the industry leaders."

"Yes, I'll admit our statements look pretty good," replied Sheri Colson, the company's vice president. "But we're doing business with a lot of companies we don't know much about and that worries me. I'll admit, though, that we're certainly moving a lot of merchandise; our inventory is actually down from last year."

A comparative balance sheet for Lomax Company containing data for the last two years follows:

Lomax Company Comparative Balance Sheet December 31, 2009 and 2008		
	2009	**2008**
Assets		
Current assets:		
Cash	$ 42,000	$ 27,000
Marketable securities....................	19,000	13,000
Accounts receivable	710,000	530,000
Inventory	848,000	860,000
Prepaid expenses	10,000	5,000
Total current assets	1,629,000	1,435,000
Long-term investments	60,000	110,000
Loans to subsidiaries	130,000	80,000
Plant and equipment	3,170,000	2,600,000
Less accumulated depreciation	810,000	755,000
Net plant and equipment..................	2,360,000	1,845,000
Goodwill................................	84,000	90,000
Total assets	$4,263,000	$3,560,000
Liabilities and Stockholders' Equity		
Current liabilities:		
Accounts payable	$ 970,000	$ 670,000
Accrued liabilities......................	65,000	82,000
Total current liabilities	1,035,000	752,000
Long-term notes	820,000	600,000
Deferred income taxes	95,000	80,000
Total liabilities	1,950,000	1,432,000
Stockholders' equity:		
Common stock.........................	1,740,000	1,650,000
Retained earnings	573,000	478,000
Total stockholders' equity	2,313,000	2,128,000
Total liabilities and stockholders' equity	$4,263,000	$3,560,000

The following additional information is available about the company's activities during 2009:
a. Cash dividends declared and paid to the common stockholders totaled $75,000.
b. Long-term notes with a value of $380,000 were repaid during the year.
c. Equipment was sold during the year for $70,000. The equipment had cost $130,000 and had $40,000 in accumulated depreciation on the date of sale.
d. Long-term investments were sold during the year for $110,000. These investments had cost $50,000 when purchased several years ago.

e. The company's income statement for 2009 follows:

Sales		$2,000,000
Cost of goods sold		1,300,000
Gross margin		700,000
Selling and administrative expenses		490,000
Net operating income		210,000
Nonoperating items:		
Gain on sale of investments	$60,000	
Loss on sale of equipment	20,000	40,000
Income before taxes		250,000
Income taxes		80,000
Net income		$ 170,000

Required:
1. Prepare a worksheet like Exhibit 15-9 for Lomax Company.
2. Using the indirect method, prepare a statement of cash flows for the year 2009.
3. What problems relating to the company's activities are revealed by the statement of cash flows that you have prepared?

PROBLEM 15-17 (Appendix 15A) Adjusting Net Income to a Cash Basis (Direct Method) [LO4]
Refer to the data for the Lomax Company in Problem 15-16. All of the long-term notes issued during 2009 are being held by Lomax's bank. The bank's management wants the income statement adjusted to a cash basis so that it can compare the cash basis statement to the accrual basis statement.

Required:
Use the direct method to convert Lomax Company's 2009 income statement to a cash basis.

PROBLEM 15-18 Missing Data; Statement of Cash Flows (Indirect Method) [LO2, LO3]
Below are listed the *changes* in Yoric Company's balance sheet accounts for the past year:

	Debits	Credits
Cash	$ 17,000	
Accounts Receivable	110,000	
Inventory		$ 65,000
Prepaid Expenses		8,000
Long-Term Loans to Subsidiaries		30,000
Long-Term Investments	80,000	
Plant and Equipment	220,000	
Accumulated Depreciation		5,000
Accounts Payable		32,000
Accrued Liabilities	9,000	
Bonds Payable		400,000
Deferred Income Taxes		16,000
Common Stock	170,000	
Retained Earnings		50,000
	$606,000	$606,000

The following additional information is available about last year's activities:
a. Net income for the year was $_____?_____.
b. The company sold equipment during the year for $15,000. The equipment originally cost $50,000 and it had $37,000 in accumulated depreciation at the time of sale.
c. Cash dividends of $20,000 were declared and paid during the year.
d. Depreciation charges for the year were $_____?_____.

e. The balances in the Plant and Equipment and Accumulated Depreciation accounts are given below:

	Ending	Beginning
Plant and Equipment.	$1,800,000	$1,580,000
Accumulated Depreciation	$680,000	$675,000

f. The balance in the Cash account at the beginning of the year was $23,000; the balance at the end of the year was $_____?_____.

g. If data are not given explaining the change in an account, make the most reasonable assumption as to the cause of the change.

Required:
Using the indirect method, prepare a statement of cash flows for the year.

Cases

RESEARCH AND APPLICATION 15–19 [LO1]

To answer this question, download Netflix Inc.'s 2005 10-K at www.hoovers.com. Once at this website, do a search for Netflix. Click on the company name and then click on the link called SEC filings. Download the 2005 10-K (which was filed in March 2006). You do not need to print the 10-K to answer the questions.

Required:
1. What is Netflix's strategy for success in the marketplace? Does the company rely primarily on a customer intimacy, operational excellence, or product leadership customer value proposition? What evidence supports your conclusion?
2. What business risks does Netflix face that may threaten the company's ability to satisfy stockholder expectations? Of the risks that you have identified, which ones are controllable and which ones are largely uncontrollable? (Hint: Focus on pages 8–20 of the 10-K.)
3. Prepare a comparative balance sheet similar to the one shown in Exhibit 15–4 (Use Netflix's data from 2004 and 2005). For each account shown on Netflix's balance sheet, calculate the change in the balance and whether the change represents a source or a use of cash.
4. Explain how each change shown in your comparative balance sheet is accounted for in Netflix's 2005 statement of cash flows.
5. Refer to the In Business box titled "Free Cash Flow: Do the Math" shown on page 699 of the textbook. Compute Netflix's free cash flow for 2005. What insights are revealed by your calculation?Suggested Reading

Chapter

16

Learning Objectives

After studying Chapter 16, you should be able to:

LO1 Prepare and interpret financial statements in comparative and common-size form.

LO2 Compute and interpret financial ratios that would be useful to a common stockholder.

LO3 Compute and interpret financial ratios that would be useful to a short-term creditor.

LO4 Compute and interpret financial ratios that would be useful to a long-term creditor.

"How Well Am I Doing?" Financial Statement Analysis

Getting Paid on Time

Rick Burrock, the managing director of a Minneapolis-based accounting firm, advises his small business clients to keep a tight rein on credit extended to customers. "You need to convey to your customers, right from the beginning, that you will work very hard to satisfy them and that, in return, you expect to be paid on time. Start by investigating all new customers. A credit report helps, but with a business customer you can find out even more by requesting financial statements . . . Using the balance sheet, divide current assets by current liabilities to calculate the current ratio. If a company's current ratio is below 1.00, it will be paying out more than it expects to collect; you may want to reconsider doing business with that company or insist on stricter credit terms." ■

BUSINESS FOCUS

Source: Jill Andresky Fraser, © 2004 Gruner + Jahr USA Publishing. First published in Inc. Magazine. Reprinted with permission.

All financial statements are historical documents. They summarize what *has happened* during a particular period. However, most users of financial statements are concerned with what *will happen* in the future. For example, stockholders are concerned with future earnings and dividends and creditors are concerned with the company's future ability to repay its debts. While financial statements are historical in nature, they can still provide users with valuable insights. These users rely on *financial statement analysis,* which involves examining trends in key financial data, comparing financial data across companies, and analyzing financial ratios to assess the financial health and future prospects of a company. In this chapter, we focus our attention on the most important ratios and other analytical tools that financial analysts use.

In addition to stockholders and creditors, managers are also vitally concerned with the financial ratios discussed in this chapter. First, the ratios provide indicators of how well the company and its business units are performing. Some of these ratios might be used in a balanced scorecard approach as discussed in Chapter 10. The specific ratios selected depend on the company's strategy. For example, a company that wants to emphasize responsiveness to customers may closely monitor the inventory turnover ratio discussed later in this chapter. Second, since managers must report to stockholders and may want to raise funds from external sources, managers must pay attention to the financial ratios used by external investors.

Limitations of Financial Statement Analysis

Although financial statement analysis is a useful tool, it has two limitations that should be mentioned before proceeding any further. These two limitations involve the comparability of financial data between companies and the need to look beyond ratios.

Comparison of Financial Data

Comparisons of one company with another can provide valuable clues about the financial health of an organization. Unfortunately, differences in accounting methods between companies sometimes make it difficult to compare their financial data. For example, if one company values its inventories by the LIFO method and another company by the average cost method, then direct comparisons of their financial data such as inventory valuations and cost of goods sold may be misleading. Sometimes enough data are presented in footnotes to the financial statements to restate data to a comparable basis. Otherwise, the analyst should keep in mind any lack of comparability. Even with this limitation in mind, comparisons of key ratios with other companies and with industry averages often suggest avenues for further investigation.

The Need to Look beyond Ratios

Ratios should not be viewed as an end, but rather as a *starting point.* They raise many questions and point to opportunities for further analysis, but they rarely answer any questions by themselves. In addition to ratios, the analyst should evaluate industry trends, technological changes, changes in consumer tastes, changes in broad economic factors, and changes within the company itself.

Statements in Comparative and Common-Size Form

LEARNING OBJECTIVE 1
Prepare and interpret financial statements in comparative and common-size form.

An item on a balance sheet or income statement has little meaning by itself. Suppose a company's sales for a year were $250 million. In isolation, that is not particularly useful information. How does that stack up against last year's sales? How do the sales relate to the cost of goods sold? In making these kinds of comparisons, three analytical techniques are widely used:

1. Dollar and percentage changes on statements (*horizontal analysis*).
2. Common-size statements (*vertical analysis*).
3. Ratios.

The first and second techniques are discussed in this section; the third technique is discussed in the remainder of the chapter. Throughout the chapter, we will illustrate these analytical techniques using the financial statements of Brickey Electronics, a producer of specialized electronic components.

Dollar and Percentage Changes on Statements

Horizontal analysis (also known as **trend analysis**) involves analyzing financial data over time. This can involve nothing more complicated than showing year-to-year changes in each financial statement item in both dollar and percentage terms. Exhibits 16–1 (page 719) and 16–2 (page 720) show Brickey Electronics' financial statements in this *comparative form.* The dollar changes highlight the changes that are the most important economically; the percentage changes highlight the changes that are the most unusual.

Horizontal analysis can be even more useful when data from a number of years are used to compute *trend percentages.* To compute **trend percentages,** a base year is selected and the data for all years are stated as a percentage of that base year. To illustrate, consider the sales and net income of McDonald's Corporation, the world's largest food service retailer, with more than 31,000 restaurants worldwide:

Topic Tackler
PLUS
16–1

	2004	2003	2002	2001	2000	1999	1998	1997	1996	1995
Sales (millions)	$19,065	$17,140	$15,406	$14,870	$14,243	$13,259	$12,421	$11,409	$10,687	$9,795
Net income (millions)	$2,279	$1,471	$893	$1,637	$1,977	$1,948	$1,550	$1,642	$1,573	$1,427

Be careful to note that the above data have been arranged with the most recent year on the left. This may be the opposite of what you are used to, but it is the way financial data are commonly displayed in annual reports and other sources. By simply looking at these data, you can see that sales increased every year, but the net income has not. However, recasting these data into trend percentages aids interpretation:

	2004	2003	2002	2001	2000	1999	1998	1997	1996	1995
Sales	195%	175%	157%	152%	145%	135%	127%	116%	109%	100%
Net income	160%	103%	63%	115%	139%	137%	109%	115%	110%	100%

In the above table, both sales and net income have been restated as a percentage of the 1995 sales and net income. For example, the 2004 sales of $19,065 are 195% of the 1995 sales of $9,795. This trend analysis is particularly striking when the data are plotted as in Exhibit 16–3 (page 720). McDonald's sales growth was impressive throughout the entire 10-year period and was closely tracked by net income for the first part of this period, but net income faltered in 1998 and then plummeted in 2001 and 2002, finally recovering dramatically in 2003 and 2004.

IN BUSINESS

PRO FORMA EARNINGS—THE FEDS CRACK DOWN

In the 1990s, many companies got into the practice of reporting "pro forma" earnings to investors and analysts instead of GAAP earnings. While there were no rules for pro forma earnings, companies typically excluded items such as depreciation, goodwill amortization, restructuring charges, unusual gains and losses, and stock-option-related compensation expenses that depress earnings. In a period in which the 100 companies in the Nasdaq 100 index reported a GAAP loss of $82.3 billion, the same companies reported pro forma profits of $19.1 billion! If you want to report a profit instead of a loss, excluding inconvenient expenses like depreciation sure helps. Because of the perception that pro forma earnings were deliberately concocted to mislead investors, Congress acted. The Sarbanes-Oxley Act of 2002 directed the SEC to issue rules that would bar companies from issuing misleading pro forma earnings reports and that would require a reconciliation between GAAP and pro forma earnings. Detailed rules were subsequently issued by the SEC that prohibited companies from: (1) giving prominence to pro forma earnings over GAAP earnings; (2) excluding from pro forma earnings any charges or liabilities that would require cash settlement; (3) excluding unusual or nonrecurring items if in fact there had been a similar unusual or nonrecurring item within the prior two years; (4) inserting pro forma earnings into GAAP financial statements; and (5) using titles in a pro forma news release that are the same as or similar to GAAP titles.

Sources: "Why Honesty Is the Best Policy," *The Economist*, March 9, 2002, pp. 9–13; and Mark P. Holtzman, Robert Fonfeder, and J. K. Yun, "Goodby 'Pro Forma' Earnings," *Strategic Finance*, November 2003, pp. 33–35.

EXHIBIT 16–1

Brickey Electronics
Comparative Balance Sheet
December 31, 2007 and 2006
(dollars in thousands)

	2007	2006	Increase (Decrease) Amount	Increase (Decrease) Percent
Assets				
Current assets:				
Cash	$ 1,200	$ 2,350	$(1,150)	(48.9)%*
Accounts receivable, net	6,000	4,000	2,000	50.0%
Inventory	8,000	10,000	(2,000)	(20.0)%
Prepaid expenses	300	120	180	150.0%
Total current assets	15,500	16,470	(970)	(5.9)%
Property and equipment:				
Land	4,000	4,000	0	0%
Buildings and equipment, net	12,000	8,500	3,500	41.2%
Total property and equipment	16,000	12,500	3,500	28.0%
Total assets	$31,500	$28,970	$ 2,530	8.7%
Liabilities and Stockholders' Equity				
Current liabilities:				
Accounts payable	$ 5,800	$ 4,000	$ 1,800	45.0%
Accrued payables	900	400	500	125.0%
Notes payable, short term	300	600	(300)	(50.0)%
Total current liabilities	7,000	5,000	2,000	40.0%
Long-term liabilities:				
Bonds payable, 8%	7,500	8,000	(500)	(6.3)%
Total liabilities	14,500	13,000	1,500	11.5%
Stockholders' equity:				
Preferred stock, $100 par, 6%	2,000	2,000	0	0%
Common stock, $12 par	6,000	6,000	0	0%
Additional paid-in capital	1,000	1,000	0	0%
Total paid-in capital	9,000	9,000	0	0%
Retained earnings	8,000	6,970	1,030	14.8%
Total stockholders' equity	17,000	15,970	1,030	6.4%
Total liabilities and stockholders' equity	$31,500	$28,970	$ 2,530	8.7%

*The changes between 2006 and 2007 are expressed as a percentage of the dollar amount for 2006. For example, Cash decreased by $1,150 between 2006 and 2007. This decrease expressed in percentage form is computed as follows: $1,150 ÷ $2,350 = 48.9%. Other percentage figures in this exhibit and Exhibit 16–2 are computed in the same way.

EXHIBIT 16–2

Brickey Electronics Comparative Income Statement and Reconciliation of Retained Earnings For the Years Ended December 31, 2007 and 2006 (dollars in thousands)			Increase (Decrease)	
	2007	2006	Amount	Percent
Sales	$52,000	$48,000	$4,000	8.3%
Cost of goods sold	36,000	31,500	4,500	14.3%
Gross margin	16,000	16,500	(500)	(3.0)%
Selling and administrative expenses:				
Selling expenses	7,000	6,500	500	7.7%
Administrative expenses...............	5,860	6,100	(240)	(3.9)%
Total selling and administrative expenses ...	12,860	12,600	260	2.1%
Net operating income	3,140	3,900	(760)	(19.5)%
Interest expense.......................	640	700	(60)	(8.6)%
Net income before taxes	2,500	3,200	(700)	(21.9)%
Income taxes (30%)	750	960	(210)	(21.9)%
Net income..........................	1,750	2,240	$ (490)	(21.9)%
Dividends to preferred stockholders, $6 per share (see Exhibit 16–1)	120	120		
Net income remaining for common stockholders	1,630	2,120		
Dividends to common stockholders, $1.20 per share......................	600	600		
Net income added to retained earnings	1,030	1,520		
Retained earnings, beginning of year.......	6,970	5,450		
Retained earnings, end of year	$ 8,000	$ 6,970		

EXHIBIT 16–3
McDonald's Corporation:
Trend Analysis of Sales and
Net Income

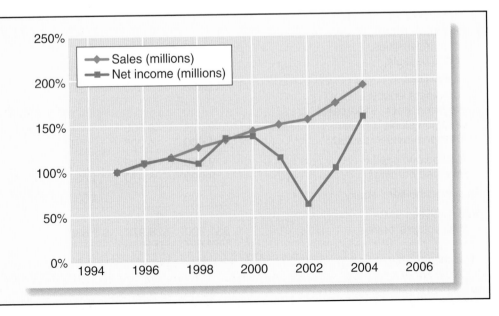

Common-Size Statements

Horizontal analysis, which was discussed in the previous section, examines changes in a financial statement item over time. **Vertical analysis** focuses on the relations among financial statement items at a given point in time. A **common-size financial statement** is a vertical analysis in which each financial statement item is expressed as a percentage. In income statements, all items are usually expressed as a percentage of sales. In balance sheets, all items are usually expressed as a percentage of total assets. Exhibit 16–4 contains a common-size balance sheet for Brickey Electronics and Exhibit 16–5 (page 722) contains a common-size income statement for the company.

EXHIBIT 16–4

Brickey Electronics Common-Size Comparative Balance Sheet December 31, 2007 and 2006 (dollars in thousands)			Common-Size Percentages	
	2007	2006	2007	2006
Assets				
Current assets:				
Cash..................................	$ 1,200	$ 2,350	3.8%*	8.1%
Accounts receivable, net...............	6,000	4,000	19.0%	13.8%
Inventory............................	8,000	10,000	25.4%	34.5%
Prepaid expenses....................	300	120	1.0%	0.4%
Total current assets	15,500	16,470	49.2%	56.9%
Property and equipment:				
Land................................	4,000	4,000	12.7%	13.8%
Buildings and equipment, net...........	12,000	8,500	38.1%	29.3%
Total property and equipment............	16,000	12,500	50.8%	43.1%
Total assets	$31,500	$28,970	100.0%	100.0%
Liabilities and Stockholders' Equity				
Current liabilities:				
Accounts payable	$ 5,800	$ 4,000	18.4%	13.8%
Accrued payables	900	400	2.9%	1.4%
Notes payable, short term..............	300	600	1.0%	2.1%
Total current liabilities..................	7,000	5,000	22.2%	17.3%
Long-term liabilities:				
Bonds payable, 8%...................	7,500	8,000	23.8%	27.6%
Total liabilities	14,500	13,000	46.0%	44.9%
Stockholders' equity:				
Preferred stock, $100, 6%	2,000	2,000	6.3%	6.9%
Common stock, $12 par	6,000	6,000	19.0%	20.7%
Additional paid-in capital..............	1,000	1,000	3.2%	3.5%
Total paid-in capital...................	9,000	9,000	28.6%	31.1%
Retained earnings....................	8,000	6,970	25.4%	24.1%
Total stockholders' equity	17,000	15,970	54.0%	55.1%
Total liabilities and stockholders' equity	$31,500	$28,970	100.0%	100.0%

*Each asset account on a common-size statement is expressed as a percentage of total assets, and each liability and equity account is expressed as a percentage of total liabilities and stockholders' equity. For example, the percentage figure above for Cash in 2007 is computed as follows: $1,200 ÷ $31,500 = 3.8%.

EXHIBIT 16–5

Brickey Electronics Common-Size Comparative Income Statement For the Years Ended December 31, 2007 and 2006 (dollars in thousands)			Common-Size Percentages	
	2007	2006	2007	2006
Sales	$52,000	$48,000	100.0%	100.0%
Cost of goods sold	36,000	31,500	69.2%	65.6%
Gross margin	16,000	16,500	30.8%	34.4%
Selling and administrative expenses:				
Selling expenses	7,000	6,500	13.5%	13.5%
Administrative expenses................	5,860	6,100	11.3%	12.7%
Total selling and administrative expenses	12,860	12,600	24.7%	26.3%
Net operating income.....................	3,140	3,900	6.0%	8.1%
Interest expense.........................	640	700	1.2%	1.5%
Net income before taxes	2,500	3,200	4.8%	6.7%
Income taxes (30%)....................	750	960	1.4%	2.0%
Net income............................	$ 1,750	$ 2,240	3.4%	4.7%

*Note that the percentage figures for each year are expressed as a percentage of total sales for the year. For example, the percentage figure for cost of goods sold in 2007 is computed as follows:
$36,000 \div $52,000 = 69.2\%$

Notice from Exhibit 16–4 that placing all assets in common-size form clearly shows the relative importance of the current assets as compared to the noncurrent assets. It also shows that significant changes have taken place in the composition of the current assets over the last year. For example, accounts receivable have increased in relative importance and both cash and inventory have declined in relative importance. Judging from the sharp increase in accounts receivable, the deterioration in the cash balance may be a result of an inability to collect from customers.

Shifting now to the income statement, in Exhibit 16–5 the cost of goods sold as a percentage of sales increased from 65.6% in 2006 to 69.2% in 2007. Or looking at this from a different viewpoint, the *gross margin percentage* declined from 34.4% in 2006 to 30.8% in 2007. Managers and investment analysts often pay close attention to this measure of profitability. The **gross margin percentage** is computed as follows:

$$\text{Gross margin percentage} = \frac{\text{Gross margin}}{\text{Sales}}$$

The gross margin percentage should be more stable for retailing companies than for other companies because the cost of goods sold in retailing excludes fixed costs. When fixed costs are included in the cost of goods sold, the gross margin percentage should increase and decrease with sales volume. With increases in sales volume, fixed costs are spread across more units and the gross margin percentage should improve.

Common-size statements are particularly useful when comparing data from different companies. For example, in 2002, Wendy's net income was $219 million, whereas McDonald's was $893 million. This comparison is somewhat misleading because of the dramatically different sizes of the two companies. To put this in better perspective, net income can be expressed as a percentage of the sales revenues of each company. Since Wendy's sales revenues were $2,730 million and McDonald's were $15,406 million, Wendy's net income as a percentage of sales was about 8.0% and McDonald's was about 5.8%. In this light, McDonald's performance did not compare favorably with Wendy's performance.

"How Well Am I Doing?" Financial Statement Analysis

723

Ratio Analysis—The Common Stockholder

A number of financial ratios are used to assess how well a company is doing from the standpoint of its stockholders. These ratios focus on net income, dividends, and stockholders' equity.

Earnings per Share

An investor buys a stock in the hope of realizing a return in the form of either dividends or future increases in the value of the stock. Since earnings form the basis for dividend payments and future increases in the value of shares, investors are interested in a company's *earnings per share.*

Earnings per share is computed by dividing net income available for common stockholders by the average number of common shares outstanding during the year. "Net income available for common stockholders" is net income minus dividends paid to the owners of the company's preferred stock.[1]

$$\text{Earnings per share} = \frac{\text{Net income} - \text{Preferred dividends}}{\text{Average number of common shares outstanding}}$$

Using the data in Exhibits 16–1 and 16–2, we see that the earnings per share for Brickey Electronics for 2007 is computed as follows:

$$\text{Earnings per share} = \frac{\$1,750,000 - \$120,000}{(500,000 \text{ shares*} + 500,000 \text{ shares})/2} = \$3.26 \text{ per share}$$

*$6,000,000 total par value ÷ $12 par value per share = 500,000 shares.

PENNIES MATTER!

IN BUSINESS

In January 2005, on-line auctioneer eBay announced that its fourth quarter earnings for 2004 rose 44% compared to the same quarter from the prior year. While eBay's fourth quarter earnings of 30 cents per share matched the company's own forecast, it came up short of Wall Street analysts' forecasts by an average of four cents per share. Consequently, eBay's stock price tumbled $15.36 in less than 24 hours. Given that eBay had about 662 million shares of common stock outstanding at the time, the company's stockholders saw more than $10 billion of wealth evaporate in one day.

EBay's experience clearly illustrates how Wall Street investors exert pressure on publicly traded companies to deliver quarterly earnings that meet expectations. Critics often urge managers to take a more long-run point of view when making decisions, but managers face the cold, hard reality that if their quarterly earnings fall short of Wall Street's expectations, their stock price will probably take a beating.

Source: Mylene Mangalindan, "EBay Posts 44% Jump in Profit; Forecast Is Tepid," *The Wall Street Journal*, January 20, 2005, p. A3.

---

[1] A complication can arise when a company has issued securities such as executive stock options or warrants that can be converted into shares of common stock. If these conversions were to take place, the same earnings would have to be distributed among a greater number of common shares. Therefore, a supplemental earnings per share figure, called diluted earnings per share, may have to be computed. Refer to an intermediate financial accounting text for details.

THE EARNINGS PER SHARE GAME

Over the last several decades, a subtle, but very important, change occurred in how managers viewed earnings per share. Instead of honestly reporting the company's earnings per share number and letting the stock market sort out the implications, top executives too often decided to manage the earnings numbers themselves. The goal was steadily growing earnings per share and beating investment analysts' earnings forecasts quarter after quarter. Cisco, for example, regularly "beat" investment analysts' earnings per share forecasts by 1 penny, quarter after quarter. The legendary investor Warren Buffet warns that if you tell Wall Street that your earnings per share will grow 17%—just as it did last year and the year before that—then your earnings had better grow by 17% or the stock market will pummel your stock. To Buffet, the expectations of continuous growth and beating analysts' estimates almost requires cheating with the accounting numbers. "No large company can grow earnings 15% quarter after quarter like that... It isn't the way business works."

Source: Andy Serwer, Janice Revell, and John Boorstin, "Dirty Rotten Numbers," *Fortune*, February 18, 2002, pp. 74–84.

Price-Earnings Ratio

The relationship between the market price of a share of stock and the stock's current earnings per share is often stated in terms of a **price-earnings ratio.** If we assume that the current market price for Brickey Electronics' stock is $40 per share, the company's price-earnings ratio would be computed as follows:

$$\text{Price-earnings ratio} = \frac{\text{Market price per share}}{\text{Earnings per share}}$$

$$= \frac{\$40 \text{ per share}}{\$3.26 \text{ per share}} = 12.3$$

The price-earnings ratio is 12.3; that is, the stock is selling for about 12.3 times its current earnings per share.

The price-earnings ratio is widely used by investors. A high price-earnings ratio means that investors are willing to pay a premium for the company's stock—presumably because the company is expected to have higher than average future earnings growth. Conversely, if investors believe a company's future earnings growth prospects are limited, the company's price-earnings ratio would be relatively low. In the late 1990s, the stock prices of some dot.com companies—particularly those with little or no earnings—were selling at levels that resulted in huge and nearly unprecedented price-earnings ratios. Many commentators cautioned that these price-earnings ratios were unsustainable in the long run—and they were right. The stock prices of almost all dot.com companies subsequently crashed.

Dividend Payout and Yield Ratios

Investors in a company's stock make money in two ways—increases in the market value of the stock and dividends. In general, earnings should be retained in a company and not paid out in dividends as long as the rate of return on funds invested inside the company exceeds the rate of return that stockholders could earn on alternative investments outside the company. Therefore, companies with excellent prospects of profitable growth often pay little or no dividend. Companies with little opportunity for profitable growth, but with steady, dependable earnings, tend to pay out a higher percentage of their cash flow from operations as dividends.

The Dividend Payout Ratio   The **dividend payout ratio** gauges the portion of current earnings being paid out in dividends. This ratio is computed by dividing the dividends per share by the earnings per share for common stock:

$$\text{Dividend payout ratio} = \frac{\text{Dividends per share}}{\text{Earnings per share}}$$

For Brickey Electronics, the dividend payout ratio for 2007 is computed as follows:

$$\text{Dividend payout ratio} = \frac{\$1.20 \text{ per share (see Exhibit 16–2)}}{\$3.26 \text{ per share}} = 36.8\%$$

There is no such thing as a "right" dividend payout ratio, although the ratio tends to be similar for companies within the same industry. As noted above, companies with ample growth opportunities at high rates of return tend to have low payout ratios, whereas companies with limited reinvestment opportunities tend to have higher payout ratios.

The Dividend Yield Ratio   The **dividend yield ratio** is computed by dividing the current dividends per share by the current market price per share:

$$\text{Dividend yield ratio} = \frac{\text{Dividends per share}}{\text{Market price per share}}$$

Since the market price for Brickey Electronics' stock is $40 per share, the dividend yield is computed as follows:

$$\text{Dividend yield ratio} = \frac{\$1.20 \text{ per share}}{\$40 \text{ per share}} = 3.0\%$$

The dividend yield ratio measures the rate of return (in the form of cash dividends only) that would be earned by an investor who buys common stock at the current market price. A low dividend yield ratio is neither bad nor good by itself.

Return on Total Assets

The **return on total assets** is a measure of operating performance. It is defined as follows:

$$\text{Return on total assets} = \frac{\text{Net income} + [\text{Interest expense} \times (1 - \text{Tax rate})]}{\text{Average total assets}}$$

Interest expense is added back to net income to show what earnings would have been if the company had no debt. With this adjustment, the return on total assets can be compared for companies with differing amounts of debt or for a single company that has changed its mix of debt and equity over time. Notice that the interest expense is placed on an after-tax basis by multiplying it by the factor $(1 - \text{Tax rate})$.

The return on total assets for Brickey Electronics for 2007 is computed as follows (from Exhibits 16–1 and 16–2):

$$\text{Return on total assets} = \frac{\$1,750,000 + [\$640,000 \times (1 - 0.30)]}{(\$31,500,000 + \$28,970,000)/2} = 7.3\%$$

Brickey Electronics has earned a return of 7.3% on average total assets employed over the last year.

Return on Common Stockholders' Equity

The **return on common stockholders' equity** is based on the book value of common stockholders' equity. It is computed as follows:

$$\text{Return on common stockholders' equity} = \frac{\text{Net income} - \text{Preferred dividends}}{\text{Average common stockholders' equity}}$$

where

$$\text{Average common stockholders' equity} = \text{Average total stockholders' equity} - \text{Average preferred stock}$$

For Brickey Electronics, the return on common stockholders' equity for 2007 is computed as follows:

$$\text{Average total stockholders' equity} = \frac{(\$17,000,000 + \$15,970,000)}{2} = \$16,485,000$$

$$\text{Average preferred stock} = \frac{(\$2,000,000 + \$2,000,000)}{2} = \$2,000,000$$

$$\text{Average common stockholders' equity} = \$16,485,000 - \$2,000,000 = \$14,485,000$$

$$\text{Return on common stockholders' equity} = \frac{\$1,750,000 - \$120,000}{\$14,485,000} = 11.3\%$$

Compare the return on common stockholders' equity above (11.3%) with the return on total assets computed in the preceding section (7.3%). Why is the return on common stockholders' equity so much higher? The answer lies in *financial leverage*.

Financial Leverage

Financial leverage results from the difference between the rate of return the company earns on investments in its own assets and the rate of return that the company must pay its creditors. If the company's rate of return on total assets exceeds the rate of return the company pays its creditors, *financial leverage is positive*. If the rate of return on total assets is less than the rate of return the company pays its creditors, *financial leverage is negative*.

We can see financial leverage in operation in the case of Brickey Electronics. Notice from Exhibit 16–1 that the company pays 8% interest on its bonds payable. The after-tax interest cost of these bonds is only 5.6% [8% interest rate × (1 − 0.30) = 5.6%]. As shown earlier, the company's after-tax return on total assets is 7.3%. Since the return on total assets of 7.3% is greater than the 5.6% after-tax interest cost of the bonds, leverage is positive, and the difference goes to the common stockholders. This explains in part why the return on common stockholders' equity of 11.3% is greater than the return on total assets of 7.3%. If financial leverage is positive, having some debt in the capital structure can substantially benefit common stockholders. For this reason, companies often try to maintain a level of debt that is considered to be normal within their industry.

Unfortunately, leverage is a two-edged sword. If assets do not earn a high enough return to cover the interest costs of debt and preferred stock dividends, then the common stockholder suffers. In that case, financial leverage is negative.

Book Value per Share

Book value per share measures the amount that would be distributed to holders of each share of common stock if all assets were sold at their balance sheet carrying amounts (i.e., book values) and if all creditors were paid off. Book value per share is based entirely on historical costs. The formula for computing it is:

$$\text{Book value per share} = \frac{\text{Total stockholders' equity} - \text{Preferred stock}}{\text{Number of common shares outstanding}}$$

LOOKING AT MCDONALD'S FINANCIALS

McDonald's Corporation provides an interesting illustration of the use of financial ratios. The data below relate to the year ended December 31, 2004. (Averages were computed by adding together the beginning and end of year amounts reported on the balance sheet, and dividing the total by two.)

Net income	$2,279 million
Interest expense	$359 million
Tax rate	28.9%
Average total assets	$26,838 million
Preferred stock dividends	$0 million
Average common stockholders' equity	$13,092 million
Common stock dividends per share	$0.55
Earnings per share	1.81
Market price per share—end of year	$32.06
Book value per share—end of year	$7.88

Some key financial ratios from the standpoint of the common stockholder are computed below:

$$\text{Return on total assets} = \frac{\$2{,}279 + [\$359 \times (1 - 0.289)]}{\$26{,}838} = 9.4\%$$

$$\text{Return on common stockholders' equity} = \frac{\$2{,}279 - \$0}{\$13{,}092} = 17.4\%$$

$$\text{Dividend payout ratio} = \frac{\$0.55}{\$1.81} = 30.4\%$$

$$\text{Dividend yield ratio} = \frac{\$0.55}{\$32.06} = 1.7\%$$

The return on common stockholders' equity of 17.4% is higher than the return on total assets of 9.4%, and therefore the company has positive financial leverage. Creditors provide about half of the company's financing; stockholders provide the remainder. (In contrast, the company's return on common stockholders' equity was 9.0% and its return on total assets was 4.8% in 2002.) Note that the market value per share is more than four times as large as the book value per share. (In contrast, the market value per share was two times as large as the book value per share in 2002.)

Source: McDonald's Corporation Annual Report for the year 2004.

The book value per share of Brickey Electronics' common stock for 2007 is computed as follows:

$$\text{Book value per share} = \frac{\$17{,}000{,}000 - \$2{,}000{,}000}{500{,}000 \text{ shares}} = \$30 \text{ per share}$$

If this book value is compared with the $40 market value of Brickey Electronics' stock, then the stock may appear to be overpriced. However, as we discussed earlier, market prices reflect expectations about future earnings and dividends, whereas book value largely reflects the results of events that have occurred in the past. Ordinarily, the market value of a stock exceeds its book value. For example, in one year, Microsoft's common stock often traded at over 4 times its book value, and Coca-Cola's market value was over 17 times its book value.

Ratio Analysis—The Short-Term Creditor

LEARNING OBJECTIVE 3
Compute and interpret
financial ratios that would be
useful to a short-term
creditor.

Short-term creditors, such as suppliers, want to be repaid on time. Therefore, they focus on the company's cash flows and on its working capital since these are the company's short-term primary sources of cash.

Working Capital

The excess of current assets over current liabilities is known as **working capital.**

$$\text{Working capital} = \text{Current assets} - \text{Current liabilities}$$

The working capital for Brickey Electronics at the end of 2007 is computed as follows:

$$\text{Working capital} = \$15,500,000 - \$7,000,000 = \$8,500,000$$

Ample working capital provides some assurance to short-term creditors that they will be paid by the company. However, maintaining large amounts of working capital isn't free. Working capital must be financed with long-term debt and equity—both of which are expensive. Therefore, managers often want to minimize working capital.

A large and growing working capital balance may not be a good sign. For example, it could be the result of unwarranted growth in inventories. To put working capital into proper perspective, it should be supplemented with the following four ratios—the current ratio, the acid-test ratio, the accounts receivable turnover, and the inventory turnover—each of which will be discussed in turn.

Current Ratio

The elements involved in the computation of working capital are frequently expressed in ratio form. A company's current assets divided by its current liabilities is known as the **current ratio:**

$$\text{Current ratio} = \frac{\text{Current assets}}{\text{Current liabilities}}$$

For Brickey Electronics, the current ratio at the end of 2007 would be computed as follows:

$$\text{Current ratio} = \frac{\$15,500,000}{\$7,000,000} = 2.21$$

Although widely regarded as a measure of short-term debt-paying ability, the current ratio must be interpreted with great care. A *declining* ratio might be a sign of a deteriorating financial condition or it might be the result of eliminating obsolete inventories or other stagnant current assets. An *improving* ratio might be the result of stockpiling inventory, or it might indicate an improving financial situation. In short, the current ratio is useful, but tricky to interpret.

The general rule of thumb calls for a current ratio of at least 2. However, many companies successfully operate with a current ratio below 2. The adequacy of a current ratio depends heavily on the *composition* of the assets. For example, as we see in the table below, both Worthington Corporation and Greystone, Inc., have current ratios of 2. However, they are not in comparable financial condition. Greystone is likely to have difficulty meeting its current financial obligations because almost all of its current assets consist of inventory rather than more liquid assets such as cash and accounts receivable.

	Worthington Corporation	Greystone, Inc.
Current assets:		
Cash	$ 25,000	$ 2,000
Accounts receivable, net	60,000	8,000
Inventory	85,000	160,000
Prepaid expenses	5,000	5,000
Total current assets (a)	$175,000	$175,000
Current liabilities (b)	$ 87,500	$ 87,500
Current ratio, (a) ÷ (b)	2	2

Acid-Test (Quick) Ratio

The **acid-test (quick) ratio** is a more rigorous test of a company's ability to meet its short-term debts than the current ratio. Inventories and prepaid expenses are excluded from total current assets, leaving only the more liquid (or "quick") assets to be divided by current liabilities.

$$\text{Acid-test ratio} = \frac{\text{Cash} + \text{Marketable securities} + \text{Accounts receivable} + \text{Short-term notes receivable}}{\text{Current liabilities}}$$

The acid-test ratio is designed to measure how well a company can meet its obligations without having to liquidate or depend too heavily on its inventory. Ideally, each dollar of liabilities should be backed by at least $1 of quick assets. However, acid-test ratios as low as 0.3 are common.

The acid-test ratio for Brickey Electronics at the end of 2007 is computed below:

$$\text{Acid-test ratio} = \frac{\$1,200,000 + \$0 + \$6,000,000 + \$0}{\$7,000,000} = 1.03$$

Although Brickey Electronics' acid-test ratio is within the acceptable range, an analyst might be concerned about several trends revealed in the company's balance sheet. Notice in Exhibit 16–1 that short-term debts are rising, while the cash balance is declining. Perhaps the lower cash balance is a result of the substantial increase in accounts receivable. In short, as with the current ratio, the acid-test ratio should be interpreted with one eye on its basic components.

IN BUSINESS

TOO MUCH CASH?

Microsoft has accumulated an unprecedented hoard of cash and cash equivalents—over $49 billion at the end of fiscal year 2003 and this cash hoard is growing at the rate of about $1 billion per month. This cash hoard is large enough to give every household in the U.S. a check for $471. What does Microsoft need all this money for? Why doesn't it pay more dividends? Microsoft executives say the cash is needed for antitrust lawsuits. Critics of the company's power, including some of its competitors, claim that the cash gives the company a huge competitive advantage. Because of this huge reserve of cash, the company can afford to lose money to enter risky new markets like the Xbox game console.

Sources: Jay Greene, "Microsoft's $49 Billion 'Problem,'" *BusinessWeek,* August 11, 2003, p. 36; and the Microsoft Annual Report for the year 2003.

Accounts Receivable Turnover

The *accounts receivable turnover* and *average collection period* ratios are used to measure how quickly credit sales are converted into cash. The **accounts receivable turnover** is computed by dividing sales on account (i.e., credit sales) by the average accounts receivable balance for the year:

$$\text{Accounts receivable turnover} = \frac{\text{Sales on account}}{\text{Average accounts receivable balance}}$$

Assuming that all of Brickey Electronics' sales were on account, its accounts receivable turnover for 2007 is computed as follows:

$$\text{Accounts receivable turnover} = \frac{\$52,000,000}{(\$6,000,000 + \$4,000,000)/2} = 10.4$$

The accounts receivable turnover can then be divided into 365 days to determine the average number of days required to collect an account (known as the **average collection period**).

$$\text{Average collection period} = \frac{365 \text{ days}}{\text{Accounts receivable turnover}}$$

The average collection period for Brickey Electronics for 2007 is computed as follows:

$$\text{Average collection period} = \frac{365 \text{ days}}{10.4} = 35 \text{ days}$$

This means that on average it takes 35 days to collect a credit sale. Whether this is good or bad depends on the credit terms Brickey Electronics is offering its customers. Many customers will tend to withhold payment for as long as the credit terms allow. If the credit terms are 30 days, then a 35-day average collection period would usually be viewed as very good. On the other hand, if the company's credit terms are 10 days, then a 35-day average collection period is worrisome. A long collection period may result from having too many old uncollectible accounts, failing to bill promptly or follow up on late accounts, lax credit checks, and so on. In practice, average collection periods ranging all the way from 10 days to 180 days are common, depending on the industry.

Inventory Turnover

The **inventory turnover ratio** measures how many times a company's inventory has been sold and replaced during the year. It is computed by dividing the cost of goods sold by the average level of inventory [(Beginning inventory balance + Ending inventory balance) ÷ 2]:

$$\text{Inventory turnover} = \frac{\text{Cost of goods sold}}{\text{Average inventory balance}}$$

Brickey's inventory turnover for 2007 is computed as follows:

$$\text{Inventory turnover} = \frac{\$36,000,000}{(\$8,000,000 + \$10,000,000)/2} = 4.0$$

The number of days needed on average to sell the entire inventory (called the **average sale period**) can be computed by dividing 365 by the inventory turnover:

$$\text{Average sale period} = \frac{365 \text{ days}}{\text{Inventory turnover}}$$

$$= \frac{365 \text{ days}}{4 \text{ times}} = 91\tfrac{1}{4} \text{ days}$$

The average sale period varies from industry to industry. Grocery stores, with significant perishable stocks, tend to turn their inventory over quickly. On the other hand, jewelry stores tend to turn their inventory over slowly. In practice, average sales periods of 10 days to 90 days are common, depending on the industry.

A company whose inventory turnover ratio is much slower than the average for its industry may have too much inventory or the wrong sorts of inventory. Some managers argue that they must buy in large quantities to take advantage of quantity discounts. But these discounts must be compared to the added costs of insurance, taxes, financing, and risks of obsolescence and deterioration that result from carrying added inventories.

Inventory turnover should increase in companies that adopt Lean Production. If properly implemented, Lean Production should result in both a decrease in inventories and an increase in sales due to better customer service.

IN BUSINESS

SETTING THE STANDARD FOR INVENTORY TURNOVER

Dell Inc. has earned a reputation as the world's most efficient computer maker—requiring very little inventory to support its sales. To keep its inventories at the lowest possible level, the company only builds computers to order and relentlessly trims the time required to build a machine. As a result, the company's turnover for the fiscal year ending January 31, 2003, was a phenomenal 99.5 times (cost of sales of $29,055 million divided by average inventories of $292 million). This translates into an average sale period of 3.7 days.

Source: Dell Inc. Annual Report for the year 2003.

Ratio Analysis—The Long-Term Creditor

Long-term creditors are concerned with a company's ability to repay its loans over the long run. For example, if a company were to pay out all of its available cash in the form of dividends, then nothing would be left to pay back creditors. Consequently, creditors often seek protection by requiring that borrowers agree to various restrictive covenants, or rules. These restrictive covenants typically include restrictions on payment of dividends as well as rules stating that the company must maintain certain financial ratios at specified levels. Although restrictive covenants are widely used, they do not ensure that creditors will be paid when loans come due. The company still must generate sufficient earnings to cover payments.

LEARNING OBJECTIVE 4
Compute and interpret financial ratios that would be useful to a long-term creditor.

Times Interest Earned Ratio

The most common measure of the ability of a company's operations to provide protection to long-term creditors is the **times interest earned ratio.** It is computed by dividing earnings *before* interest expense and income taxes (i.e., net operating income) by interest expense:

$$\text{Times interest earned} = \frac{\text{Earnings before interest expense and income taxes}}{\text{Interest expense}}$$

For Brickey Electronics, the times interest earned ratio for 2007 is computed as follows:

$$\text{Times interest earned} = \frac{\$3,140,000}{\$640,000} = 4.9$$

The times interest earned ratio is based on earnings before interest expense and income taxes because that is the amount of earnings that is available for making interest payments. Interest expenses are deducted *before* income taxes are determined; creditors have first claim on the earnings before taxes are paid.

Clearly, a times interest earned ratio of less than 1 is inadequate because interest expense exceeds the earnings that are available for paying that interest. In contrast, a times interest earned ratio of 2 or more may be considered sufficient to protect long-term creditors.

Debt-to-Equity Ratio

Long-term creditors are also concerned with a company's ability to keep a reasonable balance between its debt and equity. This balance is measured by the **debt-to-equity ratio:**

$$\text{Debt-to-equity ratio} = \frac{\text{Total liabilities}}{\text{Stockholders' equity}}$$

Brickey's debt-to-equity ratio at the end of 2007 is computed as follows:

$$\text{Debt-to-equity ratio} = \frac{\$14,500,000}{\$17,000,000} = 0.85$$

The debt-to-equity ratio indicates the relative proportions of debt and equity on the company's balance sheet. In 2007, creditors of Brickey Electronics were providing 85 cents for each $1 being provided by stockholders.

Creditors and stockholders have different views about the optimal debt-to-equity ratio. Ordinarily, stockholders would like a lot of debt to take advantage of positive financial leverage. On the other hand, because equity represents the excess of total assets over total liabilities and hence a buffer of protection for the creditors, creditors would like to see less debt and more equity.

In practice, debt-to-equity ratios from 0.0 (no debt) to 3.0 are common. Generally speaking, in industries with little financial risk, creditors tolerate high debt-to-equity ratios. In industries with more financial risk, creditors demand lower debt-to-equity ratios.

Summary of Ratios and Sources of Comparative Ratio Data

Exhibit 16–6 contains a summary of the ratios discussed in this chapter. The formula for each ratio and a summary comment on each ratio's significance are included in the exhibit.

Exhibit 16–7 (page 734) contains a listing of public sources that provide comparative ratio data organized by industry. These sources are used extensively by managers, investors, and analysts. The EDGAR database listed in Exhibit 16–7 is a particularly rich source of data. It contains copies of all reports filed by companies with the SEC since about 1995—including annual reports filed as Form 10-K.

IN BUSINESS

XBRL: THE NEXT GENERATION OF FINANCIAL REPORTING

The Securities and Exchange Commission (SEC) encourages companies to submit financial reports using a computer code known as Extensible Business Reporting Language, or XBRL for short. XBRL is a "financial reporting derivation of Extensible Markup Language, or XML—a framework that establishes individual 'tags' for elements in structured documents, allowing specific elements to be immediately accessed and aggregated."

XBRL dramatically improves the financial reporting process in two ways. First, data are tagged in accordance with a generally accepted framework. This simplifies the process of making apples-to-apples comparisons of financial results across companies. For example, "many of the components of a 'property, plant, and equipment' listing on a balance sheet . . . may be described differently by different companies, but when tagged in XBRL, a straight comparison becomes much simpler."

Second, XBRL simplifies the exchange of financial data. Without XBRL, a company's financial data are typically stored in a format that is unique to that company's specific financial software application and that cannot be easily read by other financial software. This problem is overcome with XBRL because the tagged data become "independent of the originating application and can readily be shared with any application that recognizes XBRL. This feature of XBRL makes the markup language very attractive for government regulators and financial analysts."

Sources: Glenn Cheney, "U.S. gets its XBRL in gear: SEC, FDIC OK tagged data," *Accounting Today*, March 14–April 3, 2005, pp. 26–27; Neal Hannon, "XBRL Fundamentals," *Strategic Finance*, April 2005, pp. 57–58; Ghostwriter, "From Tags to Riches," *CFO-IT*, Spring 2005, pp. 13–14.

EXHIBIT 16–6
Summary of Ratios

Ratio	Formula	Significance
Gross margin percentage	Gross margin ÷ Sales	A broad measure of profitability
Earnings per share (of common stock)	(Net income − Preferred dividends) ÷ Average number of common shares outstanding	Affects the market price per share, as reflected in the price-earnings ratio
Price-earnings ratio	Market price per share ÷ Earnings per share	An index of whether a stock is relatively cheap or relatively expensive in relation to current earnings
Dividend payout ratio	Dividends per share ÷ Earnings per share	An index showing whether a company pays out most of its earnings in dividends or reinvests the earnings internally
Dividend yield ratio	Dividends per share ÷ Market price per share	Shows the return in terms of cash dividends being provided by a stock
Return on total assets	{Net income + [Interest expense × (1 − Tax rate)]} ÷ Average total assets	Measures how well assets have been employed by management
Return on common stockholders' equity	(Net income − Preferred dividends) ÷ (Average total stockholders' equity − Average preferred stock)	When compared to the return on total assets, measures the extent to which financial leverage is working for or against common stockholders
Book value per share	(Total stockholders' equity − Preferred stock) ÷ Number of common shares outstanding	Measures the amount that would be distributed to common stockholders if all assets were sold at their balance sheet carrying amounts and if all creditors were paid off
Working capital	Current assets − Current liabilities	Measures the company's ability to repay current liabilities using only current assets
Current ratio	Current assets ÷ Current liabilities	Test of short-term debt-paying ability
Acid-test ratio	(Cash + Marketable securities + Accounts receivable + Short-term notes receivable) ÷ Current liabilities	Test of short-term debt-paying ability without having to rely on inventory
Accounts receivable turnover	Sales on account ÷ Average accounts receivable balance	Measures how many times a company's accounts receivable have been turned into cash during the year
Average collection period	365 days ÷ Accounts receivable turnover	Measures the average number of days taken to collect an account receivable
Inventory turnover	Cost of goods sold ÷ Average inventory balance	Measures how many times a company's inventory has been sold during the year
Average sale period	365 days ÷ Inventory turnover	Measures the average number of days taken to sell the inventory one time
Times interest earned	Earnings before interest expense and income taxes ÷ Interest expense	Measures the company's ability to make interest payments
Debt-to-equity ratio	Total liabilities ÷ Stockholders' equity	Measures the amount of assets being provided by creditors for each dollar of assets being provided by the stockholders

EXHIBIT 16–7
Sources of Financial Ratios

Source	Content
Almanac of Business and Industrial Financial Ratios, Aspen Publishers; published annually	An exhaustive source that contains common-size income statements and financial ratios by industry and by the size of companies within each industry.
AMA Annual Statement Studies, Risk Management Association; published annually.	A widely used publication that contains common-size statements and financial ratios on individual companies; the companies are arranged by industry.
EDGAR, Securities and Exchange Commission; website that is continually updated; www.sec.gov	An exhaustive Internet database that contains reports filed by companies with the SEC; these reports can be downloaded.
FreeEdgar, EDGAR Online, Inc.; website that is continually updated; www.freeedgar.com	A site that allows you to search SEC filings; financial information can be downloaded directly into Excel worksheets.
Hoover's Online, Hoovers, Inc.; website that is continually updated; www.hoovers.com	A site that provides capsule profiles for 10,000 U.S. companies with links to company websites, annual reports, stock charts, news articles, and industry information.
Industry Norms & Key Business Ratios, Dun & Bradstreet; published annually	Fourteen commonly used financial ratios are computed for over 800 major industry groupings.
Mergent Industrial Manual and Mergent Bank and Finance Manual; published annually	An exhaustive source that contains financial ratios on all companies listed on the New York Stock Exchange, the American Stock Exchange, and regional American exchanges.
Standard & Poor's Industry Survey, Standard & Poor's; published annually	Various statistics, including some financial ratios, are given by industry and for leading companies within each industry grouping.

Summary

The data contained in financial statements represent a quantitative summary of a company's operations and activities. Someone who is skillful at analyzing these statements can learn much about a company's strengths, weaknesses, emerging problems, operating efficiency, profitability, and so forth.

Many techniques are available to analyze financial statements and to assess the direction and importance of trends and changes. In this chapter, we have discussed three such analytical techniques—dollar and percentage changes in statements (horizontal analysis), common-size statements (vertical analysis), and ratio analysis. Refer to Exhibit 16–6 for a detailed listing of the ratios.

Review Problem: Selected Ratios and Financial Leverage

Starbucks Coffee Company is the leading retailer and roaster of specialty coffee in North America selling freshly brewed coffee, pastries, and coffee beans. Data (slightly modified) from the company's financial statements are as follows:

Starbucks Coffee Company Comparative Balance Sheet (dollars in millions)	End of Year	Beginning of Year
Assets		
Current assets:		
Cash..	$ 113	$ 71
Marketable securities...........................	107	61
Accounts receivable............................	90	76
Inventories	221	202
Other current assets............................	63	48
Total current assets	594	458
Property and equipment, net....................	1,136	931
Other assets....................................	121	103
Total assets	$1,851	$1,492
Liabilities and Stockholders' Equity		
Current liabilities:		
Accounts payable.............................	$128	$74
Short-term bank loans	62	56
Accrued payables	245	174
Other current liabilities	10	8
Total current liabilities	445	312
Long-term liabilities	30	32
Total liabilities................................	475	344
Stockholders' equity:		
Preferred stock...............................	0	0
Common stock and additional paid-in capital	792	751
Retained earnings	584	397
Total stockholders' equity	1,376	1,148
Total liabilities and stockholders' equity	$1,851	$1,492

Starbucks Coffee Company Income Statement (dollars in millions)	Current Year
Sales	$2,678
Cost of goods sold.........................	1,113
Gross margin	1,565
Selling and administrative expenses:	
Store operating expenses...................	875
Other operating expenses	93
Depreciation and amortization..............	164
General and administrative expenses.........	151
Total selling and administrative expenses	1,283
Net operating income.......................	282
Less internet investment losses................	3
Plus interest income.........................	11
Interest expense............................	0
Net income before taxes	290
Income taxes (about 37%)...................	108
Net income................................	$ 182

Required:

1. Compute the return on total assets.
2. Compute the return on common stockholders' equity.
3. Is Starbucks' financial leverage positive or negative? Explain.
4. Compute the current ratio.
5. Compute the acid-test (quick) ratio.
6. Compute the inventory turnover.
7. Compute the average sale period.
8. Compute the debt-to-equity ratio.

Solution to Review Problem

1. Return on total assets:

$$\text{Return on total assets} = \frac{\text{Net income} + [\text{Interest expense} \times (1 - \text{Tax rate})]}{\text{Average total assets}}$$

$$= \frac{\$182 + [\$0 \times (1 - 0.37)]}{(\$1,851 + \$1,492)/2} = 10.9\% \text{ (rounded)}$$

2. Return on common stockholders' equity:

$$\text{Return on common stockholders' equity} = \frac{\text{Net income} - \text{Preferred dividends}}{\text{Average common stockholders' equity}}$$

$$= \frac{\$182 - \$0}{(\$1,376 + \$1,148)/2} = 14.4\% \text{ (rounded)}$$

3. The company has positive financial leverage because the return on common stockholders' equity of 14.4% is greater than the return on total assets of 10.9%. The positive financial leverage was obtained from current and long-term liabilities.
4. Current ratio:

$$\text{Current ratio} = \frac{\text{Current assets}}{\text{Current liabilities}}$$

$$= \frac{\$594}{\$445} = 1.33 \text{ (rounded)}$$

5. Acid-test (quick) ratio:

$$\text{Acid-test ratio} = \frac{\text{Cash} + \text{Marketable securities} + \text{Accounts receivable} + \text{Short-term notes receivable}}{\text{Current liabilities}}$$

$$= \frac{\$113 + \$107 + \$90 + \$0}{\$445} = 0.70 \text{ (rounded)}$$

6. Inventory turnover:

$$\text{Inventory turnover} = \frac{\text{Cost of goods sold}}{\text{Average inventory balance}}$$

$$= \frac{\$1,113}{(\$221 + \$202)/2} = 5.26 \text{ (rounded)}$$

7. Average sale period:

$$\text{Average sale period} = \frac{365 \text{ days}}{\text{Inventory turnover}}$$

$$= \frac{365 \text{ days}}{5.26} = 69 \text{ days (rounded)}$$

8. Debt-to-equity ratio:

$$\text{Debt-to-equity ratio} = \frac{\text{Total liabilities}}{\text{Stockholders' equity}}$$

$$= \frac{\$445 + \$30}{\$1,376} = 0.35 \text{ (rounded)}$$

Glossary

(Note: Definitions and formulas for all financial ratios are shown in Exhibit 16–6. These definitions and formulas are not repeated here.)

Common-size financial statements A statement that shows the items appearing on it in percentage form as well as in dollar form. On the income statement, the percentages are based on total sales revenue; on the balance sheet, the percentages are based on total assets. (p. 721)

Financial leverage A difference between the rate of return on assets and the rate paid to creditors. (p. 726)

Horizontal analysis A side-by-side comparison of two or more years' financial statements. (p. 718)

Trend analysis See *Horizontal analysis*. (p. 718)

Trend percentages Several years of financial data expressed as a percentage of performance in a base year. (p. 718)

Vertical analysis The presentation of a company's financial statements in common-size form. (p. 721)

Questions

16-1 Distinguish between horizontal and vertical analysis of financial statement data.

16-2 What is the basic purpose for examining trends in a company's financial ratios and other data? What other kinds of comparisons might an analyst make?

16-3 Assume that two companies in the same industry have equal earnings. Why might these companies have different price-earnings ratios? If a company has a price-earnings ratio of 20 and reports earnings per share for the current year of $4, at what price would you expect to find the stock selling on the market?

16-4 Would you expect a company in a rapidly growing technological industry to have a high or low dividend payout ratio?

16-5 What is meant by the dividend yield on a common stock investment?

16-6 What is meant by the term financial leverage?

16-7 The president of a plastics company was quoted in a business journal as stating, "We haven't had a dollar of interest-paying debt in over 10 years. Not many companies can say that." As a stockholder in this company, how would you feel about its policy of not taking on debt?

16-8 If a stock's market value exceeds its book value, then the stock is overpriced. Do you agree? Explain.

16-9 A company seeking a line of credit at a bank was turned down. Among other things, the bank stated that the company's 2 to 1 current ratio was not adequate. Give reasons why a 2 to 1 current ratio might not be adequate.

Exercises

EXERCISE 16-1 Common-Size Income Statement [LO1]

A comparative income statement is given below for McKenzie Sales, Ltd., of Toronto:

McKenzie Sales, Ltd. Comparative Income Statement	This Year	Last Year
Sales	$8,000,000	$6,000,000
Cost of goods sold	4,984,000	3,516,000
Gross margin	3,016,000	2,484,000
Selling and administrative expenses:		
Selling expenses	1,480,000	1,092,000
Administrative expenses	712,000	618,000
Total expenses	2,192,000	1,710,000
Net operating income	824,000	774,000
Interest expense	96,000	84,000
Net income before taxes	$ 728,000	$ 690,000

Members of the company's board of directors are surprised to see that net income increased by only $38,000 when sales increased by two million dollars.

Required:

1. Express each year's income statement in common-size percentages. Carry computations to one decimal place.
2. Comment briefly on the changes between the two years.

EXERCISE 16-2 Financial Ratios for Common Stockholders [LO2]

Comparative financial statements for Weller Corporation for the fiscal year ending December 31 appear below. The company did not issue any new common or preferred stock during the year. A total of 800,000 shares of common stock were outstanding. The interest rate on the bond payable was 12%, the income tax rate was 40%, and the dividend per share of common stock was $0.25. The market value of the company's common stock at the end of the year was $18. All of the company's sales are on account.

Weller Corporation Comparative Balance Sheet (dollars in thousands)	This Year	Last Year
Assets		
Current assets:		
Cash	$ 1,280	$ 1,560
Accounts receivable, net	12,300	9,100
Inventory	9,700	8,200
Prepaid expenses	1,800	2,100
Total current assets	25,080	20,960
Property and equipment:		
Land	6,000	6,000
Buildings and equipment, net	19,200	19,000
Total property and equipment	25,200	25,000
Total assets	$50,280	$45,960
Liabilities and Stockholders' Equity		
Current liabilities:		
Accounts payable	$9,500	$8,300
Accrued payables	600	700
Notes payable, short term	300	300
Total current liabilities	10,400	9,300
Long-term liabilities:		
Bonds payable	5,000	5,000
Total liabilities	15,400	14,300
Stockholders' equity:		
Preferred stock	2,000	2,000
Common stock	800	800
Additional paid-in capital	2,200	2,200
Total paid-in capital	5,000	5,000
Retained earnings	29,880	26,660
Total stockholders' equity	34,880	31,660
Total liabilities and stockholders' equity	$50,280	$45,960

Weller Corporation Comparative Income Statement and Reconciliation (dollars in thousands)		
	This Year	Last Year
Sales	$79,000	$74,000
Cost of goods sold	52,000	48,000
Gross margin	27,000	26,000
Selling and administrative expenses:		
Selling expenses	8,500	8,000
Administrative expenses	12,000	11,000
Total operating expenses	20,500	19,000
Net operating income.............................	6,500	7,000
Interest expense	600	600
Net income before taxes	5,900	6,400
Income taxes	2,360	2,560
Net income	3,540	3,840
Dividends to preferred stockholders	120	400
Net income remaining for common stockholders	3,420	3,440
Dividends to common stockholders	200	200
Net income added to retained earnings..............	3,220	3,240
Retained earnings, beginning of year	26,660	23,420
Retained earnings, end of year	$29,880	$26,660

Required:
Compute the following financial ratios for common stockholders for this year:
1. Gross margin percentage.
2. Earnings per share of common stock.
3. Price-earnings ratio.
4. Dividend payout ratio.
5. Dividend yield ratio.
6. Return on total assets.
7. Return on common stockholders' equity.
8. Book value per share.

EXERCISE 16-3 Financial Ratios for Short-Term Creditors [LO3]
Refer to the data in Exercise 16–2 for Weller Corporation.

Required:
Compute the following financial data for short-term creditors for this year:
1. Working capital.
2. Current ratio.
3. Acid-test ratio.
4. Accounts receivable turnover. (Assume that all sales are on account.)
5. Average collection period.
6. Inventory turnover.
7. Average sale period.

EXERCISE 16-4 Financial Ratios for Long-Term Creditors [LO4]
Refer to the data in Exercise 16–2 for Weller Corporation.

Required:
Compute the following financial ratios for long-term creditors for this year:
1. Times interest earned ratio.
2. Debt-to-equity ratio.

EXERCISE 16-5 Trend Percentages [LO1]

Rotorua Products, Ltd., of New Zealand markets agricultural products for the burgeoning Asian consumer market. The company's current assets, current liabilities, and sales have been reported as follows over the last five years (Year 5 is the most recent year):

	Year 5	Year 4	Year 3	Year 2	Year 1
Sales	$NZ2,250,000	$NZ2,160,000	$NZ2,070,000	$NZ1,980,000	$NZ1,800,000
Cash	$NZ 30,000	$NZ 40,000	$NZ 48,000	$NZ 65,000	$NZ 50,000
Accounts receivable, net	570,000	510,000	405,000	345,000	300,000
Inventory	750,000	720,000	690,000	660,000	600,000
Total current assets	$NZ1,350,000	$NZ1,270,000	$NZ1,143,000	$NZ1,070,000	$NZ 950,000
Current liabilities	$NZ 640,000	$NZ 580,000	$NZ 520,000	$NZ 440,000	$NZ 400,000

$NZ stands for New Zealand dollars.

Required:

1. Express all of the asset, liability, and sales data in trend percentages. (Show percentages for each item.) Use Year 1 as the base year and carry computations to one decimal place.
2. Comment on the results of your analysis.

EXERCISE 16-6 Selected Financial Ratios for Common Stockholders [LO2]

Selected financial data from the June 30 year-end statements of Safford Company are given below:

Total assets	$3,600,000
Long-term debt (12% interest rate)	$500,000
Preferred stock, $100 par, 8%	$900,000
Total stockholders' equity	$2,400,000
Interest paid on long-term debt	$60,000
Net income	$280,000

Total assets at the beginning of the year were $3,000,000; total stockholders' equity was $2,200,000. There has been no change in preferred stock during the year. The company's tax rate is 30%.

Required:

1. Compute the return on total assets.
2. Compute the return on common stockholders' equity.
3. Is financial leverage positive or negative? Explain.

EXERCISE 16-7 Selected Financial Measures for Short-Term Creditors [LO3]

Norsk Optronics, ALS, of Bergen, Norway, had a current ratio of 2.5 on June 30 of the current year. On that date, the company's assets were:

Cash	Kr 90,000
Accounts receivable, net	260,000
Inventory	490,000
Prepaid expenses	10,000
Plant and equipment, net	800,000
Total assets	Kr1,650,000

The Norwegian currency is the krone, denoted here by the symbol Kr.

Required:

1. What was the company's working capital on June 30?
2. What was the company's acid-test (quick) ratio on June 30?
3. The company paid an account payable of Kr40,000 immediately after June 30.
   a. What effect did this transaction have on working capital? Show computations.
   b. What effect did this transaction have on the current ratio? Show computations.

"How Well Am I Doing?" Financial Statement Analysis

741

EXERCISE 16-8 Selected Financial Ratios [LO3, LO4]
The financial statements for Castile Products, Inc., are given below:

Castile Products, Inc. Balance Sheet December 31	
Assets	
Current assets:	
Cash	$ 6,500
Accounts receivable, net.	35,000
Merchandise inventory	70,000
Prepaid expenses	3,500
Total current assets	115,000
Property and equipment, net	185,000
Total assets	$300,000
Liabilities and Stockholders' Equity	
Liabilities:	
Current liabilities	$ 50,000
Bonds payable, 10%	80,000
Total liabilities	130,000
Stockholders' equity:	
Common stock, $5 par value . . . . $ 30,000	
Retained earnings 140,000	
Total stockholders' equity.	170,000
Total liabilities and stockholders' equity	$300,000

Castile Products, Inc. Income Statement For the Year Ended December 31	
Sales	$420,000
Cost of goods sold.	292,500
Gross margin	127,500
Selling and administrative expenses	89,500
Net operating income.	38,000
Interest expense	8,000
Net income before taxes	30,000
Income taxes (30%)	9,000
Net income.	$ 21,000

Account balances at the beginning of the year were: accounts receivable, $25,000; and inventory, $60,000. All sales were on account.

Required:
Compute financial ratios as follows:
1. Gross margin percentage.
2. Current ratio.
3. Acid-test (quick) ratio.
4. Debt-to-equity ratio.
5. Average collection period.
6. Average sale period.
7. Times interest earned.
8. Book value per share.

EXERCISE 16-9 Selected Financial Ratios for Common Stockholders [LO2]

Refer to the financial statements for Castile Products, Inc., in Exercise 16–8. In addition to the data in these statements, assume that Castile Products, Inc., paid dividends of $2.10 per share during the year. Also assume that the company's common stock had a market price of $42 at the end of the year and there was no change in the number of outstanding shares of common stock during the year.

Required:

Compute financial ratios as follows:

1. Earnings per share.
2. Dividend payout ratio.
3. Dividend yield ratio.
4. Price-earnings ratio.

EXERCISE 16-10 Selected Financial Ratios for Common Stockholders [LO2]

Refer to the financial statements for Castile Products, Inc., in Exercise 16–8. Assets at the beginning of the year totaled $280,000, and the stockholders' equity totaled $161,600.

Required:

Compute the following:

1. Return on total assets.
2. Return on common stockholders' equity.
3. Was financial leverage positive or negative for the year? Explain.

Problems

eXcel

PROBLEM 16-11 Common-Size Statements and Financial Ratios for Creditors [LO1, LO3, LO4]

Paul Sabin organized Sabin Electronics 10 years ago to produce and sell several electronic devices on which he had secured patents. Although the company has been fairly profitable, it is now experiencing a severe cash shortage. For this reason, it is requesting a $500,000 long-term loan from Gulfport State Bank, $100,000 of which will be used to bolster the Cash account and $400,000 of which will be used to modernize equipment. The company's financial statements for the two most recent years follow:

Sabin Electronics Comparative Balance Sheet	This Year	Last Year
Assets		
Current assets:		
Cash	$ 70,000	$ 150,000
Marketable securities	0	18,000
Accounts receivable, net.	480,000	300,000
Inventory.	950,000	600,000
Prepaid expenses	20,000	22,000
Total current assets	1,520,000	1,090,000
Plant and equipment, net	1,480,000	1,370,000
Total assets	$3,000,000	$2,460,000
Liabilities and Stockholders' Equity		
Liabilities:		
Current liabilities	$800,000	$ 430,000
Bonds payable, 12%	600,000	600,000
Total liabilities	1,400,000	1,030,000
Stockholders' equity:		
Preferred stock, $25 par, 8%	250,000	250,000
Common stock, $10 par	500,000	500,000
Retained earnings	850,000	680,000
Total stockholders' equity.	1,600,000	1,430,000
Total liabilities and equity	$3,000,000	$2,460,000

Sabin Electronics Comparative Income Statement and Reconciliation		
	This Year	Last Year
Sales	$5,000,000	$4,350,000
Cost of goods sold.....................	3,875,000	3,450,000
Gross margin	1,125,000	900,000
Selling and administrative expenses	653,000	548,000
Net operating income....................	472,000	352,000
Interest expense.......................	72,000	72,000
Net income before taxes	400,000	280,000
Income taxes (30%)....................	120,000	84,000
Net income...........................	280,000	196,000
Dividends paid:		
Preferred dividends	20,000	20,000
Common dividends	90,000	75,000
Total dividends paid.....................	110,000	95,000
Net income retained.....................	170,000	101,000
Retained earnings, beginning of year........	680,000	579,000
Retained earnings, end of year	$ 850,000	$ 680,000

During the past year, the company introduced several new product lines and raised the selling prices on a number of old product lines in order to improve its profit margin. The company also hired a new sales manager, who has expanded sales into several new territories. Sales terms are 2/10, n/30. All sales are on account. Assume that the following ratios are typical of companies in the electronics industry:

Current ratio..................	2.5
Acid-test (quick) ratio	1.3
Average collection period........	18 days
Average sale period............	60 days
Debt-to-equity ratio	0.90
Times interest earned	6.0
Return on total assets	13%
Price-earnings ratio	12

Required:
1. To assist the Gulfport State Bank in making a decision about the loan, compute the following ratios for both this year and last year:
   a. The amount of working capital.
   b. The current ratio.
   c. The acid-test (quick) ratio.
   d. The average collection period. (The accounts receivable at the beginning of last year totaled $250,000.)
   e. The average sale period. (The inventory at the beginning of last year totaled $500,000.)
   f. The debt-to-equity ratio.
   g. The times interest earned ratio.
2. For both this year and last year:
   a. Present the balance sheet in common-size format.
   b. Present the income statement in common-size format down through net income.
3. Comment on the results of your analysis in (1) and (2) above and make a recommendation as to whether or not the loan should be approved.

PROBLEM 16-12 Financial Ratios for Common Stockholders [LO2]

Refer to the financial statements and other data in Problem 16–11. Assume that you are an account executive for a large brokerage house and that one of your clients has asked for a recommendation about the possible purchase of Sabin Electronics' stock. You are not acquainted with the stock and for this reason wish to do some analytical work before making a recommendation.

Required:

1. You decide first to assess the well-being of the common stockholders. For both this year and last year, compute:

    a. The earnings per share. There has been no change in preferred or common stock over the last two years.

    b. The dividend yield ratio for common stock. The company's stock is currently selling for $40 per share; last year it sold for $36 per share.

    c. The dividend payout ratio for common stock.

    d. The price-earnings ratio. How do investors regard Sabin Electronics as compared to other companies in the industry? Explain.

    e. The book value per share of common stock. Does the difference between market value and book value suggest that the stock is overpriced? Explain.

2. You decide next to assess the company's rate of return. Compute the following for both this year and last year:

    a. The return on total assets. (Total assets at the beginning of last year were $2,300,000.)

    b. The return on common stockholders' equity. (Stockholders' equity at the beginning of last year was $1,329,000.)

    c. Is the company's financial leverage positive or negative? Explain.

3. Would you recommend that your client purchase shares of Sabin Electronics' stock? Explain.

PROBLEM 16-13 Effects of Transactions on Various Ratios [LO3]

Denna Company's working capital accounts at the beginning of the year are given below:

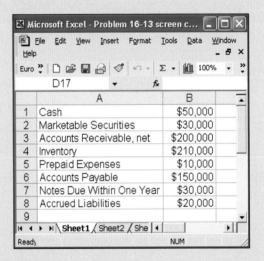

A	B
1 Cash	$50,000
2 Marketable Securities	$30,000
3 Accounts Receivable, net	$200,000
4 Inventory	$210,000
5 Prepaid Expenses	$10,000
6 Accounts Payable	$150,000
7 Notes Due Within One Year	$30,000
8 Accrued Liabilities	$20,000

During the year, Denna Company completed the following transactions:

x. Paid a cash dividend previously declared, $12,000.

a. Issued additional shares of common stock for cash, $100,000.

b. Sold inventory costing $50,000 for $80,000, on account.

c. Wrote off uncollectible accounts in the amount of $10,000, reducing the accounts receivable balance accordingly.

d. Declared a cash dividend, $15,000.

e. Paid accounts payable, $50,000.

f. Borrowed cash on a short-term note with the bank, $35,000.

g. Sold inventory costing $15,000 for $10,000 cash.

h. Purchased inventory on account, $60,000.

i. Paid off all short-term notes due, $30,000.

j. Purchased equipment for cash, $15,000.

k. Sold marketable securities costing $18,000 for cash, $15,000.

l. Collected cash on accounts receivable, $80,000.

Required:

1. Compute the following amounts and ratios as of the beginning of the year:
   a. Working capital.
   b. Current ratio.
   c. Acid-test (quick) ratio.
2. Indicate the effect of each of the transactions given above on working capital, the current ratio, and the acid-test (quick) ratio. Give the effect in terms of increase, decrease, or none. Item (x) is given below as an example of the format to use:

| | The Effect on | | |
Transaction	Working Capital	Current Ratio	Acid-Test Ratio
(x) Paid a cash dividend previously declared	None	Increase	Increase

PROBLEM 16-14 Comprehensive Ratio Analysis [LO2, LO3, LO4]

You have just been hired as a loan officer at Slippery Rock State Bank. Your supervisor has given you a file containing a request from Lydex Company, a manufacturer of safety helmets, for a $3,000,000, five-year loan. Financial statement data on the company for the last two years follow:

Lydex Company Comparative Balance Sheet	This Year	Last Year
Assets		
Current assets:		
Cash	$ 960,000	$ 1,260,000
Marketable securities....................	0	300,000
Accounts receivable, net	2,700,000	1,800,000
Inventory	3,900,000	2,400,000
Prepaid expenses	240,000	180,000
Total current assets.....................	7,800,000	5,940,000
Plant and equipment, net	9,300,000	8,940,000
Total assets...........................	$17,100,000	$14,880,000
Liabilities and Stockholders' Equity		
Liabilities:		
Current liabilities	$ 3,900,000	$ 2,760,000
Note payable, 10%	3,600,000	3,000,000
Total liabilities	7,500,000	5,760,000
Stockholders' equity:		
Preferred stock, 8%, $30 par value	1,800,000	1,800,000
Common stock, $80 par value	6,000,000	6,000,000
Retained earnings	1,800,000	1,320,000
Total stockholders' equity	9,600,000	9,120,000
Total liabilities and stockholders' equity	$17,100,000	$14,880,000

Lydex Company Comparative Income Statement and Reconciliation		
	This Year	Last Year
Sales (all on account).....................	$15,750,000	$12,480,000
Cost of goods sold.......................	12,600,000	9,900,000
Gross margin	3,150,000	2,580,000
Selling and administrative expenses	1,590,000	1,560,000
Net operating income.....................	1,560,000	1,020,000
Interest expense	360,000	300,000
Net income before taxes	1,200,000	720,000
Income taxes (30%)......................	360,000	216,000
Net income............................	840,000	504,000
Dividends paid:		
Preferred dividends	144,000	144,000
Common dividends	216,000	108,000
Total dividends paid......................	360,000	252,000
Net income retained......................	480,000	252,000
Retained earnings, beginning of year	1,320,000	1,068,000
Retained earnings, end of year	$ 1,800,000	$ 1,320,000

Helen McGuire, who just a year ago was appointed president of Lydex Company, argues that although the company has had a "spotty" record in the past, it has "turned the corner," as evidenced by a 25% jump in sales and by a greatly improved earnings picture between last year and this year. McGuire also points out that investors generally have recognized the improving situation at Lydex, as shown by the increase in market value of the company's common stock, which is currently selling for $72 per share (up from $40 per share last year). McGuire feels that with her leadership and with the modernized equipment that the $3,000,000 loan will permit the company to buy, profits will be even stronger in the future. McGuire has a reputation in the industry for being a good manager who runs a "tight" ship.

Not wanting to botch your first assignment, you decide to generate all the information that you can about the company. You determine that the following ratios are typical of companies in Lydex Company's industry:

Current ratio..................	2.3
Acid-test (quick) ratio............	1.2
Average collection period.........	30 days
Average sale period.............	60 days
Return on assets	9.5%
Debt-to-equity ratio	0.65
Times interest earned	5.7
Price-earnings ratio	10

Required:

1. You decide first to assess the rate of return that the company is generating. Compute the following for both this year and last year:
   a. The return on total assets. (Total assets at the beginning of last year were $12,960,000.)
   b. The return on common stockholders' equity. (Stockholders' equity at the beginning of last year totaled $9,048,000. There has been no change in preferred or common stock over the last two years.)
   c. Is the company's financial leverage positive or negative? Explain.
2. You decide next to assess the well-being of the common stockholders. For both this year and last year, compute:
   a. The earnings per share.
   b. The dividend yield ratio for common stock.
   c. The dividend payout ratio for common stock.

    d. The price-earnings ratio. How do investors regard Lydex Company as compared to other companies in the industry? Explain.

    e. The book value per share of common stock. Does the difference between market value per share and book value per share suggest that the stock at its current price is a bargain? Explain.

    f. The gross margin percentage.

3. You decide, finally, to assess creditor ratios to determine both short-term and long-term debt-paying ability. For both this year and last year, compute:

    a. Working capital.

    b. The current ratio.

    c. The acid-test ratio.

    d. The average collection period. (The accounts receivable at the beginning of last year totaled $1,560,000.)

    e. The inventory turnover. (The inventory at the beginning of last year totaled $1,920,000.) Also compute the average sale period.

    f. The debt-to-equity ratio.

    g. The times interest earned ratio.

4. Make a recommendation to your supervisor as to whether the loan should be approved.

PROBLEM 16-15 Common-Size Financial Statements [LO1]

Refer to the financial statement data for Lydex Company given in Problem 16–14.

Required:

For both this year and last year:

1. Present the balance sheet in common-size format.

2. Present the income statement in common-size format down through net income.

3. Comment on the results of your analysis.

PROBLEM 16-16 Effects of Transactions on Various Financial Ratios [LO2, LO3, LO4]

In the right-hand column below, certain financial ratios are listed. To the left of each ratio is a business transaction or event relating to the operating activities of Delta Company.

Business Transaction or Event	Ratio
1. Declared a cash dividend.	Current ratio
2. Sold inventory on account at cost.	Acid-test (quick) ratio
3. Issued bonds with an interest rate of 8%. The company's return on assets is 10%.	Return on common stockholders' equity
4. Net income decreased by 10% between last year and this year. Long-term debt remained unchanged.	Times interest earned
5. Paid a previously declared cash dividend.	Current ratio
6. The market price of the company's common stock dropped from 24½ to 20. The dividend paid per share remained unchanged.	Dividend payout ratio
7. Obsolete inventory totaling $100,000 was written off as a loss.	Inventory turnover ratio
8. Sold inventory for cash at a profit.	Debt-to-equity ratio
9. Changed customer credit terms from 2/10, n/30 to 2/15, n/30 to comply with a change in industry practice.	Accounts receivable turnover ratio
10. Issued a dividend to common stockholders.	Book value per share
11. The market price of the company's common stock increased from 24½ to 30.	Book value per share
12. Paid $40,000 on accounts payable.	Working capital
13. Issued a common stock dividend to common stockholders.	Earnings per share
14. Paid accounts payable	Debt-to-equity ratio
15. Purchased inventory on account.	Acid-test (quick) ratio
16. Wrote off an uncollectible account against the Allowance for Bad-Debts.	Current ratio
17. The market price of the company's common stock increased from 24½ to 30. Earnings per share remained unchanged.	Price-earnings ratio
18. The market price of the company's common stock increased from 24½ to 30. The dividend paid per share remained unchanged.	Dividend yield ratio

Required:

Indicate the effect that each business transaction or event would have on the ratio listed opposite to it. State the effect in terms of increase, decrease, or no effect on the ratio involved, and give the reason for your answer. In all cases, assume that the current assets exceed the current liabilities both before and after the event or transaction. Use the following format for your answers:

Effect on Ratio	Reason for Increase, Decrease, or No Effect
1.	
Etc.	

PROBLEM 16–17 Interpretation of Financial Ratios [LO2, LO3]

Paul Ward is interested in the stock of Pecunious Products, Inc. Before purchasing the stock, Mr. Ward would like your help in analyzing the data that are available to him as shown below:

	Year 3	Year 2	Year 1
Sales trend	128.0	115.0	100.0
Current ratio	2.5	2.3	2.2
Acid-test (quick) ratio	0.8	0.9	1.1
Accounts receivable turnover	9.4	10.6	12.5
Inventory turnover	6.5	7.2	8.0
Dividend yield	7.1%	6.5%	5.8%
Dividend payout ratio	40%	50%	60%
Return on total assets	12.5%	11.0%	9.5%
Return on common stockholders' equity	14.0%	10.0%	7.8%
Dividends paid per share*	$1.50	$1.50	$1.50

*There have been no changes in common stock outstanding over the three-year period.

Mr. Ward would like answers to a number of questions about the trend of events in Pecunious Products, Inc., over the last three years. His questions are:

a.   Is it becoming easier for the company to pay its bills as they come due?
b.   Are customers paying their accounts at least as fast now as they were in Year 1?
c.   Is the total of the accounts receivable increasing, decreasing, or remaining constant?
d.   Is the level of inventory increasing, decreasing, or remaining constant?
e.   Is the market price of the company's stock going up or down?
f.   Is the earnings per share increasing or decreasing?
g.   Is the price-earning ratio going up or down?
h.   Is the company employing financial leverage to the advantage of the common stockholders?

Required:

Answer each of Mr. Ward's questions and explain how you arrived at your answers.

PROBLEM 16–18 Ethics and the Manager [LO3]

Venice InLine, Inc., was founded by Russ Perez to produce a specialized in-line skate he had designed for doing aerial tricks. Up to this point, Russ has financed the company with his own savings and with cash generated by his business. However, Russ now faces a cash crisis. In the year just ended, an acute shortage of high-impact roller bearings developed just as the company was beginning production for the Christmas season. Russ had been assured by his suppliers that the roller bearings would be delivered in time to make Christmas shipments, but the suppliers had been unable to fully deliver on this promise. As a consequence, Venice InLine had large stocks of unfinished skates at the end of the year and had been unable to fill all of the orders that had come in from retailers for the Christmas season. Consequently, sales were below expectations for the year, and Russ does not have enough cash to pay his creditors.

Well before the accounts payable were due, Russ visited a local bank and inquired about obtaining a loan. The loan officer at the bank assured Russ that there should not be any problem getting a loan to pay off his accounts payable—providing that on his most recent financial statements the current ratio was above 2.0, the acid-test ratio was above 1.0, and net operating income was at least four times the interest on the proposed loan. Russ promised to return later with a copy of his financial statements.

Russ would like to apply for a $80,000 six-month loan bearing an interest rate of 10% per year. The unaudited financial reports of the company appear below:

Venice Inline, Inc.
Comparative Balance Sheet
As of December 31
(dollars in thousands)

	This Year	Last Year
Assets		
Current assets:		
Cash	$ 70	$150
Accounts receivable, net	50	40
Inventory	160	100
Prepaid expenses	10	12
Total current assets	290	302
Property and equipment	270	180
Total assets	$560	$482
Liabilities and Stockholders' Equity		
Current liabilities:		
Accounts payable	$154	$ 90
Accrued payables	10	10
Total current liabilities	164	100
Long-term liabilities	—	—
Total liabilities	164	100
Stockholders' equity:		
Common stock and additional paid-in capital	100	100
Retained earnings	296	282
Total stockholders' equity	396	382
Total liabilities and stockholders' equity	$560	$482

Venice Inline, Inc.
Income Statement
For the Year Ended December 31
(dollars in thousands)

	This Year
Sales (all on account)	$420
Cost of goods sold	290
Gross margin	130
Selling and administrative expenses:	
Selling expenses	42
Administrative expenses	68
Total operating expenses	110
Net operating income	20
Interest expense	—
Net income before taxes	20
Income taxes (30%)	6
Net income	$ 14

Required:
1. Based on the above unaudited financial statements and the statement made by the loan officer, would the company qualify for the loan?
2. Last year Russ purchased and installed new, more efficient equipment to replace an older plastic injection molding machine. Russ had originally planned to sell the old machine but found that it is still needed whenever the plastic injection molding process is a bottleneck. When

Russ discussed his cash flow problems with his brother-in-law, he suggested to Russ that the old machine be sold or at least reclassified as inventory on the balance sheet since it could be readily sold. At present, the machine is carried in the Property and Equipment account and could be sold for its net book value of $45,000. The bank does not require audited financial statements. What advice would you give to Russ concerning the machine?

PROBLEM 16–19 Incomplete Statements; Analysis of Ratios [LO2, LO3, LO4]
Incomplete financial statements for Pepper Industries follow:

	Pepper Industries Balance Sheet March 31	
Current assets:		
Cash	$	?
Accounts receivable, net		?
Inventory		?
Total current assets		?
Plant and equipment, net		?
Total assets.	$	?
Liabilities:		
Current liabilities	$	320,000
Bonds payable, 10%		?
Total liabilities		?
Stockholders' equity:		
Common stock, $5 par value		?
Retained earnings.		?
Total stockholders' equity.		?
Total liabilities and stockholders equity	$	?

	Pepper Industries Income Statement For the Year Ended March 31
Sales.	$4,200,000
Cost of goods sold.	?
Gross margin	?
Selling and administrative expenses	?
Net operating income.	?
Interest expense.	80,000
Net income before taxes	?
Income taxes (30%)	?
Net income.	$?

The following additional information is available about the company:
a.   All sales during the year were on account.
b.   There was no change in the number of shares of common stock outstanding during the year.
c.   The interest expense on the income statement relates to the bonds payable; the amount of bonds outstanding did not change during the year.
d.   Selected balances at the *beginning* of the current year were:

Accounts receivable	$270,000
Inventory	$360,000
Total assets.	$1,800,000

e.   Selected financial ratios computed from the statements above for the current year are:

Earnings per share	$2.30
Debt-to-equity ratio	0.875
Accounts receivable turnover	14.0
Current ratio	2.75
Return on total assets	18.0%
Times interest earned	6.75
Acid-test (quick) ratio.	1.25
Inventory turnover	6.5

Required:
Compute the missing amounts on the company's financial statements. (Hint: What's the difference between the acid-test ratio and the current ratio?)

Cases

RESEARCH AND APPLICATION 16–20   [LO1, LO2, LO3, LO4]

The questions in this exercise are based on Target Corporation. To answer the questions, you will need to download Target's 2004 annual report (the company's fiscal year ended on January 29, 2005) at http://investors.target.com/. You do not need to print the annual report to answer the questions.

Required:
1.   Prepare a five-year horizontal analysis of Target's sales and earnings from continuing operations. Use 2000 as your base year and present the trended data in dollar and percentage form as illustrated on page 718 of the textbook. What insights are revealed by the data?
2.   Prepare a common-size balance sheet as of the fiscal years ended January 29, 2005, and January 31, 2004. Use the format shown in Exhibit 16–4 within the chapter.
3.   When performing a vertical analysis of its profitability does Target use sales ($45,682 for 2004) or total revenues ($46,839 for 2004)? Why? (Hint: Look at how Target computes its gross margin rates and selling, general, and administrative expense rates on pages 17 and 18 of the annual report.)
4.   Calculate Target's earnings per share, price-earnings ratio, dividend payout ratio, dividend yield ratio, return on total assets, return on common stockholders' equity, and book value per share for the fiscal year ended January 29, 2005. Use earnings from continuing operations for all of your calculations. Assume that Target's market price per share of common stock was $49.49 as of January 29, 2005.
5.   Calculate Target's working capital, current ratio, acid-test ratio, inventory turnover ratio, and average sale period for the fiscal year ended January 29, 2005.
6.   Calculate Target's times interest earned and debt-to-equity ratio for the fiscal year ended January 29, 2005.
7.   Below are selected financial ratios for Wal-Mart Stores, Inc. for its fiscal year ended January 31, 2005. How does Target's performance compare to Wal-Mart's?

Current ratio	0.90
Acid-test ratio	0.17
Average sale period	46.6 days
Times interest earned	17.3
Debt-to-equity ratio	1.43
Return on total assets	9.3%
Price-earnings ratio	21.7

Pricing Products and Services

Learning Objectives

After studying this appendix, you should be able to:

LO1 Compute the profit-maximizing price of a product or service using the price elasticity of demand and variable cost.

LO2 Compute the selling price of a product using the absorption costing approach.

LO3 Compute the target cost for a new product or service.

Introduction

Some products have an established market price. Consumers will not pay more than this price and there is no reason for a supplier to charge less—it can sell all that it produces at this price. Under these circumstances, the company simply charges the prevailing market price for the product. Markets for basic raw materials such as farm products and minerals follow this pattern.

In this appendix, we are concerned with the more common situation in which a business is faced with the problem of setting its own prices. Clearly, the pricing decision can be critical. If the price is set too high, customers won't buy the company's products. If the price is set too low, the company's costs won't be covered.

The usual approach in pricing is to *mark up* cost.[1] A product's **markup** is the difference between its selling price and its cost and is usually expressed as a percentage of cost.

$$\text{Selling price} = (1 + \text{Markup percentage}) \times \text{Cost}$$

For example, a company that uses a markup of 50% adds 50% to the costs of its products to determine selling prices. If a product costs $10, then the company would charge $15 for the product. This approach is called **cost-plus pricing** because a predetermined markup percentage is applied to a cost base to determine the selling price.

Two key issues must be addressed with the cost-plus approach to pricing. First, what cost should be used? Second, how should the markup be determined? Several alternative approaches are considered in this appendix, starting with the approach generally favored by economists.

The Economists' Approach to Pricing

LEARNING OBJECTIVE 1
Compute the profit-maximizing price of a product or service using the price elasticity of demand and variable cost.

If a company raises the price of a product, unit sales ordinarily fall. Because of this, pricing is a delicate balancing act in which the benefits of higher revenues per unit are traded off against the lower volume that results from charging a higher price. The sensitivity of unit sales to changes in price is called the *price elasticity of demand.*

Elasticity of Demand

A product's price elasticity should be a key element in setting its price. The **price elasticity of demand** measures the degree to which a change in price affects the unit sales of a product or service. Demand for a product is said to be *inelastic* if a change in price has little effect on the number of units sold. The demand for designer perfumes sold by trained personnel at cosmetic counters in department stores is relatively inelastic. Raising or lowering prices on these luxury goods has little effect on unit sales. On the other hand, demand for a product is *elastic* if a change in price has a substantial effect on the volume of units sold. An example of a product whose demand is elastic is gasoline. If a gas station raises its price for gasoline, unit sales will drop as customers seek lower prices elsewhere.

Price elasticity is very important in determining prices. Managers should set higher markups over cost when customers are relatively insensitive to price (i.e., demand is inelastic) and lower markups when customers are relatively sensitive to price (i.e., demand is

---

[1] There are some legal restrictions on prices. Antitrust laws prohibit "predatory" prices, which are generally interpreted by the courts to mean a price below average variable cost. "Price discrimination"—charging different prices to customers in the same market for the same product or service—is also prohibited by the law.

elastic). This principle is followed in department stores. Merchandise sold in the bargain basement has a much lower markup than merchandise sold elsewhere in the store because customers who shop in the bargain basement are much more sensitive to price (i.e., demand is elastic).

The price elasticity of demand for a product or service, ϵ_d, can be estimated using the following formula.[2,3]

$$\epsilon_d = \frac{\ln(1 + \% \text{ change in quantity sold})}{\ln(1 + \% \text{ change in price})}$$

For example, suppose that the managers of Nature's Garden believe that a 10% increase in the selling price of their apple-almond shampoo would result in a 15% decrease in the number of bottles of shampoo sold.[4] The price elasticity of demand for this product would be computed as follows:

$$\epsilon_d = \frac{\ln[1 + (-0.15)]}{\ln[1 + (0.10)]} = \frac{\ln(0.85)}{\ln(1.10)} = -1.71$$

For comparison purposes, the managers of Nature's Garden believe that another product, strawberry glycerin soap, would experience a 20% drop in unit sales if its price is increased by 10%. (Purchasers of this product are more sensitive to price than the purchasers of the apple-almond shampoo.) The price elasticity of demand for the strawberry glycerin soap is:

$$\epsilon_d = \frac{\ln[1 + (-0.20)]}{\ln[1 + (0.10)]} = \frac{\ln(0.80)}{\ln(1.10)} = -2.34$$

Both of these products, like other normal products, have a price elasticity that is less than -1.

Note that the price elasticity of demand for the strawberry glycerin soap is larger (in absolute value) than the price elasticity of demand for the apple-almond shampoo. This indicates that the demand for strawberry glycerin soap is more elastic than the demand for apple-almond shampoo.

In the next subsection, the price elasticity of demand will be used to compute the selling price that maximizes the profits of the company.

The Profit-Maximizing Price

Under certain conditions, the profit-maximizing price can be determined by marking up *variable cost* using the following formula:[5]

$$\text{Profit-maximizing markup on variable cost} = \frac{-1}{1 + \epsilon_d}$$

Using the above markup, the selling price would be set using the formula:

$$\text{Profit-maximizing price} = (1 + \text{Profit-maximizing markup on variable cost}) \times \text{Variable cost per unit}$$

---

[2] The term "ln( )" is the natural log function. You can compute the natural log of any number using the LN or ln*x* key on your calculator. For example, ln(0.85) = −0.1625.

[3] This formula assumes that the price elasticity of demand is constant. This occurs when the relation between the selling price, p, and the unit sales, q, can be expressed in the following form: $\ln(q) = a + \epsilon_d \ln(p)$. Even if this is not precisely true, the formula provides a useful way to estimate a product's price elasticity.

[4] The estimated change in unit sales should take into account competitors' responses to a price change.

[5] The formula assumes that (a) the price elasticity of demand is constant; (b) Total cost = Total fixed cost + Variable cost per unit × Quantity sold; and (c) the price of the product has no effect on the sales or costs of any other product. The formula can be derived using calculus.

WHAT DID THAT SALMON DISH COST?

Restaurants mark up food costs by an average of 300% to cover their overhead and generate a profit, but the markup is not the same for all items on the menu. Some ingredients—especially prime cuts of beef and exotic seafood such as fresh scallops—are so costly that diners would not tolerate a 300% markup. So restaurants make it up on the cheap stuff—vegetables, pasta, and salmon. Why salmon? The farmed variety is only $2.50 per pound wholesale, much cheaper than prime restaurant-quality beef. At the Docks restaurant in New York City, a 10-ounce salmon dinner garnished with potatoes and coleslaw is $19.50. The actual cost of the ingredients is only $1.90.

To take another example, the ingredients of the best-selling Angus beef tenderloin at the Sunset Grill in Nashville, Tennessee, costs the restaurant $8.42. Applying the average 300% markup, the price of the meal would be $33.68. But few diners would order the meal at that price. So instead the restaurant charges just $25. In contrast, the restaurant charges $9 for its Grill vegetable plate—whose ingredients cost only $1.55.

Source: Eileen Daspin, "Entrée Economics," *The Wall Street Journal*, March 10, 2000, pp. W1 and W4.

The profit-maximizing prices for the two Nature's Garden products are computed below using these formulas:

Apple-Almond Shampoo

Profit-maximizing markup on variable cost $= \left(\dfrac{-1}{1 + (-1.71)} \right) = 1.41$

Profit-maximizing price $= (1 + 1.41)\$2.00 = \$4.82$

Strawberry Glycerin Soap

Profit-maximizing markup on variable cost $= \left(\dfrac{-1}{1 + (-2.34)} \right) = 0.75$

Profit-maximizing price $= (1 + 0.75)\$0.40 = \$0.70$

Note that the 75% markup for the strawberry glycerin soap is lower than the 141% markup for the apple-almond shampoo. The reason for this is that the purchasers of strawberry glycerin soap are more sensitive to price than the purchasers of apple-almond shampoo. Strawberry glycerin soap is a relatively common product with close substitutes available in nearly every grocery store.

Exhibit A–1 shows how the profit-maximizing markup is generally affected by how sensitive unit sales are to price. For example, if a 10% increase in price leads to a 20% decrease in unit sales, then the optimal markup on variable cost according to the exhibit is 75%—the figure computed above for the strawberry glycerin soap. Note that the optimal markup drops as unit sales become more sensitive to price.

Caution is advised when using these formulas to establish a selling price. The formulas rely on simplifying assumptions and the estimate of the percentage change in unit sales that would result from a given percentage change in price is likely to be inexact. Nevertheless, the formulas can provide valuable clues regarding whether prices should be increased or decreased. Suppose, for example, that the strawberry glycerin soap is currently being sold for $0.60 per bar. The formula indicates that the profit-maximizing price is $0.70 per bar. Rather than increasing the price by $0.10, it would be prudent to increase the price by a more modest amount to observe what happens to unit sales and to profits.

The formula for the profit-maximizing price conveys a very important lesson. If the total fixed costs are the same whether the company charges $0.60 or $0.70, they cannot be relevant in the decision of which price to charge for the soap. The optimal selling price should depend on two factors—the variable cost per unit and how sensitive unit sales are to changes in price. Fixed costs play no role in setting the optimal price. Fixed costs are relevant when

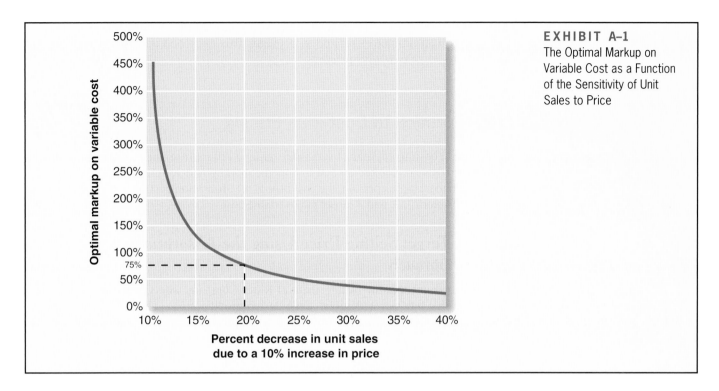

EXHIBIT A–1
The Optimal Markup on Variable Cost as a Function of the Sensitivity of Unit Sales to Price

deciding whether to offer a product but are not relevant when deciding how much to charge for the product.

We can directly verify that an increase in selling price for the strawberry glycerin soap from the current price of $0.60 per bar is warranted, based just on the forecast that a 10% increase in selling price would lead to a 20% decrease in unit sales. Suppose, for example, that Nature's Garden is currently selling 200,000 bars of the soap per year at the price of $0.60 a bar. If the change in price has no effect on the company's fixed costs or on other products, the effect on profits of increasing the price by 10% can be computed as follows:

	Present Price	Higher Price
Selling price	$0.60	$0.60 + (0.10 × $0.60) = $0.66
Unit sales	200,000	200,000 − (0.20 × 200,000) = 160,000
Sales	$120,000	$105,600
Variable cost ($0.40 per unit)	80,000	64,000
Contribution margin	$ 40,000	$ 41,600

Despite the apparent optimality of prices based on marking up variable costs according to the price elasticity of demand, surveys consistently reveal that most managers approach the pricing problem from a completely different perspective.[6] They prefer to

---

[6] One study found that 83% of the 504 large manufacturing companies surveyed used some form of full cost (either absorption cost or absorption cost plus selling and administrative expenses) as the basis for pricing. The remaining 17% used only variable costs as a basis for pricing decisions. See V. Govindarajan and Robert N. Anthony, "How Firms Use Cost Data in Pricing Decisions," *Management Accounting,* July 1983, pp. 30–36. A more recent, but less extensive, survey by Eunsup Shim and Ephraim F. Sudit, "How Manufacturers Price Products," *Management Accounting,* February 1995, pp. 37–39, found similar results.

On the other hand, a survey of small-company executives summarized in *Inc.* magazine, November 1996, p. 84, revealed that only 41% set prices based on cost. The others charge what they think customers are willing to pay or what the market demands.

mark up some version of full, not variable, costs, and the markup is based on desired profits rather than on factors related to demand. This approach is called the *absorption costing approach to cost-plus pricing*.

The Absorption Costing Approach to Cost-Plus Pricing

The absorption costing approach to cost-plus pricing differs from the economists' approach both in what costs are marked up and in how the markup is determined. Under the absorption approach to cost-plus pricing, the cost base is the absorption costing unit product cost as defined in Chapters 2, 3, and 4 rather than variable cost.

Setting a Target Selling Price Using the Absorption Costing Approach

To illustrate, assume that the management of Ritter Company wants to set the selling price on a product that has just undergone some design modifications. The Accounting Department has provided cost estimates for the redesigned product as shown below:

	Per Unit	Total
Direct materials	$6	
Direct labor	$4	
Variable manufacturing overhead	$3	
Fixed manufacturing overhead		$70,000
Variable selling and administrative expenses	$2	
Fixed selling and administrative expenses		$60,000

The first step in the absorption costing approach to cost-plus pricing is to compute the unit product cost. For Ritter Company, this amounts to $20 per unit at a volume of 10,000 units, as computed below:

Direct materials	$ 6
Direct labor	4
Variable manufacturing overhead	3
Fixed manufacturing overhead ($70,000 ÷ 10,000 units)	7
Unit product cost	$20

Ritter Company has a general policy of marking up unit product costs by 50%. A price quotation sheet for the company prepared using the absorption approach is presented in Exhibit A–2. Note that selling and administrative expenses are not included in the cost base. Instead, the markup is supposed to cover these expenses.

EXHIBIT A–2
Price Quotation Sheet—
Absorption Basis (10,000 Units)

Direct materials	$ 6
Direct labor	4
Variable manufacturing overhead	3
Fixed manufacturing overhead (based on 10,000 units)	7
Unit product cost	20
Markup to cover selling and administrative expenses and desired profit—50% of unit manufacturing cost	10
Target selling price	$30

Determining the Markup Percentage

Ritter Company's markup percentage of 50% could be a widely used rule of thumb in the industry or just a company tradition that seems to work. The markup percentage may also be the result of an explicit computation. As we have discussed, the markup over cost should be largely determined by market conditions. However, many companies base their markup on cost and desired profit. The reasoning goes like this. The markup must be large enough to cover selling and administrative expenses and provide an adequate return on investment (ROI). Given the forecasted unit sales, the markup can be computed as follows:

$$\text{Markup percentage on absorption cost} = \frac{(\text{Required ROI} \times \text{Investment}) + \text{Selling and administrative expenses}}{\text{Unit product cost} \times \text{Unit sales}}$$

To show how this formula is applied, assume Ritter Company invests $100,000 in operating assets such as equipment to produce and market 10,000 units of the product each year. If Ritter Company requires a 20% ROI, then the markup for the product would be determined as follows:

$$\text{Markup percentage on absorption cost} = \frac{(20\% \times \$100,000) + (\$2 \text{ per unit} \times 10,000 \text{ units} + \$60,000)}{\$20 \text{ per unit} \times 10,000 \text{ units}}$$

$$= \frac{(\$20,000) + (\$80,000)}{\$200,000} = 50\%$$

As shown earlier, this markup of 50% leads to a target selling price of $30 for Ritter Company. *If the company actually sells 10,000 units* of the product at this price, the company's ROI on this product will indeed be 20%. This is verified in Exhibit A–3. However, if it turns out that more than 10,000 units are sold at this price, the ROI will be greater than 20%. If less than 10,000 units are sold, the ROI will be less than 20%. *The required ROI will be attained only if the forecasted unit sales volume is attained.*

Direct materials	$ 6
Direct labor	4
Variable manufacturing overhead	3
Fixed manufacturing overhead ($70,000 ÷ 10,000 units)	7
Unit product cost	$20

Ritter Company
Absorption Costing Income Statement

Sales ($30 per unit × 10,000 units)	$300,000
Cost of goods sold ($20 per unit × 10,000 units)	200,000
Gross margin	100,000
Selling and administrative expenses ($2 per unit × 10,000 units + $60,000)	80,000
Net operating income	$ 20,000

ROI

$$\text{ROI} = \frac{\text{Net operating income}}{\text{Average operating assets}}$$

$$= \frac{\$20,000}{\$100,000}$$

$$= 20\%$$

EXHIBIT A–3
Income Statement and ROI Analysis—Ritter Company Actual Unit Sales = 10,000 Units; Selling Price = $30

COST-BASED OR MARKET-BASED PRICES?

Jerry Bernstein, the director of Emerson Electric Co.'s price improvement team, says that setting prices used to be easy: "You developed a product, looked at the costs, and said, 'I need to make X,' and you marked it up accordingly—and people would buy it." Now the company charges based on what customers are willing to pay rather than its own costs. For example, a new compact sensor for factories that measures the flow of fluids would have been priced at $2,650 based on its cost. However, careful analysis revealed that customers would be willing to pay 20% more for the sensors than the company had planned to charge. The company settled on a price of $3,150.

Source: Timothy Aeppel, "Survival Strategies: After Cost Cutting, Companies Turn Toward Price Rises," *The Wall Street Journal*, September 18, 2002, pp. A1 and A12.

Problems with the Absorption Costing Approach

The absorption costing approach makes pricing decisions look deceptively simple. All a company needs to do is compute its unit product cost, decide how much profit it wants, and then set its price. It appears that a company can ignore demand and arrive at a price that will safely yield whatever profit it wants. However, as noted above, the absorption costing approach relies on a forecast of unit sales. Neither the markup nor the unit product cost can be computed without such a forecast.

The absorption costing approach essentially assumes that customers *need* the forecasted unit sales and will pay whatever price the company decides to charge. However, customers have a choice. If the price is too high, they can buy from a competitor or they may choose not to buy at all. Suppose, for example, that when Ritter Company sets its price at $30, it sells only 7,000 units rather than the 10,000 units forecasted. As shown in Exhibit A–4, the

EXHIBIT A–4
Income Statement and ROI Analysis—Ritter Company
Actual Unit Sales = 7,000 Units; Selling Price = $30

Direct materials	$ 6
Direct labor	4
Variable manufacturing overhead	3
Fixed manufacturing overhead ($70,000 ÷ 7,000 units)	10
Unit product cost	$23

Ritter Company
Absorption Costing Income Statement

Sales ($30 per unit × 7,000 units)	$210,000
Cost of goods sold ($23 per unit × 7,000 units)	161,000
Gross margin	49,000
Selling and administrative expenses ($2 per unit × 7,000 units + $60,000)	74,000
Net operating income	$ (25,000)

ROI

$$ROI = \frac{\text{Net operating income}}{\text{Average operating assets}}$$

$$= \frac{-\$25,000}{\$100,000}$$

$$= -25\%$$

company would then have a loss of $25,000 on the product instead of a profit of $20,000.[7] Some managers believe that the absorption costing approach to pricing is safe. This is an illusion. The absorption costing approach is safe only if customers choose to buy at least as many units as managers forecasted they would buy.

Target Costing

Our discussion thus far has presumed that a product has already been developed, has been costed, and is ready to be marketed as soon as a price is set. In many cases, the sequence of events is just the reverse. That is, the company already *knows* what price should be charged, and the problem is to *develop* a product that can be marketed profitably at the desired price. Even in this situation, where the normal sequence of events is reversed, cost is still a crucial factor. The company can use an approach called *target costing.* **Target costing** is the process of determining the maximum allowable cost for a new product and then developing a prototype that can be profitably made for that maximum target cost figure. A number of companies have used target costing, including Compaq, Culp, Cummins Engine, Daihatsu Motors, DaimlerChrysler, Ford, Isuzu Motors, ITT Automotive, Komatsu, Matsushita Electric, Mitsubishi Kasei, NEC, Nippodenso, Nissan, Olympus, Sharp, Texas Instruments, and Toyota.

> LEARNING OBJECTIVE 3
> Compute the target cost for a new product or service.

The target cost for a product is computed by starting with the product's anticipated selling price and then deducting the desired profit, as follows:

$$\text{Target cost} = \text{Anticipated selling price} - \text{Desired profit}$$

The product development team is then given the responsibility of designing the product so that it can be made for no more than the target cost.

Reasons for Using Target Costing

The target costing approach was developed in recognition of two important characteristics of markets and costs. The first is that many companies have less control over price than they would like to think. The market (i.e., supply and demand) really determines price, and a company that attempts to ignore this does so at its peril. Therefore, the anticipated market price is taken as a given in target costing. The second observation is that most of a product's cost is determined in the design stage. Once a product has been designed and has gone into production, not much can be done to significantly reduce its cost. Most of the opportunities to reduce cost come from designing the product so that it is simple to make, uses inexpensive parts, and is robust and reliable. If the company has little control over market price and little control over cost once the product has gone into production, then it follows that the major opportunities for affecting profit come in the design stage where valuable features that customers are willing to pay for can be added and where most of the costs are really determined. So that is where the effort is concentrated—in designing and developing the product. The difference between target costing and other approaches to product development is profound. Instead of designing the product and then finding out how much it costs, the target cost is set first and then the product is designed so that the target cost is attained.

---

[7] It may be *impossible* to break even using an absorption costing approach when the company has more than one product—even when it would be possible to make substantial profits using the economists' approach to pricing. For details, see Eric Noreen and David Burgstahler, "Full Cost Pricing and the Illusion of Satisficing," *Journal of Management Accounting Research,* 9 (1997).

MANAGING COSTS IN THE PRODUCT DESIGN STAGE

The Boeing Company is building the airframe of its 787 Dreamliner jet using carbon fiber-reinforced plastic. While this type of plastic has been used in golf club shafts and tennis rackets, it has never been used to construct the exterior of an airplane. Boeing is excited about this innovative raw material because it allows enormous cost savings. For example, Boeing's Dreamliner should be 20% more fuel efficient than the Boeing 767 or Airbus A330, its maintenance costs should be 30% less than aluminum planes, and the number of fasteners needed to assemble its fuselage should be 80% less than conventional airplanes. In addition, aluminum airplanes require costly corrosion inspections after 6 years of service, while the Dreamliner can fly 12 years before it would need a comparable inspection. To Boeing's delight, the Dreamliner's sales have "taken off" because "customers get tremendous bang for their bucks. For $120 million—about what they paid for the comparable Boeing 767-300 back in the 1980s—airlines get an all-new aircraft that flies faster than the competition and costs substantially less to operate."

Source: Stanley Holmes, "A Plastic Dream Machine," *BusinessWeek*, June 20, 2005, pp. 32–36.

An Example of Target Costing

To provide a simple example of target costing, assume the following situation: Handy Company wishes to invest $2,000,000 to design, develop, and produce a new hand mixer. The company's Marketing Department surveyed the features and prices of competing products and determined that a price of $30 would enable Handy to sell an estimated 40,000 hand mixers per year. Since the company desires a 15% ROI, the target cost to manufacture, sell, distribute, and service one mixer is $22.50 as computed below:

Projected sales (40,000 mixers × $30 per mixer)	$1,200,000
Less desired profit (15% × $2,000,000)	300,000
Target cost for 40,000 mixers	$ 900,000
Target cost per mixer ($900,000 ÷ 40,000 mixers)	$22.50

This $22.50 target cost would be broken down into target costs for the various functions: manufacturing, marketing, distribution, after-sales service, and so on. Each functional area would be responsible for keeping its actual costs within target.

Summary

Pricing involves a delicate balancing act. Higher prices result in more revenue per unit but drive down unit sales. Exactly where to set prices to maximize profit is a difficult problem, but, in general, the markup over cost should be highest for those products where customers are least sensitive to price. The demand for such products is said to be price inelastic.

Managers often rely on cost-plus formulas to set target prices. From the economists' point of view, the cost base for the markup should be variable cost. In contrast, in the absorption costing approach the cost base is the absorption costing unit product cost and the markup is computed to cover both nonmanufacturing costs and to provide an adequate return on investment. With the absorption approach, costs will not be covered and return on investment will not be adequate unless the unit sales forecast used in the cost-plus formula is accurate. If applying the cost-plus formula results in a price that is too high, the unit sales forecast will not be attained.

Some companies take a different approach to pricing. Instead of starting with costs and then determining prices, they start with prices and then determine allowable costs. Companies that use target costing estimate what a new product's market price is likely to be based on its anticipated features and prices of products already on the market. They subtract desired profit from the estimated market price to arrive at the product's target cost. The design and development team is then given the responsibility of ensuring that the actual cost of the new product does not exceed the target cost.

Glossary

Cost-plus pricing A pricing method in which a predetermined markup is applied to a cost base to determine the target selling price. (p. 754)

Markup The difference between the selling price of a product or service and its cost. The markup is usually expressed as a percentage of cost. (p. 754)

Price elasticity of demand A measure of the degree to which a change in price affects the unit sales of a product or service. (p. 754)

Target costing The process of determining the maximum allowable cost for a new product and then developing a prototype that can be profitably made for that maximum target cost figure. (p. 761)

Questions

A-1 What is cost-plus pricing?

A-2 What does the price elasticity of demand measure? What is inelastic demand? What is elastic demand?

A-3 According to the economists' approach to setting prices, the profit-maximizing price should depend on what two factors?

A-4 Which product should have a larger markup over variable cost, a product whose demand is elastic or a product whose demand is inelastic?

A-5 When the absorption costing approach to cost-plus pricing is used, what is the markup supposed to cover?

A-6 What assumption does the absorption costing approach make about how consumers react to prices?

A-7 Discuss the following statement: "Full cost can be viewed as a floor of protection. If a company always sets its prices above full cost, it will never have to worry about operating at a loss."

A-8 What is target costing? How do target costs enter into the pricing decision?

Exercises

EXERCISE A-1 The Economists' Approach to Pricing [LO1]

Maria Lorenzi owns an ice cream stand that she operates during the summer months in West Yellowstone, Montana. Her store caters primarily to tourists passing through town on their way to Yellowstone National Park.

Maria is unsure of how she should price her ice cream cones and has experimented with two prices in successive weeks during the busy August season. The number of people who entered the store was roughly the same each week. During the first week, she priced the cones at $1.89 and 1,500 cones were sold. During the second week, she priced the cones at $1.49 and 2,340 cones were sold. The variable cost of a cone is $0.43 and consists solely of the costs of the ice cream and of the cone itself. The fixed expenses of the ice cream stand are $675 per week.

Required:

1. Did Maria make more money selling the cones for $1.89 or for $1.49?
2. Estimate the price elasticity of demand for the ice cream cones.
3. Estimate the profit-maximizing price for ice cream cones.

EXERCISE A-2 Absorption Costing Approach to Setting a Selling Price [LO2]
Martin Company is considering the introduction of a new product. To determine a selling price, the
company has gathered the following information:

Number of units to be produced and sold each year	14,000
Unit product cost	$25
Projected annual selling, general and administrative expenses	$50,000
Estimated investment required by the company	$750,000
Desired return on investment (ROI)	12%

Required:
The company uses the absorption costing approach to cost-plus pricing.
1. Compute the markup required to achieve the desired ROI.
2. Compute the selling price per unit.

EXERCISE A-3 Target Costing [LO3]
Shimada Products Corporation of Japan is anxious to enter the electronic calculator market. Management believes that in order to be competitive in world markets, the price of the electronic calculator that the company is developing cannot exceed $15. Shimada's required rate of return is 12% on
all investments. An investment of $5,000,000 would be required to purchase the equipment needed to
produce the 300,000 calculators that management believes can be sold each year at the $15 price.

Required:
Compute the target cost of one calculator.

Problems

PROBLEM A-4 Standard Costs; Absorption Costing Approach to Setting Prices [LO2]]
Wilderness Products, Inc., has designed a self-inflating sleeping pad for use by backpackers and
campers. The following information is available about the new product:
a. An investment of $1,350,000 will be necessary to carry inventories and accounts receivable and
    to purchase some new equipment needed in the manufacturing process. The company's required
    rate of return is 24% on all investments.
b. A standard cost card has been prepared for the sleeping pad, as shown below:

	Standard Quantity or Hours	Standard Price or Rate	Standard Cost
Direct materials	4.0 yards	$2.70 per yard	$10.80
Direct labor	2.4 hours	$8.00 per hour	19.20
Manufacturing overhead			
(⅙ variable)	2.4 hours	$12.50 per hour	30.0
Total standard cost per jacket.			$60.00

c. The only variable selling, general, and administrative expense will be a sales commission of
    $9 per pad. Fixed selling, general, and administrative expenses will be (per year):

Salaries	$ 82,000
Warehouse rent	50,000
Advertising and other	600,000
Total	$732,000

d. Since the company manufactures many products, no more than 38,400 direct labor-hours per year
    can be devoted to production of the new sleeping pads.
e. Manufacturing overhead costs are allocated to products on the basis of direct labor-hours.

Required:

1. Assume that the company uses the absorption approach to cost-plus pricing.
    a. Compute the markup that the company needs on the pads to achieve a 24% return on investment (ROI) if it sells all of the pads it can produce.
    b. Using the markup you have computed, prepare a price quotation sheet for a single sleeping pad.
    c. Assume that the company is able to sell all of the pads that it can produce. Prepare an income statement for the first year of activity and compute the company's ROI for the year on the pads.
2. After marketing the sleeping pads for several years, the company is experiencing a falloff in demand due to an economic recession. A large retail outlet will make a bulk purchase of pads if its label is sewn in and if an acceptable price can be worked out. What is the minimum acceptable price for this special order?

PROBLEM A-5 The Economists' Approach to Pricing [LO1]

The postal service of St. Vincent, an island in the West Indies, obtains a significant portion of its revenues from sales of special souvenir sheets to stamp collectors. The souvenir sheets usually contain several high-value St. Vincent stamps depicting a common theme, such as the life of Princess Diana. The souvenir sheets are designed and printed for the postal service by Imperial Printing, a stamp agency service company in the United Kingdom. The souvenir sheets cost the postal service $0.80 each. (The currency in St. Vincent is the East Caribbean dollar.) St. Vincent has been selling these souvenir sheets for $7.00 each and ordinarily sells about 100,000 units. To test the market, the postal service recently priced a new souvenir sheet at $8.00 and sales dropped to 85,000 units.

Required:

1. Does the postal service of St. Vincent make more money selling souvenir sheets for $7.00 each or $8.00 each?
2. Estimate the price elasticity of demand for the souvenir sheets.
3. Estimate the profit-maximizing price for souvenir sheets.
4. If Imperial Printing increases the price it charges to the St. Vincent postal service for souvenir sheets to $1.00 each, how much should the St. Vincent postal service charge its customers for the souvenir sheets?

PROBLEM A-6 The Economists' Approach to Pricing; Absorption Costing Approach to Cost-Plus Pricing [LO1, LO2]

Software Solutions, Inc., was started by two young software engineers to market SpamBlocker, a software application they had written that screens incoming e-mail messages and eliminates unsolicited mass mailings. Sales of the software have been good at 50,000 units a month, but the company has been losing money as shown below:

Sales (50,000 units × $25 per unit)	$1,250,000
Variable cost (50,000 units × $6 per unit)	300,000
Contribution margin	950,000
Fixed expenses	960,000
Net operating income (loss)	$ (10,000)

The company's only variable cost is the $6 fee it pays to another company to reproduce the software on floppy diskettes, print manuals, and package the result in an attractive box for sale to consumers. Monthly fixed selling, general, and administrative expenses are $960,000.

The company's marketing manager has been arguing for some time that the software is priced too high. She estimates that every 5% decrease in price will yield an 8% increase in unit sales. The marketing manager would like your help in preparing a presentation to the company's owners concerning the pricing issue.

Required:

1. To help the marketing manager prepare for her presentation, she has asked you to fill in the blanks in the following table. The selling prices in the table were computed by successively decreasing the selling price by 5%. The estimated unit sales were computed by successively increasing the unit sales by 8%. For example, $23.75 is 5% less than $25.00 and 54,000 units is 8% more than 50,000 units.

Selling Price	Estimated Unit Sales	Sales	Variable Cost	Fixed Expenses	Net Operating Income
$25.00	50,000	$1,250,000	$300,000	$960,000	$(10,000)
$23.75	54,000	$1,282,500	$324,000	$960,000	$ (1,500)
$22.56	58,320	?	?	?	?
$21.43	62,986	?	?	?	?
$20.36	68,025	?	?	?	?
$19.34	73,467	?	?	?	?
$18.37	79,344	?	?	?	?
$17.45	85,692	?	?	?	?
$16.58	92,547	?	?	?	?
$15.75	99,951	?	?	?	?

2. Using the data from the table, construct a chart that shows the net operating income as a function of the selling price. Put the selling price on the X-axis and the net operating income on the Y-axis. Using the chart, determine the approximate selling price at which net operating income is maximized.
3. Compute the price elasticity of demand for the SpamBlocker software. Based on this calculation, what is the profit-maximizing price?
4. The owners have invested $2,000,000 in the company and feel that they should be earning at least 2% per month on these funds. If the absorption costing approach to pricing were used, what would be the target selling price based on the current sales of 50,000 units? What do you think would happen to the net operating income of the company if this price were charged?
5. If the owners of the company are dissatisfied with the net operating income and return on investment at the selling price you computed in (3) above, should they increase the selling price? Explain.

PROBLEM A-7 Missing Data; Markup Computations: Return on Investment (ROI); Pricing [LO2]
South Seas Products, Inc., has designed a new surfboard to replace its old surfboard line. Because of the unique design of the new surfboard, the company anticipates that it will be able to sell all the boards that it can produce. On this basis, the following incomplete budgeted income statement for the first year of activity is available:

Sales (? boards at ? per boards)	$?
Cost of goods sold (? boards at ? per boards)	1,600,000
Gross margin	?
Selling, general, and administrative expenses	1,130,000
Net operating income	$?

Additional information on the new surfboard follows:
a. An investment of $1,500,000 will be necessary to carry inventories and accounts receivable and to purchase some new equipment. The company's required rate of return is 18% on all investments.
b. A partially completed standard cost card for the new surfboard follows:

	Standard Quantity or Hours	Standard Price or Rate	Standard Cost
Direct materials.	6 feet	$4.50 per foot	$27
Direct labor	2 hours	? per hour	?
Manufacturing overhead	?	? per hour	?
Total standard cost per surfboard			$?

c. The company will employ 20 workers to make the new surfboards. Each will work a 40-hour week, 50 weeks a year.

d. Other information relating to production and costs follows:

Variable manufacturing overhead cost (per board)	$5
Variable selling expense (per board).	$10
Fixed manufacturing overhead cost (total)	$600,000
Fixed selling, general, and administrative expense (total)	?
Number of boards produced and sold (per year)	?

e. Overhead costs are allocated to production on the basis of direct labor-hours.

Required:

1. Complete the standard cost card for a single surfboard.
2. Assume that the company uses the absorption costing approach to cost-plus pricing.
    a. Compute the markup that the company needs on the surfboards to achieve an 18% return on investment (ROI).
    b. Using the markup you have computed, prepare a price quotation sheet for a single surfboard.
    c. Assume, as stated, that the company is able to sell all of the surfboards that it can produce. Complete the income statement for the first year of activity, and then compute the company's ROI for the year.
3. Assuming that direct labor is a variable cost, how many units would the company have to sell at the price you computed in (2) above to achieve the 18% ROI? How many units would have to be sold to just break even?

PROBLEM A-8 Target Costing [LO3]

National Restaurant Supply, Inc., sells restaurant equipment and supplies throughout most of the United States. Management is considering adding a machine that makes sorbet to its line of ice cream making machines. Management will negotiate the price of the sorbet machine with its Swedish manufacturer.

Management of National Restaurant Supply believes the sorbet machine can be sold to its customers in the United States for $4,950. At that price, annual sales of the sorbet machine should be 100 units. If the sorbet machine is added to National Restaurant Supply's product lines, the company will have to invest $600,000 in inventories and special warehouse fixtures. The variable cost of selling the sorbet machines would be $650 per machine.

Required:

1. If National Restaurant Supply requires a 15% return on investment (ROI), what is the maximum amount the company would be willing to pay the Swedish manufacturer for the sorbet machines?
2. The manager who is flying to Sweden to negotiate the purchase price of the machines would like to know how the purchase price of the machines would affect National Restaurant Supply's ROI. Construct a chart that shows National Restaurant Supply's ROI as a function of the purchase price of the sorbet machine. Put the purchase price on the *X*-axis and the resulting ROI on the *Y*-axis. Plot the ROI for purchase prices between $3,000 and $4,000 per machine.
3. After many hours of negotiations, management has concluded that the Swedish manufacturer is unwilling to sell the sorbet machine at a low enough price so that National Restaurant Supply is able to earn its 15% required ROI. Apart from simply giving up on the idea of adding the sorbet machine to National Restaurant Supply's product lines, what could management do?

Profitability Analysis

Learning Objectives

After studying this appendix, you should be able to:

LO1 Compute the profitability index and use it to select from among possible actions.

LO2 Compute and use the profitability index in volume trade-off decisions.

LO3 Compute and use the profitability index in other business decisions.

Introduction

Perhaps more than any other information, managers would like to know the profitability of their products, customers, and other business segments. They want this information so that they know what segments to drop and add and which to emphasize. This appendix provides a coherent framework for measuring profitability, bringing together relevant materials from several chapters. After studying this appendix you should have a firm grasp of the principles underlying profitability analysis. The first step is to distinguish between *absolute profitability* and *relative profitability*.

IN BUSINESS

TRIMMING THE PRODUCT LINE

A large pharmaceutical company eliminated 20% of its products, despite protests from the marketing department. This resulted in a 5% reduction in sales, but a 60% increase in net profits. Why? The products that were dropped were *absolutely* unprofitable. The company was better off simply dropping them.

Source: Tim Allen, "Are Your Products Profitable?" *Strategic Finance,* March 2002, pp. 33–37.

Absolute Profitability

Absolute profitability is concerned with the impact on the organization's overall profits of adding or dropping a particular segment such as a product or customer—without making any other changes. For example, if Coca-Cola were considering closing down its operations in the African country of Zimbabwe, managers would be interested in the absolute profitability of those operations. Measuring the absolute profitability of an existing segment is conceptually straightforward—compare the revenues that would be lost from dropping the segment to the costs that would be avoided. When considering a new potential segment, compare the additional revenues from adding the segment to the additional costs that would be incurred. In each case, include only the additional costs that would actually be avoided or incurred. All other costs are irrelevant and should be ignored.

In practice, figuring out what costs would change and what costs would not change if a segment were dropped (or added) can be very difficult. Activity-based costing can help in identifying such costs, but all costs should be carefully analyzed to determine whether they would really change. For example, an activity-based costing study of Coca-Cola's Zimbabwe operations might include charges for staff support provided to the Zimbabwe operations by Coca-Cola's corporate headquarters in Atlanta. However, if eliminating the Zimbabwe operations would have no impact on actual costs in Atlanta, then these costs are not relevant and should be excluded when measuring the absolute profitability of the Zimbabwe operations.

For examples of the measurement of absolute profitability see "Appendix 8A: ABC Action Analysis," the sections "Decentralization and Segment Reporting" in Chapter 12 and "Adding and Dropping Product Lines and Other Segments" in Chapter 13.

KRAFT BULKS UP AND THEN SLIMS DOWN

In 2000, Kraft Foods Inc. acquired Nabisco for $19 billion. This acquisition coupled with nine others pushed Kraft's annual sales above $32 billion. Indeed, Kraft had assembled an impressive portfolio of brands including Oreo cookies, Oscar Mayer meats, Post cereals, Maxwell House Coffees, and DiGiorno pizzas, to name a few. However, Kraft's CEO, Roger K. Deromedi, has decided that it is time to slim the company down a bit. In 2004, Kraft sold its Life Savers and Altoids brands to Wm. Wrigley Jr. Co. for $1.5 billion in cash. Deromedi sold these laggard brands to enable Kraft to "concentrate on the blockbuster brands that can be tops in their categories worldwide." Presumably, Kraft considered Life Savers and Altoids to be relatively unprofitable compared to the other brands within the organization that were competing for scarce investment funds.

Source: Michael Arndt, "Why Kraft Is on a Crash Diet," *BusinessWeek*, November 29, 2004, p. 46.

Relative Profitability

Even when every segment is *absolutely* profitable, managers often want to know which segments are most and least profitable. **Relative profitability** is concerned with ranking products, customers, and other business segments to determine which should be emphasized.

Why are managers interested in ranking segments or determining the relative profitability of segments? The answer to this deceptively simple question provides the key to measuring relative profitability. The only reason to rank segments is if something forces you to make trade-offs among them. If trade-offs are not necessary, the solution is simple—keep every segment that is absolutely profitable. What would force a manager to make trade-offs among profitable segments? There is only one answer—a *constraint*. In the absence of a constraint, all segments that are absolutely profitable should be pursued. On the other hand, if a constraint is present, then by definition the company cannot pursue every profitable opportunity. Choices have to be made. Thus, measuring relative profitability makes sense only when a constraint exists that forces trade-offs. This point cannot be overemphasized; constraints are fundamental to understanding and measuring relative profitability.

How should relative profitability be measured? Divide each segment's measure of absolute profitability, which is the incremental profit from that segment, by the amount of the constraint required by the segment. For example, refer to the data below for two of the many segments within a company:

	Segment A	Segment B
Incremental profit	$100,000	$200,000
Amount of constrained resource required	100 hours	400 hours

Segment B may seem more attractive than Segment A because its incremental profit is twice as large, but it requires four times as much of the constrained resource. In fact, Segment B would not be the best use of the constrained resource because it generates only $500 of incremental profit per hour ($200,000 ÷ 400 hours), whereas Segment A generates $1,000 of incremental profit per hour ($100,000 ÷ 100 hours). Another way to look at this is to suppose that 400 hours of the constrained resource are available. Would you rather use the hours on four segments like Segment A, generating a total incremental profit of $400,000, or on one segment like Segment B, which generates $200,000 in incremental profit?

In general, the relative profitability of segments should be measured by the **profitability index** as defined below:

$$\text{Profitability index} = \frac{\text{Incremental profit from the segment}}{\text{Amount of the constrained resource required by the segment}}$$

LEARNING OBJECTIVE 1
Compute the profitability index and use it to select from among possible actions.

The profitability index is computed below for the two segments in the example:

	Segment A	Segment B
Incremental profit (a)	$100,000	$200,000
Amount of constrained resource required (b)	100 hours	400 hours
Profitability index (a) ÷ (b)	$1,000 per hour	$500 per hour

We have already encountered several examples of the profitability index in previous chapters. For example, in Chapter 14 the project profitability index was defined as:

$$\text{Project profitability index} = \frac{\text{Net present value of the project}}{\text{Amount of investment required by the project}}$$

The project profitability index is used when a company has more long-term projects with positive net present values than it can fund. In this case, the incremental profit from the segment is the net present value of the project. And since the investment funds are the constraint, the amount of the constrained resource required by the segment is the amount of investment required by the project.

As an example of the use of the profitability index, consider the case of Quality Kitchen Design, a small company specializing in designing kitchens for upscale homes. Management is considering the 10 short-term projects listed in Panel A of Exhibit B–1. The incremental profit from each project is listed in the second column. For example, the incremental profit from Project A is $9,180. This incremental profit consists of the revenues from the project less any costs that would be incurred by the company as a consequence of accepting the project. The company's constraint is the lead designer's time. Project A would require 17 hours of the lead designer's time. If all of the projects were accepted, they would require a total of 100 hours. Unfortunately, only 46 hours are available. Consequently, management will have to turn down some projects. The profitability index will be used in deciding which projects to accept and which to turn down. The profitability index for a project is computed by dividing its incremental profit by the amount of the lead designer's time required for the project. In the case of Project A, the profitability index is $540 per hour.

The projects are ranked in order of the profitability index in Panel B of Exhibit B–1. The last column in that panel shows the cumulative amount of the constrained resource (i.e., lead designer's time) required to do the projects at that point in the list and higher. For example, the 7 hours listed to the right of Project J in the cumulative column represents the sum of the 4 hours required for Project F plus the 3 hours required for Project J.

To find the best combination of projects within the limits of the constrained resource, go down the list in Panel B to the point where all of the available constrained resource is used. In this case, since 46 hours of lead designer time are available, that would be the point above the solid line drawn in Panel B of Exhibit B–1. Projects F, J, B, I, D, and A lie above that line and would require a total of exactly 46 hours of lead designer time. The optimal plan consists of accepting these six projects and turning down the others. The total incremental profit from accepting these projects would be $32,930 as shown in Panel C of Exhibit B–1. No other feasible combination of projects would yield a higher total incremental profit.[1]

We should reinforce a very important point that may be forgotten in the midst of these details. The profitability index is based on *incremental* profit. When computing the incremental

---

[1]   In this example, the top projects exactly consumed all of the available constrained resource. That won't always happen. For example, assume that only 45 hours of lead designer time are available. This small change complicates matters considerably. Because of the "lumpiness" of the projects, the optimal plan isn't necessarily to do projects F, J, B, I, and D—stopping at Project D on the list and a cumulative requirement of 29 hours. That would leave 16 hours of unused lead designer time. The best use of this time may be Project C, which has an incremental profit of $7,040. However, other possibilities exist too. Finding and evaluating all of the most likely possibilities can take a lot of time and ingenuity. When the constrained resource is not completely exhausted by the top projects on the list, some tinkering with the solution may be necessary. For this reason, the list generated by ranking based on the profitability index should be viewed as a starting point rather than as a definitive solution when the projects are "lumpy" and take big chunks of the constrained resource.

Panel A: Computation of the Profitability Index

	Incremental Profit (A)	Amount of the Constrained Resource Required (B)	Profitability Index (A) ÷ (B)
Project A	$9,180	17 hours	$540 per hour
Project B	$7,200	9 hours	$800 per hour
Project C	$7,040	16 hours	$440 per hour
Project D	$5,680	8 hours	$710 per hour
Project E	$5,330	13 hours	$410 per hour
Project F	$4,280	4 hours	$1,070 per hour
Project G	$4,160	13 hours	$320 per hour
Project H	$3,720	12 hours	$310 per hour
Project I	$3,650	5 hours	$730 per hour
Project J	$2,940	3 hours	$980 per hour
		100 hours	

Panel B: Ranking Based on the Profitability Index

	Profitability Index	Amount of the Constrained Resource Required	Cumulative Amount of the Constrained Resource Used
Project F	$1,070 per hour	4 hours	4 hours
Project J	$980 per hour	3 hours	7 hours
Project B	$800 per hour	9 hours	16 hours
Project I	$730 per hour	5 hours	21 hours
Project D	$710 per hour	8 hours	29 hours
Project A	$540 per hour	17 hours	46 hours
Project C	$440 per hour	16 hours	62 hours
Project E	$410 per hour	13 hours	75 hours
Project G	$320 per hour	13 hours	88 hours
Project H	$310 per hour	12 hours	100 hours

Panel C: The Optimal Plan

	Incremental Profit
Project F	$ 4,280
Project J	2,940
Project B	7,200
Project I	3,650
Project D	5,680
Project A	9,180
	$32,930

profit for a segment such as a product, customer, or project, only the *incremental* costs of the segment should be included. Those are the costs that could be avoided— whether fixed or variable—if the segment is eliminated. All other costs are not relevant and should be ignored—including allocations of common costs.

Volume Trade-Off Decisions

Earlier we stated that you have already encountered several examples of the profitability index in this book. One was the project profitability index in Chapter 14. The other example of the profitability index is in the section "Utilization of a Constrained Resource" in Chapter 13. That section deals with situations in which a company does not have enough capacity to satisfy demand for all of its products. Therefore, the company must produce less than the market demands of some products. This is called a volume trade-off decision because the decision, at the margin, consists of trading off units of one product for units of another. Fixed costs are typically unaffected by such decisions—capacity will be fully utilized, it is just a question of how it will be utilized. In volume trade-off decisions where fixed costs are irrelevant, the profitability index takes the special form:

$$\text{Profitability index for a volume trade-off decision} = \frac{\text{Unit contribution margin}}{\text{Amount of the constrained resource required by one unit}}$$

This profitability index is identical to the "contribution margin per unit of the constrained resource" that was used in Chapter 13 to decide which products should be emphasized. An example of a volume trade-off decision is presented in Exhibit B–2. In this example, the company makes three products that use the constrained resource—a machine that is available 2,200 minutes per week. As shown in Panel B of Exhibit B–2, producing all three products up to demand would require 2,700 minutes per week—500 more minutes than are available. Consequently, the company cannot fully satisfy demand for these three products and some product or products must be cut back.

The profitability index for this decision is computed in Panel C of Exhibit B–2. For example, the profitability index for product RX200 is $3 per minute. The comparable figure for product VB30 is $5 per minute and for product SQ500 is $4 per minute. Consequently, the correct ranking of the products is VB30 followed by SQ500, then followed by RX200.

The optimal production plan is laid out in Panel D of Exhibit B–2. The most profitable products, VB30 and SQ500, are produced up to demand and the remaining time on the constraint is used to make 200 units of RX200 (1,000 available minutes ÷ 5 minutes per unit).

The total contribution margin from following this plan is computed in Panel E of Exhibit B–2. The total contribution margin of $8,600 is higher than the contribution margin that could be realized from following any other feasible plan. Assuming that fixed costs are not affected by the decision of which products to emphasize, this plan will also yield a higher total profit than any other feasible plan.

Managerial Implications

In addition to the add-or-drop and volume trade-off decisions discussed above, the profitability index can be used in other ways. For example, which products would you rather have your salespersons emphasize—those with a low profitability index or those with a high profitability index? The answer is, of course, that salespersons should be encouraged to emphasize sales of the products with the highest profitability indexes. However, if salespersons are paid commissions based on sales, what products will they try to sell? The selling prices of products RX200, VB30, and SQ500 appear below:

	Products		
	RX200	VB30	SQ500
Unit selling price.	$40	$30	$35

If salespersons are paid a commission based on gross sales, they will prefer to sell product RX200, which has the highest selling price. But that is the *least* profitable product given the current constraint. It has a profitability index of only $3 per minute compared to $5 per minute for VB30 and $4 per minute for SQ500.

This suggests that salespersons should be paid commissions based on the profitability index and the amount of constraint time sold rather than on sales revenue. This would encourage them to sell the most profitable products, rather than the products with the highest selling prices. How would such a compensation system work? Prior to making a sales call, a salesperson would

EXHIBIT B–2
Using the Profitability Index in a Volume Trade-Off Decision

Panel A: Product Data

	RX200	Products VB30	SQ500
Unit contribution margin	$15 per unit	$10 per unit	$16 per unit
Demand per week	300 units	400 units	100 units
Amount of the constrained resource required	5 minutes per unit	2 minutes per unit	4 minutes per unit

Panel B: Total Demand on the Constrained Resource

	RX200	Products VB30	SQ500	Total
Demand per week (a)	300 units	400 units	100 units	
Amount of the constrained resource required (b)	5 minutes per unit	2 minutes per unit	4 minutes per unit	
Total amount of the constraint required per week to meet demand (a) × (b)	1,500 minutes	800 minutes	400 minutes	2,700 minutes

Panel C: Computation of the Profitability Index

	RX200	Products VB30	SQ500
Unit contribution margin (a)	$15 per unit	$10 per unit	$16 per unit
Amount of the constrained resource required (b)	5 minutes per unit	2 minutes per unit	4 minutes per unit
Profitability index (contribution margin per unit of the constrained resource) (a) ÷ (b)	$3 per minute	$5 per minute	$4 per minute

Panel D: The Optimal Plan

Amount of constrained resource available	2,200 minutes
Less: Constrained resource required for production of 400 units of VB30	800 minutes
Remaining constrained resource available	1,400 minutes
Less: Constrained resource required for production of 100 units of SQ500	400 minutes
Remaining constrained resource available	1,000 minutes
Less: Constrained resource required for production of 200 units of RX200*	1,000 minutes
Remaining constrained resource available	0 minutes

*1,000 minutes available ÷ 5 minutes per unit of RX200 = 200 units of RX200.

Panel E: The Total Contribution Margin under the Optimal Plan

	RX200	Products VB30	SQ500	Total
Unit contribution margin (a)	$15 per unit	$10 per unit	$16 per unit	
Optimal production plan (b)	200 units	400 units	100 units	
Contribution margin (a) × (b)	$3,000	$4,000	$1,600	$8,600

receive an up-to-date report indicating how much of the constrained resource is currently available and a listing of all products showing the amount of the constraint each requires and the profitability index. Such a report would appear as follows:

Marketing Data Report

	Products		
	RX200	VB30	SQ500
Unit selling price......................	$40	$30	$35
Unit variable cost	25	20	19
Unit contribution margin (a)	$15	$10	$16
Amount of the constrained resource required per unit (b)	5 minutes	2 minutes	4 minutes
Profitability index (a) ÷ (b)	$3 per minute	$5 per minute	$4 per minute

Total available time on the constrained resource: 100 minutes

The key here is to realize that the salesperson is really selling time on the constraint. A salesperson who is paid based on the profitability index will prefer to sell product VB30 since the salesperson would get credit for sales of $500 if all 100 minutes are used on product VB30 ($5 per minute × 100 minutes), whereas the credit would be only $300 for product RX200 or $400 for product SQ500.[2]

The profitability index also has implications for pricing new products. Suppose that the company has designed a new product, WR6000, whose variable cost is $30 per unit and that requires 6 minutes of the constrained resource per unit. Since the company is currently using all of its capacity, the new product would necessarily displace production of existing products. Consequently, the price of the new product should cover not only its variable cost, but it should also cover the opportunity cost of displacing existing products. What product would be displaced? Production of RX200 should be cut first because it is the least profitable existing product. And how much is a minute of the constrained resource worth if it would otherwise be used to make product RX200? A minute of the constrained resource is worth $3 per minute, the profitability index of product RX200. Therefore, the selling price of the new product should at least cover the costs laid out below:[3]

$$\begin{matrix} \text{Selling price of} \\ \text{new product} \end{matrix} \geq \begin{matrix} \text{Variable cost of} \\ \text{the new product} \end{matrix} + \left(\begin{matrix} \text{Opportunity} \\ \text{cost per unit of} \\ \text{the constrained} \\ \text{resource} \end{matrix} \times \begin{matrix} \text{Amount of the} \\ \text{constrained resource} \\ \text{required by a unit of} \\ \text{the new product} \end{matrix} \right)$$

In the case of the new product WR6000, the calculations would be:

$$\begin{matrix} \text{Selling price of} \\ \text{WR6000} \end{matrix} \geq \$30 + (\$3 \text{ per minute} \times 6 \text{ minutes}) = \$30 + \$18 = \$48$$

WR6000 should sell for at least $48 or the company would be better off continuing to use the available capacity to produce RX200.[4]

---

[2] Equivalent incentives would be provided by commissions based on total contribution margin. If all 100 available minutes are used to make product VB30, 50 units could be produced (100 minutes ÷ 2 minutes per unit), for which the total contribution margin would be $500 ($10 per unit × 50 units). Likewise, the total contribution margin for product RX200 would be $300, and the total contribution margin would be $400 for product SQ500 if all available minutes were used to make just those products.

[3] In addition, the selling price of a new product should cover any avoidable fixed costs of the product. This is easier said than done, however, since achieving this goal involves estimating how many units will be sold—which in turn depends on the selling price.

[4] If production of WR6000 eventually completely displaces production of RX200, the opportunity cost would change. It would increase to $4 per minute, the profitability index of the next product in line to be cut back.

DEALING WITH UNPROFITABLE CUSTOMERS

One retailer discovered that many of the biggest spending customers in their "loyalty" program were unprofitable because they bought only sale items and returned lots of items. The company stopped sending these customers notices of upcoming "private" sales.

Source: Larry Selden and Geoffrey Colvin, "Will this Customer Sink Your Stock?" *Fortune*, September 30, 2002, pp. 127–132.

Summary

A strong distinction should be made between absolute profitability and relative profitability. A segment is considered profitable in an absolute sense if dropping it would result in lower overall profits. Absolute profitability is measured by the segment's incremental profit, which is the difference between the revenues from the segment and the costs that could be avoided by dropping the segment.

A relative profitability measure is used to rank segments. Such rankings are necessary only if a constraint forces the organization to make trade-offs among segments. To appropriately measure relative profitability, three things must be known. First, the constraint must be identified. Second, the incremental profit associated with each segment must be computed. Third, the amount of the constrained resource required by each segment must be determined. Relative profitability is determined by the profitability index, which is the incremental profit from the segment divided by the amount of the constrained resource required by the segment. The profitability index can be used in a variety of situations, including selections of projects and volume trade-off decisions.

Glossary

Absolute profitability The impact on the organization's overall profits of adding or dropping a particular segment such as a product or customer—without making any other changes. (p. 770)

Profitability index The measure of relative profitability, which is computed by dividing the incremental profit from a segment by the amount of the constrained resource required by the segment. (p. 771)

Relative profitability A ranking of products, customers, or other business segments for purposes of making trade-offs among segments. This is necessary when a constraint exists. (p. 771)

Questions

B-1   What is meant by *absolute* profitability?
B-2   What is meant by *relative* profitability?
B-3   A successful owner of a small business stated: "We have the best technology, the best products, and the best people in the world. We have no constraints." Do you agree?
B-4   What information is needed to measure the *absolute* profitability of a segment?
B-5   What information is needed to measure the *relative* profitability of a product?
B-6   How should the relative profitability of products be determined in a volume trade-off decision?
B-7   What costs should be covered by the selling price of a new product?

Exercises

EXERCISE B-1 Ranking Projects Based on the Profitability Index [LO1]

MidWest Amusements is in the process of reviewing 10 proposals for new rides at its theme parks in cities scattered throughout the American heartland. The company's only experienced safety engineer must carefully review plans and monitor the construction of all new rides. However, she is only available to work on new rides for 1,590 hours during the year. The net present values and the amount of safety engineer time required for the proposed rides are listed below:

Proposed Ride	Net Present Value	Safety Engineer Time Required (hours)
Ride 1	$1,268,200	340
Ride 2	1,152,000	360
Ride 3	649,600	320
Ride 4	644,100	190
Ride 5	540,000	250
Ride 6	539,200	160
Ride 7	462,000	110
Ride 8	457,200	360
Ride 9	403,200	180
Ride 10	387,500	250
Total	$6,503,000	2,520

Required:
1. Which of the proposed rides should the company build this year? (Note: The incremental profit of a long-term project such as constructing a new ride is its net present value.)
2. What would be the total net present value of the rides built under your plan?

EXERCISE B-2 Volume Trade-Off Decision [LO2]
Heritage Watercraft makes reproductions of classic wooden boats. The bottleneck in the production process is fitting wooden planks to build up the curved sections of the hull. This process requires the attention of the shop's most experienced craftsman. A total of 1,800 hours is available per year in this bottleneck operation. Data concerning the company's four products appear below:

	Adirondack	Lake Huron	Oysterman	Voyageur
Unit contribution margin	$485	$268	$385	$600
Annual demand (units)	80	120	100	140
Hours required in the bottleneck operation per unit	5	4	7	8

No fixed costs could be avoided by modifying how many units are produced of any product or even by dropping any one of the products.

Required:
1. Is there sufficient capacity in the bottleneck operation to satisfy demand for all products?
2. What is the optimal production plan for the year?
3. What would be the total contribution margin for the optimal production plan you have proposed?

EXERCISE B-3 Pricing a New Product [LO3]
Seattle's Top Coffee owns and operates a chain of popular coffee stands that serve over 30 different coffee-based beverages. The constraint at the coffee stands is the amount of time required to fill an order, which can be considerable for the more complex beverages. Sales are often lost because customers leave after seeing a long waiting line to place an order. Careful analysis of the company's existing products has revealed that the opportunity cost of order filling time is $2.70 per minute.

The company is considering introducing a new product, praline cappuccino, to be made with pecan extract and molasses. The variable cost of the standard size praline cappuccino would be $0.30 and the time required to fill an order for the beverage would be 40 seconds.

Required:
What is the minimum acceptable selling price for the new praline cappuccino product?

Problems

PROBLEM B-4 Ranking Alternatives and Managing with a Constraint [LO1, LO3]

Luxus Baking Company has developed a reputation for producing superb, one-of-a-kind wedding cakes in addition to its normal fare of breads and pastries. While the wedding cake business is a major moneymaker, it creates some problems for the bakery's owner, Kari Therau, particularly in June. The company's reputation for wedding cakes is largely based on the skills of Regina Yesterman, who decorates all of the cakes. Unfortunately, last year the company accepted too many cake orders for some June weekends, with the result that Regina was worked to a frazzle and almost quit. To prevent a recurrence, Kari has promised Regina that she will not have to work more than 27 hours in any week to prepare the wedding cakes for the upcoming weekend. (Regina also has other duties at the bakery, so even with the 27-hour limitation, she would be working more than full-time in June.)

A number of reservations for wedding cakes for the first weekend in June had already been received from customers by early May. When a customer makes a reservation, Ms. Therau gets enough information concerning the size of the wedding party and the desires of the customer to determine the cake's price, the cost to make it, and the amount of time that Regina will need to spend decorating it. The reservations for the first weekend in June are listed below:

Customer	Incremental Profit	Regina's Time Required (hours)
Afonso.........	$ 195	5
Carloni	259	7
Cullins.........	105	3
Frese..........	170	5
Gerst..........	117	3
Jelovich........	124	4
Klarr	192	6
Melby	144	4
Rideau	150	5
Towner	256	8
Total	$1,712	50

For example, the Afonso cake would require 5 hours of Regina's time and would generate a profit of $195 for the bakery. Following industry practice, pricing for the cakes is based on their size and standard formulas and does not reflect how much decorating would be required.

Required:
1. Ms. Therau feels that she must cancel enough cake reservations to reduce Regina's workload to the promised level. She knows that customers whose reservations have been cancelled will be disappointed, but she intends to refer all of those customers to an excellent bakery across town. If the sole objective is to maximize the company's total profit, which reservations should be cancelled?
2. What would be the total profit if your recommendation in part (1) above is followed?
3. Assume that for competitive reasons it would not be practical for Luxus Bakery to change the pricing of its wedding cakes. What recommendations would you make to Ms. Therau concerning taking reservations in the future?
4. Assume that Luxus Bakery could change the way it prices its wedding cakes. What recommendations would you make to Ms. Therau concerning how she should set the prices of wedding cakes in the future?
5. What might Ms. Therau be able to do to keep both Regina and her customers happy while increasing her profits? Be creative. (Hint: Review the section on managing constraints in Chapter 13.)

PROBLEM B-5 Interpreting Common Practice [LO1]

In practice, many organizations measure the relative profitability of their segments by dividing the segments' margins by their revenues. The segment margin for this purpose is the segment's revenue less its fully allocated costs—including allocations of fixed common costs. For example, a hospital might compute the relative profitability of its major segments as follows:

St. Ignatius Hospital Profitability Report (in thousands of dollars)				
	Emergency Room	Surgery	Acute Care	Total
Revenue	$10,630	$21,470	$18,840	$50,940
Fully allocated cost	10,060	21,090	18,550	49,700
Margin	$ 570	$ 380	$ 290	$ 1,240
Profitability (Margin ÷ Revenue)	5.4%	1.8%	1.5%	2.4%

The hospital's net operating income for this period was $1,240,000.

Required:
1. Evaluate the use of the margin, as defined above, in the numerator of the profitability measure.
2. Evaluate the use of revenue in the denominator of the profitability measure.

PROBLEM B-6 Volume Trade-Off Decision; Managing the Constraint [LO2, LO3]
Sammamish Brick, Inc., manufactures bricks using clay deposits on the company's property. Raw clays are blended and then extruded into molds to form unfired bricks. The unfired bricks are then stacked onto movable metal platforms and rolled into the kiln where they are fired until dry. The dried bricks are then packaged and shipped to retail outlets and contractors. The bottleneck in the production process is the kiln, which is available for 2,000 hours per year. Data concerning the company's four main products appear below. Products are sold by the pallet.

	Traditional Brick	Textured Facing	Cinder Block	Roman Brick
Gross revenue per pallet	$756	$1,356	$589	$857
Contribution margin per pallet	$472	$632	$376	$440
Annual demand (pallets)	90	110	100	120
Hours required in the kiln per pallet	8	8	4	5

No fixed costs could be avoided by modifying how much is produced of any product.

Required:
1. Is there sufficient capacity in the kiln to satisfy demand for all products?
2. What is the production plan for the year that would maximize the company's profit?
3. What would be the total contribution margin for the production plan you have proposed?
4. The kiln could be operated for more than 2,000 hours per year by running it after normal working hours. Up to how much per hour should the company be willing to pay in overtime wages, energy costs, and other incremental costs to operate the kiln additional hours?
5. The company is considering introducing a new product, glazed Venetian bricks, whose variable cost would be $820 per pallet and that would require 10 hours in the kiln per pallet. What is the minimum acceptable selling price for this new product?
6. Salespersons are currently paid a commission of 5% of gross revenues. Will this motivate the salespersons to make the right choices concerning which products to sell most aggressively?

PROBLEM B-7 Customer Profitability and Managerial Decisions [LO1, LO3]
Advanced Pharmaceuticals, Inc., is a wholesale distributor of prescription drugs to independent retail and hospital-based pharmacies. Management believes that top-notch customer representatives are the key factor in determining whether the company will be successful in the future. Customer representatives serve as the company's liaison with customers—helping pharmacies monitor their stocks, delivering drugs when customer stocks run low, and providing up-to-date information on drugs from many different companies. Customer representatives must be ultra-reliable and are highly trained. Good customer representatives are hard to come by and are not easily replaced.

Customer representatives routinely record the amount of time they spend serving each pharmacy. This time includes travel time to and from the company's central warehouse as well as time spent replenishing stocks, dealing with complaints, answering questions about drugs, informing pharmacists of the latest developments and newest products, reviewing bills, explaining procedures, and so on. Some pharmacies require more hand-holding and attention than others and consequently they consume more of the representatives' time.

Recently, customer representatives have made more frequent complaints that it is impossible to do their jobs without working excessive overtime hours. This has led to an alarming increase in the number of customer representatives quitting for jobs in other organizations. As a consequence, management is considering dropping some customers to reduce the workload on customer representatives. Data concerning a representative sample of the company's customers appears below:

	Leafcrest Pharmacy	Providence Hospital Pharmacy	Madison Clinic Pharmacy	Jenkins Pharmacy
Total revenues	$272,650	$2,948,720	$1,454,880	$155,280
Cost of drugs sold...............	$211,470	$2,234,480	$1,119,440	$115,920
Customer service costs	$10,640	$74,400	$42,000	$4,480
Customer representative time........	190	1,240	560	80

Customer service costs include all of the costs—other than the costs of the drugs themselves—that could be avoided by dropping the customer. These costs include the hourly wages of the customer representatives, their sales commissions, the mileage-related costs of the customer representatives' company-provided vehicles, and so on.

Required:
1. Rank the four customers in terms of their profitability.
2. Customer representatives are currently paid $25 per hour plus a commission of 1% of sales revenues. If these four pharmacies are indeed representative of the company's customers, could the company afford to pay its customer representatives more in order to retain them?

Cases

CASE B-8 Redirecting Effort [LO2]

Vectra Corporation recently suffered its fourth straight decline in quarterly earnings—despite a modest increase in sales. Unfortunately, Vectra's industry is highly competitive, so the company is reluctant to increase its prices. However, management believes that profits would improve if the efforts of its sales force were redirected toward the company's most profitable products.

Several years ago Vectra decided that its core competencies were strategy, design, and marketing and that production should be outsourced. Consequently, Vectra subcontracts all of its production.

Vectra's salespersons are paid salaries and commissions. All of the company's salespersons sell the company's full line of products. The commissions are 5% of the revenue generated by a salesperson and average about 60% of a salesperson's total compensation. There has been some discussion of increasing the size of the sales force, but management would rather redirect the efforts of salespersons towards the more profitable products. While management is reluctant to tinker with the sales compensation scheme, revenue targets for the various products will be set for the regional sales managers based on the products that management wants to push most aggressively. The regional sales managers will be paid a bonus if the sales targets are met.

The company computes product margins for all of its products using the following formula:

> Selling price
> Less: Sales commissions
> Less: Cost of sales
> Less: Operating expenses
> Product margin

The cost of sales in the product margin formula is the amount Vectra pays to its production subcontractors. The operating expenses represent fixed costs. Each product is charged a fair share of those costs, calculated this year as 34.6% of the product's selling price.

Management is convinced that the best way to improve overall profits is to redirect the efforts of the company's salespersons. There are no plans to add or drop any products.

Required:
How would you measure the relative profitability of the company's products in this situation? Assume that it is not feasible to change the way salespersons are compensated. Also assume that the only data you have available are the selling price, the sales commissions, the cost of sales, the operating expenses, and the product margin for each product.

Credits

Photos

Logos